November 9-13, 2015
Seattle, Washington, USA

Association for Computing Machinery

Advancing Computing as a Science & Profession

ICMI'15

Proceedings of the 2015 ACM International Conference on Multimodal Interaction

Sponsored by:

ACM SIGCHI

Supported by:

OpenStream, NSF, Microsoft, VoiceBox Technologies, ArcSoft, Disney Research, Amazon Echo, Aldebaran, HRI, and Interactions

Association for
Computing Machinery

Advancing Computing as a Science & Profession

The Association for Computing Machinery
2 Penn Plaza, Suite 701
New York, New York 10121-0701

ISBN: 978-1-4503-3912-4 (Digital)

ISBN: 978-1-4503-4108-0 (Print)

Additional copies may be ordered prepaid from:

ACM Order Department
PO Box 30777
New York, NY 10087-0777, USA

Phone: 1-800-342-6626 (USA and Canada)
+1-212-626-0500 (Global)
Fax: +1-212-944-1318
E-mail: acmhelp@acm.org
Hours of Operation: 8:30 am – 4:30 pm ET

Printed in the USA

Chairs' Welcome

It is our great pleasure to welcome you to Seattle and to the **2015 ACM International Conference on Multimodal Interaction**. This year's conference continues its tradition of being the premier forum for presenting research results and experience studies on multimodal human-human and human-computer interaction. The conference focuses on theoretical and empirical foundations, component technologies, and combined multimodal processing techniques that define the field of multimodal interaction analysis, interface design, and system development. ICMI 2015 features a single-track main conference which includes: keynote speakers, technical full and short papers (including oral and poster presentations), demonstrations, exhibits, grand challenges, and doctoral symposium papers. It is followed by a day with five workshops.

The ICMI 2015 call for long and short papers attracted 127 paper submissions (84 in the long category and 43 in the short category). The papers were reviewed by a program committee led by 3 Program Chairs and composed of 25 Senior Program Committee members and a large number of technical reviewers. In a rebuttal process, the authors had the opportunity to clarify any misunderstandings and respond to questions raised in the reviews and meta-reviews. After the rebuttal phase, the program chairs held several remote meetings to discuss the papers. As a result, 24 papers were accepted for oral presentation and 28 papers were accepted for poster presentation. The acceptance rate is 19% for oral presentations and 41% overall, for short and long papers combined.

This year, the conference will host two invited keynote speeches from thought leaders in industry and academia. They are:

- *Sharing Representations for Long Tail Computer Vision Problems*, Dr. Samy Bengio, Google (USA),
- *Interaction Studies with Social Robots*, Prof. Kerstin Dautenhahn, University of Hertfordshire (UK).

In addition, Dr. Eric Horvitz, Microsoft (USA), the recipient of the ICMI 2015 Sustained Accomplishment Award, presented by the ICMI Advisory Board, will give a plenary talk entitled *Connections*. We encourage attendees to attend the keynote presentations. These valuable and insightful talks can and will guide us to a better understanding of the future of multimodal interaction.

The main ICMI conference program includes an exciting Demonstration session co-chaired by Hrvoje Benko (Microsoft, USA) and Stefan Scherer (University of Southern California, USA) that will showcase innovative implementations, systems, and technologies that incorporate multimodal interaction. The demonstration session will include 12 refereed demonstrations (out of 17 submitted), plus 5 demonstrations that accompany accepted main track papers.

The Doctoral Consortium is by now a traditional ICMI satellite event which takes place on the first day of the conference and extends our commitment to the next generation of researchers. This year, the event is co-chaired by Carlos Busso (University of Texas at Dallas, USA) and Vidhyasaharan Sethu (University of New South Wales, Australia). In this special session, a highly-accomplished mentor team and senior PhD students, selected via a rigorous review process by the Doctoral Consortium Program Committee, as well as by peer reviews from other applicants, gather to discuss research plans and progress of each student. From among 30 applications, 14 students were accepted for participation. The accepted students receive a travel grant and registration waiver to attend both the Doctoral Consortium event, and the main conference. The organizers thank the U.S. National Science Foundation (award IIS 1346655 and IIS 1443097) and conference sponsors for the financial support that makes this possible.

The Multimodal Grand Challenges were introduced to ICMI in 2012. They are designed to stimulate the community with standardized corpora competitions, and new research questions. This year's challenges are co-chaired by Cosmin Munteanu (University of Toronto, Canada) and Marcelo Worsley (Stanford University, USA), and include: the Fourth Multimodal Learning Analytics Challenge (MLA), the Third Emotion Recognition In The Wild Challenge (EMOTIW), and the Recognition of Social Touch Gestures Challenge. All three Grand Challenges will be presented on Monday, November 9th, and an overview and poster session will take place on Thursday, November 12th, during the main conference.

The ICMI workshop program was co-chaired this year by Jean-Marc Odobez (IDIAP, Switzerland) and Hayley Hung (Technical University of Delft, Netherlands). Five workshops will be held after the main conference, on Friday, November 13th. They are: the 1st Workshop on Modeling INTERPERsonal SynchrONy And infLuence (INTERPERSONAL), the ACM Workshop on Multimodal Deception Detection (WMDD), the International Workshop on Emotion Representations and Modelling for Companion Systems (ERM4CT), the 1st International Workshop on Advancements in Social Signal Processing for Multimodal Interaction (ASSP4MI), and the Workshop on Developing Portable & Context-aware Multimodal Applications for Connected Devices using W3C Multimodal Architecture (sponsored workshop).

Outstanding paper awards have also been a tradition at ICMI. This year, in addition to the traditional *Outstanding Paper* award and *Outstanding Student Paper* award, the ICMI board also established an Honorable Mention award. The Program Chairs considered the top-ranked paper submissions based on the reviews and meta-reviews and identified a set of nominations for the awards. A paper award committee was created with internationally renowned researchers in multimodal interaction. The committee reviewed the nominated papers carefully and selected the recipients of these awards, which will be announced at the banquet.

The *Sustained Accomplishment Award* is presented to a scientist who has made innovative and long-lasting contributions to our field. The award acknowledges an individual who has demonstrated vision in shaping the field, with a sustained record of research that has influenced the work of others. This year's award is presented to Dr. Eric Horvitz, Microsoft (USA), for his many contributions to multimodal interaction. The *ICMI Community Service Award* is given to an individual who has made organizational contributions that have had a major impact on the ICMI community and its annual events. Nominees will have made contributions to build and diversify our community over a period of five years or longer, including the creation of mechanisms to promote intellectual exchange and multidisciplinary or international alliances, and the expansion of opportunities for student training and participation. The 2015 ICMI Community Service award is presented to Dr. Kenji Mase, Nagoya University (Japan). Finally, this year, the ICMI Advisory Board will present two *Ten Year Technical Impact* paper awards at the banquet.

Putting together ICMI 2015 was very much a team effort. We first thank the authors for providing the content of the program. We are grateful to the entire program committee, including the program chairs, the senior program committee, the demo, challenge, doctoral consortium and workshop chairs, as well as the entire collection of reviewers, who worked very hard in reviewing papers and providing feedback to the authors. We'd like to thank other conference organization committee members who have been working very hard to make this conference a success. They include Publication Chair Lisa Anthony (University of Florida, USA); Publicity Chairs Xilin Chen (Chinese Academy of Sciences, China), Louis-Philippe Morency (Carnegie Mellon University, USA), and Christian Müller (DFKI GmbH, Germany); Sponsorship Chairs YingLi Tian (City University of New York, USA), Laurence Devillers (LIMSI, France), and Fei Wu (Zhejiang University, China); Finance Chair David McGee (Adapx, USA); Web Chair Hyunggu Jung (University of Washington,

USA); and Volunteer Chair Ankur Agrawal (University of Washington, USA). We also are grateful to our sponsor, ACM SIGCHI, and to our generous supporters, the National Science Foundation, OpenStream, Microsoft, Voicebox Technologies, ArcSoft, Disney Research, Amazon, Aldebaran, Honda Research Institute (HRI), and Interactions.

Last but not least, ICMI 2015 will host a rare event --- visiting Microsoft in the afternoon of Monday, November 9th. Attendees will be able to tour Microsoft Envisioning Center which is usually reserved for Microsoft partner executives and government dignitaries (Non-Disclosure Agreements are required). In addition, attendees will see demos from Microsoft Research (MSR), interact with MSR researchers, visit Microsoft Museum, or buy souvenirs from Microsoft Company Store. We thank local arrangement chairs Zicheng Liu and Sean Anderson for their meticulous and painstaking planning.

We hope that you will find this program interesting and thought-provoking and that ICMI 2015 will provide you with a valuable opportunity to share ideas with other researchers and practitioners from institutions around the world.

Philip R. Cohen
General Chair
Voicebox Technologies, USA

Zhengyou Zhang
General Chair
Microsoft Research, USA

Dan Bohus
Program Chair
Microsoft Research ,
USA

Radu Horaud
Program Chair
INRIA Grenoble
Rhone-Alpes, France

Helen Meng
Program Chair
Chinese University of
Hong Kong, China

Table of Contents

Oral Session 3: Language, Speech and Dialog

Session Chair: Jill F. Lehman *(Disney Research)*

Oral Session 4: Communication Dynamics

Session Chair: Louis-Philippe Morency *(Carnegie Mellon University)*

Oral Session 5: Interaction Techniques

Session Chair: Sharon Oviatt *(Incaa Designs)*

Oral Session 6: Mobile and Wearable

Session Chair: Michael Johnston *(Interactions Corporation)*

Poster Session

Session Chairs: Radu Horaud *(INRIA Grenoble Rhone-Alpes)* and Dan Bohus *(Microsoft Research)*

Demonstrations

Session Chair: Stefan Scherer *(University of Southern California)*

Grand Challenge 1: Recognition of Social Touch Gestures Challenge 2015

Grand Challenge 2: Emotion Recognition in the Wild Challenge 2015

Grand Challenge 3: Multimodal Learning and Analytics Grand Challenge 2015

Doctoral Consortium

Session Chair: Carlos Busso *(University of Texas at Dallas)*

ICMI 2015 Conference Organization

General Chairs: Zhengyou Zhang *(Microsoft Research, USA)*
Phil Cohen *(VoiceBox Technologies, USA)*

Program Chairs: Dan Bohus *(Microsoft Research, USA)*
Radu Horaud *(INRIA Grenoble Rhone-Alpes, France)*
Helen Meng *(Chinese University of Hong Kong, China)*

Workshop Chairs: Jean-Marc Odobez *(IDIAP, Switzerland)*
Hayley Hung *(Technical University of Delft, Netherlands)*

Demo Chairs: Hrvoje Benko *(Microsoft Research, USA)*
Stefan Scherer *(University of Southern California, USA)*

Multimodal Grand Challenge Chairs: Cosmin Munteanu *(University of Toronto, Canada)*
Marcelo Worsley *(Stanford University, USA)*

Doctoral Consortium Chairs: Carlos Busso *(University of Texas at Dallas, USA)*
Vidhyasaharan Sethu *(University of New South Wales, Australia)*

Publication Chair: Lisa Anthony *(University of Florida, USA)*

Publicity Chairs: Xilin Chen *(Chinese Academy of Sciences, China)*
Louis-Philippe Morency *(Carnegie Mellon University, USA)*
Christian Müller *(DFKI GmbH, Germany)*

Sponsorship Chairs: YingLi Tian *(City University of New York, USA)*
Laurence Devillers *(LIMSI, France)*
Fei Wu *(Zhejiang University, China)*

Local Organization Chairs: Zicheng Liu *(Microsoft Research, USA)*
Sean Anderson *(Microsoft Research, USA)*

Finance Chair: David McGee *(Adapx, USA)*

Web Chair: Hyunggu Jung *(University of Washington, USA)*

Volunteer Chair: Ankur Agrawal *(University of Washington, USA)*

Senior Program Committee:

Sileye Ba *(INRIA, France)*
Carlos Busso *(University of Texas at Dallas, USA)*
Jan Cech *(Czech Technical University, Czech Republic)*
Mary Czerwinski *(Microsoft Research, USA)*
David DeVault *(Institute for Creative Technologies, USA)*
Julien Epps *(University of New South Wales, Australia)*
Jonathan Gratch *(University of Southern California, USA)*
Michael Johnston *(Interactions Corporation, USA)*
Takayuki Kanda *(ATR, Japan)*
Iwan de Kok *(Bielefeld University, Germany)*
Stefan Kopp *(Bielefeld University, Germany)*
Louis-Philippe Morency *(Carnegie Mellon University, USA)*
Samer El Moubayed *(Disney Research, USA)*
Shrikanth Narayanan *(University of Southern California, USA)*
Anton Nijholt *(University of Twente, Netherlands)*
Jean-Marc Odobez *(IDIAP, Switzerland)*
Sharon Oviatt *(Incaa Designs, USA)*
Gerasimos Potamianos *(University of Thessaly, Greece)*
Emily Provost *(University of Michigan, USA)*
Elisa Ricci *(University of Perugia, Italy)*
Beat Signer *(Vrije University, Belgium)*
Rainer Stiefelhagen *(University of Karlsruhe, Germany)*
David Traum *(USC Institute for Creative Technologies, USA)*
Andy Wilson *(Microsoft Research, USA)*
Sebastian Wrede *(University of Bielefeld, Germany)*

Doctoral Consortium

Program Committee:
Roland Goecke *(University of Canberra, Australia)*
Federico Fontana *(University of Udine, Italy)*
Nicu Sebe *(University of Trento, Italy)*
Panayiotis Georgiou *(University of Southern California, USA)*
Stefan Scherer *(University of Southern California, USA)*
Merlin Suarez *(De La Salle University - Manila, Philippines)*
Nadia Bianchi-Berthouze *(University College London, UK)*
Marcelo Worsley *(University of Southern California, USA)*
David McGee *(Adapx, USA)*
Bjoern Schuller *(University of Passau, Germany)*
Dirk Heylen *(University of Twente, The Netherlands)*
Julien Epps *(The University of New South Wales, Australia.)*
Ronald Boeck *(Otto von Guericke University Magdeburg, Germany)*
Tadas Baltrusaitis *(Carnegie Mellon University, USA)*
Alessandro Vinciarelli *(The University of Glasgow, UK)*
Andrea Cavallaro *(Queen Mary University of London, UK)*
Michel Valstar *(University of Nottingham, UK)*
Yukiko Nakano *(Seikei University, Japan)*
Xaris Papageorgiou *(The Institute for Language & Speech Processing, Greece)*
Kim Hartmann *(Otto von Guericke University Magdeburg, Germany)*
Kristiina Jokinen *(University of Helsinki, Finland)*

ICMI 2015 Short and Long Paper Reviewers

Vicent Alabau
Robert Albrecht
Elisabeth Andre
Sean Andrist
Lisa Anthony
Gerard Bailly
Tadas Baltrusaitis
Timo Baumann
Christian Becker Asano
Kirsten Bergmann
Jonas Beskow
Nadia Bianchi-Berthouze
Timothy Bickmore
Brigitte Bigi
Nigel Bosch
Stephen Brewster
Frank Broz
Drazen Brscic
Alessio Brutti
Judee Burgoon
Hendrik Buschmeier
Pavel Campr
Xi Laura Cang
Géry Casiez
Theodora Chaspari
Siyuan Chen
Adrian Cheok
Michael Cohen
Nicholas Cummins
Randall Davis
Alexander De Luca
Abhinav Dhall
Sotirios Diamantas
Hamdi Dibeklioglu
Sidney D'Mello
David Dobbelstein
Séverine Dubuisson
Stefan Duffner
Bruno Dumas
Jens Edlund
Georgios Evangelidis
Katayoun Farrahi
Kenneth Alberto Funes Mora
Petra Galuscakova
Patrick Gebhard
Hans Gellersen
Kallirroi Georgila
Guillaume Gibert
Dorota Glowacka
Joseph Grafsgaard
Sidhant Gupta
Joakim Gustafson
Michael Haller
Zakia Hammal
Marc Hanheide
Seongkook Heo
Anna Hjalmarsson
Nico Hochgeschwender
Patrick Holthaus
Mohammed Ehsan Hoque
Lode Hoste
Hung-Hsuan Huang
Jing Huang
Eva Hudlicka
Gijs Huisman
Felix Hülsmann
Hayley Hung
Wolfgang Hürst
Ali Israr
Dinesh Babu Jayagopi
Kristiina Jokinen
Merel Jung
Kyriaki Kalimeri
Athanasios Katsamanis
Casey Kennington
Peter Khooshabeh
Wolf Kienzle
Yelin Kim
Maria Koutsombogera
Ayse Kucukyilmaz
Oswald Lanz
Gierad Laput
Chi-Chun Lee
Geehyuk Lee
Jill Lehman
Iolanda Leite
Luis Leiva
James Lester
Vincent Levesque
Nanxiang Li
David Lindlbauer
Patrick Lucey
Marwa Mahmoud
Maurizio Mancini
Etienne Marcheret
Soroosh Mariooryad
Nicolai Marquardt
Ioannis Marras
Marco Matassoni
Martin Matousek
Haruka Matsukura
Ali Mazalek
Angeliki Metallinou
Rada Mihalcea
Chreston Miller
Yukiko Nakano
Laurent Nguyen
Radoslaw Niewiadomski
David Novick
Mohammad Obaid
Marianna Obrist
Catharine Oertel Genannt Bierbach
Shogo Okada
Rieks op den Akker
Kazuhiro Otsuka
Philippe Palanque
Yifan Peng
Stavros Petridis
Thies Pfeiffer
Martin Pielot
Xavier Alameda Pineda
Aristodemos Pnevmatikakis
Isabella Poggi
Ronald Poppe
Benjamin Poppinga
Alexandros Potamianos
Francesc Alías Pujol
Bogdan Raducanu
Shyam Sundar Rajagopalan
Nimesha Ranasinghe
Spyros Raptis
Carsten Rocker
Luis Rodríguez
Ognjen Rudovic
Nele Russwinkel
Maha Salem
Enrique Sánchez-Lozano
Allison Sauppé
Stefan Scherer
David Schlangen
Johannes Schöning
Bjoern Schuller
Tim Schwartz
Ethan Selfridge
Vidhyasaharan Sethu
Masahiro Shiomi
Yale Song
Charles Spence
Sophie Stellmach
Matthew Stone
Svetlana Stoyanchev
Ronnie Taib
Hong Tan
Stefanie Tellex
Jacques Terken
Barry-John Theobald
Khiet Truong
Matthew Turk
Ambrish Tyagi
Michel Valstar
Florian van de Camp
Herwin van Welbergen
Jean Vanderdonckt
Radu-Daniel Vatavu
Brian Vaughan
Carlos Velasco
Torben Wallbaum
Nigel Ward
Johannes Wienke
Jason Williams
Graham Wilson
Matthias Woelfel
Marcelo Worsley
Bo Xiao
Yan Yan
Tomoko Yonezawa
Zhou Yu
Anil Yüce
Xenophon Zabulis
Massimo Zancanaro
Mi Zhang
Yin Zhou
Zhengyu Zhou

ICMI 2015 Sponsors & Supporters

Sponsors:

Association for Computing Machinery
Advancing Computing as a Science & Profession

SIGCHI

Platinum Supporters:

Openstream® — Making Communications Smarter

NSF

Microsoft

Gold Supporter:

VoiceBox TECHNOLOGIES

Silver Supporters:

ArcSoft®

Disney Research

Bronze Supporters:

amazon echo

ALDEBARAN — SoftBank Group

HRI

interactions

Sharing Representations for Long Tail Computer Vision Problems

Samy Bengio
Google
bengio@google.com

ABSTRACT

The long tail phenomena appears when a small number of objects/words/classes are very frequent and thus easy to model, while many many more are rare and thus hard to model. This has always been a problem in machine learning. We start by explaining why representation sharing in general, and embedding approaches in particular, can help to represent tail objects. Several embedding approaches are presented, in increasing levels of complexity, to show how to tackle the long tail problem, from rare classes to unseen classes in image classification (the so-called zero-shot setting). Finally, we present our latest results on image captioning, which can be seen as an ultimate rare class problem since each image is attributed to a novel, yet structured, class in the form of a meaningful descriptive sentence.

Categories and Subject Descriptors

I.2.6 [Artificial Intelligence]: Learning---connectionism and neural nets; I.2.6 [Artificial Intelligence]: Learning---parameter learning; I.4.10 [Image Processing and Computer Vision]: Image representation---statistical; I.5.1 [Pattern Recognition]: Models---neural nets, statistical.

Keywords

Embedding representations; long tail phenomena; latent representations; image description; neural nets

BIO

Samy Bengio (PhD in computer science, University of Montreal, 1993) is a research scientist at Google since 2007. Before that, he was senior researcher in statistical machine learning at IDIAP Research Institute since 1999. His most recent research interests are in machine learning, in particular large scale online learning, image ranking and annotation, music and speech processing, and deep learning.

He is action editor of the Journal of Machine Learning Research and on the editorial board of the Machine Learning Journal. He is a program chair of the International Conference on Learning Representations, ICLR, for 2015 and 2016. He was associate editor of the journal of computational statistics, general chair of the Workshops on Machine Learning for Multimodal Interactions (MLMI'2004, 2005 and 2006), program chair of the IEEE Workshop on Neural Networks for Signal Processing (NNSP'2002), chair of BayLearn (2012, 2013, 2014), and on the program committee of several international conferences such as NIPS, ICML, ECML and ICLR. More information can be found on his website: http://bengio.abracadoudou.com.

ICMI 2015, November 9-13, 2015, Seattle, Washington, USA.
ACM 978-1-4503-3912-4/15/11. DOI: http://dx.doi.org/10.1145/2818346.2818348

Interaction Studies with Social Robots

Kerstin Dautenhahn
University of Hertfordshire
k.dautenhahn@herts.ac.uk

ABSTRACT

Over the past 10 years we have seen worldwide an immense growth of research and development into companion robots. Those are robots that fulfil particular tasks, but do so in a socially acceptable manner. The companionship aspect reflects the repeated and long-term nature of such interactions, and the potential of people to form relationships with such robots, e.g. as friendly assistants. A number of companion and assistant robots have been entering the market, two of the latest examples are Aldebaran's Pepper robot, or Jibo (Cynthia Breazeal). Companion robots are more and more targeting particular application areas, e.g. as home assistants or therapeutic tools. Research into companion robots needs to address many fundamental research problems concerning perception, cognition, action and learning, but regardless how sophisticated our robotic systems may be, the potential users need to be taken into account from the early stages of development. The talk will emphasize the need for a highly user-centred approach towards design, development and evaluation of companion robots. An important challenge is to evaluate robots in realistic and long-term scenarios, in order to capture as closely as possible those key aspects that will play a role when using such robots in the real world. In order to illustrate these points, my talk will give examples of interaction studies that my research team has been involved in. This includes studies into how people perceive robots' non-verbal cues, creating and evaluating realistic scenarios for home companion robots using narrative framing, and verbal and tactile interaction of children with the therapeutic and social robot Kaspar. The talk will highlight the issues we encountered when we proceeded from laboratory-based experiments and prototypes to real-world applications.

Categories and Subject Descriptors

H.1.2 [Models and Principles]: User machine systems---human factors; H.5.1 [Information Interfaces and Presentation]: Multimedia information systems---audio input/output; I.2.9 [Artificial Intelligence]: Robotics.

Keywords

Human-robot interaction; social robots; companion robots;

BIO

Kerstin Dautenhahn, Senior Member IEEE, is Professor in the School of Computer Science at University of Hertfordshire in U.K. She received her Ph.D. degree from the Biological Cybernetics Department of the University of Bielefeld, Germany, in 1993, and has published more than 300 research articles. Prof. Dautenhahn has edited several books and frequently gives invited keynote lectures at international meetings. She has been Principal Investigator of her research team in several European and nationally funded projects. Prof. Dautenhahn is Founding Editor in Chief of the journal Interaction Studies: Social Behaviour and Communication in Biological and Artificial Systems, as well as Associate Editor of Adaptive Behaviour (Sage Publications), the International Journal of Social Robotics (Springer), IEEE Transactions on Affective Computing and the IEEE Transactions on Autonomous Mental Development. She is also on the Advisory Board of the journal AI & Society.

ICMI 2015, November 9-13, 2015, Seattle, Washington, USA.
ACM 978-1-4503-3912-4/15/11. DOI: http://dx.doi.org/10.1145/2818346.2818347

Connections
(2015 ICMI Sustained Accomplishment Award Lecture)

Eric Horvitz
Microsoft Research, Redmond, WA, USA
horvitz@microsoft.com

ABSTRACT
Our community has long pursued principles and methods for enabling fluid and effortless collaborations between people and computing systems. Forging deep connections between people and machines has come into focus over the last 25 years as a grand challenge at the intersection of artificial intelligence, human-computer interaction, and cognitive psychology. I will review experiences and directions with leveraging advances in perception, learning, and reasoning in pursuit of our shared dreams.

Categories and Subject Descriptors
I.2 [Artificial Intelligence]; H.4 [Information Systems Applications]; H.5 [Information Interfaces and Presentation].

Keywords
Human-computer interaction; Cognitive psychology; Community; Perception; Learning; Reasoning; Decision; Action.

BIO
Eric Horvitz is a Technical Fellow at Microsoft and the Managing Director of the Microsoft Research lab at Redmond. He has been pursuing research in artificial intelligence and multimodal interaction, focusing on principles and applications of machine perception, inference, and decision making. He has been elected fellow of the National Academy of Engineering NAE), ACM, AAAI, and of the American Academy of Arts and Sciences. He was inducted into the CHI Academy for contributions including "principles of mixed-initiative interaction for interleaving automated services with user actions, methods for predicting intentions and goals of users, and advances with spoken dialog systems."

In 2015, he was awarded the AAAI Feigenbaum Prize "for contributions in computational models of perception, reflection and action, and their applications." He received his Ph.D. and M.D. degrees from Stanford University. More information can be found at http://research.microsoft.com/~horvitz/.

ICMI 2015, November 9-13, 2015, Seattle, Washington, USA.
ACM 978-1-4503-3912-4/15/11.
DOI: http://dx.doi.org/10.1145/2818346.2835500

Combining Two Perspectives on Classifying Multimodal Data for Recognizing Speaker Traits

Moitreya Chatterjee
CrowdShipping Inc.
Los Angeles, CA, USA
metro.smiles@gmail.com

Sughyun Park
USC Institute for Creative Technologies
Playa Vista, CA, USA
park@ict.usc.edu

Louis-Philippe Morency
LTI, Carnegie Mellon University
Pittsburgh, PA, USA
morency@cs.cmu.edu

Stefan Scherer
USC Institute for Creative Technologies
Playa Vista, CA, USA
scherer@ict.usc.edu

ABSTRACT

Human communication involves conveying messages both through verbal and non-verbal channels (facial expression, gestures, prosody, etc.). Nonetheless, the task of learning these patterns for a computer by combining cues from multiple modalities is challenging because it requires effective representation of the signals and also taking into consideration the complex interactions between them. From the machine learning perspective this presents a two-fold challenge: a) Modeling the intermodal variations and dependencies; b) Representing the data using an apt number of features, such that the necessary patterns are captured but at the same time allaying concerns such as over-fitting. In this work we attempt to address these aspects of multimodal recognition, in the context of recognizing two essential speaker traits, namely passion and credibility of online movie reviewers. We propose a novel ensemble classification approach that combines two different perspectives on classifying multimodal data. Each of these perspectives attempts to independently address the two-fold challenge. In the first, we combine the features from multiple modalities but assume inter-modality conditional independence. In the other one, we explicitly capture the correlation between the modalities but in a space of few dimensions and explore a novel clustering based kernel similarity approach for recognition. Additionally, this work investigates a recent technique for encoding text data that captures semantic similarity of verbal content and preserves word-ordering. The experimental results on a recent public dataset shows significant improvement of our approach over multiple baselines. Finally, we also analyze the most discriminative elements of a speaker's non-verbal behavior that contribute to his/her perceived credibility/passionateness.

ICMI '15, November 09-13, 2015, Seattle, WA, USA.

http://dx.doi.org/10.1145/2818346.2820747.

Categories and Subject Descriptors

H.1.2 [**Information Systems**]: User/Machine Systems—*Human information processing*; I.5.3 [**Pattern Recognition**]: Clustering—*Algorithms, Similarity Measures*

Keywords

Generative Model; Discriminative Model; Clustering; Kernels; Ensemble; Multimodal

1. INTRODUCTION

Human communication/interaction is a complex process that involve both verbal and non-verbal cues (eye gaze, head gestures, voice pitch, etc.). Very often the motive behind initiating such a communication or interaction is to persuade others' of a person's opinion on a certain topic. Consider a public speech or an online video presenting a person's viewpoint, for instance. In such scenarios, the key to effective communication is, in Aristotle's words, the three components of *Ethos, Pathos* and *Logos* [13]. The *Ethos* of the speaker refers to his/her perceived credibility by the audience, *Pathos* emphasizes the importance of building an emotional connection with the audience by being passionate. Finally *Logos* underscores the importance of presenting a logically cogent argument. While *Logos* often entails an objective presentation of facts, the other two however, can be achieved by the effective use of both verbal and non-verbal communication channels [21].

The proliferation of video-sharing websites (YouTube, Dailymotion, etc.) has meant that more and more of human communication is taking place online. People now share their opinions of almost everything from politics to commercial products through online videos, making it more and more important to study human communication in the online domain. In this work, we therefore focus on recognizing two important speaker traits, namely the degree of *passion* and *credibility*, of a speaker in online reviews of movies. This task raises three important research questions.

The first one pertains to the machine learning component of this task. From the perspective of machine learning, this task presents a two-fold challenge. On the one hand, we need to model the variations and dependencies between the modalities (text, audio, video), since a simplistic representation of the data without capturing the inter-modality variations, would most likely fail to uncover important latent patterns [23]. On the other hand, we need to ensure that the data is represented using an apt number of effective features. A large number of features for modeling the several complex patterns in the data is both hard to design and also faces the challenge of potential over-fitting [5]. These issues raise the central research question, **Q1**: *Is there an effective technique of representing and classifying multimodal data so that the important inter-modal dependencies are captured?*

In this work, we attempt to address this challenge by proposing a novel ensemble-based classification scheme that combines discriminatory information from two different perspectives on classifying multimodal data. In the first one, we combine the features from multiple modalities in a combined space but assume conditional independence across the modalities. This avoids the task of having to learn too many parameters. In the other one, we project the data to a space of few dimensions using Multiview Canonical Correlation Analysis(MVCCA) [14], such that the correlation between the modalities is explicitly captured. We then classify using a novel non-parametric approach that relies on clustering-based kernel similarity. Our inclination towards a non-parametric approach, stems from the strong theoretical guarantees of performance that they have [9]. Figure 1 presents an overview of our approach.

The second research question pertains to effective representation of text. The conventional text representation approach for analyzing online movie reviews, Bag-of-Words [22, 10], suffers from a lack of semantic-awareness of the content and loss of word ordering [16]. Thus our concern is, **Q2**: *What constitutes an effective feature representation of text data in the context of online reviews?* As a potential solution, we explore a recent style of embedding text features, that has yet remained unexplored in the context of multimodal recognition. This technique maps semantically similar paragraphs as less-distant points in a feature space and also preserves word-ordering [16].

On the side of non-verbal behavior(acoustic, visual cues), we are faced with our third concern. By its very nature such behavior is subtle. We are therefore interested in knowing, **Q3**: *What non-verbal behavioral components allows us to discriminate between passionate/credible reviewers and those who are not?* We attempt to address this by performing an analysis of the descriptors of non-verbal behavior.

The core contribution of this paper is our attempt to answer these 3 research questions.

Our experiments on the recently released Persuasive Opinion Multimedia Corpus(POM) [22] show that our proposed solutions to all three research questions(Q1-Q3) hold promise, for the intended recognition tasks.

2. RELATED WORK

A feature-level stacking technique, called *early fusion* has widely been explored for multimodal recognition [4, 22, 24, 6]. While this technique does combine cues from multiple modalities, however, it does not explicitly model the inter-modality correlations. Furthermore a fusion of features from multiple modalities via *early fusion*, often leads to a blow-up of the number of feature dimensions. This makes it prone to over-fitting(high variance), resulting in poor generalization [5]. Many of these previous approaches resort to either dimension reduction or feature selection techniques to address this issue [24, 22]. On the contrary, we explore a novel idea of an ensemble of two classification approaches, each of which attempts to mitigate this concern in a different way. The first of these incorporates the inter-modality dependencies and variances through a Multiview Canonical Correlation Analysis(MVCCA) [14]-based technique and projects the data to a low-dimensional space, allaying concerns related to dimensionality. While the second classification technique, stacks up the features in a combined space like *early fusion* but assumes inter-modality conditional independence. This avoids the task of having to learn a large number of validated parameters.

Recently, Song et al. [23] successfully explored a technique for multimodal classification that models explicit correlation between the modalities through Canonical Correlation Analysis(CCA) [12]-based techniques. Their approach however, considers only two modalities for fusion. Our MVCCA-based approach, is an extension of CCA for more than 2 modalities. To the best of our knowledge, this application of MVCCA to multimodal (> 2) recognition is novel.

For the task of multimodal recognition, *mixed norm regularization* has shown promise [26]. In this approach, Zhuang et al. regularize data from different modalities using separate norms, viz. L_1 and L_2 respectively. We,On the other hand, in one of our classification approaches, model features from dissimilar modalities using entirely different probability distributions.

Bag-of-Words(BoW) has been a long-standing approach for capturing patterns in text for a diverse range of applications [18, 17, 10, 22]. However, an inherent weakness of this technique is that it only considers frequency of occurrence of the words and does not capture the semantic similarity between them. This might potentially result in the model being perplexed about the topic of the document if prepositions, articles, verbs, etc. occur frequently. Further, BoW also fails to preserve word ordering. We therefore investigate a recent technique for text encoding which maps the text document to a word-order preserving feature space, where semantically similar paragraphs occur as less-distant points [16].

Finally in the context of online movie reviews, Park et al. have probed into "persuasiveness" of the reviewer [22]. We on the other hand, explore "credibility" and "passion" which are two well-known attributes of an eloquent speaker [13]. The reader is referred to Mohammadi et al. for a treatise on how these attributes relate to personality traits [19].

3. DATASET

The Persuasive Opinion Multimedia(POM) Corpus is a recently introduced public dataset of 1,000 online movie review videos crawled from *ExpoTV.com* [22]. Each video consists of a speaker, presenting his/her review of a movie, facing the camera. The crawled videos are controlled for their video and audio qualities, in order to avoid noisy samples. The mean length of the videos in the corpus is 94.38 seconds. This corpus consists of just those reviews where the speaker either assigned 5-stars (most recommended) or 1 or 2-stars (least recommended) for the movie they are reviewing and these direct ratings by the speakers are made available. For 500 of these reviews, the reviewers have assigned 5-stars for the corresponding movie while the remaining 500 have been assigned 1 or 2-stars. The dataset along

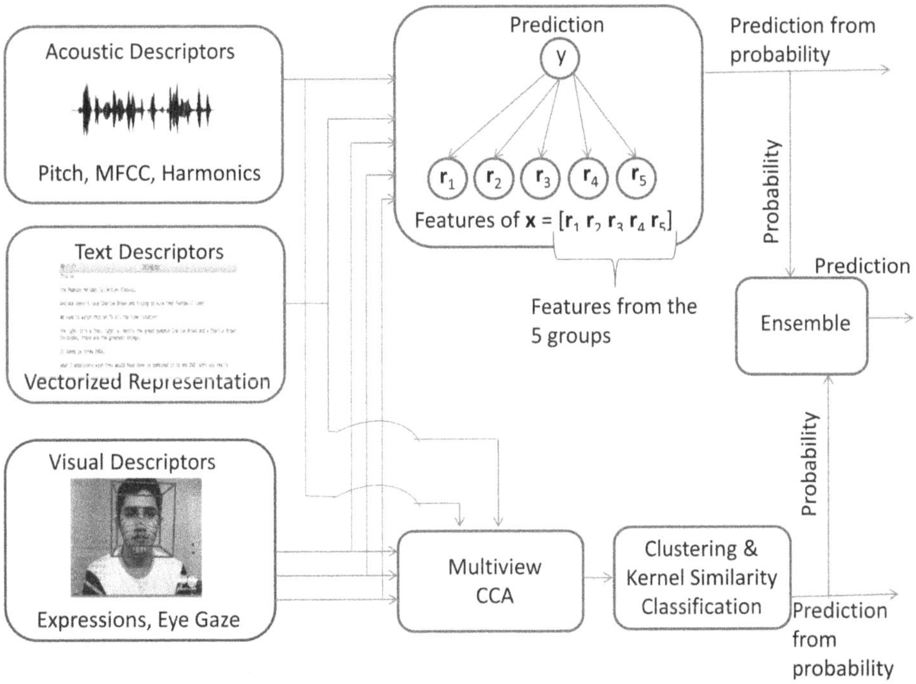

Figure 1: **The overview of our approach. We extract 5 groups of features from audio(1), text(1) and visual(3) channels. These features are then fed into two separate classification pipelines. Finally, an ensemble combines the outputs.**

with the transcriptions of what the reviewers say (including para-verbal markers such as stuttering, filled pauses, etc.) are also made available.

Each review has been annotated for various high-level subjective attributes such as "Persuasion", "Passion", "Credibility", "Confidence", etc. on a Likert-scale of 1(low) to 7(high) by 3 annotators, from Amazon Mechanical Turk. This work being targeted at exploring the qualities of an eloquent speaker, we focus exclusively on the "Passion" and "Credibility" attributes. The inter-coder agreement, as measured by Krippendorff's alpha, is 0.69 and 0.75 for "credibility" and "passion" respectively. This is suggestive of a high inter-coder agreement.

4. PROPOSED APPROACH

4.1 Computational Descriptors

We designed descriptors for the acoustic, visual and verbal modalities. They are as follows:

4.1.1 Descriptors for the Acoustic Modality

Park et al. have successfully explored a set of acoustic features for determining the degree of persuasiveness of a speaker in the context of online movie reviews [22]. We re-computed those features over the full length of the acoustic signals. It involved computing several statistical functionals for the first 5 Formants, the first 24 Mel Cepstral Frequency Coefficients (MFCCs), pitch (F0), and several voice quality measures including Normalized Amplitude Quotient (NAQ), Parabolic Spectral Parameter (PSP), Maxima Dispersion Quotient (MDQ), Quasi-Open Quotient (QOQ), difference between the first two harmonics (H1 - H2), and peak-slope. We used the mean, median, percentiles (10th, 25th, 75th, and 90th), ranges (between min and max, 10th and 90th percentiles, and 25th and 75th percentiles), and standard deviation as the statistical functionals.

4.1.2 Descriptors for the Visual Modality

On similar lines with the acoustic modality, we computed the same set of statistical functionals for automatically tracked facial features. The statistical functionals were computed for discrete emotions (anger, contempt, disgust, fear, joy, sadness, and surprise), valence (positive and negative), several Facial Action Units, eye gaze movements (up/down, left/right), and head movements (about the X, Y and Z axes). A detailed description is available in Park et al. [22]. Different from Park et al. however, we treat the head motion, eye gaze and the rest of the descriptors as three separate groups of features, i.e. we treat them as though they were descriptors from 3 separate modalities. This is because they are completely heterogeneous signals with very different amplitude variations and are computed using three different trackers, namely GAVAM[20], OKAO[3] and FACET[1].

4.1.3 Descriptors for the Verbal Modality

Modeling text using a bag-of-words (BoW) technique has been a long standing approach [18, 17]. Recently, this has also been explored in the context of assessing persuasiveness of online movie reviewers [10]. However this technique does not preserve word-ordering nor does it capture the semantic similarity among words. It treats every word independently and builds a histogram based on *term frequency*. This often results in "significant" words in the context of a certain problem being dominated by prepositions, articles or other words that tend to occur more frequently in any text document. Filtering out a pre-determined list of words or using the frequency count to trim down the vocabulary are not generalizable from one application to another.

To mitigate these weaknesses, we project the text data into a fixed 100-dimensional continuous feature space where semantically similar paragraphs across documents map as less-distant points [16, 2]. This framework is completely unsupervised and encodes every paragraph as a point in a multi-dimensional feature space. The approach works by comparing the word-ordering in a paragraph to their likelihood of occurrence in a training corpus. This likelihood is used to extract features using a Neural Language Model [7]. Finally, a linear regression like approach maps these features to a vector.

We thus have a total of five(5) sets of features, which we call *feature groups*, audio - 1, text - 1 and visual - 3.

4.2 Classification Technique

Our classification technique relies on an ensemble of two classification approaches that adopt two different perspectives for classifying multimodal data. For the subsequent explanations, we adopt the following notations. We have a set of N training samples, $\mathcal{X} = \{\mathbf{x}_i, y_i\}_{i=1}^{N}$, where every sample $\mathbf{x_i}$ is represented by a concatenation of the set of features obtained from the five feature groups, $\mathbf{x_i} = [\mathbf{r}_{i_1}, \mathbf{r}_{i_2}, ..., \mathbf{r}_{i_5}]$. y_i is the class label and $y_i \in \{+1, -1\}$. For a test sample $\mathbf{x}$, represented by $\mathbf{x} = [\mathbf{r}_1, \mathbf{r}_2, ..., \mathbf{r}_5]$, we want to assign a label y, where $y \in \{+1, -1\}$.

4.2.1 Ensemble Classifier

Our proposed ensemble classifier is a linear weighted combination of two classifiers, called the Modality-Independent Bayesian Classifier and the Similarity Classifier. These two classifiers adopt two different perspectives on classifying multimodal data. The ensemble allows us to combine the discriminative powers of both the models. For the task of classification, we compute the posterior probability for $\mathbf{x}$ as:

$$P_E = P(y = 1|\mathbf{x}) = \rho P_1 + (1 - \rho)P_2; \rho \in [0, 1] \qquad (1)$$

where P_1 and P_2 are the posterior probabilities for $\mathbf{x}$ obtained from the Modality-Independent Bayesian Classifier and the Similarity Classifier, respectively. These two classifiers are described in subsequent sections. We then, compare P_E to $P_E^c = P(y = -1|\mathbf{x}) = 1 - P_E = \rho(1 - P_1) + (1 - \rho)(1 - P_2)$ and determine which one is greater and assign the label to the test sample accordingly. ρ is chosen to maximizes the classification accuracy on the training data.

4.2.2 Modality-Independent Bayesian Classifier

Our first perspective on the data is that of conditional independence of the modalities(feature groups). This assumption is directed at addressing the issue of potential over-fitting of a large number of model parameters. Such scenarios are commonplace in early fusion settings, which attempt to model a full association among all the features across all modalities [5].

Mixed norm regularization is a classification approach that works by combining decisions from multiple modalities. For the task of learning the decision boundary, the parameters for each modality are regularized with a different norm, viz. L_1 and L_2 [26]. This allows the model to capture the variations within different modalities, to some extent. Inspired by such approaches, we model features from different feature groups using entirely different distributions. The posterior probability for $\mathbf{x}$ is computed as,

$$P(y|\mathbf{x}) \propto P(\mathbf{x}|y)P(y) = \prod_{i=1}^{5} P(\mathbf{r}_i|y)P(y),$$

This is a generative technique of modeling and its use is inspired by recent successes of such approaches for various learning tasks [15]. Our approach might reminisce the reader about the popular Naive Bayes classifier [9]. However different from that, we do not assume full conditional independence among all the features within a feature group. In fact, we represent each of the class-conditionals for every feature group, $P(\mathbf{r}_i|y)$ by a separate multidimensional Gaussian Distribution, $\mathcal{N}(\mathbf{r}_i; \mu, \Sigma)$, with a fully general covariance matrix Σ, learned from the training data. We then pick the greater of $P_1 = P(y = 1|\mathbf{x})$ and $P_1^c = P(y = -1|\mathbf{x})$ for label assignment. This results in a model that not only combines cues from multiple modalities but also drastically cuts the number of validation parameters. This P_1 is also used for the Ensemble classification by substituting it in Equation 1. We subsequently refer this approach as Cls. 1.

4.2.3 Similarity Classifier

In our second perspective, we explicitly capture the inter-modality correlations in the process of classifying. Our classification technique, is a non-paramteric one and banks on clustering and a kernel similarity ratio. The 3-step procedure for this is as follows:

- **MVCCA**: We first perform Multiview Canonical Correlation Analysis (MVCCA) to project the data to a 5-dimensional space where the 5 features groups are correlated the most [14]. This achieves two objectives: a) Maps the data to a space where the cross-modality features correlate, thereby making them more homogeneous (see Figure 2); b) Performs dimensionality reduction. The regular CCA [12] works for two feature groups by computing projection vectors for each that maximize the correlation between the two. For 3 or more feature groups however, there are several options such as maximizing the sum of correlations, maximizing the variance in the data in the projected space or minimizing the variance, minimizing the sum of squared errors, etc. [14]. Each of these approaches optimizes a different objective function. We choose to maximize the sum of correlations because of the ease of solving the corresponding optimization problem. Let $\mathcal{X} \in \mathbb{R}^{N \times (D_1 + ... + D_5)}$ be the training set of N samples, where $D_1, ..., D_5$ are the dimensions of each feature group. We compute the set of projection vectors $\mathbf{h}_1, ..., \mathbf{h}_5$ where $\mathbf{h}_1 \in \mathbb{R}^{D_1 \times 1}$ and so on s.t.:

$$\arg \max_{\mathbf{h}_1, ..., \mathbf{h}_5} \sum_{i \neq j; i,j=1}^{5} \mathbf{h}_i^T \Sigma_{ij} \mathbf{h}_j;$$

$$s.t.\ \mathbf{h}_i^T \Sigma_{ii} \mathbf{h}_i = 1;\ \forall i = 1, ..., 5,$$

where $\Sigma_{ij} \in \mathbb{R}^{D_i \times D_j}$ is the covariance matrix between feature groups i and j. This optimization is solved by the Generalized Eigen Value technique [25].

After having projected the data to a 5-d MVCCA space, we cluster the data:

- **Clustering in the MVCCA Space**: We first cluster the training data in the MVCCA space. We perform clustering using the standard Gaussian Mixture Model (GMM)-Expectation Maximization (EM) technique [8] followed by

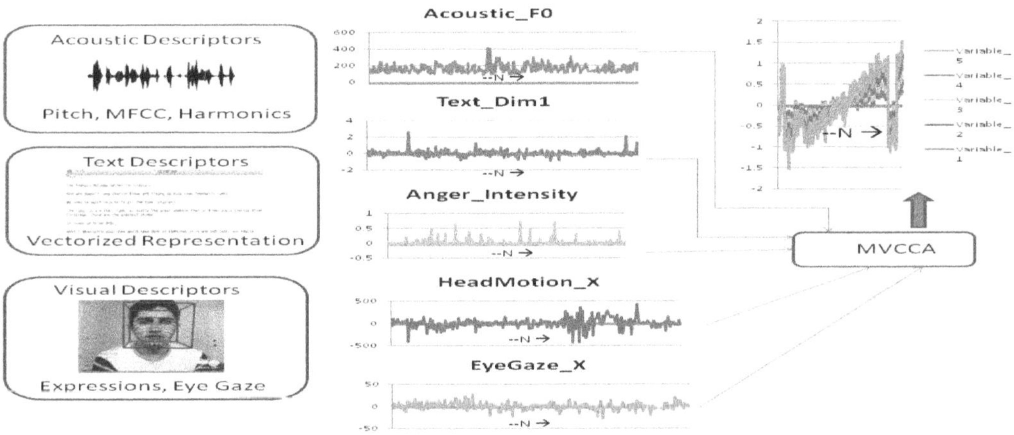

Figure 2: **This figure shows how signals from multiple groups(5 for our case) are projected into a common space where their mutual correlation is the highest. This is for our experiments with "passion."**

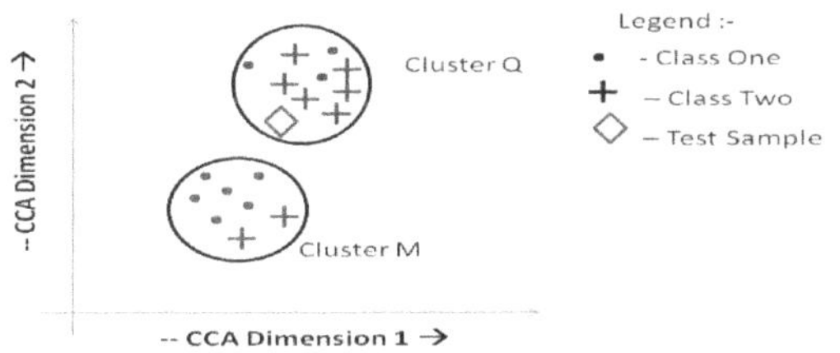

Figure 3: **The test sample is assigned to Cluster Q and thus all samples in Cluster M may be discarded for classification.**

the crisp assignment of every sample to a cluster, i.e. every Gaussian component is considered as one cluster and every sample is assigned to exactly one cluster. The number of mixture components are automatically chosen based on whichever number, in the range of 1 to 20, minimizes the Akaike Information Criterion (AIC) scores.

Now that we have our clusters on the training data in place, we assign each test sample $\mathbf{x}$ (projected in MVCCA space) to one of these clusters based on the most probable candidate. Assuming there are T clusters, this step may be defined as:

$$\arg \max_{i=\{1,\ldots,T\}} P(\mathbf{x}; \mu_i, \Sigma_i),$$

where μ_i, Σ_i are the mean and the covariance matrix of the Gaussian distribution corresponding to the ith cluster.

Our motivation for clustering the data is two-fold: a) Our classification technique for the Similarity Classifier is non-parametric, quite like k-Nearest Neighbor(kNN) [9]. However, unlike kNN, which is constrained to choose a fixed number of neighbors for decision making(k), we dynamically assign all the training samples in the same cluster as the test, to be the test sample's "neighbors". Clustering incorporates this flexibility.; b) Speed-gain in the process of classification.

• **Classification**: For the final classification, we adopt a non-parametric approach. Our reason for being inclined towards such an approach is because theoretically, the empirical risk for non-parametric classifiers is bounded to be within twice that of a hypothetical optimal classifier [9]. This gives an assurance in terms of classification performance of such algorithms. For classifying the test sample, we look into that subset of training samples that are in the same cluster as the test (say Q). The training samples in Cluster Q have the most similar feature appearance as the test and thus we discard all other training samples. This prevents the dissimilar training samples from influencing the inference process and also adds to the computational speed of our algorithm (see Figure 3). Now we compute a normalized similarity score between the test sample and the samples of each of the classes in cluster Q and see to which one it is more similar. In order to capture non-linear similarity patterns, we compute this similarity using kernel mappings. The normalization allows for a probabilistic interpretation of the similarity score. The posterior probability for the test sample $\mathbf{x}$ is computed by using the kernel similarity ratio as follows:

$$P_2 = P(y=1|\mathbf{x}) = \frac{\sum_{\mathbf{x}_i \in \mathcal{X}, \mathbf{x}_i \in Q, y_i=1} K_{Gauss}(\mathbf{x}, \mathbf{x_i}; \Sigma_Q)}{\sum_{\mathbf{x}_i \in \mathcal{X}, \mathbf{x}_i \in Q} K_{Gauss}(\mathbf{x}, \mathbf{x_i}; \Sigma_Q)},$$

where

$$K_{Gauss}(\mathbf{x}, \mathbf{x_i}; \Sigma_Q) = \exp(-\mathbf{x}^T(\Sigma_Q + \lambda I)^{-1}\mathbf{x_i}/2),$$

is a Gaussian kernel whose variance (Σ_Q) is the variance of the Gaussian distribution that was fitted to cluster Q in the previous step, I is the identity matrix and λ is the regularization term, typically with a very low value. Label assignment is done by comparing P_2 with $P_2^c = 1 - P_2$ and choosing the higher one. This P_2 is also plugged into Equation 1 for computing the ensemble classifier. We subsequently refer to this approach as Cls. 2.

5. EXPERIMENTS

5.1 Ground-Truth Labels

This work aims at exploring the differences in verbal and non-verbal behavior between highly passionate and credible reviewers and their counterparts on the other side of the spectrum. For our experiments, one for passion and the other for credibility, we therefore choose only those videos that had a mean annotator rating of 5.5 or more(highly passionate/credible) or 2.5 or less(weakly passionate/credible). For our experiments with passion, this resulted in a total of 291 videos(116 passionate and 175 phlegmatic) while for credibility, we ended up with a total of 233 videos(122 of the reviews deemed highly credible and 111 as not).

5.2 Methodology

We performed experiments to address our three research questions (Q1-Q3).

To address Q1, we conduct two separate classification experiments for recognizing "passion" and "credibility". Our experiments for passion and credibility, are based on the ground-truth labels obtained using the procedure described above. We perform *speaker and movie-independent* 5-fold cross-validation experiments, with separate training (4 partitions) and test partition (1 partition) for each. Thus we perform, 5 separate classification experiments for each of passion and credibility and report the mean classification accuracy. Our approach consists of two separate classifiers and one ensemble of the two(Cls. 1, Cls. 2 and Ensemble respectively) that were used for the classification tasks. The parameters of the models such as the mean and the covariance matrices of the Gaussian distributions, the covariance matrix of the Gaussian kernel used in Cls. 2 or ρ in Equation 1, were all directly estimated from the training data. The regularization parameter λ of the Gaussian kernel, $K_{Gauss}(.,.)$ was preset to 10^{-9}. We also measured the correlation between the predictions from Cls. 1 & Cls. 2 to see how often they predicted the same label.

We compared our approach with several baselines for both the classification tasks. Firstly, we explored the efficacy of unimodal classifiers, using features from each of the 5 feature groups separately and the popular polynomial(poly) kernel Support Vector Machine(SVM) [9] as the classifier(Audio, Text/Doc2Vec, Facet, Gavam, Okao). This also allows us to test the effectiveness of the feature encoding scheme for the text modality, which is our second research objective (Q2).

Next, we explored traditional multimodal classification approaches as baselines, stacking up(early fusion) of features of the modalities followed by a poly kernel SVM classifier(MM Full) and a Naive Bayes classifier(MM Full_NB). The MM Full_NB setting allows us to test if a full conditional independence assumption across all the features is effective or not. We also investigated the effect of dimension reduction techniques. For this, we first performed early fusion of features, then projected the data down to a 5-dimensional space(because Cls. 2 also projects into 5-dim.) using Principal Component Analysis(PCA) and then used a poly kernel SVM classifier for classification(MM Proj).

We also tried several baseline approaches using the features projected in the MVCCA space. First, we used a poly kernel SVM classifier on the data projected on to the MVCCA space, as a baseline(CCA). Further in the last step of Cls. 2, we compute a kernel-similarity ratio for the classification. An alternative classification technique would be to assign the test sample, the label of the majority class of the cluster to which the test sample is assigned. We therefore, also explore this as a baseline(Cls_F). Our final baseline classifier, is the majority vote classifier on the ground-truth(Baseline/ Majority Baseline).

The hyper-parameters for the poly kernel SVMs are determined using 4-fold cross-validation(with 1-partition for validation/ development) on the training data for each of our experiments.

Moreover, we also performed two sample t-tests between our proposed approaches and the baselines to test for statistical significance in classification performance.

For task Q3, where we intend to explore what non-verbal characteristics contribute most significantly to the perfor-

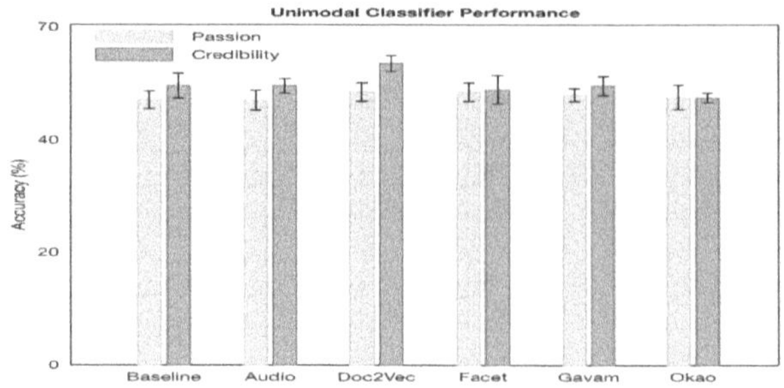

Figure 4: **Accuracies for different Unimodal Classifiers.**

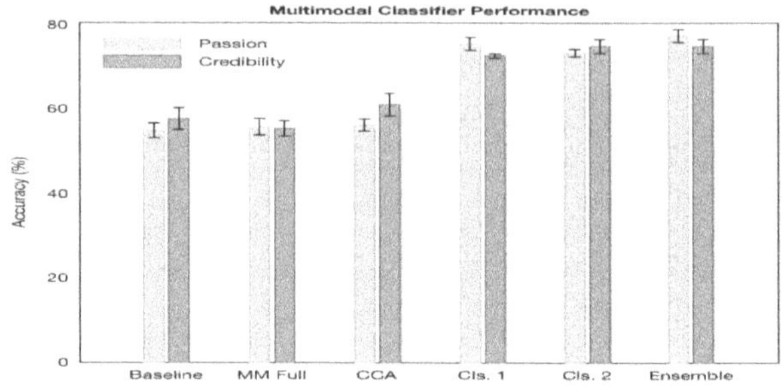

Figure 5: **Accuracies for different Multimodal Classifiers.**

mance of our model, we ranked the non-verbal features, in their original feature space, by their Information Gain(IG) scores [9]. A more discriminatory feature is expected to have a higher IG score. We report the most significant feature from each feature group for both "passion" and "credibility".

6. RESULTS AND DISCUSSION

6.1 Classification Experiments

6.1.1 Unimodal Classifiers

The performance of the unimodal classifiers (see Table 1) show that the classifier for the text modality performs either better or no-worse than the other unimodal classifiers for both credibility and passion. Since all the unimodal classifiers use the same poly kernel SVM classifier and differ only in the features used, we therefore conclude, that our semantic-similarity based feature encoding for text is the most effective amongst all cues individually, for our recognition tasks. This, presents a probable solution to Q2. Figure 4 presents a visualization of the performance of the unimodal classifiers.

6.1.2 Multimodal Classifiers

The major observation that emerges from the classification results of the multimodal classifiers for both passion and credibility, is that combining cues from multiple modalities, in a judicious fashion, adds more discriminatory power as compared to considering cues from just one modality(Table 1). We observe this from the performance of our proposed multimodal approaches(Cls. 1, Cls. 2 and Ensemble), which significantly outperform all unimodal baseline classifiers. Table 1 also shows the significance levels for the classification results. Further, the Pearson's correlation measure between the predicted labels of Cls. 1 and Cls. 2 across the 5-folds, was 0.2028 for "passion" and 0.319 for "credibility". Thus the two predictions were only moderately correlated, thereby suggesting that Cls. 1 and Cls. 2 exploit somewhat different patterns in the data for inference.

Our experiments reveal that not all techniques of combining cues from multiple modalities are equally effective.

In the MM Full setting we perform an early fusion of all the features, in an attempt to model the dependencies between the features of the various feature groups and then classify using a SVM. Again MM Full_NB, presents the complete contrastive setting where we classify using the Naive Bayes classifier, thereby assuming full conditional independence. Our experiments show that neither approaches are ideal for classification, in our context. A sweet-spot between these two extreme assumptions, where we assume conditional-independence between just the feature groups in the combined feature space is more effective. The performance of Cls. 1 compared to MM Full or MM Full_NB shows this. Furthermore, to assuage concerns regarding the issue of high dimensionality of the early fusion feature space leading to over-fitting, we used a PCA baseline(MM Proj). However, it also provides no significant performance improvement because PCA treats all the features from the same perspective. It is incognizant of the fact that the concatenated set of features is a heterogeneous mixture of signals from multiple sources, each with different levels of noise in them. It gives equal importance to all the features and thus, fails to combine the cues effectively.

Another different approach to modeling multimodal data is to explicitly capture the dependencies between every feature group but in a space of few dimensions. MVCCA attempts to address this concern. For our experiments, this results in atleast a marginal gain in performance, over multimodal classification techniques that rely on a modality-unaware dimensionality reduction. We see this when we compare CCA, Cls_F and Cls.2 approaches to MM Proj (atleast a gain of 0.67%).

We also investigated the role of clustering and non-parametric classification techniques in this correlated space. Our experiments divulged that such an approach of clustering followed by classification by assigning the majority class of a cluster(Cls_F) is almost at a-par with a kernel SVM classifier that uses the features directly from the correlated space(CCA). Here we must note that a kernel SVM, is able to capture non-linear patterns in the feature space through the use of a kernel, which is an inherent weakness of the Cls_F model where we simply assign the majority class. Once this weakness is mitigated in our clustering-based model(Cls. 2), we notice a statistically significant performance boost over other unimodal/multimodal baseline classification techniques. This is observable when comparing Cls. 2 with other approaches.

Finally, the linear ensemble of Cls. 1 and Cls. 2 allows us to combine their respective inferences on the data. This brings together the best of both worlds, giving us a performance that is either better or no worse than Cls. 1 or Cls. 2 individually and is better than all other baselines. The parameter ρ allows us to prefer one classifier over the other. For our classification experiments with "passion" the mean ρ across the 5-folds was 0.7280, suggesting the ensemble favored Cls. 1 over Cls. 2. Indeed, even in terms of the classification accuracy on the test-set, for "passion", Cls. 1 is clearly better. For "credibility", the mean ρ across the 5-folds was 0.2040, suggesting the ensemble's tilt towards Cls. 2. Again this in agreement with the results on the test set. We are thus, able to answer Q1.

Figure 5 presents a visualization of the performance of the proposed multimodal classification approaches and a selected set of multimodal baselines.

6.2 Feature Analysis

Our experiments on analyzing the discriminatory power of the non-verbal behaviors of the speaker, our third research goal, brings several interesting observations to light. Tables 2,3 list the most discriminative feature from each category based on their IG scores for "passion" and "credibility" respectively. The higher the score the more discriminative is the feature.

Table 2: **Most discriminative non-verbal descriptors of Passion as measured by Information Gain**

Modality	Statistical Functional	Feature	IG Score
Audio	Standard Deviation	MFCC_5	0.0400
Facet	Standard Deviation	AU 28	0.0200
Gavam	Standard Deviation	Ang. D_Z	0.0100
Okao	75th Percentile	Gaze_LR	0.0311

From the acoustic modality we find the lower(5th or the 6th order) MFCC coefficients to be significant. This is in line with our expectations, since they have denser resolutions and are more robust to noise [22].

From amongst the descriptors obtained from Facet, Action Unit(AU) 28 assumes significance.

Table 3: **Most discriminative non-verbal descriptors of Credibility as measured by Information Gain**

Modality	Statistical Functional	Feature	IG Score
Audio	Standard Deviation	MFCC_6	0.0025
Facet	Standard Deviation	AU 28	0.0046
Gavam	Standard Deviation	Ang. D_Z	0.0032
Okao	Standard Deviation	Gaze_UD	0.0009

The most significant descriptor from Gavam is Angular Diplacement around Z-axis. This corresponds to in-plane head motion and is suggestive of the more expressive gesturing of "passionate", engaging and "credible" speakers.

Finally, we surmise that the most differentiating descriptor from OKAO, namely Gaze deviations up/down(UD) or left/right(LR) hint at the wavering engagement(eye contact) with the audience that is characteristic of non-passionate or inexperienced speakers.

7. CONCLUSIONS & FUTURE WORK

In this work, we attempted to answer 3 research questions in the context of classifying reviewer "passion"(*Pathos*) and "credibility"(*Ethos*). As an answer to the first, we proposed two multimodal classifiers that made polar-opposite assumptions, and both were shown to be effective independently and a linear ensemble of the two was shown to hold promise. We thus, conclude that indeed multimodal cues add discriminatory power compared to just unimodal cues. However, the technique of fusion of these cues plays a pivotal role for achieving good performance. An analysis of the unimodal classifiers showed that the most effective unimodal classifier

Table 1: **Classification Performance of our proposed approach and multiple baselines for Credibility and Passion. The numbers in parenthesis "()" indicate the standard error levels. "[*symb*,*symb*,*symb*]" indicates statistical significance levels between Cls. 1, Cls. 2 and the Ensemble respectively and the current baseline classifier. *symb* could be either $\diamond, \triangle, *$ for p-value < 0.001, 0.01 and 0.05 respectively.**

		Passion	Credibility
Majority Baseline		54.55%(1.77) [◇,◇,◇]	57.38%(2.55) [◇,◇,◇]
Unimodal	Audio	54.46%(2.00) [◇,◇,◇]	57.39%(1.45) [◇,◇,◇]
	Doc2vec	**56.15%**(1.88) [◇,◇,◇]	**61.98%**(1.62) [◇,◇,◇]
	Facet	56.15%(1.88) [◇,◇,◇]	56.65%(2.89) [◇,◇,◇]
	Gavam	55.54%(1.32) [◇,◇,◇]	57.39%(1.95) [◇,◇,◇]
	Okao	55.10%(2.51) [◇,◇,◇]	55.02%(0.97) [◇,◇,◇]
Multimodal	MM Full	55.40%(1.95) [◇,◇,◇]	55.05%(1.79) [◇,◇,◇]
	MM Full_NB	57.04%(2.66) [◇,◇,◇]	57.36%(3.18) [△,△,△]
	MM Proj	55.17%(1.45) [◇,◇,◇]	59.69%(4.59) [*,*,*]
	CCA	55.84%(1.36) [◇,◇,◇]	60.63%(2.70) [△,△,△]
	Cls_F	57.21%(1.64) [◇,◇,◇]	59.70%(0.62) [◇,◇,◇]
	Cls. 1	74.93%(1.51)	72.11%(0.50)
	Cls. 2	72.78%(0.92)	**74.38%**(1.64)
	Ensemble	**76.85%**(1.50)	**74.38%**(1.64)

was the one corresponding to the text modality, where we represented the text in a space that captures semantic similarity and preserves word-ordering. This seemed to be a promising response to our second research question. As a response to the third research question, we looked into what non-verbal cues were discriminatory. Finally we note, that all our algorithms generalized well for both "passion" and "credibility", giving comparable performance.

For future work, we intend to extend our proposed approach for multi-label classification, try it on other multimodal recognition tasks, and explore feature-selection techniques. On the lines of Chatterjee et al. we also intend to investigate the effect of considering meta-information in the problem context, such as reviewer rating of the movie, for the task of classification [10, 11].

Acknowledgements: This material is based upon work supported by U.S. Army Research Laboratory under contract number W911NF-14-D-0005. Any opinions, findings, and conclusions or recommendations expressed in this material are those of the author(s) and do not necessarily reflect the views of the Government, and no official endorsement should be inferred.

8. REFERENCES

[1] Facet. url: http://www.emotient.com/cert.

[2] Gensim. url:https://radimrehurek.com/gensim/.

[3] Okao vision. url: http://www.omron.com/technology/core.html.

[4] M. Abouelenien et al. Deception detection using a multimodal approach. In *16th ACM ICMI*, 2014.

[5] E. Alpaydin. *Introduction to machine learning*. MIT press, 2014.

[6] O. Aran and D. Gatica-Perez. One of a kind: Inferring personality impressions in meetings. In *ACM ICMI*, 2013.

[7] Y. Bengio, R. Ducharme, P. Vincent, and C. Janvin. A neural probabilistic language model. *The Journal of Machine Learning Research*, 3, 2003.

[8] C. M. Bishop. Mixture models and the em algorithm. *Microsoft Research, Cambridge*, 2006.

[9] C. M. Bishop et al. *Pattern recognition and machine learning*, volume 4. springer New York, 2006.

[10] M. Chatterjee, S. Park, H. S. Shim, K. Sagae, and L.-P. Morency. Verbal behaviors and persuasiveness in online multimedia content. *SocialNLP 2014*.

[11] M. Chatterjee, G. Stratou, S. Scherer, and L.-P. Morency. Context-based signal descriptors of heart-rate variability for anxiety assessment. In *39th IEEE ICASSP*, 2014.

[12] H. Hotelling. Canonical correlation analysis (cca). *Journal of Educational Psychology*, 1935.

[13] G. A. Kennedy. *On rhetoric: A theory of civic discourse.* OUP, 1991.

[14] J. R. Kettenring. Canonical analysis of several sets of variables. *Biometrika*, 1971.

[15] V. Lavrenko, R. Manmatha, and J. Jeon. A model for learning the semantics of pictures. In *NIPS*, 2003.

[16] Q. Le and T. Mikolov. Distributed representations of sentences and documents. In *ICML*, 2014.

[17] D. D. Lewis and W. A. Gale. A sequential algorithm for training text classifiers. In *17th ACM SIGIR*, 1994.

[18] T. M. Mitchell. Machine learning. wcb, 1997.

[19] G. Mohammadi et al. Who is persuasive? the role of perceived personality and communication modality in social multimedia. In *15th ACM ICMI*, 2013.

[20] L. Morency et al. Generalized adaptive view-based appearance model: Integrated framework for monocular head pose estimation. In *8th IEEE FG*, 2008.

[21] N. Morgan. How to become an authentic speaker, harvard business review, url: https://hbr.org/2008/11/how-to-become-an-authentic-speaker.

[22] S. Park, H. S. Shim, M. Chatterjee, K. Sagae, and L.-P. Morency. Computational analysis of persuasiveness in social multimedia: A novel dataset and multimodal prediction approach. In *Proceedings of the 16th ACM ICMI*, 2014.

[23] Y. Song, L.-P. Morency, and R. Davis. Multimodal human behavior analysis: learning correlation and interaction across modalities. In *14th ACM ICMI*, 2012.

[24] R. Subramanian, Y. Yan, J. Staiano, O. Lanz, and N. Sebe. On the relationship between head pose, social attention and personality prediction for unstructured and dynamic group interactions. In *Proceedings of the 15th ACM ICMI*, 2013.

[25] J. Vıa, I. Santamarıa, and J. Pérez. Canonical correlation analysis (cca) algorithms for multiple data sets: Application to blind simo equalization. In *13th EUSIPCO*, 2005.

[26] Y. T. Zhuang et al. Supervised coupled dictionary learning with group structures for multi-modal retrieval. In *AAAI*, 2013.

Personality Trait Classification via Co-Occurrent Multiparty Multimodal Event Discovery

Shogo Okada [1]
okada@dis.titech.ac.jp

Oya Aran [2]
oaran@idiap.ch

Daniel Gatica-Perez [2,3]
gatica@idiap.ch

[1] Tokyo Institute of Technology, Yokohama, Japan
[2] Idiap Research Institute, Martigny, Switzerland
[3] Ecole Polytechnique Federale de Lausanne (EPFL), Lausanne, Switzerland

ABSTRACT

This paper proposes a novel feature extraction framework from mutli-party multimodal conversation for inference of personality traits and emergent leadership. The proposed framework represents multi modal features as the combination of each participant's nonverbal activity and group activity. This feature representation enables to compare the nonverbal patterns extracted from the participants of different groups in a metric space. It captures how the target member outputs nonverbal behavior observed in a group (e.g. the member speaks while all members move their body), and can be available for any kind of multiparty conversation task. Frequent co-occurrent events are discovered using graph clustering from multimodal sequences. The proposed framework is applied for the ELEA corpus which is an audio visual dataset collected from group meetings. We evaluate the framework for binary classification task of 10 personality traits. Experimental results show that the model trained with co-occurrence features obtained higher accuracy than previously related work in 8 out of 10 traits. In addition, the co-occurrence features improve the accuracy from 2% up to 17%.

Categories and Subject Descriptors

I.5.2 [**Pattern Recognition**]: Design Methodology—*Feature evaluation and selection*; H.2.8 [**Database Applications**]: Data mining

General Terms

Algorithms, Experimentation

Keywords

Personality trait, Inference, Data mining, Multiparty interaction

1. INTRODUCTION

Automatic nonverbal analysis of small group interaction promises many kinds of applications. In recent years, one challenge in this research is to infer high level characteristics of participants as target variables, such as roles, attitude in conversation, emerging leadership, and personality traits, by combining audio and visual information observed from people. In these works, data-driven approaches are often used to model relationships between nonverbal behavior observed from start to end of an interaction and target variables such as personality traits, leadership, etc. A key factor for success is to extract various types of nonverbal features that have possibility to infer the target variable. To extract effective features for inference of these target variables, previous works have proposed static features from audio and visual data defined based on knowledge of social science.

Common aspects in these features are that these statistics are calculated by accumulating each event observed in the whole meeting. On the other hand, conversational nonverbal patterns exist at multiple time scales [7], ranging from fine-grain features such as presence of speech and head gesture patterns, to conversational context patterns where multiple events co-occur simultaneously, such as events in which listeners nod when a speaker explains something with gestures. Using co-occurrence patterns between modalities yields two main advantages for modeling personality traits. First, it is possible to improve the inference accuracy of the trait value based on rich feature set extracted by capturing the interaction between modalities. Second, discovering key context patterns linking personality traits helps us understand effective conversational contexts to predict the trait variables. For example, when co-occurrence events (gaze and utterance) are observed in a group conversation, emergent leaders likely speak while gazing to people [20].

In this paper, we propose a co-occurrent event mining framework from multiparty and multimodal interaction data to infer personality traits. Figure 1 shows the overview of the proposed framework. The goal is to find patterns between modalities and multiple people: segments of utterance, speech, gaze, head gestures and body gestures. To apply co-occurrence mining for group conversations,

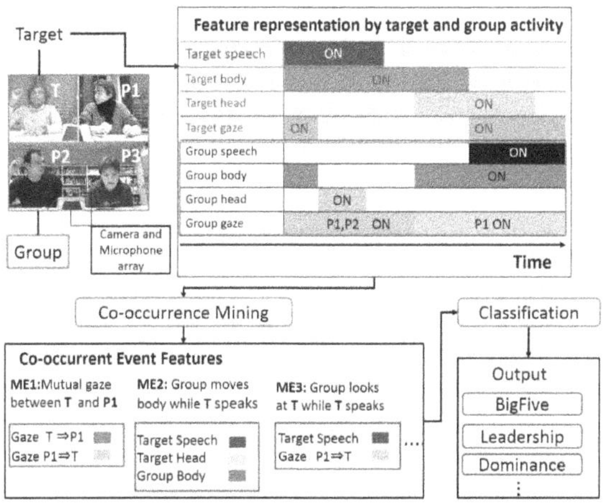

Figure 1: Overview of proposed framework

ICMI 2015, November 9–13, 2015, Seattle, WA, USA.
© 2015 ACM. ISBN 978-1-4503-3912-4/15/11 ...$15.00.
DOI: http://dx.doi.org/10.1145/2818346.2820757.

we need to tackle the problem of how to compare the data collected from groups which are composed of different members in one metric space. Here, we separate the multimodal signals from each participant into signals observed from (1) a group member and (2) the other group members. This data representation captures what an individual member does (speak, look, and move) when the other members do certain actions. The data representation enables to compare multimodal activities of individual members and captures the context in which the individual members acts in group interaction each time. After data representation, multiparty multimodal data is converted to 2-D time-series dataset. A pairwise event discovery algorithm based on graph mining is applied to find co-occurrent events and discovered patterns are used as features for the inference.

In this research, we use the ELEA (Emerging LEadership Analysis) corpus including 27 group interactions composed of 3 or 4 members. This dataset includes audio and visual data and personality traits scored from group members and external observers, such as BigFive personality impressions, and perceived leadership [20]. The Big Five model has been proposed in psychology as one capable of capturing the construction of personality [11]. In experiments, we perform binary trait level classification to evaluate our approach with previous work. Experimental results show that co-occurrent event features improve the accuracy in 8 out of 10 traits.

There are two main contributions in our paper. First, we perform co-occurrence mining in multimodal and multiparty interaction for inference of personality trait, which is an unexplored problem setting. Second, we show that using conversational context features, extracted based on co-occurrence of patterns improves the classification accuracy of several personality traits.

We present related work in Section 2. In Section 3, we present data used for inference of personality traits. Section 4 explains the method for feature representation. Section 5 explains the mining framework. Section 6 and section 7 present the experimental setting and the evaluation of our framework, respectively. We discuss the results in Section 8 and conclude this study in Section 9.

2. RELATED WORK

Our research is related to the topics of personality trait modeling, interaction mining, and multimodal recognition using contextual information.

2.1 Personality trait inference in group

There is an increasing interest towards inferring higher level concepts such as individual traits, leadership from low level, multimodal signals observed in multiparty interaction. We focus on personality trait modeling in group meetings and in this section we present related research emphasizing group interaction, without including works modeling a single person (e.g.[5]) and works modeling these concepts from dyadic interaction (e.g.[15]).

In multiparty interaction, different works looked at different variables including social roles and, personality traits. [23] proposed an approach to detect functional roles played by participants in group conversation. [22] proposed approaches for speaker role recognition in group conversation. [18] presents an analysis on personality prediction of each participant using self-reported questionnaires. [20] presents an analysis on emergent leadership in meetings. [2] presents an analysis on prediction of participant's personality trait impressions formed by external observers.

In this research, feature extraction from audio and visual data corpus is a key technique. [20] points that when the count of speech turns and the speech length of a member are larger than that of the other members, the member is likely perceived as a leader from the group members. [2] reports that the energy of the speech signal is effective to predict openness to experience, which is a BigFive personality trait. From visual data, body gestures, head gestures, and gaze are also known as important features. In particular, the amount and frequency of body motion are captured as Motion Energy Images (MEI) calculated using difference of images in time. Head gesture and gaze are approximated using head posture and motion. [10] points to visual focus of attention as a key feature to link impressions from group members. [17] also points to gaze states as effective feature to detects important statements.

In a common approach of these works, audio and visual features are calculated thorough mean, medium, min, max and X percentile from various amounts of statistics (count and length) from each pattern observed for the whole meeting or for a part of the meeting [2], [20], [17]. These feature sets are used as input data to train inference models. Though this approach often can fuse total statistics of patterns observed within a duration time, it can not capture co-occurence between multi modal patterns at each time. For example, extracting co-occurrent events between an utterance and a body motion pattern as a feature is useful to model personality traits if the utterance accompanying body gesture will make a stronger impression to the listener than utterance without the gesture. Kendon points out that it is important to analyze co-occurring multi modal patterns to understand multimodal conversation phenomenon [12]. Our objective of this study is to improve the inference accuracy of personality traits by extracting co-occurence features, which are not explored in many previous work. We explicitly discover frequent co-occurrent events from 49-dimensional time-series data observed in multimodal multiparty interaction data by using a graph clustering algorithm.

2.2 Unsupervised interaction analysis

Supervised learning is used in existing works to infer personality traits. On the other hand, unsupervised learning approaches can often find intermediate representations that help understand these higher concepts [10].

The work in [9],[10] use Latent Dirichlet Allocation (LDA) to mine context features in groups. In [10], group features called group looking (or speaking) cues are defined manually for input to LDA. Context features are extracted as topics (clusters) generated by LDA. In contrast, co-occurrence clustering as we propose here is done to discover combinations of each modal pattern, and group features are extracted automatically. The work in [4] models influence from a member to the other members by relating interactions of nonverbal pattern between group members to transition between hidden states (e.g. whose utterance starts after whose utterance) in a Markovian formulation.

In [10],[4], feature extraction is done per group to analyze these group nonverbal patterns and group performance or group composition. On the other hand, we need to compare between individuals belonging to different groups to model personality traits. We thus propose a novel data representation method to apply to a mining framework by separating nonverbal patterns of a member and those of the other members.

In [9], co-occurrence statistics are calculated in each time slice (from 30 seconds to 5 minutes) from visual focus of attention and speech state. However, exact co-occurrence patterns such as "x th utterance is overlapped with y th body movement pattern" are not extracted. In our study we discover such multimodal patterns in finer time scale to apply to the inference of personality traits. Mining a large and more diverse set of co-occurrent events is important to discover effective features however this has been unexplored in previous work.

A data mining framework has also been applied for other kind of multimodal datasets. The work in [13] applied frequent sequence mining as a feature extraction method in predicting user states (anxious, challenging, exciting, and so on) while playing games by using physiological signals, game play information, and user keystrokes. The work in [14] enhanced this framework as an unsupervised feature learning framework using deep learning. In contrast to user's playing games, we tackle in this research multimodal multiparty interaction. In general, the phenomena observed from multiparty interaction is more complex than that observed from a single participant.

3. MULTIMODAL DATA CORPUS

3.1 Dataset and tasks

We used a subset from the Emergent LEAder (ELEA) corpus [20] for this study. The subset consists of audio-visual (AV) recordings of 27 meetings, in which the participants perform a winter survival task with no roles assigned.

The participants in the task, as the survivors of an airplane crash, were asked to rank 12 items to take with them to survive as a group. Participants first ranked the items individually, then as a group. The task itself promotes interactions among the participants.

Participants discuss while being seated around a table. For sensing infrastructure, Dev-Audio Microcone, a commercial portable microphone array (green square in the left picture on Figure 1) is used to collect the audio. Two wide-angle web cameras (right blue square on Figure 1) are used for the video setup.

While the corpus was originally designed to study leadership, the personality of each individual can be made evident through the discussion and negotiation parts of the interaction. There are 102 participants in total (six meetings with three participants and 21 meetings with four participants). Each meeting lasts around 15 minutes. The synchronization of audio and video was done manually by aligning the streams using the clapping activity. More details about the ELEA AV corpus can be found in [19]. Figure 1 shows a snapshot from the data.

3.2 Personality trait impression annotations

The ELEA corpus includes personality annotation data as a result of scoring each participant via questionnaires.

Big-Five Trait Impressions from external observers: Personality impressions of the participants by the external observers were collected in [2]. These annotations include scores for the BigFive: Extraversion (Ext), Agreeableness (Agr), Conscientiousness (Con), Emotional stability (Emo), and Openness to Experience (Ope). More details about modeling can be found in [11].

The Ten Item Personality Inventory (TIPI) was used to measure the BigFive personality traits of the participants [8]. It includes two questions per trait, answered on a 7-point Likert scale. The questionnaire was done for each participant, on a one-minute segment from the meeting, which corresponds to the segment that includes the participant's longest speaking turn, and isolating the video of each participant (Only a single participant is visible). The audio on the other hand is intact and contains speech from all participants in that segment. More details can be found in [2].

Dominance and Leadership Impressions from group members The ELEA corpus also includes scores for traits relevant to the functioning of individuals with respect to dominance and leadership. After the meeting task, participants filled out a Perceived Interaction Score, that captures perceptions from participants during the interaction, in which they score every participant in the group through four items related to the following concepts: perceived leadership (PLead), perceived dominance (PDom), perceived competence (PCom) and perceived liking (PLike). Afterwards a dominance ranking (RDom) is calculated. PLead captures whether the person directs the group, imposes his or her opinion. PDom captures whether the person dominates, or is in a position of power.

Participants were asked to rank the group, giving 1 to the most dominant participant, and 3 or 4 for the less dominant, such that they have to include themselves in the ranking. More details can be found in [20].

4. MULTIMODAL FEATURE REPRESENTATION

We propose a feature representation to compare nonverbal patterns that are observed from each participant in a group. In the feature representation, we define two kinds of features as

$$NF = \{NF_m, NF_{/m}\},$$
$$NF_m = \{nf_{m,1}, \ldots, nf_{m,t}, \ldots, nf_{m,T}\}, \quad (1)$$

where NF_m, $NF_{/m}$ is time-series binary data composed of $nf_{m,t}$ and $nf_{/m,t}$, respectively, $nf_{m,t}$ is tth segment observed from a particular member m in a group and $nf_{/m,t}$ is tth segment observed from the group members except the member m. The tth event has a time length and corresponds a segment of "ON" in Figure 1. We defined an event as a segment where the feature is active. T_{ns} is the number of nonverbal patterns NF observed in the whole meeting.

On one hand, $nf_{m,t}$ represents nonverbal features extracted from mutilmodal nonverbal signals observed from an individual participant such as speech utterances, body and head motion and gaze patterns. On the other hand, $nf_{/m,t}$ represents group nonverbal features extracted from signals which are observed from all group members except the participant m. The representation captures how the participant acts when the other members execute any nonverbal activity as a joint probability of each activity by simultaneously observing nonverbal activities both of the individual participant and the other group members.

We define co-occurrence patterns as multimodal events overlapped in time. Our approach requires transforming the continuous signals (pitch, energy, and image template features) into sequences of events. In section 5, we present our data mining algorithm to find frequent co-occurrence events. In this section, we present the input audio and visual signals. The features are summarized in Table 2. We refer the reader to related papers for detailed information on audio-visual feature extraction.

4.1 Audio features

4.1.1 *Speaking turn features*

Binary segmentation is performed to capture the speaking status ST of each participant. This binary segmentation is provided by the microphone array that is used for the audio recordings, which is used for speaker diarization [20]. We define a set of segments where the speech status is on, as speaking turn set ST. The speaking turn set of each participant m in the group is denoted ST_m.

We define three type of features, $SO1$, $SO2$, $Ssil$, as group speaking turn features $ST_{/m}$. $SO1$ is a set of segments where the speech state of one group member (except m) is on. $SO2$ is a set of segments where the speech states of more than two members except m are on. $Ssil$ is a set of segments where the speech states of all members are off.

4.1.2 *Prosodic features*

Prosodic features are extracted for each individual member. Based on the binary speaker segmentation, we obtain the speech signal for

Figure 2: Multimodal feature set

ID	Features	Symbol	Description
F_1	Speaking Status (*ST*)	*ST*	Speech segments of the target person
		*SO*1	One person other than target speaks
		*SO*2	More than two people speak.
		Ssil	Silent segment
F_2	Pitch (*PI*)	*PUp, PDo*	Sign of difference between utterance t and utterance $t-1$
		PCL, PCM, PCH	Cluster index (low medium and high level) after clustering
		PCNL, PCNM, PCNH	Cluster index after clustering of normalized value
F_3	Energy (*EN*)	*EUp, EDo*	Sign of difference between utterance t and utterance
		ECL, ECM, ECH	Cluster index after clustering
		ECNL, ECNM, ECNH	Cluster index after clustering of normalized value
F_4	Head Motion (*H*)	*HMT*	Motion segments of target person
		*HMO*1	One person other than target moves
		*HMO*2	More than two people move
		HMsil	Still motion segment
F_5	Body Motion (*B*)	*BMT*	Motion segments of target person
		*BMO*1	One person other than target moves
		*BMO*2	More than two people move
		BMsil	Still motion segment
F_6	MEI (*MT*)	*MUp, MDo*	Sign of difference between segments
		MCL, MCM, MCH	Cluster index after clustering
		MCNL, MCNM, MCNH	Cluster index after clustering of normalized MEI
F_7	Gaze (*G*)	*GT*	Target person looks at person
		GTSp	Target person looks at speaker
		*GOT*1	One person looks at the target
		*GOT*2	More than two people look at the target
		MGT	Mutual gaze between target and another person
		MGO	Mutual gaze between two people other than target

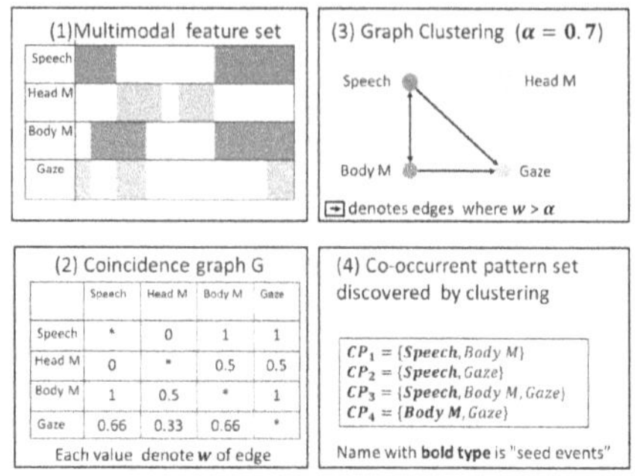

Figure 3: Example of multimodal pattern mining (A case of 4 dimentional patterns)

each participant. Overlapping speech segments are discarded, and only the segments with the participant being the sole speaker are considered for further processing. Two prosodic speech features, energy and pitch, are computed on the signal.

We convert energy and pitch into a sequence of significant increments and decrements of the signal. We calculate the sign of the difference between statistics of utterance j and utterance $j+1$. It is assumed that prosodic features change due to various reasons. For example, when a participant is likely excited, the energy of his/her utterance may increase after hearing an utterance of other participants. Based on this, we extract the sign of the difference for a prosodic signal as a feature.

Pitch samples pi_j are extracted from utterance j. We perform a statistical t-test between pi_j and pi_{j+1}. If significance exists and the mean of pi_{j+1} is larger than the mean of pi_j, we add utterance $j+1$ to a set *PUp* of utterance segments whose pitch of the current utterance is larger than that of the past utterance. We do something similar for significant decreasing differences generating a set *PDo* of utterance segments whose pitch of current utterance is small than that of past utterance. A t-test is done between energy samples en_j, en_{j+1} in the same manner. We extract an utterance segment set *EUp* where energy is increased more than past utterance, and an utterance segment set *EDo* where energy is decreased more than past utterance.

Next, we perform clustering to convert energy and pitch signals into categorical data. Clustering is done using utterances ST_m of all participants. The procedure of clustering is as follows.

1. Calculate statistics (max, min, average) of all prosodic values in each utterance as input samples for clustering.
2. K-means clustering is done using the data samples calculated from all participants.
3. Each utterance is converted to cluster index.

We set the number of clusters as 3, corresponding to low level (*CL*), medium level (*CM*) and high level (*CH*) cluster. Utterance segments clustered by pitch value are added into feature sets *PCL*, *PCM*, *PCH*. Utterance segments clustered by energy value are added into feature sets *ECL*, *ECM*, *ECH*. We also normalize the prosodic value within segments for each participant considering individual differences, and perform clustering in the same manner.

Utterance segments clustered by normalized pitch value are added into feature sets *PNCL*, *PNCM*, *PNCH*. Utterance segments clustered by normalized energy value are added into feature sets *ENCL*, *ENCM*, *ENCH*. This feature set also captures the variance of each participant. We summarize the feature set for pitch and as $PI = \{PUp, PDo, PCL, PCM, PCH, PNCL, PNCM, PNCH\}$, $EN = \{EUp, EDo, ECL, ECM, ECH, ENCL, ENCM, ENCH\}$. These feature sets, *PI* and *EN*, are calculated for the individual participants.

4.2 Visual features

4.2.1 Visual activity features

Visual activity features characterize the bodily activity of the participant. We used two different approaches to extract activity features. The first approach is based on head and body tracking and optical flow, which provides the binary head and body activity status and the amount of activity as well. As done for speech states, binary segmentation is done and an activity state set is extracted for head and body motion.

We define a set of segments where the body or head status is on, as the body activity set *B* and the head activity set *H*. We also define three types of features: *BO*1, *BO*2, *Bsil*, as group body activity features $B_{/m}$, and three types of features *HO*1, *HO*2, *Hsil*, as group head activity features $H_{/m}$ in the same manner for *ST*.

4.2.2 Motion template based features

As a second approach, we have used Motion Energy Images (MEI) [6] as descriptors of body activity. We used the length of the meeting segment to normalize the images. Motion Energy Images (MEI) are obtained by integrating each difference image from whole video clip. Significant changes of MEI have the possibility to capture behaviors related to personality traits.

Here, we calculate time-series changes of MEI with a sliding window method over the whole meeting. Time-series data of MEI is continuous and we have to segment to categorical patterns. We follow this procedure. 1: Difference images are calculated in between each frame. 2: Calculate motion energy image in windows of 1sec duration. 3: Calculate time-series MEI features with sliding windows. 4: Detect peaks of the time-series after smoothing. 5: Extract segments of MEI as intervals between peaks. 6: Follow the same procedure as that of prosody features to extract MEI-related features.

Motion template feature set *MT* is defined from segments of MEI. We extract a segment set *MUp*, where current MEI energy segment has increased compared to the past segment, and a segment set *MDo*, where MEI energy has decreased compared to the past segment. MEI segments after clustering are added into feature sets *MCL*, *MCM*, *MCH*. Furthermore, after normalization with respect to each participant, MEI energy segments after clustering are added into feature sets *MNCL*, *MNCM*, *MNCH*. We summarize the feature set for motion template as
$MT = \{MUp, MDo, MCL, MCM, MCH, MNCL, MNCM, MNCH\}$,
Feature set *MT* is calculated for the individual participants.

4.2.3 Visual focus of attention features

Visual focus of attention (VFOA) features were extracted and shared by the authors in [19], where a probabilistic framework was used to estimate the head location and pose jointly based on a state space formulation. We define a set of segments *GT* where the target participant looks at the other participants through the meeting. We also define a set of segments *GTSp* where the target participant looks at the speaker. Looking at speaker is an important signal of the listener's interest and politeness [21]. We further define two features $GOT1, GOT2$ as group attention features $G_{/m}$. $GOT1$ is a set of segments where one member looks at the member *m*. $GOT2$ is a set of segments where more than two members looks at the member *m*.

Mutual gazing is also an important feature [10]. Therefore, we explicitly define the segment set for mutual gazing (although mutual gazing is defined as co-occurrence pattern with *GT* and $GOT1,2$). We prepare two group features for mutual gazing. *MGT* is a set of segments where one member *x* looks at the member *m* and vice versa. *MGO* is a set of segments where two members y, z except the member *m* look at each other.

5. CO-OCCURRENT MULTIMODAL PATTERN MINING

In this section, we present our mining algorithm to discover co-occurrent patterns between modalities. The goal of this algorithm is to find frequent co-occurring segments from the feature sets in section 4. Co-occurrent pattern discovery is done using a graph clustering algorithm. These multimodal patterns sometimes capture the characteristics of conversation scenes more than single modal patterns. We adopt the star algorithm proposed in [3] to efficiently discover time-series co-occurring patterns from continuous time-series data for our purpose. Figure 3 shows an example of the mining algorithm. The procedure is as follows.

Input: Multimodal feature sets: *ST*, *PI*, *EN*, *H*, *B*, *MT*, *G* ((1) in Figure 3)
Output: Co-occurrent pattern set: *CP*

Step1: Construct a coincidence graph *G*. *G* is a directed graph $G = (V, E)$, Vertex *V* contains the features, *E* are the weight values calculated based on coincidence frequency between segments nf. Co-occurent pattern set *CP* is initialized as an empty set $\emptyset$ and number *n* of patterns in the set is 0.

Step2: A feature NF_k (Equation 1) in the feature set is represented by a vertex v_k. The weight value $w_{k,l}$ is represented by an edge $e_{k,l}$ (edge connecting vertex *k* to vertex *l*) is calculated as $w_{k,l} = overlap(NF_k, NF_l)/N_k$, where $overlap(NF_k, NF_l)$ is the total number of count that there is a temporal overlap between occurrences of NF_k and NF_l ((2) in Figure 3). Here, NF_k is different than NF_l (e.g. $\{NF_k, NF_l\}$ correspond to $\{ST, GT\}$, $\{SO1, HMT\}$, etc.).

For example, $overlap(ST, BT) = 80$, where 80 of total events (nf in Equation 1) in the speaking turns of the target person *ST* are overlapped temporally with the body motion segments *BT*. N_k is the number of total segments in NF_k.

Step3: Features NF_k and NF_l is grouped if weight value is more than threshold α ((3) in Figure 3). A set $\{NF_k, NF_l\}$ is extracted as a Multimodal co-occurent pattern CP_{n+1} and *n* is updated to $n+1$. Here NF_k is defined as a seed modality of the pattern CP_n. This step is done for all pairs of NF_k and NF_l.

Step4: Patterns in *CP*, which are newly discovered in Step3 are added as new features to Vertex *V* ((4) in Figure 3).

Step5: Coincidence graph is updated by re-calculating weight between CP_n and all of *NF*.

Step6: Step3 - Step5 are iterated until all the weights in *E* is less than α.

α ($0 < \alpha < 1$) is used to determine the minimum between two segments. To find many kind of features for inference, we detect various sub-graphs (e.g. Co-occurrence of 2 pairs $\{ST, GT\}$, 3 pairs $\{ST, GT, BO1\}$, etc) from the coincidence graph in Step4. If we set α as a small value, a large amount of patterns are discovered. In this study, The alpha is set manually as $\alpha = 0.8$ by considering balance of number of mined features and number of training samples.

After the mining process, total count that CP_n is observed in the whole meeting is used as a feature value for inference of personality traits. The value of feature CP_n for a particular member *m* in a group is calculated as the total count that CP_n is observed in whole meeting in the group (in feature sets $\{NF_m, NF_{/m}\}$).

6. EXPERIMENTAL SETTING

To evaluate the effectiveness of the proposed co-occurrence features, we compare the inference accuracy by a model trained using co-occurrence features with the accuracy by the same model trained using multimodal features used in previous work [2]. The personality traits include 10 variables as described in Section 3: personality trait impressions including 5 variables: Extraversion, Agreeableness, Conscientiousness, Emotional Stableness, Opennes to Experience and perceived impressions including 5 variables: Leadership, two versions of Dominance (ranked and scored), Competence, Likeness.

6.1 Setting of Co-occurrence features

Each feature corresponds to the count (frequency) of each mined event and Counts of *CP* are concatenated into one vector. The total number of dimensions is equal to the total number of mined co-occurrence events. As our dataset is rather small (102 samples) compared to the total number of mined events, we reduce the abundant mined features by the different heuristic methods.

First, we calculate cosine similarity (maximum 1 and minimum 0) between vectors of the feature value in all data samples. We merged the pairs where the similarity is more than 0.99. Second, we count the number of co-occurring events per modality, finding that this number for pitch, energy and MEI is huge because these features are likely to overlap with other patterns. We perform PCA for co-occurring features with pitch, energy and MEI. We use the cumulative energy ratio (which is the value obtained by dividing the sum of j eigenvalues by the sum of all eigenvalues) to decide the number of features, setting the cumulative energy ratio to 0.90. Totally, the number of features is reduced to 188 from 184143.

6.2 Setting of baseline feature set

A multimodal feature set is proposed in a previous research [2], which has been used for inference of personality traits by accumulating the statistics over whole meetings. This feature set has 37 dimensions, and is composed of speaking turn, energy, pitch, visual activity, MEI, and gaze features. The features are extracted from both target and others for gaze, and from only target for other modalities. These features are well engineered because these feature set includes various kind of statistics. For these features, the min, max, mean, medium, standard deviation, quantile value, count (e.g. of speaking turns) and total time length (e.g. speaking length) were calculated. The original feature set used in [2] was kindly shared for comparison purposes.

6.3 Inference task and Classification model

In [2], regression and classification tasks are tested to infer personality traits from nonverbal features. The authors of [2] reported that it is difficult to regress personality traits except the extraversion trait, because R^2 values from regression results via leave-one-out validation, are less than 0.1 for each trait. Based on these results we decide to perform classification of binary levels of personality traits. In the classification task, trait values are converted to binary values (high or low) by thresholding using median value, e.g. to represent people scoring high/low in extraversion, respectively. The trained model is evaluated by classification accuracy of test data.

To precisely compare the results obtained in [2], we followed the evaluation procedure and used ridge regression model and linear SVM as classification models in same manner with experiment in [2]. For training a ridge regression classifier, the original personality impression scores is used and the median score is used as the threshold for prediction (this method is called R_{SCR} in [2]).

In the experiments below, we use leave-one-out cross validation and report the average accuracy over all folds. We normalize the data such that each feature has zero mean and one standard deviation. The ridge parameter in ridge regression model is optimized using a cross validation scheme, with values in the range of [2, 150]. The parameters of SVM are optimized similarly with a nested cross validation scheme, with C parameter values selected from [0, 0.01, 0.1, 1].

7. EXPERIMENTAL RESULTS

Table 1 shows the classification accuracy, and the bold values indicate the highest accuracy. Only accuracies above 62.7% are considered significantly better (with 99% confidence level) than the 50% random assignment baseline.

First to fifth rows in Table 1 shows the classification results for BigFive impressions from external observers, and sixth to tenth rows in Table 1 shows the personality traits perceived from the group members. Each column corresponds to a personality trait and rows correspond to feature sets and classification methods. In each feature set, Co-occurrence feature denotes our proposal, Baseline denotes the feature set defined in [2].

For extraversion and agreebleness, we obtain best accuracies as high as 67.6% using SVM, 68.6% using Ridge Regression, with proposed features, respectively. In contrast, [2] reports that the results for BigFive are significantly different than the random baseline for only extraversion with all features. In particular, the model trained with co-occurrence features improve the Agreeableness accuracy in about 10% compared to the feature set proposed in [2]. In addition, though the results for conscientiousness and emotion stability are not significantly different than the random baseline, the use of both features ((3) Fusing) improves the accuracy about 3% and 2% respectively more than that with the feature set proposed in [2]. For Opennes to Experience, we obtained the best accuracy as high as 61.7% using the model trained with the feature set of [2].

For both perceived competence and ranked dominance, we obtain better than the feature set defined in [2] as high as 66.6% and 64.7% using Ridge regression with proposed features. On the other hand, for perceived dominance and perceived likeness, the result of model with feature set in [2] is better. For perceived leadership, the results with feature set in [2] and our feature set are equal (72.5%).

Furthermore, the better classification model varies for each trait. Ridge regression is effective for agreeableness, emotion stability, perceived dominance, perceived competence. Linear SVM is effective for extraversion, conscientiousness, openness to experience, perceived likeness. Results with both classification models are equal for perceived leadership, ranked dominance. In summary, the proposed co-occurrence features obtained best results for 5 traits, which are significantly better than the random baseline, and obtained equal or the better results than the feature set defined in [2] for 7 traits.

8. DISCUSSION

8.1 Contribution of specific co-occurrence

In this section, we analyze the contribution of specific co-occurrence features to classification performance. Mined co-occurrence can be classified into two types. One is defined as a combination of modalities of the subject (target) participant, such as "speaking with head gesture". We call this feature set as "Self Context". The second type is defined as a combination of nonverbal patterns observed from multiple people, such as mutual gaze. We form the "Self Context" event set by removing the second type events from all events.

Next, multimodal features can be also classified into two types. One is the feature set extracted from "On/Off Features" : Speech turn ST, Body motion B, Head motion H, Gaze state G ($F_{1,4,5,7}$ in Table 2) which means whether or not the pattern is observed. The second is the categorical feature set (including three levels: High, Middle, Low, change of time-series) extracted from continuous data: audio pitch P, audio energy E, motion energy image M. The feature set extracted from signal dataset:$\{P, E, M\}$ ($F_{2,3,6}$ in Table 2) can extract detailed information. We obtain the feature event set by removing the events composed from a combination of signal dataset from all events. Table 2 shows the classification results with each co-occurrence feature set: "Self Context", "On/Off Features", and All (Both on/off and categorical features). The table also shows the best results obtained with baseline feature set in Table 1.

From Table 2, classification accuracy using all co-occurrence features is the best for agreeableness and perceived competence. On the other hand, the table shows that best classification model is obtained with features extracted from on/off features for conscientiousness, perceived leadership, ranked dominance and with "Self Context" for emotional stability. For extraversion and perceived dominance, the results with features extracted from on/off features and "Self Context" are equal and best with 69.6% and 67.6%, respectively.

The proposed co-occurrence features with on/off data obtained best results for 5 traits, which are significantly better than the ran-

Table 1: Classification accuracy for 10 personality traits (Ridge and L-SVM denote Ridge regression based classifier and Linear SVM respectively)

		Extra-version	Agree-ableness	Conscien-tiousness	Emotional stability	Opennes to Experience	Perceived Leadership	Perceived Dominance	Perceived Competence	Perceived Likeness	Ranked Dominance
(1) Baseline [2]	Ridge	66.67	58.82	51.96	51.96	54.90	**72.55**	**65.69**	52.94	60.78	51.96
	L-SVM	63.44	52.94	52.94	53.92	**61.73**	67.65	60.78	52.94	**64.71**	48.04
(2) Co-occurrence Features	Ridge	64.71	**68.63**	53.92	53.92	57.84	69.61	57.84	**66.67**	53.92	**64.71**
	L-SVM	**67.65**	64.71	50.00	46.08	48.04	**72.55**	61.76	64.71	53.92	**64.71**
(3) Fusing (1) + (2)	Ridge	57.84	60.78	50.98	**55.88**	53.92	67.64	56.86	64.71	55.88	59.80
	L-SVM	66.67	55.88	**55.88**	48.04	43.14	59.80	63.73	59.80	54.90	55.88

Table 2: Classification accuracy for 10 personality traits with various kinds of co-occurence features (Co-occurence features (Self Context, On/Off Features and All) VS Best of baseline [2])

Co-occurrence Features		Extra-version	Agree-ableness	Conscien-tiousness	Emotional stability	Opennes to Experience	Perceived Leadership	Perceived Dominance	Perceived Competence	Perceived Likeness	Ranked Dominance
(1-1) Self context	Ridge	**69.61**	60.78	47.06	47.06	52.94	62.75	60.78	60.78	54.90	62.75
	L-SVM	56.86	65.69	42.16	**56.86**	54.90	64.71	**67.65**	55.88	59.80	58.82
(1-2) On/Off Features ($F_{1,4,5,7}$ in Table 2)	Ridge	**69.61**	63.73	**59.80**	55.88	57.84	**74.51**	52.94	59.80	50.98	**68.63**
	L-SVM	60.78	56.86	50.98	48.04	56.86	69.61	**67.65**	58.82	43.14	63.73
(1-3) All ((2)in Table 1)	Ridge	64.71	**68.63**	53.92	53.92	57.84	69.61	57.84	**66.67**	53.92	64.71
	L-SVM	67.65	64.71	50.00	46.08	48.04	72.55	61.76	64.71	53.92	64.71
Best of Baseline [2]		66.67	58.82	52.94	53.92	**61.73**	72.55	65.69	52.94	**64.71**	51.96

dom baseline, and obtained equal or better results than the feature set defined in [2] for 8 traits. The feature set also improves the accuracy about 7%and 3% for conscientiousness and emotion stability respectively more than best accuracy with the feature set proposed in [2]. This results shows that combinations of only on/off features contribute positively to classification performance in general.

In summary, the proposed co-occurrence features with all features, on/off features and self context features obtained equal or better results than the feature set defined in [2] for 7, 8, 6 traits in 10 traits, respectively. These results show the promise of our approach to improve the inference accuracy of personality traits compared to simple feature sets obtained by accumulated statistics of nonverbal patterns observed from a whole meeting.

8.2 Analysis of Co-occurrence features

We analyze the relationship between these co-occurrence events and each personality trait by correlation analysis. We use the Pearson product-moment correlation for relationship analysis between each trait and the mined patterns with threshold $\alpha = 0.7$.

We discuss for the results of correlation analysis for extraversion, which co-occurrence events were more effective than previous work. Note that there are correlations with other traits as well, but are omitted for space reasons. As the result of correlation analysis, a total of 27586 events (including overlap of events between traits) have significant correlation with $p < 0.1$ for extraversion among 28427 mined events.

To visualize event co-occurrence, we show the co-occurrence matrix in Figure 4, where each value shows the count of each event which has significant correlation with the extraversion trait. Each column corresponds to the type of "seed events" (i.e. the event is used as reference of starting point in mining process) and each row corresponds to the type of event co-occuring with the seed events. In each matrix, red and blue region denotes total frequency of co-occurrence events which has significant positive and negative correlations, respectively. If there are N events such as ith pattern (e.g. ST) co-occurs to jth and kth patterns in co-occurrence events which are positively correlated with extraversion, value (i,i), (i,j), (i,k) in the matrix is N (colored with red) in Figure 4, and these values are $-N$ (colored with blue) where these events have negative correlation. The symbol > 99 denotes when the value is larger than 99. The symbol in each column and row corresponds to that in Table 2. We observe high co-occurrence of nonverbal patterns and the co-occurrence patterns significantly correlated to extraversion from Figure 4. These patterns relate to the traits differently. Some patterns are positively correlated and some patterns are negatively correlated. In the following paragraphs, we observe the relationship of the correlation between co-occurrence patterns and the trait.

Speech (col.1-4): In red regions, speech turn of target persons (ST) is likely to co-occur with that of the others ($SO1$), head motion of target (HMT) and the other. In blue regions, silence ($Ssil$) is likely to co-occur with head motion of others ($HMO1$) and still body motion ($BMsil$) The results show that participants who are perceived as extraverted likely speak with head gestures, start to speak while another member speaks and is given focus of attention by the other members. When there is a participant who is not perceived as extraverted in a group, more silent segments are observed during the interaction.

Head and Body motion (col.5-12): Events co-occurred with head motion are negatively correlated to extraversion (blue). On the contrary, events co-occurred with body motion are positively correlated to extraversion (red).

Gaze (col.13-18): Participants who are perceived as extraverted are likely to look at another person (GT) and receive attention from another person ($GOT1,2$). When there is a participant who is not perceived as extraverted, mutual gazing between the others are likely observed.

8.3 From co-occurence to time-series

Through the experiments, we showed that co-occurence features are effective to predict personality traits. The result leads to an open question. The annotators of personality traits do not observe all of visual interaction patterns between the target participant and the group; nevertheless, the patterns improve the classification of the traits. A hypothesis is that personality or nonverbal behavior of the target influences the nonverbal behavior of the other participants.

As an approach to answer the question, we should analyze the time-series structure of co-occurence patterns (e.g. a group head gesture is observed after (or before) the target's utterance), the interval between patterns and their possible causal relations. This structure might reveal which individual patterns influences (or is influenced by) the group activity. Therefore, a future direction in this research is to analyze the structure in multimodal multiparty

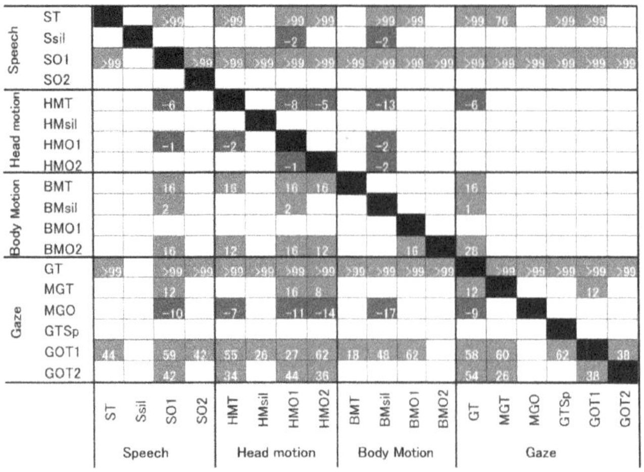

Figure 4: Co-occurrence matrix between multimodal features, where each value is the count of the co-occurrence pattern having significant correlation ($p < 0.1$) with extraversion trait, symbol > 99 denotes when the value is larger than 99 and red (blue) color denotes positive (negative) correlation pair.

conversation with reference of time-series reasoning algorithms [1] and an effective search method for structural temporal multimodal data [16].

9. CONCLUSIONS

We presented a novel feature extraction framework from mutli-party multimodal conversation for inference of personality traits. Our framework represents multimodal features as the combination of each participants' nonverbal activity and also the group activity. Frequently co-occurring events are discovered using graph clustering. We applied the framework for inference of 10 personality trait impressions on the ELEA corpus. Experimental results show that classifiers trained with co-occurring features produced higher accuracy than other features proposed in recent works for 8 of the traits and are statistically better than random for a total of 6 traits of personality traits. In addition, co-occurrence features provide improvement on the classification accuracy ranging from 2% to 17%.

Our feature representation captures the interplay between the nonverbal behavior of an individual and her/his interactions, and can be used for feature extraction for other types of conversation (e.g. dyadic interaction). To validate the versatility of proposed framework, we plan to apply this framework for multimodal datasets observed from other kind of conversations to infer various types of higher attributes such as conversational roles and persuasiveness in the same manner. We also plan to enhance this framework to time-series structure mining. To improve the classification accuracy, using label information for mining is also part of future work (e.g. discriminative feature extraction).

10. ACKNOWLEDGMENTS

We thank the support of the SNSF through the SOBE (PZ00P2 136811), UBImpressed projects and JSPS KAKENHI (25730132, 15K00300, 25280076).

11. REFERENCES

[1] J. F. Allen. Maintaining knowledge about temporal intervals. *Communications of the ACM*, 26(11):832–843, 1983.

[2] O. Aran and D. Gatica-Perez. One of a kind: Inferring personality impressions in meetings. In *Proc. of ACM ICMI*, ICMI '13, pages 11–18. ACM, 2013.

[3] J. Aslam, K. Pelekhov, and D. Rus. A practical clustering algorithm for static and dynamic information organization. In *Proc. of ACM-SIAM Symposium on Discrete Algorithms*, SODA '99, pages 51–60, 1999.

[4] U. Avci and O. Aran. Effect of nonverbal behavioral patterns on the performance of small groups. In *Proc. of workshop on Understanding and Modeling Multiparty, Multimodal Interactions*, pages 9–14. ACM, 2014.

[5] O. Celiktutan, F. Eyben, E. Sariyanidi, H. Gunes, and B. Schuller. Maptraits 2014 - the first audio/visual mapping personality traits challenge - an introduction: Perceived personality and social dimensions. In *Proc. of ACM ICMI*, ICMI '14, pages 529–530, New York, NY, USA, 2014. ACM.

[6] J. W. Davis and A. F. Bobick. The representation and recognition of human movement using temporal templates. In *Proc. of IEEE CVPR*, pages 928–934. IEEE, 1997.

[7] D. Gatica-Perez. Automatic nonverbal analysis of social interaction in small groups: A review. *Image Vision Computing*, 27(12):1775–1787, nov 2009.

[8] S. D. Gosling, P. J. Rentfrow, and W. B. Swann. A very brief measure of the big-five personality domains. *Journal of Research in Personality*, 37:504–528, 2003.

[9] D. Jayagopi and D. Gatica-Perez. Mining group nonverbal conversational patterns using probabilistic topic models. *IEEE Trans. on Multimedia*, 12(8):790–802, 2010.

[10] D. B. Jayagopi, D. Sanchez-Cortes, K. Otsuka, J. Yamato, and D. Gatica-Perez. Linking speaking and looking behavior patterns with group composition, perception, and performance. In *Proc. of ACM ICMI*, pages 433–440, 2012.

[11] O. P. John and S. Srivastava. The big five trait taxonomy: History, measurement, and theoretical perspectives. *Handbook of personality: Theory and research*, 2(1999):102–138, 1999.

[12] A. Kendon. *Gesture: Visible Action as Utterance*. Cambridge University Press, 2004.

[13] H. P. Martínez and G. N. Yannakakis. Mining multimodal sequential patterns: A case study on affect detection. In *Proc. of ACM ICMI*, pages 3–10. ACM, 2011.

[14] H. P. Martínez and G. N. Yannakakis. Deep multimodal fusion: Combining discrete events and continuous signals. In *Proc. of ACM ICMI*, pages 34–41, 2014.

[15] A. Metallinou, A. Katsamanis, and S. Narayanan. Tracking continuous emotional trends of participants during affective dyadic interactions using body language and speech information. *Image and Vision Computing*, 31(2):137–152, feb 2013.

[16] C. Miller, L.-P. Morency, and F. Quek. Structural and temporal inference search (stis): Pattern identification in multimodal data. In *Proc. of ACM ICMI*, pages 101–108, 2012.

[17] F. Nihei, Y. I. Nakano, Y. Hayashi, H.-H. Hung, and S. Okada. Predicting influential statements in group discussions using speech and head motion information. In *Proc. of ACM ICMI*, ICMI '14, pages 136–143, 2014.

[18] F. Pianesi, N. Mana, A. Cappelletti, B. Lepri, and M. Zancanaro. Multimodal recognition of personality traits in social interactions. In *Proc. of ACM ICMI*, ICMI '08, pages 53–60. ACM, 2008.

[19] D. Sanchez-Cortes, O. Aran, D. B. Jayagopi, M. S. Mast, and D. Gatica-Perez. Emergent leaders through looking and speaking: from audio-visual data to multimodal recognition. *Journal on Multimodal User Interfaces*, 7(1-2):39–53, 2013.

[20] D. Sanchez-Cortes, O. Aran, M. S. Mast, and D. Gatica-Perez. A nonverbal behavior approach to identify emergent leaders in small groups. *IEEE Trans. on Multimedia*, 14(3):816–832, 2012.

[21] L. A. Turner, L. H. Perry, and H. M. Sterk. *Constructing and reconstructing gender: The links among communication, language, and gender*. SUNY Press, 1992.

[22] A. Vinciarelli. Speakers role recognition in multiparty audio recordings using social network analysis and duration distribution modeling. *IEEE Trans. on Multimedia*, 9(6):1215–1226, 2007.

[23] M. Zancanaro, B. Lepri, and F. Pianesi. Automatic detection of group functional roles in face to face interactions. In *Proc. of ACM ICMI*, pages 28–34. ACM, 2006.

Evaluating Speech, Face, Emotion and Body Movement Time-series Features for Automated Multimodal Presentation Scoring*

Vikram Ramanarayanan
ETS Research
90 New Montgomery St
San Francisco, CA
vramanarayanan@ets.org

Chee Wee Leong
ETS Research
600 Rosedale Road
Princeton, NJ
cleong@ets.org

Lei Chen
ETS Research
600 Rosedale Road
Princeton, NJ
lchen@ets.org

Gary Feng
ETS Research
600 Rosedale Road
Princeton, NJ
gfeng@ets.org

David Suendermann-Oeft
ETS Research
90 New Montgomery St
San Francisco, CA
suendermann-oeft@ets.org

ABSTRACT

We analyze how fusing features obtained from different multimodal data streams such as speech, face, body movement and emotion tracks can be applied to the scoring of multimodal presentations. We compute both time-aggregated and time-series based features from these data streams—the former being statistical functionals and other cumulative features computed over the entire time series, while the latter, dubbed histograms of cooccurrences, capture how different prototypical body posture or facial configurations co-occur within different time-lags of each other over the evolution of the multimodal, multivariate time series. We examine the relative utility of these features, along with curated speech stream features in predicting human-rated scores of multiple aspects of presentation proficiency. We find that different modalities are useful in predicting different aspects, even outperforming a naive human inter-rater agreement baseline for a subset of the aspects analyzed.

Keywords

multimodal analysis, speech recognition, emotion tracking, motion capture, face tracking, presentation assessment

1. INTRODUCTION

Accurate assessment of performance in presentational skills is gaining importance in educational institutions and within workplaces, where the effectiveness and delivery of presentation tasks are critical in securing teacher licensure, job offers, business contracts, etc. Multimodal data capture techniques based on video, audio and motion feeds provide a rich source of information for such assessment, but the complexity of these data streams brings with it a need for signal analysis tools to automatically process and make sense of this data.

Researchers have made many advances towards understanding and modeling these multimodal data streams. For example, Naim et al. [10] analyzed job interview videos of internship-seeking students and found, using machine learning techniques, that prosody, language and facial expression features were good predictors of human ratings of desirable interview traits such as excitement, friendliness or engagement. Nguyen et al. [11] proposed a computational framework to predict the hiring decision using non-verbal behavioral cues extracted from a dataset of 62 interview videos. While there is much work on automatic recognition of one or more social cues and verbal and nonverbal behavioral traits in the speech and larger multimodal analysis communities (see for example [9, 12, 14, 15]), this problem has been also been highlighted as a particularly important one, evidenced by a number of challenges at international conferences on related topics [17, 18]. Recently [2] also presented a framework for collecting multimodal data of subjects giving presentations for purposes of automated assessment. They further presented preliminary results suggesting that basic features in the speech content and delivery, and movements related to the head, body and hands significantly predicted holistic human ratings of public speaking skills. While those works focus on (i) time-aggregated, and (ii) hand-selected features that can each have an explicit interpretation, in this paper we focus on time-series features that are also motivated from an interpretability standpoint, but are relatively high-dimensional, since they have to encapsulate information about the evolution of the entire time-series. In addition, we build upon and extend this work to predict not only a holistic score of presentation proficiency, but other aspects as well, using a combination of features derived from speech, visual and Kinect data.

ICMI '15 November 09 - 13, 2015, Seattle, WA, USA

ACM 978-1-4503-3912-4/15/11 ...$15.00.
DOI: http://dx.doi.org/10.1145/2818346.2820765

Table 1: *Performance standards adapted from the Public Speaking Competence Rubric (PSCR) [16] that human raters were asked to score each multimodal presentation on.*

Score Dimension	Shorthand	Description of Item Competency
1	Intro	Formulate an introduction that orients the audience to the topic and speaker
2	Org	Use an effective organizational pattern
3	Conc	Develop a conclusion that reinforces the thesis and provides psychological closure
4	WC	Demonstrate a careful choice of words
5	VE	Effectively use vocal expression and paralanguage to engage the audience
6	NVB	Demonstrate nonverbal behavior that reinforces the message
7	AudAdap	Successfully adapt the presentation to the audience
8	VisAid	Skillfully make use of visual aids
9	Persuasion	Construct an effectual persuasive message with credible evidence
10	Holistic	Overall holistic performance

Despite the research advances made so far in multimodal signal analysis and presentation scoring, there is little work that explicitly models the temporal evolution of these signals and exploits this information for presentation scoring and understanding. Explicitly modeling temporal information in such data is important because a person's presentation competency need not stay constant over the course of the presentation – he/she could get fatigued over time, or be more nervous at the very beginning (resulting in repetitive, cyclic fidgeting behavior), but gradually settle into a comfort zone later. For similar reasons his/her body language and emotional state can also fluctuate over the time series. However, current feature extraction approaches that aggregate information across time are not able to explicitly model temporal cooccurrence patterns; consider for instance that a certain prototypical body posture follows a second particular posture in a definitive pattern during certain parts of the presentation. Capturing such patterns might help us (i) explicitly understand the predictive power of different features (such as the occurrence of a given emotion) in temporal context (such as how often did this emotional state occur given the previous occurrence of another emotional state), thus allowing us to (ii) obtain features that are more interpretable. It is this gap that we attempt to bridge in this study. Specifically, we propose a feature based on histograms of cooccurrences [19, 20, 13] that models how different "template" body postures or facial expressions co-occur within different time lags of each other in a particular time series. Such a feature explicitly takes into account the temporal evolution of face/body posture and facial features in different presentation contexts. This feature has been previously shown to perform well on phone classification tasks [13] as well as for unsupervised pattern discovery [19, 20]. We aim to explore how much of a benefit such time-series-based modeling can provide in assessment of presentation and interview performance.

The rest of the paper is organized as follows: Section 2 goes into the details of the multimodal data corpus, including the tasks, data collection and processing, and human scoring of different aspects of presentation proficiency. We then describe the different Kinect and speech-based features in Section 3, followed by the results of the regression experiments for presentation score prediction using these features in Section 4.

2. DATA

2.1 Assessment Tasks and Multimodal Data Collection

Five public speaking tasks were utilized for data collection. Among these tasks, the first one, task A, was an "ice-breaker", in which the speaker introduced him or herself; this task is not analyzed due to the personally identifiable information involved. Tasks B and C were modeled after prepared informational speeches, in which the speaker was given a pre-prepared slide deck and up to 10 minutes to prepare for the presentation. Task B was a business presentation, where the speaker was to present a financial report. Task C is a simulated teaching task on a topic targeting middle school students. The other two tasks were persuasive and impromptu speeches. Task D asked speakers to consider a movie they did not like but nonetheless recommend it to others. Task E asked speakers to consider a place inconvenient to live in and discuss the benefits of living there. Note that there has no visual aid for for Tasks D and E. Figures 1 and 2 show examples of the different multivariate data streams recorded.

We collected multimodal data using the following equipment and software tools: (a) Microsoft Kinect (Windows Version 1) for recording *3D* body motions, (b) Brekel Pro Body Kinect tracking software (v1.30 64 bit version) for recording 58 body joints' motion traces in the Biovision hierarchical data format (BVH), and (c) a JVC Everio GZ-HM35BUSD digital camcorder for audio/video recording. Note that the camcorder was mounted together with Kinect on a tripod. Both Kinect and camcorder were placed 1.83m away from the front of the speaking zone that was marked on the ground. Additionally, during Task B and C, a SMART Board projector system was used to show the PowerPoint slides.

17 volunteers were recruited from within a non-profit organization, with ten male participants and seven female participants. Seven of the participants were experienced public speakers from the Toastmasters Club. The rest varied widely in their experience in public speaking. After being familiarized with the recording equipment, participants were informed that they were expected to speak for 4 to 5 minutes for Task B and C and 2 to 3 minutes for Task D and E. For Tasks B and C, which involved PowerPoint slides, they were given 10 minute to prepare for their presentation. They

Figure 1: Example of face tracking.

were not allowed to bring notes during the presentation. In Task D and E, the participants were given no preparation time. They would start speaking as soon as they were given the topic of the impromptu speech. Before each recording, the speaker was asked to clap, which served as a signal synchronizing the multimodal data. Data from 3 speakers were lost due to equipment failure. In total, we obtained 56 presentations from 14 speakers (4 per speaker) with complete multimodal recordings. After getting raw recordings from our lab sessions, the motion and video data streams were synchronized.

2.2 Human Rating

Since the ultimate goal of this study will be developing a valid assessment for measuring public speaking skills via presenters' multimodal behaviors, we chose the Public Speaking Competence Rubric (PSCR) [16] as an assessment rubric due to its favorable psychometric properties. Using the PCSR tailored to our tasks, human raters scored these presentation videos along 10 dimensions that represent various aspects of presentation proficiency on a five-point Likert scale from 0 to 4 [16]. See Table 1 for the complete list of scoring dimensions.

Five raters were recruited from within an educational testing company. Two expert raters had background in oral communication/public speaking instruction at the higher education level. The other three (non-expert raters) had extensive experience in scoring essays, but not in scoring public speaking performances. For reliability purposes, the presentations were double-scored. In the event that the scores between two raters were discrepant, the following adjudication process was used to generate final scores. If the first two raters *did not* agree with each other, a third rater (expert) was brought in to make another judgment, and the final score assigned was the average of all three scores. However, in the event that the first two raters agreed with each other, that score was used as the final score.

2.3 Head pose and eye gaze

A successful presentation entails speaker engagement with the audience, which translates to head postures and eye gazes that are necessarily directed towards the audience. Here, we extract a set of features that target these aspects of the presentation. Head postures are approximated using the rotation attribute (i.e., pitch, yaw, and roll) of the head through Visage's SDK FaceTrack[1], a robust head and face tracking engine. See Figure 1. The tracking is activated if and only if the detector has detected a face in the current frame. Additionally, gaze directions are approximated through the *gazeDirectionGlobal* attribute of the Visage tracker SDK, which tracks gaze directions taking into account both head pose and eye rotation. Note that, different from head rotation, gaze directions represent estimated "eyeball" directions regardless of head postures, and can potentially measure a speaker's level of engagement with the audience. Thus, for each presentation, we used the time evolution of basic head pose measurements (Cartesian X, Y, Z coordinates along with pitch, yaw, and roll) as well as gaze tracking information over the entire presentation to extract features.

[1]http://www.visagetechnologies.com

2.4 Emotion tracking

Facial expressions from presenters also contribute to an effective presentation. Therefore, we utilized an off-the-shelf emotion detection toolkit, Emotient's FACET SDK[2], to analyze facial expressions. FACET outputs the intensity (ranging from 0 to 1) and confidence values for seven primary emotions (i.e., anger, contempt, disgust, joy, fear, sadness and surprise). See Figure 2. We primarily focus on the time-evolution of the estimated intensities of different emotional states for each presentation in order to compute features. Note that we faced certain technical challenges during emotion intensity tracking, such as: (a) the presenters' faces were relatively small as compared to the screen size due to the large distance from the camera, (b) considerable background brightness from using a SmartBoard during the informative task, and (c) that presenters frequently turned their heads during their presentations, which sometimes resulted in inaccurate tracking output. However, since we are considering the entire time series of emotion data as opposed to any one particular frame, we hope to minimize the effects of tracking errors.

3. METHOD

3.1 Computing time-aggregated Kinect features

For time-aggregated Kinect features, we computed statistical functionals of certain body point markers that correlated the best with the human-rated holistic scores and that captured the degree of locomotion and hand movement. A basic feature set was extracted based on the statistical functionals (such as the mean and standard deviations of the hip markers, hand movement markers and their speeds).

3.2 Computing histograms of co-occurrences (HoC) features

Recall that one of the primary goals of this work is to investigate the efficacy of time-series features computed on different multimodal time series vis-a-vis scoring of multimodal presentations. The motivation is that explicitly examining and modeling the evolution of each of these time series will result in richer features as opposed to time-aggregated features. With this in mind, we elucidate below a general methodology to compute such a feature called histograms of cooccurrences (or HoC) that can be applied to any multivariate time-series – in this paper we compute this feature for the Kinect, Face/Gaze and Emotion data streams. Note that we compute *one* high-dimensional HoC feature vector for each time-series; this is particularly useful in cases like ours, where we have one rating for an entire time-series. Further, the advantage of this feature vector over conventional time-aggregated one is that it explicitly encapsulates information regarding temporal co-occurrence patterns; so, for example, it would model how often a certain prototypical body posture (such as folded hands) follows a second prototypical posture (say, an open stance) in a definitive pattern during different parts of the presentation.

So that being said, the idea behind the histogram of cooccurrence (HoC) feature is to count the number of times different prototypical body postures co-occur with each other *at different time lags* over the course of the time series. As

[2]http://www.emotient.com

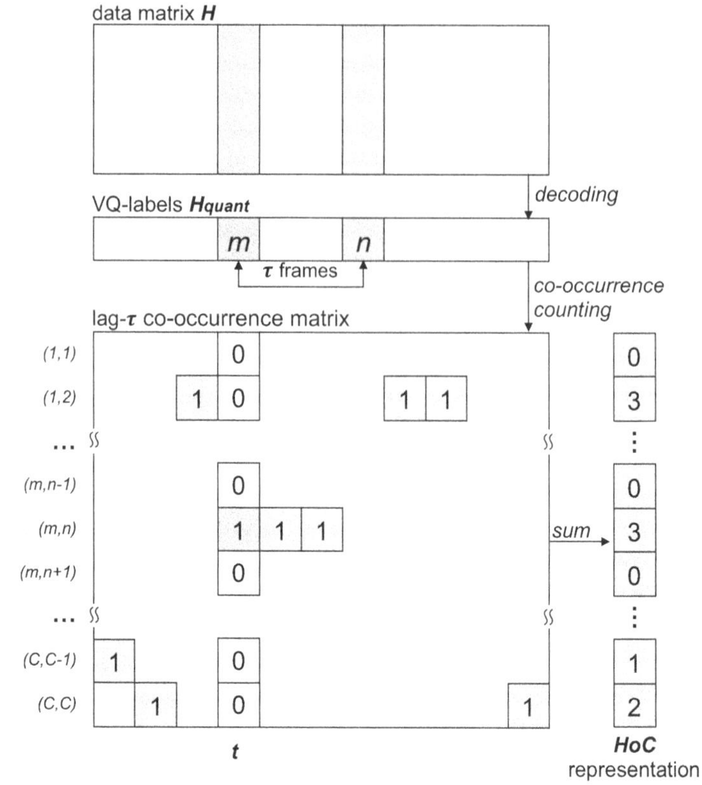

Figure 3: Schematic depiction of the computation of histograms of cooccurrences (HoC) (adapted from [13]). For a chosen lag value, τ, and a time step t, if we find labels m and n occurring τ time steps apart (marked in gold), we mark the entry of the lag-τ cooccurrence matrix corresponding to row (m, n) and the tth column with a 1 (corresponding entry also marked in gold). We sum across the columns of this matrix (across time) to obtain the lag-τ HoC representation.

to what these prototypical body postures are – while this is an interesting research question in itself, for the purposes of this paper we use cluster centroids derived from simple K-means clustering on the space of body postures (in the training dataset) as prototypical body postures. We experimented with different cluster sizes $(16, 32, 64)$ and found that 32 clusters gave us the best empirical performance on the prediction task described below.

Once we perform this clustering, we can replace each frame of the input time series data matrix $\mathbf{H}$ with the best matching cluster label (corresponding to the cluster to which it belongs). This way, the data matrix is now represented by a single row vector of cluster labels, $\mathbf{H}_{quant}$. A HoC-representation of *lag* τ is then defined as a vector where each entry corresponds to the number of times all pairs of cluster labels are observed τ frames apart. In other words, we construct a vector of lag-τ co-occurrences where each entry (m, n) signifies the number of times that the input sequence of activation frames is encoded into a cluster label m at time t (in the row vector H_{quant}), while encoded into cluster label n at time $t + \tau$ [19, 20, 13]. By stacking all (m, n) combinations, each interval can be represented by a

Table 2: *Speaking proficiency features extracted by our speech rating engine, SpeechRater.*

Category	Sub-category	# of Features	Example Features
Prosody	Fluency	24	This category includes features based on the number of words per second, number of words per chunk, number of silences, average duration of silences, frequency of long pauses ($\geq$ 0.5 sec.), number of filled pauses (*uh* and *um*). See [22] for detailed descriptions of these features.
	Intonation & Stress	11	This category includes basic descriptive statistics (mean, minimum, maximum, range, standard deviation) for the pitch and power measurements for the utterance.
	Rhythm	26	This category includes features based on the distribution of prosodic events (promincences and boundary tones) in an utterance as detected by a statistical classifier (overall percentages of prosodic events, mean distance between events, mean deviation of distance between events) [22] as well as features based on the distribution of vowel, consonant, and syllable durations (overall percentages, standard deviation, and Pairwise Variability Index) [5].
Pronunciation	Likihood-based	8	This category includes features based on the acoustic model likelihood scores generated during forced alignment with a native speaker acoustic model [6].
	Confidence-based	2	This category includes two features based on the ASR confidence score: the average word-level confidence score and the time-weighted average word-level confidence score [7].
	Duration	1	This category includes a feature that measures the average difference between the vowel durations in the utterance and vowel-specific means based on a corpus of native speech [6].
Grammar	Location of Disfluencies	6	This category includes features based on the frequency of between-clause silences and edit disfluencies compared to within-clause silences and edit disfluencies [3],[4].
Audio Quality	–	2	This category includes two scores based on MFCC features that assess the probability that the audio file has audio quality problems or does not contain speech input [8].

single column vector where the elements express the sum of all C^2 possible lag-τ co-occurrences (where C is the number of clusters; in our case, 32). See Figure 3 for a schematic of the HoC feature computations. We can repeat the procedure for different values of τ, and stack the results into one "supervector". Note however, that the dimensionality of the HoC feature increases by a factor of C^2 for each lag value τ that we want to consider. In our case, we empirically found that choosing four lag values of 1 to 10 frames (corresponding to 100-1000ms) gave an optimal prediction performance on regression experiments described below.

3.3 Computing speech features

Regarding measuring speech delivery skills demonstrated in public speaking, we included features widely used in automated speech scoring research area, covering diverse measurements among lexical usage, fluency, pronunciation, prosody, and so on. In particular, following the feature extraction method described in [6], we used *SpeechRater*, a speech rating system that processes speech and its associated transcription to generate a series of features on the multiple dimensions of speaking skills, e.g., speaking rate, prosodic variations, pausing profile, and pronunciation, which typically is measured by Goodness of Pronunciation (GOP) [21] or its derivatives. For more details on these features, please see Table 2.

3.4 Regression experiments

We used linear support vector machines (SVM) to perform regression experiments [1] on each of the 10 scoring dimensions with leave-one-speaker-out (or 14-fold) cross-validation. We experimented with both linear as well as radial basis function (RBF) kernels and empirically found that the former performed better on the prediction task. This could be due to the large dimensionality of the HoC feature space. We further tuned hyperparameters using a grid-search method.

4. OBSERVATIONS AND RESULTS

Table 3 lists the performance of various feature sets in predicting different human-rated dimensions of the multimodal presentation. We compare the performance of several feature sets—speech features obtained from SpeechRater, time-aggregated Kinect features, time-series HoC-based Kinect, Face and Emotion features as well as their combinations—as measured by the magnitude of Pearson correlation with the final human-adjudicated score. We also present, the Pearson correlations between the first and second human raters (denoted for $\rho_{R_1R_2}$), and finally, for benchmarking purposes, the Pearson correlation between each of the *individual* human raters' scores and the final human-adjudicated score. These last two correlation numbers can be thought of as a upper bound on the prediction performance.

Table 3: *Performance of various feature sets in predicting ten different aspects of multimodal presentation proficiency. The numbers represent Pearson correlations with the final human-adjudicated score (except for the row enclosed by dashed lines, which represents Pearson correlations between scores predicted by human raters 1 and 2, $\rho_{R_1R_2}$). The best machine score in each dimension relative to $\rho_{R_1R_2}$ are marked in* **bold**. *Also shown as a reference benchmark, is the Pearson correlations between each of the raters (1,2) and the final human-adjudicated score.*

Rater	Feature Set	1 Intro	2 Org	3 Conc	4 WC	5 VE	6 NVB	7 AudAdap	8 VisAid	9 Persuasion	10 Holistic
Machine	Kinect HoC	0.13	0.14	0.16	**0.23**	0.01	0.25	0.06	0.66	0.24	0.03
	Kinect Aggregated	0.12	**0.53**	0.09	0.08	0.16	0.26	0.31	0.03	0.11	0.12
	Speech	0.28	0.34	0.03	0.12	0.37	0.22	0.30	0.75	**0.48**	0.44
	Kinect Both	0.13	0.35	0.19	**0.23**	0.01	0.27	0.18	0.69	0.25	0.01
	Speech + Kinect	0.20	0.17	0.16	0.16	0.23	0.08	0.07	0.82	0.34	0.31
	Face HoC	**0.45**	0.39	0.09	0.09	0.33	0.39	**0.47**	0.16	**0.49**	**0.69**
	Emotion HoC	0.21	0.14	0.49	0.20	0.06	**0.65**	0.26	0.01	0.13	0.03
	Speech + Face HoC	0.39	0.01	**0.52**	0.05	0.25	0.05	0.13	0.03	0.27	0.03
	Speech + Emo HoC	0.36	0.04	0.47	0.15	0.03	0.01	0.07	0.03	0.32	0.02
	All	0.15	0.18	0.18	0.09	0.29	0.08	0.06	0.79	0.34	0.36
Inter-rater agreement, $\rho_{R_1R_2}$		0.24	0.33	0.48	0.11	**0.60**	0.40	0.15	**0.88**	0.02	0.39
Human	Rater 1	0.70	0.76	0.86	0.79	0.89	0.82	0.70	0.94	0.69	0.81
	Rater 2	0.80	0.83	0.83	0.61	0.86	0.83	0.73	0.97	0.63	0.82

Let us first look at the human-rater correlations. Consider the the human inter-rater agreement $\rho_{R_1R_2}$ which is the correlation between the ratings of the first and second human raters, who need not be experts in the field. We observe only two cases where $\rho_{R_1R_2}$ is greater than 0.5, and these are also the only cases where $\rho_{R_1R_2}$ outperforms machine correlations. This exemplifies the inherent subjectivity and difficulty involved in scoring various aspects of presentation proficiency – non-expert human raters tend to disagree when it comes to rating aspects of performance such as word choice, persuation and audience adaptability, for example, which are higher-level constucts that are not easily defined. However, the correlations between each of these raters' scores and the *final* rating for each scoring dimension are much higher, and close to 1 in many cases. Recall that the final score was adjudicated by an human expert with substantial prior experience in the field after considering the ratings of raters 1 and 2, and that this score need not be a simple average of those scores[3]. This suggests that although non-experts are able to score some aspects of presentation proficiency in line with how an expert would, a substantial amount of expertise is required for the scoring task. In other words, this is a non-trivial problem for not only machines to solve, but naive humans as well.

Let us now focus on the last four scoring dimensions – for instance, the 8th score, representing skillful use of visual aids, is predicted with correlations coming close to the human inter-rater agreement correlation $\rho_{R_1R_2}$. Kinect HoC features and SpeechRater features are particularly useful in this regard, and a combination of these features provides the best correlation of 0.82. This suggests that features that capture temporal information about body movement and speech are very useful in predicting how well subjects use visual aids in presentations, which makes intuitive sense. Further, we see that the 7th, 9th and 10th score dimensions, representing audience-adaptation, persuasiveness, and overall holistic performance respectively, are predicted well by face and gaze (time-series) features in particular. This, again, stands to reason – maintaining an appropriate head posture and direction of one's gaze are important for communicating effectively and persuasively to a given audience. Note also that in these cases the machine correlations are higher than the human agreement correlation $\rho_{R_1R_2}$. Notice that in some of these cases feature combinations may perform worse than the standalone features themselves – this could be due to the relatively larger dimension of the feature fusion (this is especially true in the case of the HoC features, which are sparse and have of the order of 10000 dimensions).

We see that time-series features computed over the intensities of different emotional states (estimated from facial expressions) perform much better than other features in predicting the 6th set of scores (non-verbal behavior). This reconfirms earlier findings in the literature that emotional state information is an important predictor of non-verbal aspects of performance (for example, [10, 9]). While speech and face/gaze features are useful features in predicting the 5th scoring dimension (vocal expression), these correlations are not as high as the human agreement correlation $\rho_{R_1R_2}$.

As far as the other four scoring dimensions are concerned, although our features perform much better than the baseline in all cases, these may not be readily interpretable – since these scores capture higher-level meta-characteristics of the presentation such as quality of introduction, conclusion, organization skill and word choice – and so it may not be clear why these scores perform well at the present time. Indeed, that we observe that speech and face/gaze features perform well on scoring dimensions #1 and #3 while combinations of our Kinect features perform well on scoring dimensions #2 and #4 might suggest that these features capture important behavioral aspects of these meta-characteristics, but understanding and interpreting the reason why is out of the scope of the current paper. Future work will focus on more tailored features in order to predict these scores in an interpretable

[3]Nonetheless, notice that the final adjudicated score is some nonlinear functional of the individual rater scores would result in a bump in correlation values.

manner. For example, these could be features that specifically look at the semantic/syntactic content of the speech for word choice, or that look at the beginning and ending portions of the time-series so as to focus on the introduction and conclusion.

5. CONCLUSIONS

We have presented a comparative analysis of three different feature sets – time-aggregated Kinect features, time-series (or histograms of cooccurrence) Kinect features and SpeechRater features (this combines information from both across and within time-series) – in predicting different human-rated scores of presentation proficiency. We found that certain scoring dimensions were better predicted by speech features, some on Kinect features, and others on combinations of all features. We further observed that these features allowed us to achieve prediction performance near human inter-rater agreement for a subset of these scores. Although there is much room for improvement along the lines of better, more interpretable and predictive features as well as machine learning algorithms and methods (indeed, we have only experimented with support vector regression here), these experiments provide us significant insight into understanding how to design better techniques for automated assessment and scoring of public speaking and presentation proficiency.

6. ACKNOWLEDGEMENTS

The authors would like to thank Christopher Kitchen, Jilliam Joe, and Chong Min Lee for their help in developing, organizing and supervising the data collection and rating process as well as the processing of speech data.

7. REFERENCES

[1] C. Chang and C. Lin. LIBSVM: a library for support vector machines. *ACM Transactions on Intelligent Systems and Technology (TIST)*, 2(3):27, 2011.

[2] L. Chen, G. Feng, J. Joe, C. W. Leong, C. Kitchen, and C. M. Lee. Towards automated assessment of public speaking skills using multimodal cues. In *Proceedings of the 16th International Conference on Multimodal Interaction*, pages 200–203. ACM, 2014.

[3] L. Chen, J. Tetreault, and X. Xi. Towards using structural events to assess non-native speech. In *Proceedings of the 5th Workshop on Innovative Use of NLP for Building Educational Applications, NAACL-HLT*, Los Angeles, CA, 2010. Association for Computational Linguistics.

[4] L. Chen and S.-Y. Yoon. Application of structural events detected on ASR outputs for automated speaking assessment. In *Proceedings of Interspeech*, 2012.

[5] L. Chen and K. Zechner. Applying rhythm features to automatically assess non-native speech. In *Proceedings of Interspeech*, 2011.

[6] L. Chen, K. Zechner, and X. Xi. Improved pronunciation features for construct-driven assessment of non-native spontaneous speech. In *Proceedings of NAACL-HLT*, 2009.

[7] D. Higgins, X. Xi, K. Zechner, and D. M. Williamson. A three-stage approach to the automated scoring of spontaneous spoken responses. *Computer Speech and Language*, 25(2):282–306, 2011.

[8] J. H. Jeon and S.-Y. Yoon. Acoustic feature-based non-scorable response detection for an automated speaking proficiency assessment. In *Proceedings of Interspeech*, pages 1275–1278, 2012.

[9] A. Kapoor and R. W. Picard. Multimodal affect recognition in learning environments. In *Proceedings of the 13th annual ACM international conference on Multimedia*, pages 677–682. ACM, 2005.

[10] I. Naim, M. I. Tanveer, D. Gildea, and M. E. Hoque. Automated prediction and analysis of job interview performance: The role of what you say and how you say it.

[11] L. Nguyen, D. Frauendorfer, M. Schmid Mast, and D. Gatica-Perez. Hire me: Computational inference of hirability in employment interviews based on nonverbal behavior. *IEEE transactions on multimedia*, 16(4):1018–1031, 2014.

[12] F. Pianesi, N. Mana, A. Cappelletti, B. Lepri, and M. Zancanaro. Multimodal recognition of personality traits in social interactions. In *Proceedings of the 10th international conference on Multimodal interfaces*, pages 53–60. ACM, 2008.

[13] V. Ramanarayanan, M. Van Segbroeck, and S. Narayanan. Directly data-derived articulatory gesture-like representations retain discriminatory information about phone categories. *Computer Speech and Language*, in press.

[14] R. Ranganath, D. Jurafsky, and D. A. McFarland. Detecting friendly, flirtatious, awkward, and assertive speech in speed-dates. *Computer Speech & Language*, 27(1):89–115, 2013.

[15] D. Sanchez-Cortes, J.-I. Biel, S. Kumano, J. Yamato, K. Otsuka, and D. Gatica-Perez. Inferring mood in ubiquitous conversational video. In *Proceedings of the 12th International Conference on Mobile and Ubiquitous Multimedia*, page 22. ACM, 2013.

[16] L. M. Schreiber, G. D. Paul, and L. R. Shibley. The development and test of the public speaking competence rubric. *Communication Education*, 61(3):205–233, 2012.

[17] B. Schuller, A. Batliner, S. Steidl, F. Schiel, and J. Krajewski. The interspeech 2011 speaker state challenge. In *Proceedings INTERSPEECH 2011, 12th Annual Conference of the International Speech Communication Association*, pages 3201–3204, 2011.

[18] B. Schuller, S. Steidl, A. Batliner, E. Nöth, A. Vinciarelli, F. Burkhardt, R. Van Son, F. Weninger, F. Eyben, T. Bocklet, et al. The interspeech 2012 speaker trait challenge. In *INTERSPEECH*, 2012.

[19] H. Van hamme. HAC-models: a novel approach to continuous speech recognition. In *Interspeech*, 2008.

[20] M. Van Segbroeck and H. Van hamme. Unsupervised learning of time–frequency patches as a noise-robust representation of speech. *Speech Communication*, 51(11):1124–1138, 2009.

[21] S. M. Witt. *Use of Speech Recognition in Computer-assisted Language Learning*. PhD thesis, University of Cambridge, 1999.

[22] K. Zechner, D. Higgins, X. Xi, and D. M. Williamson. Automatic scoring of non-native spontaneous speech in tests of spoken english. *Speech Communication*, 51(10):883–895, 2009.

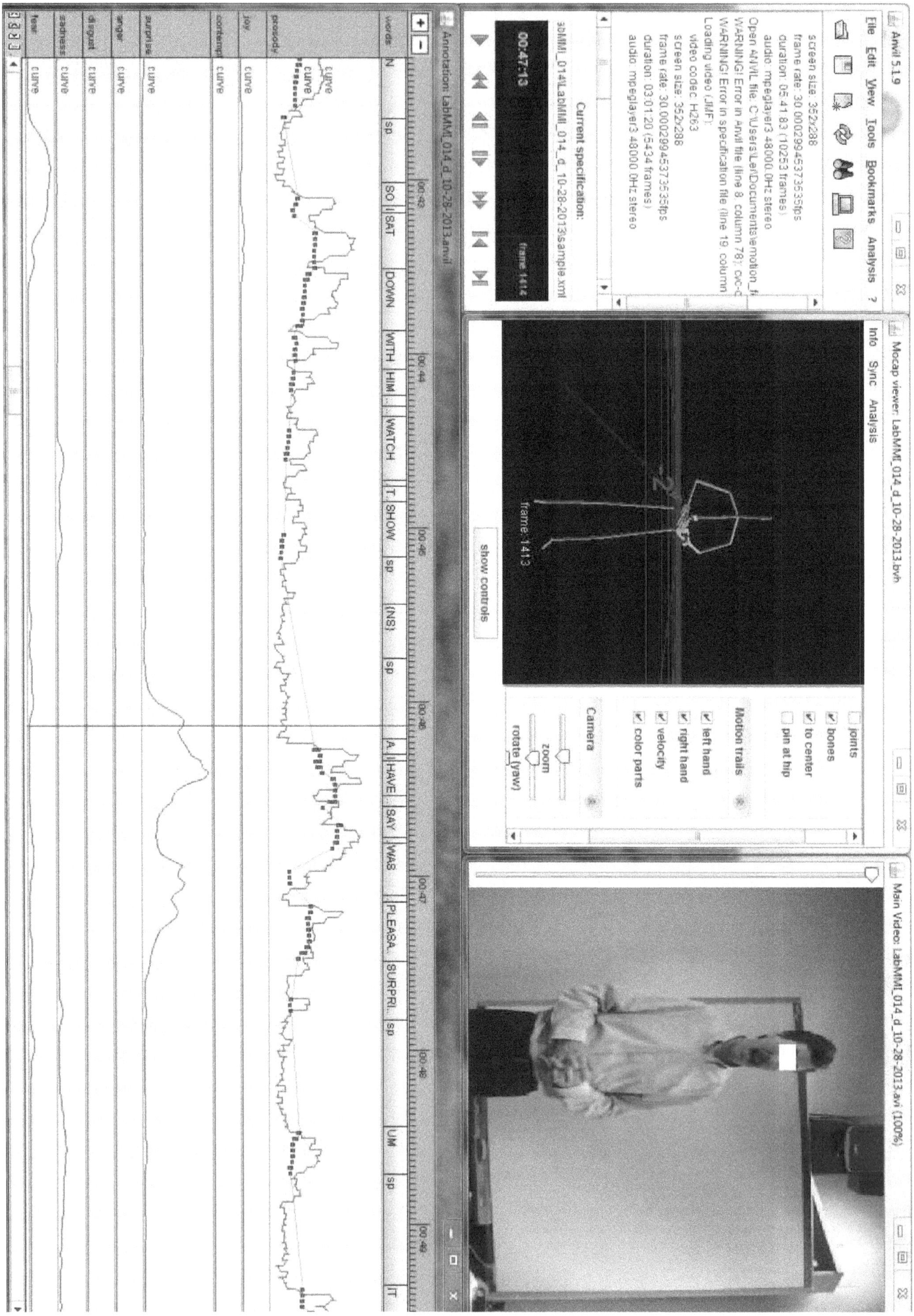

Figure 2: Example figure showing all data streams.

Gender Representation in Cinematic Content: A Multimodal Approach

Tanaya Guha Che-Wei Huang Naveen Kumar, Yan Zhu, Shrikanth S. Narayanan
Signal Analysis and Interpretation Lab (SAIL)
University of Southern California, Los Angeles
tanaya@sipi.usc.edu,{cheweihu,komathnk,zhuyan}@usc.edu,shri@sipi.usc.edu

ABSTRACT

The goal of this paper is to enable an objective understanding of gender portrayals in popular films and media through multimodal content analysis. An automated system for analyzing gender representation in terms of screen presence and speaking time is developed. First, we independently process the video and the audio content of a given movie, to estimate gender distribution of screen presence at shot level, and of speech at utterance level. A measure of the movie's excitement or intensity is computed using audio-visual features for every scene. This measure is used as a weighting function to combine the shot/utterance level gender distribution to compute gender representation for the entire movie. Detailed results and analyses are presented on seventeen full length Hollywood movies.

Keywords

Content analysis, gender representation, movie, multimodal.

1. INTRODUCTION

Automated analysis of multimedia content has become indispensable for organizing, indexing and navigating through vast amount of data. More recently, research in this area is being driven by the needs of facilitating and improving personal and social activities, insight generation, and interaction experience. Emphasizing the assistive, human-centric role that technology plays, this paper extends the application of multimedia content analysis to computational social science and media informatics. Specifically, our focus is on enabling an objective understanding of gender portrayals and biases in films. Thought leaders from the Hollywood movie industry, such as Geena Davis, have noted the presence of such inherent biases, and have both inspired research and championed steps for addressing them[1], including the work of this paper. Notably, this had led to research by social scientists and media experts who have repeatedly noted that women are highly underrepresented in popular films and media [12, 11]. Women comprise only 20-30% of all speaking characters in movies, and have much less screen presence and dialogs compared to their male counterparts [12]. To conduct such studies, researchers analyze large volume of media content *by hand*. This is extremely tedious, and calls for automated analysis. More importantly, automated content analysis can create opportunities for deeper, nuanced interpretation and analyses of multimodal content, which may not be even possible by manual inspection. For example, a recent work on automatic text analysis has reported significant differences between genders, and predictable gender patterns in terms of the language being used in movies [10]. .

In this paper, we propose to automatically quantify gender representation in movies from multimodal cues. Motivated by the aspects that media researchers and practitioners consider important, we automatically estimate *on-screen time* (from video) and *speaking time* (from audio) for male and female characters in movies. Since all parts of a movie are not equally important, it is reasonable to think that a character's presence (visual or audio) in the key parts of a movie is more important than that in less important parts. To capture this, we compute a measure of the movie's excitement (*scene intensity*) for every scene from video and music features. The raw on-screen and speaking time are then weighted by the corresponding scene intensity score to obtain a better understanding of gender representation in movies. We compute gender distribution on 17 popular Hollywood movies. Additionally, we perform various audio-visual analyses to study any inherent trends and biases in gender representation.

The objective of this work is twofold: (i) to provide a quantitative understanding of gender representation in media, and (ii) to build a scalable system that can scan large volume of data and automatically estimate quantities that are difficult to compute by hand.

2. PROPOSED APPROACH

Our gender representation framework has three main components: (i) on-screen time and (ii) speaking time estimation, and (iii) scene intensity computation.

2.1 On-Screen time estimation

Analyzing visual content in movies is extremely challenging, because the characters in movies exhibit significant variation in their appearances due to changes in scale, pose, illumination, expressions, camera angle etc. [1]. Our first task

[1]seejane.org

ICMI 2015, November 9–13, 2015, Seattle, WA, USA.
 ISBN 978-1-4503-3912-4/15/11 ...$15.00.
DOI: http://dx.doi.org/10.1145/2818346.2820778 .

Figure 1: Examples of success and failure of the face detector in movie frames.

is to estimate the total time during which at least one female actor is present on screen, and the same when at least one male actor appears on screen. An obvious step is to detect and track all faces that appear on screen. However, popular face detectors, such as the Viola-Jones face detector [13], can reliably detect faces under limited conditions (e.g. frontal poses). Employing multipose face detectors [7] may increase accuracy, but they are not as efficient. Frame-to-frame tracking of multiple faces for long duration is also computationally expensive.

To mitigate the above issues, we cast screen time computation as a video shot labeling problem. A video shot is defined as a contiguously recorded sequence of frames. We assume that the same actors are present through out the duration of a shot. Hence, even if we can detect an actor only in a few frames within a shot, the actor's on-screen time includes the entire duration of the shot. Under this setting, computing gender-specific screen time requires detecting at least one face of each gender present in a shot. Our system next attempts to determine whether a given shot is a *male only* (`M`), *female only* (`F`) or a *male and female* (`MF`) shot by running a gender classifier on the detected faces. Our video processing framework comprises the following steps:

1) Partition into shots: First, we partition a given movie into N shots: $S_1, S_2, .., S_N$ with duration $t(1), t(2), ...,$ $t(N)$ sec. We perform shot detection using an open source tool called the *ffmpeg*. This tool identifies the shot boundaries in a video stream by computing pixel-by-pixel differences between consecutive frames, and applying a threshold thereafter. Such pixel-based methods are robust to shot changes, and are popular in video processing literature [15]. We use a low threshold ($= 0.2$) value so that N is large (typically, 700 - 1500). Any S_i with $t(i) < 1$ sec is considered a false positive, and is merged with S_{i-1}.

2) Face detection: For each shot, a frontal face detector [13] is run on every frame. If at a frame, no face is detected, a profile face detector [13] is run on that frame (see Fig. 1 for examples of face detection). Our system is thus restricted to detect only the frontal and profile faces. Recall that we want to assign a label (`M`, `F` or `MF`) at shot level. Hence, the minimum requirement at this stage is to detect at least one human face of each gender present in the shot. If for a shot, no face is detected at all, it is labeled *empty*, and is not processed further.

3) False positives removal: Despite the high reliability of the face detector, false faces are detected. To remove false faces, a facial landmark point detection method [1] is used to localize 9 landmark points on eyes, nose and mouth corners (see Fig. 2) on each face. Originally developed for capturing mouth movement, this method returns a confidence score (c_v) as a measure of reliability of the localization. The idea is that in true faces, the landmark points will be localized

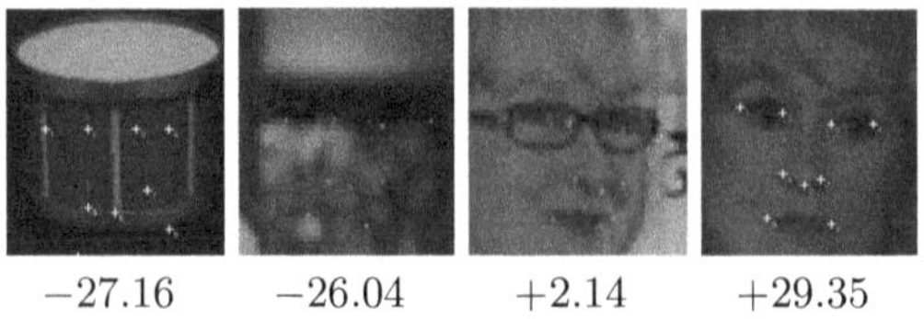

Figure 2: Examples of confidence score for localizing landmark points on false and true faces.

Table 1: Shot-level face detection accuracy in %.

	Face detected	*No face detected*
Face exists	73.91	26.09
No face exists	6.82	93.18

Table 2: Comparison of manual and automatically computed on-screen time (hh:mm:ss).

		Manual	*Estimated*
On-screen time	M	01:15:30	01:13:16
	F	01:08:18	00:59:11

with higher reliability, but for false faces c_v will be significantly low (see Fig. 2). If, for a face, c_v is greater than an empirically set threshold, it is considered to be a true face, and discarded otherwise.

4) Gender identification and Shot labeling: Our gender identification system is trained on the Labeled Faces in the Wild (LFW) database [5]. A subset of $6,000$ images (roughly equal male and female faces) are chosen from this database. Local Binary Pattern (LBP) [8] features (64 dimensional) are extracted from all faces. These features are used to train a binary Support Vector Machine (SVM) classifier with the radial basis function kernel. The overall gender classification accuracy on the LFW database is 90.85% (5-fold cross validation), with 99.42% accuracy for male, and 98.73% for female faces. This pretrained SVM is used to identify gender of the faces detected in movies. Consider n true faces extracted from a given shot S_i, where m faces are identified as male, and $n - m$ as female. A simple rule is used to label each shot: if $\frac{m}{n} \geq 0.9$, S_i is labeled `M`, i.e. $\ell_i \leftarrow$ `M` where ℓ_i is the label of S_i; for $\frac{n-m}{n} \geq 0.9$, $\ell_i \leftarrow$ `F`. Else, $\ell_i \leftarrow$ `MF`, implying the presence of both genders on screen. Each non-empty shot is thus labeled either `M`, `F` or `MF`. Total screen time for the female actors is $F_{scrn} = \sum_j t(j : \ell_j \in \{\texttt{F}, \texttt{MF}\})$. Similarly, the total screen time for the male actors is $M_{scrn} = \sum_j t(j : \ell_j \in \{\texttt{M}, \texttt{MF}\})$.

Validation: To evaluate the proposed system, we manually annotated 734 shots of duration ~2 hours in total. An annotator labeled each shot as (`M`, `F` or `MF`), according to the presence of male and female actors. Shots with no recognizable human face (e.g. small faces or actors not facing the camera) are labeled *empty*. The performance of our video processing system is evaluated against the manual annotations at the *shot level*.

After running the face detector, false faces are removed by thresholding at $c_v \geq -20$. This step reduces the false positives from 15.9% to 6.8%. Face detection performance after false face removal is presented in Table 1. Gender identification accuracy is computed in terms of precision and recall. The average precision is 0.72 and average recall is 0.86. The error of misclassifying an `M` shot as an `F` shot is

Table 3: Acoustic gender identification results (in %) on 557 utterances.

		Computed labels	
		M	F
True labels	M	75.81	24.19
	F	12.17	87.83

Table 4: Comparison of manual and automatically computed speaking time (mm:ss).

		Manual	*Estimated*
Speaking time	M	17:09	14:18
	F	09:07	11:57

10.53%, and that of F as M is 13.77%. Overall screen time results are presented in Table 2.

2.2 Speaking time estimation

Our next task of computing speaking time of male and female characters in movies follows the steps below.

1) Speech region segmentation: Voice activity detection (VAD) is a crucial first step to automatic speech processing. Despite the availability of many algorithms, robust VAD in movie and web media content is extremely challenging due to highly noisy and non-stationary acoustic environment [3]. We use a VAD algorithm implemented in the OpenSMILE toolkit [2], where a long short-term memory recurrent neural network is trained, and tested on Hollywood films [3]. This algorithm is chosen because it exhibits high performance on movie data. The VAD is followed by a Bayesian information criterion (BIC)-based speaker segmentation to ensure each utterance is speaker-homogeneous.

2) Acoustic gender identification: Two key features in acoustic gender identification are *pitch* and the *Relative spectral transform - perceptual linear prediction* (RASTA-PLP) [14, 9]. Two Gaussian mixture models (GMM), pertaining to male and female speech, are trained on the TIMIT database [4], containing 6300 clean utterances from different speakers. Pitch, and 11-dimensional RASTA-PLP features are extracted, and used to train the GMM with 8 mixture components and a full shared covariance. The number of components and the type of covariance are chosen by cross validation. Using (randomly chosen) 75% of the samples as the training set, and the rest as the test set, we achieved 97.68% accuracy on female utterances, 98.12% on male utterances, with overall classification accuracy of 97.98%. The pretrained GMMs are then used to classify utterances from movies. To compute gender-specific speaking time, we assign a gender label (M or F) to each utterance. For each utterance, its likelihoods of being spoken by a male $P(\text{speech}|\texttt{M})$, and that by a female character $P(\text{speech}|\texttt{F})$, are computed. A gender label is assigned accordingly.

Validation: Our audio processing system is evaluated on a labeled database that we created. This database contains 557 utterances from the movie *Hope Springs*. An annotator manually assigned a label of M or F to each utterance. The gender identification system is then run on this database and results are compared against the manual annotations. Classification results in Table 3 indicates reasonable accuracy of our system on this challenging corpus. Table 4 presents overall comparison of manual and estimated speaking time.

2.3 Scene intensity and Gender representation

Scene intensity, in the context of this work, can be understood as a measure of excitement or activity in a movie scene. Measuring the excitement induced by a scene can be a challenging problem in itself. Motivated by the ideas like tempo or story intensity popularly used in content analysis [6], we compute a multimodal measure of scene intensity based on various low-level features.

For a given movie, we compute two visual features: *shot length* and *motion energy*. Following the procedure mentioned in section 2.1, we partition a movie into its constituent shots, and compute a feature vector $\mathcal{S}$ where the ith element is the number of frames in the ith shot. Motion energy at a video frame is computed as the total motion the frame has undergone with respect to its previous frame. Motion is estimated based on optical flow vector method. Motion energy feature $\mathcal{M}$ is computed at shot level by averaging across all frames in a shot. Since music plays a key role in communicating excitement to the audience, we extract a feature called *harmonicity* that detects the presence of music in a movie's audio stream. At a time instant, it is measured as the average periodicity in its neighborhood. The harmonicity feature $\mathcal{H}$ at shot level is computed by averaging its values over the entire duration of a shot. These three features, computed at shot level, are normalized to have zero mean and unit standard deviation. When combined linearly with equal weights [6], we obtain a measure of excitement at shot level. Let the intensity of the ith shot be denoted as $\mathcal{I}(i)^{(sh)}$. A scene in a movie is usually comprised a number of shots, and the scene boundaries can be detected using *ffmpeg*. Scene intensity for the kth scene $\mathcal{I}(k)^{(sc)}$ is computed as follows:

$$\mathcal{I}(k)^{(sc)} = \sum_{shot\ i \in scene\ k} \mathcal{I}(i)^{(sh)} \quad (1)$$

A high value of $\mathcal{I}(k)^{(sc)}$ indicates that a scene is more exciting, and is likely to be a key scene in a movie. Gender representation percentages are first computed at the scene level. Let the female representation (on-screen or speaking time) percentage for the jth scene be $\mathcal{G}(j)^{(f)(sc)}$. The scene intensity scores, $\mathcal{I}(k)^{(sc)}$, are then used to weight scene-level gender percentages to compute overall gender representation $\mathcal{G}^{(f)(sc)}$ as shown in Eq.(2).

$$\mathcal{G}^{(f)} = \sum_{scene\ j} \mathcal{I}(j)^{(sc)}\mathcal{G}(j)^{(f)(sc)} / \sum_{\forall scenes} \mathcal{I}^{(sc)} \quad (2)$$

3. RESULTS

Our audio and video processing systems are first run on the 17 full-length Hollywood movies independently, to estimate gender distributions of screen and speaking time. To explore any structure among movies on the basis of gender representation, a clustering attempt is made. Let F_{scrn}, F_{spk} denote the percentages of female screen and speaking time in a movie. Using these two measures, a feature vector $\mathbf{F} = [F_{scrn}, F_{spk}]$ is obtained for each movie. The movies are then subject to agglomerative hierarchical clustering, where the distance between two movies is the ℓ_2 distance between their features. The distance between two clusters (linkage criterion) is measured by weighted pair group with average. Applying a threshold at the 70% of the maximum distance, three clear clusters are observed (Fig. 3) indicating

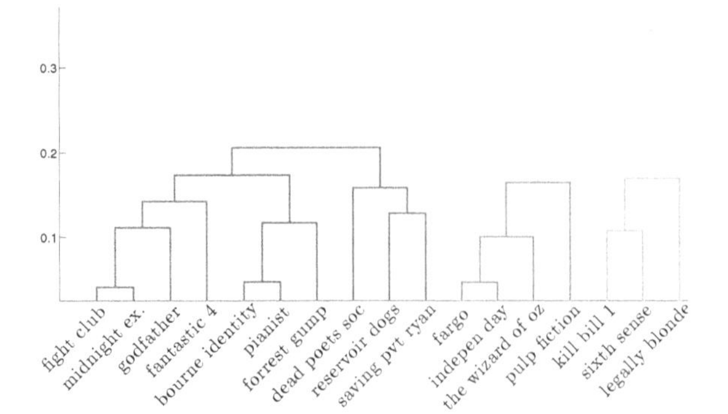

Figure 3: Agglomerative clustering of 17 movies on the basis of gender representation showing three clear clusters.

Table 5: Results of audiovisual co-occurance analysis normalized by speech (top)

Speech \ Face	None	M	F
None	0.26	0.49	0.24
M	0.20	0.51	0.28
F	0.16	0.50	0.33

similarity among the movies in terms of quantitative gender representation.

Audiovisual cooccurance analysis: A joint analysis of the audio and video streams is important to understand and compare gender representation across modalities. This joint analysis use the two output streams of gender labels obtained from the audio and video processing systems. We compute co-occurance scores (across all movies) of M/F appearance on screen with M/F speech (results in Table 5). A few interesting observations from Table 5: (i) in case of no speech, men are more likely to appear on-screen than women, (ii) when dialogs are spoken by women, male faces are still more likely to appear on-screen than females. Alternately, when a female actor appears on screen, male and female speech have equal probability.

Next, we perform scene detection on each movie. Scene intensity is computed, and weighted average of the on-screen /speaking time are computed as quantitative measure of gender portrayal as described in section 2.3. Results in Fig. 4 suggests that *Bourne Identity, Fargo, Fight Club* and *Reservoir Dogs* have lower female representation compared to others. A summary of the gender representation results is presented in Table 6.

4. CONCLUSIONS

A multimodal framework for quantifying gender representation in movies is proposed. At this preliminary stage, our system computes simple quantities like on-screen and speaking time. These quantities are analyzed, and combined with scene intensity information to show how an objective understanding of gender representation in media can be developed. Our system is scalable, and can handle large number of movies.

Acknowledgment

The authors are grateful to Madeline Di Nonno (Geena Davis Institute on Gender in Media), Hartwig Adam (Google), Stacy Smith and Marc Choueiti (USC), and support from NSF and Google.org.

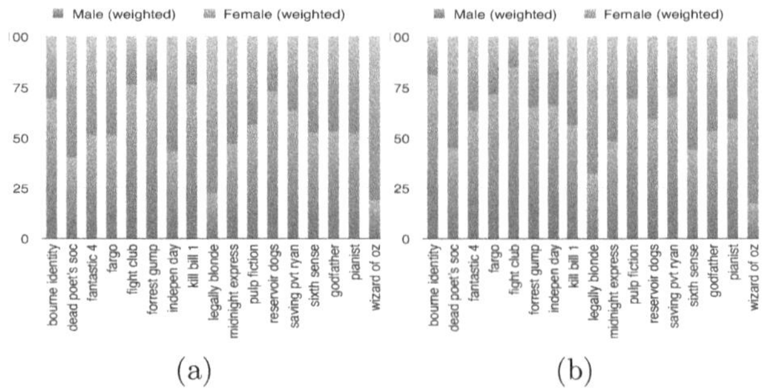

Figure 4: Scene intensity-weighted gender distribution (in %) for (a) on-screen time, (b) speaking time.

Table 6: Summary of gender representation results

Measures	*Avg. female representation*
On-screen time	36.19%
Speaking time	41.06%
On-screen time (weighted)	45.12%
Speaking time (weighted)	42.17%

5. REFERENCES

[1] Arandjelovic, O., and Zisserman, A. Automatic face recognition for film character retrieval in feature-length films. In *CVPR* (2005), pp. 860–867.

[2] Eyben, F., Weninger, F., Gross, F., and Schuller, B. Recent developments in opensmile, the munich open-source multimedia feature extractor. In *ACM Mutimedia* (2013).

[3] Eyben, F., Weninger, F., Squartini, S., and Schuller, B. Real-life voice activity detection with lstm recurrent neural networks and an application to hollywood movies. In *ICASSP* (2013).

[4] Garofolo, J., Lamel, L., Fisher, W., Fiscus, J., Pallett, D. S., Dahlgren, N. L., and ZueE, V. Timit acoustic-phonetic continuous speech corpus. Linguistic Data Consort. Philadelphia.

[5] Gary, B. H., Manu, R., Tamara, B., and Erik, L. Labeled faces in the wild: A database for studying face recognition in unconstrained environments. Tech. Rep. 07-49, UMass, Amherst, Oct 2007.

[6] Guha, T., Kumar, N., Narayanan, S., and Smith, S. Computationally deconstructing movie narratives: an informatics approach. In *ICASSP* (2015).

[7] Li, S. Z., and Zhang, Z. Floatboost learning and statistical face detection. *IEEE Trans. PAMI 26*, 9 (2004), 1112–1123.

[8] Ojala, T., Pietikainen, M., and Maenpaa, T. Multiresolution gray-scale and rotation invariant texture classification with local binary patterns. *IEEE Trans. PAMI 24*, 7 (2002), 971–987.

[9] Parris, E., and Carey, M. Language independent gender identification. In *ICASSP* (1996), pp. 685–688.

[10] Ramakrishna, A., Malandrakis, N., Staruk, E., and Narayanan, S. S. A quantitative analysis of gender differences in movies using psycholinguistic normatives. In *EMNLP* (2015).

[11] Smith, S. L., and Choueiti, M. Gender disparity on screen and behind the camera in family films; the executive report.

[12] Smith, S. L., and Cook, C. A. Gender stereotypes: An analysis of popular films and tv.

[13] Viola, P., and Jones, M. Rapid object detection using a boosted cascade of simple features. In *CVPR* (2001), pp. I–511.

[14] Y. Zeng, Z. Wu, T. F., and Chan, W. Robust gmm based gender clas- sification using pitch and rasta-plp parameters of speech. In *Proc. ICMLC* (2006), p. 3376âĂŞ3379.

[15] Yuan, J., Wang, H., Xiao, L., Zheng, W., Li, J., Lin, F., and Zhang, B. A formal study of shot boundary detection. *IEEE Trans. CSVT 17*, 2 (2007), 168–186.

Effects of Good Speaking Techniques on Audience Engagement

Keith Curtis
ADAPT Centre
School of Computing
Dublin City University
Dublin, Ireland
kcurtis@computing.dcu.ie

Gareth J. F. Jones
ADAPT Centre
School of Computing
Dublin City University
Dublin, Ireland
gjones@computing.dcu.ie

Nick Campbell
ADAPT Centre
School of Computer Science and Statistics
Trinity College Dublin
Dublin, Ireland
nick@tcd.ie

ABSTRACT

Understanding audience engagement levels for presentations has the potential to enable richer and more focused interaction with audio-visual recordings. We describe an investigation into automated analysis of multimodal recordings of scientific talks where the use of modalities most typically associated with engagement such as eye-gaze is not feasible. We first study visual and acoustic features to identify those most commonly associated with good speaking techniques. To understand audience interpretation of good speaking techniques, we angaged human annotators to rate the qualities of the speaker for a series of 30-second video segments taken from a corpus of 9 hours of presentations from an academic conference. Our annotators also watched corresponding video recordings of the audience to presentations to estimate the level of audience engagement for each talk. We then explored the effectiveness of multimodal features extracted from the presentation video against Likert-scale ratings of each speaker as assigned by the annotators. and on manually labelled audience engagement levels. These features were used to build a classifier to rate the qualities of a new speaker. This was able classify a rating for a presenter over an 8-class range with an accuracy of 52%. By combining these classes to a 4-class range accuracy increases to 73%. We analyse linear correlations with individual speaker-based modalities and actual audience engagement levels to understand the corresponding effect on audience engagement. A further classifier was then built to predict the level of audience engagement to a presentation by analysing the speaker's use of acoustic and visual cues. Using these speaker based modalities pre-fused with speaker ratings only, we are able to predict actual audience engagement levels with an accuracy of 68%. By combining with basic visual features from the audience as whole, we are able to improve this to an accuracy of 70%.

ICMI 2015, November 9–13, 2015, Seattle, WA, USA.

ACM 978-1-4503-3912-4/15/11 ...$15.00.
DOI: http://dx.doi.org/10.1145/2818346.2820766 .

Categories and Subject Descriptors

H.5.1 [**Information Interfaces and Presenation**]: Multimedia Information Systems; I.5.4 [**Pattern Recognition**]: Applications

Keywords

Classification; Engagement; Interest; Public Speaking; Multimodal Corpus

1. INTRODUCTION

The identification of multimodal content observed to be most engaging or interesting from a user perspective has many potential applications, such as for identifying elements for inclusion in video summarisation, browsing and retrieval. The efficiency of user interaction with multimodal content can potentially be increased if users are directed to these regions. In this investigation we aim to provide a mechanism to predict content of interest to the user based on analysis of content delivery and audience reaction.

Previous work [2, 22, 6, 14] in engagement detection has focussed mainly on annotation and detection of engagement in conversation. Others [27, 17] have worked on engagement detection in multimodal learning environments. Other studies [5, 10] have examined engagement detection in human-robot conversation. In our work we study audience engagement with presentations given in academic conferences. Meanwhile, previous studies on good public speaking techniques [25, 24, 9] have focussed on extracting the most influential, mainly acoustic, features associated with good public speaking skills. Other work [18] has been performed on detection of emotional speech.

We study the features of speech which humans consider to be good speaking techniques and attempt to train a classifier on these. In this we examine the relationship between speaking techniques and audience level engagement in scientific talks. In order to define 'good' speaking techniques, a pool of annotators rated the strengths of speakers at an international conference related to speech. We analyse correlations between features of speaking techniques and audience level engagement. A classifier was trained to automatically rate the strengths of a presenter. We then show how these ratings can be used to predict the level of engagement of the audience with the talk in progress.

In this investigation we address two research questions. 'Can we build a classifier to automatically rate how 'good' a public speaker is?' 'Can we build a classifier to automatically predict the level of audience engagement with a public presentation by utilizing speaker based and basic visual audience-based modalities?'

We address the first question by asking human annotators to label a corpus of scientific talks. The annotators were asked to watch randomly selected video segments of talks and to rate the speaker on a scale from 1 to 8, basing their judgements according to both acoustic and visual stimuli.

We demonstrate how to predict audience engagement in a situation where eye gaze information is not available. We do this by studying the speakers use of speaking techniques shown to influence audience engagement. We then predict audience engagement levels based on the strengths of the speaker. We show how this prediction is more accurate than visual based estimation methods only when gaze information is not available. We show how this information can then be combined with basic visual features to improve classification accuracy for audience engagement.

Following this we address our second research question by studying the relationship between speaker ratings and audience level engagement ratings. Acoustic and visual based features were extracted from video of the speaker from each presentation. A classifier was then trained to automatically rate the qualities of each speaker. We achieved accuracy results of 52% over the base 8-class range and accuracy of 73% over a combined 4-class range.

Visual based features were extracted from audience video of each presentation and used to train a classifier to predict levels of engagement using the ratings and speaking techniques from each speaker in tandem with visual classifiers of motion and positive facial detections. Accuracy results of 70% were achieved over a base 4-class range.

The remainder of this paper is structured as follows: Section 2 describes related work in the areas of speaking technique and engagement. Section 3 describes the design and construction of the multimodal corpus used in this research and the multimodal features extracted. In section 4 we discuss the experiments performed while section 5 outlines our results and analysis. Conclusions are offered in section 6 of this paper.

2. RELATED WORK

In this section we provide a review of existing research related to our work. We look first at investigations examining what constitutes good speaking techniques. Previous work has studied what people popularly perceive to be 'good' public speaking skills and evaluated the correlation with these features and human judgements. We also look at previous work in the area of engagement detection, most commonly performed in a multimodal meetings context. Separate studies have looked at engagement detection, most commonly in meetings and usually through the modalities of eye-gaze and facial expressions.

2.1 Public Speaking Studies

The qualities of 'good' public speaking have been explored in a number of previous studies. Strangert and Gustafson [25] looked at qualities of a good public speaker from the context of political speech. Human annotators listened to clips of political speeches from the Swedish parliament and rated the qualities of each speaker on a 5-point scale based on 13 statements about the speaker. Statements took the form *The speaker is ...* followed by one of 13 positive or negative adjectives including *insecure, powerful etc.*. Acoustic measurements were taken to identify the most important features of the speech signal from which the f0 value, particularly range, shows to correlate with positive statements about speakers.

An assessment of good public speaking skills was performed by Chen et al. [9] who extracted multimodal cues and evaluated the linear correlation with human holistic scores, gathered from 5 human raters who scored presentations according to 10 dimensions including vocal expression and nonverbal behaviour. In this work they found that simple multimodal features of the speech content, speech delivery (fluency, pronunciation, prosody) and non-verbal behaviours (head, body and hand movements) together can significantly predict human scores on presentation performance. Liscombe et al. [18] trained a classifier on emotional speech using acoustic features including the min, max mean, range and standard deviation of f0 and amplitude measurements and hand-labelled features including spectral tilt and type of accent. In this work they used an emotional speech corpus compiled using 8 professional actors. Subjects listened to emotional speech samples and expressed a judgement on the emotion being expressed. They suggest that spectral tilt and type of phrase accent and boundary tone, may be useful in discriminating between positive or negative emotion.

A multimodal virtual audience platform was developed by Batrinca et al. [1] for public speaking training. They used professional public speakers invited from toastmasters to rate the qualities of presentations using audio and visual stimuli. A dataset of 14 presenters giving a 5-15 minute presentation in front of a virtual audience was used. They found several expert estimates of non-verbal behaviour to be significantly correlated with an overall assessment of a presenter's performance.

2.2 Audience Engagement

Conversational engagement in multiparty video conversation has been studied by Bednarik et al. [2] with their emphasis on eye gaze. In this work they used 6 levels of engagement (no interest, following, responding, conversing, influencing, managing) annotated over 15 second intervals using two annotators, in which they focused on the individual within the group rather than the group as a whole. In this work they found that gaze behaviour differs during distinct levels of conversational engagement, with the number of unique faces attended at its maximum during the influencing level of conversational engagement, and the number of switches between faces at its maximum during the following level of engagement. Both these figures were at a minimum during the no interest level of engagement.

Group involvement was contrasted with individual engagement by Bonin et al. [6] who annotated conversational engagement at an individual level and also the engagement of the group as a whole, in which no prior examples of engagement levels were provided to annotators. This work was extended by Oertel and Salvi [22] who used eye gaze to relate group involvement to individual engagement in which participants rated their own engagement levels. They found that it is possible to estimate individual engagement and group involvement by analysing the participants eye-gaze patterns. Oertel et al. [21] studied automatic detection of involvement in conversation through measuring body movements and voice features. In this they found that the Intensity cue shows an increasing slope with higher interest levels showing a correlation with high intensity and high interest levels.

Grafsgaard et al. [15] analysed the additive effect of multimodal features for predicting engagement, frustration and learning in the study of introductory computer programming tutoring in which tutors communicated with students through a text-based interface. They found large improvements from the unimodal set (dialogue or nonverbal behaviour or task actions) to the bimodal set (dialogue and task actions) and from the bimodal set to the trimodal set (dialogue, nonverbal behaviour and task actions). The complete trimodal set of features was the most predictive.

Group engagement detection in multimodal meetings was performed by Gatica-Perez et al. [14]. Annotators were asked to label 15 second intervals from 4 party meetings according to 5 levels of group interest-level ranging from very low to very high with 3 being neutral. In this work they extracted audio (energy, pith and speaking rate) and visual (person motion, person pose) features from the multimodal corpus using microphone arrays and lapel microphones for audio features and colour blobs for visual features. HMMs were used to detect segments of high and neutral group interest levels. In this work they found that audio only modalities performed better than visual only modalities. McCowan et al. [20] used HMMs to compare the relationship between individual and group level engagement. In this they made use of visual and acoustic features including (hand blob, combined motion, presentation blob, speech activity, speech pitch, speech energy and speech rate) with no eye gaze information. They found that it is important to model the correlation between the behaviour of different participants and that there is evidence of asynchrony between participants acting within the group actions.

Student engagement was studied by Whitehill et al. [27] from analyses of facial expressions. Undergraduate students had their faces recorded while using a cognitive skills training application installed on an iPhone. Undergraduate and graduate students of computer science and psychology to rate the engagement level of each student when using the software application based on their recorded facial expressions. They found that observers relied on head pose and elementary facial actions like brow raise and eye closure. Video analysis was performed by Jang et al [17] to build a classifier for detection of engagement levels in children while using a robot based math game. Each video was coded by three annotators redundantly. A number of social signals including gaze, posture, behaviour, speech and facial expression were annotated by the raters. In their evaluation they found that a C4.5 decision tree with time window length of 1 second performed best, while a window length of 2 seconds gave the next best performance.

2.3 Current Study

Our work combines these two areas by first studying aspects of what people consider to be good public speaking techniques. Similar to previous work we evaluate the correlation between multimodal features and human scoring. We use the results of this study to train a classifier to automatically rate the qualities of public speakers based on human judgements of what actually represents a good public speaker. Following this we extend previous work by exploring the relationship between these 'good' speaking techniques and actual audience engagement levels by calculating linear correlations between visual and acoustic features and human ratings for both speaking ratings and audience engagement levels. We then train a classifier to predict audience engagement levels based on the use of speaking techniques found to correlate positively with audience engagement. We also study the use of basic visual features from the audience to improve classifications for engagement levels.

Figure 1: Video Annotation application - screen shot

3. MULTIMODAL CORPUS

In order to carry out this study we gathered a multimodal corpus by collecting video recordings of academic talks which were subsequently manually annotated with details of speaker quality and audience engagement. The presentations were recorded at an international conference related to speech held in May 2014. We made separate video recordings of the presenter and of the audience during each session. High quality audio was recorded separately and synched to the video recordings. Sessions were recorded on two SONY HDR-XR500 cameras. Video was recorded in 1080p at 29.97 fps with H264 codec. Audio was recorded in Dolby Digital 48kHz, 16 bit stereo. The recording standard used was AVCHD. The majority of presentations were standard podium presentations by a single speaker in front of a seated audience. Two presentations from the dataset consisted of two speakers.

A camera was located within the gallery of the auditorium and set to record the speaker and their presentation slides. A further camera was located on the stage behind the speaker facing towards the audience in order to record the audience from each talk. PDFs and back-up recordings from each presenter's slides were also collected.

A total of The corpus consists of dual video recordings from the presenter and audience of 31 scientific talks, totalling 520 minutes of conference video were collection. Taking account of the recordings of the speakers and their audiences, this gave us a total of 1040 minutes of video requiring human annotation.

3.1 Human Annotation

To rate the audience engagement level for this video segment based on a Likert scale from 1 to 4, annotators were asked to watch 30 second video segments, selected at random

Figure 2: Audience View

Figure 3: Presenter Close-up view

from the collection. Prior to performing the engagement rating, participants were provided with example labelled video segments from each of the 4 engagement levels. Annotators were also requested to provide an estimate of the attendance level at each talk, estimated on a scale from 1 to 5.

Annotation of video segments was performed using a web based application which played video segments. Annotation records from each annotator were recorded which later allowed us to analyse annotator ratings. Annotators were recruited from a pool of research students, support staff and research engineers across Dublin City University and Trinity College Dublin. There consisted an equal balance of native English speakers and non-native speakers. Some, but not all, annotators had prior experience of work on spoken content. Each video segment was annotated once, thus further steps were taken to eliminate bias as outlined below.

In a following human annotation study, participants were asked to watch 30 second video segments of the speaker, selected at random, and to rate the speaker according to their level of agreement with the following statement 'This is a good speaker who is able to capture the attention of the audience and bring the presentation to life.' Annotators were asked to base their judgements on both acoustic and visual stimuli. Human judgements were provided on a Likert scale from 1 to 8 with 1 being the weakest level of agreement with the given statement and 8 being the strongest level of agreement.

Presentation recordings were cropped in order to exclude each presenter's slides, for speaker ratings annotation, in order to ensure that judgements were based on the speaking techniques employed by each presenter as opposed to the quality of the presentation content as represented in the slides.

3.2 Verification and Normalisation

Three data processing steps were carried out to prepare the data in order to reduce annotator bias and apply smoothing to the human annotations.

Obvious outliers were first removed from the data set, and re-annotated by different annotators. Outliers were defined as segments whose labels did not appear to reasonably match up with nearby segment annotations. For example, if we had a sequence of video segments receiving an engagement rating of 3 followed by a segment receiving an engagement rating of 1, this final segment was re-annotated. This procedure was based on the assumption that engagement levels will not vary significantly over a short time frame.

The next step was to normalisation of segment labels to account for annotator bias. This was achieved by analysing the ratings for each annotator and applying either a lowering or raising to the annotator's labels to bring each annotators ratings in line with with other annotations. For example, some annotators were found to have an annotation range from 2 to 5 while others were found to have a range from 3 to 7. By analysing annotations we were able to adjust ratings to be within the consistent range.

The final stage involved Time Windowing. Video segments were aligned into time windows each 90 seconds in length and in steps of 30 seconds. In order to find the label for each 90 second time window we took the mean of labels for each video segment within this time window. This procedure was performed in order to smooth the annotations and reduce the effect of annotator bias.

3.3 Multimodal Feature Extraction

A set of visual and acoustic features was extracted from the multimodal corpus of scientific talks. Acoustic and visual features were used for our speaker rating classifier, while visual features were extracted for our audience engagement classifier. Acoustic features were extracted using Praat [4] while visual features were extracted using OpenCV [7].

3.3.1 Speaker-Based Acoustic Features

Pitch values were extracted using AutoBi Pitch Extractor [23]. We use default min and max values of 50 and 400 respectively. We used the max, range, mean and standard deviation of extracted pitch values for our experiments in order to account for variables in pitch values throughout the segment.

Intensity was extracted using AutoBi Intensity Extractor described by Rosenberg [23]. As for pitch we used the max, range, mean and standard deviation of Intensity values. This generated an Intensity contour using default parameters of a minimum Intensity of 75dB and a timestep of 100ms. These values were chosen as they represent commonly used default values for Intensity extraction using AutoBi.

Speech Rate, defined as the number of syllables per duration, and **Articulation Rate**, defined as the number of syllables per phonation time, were extracted for each talk using the Praat script described by De Jong and Wempe

[11]. These features were extracted as previous work has shown them to be useful features for evaluation of speaking performance.

3.3.2 *Speaker-Based Visual Features*

Head movement was extracted using Robust Facial Detection described by Viola and Jones [26]. For this task we used a Head and Shoulder cascade, provided by Castrillón-Santana et al. [8], to detect the presenters head and return the pixel values for the location of the speakers head at that point in time. We then extracted head movement by taking the Euclidean distance between pixel points in corresponding frames. We took the mean and standard deviation of head movement per second to give consistency to values regardless of the segment length. For this task we used the head and shoulder detector rather than the standard frontal face detector as the latter is likely to fail if the speaker turns to the side due to the nature of frontal face cascades which require the person to be facing forward showing their full face to the camera.

Speaker Motion was extracted using an optical flow implementation in OpenCV described by Lucas and Kanade [19]. We calculated the total pixel motion changes from frame to frame to put more weight on directional changes in motion and take the mean and standard deviation in overall speaker motion. This is to account for change of direction in motion and represent variances of these values.

3.3.3 *Audience-Based Visual Features*

Face Counts were extracted using a facial detector[26] on a trained frontal face cascade, provided by Castrillón-Santana et al. [8], over the audience video to detect faces that were facing forwards towards the speaker or the slides. This method is based on the theory that positive frontal face detections are more likely if the person is facing forwards. The total number of positive detections per second were counted and the mean and standard deviation of these values were calculated per video segment to give consistency to values regardless of the segment length.

Audience Motion was extracted in a similar way to Speaker Motion described above. As above we took the mean and standard deviation in audience level motion. We calculate pixel motion changes through frames to account for change of direction in motion and represent variances of these values.

Attendance rate, or, the number of people in attendance for talks, was estimated by taking as a region of interest a vacant seat in the gallery and calculating Red, Green and Blue High and Low values from the region of interest. This method assumes all seats are of the same colour. In the multimodal corpus used for this study all seats were blue. Pixels which had values falling within this range were counted which could then be used to give an estimate of attendance. To obtain attendance values for each presentation, pixel counts were sampled over every minute of video. The next stage involved recording the high and low values, taken as low and high level of attendance. The mean of all samples from the talk was then recorded. This mean value was then divided by the range between high and low values to give an added value figure. An Integer value of 4, representative of the range from low and high attendance estimates 1 to 5, was then divided by this added value figure and the result incremented by 1. We then subtracted this from our high value of 5 and finally as a normalization unit we take the value of the added value figure, divide by 5, representative of the attendance range, and add this result to our final added value figure which is then divided by the average attendance figure multiplied by 100 to obtain attendance estimates as a percentage figure.

To evaluate the attendance estimator we took the average attendance provided by our human annotators as our ground-truth and evaluated the closeness of our estimates with this ground-truth. By selecting a region of interest only once at the start of the video collection we achieved an accuracy of 88.04%.

4. EXPERIMENTAL INVESTIGATION

In this section we describe the experiments we have performed. We first describe the classifier we have used for classification and our reasons for using this. Following this we describe our experiments performed in order to discover the strength of each modality for speaker ratings and engagement prediction. We then describe the classification experiments performed.

While previous work in this regard, as cited above, has tended to use a regression model for classification, human annotation on speaker ratings and engagement level in this study are rated on a Likert scale. As pointed out by Blaikie [3] and Jamieson [16], Likert scales fall within the ordinal level of measurement. While ratings on a Likert scale have a rank order, intervals between values cannot be presumed equal. For this reason we treated this problem as an Ordinal Classification problem rather than as a standard regression problem.

In order to investigate the effects of individual speaker acoustic modalities on audience engagement, we calculated the Pearson Linear Correlation between acoustic modalities and corresponding engagement level. This was performed for the range, mean and standard deviation of speaker Pitch and Intensity. Calculations were performed over the entire data set to discover the true correlation with human annotations. We also calculated the Linear Correlation between Speaker Ratings and corresponding audience Engagement Level to investigate the relationship between what people perceived to be good speaking techniques and the actual engagement of the audience at that time.

We trained a classifier to automatically rate the qualities of the speaker, and estimate the audience engagement levels using Weka data mining workbench [13]. Classification was performed using Ordinal Class Classifier as described by Frank and Hall [12] and evaluated using 10-fold cross validation. For speaker ratings classification we used the base 8 point Likert scale as used for annotation. We then combined classes to form a 4 point scale to investigate the effects on accuracy rates. Audience engagement classification used the base 4 point Likert scale used for annotation.

Individual speaker modalities including Pitch (max, range, mean, standard deviation), Intensity (max, range, mean, standard deviation), Head Movement (total, range, mean, standard deviation) and overall Speaker Motion (range, mean, standard deviation) were pre-fused for classification by including all modalities within the training set. For Audience level engagement classification we pre-fused visual modalities of the audience including Audience Motion (mean, standard deviation) Frontal Face Counts (mean per second, standard deviation per second) and Attendance (per talk) in addition to speaker ratings and individual speaker acoustic modalities above. Individual modalities were then removed from the training set to investigate their effects on classification accuracy.

5. RESULTS AND DISCUSSION

We now demonstrate results from these preliminary studies. Table 1 shows the linear correlation scores between multimodal speaker-based features and annotated speaker ratings. Table 2 shows the linear correlation scores between multimodal speaker based features and audience engagement level. Following this, table 3 shows the linear correlation between our annotated speaker ratings and audience engagement levels. Table 4 shows our Speaker Ratings classification results on an 8-class scale for audio modalities only, visual modalities only and audio and visual modalities combined. In table 5 we present our Speaker Ratings Classification results after classes have been combined to make a 4 class problem. We again demonstrate results from acoustic modalities only followed by visual modalities only followed by visual and acoustic modalities combined. Finally, Table 6 presents results from our Audience Engagement Classifier. As annotations received for audience engagement level mainly reside from 2 to 4, labels 1 and 2 have been combined to make a three class problem. We first present results using Audience Visual modalities only, followed by speaker based modalities for prediction only followed by results combining audience visual modalities with speaker based modalities which are shown in table 2 to have an impact on engagement levels.

We use the majority class classifier for baselines for tables 4, 5 and 6 which indicates the accuracy of a classifier which classifies all intances to the majority class. In table 6, we also present results for Intensity-only modality. Of the most important modalities for speaker ratings classification, we can see that Speech Rate and Articulation Rate have a big influence in how strong a presenter annotators perceived this speaker to be, as can be seen by inspecting Table 1. Visual modalities such as overall speaker movement normalised by head movement appear to have a big influence while head movement by itself does not appear to have a strong effect, with a slight negative linear correlation suggesting that too much head movement may actually put listeners off.

In Table 2 we can see that a number of speaker based acoustic and visual modalities have an important influence over audience engagement levels. The most influential of these is clearly Intensity mean and max values. Intensity range and standard deviation values are also effective, however these do not appear to be as important as the max and mean values. Articulation rate also shows to an important modality for prediction of audience engagement which is highlighted in Table 2. Of the visual modalities the mean speaker motion normalised by head movement shows to be quite influential however head movement alone does not appear to be anywhere near as effective as overall speaker motion for prediction of engagement, suggesting that speaker motion should be comprised of overall body motion and gesturing rather than head movement on it's own.

The weak positive linear correlation between speaker ratings and engagement annotations, as demonstrated in Table 3, suggests that there may be a difference between what people popularly perceive to be good public speaking techniques and what is more likely to capture the attention of the

Table 1: Speaker Ratings Linear Correlation

Multimodal Feature	$r =$
Pitch Mean	-0.135
Pitch Max	**0.185**
Pitch Range	**0.190**
Pitch Std Dev	-0.044
Intensity Mean	**0.374**
Intensity Max	**0.336**
Intensity Range	**0.218**
Intensity Std Dev	0.141
Speech Rate	**0.313**
Articulation Rate	**0.459**
Face Movement Range	-0.065
Face Movement Mean	**-0.233**
Face Movement Std Dev	-0.106
Face Movement Total	**-0.210**
Speaker Motion Range	**0.302**
Speaker Motion Mean	**0.558**
Speaker Motion Std Dev	**0.415**

Table 2: Engagement Level Linear Correlation

Multimodal Feature	$r =$
Pitch Mean	0.014
Pitch Max	0.067
Pitch Range	0.062
Pitch Std Dev	0.044
Intensity Mean	**0.318**
Intensity Max	**0.352**
Intensity Range	**0.191**
Intensity Std Dev	**0.194**
Speech Rate	-0.021
Articulation Rate	**0.135**
Face Movement Range	0.040
Face Movement Mean	-0.033
Face Movement Std Dev	0.013
Face Movement Total	-0.044
Speaker Motion Range	-0.004
Speaker Motion Mean	**0.128**
Speaker Motion Std Dev	0.044

Table 3: 8-Class Speaker Ratings Classifier

Modalities	Accuracy	MAE	RMSE
Baseline	**30.194**	**1.129**	**1.527**
Audio Only	51.177	0.141	0.308
Visual Only	37.052	0.174	0.323
Audio and Visual	52.099	0.133	0.309

Table 4: 4-Class Speaker Ratings Classifier

Modalities	Accuracy	MAE	RMSE
Baseline	**43.808**	**0.658**	**0.922**
Audio Only	72.364	0.177	0.339
Visual Only	61.208	0.237	0.368
Audio and Visual	73.081	0.161	0.336

Table 5: Audience Engagement Classifier

Modalities	Accuracy	MAE	RMSE
Baseline	**62.436**	**0.376**	**0.615**
Speaker Intensity Only	65.302	0.240	0.353
Audience Visual Only	66.121	0.221	0.355
Speaker Based Prediction	68.270	0.202	0.357
Speaker & Aud. Visual	70.317	0.180	0.352

Table 6: Speaker Ratings - Engagement Linear Correlation

Label	Label	$r =$
Speaker Ratings	Audience Engagement	**0.227**

audience. The most obvious of these appears to be Articulation Rate which has a strong positive linear correlation with Speaker Ratings but a much weaker correlation with audience engagement ratings. Similarly the use of gesturing and other speaker movements tended to attract positive speaker ratings but again shows a much weaker correlation with actual audience engagement. Nevertheless, the r score of 0.227 suggests a linear correlation which can be fused with pre-extracted multimodal speaker based features to help with prediction of audience engagement levels.

Speaker Intensity on the other hand, measured here by loudness, shows a very similar positive linear correlation with speaker ratings and with audience engagement levels as can be seen from looking at Table 2 and Table 3. From this we can use mean and max speaker Intensity as a basis for the prediction of audience engagement levels. In addition to mean and max Intensity, Articulation Rate, Mean Speaker Motion and predicted speaker ratings can be used to predict audience engagement to an accuracy of 68%. By using mean facial counts per second, mean audience motion and extracted attendance rates we are able to improve classification accuracy to 70%. Table 6 shows results for Intensity Mean, Range, Max and Standard Deviation values only.

Our findings on the importance of Speech Rate, Articulation Rate and Body Movement in particular correlate to the findings of Chen et al. [9], which showed that speech delivery and nonverbal behaviours can significantly predict human scores on presentation performance.

Our results for intensity relate directly to the findings of Oertel et al. [21], in which increasing levels of intensity correspond to increasing levels of involvement. Our findings on body movement can also be related to this previous work in which individual sessions show increasing levels of body movement corresponding to levels of involvement, whilst other sessions do not. This bears some resemblance to our results which show importance of mean body motion but not of the standard deviation and range of movement.

Based on the linear correlations as demonstrated above we trained our speaker ratings classifier on the following visual and acoustic modalities: Pitch max and range, intensity max and mean, mean head movement, mean and standard deviation of speaker motion normalised by head movement, speech rate and articulation rate. Our combined audience visual and speaker modality based audience engagement prediction classifier is trained on the following modalities: Speak Rating outputs, audience motion normalised by attendance rate, overall audience motion, face counts normalised by attendance rate, speaker max and mean Intensity levels, mean speaker motion, Articulation rate and attendance rates. The best modalities for classification are bold printed on our results tables above.

6. CONCLUSIONS

In this paper we report on the development of a multimodal corpus of academic talks that has been annotated according to the quality of speakers and the estimated level of audience engagement. We studied the effects of acoustic and visual speech modalities on what human annotators perceived to be good speaking techniques. Based on our corpus, we have studied the correlation between these 'good' speaking techniques and direct audience engagement levels with the talk in progress and have also studied the correlation between annotated speaker ratings and actual audience engagement levels. We have trained a classifier to automatically rate the qualities of each public speaker. Following this we showed how these speaker-based acoustic and visual modalities can be used for automatic prediction of audience engagement levels in a scenario where typical modalities associated with engagement detection such as eye-gaze are not feasible. By using visual information from the audience, the accuracy of these predictions can be improved.

Our results are very promising and demonstrate the ability to predict levels of audience engagement based on the speaking techniques employed by the presenter. This work is a proof of concept performed on a small dataset comprised of 9 hours of presentation and audience recordings from an academic conference. Further work will look to experiment with this method on larger datasets.

The weak linear correlation between speaker ratings and audience engagement may be due to a larger than anticipated influence of the actual presentation content. This study does not consider the influence of the actual presentation content. In the future, we will investigate this further. It will also be interesting to investigate how prosodic and visual cues are used by speakers to provide extra emphasis on parts of a presentation that they consider to be most important and how these cues can be used to automatically detect areas of extra emphasis in order to provide a natural time-point for playback. We will also investigate the potential to correlate these features of emphasis with actual audience engagement levels.

7. ACKNOWLEDGMENTS

This research is supported by Science Foundation Ireland through the CNGL Programme (Grant 12/CE/I2267) in the ADAPT Centre (www.adaptcentre.ie) at Dublin City University. We would like to thank all of our human annotators for participating in this study.

8. REFERENCES

[1] L. Batrinca, G. Stratou, A. Shapiro, L.-P. Morency, and S. Scherer. Cicero-towards a multimodal virtual audience platform for public speaking training. In *Intelligent Virtual Agents*, pages 116–128. Springer, 2013.

[2] R. Bednarik, S. Eivazi, and M. Hradis. Gaze and conversational engagement in multiparty video conversation: an annotation scheme and classification of high and low levels of engagement. In *Proceedings of*

the 4th workshop on eye gaze in intelligent human machine interaction, page 10. ACM, 2012.
[3] N. Blaikie. *Analyzing quantitative data: From description to explanation.* Sage, 2003.
[4] P. Boersma and D. Weenink. Praat, a system for doing phonetics by computer. 2001.
[5] D. Bohus and E. Horvitz. Managing human-robot engagement with forecasts and... um... hesitations. In *Proceedings of the 16th International Conference on Multimodal Interaction*, pages 2–9. ACM, 2014.
[6] F. Bonin, R. Bock, and N. Campbell. How do we react to context? annotation of individual and group engagement in a video corpus. In *Privacy, Security, Risk and Trust (PASSAT), 2012 International Conference on and 2012 International Confernece on Social Computing (SocialCom)*, pages 899–903. IEEE, 2012.
[7] G. Bradski and A. Kaehler. *Learning OpenCV: Computer vision with the OpenCV library.* " O'Reilly Media, Inc.", 2008.
[8] M. Castrillón-Santana, O. Déniz-Suárez, L. Antón-Canalís, and J. Lorenzo-Navarro. Face and facial feature detection evaluation performance evaluation of public domain haar detectors for face and facial feature detection. 2008.
[9] L. Chen, G. Feng, J. Joe, C. W. Leong, C. Kitchen, and C. M. Lee. Towards automated assessment of public speaking skills using multimodal cues. In *Proceedings of the 16th International Conference on Multimodal Interaction*, pages 200–203. ACM, 2014.
[10] L. J. Corrigan, C. Basedow, D. Küster, A. Kappas, C. Peters, and G. Castellano. Mixing implicit and explicit probes: finding a ground truth for engagement in social human-robot interactions. In *Proceedings of the 2014 ACM/IEEE international conference on Human-robot interaction*, pages 140–141. ACM, 2014.
[11] N. H. De Jong and T. Wempe. Praat script to detect syllable nuclei and measure speech rate automatically. *Behavior research methods*, 41(2):385–390, 2009.
[12] E. Frank and M. Hall. A simple approach to ordinal classification. In *12th European Conference on Machine Learning*, pages 145–156. Springer, 2001.
[13] E. Frank, M. Hall, G. Holmes, R. Kirkby, B. Pfahringer, I. H. Witten, and L. Trigg. Weka-a machine learning workbench for data mining. In *Data Mining and Knowledge Discovery Handbook*, pages 1269–1277. Springer, 2010.
[14] D. Gatica-Perez, I. A. McCowan, D. Zhang, and S. Bengio. Detecting group interest-level in meetings. In *IEEE Int. Conf. on Acoustics, Speech, and Signal Processing (ICASSP)*, number EPFL-CONF-83257, 2005.
[15] J. F. Grafsgaard, J. B. Wiggins, A. K. Vail, K. E. Boyer, E. N. Wiebe, and J. C. Lester. The additive value of multimodal features for predicting engagement, frustration, and learning during tutoring. In *Proceedings of the 16th International Conference on Multimodal Interaction*, pages 42–49. ACM, 2014.
[16] S. Jamieson et al. Likert scales: how to (ab) use them. *Medical education*, 38(12):1217–1218, 2004.
[17] M. Jang, C. Park, H.-S. Yang, J.-H. Kim, Y.-J. Cho, D.-W. Lee, H.-K. Cho, Y. Kim, K. Chae, and B.-K. Ahn. Building an automated engagement recognizer based on video analysis. In *Proceedings of the 2014 ACM/IEEE international conference on Human-robot interaction*, pages 182–183. ACM, 2014.
[18] J. Liscombe, J. Venditti, and J. B. Hirschberg. Classifying subject ratings of emotional speech using acoustic features. 2003.
[19] B. D. Lucas, T. Kanade, et al. An iterative image registration technique with an application to stereo vision. In *IJCAI*, volume 81, pages 674–679, 1981.
[20] I. McCowan, D. Gatica-Perez, S. Bengio, G. Lathoud, M. Barnard, and D. Zhang. Automatic analysis of multimodal group actions in meetings. *Pattern Analysis and Machine Intelligence, IEEE Transactions on*, 27(3):305–317, 2005.
[21] C. Oertel, C. De Looze, S. Scherer, A. Windmann, P. Wagner, and N. Campbell. Towards the automatic detection of involvement in conversation. In *Analysis of Verbal and Nonverbal Communication and Enactment. The Processing Issues*, pages 163–170. Springer, 2011.
[22] C. Oertel and G. Salvi. A gaze-based method for relating group involvement to individual engagement in multimodal multiparty dialogue. In *Proceedings of the 15th ACM on International conference on multimodal interaction*, pages 99–106. ACM, 2013.
[23] A. Rosenberg. Autobi-a tool for automatic tobi annotation. In *INTERSPEECH*, pages 146–149, 2010.
[24] E. Strangert. What makes a good speaker? subjective ratings and acoustic measurements. In *Proceedings from Fonetik 2007: speech, music and hearing, quarterly progress and status report, TMH-QPSR, Vol 50, 2007*, pages 29–32, 2007.
[25] E. Strangert and J. Gustafson. What makes a good speaker? subject ratings, acoustic measurements and perceptual evaluations. In *INTERSPEECH*, volume 8, pages 1688–1691, 2008.
[26] P. Viola and M. J. Jones. Robust real-time face detection. *International journal of computer vision*, 57(2):137–154, 2004.
[27] J. Whitehill, Z. Serpell, Y.-C. Lin, A. Foster, and J. Movellan. The faces of engagement: Automatic recognition of student engagement from facial expressions. 2014.

Multimodal Public Speaking Performance Assessment

Torsten Wörtwein
KIT Institute of Anthropomatics and Robotics
Karlsruhe, Germany
uncwt@student.kit.edu

Mathieu Chollet
USC Institute for Creative Technologies
Playa Vista, CA, USA
chollet@ict.usc.edu

Boris Schauerte
KIT Institute of Anthropomatics and Robotics
Karlsruhe, Germany
boris.schauerte@kit.edu

Louis-Philippe Morency
CMU Language Technologies Institute
Pittsburgh, PA, USA
morency@cs.cmu.edu

Rainer Stiefelhagen
KIT Institute of Anthropomatics and Robotics
Karlsruhe, Germany
rainer.stiefelhagen@kit.edu

Stefan Scherer
USC Institute for Creative Technologies
Playa Vista, CA, USA
scherer@ict.usc.edu

ABSTRACT

The ability to speak proficiently in public is essential for many professions and in everyday life. Public speaking skills are difficult to master and require extensive training. Recent developments in technology enable new approaches for public speaking training that allow users to practice in engaging and interactive environments. Here, we focus on the automatic assessment of nonverbal behavior and multimodal modeling of public speaking behavior. We automatically identify audiovisual nonverbal behaviors that are correlated to expert judges' opinions of key performance aspects. These automatic assessments enable a virtual audience to provide feedback that is essential for training during a public speaking performance. We utilize multimodal ensemble tree learners to automatically approximate expert judges' evaluations to provide post-hoc performance assessments to the speakers. Our automatic performance evaluation is highly correlated with the experts' opinions with $r = 0.745$ for the overall performance assessments. We compare multimodal approaches with single modalities and find that the multimodal ensembles consistently outperform single modalities.

Categories and Subject Descriptors

H.5.1 [**Multimedia Information Systems**]: Artificial, augmented, and virtual realities

General Terms

Algorithms, Human Factors, Measurement, Performance, Experimentation

Keywords

Public Speaking; Machine Learning; Nonverbal Behavior; Virtual Human Interaction

ICMI 2015, November 9–13, 2015, Seattle, WA, USA.

ACM 978-1-4503-3912-4/15/11 ...$15.00.
DOI: http://dx.doi.org/10.1145/2818346.2820762 .

1. INTRODUCTION

Recent developments in nonverbal behavior tracking, machine learning, and virtual human technologies enable novel approaches for interactive training environments [7, 3, 30]. In particular, virtual human based interpersonal skill training has shown considerable potential in the recent past, as it proved to be effective and engaging [15, 25, 2, 12, 4]. Interpersonal skills such as public speaking are essential assets for a large variety of professions and in everyday life. The ability to communicate in social and public environments can greatly influence a person's career development, help build relationships, resolve conflict, or even gain the upper hand in negotiations. Nonverbal communication expressed through behaviors, such as gestures, facial expressions, and prosody, is a key aspect of successful public speaking and interpersonal communication. This was shown in many domains including healthcare, education, and negotiations where nonverbal communication was shown to be predictive of patient and user satisfaction as well as negotiation performance [27, 8, 22]. However, public speaking with good nonverbal communication is not a skill that is innate to everyone, but can be mastered through extensive training [12].

We propose the use of an interactive virtual audience for public speaking training. Here, we focus primarily on the automatic assessment of nonverbal behavior and multimodal modeling of public speaking behavior. Further, we assess how nonverbal behavior relates to a number of key performance aspects and the overall assessment of a public speaking performance. We aim to identify nonverbal behaviors that are correlated to expert judges' opinions automatically in order to enable a virtual audience to provide feedback during a public speaking performance. Further, we seek to model the performance using multimodal machine learning algorithms to enable the virtual audience to provide post-hoc performance assessments after a presentation in the future. Lastly, we compare subjective expert judgements with objective manually transcribed performance aspects of two key behaviors, namely the use of pause fillers and the ability to hold eye contact with the virtual audience. In particular, we investigate three main research questions:

Q1: What nonverbal behaviors are correlated with expert judgements of certain performance aspects of public speaking to enable online feedback to the trainee?

Q2: Is it possible to automatically approximate public speaking performance assessments of expert judges using multimodal machine learning to provide post-hoc feedback to the trainee?

Q3: Are expert judges objective with their assessments, when compared to ground truth manual annotations of two key behaviors and how do automatic behavior assessments compare?

2. RELATED WORK

In general, excellent and persuasive public speaking performances, such as giving a presentation in front of an audience, are not only characterized by decisive arguments or a well structured train of thoughts, but also by the nonverbal characteristics of the presenter's performance, i.e. the facial expressions, gaze patterns, gestures, and acoustic characteristics. This has been investigated by several researchers in the past using political speakers' performances. For example researchers found that vocal variety, as measured by fundamental frequency (f_0) range and maximal f_0 of focused words are correlated with perceptual ratings of a good speaker within a dataset of Swedish parliamentarians [29, 24]. Further, manual annotations of disfluencies were identified to be negatively correlated with a positive rating.

In [26], the acoustic feature set, used in [29], was complemented by measures of pause timings and measures of tense voice qualities. The study shows that tense voice quality and reduced pause timings were correlated with overall good speaking performances. Further, the authors investigated visual cues, in particular motion energy, for the assessment of the speakers' performances. They found that motion energy is positively correlated with a positive perception of speakers. This effect is increased when only visual cues are presented to the raters.

A specific instance of public speaking are job interviews. In [21] researches have tried to predict the *hireability* in job interviews. Based on a dataset of 43 job interviews, the following non-verbal behaviors were used to estimate the *hireability*: manual annotations of body activity (gestures and self-touches), hand speed and position (on table height or on face height), and the speaking status to mask the temporal features. The most useful feature was the activity histogram from the hand position and speed.

Within this work we employ a virtual audience for public speaking training. Virtual humans are used in a wide range of social and interpersonal skill training environments, such as job interview training [2, 14], public speaking training [4, 23], and intercultural communicative skills training [18].

In [4], the use of a virtual audience and the automatic assessment of public speaking performances was investigated for the first time. A proof-of-concept non-interactive virtual public speaking training platform named Cicero was introduced. Three main findings were reported: nonverbal behaviors of only 18 subjects, such as flow of speech, vocal variety, were significantly correlated with an overall assessment of a presenter's performance as assessed by public speaking experts. A simple support vector regression approach showed promising results of automatic approximation of the experts' overall performance assessment with a significant correlation of r = 0.617 (p = 0.025), which approaches the correlation between the experts' opinions (i.e. r = 0.648).

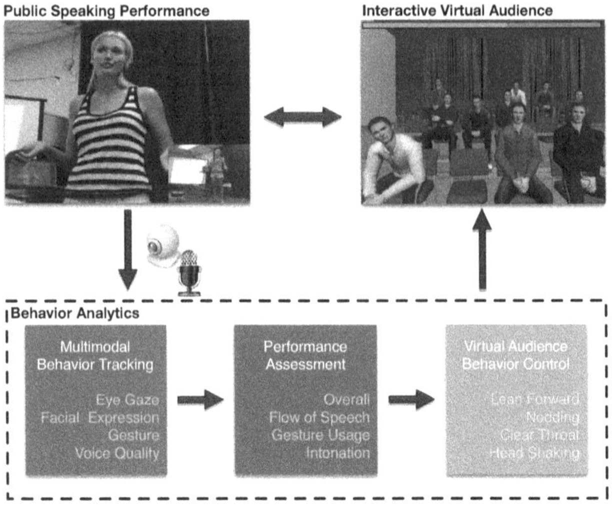

Figure 1: Depiction of the virtual human driven public speaking training interaction loop. The trainee's performance is automatically assessed within the behavior analytics framework. Multimodal nonverbal behavior is tracked, the performance is automatically assessed using machine learning approaches and the virtual audience provides audiovisual feedback to the trainee based on training strategies.

Within the present work, we aim to further improve these promising results using more sophisticated machine learning approaches. In addition, the present work is concerned with the assessment of *individual speaker improvement after training* rather than how well they present in comparison to other speakers. The present work is to the best of our knowledge the first to identify within-subject improvements and how they relate to changes in nonverbal behavior from one presentation to the other. Previous work did either not focused specifically on public speaking performance, did not investigate a data-driven comparison of presentations, or did not solely rely on automatically extracted features. Therefore, we focus on automatic features indicating differences in public speaking performances between presentations.

3. INTERACTIVE VIRTUAL AUDIENCE

We developed an interactive learning framework based on audiovisual behavior sensing and learning feedback strategies (cf. Figure 1). In particular, the speaker's audiovisual nonverbal behavior was registered in the architecture and feedback was provided to the speaker via the learning feedback strategies. We investigated three such strategies: (1) no feedback, i.e. the control condition, (2) direct visual feedback, and (3) nonverbal feedback from the virtual audience itself. Within this work, however, we solely focus on the performance of the speakers rather than the effect of learning strategies.

During training, the interactive virtual characters were configured with a feedback profile as our learning strategies. These profiles define behaviors the virtual characters will enact when specific conditions were met. Thus, the virtual characters can be used to provide natural, nonverbal feedback to the users according to their performance [5]. In our case, the characters can change their postures (leaning forward and being attentive, standing straight on their chairs, and leaning backwards in a very relaxed manner), and also nod or shake their head regularly. Positive behaviors (leaning forward, nodding regularly) were assigned to trigger when the speaker's performance is good, while negative behaviors (leaning backwards, head shake) would trigger when the speaker's performance is bad. Threshold values for these triggers were randomly sampled for each virtual character so that the virtual characters would not behave simultaneously. Alternatively, we can provide color-coded *direct visual feedback*. A color-coded bar allows us to display the internal value of a behavioral descriptor directly, giving immediate feedback to the speaker about his or her performance.

To provide the learning framework with perceptual information on the speaker's performance, we made use of a wizard of Oz interface in order to ensure correct detection of the target behaviors (i.e. eye contact and pause fillers). In the future, we will utilize automatic audiovisual behavior tracking and machine learned models, investigated in this work, to automatically assess the speaker's performance, as suggested in [4]. Within the architecture, the perceptual information was aggregated into public speaking performance descriptors that directly influenced either the virtual audience's nonverbal behavior as feedback or the direct visual overlays.

4. METHODS

4.1 Experimental Design

As an initial study, we had users train with our virtual audience prototype with a pre- to post-training test paradigm, i.e. we compare learning outcomes between a pre-training performance and a post-training performance. By following this paradigm, we can assess speakers' relative performance improvement while compensating for their initial public speaking expertise.

4.1.1 Study Protocol

Participants were instructed they would be asked to present two topics during 5-minute presentations and were sent material (i.e. abstract and slides) to prepare the day of the study. Before recording the first presentation, participants completed questionnaires on demographics, self-assessment, and public-speaking anxiety. Each participant gave four presentations. The first and fourth consisted of the pre-training and post-training presentations, where the participants were asked to present the same topic in front of a passive virtual audience. Between these two tests, the participants trained for *eye contact* and *avoiding pause fillers* in two separate presentations, using the second topic. We specifically chose these two basic behavioral aspects of good public speaking performances following discussions with Toastmasters[1] experts. In addition, these aspects are clearly defined and can be objectively quantified using manual annotation enabling our threefold evaluation. In the second and third presentations, the audience was configured to use condition dependent different feedback strategies: no feedback, direct feedback through a red-green bar-indicator, or through non-verbal behavior of the audience. The condition was randomly assigned to participants when they came in. Please note, this work does not rely on these conditions. All three research questions focus on the pre- and post-training presentation.

[1]`http://www.toastmasters.org/`

The virtual audience was displayed using two projections to render the audience in life-size. The participants were recorded with a head mounted microphone, with a Logitech web camera capturing facial expressions, and a Microsoft Kinect placed in the middle of the two screens capturing the body of the presenter.

4.2 Participants and Dataset

Participants were recruited from Craigslist[2] and paid USD 25. In total, 47 people participated (29 male and 18 female) with an average age of 37 years ($SD = 12.05$). Out of the 47 participants 30 have some college education.
Two recordings had technical problems leaving a total of 45 participants On average the pre-training presentations lasted for 237 seconds ($SD = 116$) and the post-training presentation 234 seconds ($SD = 137$) respectively. Overall, there is no significant difference in presentation length between pre- and post-training presentations.

Experts

To compare the pre- with the post-training presentations, three experienced experts of the worldwide organization of Toastmasters were invited and paid USD 125. Their average age is 43.3 year ($SD = 11.5$), one was female and two were male. The experts rated their public speaking experience and comfort on 7-point Likert scales. On average they felt very comfortable presenting in front of a public audience ($M = 6.3$, with 1 - not comfortable, 7 - totally comfortable). They have extensive training in speaking in front of an audience ($M = 6$, with 1 - no experience, 7 - a lot of experience).

4.3 Measures

To answer our research questions we need different measures. For **Q1** as well as **Q2** we need an expert assessment and automatically extracted features. In addition to an expert assessment, **Q3** requires manually annotated behaviors.

4.3.1 Expert Assessment

Three Toastmasters experts, who were blind to the order of presentation (i.e. pre-training vs. post-training), evaluated whether participants improved their public speaking skills. Experts viewed videos of the presentations. The videos are presented pairwise for a direct comparison in a random order. Each video showed both the participant's upper body and facial expressions (cf. Figure 1). Each expert evaluated the performance differences for all pairs on 7-point Likert scales for all ten aspects. In particular, they assessed performance aspects derived from prior work on public speaking assessment [27, 4, 26, 24] and targeted discussions with experts apply more to the pre- or post-training presentation[3]:

1. Eye Contact
2. Body Posture
3. Flow of Speech
4. Gesture Usage
5. Intonation
6. Confidence Level
7. Stage Usage
8. Avoids pause fillers
9. Presentation Structure
10. Overall Performance

The pairwise agreement between the three experts is measured by the absolute distance between the experts' Likert

[2]`http://www.craigslist.org/`
[3]Aspect definitions and a dummy version of the questionnaire are available: `http://tinyurl.com/ovtp67x`

scale ratings. The percentage of agreement with a maximal distance of 1 ranges between 63.70% and 81.48% for all 10 aspects, indicating high overall agreement between raters.

4.3.2 Objective measures

To complement expert ratings, we evaluated public speaking performance improvement using two objective measures, namely *eye contact* and the *avoidance of pause fillers*. The presenters were specifically informed about these two aspects in the training presentations for all three conditions. In order to create objective individual baselines, we annotated both measures for all pre-training and post-training test presentations. Two annotators manually marked periods of *eye contact* with the virtual audience and the occurrence of *pause fillers* using the annotation tool ELAN [28]. For both aspects we observed high inter-rater agreement for a randomly selected subset of four videos that both annotators assessed. The Krippendorff α for eye contact is $\alpha = 0.751$ and pause fillers $\alpha = 0.957$ respectively. Krippendorff's α is computed on a frame-wise basis at 30 Hz.

For eye contact we computed a ratio for looking at the audience $\in [0, 1]$, with 0 = never looks at the audience and 1 = always looks at the audience, over the full length of the presentation based on the manual annotations. The number of pause filler words were normalized by the duration of the presentation in seconds.

The improvement is measured by the normalized difference index *ndi* between the pre-training and post-training test presentations for both objectively assessed behaviors and was calculated by

$$ndi = \frac{post - pre}{post + pre}. \tag{1}$$

4.3.3 Automatic Behavior Assessment

In this section the automatically extracted features and the used machine learning algorithms are introduced. The following features of the pre- and post-training presentations are combined with equation 1 to reflect improvement or the lack thereof.

Acoustic Behavior Assessment.

For the processing of the audio signals, we use the freely available COVAREP toolbox (v1.2.0), a collaborative speech analysis repository [6]. COVAREP provides an extensive selection of open-source robust and tested speech processing algorithms enabling comparative and cooperative research within the speech community.

All following acoustic features are masked with voiced-unvoiced (VUV) [9], which determines whether the participant is voicing, i.e. the vocal folds are vibrating. After masking, we use the average and the standard deviation of the temporal information of our features. Not affected by this masking is VUV itself, i.e. the average of VUV is used as an estimation of the ratio of speech to pauses.

Using COVAREP, we extract the following acoustic features: the maxima dispersion quotient (MDQ) [17], peak slope (PS) [16], normalized amplitude quotient (NAQ) [1], the difference in amplitude of the first two harmonics of the differentiated glottal source spectrum (H1H2) [31], and the estimation of the R_d shape parameter of the Liljencrants-Fant glottal model (RD) [11]. Beside these features we also use the fundamental frequency (f_0) [9] and the first two KARMA filtered formants (F_1, F_2) [20]. Additionally, we use the first four Mel-frequency cepstral coefficients ($MFCC_{0-3}$) and extract the voice intensity in dB.

Visual Behavior Assessment.

Gestures are measured by the change of upper body joints' angles from the Microsoft Kinect. Therefore, we take the sum of differences in angles (from the following joints: shoulder, elbow, hand, and wrist). To eliminate noise, we set the difference to zero when not both hands are above the hips. To avoid assigning too much weight to voluminous gestures, we truncate the differences when the difference is higher than a threshold, which we calculated from manual gesture annotations of 20 presentations. In the end, we use the mean of the absolute differences as an indicator for gesturing during the presentation.

We evaluate eye contact with the audience based on two eye gaze estimations. The eye gaze estimation from OKAO [19] head orientation from CLNF [3] are used separately to classify whether a participant is looking at the audience or not. The intervals for the angles, which we use to attest eye contact, are calculated from our eye contact annotations. Finally, we use the ratio of looking at the audience relative to the length of the presentation as a feature.

Emotions, such as anger, sadness, and contempt, are extracted with FACET [10]. After applying the confidence provided by FACET, we take the mean of the emotions' intensity as features.

Machine Learning.

To approximate the experts' combined performance assessments we utilize a regression approach with the experts' averaged ratings as targets for all ten aspects. For this, we use Matlab's implementation of a least squared boosted regression ensemble tree. We evaluate our predictions with a leave one speaker out cross-evaluation. Since we have relatively many features with respect to the number of participants, we use the forward feature selection to find a subset of features using the speaker independent validation strategy. This kind of feature selection starts with an empty set of features and iteratively adds the feature that decreases together with the chosen features a criterion function the most. The resulting feature subset might not be optimal. As a criterion function we use $(1 - \text{corr}(\hat{y}, y))^2$, where $\hat{y}$ are the predictions of the leave one speaker out cross-evaluation and y the ground truth.

5. RESULTS

5.1 Q1 - Behavioral Indicators

We report correlation results with the linear Pearson correlation coefficient along with the degrees of freedom and the p-value. Table 1 summarizes the features, which change between the pre- and post-training presentation measured by *ndi* (Eq. 1) strongly correlates with aspects of public speaking proficiency. We list only detail statistical findings for a reduced number of aspects due to space restrictions. Please note, this table and the following paragraphs are not complete in respect to all aspects nor do they mention all features. For a complete list of all aspects and correlating features see Table 1 of the supplementary material.

Eye Contact: Experts' eye contact assessments slightly correlate with an increase of the average eye contact as

Table 1: Overview of correlating features for each improvement aspect. Arrows indicating the direction of the correlation, i.e. ↑ means positive correlation and ↓ means negative correlation.

Improvement Aspect	Correlating Behavior
Eye Contact	↑ eye contact ↓ contempt ↓ VUV std ↓ H1H2 std
Flow of Speech	↑ voice intensity variation ↑ peak slope std ↑ $MFCC_0$ std ↓ H1H2 std ↓ $MFCC_0$ mean ↓ VUV std
Gesture Usage	↑ ratio of speech and pauses ↑ gesture ↑ MDQ mean
Intonation	↑ pitch mean ↑ peak slope std ↑ vocal expressivity ↓ peak slope mean
Confidence	↑ F_1 mean ↑ vocal expressivity ↑ ratio of speech and pauses ↑ pitch mean ↓ $MFCC_0$ mean ↓ peak slope mean
Pause Fillers	↑ peak slope std ↓ contempt ↓ VUV std
Overall Performance	↑ peak slope std ↓ H1H2 std ↓ contempt ↓ VUV std

assessed by OKAO ($r(43) = 0.24$, $p = 0.105$). Also, assessed contempt facial expressions correlate negatively with the eye contact assessment ($r(43) = -0.33$, $p = 0.029$). We identify two negatively correlating acoustic features, namely a decrease of the standard deviation of VUV ($r(43) = -0.34$, $p = 0.024$) and a decrease of the standard deviation of H1H2 ($r(43) = -0.45$, $p = 0.002$).

Flow of Speech: Experts' flow of speech assessment correlates only with acoustic features. They include an increase of the standard deviation of the voice intensity ($r(43) = 0.31$, $p = 0.039$), a decrease of the average of $MFCC_0$ ($r(43) = -0.36$, $p = 0.015$) as well as an increase of the standard deviation of it ($r(43) = 0.35$, $p = 0.019$). Beside these features also a decrease in the standard deviation of VUV ($r(43) = -0.39$, $p = 0.008$), a decrease in the standard deviation of H1H2 ($r(43) = -0.33$, $p = 0.026$), and an increase in the standard deviation of PS ($r(43) = 0.31$, $p = 0.040$) correlated with *flow of speech*.

Confidence: Experts' confidence assessment correlates with several acoustic features. It correlates with an increasing average pitch ($r(43) = 0.32$, $p = 0.034$), an increase of mean of VUV ($r(43) = 0.32$, $p = 0.031$), a decrease of VUV standard deviation ($r(43) = -0.40$, $p = 0.006$), the decrease of the standard deviation of H1H2 ($r(43) = -0.36$, $p = 0.016$), and a decrease of the average PS ($r(43) = -0.32$, $p = 0.034$). In addition to these features, an increase of the standard deviation of $MFCC_2$ ($r(43) = 0.30$, $p = 0.044$) correlate with *confidence*, too. Lastly, the following formants correlate with *confidence* of the first formant an increase in the average ($r(43) = 0.34$, $p = 0.021$) as well as an increase of the standard deviation ($r(43) = 0.31$, $p = 0.037$) and of the bandwidth from the second formant a decrease of the average ($r(43) = -0.32$, $p = 0.033$) as well as a decrease of the standard deviation ($r(43) = -0.40$, $p = 0.007$).

Avoids Pause Fillers The assessed avoidance of pause fillers correlates with a decrease of the standard deviation of VUV ($r(43) = -0.52$, $p < 0.001$) and an increase of PS's standard deviation ($r(43) = 0.32$, $p = 0.030$). Furthermore, it correlates with two visual features, namely being less contempt ($r(43) = -0.36$, $p = 0.016$) and having more neutral facial expressions ($r(43) = 0.35$, $p = 0.019$).

Overall Performance: Finally, the assessed overall performance correlates with showing less contempt facial expressions ($r(43) = -0.32$, $p = 0.030$) and the following acoustic features: a decrease of the standard deviation of VUV ($r(43) = -0.46$, $p = 0.002$), a decrease of the standard deviation of H1H2 ($r(43) = -0.31$, $p = 0.039$), an increase in PS' standard deviation ($r(43) = 0.36$, $p = 0.015$), and a decrease of the bandwidth from the second formant ($r(43) = -0.30$, $p = 0.042$).

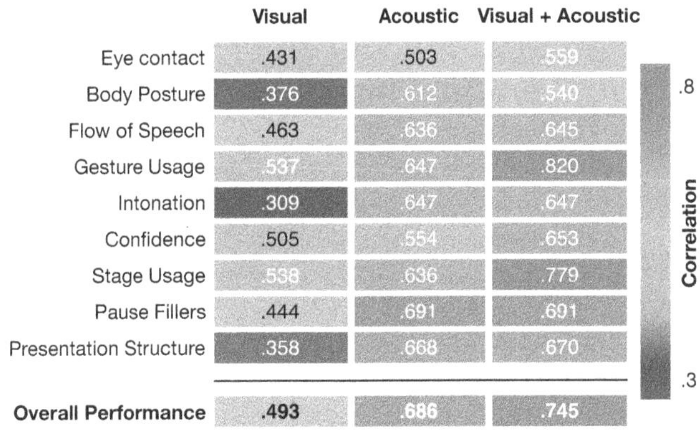

Figure 2: Color coded visualization of the Pearson correlation between the expert assessments of all evaluated aspects and the automatic prediction using both single modalities and both combined.

5.2 Q2 - Automatic Assessment

In Figure 2 we report Pearson's correlation results for every aspect using the three feature sets (*visual*, *acoustic*, and *acoustic+visual*). As seen in Figure 2, the acoustic+visual feature set outperforms the other two modalities consistently. We present the p-values of two-tailed t-tests and Hedges' g values as a measure of the effect size. The g value denotes the estimated difference between the two population means in magnitudes of standard deviations [13].

In addition to correlation assessments, we investigate mean absolute errors of our automatic assessment using tree ensembles. As a comparison performance we use the mean over all expert ratings for every aspect and all participants as a constant baseline and compare it with the automatic assess-

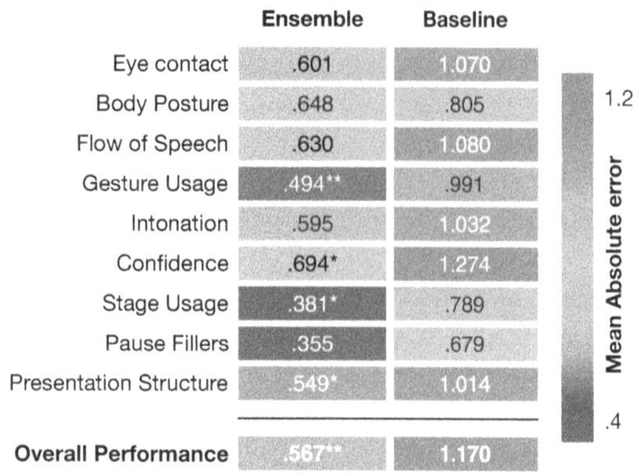

Figure 3: Color coded visualization of the mean absolute error of the ensemble tree approach and the baseline assessment. Significant improvements are marked with * ($p < 0.05$) and ** ($p < 0.01$).

ment using the mean absolute error. Our prediction errors ($M = 0.55$, $SD = 0.42$) are consistently lower compared to the baseline errors ($M = 0.74$, $SD = 0.57$) and significantly better ($t(898) = 0.50$, $p < 0.001$, $g = -0.372$) across all aspects. Additionally, for *overall performance* alone the automatic assessment ($M = 0.57$, $SD = 0.46$) is also significantly better than the baseline ($M = 0.88$, $SD = 0.61$; $t(88) = 0.54$, $p = 0.008$, $g = -0.566$). For a full comparison of all aspects between our prediction errors and the constant prediction errors see Figure 3.

When we compare the different modalities, i.e. acoustic and visual features separately as well as jointly, we identified the following results: *Acoustic* features only ($M = 0.59$, $SD = 0.45$; $t(898) = 0.50$, $p = 0.002$, $g = -0.202$) and *acoustic+visual* features ($M = 0.55$, $SD = 0.42$; $t(898) = 0.48$, $p < 0.001$, $g = -0.297$) significantly outperform the *visual* ($M = 0.70$, $SD = 0.54$) features. We do not observe a significant difference between *acoustic* and *acoustic+visual* ($t(898) = 0.44$, $p = 0.140$, $g = 0.099$).

5.3 Q3 - Expert Judgments

We annotated eye contact and pause filler words in all pre- and post-training presentations, see Section 4.3. For the eye contact annotation, we use the normalized value of the annotated aspect, the annotated period divided by the length of the presentations. The count of pause filler words is used directly as a score. Thereby, we have scores of the annotated aspects representing the annotated behavior in the pre- and post-training presentation.

To have a score comparable to the expert assessment, we use equation 1 to combine the scores of the pre- and post-training presentation. We do not observe a significant correlation between the experts' eye contact assessment and the annotated eye contact ($r(43) = 0.20$, $p = 0.197$) as well as no correlation between the pause filler annotations and the assessed pause fillers ($r(43) = -0.05$, $p = 0.739$). However, we observe a strong correlation between the automatic measures of eye contact using OKAO ($r(88) = 0.62$, $p < 0.001$) and CLNF ($r(88) = 0.66$, $p < 0.001$) and the manually annotated eye contact.

6. DISCUSSION

6.1 Q1 - Behavioral Indicators

Our first research question aims at identifying within-subject nonverbal behavioral changes between pre- and post-training presentations and how they relate to expert assessments. All reported behaviors are automatically assessed and changes are identified using the *ndi* (see Section 4). We correlate the observed behavioral changes with expert assessed performances in all ten aspects. Our findings confirm that large portions of a public speaking performance improvements are covered by nonverbal behavior estimates.

As summarized in Table 1, we can identify a number of multimodal nonverbal behaviors that are correlated with expert assessments for the investigated aspects as well as for overall performance improvement (due to space restrictions we excluded three aspects from our analysis). For several aspects, such as *intonation* and *gesture usage* prior intuitions are confirmed. For example vocal expressivity, increased tenseness (as measured by peak slope), and pitch are correlated with an improvement in the assessment of intonation. Further, the increased usage of gestures from pre- to post-training presentations is correlated with an assessed improvement of gesture usage. In addition, multifaceted aspects such as *confidence* show a broad spectrum of automatic measures that are correlated, both positively and negatively. For the assessment of *overall performance*, we identified that the use of contempt facial expressions is negatively correlated with performance improvement. This could be interpreted that if the presenter accepted the virtual audience and engaged in training they gained more from the experience. Further, changes in pause to speech ratio and increased variability in the voice as measured with peak slope correlate with overall performance improvement. Change of the standard deviation of VUV negatively correlates most prominently with a number of aspects. As VUV is a logical vector, i.e. whether a person is voicing or not, the standard deviation is similar to the entropy. This indicates that a decrease in speaking variety or the development of a more regular flow of speech, is a key feature of public speaking performance improvement.

As shown in Figure 1, we plan to incorporate the identified automatic measures of behavioral change as input to control the virtual audience online feedback. We anticipate to use both targeted feedback behavior, such as a virtual audience member clears its throat to signify that it feels neglected by lack of eye contact, as well as complex feedback covering multiple aspects. The exact types of behavioral online feedback need to be further investigated in future studies; it is important that the behaviors of the virtual audience are clearly identifiable. Only then will the trainee be able to reflect on his or her behavior during training and ultimately improve.

6.2 Q2 - Automatic Assessment

In order to answer the second research question, we conducted extensive unimodal and multimodal experiments and investigate ensemble trees to automatically approximate the experts' assessments on the ten behavioral aspects. Figure 2 summarizes the observed correlation performance of our automatic performance assessment ensemble trees. In addition, we investigate mean absolute errors for the regression output of the ensemble trees compared to an average baseline. For both performance measures, i.e. correlation and mean absolute error, we observe that multimodal features consistently outperform unimodal feature sets. In particular, complex behavioral assessments such as the overall performance and confidence of the speaker benefit from features of multiple modalities. Out of the single modalities the acoustic information seems to be most promising for the assessment of performance improvement. However, we are confident that with the development of more complex and tailored visual features similar success can be achieved. When compared to the baseline, the ensemble tree regression approach significantly improves baseline assessment for several aspects including overall performance.

One of the main reasons for choosing ensemble trees as the regression approach of choice is the possibility to investigate the selected features to achieve the optimal results. This enables us to investigate behavioral characteristics of public speaking performance improvement in detail. For the overall performance estimation the multimodal ensemble tree selected negative facial expressions, pause to speech ratio, average RD measure, average second and third formants, as well as the second formant's bandwidth. This selection shows the importance for both the facial expressions and the voice characteristics for the assessment of performance improvement. Overall the ensemble trees' output is correlated with the experts' assessment at $r > 0.7$, which is a considerably high correlation and a very promising result.

In the future, we plan to use these automatic performance improvement estimates to give the trainees targeted post-hoc feedback on what aspects did improve and which need further training. Similar to the work in [14], we plan to provide a visual performance report to the trainee as a first step. In addition, such visual reports can be enhanced by a virtual tutor that guides the trainee through the assessment and possibly replays several scenes from the presentation and provides motivational feedback to the trainee.

6.3 Q3 - Expert Judgments

When investigating the third research question, we identified a considerable difference between the manual ground truth labels of two key behaviors and experts' subjective opinions. In particular, we found that there is no correlation between the experts' assessment of the used number of pause fillers and the actual number of pause fillers uttered by the presenters. We also found no correlation between the assessment of eye contact and the manually annotated times of actual eye contact of the presenter with the virtual audience. However, we found a strong correlation between the automatic measures of eye contact with the manual annotation. This finding could explain why the automatically assessed eye contact only slightly correlates with the experts' assessment (see Section 5.1).

It is possible to argue that the experts did not accurately count the number of pause fillers during their assessments and if they had been provided with the exact numbers their assessment would have changed, however, this probably does not hold for the more complex behavior of eye contact. While both the manual annotation and the automatic assessment of eye contact are crude measures of the time a presenter looks at an audience, the experts might inform their decision on a much more complex basis. In particular, we believe that eye gaze patterns such as slowly swaying the view across the entire audience vs. staring at one single person for an entire presentation might be strong indicators of excellent or poor gaze behaviors. A distinction between such behaviors is not possible using the utilized crude measures. As mentioned earlier, we plan to investigate more tailored behavioral descriptors in the near future.

7. CONCLUSION

Based on the three research questions investigated in this work we can identify the following main findings: **Q1** We could identify both visual and acoustic nonverbal behaviors that are strongly correlated with pre- to post-training presentation performance improvement and the lack thereof. In particular, facial expressions, gestures, and voice characteristics are identified to correlate with performance improvement as assessed by public speaking experts from the Toastmasters organization. **Q2** Based on the automatically tracked behaviors, we investigated machine learning approaches to approximate the public speaking performance on ten behavioral aspects including the overall performance. We showed that the multimodal approach utilizing both acoustic and visual behaviors consistently outperformed the unimodal approaches. In addition, we found that our machine learning approach significantly outperforms the baseline. **Q3** Lastly, we investigated manual ground truth assessments for eye contact and number of pause fillers used in pre- and post-training presentations and how they relate to expert assessments. We could identify a considerable difference between expert assessments and actual improvement for the two investigated behaviors. This indicates that experts base their assessments on more complex information than just the amount spent looking at the audience or the number of pause fillers uttered, but rather identify patterns of behaviors showing proficiency. We plan to investigate such more complex patterns of behaviors in the near future and confer with our public speaking experts to inform us on their decision process.

Overall, our findings and results are promising and we believe that this accessible technology has the potential to impact training focused on the nonverbal communication aspects of in fact a wide variety of interpersonal skills, including but not limited to public speaking.

Acknowledgment

This material is based upon work supported by the National Science Foundation under Grants No. IIS-1421330 and U.S. Army Research Laboratory under contract number W911NF-14-D-0005. Any opinions, findings, and conclusions or recommendations expressed in this material are those of the author(s) and do not necessarily reflect the views of the National Science Foundation or the Government, and no official endorsement should be inferred.

8. REFERENCES

[1] P. Alku, T. Bäckström, and E. Vilkman. Normalized amplitude quotient for parameterization of the glottal flow. *Journal of the Acoustical Society of America*, 112(2):701–710, 2002.

[2] K. Anderson and et al. The TARDIS framework: Intelligent virtual agents for social coaching in job interviews. In *Proceedings of International Conference on Advances in Computer Entertainment*, pages 476–491, 2013.

[3] T. Baltrusaitis, P. Robinson, and L.-P. Morency. Constrained local neural fields for robust facial

landmark detection in the wild. In *International Conference on Computer Vision Workshops*, pages 354–361, 2013.

[4] L. Batrinca, G. Stratou, A. Shapiro, L.-P. Morency, and S. Scherer. Cicero - towards a multimodal virtual audience platform for public speaking training. In *Proceedings of Intelligent Virtual Agents 2013*, pages 116–128. Springer, 2013.

[5] M. Chollet, G. Stratou, A. Shapiro, L.-P. Morency, and S. Scherer. An interactive virtual audience platform for public speaking training. In *Proceedings of International Conference on Autonomous Agents and Multiagent Systems*, pages 1657–1658, 2014.

[6] G. Degottex, J. Kane, T. Drugman, T. Raitio, and S. Scherer. Covarep - a collaborative voice analysis repository for speech technologies. In *Proceedings of International Conference on Acoustics, Speech and Signal Processing*, pages 960–964, 2014.

[7] D. DeVault and et al. Simsensei kiosk: A virtual human interviewer for healthcare decision support. In *Proceedings of Autonomous Agents and Multiagent Systems*, pages 1061–1068, 2014.

[8] M. R. DiMatteo, R. D. Hays, and L. M. Prince. Relationship of physicians' nonverbal communication skill to patient satisfaction, appointment noncompliance, and physician workload. *Health Psychology*, 5(6):581, 1986.

[9] T. Drugman and A. Abeer. Joint robust voicing detection and pitch estimation based on residual harmonics. In *Proceedings of Interspeech 2011*, pages 1973–1976, 2011.

[10] Emotient. FACET SDK, 2014. `http://www.emotient.com/products`.

[11] G. Fant, J. Liljencrants, and Q. Lin. The LF-model revisited. transformations and frequency domain analysis. *Speech Transmission Laboratory, Quarterly Report, Royal Institute of Technology*, 2(1):119–156, 1995.

[12] J. Hart, J. Gratch, and S. Marsella. *How Virtual Reality Training Can Win Friends and Influence People*, chapter 21, pages 235–249. Human Factors in Defence. Ashgate, 2013.

[13] L. V. Hedges. Distribution theory for glass's estimator of effect size and related estimators. *Journal of Educational Statistics*, 6(2):107–128, 1981.

[14] M. Hoque, M. Courgeon, J.-C. Martin, M. Bilge, and R. Picard. Mach: My automated conversation coach. In *Proceedings of International Joint Conference on Pervasive and Ubiquitous Computing*, 2013.

[15] W. L. Johnson, J. W. Rickel, and J. C. Lester. Animated pedagogical agents: Face-to-face interaction in interactive learning environments. *International Journal of Artificial Intelligence in Education*, 11(1):47–78, 2000.

[16] J. Kane and C. Gobl. Identifying regions of non-modal phonation using features of the wavelet transform. In *Proceedings of Interspeech 2011*, pages 177–180, 2011.

[17] J. Kane and C. Gobl. Wavelet maxima dispersion for breathy to tense voice discrimination. *Audio, Speech, and Language Processing, IEEE Transactions on*, 21(6):1170–1179, 2013.

[18] H. C. Lane, M. J. Hays, M. G. Core, and D. Auerbach. Learning intercultural communication skills with virtual humans: Feedback and fidelity. *Journal of Educational Psychology Special Issue on Advanced Learning Technologies*, 105(4):1026–1035, 2013.

[19] S. Lao and M. Kawade. Vision-based face understanding technologies and their applications. In *Proceedings of the Conference on Advances in Biometric Person Authentication*, pages 339–348, 2004.

[20] D. D. Mehta, D. Rudoy, and P. J. Wolfe. KARMA: Kalman-based autoregressive moving average modeling and inference for formant and antiformant tracking. *Journal of the Acoustical Society of America*, 132(3):1732–1746, 2011.

[21] L. S. Nguyen, A. Marcos-Ramiro, M. Marrón Romera, and D. Gatica-Perez. Multimodal analysis of body communication cues in employment interviews. In *Proceedings of the International Conference on Multimodal Interaction*, pages 437–444, 2013.

[22] S. Park, P. Shoemark, and L.-P. Morency. Toward crowdsourcing micro-level behavior annotations: the challenges of interface, training, and generalization. In *Proceedings of the 18th International Conference on Intelligent User Interfaces*, pages 37–46. ACM, 2014.

[23] D.-P. Pertaub, M. Slater, and C. Barker. An experiment on public speaking anxiety in response to three different types of virtual audience. *Presence: Teleoperators and Virtual Environments*, 11(1):68–78, 2002.

[24] A. Rosenberg and J. Hirschberg. Acoustic/prosodic and lexical correlates of charismatic speech. In *Proceedings of Interspeech 2005*, pages 513–516, 2005.

[25] J. Rowe, L. Shores, B. Mott, and J. C. Lester. Integrating learning and engagement in narrative-centered learning environments. In *Proceedings of the Tenth International Conference on Intelligent Tutoring Systems*, 2010.

[26] S. Scherer, G. Layher, J. Kane, H. Neumann, and N. Campbell. An audiovisual political speech analysis incorporating eye-tracking and perception data. In *Proceedings of the Eight International Conference on Language Resources and Evaluation*, pages 1114–1120. ELRA, 2012.

[27] L. M. Schreiber, D. P. Gregory, and L. R. Shibley. The development and test of the public speaking competence rubric. *Communication Education*, 61(3):205–233, 2012.

[28] H. Sloetjes and P. Wittenburg. Annotation by category: ELAN and ISO DCR. In *Proceedings of the International Conference on Language Resources and Evaluation*, 2008.

[29] E. Strangert and J. Gustafson. What makes a good speaker? subject ratings, acoustic measurements and perceptual evaluations. In *Proceedings of Interspeech 2008*, pages 1688–1691, 2008.

[30] W. Swartout, R. Artstein, E. Forbell, S. Foutz, H. C. Lane, B. Lange, J. Morie, A. Rizzo, and D. Traum. Virtual humans for learning. *AI Magazine*, 34(4):13–30, 2013.

[31] I. Titze and J. Sundberg. Vocal intensity in speakers and singers. *Journal of the Acoustical Society of America*, 91(5):2936–2946, 1992.

I Would Hire You in a Minute: Thin Slices of Nonverbal Behavior in Job Interviews

Laurent Son Nguyen
Idiap Research Institute
École Polytechnique Fédérale de Lausanne
Switzerland
lnguyen@idiap.ch

Daniel Gatica-Perez
Idiap Research Institute
École Polytechnique Fédérale de Lausanne
Switzerland
gatica@idiap.ch

ABSTRACT

In everyday life, judgments people make about others are based on brief excerpts of interactions, known as thin slices. Inferences stemming from such minimal information can be quite accurate, and nonverbal behavior plays an important role in the impression formation. Because protagonists are strangers, employment interviews are a case where both nonverbal behavior and thin slices can be predictive of outcomes. In this work, we analyze the predictive validity of thin slices of real job interviews, where slices are defined by the sequence of questions in a structured interview format. We approach this problem from an audio-visual, dyadic, and nonverbal perspective, where sensing, cue extraction, and inference are automated. Our study shows that although nonverbal behavioral cues extracted from thin slices were not as predictive as when extracted from the full interaction, they were still predictive of hirability impressions with R^2 values up to 0.34, which was comparable to the predictive validity of human observers on thin slices. Applicant audio cues were found to yield the most accurate results.

Categories and Subject Descriptors

H.1.2 [**Information Systems**]: User/Machine Systems—*Human factors*

Keywords

Social computing; job interview; thin slices; nonverbal behavior; hirability; first impressions; multimodal interaction

1. INTRODUCTION

In our everyday lives, many decisions or judgments people make about others are made based on inferences arising from brief interactions. Social psychology research has shown that the proverb "first impressions are the ones lasting" holds true up to a certain extent: humans are quite accurate at making inferences about others, even if the information is minimal [5]. Short segments of interactions, typically under five minutes, are commonly referred to as thin slices [5]. Surprisingly, such minimal displays of behavior can be predictive of social constructs (*e.g.*, personality, competence) and outcomes (*e.g.* teacher ratings) [5]. As an extreme example of thin-slicing, inferences of competence by naïve raters based on simple photographs were strongly correlated with election outcomes [31].

Used in virtually every organization for the personnel selection process, job interviews are a prototypical situation in which first impressions play a crucial role; indeed, the hiring decision is most often based on how the job applicant was perceived by the recruiter. Employment interviews consist of an interpersonal interaction between at least two protagonists (the applicant and one or more interviewers). Because protagonists are strangers, recruiters have access to very little information (usually, the verbal and nonverbal elements of the interaction, as well as the resume), which makes job interviews close to what psychologists refer to as *zero-acquaintance interactions* [4], and nonverbal behavior is known to play a key role in the formation of first impressions [17].

In this work, we investigate the use of job interview thin slices for the task of automatically inferring hirability first impressions. To the best of our knowledge, no computational study has examined the role of thin slices in this type of interactions. We believe that job interviews are an interesting setting to investigate the interplay between thin slices and nonverbal behavior. This study specifically aims to address the following research questions:

- Q1 Can a short excerpt of the interview be predictive of the hirability ratings based on the full interview?
- Q2 If so, what are the most predictive slices?
- Q3 What are the cues used for prediction, and are they consistent across slices?
- Q4 Is the interaction during interview questions predictive of hirability compared to the interview answers?

We approach these research questions from a nonverbal perspective where sensing, cue extraction, and prediction are automated. Our study shows that although nonverbal behavioral cues extracted from thin slices were not as predictive as when extracted from the full interaction, they were still predictive of hirability impressions, with R^2 values up to 0.34. Automatically extracted nonverbal cues were found to yield comparable results to slice annotations in the task of predicting hirability impressions based on the full interview.

We believe that the answers to these questions could be applied to real-life application scenarios such as automated

ICMI'15, November 09 – 13, 2015, Seattle, WA, USA

ACM 978-1-4503-3912-4/15/11 ...$15.00.
http://dx.doi.org/10.1145/2818346.2820760.

interview training systems or HR assistive services by providing insights on (1) what questions and/or what moments in the interviews are most predictive of the outcome, (2) the amount of behavioral information necessary to obtain an accurate inference, and (3) what cues are predictive and how consistent they remain when thin-sliced.

This paper is structured as follows. In Section 2, we discuss the work related to thin slices and job interviews both in the psychology and computing domains. In Section 3, we present the dataset and the annotations used for this study. In Section 4, we discuss the nonverbal cues automatically extracted for both the applicant and the interviewer. In Section 5, we present the automatic inference task and discuss the results. We finally conclude in Section 6.

2. RELATED WORK

2.1 Related work in psychology

Thin slice research in social psychology has examined the amount of information that could be inferred from short excerpts of behavior by unacquainted judges. To this end, the concept of *observer predictive validity* has been used as an assessment of the relationship between thin slice ratings and the ground truth, defined by direct measurements, self-reports, or impressions obtained from the full interaction, depending on the abstraction level of the social construct being judged [3]. Although the most widely used measure for predictive validity is the correlation between thin slice ratings and the ground truth, other metrics exist, such as the amount of agreement among raters. Works in social psychology have shown that thin slices could be predictive of a broad array of social outcomes, such as individual performance (teaching, job performance, health care), relationships (type and quality of relationships), and individual differences (personality, gender, sexual orientation) [3]. Social psychology research has also investigated the predictive validity of thin slices depending on the channels of communication; the nonverbal channel was shown to play an important role in the formation of these first impressions in such brief excerpts of social interactions [5, 3].

Employment interviews have been a major research topic in social psychology for decades. In particular, previous works have investigated the reliability (*i.e.*, the level of agreement among judges for rating applicants) [15] and validity (*i.e.*, the amount of correlation between interview ratings and job performance) [27] of employment interviews, as well as the relationship between high-level social variables (*e.g.*, personality traits, general intelligence) and job performance [28, 7]. Particular attention has been put on the impact of the applicant's nonverbal behavior on the job interview outcome, and results have shown that applicants who employed more eye contact, smiled more, nodded more, produced more facial expressions, and were more oriented towards the interviewer were generally more likely to be hired, and were perceived as more competent, motivated, and more successful than applicants who did not [13, 25, 6, 16].

Surprisingly, only a few studies have investigated the effect of impressions from thin slices on job interview outcomes. In an unpublished Master's thesis [14], unacquainted judges rated short pre-interview thin slices, defined by the 10 seconds following the moment when the job applicant took his seat; thin slices ratings were observed to be significantly correlated with the full interview ratings. Another work [30] examined the relationships of hiring recommendations based on thin slices and full interviews, and ratings based on 12-second silenced snippets of video were correlated with full interview ratings. Impressions of social skills (*e.g.*, attentive, anxious, confident, etc.) based on thin slices were observed to be associated with full interview ratings, whereas manually annotated visual nonverbal behaviors (*e.g.*, head nods, smiles, fidgets, etc.) did not show any significant correlation.

2.2 Related work in computing

Several computational studies have examined the use of thin slices in contexts similar to job interviews. The work in [11] studied the relationship between nonverbal behavior and outcomes in a simulated dyadic negotiation scenario, focusing on the first five minutes of the interaction. In [8], personality traits were predicted from self-presentations ranging from 30 to 120 seconds in a human-computer setting. Other computational studies have investigated the use of thin slices for the prediction of social constructs as diverse as interest [19], personality [9, 26], attraction [19], emergent leadership [29], or individual performance [18] in face-to-face interactions. In most of these works [19, 8, 18], the concept of thin slices was used because the interactions were inherently short, and both the extracted behavioral features and the annotations of social variables stemmed from the full interactions. However, the study in [29] investigated the effect of slice durations on the prediction accuracy by extracting behavioral features from the slice of interest and using them to infer the social variables annotated from the full interaction, and observed that an asymptote was reached around the middle of the interaction.

Despite the importance of job interviews in the personnel selection process, to our knowledge only a few studies have analyzed this type of interactions from a computational perspective. In previous works, we have investigated the use of automatically extracted nonverbal cues (speaking turns, prosody, head nods, visual activity) to infer five types of hirability variables in a dataset of real job interviews [21]. In another study, we examined the relationship between visual body activity and personality and hirability using a mixture of automatically and manually extracted features [22]. Naim *et al.* [20] collected a dataset of 69 internship-seeking students participating to mock interviews, and extracted nonverbal and lexical features for the prediction of various social variables (*e.g.*, hiring recommendation, engagement, friendliness) and perceived behaviors (*e.g.*, smile, eye contact, speaking rate). Last, Chen *et al.* [10] proposed a multimodal method to recognize job applicants' affective states from 20 acted video interviews. To our knowledge, no previous study has investigated employment interviews from a thin-slice perspective.

3. DATASET

3.1 Job interview dataset

We used the dataset of 62 real job interviews collected in [21]. Applicants were applying for a paid marketing job in which they had to convince people on the street to participate to psychology studies (USD200 for four hours of effective work). The interviews were dyadic, where one applicant and one interviewer were seated at opposite sides of a table. All interviews were conducted by the same person, a researcher in organizational psychology.

No binary hiring outcome was given as such; all applicants were hired for the job regardless of their performance during the interview. However, applicants were performing at their best because they were believing that the interview outcome was depending on their performance. The interviewer did not rate the applicants, but video recordings of the interviews were sent to human resource professionals for rating (see Sections 3.3.1 and 3.3.2 for details).

The job interviews were structured, meaning that the sequence of questions/answers was constant across interviews, ensuring that comparisons could be made across job applicants. The interview structure was the following:

1. Short self-presentation.
2. Motivation to apply for the job.
3. Importance of scientific research.
4. Past experience where communication skills were required.
5. Past experience where persuasion skills were required.
6. Past experience of conscientious work.
7. Past experience where stress was correctly managed.
8. Strong/weak points about self.

The interview dataset contains audio-video data for both the applicant and the interviewer. RGB video was recorded at 26.6 frames per second with a 1280×960 resolution. Cameras were nearly frontal, filming the upper part of the body. For audio, a Microcone microphone array was used, which provides semi-automatic speaker segmentation in addition to recording audio at 48kHz [1].

3.2 Definition of thin slices

Most previous studies in thin slices used segments of fixed duration, which is valid for the case of unstructured interactions, but generates an undesirable bias when the interaction is structured such as in our case. To prevent this, we decided to make use of the structured nature of the interviews by annotating the timings of the eight specific question/answer segments of the job interview. Additionally, in order to compare the behavioral predictive power of question *vs.* answer segments, we further annotated the timing of questions and answers. The annotations of timings were completed by one of the authors. In summary, three thin-slice cases were used: whole-slice, question-only, and answer-only (see Table 1).

Statistics of slice durations are shown in Table 2. We first observe that the longest slice (whole-slice) was the first question (self-presentation), which can be explained by the fact that the question was significantly longer than the other ones because it included the job description. The low variance in duration for the question-only case can be explained by the fact that the interviewer was instructed to follow a script. In terms of answers, six had an average duration over 50 seconds. The shortest answer was the motivation to apply for the job, and this can be explained by the fact that some applicants had already mentioned their motivation in the first question (self-presentation).

3.3 Hirability impressions

3.3.1 Hirability impressions from the full interview

Hirability impressions were annotated by a pool of five human resources (HR) professionals, who watched the full videos of the applicant including the audio track. All interviews were annotated in total by three raters. The HR professionals were asked to rate the applicants' overall performances, and gave a score on a 10-point Likert scale, where 1 was the minimum score, and 10 the maximum score. To avoid bias, no specific instruction was given on what behaviors to focus on so that they could focus on their own internal representations.

Table 1: Definition of the three thin slice cases used for the eight slices of the structured interview.

TS case	t_{start}	t_{end}
Question-only	Question start	Question end
Answer-only	Answer start	Answer end
Whole-slice	Question start	Answer end

Inter-rater agreement proved to be high among HR professionals, with $ICC(1,1) = 0.501$ and $ICC(1,k) = 0.751$, using the intraclass correlation coefficient. Four other hirability scores related to questions 4-7 of the interview were annotated, but were not used in this study as they were highly correlated with the hiring decision score ($r \in [0.610, 0.916]$, using Pearson's correlation coefficient).

3.3.2 Hirability impressions from thin slices

To assess the accuracy of human raters when exposed to short excerpts of interactions *vs.* when they have access to the full interviews, we collected annotations for each interview slice. To this end, a pool of four human resource professionals rated each individual slice (whole-slice, *i.e.* including question and answer), including both audio and video. In total, each rater watched two slices from the same interview; the two slices were ensured not to be subsequent such that the hirability impression on the second slice was not too heavily influenced by the first one. In order to avoid bias, the professional raters were different from the ones who annotated the full interviews (Section 3.3.1), but had similar backgrounds.

To assess agreement among judges, all 8 slices were viewed by a second rater for 10 interviews. Inter-rater agreement was computed for each slice using Pearson's pairwise correlation coefficient, and results are displayed in Figure 1 (1); the inter-rater agreement for the full interview (using the average Pearson's correlation coefficient as measure) is also displayed. Although the number of double-coded videos for each slice was relatively low, it provides a good insight on the reliability of judges in forming first impressions from short excerpts of interviews. Inter-rater agreement for slice 4 (communication skills) and slice 8 (strong/weak points) was observed to be low, which suggests that these slices were more difficult to annotate. Other slices had agreements ranging from $r = 0.50$ to $r = 0.85$.

3.3.3 Observer predictive validity

We then computed the pairwise correlations between slice and full interview annotations, using Pearson's correlation coefficient. Slice-full correlations are displayed in Figure 1 (2). In social psychology related works [3], this measure is often used to quantify the observer predictive validity of the slice, which corresponds to the amount of information that an unacquainted judge can infer from a short excerpt of behavioral stream compared to the full interaction. Slice-full correlations ranged from $r = 0.25$ to $r = 0.69$. We observe that not all slices showed the same observer predictive validity: slice 2 (motivation for the job) and slice 4

Table 2: Statistics on the duration of slices: mean and standard deviation (in seconds). N = 62.

		Question-only		Answer-only		Whole-slice	
Slice	Slice description	mean [s]	std [s]	mean [s]	std [s]	mean [s]	std [s]
1	Self-presentation	64.5	6.1	63.4	34.8	128.0	36.2
2	Motivation for the job	3.3	0.5	35.3	18.4	38.6	18.3
3	Importance of research	5.4	0.7	46.4	20.8	51.8	20.8
4	Communication skills	31.2	2.3	64.2	33.3	95.4	33.7
5	Persuasion skills	20.7	1.5	60.7	32.9	81.5	33.2
6	Conscientiousness	27.8	1.9	55.4	34.6	83.3	34.7
7	Stress resistance	15.4	1.1	60.8	43.2	76.2	43.0
8	Strong/weak points	6.0	0.7	71.6	32.5	77.6	32.3

(communication skills) were found to be less strongly correlated with the full interview rating ($r = 0.36$ and $r = 0.25$, resp.) than other slices. The low predictive validity of slice 4 (communication skills) can be explained by the fact that the agreement among judges for this slice was low ($r = 0.05$). For slice 2 (motivation for the job), although the inter-rater agreement was high ($r = 0.84$) the slice showed poor observer predictive validity. This finding can be explained by the fact that some job applicants stated their motivation to apply for the job in the previous question (self-presentation) and provided a short answer (*e.g.*, "As I already told you...") for slice 2, possibly earning low thin-slice hirability ratings due to this.

As a last step, we computed the squared value of the slice-full correlations. The obtained R^2 value accounts for the variance explained by an ordinary least squares linear model using the slice annotation as only predictor, with no cross-validation. In other words, this number represents the amount of explained variance by holding the rating based on the thin slice, and can be used for the comparison with automated methods in a regression task. The R^2 values for each slice are displayed in Figure 1 (3). We observe that the obtained R^2 values range from $R^2 = 0.06$ (communication skills) to $R^2 = 0.47$ (stress resistance).

4. BEHAVIORAL FEATURES

4.1 Extracted features

In order to obtain a behavioral representation of the interaction between the applicant and the interviewer during interview slices, we automatically extracted nonverbal cues from the audio and visual modalities for both protagonists. The extracted nonverbal cues were based on their relevance in the nonverbal communication literature [12, 16, 17] and the available computational tools. Other behavioral cues (*e.g.* gaze, facial expressions, verbal content) could also be extracted to get a more complete representation of the interaction, but we limited ourselves to the set of features listed below. The analysis of other behavioral cues will be the focus of future work.

All features were extracted for the eight interview questions (see Section 3) and the three thin slice cases (see Table 1), and were normalized with respect to slice duration. Additionally, the features were also extracted for the full interview. The list of all extracted nonverbal features is displayed in the **supplementary material**.

4.1.1 Audio features

Speaking activity features such as fluency or speaking time were shown to have an impact on hirability ratings [12]. All speaking activity cues were based on the speaker segmentations provided by the Microcone device [1]. The following cues were extracted (in brackets, we list the statistics used as features):

- *Speaking time* was obtained by summing all speaking turn durations in the slice of interest.
- *Speaking turns* were defined as speaking segments longer than 2 seconds in the slice of interest (number of turns, average, standard deviation, and maximum of turn durations).
- *Pauses* were defined as non-speaking gaps of duration smaller than 2 seconds (number of pauses).
- *Silence* was defined as moments when none of the protagonist was speaking (number of events and total duration).
- *Overlapping speech* was defined as events when both protagonists were speaking at the same time (number of events and total duration).
- *Short utterances* were defined as speaking segments of duration smaller than 2 seconds (number of events).
- *Audio backhannels* were defined as short utterances when the other person was speaking (number of events).

Prosody relates to the variations of tone that accompany speech and includes pitch (voice fundamental frequency), speaking rate (speed at which syllables are burst), and energy (voice loudness) [17]. These cues were shown to be correlated with hirability ratings in psychology studies [12]. We used the speech feature extraction code [2] from the MIT Media Lab. For speech energy, pitch, and voiced rate, we extracted the mean, standard deviation, minimum, maximum, entropy, median, and quartiles.

4.1.2 Visual features

Overall visual motion quantifies the amount of visual information displayed by the protagonist throughout the slice of interest and is an indicator of kinetic expressiveness. To compute it, we used Weighted Motion Energy Images (WMEI) developed in [9] which summarizes the motion during a time segment into a single grayscale image, each pixel intensity corresponding to the visual activity at this location. Statistics from WMEI images were then extracted: mean, median, standard deviation, minimum, maximum, entropy, and quartiles.

Head-region visual motion quantifies the amount of motion displayed in the face region. We used the parametric optical flow method developed in [24] located in the face bounding box to extract the head-region optical flow. Statistics from this time-series were then computed: mean, median, standard deviation, maximum, entropy, and quartiles.

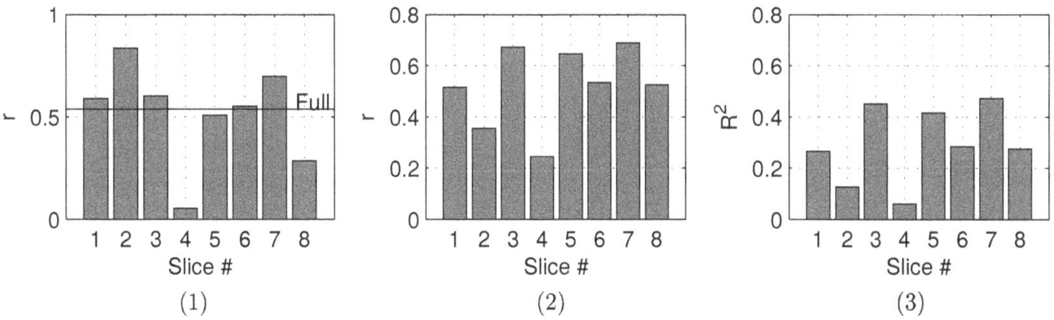

Figure 1: (1) Slice-level inter-rater agreement (N = 10), using Pearson's correlation as agreement measure. The solid line denotes the average correlation between the three raters on the full interview (N = 62). (2) Pearson's correlation between thin slice and full-interview annotations (N = 62). (3) R^2 values for each slice (squared of values displayed in (2)), corresponding to the prediction accuracy using only the slice annotations and OLS regression model (N = 62).

Head nods were extracted using the method developed in [23]; total nodding time and number of events were then extracted from the obtained binary time-series.

4.1.3 Multimodal features

Visual backchannels were defined as an event where one protagonist was nodding while the other person was speaking; they are often used to signal agreement and enhancing communicative attention [17]. Total backchanneling time and number of events were used as features.

Nodding while speaking were defined as events when a protagonist was nodding while he was speaking. In terms of communicative behavior, nodding while speaking can *inter alia* be used to elicit feedback from the listener [17]. Total nodding-while-speaking time and number of events were computed.

4.2 Correlation analysis

Pairwise correlations between single behavioral cues extracted from thin slices and hirability impressions obtained from the full interview were computed. Due to space constraints, the correlation values are not displayed here but can be found in the **supplementary material**.

4.2.1 Applicant cues

Some applicant audio features were found to be consistently and significantly correlated with the full interview hiring decision across slices. This is the case of the prosodic cues related to energy (median and lower quartile), voiced rate (mean, std, median, and upper quartile), and pitch (std, median, and lower quartile), which were found to be associated with the hiring decision score, when extracted from both the full interview and most thin slices.

For applicant cues based on speaker segmentations, the number of turns, silence features (although also related to the interviewer), and short utterances were observed to be negatively correlated with the hiring decision score across slices and for the full interview case; applicant average turn duration was positively associated with the interview outcome for the full interview and some slices. This observation suggests that these behavioral cues were consistently displayed by job applicants. This was however not the case of applicant speaking time, which was positively associated with the hiring decision for the full interview case, but negatively correlated for most thin slices. This is an interesting result because speaking time has been shown to be a robust predictor of other social constructs including personality [17].

To a lesser degree, applicant vertical head motion (mean and median) was positively associated with the hiring decision score, independently from the fact that they were extracted from the full interview or the thin slices. Otherwise, no applicant visual behavioral cue was consistently correlated with the interview outcome.

In terms of the number of significantly correlated features with the hiring decision score, all slices were not equal. Slice 4 (communication skills) was the slice from which the larger number of applicant cues significantly correlated with the hiring decision were extracted (32 significantly correlated cues whereas other slices ranged from 18 to 25). This finding is paradoxical because this slice was the one showing the lowest observer predictive validity ($r = 0.25$), and was also the slice where the agreement among raters was the lowest ($r = 0.05$).

4.2.2 Interviewer cues

Interviewer pitch standard variation was observed to be consistently and negatively associated with the hiring decision score across slices. This suggests that the interviewer had a more monotonous tone of voice in presence of highly hirable job applicants, and that this behavior was displayed throughout the totality of the job interview, with the exception of slice 1 (self-presentation).

Interviewer short utterances were also observed to be negatively and consistently correlated with the interview hiring decision score. This finding corroborates the findings of [21]: the short utterances stemmed from short back-and-forth exchanges between the applicant and the interviewer and could be seen as clarifications asked by the job applicant. These short utterances were perceived negatively by raters, and the effect can be observed throughout the full interview.

Interestingly, head-nod-related cues (number of nods, nodding time, visual back-channels) were positively and significantly correlated to the hiring decision score when extracted from the full interaction; however, this tendency was reversed when the cues were extracted from thin slices. One possible hypothesis to explain this finding could be that these features were unstable when extracted over short periods, due to the relative sparsity of head nods. This issue of temporal stability needs to be examined in more detail.

5. INFERENCE

5.1 Experiments

We defined the prediction task as a regression task, where the goal was to infer the hirability scores annotated from the full interview, using behavioral features extracted from thin slices as input. As a possible prediction task, inferring the hirability impressions obtained from thin slices was also considered, but we decided not to address this task as we strongly believe that inferring slice impressions is not as useful as predicting the full interview outcome.

For inference, several regression techniques were tested (ridge regression, random forest, LASSO, ordinary least squares). Ridge regression with no dimensionality reduction was found to consistently yield the best prediction accuracies, therefore results obtained with other methods are not presented here. We used leave-one-interview-out cross validation, using all interviews except one for training, and the remaining one to evaluate our method. Prior to the inference step, highly skewed features ($skewness > 1$) were transformed using log-transformation ($z = log(1 + x)$, where x and z denote the original and log-transformed feature, respectively); also, all behavioral features were normalized using the z-score, such that they had zero mean and unity variance.

We ran the inference task for all eight interview slices and for all three thin slice case (see Table 1), for a total of 24 slice-cases. Furthermore, to investigate what group of cues were predictive of hirability, we did the same experiment using feature groups based on modality and person of interest. Modality-based feature groups included 'audio', 'video', and 'all' (*i.e.*, the combination of audio, video, and multimodal features). Person-based feature groups included 'applicant', 'interviewer', and 'dyad' (*i.e.*, the combination of applicant and interviewer features).

As an evaluation measure, we used the coefficient of determination R^2, which accounts for the amount of total variance explained by the model under analysis; it is a metric often used in both psychology and social computing when dealing with regression tasks. Note that the use of adjusted R^2 often used in psychology is unnecessary here because we use a cross-validation framework which by construction separates the training from the test sets; indeed, the purpose of the adjusted R^2 is to account for an increase in the number of predictors when fitting a ordinary least-squares model to a variable.

5.2 Results and discussion

Q1: Prediction from thin slices

The prediction results obtained for each thin slice, person-based feature groups, modality-based feature groups, and thin slice cases, as well as the results obtained using the full interview are shown in Figure 2. The results show that all slices could be predictive of hirability ratings up to a certain level. This finding provides an answer to Q1, our first research question: a short excerpt of a job interview can be predictive of hirability. The best results obtained from thin slices were competitive compared to the observer predictive validity, with R^2 of up to 0.34. However, in most cases the results obtained from thin slices were less accurate than the ones yielding from the full interview, suggesting that a larger amount of behavioral information remains beneficial for a better prediction.

Q2: Most predictive slices

For feature groups yielding positive prediction results for thin slices, no slice clearly stood out either negatively or positively. For the 'dyad:all' feature group, the second half of the interview (slices 5-8) tended to be slightly less predictive than the first half, but this was not observed for the other feature groups. Hence, no firm conclusion can be drawn on which question of the job interview elicited the most discriminative behavior for the prediction of hirability. These findings answer Q2, our second research question: no slice was clearly more predictive than the others.

Q3: Predictive cues

We observe that the predictive validity of thin slices was dependent on both the modality and the person of interest. Applicant and dyad audio features extracted for the full interview were predictive of hirability ratings ($R^2 = 0.39$ for both). For thin slices, their prediction accuracy was consistent across segments of the interview. Interviewer audio cues were somewhat predictive for the full interview ($R^2 = 0.17$), but the validity of thin slices was not observed, as only slices 3, 4, 6, and 8 yielded mildly positive results. Visual features taken for the full interview were predictive of hirability for the dyad case ($R^2 = 0.28$), but were not predictive when thin-sliced, suggesting that these cues require longer temporal support to be predictive of the interview outcome. Applicant and interviewer visual features taken separately were not predictive of hirability for both the full interview and the thin slices. For head nods taken separately (not shown in Figure 2), interviewer and dyad nods were predictive when extracted from the full interview ($R^2 = 0.43$ and 0.40, resp.), but prediction accuracy dropped below zero for thin slices. This finding can be explained by the results obtained in Section 4.2, where interviewer heads nods extracted from the full interview were observed to be positively correlated with the hiring decision, while the ones obtained from thin slices were negatively correlated. This inconsistency in the display of head nods by the interviewer was responsible for the performance drop observed when using thin slices. These observations answer Q3, our third research question: only applicant and dyad audio cues were consistently predictive of hirability across slices.

Q4: Interview question vs. answers

In terms of thin slice cases, question-only segments were consistently not predictive of hirability, with frequent negative R^2 and quasi-constant poorer results compared to answer-only or whole-slice segments. The short duration of questions (see Table 2) fails to fully explain this finding, as the longest question (slice 1) was in no way more predictive than shorter answers. Along the same lines, whole-slices were not more predictive than answer-only segments, underlining the finding that questions did not add behavioral information to answers. These findings answer Q4, our fourth research question investigating the differences between questions and answers in terms of behavioral predictive validity: hirability ratings were not influenced by the listening behavior of applicants, but stemmed almost entirely from answers.

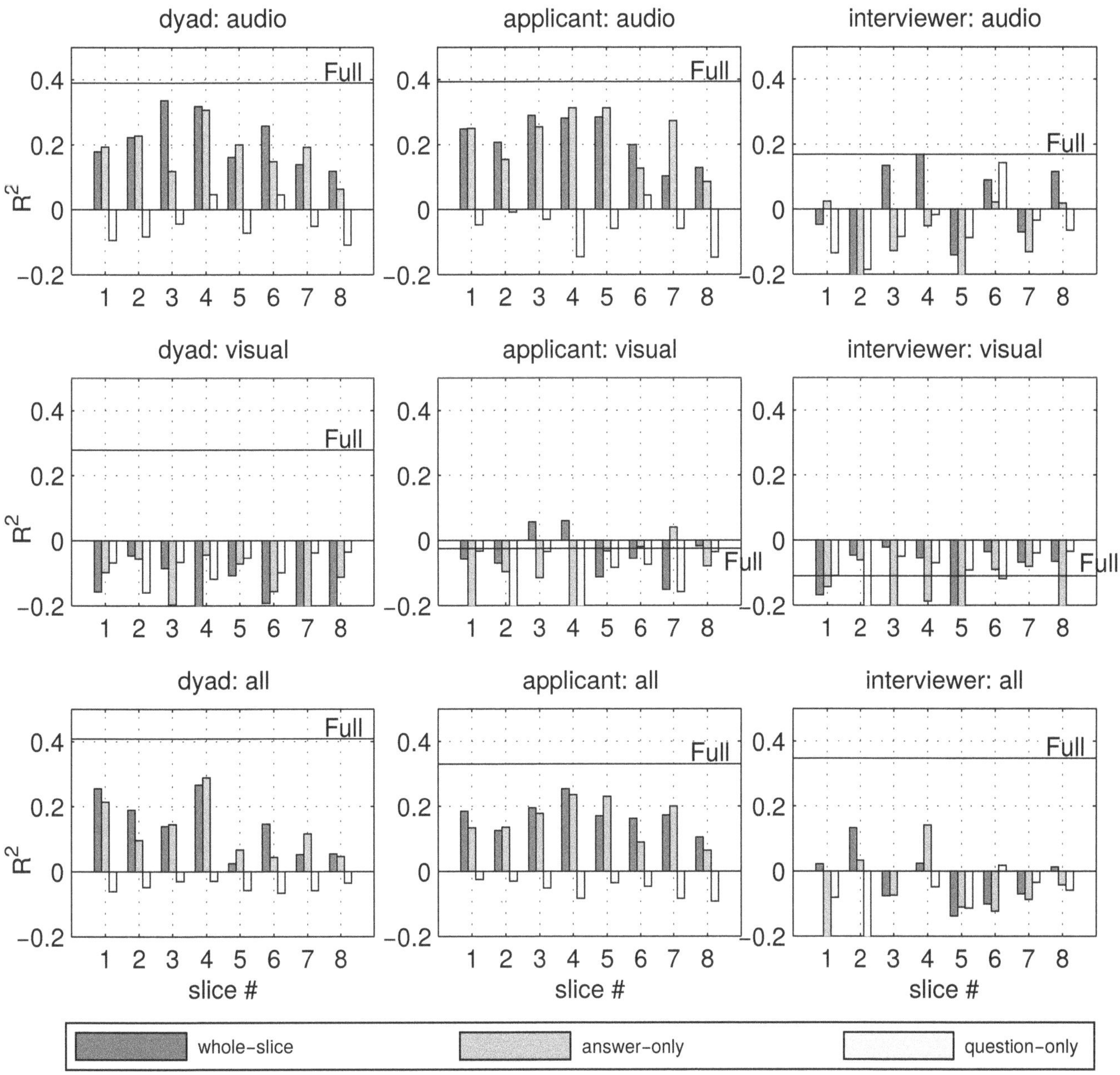

Figure 2: R^2 results from thin slices for person-based feature groups (columns), modality-based feature groups (rows), and thin slice cases (dark green for whole-slice, light green for answer-only, and yellow for question-only). The solid line refers to the prediction result obtained using the full interaction. N = 62. Best viewed in color.

6. CONCLUSION

We analyzed thin slices of job interviews, where slices were defined by the specific questions of the interview structure. To our knowledge, this work constitutes the first computational attempt at understanding the effect of thin-slicing in job interviews. Among the main results, we found that predicting hirability from automatically extracted nonverbal cues from the full interview yielded results similar to using annotations obtained by human resource professionals based on thin slices. Features extracted from thin slices were found to be not as predictive as the full interview, but they were still predictive of the interview outcome: the best results obtained from thin slices were competitive compared to the observer predictive validity, with R^2 of up to 0.34. These results align with the previous findings in social psychology stating that nonverbal behavior plays an important role in the formation of first impressions, especially when the amount of information is low [17].

No slice clearly stood out in terms of predictive validity: all slices yielded comparable results, suggesting that the observed nonverbal behavior did not drastically change from one slice to another. We also examined the accuracy stemming from person- and modality-based feature groups, and applicant audio features yielded the most accurate results, while visual cues were quite unpredictive of hirability. One possible explanation for these results is the relatively limited number of behavioral channels analyzed in this work. Other types of behaviors such as gaze, gestures, facial expressions, smiles, and verbal content were shown to play an important role in the impression formation process [17] and might shed light on Q2, what questions/slices are the most predictive. This will be investigated in detail in future work.

Questions taken alone were found to consistently yield negative results, whereas answers predicted the hiring decision score to a lesser degree than using the full interview; moreover, adding the questions to the answers (*i.e.* using the whole-slice case) did not significantly improve the predictive validity, which suggests that raters made their impression based on the applicant's speaking behavior.

Beyond employment interviews, one of the challenges in thin slice research is the amount of temporal support necessary for each behavioral feature to be predictive of the outcome of the full interaction or the social construct of interest. In other words, some cues require to be aggregated over a longer period than others. Here, this was the case of the interviewer's nodding behavior which was predictive of hirability when extracted from the full interaction, but not from thin slices. To our knowledge, apart from the correlation between a thin-sliced feature and its full-interaction counterpart, no metric assessing the necessary amount of temporal support for a given feature exists; we believe that this would be beneficial for the field.

Acknowledgments

This work was funded by the UBIMPRESSED project of the Sinergia interdisciplinary program of the Swiss National Science Foundation (SNSF). Special thanks to Marianne Schmid-Mast and Denise Frauendorfer (Université de Lausanne) for the collaboration on experimental design and data collection.

7. REFERENCES

[1] Microcone: intelligent microphone array for groups [online]. Available: http://www.dev-audio.com/products/microcone/.

[2] Speech feature extraction code [online]. Available: http://groupmedia.media.mit.edu/data.php.

[3] N. Ambady, F. Bernieri, and J. Richeson. Toward a histology of social behavior: Judgmental accuracy from thin slices of the behavioral stream. *Advances in Experimental Social Psychology*, 2000.

[4] N. Ambady, M. Hallahan, and R. Rosenthal. On Judging and Being Judged Accurately in Zero-Acquaintance Situations. *J. of Personality and Social Psychology*, 1995.

[5] N. Ambady and R. Rosenthal. Thin slices of expressive behavior as predictors of interpersonal consequences: A meta-analysis. *Psychological Bulletin*, 1992.

[6] N. Anderson and V. Shackleton. Decision making in the graduate selection interview: A field study. *J. of Occupational Psychology*, 1990.

[7] M. Barrick and M. Mount. The Big Five personality dimensions and job performance: A meta-analysis. *J. of Personnel Psychology*, 1991.

[8] L. Batrinca, N. Mana, B. Lepri, F. Pianesi, and N. Sebe. Please, tell me about yourself: automatic personality assessment using short self-presentations. *Proc. ICMI*, 2011.

[9] J. Biel, O. Aran, and D. Gatica-Perez. You are known by how you vlog: Personality impressions and nonverbal behavior in YouTube. In *Proc. ICSWM*, 2011.

[10] L. Chen, M. Martin, and M. Ma. An initial analysis of structured video interviews by using multimodal emotion detection. In *Proc. Workshop on Emotion Representations and Modelling for HCI Systems*, 2014.

[11] J. Curhan and A. Pentland. Thin slices of negotiation: Predicting outcomes from conversational dynamics within the first 5 minutes. *J. of Applied Psychology*, 2007.

[12] T. DeGroot and S. Motowildo. Why visual and vocal interview cues can affect interviewers' judgments and predict job performance. *J. of Applied Psychology*, 1999.

[13] R. Forbes and P. Jackson. Non-verbal behaviour and the outcome of selection interviews. *J. of Occupational Psychology*, 1980.

[14] N. Gada-Jain. Intentional synchrony effects on job interview evaluation. Master's thesis, University of Toledo, 1999.

[15] A. Huffcut, J. Conway, P. Roth, and N. Stone. Identification and meta-analytic assessment of psychological constructs measured in employment interviews. *J. of Applied Psychology*, 2001.

[16] A. Imada and M. Hakel. Influence of nonverbal communication and rater proximity on impressions and decisions in simulated employment interviews. *J. of Applied Psychology*, 1977.

[17] M. Knapp and J. Hall. *Nonverbal communication in human interaction*. Wadsworth, Cengage Learning, 2009.

[18] B. Lepri, N. Mana, A. Cappelletti, and F. Pianesi. Automatic prediction of individual performance from "thin slices" of social behavior. In *Proc. ICMI*, 2009.

[19] A. Madan. *Thin Slices of Interest*. PhD thesis, Massachusetts Institute of Technology, 2005.

[20] I. Naim, M. Tanveer, D. Gildea, and M. E. Hoque. Automated prediction and analysis of job interview performance: The role of what you aay and how you say it. In *Proc. FG*, 2015.

[21] L. Nguyen, D. Frauendorfer, M. Schmid Mast, and D. Gatica-Perez. Hire me: Computational inference of hirability in employment interviews based on nonverbal behavior. *IEEE Trans. on Multimedia*, 2014.

[22] L. Nguyen, A. Marcos-Ramiro, M. Marrón Romera, and D. Gatica-Perez. Multimodal analysis of body communication cues in employment interviews. In *Proc. ICMI*, 2013.

[23] L. Nguyen, J.-M. Odobez, and D. Gatica-Perez. Using self-context for multimodal detection of head nods in face-to-face interactions. In *Proc. ICMI*, 2012.

[24] J.-M. Odobez and P. Bouthemy. Robust multiresolution estimation of parametric motion models. *J. of Visual Communication and Image Representation*, 1995.

[25] C. Parsons and R. Liden. Interviewer perceptions of applicant qualifications: A multivariate field study of demographic characteristics and nonverbal cues. *J. of Applied Psychology*, 1984.

[26] F. Pianesi, N. Mana, A. Cappelletti, B. Lepri, and M. Zancanaro. Multimodal recognition of personality traits in social interactions. In *Proc. ICMI*, 2008.

[27] R. Posthuma, F. Morgeson, and M. Campion. Beyond employment interview validity: A comprehensive narrative review of recent research and trends over time. *J. of Personnel Psychology*, 2002.

[28] S. Rothmann and E. Coetzer. The big five personality dimensions and job performance. *J. of Industrial Psychology*, 2003.

[29] D. Sanchez-Cortes, O. Aran, M. Schmid Mast, and D. Gatica-Perez. A nonverbal behavior approach to identify emergent leaders in small groups. *IEEE Trans. on Multimedia*, 2012.

[30] G. Schmidt. The effect of thin slicing on structured interview decisions. Master's thesis, University of South Florida, 2007.

[31] A. Todorov, A. Mandisodza, A. Goren, and C. Hall. Inferences of competence from faces predict election outcomes. *Science*, 2005.

Deception Detection using Real-life Trial Data

Verónica Pérez-Rosas
Computer Science and Engineering
University of Michigan
Ann Arbor, MI 48109, USA
vrncapr@umich.edu

Mohamed Abouelenien
Computer Science and Engineering
University of Michigan
Ann Arbor, MI 48109, USA
zmohamed@umich.edu

Rada Mihalcea
Computer Science and Engineering
University of Michigan
Ann Arbor, MI 48109, USA
mihalcea@umich.edu

Mihai Burzo
Mechanical Engineering
University of Michigan, Flint
Flint, MI 48502, USA
mburzo@umich.edu

ABSTRACT

Hearings of witnesses and defendants play a crucial role when reaching court trial decisions. Given the high-stake nature of trial outcomes, implementing accurate and effective computational methods to evaluate the honesty of court testimonies can offer valuable support during the decision making process. In this paper, we address the identification of deception in real-life trial data. We introduce a novel dataset consisting of videos collected from public court trials. We explore the use of verbal and non-verbal modalities to build a multimodal deception detection system that aims to discriminate between truthful and deceptive statements provided by defendants and witnesses. We achieve classification accuracies in the range of 60-75% when using a model that extracts and fuses features from the linguistic and gesture modalities. In addition, we present a human deception detection study where we evaluate the human capability of detecting deception in trial hearings. The results show that our system outperforms the human capability of identifying deceit.

Categories and Subject Descriptors

I.2 [**Artificial Intelligence**]: Miscellaneous

Keywords

multimodal; verbal; non-verbal; real-life trial; deception detection

1. INTRODUCTION

With thousands of trials and verdicts occurring daily in courtrooms around the world, the chance of using deceptive statements and testimonies as evidence is growing. Given the high-stake nature of trial outcomes, implementing accurate and effective computational methods to evaluate the honesty of provided testimonies can offer valuable support during the decision making process.

ICMI 2015, November 9–13, 2015, Seattle, WA, USA.

DOI: http://dx.doi.org/10.1145/2818346.2820758

The consequences of falsely accusing the innocents and freeing the guilty can be severe. For instance, in U.S. along there are tens of thousand of criminal cases filed every year. In 2013, there were 89,936 criminal cases filings in U.S. District Courts and in 2014 the number was 80,262. [1] Moreover, the average number of exonerations per year increased from 3.03 in 1973-1999 to 4.29 between 2000 and 2013. The National Registry of Exonerations reported on 873 exonerations from 1989 to 2012, with a tragedy behind each case [17]. Hence, the need arises for a reliable and efficient system to detect deceptive behavior and discriminate between liars and truth tellers.

In criminal settings, the polygraph test has been used as a standard method to identify deceptive behavior. This becomes impractical in some cases, as this method requires the use of skin-contact devices and human expertise. In addition, the final decisions are subject to error and bias [41, 15]. Furthermore, using proper countermeasures, offenders can deceive these devices as well as the human experts. Given the difficulties associated with the use of polygraph-like methods, learning-based approaches have been proposed to address the deception detection task using a number of modalities, including text [13] and speech [20, 29]. Unlike the polygraph method, learning-based methods for deception detection rely mainly on data collected from deceivers and truth-tellers. The data is usually elicited from human contributors, in a lab setting or via crowdsourcing [28, 33], for instance by asking subjects to narrate stories in deceptive and truthful manner [28], by performing one-on-one interviews, or by participating in "Mock crime" scenarios [33]. However, an important drawback identified in this data-driven research on deception detection is the lack of real data and the absence of true motivation while eliciting deceptive behavior. Because of the artificial setting, the subjects may not be emotionally aroused thus making it difficult to generalize findings to real-life scenarios.

In this paper, we describe what we believe is a first attempt at building a multimodal system that detects deception in real-life trial data using text and gestures modalities. While there is research work that has used court trial transcripts to identify deceptive statements [14], we are not aware of any previous work that took into consideration modalities other than text for deception detection on trial court data.

[1] www.uscourts.gov

We present a novel dataset consisting of 121 deceptive and truthful video clips, from real court trials. We use the transcription of these videos to extract several linguistic features, and we manually annotate the videos for the presence of several gestures that are used to extract non-verbal features. We then build a system that jointly uses the verbal and non-verbal modalities to automatically detect the presence of deception. Our experiments show that the multimodal system can identify deception with an accuracy in the range of 60-75%, which is significantly above the chance level. As deception detection research suggests that humans perform slightly above the chance level, we also place our results in context by performing a study where humans evaluate the presence of deception in court statements in single or multimodal data streams. Results show that our system outperforms humans on this task.

2. RELATED WORK

2.1 Verbal Deception Detection

To date, several research publications on verbal-based deception detection have explored the identification of deceptive content in a variety of domains, including online dating websites [39, 18], forums [42, 23], social networks [21], and consumer report websites [31, 24]. Research findings have shown the effectiveness of features derived from text analysis, which frequently includes basic linguistic representations such as n-grams and sentence count statistics [28], and also more complex linguistic features derived from syntactic CFG trees and part of speech tags [13, 43]. Some studies have also incorporated the analysis of psycholinguistics aspects related to the deception process. Research work has relied on the Linguistic Inquiry and Word Count (LIWC) lexicon [34] to build deception models using machine learning approaches [28, 4] and showed that the use of psycholinguistic information was helpful for the automatic identification of deceit. Following the hypothesis that deceivers might create less complex sentences in an effort to conceal the truth and being able to recall their lies more easily, several researchers have also studied the relation between text syntactic complexity and deception [44].

While most of the data used in related research was collected under controlled settings, only few works have explored the used of data from real-life scenarios. This can be partially attributed to the difficulty of collecting such data, as well as the challenges associated with verifying the deceptive or truthful nature of real-world data. To our knowledge, there is very little work focusing on real-life high-stake data. The work closest to ours is presented by Fornaciari and Poesio [14], which targets the identification of deception in statements issued by witnesses and defendants using a corpus collected from hearings in Italian courts. Following this line of work, we present a study on deception detection using real-life trial data and explore the use of multiple modalities for this task.

2.2 Non-verbal Deception Detection

Earlier approaches on non-verbal deception detection relied on polygraph tests to detect deceptive behavior. These tests are mainly based on physiological features such as heart rate, respiration rate, and skin temperature. Several studies [41, 15, 10] indicated that relying solely on such physiological measurements can be biased and misleading. Chittaranjan et al. [7] created an audio-visual recordings of the "Are you a Werewolf?" game in order to detect deceptive behaviour using non-verbal audio cues and to predict the subjects' decisions in the game. In order to improve lie detection in criminal-suspect interrogations, Sumriddetchkajorn and Somboonkaew [37] developed an infrared system to detect lies by using thermal variations in the periorbital area and by deducing the respiration rate from the thermal nostril areas. Granhag and Hartwig [16] proposed a methodology using psychologically informed mind-reading to evaluate statements from suspects, witnesses, and innocents.

For hand gestures, blob analysis was used to detect deceit by tracking the hand movements of subjects [25, 40], or using geometric features related to the hand and head motion [27]. Caso et al. [6] identified several hand gestures that can be related to the act of deception using data from simulated interviews. Cohen et al. [8] found that fewer iconic hand gestures were a sign of a deceptive narration, and Hillman et al. [19] determined that increased speech prompting gestures were associated with deception while increased rhythmic pulsing gestures were associated with truthful behavior. Also related is the taxonomy of hand gestures developed by Maricchiolo et al. [26] for applications such as deception detection and social behavior.

Facial expressions also play a critical role in the identification of deception. Ekman [11] defined micro-expressions as relatively short involuntary expressions, which can be indicative of deceptive behavior. Moreover, these expressions were analyzed using smoothness and asymmetry measurements to further relate them to an act of deceit [12]. Tian et al. [38] considered features such as face orientation and facial expression intensity. Owayjan et al. [32] extracted geometric-based features from facial expressions, and Pfister and Pietikainen [36] developed a micro-expression dataset to identify expressions that are clues for deception.

Recently, features from different modalities were integrated in order to find a combination of multimodal features with superior performance [5, 22]. A multimodal deception dataset consisting of linguistic, thermal, and physiological features was introduced in [35], which was then used to develop a multimodal deception detection system [2]. An extensive review of approaches for evaluating human credibility using physiological, visual, acoustic, and linguistic features is available in [30].

To our knowledge, no work to date has considered the problem of deception detection on multimodal real-life trial data, which is the task that we are addressing in this paper.

3. DATASET

Our goal is to build a multimodal collection of occurrences of real deception during court trials, which will allow us to analyze both verbal and non-verbal behaviors in relation to deception.

3.1 Data Collection

To collect the dataset, we start by identifying public multimedia sources where trial hearing recordings were available, and deceptive and truthful behavior could be fairly observed and verified.

We specifically target trial recordings on which some of the constraints imposed by current data processing technologies could be enforced: the defendant or witness in the video should be clearly identified; her or his face should be visible enough during most of the clip duration; visual quality should be clear enough to identify the facial expressions; and finally, audio quality should be clear enough to hear the voices and understand what the person is saying.

We considered three different trial outcomes that helped us to correctly label a certain trial video clip as deceptive or truthful: guilty verdict, non-guilty verdict, and exoneration. Thus, for guilty verdicts, deceptive clips are collected from a defendant in a trial and truthful videos are collected from witnesses in the same trial. In some cases, deceptive videos are collected from a suspect denying a crime he committed and truthful clips are taken from the same suspect when answering questions concerning some facts that were verified by the police as truthful. For the witnesses, testimonies that were verified by police investigations are labeled as truthful

Figure 1: Sample screenshots showing facial displays and hand gestures from real-life trial clips. Starting at the top left-hand corner: deceptive trial with forward head movement (*Move forward*), deceptive trial with both hands movement (*Both hands*), deceptive trial with one hand movement (*Single hand*), truthful trial with raised eyebrows (*Eyebrows raising*), deceptive trial with scowl face (*Scowl*), and truthful trial with an up gaze (*Gaze up*).

Truthful	Deceptive
We proceeded to step back into the living room in front of the fireplace while William was sitting in the love seat. And he was still sitting there in shock and so they to repeatedly tell him to get down on the ground. And so now all three of us are face down on the wood floor and they just tell us "don't look, don't look" And then they started rummaging through the house to find stuff...	No, no. I did not and I had absolutely nothing to do with her disappearance. And I'm glad that she did. I did. I did. Um and then when Laci disappeared, um, I called her immediately. It wasn't immediately, it was a couple of days after Laci's disappearance that I telephoned her and told her the truth. That I was married, that Laci's disappeared, she didn't know about it at that point.

Table 1: Sample transcripts for deceptive and truthful clips in the dataset.

whereas testimonies in favor of a guilty suspect are labeled as deceptive. Exoneration testimonies are collected as truthful statements.

Examples of famous trials included in the dataset are the trials of Jodi Arias, Donna Scrivo, Jamie Hood, Andrea Sneiderman, Mitchelle Blair, Amanda Hayes, Crystal Mangum, Marissa Devault, Carlos Miller, Michael Dunn, Bessman Okafor, Jonathan Santillan, among other trials. Clips containing exonerees testimonies are obtained from "The Innocence Project" website.[2]

Given our goals and constraints, data collection ended up being a lengthy and laborious process consisting of several iterations of Web mining, data processing and analysis, and content validation.

The final dataset consists of 121 videos including 61 deceptive and 60 truthful trial clips. The average length of the videos in the dataset is 28.0 seconds. The average video length is 27.7 seconds and 28.3 seconds for the deceptive and truthful clips, respectively. The data consists of 21 unique female and 35 unique male speakers, with their ages approximately ranging between 16 and 60 years.

3.2 Transcriptions

Our goal is to analyze both verbal and non-verbal behavior to understand their relation to deception.

Gesture Category	Agreement	Kappa
General Facial Expressions	66.07%	0.328
Eyebrows	80.03%	0.670
Eyes	64.28%	0.465
Gaze	55.35%	0.253
Mouth Openness	78.57%	0.512
Mouth Lips	85.71%	0.690
Head Movements	69.64%	0.569
Hand Movements	94.64%	0.917
Hand Trajectory	82.14%	0.738
Average	75.16%	0.571

Table 2: Gesture annotation agreement

All the video clips are transcribed via crowd sourcing using Amazon Mechanical Turk. We specifically asked transcribers to include word repetitions and fillers such as *um*, *ah*, and *uh*, as well as indicate intentional silence using ellipsis. Obtained transcriptions were manually verified to avoid spam and ensure their quality. The final set of transcriptions consists of 8,055 words, with an average of 66 words per transcript. Table 1 shows transcriptions of sample deceptive and truthful statements.

[2]http://www.innocenceproject.org/

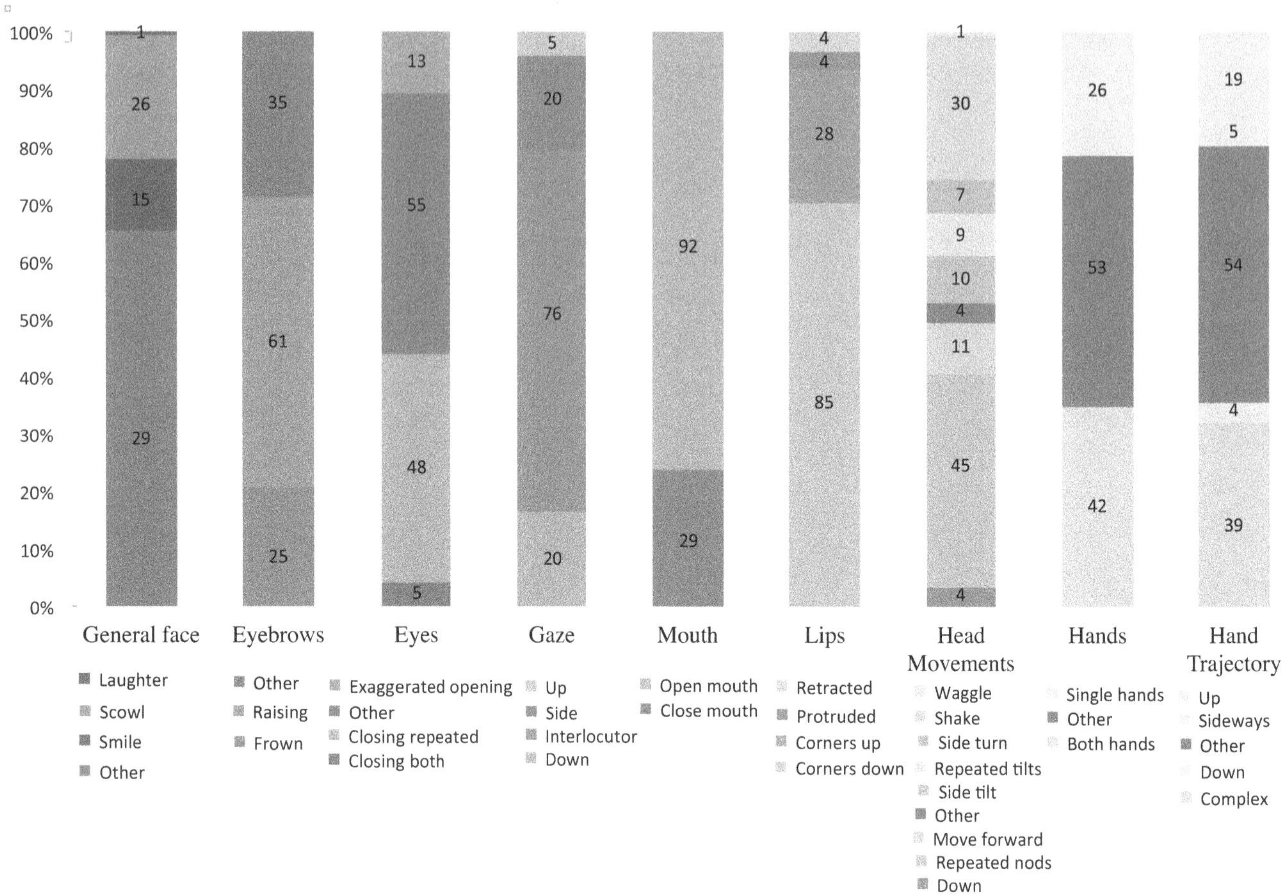

Figure 2: Distribution for nine facial displays and hand gestures

3.3 Non-verbal Behavior Annotations

We annotate the gestures[3] observed during the interactions in the video clips. Since our data occurs in interview-based scenarios where deceivers and truth-tellers are interacting with the interviewers, we decided to annotate the gesture behavior using a scheme that has been specifically designed for interpersonal communication.

We specifically focus on the annotation of facial displays and hand movements, as they have been previously found to correlate with deceptive behavior [9]. The gesture annotation is performed using the MUMIN coding scheme [3], which is a standard multimodal annotation scheme for interpersonal interactions.

In the MUMIN scheme, facial displays consist of several different facial expressions associated with overall facial expressions, eyebrows, eyes and mouth movements, gaze direction, as well as head movements. In addition, the scheme includes a separate category for general face displays, which codes four facial expressions: smile, laughter, scowl, and other. Hand movements are also labeled in terms of handedness and trajectory. Figure 2 shows the nine gesture categories considered during the annotation.

The multimodal annotation was performed by two annotators using the Elan software. During the annotation process, annotators were allowed to watch each video clip as many times as they needed. They were asked to identify the facial displays and hand gestures that were most frequently observed or dominating during the entire clip duration. For each video clip, the annotators had to choose one label for each of the nine gestures listed in Figure 2. Annotations were performed at video level in accordance with the overall judgment of truthfulness and deceitfulness, which is based on the whole video content. During the annotation process, annotators chose only one label per gesture for every video clip.

Note that the "Other" category indicates cases where none of the other gestures was observed. For instance, in the case of gestures associated with hand movements, the "Other" label also accounted for those cases where the speaker's hands were not moving or were not visible.

Before all the video clips were annotated for gestures, we measured the inter-annotator agreement in a subset of 56 videos. Table 2 shows the observed annotation agreement between the two annotators, along with the Kappa statistic. The agreement measure represents the percentage of times the two annotators agreed on the same label for each gesture category. For instance, 80.03% of the time the annotators agreed on the labels assigned to the *Eyebrows* category. On average, the observed agreement was measured at 75.16%, with a Kappa of 0.57 (macro-averaged over the nine categories). Differences in annotation were reconciled through discussions. After this, the remaining videos were split between the two annotators, and were labeled by only one annotator. Figure 2 shows

[3] As done in the Human-Computer Interaction community, we use the term "gesture" to broadly refer to body movements, including facial expressions and hand gestures.

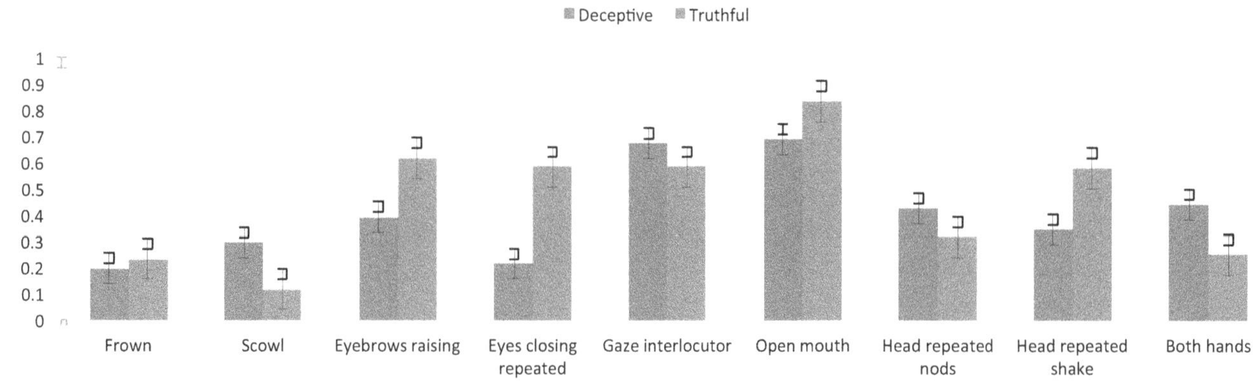

Figure 3: Distribution of non-verbal features for deceptive and truthful groups

the final frequency counts associated with each of the nine gestures considered during the annotation.

4. FEATURES OF VERBAL AND NON-VERBAL BEHAVIORS

Given the multimodal nature of our dataset, we focus on both the linguistic and gesture components of the recordings included in our collection. In this section, we describe the sets of features extracted from each modality, which will then be used to build classifiers of deception.

4.1 Verbal Features

The verbal features consist of unigrams and bigrams derived from the bag-of-words representation of the video transcripts. These features are encoded as word and word pairs frequencies and include all the words present in the transcripts with frequencies greater than 10. The frequency threshold cut was chosen using a small development set.

Previous work has also considered features derived from semantic lexicons, e.g., LIWC [34]. However, while these are great features to consider in order to gain insights into the semantic categories of words that represent useful clues for deception, their performance is often similar to that of the n-grams features [2]. Since in our current work we are not focusing on the insights that can be gained from linguistic analyses, we are not using these features in our current experiments.

4.2 Non-verbal Features

The non-verbal features are derived from the annotations performed using the MUMIN coding scheme as described in Section 3.3. We create a binary feature for each of the 40 available gesture labels. Each feature indicates the presence of a gesture only if it is observed during the majority of the interaction duration. The generated features represent nine different gesture categories covering facial displays and hand movements.

Facial Displays. These are facial expressions or head movements displayed by the speaker during the deceptive or truthful interaction. They include all the behaviors listed in Figure 2 under the General Facial Expressions, Eyebrows, Eyes, Mouth Openness, Mouth Lips, and Head Movements.

Hand Gestures. The second broad category covers gestures made with the hands, and it includes the Hand Movements and Hand Trajectories listed in Figure 2.

Feature Set	DT	RF
Unigrams	60.33%	56.19%
Bigrams	53.71%	51.20%
Facial displays	70.24%	76.03%
Hand gestures	61.98%	62.80%
Uni+Facial displays	66.94%	57.02%
All verbal	60.33%	50.41%
All non-verbal	68.59%	73.55%
All features	75.20%	50.41%

Table 3: Deception classifiers using individual and combined sets of verbal and non-verbal features.

5. EXPERIMENTS

We start our experiments with an analysis of the non-verbal behaviors occurring in deceptive and truthful videos. We compare the percentage of each behavior as observed in each class. For instance, there is a total of 61 videos in the dataset that include the Eyebrows raising feature (as shown in Figure 2), out of which 24 are part of the deceptive set of 61 videos, and 37 are part of the truthful set (60 videos). Hence, the percentages of existence of this feature are 39% in the deceptive class and 61% in the truthful class. Figure 3 shows the percentages of all the non-verbal features for which we observe noticeable differences for the deceptive and truthful groups. As the figure suggests, eyebrow and eye gestures help differentiate between the deceptive and truthful conditions. For instance, we can observe that truth-tellers appear to raise their eyebrows (Eyebrows raising), shake their head (Head repeated shake), and blink (Eyes closing repeated) more frequently than deceivers. Interestingly, deceivers seem to blink and shake their head less frequently than truth-tellers.

Motivated by these results, we proceed to conduct further experiments to evaluate the performance of the extracted features using a machine learning approach.

We run our learning experiments on the trial dataset introduced earlier. Given the distribution between deceptive and truthful clips, the baseline on this dataset is 50.4%. For each video clip, we create feature vectors formed by combinations of the verbal and non-verbal features described in the previous section.

We build deception classifiers using two classification algorithms: Decision Trees (DT) and Random Forest (RF).[4] We run several

[4]We use the implementation available in the Weka toolkit with the default parameters.

comparative experiments using leave-one-out cross-validation. Table 3 shows the accuracy figures obtained by the two classifiers on the major feature groups described in Section 4. As shown in this table, the combined classifier that uses all the features (using Decision Trees) and the individual classifier that relies on the facial displays features (using Random Forest) achieve the best results. We also evaluate classifiers that rely on combined sets of features, with the non-verbal features clearly outperforming the verbal features.

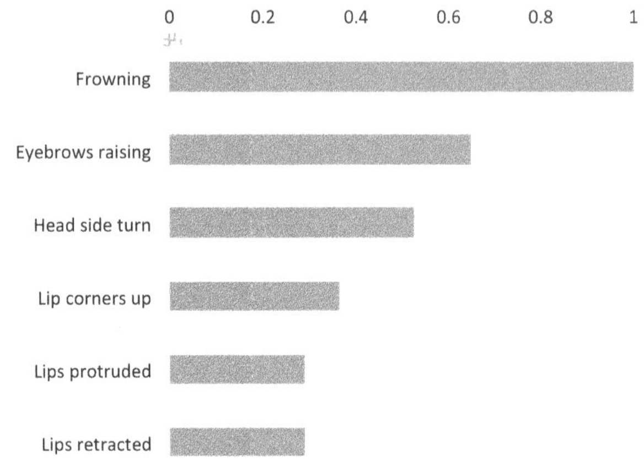

Figure 4: Weights of top non-verbal features

5.1 Analysis of Feature Contribution

To better understand the contribution of the different feature sets to the overall classifier performance, we conduct an ablation study where we remove one group of features at a time. Given that Decision Trees had the most consistent performance across different settings in our initial set of experiments, we run all our analysis experiments only using this classifier.

Table 4 shows the accuracies obtained when one feature group is removed and the deception classifier is built using the remaining features. From this table we made interesting findings for the combined model. Not surprisingly, the facial displays seem to contribute the most to the classifier performance, followed by the unigram features. This further suggests that a better feature fusion method may be beneficial, and we plan to explore this in future work.

For a closer look at the contribution of individual features included in the group of *Facial Displays*, we determine and compare the weights assigned by the learning algorithm to the features in this group, as shown in Figure 4.[5] The five most predictive features are the presence of frowning (Frowning), eyebrows movement (Eyebrows raising), lip gestures (Lip corners up, Lips protruded, Lips retracted), and head turns (Head side turn). These gestures were frequently portrayed by defendants and witnesses while being interrogated.

6. HUMAN PERFORMANCE

An important remaining question is concerned with the human performance on the task of deception detection. An answer to this question can shed light on the difficulty of the task, and can also place our results in perspective.

[5]In the figure, the features are normalized with respect to the largest feature weight.

Feature Set	DT
All	**75.20%**
– Hand gestures	71.90%
– Facial displays	59.50%
– Bigrams	66.94%
– Unigrams	61.98%

Table 4: Feature ablation study.

Modality	Agreement	Kappa
Text	59.80%	0.071
Audio	62.00%	0.196
Silent video	51.50%	0.014
Full video	57.60%	0.127

Table 5: Agreement among three human annotators on text, audio, silent video, and full video modalities.

We conduct a study where we evaluate the human ability to identify deceit on trial recordings when exposed to four different modalities: *Text*, consisting of the language transcripts; *Audio*, consisting of the audio track of the clip; *Silent video*, consisting of only the video with muted audio; and *Full video*, where audio and video are played simultaneously.

We create an annotation interface that shows an annotator instances for each modality in random order, and ask him or her to select a label of either "Deception" or "Truth" according to his or her perception of truthfulness or falsehood. The annotators did not have access to any information that would reveal the true label of an instance. The only exception to this could have been the annotators' previous knowledge of some of the public trials in our dataset. A discussion with the annotators after the annotation took place indicated however that this was not the case.

To avoid annotation bias, we show the modalities in the following order: first we show either *Text* or *Silent video*, then we show *Audio*, followed by *Full video*. Note that apart from this constraint, which is enforced over the four modalities belonging to each video clip, the order in which instances are presented to an annotator is random.

Three annotators labeled all 121 video clips in our dataset. Since four modalities were extracted from each video, each annotator annotated a total of 484 instances. Annotators were not offered a monetary reward and we considered their judgments to be honest as they participated voluntarily in this experiment. Table 5 shows the observed agreement and Kappa statistics among the three annotators for each modality.[6] The agreement for most modalities is rather low and the Kappa scores show mostly slight agreement. As noted before [31], this low agreement can be interpreted as an indication that people are poor judges of deception.

We also determine each annotator performance for each modality. The results, shown in Table 6, additionally support the argument that human judges have difficulty performing the deception detection task. Not surprisingly, human detection of deception on silent video is more challenging than the rest of the modalities due to the lesser amount of deception cues available to the raters. An interesting, yet perhaps unsurprising observation is that the human performance increases with the availability of modalities. The

[6]Inter-rater agreement with multiple raters and variables. `https://mlnl.net/jg/software/ira/`

	Text	Audio	Silent video	Full video
A1	54.55%	51.24%	45.30%	56.20%
A2	47.93%	55.37%	46.28%	53.72%
A3	50.41%	59.50%	47.93%	59.50%
Sys	60.33%	NA	68.59%	75.20%

Table 6: Performance of three annotators (A1, A2, A3) and the developed automatic system (Sys) on the real-deception dataset over four modalities.

poorest accuracy is obtained in *Silent video*, followed by *Text*, *Audio*, and *Full video* where the judges have the highest performance.

Overall, our study indicates that detecting deception is indeed a difficult task for humans and further verifies previous findings where human ability to spot liars was found to be slightly better than chance [1]. Moreover, the performance of the human annotators appears to be significantly below that of our system.

7. CONCLUSIONS

In this paper we presented a study of multimodal deception detection using real-life high-stake occurrences of deceit. We introduced a novel dataset from public real trials, and used this dataset to perform both qualitative and quantitative experiments. Our analysis of non-verbal behaviors occurring in deceptive and truthful videos brought insight into the gestures that play a role in deception. We also built classifiers relying on individual or combined sets of verbal and non-verbal features, and showed that we can achieve accuracies in the range of 60-75%. Additional analyses showed the role played by the various feature sets used in the experiments.

We also performed a study of human ability to spot liars in single or multimodal data streams. The study revealed high disagreement and low deception detection accuracies among human annotators. Our automatic system outperformed humans using different modalities with a relative percentage improvement of up to 51%.

To our knowledge this is the first work to automatically detect instances of deceit using both verbal and non-verbal features extracted from real trial recordings. Future work will address the use of automatic gesture identification and automatic speech transcription, with the goal of taking steps towards a real-time deception detection system.

The dataset introduced in this paper is available upon request.

Acknowledgments

We are grateful to Hagar Mohamed, Aparna Garimella, Shibamouli Lahiri, and Charles Welch for assisting us with the data collection and the human evaluations. This material is based in part upon work supported by National Science Foundation awards #1344257 and #1355633, by grant #48503 from the John Templeton Foundation, and by DARPA-BAA-12-47 DEFT grant #12475008. Any opinions, findings, and conclusions or recommendations expressed in this material are those of the authors and do not necessarily reflect the views of the National Science Foundation, the John Templeton Foundation, or the Defense Advanced Research Projects Agency.

8. REFERENCES

[1] M. Aamodt and H. Custer. Who can best catch a liar? a meta-analysis of individual differences in detecting deception. *Forensic Examiner*, 15(1):6–11, 2006.

[2] M. Abouelenien, V. Pérez-Rosas, R. Mihalcea, and M. Burzo. Deception detection using a multimodal approach. In *Proceedings of the 16th International Conference on Multimodal Interaction*, ICMI '14, pages 58–65, Istanbul, Turkey, 2014. ACM.

[3] J. Allwood, L. Cerrato, K. Jokinen, C. Navarretta, and P. Paggio. The mumin coding scheme for the annotation of feedback, turn management and sequencing phenomena. *Language Resources and Evaluation*, 41(3-4):273–287, 2007.

[4] A. Almela, R. Valencia-García, and P. Cantos. Seeing through deception: A computational approach to deceit detection in written communication. In *Proceedings of the Workshop on Computational Approaches to Deception Detection*, pages 15–22, Avignon, France, April 2012. Association for Computational Linguistics.

[5] J. Burgoon, D. Twitchell, M. Jensen, T. Meservy, M. Adkins, J. Kruse, A. Deokar, G. Tsechpenakis, S. Lu, D. Metaxas, J. Nunamaker, and R. Younger. Detecting concealment of intent in transportation screening: A proof of concept. *IEEE Transactions on Intelligent Transportation Systems*, 10(1):103–112, March 2009.

[6] L. Caso, F. Maricchiolo, M. Bonaiuto, A. Vrij, and S. Mann. The impact of deception and suspicion on different hand movements. *Journal of Nonverbal Behavior*, 30(1):1–19, 2006.

[7] G. Chittaranjan and H. Hung. Are you awerewolf? detecting deceptive roles and outcomes in a conversational role-playing game. In *2010 IEEE International Conference on Acoustics Speech and Signal Processing (ICASSP)*, pages 5334–5337, March 2010.

[8] D. Cohen, G. Beattie, and H. Shovelton. Nonverbal indicators of deception: How iconic gestures reveal thoughts that cannot be suppressed. *Semiotica*, 2010(182):133–174, 2010.

[9] B. Depaulo, B. Malone, J. Lindsay, L. Muhlenbruck, K. Charlton, and H. Cooper. Cues to deception. *Psychological Bulletin*, pages 74–118, 2003.

[10] M. Derksen. Control and resistance in the psychology of lying. *Theory and Psychology*, 22(2):196–212, 2012.

[11] P. Ekman. *Telling Lies: Clues to Deceit in the Marketplace, Politics and Marriage*. Norton, W.W. and Company, 2001.

[12] P. Ekman. Darwin, deception, and facial expression. *Annals of the New York Academy of Sciences*, 1000(EMOTIONS INSIDE OUT: 130 Years after Darwin's The Expression of the Emotions in Man and Animals):205–221, 2003.

[13] S. Feng, R. Banerjee, and Y. Choi. Syntactic stylometry for deception detection. In *Proceedings of the 50th Annual Meeting of the Association for Computational Linguistics: Short Papers - Volume 2*, ACL '12, pages 171–175, Stroudsburg, PA, USA, 2012. Association for Computational Linguistics.

[14] T. Fornaciari and M. Poesio. Automatic deception detection in Italian court cases. *Artificial Intelligence and Law*, 21(3):303–340, 2013.

[15] T. Gannon, A. Beech, and T. Ward. *Risk Assessment and the Polygraph*, pages 129–154. John Wiley and Sons Ltd, 2009.

[16] P. A. Granhag and M. Hartwig. A new theoretical perspective on deception detection: On the psychology of instrumental mind-reading. *Psychology, Crime & Law*, 14(3):189–200, 2008.

[17] S. Gross and R. Warden. Exonerations in the united states, 1989 - 2012. Technical report, National Registry of Exonerations, 2012.

[18] R. Guadagno, B. Okdie, and S. Kruse. Dating deception: Gender, online dating, and exaggerated self-presentation. *Comput. Hum. Behav.*, 28(2):642–647, Mar. 2012.

[19] J. Hillman, A. Vrij, and S. Mann. Um ... they were wearing ...: The effect of deception on specific hand gestures. *Legal and Criminological Psychology*, 17(2):336–345, 2012.

[20] J. Hirschberg, S. Benus, J. Brenier, F. Enos, S. Friedman, S. Gilman, C. Gir, G. Graciarena, A. Kathol, and L. Michaelis. Distinguishing deceptive from non-deceptive speech. In *In Proceedings of Interspeech 2005 - Eurospeech*, pages 1833–1836, 2005.

[21] S. Ho and J. M. Hollister. Guess who? an empirical study of gender deception and detection in computer-mediated communication. *Proceedings of the American Society for Information Science and Technology*, 50(1):1–4, 2013.

[22] M. Jensen, T. Meservy, J. Burgoon, and J. Nunamaker. Automatic, multimodal evaluation of human interaction. *Group Decision and Negotiation*, 19(4):367–389, 2010.

[23] A. N. Joinson and B. Dietz-Uhler. Explanations for the perpetration of and reactions to deception in a virtual community. *Social Science Computer Review*, 20(3):275–289, 2002.

[24] J. Li, M. Ott, C. Cardie, and E. Hovy. Towards a general rule for identifying deceptive opinion spam. In *Proceedings of the 52nd Annual Meeting of the Association for Computational Linguistics*, Baltimore, Maryland, June 2014.

[25] S. Lu, G. Tsechpenakis, D. Metaxas, M. Jensen, and J. Kruse. Blob analysis of the head and hands: A method for deception detection. In *Proceedings of the 38th Annual Hawaii International Conference on System Sciences (HICSS'05)*, HICSS '05, pages 20–29, Washington, DC, USA, 2005. IEEE Computer Society.

[26] F. Maricchiolo, A. Gnisci, and M. Bonaiuto. Coding hand gestures: A reliable taxonomy and a multi-media support. In A. Esposito, A. Esposito, A. Vinciarelli, R. Hoffmann, and V. Muller, editors, *Cognitive Behavioural Systems*, volume 7403 of *Lecture Notes in Computer Science*, pages 405–416. Springer Berlin Heidelberg, 2012.

[27] T. Meservy, M. Jensen, J. Kruse, D. Twitchell, G. Tsechpenakis, J. Burgoon, D. Metaxas, and J. Nunamaker. Deception detection through automatic, unobtrusive analysis of nonverbal behavior. *IEEE Intelligent Systems*, 20(5):36–43, September 2005.

[28] R. Mihalcea and C. Strapparava. The lie detector: Explorations in the automatic recognition of deceptive language. In *Proceedings of the Association for Computational Linguistics (ACL 2009)*, Singapore, 2009.

[29] M. Newman, J. Pennebaker, D. Berry, and J. Richards. Lying words: Predicting deception from linguistic styles. *Personality and Social Psychology Bulletin*, 29, 2003.

[30] J. Nunamaker, J. Burgoon, N. Twyman, J. Proudfoot, R. Schuetzler, and J. Giboney. Establishing a foundation for automated human credibility screening. In *2012 IEEE International Conference on Intelligence and Security Informatics (ISI)*, pages 202–211, June 2012.

[31] M. Ott, Y. Choi, C. Cardie, and J. Hancock. Finding deceptive opinion spam by any stretch of the imagination. In *Proceedings of the 49th Annual Meeting of the Association for Computational Linguistics: Human Language Technologies - Volume 1*, HLT '11, pages 309–319, Stroudsburg, PA, USA, 2011. Association for Computational Linguistics.

[32] M. Owayjan, A. Kashour, N. AlHaddad, M. Fadel, and G. AlSouki. The design and development of a lie detection system using facial micro-expressions. In *2012 2nd International Conference on Advances in Computational Tools for Engineering Applications (ACTEA)*, pages 33–38, Dec 2012.

[33] I. Pavlidis, N. Eberhardt, and J. Levine. Human behaviour: Seeing through the face of deception. *Nature*, 415(6867), 2002.

[34] J. Pennebaker and M. Francis. Linguistic inquiry and word count: LIWC, 1999. Erlbaum Publishers.

[35] V. Perez-Rosas, R. Mihalcea, A. Narvaez, and M. Burzo. A multimodal dataset for deception detection. In *Proceedings of the Conference on Language Resources and Evaluations (LREC 2014)*, Reykjavik, Iceland, May 2014.

[36] T. Pfister and M. Pietikäinen. Electronic imaging & signal processing automatic identification of facial clues to lies. *SPIE Newsroom*, January 2012.

[37] S. Sumriddetchkajorn and A. Somboonkaew. Thermal analyzer enables improved lie detection in criminal-suspect interrogations. In *SPIE Newsroom: Defense & Security*, 2011.

[38] Y. Tian, T. Kanade, and J. Cohn. Facial expression analysis. In *Handbook of Face Recognition*, pages 247–275. Springer New York, 2005.

[39] C. Toma and J. Hancock. Reading between the lines: linguistic cues to deception in online dating profiles. In *Proceedings of the 2010 ACM conference on Computer supported cooperative work*, CSCW '10, pages 5–8, New York, NY, USA, 2010. ACM.

[40] G. Tsechpenakis, D. Metaxas, M. Adkins, J. Kruse, J. Burgoon, M. Jensen, T. Meservy, D. Twitchell, A. Deokar, and J. Nunamaker. Hmm-based deception recognition from visual cues. In *IEEE International Conference on Multimedia and Expo, 2005. ICME 2005*, pages 824–827, July 2005.

[41] A. Vrij. *Detecting Lies and Deceit: The Psychology of Lying and the Implications for Professional Practice*. Wiley series in the psychology of crime, policing and law. Wiley, 2001.

[42] D. Warkentin, M. Woodworth, J. Hancock, and N. Cormier. Warrants and deception in computer mediated communication. In *Proceedings of the 2010 ACM conference on Computer supported cooperative work*, pages 9–12. ACM, 2010.

[43] Q. Xu and H. Zhao. Using deep linguistic features for finding deceptive opinion spam. In *Proceedings of COLING 2012: Posters*, pages 1341–1350, Mumbai, India, December 2012. The COLING 2012 Organizing Committee.

[44] M. Yancheva and F. Rudzicz. Automatic detection of deception in child-produced speech using syntactic complexity features. In *Proceedings of the 51st Annual Meeting of the Association for Computational Linguistics (Volume 1: Long Papers)*, pages 944–953, Sofia, Bulgaria, August 2013. Association for Computational Linguistics.

Exploring Turn-taking Cues in Multi-party Human-robot Discussions about Objects

Gabriel Skantze
KTH Speech Music and Hearing
Lindstedtsv. 24
10044 Stockholm, Sweden
+46-8-7907874
skantze@kth.se

Martin Johansson
KTH Speech Music and Hearing
Lindstedtsv. 24
10044 Stockholm, Sweden
+46-8-7907874
vhmj@kth.se

Jonas Beskow
KTH Speech Music and Hearing
Lindstedtsv. 24
10044 Stockholm, Sweden
+46-8-7907874
beskow@kth.se

ABSTRACT
In this paper, we present a dialog system that was exhibited at the Swedish National Museum of Science and Technology. Two visitors at a time could play a collaborative card sorting game together with the robot head Furhat, where the three players discuss the solution together. The cards are shown on a touch table between the players, thus constituting a target for joint attention. We describe how the system was implemented in order to manage turn-taking and attention to users and objects in the shared physical space. We also discuss how multi-modal redundancy (from speech, card movements and head pose) is exploited to maintain meaningful discussions, given that the system has to process conversational speech from both children and adults in a noisy environment. Finally, we present an analysis of 373 interactions, where we investigate the robustness of the system, to what extent the system's attention can shape the users' turn-taking behaviour, and how the system can produce multi-modal turn-taking signals (filled pauses, facial gestures, breath and gaze) to deal with processing delays in the system.

Categories and Subject Descriptors
H.1.2 [User/Machine Systems]: *Human Information Processing*; H.5.2 [User Interfaces]: *Natural Language, Evaluation/methodology*; I.4.8 [Scene Analysis]: *Sensor Fusion*

General Terms
Algorithms, Experimentation, Human Factors

Keywords
Multi-party turn-taking; Human-robot interaction; Gaze; Attention

1. INTRODUCTION
Robots of the future are envisioned to help people perform tasks, not only as mere tools, but as autonomous agents interacting and solving problems together with humans. Such interaction will have several characteristics that make the modelling of the dialog challenging. Firstly, the robot should be able to solve problems together with several humans (and possibly other robots) at the same time, which means that we need to model *multi-party* interaction. Secondly, joint problem solving is in many cases *situated*, which means that the spoken discourse will involve references to, and manipulation of, objects in the shared physical space. Thirdly, the robot should not just be able to execute actions commanded by humans, but it should also be able to engage in collaborative *discussions* and *negotiation*, since the robot and the humans may have different beliefs.

The aim of this paper is two-fold: First, to present a dialog system that exhibits these characteristics, and is robust enough to be tested "in the wild", interacting with hundreds of adults and children. Second, to use a large corpus collected with the system to explore how the system can regulate the turn-taking in multi-party situated interaction, using multi-modal turn-taking signals such as filled pauses, facial gestures, breath and gaze.

Figure 1: Two children interacting with Furhat.

The system was exhibited at the Swedish National Museum of Science and Technology, in November 15-23, 2014. As can be seen in Figure 1, two visitors at a time could play a collaborative game together with the robot head Furhat, which has an animated face back-projected on a translucent mask, as well as a mechanical neck [1]. On the touch table between the players, a set of cards are shown. The two visitors and Furhat are given the task of sorting the cards according to some criterion. For example, the task could be to sort a set of inventions in the order they were invented, or a set of animals based on how fast they can run. This is a collaborative game, which means that the visitors have to discuss the solution together with Furhat. However, Furhat does not have perfect knowledge about the solution. Instead, Furhat's behaviour is motivated by a randomized belief model. This means that visitors have to determine whether they should trust Furhat's belief or

ICMI '15, November 09 - 13, 2015, Seattle, WA, USA

ACM 978-1-4503-3912-4/15/11...$15.00
DOI: http://dx.doi.org/10.1145/2818346.2820749

not, just like they have to do with each other. Thus, Furhat's role in the interaction is similar to that of the visitors, as opposed to for example a tutor role which is often given to robots in similar settings [2].

To model such dialog on a deeper semantic and pragmatic level is indeed a challenging task, given the current limitations of conversational speech recognition. However, our main goal here is to create a believable dialog agent that can be used as a test-bed for studying turn-taking and attention in dialog. Our approach has therefore been to exploit the redundancy offered by the multimodal nature of the interaction, where for example the movement of the cards can be used together with the noisy speech recognition to infer which objects are being discussed. The multi-party setup also allows the visitors to have a meaningful discussion with each other even in cases where Furhat's understanding is limited.

The paper is organized as follows: We will start with a review of previous work done on turn-taking in multi-party situated interaction, as a background for our data analysis. After this, we will provide a detailed description of how the system was implemented, in order to manage turn-taking and attention to users and objects in the shared physical space. Using the data collected from the museum, we will first analyse the robustness of the system. We will then explore how the system can utilize multi-modal cues to regulate turn-taking. Since the system's behaviour was systematically manipulated at the museum, we can now measure how the system's turn-taking and turn-yielding cues affect the users' turn-taking behaviour.

2. BACKGROUND

In order to minimize overlapping speech, speakers in dialog have to synchronize their turn-taking [3]. To do so, speakers make use of turn-holding and turn-yielding cues, including prosody, syntax and gestures [4, 5, 6]. For example, when an utterance ends with a flat final pitch, syntactic incompleteness, or a filled pause, this indicates that the speaker wants to hold the floor. If the utterance ends with a rising or falling pitch, and is syntactically complete, it is typically a strong cue to yield the floor. As more turn yielding cues are presented together, the likelihood that the listener will try to take the turn increases. Thus, in order for a robot to appropriately take the turn in interaction with humans, it should not only be able to detect these cues, but also display appropriate cues to signal that it wants to keep or yield the floor. For example, if there is a delay in the processing of the user's utterance, and the system does not immediately respond, there is a risk that the user does not know that the system wanted to take the turn, and therefore continues to speak, which might result in overlapping speech. In such cases, the system can benefit from starting to speak before the processing is complete [7], and display a turn-holding cue such as a filled pause. In face-to-face interaction, humans also use other turn-taking cues, such as gaze and facial gestures. The speaker typically gazes away from the listener during longer utterances, and then gazes back at the listener to yield the turn near the end of the utterance [8]. The listener typically looks at the speaker to signal that she wants to take the turn, then gazes away to signal that she has taken the floor. There are also other cues that indicate that a speaker is about to claim the floor, such as audible and/or visible inhalation [9]. In this study, we will use the data collected at the museum to explore if a robot could utilize such cues to signal that it is about to speak, in order to avoid overlaps. We are not aware of any previous studies that have done so on a wider range of multi-modal cues.

Multi-party interaction differs from dyadic interaction in several ways. In dyadic interaction, there are only two different roles that the speakers can have: speaker and listener. In multi-party interaction, speakers may take on several different roles, such as *side participant*, *overhearer* and *bystander* [10]. Also, in dyadic interaction, it is always clear who is to speak next at turn shifts. In multi-party interaction, this has to be coordinated somehow. The most obvious signal is to use gaze to select the next speaker [11]. Thus, for multi-party interaction between a robot and several users, the robot has to both detect the gaze of the users, and properly use its gaze to select the next speaker. However, it is not trivial to utilize eye gaze tracking in many practical settings, due to the need for calibration, limitations in field-of-view, and sensitivity to blinking and occlusion. Many systems therefore rely on head pose tracking, which is a simpler and more robust approach, but which cannot capture quick glances or track more precise gaze targets. Despite this, previous studies have found head pose to be a fairly reliable indicator of visual focus of attention in multi-party interaction, given that the targets are clearly separated [12, 13, 14].

Several previous studies have found that agents can shape the turn-taking and assignment of participant roles in multi-party interaction by the use of its gaze [10, 15, 16]. For the system to utilize gaze to select the next speaker, it must be clear who the agent is looking at. A problem with animated agents on 2D displays is that it is impossible for the user to see exactly where the agent is looking, a problem typically referred to as the Mona Lisa effect [1]. This is because the agent and user don't share the same physical space. Thus, in a multi-party setting, this means that the agent cannot establish exclusive mutual gaze with one of the users, and in situated interaction the object that is the target of the gaze cannot be inferred. However, in previous studies, we have shown that if an animated face is back-projected on a 3D mask, as done with the Furhat robot head used here, the turn-yielding accuracy is improved [1], and humans can utilize the robot's gaze to disambiguate references to objects to achieve joint attention [17].

In this study we will also investigate the effect of the system's target of attention on who will respond. However, this study is different from the previous studies reported above in two regards. First, the robot has a similar role as the speakers, thus it does not have a clear "function" (i.e., acting as a tutor or quiz host). In a previous Wizard-of-Oz study on multi-party human-robot discussion, where the robot had a task that is very similar to the one used here, we found that the addressee of many utterances is not so easy to determine [18]. Many utterances in more conversational settings are not targeted towards a specific person, but rather as open statements or questions. Second, the discussion in our task necessarily involves references to objects in the physical surroundings. In such settings, speakers also naturally look at these objects. The speaker's gaze can therefore be used by the listener as a cue to the speaker's current focus of attention, so-called joint attention [19].This has been shown to clearly affect the extent to which humans otherwise gaze at each other to yield the turn [20]. In a study on modelling turn-taking in three-party poster conversations, it was found that the participants almost always looked at the shared poster [21]. It is also important to note that objects do not only attract attention in conversation, placing or moving an object can also be regarded as a communicative act in itself [22]. We therefore think that it is important to also study the effect of the system's turn-yielding signals in dialog which involves references to object in the shared space, as we have done here.

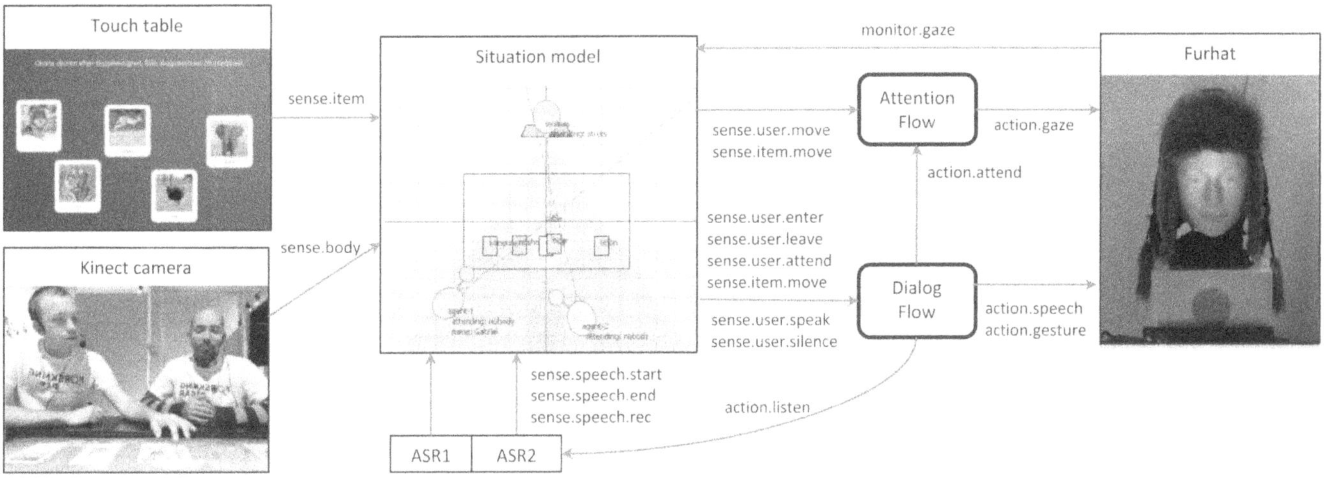

Figure 2: Overview of the different components and some of the events flowing in the system

3. SYSTEM DESCRIPTION

3.1 Overview

When two visitors are seated, Furhat starts the interaction by asking them for their names and whether they know each other. Then five cards are shown on the table and Furhat describes the sorting criterion, after which the discussion starts. When the task has been discussed for some time, a button is shown on the table that can be pressed to reveal the solution. Furhat will then comment on the solution, comparing it with his own belief. After that, the players can play another round if they wish. An excerpt from an interaction is shown in Figure 3[1]. After having played two rounds, the visitors were encouraged by Furhat to allow others to play. The system only manipulates the cards when switching between tasks – only the players can move the cards during the discussion. The tasks are defined in an XML-file, which includes the name of the objects, their true ranking values, the terms used for comparing them ("smaller", "older", etc.), etc. Thus, the game is very easy to extend with new tasks.

The system was implemented using the open source framework IrisTK[2] [23], which provides an event-driven modularized architecture for real-time multi-modal dialog processing. IrisTK comes with modules for vision, speech recognition, situation modelling, speech synthesis, dialog management, and the Furhat robot head. The main modules and events used in the museum setup are illustrated schematically in Figure 2. As can be seen, there are three main types of events: **sense** events which provide sensory data to the system, **action** events which make modules execute certain actions, and **monitor** events which a module generates before, after, or while it executes an action. The monitor events are essential for synchronization and sequencing of actions. Apart from generating sense events or reacting to sense events, modules can also act as *interpreters* (mapping low level sense events to high level sense events), *generators* (mapping high level action events to low level action events), and *controllers* (mapping sense events to action events). IrisTK also provides an XML-based formalism (IrisFlow) for rapidly developing controller modules, based on the notion of Harel statecharts [24]. As can be seen in Figure 2, we use two such controller modules running in parallel: one for dialog management and one for attention. Thus, IrisFlow can be used to script both higher-level and lower-level behaviours.

3.2 Input processing and Situation model

The location and rotation of the users' heads, as well as their hand movements, are tracked using a Kinect camera (v2). Although the system can be configured to use the array microphone in the Kinect camera, we used close talking microphones in the museum. The main motivation for this is that the Kinect array microphone cannot separate the sound sources from the two users and we wanted to be able to run parallel speech recognizers for both users in order to capture overlapping speech (for both online and offline analysis). Also, the array microphone does not work so well in very noisy environments, especially not the sound source localisation, which is essential for maintaining a multi-party dialog. The speech recognition is done with two parallel cloud-based large vocabulary speech recognition modules[3], which allows Furhat to understand the users even when they are talking simultaneously. Since the speech is of a very conversational nature, the WER is typically very high (around 60%). However, as we will see in the evaluation, this is mainly due to errors in function words, and less due to errors in content words. Therefore, a deeper syntactic parsing is not applicable here. Instead, during the discussion phase, the system uses robust phrase spotting to find whether one or more cards are mentioned, whether there is a superlative ("fastest", "smallest"), whether the users think they are done, and whether the phrase is affirmative or not.

As can be seen in Figure 2, the Situation model takes low-level events from the different sensors (Kinect, Touch table and ASR), creates a 3D representation of the situation, and then generates high-level events for the combined sensory data. The individual sensors themselves only provide information relative to their own coordinate systems, but since the Situation model keeps information about the position of the different sensors, it can then translate these coordinates into a common 3D space. Also, if there are several sensors tracking the same users and objects, the Situation model can merge these streams into one coherent model, and map sensory events to a common set of user id:s. This way, speech recognition results from the microphones can be mapped to the right users based on their location, regardless of whether it is a microphone array or a close-talking microphone. Another task

[1] A video of the complete interaction can be seen at https://www.youtube.com/watch?v=5fhjuGu3d0I

[2] http://www.iristk.net

[3] http://dragonmobile.nuancemobiledeveloper.com/

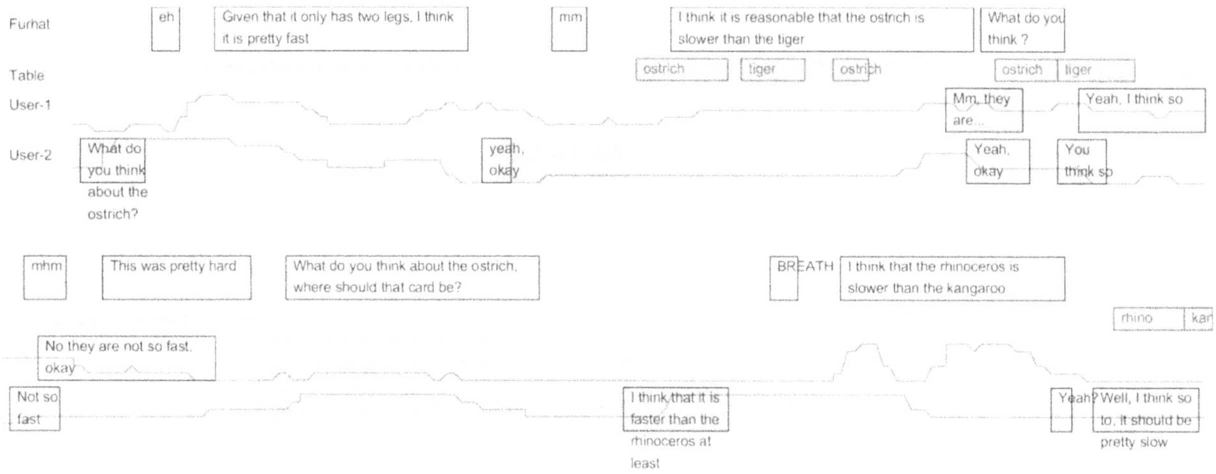

Figure 3: Dialogue fragment from an interaction (translated from Swedish). Shaded (green) track shows where Furhat's attention is directed. Card movements are illustrated in blue. Users' head poses are illustrated with red plots, where a high y-value means the angular distance towards Furhat is small.

of the Situation model is to keep track of when users enter and leave the interaction spaces of system agents (illustrated with grey circles in Figure 2), and generate appropriate engagement and disengagement events. (Although we only use one system agent here, the model allows for multi-agent systems). Finally, when cards are being introduced or moved on the digital table, the Situation model translates the 3D coordinates, and computes which items are being moved the most (which means that they should be considered to be in focus).

3.3 Turn-taking and Attention

As can be seen in Figure 2, the higher level sensory data is sent from the Situation model to the Dialog Flow and The Attention Flow. The task of the Dialog Flow is to manage the turn-taking and to generate responses from Furhat, whereas the Attention Flow keeps Furhat's attention to a specific target. A simplified scheme of the turn-taking is illustrated in Figure 4. As can be seen, the system is typically either in a Speaking state or a Listening state. In the Listening state, the Dialog Flow instructs the two speech recognizers to start listening for speech using a certain silence timeout threshold. If a start-of-speech is detected from one recognizer, a message is sent to the Attention Flow to attend to that user (using the id generated by the Situation model) and to Furhat to raise the eye brows, in order to signal that he is attending to the spoken input. There might also be a second start-of-speech if the other user starts speaking before the first speaker has stopped. When end-of-speech is detected (for both users), the system checks the Situation model to see whether the user was attending Furhat (as indicated by head pose) during some part of the utterance. If so, the system generates a **turn-taking cue** (such as a filled pause, inhaling or shifting the gaze away). Otherwise, it produces a **backchannel** (such as "mhm") to indicate that Furhat is listening while the users are talking to each other. As discussed in the Background, the reason for producing a turn-taking cue is to prevent that the user continues speaking, since the cloud-based recognizers take about 500-1000ms to return the result. During the field trial at the museum, we experimented with different combinations of turn-taking cues, as will be described in 4.2.

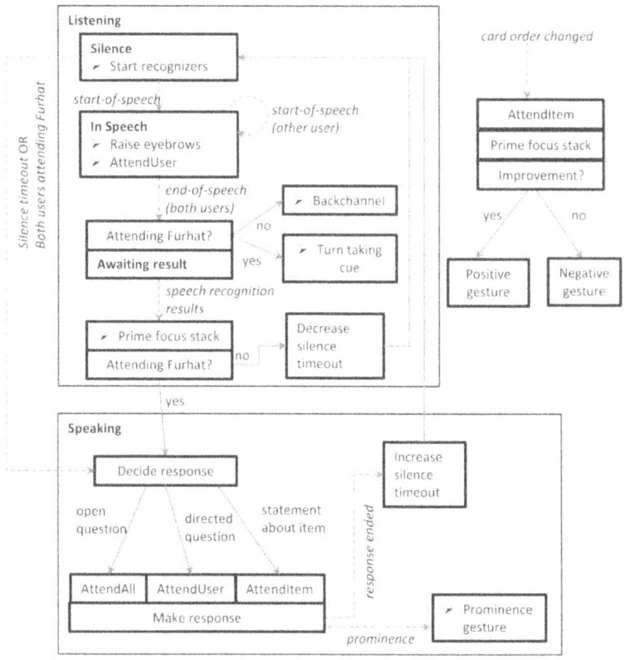

Figure 4: General scheme for managing attention and turn-taking

Once the speech recognition results are received, the attention of the users is checked again. If still no attention has been given to Furhat, the system continues to listen for more speech. However, the silence timeout is decreased. This way, Furhat will eventually take the turn if he is not addressed for some time. When the system responds, either because of a silence timeout or because Furhat was addressed, it sends an action event to the Attention Flow to shift Furhat's attention depending on the type of utterance, for example an open question to both users, a specific question to one of the users, or a statement about one of the cards. As illustrated in Figure 4, Furhat also shifts the attention to an item if the card order changes. This can also generate a positive or negative gesture in Furhat's face depending on whether the new card order is an improvement or not, according to Furhat's belief model (as described in the next section).

As can be seen in Figure 2, the Attention Flow receives continuous events about users and items moving from the Situation model, and sends continuous action.gaze events so that Furhat's attention to a certain target is maintained. There are four states the Attention Flow can be in (as instructed by the Dialog Flow): **Idle** (looking down, waiting for someone to interact with), **AttendingItem** (looking at one of the cards), **AttendingUser** (looking at one of the users), or **AttendingAll** (shifting the gaze between the users). The 3D position of the target is transformed into neck and gaze movement of Furhat (taking Furhat's position in the Situation model into account). If a shift in gaze is small, only the eyes move, otherwise the eyes move first, after which the neck movement follows.

3.4 Belief model

Since Furhat's role should be similar to that of the visitors', and therefore not have perfect knowledge, his behaviour is motivated by a randomized belief model. This is a much more generic and flexible solution than programming the system with a fixed set of tasks and response sets. It is important that this belief model reflects both Furhat's belief about how the items should be ordered, but also his confidence in this belief. Moreover, the model should be able to generate consistent comparisons between items, so that if A is believed to be smaller than B and B smaller than C, A should be smaller C with a higher confidence than for the other comparisons. To meet these requirements, we first model Furhat's belief in the correct value for each item (B_i) as a deviation from the true value (T_i):

$$B_i = T_i + Ignorance * rand(-1,1) * SD_{\bar{T}} \quad (1)$$

Ignorance is a constant that can be tuned to adjust how knowledgeable Furhat should be in general, *rand*(-1,1) is a random value between -1 and 1, and $SD_{\bar{T}}$ is the standard deviation between the true values of the items that are to be sorted. We also model Furhat's confidence in each belief as a *Belief Deviation* (BD_i):

$$BD_i = Uncertainty * rand(-1,1) * SD_{\bar{T}} \quad (2)$$

Uncertainty is a constant that can be tuned to adjust how confident Furhat should be in general. Thus, by adjusting the *Ignorance* and *Uncertainty* constants, we can tune Furhat's personality (e.g., knowledgeable but unconfident, or rather ignorant but with a very high confidence). After testing out different values, it turned out that setting both these constants to 1 gave a balanced result, roughly similar to an average adult.

This belief model can then be used to allow Furhat to compare two cards using a Z-test (treating *BD* as a standard deviation):

$$Z_{i,j} = \frac{|B_i - B_j|}{\sqrt{BD_i^2 + BD_j^2}} \quad (3)$$

The Z-value can then be transformed to a p-value (probability score) using the cumulative standard distribution. This p-value can then be mapped to natural language in order to express Furhat's confidence in his belief.

As an example, let's say Furhat compares the top speed of an elephant (T=40km/h, B=48, BD=13), a tiger (T=64km/h, B=71, BD=13) and an ostrich (T=70km/h, B=79, BD=10). This model could generate the following comparisons (using the task templates): *"I'm certain that the ostrich is faster than the elephant"* (p=0.96), *"This is a guess, but perhaps the tiger is faster than the elephant"* (p=0.88), and *"I have no idea whether the ostrich or tiger is faster"* (p=0.69).

3.5 Generating responses

As described in 3.2 above, due to the high WER (especially for function words), the syntactic and semantic analysis is very limited. For example, we do not distinguish between questions and statements, but instead try to design the responses to be agnostic to this. However, in order to provide meaningful comments about the cards being discussed, the system must be able to track which cards are being talked about, both when the users address Furhat and when they talk to each other. In order to do so, the Dialog Flow maintains a *focus stack* with the five cards. As can be seen in Figure 4, cards are primed (moved to the top) in the focus stack when their names are detected in the speech recognition. Also, each time the card order changes, the card that has moved the most is primed. Thanks to this multi-modal redundancy, the system can often generate meaningful responses, even when the speech recognition fails or deictic references are used.

Figure 5 illustrates the basic scheme for selecting a response during the discussion phase. To make the response varied, IrisFlow easily allows for several alternative responses which the system randomly chooses from, making sure there are no consecutive repetitions. In the task specification, each item may also be associated with canned comments ("The ostrich has pretty long legs") and/or questions that Furhat can ask the users ("have you ever seen a real lion?"), with an associated self-response for the next turn ("I have never been to a Safari").

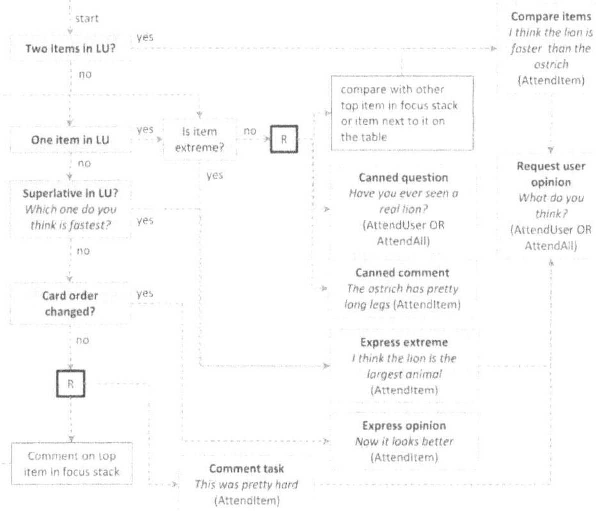

Figure 5: Simplified flow chart for generating system response (R = Random choice, LU = Last user utterance)

4. LARGE SCALE FIELD TRIAL

During the 9 days the system was exhibited at the Swedish National Museum of Science and Technology, we recorded data from 373 interactions with the system, with an average length of 4.5 minutes. Due to the setting in a museum, the dataset contains mixed user groups: both adults playing with each other (40%), children playing with adults (27%), and children playing with each other (33%). After completing one game, the players could choose to continue playing. 58 % of the pairs who completed the first game chose to do so (61% for children and 64% for adults together with children), which indicates that the game was fun.

Using this data, we will first analyse the overall performance of the system, and then analyse how Furhat's attention and turn-taking behaviour affects the interaction. For statistical analysis, we have used two-tailed tests and chosen an alpha level of 0.05.

4.1 System robustness

As discussed previously, to implement a system that can engage in discussion with both children and adults in a real setting is a challenging task. It is therefore interesting to investigate how robust the system actually is. To do so, we randomly selected 9 dialogs which we transcribed and annotated. The overall mean ASR WER was high: 63.4%, with a high standard deviation (38.3%): minimum 33.9% and maximum 94.3% (a dialog involving two very young girls, about 5 years old). Looking only at utterances involving at least one concept, the Concept Error Rate (CER) was 42.1%, indicating that content words (such as names of items) are indeed more easily recognized than other words.

In another study on the same data set [25], we have also manually annotated the end of each user speech segment depending on whether the system should have responded to them or not, on a four grade scale: DON'T, IFNEEDED, GOOD, and OBLIGED. DON'T represents cases where the users are not yielding the turn or are directly addressing each other, whereas OBLIGED are cases where a user is directly yielding the turn to Furhat, and the other cases are somewhere in between. The count of speech segments and the respective CER for each category is presented in Figure 6. As can be seen, there are many cases which fall in the two middle categories, which shows that the discussion is of an open nature, and that the addressee of utterances is not so easy to determine. 17.4% of the system responses were done at inappropriate locations, which indicates that there is room for improvement when it comes to the timing of the system responses. Also, the CER is clearly lowest when the users are directly addressing the system. However, DON'T has a lower CER than IFNEEDED, which indicates that the users probably are speaking more clearly when directly addressing someone (the other user or the system), than otherwise.

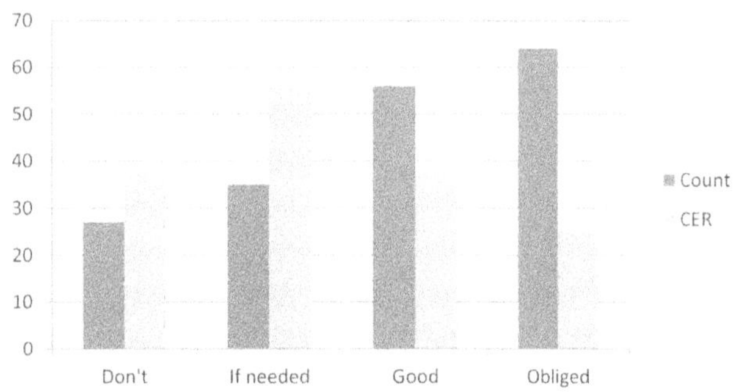

Figure 6: Count of speech segments and CER for the different turn-taking categories.

Each correctly timed system response (i.e., all except DON'T), were then annotated based on whether the response was appropriate or not. It turned out that 82.6% of them were appropriate, which is a surprisingly high number, given the relatively high CER. This indicates that the use of a focus stack (which tracks both previous speech activity and card movements) indeed helps the system to give appropriate responses.

4.2 Taking the turn

As described in 3.3, when the end of a system-directed utterance ended, the system used different turn-taking cues in order to prevent the user from continuing speaking while the speech was being recognized by the cloud-based recognizers. This is schematically illustrated in Figure 7. After 500ms of silence at the end of the user utterance, a turn-taking cue (TTC) is generated. In the museum, we explored different combinations of cues that humans have been found to use. As discussed in the background section, humans often **gaze away** when they are about to take the turn. This behaviour was randomly used as a cue in 50% of the cases, and was contrasted with **keeping the gaze** towards the user in the other cases. In combination with this, we randomly selected between four different facial/verbal cues: (1) **filled pause** ("eh"), (2) a short **breath**, (3) **smile**, or (4) **none** of these. The breath was done by opening Furhat's mouth a bit and playing a recorded inhalation sound (although it is questionable whether it was possible to hear in the noisy setting). Although smiling is not an obvious turn-taking cue, the purpose of the smile was to silently signal that the system somehow had reacted to the user's utterance. Thus, in total, we used 8 different combinations of cues.

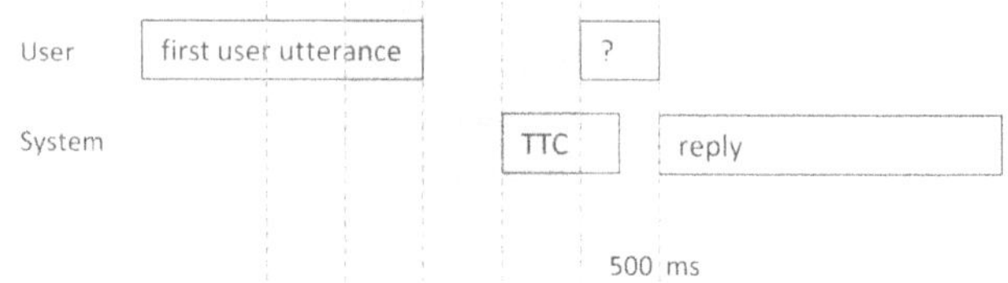

Figure 7: Using turn-taking cues (TTC) to claim the turn

In total, the system produced 1739 turn-taking cues in the complete data set. Of these, we selected the 991 cases where both users actually looked at Furhat (as estimated by their head pose), somewhere during the darkened region in Figure 7. This was done to ensure that they actually had a chance to perceive the turn-taking cue. To measure the effect of the cue, we then calculated the probability of user speech in a window 1000-1500ms after the end of the utterance (marked with "?" in Figure 7). The result is presented in Figure 8.

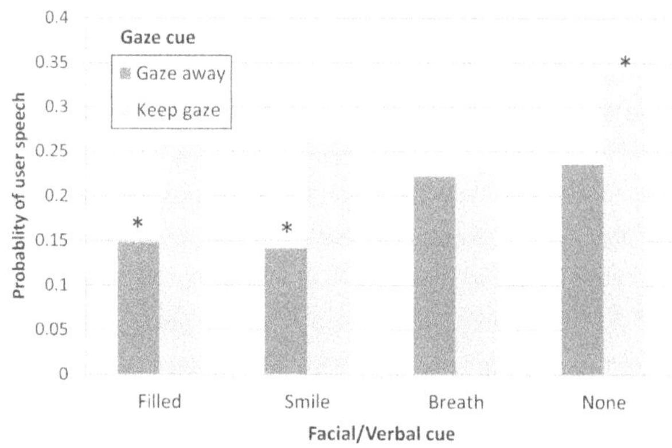

Figure 8: Effects of turn-taking cues. Significant deviations from overall distribution (adj.std.res.) are marked with (*).

A chi-square test shows that there is a significant main effect on the use of gaze ($p<0.001$), where gazing away has an inhibiting effect on the likelihood that the user will continue speaking. Looking at facial/verbal cues alone, all cues are significantly more inhibiting than no cue ($p=0.042$). However, the strongest effect is achieved by combining these cues, where a filled pause or a smile in combination with gazing away give significantly lower probability that the user will speak, and no cues give a significantly higher probability ($p=0.005$). Whereas no cue gives a fairly high probability of the user continuing speaking (33.8%), this can be reduced to 14.8% with the right cues. This indicates that the cues humans use for coordinating turn-taking can be transferred to a human-like robot and have similar effects.

4.3 Yielding the turn

Next, we wanted to explore the effect of Furhat's attention on the users' turn-taking behaviour. In this analysis, we focus on questions from the system, since the target of Furhat's attention was designed to vary randomly for these utterances. In total, there were 2454 questions posed by Furhat in the complete dataset. We can distinguish four attention targets: Furhat could either keep attending to the **Previous Speaker (PS)** who was speaking before Furhat, switch to the **Other Speaker (OS)**, to **Both** users (shifting the gaze between them), or to some of the cards on the **Table**. We then look at which of the users responds: the Previous Speaker (PS), the Other Speaker (OS), Both users at the same time, or **None** of them (within 3 seconds). The distributions are shown in Figure 9. As can be seen, Furhat's attention has a strong influence on who will respond ($p<0.001$). Separate comparisons were also performed between PS and OS, and between Both and Table. The standardized residuals of these tests show several significant differences (marked with ">" in the figure). First, we can note that by attending to one specific user (PS and OS), there is a high probability that this user will take the turn. But we can also note that the None category is reduced after a switch, which means that there is a bigger chance of getting a response if both users are involved in the discussion by switching addressee. Also, attending Both speakers when yielding the turn is more likely to result in simultaneous responses from the users, compared to when Furhat looks down at the Table. When Furhat looks down, it is instead more likely that the previous speaker will continue speaking.

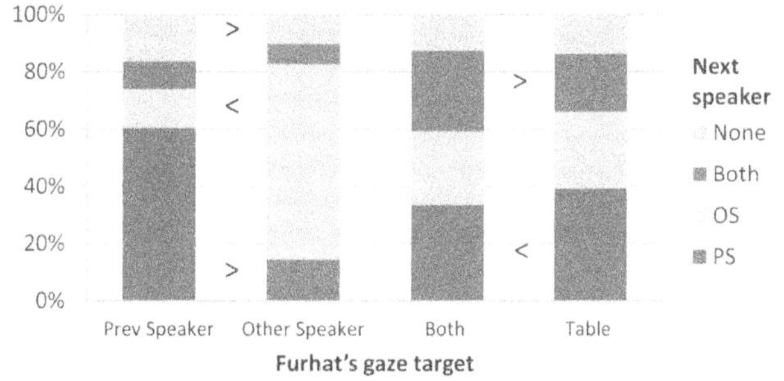

Figure 9: Users' turn-taking behaviour after questions from Furhat, depending on Furhat's attention.

Next, we wanted to investigate how the users' attention affects their likelihood to take the turn. As described in the Background, a listener typically looks at the speaker when she wants to take the turn. Also, in order to see where the speaker's attention is targeted, the listener of course has to look at her. Thus, mutual gaze between the speaker and addressee should increase the likelihood of turn-transition. Using user head pose data, we analysed the first two gaze targets in Figure 9 (PS and OS) by splitting them depending on whether the addressee was looking back at Furhat or not. The result is shown in Figure 10. The distributions were significantly different depending on where the users were looking ($p<0.05$). As can be seen, if the targeted user is looking back at Furhat, that user is more likely to take the turn. Thus, in order for the robot to efficiently yield the turn to a user, it should first ensure that the user is looking back at the robot. However, it should also be noted that Furhat's attention still has a clear effect even when the users' head pose are not directed towards Furhat. This indicates that the users might still glance at Furhat without turning their head (as captured by the Kinect camera).

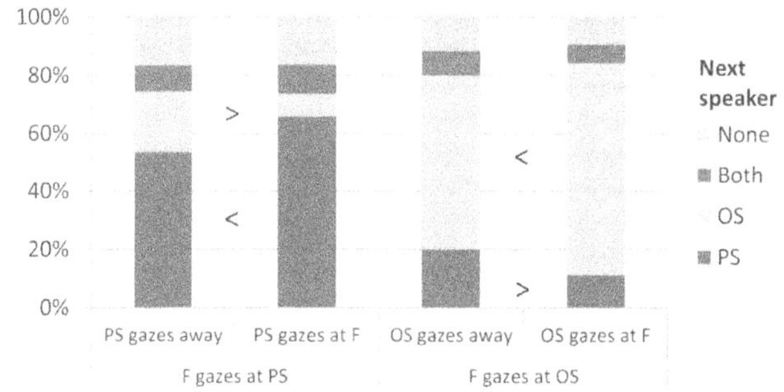

Figure 10: Users' turn-taking behaviour after questions from Furhat, depending on Furhat's *and* users' attention

As described above, when the system detected that the user's attention was not directed towards Furhat at the end of the user's utterance, a backchannel was produced to signal that Furhat was still listening, thus acting as a *side participant* [10]. However, sometimes he also switched attention to the other speaker during the backchannel. Although the pre-condition for making a backchannel was that the users' main focus of attention was not towards Furhat (as determined by the head pose tracker), this behaviour still had a significant effect on the turn-taking ($N=980$, $p=0.013$), as can be seen in Figure 11. This is interesting, as it shows that even when the robot acts as a passive side participant, it can still influence the turn-taking between the users. When the robot switches its target of attention to the other speaker, this user is more likely to continue speaking. As can be seen, this is at the expense of None, which means that the chances of keeping the conversation going is bigger if Furhat actively switches the target of attention while giving backchannels.

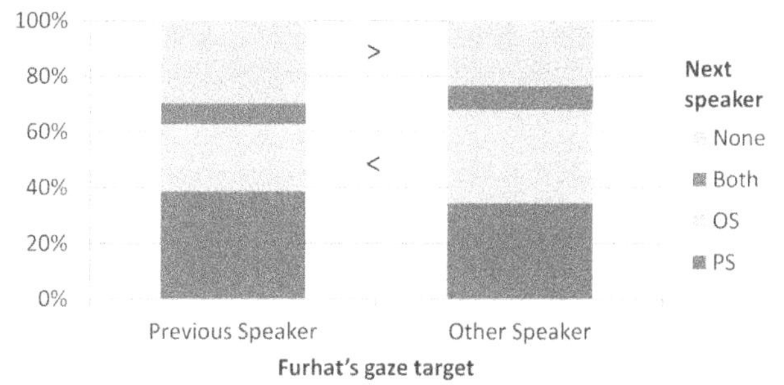

Figure 11: Users' turn-taking behaviour after backchannels from Furhat, depending on Furhat's attention

5. DISCUSSION AND CONCLUSIONS

In this paper, we have presented a dialog system that was exhibited in a museum setting, interacting with hundreds of children and adults in multi-party discussions. The discussion also involves references to objects in the shared physical space, which is interesting from a turn-taking perspective, as they also attract the interlocutors' attention. Despite the challenging setting and task, the system most often managed to provide appropriate responses. This is likely due to the multi-modal redundancy exploited in the setup, where both card movements and speech recognition was used to allow the system to track which objects were being discussed.

By systematically manipulating the robot's behaviour and analysing the data collected at the museum, we found that human-like turn-taking cues can effectively be used to signal that the system is claiming the floor, by letting the robot gaze away, while smiling or producing a filled pause. The robot's attention also has a big influence on which of the users will take the turn, but the robot should monitor the users' attention in order to achieve mutual gaze to effectively yield the turn. Even when the robot is just acting as a passive side participant, its attention matters for which of the users is more likely to continue speaking.

In the current setting, most of Furhat's behaviour is motivated by hand-crafted policies that were tuned during extensive testing. However, we think that the setup described in this paper serves as a very useful test-bed for collecting data on situated interaction (as we have done), and then use this data to build data-driven models for Furhat's behaviour. The test-bed will then allow us to evaluate these models in the same setting that the data was collected. As we saw in the evaluation, there is definitely room for improvement when it comes to the timing of system responses. As reported elsewhere [25], we have also used the annotated data to build a data-driven turn-taking model based on a large range of multimodal cues (e.g. head pose, words, prosody, card movement). Another interesting problem is to build more sophisticated models for Furhat's visual focus of attention.

One very important component in the system is the Situation model, which merges several sensor streams from different modalities, and allows Furhat to keep the attention to both objects and users in the 3D space. To test the generalizability of the model, an interesting next step would be to try it out in a multi-agent setting, and in scenarios where the discussion involves references to physical objects (tracked with vision or RFID). Since IrisTK is open source, other researchers should be able to re-use many of the components and mechanisms described in this paper to implement similar applications.

The exhibition at the museum also showed that both children and adults enjoyed the game, with several of them coming back to play more. We therefore think that the game could be a useful application in its own right, for example in an educational setting. The simple game concept (sorting of cards) allows the content to be easily customized for a particular topic.

6. ACKNOWLEDGMENTS

This work is supported by the Swedish research council (VR) project *Incremental processing in multimodal conversational systems* (2011-6237). Thanks to everyone helping out with the exhibition: Saeed Dabbaghchian, Björn Granström, Joakim Gustafson, Raveesh Meena, Kalin Stefanov and Preben Wik.

7. REFERENCES

[1] Al Moubayed, S., Skantze, G., & Beskow, J. (2013). The Furhat Back-Projected Humanoid Head - Lip reading, Gaze and Multiparty Interaction. *International Journal of Humanoid Robotics, 10*(1).

[2] Al Moubayed, S., Beskow, J., Bollepalli, B., Hussen-Abdelaziz, A., Johansson, M., Koutsombogera, M., Lopes, J., Novikova, J., Oertel, C., Skantze, G., Stefanov, K., & Varol, G. (2014). Tutoring Robots: Multiparty multimodal social dialogue with an embodied tutor. In *Proceedings of eNTERFACE2013*. Springer.

[3] Sacks, H., Schegloff, E., & Jefferson, G. (1974). A simplest systematics for the organization of turn-taking for conversation. *Language, 50*, 696-735.

[4] Duncan, S. (1972). Some Signals and Rules for Taking Speaking Turns in Conversations. *Journal of Personality and Social Psychology, 23*(2), 283-292.

[5] Koiso, H., Horiuchi, Y., Tutiya, S., Ichikawa, A., & Den, Y. (1998). An analysis of turn-taking and backchannels based on prosodic and syntactic features in Japanese Map Task dialogs. *Language and Speech, 41*, 295-321.

[6] Gravano, A., & Hirschberg, J. (2011). Turn-taking cues in task-oriented dialogue. *Computer Speech & Language, 25*(3), 601-634.

[7] Skantze, G., & Hjalmarsson, A. (2013). Towards Incremental Speech Generation in Conversational Systems. *Computer Speech & Language, 27*(1), 243-262.

[8] Kendon, A. (1967). Some functions of gaze direction in social interaction. *Acta Psychologica, 26*, 22-63.

[9] Ishii, R., Otsuka, K., Kumano, S., & Yamato, J. (2014). Analysis of Respiration for Prediction of "Who Will Be Next Speaker and When?" in Multi-Party Meetings. In *Proceedings of ICMI* (pp. 18-25). New York, NY: ACM.

[10] Mutlu, B., Kanda, T., Forlizzi, J., Hodgins, J., & Ishiguro, H. (2012). Conversational Gaze Mechanisms for Humanlike Robots. *ACM Trans. Interact. Intell. Syst., 1*(2), 12:1-12:33.

[11] Vertegaal, R., Slagter, R., van der Veer, G., & Nijholt, A. (2001). Eye gaze patterns in conversations: there is more to conversational agents than meets the eyes. In *Proceedings of ACM Conf. on Human Factors in Computing Systems*.

[12] Katzenmaier, M., Stiefelhagen, R., Schultz, T., Rogina, I., & Waibel, A. (2004). Identifying the Addressee in Human-Human-Robot Interactions based on Head Pose and Speech. In *Proceedings of ICMI*. PA, USA: State College.

[13] Stiefelhagen, R., & Zhu, J. (2002). Head orientation and gaze direction in meetings. In *CHI '02 Extended Abstracts on Human Factors in Computing Systems* (pp. 858-859).

[14] Ba, S. O., & Odobez, J-M. (2009). Recognizing visual focus of attention from head pose in natural meetings. *IEEE Transactions on Systems, Man, and Cybernetics, Part B: Cybernetics, 39*(1), 16-33.

[15] Bohus, D., & Horvitz, E. (2010). Facilitating multiparty dialog with gaze, gesture, and speech. In *Proceedings of ICMI*. Beijing, China.

[16] Skantze, G., Al Moubayed, S., Gustafson, J., Beskow, J., & Granström, B. (2012). Furhat at Robotville: A Robot Head Harvesting the Thoughts of the Public through Multi-party Dialogue. In *Proceedings of IVA-RCVA*. Santa Cruz, CA.

[17] Skantze, G., Hjalmarsson, A., & Oertel, C. (2014). Turn-taking, Feedback and Joint Attention in Situated Human-Robot Interaction. *Speech Communication, 65*, 50-66.

[18] Johansson, M., Skantze, G., & Gustafson, J. (2013). Head Pose Patterns in Multiparty Human-Robot Team-Building Interactions. In *Proceedings of ICSR*. Bristol, UK.

[19] Velichkovsky, B. M. (1995). Communicating attention: Gaze position transfer in cooperative problem solving. *Pragmatics and Cognition, 3*, 199–224.

[20] Argyle, M., & Graham, J. A. (1976). The central Europe experiment: Looking at persons and looking at objects. *Environmental Psychology and Nonverbal Behavior, 1*(1), 6-16.

[21] Kawahara, T., Iwatate, T., & Takanashi, K. (2012). Prediction of Turn-Taking by Combining Prosodic and Eye-Gaze Information in Poster Conversations.. In *Interspeech 2012*.

[22] Clark, H. H. (2005). Coordinating with each other in a material world. *Discourse studies, 7*(4-5), 507-525.

[23] Skantze, G., & Al Moubayed, S. (2012). IrisTK: a statechart-based toolkit for multi-party face-to-face interaction. In *Proceedings of ICMI*. Santa Monica, CA.

[24] Harel, D. (1987). Statecharts: A visual formalism for complex systems. *Science of Computer Programming, 8*, 231-274.

[25] Johansson, M., & Skantze, G. (2015). Opportunities and Obligations to Take Turns in Collaborative Multi-Party Human-Robot Interaction. In Proceedings *of SIGDIAL*. Prague, Czech Republic.

Visual Saliency and Crowdsourcing-based Priors for an In-car Situated Dialog System

Teruhisa Misu
Honda Research Institute
375 Ravendale Drive Suite B
Mountain View, CA, 94043
tmisu@honda-ri.com

ABSTRACT

This paper addresses issues in situated language understanding in a moving car. We propose a reference resolution method to identify user queries about specific target objects in their surroundings. We investigate methods of predicting which target object is likely to be queried given a visual scene and what kind of linguistic cues users naturally provide to describe a given target object in a situated environment. We propose methods to incorporate the visual saliency of the visual scene as a prior. Crowdsourced statistics of how people describe an object are also used as a prior. We have collected situated utterances from drivers using our research system, which was embedded in a real vehicle. We demonstrate that the proposed algorithms improve target identification rate by 15.1%.

Categories and Subject Descriptors

H.5.1 [**Information Interfaces and Presentation**]: Multimedia Information Systems—*Audio input/output*; H.5.2 [**Information Interfaces and Presentation**]: User Interfaces—*Natural language*; I.2.10 [**Artificial Intelligence**]: Vision and Scene Understanding—*Perceptual reasoning*

Keywords

Situated dialog; In-car interaction; Visual saliency; Crowdsourcing; Multimodal interaction

1. INTRODUCTION

Recent advances in sensing technologies have allowed researchers to explore applications that require clear awareness of a system's dynamic context and physical surroundings. Such applications include multi-participant conversation systems [1] and human-robot interaction systems [2, 3]. The general problem of understanding and interacting with human users in such environments is referred to as *situated interaction*. In this study, we address an environment in which situated interactions take place, i.e., a moving car. Previous studies that have analyzed in-car interactions between an expert co-pilot and a driver [4] have shown that people frequently use referring expressions about their surroundings (e.g., *What is that big building on the right?*). In addition, conversations between a driver and a passenger focus on the surrounding objects. (e.g., *Take a left turn in front of that blue restaurant.*). Therefore, we believe that a method to find a link between the user utterance and physical object in the surrounding environment (situated query understanding) is a key technology to facilitate driver-vehicle and driver-passenger communications.

ICMI 2015, November 9–13, 2015, Seattle, WA, USA.

ACM 978-1-4503-3912-4/15/11 ...$15.00.
DOI: http://dx.doi.org/10.1145/2818346.2820748 .

Data fusion from various media inputs is vital to achieve such situated query understanding for in-car interactions. Driver behavioral signal understanding is a popular approach. Cohen et al. [4] showed that many people do not necessarily present a detailed description of the target, but simply say "what's that". Drivers use multimodal cues such as head-pose or gestures to indicate their target. In practice, however, head-pose and/or eye-gaze signals can be problematic. First, head-pose or eye-gaze detection in changing lighting conditions (e.g., outdoors) is difficult, because the estimation algorithm relies on a camera image. Second, mapping between eye-gaze behavior and user intention is not straightforward in interactions in a rapidly changing environment while driving, in which eye fixations are unusual activities. Third, eye-gaze estimation fundamentally requires calibration because the optical axis of the human eye differs by individual offset from the visual axis, which is the true gaze direction [5]; Therefore, a calibration-free method is preferred.

Linguistic information, such as the color and position of the target object is one of the most informative cues for situated reference resolution; however, such linguistic information lacks practicality. Computer vision-based techniques have been applied to acquire property/category information of objects in an environmental context. Most conventional studies have considered relatively simple scenes containing single color objects without occlusions or complex backgrounds. However, scene recognition in the real world remains challenging and error-prone. Although public point-of-interest (POI) databases (DB) (e.g., The Google Places API[1] and Yelp API[2]) include properties for search purposes (i.e., name, geolocation, category, and cuisine), the DBs do not include properties that people are likely to use in an environmental context (e.g., color, equipment, and position).

[1] https://developers.google.com/places/
[2] http://www.yelp.com/developers/

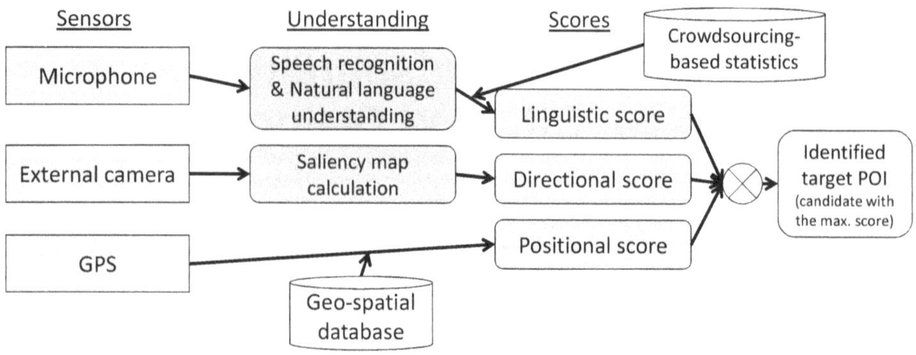

Figure 1: System overview (POI identification)

In addition, subjective information (e.g., size) is difficult to obtain with image recognition techniques.

To address the above issues, we introduce two priors for in-car situated dialog systems. One is based on visual saliency, which is defined as a quality that makes some region of an image stand out relative to its neighbors. We assume that one reason we sometimes do not necessarily use explicit linguistic/multimodal cues is that we can achieve saliency-based joint attention naturally. We incorporate visual saliency as a directional prior. The other prior used in this study is linguistic cues that people are likely to provide given the POI in an environmental context. We use crowdsourcing to collect such statistics, We show that these priors using visual saliency and crowdsourcing can improve target POI identification.

2. RELATED WORK

The ability to achieve grounding in a situated environment is a key function to achieve a natural interaction between humans and machines. Most previous studies have been performed in the context of human-robot interaction.

Analyses of human-human situated dialog have proved that apparent and position cues are important to understand user utterances that describe the situated surroundings [6]. In a real-world situation, although the effectiveness of such cues has been confirmed [7, 8], it is almost impossible to manually annotate all objects in the environment with the properties of the objects. Thus, researchers have applied computer vision techniques to annotate objects in a scene [9, 10, 11]. Although most studies have focused on relatively simple scenes containing single color objects, without occlusions or complex backgrounds, a real-world object annotation and category acquisition task remains a research challenge. In this work, we introduce a more accurate yet feasible solution to obtain object properties, i.e., crowdsourcing. We assume this strategy is especially realistic for a POI identification task for targets located along roads, because unlike situations human-robot interaction take place (e.g., a smart home environment), POI (e.g., restaurants and businesses) properties do not change in a short period. Although several studies have used crowdsourcing to obtain environmental [12, 13], we verify its application to a target identification task.

Another approach to achieve situated reference resolution is the incorporation of user behavior information. Recent advancements in gaze and face direction estimation techniques have led to successes in user behavior understanding. A number of studies have analyzed the relationship between gaze and user intention, such as user focus [14], addressee identification [15], and reference expression understanding [16, 17, 18, 19, 20]. These studies have confirmed that a system's target identification performance is enhanced by considering user eye fixation; however, their results are not directly applicable to an interaction in a rapidly changing environment while driving in which eye fixations are unusual activities. Kim and Misu [21] proposed a model using head-pose trajectory, however, they also indicated that head-pose patterns are user dependent. In this study, we do not track user behavior. Instead, we track an external scene and detect objects that may affect user behavior (grab user attention). In other words, we use visual saliency [22] which is often used to predict visual search behavior. Although typical applications of visual saliency include automatic target detection [23] and landmark selection for robots [24], our contribution is the application of visual saliency to user intention detection in a situated interactive dialog system.

In summary, we address the following research questions in dealing with situated reference resolution in vehicles, and demonstrate the effectiveness of the proposed methods through data collection and analyses.

1. Can we determine a user calibration-free multi-modal cue to identify driver intention using visual saliency?
2. Is crowdsourcing effective to obtain the categories/properties of real-world objects? How useful is the data in a target identification task compared to public and ideal DBs.

3. SYSTEM ARCHITECTURE

Our primary goal is to achieve a situated intelligent in-car assistant that can answer user queries/questions that contain object references regarding POIs. The experimental system uses three main input modalities, i.e., speech, geolocation, and video of the external scene. Speech is the primary input modality and is used to trigger interactions with the system. User speech is recognized, and requested concepts and values are then extracted. Images from external camera and geolocation data are used to identify the target POI of the user query combined with speech information.

Our logic to identify the user intended POI comprises listing and scoring candidate POIs followed by selecting the POI

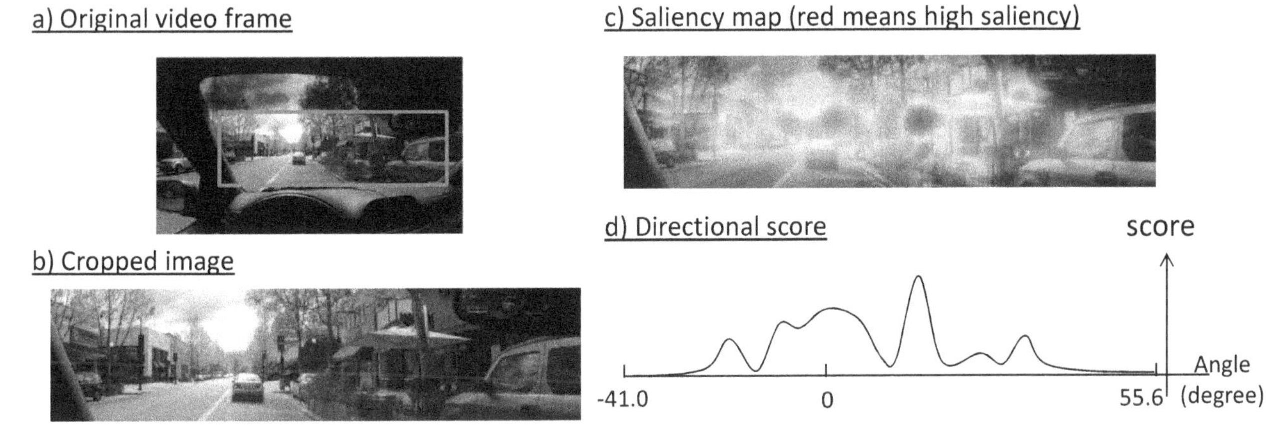

Figure 2: Example saliency map and directional score calculation

with the highest score. An overview of the system and its process flow is illustrated in Figure 1.

The system first performs a POI look-up based on the geolocation information at the time of start-of-speech. The search range for candidate POIs is 200 m direct distance. This is followed by the target identification process, which uses the following scores.

1. Directional score
   The directional score depends on the angle from the car to the POI. Weights for the angles are calculated using a saliency map based on the image captured by the external camera.

2. Linguistic (POI category/property-based) score
   The linguistic score is based on the degree of matching between user-provided linguistic cues and the properties of the POI. Crowdsourcing-based likelihoods that represent how likely it is that a POI will be described using a specific linguistic cue are considered.

3. Positional score
   The positional score is calculated on the basis of the axial and lateral distances from the car to the POI.

The overall score for the candidate POI is given by multiplying these three scores. Further details about the scores are given in the following sections.

Here we define the parameters used to calculate these scores (Figure 3). In Figure 3, the horizontal-axis is the lateral distance (i.e., the distance in the direction orthogonal to the heading with a positive value indicating right) and the vertical-axis is the axial distance. The relative angle θ is defined as an arctangent of the axial distance divided by lateral distance, i.e., θ with a negative value indicates that the POI is to the left of the car.

3.1 Directional (saliency-based) score

The directional score is defined using visual saliency. We give a higher prior to POIs with "salient" appearances based on the assumption that users are likely to query POIs that are likely to grab the user's visual attention. We consider that such saliency is especially effective to understand user queries while driving, because driving is a primary task that requires significant cognitive load and making a query is a secondary task. Thus, queries are performed on the basis of the user's intuition rather than deep consideration.

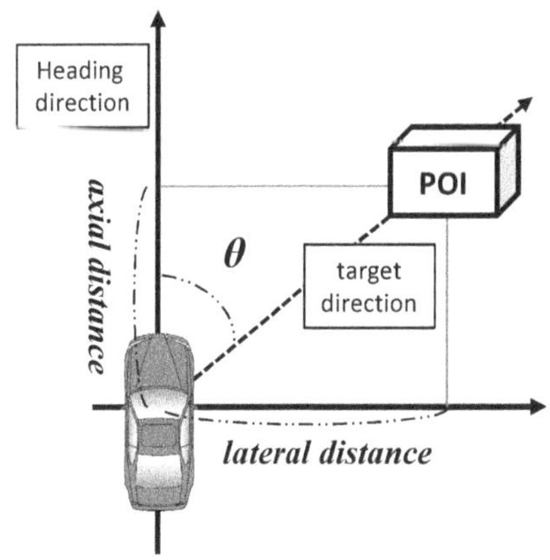

Figure 3: Parameters used for score calculate

To achieve the above strategy, we calculate a saliency map from an image captured by the external camera recorded from the driver's perspective (the camera is located right beside the driver's head) and assign a high prior to POIs which are located in the direction where salient objects exist. To synchronize the image with the car position, we use video frames that correspond to GPS time stamps. We used a 1-Hz GPS; thus, one video frame per second is used for the score calculation. The score calculation for the video frames comprises the following three steps. An example calculation of the saliency map and its conversion to a prior is illustrated in Figure 2. First, we crop the original image (a) to fit the region within the windshield (b). We then apply a graph-based visual saliency algorithm [25] that uses a bottom-up approach for saliency map calculation. The algorithm finds regions that are sufficiently different from their surroundings. The difference is measured by the contrast, intensity and orientation of the image. The size of the saliency map is set to 128 × 38. Each element of the saliency map (i.e., an element of the matrix representing the saliency of the region) is normalized in the range 0 to 1 (c). Note that saliency based on motion and semantic information (e.g., the type of object in the image) is not considered. The prior for POI directions is given by the average of each column of the saliency map (d).

We also consider a timing factor. A previous study [21] has indicated a discrepancy between driver head-pose direction and speech timing. In most cases, head-pose motion is followed by the start-of-speech.) This may imply that most users identify a target POI, and then begin querying that POI. Therefore, based on the hypothesis that the user target is a salient POI identified several seconds before the start-of-speech, we consider this time interval when calculating the directional score.

The directional score Dir_i^t of POI i for a query made at time t is defined as follows:

$$Dir^t(POI_i) = \frac{1}{d} \sum_{n=t-d}^{t} Sal(\theta_i^n). \tag{1}$$

Here, d is the time interval in seconds that is considered for the directional score calculation (e.g., d = 2 implies that the system uses saliency maps from 2 s before the start-of-speech). The effect of d is discussed in Section 5.1. θ_i^n denotes the relative angle to the POI i from the car at time n (Figure 3). $Sal()$ is a function to obtain the prior from the saliency map. If the direction to the POI is within the (cropped) video angle range [3] the score for the direction (by selecting the closest angle to the POI direction from the 128 directions) is used. Otherwise, a constant value α is used[4].

Furthermore, we incorporate linguistic cues for the directional score calculation (**LR filtering**). We use positions cues (e.g. on the right/left) for the calculation, and use the saliency of the specified directions only (i.e., we ignore saliency of directions that are not specified by the user). In other words, if the user specifies that the target POI is on the *right*, $Sal()$ returns α if θ of the candidate POI is negative. Similarly, $Sal()$ returns α for a positive degree when *left* is specified by the user utterance.

3.2 Linguistic (POI property-based) score

The linguistic score is calculated on the basis of the similarity between the user query and the POI vector that represents the likelihood that the POI is described. In this work, we used six linguistic cue categories. "B-category" refers to businesses. Typical values include *restaurant* and *café*. "Cuisine" identities restaurant type, such as *Chinese*, *Mexican*, or *ice cream*. Color information about buildings and signs is in the "Color" category, and expressions about the size, width, and height of POIs are in the "Size" category. The "Equipment" category describes building facilities, such as *outside seating* and *awnings*. The "RoadPosition" category represents expressions that refer to the relative positions of the target POIs to roads (e.g., *on the corner*).

3.2.1 Score calculation

The linguistic score for the candidate POI i given user query q_k is calculated as the product of the category likelihoods regarding POI i.

$$Ling(POI_i|q_k) = \prod_{c} Pr(v_k^c|POI_i) \tag{2}$$

Here v_k^c denotes the value of category c included in user query q_k. Using user queries collected by crowdsourcing is

Figure 4: Sample image for street-view HIT

described later. $Pr(v_k^c|POI_i)$ is defined as follows:

$$Pr(v_k^c|POI_i) = \begin{cases} \frac{count(v_k^c)}{N_i} & \text{if} \quad v_k^c \in q_k \\ \beta & \text{otherwise} \end{cases}. \tag{3}$$

N_i denotes the number of queries describing POI i and *count*() is the number of queries containing the value in the collected queries using crowdsourcing. For example, we assume a user query is "Tell me about that blue restaurant." Here the user query contains two keywords, i.e., *blue* and *restaurant*. These keywords belong to "Color" and "B-category," respectively. If crowdsourcing-based statistics about POI_i indicate that 20% of users describe this POI as blue and 40% describe as restaurant, the linguistic score for the POI_i is $0.2 \times 0.4 \times \beta^4$. (where β is a penalty for category with a null value[5].

3.2.2 Data collection by crowdsourcing

To obtain statistics for each POI, we used Amazon Mechanical Turk crowdsourcing platform[6] to collect data. With this platform, crowd workers (called Turkers) perform tasks called human intelligent tasks (HITs) posted by requesters. We prompted Turkers using a street-view application. We constructed a data collection page using the Google Street-View API. We displayed an image with a pin on the target POI and asked Turkers to write a natural language query based on that image. we provided the Turkers with the following scenario as a part of our instructions[7].

You are driving with a passenger. While driving, you want to know about the place shown in the pinned image (i.e., the business nearest the pin). The passenger is a local and you are sure that they know what the place is.

We also attached a sample photo with the following three sample utterances:

- Please tell me about that place on the right.
- What is that blue building on the corner?
- I would like to know about the cafe with the blue awning.

The default viewpoint is set to approximately 30 m from the POI position. We set the view-points semi-automatically. First, we set viewpoints using street information obtained from OpenStreetMap[8] road data. Then,

[3]from -41.0 degree to 55.6 degree in our setting
[4]We empirically set α to 0.01.

[5]We empirically set β to 0.01.
[6]www.mturk.com
[7]URL: https://dogmatix.honda-ri.com:8443/describePOI2/preview.html
[8]www.openstreetmap.org

Table 1: Crowd worker-provided linguistic cues

Linguistic cue category	Percentage used (%)
B-category (e.g., restaurant, cafe)	20.1
Color (e.g., green, yellow)	17.8
Cuisine (e.g., Chinese, Japanese, Mexican)	7.8
RoadPosition (e.g., corner)	8.1
Equipment (e.g., awning, outside seating)	13.3
Size (e.g., big, small, huge)	4.4

we check and modify the views. A sample image[9] is shown in Figure 4. We asked Turkers to construct one query per target POI. The HIT contained five target POIs, each of which were randomly selected from 78 candidates. We paid five cents for completion of the HIT. Note that not all Turkers submitted five queries.

We analyzed the collected data focusing on the number of words provided by the Turkers who acted as drivers. We collected 37,587 queries. The average number of words per query was 8.56. After collecting the queries, we examined 2,000 queries to determine correctness. We categorized errors into two types. Task errors occurred when crowd workers did not follow instructions when constructing their queries. Typically, Turkers would inquire about non-business targets, such as bus stops, plants, or cars on the road. Others inquired about the city of Mountain View and routes. For the street-view and video HITs, the task errors rate was 10.9%. POI errors occurred when Turkers who completed street-view HIT inquired about businesses neighboring those marked with pins. In total, 4.9% of the queries contained POI errors.

Categories and values were then extracted from the collected utterances. Table 1 shows the statistics for the categories in the collected queries. $Pr(v_k^c|POI_i)$ is calculated on the basis of the statistics per POI[10]. For example, for the green restaurant on the left in Figure 4, 18.5% of queries included "green" in the color category, 30.5% described the POI as "coffee shop," 14.2% described it as a "restaurant," and 25.6% indicated that it was on the corner. For the business on the right with the green awnings, 23.3% of the workers described as having "awnings," 14.7% said it was a "bookstore," 3.2% and 2.6% described it as a "restaurant" or a "coffee shop," respectively.

3.3 Positional score

The positional score is given on the basis of the relationship between the car and the target POI. An issue peculiar to the assigned task is that it is very time sensitive, because the spatial relationship between the car and the target changes while the user is speaking. Based on our previous analysis [26, 27], which reported that the POI position is less dependent on users and scenes at the start-of-speech timing than the speech recognition result is obtained, we used the relationship between the car and the target POI at the start-of-speech.

[9]Due to copyright issues, this is not the image used for the HIT.

[10]We did not exclude erroneous utterances due to the cost of manual checking.

We applied a Gaussian mixture model (GMM) with diagonal covariance matrices over the input parameter space to model the relationship between POI position $\mathbf{x_i}$ and the positional score [27]. The positional score $Pos(\mathbf{x_i})$ is expressed as follows:

$$Pos(\mathbf{x_i}) = \sum_{k=1}^{K} \pi_k \mathcal{N}(\mathbf{x}_i|\boldsymbol{\mu}_k, \boldsymbol{\Sigma}_k). \quad (4)$$

Here $\mathbf{x_i}$ is a d-dimensional data vector (input parameters), π_k, where $k = 1, \ldots, K$, are the mixture weights, and $\mathcal{N}(\mathbf{x}_i|\boldsymbol{\mu}_k, \boldsymbol{\Sigma}_k)$ are the component Gaussian densities. Each component density is a d-variate Gaussian function of the following form:

$$\mathcal{N}(\mathbf{x}_i|\boldsymbol{\mu}_k, \boldsymbol{\Sigma}_k) = \frac{1}{(2\pi)^{d/2}|\Sigma_k|^{1/2}} \exp\left\{-\frac{1}{2}(\mathbf{x}_i - \boldsymbol{\mu}_k)'\Sigma_k^{-1}(\mathbf{x}_i - \boldsymbol{\mu}_k)\right\}, \quad (5)$$

with mean vector $\boldsymbol{\mu}_k$ and diagonal covariance matrix $\boldsymbol{\Sigma}_k$. The mixture weights sum to 1 ($\Sigma_{k=1}^{K}\pi_k = 1$). We used two input parameters ($d = 2$), i.e., the lateral and axial distances of POI i at the start-of-speech.

We used two GMM settings. The first was a simple GMM that did not consider linguistic information (**Baseline GMM**). We empirically set the number of Gaussian components to $K = 6$. The other setting was position cue-dependent (**LRN-GMM**), i.e., we prepared three sets of GMMs for left, right, and no position cue cases. The system selects which GMM to apply on the basis of the position-cue in the user query. Following previous report [27], we empirically set the number of Gaussian components to 2 $K = 2$ for each position cue-dependent GMM.

4. DATA COLLECTION

We collected data using a test route that passed through downtown Mountain View. We constructed DB that contained 78 POIs including businesses, restaurants, and other companies on Castro Street. Each DB entry (i.e., POI) had a name, geolocation, category, and property information (Section 3.2). POI geolocation was represented as a latitude-longitude pair (e.g., 37.4010,-122.0539). The route took approximately 15 min to drive. On average, each POI had on average 7.2 other POIs within 50 m.

We collected data from 14 subjects. Each participant was asked to drive (roundtrip) the test route and construct queries about the surrounding businesses. Queries regarding businesses that do not exist in our DB (typically a vacant store) were excluded. We collected 206 queries with valid target POIs. Example user utterances included "What is that blue restaurant on the right?" "How about this building to my right with outside seating?" and "What kind of the restaurant is that on the corner?". The queries were transcribed, and user-intended POIs were manually annotated by confirming the intended target POI with the subjects after data collection based on a video taken during the drive.

5. EXPERIMENTS

We used manual transcriptions and natural language understanding results of user queries to focus our evaluations on the issues listed in Section 1. We evaluated the POI identification performance based on cross-validation. We used the data from 13 users to train the GMM parameters. We

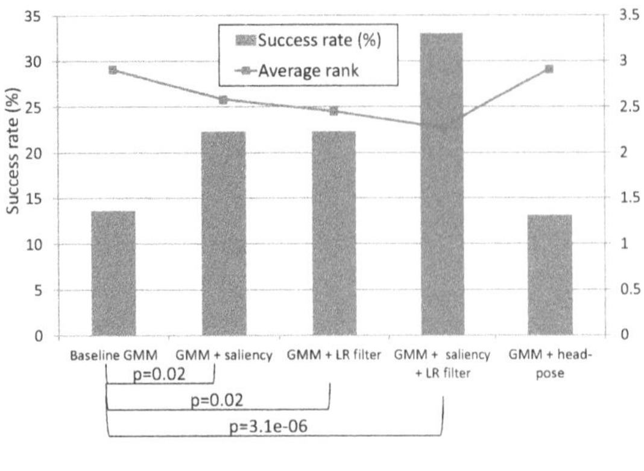

Figure 5: Effect of using saliency-based prior

trained the model parameters of the GMM $(\boldsymbol{\pi}, \boldsymbol{\mu}, \boldsymbol{\Sigma})$ using the EM algorithm [28].

We did not set a rejection threshold. We judged that the system successfully understood a user query when the posterior of the target (user-intended) POI was the highest. The chance rate, given by the average of the inverse number of candidate POIs in the POI lookup, was 6.0%.

5.1 Effect of visual saliency

We investigated the effect of the directional score on the basis of the visual saliency-based prior (Section 3.1). Figure 5 illustrates the effect of the saliency-based prior with the **baseline GMM**. The time interval parameter n was set to 4. The linguistic score (except the position cues for LR filtering) was not used for the POI identification.

Figure 5 shows the results. As can be seen, visual saliency-based directional score (**Base GMM + saliency**) improved the target identification rate by 8.7% absolute over the case using the baseline GMM only. Note that while simply applying the LR filter [11] (**GMM + LR filtering**) improved performance, performance was even higher when the LR filter was combined with the saliency-based score (**Base GMM + saliency + LR filtering**), achieving a significant improvement of 19.4% over the baseline method. We also observed that the average rank of the user-intended POI improved significantly.

Next, we compared the saliency-based prior with the driver's head-direction-based prior. We used the $HD()$ function rather than the $Sal()$ in Equation 1. $HD()$ is defined as a Gaussian kernel to measure the distance between the POI direction θ_i^n and head-pose direction[12] $head_n$ at time n.

$$HD(\theta_i^n, head^n) = \frac{1}{\sqrt{2\pi\sigma^2}} \exp\left(-\frac{(\theta_i^n - head^n)^2}{2\sigma^2}\right) \quad (6)$$

Here σ is a parameter of the kernel empirically set to 3.0 to maximize the success rate. This result is also illustrated in Figure 5. As observed, using the head-direction function did not improve target identification rate. This result agrees with the result of a previous study [27], which using low frequency (1 Hz) head-pose information does not necessarily contribute to target identification rate improvement[13].

[11] The directional score 0.5 is given when the target POI is within the field of view, otherwise α is given. Filtering using position cues (LR filtering) is also applied.

[12] Using a 3D depth sensor (PrimeSense Carmine 1.09) and the Point Cloud Library, the system estimated the head-pose direction at 1 Hz.

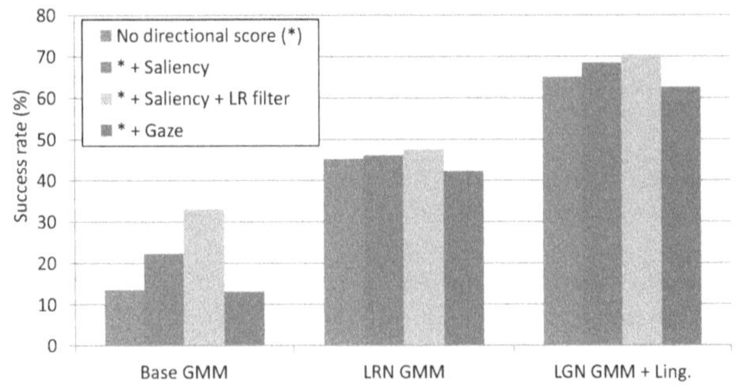

Figure 6: Incorporation of position-cue-dependent GMM and linguistic information

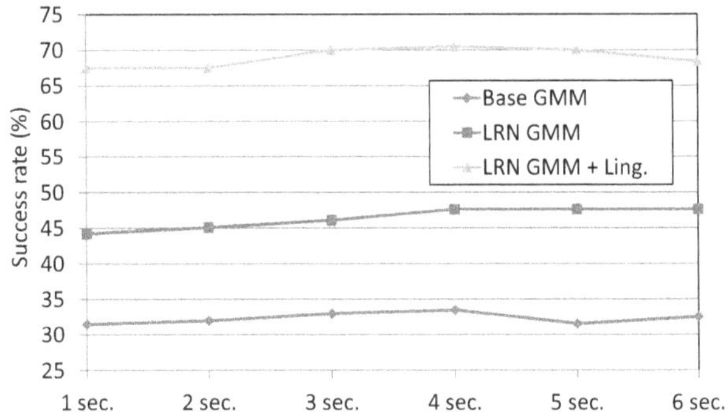

Figure 7: Effect of interval used for directional score calculation

We also evaluated the effect of the saliency-based directional score combined with the LRN GMM and the linguistic score (using the **mixed DB**, which is explained in Section 5.2). These results are illustrated in Figure 6. The improvements under those conditions were not larger than those under the Baseline GMM condition; however adequate improvement was achieved.

Finally, we analyzed the effect of interval parameter n (how long visual context should be considered) when calculating the directional score. Because the GPS input is 1 Hz, n coincides to the number of video frames used to calculate the directional score. We plotted the relationship between time interval n and success rate in Figure 7. The results suggest that using a longer ($n > 3$) interval improved the success rate. This validates our hypothesis that that users identify a target POI, and then begin querying that POI.

5.2 Effect of crowdsourcing-based DB

First, we analyzed the linguistic cues provided by the users. Table 2 lists the percentage of user utterances containing each cue type. Note that "CarPosition" is not used to calculate linguistic score but is used for directional and positional scores.

Compared to the data collected using crowdsourcing, the percentages of "B-category," "Cuisine, " and "Size" are about twice as frequent. As can be seen, users provided POI positions relative to the car (right and left) quite often. Nearly

[13] They extended their work and showed that using 10 Hz input can performance [21].

Table 2: User-provided linguistic cues

Linguistic cue category	Percentage used (%)
CarPosition (on the right/left)	68.0
B-category (e.g. restaurant, cafe)	37.9
Color (e.g. green, yellow)	19.9
Cuisine (e.g. Chinese, Japanese, Mexican)	12.6
RoadPosition (e.g. corner)	9.2
Equipment (e.g. awning, outside seating)	8.7
Size (e.g., big, small, huge)	8.2

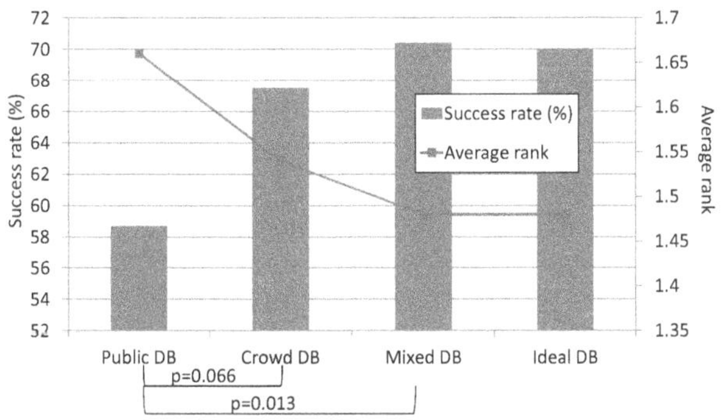

Figure 8: Effect of using crowdsourcing-based prior

70% of the queries included this type of cue. This might be the reason why we achieved significant improvement by applying the LRN GMM (Figure 6).

We then analyzed the effect of using a crowdsourcing-based DB. Here we compared the following cases.

1. **Public DB** (baseline)
   Assuming a public database, we used "B-category" and "Cuisine" categories only. The likelihood $Pr(v^c|POI_i)$ was set to 1.0 if the POI corresponded to those categories. The other categories were not used for the score calculation.

2. **Crowdsourcing DB**
   We used the data collected using our crowdsourcing method. The likelihood was set on the basis of the frequency of the category value that the crowd workers provided as described in Section 3.2.

3. **Mixed DB**
   Assuming that both public and crowdsourcing DBs are available, we used the likelihoods of **Public DB** for "B-category" and "Cuisine" and used the likelihoods of **Crowdsourcing DB** for the other categories.

4. **Ideal DB** (reference)
   We assumed an ideal DB that contains every property actually described by the users. The likelihoods $Pr(v^c|POI_i)$ for all values were set to 1.0.

The results are shown in Figure 8. The LRN GMM and the visual-saliency-based directional score were also applied for this comparison. As observed, using a crowdsourcing-based DBs (**Crowdsourcing DB**) improved the target identification rate by 8.8% over the baseline **Public DB**. This confirmed that using apparent and positional linguistic cues is vital for the target POI identification in this task. By combining the crowdsourcing-based DB with the public DB (**Mixed DB**), we achieved a large ($p = 0.013$) improvement over the baseline. This indicates that accurate category and cuisine information can be recognized more accurately by the user under the real condition than the crowdsourcing condition. This is probably because of the resolution of the image in the crowdsourcing setting (reading characters on buildings/awnings/signs might be easier while real actually driving). In addition, the performance of the mixed database (70.5%) was comparable to the case using ideal DB, indicating that category information concerning appearance and POI position collected by crowdsourcing is as informative as the ideal case.

Overall, we achieved a significant ($p = 0.0007$) improvement of 15.1% in the target identification rate by using both saliency and crowdsourcing-based priors when combined with LRN GMM (Public DB w/o directional score vs. Mixed DB w/ directional score). The improvement was more significant when we used the Baseline GMM (28.6-60.2%). While a 70.5% in success rate is not satisfactory, the success rate improves to 86.9% if we consider second rank candidates. Using second rank candidates, we can obtain adequate performance when combined with an interactive presentation method. e.g., "Restaurant A is on your right and restaurant B is on your left."

6. DISCUSSION

The major limitation of our work comes from the small amount of data we were able to collect. It is unclear how our results can be generalized to other sites, POI densities, and sensor performance. Results might depend on experimental conditions such as weather and lighting conditions. Thus, adaptation of the proposed method's statistics must be explored.

While robustness to different experimental conditions was not proved in this study, we believe that one advantage of using visual saliency is that it can reflect the lighting conditions of the actual surroundings. For example, under a back-lit condition, color might not be the primary factor in the saliency calculation. This might also be the case for drivers. On the other hand, the saliency map calculation for driving scenes remains a focus of future work. Although we applied a general-purpose algorithm for saliency map calculation, regions that attract driver attention might differ from those that attract attention while looking at a still picture. Using a traffic context, such as considering the surrounding cars and pedestrians, may lead to improved saliency calculation while driving.

Our experiment used 1-Hz head-pose input data; however this data does not contribute to any improvement. Thus incorporation of head-pose/gaze behavior should also be further investigated. We believe that using better sensor input will lead to better understanding of driver intention. In addition, consideration of driving behavior [29] may be a key factor in understanding driver head-pose/gaze behavior. We will need to distinguish between driving-task gaze/head-pose behaviors and POI query task behaviors.

Another area of further exploration is methods to obtain more meaningful statistics through crowdsourcing. One involves instructions for crowd workers. We used only one image and angle to obtain statistics about the target POI;

however, using multiple angles and lighting conditions will likely yield more realistic statistics. The other involves post-processing, especially elimination of erroneous crowdworker-provided information. For example, we believe better statistics can be obtained through comparison with neighboring POIs.

7. CONCLUSION

We have investigated methods for identifying user-intended target objects for situated dialog systems in a car. We have introduced two priors for the identification task using visual saliency and crowdsourcing-based statistics. The effectiveness of the proposed methods was confirmed on the basis of evaluations using a target POI identification task with our in-car dialog system. This paper has addressed a focused application of identifying driver intended POIs; however, the methodology used in this paper is widely applicable to tasks that involve in-car situated interactions. For example, identification and illustration of passenger intention (e.g., "turn right at that building") on a navigation display will decrease driver distraction. Extension of the framework to non-stationary target objects (e.g., cars and pedestrians) will enable many other applications. Thus, we believe that the proposed methodologies are applicable to many other tasks.

8. REFERENCES

[1] D. Bohus and E. Horvitz. Models for Multiparty Engagement in Open-World Dialog. In *Proc. SIGDIAL*, pages 225–234, 2009.

[2] S. Tellex, T. Kollar, S. Dickerson, M. Walter, A. Banerjee, S. Teller, and N. Roy. Understanding natural language commands for robotic navigation and mobile manipulation. In *Proc. AAAI*, 2011.

[3] K. Sugiura, N. Iwahashi, H. Kawai, and S. Nakamura. Situated spoken dialogue with robots using active learning. *Advance Robotics*, 25(17):2207–2232, 2011.

[4] D. Cohen, A. Chandrashekaran, I. Lane, and A. Raux. The HRI-CMU corpus of situated in-car interactions.

[5] D. Hansen and Q. Ji. In the eye of the beholder: A survey of models for eyes and gaze. *IEEE Trans. on Pattern Analysis and Machine Intelligence*, 32(3):478–500, 2010.

[6] A. Cremers. Object reference in task-oriented keyboard dialogues. In *Multimodal Human-Computer Communication*, volume 1374, pages 279–293. 1998.

[7] A. Tom and M. Denis. Referring to Landmark or Street Information in Route Directions: What Difference Does It Make? In *Spatial Information Theory. Foundations of Geographic Information Science (LNCS)*, pages 97–100, 2003.

[8] J. Götze and J. Boye. Deriving salience models from human route directions. In *Proc. CoSLI-3*, pages 7–12, 2013.

[9] D. Roy. Integration of speech and vision using mutual information. In *Proc. ICASSP*, pages 2369–2372, 2000.

[10] T. Nakamura, T. Nagai, and N. Iwahashi. Grounding of word meanings in multimodal concepts using LDA. In *Proc. IROS*, pages 3943–3948, 2009.

[11] C. Liu, R. Fang, and J. Chai. Towards mediating shared perceptual basis in situated dialogue. In *Proc. SIGDIAL*, pages 140–149, 2012.

[12] R. Meena, J. Boye, G. Skantze, and J. Gustafson. Crowdsourcing street-level geographic information using a spoken dialogue system. In *Proc. SIGDIAL*, pages 2–11, 2014.

[13] T. Misu. Crowdsourcing for situated dialog systems in a moving car. In *Proc. Interspeech*, pages 125–129, 2014.

[14] R. Yonetani, H. Kawashima, T. Hirayama, and T. Matsuyama. Gaze probing: Event-based estimation of objects being focused on. In *Proc. ICPR*, pages 101–104, 2010.

[15] Y. Nakano, N. Baba, H. Huang, and Y. Hayashi. Implementation and evaluation of a multimodal addressee identification mechanism for multiparty conversation systems. In *Proc. ICMI*, pages 35–42, 2013.

[16] A. Koller, K. Garoufi, M. Staudte, and M. Crocker. Enhancing referential success by tracking hearer gaze. In *Proc. SIGDIAL*, pages 30–39, 2012.

[17] J. Chai and Z. Prasov. Fusing eye gaze with speech recognition hypotheses to resolve exophoric reference in situated dialogue. In *Proc. EMNLP*, 2010.

[18] C. Kennington, S. Kousidis, and D. Schlangen. Interpreting situated dialogue utterances: an update model that uses speech, gaze, and gesture information. In *Proc. SIGDIAL*, 2013.

[19] A. Prokofieva, M. Slaney, and D. Hakkani-Tur. Probabilistic features for connecting eye gaze to spoken language understanding. In *Proc. ICASSP*, 2015.

[20] C. Kennington, R. Iida, T. Tokunaga, and D. Schlangen. Incrementally tracking reference in human/human dialogue using linguistic and extra-linguistic information. In *Proc. HLT/NAACL*, pages 272–282, 2015.

[21] Y. Kim and T. Misu. Identification of the driver's interest point using a head pose trajectory for situated dialog systems. In *Proc. ICMI*, pages 92–95, 2014.

[22] L. Itti and C.Koch. Computational modeling of visual attention. *Nature Reviews Neuroscience*, 2, 2001.

[23] L. Itti and C. Koch. A saliency-based search mechanism for overt and covert shifts of visual attention. *Vision Research*, 40:1489–1506, 2000.

[24] S. Frintrop, P. Jensfelt, and H. Christensen. Attentional landmark selection for visual slam. In *Proc. IROS*, 2006.

[25] J. Harel, C. Koch, and P. Perona. Graph-Based Visual Saliency. In *Proc. NIPS*, pages 545–552, 2006.

[26] T. Misu, A. Raux, R. Gupta, and I. Lane. Situated language understanding at 25 miles per hour. In *Proc. SIGDIAL*, pages 22–31, 2014.

[27] T. Misu, A. Raux, I. Lane, and R. Gupta. Situated language understanding for a spoken dialog system within vehicles. *Computer Speech and Language.*

[28] C. Bishop. *Pattern Recognition and Machine Learning.* Springer, 2006.

[29] S. Kousidis, C. Kennington, T. Baumann, H. Buschmeier, S. Kopp, and D. Schlangen. A multimodal in-car dialogue system that tracks the driver's attention. Proc. ICMI, pages 26–33, 2014.

Leveraging Behavioral Patterns of Mobile Applications for Personalized Spoken Language Understanding

Yun-Nung Chen Ming Sun Alexander I. Rudnicky Anatole Gershman
School of Computer Science, Carnegie Mellon University
5000 Forbes Avenue, Pittsburgh, PA 15213, USA
{yvchen, mings, air, anatoleg}@cs.cmu.edu

ABSTRACT

Spoken language interfaces are appearing in various smart devices (e.g. smart-phones, smart-TV, in-car navigating systems) and serve as intelligent assistants (IAs). However, most of them do not consider individual users' behavioral profiles and contexts when modeling user intents. Such behavioral patterns are user-specific and provide useful cues to improve spoken language understanding (SLU). This paper focuses on leveraging the app behavior history to improve spoken dialog systems performance. We developed a matrix factorization approach that models speech and app usage patterns to predict user intents (e.g. launching a specific app). We collected multi-turn interactions in a WoZ scenario; users were asked to reproduce the multi-app tasks that they had performed earlier on their smart-phones. By modeling latent semantics behind lexical and behavioral patterns, the proposed multi-model system achieves about 52% of turn accuracy for intent prediction on ASR transcripts.

Categories and Subject Descriptors

I.2.7 [**Natural Language Processing**]: Language Parsing and Understanding—*speech and behavioral patterns*

Keywords

Spoken Language Understanding; Spoken Dialogue System; Intelligent Assistant; Behavioral Patterns; Matrix Factorization

1. INTRODUCTION

Spoken dialogue systems (SDS) are developed in smart-devices and allow users to launch apps via spontaneous speech. The key component of an SDS is a spoken language understanding (SLU) model, which predicts users' intended apps by understanding input utterances. However, language ambiguity often makes prediction difficult, for example, two apps "Email" and "Message" are both plausible by hearing an utterance "*Send to Alex*". This work improves the prediction performance base on our observation that the intended apps usually depend on 1) the preference of individual users (some people prefer "Message" to "Email") and 2) behavioral patterns in the app level ("Message" is more likely to follow "Camera" and "Email" is more likely to follow "Excel").

Typical intelligent assistants (IAs) treat each task (e.g. restaurant search, messaging, etc) independent of each other, where only current utterances are considered to decide the desired apps in SLU [3]. Some IAs modeled user intents by keeping the contexts from the previous utterances, but they did not consider behavioral patterns of individual users [1]. To improve understanding, some studies utilized the non-verbal contexts like eye gaze and head nod as cues to resolve the referring expression ambiguity and to improve driving performance respectively [7, 9]. Considering that human users often interact with their phones to carry out complicated tasks that span multiple domains and apps, user behavioral patterns as additional non-verbal signals may provide deeper insights into user intent [11, 2]. For example, if a user always texts his friend via "Message" instead of "Email" right after finding a good restaurant via "Yelp", such behavioral pattern helps disambiguate the intended apps of the utterance "*Send to Alex*". Therefore, this paper investigates if user behavioral patterns improve understanding along with three-fold contributions:

- We are among the first to model personalized SLU combining with contextual app behaviors.
- We propose a novel matrix factorization (MF) approach to model the implicit semantics based on users' lexical and behavioral patterns.
- Combining lexical and behavior features helps disambiguate users' intended apps for intent prediction.

2. DATA COLLECTION

To captures how users converse in the course of multi-app tasks, we conducted a longitudinal study with 14 participants to investigate how people structure and perform such tasks via speech. This user study investigated users' behavior across multiple domains/apps. Users were provided with an Android app that logs all their app invocation, as well as the time and the location. Logs were uploaded by participants on a daily basis with privacy control. Participants were invited to lab regularly to perform the following annotations as to the nature of their activities.

1. **Task Structure** — link applications that served a common goal.
2. **Task Description** — type in a brief description of the goal or intention of the task.

ICMI 2015, November 9–13, 2015, Seattle, WA, USA.
 ISBN 978-1-4503-3912-4/15/11 ...$15.00.
DOI: http://dx.doi.org/10.1145/2818346.2820781.

Meta TASK59; 20150203; 1; Tuesday; 10:48

Desc play music via bluetooth speaker

App com.android.settings → com.lge.music

Dialogue

$\mathbf{W}_1$: Ready.

$\mathbf{U}_1$: Connect my phone to bluetooth speaker. SETTINGS

$\mathbf{W}_2$: Connected to bluetooth speaker.

$\mathbf{U}_2$: And play music. MUSIC

$\mathbf{W}_3$: What music would you like to play?

$\mathbf{U}_3$: Shuffle playlist. MUSIC

$\mathbf{W}_4$: I will play the music for you.

Figure 1: Multi-app task dialogue example

For example, in the upper part of Figure 1, "Settings" and "Music" are linked together since they were used for the goal of "play music via bluetooth speaker".

Then users were shown tasks annotated by themselves earlier along with the meta-data (date, location, and time), the task description they furnished earlier, and the apps that had been grouped (Meta, Desc, App lines in Figure 1). Subsequently they were asked to use a wizard system to perform the annotated task by speech in an office environment. The wizard was instructed to respond directly to participant's goal-directed requests and to not accept out-of-domain inputs. The participants were informed that they do not need to follow the order of the applications used on their smartphones. Other than for being on-task, we did not constrain what users could say.

Conversations between users (U) and the wizard (W) were recorded, segmented into utterances and transcribed by human and a Cloud speech recognizer. One example dialogue is shown in Fig. 1. Each user utterance was further associated with the apps that are able to handle it. As in Fig. 1, "Settings" would deal with the utterance "*Connect my phone to bluetooth speakers*" (U_1), and "Music" would take care of music related utterances such as "*And play music*" (U_2) and "*Shuffle playlist*" (U_3).[1]

3. SPOKEN LANGUAGE UNDERSTANDING

The goal of our SLU model is to predict apps that are more likely to handle the user requests given input utterances and behavioral contexts. Considering that multi-app tasks are usually user-specific, for each user we build a personalized SLU component to model his/her intents by framing the task as a multi-class classification task, where we estimate the probability of each intent/app given the interaction at each turn t. The extracted features include word patterns in the utterance u_t along with its behavioral history $h_t = \{a_1, ..., a_{t-1}\}$, where the behavioral history is a set of apps previously launched in the ongoing dialogue. The following approaches focus on estimating $P(a_t \mid u_t, h_t)$ for intent prediction.

We perform 1) a standard multinomial logistic regression (MLR) to model explicit semantics, which uses a maximum likelihood estimation approach by the gradient ascent to estimate $P(a_t \mid u_t, h_t)$, and 2) a matrix factorization (MF) to additionally model implicit feedback described below.

[1]Dataset available at `http://AppDialogue.com`

3.1 Matrix Factorization (MF)

The matrix factorization (MF) technique has been explored in different domains, and is credited as the most useful technique for recommendation systems [8]. An MF model considers the unobserved patterns and estimates their probabilities instead of viewing them as negative, which is able to model the implicit information [4].

We use MF to build personalized SLU models considering the ability to model 1) noisy data, 2) latent information, and 3) long-range dependencies between observations. Fig. 2 illustrates the matrix, where an example testing utterance "*Send it to alice*" only contains the observed word "*send*", but the MF model is able to estimate higher probability for the intended app "IM (Instant Message)" than the one of "Email" by learning the latent semantics carried by behavior history ("Camera" in history infers semantics about "*tell*").

In our model, we use U to denote the set of user utterances, which contains word patterns W and observed behavior history $H = \{h_t\}$, and A as a set of intents for prediction (a predicted intent corresponds to an app). The pair of an utterance and a word/history/app pattern, $\langle x, y\rangle$, is a *fact*, where $x \in U$ and $y \in \{W \cup H \cup A\}$. The input to our model is a set of observed facts $\mathcal{O}$, and the observed facts for a given utterance is denoted by $\{\langle x, y\rangle \in \mathcal{O}\}$. The goal of our model is to estimate, for a given utterance x and a given lexical/behavioral/intent feature y, the probability, $p(M_{x,y} = 1)$, where $M_{x,y}$ is a binary random variable that is true if and only if y is the lexical/behavioral pattern or predicted intent for the utterance x. We introduce a series of exponential family models using a natural parameter $\theta_{x,y}$ and a logistic sigmoid function:

$$p(M_{x,y} = 1 \mid \theta_{x,y}) = \sigma(\theta_{x,y}) = \frac{1}{1 + \exp(-\theta_{x,y})}. \quad (1)$$

We construct a matrix $M_{|U|\times(|W|+|H|+|A|)}$ with observed facts to integrate lexical and behavioral information together.

3.1.1 Feature Matrix

To model the content of user utterances, we first build a word pattern matrix F_w with binary values based on observations, where each row represents an interaction and each column refers to an observed word occurring in the utterances. In other words, F_w carries the basic word vectors for all interactions. Similarly, we build a behavioral history matrix F_h for utterances, where each row represents an utterance and each column refers to a set of previously observed apps in the dialogue.

To link the feature patterns with the corresponding apps, an intended app matrix F_a is constructed, where each column is an intent for launching a specific app. Hence, the entry is 1 for the intended app, and 0 otherwise. The feature model M is built from these three matrices: $M = [\ F_w \quad F_h \quad F_a\ ]$, which is illustrated in Fig. 2.

3.1.2 Parameter Estimation

The proposed model is parametrized through weights and latent component vectors, where the parameters are estimated by maximizing the log likelihood on observed data [5].

$$\begin{aligned}\theta^* &= \arg\max_{\theta} \prod_{x\in U} p(\theta \mid M_x) = \arg\max_{\theta} \prod_{x\in U} p(M_x \mid \theta) p(\theta) \\ &= \arg\max_{\theta} \sum_{x\in U} \ln p(M_x \mid \theta) - \lambda_\theta, \quad (2)\end{aligned}$$

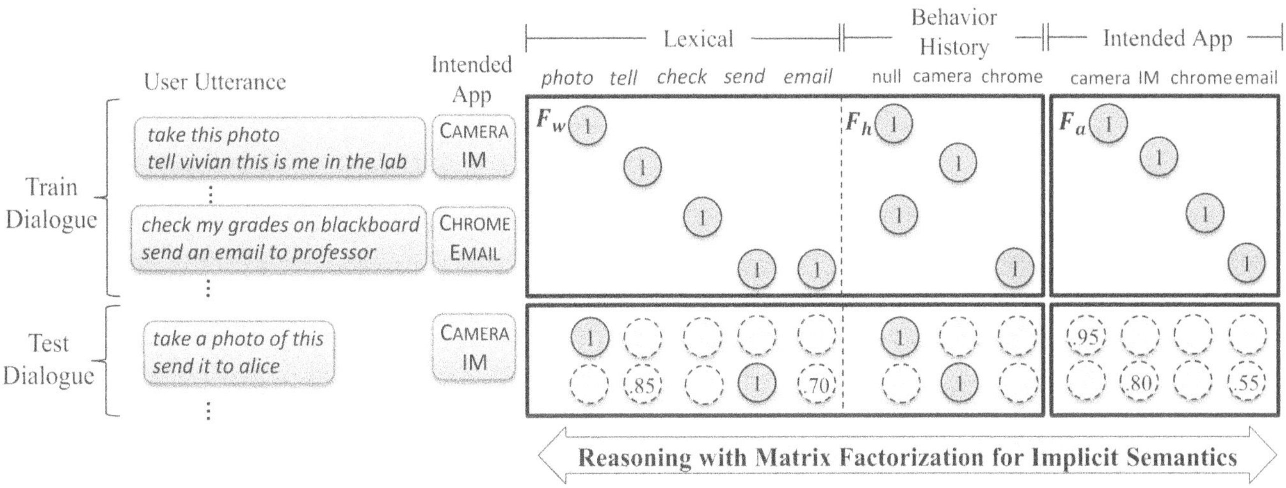

Figure 2: Our MF method completes a partially-missing matrix for implicit semantics modeling. Dark circles are observed facts, and shaded circles are latent and inferred facts. Reasoning with MF considers latent semantics to predict intents based on user utterance contents and app behavior history.

where M_x is the vector corresponding to the utterance x (a row in the matrix), because we assume that each utterance is independent of others.

To avoid treating unobserved facts as designed negative facts, we consider our positive-only data as *implicit feedback*. Bayesian Personalized Ranking (BPR) is a optimization criterion that learns from implicit feedback for MF, which uses a variant of the ranking: giving observed true facts higher scores than unobserved (true or false) facts [10].

To estimate the parameters in (2), we create a dataset of *ranked pairs* from M: for each utterance x (e.g. "*take this photo*" in Fig. 2), we create pairs of observed and unobserved facts: $f^+ = \langle x, y^+ \rangle$ and $f^- = \langle x, y^- \rangle$, where y^+ corresponds to an observed lexical/behavioral/app feature (e.g., "*photo*" for lexical, "*null*" for behavior, "*camera*" for intended app); y^- corresponds to an unobserved feature (e.g. "*tell*", "*camera*", "*email*"). Then for each pair $\langle f^+, f^- \rangle$, we want our model to maximize the margin between $p(f^+)$ and $p(f^-)$ i.e., the difference between θ_{f^+} and θ_{f^-} according to (1). BPR maximizes the summation of each ranked pair with the objective:

$$\sum_{x \in U} \ln p(M_x \mid \theta) = \sum_{f^+ \in O} \sum_{f^- \notin O} \ln \sigma(\theta_{f^+} - \theta_{f^-}), \qquad (3)$$

which is an approximation to the per interaction AUC (area under the ROC curve), which correlates to well-ranked intents per utterance.

To maximize the objective in (3), we employ a stochastic gradient descent (SGD) algorithm [10]. For each randomly sampled observed fact $\langle x, y^+ \rangle$, we sample an unobserved fact $\langle x, y^- \rangle$, which results in $|O|$ fact pairs $\langle f^+, f^- \rangle$. Then we perform an SGD update using the gradient of the corresponding objective function using sampled pairs for MF [6].

Finally we can obtain the estimated probabilities of all lexical, behavioral, and intent-related features given the current dialogue turn. In this paper, we are interested in probabilities of intended apps $P(a_t \mid u_t, h_t)$, but as shown in Fig. 2, hidden semantics (e.g. "*tell*", "*email*") can also be inferred from "*send it to alice*" in this model.

4. EXPERIMENTS

In our experiments, we collected smart-phone app usage data from 14 participants with Android OS version 4. The total number of multi-app spoken dialogues is 533 with 1,607 utterances (on average 3 user utterances per dialogue). Among these dialogues, we have 455 multi-turn dialogs (82.3%), presenting the richness of behavioral features. The word error rate from Google automatic speech recognition (ASR) is reported as 25% without further text normalization.

We group 70% of each user's multi-app dialogues into a training set, and use the rest 30% as a testing set. For each user, we build a personalized SLU model with his/her own training data to estimate the probability distribution of all intended apps for each dialogue turn. To evaluate the prediction performance, we compute turn accuracy (ACC) as the percentage that our top 1 predictions match the correct apps. For a soft prediction, we also evaluate the performance by mean average precision (MAP), which considers the whole ranking list of all apps corresponding to each utterance. Table 1 shows the experiments performed on both ASR and manual transcripts.

The baselines here apply maximum likelihood estimation (MLE) to predict intents according to the observed distribution in the training data, where the prediction accuracy is around 20%. The reasons of the poor performance includes: 1) This intent prediction task here is different from traditional one, because a correct prediction is a single app that the user plan to use; hence this task is more difficult. For example, in traditional intent prediction task, "Messager" and "Gmail" belong to the same intent "communication", so deciding a single intended app is more challenging than deciding an intent. 2) The total number of intents/apps in our dataset is relatively large, because we do not limit the apps that users can use, where the average number of apps per user is 15.8 and total number is 133.

To compare the performance between features, we show the results using lexical and behavioral features individually for intent prediction. We can see that lexical features achieve better performance than behavioral features alone, indicating that the majority of utterances contains explicit

Table 1: User intent prediction on turn accuracy (ACC) and mean average precision (MAP) (%). † means that all features perform significantly better than lexical/behavioral features alone; § means that integrating with MF significantly improves the MLR model (t-test with $p < 0.05$).

Approach			ACC					MAP				
			Lexical		Behavioral	All		Lexical		Behavioral	All	
			ASR	Trans		ASR	Trans	ASR	Trans		ASR	Trans
(a)	MLE	User-Indep			13.5					19.6		
(b)		User-Dep			20.2					27.9		
(c)	MLR	User-Indep	42.8	47.7	14.9	$46.2^{\dagger}$	48.8	46.4	51.3	18.7	$50.1^{\dagger}$	53.1
(d)		User-Dep	48.2	51.6	19.3	$50.1^{\dagger}$	52.8	52.1	55.5	25.2	$53.9^{\dagger}$	56.6
(e)	(c) + Personalized MF		47.6	49.1	16.4	$50.3^{\dagger\S}$	$53.5^{\dagger\S}$	51.1	53.3	20.3	$54.2^{\dagger\S}$	$57.6^{\dagger\S}$
(f)	(d) + Personalized MF		48.3	51.3	20.6	$\mathbf{51.9}^{\dagger\S}$	$\mathbf{54.0}^{\dagger}$	52.7	55.4	26.7	$\mathbf{55.7}^{\dagger\S}$	$\mathbf{57.7}^{\dagger\S}$

expressions that are predictable. In addition, combining behavior history and lexical features performs best in terms of two measures. For ASR results, adding behavioral features significantly improves ACC from 48% to 50% and MAP from 52% to 54% (row (d)).

To evaluate the effectiveness of modeling latent semantics through MF, Table 1 also shows the performance of the MLR model integrated with personalized MF estimation in the rows (e)-(f)[2]. For both user-independent and user-dependent MLR results, additional integrating an MF model outperforms almost all MLR models, especially for all features (significant improvement with $p < 0.05$ in t-test), because MF is able to model the latent semantics under lexical and behavioral patterns. However, for manual results, integrating with the MF model does not perform better when using only lexical features (from 51.6% to 51.3% on ACC and from 55.5% to 55.4% on MAP), probably because manually transcribed utterances contain more clear and explicit semantics, and learning latent semantics does not improve the performance.

Comparing the results for ASR and manual transcripts, we observe that the performance is worse when the user utterances contain recognition errors, because the explicit expression contains more noises and they may result in worse prediction. The benefit of MF techniques on ASR results is more significant (3.6% and 3.3% relative improvement of ACC and MAP respectively) than under manual transcripts, showing the effective capability of MF about modeling latent semantics in noisy data. Additionally, user-dependent results are better than user-independent results, showing that different users use mobile phones in different ways, so modeling personalized SLU is able to effectively improve intent prediction. Finally, our experiments show the feasibility of disambiguating spoken language inputs for better intent prediction using behavioral patterns. The best prediction on ASR achieves 51.9% of ACC and 55.7% of MAP.

5. CONCLUSION

This paper presents an MF model that exploits both lexical and behavioral features for SLU in dialogue systems. The proposed model considers implicit semantics to enhance intent inference given the noisy ASR inputs. Also we are able to model users' behavioral patterns and their app preference, and further to better predict user intents in a smart-phone intelligent assistant setting (e.g. requesting an app). The resulting multi-model personalized system effectively improves intent prediction performance, achieving about 52% on turn accuracy and 56% on mean average precision for ASR transcripts with 25% word error rate.

[2] Using an MF model alone does not perform better compared to MLR (performing around 20-30% on ACC and MAP), because MF takes latent information into account and has weaker capability of modeling explicit observations.

6. REFERENCES

[1] A. Bhargava, A. Celikyilmaz, D. Hakkani-Tur, and R. Sarikaya. Easy contextual intent prediction and slot detection. In *ICASSP*, 2013.

[2] A. Celikyilmaz, Z. Feizollahi, D. Hakkani-Tür, and R. Sarikaya. Resolving referring expressions in conversational dialogs for natural user interfaces. In *EMNLP*, 2014.

[3] Y.-N. Chen and A. I. Rudnicky. Dynamically supporting unexplored domains in conversational interactions by enriching semantics with neural word embeddings. In *SLT*, 2014.

[4] Y.-N. Chen, W. Y. Wang, A. Gershman, and A. I. Rudnicky. Matrix factorization with knowledge graph propagation for unsupervised spoken language understanding. In *ACL-IJCNLP*, 2015.

[5] M. Collins, S. Dasgupta, and R. E. Schapire. A generalization of principal components analysis to the exponential family. In *NIPS*, 2001.

[6] Z. Gantner, S. Rendle, C. Freudenthaler, and L. Schmidt-Thieme. MyMedialite: A free recommender system library. In *RecSys*, 2011.

[7] D. Hakkani-Tür, M. Slaney, A. Celikyilmaz, and L. Heck. Eye gaze for spoken language understanding in multi-modal conversational interactions. In *ICMI*, 2014.

[8] Y. Koren, R. Bell, and C. Volinsky. Matrix factorization techniques for recommender systems. *Computer*, (8):30–37, 2009.

[9] S. Kousidis, C. Kennington, T. Baumann, H. Buschmeier, S. Kopp, and D. Schlangen. A multimodal in-car dialogue system that tracks the driver's attention. In *ICMI*, 2014.

[10] S. Rendle, C. Freudenthaler, Z. Gantner, and L. Schmidt-Thieme. BPR: Bayesian personalized ranking from implicit feedback. In *UAI*, 2009.

[11] C. Shin, J.-H. Hong, and A. K. Dey. Understanding and prediction of mobile application usage for smart phones. In *UbiComp*, 2012.

Who's Speaking? Audio-Supervised Classification of Active Speakers in Video

Punarjay Chakravarty
ESAT-PSI
KU Leuven
iMinds MMT
pchakrav@esat.kuleuven.be

Sayeh Mirzaei
Department of Electrical Engineering
Amirkabir University of Technology
sayeh.mirzaei@esat.kuleuven.be

Tinne Tuytelaars
ESAT-PSI
KU Leuven
iMinds MMT
tinne.tuytelaars@esat.kuleuven.be

Hugo Van hamme
ESAT-PSI
KU Leuven
hugo.vanhamme@esat.kuleuven.be

ABSTRACT

Active speakers have traditionally been identified in video by detecting their moving lips. This paper demonstrates the same using spatio-temporal features that aim to capture other cues: movement of the head, upper body and hands of active speakers. Speaker directional information, obtained using sound source localization from a microphone array is used to supervise the training of these video features.

Categories and Subject Descriptors

H.5.1 [**Multimedia Information Systems**]: Audio input/output; I.2.10 [**Vision and Scene Understanding**]: Video analysis; I.4.8 [**Scene Analysis**]: Sensor fusion

General Terms

Algorithms, Human Factors

Keywords

Ambient Intelligence & Smart Environments; Human-Robot Interaction; Multimodal Fusion and Integration

1. INTRODUCTION

Existing research for active speaker detection [2, 3, 6] has focussed on tracking the face and correlating lip movement with speech. While this method will work for high quality, high resolution frontal shots of people, it will not always be ideal when the speaker presents a profile view to the camera or her hands occlude her lips while speaking or when she is too far from the camera for her lips to be detected by facial feature detectors.

ICMI '15, November 09-13, 2015, Seattle, WA, USA
Copyright 2015 ACM ISBN 978-1-4503-3912-4/15/11
DOI: http://dx.doi.org/10.1145/2818346.2820780 ...$15.00.

This research tries to use spatio-temporal action recognition features, also called dense trajectory features [10] to pick up subtle clues accompanying a person's speech, like the movement of the head and hands. We use audio to supervise the training of the video features. Microphone pairs are standard on a lot of modern laptops, and we use a pair of laptop-embedded microphones for localizing the bearing direction of the active speaker, which is associated with an upper body detection in video. Audio is used to label dense trajectory features extracted from within upper body tracks of people as speaking vs non-speaking, and these labelled examples are used to train an active speaker classifier using video alone.

The problem of determining who is speaking in video is useful for a number of applications. It could be a starting point for video diarization, the process of annotating speakers in video. Human-Computer Interaction (HCI) systems would benefit from determining who is speaking, so that the robot or computer can respond to the specific interlocuter when more than one person is present in the system's interaction environment. Video conferencing systems could use active speaker detection to highlight one amongst a group of meeting attendees at a table and only transmit the video of the person who is doing the talking.

There has been some research on combining features detected from audio with features detected from video to both identify a specific speaker, and for speech recognition. An early example of this is by Cutler et al. [2], who use a single microphone and camera system to detect the correlation between audio and video data corresponding to speech. Correlation between Mel-cepstrum coefficients in the audio signal and frame differencing around the lips on successive frames are used to identify specific utterances in the speech.

Audio and video features have also been fused to distinguish between speakers. Li et al. [6] used Canonical Correlation Analysis (CCA) to find the commonality between synced audio and visual features. CCA calculates basis vectors that are used to project audio and video feature vectors onto a common subspace, following which the concatenated feature vector is used to train a classifier to distinguish between speakers.

Video annotation using speaker detection was demonstrated by Everingham et al. [3]. They annotate a TV series, Buffy the Vampire Slayer, by matching the script to the subtitles. Characters are tracked using similarities in face and clothing and the detection of active speakers is used as an additional cue to link speakers in the script to faces in the video. Frame-differencing in a rectangular window around the lip features in a tracked face is used to determine movement of the lips, and faces with lips that move above a threshold value are determined to be speaking.

The detection of active speakers has been used for automatic editing of classroom video. Hariharan et al. [5] use a microphone array to localize a questioner with a Time Difference of Arrival (TDOA) algorithm, and combine this with video detection of the raised hand of the questioner.

Zhang et al. [11] describe a meeting room video conferencing system that automatically detects the speaker and concentrates the transmitted video on the speaker. A circular mic array and a panoramic camera system are used to localize active speakers around a table. Instead of having separate audio and video classifiers, they feed information from both sources into an Adaboost classifier. Weak classifiers - functions of the audio sound source localization and image-based frame differencing are used in a boosting framework to determine the region of interest of an active speaker in panoramic video.

More recently, Cech et al. [1] have used audio-visual cues to focus the attention of Nao, a child-sized humanoid robot equipped with a microphone array and a stereo camera pair, on specific speakers in its environment. They also use TDOA to get the azimuth and elevation of the active speaker, which is then coupled with face detections in the stereo camera pair.

In contrast, our work uses audio to supervise the training of spatio-temporal features from the face and upper body that accompany a person's speech. Section 2 describes the setup of the system used for capturing the audio-visual data, the audio sound source localization and the video feature training, followed by experimental results and analysis.

2. SYSTEM DESCRIPTION

Experimental Setup.

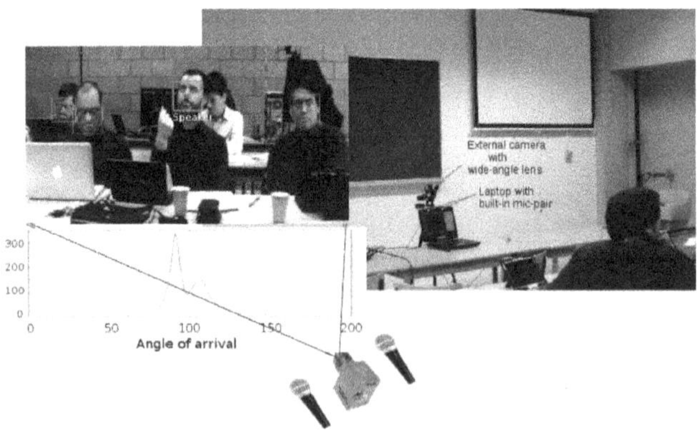

Figure 1: Hardware: wide angle camera & microphone pair in laptop. GCC-PHAT metric plotted against bearing of targets. Largest peak above a threshold is associated with face/upper body detections, and this face/upper body is identified as speaking.

The audio-visual (one camera, one microphone pair) recordings were conducted in a natural setting - a student presentation session at university. 7 recordings were made, for 7 different presentations, to a jury of examiners. Each recording comprised of roughly 25 minutes of presentation, followed by 5 minutes of questions. A laptop with its in-built microphone pair was used for recording the audio, along with an external camera with a wide-angle lens, to capture the video. The setup was pointed towards the jury, with the 3 members in the first row dominating the view. The audio-based speaker bearing estimation software was run in real-time and the video was stored frame-by-frame, along with a bearing angle of the speaker for each frame. The detection and tracking of the upper bodies, the extraction of the dense trajectory features from within the upper body bounding boxes for each track, and the training of the classifier was done off-line. The following paragraphs explain these algorithms in more detail.

Audio Sound Source Localization.

The audio signal at the microphones is a mixture of several different sound sources, due to speakers speaking at the same time, background noise or reverberation effects. The separation of these sound sources is called Blind Source Separation (BSS), which is traditionally done by clustering of the Fourier Transform coefficients in each Time Frequency (TF) cell of the Short Term Fourier Transform (STFT) of the signals. However, this requires two assumptions - the number of sources be known in advance, and signal sparsity, i.e., the source represenations do not overlap in the TF domain. The number of sources is not always known, and the sparsity assumption is violated in the presence of noise or when sources overlap. We use the approach proposed by Mirzaei et al. [7], where an angular spectrum is derived for estimating the number of sources as well as the direction of arrival of the sources. A non-linear function of the Generalized Cross Correlation - Phase transform (GCC-PHAT) between the two signals is calculated in each TF bin, against all angles of arrival of the source signal with respect to the microphone baseline direction. The dominant peak in this function above a threshold gives the direction of the sound source (Figure 1). This method is particularly useful when the microphone baseline is small compared to the distance to the sound sources, as is the case in our setup.

Video Person Tracking.

An upper body detector from Ferrari et al. [4] is run on each frame of the video and a multi-target tracker is used to cluster these detections in space and time. A track is initialized at persistent detections, and is updated with a new detection at each frame. Detections are associated with tracks based on proximity and bounding box size. A simple alpha filter update rule suffices in this case - the track's updated position is based on a weighted linear combination of the previous state and the new observation (detection) associated with it. A track not associated with any detections for a pre-defined number of frames is deleted.

Dense Trajectories for Active Speaker Classification.

Dense Trajectories pooled by a Fisher vector (FV) [9] representation, and subsequently trained with Support Vector Machine (SVM) classifiers, is a standard, state-of-the-art pipeline used for action recognition [10], and we use the same for active speaker detection. Dense trajectory features inside the upper body bounding boxes of each person track are categorized as speak and non-speak trajectories, as classified by audio sound source separation. To this end, the sound source separation gives, for each frame, the bearing value of the highest intensity sound at that frame. These bearing values are associated with the upper body detections, and a detection is marked as speaking/non-speaking depending on this association. A simple linear transformation (requiring no special calibration) is used between the bearing range of the audio and the image width - this transforms a bearing value to a column index.

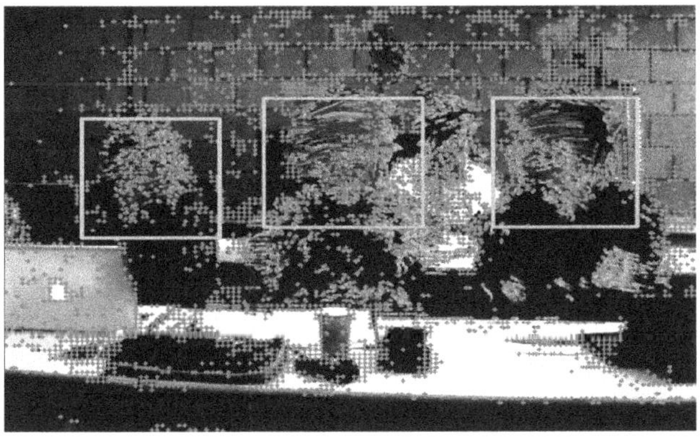

Figure 2: Dense Trajectories within upper bodies

Each dense trajectory track is calculated from 15 successive frames and has associated with it the mean pixel location of the trajectory, and Histogram of Gradients (HoG), Histogram of Flow (HoF) and Motion Boundary Histogram (MBH) features [10]. The feature vectors are each reduced to half their original dimensionality using Principal Components Analysis (PCA). For the FV encoding, we use a Gaussian Mixture Model (GMM) with 256 components. Trajectories that start at the same frame and are inside the bounding box of the upper body of a track are pooled using the FV representation. FVs for the HoG, HoF and MBH features are separately calculated and concatenated to give a 101,376 dimensional FV representing all the features along all trajectories within a sequence of 15 contiguous upper body detections, and the label of the starting frame of these trajectories - speaking/non-speaking is used as the label for the FV. FVs from speaking frames are used as positive training samples and those from non-speaking frames are used as negative training samples, and a linear SVM classifier is trained using these samples. Intra-class L2-normalization of the FV and a final power and L2 normalization of the whole vector are performed before the classification step. These are techniques that have been shown to significantly boost the performance of action recognition classifiers and are considered best practice [8]. Figure 3 illustrates the steps in the training pipeline.

Results.

7 audio-visual recordings are used: each recording has roughly 25 minutes of presentation by the student (during which the jury mostly remains silent, but occasionally whispers amongst themselves), and 5 minutes of questioning by the jury. The active speaker classifier is trained using Leave-One-Out-Cross-Validation (LOOCV) - trained on 6 presentations and tested on the 7th, and this is repeated 7 times,

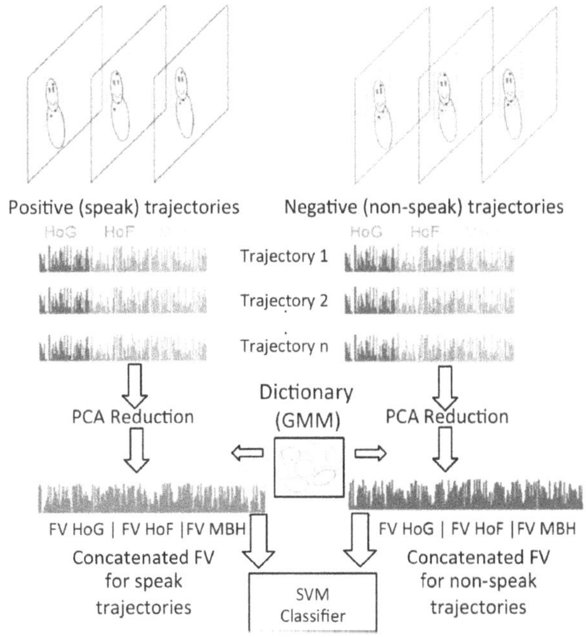

Figure 3: Active speaker classifier training pipeline

based on the recording that is used for testing.

The speaking/non-speaking labelling generated by the audio sound source localization is noisy - see column 1 in the table in Figure 4. This is corrected manually to obtain ground truth labels for speak/non-speak frames in all the videos. Only the 3 speakers sitting in the first row are considered in the experiments, as speakers behind them are partly or fully occluded. The video-based spatio-temporal dense trajectories classifier is trained using both the cleaned up (ground truth) and noisy frame labels from audio - let's call these results video-clean, and video-noisy respectively. Finally, a baseline method, based on lip movement detection (video-lips) within tracked faces [3] is used for comparison. The Receiver Operating Characteristic (ROC) curves (Figure 4), plots of the true positive rate (TPR) vs the false positive rate (FPR), show the results of the video-clean and video-noisy classifiers. It can be seen that even using the noisy training data, the video-based classifier can distinguish speaking vs non-speaking better than the baseline lip-movement based method. Furthermore, the mean Equal Error Rate (EER) for video-noisy is 0.66 and for video-clean is 0.69 - this shows that the supervision from audio is sufficient to train the video classifier, with slight improvement using training with ground truth. Both the audio and lip-movement based active speaker classifiers present a binary classification result, as opposed to a real-valued score for the video-based classifiers video-clean and video-noisy. Consequently, only a single (TPR, FPR) pair is available for audio and video-lips, shown as dots and stars respectively in the ROC curves of Figure 4. One anomalous result is the low EER value for video-clean, fold 5, and at the time of writing, it is not clear why this is so. When a speaker is silent he often sits with his fingers obscuring his lips, resulting in false-positives and poor performance for the video-lips baseline method.

fold	audio	video-clean	video-noisy	video-lips
1	(64,7)	(75,24)	(72,28)	(27,21)
2	(77,2)	(75,24)	(72,28)	(30,19)
3	(50,3)	(72,27)	(65,35)	(40,25)
4	(39,4)	(71,29)	(64,36)	(37,24)
5	(60,2)	(54,46)	(70,29)	(19,25)
6	(17,3)	(67,32)	(61,39)	(34,21)
7	(26,2)	(71,29)	(61,39)	(30,19)

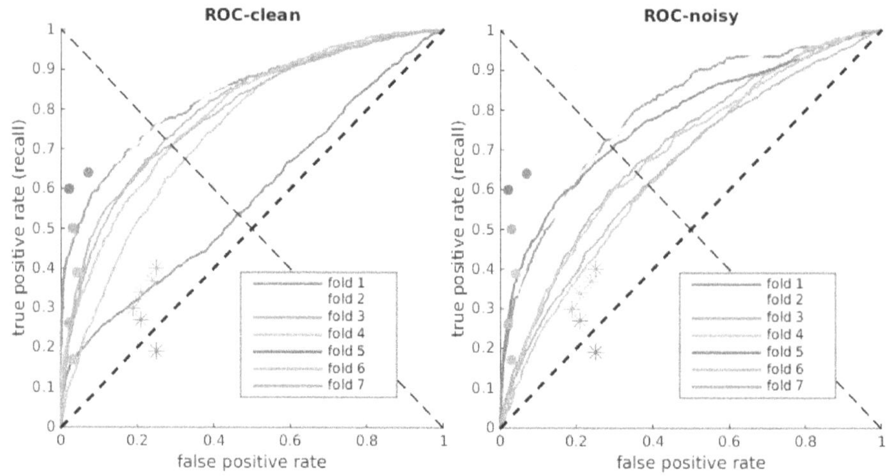

Figure 4: Left: True and False Positive rates (TPR, FPR) in % for audio, spatio-temporal video classifiers (video-clean and video-noisy) and lip-movement based methods (video-lips) across the 7 cross-validation folds. Middle: ROC curves for video-clean. Right: ROC curves for video-noisy. Circles and stars show (TPR, FPR) pairs for audio and video-lips.

3. CONCLUSIONS

This work presents to our knowledge, the first attempt at detecting active speakers in video using action recognition features. Whereas earlier work has used the movement of the lips for detecting speakers in video, our work trains a classifier on spatio-temporal action recognition features to pick up face and upper body movements and gesticulations accompanying a person's speech.

Our other contribution is the use of audio sound source localization (from a microphone array) to supervise the labelling of speaking vs non-speaking parts of the video. We use a microphone pair in a laptop to capture the sound data, and the bearing of the speaker calculated from the time difference of arrival of the sound is associated with upper bodies detected and tracked in video. Upper body tracks and dense trajectory features within them are labelled as speaking and non-speaking and the samples, quantized and pooled with a Fisher vector representation are fed into a SVM classifier. We obtain a mean Equal Error Rate (EER) of 0.66 with supervision from audio over 7 experiments (3.5 hours of audio-visual data), tested using Leave One Out Cross Validation (LOOCV). Training on ground truth labels give a slight improvement - an EER of 0.69.

Future work will focus on training the classifier in a single audio channel setting, which is the case for the vast majority of videos available. Voice Activity Detection will tell us whether or not there is speech in a frame, and the particular person that is speaking will be learnt as a latent variable in a Latent SVM framework. Methods for fusing audio and video for more reliable detection will also be investigated.

4. ACKNOWLEDGMENTS

This work has been supported by the KU Leuven GOA project CAMETRON.

5. REFERENCES

[1] J. Cech, R. Mittal, A. Deleforge, J. Sanchez-Riera, X. Alameda-Pineda, and R. Horaud. Active-speaker detection and localization with microphones and cameras embedded into a robotic head. In *IEEE-RAS International Conference on Humanoid Robots*, 2013.

[2] R. Cutler and L. Davis. Look who's talking: Speaker detection using video and audio correlation. In *IEEE International Conference on Multimedia and Expo (ICME)*, volume 3, pages 1589–1592, 2000.

[3] M. Everingham, J. Sivic, and A. Zisserman. Taking the bite out of automatic naming of characters in TV video. *Image and Vision Computing*, 27(5), 2009.

[4] V. Ferrari, M. Marin-Jimenez, and A. Zisserman. Progressive search space reduction for human pose estimation. In *CVPR*, June 2008.

[5] B. Hariharan, H. S, and U. Gopalakrishnan. Multi speaker detection and tracking using audio and video sensors with gesture analysis. In *Tenth International Conference on Wireless and Optical Networks (WOCN)*, pages 1–5, 2013.

[6] D. Li, C. M. Taskiran, N. Dimitrova, W. Wang, M. Li, and I. K. Sethi. Cross-modal analysis of audio-visual programs for speaker detection. In *IEEE 7th Workshop on Multimedia Signal Processing, MMSP*, pages 1–4, 2005.

[7] S. Mirzaei, H. Van hamme, and Y. Norouzi. Blind audio source separation of stereo mixtures using bayesian non-negative matrix factorization. In *Signal Processing Conference (EUSIPCO)*, pages 621–625, Sept 2014.

[8] X. Peng, L. Wang, X. Wang, and Y. Qiao. Bag of visual words and fusion methods for action recognition: Comprehensive study and good practice. *CoRR*, abs/1405.4506, 2014.

[9] F. Perronnin, J. Sánchez, and T. Mensink. Improving the fisher kernel for large-scale image classification. In *ECCV*, pages 143–156, Berlin, Heidelberg, 2010.

[10] H. Wang and C. Schmid. Action Recognition with Improved Trajectories. In *ICCV*, pages 3551–3558, Sydney, Australia, Dec. 2013.

[11] C. Zhang, P. Yin, Y. Rui, R. Cutler, P. A. Viola, X. Sun, N. Pinto, and Z. Zhang. Boosting-based multimodal speaker detection for distributed meeting videos. *IEEE Transactions on Multimedia*, 10(8):1541–1552, 2008.

Predicting Participation Styles using Co-occurrence Patterns of Nonverbal Behaviors in Collaborative Learning

Yukiko I. Nakano
Seikei University
Musashino, Tokyo 180-8633 Japan
y.nakano@st.seikei.ac.jp

Sakiko Nihonyanagi
Seikei University
Musashino, Tokyo 180-8633 Japan
nihonyanagi.s@gmail.com

Yutaka Takase
Seikei University
Musashino, Tokyo 180-8633 Japan
yutaka-takase@st.seikei.ac.jp

Yuki Hayashi
Osaka Prefecture University
Sakai, Osaka 599-8531 Japan
hayashi@kis.osakafu-u.ac.jp

Shogo Okada
Tokyo Institute of Technology
Yokohama, Kanagawa 226-8502 Japan
okada@dis.titech.ac.jp

ABSTRACT
With the goal of assessing participant attitudes and group activities in collaborative learning, this study presents models of participation styles based on co-occurrence patterns of nonverbal behaviors between conversational participants. First, we collected conversations among groups of three people in a collaborative learning situation, wherein each participant had a digital pen and wore a glasses-type eye tracker. We then divided the collected multimodal data into 0.1-second intervals. The discretized data were applied to an unsupervised method to find co-occurrence behavioral patterns. As a result, we discovered 122 multimodal behavioral motifs from more than 3,000 possible combinations of behaviors by three participants. Using the multimodal behavioral motifs as predictor variables, we created regression models for assessing participation styles. The multiple correlation coefficients ranged from 0.74 to 0.84, indicating a good fit between the models and the data. A correlation analysis also enabled us to identify a smaller set of behavioral motifs (fewer than 30) that are statistically significant as predictors of participation styles. These results show that automatically discovered combinations of multiple kinds of nonverbal information with high co-occurrence frequencies observed between multiple participants as well as for a single participant are useful in characterizing the participant's attitudes towards the conversation.

Categories and Subject Descriptors
H5.3 [Information Interfaces and Presentation]: Group and Organization Interfaces - Synchronous interaction

General Terms
Human Factors; Design; Measurement

ICMI '15, November 09-13, 2015, Seattle, WA, USA.
Copyright 2015 ACM. ISBN 978-1-4503-3912-4/15/11 ...$15.00.
DOI: http://dx.doi.org/10.1145/2818346.2820764

Keywords
Co-occurrence behavior patterns; participation styles; nonverbal behaviors; collaborative learning

1. INTRODUCTION
The observation of group communications has shown that some individuals proactively participate in a conversation, whereas others seem to have a passive attitude about engaging in the conversation. Assessing such group communication participation styles is useful for predicting the performance of individual participants in a group. However, participation styles may not only be determined by the behaviors of the respective participant, they may also be affected by the behaviors of other participants because conversation is a co-constructive activity between multiple participants. Suppose an evaluator observes a target participant as a speaker and other participants in the group do not listen to the speaker or ignore his/her speech. In such a case, the speaker is perceived as not being positively engaged in the conversation. On the other hand, if the other participants pay full attention to the speaker while listening, observers may have the impression that the speaker is proactively contributing to the communication and to managing the conversation.

Therefore, one of the key issues for assessing participation style is to identify predictors by determining the set of behavioral traits which simultaneously occur when the group is communicating. In studies on multimodal communication, it has been shown that multimodal features, such as gazing at a person while speaking or listening, are useful in modeling and estimating a participant's characteristics. However, the combinations of modalities for constructing multimodal features have typically been determined manually. If the number of modalities is large and the variation in the behavior significant, it is not realistic to find useful multimodal features from all the possible combinations of behavioral patterns. To find useful multimodal features in a systematic and efficient way, we exploit the multidimensional motif discovery algorithm proposed by Vahdatpour et al. [21]. This algorithm enables the discovery of meaningful co-occurrence behavioral patterns while limiting the number of patterns to be found. Thus, it is expected that by applying this algorithm to a multimodal corpus, a limited number of meaningful behavioral co-occurrence patterns can be automatically extracted, even though the corpus contains various pieces of information from several modalities.

Thus, in this study, we considered conversations in a collaborative learning situation in which glasses-type eye-trackers and digital pens were used to measure the gaze and writing behaviors of three participants. The possible combinations of the behavior associated with these two modalities were used to extract the high co-occurrence combinations, which we refer to as multimodal motifs, using an unsupervised method. Then, we examined whether these patterns were useful in predicting the participation styles. We focused on collaborative learning because this participation style is an important factor in assessing attitudes toward learning.

To accomplish our research goal, this study addressed the following issues:

- Collecting of a multimodal corpus that includes precise eye gaze data using head-mounted eye-trackers and writing action detected by a digital pen.
- Extraction of behavioral co-occurrence patterns of the gaze and writing actions by three participants.
- Proposing of prediction models for participation styles, such as passive and proactive, using extracted nonverbal behavioral patterns and then evaluating the prediction models.

The remainder of this paper is organized as follows. Previous work on multimodal corpus analysis and group conversations is reviewed in Section 2. In Section 3, we describe our collection of the corpus of collaborative learning situations. The extraction of behavioral co-occurrence patterns is discussed in Section 4. In Section 5, we describe how we conducted the assessment of the participation style using video observation. In Section 6, we present regression models which can be used to predict the participation styles.

2. RELATED WORK

In recent years, the data mining approach, in which behaviors are measured by using equipment and applying statistical methods to analyze the data, has drawn attention in learning settings, such as educational software and computer supported collaborative learning (CSCL) [3]. They measured the leaners' activities, such as speech, writing, and logs of student-computer interactions. The goal of these studies was to obtain a better understanding of students' characteristics or states, such as their current knowledge, motivations, meta-cognitions, and attitudes. For example, in a "grand-challenge" for multimodal learning analytics [16], Oviatt et al. [17] investigated students' speech and digital pen input while small groups collaborated on solving math problems to identify domain experts. Enhanced student models were expected to improve the ability of the systems to support learning.

Some of the studies emphasized the analysis of human interaction and communicative behaviors in CSCL environments [4]. Dillenbourg et al. [6] analyzed interaction in online educational environments based on the theory of grounding [5]. Soller [19] proposed Collaborative Learning Conversation Skills, including the support of group cohesion and the ability to appreciate other members' comments. It also reported that learners' active learning skills were roughly proportional to their degree of participation in the group conversation. These studies suggest that in order to support social interaction by intelligent collaborative learning systems, sensing communication signals and predicting the participation attitudes of the leaners are indispensable. However, they did not employ a data mining approach to investigate and model the interaction in collaborative learning.

In contrast, there are many studies on multimodal interaction which analyzed a number of nonverbal behaviors (e.g., prosody, gestures, gaze, and facial expressions) and employed machine learning techniques to predict the characteristics of the participants, such as dominance, personality, and roles in the communication process [1, 7, 9, 18]. Although these previous studies analyzed group discussions, the participants' characteristics on which these studies focused are closely related to the conversation skills required during collaborative learning. However, in addition to analyzing behavioral patterns in group discussions, such as speaking turns, speech length, and pitch as audio features, and attention given/received, and head/body activities as visual features, in collaborative learning situations, writing behavior is frequently observed and looking at the notes is a popular gaze behavior. More importantly, in collaborative learning, the difference in participants' knowledge level may affect their interaction.

Thus, this study shares with previous studies the same research goal of analyzing multimodal data, but we are more interested in investigating interactions among participants in learning groups in which knowledgeable and novice learners studied together, and in characterizing the learners with respect to their contributions, roles, and attitudes during the interaction. In addition, we employ a data mining approach, wherein we collected a large amount of human behavior sensing data and investigate the multimodal corpus using data mining techniques.

In the analysis of multimodal face-to-face interaction [1, 2, 7, 9, 18], it was noted that both single modal features for audio and visual information and multimodal features, which used combinations of features from different modalities, contributed to improving the performance of the prediction models. Thus, identifying useful behavioral patterns is an important issue that contributes to improving prediction performance. Studies by Jayagopi et al. [10, 11] used LDA to find a set of nonverbal behaviors that characterized the discussion group, such as extraverted and hierarchical. Song et al. [20] also used latent variables to find highly correlated behaviors. One study strived to discover and research behavioral patterns human observers intuitively recognize [15]. In their study, a human expert provided a seed pattern and their mechanism detected similar patterns based on temporal inference on multiple sequences of behaviors. As another direction, Martinez and Yannakakis [14] attempted to automatically generate a set of multimodal features by applying deep learning as a method for training multimodal fusion. However, their goal was to predict the preference of game players, rather than modeling multimodal-multiparty interaction.

Based on the discussion above, this study aims to predict an individual learner's characteristics in terms of participation style in collaborative learning. To this end, we focus on the co-occurrence of multiple behaviors by multiple participants, and automatically identify simultaneous behaviors as the co-occurrence behavioral patterns or multimodal motifs which contribute to prediction of the learner's participation attitude toward collaborative learning.

3. DATA COLLECTION

3.1 Collaborative Learning Situation

We conducted an experiment to collect multimodal behavior data during collaborative learning. Thirty university students (20 males and 10 females) participated in the experiment. Out of the 30 subjects, 20 of them were students from a computer and information science department, and 10 were from other departments, such as literature or economics. Each learning group comprised two participants from the computer science department and one from another department. Therefore, each learning group consisted of three participants, and ten groups were created for the experiments.

Each group was instructed to complete exercises in the field of computer and information science in two sessions. A snapshot of the experiment is shown in Figure 1. In the first session (Exercise 1), the subjects were instructed to solve a radix conversion problem. In the second session (Exercise 2), they were engaged in a discussion on cloud computing by exchanging opinions for knowledge sharing. In such a situation, the two participants from the computer and information science department knew more about the task than the participant from another department. Thus, we referred to participants who majored in computer and information science as "knowledgeable participants," whereas participants whose major was in another field were deemed "novice participants." To avoid a situation in which none of the participants progressed in their learning, we informed the knowledgeable learners of the type of exercises to be assigned. We instructed them to review the exercise domain in advance. The participants were instructed to write on paper the calculation process and answers for Exercise 1 and to write useful comments for Exercise 2.

3.2 Data

The purpose of this study was to analyze communication between the participants; therefore, we used only data from Exercise 2, in which the subjects were instructed to discuss with each other. We collected the gaze, speech, and writing-action data of the participants during their collaborative learning communications. The average duration of a conversation for Exercise 2 was 817 seconds.

(i) Eye tracking data: Each participant wore a Tobii Glasses eye tracker[1] to measure their gaze. The tracking frame rate was 30 fps. These wearable glasses are equipped with a camera capable of capturing the scene (640 × 480 pixels at 30 Hz). The gaze point in a given scene was measured as x-y coordinates. Then, user perspective videos, in which the gaze targets were overlaid on a picture of the scene, were created using Tobii Studio, the analysis software for Tobii eye trackers. By reviewing the gaze-overlaid videos, we manually annotated the gaze targets as either gazing at another participant or at their notes. The eye-tracking data for the three participants were synchronized by specifying an offset at the beginning of the conversation. Figure 2 shows how synchronized multi-user eye-tracking works.

(ii) Speech data: Each participant's voice was recorded using a microphone. The audio data stream was transmitted via an audio interface device and independently recorded as audio data (file format: wav; channel(s): 1; sampling rate: 16,000 Hz). For detecting speech intervals, we used the Julius speech recognition adintool software[2], which segments the audio data based on the amplitude level. If the pause between two speech intervals by the same speaker was shorter than 0.1 seconds, these two intervals were combined as one speech interval. Speech timestamps were

Figure 1. Snapshot of interaction in a collaborative learning situation. The learner in the center is the novice and the other two are knowledgeable learners.

Figure 2. Multi-user eye tracking. Gaze-overlaid (red dots indicate the gaze points) videos from three participants (knowledgeable learner: A, C, novice learner: B) and an overview video are shown synchronously.

also synchronized with the gaze data using the beep-sound recorded in both audio and gaze-overlaid video.

In addition, we defined 23 speech-act types based on the SWBD-DAMSL coding scheme [12]. These included statement, question, and acknowledgement. We annotated one of these speech act tags for each speech interval, and the inter-coder agreement of the speech act tags was sufficiently high (Cohen's κ = 0.69). We assumed that in this experiment, knowledgeable learners provided their knowledge through information-providing utterances categorized as a statement. Thus, we analyzed all participants' behaviors during information providing utterances by the knowledgeable learners, and predicted the participation styles of the knowledgeable learners using these data. To verify the validity of focusing on this type of utterance, we compared the number of information-providing statements between the knowledgeable learners and novice learners. As a result of the t-test, the average number of information-providing statements differed between the knowledgeable learners and novice learners ($t(28) = 3.982$, $p < 0.01$). This suggests that the two knowledgeable learners in a learning group had a greater opportunity to instruct or provide knowledge to the novice learner.

(iii) Writing action: Each participant used a digital pen. The pen device had a normal ballpoint-type tip to enable the participants to record their notes on paper. Moreover, the pen was recognized as a wireless computer mouse; the writing action was sensed when the mouse was clicked (i.e., when the pen top was pressed on the paper). We used the mouse mode to determine whether participants were writing; this was expressed as mouse-clicking actions based on the pressure-sensitive information collected by the device. In addition, with the purpose of synchronizing each participant's writing data, we implemented a digital-pen capturing

[1] http://www.tobii.com/

[2] http://julius.osdn.jp/

		...	t_9	t_{10}	t_{11}	...					
b_1	T/S_gazeAt_O/NS	...	0	1	1	1	1	0	0	0	...
b_2	T/S_gazeAt_Note.O/NS	...	0	0	0	1	1	1	0	0	...
b_3	NV_writing	...	0	1	0	0	0	0	1	1	...
...	...										
b_{34}	O/S_gazeAt_Note.NV	...	0	0	0	0	0	0	0	0	...

Figure 3. Example of discretized data

tool that transferred the pen-pressed/released data to a server program, where a unique timestamp was assigned.

For each conversation, the data of all three participants were integrated into one annotation file in Anvil format [13]. This enabled us to analyze the co-occurrence of multimodal behaviors by multiple participants while observing the interaction videos.

4. MULTI-MODAL MULTI-USER DATA

In this section, we first describe how we discretized the data collected as described above. We then present a method for constructing behavioral patterns from these data.

4.1 Data Discretization

As the first step in analyzing the collected data, we defined behavioral categories by distinguishing the status of the two knowledgeable learners in each group; i.e., either a speaker or not a speaker of a given information-providing statement. In addition to a label for the novice participant, we defined the following five labels:

- T/S: The target knowledgeable participant (T) as a speaker (S).
- T/NS: The target knowledgeable participant (T) as a non-speaker (NS).
- O/S: The other knowledgeable participant (O) as a speaker (S).
- O/NS: The other knowledgeable participant (O) as a non-speaker (NS).
- NV: A novice participant.

In addition, we defined the following three behavioral labels:

- *x*_gazeAt_*y*: Participant *x* is gazing at participant *y*.
- *x*_gazeAt_Note.*y*: Participant *x* is gazing at participant *y's* note.
- *x*_writing: Participant *x* is writing a note.

Using these participant labels, we defined 34 types of nonverbal behaviors by listing up all the possible combinations of participant labels and behavioral labels shown above. For example, in the behavioral category "T/S_gazeAt_O/NS", "T/S" means that the target knowledgeable participant (T) was the speaker (S), and "O/NS" means that the other knowledgeable participant (O) was not the speaker (NS). Thus, "T/S_gazeAt_O/NS" means that the target knowledgeable participant as the speaker (T/S) was gazing at the other knowledgeable participant who was not the speaker (O/NS). Then, we divided the data into 0.1-second intervals. For each of the 34 types of behaviors, we assigned 1 if the behavior was observed in a given time interval and 0 if the behavior was not observed. As a result, a behavioral data vector consisting of a 0 or 1 as the value for the 34 types of behaviors was created for each time interval. Figure 3 shows how we created behavioral data vectors. For example, the first behavioral category was "T/S_gazeAt_O/NS" (i.e., the target knowledgeable participant, who was the speaker, was gazing at the other knowledgeable participant, who was not the speaker). Because this behavior was observed in the current interval (t_{10}), the value of this category was 1. The next category was "T/S_gazeAt_Note.O/NS" (i.e., the target knowledgeable participant, who was the speaker, was gazing at a note written by the other knowledgeable participant, who was not the speaker). Since this behavior was not observed in the current interval (t_{10}), the value of this category was 0. The third example was "NV_writing" (i.e., the novice participant was writing a note). This behavior was observed in t_{10}, and the assigned value was 1.

For the behavior data vector of this time interval, the first and third dimension values were 1. If one of the values of these 34 bits was different, it marked a different behavioral data vector. In our corpus, we found more than 3,000 behavior category combinations in total. However, some of the combinations were too complex to interpret. Therefore, it was necessary to extract fewer meaningful co-occurrence patterns that characterized the group interaction.

4.2 Multimodal Motif Construction

As the variations of behavioral data vectors were too numerous and some of the patterns were too complex to interpret, we exploited the multi-dimensional motif discovery algorithm proposed by Vahdatpour et al. [21], which enabled us to find meaningful co-occurrence behavioral patterns while limiting the number of patterns to be found.

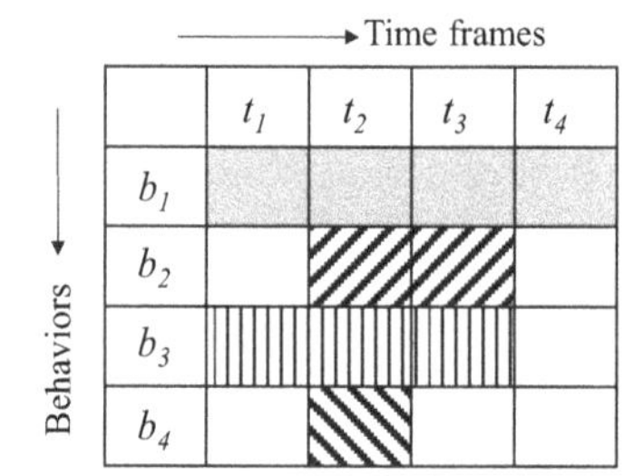

Figure 4. Example of discretized multimodal data

We briefly explain the algorithm. For a set of behavior data vectors for time frames, $T=\{t_1,...t_i\}$, where i is the number of frames and $i = 1,...n$, each data vector consists of a set of behavior data (the value is 0 or 1), $B=\{b_1,...b_j\}$, where $j = 1,...m$. Figure 4 shows a simplified example, which consists of four time frames, t_1 to t_4, and each of them consists of four kinds of behavior: b_1, b_2, b_3, and b_4. The figure illustrates that b_1 and b_3 are observed in frame t_1. Although the combinations of the types of behaviors observed in frame t_1 to t_4 are all different, some of them are partially matched. The combination of b_1 and b_3 is observed in frames t_1, t_2, and t_3, and the combination of b_1, b_2, and b_3 is shared in frames t_2 and t_3. By applying the multi-dimensional motif discovery algorithm [21], subparts of behavior combinations with a higher co-occurrence probability are preferred for extraction as a motif.

The algorithm consists of the following four steps:

[Step 1] In a sorted list of behaviors, calculate a co-occurrence matrix based on the co-occurrence ratios. The co-occurrence ratio for b_i and b_j is calculated as

$$C_{ij} = co\text{-}occurrence\ (b_i,\ b_j)\ /\ occurrence\ (b_i)$$

where *co-occurrence* (b_i, b_j) is the total number of times that both b_i and b_j are observed in the same frame, and *occurrence* (b_i) is the total number of frames in which b_i is observed. As shown in Figure 4, b_1 occurred in all four frames. Thus, *occurrence* (b_1) is 4. Next, we consider the row for b_2. Because b_2 co-occurs with b_1 for frames t_2 and t_3, the *co-occurrence* (b_1, b_2) is 2. Thus, C_{12} is 0.5. By calculating the co-occurrence ratio for the other behaviors, a 4 ×4 co-occurrence matrix is created.

[Step 2] Sort the co-occurrence matrix based on the total number of b_i (*occurrence* (b_i)). Thus, the matrix is sorted as shown in Figure 5.

	b_1	b_2	b_3	b_4
b_1	1	0.5	0.75	0.25
b_2	1	1	1	0.5
b_3	1	0.66	1	0.33
b_4	1	1	1	1

Figure 5. Co-occurrence matrix

[Step 3] If the co-occurrence ratio (C_{ij}) is greater than the threshold, *th*, then add b_j to motif S_i, which is the co-occurrence pattern for b_i.

Assume that threshold *th* is set to 0.5. As shown in Figure 6, in this example, C_{11}, C_{12}, and C_{13} are 1, 0.5, and 0.75, respectively, and they are higher than the threshold *th*, the algorithm generates a motif (b_1, b_2, b_3). If the co-occurrence ratios with other behaviors, such as C_{12} and C_{13}, do not exceed the threshold, b_i constructs one motif with no combination of other behaviors.

Co-occurrence patterns extracted (*th*=0.5): $S_1=(b_1, b_2, b_3)$ …

	b_1	b_2	b_3	b_4
b_1	1	0.5	0.75	0.25
b_3	1	0.66	1	0.33
b_2	1	1	1	0.5
b_4	1	1	1	1

Figure 6. Sorted co-occurrence matrix

[Step 4] Update the co-occurrence matrix by removing the behaviors included in motif S_i.

The algorithm outputs all non-empty motifs by repeating Steps 2 to 4.

The advantage of this algorithm in finding patterns of nonverbal behaviors is that it can ignore less frequent combinations, which may be produced because of misrecognition by the sensors or slight misalignment of timing between the modalities.

We applied the algorithm shown above to ten conversations in Exercise 2 (described in Section 3). Threshold *th* was set to 0.2. The lower the parameter *th* is, the more motifs are generated. By collecting all patterns produced in each conversation and removing the redundant patterns, we finally determined 122 patterns, which was much less than the variations of the original behavior data vectors.

Table 1. Basic statistics for assessment of participation styles

	min	max	average	std
Passive participation	2.91	5.86	4.18	0.725
Receptive participation	4.44	5.78	5.08	0.353
Conversation management	1.78	6.03	4.18	1.028
Proactive participation	2.03	5.50	4.27	0.853

For example, a co-occurrence pattern, "O/NS_gazeAt_T/S + NV_gazeAt_T/S" was the combination of "O/NS_gazeAt_T/S" and "NV_gazeAt_T/S". This pattern indicated that, while the target knowledgeable participant was speaking, the other knowledgeable participant and the novice participant both gazed at the target participant. It is notable that most of the multimodal motifs produced were very clear and easy to understand.

5. EVALUATIING PARTICIPATION STYLES BY OBSERVING VIDEOS

In order to evaluate the participation styles of the subjects, we used Communication Participation Style[8] Scales (COMPASS), which were developed in a social-psychological study in Japan. This scale contains four factors: conversation management, proactive participation, receptive participation, and passive participation. Each of them is measured by four question items, and the questionnaire consists of 16 questions with a seven-point Likert scale. Subjects with a higher score in "conversation management" tend to serve as the chairperson. They manage the conversation and encourage others to contribute. Subjects with a higher score in "proactive participation" tend to describe their ideas without hesitation and claim their opinions. On the other hand, "receptive participation" is the behavioral tendency of listening to the others and trying to understand what they are saying. If a participant has a higher score in "passive participation", he/she is not engaged in the conversation but rather behaves as a bystander.

We split in half each of the ten conversations analyzed in Section 4 and created 20 video clips. The length of each video was approximately 400 seconds. We recruited nine subjects who did not participate in the data collection experiment, and asked them to evaluate the knowledgeable participants in the videos using the COMPASS questionnaire. The order in which the videos were played differed depending on the evaluator. Since there were two knowledgeable participants in each group, the evaluators completed the questionnaire for each of them. We collected 360 answer sheets and obtained COMPASS scores for 40 knowledgeable participants in total. The score of each factor was computed as the average of four question items. The basic statistics of the rating results are shown in Table 1. Cronbach's alpha values for Passive participation, Receptive participation, Conversation management, and Proactive participation were 0.91, 0.89, 0.97, and 0.94 respectively, showing that the COMPASS scale is highly reliable. In the next section, we analyze the correlation between the COMPASS scores and co-occurrence behavioral patterns. We also create regression models that estimate the COMPASS scores from the co-occurrence behavioral patterns.

6. CORRELATION ANALYSIS

We examined the possibility of estimating participation styles evaluated using COMPASS based on behavioral patterns by conducting a correlation analysis between the frequency of behavioral patterns and the COMPASS scores. Table 2 shows the Pearson correlation coefficients. The table only shows 26 patterns that have statistically significant correlation ($p < 0.05$) with at least one of the COMPASS factors.

"Passive participation" correlated negatively with many of the patterns, specifically with those including O/NS_gazeAt_T/S. In contrast, it had positive correlations only with O/S_gazeAt_ Note.O/S and O/S_gazeAt_NV. This indicates that a participant gave the impression of passive participation when he/she was not gazed at by the other knowledgeable participant, even while speaking, and that the other knowledgeable participant gazed at his/her own notes or the novice participant. "Conversation management" and "proactive participation" were highly correlated; the correlation coefficient was 0.929. Therefore, many of the patterns that were highly correlated with "conversation management" had a high correlation with "proactive participation". NV_gazeAt_T/S showed the strongest correlation with both styles: 0.533 with "conversation management" and 0.523 with "proactive participation". This suggests that attracting and holding the novice participant's attention while speaking is important for becoming the leader of the conversation. "Receptive participation" correlated with different behavioral patterns from other participation styles. It had strong correlations with patterns resulting from the target participant receiving attention from other participants and the target participant paying attention to the others' notes.

Approximately half of the statistically significant behavioral patterns were combinations of multiple types of behaviors. This suggests that finding meaningful co-occurrence patterns contributes to improving knowledge about the given communication in collaborative learning. It was also found that highly correlated behavioral patterns differed depending on the participation styles. This suggests that different prediction models with different predictors should be defined for each participation style.

7. ESTIMATING SCORES FOR PARTICIPATION STYLES

Based on the analysis in the previous section, we propose models for estimating the scores for each participation style. For this purpose, we employed linear regression analysis. We created models using only individual behavioral patterns (single-dimensional motifs) as well as models using both individual and multiple behavior co-occurrence patterns (multi-dimensional motifs). In order to select variables for avoiding multi-collinearity, which may produce contradictive models, we employed a stepwise method that combines forward selection and backward elimination. The criteria of the predictor selection decision were based on F-tests ($p \leqq 0.08$ for adding a variable; $p \leqq 0.1$ for eliminating a variable).

Table 3 lists the correlation coefficients, with the numbers in parentheses showing the coefficient of determination (adjusted R^2) values that indicate the overall fit of the model. For "passive participation" and "receptive participation", the models using behavioral co-occurrence patterns were superior to those using only individual behaviors. The correlation coefficients were more than 10% higher. However, for "conversation management" and "proactive participation" the models were slightly improved for those models using co-occurrence patterns. The main reason for this result is that, in "conversation management" and "proactive participation", fewer co-occurrence patterns were selected compared to "passive participation" and "receptive participation", and this contributes less to model improvements by using co-

Table 2. Results of correlation analysis. Significant positive correlations are shown in bold, and negative correlations are underlined

	Pass. prt.	Recept. prt.	Conv. mng.	Proact. prt
O/NS_gazeAt_T/S	-.530**	.292	**.473****	**.455****
O/NS_gazeAt_T/S+ NV_gazeAt_T/S	-.435**	.325	**.430****	**.417***
O/NS_gzeAt_Note.T/S	-.425**	-.020	**.378***	**.364***
T/S_gazeAt_O/NS	-.464**	.049	.301	**.420***
T/S_gazeAt_O/NS+ NV_Writing+ NV_gazeAt_Note.NV	-.391*	-.083	.246	.300
T/S_gazeAt_O/NS+ O/NS_gazeAt_T/S+ NV_gazeAt_Note.NV	-.366*	.053	.184	.321
NV_gazeAt_O/NS	-.390*	-.203	.127	.225
O/NS_gazeAt_NV+ NV_gazeAt_O/NS	-.382*	-.169	.128	.190
O/NS_gazeAt_T/S+ T/S__gazeAt_O/NS+ NV_gazeAt_Note.NV	-.366*	.053	.184	.321
O/S_gazeAt_Note.O/S	**.359***	.096	.010	-.195
O/S_gazeAt_NV	**.378***	.182	-.101	-.115
NV_gazeAt_T/S	-.367*	**.463****	**.533****	**.523****
O/NS_gazeAt_T/S+ T/S_gazeAt_NV+ NV_gazeAt_T/S	-.381*	.285	**.508****	**.417***
T/S_gazeAt_Note.NV	-.393*	.293	**.412***	**.390***
T/S_gazeAt_NV+ NV_gazeAt_T/S	-.090	.284	**.409***	**.346***
T/S_gazeAt_NV	-.340*	.029	**.370***	.324
T/S_gazeAt_Note.O/NS	-.236	.242	**.348***	.297
T/NS_gazeAt_Note.NV	.107	**.534****	.240	.179
T/S_gazeAt_Note.O/NS+ O/NS_Writing+ NV_Writing+ NV_gazeAt_Note.NV	-.034	**.427****	.170	.094
O/NS_Writing+ T/S_gazeAt_Note.O/NS	-.099	**.427****	.154	.191
T/S_gazeAt_Note.NV + O/NS_gazeAt_T/S+ NV_gazeAt_T/S	-.190	**.406***	.252	.193
O/NS_Writing	.040	**.443****	.007	-.017
O/NS_Writing+ T/S_gazeAt_Note.T/S+ NV_Writing	.103	**.375***	-.006	.062
NV_gazeAt_O/S	.143	**.415***	.174	.144
O/S_Writing+ T/NS_gazeAt_Note.O/S	-.066	**.364***	.354*	.264
O/S_gazeAt_T/NS	.091	**.378***	-.058	-.016

*: $p < 0.05$ **: $p < 0.01$

Table 3. Correlation coefficient and adjusted R^2

	Single- dimensional motifs	Single- and multi-dimensional motifs
Pass. prt.	.735 (.497)	.844 (.652)
Recept. prt	.684 (.417)	.816 (.596)
Conv. mng	.694 (.433)	.738 (.485)
Proact. prt.	.710 (.440)	.742 (.492)

occurrence patterns. Nevertheless, the models were improved for all participation styles, which suggests that co-occurrence patterns are indispensable in estimating scores for participation styles.

Now we discuss in greater detail the models that use co-occurrence patterns. Table 4 shows the standardized partial regression coefficients (std_beta) for predictors selected by the stepwise method. The std_beta values were computed by applying regression analysis after standardizing all the variables to a mean of 0 and a variance of 1. Therefore, they are useful in discussing the importance of the variables because they can be compared to each other even when the units of measurement of each parameter are different.

In "passive participation", two co-occurrence patterns were found to have larger positive std_beta values. In O/S_gazeAt _T/NS+NV_Writing+NV_gazeAt_Note.NV, the other participant was speaking while gazing at the target participant; however, the novice participant was writing without looking at the knowledgeable participants. In T/NS_gazeAt _O/S+O/S_gazeAt_NV+NV_gazeAt_O/S, the other knowledgeable participant and novice participant exchanged glances with each other but not with the target participant, even though he/she was looking at the other knowledgeable participant. On the other hand, the predictor with the largest negative std_beta value was O/NS_gazeAt_T/S, suggesting that it was less likely that the other knowledgeable participant would gaze at the target participant who was speaking. These results suggest that participants believed that a person was passively participating in a conversation when he/she was actually not actively speaking and was given less attention from other individuals.

For "receptive participation", the patterns that accompanied the behavior of paying attention to others or the notes of the other participants had larger positive std_beta values. This suggests that the target participant was perceived to be engaged in understanding the others when both the target participant and the others displayed attentive behaviors, such as focusing attention on the others and on their notes.

Third, in "conversation management", clear bi-directional behaviors were identified: NV_gazeAt_T/S and T/S_gazeAt_NV. Therefore, in a collaborative learning situation, a person is perceived as a leader of the conversation if he/she is paying attention to the novice participant while speaking and the novice participant is also looking at the target person. On the other hand, in "proactive participation" all the participants paid attention to each other while the target participant was speaking, whereas in "receptive participation," paying attention to others' notes is more important than looking at their faces. Note that as discussed in Section 6, "conversation management" and "proactive participation" are highly correlated, and they are more dependent on single-dimensional motifs than multi-dimensional motifs.

8. CONCLUSIONS AND FUTURE WORK

With a goal of estimating participation styles in communication, this paper presents a corpus analysis for identifying nonverbal behavioral motifs, which includes individual behaviors and co-occurrence patterns of behaviors. First, we collected the eye gaze and writing actions for three participants in a synchronized manner, and discretized the behavioral data in 0.1-second time intervals. Then, we extracted 122 motifs using a multi-dimensional motif discovery algorithm. Based on the frequency of these motifs, we created regression models for estimating scores concerning four participation styles. The multiple correlation coefficients were 0.74 to 0.84, indicating a good fit with the data. Based on the regression analysis, we also identified several behavioral motifs as statistically significant predictors for each participation style. These motifs were sufficiently consistent and comprehensible for discussing the meaning of the behavior combinations.

While this study focused on collaborative learning interaction, the participation styles defined in COMPASS and the method of constructing multi-dimensional motifs are applicable to other domains. The contribution of this study is to identify useful behavioral motifs for predicting participation styles in collaborative learning interaction. An interesting future direction is to apply the same method to other domains of communication, such as group discussion for non-educational purposes, and

Table 4. Regression models with standardized partial regression coefficients (std_beta)

Passive		Receptive		Conv. management		Proactive	
O/NS_gazeAt_T/S	-0.434	T/NS_gazeAt_Note.NV	0.544	NV_gazeAt_T/S	0.554	NV_gazeAt_T/S	0.393
O/NS_gazeAt_Note.NV	-0.229	T/S_gazeAt_Note.O/NS + O/NS_Writing+ NV_Writing+ NV_gazeAt_Note.NV	0.386	T/S_gazeAt_NV	0.364	T/S_gazeAt_O/NS	0.320
NV_gazeAt_O/NS	-0.205	O/S_gazeAt_T/NS+ NV_gazeAt_O/S	0.304	T/S_Writing	0.364	O/NS_gazeAt_NV	0.335
O/S_gazeAt_T/NS+ NV_Writing+ NV_gazeAt_Note.NV	0.378	NV_gazeAt_Note.T/S	0.341	T/NS_GazeAt_O/S+ O/S_gazeAt_Note.NV+ NV_gazeAt_O/S	0.231	O/NS_gazeAt_Note.T/S	0.283
T/NS_gazeAt_O/S+ O/S_gazeAt_NV+ NV_gazeAt_O/S	0.333	O/S_gazeAt_Note.T/NS + T/NS_Writing+ NV_Writing+ NV_gazeAt_Note.NV	-0.217				
T/S_gazeAt_Note.NV	-0.299	NV_gazeAt_T/NS	0.212				

compare the motifs with those found in this study. This would enable us to discuss the domain-specific motifs in collaborative learning interaction, and the general motifs in multi-party interaction.

Another important future direction of this work would be to improve the models, specifically for "conversation management" and "proactive participation", for which the values of R^2 were lower than the other two styles. One solution would be to find and add more useful information. For "proactive participation", the evaluation questions asked about the content of the utterance. Therefore, only considering the nonverbal behaviors may not be sufficient. We expect that by adding linguistic information, the models will be improved. It may also be useful to add more nonverbal information, such as head and body motion measured by acceleration sensors and prosodic features in speech. Furthermore, we would like to apply the findings of this study to assist collaborative learning activities in improving the effectiveness of the learning.

9. ACKNOWLEDGEMENTS

This work was supported by JST CREST and JSPS KAKENHI Grant Number 25280076.

10. REFERENCES

[1] Aran, O. and Gatica-Perez, D. *One of a Kind: Inferring Personality Impressions in Meetings*. in Proceedings of *the 15th ACM on International conference on multimodal interaction (ICMI2013)*. p. 11-18, 2013.

[2] Bailly, G., Raidt, S., and Elisei, F. *Gaze, conversational agents and face-to-face communication.* Speech Communication. **52**(6): p. 598-612, 2010.

[3] Baker, R.S.J.d. and Yacef, K. *The State of Educational Data Mining in 2009: A Review and Future Visions.* Journal of Educational Data Mining. **1**(1): p. Article 1, 2009.

[4] Cakir, M.P. and Stahl, G. *Interaction analysis of dual-interaction CSCL environments*. in Proceedings of *the 9th international conference on Computer supported collaborative learning - Volume 1*. Rhodes, Greece: International Society of the Learning Sciences, p. 3-12, 2009.

[5] Clark, H.H. and Brennan, S.E. *Grounding in communication*, in *Perspectives on socially shared cognition*, Resnick, L.B., Levine, J.M., and Teasley, S.D., Editors. American Psychological Association: Washington DC. p. 127-149, 1991.

[6] Dillenbourg, P. and Traum, D. *Sharing solutions: Persistence and grounding in multimodal collaborative problem solving.* Journal of the Learning Sciences. **15**(1): p. 121-151, 2006.

[7] Dong, W., Lepri, B., Cappelletti, A., Pentland, A.S., Pianesi, F., and Zancanaro, M. *Using the influence model to recognize functional roles in meetings*. in Proceedings of *the 9th international conference on Multimodal interfaces*. Nagoya, Aichi, Japan: ACM, p. 271-278, 2007.

[8] Fujimoto, M. *COMPASS indicates participants' communication participation styles.* The Japanese Society of Social Psychology. **23**(3): p. 290-297, 2008.

[9] Jayagopi, D.B., Hung, H., Yeo, C., and Gatica-Perez, D. *Modeling Dominance in Group Conversations from Nonverbal Activity Cues.* IEEE Trans. on Audio, Speech, and Language Processing. **17**(3): p. 501-513, 2009.

[10] Jayagopi, D.B. and Gatica-Perez, D. *Mining Group Nonverbal Conversational Patterns Using Probabilistic Topic Models.* IEEE Transactions on Multimedia. **12**(8): p. 790 - 802, 2010.

[11] Jayagopi, D.B., Sanchez-Cortes, D., Otsuka, K., Yamato, J., and Gatica-Perez, D. *Linking Speaking and Looking Behavior Patterns with Group Composition, Perception, and Performance.* in Proceedings of *the 14th ACM international conference on Multimodal interaction (ICMI2012)*. p. 433-440, 2012.

[12] Jurafsky, D., Shriberg, L., and Biasca, D., *Switchboard SWBD-DAMSL Shallow Discourse-Function Annotation Coders Manual*, in *Institute of Cognitive Science Technical Report*. p. 1–61., 1997.

[13] Kipp, M. *Anvil - A Generic Annotation Tool for Multimodal Dialogue*. in Proceedings of *the 7th European Conference on Speech Communication and Technology*. p. 1367-1370, 2001.

[14] Martínez, H.P. and Yannakakis, G.N. *Deep Multimodal Fusion: Combining Discrete Events and Continuous Signals*. in Proceedings of *ICMI '14 Proceedings of the 16th International Conference on Multimodal Interaction*. Istanbul, Turkey: ACM, p. 34-41, 2014.

[15] Miller, C.A., Quek, F.K.H., and Morency, L.-P. *Interactive relevance search and modeling: support for expert-driven analysis of multimodal data.* in Proceedings of *Proceedings of the 15th ACM on International conference on multimodal interaction*. p. 149-156, 2013.

[16] Oviatt, S., Cohen, A., and Weibel, N. *Multimodal learning analytics: description of math data corpus for ICMI grand challenge workshop*. in Proceedings of *the 15th ACM on International conference on multimodal interaction*. Sydney, Australia: ACM, p. 563-568, 2013.

[17] Oviatt, S. and Cohen, A. *Written Activity, Representations and Fluency as Predictors of Domain Expertise in Mathematics*. in Proceedings of *the 16th International Conference on Multimodal Interaction*. Istanbul, Turkey: ACM, p. 10-17, 2014.

[18] Sanchez-Cortes, D., Aran, O., Jayagopi, D.B., Mast, M.S., and Gatica-Perez, D. *Emergent leaders through looking and speaking: from audio-visual data to multimodal recognition.* Journal on Multimodal User Interfaces. **7**(1-2): p. 39-53, 2013.

[19] Soller, A. *Supporting Social Interaction in an Intelligent Collaborative Learning System.* International Journal of Artificial Intelligence in Education (IJAIED). **12**: p. 40-62, 2001.

[20] Song, Y., Morency, L.-P., and Davis, R. *Multimodal Human Behavior Analysis: Learning Correlation and Interaction Across Modalities*. in Proceedings of *the 14th ACM International Conference on Multimodal Interaction*. Santa Monica, California, USA: ACM, p. 27-30, 2012.

[21] Vahdatpour, A., Amini, N., and Sarrafzadeh, M. *Toward unsupervised activity discovery using multi-dimensional motif detection in time series*. in Proceedings of *the 21st international jont conference on Artifical intelligence*. Pasadena, California, USA: Morgan Kaufmann Publishers Inc. , p. 1261-1266, 2009.

Multimodal Fusion using Respiration and Gaze for Predicting Next Speaker in Multi-Party Meetings

Ryo Ishii
NTT Communication Science Laboratories, NTT Corporation
3-1, Morinosato-Wakamiya, Atsugi-shi Kanagawa, Japan
ishii.ryo@lab.ntt.co.jp

Shiro Kumano
NTT Communication Science Laboratories, NTT Corporation
3-1, Morinosato-Wakamiya, Atsugi-shi Kanagawa, Japan
kumano.shiro@lab.ntt.co.jp

Kazuhiro Otsuka
NTT Communication Science Laboratories, NTT Corporation
3-1, Morinosato-Wakamiya, Atsugi-shi Kanagawa, Japan
otsuka.kazuhiro@lab.ntt.co.jp

ABSTRACT

Techniques that use nonverbal behaviors to predict turn-taking situations, such as who will be the next speaker and the next utterance timing in multi-party meetings are receiving a lot of attention recently. It has long been known that gaze is a physical behavior that plays an important role in transferring the speaking turn between humans. Recently, a line of research has focused on the relationship between turn-taking and respiration, a biological signal that conveys information about the intention or preliminary action to start to speak. It has been demonstrated that respiration and gaze behavior separately have the potential to allow predicting the next speaker and the next utterance timing in multi-party meetings. As a multimodal fusion to create models for predicting the next speaker in multi-party meetings, we integrated respiration and gaze behavior, which were extracted from different modalities and are completely different in quality, and implemented a model uses information about them to predict the next speaker at the end of an utterance. The model has a two-step processing. The first is to predict whether turn-keeping or turn-taking happens; the second is to predict the next speaker in turn-taking. We constructed prediction models with either respiration or gaze behavior and with both respiration and gaze behaviors as features and compared their performance. The results suggest that the model with both respiration and gaze behaviors performs better than the one using only respiration or gaze behavior. It is revealed that multimodal fusion using respiration and gaze behavior is effective for predicting the next speaker in multi-party meetings. It was found that gaze behavior is more useful for predicting turn-keeping/turn-taking than respiration and that respiration is more useful for predicting the next speaker in turn-taking.

Categories and Subject Descriptors

H.1.2 [User/Machine systems]: Human information processing

ICMI 2015, November 9–13, 2015, Seattle, WA, USA.
 ISBN 978-1-4503-3912-4/15/11 ...$15.00.
DOI: http://dx.doi.org/10.1145/2818346.2820755.

Keywords

Respiration, gaze behavior, multi-party meetings, next-speaker prediction, turn-taking

1. INTRODUCTION

Face-to-face communication is one of the most basic forms of communication in daily life, and group meetings are held for conveying information, understanding others' intentions, and making decisions. To design better communication systems that can enhance our communication beyond conversation in loco and to develop social agents/robots that interact naturally with humans in conversations, it is critical to fully understand the mechanisms of human communication. Therefore, ways to automatically analyze multi-party meetings have been actively researched in recent years [6, 21].

Turn-taking, the situation where the speaker changes, is especially important. The participants in multi-party meetings need to predict the end of the speaker's utterance and who will start speaking next and to consider a strategy for good timing with respect to who will speak next in multi-party meetings. If a model can predict the next speaker and the start time of the next speaker's utterance, the model will lay the foundation for the development of natural conversational systems in which conversational agents speak with natural timing and of teleconference systems that avoid utterance collisions with time delays by appraising who will speak to participants.

Studies in sociolinguistics have reported that verbal and nonverbal behavior, such as gaze behavior, have an important association with the next speaker and the start of the next utterance [16, 23]. For automatically detecting or predicting who becomes the next speaker at the time of turn-taking in the engineering field, we have proposed using gaze behavior to predict the next speaker [8] and the start of the next utterance [8, 9]. Moreover, it has been shown that meeting participants' respiration has potential to allow predicting the next speaker [10].

It is desirable that more robust and high-precision prediction models be realized by mulitimodal fusion using multimodal information. Respiration conveys information about the intention or preliminary action to start to speak. Gaze behavior plays the role of transferring the speaking turn between humans. With the goal of building a high-performance prediction model, we integrated respiration and gaze behavior, which are completely different in quality, as a multimodal fusion to create models for predicting the next speaker in multi-party meetings. Then we evaluated whether multitimodal fusion of respiration and gaze behavior is effective for predicting the next speaker in multi-party meetings.

No previous research has dealt with multimodal fusion of respiration and gaze behavior in the field of meeting analysis. This research opens up new possibilities for multimodal fusion of respiration and nonverbal physical information such as gaze behavior.

In this work, we first collected utterance, gaze behavior, and respiration data for participants in multi-party meetings. Using the data, we implemented a model for predicting the next speaker at the end of an utterance. The model includes a two-step processing. The first processing is to predict whether turn-keeping or turn-taking happens. The second is to predict the next speaker in turn-taking. We constructed prediction models that use either respiration or gaze behavior and both respiration and gaze behavior as features and compared their performance. The results suggest that the model with both respiration and gaze latter behaviors performs better, which would indicate than the one using only respiration or gaze behavior. Thus, it is revealed that multimodal fusion using respiration and gaze behavior is effective for predicting the next speaker in multiparty meetings. In addition, it was found that gaze behavior is more useful for predicting turn-keeping/turn-taking than respiration and that respiration is more useful for predicting the next speaker in turn-taking.

This paper is organized as follows. Section 2 reviews related work and highlights our approach. Section 3 describes the corpus data in multi-party meetings. Section 4 and 5 cover the construction and evaluation of the prediction models. Section 6 discusses the potential of multimodal fusion in detail. Section 7 concludes the paper and mentions future work.

2. RELATED WORK

Most of the work related to elucidating the mechanism of the delivery of the turn in conversation has been performed in the field of sociolinguistics. Sacks et al. [23] proposed a turn-taking model in which turn-taking can only happen at transition relevance points near the end of utterances.

Several studies have explored the idea of automatically detecting whether turn-taking takes place or not in multiparty meetings by means of speech processing [2, 3, 5, 12, 18, 19, 24] and by using visual nonverbal behaviors such as gaze behavior [2, 3, 12] and physical motion [2, 3, 4] near the end of an utterance.

In addition to the prediction of turn-taking, some studies have tried to predict who will become the next speaker at the time of turn-taking and the start time of the next utterance. Kawahara et al. [14] proposed a next-speaker detection model using gaze behavior and nodding in three-person poster conversations. We proposed a prediction model that features three processing steps to predict whether turn-taking or turn-keeping will occur, who will be the next speaker in turn-taking, and the timing of the start of the next speaker's utterance using gaze transition patterns, which have an n-gram of gaze objects that include mutual gaze information [8, 9, 11]. Moreover, we explored respiration for the first time in the field of multi-party meeting analysis and demonstrated the relationship between respiration and turn-taking [10]. We revealed that a speaker inhales more rapidly and quickly right after the end of a unit of utterance in turn-keeping. The listener who will become the next speaker takes a bigger breath toward speaking in turn-taking than listeners who will not become the next speaker. The results suggested that the characteristics of the speaker's inhalation right after his/her utterance and listeners' inhalation near the end of the utterance have potential to be useful for predicting the next speaker and the start time of the next utterance in multi-party meetings.

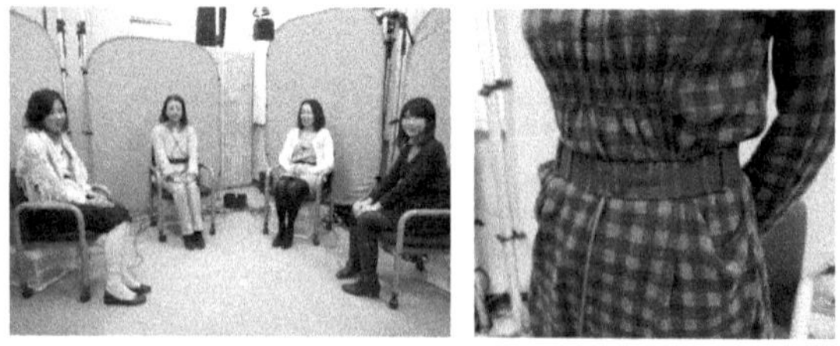

Figure 1: Sample scene of multi-party meeting and band respiratory sensor wrapped on participant's body.

In summary, previous research separately focused on gaze behavior and respiration for predicting the next speaker and the start time of the next utterance in multi-party meetings. In regard to respiration, despite the fact that the characteristics of participants' inhalations have potential to be useful for predicting the next speaker and the start time of the next utterance, a prediction model using respiration has not been constructed yet. It is hoped that the multimodal fusion of various physical nonverbal behaviors and biological information will enable the prediction of the next speaker in multi-party meetings.

With the goal of building a high-precision model for predicting the next speaker and the start time of the next utterance, we here focus on the multimodal fusion of respiration and gaze behavior, which has not been examined in previous work on prediction models for turn-taking, the next speaker, and the start time of the next utterance in multi-party meetings.

3. CORPUS DATA

To collect a conversation corpus in multi-party meetings for creating the prediction model of the next speaker using respiration and gaze behavior in multi-party meetings, we recorded eight natural four-persons meetings held by eight groups of four different persons (16 people in total). The four participants were in their 20's and 30's, and this was the first time they had met. They faced each other and sat down (See Fig. 1). We labeled the participants from left to right as P1, P2, P3, and P4. They argued and gave opinions in response to highly divisive questions like "Is marriage the same as love?" and needed to draw a conclusion within ten minutes.

We recorded the participants' voices with a pin microphone attached to their chest and made a video recording of the entire scene and took bust shots of each participant (recorded at 30 Hz). We recorded each participant's respiration information using a NeXus-10 MARKII [20]. The respiration sensor of the system records the depth of breathing with the belt wrapped around participant's body (See Fig. 1) and outputs a value of the degree of breathing depth (called the "RSP value" hereafter) at 128 Hz. A high RSP value means that the person keeps taking air into the lungs. In contrast, a low one indicates the absence of air in the

Table 1: Overview of the 36 features we used for creating the prediction model of the next speaker in multi-party meetings.

Modality	Number	Features
Speaking state	4	Speaking state of P1, P2, P3, and P4
Respiration	24	INT, MAX, AMP, DUR, SLO_{early}, and SLO of P1, P2, P3, and P4
Gaze Behavior	8	$GTP_{Wolabel}$ and GTP_{Wlabel} of P1, P2, P3, and P4

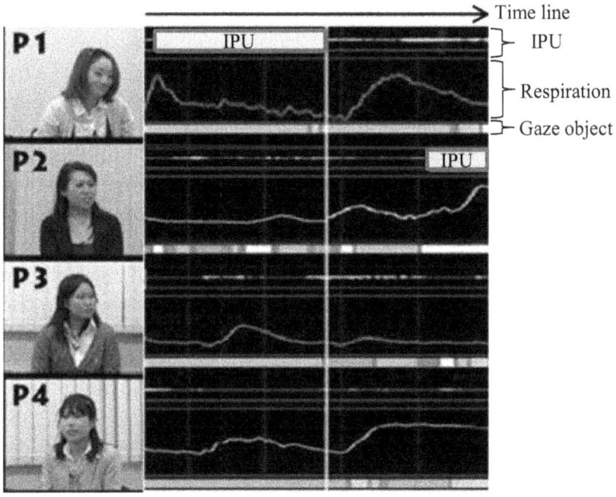

Figure 2: Example of corpus in multi-party meeting.

lungs. A scene with the respiration sensor wrapped around a participant's body is shown in Fig. 1. We collected data for four meetings whose length was about 12 minutes each (total of about 100 minutes) and built a multimodal corpus consisting of the following verbal and nonverbal behaviors and biological information from the recorded data:

- Utterance: We built the utterance unit using the inter-pausal unit (IPU) [17]. The utterance interval was extracted manually from the speech wave. The portion of an utterance followed by 200 ms of silence was used as the unit of one utterance. From the created IPU, supportive responses [13] were excluded and an utterance unit continued by the same person was considered as one utterance turn. And pairs of IPUs that adjoined in time and groups of IPUs at the time of turn-keeping and turn-taking were created. Data for speech overlap situations, i.e., when a listener interrupted during a speaker's utterance or two or more participants spoke simultaneously in turn-taking, were excluded from the pairs of IPUs for analysis. Eventually, the numbers of the created groups of IPUs were 1479 at the time of turn-keeping and 128 at the time of turn-taking.
- Respiration: The RSP value output from the NeXus-10 MARKI has a different magnitude for each participant. To correct for the individual differences, the RSP value of each participant was normalized by the mean value μ and standard deviation value δ of each participant. Specifically, the RSP value of each participant was normalization on the basis of the values of $\mu + \delta$ and $\mu - \delta$ of each participant. In this way, we were able to treat each participants RSP value data for the analysis on the same scale.
- Gaze object: A skilled annotator annotated the gaze object manually using bust/head and overhead views in each frame of the videos. The objects of gaze were the four participants (labeled P1, P2, P3, and P4, as mentioned above) and non-persons, i.e., the walls or floor.

All of the above-mentioned data were integrated at 30 Hz for visual display using the NTT Multimodal Meeting Viewer (called "NTT MM-Viewer") [22] (See Fig. 2). The viewer enables us to annotate the multimodal data frame by frame and observe the data intuitively.

4. MULTIMODAL FEATURES

4.1 Guidelines for creating prediction model

The goal of our research is to create a model that predicts the next speaker using respiration and gaze behavior. Our work on respiration demonstrated that inhalations of the speaker and listeners near the end of an utterance have the potential to allow predicting the next speaker in multi-party meetings [10]. Our other work attempted to create a prediction model that can predict the next speaker 200 ms after end of an utterance using gaze behavior [8]. We built an utterance unit using the IPU [17]. The IPU is determined only on the basis of whether the speaker is uttering or not. This simple definition is suitable for real-time processing, though this paper deals with off-line processing. Specifically, the portion of an utterance followed by 200 ms of silence was used as the unit of one utterance. In generating an IPU, 200 ms is required after the actual end of an utterance. Therefore, we devised a model to predict the next speaker at the time the IPU is created, i.e., at 200 ms after the end of the IPU. In a similar manner, we also tried to create a prediction model that predicts the next speaker 200 ms after the end of IPU. For predicting the next speaker, we created a prediction model that has a two-step processing in a way similar to that in our previoius work [8]. The first processing is to predict whether turn-keeping or turn-taking happens; the second is to predict the next speaker in turn-taking. In a way similar to that in the related work, we also created prediction models that can predict the next speaker with either respiration or gaze behavior and with both respiration and gaze behaviors near the end of utterance as features. We compared their performance to evaluate whether multimodal fusion is effective.

Table 1 summarizes the features of respiration and gaze behavior. The features of the speaking state show the binary format that concerns information about the person taken into consideration, whether as speaker or listener. Hereafter in this section, we describe how we extracted the features of respiration and gaze behavior.

4.2 Features of Respiration

We analyzed the differences in the inhalation of the speaker right after the end of the speaker's IPU and the inhalation of listeners right before the start of the next speaker's IPU be-

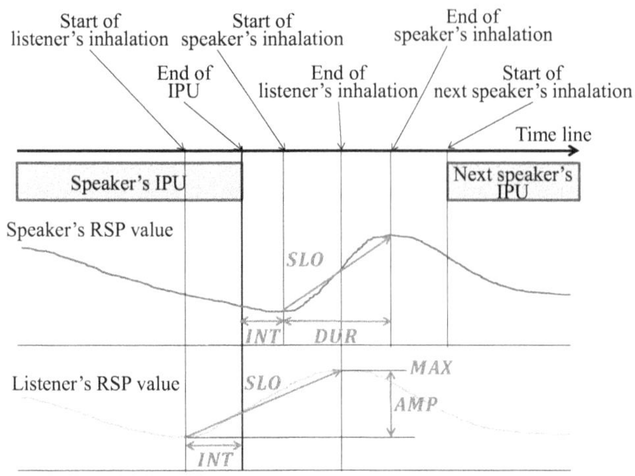

Figure 3: Analytic inhalation parameters.

tween turn-taking and turn-keeping [10]. We found that the following three inhalation-phase parameters of the speaker differ between turn-keeping and turn-taking (See Fig. 3).

- INT: Interval between end time of speaker's IPU and start time of inhalation.
- DUR: Duration of inhalation phase.
- SLO: Mean value of slope of RSP value per second during inhalation phase.

In detail, we found that INT and DUR of the speaker's inhalation in turn-keeping are shorter than in turn-taking and that SLO of the speaker's inhalation in turn-keeping is bigger than in turn-taking. The results suggested that a speaker inhales more rapidly and quickly right after the end of a unit of utterance in turn-keeping.

As the result of the analysis of listeners' inhalation, we found that the following four inhalation-phase parameters of the listener differ between turn-keeping and turn-taking (See Fig. 3).

- INT: Interval between end time of speaker's IPU and start time of inhalation.
- MAX: RSP value at the end of inhalation phase, i.e., maximum RSP value of inhalation phase.
- AMP: Amplitude of RSP value of inhalation phase.
- SLO: Mean value of slope of RSP value per second during inhalation phase.

In detail, we found that INT of inhalation of the listener who will become the next speaker in turn-taking is shorter than that for listeners in turn-keeping and turn-taking and that MAX, AMP, and SLO of the listener who will become the next speaker in turn-taking are bigger than those for listeners who will not become the next speaker in turn-keeping and turn-taking. The results suggested the listener who will be next speaker starts taking a breath near the time of end of speaker's utterance and takes a bigger breath toward speaking in turn-taking than listeners who will not become the next speaker.

On the basis of these results, we extracted the speaker's inhalation right after the end of the speaker's IPU and listener's inhalation near the end of the IPU until 200 ms after the end of the IPU. We use the INT, MAX, AMP, DUR, and SLO of their inhalation. But not all of the inhalation parameters were collected during the 200 ms after the end of the IPU. In particular — For instance, MAX, AMP, DUR and SLO can be collected after the inhalation ends. Regarding SLO, we collected the slope of the RSP value during a period of 100 ms between the start of inhalation and 100 ms after the start of inhalation, called SLO_{early}, in addition to SLO.

To extract the inhalation-phase in detail, we extracted a point where two RSP values right before the point continuously decreased and two RSP values right after it continuously increased as the start of the inhalation phase. We extracted a point after the start of the inhalation phase where two RSP values right before the point continuously increased and two RSP values right after it continuously decreased as a the end of the inhalation phase.

The average start time of the next speaker's inhalation in turn-taking is 297 ms before the end of the speaker's IPU. To extract the inhalation of listeners in detail, we treated the data in the interval between 2000 ms before the end of speaker's IPU and 200 ms after the end of the speaker's IPU as analysis data. We extracted the last inhalation of all inhalations during that interval. The content of any respiration feature not extracted was set at the average value of the feature.

4.3 Features of gaze behavior

It is known that gaze behavior is an important cue for smooth turn-taking. For example, Kendon [16] has demonstrated that the next speaker looks away when he/she starts to speak after having made eye contact with the current speaker in two-person meetings. We focused on the gaze transition pattern (GTP), which is a temporal transition of participant's gaze behavior near the end of utterances [8, 9]. We expressed it as an n-gram, which wedefined as a sequence of gaze direction shifts. We demonstrated that the GTP is effective for predicting the next speaker in multiparty meetings. We used the GTP as a feature of gaze behavior to predict the next speaker. For GTP generation, we focused on the gazed object for 1200 ms: 1000 ms before the utterance of the utterance and 200 ms after it. In this research, we created the following two kinds of GTPs from each participant's gaze behavior during the 1200 ms.

- $GTP_{Wolabel}$: A gaze transition pattern whose composition element is a person or non-person.
- GTP_{Wlabel}: A gaze transition pattern whose composition element of person is classified as "speaker", "listener", or "non-person" and labeled. At this time, the existence of mutual gaze was taken into consideration from the knowledge [16] that a mutual gaze takes place in two-person dialogs at the time of a turn-taking. The gaze behavior was classified into the following five gaze labels:
  - -S: Person looks at a speaker without mutual gaze (speaker doesn't look at the listener.).
  - -S_M: Person looks at the speaker with mutual gaze (speaker looks at a listener.).
  - -$L_1 \sim L_3$: Person looks at another listener without mutual gaze. L_1, L_2 and L_3: These indicate different listeners.
  - -$L_{1M} \sim L_{3M}$: Person looks at another listener with mutual gaze. L_{1M}, L_{2M} and L_{3M}: These indicate different listeners.

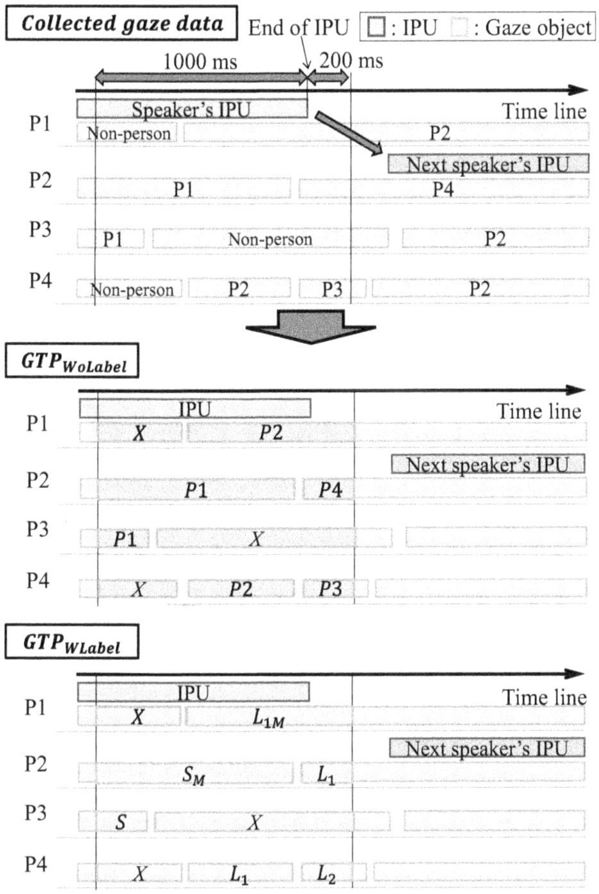

Figure 4: Example of generation of $GTP_{Wolabel}$ and GTP_{Wlabel}.

-X: Person looks at non-persons, such as the floor or ceiling.

Figure 4 shows how the $GTP_{Wolabel}$ and GTP_{Wlabel} are constructed: P1 finishes speaking and then P2 starts to speak. P1 gazes at P2 after she gazes at a non-person during the interval of analysis. Then, P1's $GTP_{Wolabel}$ is X-$P2$. When P1 looks at P2, P2 looks at P1; namely, there is mutual gaze. Therefore, P1's GTP_{Wlabel} is X-L_{1M}. P2 looks at P4 after making eye contact with P1. Then, P2's $GTP_{Wolabel}$ and GTP_{Wlabel} are $P1$-$P4$ and S_M-L_1. P3 looks at a non-person after looking at P1. Then, P3's $GTP_{Wolabel}$ and GTP_{Wlabel} are $P1$-X and S-X. P4 looks at P2 and P3 after looking at a non-person. Then, P2's $GTP_{Wolabel}$ and GTP_{Wlabel} are X-$P2$-$P3$ and X-L_1-L_2.

5. PREDICTION MODEL OF NEXT SPEAKER BY MULTIMODAL FUSION

5.1 Prediction of turn-keeping or turn-taking

As a first processing to predict the next speaker, we created a prediction model to predict whether turn-keeping or turn-taking will happen in multi-party meetings. We evaluated how useful multimodal fusion with respiration and gaze behavior is for predicting turn-keeping/turn-taking. We constructed prediction models with either respiration or gaze behavior and with both respiration and gaze behaviors as features and compared their performance.

Table 2: Performance of prediction models of turn-keeping/turn-taking.

Models	F-measure
Chance level	0.500
Respiration model	0.648
Gaze model	0.697
Respiration+Gaze model (Early fusion)	0.723
Respiration+Gaze model (Late fusion)	0.752

We constructed the prediction models using a support vector machine (SVM), in which the method is SMO [15] implemented in the Weka data mining tool [1], and evaluated the performance of the models. The settings of the SVM — the RBF (radial basis function) kernel, C (cost parameter), and γ (hyper parameter of the RBF kernel—are determined by a grid search technique. The class is binary format data which has turn-taking and turn-keeping.

We implemented the following four prediction models.

- Respiration model: The model uses the 24 features of respiration and four features of the speaking state.
- Gaze model: The model uses the eight features of gaze behavior and four features of the speaking state.
- Respiration+Gaze model (Early fusion): The model uses all the features: the 24 features of respiration, eight features of gaze behavior, and four features of the speaking state.
- Respiration+Gaze model (Late fusion): The model calculates the occurrence probability of turn-keeping and turn-taking by multiplying the occurrence probability output from the Respiration model and Gaze model.

We employed ten-fold cross validation with 256 data, which includes 128 data obtained by sampling from 1479 data in turn-taking to remove the bias of the number of data and 128 data used in turn-taking.

The F-measure of each prediction model is shown in Table 2. In the overall evaluation, the F-measure of the Respiration+Gaze model (Late fusion) is 0.752, which is the best performance among all the models. The F-measure of the Respiration+Gaze model (Early fusion) is 0.723, which is the second highest performance among the models. These results suggest that multimodal fusion using the parameters of respiration and gaze behavior contribute to predicting turn-keeping/turn-taking in multi-party meetings. A comparison of the Respiration model and the Gaze model shows that the latter performs better (0.697) than former (0.648). This suggests that gaze behavior is a stronger predictor of turn-keeping/turn-taking than respiration.

The evaluation of the worth of a feature, determined by measuring the information gain with respect to the class for the Respiration+Gaze model (Early fusion), in Table 3 supports the preceding discussion. Table 3 shows the top ten features ranked by information gain. It shows that the top seven useful features are relevant to $GTP_{Wolabel}$ or GTP_{Wlabel}. This suggests that the gaze transition pattern is the most dominant information in this model. Note that the AMP of P1 (eighth rank), MAX of P1 (nine rank), and

Table 3: Results of information gain feature evaluation of Respiration+Gaze model (Early fusion) to predict turn-keeping/turn-taking.

Rank	Information gain ratio	Feature
1	0.166	$GTP_{Wolabel}$ of P1
2	0.138	$GTP_{Wolabel}$ of P3
3	0.131	GTP_{Wlabel} of P3
4	0.124	GTP_{Wlabel} of P1
5	0.1156	$GTP_{Wolabel}$ of P2
6	0.112	$GTP_{Wolabel}$ of P4
7	0.108	GTP_{Wlabel} of P2
8	0.107	AMP of P1
9	0.090	MAX of P1
10	0.0819	SLO of P2

Table 4: Performance of prediction models for next speaker in turn-taking.

Models	F-measure
Chance level	0.333
Respiration model	0.477
Gaze model	0.456
Respiration+Gaze model (Early fusion)	0.500
Respiration+Gaze model (Late fusion)	0.523

SLO of P2 (tenth rank) are features of respiration. This result suggests that the features of respiration also useful for predicting turn-keeping/turn-taking.

5.2 Prediction of next speaker in turn-taking

As a second processing to predict the next speaker, we created prediction models to predict the next speaker in turn-taking. We evaluated how useful multimodal fusion with respiration and gaze behavior is for predicting the next speaker in turn-taking. We constructed prediction models with either respiration or gaze behavior and with both respiration and gaze behaviors as features and compared their performance.

We constructed the prediction models using the SVM and evaluated their performance in the same way as in Section 5.1. The data used in the SVM contains the next speaker as a class. We implemented the four prediction models in the same way as in Section 5.1.

We employed ten-fold cross validation with the 128 turn-taking data from our corpus. The F-measure of each prediction model is shown in Table 4. The chance level is 0.333 because there are three next-speaker candidates in turn-taking. In the overall evaluation, the F-measure of the Respiration+Gaze model (Late fusion) is 0.523, which is the best performance among the models. The F-measure of the Respiration+Gaze model (Early fusion) is 0.500, which is the second highest performance among the models. These results suggest that the multimodal fusion using the parameters of respiration and gaze behavior contributes to predicting the next speaker in turn-taking in multi-party meetings. A comparison of the Respiration model and the Gaze model shows that former performs better (0.477) than the latter (0.456). This suggests that respiration is a strong predictor of the next speaker in turn-taking alone.

Table 5: Results of information gain feature evaluation of Respiration+Gaze model (Early fusion) to predict nextspeaker in turn-taking.

Average rank	Average information gain ratio	Feature
1.4 ± 0.49	0.631 ± 0.029	GTP_{Wlabel} of P1
2.8 ± 0.98	0.584 ± 0.036	$GTP_{Wolabel}$ of P4
2.8 ± 1.08	0.593 ± 0.018	GTP_{Wlabel} of P3
3.1 ± 1.14	0.581 ± 0.031	SLO of P3
7.8 ± 2.23	0.498 ± 0.031	SLO of P1
7.9 ± 3.96	0.497 ± 0.059	MAX of P1
8.4 ± 2.06	0.483 ± 0.026	GTP_{Wlabel} of P4
8.9 ± 1.45	0.484 ± 0.020	MAX of P3
9.2 ± 2.44	0.473 ± 0.022	$GTP_{Wolabel}$ of P1
9.2 ± 2.86	0.473 ± 0.033	AMP of P3

The evaluation of the worth of a feature, determined by measuring the information gain with respect to the class for the Respiration+Gaze model (Early fusion), in Table 5 supports the preceding discussion. Table 5 shows the top ten features ranked by information gain. It shows that the top three useful features are the GTP_{Wlabel} of P1, $GTP_{Wolabel}$ of P4, and GTP_{Wlabel} of P3. These results suggest that GTP_{Wlabel} and $GTP_{Wolabel}$ are the most dominant information in the multimodal fusion model using respiration and gaze behavior. Note that the SLO of P3 (ranked fourth), SLO of P1 (ranked fifth), MAX of P1 (ranked sixth), MAX of P3 (ranked eighth), and AMP of P3 (ranked tenth) are the features of respiration. These results suggest that the features of respiration, such as SLO, MAX, and AMP, are also useful for predicting the next speaker in turn-taking. We revealed that the SLO, MAX, and AMP of inhalation differ between the listener who will become the next speaker and listeners who will not become the next speaker in turn-taking [10]. Our results are consistent with the knowledge obtained in related work. Comparing the information gain rate for predicting turn-keeping/turn-taking shows that the rank of the features of respiration is higher for predicting the next speaker in turn-taking.

6. DISCUSSION

We discuss the kind of situation where multimodal fusion using respiration and gaze behavior is useful for predicting the next speaker in multi-party meetings. We introduce one of the successful cases of multimodal fusion. Fig. 5 shows a conversational scene of turn-taking from P4 to P1. We discuss how the multimodal fusion is useful for predicting whether P1 will be the next speaker in this situation. The inhalation phase of each participant is shown by the yellow area in Fig. 5. In this situation, the result for the Respiration model is that turn-keeping will happen next. The result is not correct. The result for the Gaze model is that turn-taking will happen and P2 will be the next speaker. This prediction of turn-taking is correct. However, the next-speaker prediction is not correct. Therefore, the prediction model using only respiration or gaze behavior could not predict the next speaker correctly. In contrast, the result for

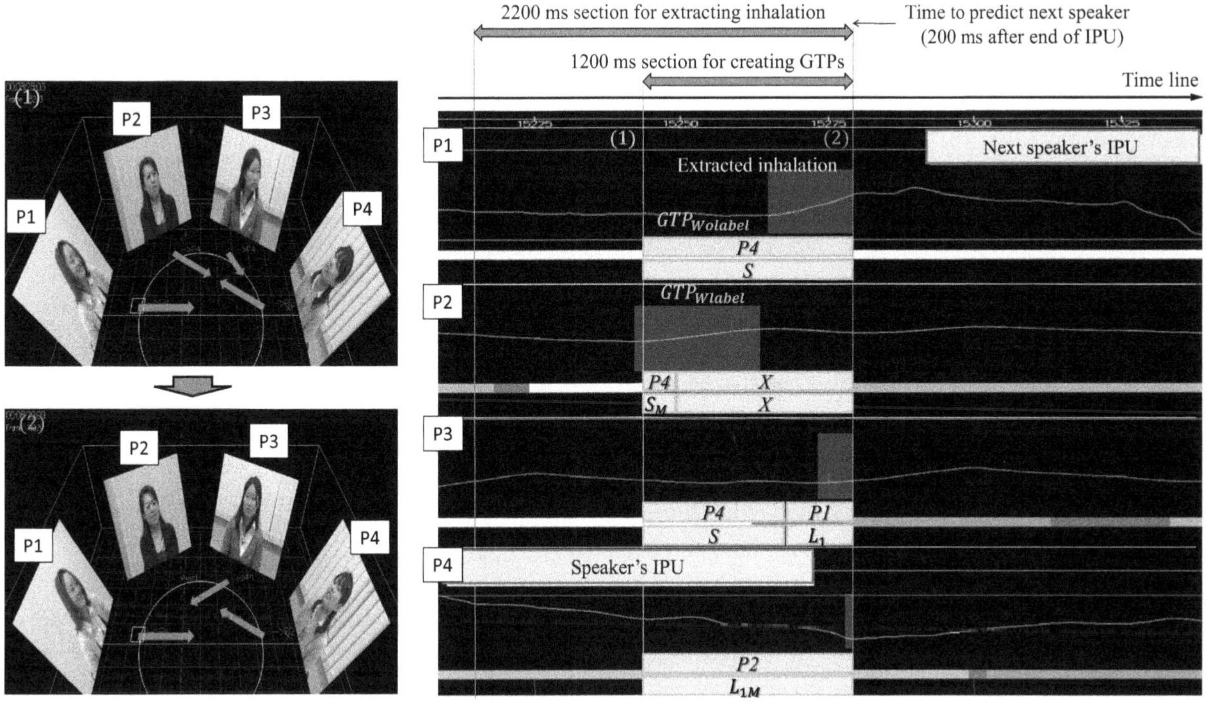

Figure 5: Sample situation of turn-taking with respiration and gaze behavior of each participant. Left: images captured by NTT MM-viewer that show each participant's face arranged in the sitting position and gaze object visually at the time of (1) and (2). Right: image captured by NTT MM-viewer that show each participant's RSP value and gaze object whose colors indicate each person gazed at.

the Respiration+Gaze model (Early fusion) and Respiration+Gaze model (Late fusion) is that turn-taking will happen and P1 will be a next speaker. This result is completely correct. Next, we discuss the kind of situation where the multimodal fusion using respiration and gaze behavior is useful for predicting the next speaker correctly.

Regarding the gaze behaviors during the 1200-ms section for creating GTPs, first, all listeners, P1, P2, and P3, look at P4, who is the speaker [see Fig. 5 (1)]. Finally, P1 continues to look at P4, P2 looks away from P4, P3 looks at P1 after looking at P4, and P4 continues to look at P2. In this case, the $P4$, $P4$-X, $P4$-$P1$, and $P2$ are created as $GTP_{Wolabel}$ of P1, P2, P3, and P4. The S, S_M-X, S-L_1, and L_{1M} are created as GTP_{Wlabel} of P1, P2, P3, and P4. The S_M-X of GTP_{Wlabel}, which means a listener looks away after making eye contact with the speaker, is typically seen in turn-taking situations. And the listener whose GTP_{Wlabel} is S_M-X will become the next speaker with a high probability [8]. For this reason, the Gaze model predicts that turn-taking will happen and P1 will be a next speaker.

Gaze behavior is an important interaction between humans for transferring the speaking turn. However, the transfer of the speaking turn will not always go as well as it did this time in multi-party meetings. In fact, P4 probably tried to give the turn to P2, but P2 didn't grab it.

On one hand, comparing the features of inhalation extracted between three listeners such as P1, P2, and P3, shows that SLO_{early} of P1 is the biggest among listeners. The SLO_{early} of P1, P2, and P3 may be useful for predicting the next speaker in turn-taking in this scene. The respiration conveys information about the intention or preliminary action to start to speak. As shown in the results of the evaluation of the prediction models in Section 5.2, the inhalation's characteristics are more helpful in predicting the next speaker in turn-taking than the gaze behavior's characteristics.

This is only one instance among many. There are many other situations in turn-taking and turn-keeping. We think that our implemented prediction model could made good use of the features of the different characteristics of respiration and gaze behavior acquired in various situations of turn-keeping and turn-taking by the machine learning technique. An analysis of the kinds of situations where the prediction model cannot predict the next speaker would be extremely fascinating.

We think that it is important to analyze phenomena and human interactions in multi-party meetings using multimodal information comprising physical nonverbal behavior and biological information such as respiration, which are completely different in quality. The present results will lead to new possibilities for the multimodal fusion of information extracted from different modalities, such as physical behavior and biological signals, and that are different in quality to demonstrate the mechanisms of human interactions and human states in the research of meeting analysis.

7. CONCLUSION AND FUTURE WORK

We integrated respiration and gaze behavior as a multimodal fusion to create models for predicting the next speaker in multi-party meetings. We implemented a model that predicts the next speaker at the end of an utterance using information about respiration and gaze behavior. The model entails a two-step processing. The first is to predict whether turn-keeping or turn-taking happens; the second is to predict the next speaker in turn-taking. We constructed prediction models with either respiration or gaze behavior and with both respiration and gaze behaviors as features and compared their performance. The results suggest that gaze behavior is more useful for predicting turn-keeping/turn-taking than respiration and that respiration is more useful for predicting the next speaker in turn-taking. The model with both respiration and gaze behaviors performs better than the one using only respiration or gaze behavior. Thus, it is revealed that multimodal fusion using respiration and gaze behavior is effective for predicting the next speaker in multi-party meetings. Our results will lead to new possibilities for multimodal fusion of information extracted from different modalities, such as physical behavior and biological signal, and that are different in quality to demonstrate the mechanism of human interactions and human states in the research of meeting analysis.

In future work, with the goal to demonstrate the mechanism of multi-party turn-taking and achieve highly accurate prediction, we plan to focus on the other modalities, such as head movement [7] and create a prediction model with multimodal fusion.

8. REFERENCES

[1] R. R. Bouckaert, E. Frank, M. A. Hall, G. Holmes, B. Pfahringer, P. Reutemann, and I. H. Witten. WEKA–experiences with a java open-source project. J. Machine Learning Research, 11:2533–2541, 2010.

[2] L. Chen and M. P. Harper. Multimodal floor control shift detection. In Proceedings of International Conference Multimodal Interaction, pages 15–22, 2009.

[3] I. de Kok and D. Heylen. Multimodal end-of-turn prediction in multi-party meetings. In Proceedings of International Conference Multimodal Interaction, pages 91–98, 2009.

[4] A. Dielmann, G. Garau, and H. Bourlard. Floor holder detection and end of speaker turn prediction in meetings. In ISCA, pages 2306–2309, 2010.

[5] L. Ferrer, E. Shriberg, and A. Stolcke. Is the speaker done yet? faster and more accurate end-of-utterance detection using prosody in human-computer dialog. In ICSLP, volume 3, pages 2061–2064, 2002.

[6] D. Gatica-Perez. Analyzing group interactions in conversations: a review. In MFI, pages 41–46, 2006.

[7] R. Ishii, S. Kumano, and K. Otsuka. Predicting next speaker using head movement in multi-party meetings. In Proceedings of International Conference on Acoustics, Speech, and Signal Processing (ICASSP), 2015.

[8] R. Ishii, K. Otsuka, S. Kumano, M. Matsuda, and J. Yamato. Predicting next speaker and timing from gaze transition patterns in multi-party meetings. In Proceedings of International Conference Multimodal Interaction, pages 79–86, 2013.

[9] R. Ishii, K. Otsuka, S. Kumano, and J. Yamato. Analysis and modeling of next speaking start timing based on gaze behavior in multi-party meetings. In ICASSP, pages 694–698, 2014.

[10] R. Ishii, K. Otsuka, S. Kumano, and J. Yamato. Analysis of respiration for prediction of "who will be next speaker and when?" in multi-party meetings. In Proceedings of International Conference Multimodal Interaction, pages 18–25, 2014.

[11] R. Ishii, K. Otsuka, S. Kumano, and J. Yamato. Analysis of timing structure of eye contact in turn-changing. In Proceedings of International Conference on Multimodal Interaction (ICMI), Workshop on Eye gaze in intelligent human machine interaction, pages 15–20, 2014.

[12] K. Jokinen, H. Furukawa, M. Nishida, and S. Yamamoto. Gaze and turn-taking behavior in casual conversational interactions. J. TiiS, 3(2):12, 2013.

[13] N. Jovanovic, R. op den Akker, and A. Nijholt. Addressee identification in face-to-face meetings. In Conf. European Chapter of the ACL, 2006.

[14] T. Kawahara, T. Iwatate, and K. Takanashii. Prediction of turn-taking by combining prosodic and eye-gaze information in poster conversations. In ISCA, 2012.

[15] S. S. Keerthi, S. K. Shevade, C. Bhattacharyya, and K. R. K. Murthy. Improvements to platt's smo algorithm for svm classifier design. Neural Computation, 13(3):637–649, 2001.

[16] A. Kendon. Some functions of gaze direction in social interaction. ActaPsychologica, 26:22–63, 1967.

[17] H. Koiso, Y. Horiuchi, S. Tutiya, A. Ichikawa, and Y. Den. An analysis of turn-taking and backchannels based on prosodic and syntactic features in japanese map task dialogs. In Language and Speech, volume 41, pages 295–321, 1998.

[18] K. Laskowski, J. Edlund, and M. Heldner. A single-port non-parametric model of turn-taking in multi-party conversation. In ICASSP, pages 5600–5603, 2011.

[19] G.-A. Levow. Turn-taking in mandarin dialogue: Interactions of tones and intonation. In SIGHAN, 2005.

[20] MIND MEDIA "NeXus-10 MARKII". http://www.mindmedia.info/CMS2014/products/systems/nexus-10-mkii.

[21] K. Otsuka. Conversational scene analysis. IEEE Signal Processing Magazine, 28:127–131, 2011.

[22] K. Otsuka, S. Araki, D. Mikami, K. Ishizuka, M. Fujimoto, and J. Yamato. Realtime meeting analysis and 3d meeting viewer based on omnidirectional multimodal sensors. In Proceedings of International Conference on Multimodal Interaction (ICMI), pages 219–220, 2009.

[23] H. Sacks, E. A. Schegloff, and G. Jefferson. A simplest systematics for the organisation of turn taking for conversation. Language, 50:696–735, 1974.

[24] D. Schlangen. From reaction to prediction experiments with computational models of turn-taking. In ISCA, pages 17–21, 2006.

Deciphering the Silent Participant

On the Use of Audio-Visual Cues for the Classification of Listener Categories in Group Discussions

Catharine Oertel
KTH
Royal Institute of Technology
Linstedtsvägen 44
Stockholm, Sweden
catha@kth.se

Kenneth A. Funes Mora
Idiap Research Institute
École Polytechnique Fédérale de Lausanne (EPFL)
Switzerland
kfunes@idiap.ch

Joakim Gustafson
KTH
Royal Institute of Technology
Linstedtsvägen 44
Stockholm, Sweden
jocke@speech.kth.se

Jean-Marc Odobez
Idiap Research Institute
École Polytechnique Fédérale de Lausanne (EPFL)
Switzerland
odobez@idiap.ch

ABSTRACT

Estimating a silent participant's degree of engagement and his role within a group discussion can be challenging, as there are no speech related cues available at the given time. Having this information available, however, can provide important insights into the dynamics of the group as a whole. In this paper, we study the classification of listeners into several categories (attentive listener, side participant and bystander). We devised a thin-sliced perception test where subjects were asked to assess listener roles and engagement levels in 15-second video-clips taken from a corpus of group interviews. Results show that humans are usually able to assess silent participant roles. Using the annotation to identify from a set of multimodal low-level features, such as past speaking activity, backchannels (both visual and verbal), as well as gaze patterns, we could identify the features which are able to distinguish between different listener categories. Moreover, the results show that many of the audio-visual effects observed on listeners in dyadic interactions, also hold for multi-party interactions. A preliminary classifier achieves an accuracy of 64%.

Categories and Subject Descriptors

H5.3 [**Information Interfaces and Presentation**]: Group and Organisation Interfaces—*Theory and models*

Keywords

listener categories; non-verbal cues; eye-gaze

ICMI'15, November 09-13, 2015, Seattle, WA, USA

ACM 978-1-4503-3912-4/15/11 ...$15.00.
http://dx.doi.org/10.1145/2818346.2820759.

1. INTRODUCTION

1.1 Motivation

In recent years, there has been a growing interest in studying the interaction between humans and robots [22, 27, 16]. In particular, in order for a human and machine to seamlessly communicate, a good understanding and modelling of the turn-taking phenomenon that underpin human communication [17] is essential. In this direction, there have been several attempts at building statistical or computational models of how turn-taking is coordinated (e.g., [21, 20]). On the output side, several virtual avatar systems have made use of a combination of cues from speech, posture shifts and head movements in order to generate convincing interactive behaviours including active listener ones [19, 7].

Yet, turn-taking modelling in itself is not sufficient when it comes to designing collaborative robots which detect and react appropriately to different dynamics in interactions. For example, participants might loose interest in the conversation. They might disengage and avert their attention and then suddenly, due to a shift in topic, re-engage again. All of these dynamics are encoded in multi-modal social signals that need to be well understood and decoded to make the appropriate interaction move. There are several studies which try to model the engagement of the individual participant andor the general involvement of the group e.g. [25, 12]. To our knowledge there is however, no study which focuses on the listener in a multi-party setting and tries to model the dynamics in listener states.

One can think of many applications where it would be useful to characterize the members of a group discussion that are not currently speaking. One is embodied or virtual tutors in collaborative settings with groups of students e.g. as in [18, 31]. Knowing more about the cognitive state of the participant could help to for example better target teacher interventions. A complicating factor for these kinds of applications is that a system in such contexts would need to handle multiple users and open domains [8]. The use of more robust low level cues could be therefore advantageous in such scenarios.

In the current paper, we therefore focus on the analysis of low-level audiovisual cues to characterize and classify silent participants in multiparty interactions.

1.2 Background and related work

In the following section, we are going to give a brief overview on literature concerning participation categories as well as research on audio-visual cues in conjunction with interaction modelling.

1.2.1 Participation Categories

Clark [9] building on Goffman [14] described participation categories in the following way. First of all he distinguishes between participants and non-participants. The former include all people taking part in the conversation, such as the speaker, the current addressee, but also people which are not currently being addressed but still belong to the circle of ratified participants; they are referred to as side–participants. Clark calls everyone else an "overhearer", "Overhearers" can be divided into two sub–categories namely "bystanders" and "eavesdroppers". A"Bystander" is a person who is openly present, but not part of the conversation whereas an "Eavesdropper" is overhearing the conversation without the other participants' awareness.

In the current paper, we are building up on these definitions but are adapting them for the specific task of listener classification. Therefore, we are exchanging the term addressee for "attentive listener"', and are otherwise only using the terms "side-participants" and "bystanders" in order to distinguish between different listener types. For the exact definition of listener categories given to the annotators please refer to section 2.4

1.2.2 Gaze Patterns

Concerning visual cues or more specifically gaze patterns we know from dyadic interactions that the speaker and listener are asymmetrical in that the listener looks at the speaker for long periods of time, while the speaker looks at the listener in short, but rather frequent periods [3]. Vertegaal [30] also found this pattern in multiparty interaction where participants gazed at an interlocutor 1.6 times more often while listening than while speaking. This means that it typically is the speaker that controls when mutual gaze occurs. Bavelas et al [4] found that listeners' verbal and nonverbal feedback was most common during periods of mutual gaze (gaze window). They also found that listener feedbacks often led to gaze aversion from the speaker, thus ending the periods of mutual gaze.

Gaze patterns are also reported to be related to participants' engagement level. Oertel and Salvi [26] for instance found that modelling whether participants were gazing at other participants or downwards described well the engagement level of participants. Moreover, Bednarik et al [5] found that participants with low engagement levels had long gaze durations at the same interlocutors (few gaze target shifts), while the engaged participants had shorter on-target gaze durations, but at a larger number of interlocutors (many gaze target shifts).

1.2.3 Verbal and Non-verbal backchannels

Up to this point in time, only few studies have been carried out exploring the relationship between visual and verbal backchannels. Truong et al. [29] for example find that in face-to-face conversation eye-gaze appears to be a cue for backchannels. They show that mutual gaze occurs significantly more often during visual backchannels. In a preliminary study Bertrand et. al.[6] noticed that when the speaker is gazing at the interlocutor, the latter produces a succession of gestural BCs. In their data they however did not find gestural backchannels followed by vocal backchannels during speaker's gaze towards the interlocutor.

None of these studies to our knowledge, however, investigates the occurrences of verbal and visual backchannel in relation to various listener types.

1.2.4 Dyadic versus multiparty conversations

Multiparty interaction differ from dyadic interaction in several regards [28]. One distinguishing feature is that in dyadic interactions there are only two different roles that and interlocutor can take on: speaker and listener. In multiparty interaction, humans may take on many different roles, such as speaker, addressee, side-participant and bystander or overhearers, as described above [9].

1.3 Contribution and paper organization

In the current paper we investigate human assessments of the listener categories attentive listeners, side-participants and bystanders and relate these to third-party assessment of listener's degree of engagement. First, we investigate whether gaze patterns found for dyadic interactions also hold for multi-party interactions. Second, we investigate to what degree it is possible to distinguish between different listener roles using only the low-level audio-visual cues *speech/no-speech*, *gaze* and *audiovisual backchannels*. Finally, we propose to use the different cues to train a classifier aiming at classifying the different listener categories and report on these results. The rest of the paper is organized as follows. In section 2 we present our corpus and thin slice perceptual test experiments. In section 3, we present the feature extracted from the corpus. Section 4 present our results while section 5 concludes the work.

2. OBSERVER ANNOTATIONS

In this section, we describe and motivate the experimental protocol used to collect people impressions on listeners. We start by describing the corpus of interactions we used, and then introduce the different elements of the web-based annotation experiments.

2.1 Corpus

In order to be able to investigate group dynamics we recorded a corpus of four-party interactions with a large number of sensors [24]. The main features are briefly summarized below.

Set-up and sensors. The set-up is shown in Fig. 1. Four people are interacting around a table, and their behaviours are recorded using several per-participant synchronized sensors: close-talking microphones, Windows Kinect 1 sensors positioned at around 0.8 meters of participants, and high resolution GoPro cameras.

Figure 1: The interaction setup.

Figure 2: Annotation input. Observers were provided with a 15 second video clip, as shown above.

Scenario. The multiparty conversation data is in the domain of group-interviews. More precisely, each interview session involved four participants: an interviewer also called moderator (post-doc) and three interviewees (PhDs). All participants were made aware of the interview goals: PhD students were told that the moderator's purpose in the interview would be to find out who would be the most qualified for a prestigious scholarship. They were told that the interviewer could either choose all of them, two, one or none.

The interviews consisted of different phases, with different interaction dynamics: self-introduction, PhD work description along with potential impact on society, and brainstorming on proposing a joint project. It has to be noted that the group never splits into subgroups. There are only few stretches of speech in which participants overlap, but these stretches are mainly due to simultaneous speaker speech and listener feedback. There are some stretches of one-to-one interactions, however, these cannot be called "dyadic" as such. A typical example of such a situation would be the participants are formally introducing themselves to the moderator, where, in actual fact, the participants do not only introduce themselves to the moderator but to the group as a whole. There was also quite some variation in the moderators behaviour. Some moderators behaved as "Attentive Listeners" while others purely as "Bystanders".

Dataset. The corpus consists of five interactions of groups of four. Each interaction lasted for about an hour, which results in approximately 5 hours of recordings of multimodal and multiparty data.

2.2 Thin slices

To obtain annotations about listeners, we adopt a thin slice approach [1]. Sample video clips containing at least one non-speaking person are extracted from the corpus and shown to the annotators who then have to fill a questionnaire. The slice duration was selected as a compromise between having segments long enough to base judgement on sufficient evidence, and short enough to avoid mixed behaviours. Following previous works on engagement [5] or interest-level inference [13], we opted for a duration of 15 seconds.

2.3 Visual clip content

The video content displayed to annotators is shown in Fig. 2. It is composed of the video data from the Kinect sensors of each participant, transformed and joined together in order to provide viewers with a feeling of the 3D setup, and in particular get a better grasp of the gaze attention targets. A top-view table layout at the bottom of the display further allows to identify the geometric relation between participants as well as the listener to annotate.

As an important aspect of the experiment, no audio was added to the video content. This served two main purposes. First, this removed the influence of the semantic speech content on the understanding of the listeners' types, and helped viewers to concentrate on the non verbal behaviour content. Note however that the video resolution was high enough for people to identify who was speaking. Secondly, since annotators would watch several windows from the same interactions, this was avoiding people to identify the role played by participant, and in particular, the moderator role.

2.4 Questionnaire, protocol and annotators

Our primary goal was to obtain annotations about the listener type in each clip. As motivated earlier the proposed categories and their definition as given to annotators were the following:

- Attentive Listener (ALi): An attentive listener is a person, who is most likely to start speaking after the current speaker.
- Side Participant (SPa): A side participant is a person who is part of the group of potential future speakers, but is probably not the next speaker.
- Bystander (Bys): A bystander is a person who the group of potential future speakers is aware of, but who they do not expect to speak in the near future. The bystander acts as an observer rather than a potential future speaker.

In addition, to assess whether the perception of the listener type matched other dimensions, the following ratings were also asked:

- Engagement (Eng): rate the listener's degree of engagement in the conversation using the seven point scale, ordered from not engaged (1) to highly engaged (7);
- Expected time to speak (ETS): rate at what point in time you expect the listener to speak next using the seven point scale: now (1); soon in the next 30 seconds (3); within the next minute (5) never (7).

Finally, besides the description of the overall task, interaction setup, and questions and ratings, annotators were also instructed to preferably watch the clip at least twice, e.g. once focusing on the specified participant and the second time focusing on the group, and only afterwards make their ratings. In addition, 5 samples selected to present a diversity of listener behaviours were asked to be annotated (but not used in analysis) to have users getting accustomed to the content and display. In total there was a pool of 25 annotators. They were not compensated for the time spent. We allotted round 40 minutes worth of annotations per annotator. All of the annotators were naive to the research topic and mainly sampled from a pool of post-graduate students who shared a similar cultural background to that of the participants.

2.5 Annotation window selection

As not all the 5 hours of data can be annotated, windows were selected to maximize diversity of situation and listeners as follows. In each window, the role of each participant was defined as the moderator (Mo), and for each interviewee, as speaker (Sp) if they spoke (which excluded backchannels), or as listener. The latter was further separated as La and Lb listeners according to whether the duration between the last time that they spoke and the start of the window (denoted **LT**) was lower or greater than 20 seconds. Window were then assigned a category according to the role combinations of the 3 interviewees: (Sp,La,La), (Sp,La,Lb), (Sp,Lb,Lb), (Sp,Sp,La), (Sp,Sp,Lb).

Using these definitions, 600 windows were sampled according to the following rules: i) windows where speakers spoke for less than 3 seconds were discarded; ii) windows were sampled uniformly across the 5 interviews and the 5 category types; iii) given a window, the listener to be annotated was sampled uniformly amongst the pool of listeners, which included the moderator.

3. DATA PROCESSING

In the following subsections we first describe the audio and visual cues which were extracted automatically or semi-automatically by processing the audio-visual data. In a second step, we introduce the different features that were computed from these cues to characterize the listeners in each temporal window of the thin slice experiments.

3.1 Automatic and semi-automatic cue extraction

3.1.1 *Speaking turns and audio backchannels*

Voice Activity Detection Voice Activity Detection (VAD) of the interlocutors was carried using a speech recognizer. The obtained voicing segments were manually checked by a phonetician for their accuracy. In the current paper we distinguish between two types voicing segments: "backchannels" and "normal speech". A voicing segment had to fulfil two conditions to be annotated as a backchannel: 1) it had to be a very short utterance as defined by [15] and 2) it had to be surrounded by "other speech". All other segments were classified as "normal speech".

Turn Detection Turns are inferred from the speaking activity. Only one participant can hold the floor at a given time time. A turn is then maintained until another participant talks for more than 1 second. In that case, the turn is assigned to that participant from the moment he/she starts speaking. The time in between is not assigned to any participant. In the case of an overlap, i.e., the turn is handed to the second participant only if the first participant stops talking before the second finishes. In that case, the turn change is defined at the instant the first participant ends talking.

3.1.2 *Gaze annotations and labels.*

As manual annotation of gaze is tedious, we followed a similar approach to [10] that was shown to provide up to 90% gaze coding accuracy in dyadic interactions. We extended this method to the group case, and used as gaze estimation method the code of an improved version of [11].

First, we calibrated the setup to obtain a single world coordinate system in which it is possible to refer all measured quantities. This was achieved in a similar way than [10], by exploited fitting planes to wall measures and the prior on sensor pose and locations.

Multi-party gaze coding. Looking at other participants from participant i was measured by leveraging the availability of 3D information as follows. We defined a gaze reference vector $\hat{\mathbf{v}}_i^k$ for looking at each other person k. Provided that the gaze estimation output is $\mathbf{v}_i^{\mathbf{h}}$, we define the gaze angle from the participant k as:

$$\psi_i^k = \arccos\left(\mathbf{v}_i^{\mathbf{h}} \cdot \hat{\mathbf{v}}_i^k\right) \tag{1}$$

from which we can derive the gaze target T_i for the participant i as:

$$T_i = \begin{cases} c & \text{if } \psi_i^c < \tau \\ -1 & \text{otherwise} \end{cases}, \tag{2}$$

where $c = \arg\min_k\{\psi_i^k\}$, i.e., the closest participant in terms of gaze direction, and "-1" is the *background* class, which indicates that the participant is not looking at any of the targets.

Final gaze label set. So far we have discriminated between looking at any of the participant or elsewhere (background). However, further splitting the background class into sub-classes such as: "up", "down", or "mid-targets" could be informative, as, for instance, [2] showed that different gaze-away directions could be more characteristic of different functions (turn taking, management, cognitive load, intimacy, etc). In the current case, we further added looking down as a label which may indicate disengagement. This was obtained by monitoring the pitch angle in the world coordinate system. So, in summary, the gaze of people was labelled according to the following set $\mathcal{G}$ of labels: each of the three other participants, Up, Down, Others.

3.1.3 *Visual backchannel (nodding)*

To annotate the visual backchannels, we used an approach similar to [23] developed for nodding recognition from video data. More precisely, we used the head orientation (pan, tilt, roll) from the head pose tracker to derive head pose dynamics. The resulting time-series were used as input to a set of Gabor filters and then classified as nod or not nod using a SVM classifier using radial-basis functions. While the method has difficulties to identify nods of speakers, its reliability to infer nods from listeners is usually high, with an accuracy of more than 80% measured on natural interactions.

3.2 Listener characterization

To characterize the listeners and interaction situations, we extracted for each listeners and for each clip a set of audio-visual (AV) features related to gaze and backchannels. More precisely, we computed:

- Visual backchannels (VisBack): the number of nods detected in the window duration;

- Audio backchannels (AudioBack): the number of verbal backchannel uttered by the listener in the window duration;
- Gaze at speaker(s) (GazeAtSpeak): percentage of window frames in which the listener is looking at the person currently speaking;
- Gaze received from speaker(s) (GazeFromSpeak): percentage of window frames in which the actual speaker look at the listener;
- Mutual gaze with speaker (MutGazeSpeaker): percentage of window frames in which the listener and the current speaker look at each other;
- Gaze down (GazeDown): defined as the percentage of window frame where the listener look down/in front of him. Similarly to Andrist et al [2] who showed that different gaze-away directions could be more characteristic of different functions, here we hypothesized that looking down (rather than elsewhere or at any participant) could be a visible indicator of bystanders or side participants disengagement.

4. RESULTS AND DISCUSSIONS

In this Section we present our results. We first comment on the results of the perception annotations. In Section 4.2, we analyse which of the cues distinguish the different listener types, and comment on the relationship with findings in the literature. In Section 4.3, we analyse verbal and visual backchannel during periods of mutual gaze. We relate those findings to findings reported for dyadic findings in the literature. Finally, in Section 4.4, we present some classification results.

4.1 Perception Test Analysis

Video frames were annotated by different amount of people, ranging from 5 to no annotators. The majority of video samples received 4 annotations. We only considered the samples which received at least 3 annotations, and assigned them to different categories according to the annotation configuration: single class (ALi, SPa, Bys) if at least 3 annotators agreed on this class. In-between categories if there was a tie between the 2 categories, and no vote for the 3rd one. This corresponds only to 2-2 ties in 4 annotator samples. The "no majority" class was assigned to the other cases.

Results are shown in Table 1. As can be seen, in 67.9% of the cases, there was a majority for a class. In addition, in the case of ties, these corresponded mainly to the plausible ones: ALi-SPa and SPa-Bys for 15% of the cases, as opposed to confusing an attentive listener with a bystander (ALi-Bys). Samples with at least one vote in each category were observed in 15% of the cases.

These results show that 1) people are usually able to agree on different listener categories; 2) do so based on visual information alone; and 3) these categories form some kind of continuum. Indeed, as will generally be shown below, the measured cues for these in-between categories often correspond to values falling in between the values taken by their 'pure' listener counterparts.

We further analysed the variation of a) Eng and b) ETS for the different listener categories. Results are depicted in Figure 3. ANOVA tests revealed that the listener categories had an effect on both ENG F(4,314)=114.8 ($p<0.001$) as well as ETS F(4,314) = 309.2 ($p<0.001$). A Bonferroni post-hoc test corroborated that the ALi was rated significantly higher in terms of ENG than the SPa ($p<0.001$), which was himself rated significantly higher than the Bys ($p<0.001$). Similarly, the ALi was estimated to speak significantly sooner than the SPa($p<0.001$) and the SPa significantly sooner than the Bys($p<0.001$).

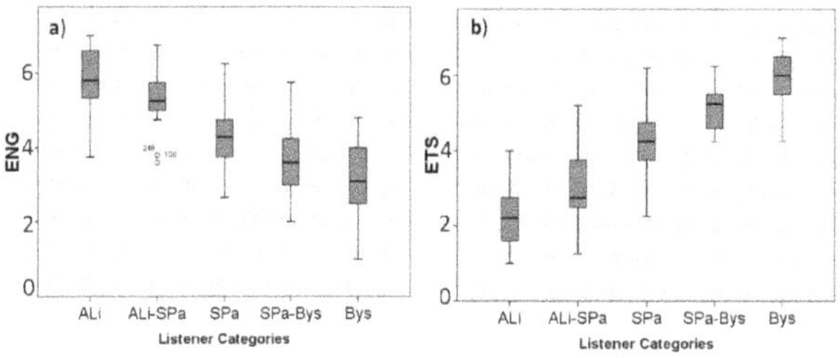

Figure 3: Eng and ETS results for different listener categories.

These results show that, as expected, observers were consistent in evaluating the degree of engagement and the time-to-speak. Still, the large variance measured also shows that there was quite some variability amongst them in general.

4.2 AV Analysis of Prototypical Listeners

Methodology. In this section, we evaluate how much different audio, visual, or audio-visual cues are characteristic of listeners. To do so, we compute the mean and standard deviations of the cue for each of the annotation configuration (five first columns of Table 1). Note that this comprises the in-between listener categories configuration, to better illustrate that cue values measured in these cases are indeed a mix of the values measured from the prototypical samples. Note however that to test the significance of the potential differences of the cues between the different prototypical listeners, we applied significance tests only on the purer samples (i.e having at least 3 agreeing annotators).

Gaze pattern analysis. We first evaluate how much gaze is different across the listener categories. Figure 4 depicts gaze distributions for the different features. Surprisingly, an ANOVA test revealed that there was no significant effect of the listener categories on the amount of "Gaze At Speaker", indicating that observers did not distinguish listeners based on their lack of attention to the speaker. However, there was a significant effect of the listener category on the amount of gaze from the active speaker F(4,314)=34.5, $p<0.001$. A Bonferroni post-hoc test revealed that the ALi receives significantly more gaze from the speaker than the SPa ($p<0.001$), and the SPa more than the Bys ($p<0.001$). Moreover, there was significant effect of the listener categories on the Mutual Gaze with the Speaker F(4,314)=20.2 $p<0.001$. A Bonferroni post-hoc test revealed that the ALi had significantly more mutual gaze with the speaker than the SPa($p<0.001$) and that SPa has share significantly more mutual gaze with the speaker than the Bys ($p<0.01$).

Overall, this is in line with Vertegaal [30] who found that in multiparty interaction participants gazed at an interlocutor 1.6 times more often while listening than while speaking, meaning that it typically is the speaker that controls when mutual gaze occurs. However, it also extends Vertegaal's findings in that it further describes the gaze distribution between the speaker and different listener categories. While our findings confirm that it is indeed the speaker who controls when mutual gaze occurs, they also show that the

Table 1: Distribution of samples across the different annotation configuration (denoted AConfig). NotEnAnnot stands for not enough annotation (i.e. the sample was annotated by less than 3 people). The percentages are given with respect to the number of samples with enough annotation.

AConfig	ALi	SPa	Bys	ALi-SPa	SPa-Bys	ALi-Bys	No Maj.	NotEnAnnot
Amount	62 (16.1 %)	82 (21.2%)	118 (30.6%)	21 (5.4%)	37 (9.6%)	7 (1.8%)	59 (15.3%)	214

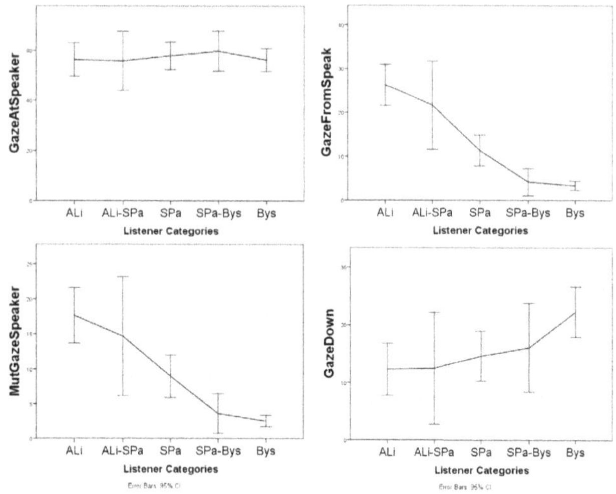

Figure 4: Gaze in Prototypical Listener Categories. See Section 3.2 for the definition of these measures.

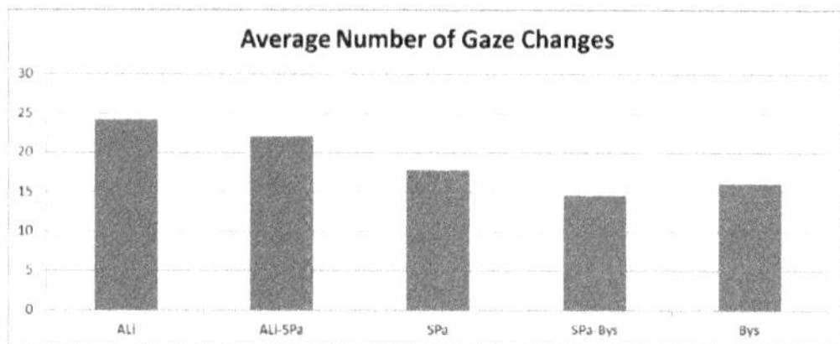

Figure 5: Number of Gaze Changes

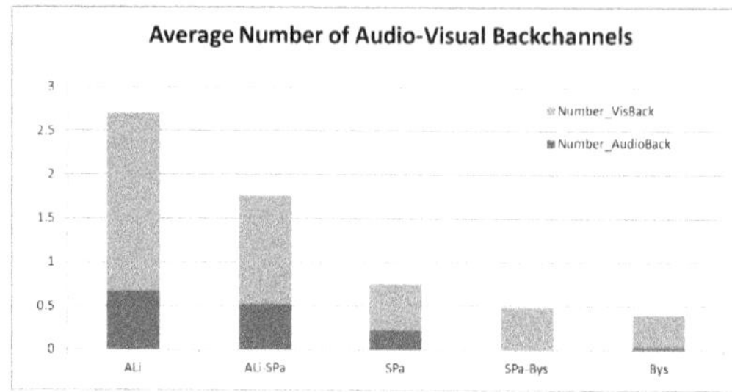

Figure 6: Number of Audio and Visual Backchannels

speaker does not establish mutual gaze with all possible interlocutors equally but establishes mutual gaze most often with the ALi, who is the listener who is the most engaged of all listeners, and also indeed the one who most probably has spoken last (as will be shown later, cf Fig. 7).

Finally, there was a significant effect of the listener categories on GazeDown $F(4,314)=2.9$. A Bonferroni posthoc test revealed that the ALi looks significantly less down than the Bys($p<0.05$). This is in line but also extends the findings of [26]. Oertel and Salvi found that in comparison to any other feature, "presence" (the feature describing whether participants were gazing at other participants or averting their gaze upwards or downwards) was the feature which distinguished best between low and high group involvement. We make a similar finding in that, also in this study, the more engaged participants are the ones who look more towards other participants than averting their gaze downwards. However, Oertel and Salvi did not distinguish between speakers and different listener categories and when participants are estimated to speak again. Interestingly, this study thus adds that silent participants who are more often averting their gaze downwards are judged to speak further in the future than silent participants who gaze towards another participant.

Gaze changes. Figure 5 depicts the number of gaze changes per listener category. As can be seen the Attentive Listener has the highest number of gaze changes, followed by the Side Participant and then finally by the Bistander. Although there is an apparent trend the χ 2 test does not show a significant effect.

Nevertheless, this trend, while not significant, is in line with findings of Bednarik et al [5] who found that participants with low engagement level had long gaze durations at the same interlocutors (few gaze target shifts), while the engaged participants had shorter on-target gaze durations, but at a higher number of interlocutors (many gaze target shifts). The fact that the number of gaze changes across listener categories, and indirectly listener engagement level, was not significant in our study might be due to two reasons. First of all, given the limited group size (three main interlocutors engaged in the conversation in general), showing too obviously disengagement might have been perceived as being rude by the others and might have lead the participants to try and minimize such disengagement cue. The second reason might be due to the fact that participants knew that they were being monitored and evaluated by the moderator and thus should try to appear as best as they could.

Backchannels. Figure 6 depicts the number of audio and visual backchannels per listener category. It can be observed that both the number of non-verbal backchannels A χ 2 (36, N=319)=107.338 ($p<0.001$) as well as verbal backchannels decreases significantly χ 2 (20, N=319)=74.070 ($p<0.001$) from Attentive Listener to Bystander. It is also noticeable that in all listener categories the number of visual backchannels is higher than the number of verbal ones. This fact is most pronounced for the Attentive Listener.

4.3 Backchannels during Mutual Gaze

Given the differences observed in amount of backchannels, we further analysed during which periods the production of backchannel in the corpus was more important. Following Bavelas et al [4] who found that listeners' production of verbal and non-verbal feedback was around height times higher than change during mutual gaze in dyadic situations, we extended this work to our multi-party case and counted the

Table 2: Listener backchannel behaviours according to the gaze activity with respect to the "active" speaker I) Mutual gaze between the listener and the speaker. II) The listener gazes at the speaker. III) The speaker gazes at the listener. IV) Other. Table a) shows the estimated number of backchannels per minute; b) reports the total count of backchannels in all 5 interviews; while c) reports the total cumulated time of the different gaze situations states.

a)

Modality	I	II	III	IV	Chance
Audio	2.728	0.378	2.627	0.508	0.59
Visual	5.233	1.601	4.970	3.327	2.44
AudioVisual	7.960	1.980	7.597	3.835	3.03

b)

Modality	I	II	III	IV
Audio	147	90	83	69
Visual	282	381	157	452
AudioVisual	429	471	240	521

c)

	I	II	III	IV
-	3233.5	14274.8	1895.4	8151.7

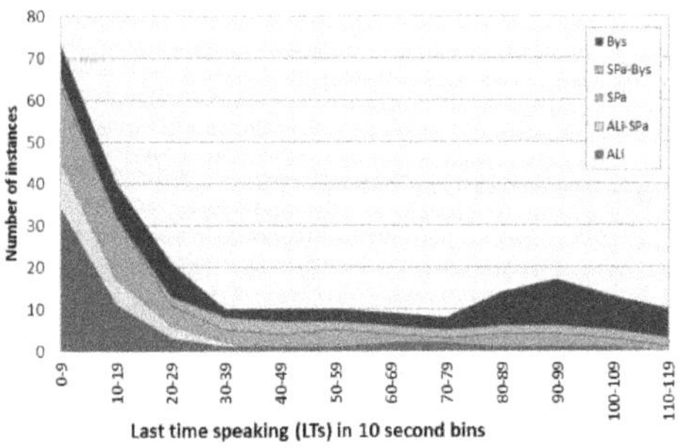

Figure 7: LTS Distribution

number of backchannels happening during specific periods of gaze patterns between the speaker and listener, as reported in Table 2. Using these numbers, we found out that in our data, the same effect was observable, though less pronounced: comparing columns (I) and the Chance one in Table 2a, we can note that it is 4.6 times higher than chance to have an audio verbal backchannel during mutual gaze, and 2.14 times higher for the visual (i.e. nods) one.

However, from Table 2a, an interesting finding that actually differs from Bavelas is that, in fact it is the speaker's gaze, that controls the amount of backchannels: backchannels are most common when the speaker looks at the listener - regardless if the backchanneling listener is gazing back at the speaker or not (around 7 AV backchannel per minute on average), whereas the least amount of backchannels (around 2 per minute) are obtained when the backchanneling listener gazes at the speaker, who looks at somebody else.

4.4 Predicting Listener Categories

In this section, we present our early experiment on classifying the different listeners.

Prediction using LT, defined as the duration between the last time when the listener last spoke and the start of the analysis window. Indeed, one hypothesis of the study was that the more recently a listener had spoken, the more attentive he would be. Surprisingly, given that observers did not have this information, this hypothesis was verified in practice. Figure 7 illustrates the distribution of LTs across the different listener categories. It can be observed that the greatest accumulation of ALis can be found in the period between 0 to 30 seconds, whereas the reverse is true for Bys. The majority of listeners rated as Bystanders spoke last between 70 to 120 seconds before the start of the analysis window. The distribution of SPa is more evenly spread with a slightly higher percentage in the period of 0 to 30 seconds. We used LT alone to perform classification using a decision tree. We obtained a classification accuracy of 52.8%.

SVM prediction. To test whether the found effects of the different cues depending on the prototypical listener categories would also be sufficient for classification, we used Support Vector Machine (SVM) classifiers based on the RBF kernel. We applied a grid-search with 10-fold cross validation to identify the hyper-parameters. We used one-vs-one classifiers. As features, in addition to LT, we used all those discussed in the above sections which were shown to have a significant effect (GazeFromSpeak, MutGazeSpeaker, MutGazeListeners, GazeDown, AudioBack, VisBack). We obtained an accuracy of 64.4%. It has to be noted, however, that a complicating factor was the fact that listener categories were not evenly balanced in terms of sample size. The sample size of Bys instances, for example, was higher than the sample size of the SPas. Moreover, the category of SPa lay in-between the other two categories which made classification of the category of Spa more challenging. When evenly balancing the classes in terms of sample size, by reducing the sample set to 62 samples per class, the accuracy is reduced to 54.1%, which corresponds to an 21% improvement over majority class classification (33.3% acc.), which was nevertheless disappointing.

5. CONCLUSION AND DISCUSSION

This paper investigated the characterization of listeners categories in multi-party situations. To this end, we relied on a corpus that we recorded using a range of sensors (close-talking microphones, Kinect), allowing for the automatic retrieval of accurate voice activity, eye gaze and visual backchannels annotations. This avoided the need for costly and time consuming manual annotations. We further proposed a thin-slice approach to collect observer annotations about three listener categories. Results showed that observers usually agreed on their labelling, making it possible to identify these categories from discriminative low-level audio visual cues. The advantage of low-level cues in comparison to high-level is that they are more robust and domain independent.

Our work builds on research carried out for dyadic scenarios, and extends it the multi-party case, using substantially more amounts of data than reported in previous findings about listeners. For instance, we extend Vertegaal's findings by further describing the gaze distribution between the speaker and different listener categories, and showed that silent participants who are more often averting their gaze downwards are judged to speak further in the future than silent participants who gaze towards another participant. Or we were able to extend to the multiparty case Bavelas findings that listener backchannel occur more during mutual gaze between a speaker and a listener. Indeed, in this later case, as one specific finding of our work, we showed that what might matter even more to trigger listener's backchannels is the speaker gaze, regardless of the listener's own gaze. Finally, a preliminary classifier achieves an accuracy of 64.4% in distinguishing between prototypical listener categories.

The work can be improved in several ways. For instance, while we believe that the audio-visual models of listeners we have extracted are quite representative of listeners in general discussions, it would be interesting to verify whether they hold (and which feature are affected) in other settings (e.g. standing people) or other scenarios. On the classification side, performance could be increased by increasing the sample size, by adding prosodic analysis of the verbal backchannels, by extending the feature sets to include further multi-modal cues (and better characterizing the dynamics as compared to the aggregation statistics currently used), or by studying the impact of changing the analysis window size.

Acknowledgments. The authors would like to acknowledge the support from the Swedish Research Council Project VR(2013-4935) and the Swiss National Science Foundation (Project G3E, 200020_153085) `www.snf.ch`.

6. REFERENCES

[1] N. Ambady, F. J. Bernieri, and J. A. Richeson. Toward a histology of social behavior: Judgmental accuracy from thin slices of the behavioral stream. *Advances in experimental social psychology*, 32:201–271, 2000.

[2] S. Andrist, X. Z. Tan, M. Gleicher, and B. Mutlu. Conversational gaze aversion for humanlike robots. *Proceedings of the 2014 ACM/IEEE international conference on Human-robot interaction - HRI '14*, pages 25–32, 2014.

[3] M. Argyle and M. Cook. Gaze and mutual gaze. 1976.

[4] J. B. Bavelas and J. Gerwing. The listener as addressee in face-to-face dialogue. *International Journal of Listening*, 25(3):178–198, 2011.

[5] R. Bednarik, S. Eivazi, and M. Hradis. Gaze and conversational engagement in multiparty video conversation: an annotation scheme and classification of high and low levels of engagement. In *Proceedings of the 4th workshop on eye gaze in intelligent human machine interaction*, page 10. ACM, 2012.

[6] R. Bertrand, G. Ferré, P. Blache, R. Espesser, and S. Rauzy. Backchannels revisited from a multimodal perspective. In *Auditory-visual Speech Processing*, pages 1–5, 2007.

[7] E. Bevacqua, M. Mancini, and C. Pelachaud. A listening agent exhibiting variable behaviour. In *Intelligent Virtual Agents*, pages 262–269. Springer, 2008.

[8] D. Bohus and E. Horvitz. Dialog in the open world: platform and applications. In *Proceedings of the 2009 international conference on Multimodal interfaces*, pages 31–38. ACM, 2009.

[9] H. H. Clark. *Using language*, volume 1996. Cambridge university press Cambridge, 1996.

[10] K. A. Funes Mora, L. S. Nguyen, D. Gatica-Perez, and J.-M. Odobez. A Semi-Automated System for Accurate Gaze Coding in Natural Dyadic Interactions. In *ICMI*, Sydney, Dec. 2013.

[11] K. A. Funes Mora and J.-M. Odobez. Gaze Estimation From Multimodal Kinect Data. In *Computer Vision and Pattern Recognition Workshops*, pages 25–30, June 2012.

[12] D. Gatica-Perez, I. McCowan, and S. Bengio. Detecting Group Interest-Level in Meetings. In *Proceedings. (ICASSP '05). IEEE International Conference on Acoustics, Speech, and Signal Processing, 2005.*, volume 1, pages 489–492. Ieee, 2005.

[13] D. Gatica-Perez, I. A. McCowan, D. Zhang, and S. Bengio. Detecting group interest-level in meetings. In *IEEE Int. Conf. on Acoustics, Speech, and Signal Processing (ICASSP)*, 2005.

[14] E. Goffman. *Interaction Ritual: Essays in Face to Face Behavior*. AldineTransaction, 1967.

[15] M. Heldner, J. Edlund, A. Hjalmarsson, and K. Laskowski. Very short utterances and timing in turn-taking. In *INTERSPEECH*, pages 2837–2840, 2011.

[16] T. Kanda, R. Sato, N. Saiwaki, and H. Ishiguro. A two-month field trial in an elementary school for long-term human–robot interaction. *Robotics, IEEE Transactions on*, 23(5):962–971, 2007.

[17] A. Kendon. Some functions of gaze-direction in social interaction. *Acta psychologica*, 26:22–63, 1967.

[18] I. Leite, M. McCoy, D. Ullman, N. Salomons, and B. Scassellati. Comparing models of disengagement in individual and group interactions. In *Proceedings of the Tenth Annual ACM/IEEE International Conference on Human-Robot Interaction*, pages 99–105. ACM, 2015.

[19] R. Maatman, J. Gratch, and S. Marsella. Natural behavior of a listening agent. In *Intelligent Virtual Agents*, pages 25–36. Springer, 2005.

[20] R. Meena, G. Skantze, and J. Gustafson. Data-driven models for timing feedback responses in a map task dialogue system. *Computer Speech & Language*, 28(4):903–922, 2014.

[21] L.-P. Morency, I. de Kok, and J. Gratch. A probabilistic multimodal approach for predicting listener backchannels. *Autonomous Agents and Multi-Agent Systems*, 20(1):70–84, 2010.

[22] B. Mutlu and J. Forlizzi. Robots in organizations: the role of workflow, social, and environmental factors in human-robot interaction. In *Human-Robot Interaction (HRI), 2008 3rd ACM/IEEE International Conference on*, pages 287–294. IEEE, 2008.

[23] L. Nguyen, J.-M. Odobez, and D. Gatica-Perez. Using Self-Context for Multimodal Detection of Head Nods in Face-to-Face Interactions. In *ACM Int Conf. on Multimodal Interaction (ICMI), Santa Monica*, Oct. 2012.

[24] C. Oertel, K. Funes, S. Sheikhi, J.-M. Odobez, and J. Gustafson. Who will get the grant ? In *Int. Conf. on Multimodal Interaction Workshop on Understanding and modeling multiparty, multimodal interactions*, 2014.

[25] C. Oertel and G. Salvi. A gaze-based method for relating group involvement to individual engagement in multimodal multiparty dialogue. In *Proceedings of the 15th ACM on International conference on multimodal interaction - ICMI '13*, pages 99–106, New York, New York, USA, 2013. ACM Press.

[26] C. Oertel and G. Salvi. A gaze-based method for relating group involvement to individual engagement in multimodal multiparty dialogue. In *International Conference on Multimodal Interaction*, 2013.

[27] A. M. Sabelli, T. Kanda, and N. Hagita. A conversational robot in an elderly care center: an ethnographic study. In *Human-Robot Interaction (HRI), 2011 6th ACM/IEEE International Conference on*, pages 37–44. IEEE, 2011.

[28] D. Traum and J. Rickel. Embodied agents for multi-party dialogue in immersive virtual worlds. In *Proceedings of the first international joint conference on Autonomous agents and multiagent systems: part 2*, pages 766–773. ACM, 2002.

[29] K. P. Truong, R. Poppe, I. de Kok, and D. Heylen. A multimodal analysis of vocal and visual backchannels in spontaneous dialogs. In *Proc. INTERSPEECH, Florence*. International Speech Communication Association, 2011.

[30] R. Vertegaal. The gaze groupware system: mediating joint attention in multiparty communication and collaboration. In *Proceedings of the SIGCHI conference on Human Factors in Computing Systems*, pages 294–301. ACM, 1999.

[31] R. Zhao, A. Papangelis, and J. Cassell. Towards a dyadic computational model of rapport management for human-virtual agent interaction. In *Intelligent Virtual Agents*, pages 514–527. Springer, 2014.

Retrieving Target Gestures Toward Speech Driven Animation with Meaningful Behaviors

Najmeh Sadoughi, Carlos Busso
Multimodal Signal Processing (MSP) Laboratory
The University of Texas at Dallas, Richardson TX 75080, USA
Emails: nxs137130@utdallas.edu, busso@utdallas.edu

ABSTRACT

Creating believable behaviors for *conversational agents* (CAs) is a challenging task, given the complex relationship between speech and various nonverbal behaviors. The two main approaches are rule-based systems, which tend to produce behaviors with limited variations compared to natural interactions, and data-driven systems, which tend to ignore the underlying semantic meaning of the message (e.g., gestures without meaning). We envision a hybrid system, acting as the behavior realization layer in rule-based systems, while exploiting the rich variation in natural interactions. Constrained on a given target gesture (e.g., head nod) and speech signal, the system will generate novel realizations learned from the data, capturing the timely relationship between speech and gestures. An important task in this research is identifying multiple examples of the target gestures in the corpus. This paper proposes a data mining framework for detecting gestures of interest in a motion capture database. First, we train One-class *support vector machines* (SVMs) to detect candidate segments conveying the target gesture. Second, we use *dynamic time alignment kernel* (DTAK) to compare the similarity between the examples (i.e., target gesture) and the given segments. We evaluate the approach for five prototypical hand and head gestures showing reasonable performance. These retrieved gestures are then used to train a speech-driven framework based on *dynamic Bayesian networks* (DBNs) to synthesize these target behaviors.

Categories and Subject Descriptors

H.5.2 [**Information Interfaces and Presentation**]: User Interfaces—*Conversational Agent*

Keywords

Gesture retrieval, conversational agents, speech-driven animations

ICMI'15, November 09-13, 2015, Seattle, WA, USA.
© 2015 ACM ISBN 978-1-4503-3912-4/15/11 ...$15.00.
DOI: http://dx.doi.org/10.1145/2818346.2820750.

1. INTRODUCTION

Verbal and nonverbal behaviors are an important aspect of human communications. While speech provides verbal communication, people use gestures to clarify, complement and emphasize their intentions and thoughts. Gestures may convey the same meaning as speech, or they can complement and enrich the message [22]. While 90% of gestures occur while speaking [22], nonverbal behaviors can occur while the subject is listening, providing suitable feedback to the speaker (e.g., backchannel communication). *conversational agents* (CAs) aiming to replicate human-like behaviors should carefully model the complex relationship between gestures and speech.

There are two main approaches used to synthesize human-like gestures: rule-based systems, and data-driven methods [11]. Both approaches have advantages and disadvantages. Rule-based systems derive animations relying on semantic analysis of speech, creating appropriate rules to synthesize behaviors that respond to the message [8, 15]. Since rule-based systems do not capture the large variability of gestures and its dependency on speech, these approaches, may result in movements that seem repetitive and not closely synchronized with the prosodic structure in speech [11]. Data-driven approaches learn the behaviors from available recordings, capturing a larger range of variability in the behaviors. Gestures are tightly connected with prosody (energy, intonation, duration) [6]. Therefore, previous studies have used speech prosody features to derive the gestures of the speaker [4,5,10,17,18,20]. While gestures generated by these methods may be perfectly synchronized with speech, they may not appropriately respond to the underlying content in the message (e.g., nodding for negations). In these cases, the CA will convey behaviors without meaning, reducing the role of gestures in the communication. There are studies that combine the rule-based and data-driven approaches to create the behaviors [21, 26, 29].

Kopp et al. [15] proposed a three layer framework for an *embodied conversational agent* (ECA) composed of intent planning, behavior planning, and behavior realization. The last layer generates the behavior, determining the parameters associated with the amplitude and the synchronization points of the behavior in time. We envision a behavior realization system that bridges gap between the rule-based systems and data-driven approaches, exploiting their benefits and overcoming their limitations. For a given message, our proposed model will generate speech-driven gestures that are constrained by specific behaviors associated with the semantic context (e.g., head shakes for negations). We aim to produce non-repetitive realization of target gestures. A key step toward this approach is generating enough examples for these target gestures to train the models (e.g., head nods, head shakes).

This study provides a flexible framework to retrieve arbitrary number of gestures in the data. We focus on gestures corresponding to movements of head and hands. Starting from few examples of the target prototypical gestures, the framework searches for similar gestures in the database using a two step approach. First, we train a One-class *support vector machines* (SVMs) to effectively reduce the number of candidates for the target gesture. Second, candidate segments are evaluated with a *dynamic time alignment kernel* (DTAK) framework, which estimates the similarity between the target gestures and the available examples. We demonstrate the performance of the system with prototypical behaviors for three hand and two head gestures, achieving precision ranging from 67% to 92%. After retrieving the examples, we analyze the relationship between the detected gestures and the underlying discourse functions of the message (i.e., discourse functions are semantic functions in the message such as *question*, *affirmation*, and *negation*). The study reveals systematic patterns where discourse functions produce characteristic distribution of these prototypical gestures. We also discuss our proposed approach to generate these prototypical gestures using speech-driven framework based on *dynamic Bayesian networks* (DBNs).

2. RELATED WORK

2.1 Rule-Based versus Data-Driven Systems

To design believable CAs, we need to incorporate naturalistic behaviors that replicate the complex relationship between human gestures and speech. These behaviors need to be semantically connected with the message and carefully synchronized with the prosodic structure in speech.

Studies have proposed approaches to synthesize behaviors from data. Among data-driven systems, speech prosodic features are particularly useful to generate gestures [3,4,7, 17,18,20]. Beat gestures are commonly used to emphasize words according to their role in the message [22]. Given that prosody is also used to fulfill the same task (i.e., emphasizing and parsing the message), it is not surprising to observe a high correlation between speech features and gestures [6]. However, other types of gestures such as iconic and metaphoric gestures are intrinsically related to the message's content. Although prosody features can provide emotional, emphatic and energy related cues to create gestures that are tightly synchronized with speech, additional information is needed to create gestures responding to the underlying content of the message.

There are several studies where the authors have used rules to animate behaviors [1,8,15]. These approaches require to define the behaviors, which may result in repetitive behaviors [11]. Furthermore, creating naturalistic synchrony between speech and behaviors is a challenge.

There are studies that have combined these two approaches. Stone et al. [29] designed a system that searches throughout a speech and motion capture dataset for suitable combination of speech and motion units in the corpus conveying similar meaning and planned behaviors. Their system utilizes a dynamic programming scheme which simultaneously solves the selection of speech and motion units. Marsella et al. [21] developed a framework that creates appropriate gestures depending on the content of speech. It uses speech prosody features to capture the emphasis and emotional state of the speaker. Sadoughi et al. [26] proposed a DBN to constrain a speech driven animation based on semantic labels (e.g., *Question* and *Affirmation*.

2.2 Gesture Segmentation and Classification

An important contribution of this study is a flexible system to retrieve segments in the data conveying target gestures. We will use these segments to constrain the behaviors synthesized by our speech-driven animation. In this context, there are several studies on gesture detection, segmentation and classification that are relevant to this study, which we review in this section.

Zhou et al. [32] proposed the *hierarchical aligned cluster analysis* (HACA) algorithm to dynamically segment and cluster motion capture data into movement primitives. HACA combines a dynamic algorithm with DTAK to automatically segment and identify clusters with similar behaviors. DTAK, which we describe in Section 4.3, estimates the similarity between two sequences. Bozkurt et al. [2] used *parallel hidden Markov models* (PHMMs) to find primitives for hand movements. PHMM is an unsupervised framework composed of several branches with equal number of states, each representing a primitive. They used PHMM to simultaneously segment and cluster the motion capture data. In these two approaches the data is segmented into gesture primitives that are automatically generated using unsupervised frameworks. For our problem, these approaches are less effective since we do not have control to define primitives similar to the target gestures.

Studies have formulated this problem as gesture classification. Joshi et al. [12] presented a framework for gesture classification and segmentation. Starting from a vocabulary of predefined gestures, the system trained a random forest model using a database of video and depth map of the joints. During testing, they use a multi-scale sliding window framework for classification, performing a forward search to segment and classify the target gestures.

There are also some studies on gesture detection. Kovar et al. [16] developed a framework that searches a motion capture data for gestures. They use dynamic time alignment to find the distance between segments and each queried gesture. The retrieved samples are the ones with distances below a threshold. They used these samples to expand the variations of the queries, which are used to repeat the search. Nickel et al. [23] presented a system that identifies pointing gestures and the direction of pointing, on stereo camera data. They trained HMMs for each phase of this gesture (onset, hold and offset). They detected the gesture wherever they find three points in time such that the probability of the first point being in the beginning phase and the last point being in the ending phase was higher than the probabilities of these points belonging to the ending and beginning phase, respectively. Wang et al. [31] proposed a framework to detect three gestures used as commands for a smart-board (lining, pointing, and circling). Their framework is based on HMMs, and they identify the gestures if the confidence value for the gesture is higher than a threshold.

2.3 Contribution of this Study

This study proposes a framework to detect prototypical

(a) So-What (b) To-Fro (c) Regress

Figure 1: Examples of the target hand gestures used in this study.

gestures, which are then analyzed as a function of their underlying discourse functions. The contributions of this paper are as follows. First, we design a framework that mines a motion capture database to find similar gestures to arbitrary number of target gestures. Second, we study the relationship between the retrieved gestures and discourse functions. This analysis is tangible, capturing characteristic patterns of typical behaviors produced by the head and hands. Third, we propose a speech-driven framework based on DBN to illustrate how the retrieved samples can be used to synthesize behaviors constrained by the target gesture. This framework can create a link between rule-based and data-driven systems.

3. DATA

This study relies on the MSP-AVATAR corpus [27]. This corpus is rich in nonverbal behaviors and discourse functions. The corpus provides dyadic interactions with improvisations, where the scenarios are carefully designed to create behaviors associated with the following discourse functions: contrast, confirmation/negation, question, uncertainty, suggest, giving orders, warn, inform, large/small, and pronouns (i.e., uttering pronouns such as "I", "you", and "they"). These discourse functions were selected following the work of Poggi et al. [25] and Marsella et al. [21]. This database also includes the labels for discourse functions, providing a suitable resource for the analysis of nonverbal behaviors and their relationship to mid level representation of speech semantics in the form of discourse functions. This corpus comprises video and audio recordings from six actors during four dyadic sessions. In each dyadic recording only one actor was recorded using the motion capture system, providing detailed facial and upper body motion information for four actors. The details of the corpus are described in Sadoughi et al. [27]. This study uses the recordings of one actress, consisting of 22 sessions (66 minutes).

To train and evaluate our approach, we need to first define our behaviors of interest. Since the corpus contains motion capture data from the upper-body joints of the actors, we consider target behaviors from prototypical hand and head gestures. The selection of the target gestures was influenced by the work of Kipp [14], which are listed in Table 1. These gestures are defined as follow:

Head Shake: gesture defined by one or more head yaw rotation.

Head Nod: gesture defined by one or more head pitch rotation.

So-What: gesture defined by outward movement of the hands such that the hands show open palms at the end of the arc (Fig. 1(a)).

To-Fro: gesture defined by the movements of both hands from one side to the other side (Fig. 1(b)).

Regress: gesture defined by the movement of both hands in circles in the direction toward the body (Fig. 1(c)).

Table 1: List of prototypical gestures considered in this study. The set $Samples_{Examples}$ consists of the samples identified in the corpus used to retrieve similar gestures. The set $Samples_{Test\&Dev}$ consists of the samples annotated on the sessions used as development and testing.

Behavior	Region	$\#Samples_{Examples}$	$\#Samples_{Test\&Dev}$
Shake	Head	27	115
Nod	Head	24	138
So-What	Hand	14	21
To-Fro	Hand	27	29
Regress	Hand	26	73

Head gestures are described with yaw, pitch and roll angles (3D vector). Hand gestures are described by the movements of the arm and forearm. We use three degrees of freedom per joint representing its Euler angles, resulting in 12D vector (2 arms × 2 joints × 3 angles). In all the experiments we z-normalized all the angles across the whole data.

We used ANVIL [13] to annotate some of the target behaviors in the videos. We split the 22 sessions into two partitions of 19 and 3 sessions. From the first partition, we manually identify between 14 and 27 examples per target behavior, forming our $Samples_{Examples}$ set (Table 1 lists the exact number of examples). To evaluate the performance of the system, we fully annotated three videos for hand and head gestures ($Samples_{Test\&Dev}$ set). Non overlapped sets in this partition are used as develop and test sets. Table 1 lists the actual number of behaviors associated with each target gesture in the $Samples_{Test\&Dev}$ set.

4. FRAMEWORK

This section describes the proposed method to retrieve behaviors in the database that are similar to the few examples provided for training. Figure 2 shows the overall architecture of the system. The key challenge in this data mining task is that gestures can have different durations and be located at any time in the signal. Therefore, we need to jointly solve the problems of segmenting and detecting the gestures. An exhaustive search is not computationally possible, so assumptions are needed to reduce the search space. We implement a temporal reduction to decrease the length of the data and examples. Then, we use multi scale windows to evaluate the presence of the gestures. The behaviors in the windows are compared with the examples using two ap-

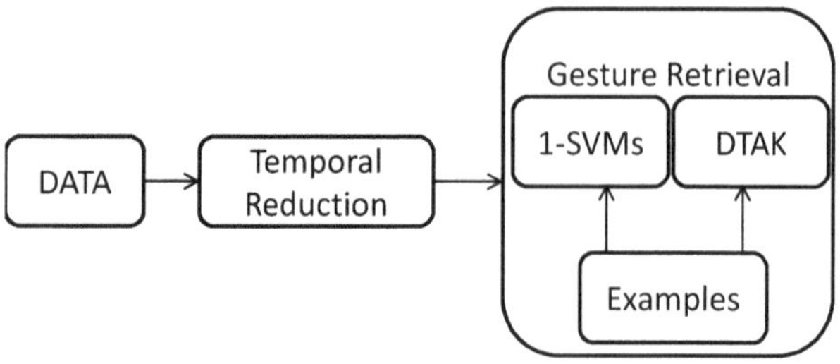

Figure 2: Block diagram of the proposed framework for gesture detection.

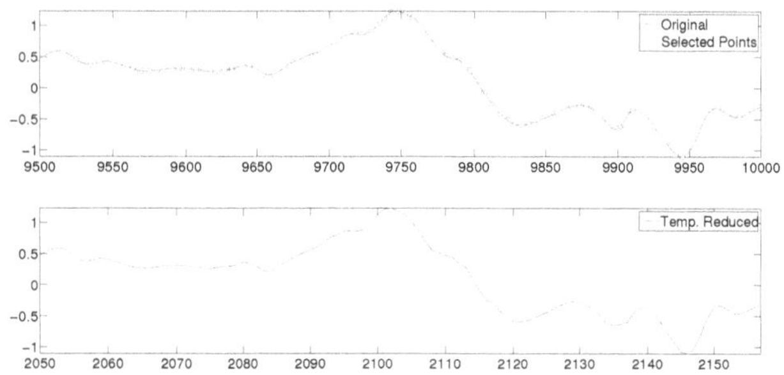

Figure 3: Example comparing the original signal and its temporally reduced version.

proaches. First, we use one class SVMs trained with limited examples. This method discards most of the segments, leaving only candidates segments, which are further evaluated using DTAK. This section explains these steps in details.

4.1 Temporal Reduction

The first step in the process is to simplify the representation of the data, making the search faster. The motion capture data is sampled at 120 fps, where the trajectories convey redundant information. Therefore, it is not practical to run the search algorithm on the original motion capture data. Instead, we remove redundant information from the frames. Zhou et al. [33] proposed an approach for temporal reduction using the K-means algorithm, where the frames were grouped in clusters capturing major transitions in the movements. Then, they applied nonuniform sampling keeping only the transitions between clusters and intermediate frames when the segments were too long. Our proposed approach builds upon this framework. K-means is sensitive to initialization – it can reach local optimum depending on the initial clusters. For each trajectory in the data, we propose to use the *Linde-Buzo-Gray vector quantization* (LBG-VQ) technique [19], setting the number of codebooks to 32. We remove consecutive frames assigned to the same cluster. We keep all the transitioning frames. Furthermore, if more than five consecutive frames are discarded, we keep intermediate frames, following the setting suggested by Zhou et al. [32]. Figure 3 shows an example for temporal reduction showing the same pattern as the original trajectory but with 20% of the frames.

4.2 Gesture Segmentation

The proposed approach simultaneously solves the segmentation and detection of the target gestures. We separately implement the approach for each of the five gestures considered in this study. The segmentation consists of defining multi scale windows, where we search for the gestures. This framework is inspired by the approach proposed by Joshi et al. [12]. We define a window of size L_w frames (after temporal reduction). We set the size of the window two times the longest gesture available in the training data. Within this window, we search for segments using the following approach. First, we define the minimum ($L_{\min}$) and maximum ($L_{\max}$) lengths of the target gesture. Starting from the beginning of the window, we create a segment of length $L_{\min}$, which is incrementally increased by Δ frames until reaching $L_{\max}$ (top diagram in Fig. 4). Then, we repeat the approach, by shifting the starting point of the segments by five frames within the window (middle diagram in Fig. 4). This approach is repeated till reaching the end of the window (bottom of diagram in Fig. 4). At this point, we slide the window keeping 75% overlapped frames, aiming to capture all possible segments containing the target gesture.

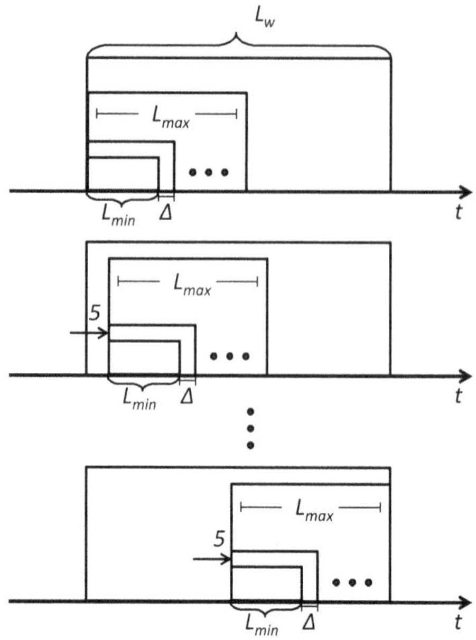

Figure 4: Multi scale window approach for segmentation.

We limit the search space with L_{min} and L_{max}. For a given target gesture, L_{min} equals to 90% of the minimum length of the training samples. Likewise, L_{max} equals to 1.3 times the maximum length of the training samples. The increment frames between iteration is empirically set to $\Delta = (L_{max} - L_{min})/30$. We evaluate the presence of the target gesture in each of the candidate segments using the approach described in Section 4.3. We may detect multiple segments within each window, which may be overlapped. Among the selected gestures in the window, wherever there is an overlap, we select the one with the maximum similarity to the target gesture.

4.3 Gesture Detection

The next step is to determine whether the target gesture is included in the a given segment. Given the large number of segments generated by the multi scale window framework, we implement a two-step approach, where the first step is fast and efficient to discard irrelevant segments, and the second step is accurate to compare candidate segments with the examples of the target gesture.

The first approach is implemented with one-class SVM with linear kernel [28]. One-class SVM finds a hyperplane that separates the positive samples. This formulation results in a binary function assigning 1 to a small region in the feature space around the positive samples. This framework is ideal for this problem, since it is fast and does not require to define negative samples per gesture. We implement the classifier with LIBSVM [9]. Given the limited number of samples, we train a one-class SVM for each dimension of the feature vector (3 for head gestures, 12 for hand gestures). Instead of using the actual values of the angles, we estimate their standard deviation which are used as features. The standard deviation of the angle captures the dynamic behavior of the gesture. Using only this feature allows us to discard segments without movements or with behaviors that are significantly different from the target gesture. As expected, not all the angles characterizing the target gesture are useful. To select the features, and therefore the classifiers, we use the examples from the training set ($Samples_{Examples}$) using one-sample-out, cross-validation method, where in each fold we train the one-class SVMs with all the samples, excepting the one used for evaluating the performance (notice that samples from the $Samples_{Test\&Dev}$ set are not used). Then, we fused the classifiers using AND operation. If the overall accuracy on the training samples is lower than 85%, we sort the features in descending order according to their overall accuracy. Then, we sequentially remove bad classifiers one by one, till reaching our target 85% accuracy. Notice that these classifiers do not need to have high accuracy. In fact, increasing the accuracy may results in increase of false negative rates, where target gestures are not detected. We can have false positive segments, which can be rejected in the second step.

The second approach is implemented with DTAK, which compares the candidates segments and each of the training examples. DTAK gives a measure of similarity between two segments regardless of their durations [24]. It defines a distance measurement that satisfies the triangular inequality, making it a better fit than *dynamic time warping* (DTW) [32]. Given two sequences X and Y of length l_x and l_y ($X = [x_i, x_2, ..., x_{l_x}]$, $Y = [y_i, y_2, ..., y_{l_y}]$), DTAK computes the similarity between them using the recursive formula given in Equation 1. The variable $u_{i,j}$ is an element of the matrix $U \in \mathbb{R}^{n_{l_x} \times n_{l_y}}$, which contains the accumulated similarity. The first element of the matrix U is initialized as $u_{1,1} = 2K_{1,1}$. $K_{i,j}$ is the kernel capturing the similarity between frames x_i and y_j. The rest of the element in U are found recursively using Equation 1. For DTAK, we use the implementations provided by Zhou et al. [32].

$$\tau(X,Y) = \frac{u_{l_x,l_y}}{l_x + l_y}, \qquad u_{i,j} = \max \begin{cases} u_{i-1,j} + K_{i,j} \\ u_{i-1,j-1} + 2K_{i,j} \\ u_{i,j-1} + K_{i,j} \end{cases} \quad (1)$$

$$K_{i,j} = \exp\left(-\frac{\|x_i - y_j\|^2}{2\sigma^2}\right) \quad (2)$$

This study uses Gaussian kernel (Equation 2). If we set the standard deviation of the kernel close to zero, ($\sigma \approx 0$), the similarity between the two sequences will be low, unless we find an exact match. If σ is too large, it will converge to 1 regardless of the distance between the two sequences. We need to set σ such that it provides a good resolution for this problem. We notice that σ equal to 0.1 gives reasonable performance.

Notice that we have multiple examples per gesture. This framework compares each of the examples with the segment. As a measure of similarity between a segment and the target gesture, Zhou et al. [32] proposed the mean of individual similarities. Instead, we consider the median of the individual similarities obtained across examples (median is less sensitive to outliers than mean). DTAK provides a score with the similarity of the segments and the target gestures. We define a threshold for this metric to make the final decision about a segment. To fix the threshold, we use a three-fold, cross-validation approach on the $Samples_{Test\&Dev}$ data to define the develop (two partitions) and test (one partition) set. We find the threshold that maximizes the F-score on the developing set. To find the F-score, we estimate the precision and recall scores. We consider a true detection, when there is an overlap between the selected segment and the ground truth detection. We consider a false negative when we fail to detect a target gesture. We use the selected thresholds on the corresponding test sets, and evaluate the result. We use the mean of the thresholds found in the three folds to detect gesture in the rest of the data.

Table 2: The precisions and recall of the detected gestures on the test set.

Region	Behavior	19 sessions	$Samples_{Test\&Dev}$	
		Precision [%]	Precision [%]	Recall [%]
Head	Shake	91.32	95.65	42.31
	Nod	85.04	87.10	61.36
Hands	So-What	79.69	76.92	47.62
	To-Fro	59.52	67.86	67.86
	Regress	71.77	78.85	57.75

5. EXPERIMENTAL EVALUATION

We evaluate the proposed approach over the entire data (22 sessions). In total, we retrieve 287 head shakes, 535 head nods, 114 So-What gestures, 223 To-Fro gestures, and 262 Regress gestures. The first evaluation of the proposed approach was to measure the precision over all the sessions, excepting the three sessions used for developing and testing (i.e., 19 sessions). To find the precision, we reviewed the retrieved gestures, to annotate whether they contain the target gesture. When the gestures were correctly detected, we count them as true positives. Otherwise, we count them as false positives. Table 2 shows the results ("19 sessions column). Over 85% of the head gestures successfully convey the target behaviors. While the precision rates decrease for hand gestures, the performance is still over 67%. Head movements are easier to distinguish than hand gestures (3D vectors vs. 12D vectors). Furthermore, there is more confusion given the complexity of hand gestures. In spite of these challenges, these precision rates are very promising.

Evaluating the performance of the system in term of recall rates is more challenging, since we need to account for the gestures that our system fails to identify. For this purpose,

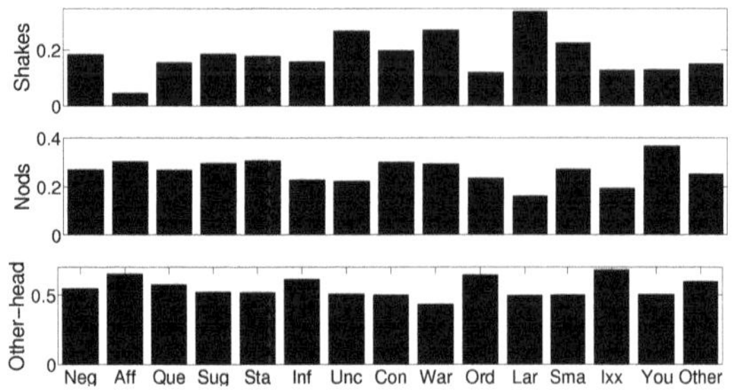

Figure 5: The distribution of the head gestures across discourse functions. Neg: Negation, Aff: Affirmation, Que: Question, Sug: Suggestion, Sta: Statement, Inf: Information, Unc: Uncertainty, Con: Contrast, War: Warn, Ord: Order, Lar: Large, Small: Small, Ixx: I-deictic, You: You-deictic and Other: Other-deictic.

we use the three test sessions, since they are fully annotated. We consider a false negative when a gesture in the annotation is not detected by our system. Table 2 gives the results for precision and recall rates over test set ($Samples_{Test\&Dev}$ columns). In general, the recall rates are lower than the precision rates indicating that some of the gestures are not detected by the system. For head movements, the recall rates are over 42%, and the precision rates are over 85%. The recall rates are over 57% for *To-Fro* and *Regress* gestures. The precision rates are higher than 65% for all hand gestures

After retrieving the target gestures, we study their distribution along the discourse functions. Figures 5 and 6 show the results for head and hand gestures, respectively. We plot the distribution for each gesture by counting the number of overlapped frames between discourse functions and target gestures. Wherever there is a confusion in a given region (hand or head), we keep the gesture with the highest similarity. We also consider the frames without target gestures ("Other-head", "Other-hand"). These numbers are normalized by the total number of frames associated with a given discourse function (head or hand). Therefore, the sum of the bins corresponding to each discourse function adds to one in both figures.

These results reveal some interesting relationships between these gestures and discourse functions. Figure 5 shows that *Shakes* happen more often during *Large*, *Contrast* and *Warn.* Also, the subject shakes her head more often during *Negations* than during *Affirmation.* We observe that *Nods* happen more often in *You*, *Statement*, *Affirmation* and *Contrast.* In addition, *Nodes* occur more often in *Affirmation* than in *Negation.* For hand gestures, Figure 6 shows that *So-What* happens quite often during *Question*, *Uncertainty* and *Large.* *To-Fro* happens more often when the person is using pronouns referring to *Other* and during *Inform.* *Regress* happens more frequently in *Small*, *Contrast*, *You*, and *Suggest.* These results show that there is a connection between discourse functions and behaviors.

6. SPEECH-DRIVEN ANIMATIONS

We are retrieving gestures to generate speech-drive animations with meaningful behaviors. Our goal is to automatically identify realizations of target gestures in the corpus to synthesize novel versions of these behaviors. After retrieving target gestures from the data, we train a model with these samples to evaluate whether we can capture the characteristics of these behaviors during synthesis. This section describes our approach.

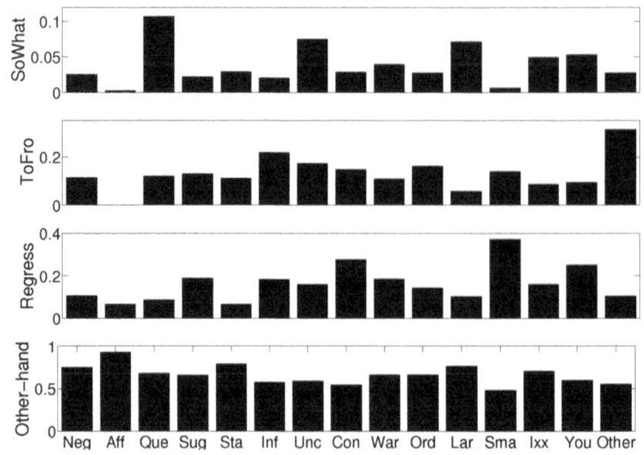

Figure 6: The distribution of the hand gestures across discourse functions. Neg: Negation, Aff: Affirmation, Que: Question, Sug: Suggestion, Sta: Statement, Inf: Information, Unc: Uncertainty, Con: Contrast, War: Warn, Ord: Order, Lar: Large, Small: Small, Ixx: I-deictic, You: You-deictic and Other: Other-deictic.

DBNs have been used in other studies to derive animations based on speech prosody features [20, 26]. This study designs a DBN inspired by the constrained DBN proposed in Sadoughi et al. [26]. We propose an improved version of this DBN displayed in Figure 7. The base structure of the model is similar. Ignoring the *Gesture* node, the model consists of a hidden variable representing the state configuration of the model ($H_{h\&s}$). This variable plays the role of a codebook capturing the relationship between prosodic features (*Speech* node) and the target behavior (*Head* or *Hand* node). For a given speech observation, we propagate the evidence through the network, synthesizing the most likely behaviors.

Sadoughi et al. [26] proposed to constrain the models by adding a child node to the state variable $H_{h\&s}$. This node represented the underlying discourse function of the message, which constrained the behaviors (in our work, the constrains are not discourse function, but the actual target behaviors). In this study, we consider the constraint as the cause of the hidden state $H_{h\&s}$ (Figure 7). The target gesture constrains the relationship between speech and gestures. This modification allows the network to learn the prior probabilities of different categories separate from their effects on the variable $H_{h\&s}$. When the number of states is big enough to cover feasible range of behaviors, the characteristics of the constraints can be learned better, even when the data is unbalanced. This network will learn the shared states using the entire data, and the transition probabilities between the states using the constraints. We train the network using full observation, i.e. we have speech prosody features, motion capture data and constraints (i.e., target gesture). To synthesize the behaviors, we run inference on the network using partial observation (just speech and constraints).

We separately train the proposed DBN for head and hand gestures. We consider 16 states for each. The constraints are discrete values which correspond to the presence of a behavior at each time frame. For a given gesture, we use all the retrieved samples, even if they are incorrect. For head gestures the *Gesture* variable has three states (shake, nod, without-constraint), and for hand gesture it has four states (So-What, To-Fro, Regress, without-constraint). We use the data when the subject is speaking to train the DBN, since we aim to synthesize animations based on speech. Following previous studies [4, 20, 26], speech features are the fundamental frequency (F0) and energy, and their first and second order derivatives. We interpolate the F0 contour to avoid discontinuities in our model. We calculate F0 and energy in windows of 16.67 ms. Since the sampling rate of the motion capture data is 120 Hz, we interpolate the speech features to match the frequency of the motion capture data.

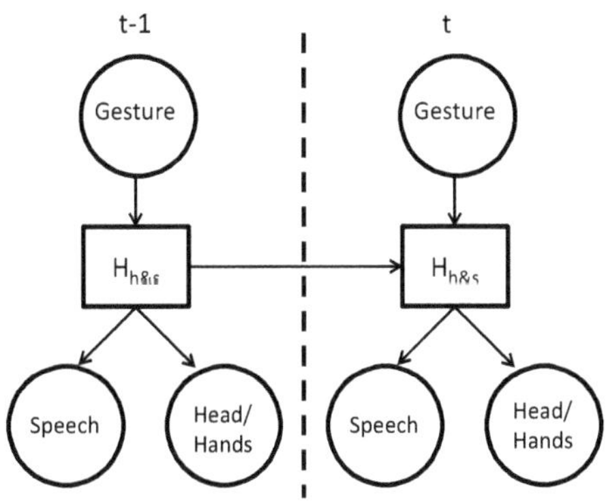

Figure 7: The structure of the DBN which is designed to capture the joint states of speech and movements while constrained on target gestures.

We synthesize animations with the Smartbody toolkit [30]. Using the same sentences, we constrain the DBN with a single behavior at a time, to observe whether the models were able to capture the characteristics of the target gestures. When the person is silent, we create animations without backchannel by simply using the average posture of the person. We smooth the behaviors using the quaternion interpolation of Euler angles used by Busso et al. [5]. We provide a video as a supplemental material with examples of animations driven by speech that are constrained on target gestures by the proposed models. The video shows that the models are in general successful in capturing the target behaviors. When we constrain the animation with head nods or head shakes, the CA displays multiple instances of these gestures. For hand movements, the models were successful in capturing *Regress*. The videos constrained on *So-What* generates more samples of this behavior than during other videos. For *To-Fro*, the approach was less successful. This result may be explained by the limited number of instances retrieved by the system, and the complexity of the behavior.

7. CONCLUSIONS

This paper proposed a framework to automatically detect target gestures defined by few examples in a motion capture database. We considered two head gestures and three hand gestures. The approach jointly solved the segmentation and detection of gestures by using multi scale windows, and a two-step detection framework. The first step efficiently reduced the number of candidate segments using one-class SVM. The second step determined the similarity between segments and the given examples using DTAK. The advantage of this framework is its flexibility to retrieve any gesture. The only requirement is to collect few examples of the target behaviors. We used the retrieved samples to synthesize novel realizations of these gestures using speech-driven animations constrained by these target behaviors. The paper demonstrated that rule-based and data-driven systems can be combined in a principled manner producing gestures with meaning, capturing the variability observed in natural nonverbal behaviors.

There are many opportunities to extend this work. An interesting question is to explore the minimum number of examples per gesture required to achieve acceptable detection rates. Likewise, the framework was evaluated with motion capture data from a single subject in the corpus. We are studying adaptation schemes to generalize the models to retrieve similar gestures from different subjects. We trained a speech driven animation model constrained on the target behaviors. The training data relied on the gestures detected by our framework. The videos show that we were still able to capture the patterns of most of the gesture, even when the detection framework was not perfect. It is not clear how much these errors affect the performance of the speech-driven models. Other statistical models may be more robust against these errors, which can lead to better realization of the behaviors.

8. ACKNOWLEDGMENTS

This work was funded by NSF grant IIS-1352950.

9. REFERENCES

[1] E. Bevacqua, M. Mancini, R. Niewiadomski, and C. Pelachaud. An expressive ECA showing complex emotions. In *Proceedings of the Artificial Intelligence and Simulation of Behaviour (AISB 2007) Annual Convention*, pages 208–216, Newcastle, UK, April 2007.

[2] E. Bozkurt, S. Asta, S. Ozkul, Y. Yemez, and E. Erzin. Multimodal analysis of speech prosody and upper body gestures using hidden semi-Markov models. In *IEEE International Conference on Acoustics, Speech and Signal Processing (ICASSP 2013)*, pages 3652–3656, Vancouver, BC, Canada, May 2013.

[3] M. Brand. Voice puppetry. In *Proceedings of the 26th annual conference on Computer graphics and interactive techniques (SIGGRAPH 1999)*, pages 21–28, New York, NY, USA, 1999.

[4] C. Busso, Z. Deng, M. Grimm, U. Neumann, and S. Narayanan. Rigid head motion in expressive speech animation: Analysis and synthesis. *IEEE Transactions on Audio, Speech and Language Processing*, 15(3):1075–1086, March 2007.

[5] C. Busso, Z. Deng, U. Neumann, and S. Narayanan. Natural head motion synthesis driven by acoustic prosodic features. *Computer Animation and Virtual Worlds*, 16(3-4):283–290, July 2005.

[6] C. Busso and S. Narayanan. Interrelation between speech and facial gestures in emotional utterances: a single subject study. *IEEE Transactions on Audio, Speech and Language Processing*, 15(8):2331–2347, November 2007.

[7] Y. Cao, W. Tien, P. Faloutsos, and F. Pighin. Expressive speech-driven facial animation. *ACM*

Transactions on Graphics, 24(4):1283–1302, October 2005.

[8] J. Cassell, C. Pelachaud, N. Badler, M. Steedman, B. Achorn, T. Bechet, B. Douville, S. Prevost, and M. Stone. Animated conversation: Rule-based generation of facial expression gesture and spoken intonation for multiple conversational agents. In *Computer Graphics (Proc. of ACM SIGGRAPH'94)*, pages 413–420, Orlando, FL,USA, 1994.

[9] C.-C. Chang and C.-J. Lin. LIBSVM: a library for support vector machines. *ACM Transactions on Intelligent Systems and Technology (TIST)*, 2(3):27:1–27, April 2011.

[10] C.-C. Chiu and S. Marsella. How to train your avatar: A data driven approach to gesture generation. In *Intelligent Virtual Agents*, pages 127–140, Reykjavik, Iceland, Sep 2011.

[11] M. E. Foster. Comparing rule-based and data-driven selection of facial displays. In *Workshop on Embodied Language Processing, Association for Computational Linguistics*, pages 1–8, Prague, Czech Republic, June 2007.

[12] A. Joshi, C. Monnier, M. Betke, and S. Sclaroffo. A random forest approach to segmenting and classifying gestures. In *IEEE International Conference on Automatic Face and Gesture Recognition (FG 2015)*, Ljubljana, Sloveni, May 2015.

[13] M. Kipp. ANVIL - a generic annotation tool for multimodal dialogue. In *European Conference on Speech Communication and Technology (Eurospeech)*, pages 1367–1370, Aalborg, Denmark, September 2001.

[14] M. Kipp. *Gesture Generation by Imitation: From Human Behavior to Computer Character Animation.* PhD thesis, Universität des Saarlandes, Saarbrücken, Germany, December 2003.

[15] S. Kopp, B. Krenn, S. Marsella, A. N. Marshall, C. Pelachaud, H. Pirker, K. R. Thórisson, and H. Vilhjálmsson. Towards a common framework for multimodal generation: The behavior markup language. In *International Conference on Intelligent Virtual Agents (IVA 2006)*, pages 205–217, Marina Del Rey, CA, USA, August 2006.

[16] L. Kovar and M. Gleicher. Automated extraction and parameterization of motions in large data sets. In *ACM Transactions on Graphics (TOG)*, volume 23, pages 559–568, LA,US, Aug 2004.

[17] B. H. Le, X. Ma, and Z. Deng. Live speech driven head-and-eye motion generators. *IEEE Transactions on Visualization and Computer Graphics*, 18(11):1902–1914, November 2012.

[18] S. Levine, P. Krähenbühl, S. Thrun, and V. Koltun. Gesture controllers. *ACM Transactions on Graphics*, 29(4):124:1–124:11, July 2010.

[19] Y. Linde, A. Buzo, and R. Gray. An algorithm for vector quantizer design. *IEEE Transactions on Communications*, 28(1):84–95, Jan 1980.

[20] S. Mariooryad and C. Busso. Generating human-like behaviors using joint, speech-driven models for conversational agents. *IEEE Transactions on Audio, Speech and Language Processing*, 20(8):2329–2340, October 2012.

[21] S. Marsella, Y. Xu, M. Lhommet, A. Feng, S. Scherer, and A. Shapiro. Virtual character performance from speech. In *ACM SIGGRAPH/Eurographics Symposium on Computer Animation (SCA 2013)*, pages 25–35, Anaheim, CA, USA, July 2013.

[22] D. McNeill. *Hand and Mind: What gestures reveal about thought.* The University of Chicago Press, Chicago, IL, USA, 1992.

[23] K. Nickel and R. Stiefelhagen. Pointing gesture recognition based on 3D-tracking of face, hands and head orientation. In *International Conference on Multimodal Interfaces (ICMI 2003)*, pages 140–146, Vancouver, BC, Canada, November 2003.

[24] H. Noma and K. Shimodaira. Dynamic time-alignment kernel in support vector machine. *Advances in neural information processing systems*, 14:921, 2002.

[25] I. Poggi, C. Pelachaud, F. de Rosis, V. Carofiglio, and B. de Carolis. Greta. a believable embodied conversational agent. In O. Stock and M. Zancanaro, editors, *Multimodal Intelligent Information Presentation*, Text, Speech and Language Technology, pages 3–25. Springer Netherlands, Dordrecht, The Netherlands, February 2005.

[26] N. Sadoughi, Y. Liu, and C. Busso. Speech-driven animation constrained by appropriate discourse functions. In *International conference on multimodal interaction (ICMI 2014)*, pages 148–155, Istanbul, Turkey, November 2014.

[27] N. Sadoughi, Y. Liu, and C. Busso. MSP-AVATAR corpus: Motion capture recordings to study the role of discourse functions in the design of intelligent virtual agents. In *1st International Workshop on Understanding Human Activities through 3D Sensors (UHA3DS 2015)*, Ljubljana, Slovenia, May 2015.

[28] B. Schölkopf, R. Williamson, A. Smola, J. Shawe-Taylor, and J. Platt. Support vector method for novelty detection. In *NIPS*, volume 12, pages 582–588, 1999.

[29] M. Stone, D. DeCarlo, I. Oh, C. Rodriguez, A. Stere, A. Lees, and C. Bregler. Speaking with hands: Creating animated conversational characters from recordings of human performance. *ACM Transactions on Graphics (TOG)*, 23(3):506–513, August 2004.

[30] M. Thiebaux, S. Marsella, A. N. Marshall, and M. Kallmann. Smartbody: Behavior realization for embodied conversational agents. In *Proceedings of the 7th international joint conference on Autonomous agents and multiagent systems-Volume 1*, volume 1, pages 151–158, Estoril, Portugal, May 2008.

[31] F. Wang, C.-W. Ngo, and T.-C. Pong. Simulating a smartboard by real-time gesture detection in lecture videos. *IEEE Transactions on Multimedia*, 10(5):926–935, August 2008.

[32] F. Zhou, F. D. la Torre, and J. K. Hodgins. Hierarchical aligned cluster analysis for temporal clustering of human motion. *IEEE Transactions on Pattern Analysis and Machine Intelligence*, 35(3):582–596, March 2013.

[33] F. Zhou, F. Torre, and J. K. Hodgins. Aligned cluster analysis for temporal segmentation of human motion. In *Automatic Face & Gesture Recognition, 2008. FG'08. 8th IEEE International Conference on*, pages 1–7. IEEE, 2008.

Look & Pedal: Hands-free Navigation in Zoomable Information Spaces through Gaze-supported Foot Input

Konstantin Klamka[1], Andreas Siegel[1], Stefan Vogt[1],
Fabian Göbel[1], Sophie Stellmach[2], Raimund Dachselt[1]

[1]Technische Universität Dresden
Dresden, Germany
{first.last}@tu-dresden.de

[2]Microsoft Corporation
Redmond, WA, USA
stellmach@acm.org

ABSTRACT

For a desktop computer, we investigate how to enhance conventional mouse and keyboard interaction by combining the input modalities gaze and foot. This multimodal approach offers the potential for fluently performing both manual input (e.g., for precise object selection) and gaze-supported foot input (for pan and zoom) in zoomable information spaces in quick succession or even in parallel. For this, we take advantage of fast gaze input to implicitly indicate where to navigate to and additional explicit foot input for speed control while leaving the hands free for further manual input. This allows for taking advantage of gaze input in a subtle and unobtrusive way. We have carefully elaborated and investigated three variants of foot controls incorporating one-, two- and multidirectional foot pedals in combination with gaze. These were evaluated and compared to mouse-only input in a user study using Google Earth as a geographic information system. The results suggest that gaze-supported foot input is feasible for convenient, user-friendly navigation and comparable to mouse input and encourage further investigations of gaze-supported foot controls.

Categories and Subject Descriptors

H.5.2 [**Information interfaces and presentation**]: User Interfaces: Input devices and strategies.

Keywords

Multimodal interaction; foot input; gaze input; eye tracking; gaze-supported interaction; navigation; pan; zoom

1. INTRODUCTION

In common computer desktop workspaces, the interaction is usually limited to mouse and keyboard input. Especially complex tasks, which are common in a variety of application areas, e.g., in geographic information systems (GIS), often require to switch between interaction modes (e.g. *navigation* and *manipulation*). If the user wants to drag an object to a remote point of the map, the mouse controls used for dragging can no longer be used for panning, and parallel navigation would be welcome. While the hands are occupied, other modalities such as gaze and foot input remain unused, although they show high potential to support and enhance conventional computer interaction.

ICMI 2015, November 9–13, 2015, Seattle, WA, USA.
 ISBN 978-1-4503-3912-4/15/11 ...$15.00.
DOI: http://dx.doi.org/10.1145/2818346.2820751.

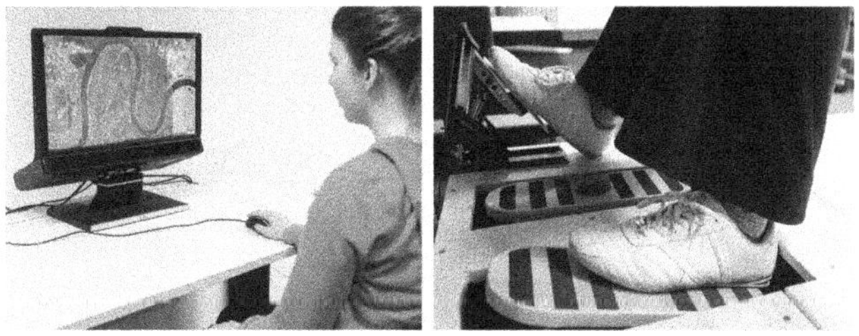

Figure 1: Envisioned setup: A single user works in a common computer desktop environment and can benefit from additional gaze and foot input for fluently navigating through zoomable information spaces while leaving the hands free for other tasks.

On the one hand, gaze input is suitable as fast and implicit pointing modality, however, lacks precision and should be used with care to avoid overwhelming the user. On the other hand, foot input allows for parallel explicit input controls, for example, to quickly confirm an action or to gradually adjust movement speeds, while it is less appropriate for precise pointing tasks [14, 18]. Thus, while our eye gaze is ideal to quickly indicate a user's current point of interest, foot interaction is well suited for parallel hands-free input controls [17]. This allows for using gaze input in a subtle and unobtrusive way, while still maintaining a fast and convenient interaction by addressing prevalent challenges associated with gaze interaction such as the *Midas Touch* problem [15] (i.e., involuntarily issuing a command via gaze). Although Pearson and Weiser [19] have already indicated the promising potential for combining gaze and foot input in the mid 1980s, further investigations of this multimodal input combination are still required.

This paper focuses on the exploratory investigation of a novel way of multimodal interaction, namely a combination of gaze, foot and manual input, and contributes to a better understanding of how to exploit the unique benefits of gaze and foot input in concert with manual controls. As an example, users could perform high precision *(primary)* interaction tasks with their hands to precisely select and manipulate objects or for fast text entry. Meanwhile, gaze and foot input could support *(secondary)* navigation tasks in zoomable information spaces for browsing through geographic data in GIS or for panning and zooming in an image editor. For example, while editing or annotating a picture, the user may want to get a closer look at details by further zooming in or moving the currently manipulated graphical content towards the center of the screen (i.e., pan the image) without the need to move the hands from mouse or keyboard or to switch system modes. With *primary* tasks we refer to interactions that may require high input precision and concentration and which are considered more suitable for manual input. *Secondary* tasks are supporting activities and should be executable with low mental and physical effort to avoid unnecessarily distracting users from their primary task.

Motivated by this, we investigate how pan and zoom actions can be performed through a combination of gaze-supported input [25] and foot controls in a desktop computer setup along with additional manual mouse input for primary interaction tasks (namely interacting with markers on a virtual geographic map) as illustrated in Figure 1. We carefully elaborated and examined several combinations of gaze input with different types of foot pedals ranging from common one-directional car-like pedals, two-directional rocking pedals to multi-dimensional foot joysticks. In our iterative design process, we developed several prototypes and evaluated them in two user studies. To summarize, in this work, we contribute to a better understanding of gaze-supported foot navigation, including:

- **Novel input:** We contribute a novel multimodal combination of implicit gaze and explicit foot input for navigation tasks combined with manual input for further tasks.
- **Feasibility:** We successfully demonstrate that gaze-supported foot input is feasible for navigation and explore particular design choices to improve performance and usability.
- **Usability:** We present a combination of gaze and foot input that was assessed very positively and is interesting for further investigations (e.g. in other application contexts).
- **Challenges:** We discuss several design considerations and potential risks for gaze-supported foot interaction that provide a foundation for on-going work.

2. GAZE-BASED PAN AND ZOOM

Our eye gaze presents an implicit and quick way to indicate interest and provides one of the fastest possible pointing methods, as our gaze reaches a target prior to a manual pointer without even thinking about it [15, 26]. For navigation controls, this can be used to quickly enlarge looked-at content either locally (zoom lenses) (e.g., [3, 16, 25]) or globally across the entire screen space [1, 4, 12, 23].

Several works have investigated how to use gaze input for pan and zoom. For instance, Hansen et al. [12] use a scalable rectangular mask superimposed over the screen with an inner zone to *pan & zoom* and an outer zone toward the screen border to *only pan*. So, if looking at the pan area, the currently viewed target will move towards the center of the screen. They use gaze-only input, which makes it difficult to adjust movement speed or to quickly zoom in and back out. Similarly, Adams et al. [1] use distinct pan regions at each screen border that are associated with a particular pan direction and speed. They compare four different pan and zoom input techniques including gaze-based panning in combination with different input techniques for zooming, such as mouse clicks, head movements towards or away from the screen, and gaze-based dwelling. While none of the gaze-based methods proved to be as efficient as conventional mouse input, user feedback for the novel techniques was encouraging.

Zhu et al. [28] present a panning-only gaze user interface for remotely controlling a camera for which the captured camera image is displayed on a desktop screen. The panning direction depends on the vector between screen center and current gaze point, whereby the panning speed refers to the length of this vector. This approach allows for continuously moving the currently viewed target towards the screen center similar to the work from Hansen et al. [12] and Adams et al. [1].

Stellmach and Dachselt [23] investigate five gaze-supported pan and zoom variants in combination with a mouse scroll wheel, single touch gestures, and tilting of a handheld smartphone. In particular gaze-based pivot zooming [25], the implicit use of gaze to indicate where to zoom in, was positively highlighted by participants in their user study. This refers to the *fixed point zoom* proposed by Furnas and Bederson [10] for which a selected pivot (e.g., the point-of-regard) remains at a fixed display location during zooming, in contrast to *central zoom* for which the zoom pivot is always at the screen center. In addition, Stellmach and Dachselt [23] point out that while gaze-directed panning was positively assessed for slow exploration of an area, quick gaze-directed movements sometimes lead to disorientation and motion sickness for the user [23].

3. FOOT-BASED NAVIGATION

Already in the 1980s, Pearson and Weiser [19] have proposed using our feet as supporting input to overcome interruptions of the user's workflow due to shifting the hand between mouse and keyboard. In this context, several studies indicate that feet are rather suitable for low accuracy interaction tasks, such as scrolling [14, 18]. Various works have investigated foot controls for navigating in virtual environments, e.g., using floor pads [5, 17], a Wii Balance Board™ [9, 20], and treadmills [8, 22]. Several works also address *multimodal* foot input, e.g., with multi-touch gestures [7, 20], but none with gaze input. However, Pearson and Weiser have already mentioned the potential of combining gaze and foot input, but did not further investigate this approach due to expensive and cumbersome eye tracking equipment at that time [19].

Two general types of foot input can be distinguished: *discrete* (e.g., taps and kicks) and *continuous* (e.g., gradually pushing down a foot pedal). According to Crossan et al. [6], single and double foot taps can be used for conveniently navigating in a menu (e.g., on a mobile device). Scott et al. [21] examine differences between toe and heel tapping and conclude that users find toe tapping more comfortable. Beckhaus et al. [5] compare discrete foot taps on a dance pad with continuous input from leaning into certain directions on a chair. While both techniques were assessed as easy to understand, the chair variant was preferred, because it was more enjoyable to use and more flexible for quickly performing several movements.

An example for *continuous* foot input is presented by Alexander et al. [2] investigating *distance-based* and *velocity-based* foot movements (kicks) to pan on a mobile map. They conclude that continuous velocity-based foot input requires less physical effort, provides higher control, is faster and more accurate. Further examples for continuous foot navigation are presented by Haan et al. [9] and Schöning et al. [20] using a Wii Balance Board™. Users can steer by shifting their weight in the corresponding direction. Haan et al. point out that users had problems stopping a movement in time, because quick weight shifts were difficult. Schöning et al. [20] combine foot with multi-touch interaction for more precise navigation of spatial data on a large-sized display. For example, a user can zoom in by pointing with the hand to a location on the map and lean forward on the Balance Board™. In addition, it is possible to pan the map towards the direction in which a user shifted his/her weight. While their initial evaluation suggests that the proposed interaction technique allows a smooth navigation, the lacking haptic feedback of the Balance Board™ led to overshooting problems.

In a nutshell, several works have highlighted the promising potential of gaze- and foot-supported navigation. For this, fast and simple ways to activate and deactivate gaze input and to smoothly control movement speeds are required. While continuous rate-based foot input is promising for this, the need for haptic feedback has been pointed out. Foot pedals, as familiar foot controls, provide this feature and have not yet been thoroughly investigated for gaze-supported foot navigation.

4. GAZE-SUPPORTED FOOT NAVIGATION

Gaze-supported foot navigation shows high potential for conveniently performing pan and zoom actions, while leaving the hands free for additional manual input. However, as this multimodal combination has not yet been investigated before, we are faced with the question in which way foot and gaze input may complement each other well to offer convenient and fast pan and zoom control. While gaze input is suitable as a fast, implicit and coarse pointing modality, foot input seems well suited for trigger actions, as it allows parallel explicit input controls. In the following, we first describe several of our design considerations for our investigation of *gaze-supported foot navigation*. Secondly, we describe our three elaborated setups that combine gaze input with different variants of foot pedals.

4.1 Design Considerations

For our design, we assume an ordinary desktop computer setup with a single user who sits on a chair and works with mouse and keyboard in an application that requires both *primary* interaction tasks (e.g., object selection and positioning) and *secondary* navigation tasks (pan and zoom).

Gaze input is used to define the position where to zoom in (or out) and to indicate the pan direction (e.g., also see [23, 28]), while foot input is used to control pan and zoom speeds. Please note that a negative zoom speed is interpreted as zoom *out*. For this, we take advantage of multiple cursors for manual and gaze input. This avoids a conflict between the mouse cursor required for selecting content and a secondary pointer to indicate the steering direction. Hence, the mouse cursor is not influenced by gaze or foot input.

In the following, we discuss how to address certain challenges associated with gaze input and several design aspects for convenient gaze- and foot-supported interaction.

4.1.1 Gaze Interaction

One major challenge is the *Midas Touch* problem [15]: the unintentional triggering of an action by merely looking at a control element. By combining implicit gaze with explicit foot input, we can provide the user with the ability to clearly and conveniently communicate when to perform a certain action. Also, if no foot input is performed, the user can freely look around without accidentally triggering an action.

Another major challenge is the *double role* of our eye gaze for orientation and control [24]. This is particularly critical for *fast* gaze-controlled panning movements [23], as the user needs to orientate him-/herself in the scene, while also trying to control the pan direction and speed with his/her gaze. To address this issue, we investigate different combinations of gaze and foot input to release the eyes for free observation. On the one hand, this includes the above mentioned approach: The user can quickly switch between gaze control and pure observation mode if not performing any foot input. This gives the user more control, as s/he can quickly stop if feeling lost. On the other hand, both *pan direction* and *speed* can be controlled via foot input to completely free the eyes for observation and orientation.

Another challenge is how to cope with *inaccurate* and *unreliable* gaze data. Jittery gaze data can be counteracted by smoothing tracked data. Offsets are more difficult to address and thus, low-precision pointing tasks are recommend for convenient and fast gaze input. Therefore, only actions that do not require high precision should be controlled via eye gaze. If the tracked gaze point is completely lost (e.g., due to tracking problems), we use the last valid gaze point.

4.1.2 Foot Interaction

For the design of *convenient* yet effective foot navigation in our envisioned desktop scenario (cf. Figure 1), we take several design goals into account. Firstly, the foot controls should require *low effort* for prolonged use. Thus, excessive foot movements should be avoided. Secondly, the foot controls should offer *high control* to the user for smoothly steering through a virtual scene, for example, to easily perform fast movements or to quickly stop to avoid overshooting. Thirdly, the foot controls should be *easy to use*, yet *fast* and (sufficiently) *precise*.

Based on these design goals, we consider foot pedals as promising, because many people are already familiar with them (e.g. from driving a car). They offer high control for fast and precise navigation by allowing *continuous rate-based* input to gradually adjust movement speeds and/or directions and by offering haptic feedback when stepping on a pedal. In addition, high-resolution input devices allow a precise and smooth mapping of foot movements to navigation tasks. Furthermore, foot pedals are *unobtrusive*, as they can be installed in the desktop environment, instead of attaching any equipment to the user's body. Thus, similar to a car scenario, a user can simply sit down and start interacting with the system without any further preparations.

4.2 Foot Input Devices

Based on the described design considerations, we selected pedals that match the pan+zoom techniques best in terms of degrees of freedom, resting position and possible mappings. We elaborated a range of stationary foot pedals, ranging from one-, two- to multi-directional foot pedals which are described in the following.

4.2.1 One-directional Foot Pedals

First, we consider commercial *foot pedals*, building on people's familiarity with common car pedals (see Figure 3a). They offer the most constrained interaction by only allowing a one-directional movement: Pushing the pedal forward or releasing it. Haptic feedback is provided by its increasing resistance. The aluminium pedals are robust and offer various adjustment possibilities to adapt to different user preferences, e.g., the tilt angle, order and orientation of pedals. The pedals provide an input range of 1024 distinct values (10-bit resolution) allowing a continuous and fine-grained speed control.

4.2.2 Two-directional Foot Pedal: Foot-Rocker

To allow for more freedom of foot movement compared to commercial car foot pedals, we designed the *Foot-Rocker* (see Figure 3b). It extends the one-directional movement of the commercial pedals by adding a second direction, allowing a back and forth tilting mo-

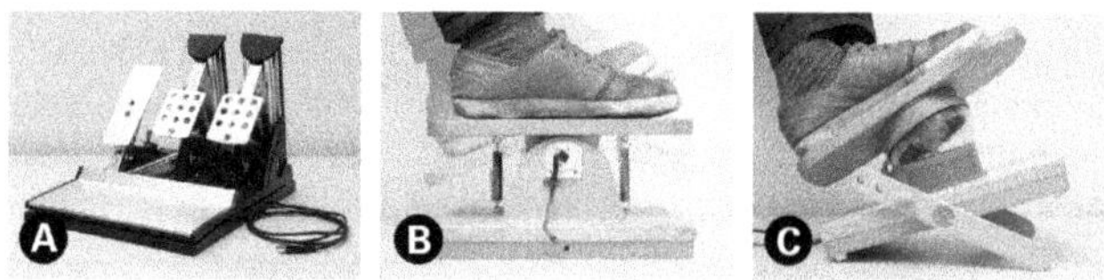

Figure 3: a) One-directional Pedals, b) Two-directional Foot-Rocker and c) Multi-directional Foot-Joystick.

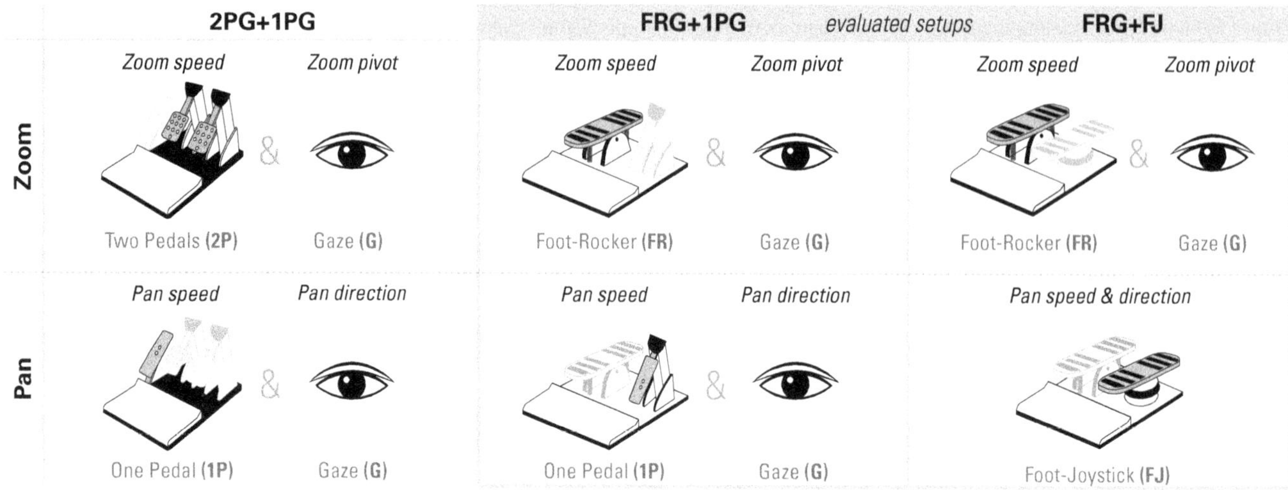

Figure 2: Investigated gaze- & foot-supported pan-and-zoom combinations.

tion. We constructed the *Foot-Rocker* with a fixed centered axis that can be tilted by about 20°, returning to the neutral position with the help of springs. Due to its prototypical character, the joystick sometimes suffers from little stiffness and slightly incomplete returns to the neutral position.

4.2.3 Multi-directional Foot Pedal: Foot-Joystick

We also designed and built *Foot-Joystick*, which extends input capabilities even further. Its ball joint mounted pedal construction provides the user with two degrees of freedom and a deviation angle of 20° in all directions from a predefined neutral position (see Figure 3c) which is also maintained by springs.

4.3 Foot Input Setups

Based on the described foot input variants, we elaborated several gaze and foot input combinations to control pan and zoom directions and speeds in an iterative design process. In the following, the three most promising gaze-supported foot navigation techniques are described in detail. In the remaining paper, the zoom-and-pan techniques are abbreviated with a two-part notation [zoom]+[pan] as listed in Figure 2.

4.3.1 Two Pedals & Gaze + One Pedal & Gaze (2PG+1PG)

The first setup consists of three commercial foot pedals. The user can zoom towards/away from a looked-at area (see gaze-pivot zooming [25]) by pushing the right/middle pedal. Simultaneously, the user can pan towards the current gaze position by pressing the left pedal, which is used for activation and increasing panning speed. It is noteworthy that this setup uses an asymmetric mapping of zoom directions.

4.3.2 Foot-Rocker & Gaze + One Pedal & Gaze (FRG+1PG)

To avoid the potential disadvantage of the first setup and to allow a symmetric mapping of zoom directions, we combine a single pedal with the two-directional foot pedal (the *Foot-Rocker*) in the second setup. Zoom in/out can be performed by tilting the *Foot-Rocker* forward/backward: The current gaze position indicates the zoom target while the tilt angle defines the zooming speed. Panning is performed in the same way as in the first setup using a combination of gaze-directed movement accelerated with the single pedal.

4.3.3 Foot-Rocker & Gaze + Foot-Joystick (FRG+FJ)

Analogue to the second setup, the *Foot-Rocker* is used for zooming towards/away from looked-at content. For panning, we use the *Foot-Joystick*: Pushing the Foot-Joystick to a certain direction results in pan movements in the same direction. The stronger a user tilts the Foot-Joystick, the faster is the panning speed. Thus, in this setup, panning direction and speed are both controlled without additional gaze input.

5. USER STUDY

As a first evaluation step in our iterative design process, we gathered early user feedback. For this, we presented the described prototypes in a hands-on-demonstration at CHI 2013 (Interactivity and workshop) and at several public science events at our university. Visitors could test the gaze-supported foot interaction prototypes and freely explore the virtual world presented in Google Earth without a particular task [11]. To further improve the designs, participants were asked to rate the interaction regarding six usability statements on a 5-point Likert scale (1 - strong disagreement; 5 - strong agreement): Convenience, ease of pan, ease of zoom and ease of navigation, as well as feasibility of additional hand input and the ability to achieve intended goals. We also collected supplementary user comments.

54 people (8 females, 46 males; including 42 HCI experts) provided feedback after testing either **2PG+1PG** or **FRG+FJ**, whereby 20 users tested both. The **FRG+1PG** setup was not tested, as the setup rearrangement was too time-consuming at the public demonstrations.

The overall results from the early user feedback affirm the promising potential for our proposed gaze-supported foot navigation techniques. The participants could easily understand the underlying concepts and were able to use them without the need of additional practice. However, the asymmetrical zooming with two individual pedals (one for zoom in, one for zoom out) was criticized for **2PG+1PG**. Instead users preferred the *Foot-Rocker* for zooming, allowing to tilt the single pedal forward and backward. Therefore, we decided to refrain from the **2PG+1PG** setup for further investigations and to rather concentrate on further enhancing and evaluating our own custom-made foot input prototypes, as both setups **2PG+1PG** and **FRG+1PG** follow the same principles. In the following, we describe a second, more structured user study to investigate **FRG+1PG** and **FRG+FJ** in more depth and compare them to mouse-based navigation (**M**).

5.1 Participants

Twelve unpaid participants (6 female) between 21 and 29 ($M = 25$, $SD = 2.52$) with normal or corrected-to-normal vision volunteered in our study. Participants were interested in the topic and were recruited via a mailing list, 10 of them were computer science students.

5.2 Apparatus

We used a Tobii TX300 binocular eye tracker (at 120 Hz, accuracy of 0.4° under ideal conditions) with an integrated 23" LCD screen (1920x1080 resolution) and a standard office mouse in MS Windows 7 with default cursor speed. To stabilize the gaze cursor position and thus to address jittery gaze data, we used the speed reduction technique [27]. The *Foot-Rocker* and *Foot-Joystick* were installed on the left and right side at floor level in front of the participant's chair. For this, the foot devices were integrated in a floor panel on which the chair was standing (see Figure 1, right). The standard office desk was lifted the same way, maintaining a common table height of approximately 72 cm. The single pedal device was screw-mounted on the platform, 8 cm right from the *Foot-Joystick* device at the platform's far end.

The basic task in this study was to navigate to certain locations in Google Earth and to click on predefined markers (see Figure 4). For this, we integrated the Google Earth Plugin in our software to test the three navigation conditions *Foot Rocker Gaze + One Pedal Gaze* (**FRG+1PG**), *Foot Rocker Gaze + Foot Joystick* (**FRG+FJ**) and *mouse-only* (**M**). Markers were set as map overlays using the Google Earth Plugin API (see Figure 4). In the **M** condition, the default Google Earth pan and zoom methods were used: The user could directly zoom towards the current mouse cursor position (*pivot zoom*) by scrolling the mouse wheel. Panning was realized by clicking the left mouse button and moving the mouse to drag or flick the view (*flick gesture*). Use of the right button was not allowed to prevent unwanted rotation movements, which are not possible with the *gaze-supported foot navigation* (**GF**) setups.

5.3 Tasks

The study includes seven tasks, which participants were asked to carry out (see Table 1). These are divided into three types: *pointing* (requiring only zoom), *combined* (intended for pan and zoom) and *tracking* (basically intended for pan). Each required the participants to navigate to several locations on the geographic map and click on graphical markers. In all three conditions, marker selection was performed with the mouse, but the navigation technique varied. The markers were always visible but only selectable below a predefined altitude, indicated by switching marker colors as shown in Figure 4. The activation altitude varied to enforce certain amounts of pan and zoom actions. For instance, the simple *pointing tasks* started from above the Atlantic Ocean and mainly required zooming in and activating a single marker, while *combined tasks* required several pan and zoom steps, and *tracking tasks* demanded longer pan movements. For *combined* and *tracking* tasks, several marker activations were necessary for which the number and placement of markers varied (see Table 1) and for which the start position was above the target area.

Type	Task Description
Pointing *(Zoom)*	Navigate to **New York** and select one marker
	Navigate to the city center of **Berlin** and select one marker
Combined *(Zoom + Pan)*	Navigate to 3 different sights in **Paris** and mark them
	Follow the curvy course of a designated **river** by clicking 5 markers
	Mark the border of **Utah** by clicking 6 markers
Tracking *(Pan)*	Follow the border between the US and **Mexico** by clicking 7 markers
	Follow the railroad track between the North Sea island **Sylt** and the German mainland by the help of 12 markers

Table 1: Overview of the seven tasks participants had to carry out.

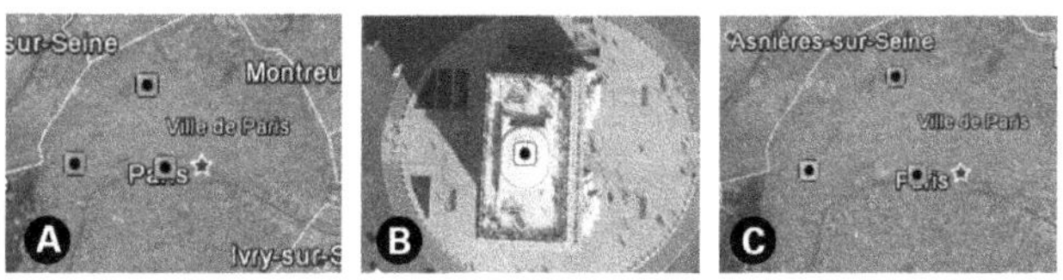

Figure 4: The three different marker color states: a) Not clickable (red), b) clickable (white), c) activated (green).

5.4 Procedure

Each participant was asked to test all three input conditions (within-subject design). The order for testing the conditions was counterbalanced across participants. For each condition the same procedure was followed: In the **GF** conditions, a nine-point eye tracking calibration was performed at the beginning. First, the participants could acquaint themselves with the respective input condition in a free training until they felt sufficiently prepared (on average not more than 3 minutes). Subsequently, they were asked to achieve the described study tasks in the order listed in Table 1 which relates to an increasing complexity (i.e., starting with simple *pointing* and finishing with complex *tracking* tasks). For this, in the **GF** conditions, gaze and feet are used as supporting input modalities in addition to manual mouse input.

A short instruction was presented to the participant before each task on the screen. Each trial concluded with a NASA-TLX usability questionnaire. After testing all three setups, participants answered a final post-study questionnaire. The overall procedure took on average 45 minutes per participant.

5.5 Measures

As performance measure, we gathered task completion times (TCT). The time measurement started with the participant confirming the task instruction on the screen and stopped when the last marker was activated. In addition, user input data was logged, such as mouse clicks, as well as gaze and foot data to later analyze users' interaction strategies. A Raw TLX [13] was conducted after finishing all tasks with a given input condition to rate the perceived task load. Participants also rated their level of visual fatigue, concentration and motivation on 5-point Likert scales before and after testing each of the three input conditions. Finally, the participants were asked to assess several usability aspects in a post-study questionnaire: ease of navigation, ease of panning, ease of zooming, perceived interaction speed, accuracy of task performance and convenience of interaction. The rating was based on a 5-point scale with contrasting input conditions on each end (e.g., 1 - **GF** to 5 - **M**, as shown in Figure 7). This was intended for a relative comparison of **GF** with **M** as well as the two **GF** techniques among each other. In the final questionnaire, participants were also asked for their favorite setup, for the influence of the prototypical character of the setups and whether they can imagine to use gaze-supported foot interaction in everyday work in the context of zoomable information spaces or in different application contexts.

6. RESULTS

We did not expect our novel interaction techniques to outperform conventional mouse-only interaction as it is in place for decades and well established. However, we expected Gaze-supported Foot Navigation to be comparable with traditional interaction for primary task work and to improve user experience and usability due to a more natural interaction for secondary task navigation.

6.1 Task Completion Time

For all input conditions, the mean task completion times ($TCTs$) increased for more complex tasks (see Figure 5). We applied a non-parametric Friedman test and post-hoc analysis (Bonferroni corrected). For the pointing tasks, that mainly require zoom, $TCTs$ in both **GF** conditions were on average shorter by 14% than in the **M** condition (not statistically significant though). An increasing amount of panning actions involved in the *combined* and *tracking tasks* resulted in longer $TCTs$ using **GF** navigation compared to **M**. From the three *combined tasks*, significant differences only occurred for the *river* task. For both *tracking tasks*, we detected significant differences between all conditions, whereby users were fastest with **M**. Further examination of logged input data showed no evidence that this is related to switching between mouse and foot devices, as there was only little discontinuity between mouse clicking and navigation actions. Instead the differences arise from the different panning speeds used in the three input conditions. While **M** allowed fast flicking gestures, users were more careful to pan with their gaze and feet, thus leading to slower panning and longer $TCTs$.

6.2 Pan and Zoom Strategies

We used input log data to identify different pan and zoom strategies and their potential impact on task completion times. In both **GF** and **M** conditions, all users sequentially performed navigation actions and mouse clicks. Interestingly, participants constantly moved the mouse in both **GF** setups during navigation actions: Users were hovering over the target positions or followed the panning path by dragging the mouse cursor along it. Participants used panning more often in the **FRG+1PG** setup compared to **FRG+FJ**. In the latter condition several participants changed their strategy after a while and rather preferred to use gaze-directed zooming instead of panning with the *Foot-Joystick*. In fact, we noticed that participants took longer to pan using gaze and feet than using gaze-directed zoom. For the *tracking tasks*, this led to changing performances between both **GF** setups. The change of strategy had a bigger influence on the $TCTs$ in the longer Sylt task.

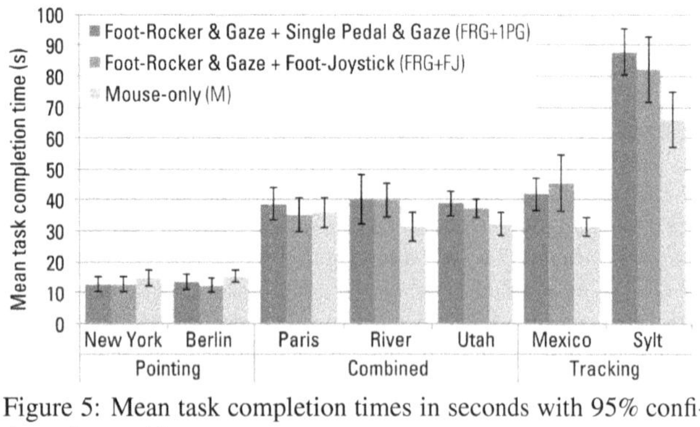

Figure 5: Mean task completion times in seconds with 95% confidence interval bars.

6.3 Workload Rating

As shown in Figure 6, mean TLX ratings did not show large differences between the three interaction techniques although the **M** condition receives lower (better) ratings in most categories. Especially for aspects such as *mental demand* this is not surprising due to the high familiarity with mouse input and the novelty as well as higher complexity of multimodal interaction (manual input + gaze and feet input vs. manual input) or the prototypical character of the **GF** setups. Thus, *physical demand* and *effort* were similarly perceived higher for the novel setups. While the user assessments are least diverged with regard to *performance* for **FRG+1PG**, participants were still more satisfied with their performance using the mouse. *Frustration* with mouse input was perceived similarly low as with **FRG+1PG**. **FRG+FJ** reached much higher ratings, however they were still good. With a deeper analysis of the *frustration scores* for **FRG+FJ** ($M = 8.17, SD = 5.64$), two groups can be distinguished: 7 participants were little frustrated ($M = 3.85$), while the other 5 participants seemed to have difficulties operating the *Foot-Joystick* ($M = 14.2$). In comparison, **M** and **FRG+1PG** did not show such differences: $M_M = 4.75, SD_M = 3.65$ and $M_{FRG+1PG} = 5.50, SD_{FRG+1PG} = 3.09$. Additionally, the evaluation of potential visual fatigue, concentration and motivation showed no effects.

6.4 Quantitative Comparison

After testing all three input conditions, participants were asked to assess several usability aspects (e.g., perceived interaction speed, precision and convenience) on a preference scale ranging between two given input techniques as shown in Figure 7. On the one hand, the two gaze-supported foot navigation techniques were compared to each other (see Figure 7, right scale). On the other hand, gaze-supported foot input in general was compared to mouse-only navigation (see Figure 7, left scale).

For the comparison between gaze-supported foot and mouse input, participants showed an overall preference toward the novel **GF** interaction techniques (cf. Figure 7), in particular with respect to *Ease of Zoom* and *Convenience*. In fact, 11 participants (91.67%) preferred **GF** zooming (7 of them strongly preferred it), while only one participant preferred mouse zooming. Nine participants (75%) stated that **GF** navigation was more *convenient* than mouse interaction. Only two participants (16,7%) indicated to (slightly) prefer **M** in terms of convenience mainly due to their familiarity with mouse input and due to difficulties with panning using the *Foot-Joystick*, which was found cumbersome by several participants. With regard to *Ease of Navigation*, 8 participants (66,67%) tended towards **GF** (2 with a strong preference). Eight users (66,67%) felt being faster with **GF** navigation, which interestingly contradicts the task

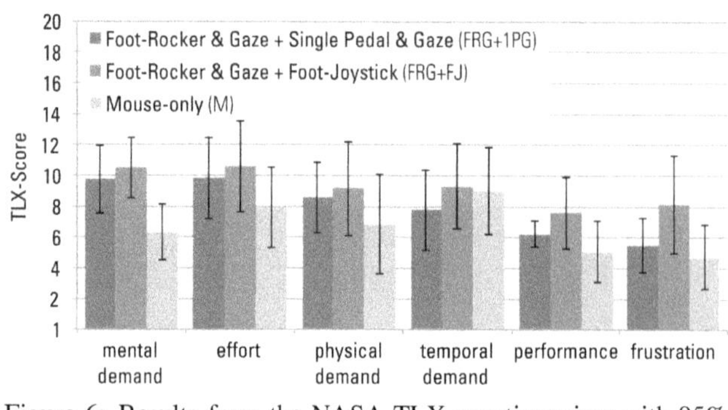

Figure 6: Results from the NASA-TLX questionnaires with 95% confidence interval bars (the lower, the better).

completion time measurements in many cases. The lowest rated usability aspect for **GF** is *accuracy*, for which users interestingly still tended towards **GF** compared to **M**. While gaze- and foot input is in general considered less precise than mouse input, this may indicate that input precision was nevertheless appropriate as pan and zoom tasks do not require high precision after all.

Comparing the two **GF** techniques, participants tended towards **FRG+1PG** for all questioned usability aspects (see Figure 7) which was probably mainly due to the circumstance that panning with the *Foot-Joystick* was sometimes described as cumbersome. While gaze-based panning (for **FRG+1PG**) was also not ideal, as it was described as exhausting to control the pan direction using the eyes over time, it was assessed easier than the foot-based panning: 10 participants (83.3%) preferred **FRG+1PG**. Even though the zoom technique was the same (*Foot-Rocker* & Gaze), four participants (33.3%) rated zooming easier in the **FRG+1PG** setup.

6.5 Post-Study User Feedback

Ten participants (83.33%) named one of the **GF** techniques as their favorite setup in the final questionnaire. Six preferred **FRG+1PG**, 4 preferred **FRG+FJ**, and 2 preferred **M**. These results are somewhat surprising, as 75% of participants also stated that their rating was negatively influenced by the prototypical character of the setups. Nevertheless, *Gaze-supported Foot Navigation* shows promising potential for the future: 10 participants can imagine to use **GF** interaction for exploring zoomable information spaces and even 11 participants (91.6%) would use it in different application contexts, e.g., for computer-aided design (CAD).

7. DISCUSSION

Based on our careful design and evaluation, we could highlight the promising potential of gaze-supported foot input for steering in zoomable information spaces. Although our tested **GF** setups still leave room for further improvements (e.g., more fluent control of the *Foot-Joystick*), participants were able to beat mouse input for tasks which primarily required zoom. However, this result is not statistically significant. It nevertheless underlines the interesting possibility to augment conventional mouse & keyboard input with gaze-supported foot controls. The particular advantage of our approach is to decouple the movement control (for pan and zoom) by allowing direction control via continuous gaze input and speed control via continuous rate-based foot input. Several improvements were suggested to further enhance our proposed setups, such as the *Foot-Joystick's* stiffness and problematic return to its neutral position. The *Foot-Rocker* could also be further improved for a more ergonomic design, integrating more sophisticated and robust metal pedals and more persistent springs that reliably move the two-directional pedal (*Foot-Rocker*) back to its neutral position. In the following, we discuss in more detail how well gaze and foot controls are suited for performing pan and zoom actions.

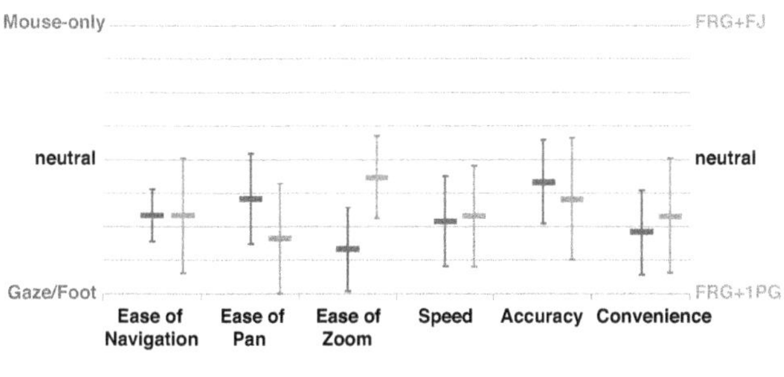

Figure 7: Two diagrams shown in one: User preference towards *Mouse (M) vs. Gaze+Foot (GF)* (magenta) and Foot-Rocker & Gaze + One Pedal & Gaze ***(FRG+1PG)*** vs. Foot-Rocker & Gaze + Foot-Joystick ***(FRG+FJ)*** (blue) with 95% confidence interval bars.

7.1 Zooming

While participants have already been very familiar with mouse-based zoom, most participants preferred the gaze-supported foot zooming. The clear tendency toward this novel way of interaction highlights its suitability for this particular interaction task and encourages further investigations.

The main benefits of this novel input are that the user can smoothly zoom in towards currently looked-at content (*gaze-based zoom direction*) and can continuously and gradually adapt the zooming speed using the foot pedal (*foot-based zoom speed*). Our preliminary study indicated that the one-directional foot pedal is less suited for convenient and quick back and forth zooming, as the user would need to frequently switch pedals or would require an additional mode switch to change between forward and backward movement. The two-directional pedal with it's symmetrical zoom mapping offered a fast and reliable way to address this issue and was the participants clear favorite. The user could remain with his/her foot on the pedal and perform continuous forward or backward tilting to zoom in and out.

7.2 Panning

While both gaze- and foot-based panning were positively assessed, and all participants could achieve the given tasks with the respective input conditions, the user feedback indicates that both input techniques have not yet been ideal for panning. In line with findings from Stellmach and Dachselt [23], gaze-directed panning works well for small pan actions (e.g., for following the curvy course of a river or country border), but can quickly become distracting and tiring for fast or long pan movements due to the *double role* of our eye gaze (for active control and passive observation). The foot-based panning with the *Foot-Joystick* was aimed at addressing this issue. However, users were very careful and hesitant when using their feet for panning or they preferred to zoom out and then back in towards an intended target by looking at it instead. We mainly attribute these findings to the limited technological maturity of our *Foot-Joystick* prototype and the interaction technique's novelty and subsequent unfamiliarity to users. Thus, further improvements and investigations of the *Foot-Joystick* are required to better assess its potential for smooth foot-based pan controls.

7.3 Future Prospects

While we have concentrated on a fundamental investigation of gaze-supported foot controls on supporting navigation tasks in a stationary desktop setup, we see a high potential for further studies of this novel input combination. Since our results yet show users like the new technology – although the mouse is as fast or even faster – it is interesting to investigate how further practice might improve task completion times and workload ratings. Moreover, future work could take other application contexts and domains into account. On the one hand, further interaction tasks could be considered, such as convenient gaze- and foot-supported scrolling of documents or quick object selections. For example, users could quickly switch between chat windows by looking at a window and tapping a foot while leaving the hands on the keyboard for typing. On the other hand, different user contexts could be considered that require a higher mobility, such as the flexible interaction with wall-sized displays.

8. CONCLUSION

In this paper, we have contributed to a better understanding of how gaze and foot input can be conveniently combined to steer in zoomable information spaces, leaving the hands free for other interaction tasks (e.g. precise object selection and manipulation or fast text entry). We initially investigated the design space, carefully elaborated three prototypes and contributed an evaluation in a real-world context.

For our investigation, we have focused on a computer desktop workplace with stationary foot pedal constructions beneath it and an integrated table-mounted eye tracker. We have carefully developed novel ways for convenient and fluent gaze- and foot-supported pan and zoom controls benefiting from implicit gaze input with explicit foot controls. We have designed and examined one-, two- and multi-directional foot pedals. Our main intention was to augment conventional mouse & keyboard interaction by managing hands-free pan and zoom operations only using gaze and feet.

Based on our evaluations, we could successfully demonstrate that gaze-supported foot navigation has not only the potential to beat familiar mouse input (in certain conditions it already did and further improvements have been suggested), but a majority of participants already preferred gaze-supported foot navigation compared to mouse-only input. The positive results for our proposed techniques, in particular the symmetrical pedal combined with gaze-directed zoom, encourage further investigations in this area considering additional interaction tasks and user contexts. While our investigations have been focused on spatial navigation in GIS applications, gaze-supported foot controls could, for example, also be used for document scrolling or for quick target selections merely by looking at a target and stepping on a foot pedal.

9. REFERENCES

[1] N. Adams, M. Witkowski, and R. Spence. The inspection of very large images by eye-gaze control. In *Proc. of AVI '08*, pages 111–118. ACM, 2008.

[2] J. Alexander, T. Han, W. Judd, P. Irani, and S. Subramanian. Putting your best foot forward: investigating real-world mappings for foot-based gestures. In *Proc. of CHI '12*, pages 1229–1238. ACM, 2012.

[3] M. Ashmore, A. T. Duchowski, and G. Shoemaker. Efficient eye pointing with a fisheye lens. In *Proc. of GI '05*, pages 203–210, 2005.

[4] R. Bates, H. Istance, M. Donegan, and L. Oosthuizen. Fly where you look: Enhancing gaze based interaction in 3D environments. In *Proc. of COGAIN '05*, pages 30–32, 2005.

[5] S. Beckhaus, K. Blom, and M. Haringer. Intuitive, hands-free travel interfaces for virtual environments. In *Proc. of IEEE VR '05, Workshop "New directions in 3D User Interfaces"*, pages 57–60. Shaker Verlag, 3 2005.

[6] A. Crossan, S. Brewster, and A. Ng. Foot tapping for mobile interaction. In *Proc. of BCS '10*, pages 418–422. British Computer Society, 2010.

[7] F. Daiber, J. Schöning, and A. Krüger. Whole body interaction with geospatial data. In *Smart Graphics*, volume 5531 of *Lect. Notes in CS*, pages 81–92. Springer, 2009.

[8] R. Darken, W. Cockayne, and D. Carmein. The omni-directional treadmill: a locomotion device for virtual worlds. In *Proc. of UIST '97*, pages 213–221. ACM, 1997.

[9] G. de Haan, E. J. Griffith, and F. H. Post. Using the wii balance board as a low-cost vr interaction device. In *Proc. of VRST '08*, pages 289–290. ACM, 2008.

[10] G. Furnas and B. Bederson. Space-scale diagrams: Understanding multiscale interfaces. In *Proc. of CHI '95*, pages 234–241. ACM Press, 1995.

[11] F. Göbel, K. Klamka, A. Siegel, S. Vogt, S. Stellmach, and R. Dachselt. Gaze-supported foot interaction in zoomable information spaces. In *Proc. of CHI EA '13*, pages 3059–3062, New York, NY, USA, 2013. ACM.

[12] D. W. Hansen, H. H. T. Skovsgaard, J. P. Hansen, and E. Møllenbach. Noise tolerant selection by gaze-controlled pan and zoom in 3d. In *Proc. of ETRA '08*, pages 205–212. ACM, 2008.

[13] S. G. Hart. Nasa-task load index (nasa-tlx); 20 years later. In *Proc. of the HFES Annual Meeting*, volume 50, pages 904–908. Sage Publications, 2006.

[14] E. R. Hoffmann. A comparison of hand and foot movement times. *Ergonomics*, 34(4):397–406, 1991.

[15] R. Jacob. The use of eye movements in human-computer interaction techniques: what you look at is what you get. *ACM TOIS*, 9(2):152–169, 1991.

[16] C. Lankford. Effective eye-gaze input into windows. In *Proc. ETRA '00*, pages 23–27. ACM, 2000.

[17] J. J. LaViola, Jr., D. A. Feliz, D. F. Keefe, and R. C. Zeleznik. Hands-free multi-scale navigation in virtual environments. In *Proc. of I3D '01*, pages 9–15. ACM, 2001.

[18] T. Pakkanen and R. Raisamo. Appropriateness of foot interaction for non-accurate spatial tasks. In *Proc. of CHI EA '04*, pages 1123–1126. ACM, 2004.

[19] G. Pearson and M. Weiser. Of moles and men: the design of foot controls for workstations. *SIGCHI Bull.*, 17(4):333–339, Apr. 1986.

[20] J. Schöning, F. Daiber, A. Krüger, and M. Rohs. Using hands and feet to navigate and manipulate spatial data. In *CHI EA '09*, pages 4663–4668. ACM, 2009.

[21] J. Scott, D. Dearman, K. Yatani, and K. N. Truong. Sensing foot gestures from the pocket. In *Proc. of UIST '10*, pages 199–208. ACM, 2010.

[22] M. Slater, A. Steed, and M. Usoh. The virtual treadmill: A naturalistic metaphor for navigation in immersive virtual environments. In *Virtual Environments '95*, Eurographics, pages 135–148. Springer Vienna, 1995.

[23] S. Stellmach and R. Dachselt. Investigating gaze-supported multimodal pan and zoom. In *Proc. of ETRA '12*, pages 357–360. ACM, 2012.

[24] S. Stellmach and R. Dachselt. Still looking: Investigating seamless gaze-supported selection, positioning, and manipulation of distant targets. In *Proc. of CHI '13*, pages 285–294. ACM, 2013.

[25] S. Stellmach, S. Stober, A. Nürnberger, and R. Dachselt. Designing gaze-supported multimodal interactions for the exploration of large image collections. In *Proc. of NGCA '11*, pages 1–8. ACM, 2011.

[26] C. Ware and H. H. Mikaelian. An evaluation of an eye tracker as a device for computer input. In *Proc. of SIGCHI+GI '87*, pages 183–188, 4 1987.

[27] X. Zhang, X. Ren, and H. Zha. Improving eye cursor's stability for eye pointing tasks. In *Proc. of CHI '08*, pages 525–534. ACM, 2008.

[28] D. Zhu, T. Gedeon, and K. Taylor. Moving to the centre: A gaze-driven remote camera control for teleoperation. *Interact. Comput.*, 23:85–95, 1 2011.

Gaze+Gesture: Expressive, Precise and Targeted Free-Space Interactions

Ishan Chatterjee[1] Robert Xiao[2] Chris Harrison[2]

[1]Harvard University
Electrical Engineering
29 Oxford Street, Cambridge, MA 02138
ishanchatterjee@college.harvard.edu

[2]Carnegie Mellon University
Human-Computer Interaction Institute
5000 Forbes Avenue, Pittsburgh, PA 15213
{brx, chris.harrison}@cs.cmu.edu

ABSTRACT
Humans rely on eye gaze and hand manipulations extensively in their everyday activities. Most often, users gaze at an object to perceive it and then use their hands to manipulate it. We propose applying a multimodal, gaze plus free-space gesture approach to enable rapid, precise and expressive touch-free interactions. We show the input methods are highly complementary, mitigating issues of imprecision and limited expressivity in gaze-alone systems, and issues of targeting speed in gesture-alone systems. We extend an existing interaction taxonomy that naturally divides the gaze+gesture interaction space, which we then populate with a series of example interaction techniques to illustrate the character and utility of each method. We contextualize these interaction techniques in three example scenarios. In our user study, we pit our approach against five contemporary approaches; results show that gaze+gesture can outperform systems using gaze or gesture alone, and in general, approach the performance of "gold standard" input systems, such as the mouse and trackpad.

Categories and Subject Descriptors
H.5.2 [**Information interfaces and presentation (e.g., HCI)**]: User Interfaces – *input devices and strategies*.

Keywords
Eye tracking; touch-free interaction, free-space gestures; input technologies; interaction techniques; sensors; pointing; cursor.

1. INTRODUCTION
Eye tracking and free space gesturing have individually been explored as methods for control in interactive systems. Like all input approaches, they have strengths and weaknesses. For example, eye movement is extremely quick, precise, and generally requires low effort (see e.g., [39] for an extended discussion). Further, gaze naturally corresponds to a user's focus of attention, which can be used for directed control of user interfaces (e.g., selection), or monitored passively to track a user's attention over time.

Unfortunately, eye tracking continues to be relatively inaccurate – on the order of ±1 degree, which translates to centimeter inaccuracies for monitors roughly 0.5 meters away. This is due to both natural jitter of the eyes and sensing limitations [27]. This precludes common fine-grained operations, such as clicking buttons, selecting text and opening menus. Although superior accuracies can be achieved with head-worn setups, these can be intrusive and generally cumbersome [26]. Furthermore, as the eyes are primarily used for sensory input, it is fatiguing to use them for manipulation tasks such as continuous gestures [44]. This significantly limits the modal expressivity of gaze, with systems often relying on winks, blinks and dwells to trigger interactive functions [10, 44].

Conversely, our hands excel at continuous manipulation and can occupy a wide variety of poses (i.e., gestures), which can be used to trigger interactive functions. This capability is not surprising given that our hands are our chief means for manipulating the world around us [7, 21, 42]. However, by operating in free-space (i.e., in the air), we lose many of the tactile affordances and visual references that make our hands dexterous at small scales. This makes targeting, for example, considerably more time consuming and fatiguing as compared to operating on a touchscreen. Previous free-space gesturing systems often mitigate this by having a low control-device (CD) gain [6], but this in turn means the hands must traverse a larger volume, compounding issues of fatigue.

To summarize, gaze is particularly well suited to rapid, coarse, absolute pointing, but lacks natural and expressive mechanisms to support modal actions. Conversely, free space gesturing is slow and imprecise for pointing, but has unparalleled strength in gesturing, which can be used to trigger a wide variety of interactive functions. Thus, these two modalities are highly complementary. By fusing gaze and gesture into a unified and fluid interaction modality, we can enable rapid, precise and expressive free-space interactions that mirror natural use. Moreover, although both ap-

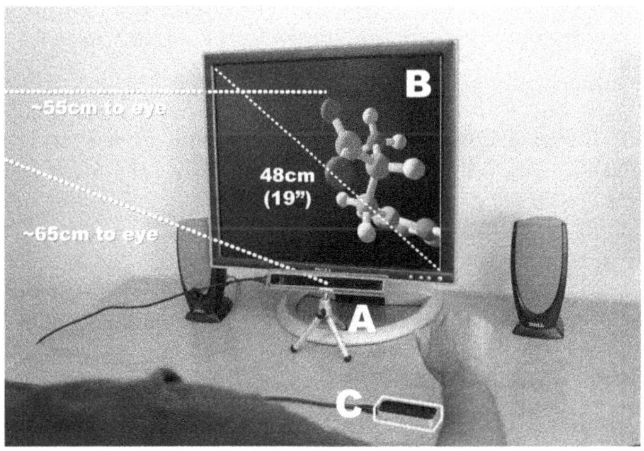

Figure 1. The apparatus used for our example interaction techniques and evaluation. The eye tracker (A) is located beneath the monitor (B), while the hand tracker (C) lies under the user's hand.

ICMI '15, November 09 - 13, 2015, Seattle, WA, USA

ACM 978-1-4503-3912-4/15/11...$15.00
DOI: http://dx.doi.org/10.1145/2818346.2820752

proaches are independently poor for pointing tasks, combining them can achieve pointing performance superior to either method alone. This opens new interaction opportunities for gaze and gesture systems alike.

There are two main contributions of this work. Foremost, we present a series of gaze+gesture interaction techniques, contextualized in three example application scenarios. To help explore the interaction design space of gaze and free-space gesture, our development efforts were guided by an interaction taxonomy we extended from Stellmach and Dachselt's [38] work on gaze and direct touch. Secondly, we present a user study that rigorously compares gaze+gesture against five contemporary approaches. Such an *apples-to-apples* comparison is vital, as the present literature employs a variety of study designs that generally preclude direct comparison. The results of this study suggest our approach has a similar index of performance to "gold standard" input methods, such as mouse, and can target small elements that are generally inaccessible to gaze-only or gesture-only systems.

2. RELATED WORK

Related work to our gaze+gesture system can be divided into three primary categories: gesture-centric input approaches, multimodal gaze-based interactions and gaze-and-gesture input systems.

2.1 Multimodal Gesture Input

Compared with touch, keyboard or mouse input, hand gesture input can better utilize the expressive power of the human hand to enable rich interactions. For instance, hands excel at 3D manipulation tasks, leading to a profusion of hand-gesture based 3D input techniques (see e.g., [16, 18]). Thus, automatic tracking of hands in free-space has long been sought after. Early systems used mechanical gloves [47] or wearable sensors [36], but it is now possible to avoid instrumenting the user using e.g., computer vision [8].

Perhaps due to the expressive nature of gesture input, multimodal gesture-centric systems are much less common. By far, the most common multimodal pairing for gesture input is speech. As shown in e.g., Put-That-There [2], the flexible, free-form nature of speech input can complement the more directed nature of gesture input. Researchers have also paired free-space gesturing with touch [41], pen input [17] and EMG sensing [45].

2.2 Multimodal Gaze Input

Computerized eye trackers were first used interactively in seminal work such as the 1989 Erica system [13], which was designed to enable paralyzed users to select menu items using only eye gaze.

Fundamentally, pure-gaze input approaches tend to suffer from "Midas Touch" issues [15] due the lack of a natural input delimiter. To alleviate this, gaze is often combined with another input modality, e.g., mice [44], keyboards [19], voice [34], touch input [28], [38], head movements [35] and even facial EMG [23]. Gaze can be used to rapidly target items, which are then selected by using the second input modality. As Zhai et al. [44] showed, such a hybrid approach can significantly enhance the performance of an input system, as compared to either approach alone. This approach can also compensate for gaze inaccuracies by relying on the more accurate modality (e.g., mouse) for the final selection of targets.

More recently, with the proliferation of touchscreen devices, gaze and touch input systems have become an active area of research. Gaze-Touch [28] combines gaze interaction with touch screen input, focusing primarily on selection and spatial manipulation of objects, such as dragging, scaling, rotating and grouping. Modal gestures are partially explored, but are limited to finger chording. Finally, there is no mechanism presented for targeting objects smaller than the gaze tracker's accuracy limits. Stellmach and Dachselt further explored gaze and touch in [37, 38], with the use of an eye tracker and a handheld touchscreen device, presenting interaction techniques for manipulating both small and large objects. Of note, although both papers evaluate their individual technique, neither compares against other techniques, an issue we attempt to rectify in our study design.

Importantly, our work differs from the prior gaze+touch work in that it explores the interaction design space of two non-tactile input methods. Free-space gesture is well established as being different than direct touch [40], with unique challenges and benefits, and so the interactions and methods also naturally differ. Touch has the advantage of absolute positioning with respect to the touchscreen borders, while mid-air gestures only offer relative positioning. Additionally, touch has superior physical affordances and an innate ability to clutch [40]. However, mid-air gestures can be more expressive as the free-space gesture set is larger than that of conventional, planar touch interfaces.

2.3 Gaze and Free-Space Gesture Input Systems

Despite the appearance of inexpensive eye trackers (such as the Eye Tribe Tracker [9]) and consumer-level gesture trackers (such as the Microsoft Kinect [24] and Leap Motion Controller [20]), comparatively little work has been done on combining gaze with free-space gesture input. Chen [4] examines the role of gaze and gesture in human communication. Pouke et al. [29] demonstrate a system that uses gaze input to select large targets on a screen, and a hand-worn accelerometer to sense discrete gestures. This system did not compensate for gaze-tracking inaccuracies, leading to poor results. Yoo et al. [43] describe an approach using a head tracker and depth camera to enable targeted interactions with large targets on a wall-sized display. Hales et al. [11] present a system in which users select physical objects by gazing at markers printed on them, and use hand gestures to interact or control them.

Our present system advances upon this prior gaze and gesture work in four significant ways. First, we provide interaction techniques for selecting objects of any scale, even those that are below the minimum threshold of gaze accuracy. Second, we enable continuous free-space manipulations with our gestures, whereas past systems focused on discrete hand gestures. Third, we use a structured taxonomy to guide the creation of interaction techniques, in which we situate familiar digital tasks. Finally, we conducted an evaluation benchmarking our technique against several of the aforementioned techniques, and against common input devices.

3. SYSTEM

As a vehicle for exploration, we developed a proof of concept system using off the shelf components. Importantly, we chose to use minimally invasive, low-cost, consumer-grade devices. Although offering lower accuracy compared to professional systems (e.g., head mounted cameras), they are the types of sensors that are most likely to be integrated into consumer electronics – and thus user experiences – in the near future.

Specifically, we use an off-the-shelf, $99 Eye Tribe Tracker [9]. This device consists of an infrared emitter (to illuminate the eyes) and a pair of cameras inside a bar-shaped case, mounted on a miniature tripod. This is positioned below a conventional 19" LCD monitor, set back ~55cm from the user's chest (Figure 1). Following a per-session calibration, the Eye Tribe software produces a stream of screen-space X/Y gaze coordinates at 30 FPS.

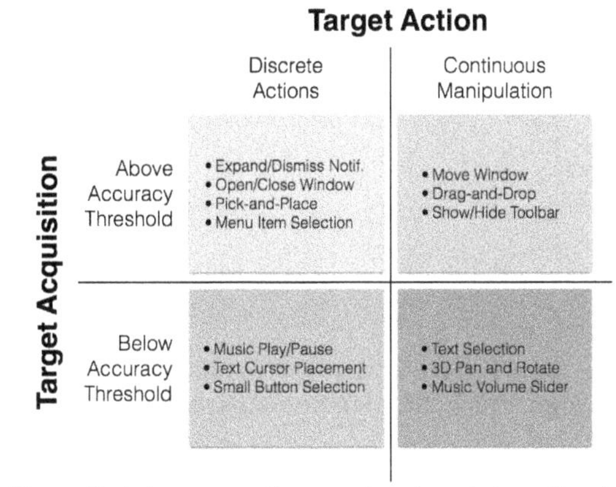

Figure 2. A taxonomy for gaze+gesture interaction techniques, showing sample interactions in each division.

To track users' free-space hand movements and gestures, we use an off-the-shelf, $80 Leap Motion Controller [20]. This hand tracker also uses infrared light (to illuminate the skin) and a pair of cameras. We use the Leap Motion software to obtain continuous 3D hand pose estimation, and employ their API to detect predefined gestures, such as pinching. Our interactions only used relative motions of the hand, and thus we did not need to calibrate the Leap Motion against the eye tracker or the display. We situate this device to the front and right of the computer monitor in order to capture the movement of the user's right hand, and to avoid occluding the eye tracker with the hands.

Finally, we used a desktop computer running Windows 8.1 to run our software, example applications and user study, which were developed in C++ using the respective device SDKs and the OpenFrameworks graphics library. It should be noted, however, this desktop setup was chiefly for prototyping and experimentation purposes, and that our techniques and exploration are applicable to other gaze+gesture contexts, such as large, vertical displays.

4. INTERACTION TECHNIQUES

Our approach divides interactive tasks between the visual and gestural channel in a natural fashion. The eyes, possibly in conjunction with the hands, specify the user's focus or target area (*target acquisition phase*), followed by the hands performing gestural actions or spatial manipulations on the virtual objects (*target action phase*). Emphasizing user comfort, we avoid interaction techniques requiring continuous gaze, as it is fatiguing and unnatural [15]. Thus, gaze is never used in the *target action phase*. To guide our work, we started with a taxonomy of the interaction design space from prior work on gaze+touch systems and extended it to include the capabilities of our free-space gesture tracking.

4.1 Target Acquisition Phase

Inaccuracies and noise inherent in gaze tracking systems results in a target size threshold, below which targets cannot be accurately determined by gaze alone. As noted in Stellmach and Dachselt [38] and Zhai et al. [44] there exists an area around the detected gaze position in which one can be reasonably sure the intended target resides. This natural demarcation forms a size threshold for targets: targets larger than e.g. the 95% confidence interval around the gaze position can be selected by gaze alone, while targets smaller than this size threshold require additional information from the other input modality to be accurately selected. Therefore, we split targets into two categories: those *above* the accuracy threshold (only coarse targeting required) and *below* the accuracy threshold (finer targeting possibly required), similar to the method described in Stellmach and Dachselt [38]. Although eye tracker accuracy will improve with better technology, there will always be an upper limit on accuracy due to intrinsic eye behavior such as tremors and microsaccades, and so this distinction will continue to be relevant.

4.1.1 Above Accuracy Threshold

When the gaze target is larger than the eye tracker's accuracy threshold, the target can be immediately determined using gaze information alone. Typical above-threshold targets include large icons and buttons, sliders, windows, text paragraphs, and screen edges. The subsequent hand gesture therefore acts directly on the target. In some cases, the intended target can be ambiguous, not because of size, but because of z-ordering or hierarchy – for example a file icon and the window containing that file. To disambiguate, we use different gestures (e.g. using a pinch for icons and a grab for windows), though other strategies are possible.

4.1.2 Below Accuracy Threshold

When the desired target is smaller than the eye tracker's accuracy threshold, the application must disambiguate between proximate targets in some way. Typical below-threshold targets include individual text characters, map positions and small buttons.

We devised three *target disambiguation* strategies, some of which utilize gesture input in addition to the gaze input. 1) *Loose targeting*: an application can choose to accept "loose" targeting, which is appropriate if a precise target is not critical, e.g. when choosing a focal point for zooming a map. 2) *Contextualization*: different gestures can be used to disambiguate between multiple possible targets. For example, the controls on a music player might lie below the accuracy threshold. In this case, we can disambiguate between "previous", "play", and "next" controls on a music player by using left swipe, click, and right swipe gestures respectively. Finally, 3) *fine selection*: we can resort to a high-precision mode

Figure 3. We built three example scenarios as a sandbox for our interaction techniques. Left-to-right: desktop, word processor, and 3D model viewer. Please also see the Video Figure.

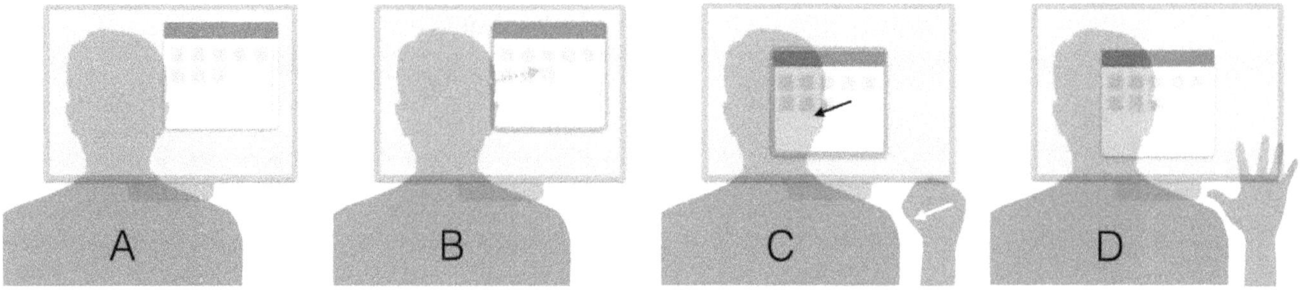

Figure 4. An example of an above gaze threshold interaction using continuous hand gesture interaction. (A) User is working. (B) User looks at window they wish to move. (C) User performs a grab gesture, after which the window tracks with the hand until (D) the fist is released.

that uses a low CD-gain manipulation gesture (e.g. pinch and drag) to adjust the selection (e.g. to precisely position a cursor within text).

4.2 Target Action Phase

Once a UI target has been accurately selected, a subsequent selection or manipulation can be performed. As noted above, continuous gaze control is uncomfortable and therefore only gesture is used for the *action phase*. These gestures manifest in one of two ways: for *discrete actions* (e.g. pinching, swiping, grabbing) or *continuous manipulation* (e.g. moving, dragging, rotating).

4.2.1 Discrete Actions

A discrete hand gesture is a single event triggered by a specific hand pose or motion. These gestures can be used for actions commonly associated with clicks and taps on traditional interfaces, e.g. opening and closing documents, activating buttons, and dismissing dialogs. Typical discrete gestures include closing or opening the fingers (e.g., touching two fingers for "pinching", making a fist for "grabbing"), threshold-crossing movements with the hand (e.g., moving horizontally for "swiping", vertically for "clicking"), or rapid movements with one or more fingers (e.g., "flicking" movements). Discrete hand gestures are therefore suited to the purpose of target selection such as button press or triggered actions (e.g. see music player play/pause example).

4.2.2 Continuous Manipulation

Continuous manipulation with the hands consists of relative movements and provides continuous positional information in three dimensions. We preface these manipulations with an activation gesture (e.g., pinching, grabbing), which establishes the origin point for the manipulation and enables clutching. Common continuous manipulations include moving the hand while pinching or grabbing (for e.g., "dragging" items or "panning" a scene), translating and rotating the hands in 3D (to manipulate a virtual camera or object), and spreading two hands for "zooming". Continuous manipulation gestures are therefore suited to the purpose of fluid target positioning and manipulation.

4.3 Taxonomy

Using this interactive breakdown, a 2x2 taxonomy naturally arises (Figure 2). On one axis, we have the *target acquisition phase*, which specify targets either above or below its accuracy threshold. On the other axis, the *target action phase* consists of discrete gesturing and continuous manipulation. Figures 4 through 7 offer examples for each quadrant of the taxonomy.

5. EXAMPLE APPLICATIONS

Using our taxonomy as a guide, we created a series of exemplary interaction techniques to illustrate the potential and flexibility of our approach. To contextualize these interactions, we embed them within three illustrative scenarios – a desktop environment, word processor, and 3D object viewer (Figure 3). See the Video Figure for a real-time demonstration. We can envision these techniques augmenting both classic desktop computing experiences (e.g., with a keyboard), as well as large wall displays, kiosks, or distant displays, where keyboards and mice are impractical.

For each scenario, we show how these interaction techniques can be used to e.g., select, navigate, and otherwise manipulate content in rapid and expressive ways. Each application is a fully implemented prototype (i.e., all described actions are available at every moment in time), though obviously not all possible functions are implemented. Finally, we note that the particular designs of these applications were adjusted to demonstrate a variety of functionalities, and do not represent idealized systems. Designing a practical

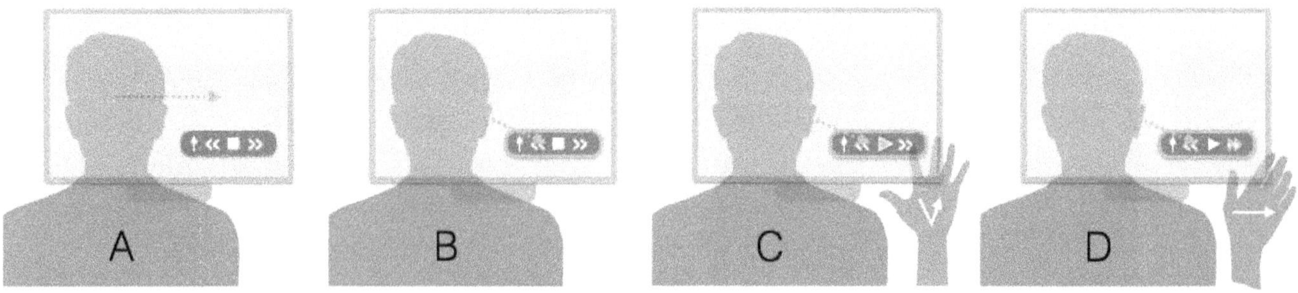

Figure 5. An example of a below gaze threshold interaction using discrete hand gesture. (A) While user is working, he wishes to play some music. (B) User looks at the music player play button (currently stopped). (C) Buttons on the music player are too small for gaze targeting alone, so gestures are employed to resolve the ambiguity. In this case, a downward bounce of the hand toggles between pause and play. (D) User advances to the next song with a right hand swipe.

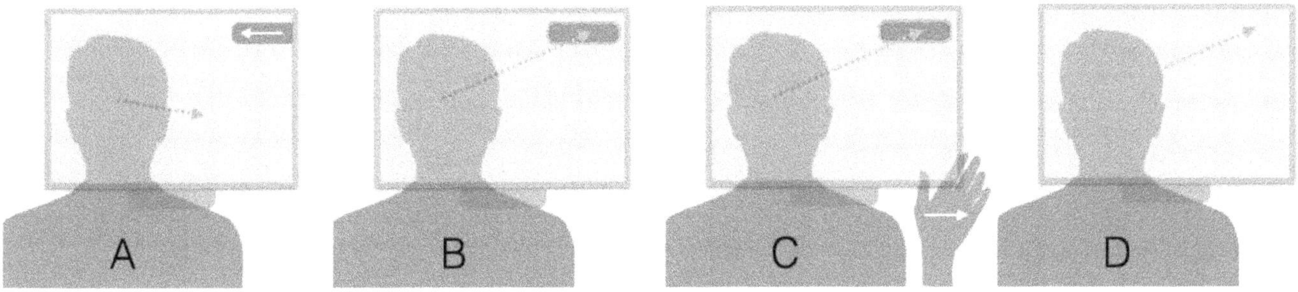

Figure 6. An example of an above gaze threshold interaction using discrete hand gesture. (A) While user is working, a notification window slides in from the top right. (B) User looks at (i.e., reads) notification. (C) User decides to dismiss notification, and performs a rightward hand swipe. (D) Notification is dismissed.

gaze+gesture system would require an in-depth examination of how all of the gestures would interplay across applications to form cohesive and intuitive experiences. We provide these example scenarios not necessarily as end-user applications, but more as a vehicle to frame to the individual application techniques, offer a familiar context, and to provide a label by which to refer to the individual interactions (such as in Figure 2).

5.1 Desktop Scenario

We included several GUI elements in our desktop scenario (Figure 3, left). Foremost, we have icons and windows. To disambiguate between file and window selection, two different gestures are used. A "grab" gesture (making a fist) selects the gazed-at window (Figure 4, B), which can then be moved by translating the hand in space (Figure 4, C) and closed with a downward movement. Alternatively, by using a "pinch" gesture with the thumb and index finger, the gazed-at file is selected. Once selected, the file can be dragged by translating the hand, or opened with an upward motion. Of note, if the gaze area contains no windows or files, the action is ignored. Lastly, we also implemented a "pick and place" method where instead of dragging a file to a destination, the user can simply pinch to select the file, look at where they want the file to go, and release the pinch, instantly transporting it.

We also provide a minimized music player, the buttons of which (purposely) lie below the gaze accuracy threshold (Figure 5). To trigger functionality, different gestures must be used. Here, we use left and right swipes to move to the previous and next track respectively. A downward hand bounce toggles pause and play. Pinching plus lateral translations of the hand adjusts the volume.

Finally, the scenario also includes slide-in notifications, which, once looked at, can be opened with a left swipe or dismissed with a right swipe (Figure 6).

5.2 Word Processor Scenario

We created a basic text editor which uses gaze+gesture. Users can move the text cursor by gazing at the target location and pinching to coarsely position the cursor (Figure 7, A and B). Users then drag to perform fine adjustment on the cursor position, allowing character level positioning (Figure 7, C). After placing the cursor, the user may select text in two ways. 1) To select a small region of text, the user can briefly unpinch and then drag to select. 2) To select a large region of text, the user can unpinch, gaze elsewhere, and then double-pinch and drag to define the end position of the text selection.

Once text has been selected, the user can flick two fingers upwards to summon a contextual menu, displaying common operations such as bold, italicize, highlight, copy, cut, etc. Gazing at a menu item highlights it, and flicking the fingers upwards again selects the operation. Alternatively, flicking the fingers downwards cancels the menu. Because the menu is only made visible on demand and selection is done with a quick glance, it can be as large as needed.

5.3 3D Model Viewer Scenario

To demonstrate how gaze+gesture works in 3D contexts, we created a molecule viewer. Users can select, view and explore different molecules, and inspect details within the structure (e.g. atoms).

A toolbar on the right side of the screen provides access to a database of molecules. The user summons it by gazing at the right edge of the screen, using a grab gesture, and pulling leftward. Users select a molecule from the toolbar by gazing at the desired item and pinch-dragging it to the main viewing area. The toolbar can likewise be closed by gazing, grabbing and swiping right.

When looking at molecules, the closest atom to the gaze location is highlighted. Users can translate and rotate the molecule in 3D

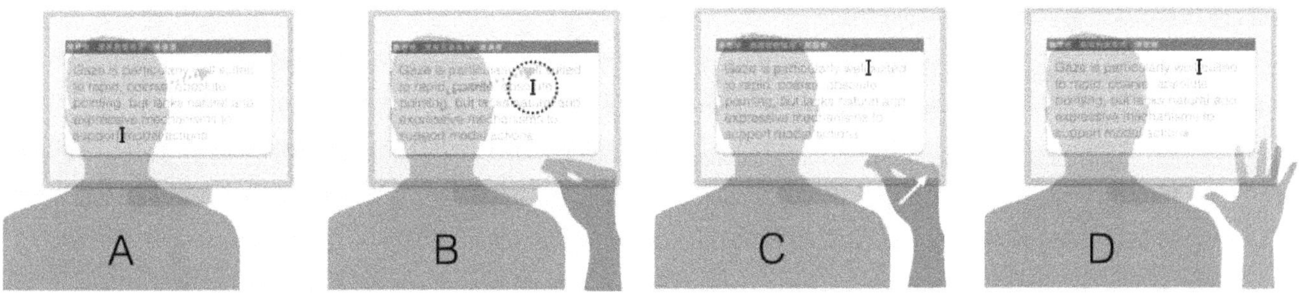

Figure 7. An example of a below gaze threshold interaction using continuous hand gesture interaction to reposition a cursor. (A) The user wishes to reposition the cursor, and gazes at the destination. (B) He pinches his hand, and the cursor is moved to the approximate gaze location (uncertainty shown as a dotted circle). (C) By translating the pinched hand, the user can finely manipulate the cursor position. (D) When satisfied with the position, the pinch is released. The user can e.g., resume typing.

space by grabbing with one or two hands. A bimanual two-finger pinch gesture is used to zoom the entire view about the gaze point. This allows for much smoother navigation to the specific section of the model within the user's focus. Finally, a single pinch is used to bring up additional information about an atom.

5.4 Evaluation

To better understand the pointing performance of gaze+ gesture, we ran a Fitts-style study. Of note, the diversity of study designs and targeting tasks make direct comparisons between pointing techniques difficult, especially when they are multimodal. Replicating others' apparatuses is equally problematic. As such, we endeavored to include a suite of comparative techniques, drawn from the literature and popular use to better ground our results and discussion [3, [10], 15, 21, 25, 30, 39].

Specifically, we include two gaze-driven techniques, one gesture-only technique, the mouse, and the trackpad. Although we described several techniques using gaze+gesture, we chose to evaluate our post-gaze, fine adjustment method. We hypothesized this would allow for rapid distance traversals whilst simultaneously permitting small-scale targeting (i.e., best of both worlds), which is where current gaze and gesture systems struggle.

Of note, there is an ongoing debate over whether Fitts' Law applies to gaze input, with research arguing both for [25, 39, 41] and against [5, 33]. Thus we caution that the raw numerical results generated from the study may not represent the intrinsic performance index needed to enable between-paper comparisons. Nonetheless, they do serve as a useful *relative* measure of performance within this study, with which we use to assess our results.

5.5 Participants

Twenty-two participants were recruited. Three participants' data were dropped: two due the inability of the Leap SDK to recognize participants' pinching gesture, and one that was a performance outlier (>3 SD above mean). Out of the 19 participants analyzed, 8 were female and 17 were right-handed; mean age was 25.8. None had prior experience with an eye tracker or free hand gesture control. Due to calibration issues with the Eye Tribe Tracker, we could not recruit users who wore glasses.

5.6 Conditions

In addition to testing gaze+gesture, we evaluated five additional input methods that we felt were interesting and relevant points of comparison or strong baselines. Appropriate gain values were informed by pilot studies.

- ***Mouse***: The mouse has repeatedly been shown to be an excellent pointing device (e.g. [1, 3]), and as such, serves as a gold standard baseline. Targets were selected by clicking.
- ***Trackpad***: Though it is less efficient than a mouse, the trackpad is an equally ubiquitous input mechanism, and so also serves as an aggressive baseline. Targets were selected by clicking down on the pad.
- ***Gaze+Dwell***: Gaze coupled with dwell for selection has been used in e.g., [15, 21, 25, 39]. We use a 500ms dwell time, which was shown to have the highest performance out of dwell-based methods in [22]. Gaze controls absolute cursor location; no clutching is required.
- ***Gaze+Blink***: Gaze plus blink for selection was used in e.g., [10, 30]. We evaluated a range of blink durations from the literature [30] during piloting, and settled on a blink duration of 100ms as a trigger as it was found to have the lowest false positive rate and overall fastest time. Gaze again controls absolute cursor location, without clutching.
- ***Gesture+Dwell***: Many systems have used free-space pointing or translation plus a dwell for selection (see e.g., [12, 31]). We used a 500ms dwell for selection. The Leap's field of view is insufficient to address the entire screen at a useable CD gain. Thus, a clutching mechanism is needed, for which we use a pinch gesture. When pinched, 1cm of hand movement corresponds to ~40px of cursor movement. When un-pinched, the hand is not tracked, enabling clutching.
- ***Gaze+Gesture***: When the hand is un-pinched, the approximate gaze position is shown as a blue outlined box superimposed on screen (Figure 8). When the hand is pinched, cursor appears at the center of the blue box, and the blue outline is hidden. The cursor can then be controlled by gesture, with 1cm of hand movement corresponding to ~20px of cursor movement.

5.7 Apparatus and Calibration

For conditions utilizing gaze, gesture, or both modalities, we use the apparatus described in the Implementation section (Figure 1). For the mouse and trackpad conditions, the input device was placed on the table. Users were seated 55 cm in front of a 19" (48 cm) 1280 x 1024 LCD monitor. At this distance, 32px corresponded to approximately 1° of visual arc. Our study software mediated all input for cursor control, displayed graphics, and logged study data.

No calibration was needed for gesture tracking. Calibrating the gaze tracker consisted of looking at nine targets on the screen, taking about 14 seconds to complete. The calibration procedure was repeated until the calibration routine reported a "four star" or "five star" (best possible) calibration result, corresponding to maximum inaccuracies of < 0.7° and < 0.5° respectively (as claimed by the Eye Tribe documentation). Users usually had to calibrate one to three times to achieve this result. In practice, we found accuracy to be closer to ±3°. Though participants were asked to hold their position and posture as best possible, we did not institute any strict rules.

5.8 Procedure

We use the ISO 9241-9 Fitts' study standard procedure [14] as it is widely used to produce targeting performance data comparable across studies. Each participant tested all six input methods (described above) in a random order. For each input method, users were presented with all combinations of target widths (1.5, 3.0 and 4.5cm) and target distances (7.5, 15, 22.5, 30cm). Each block pre-

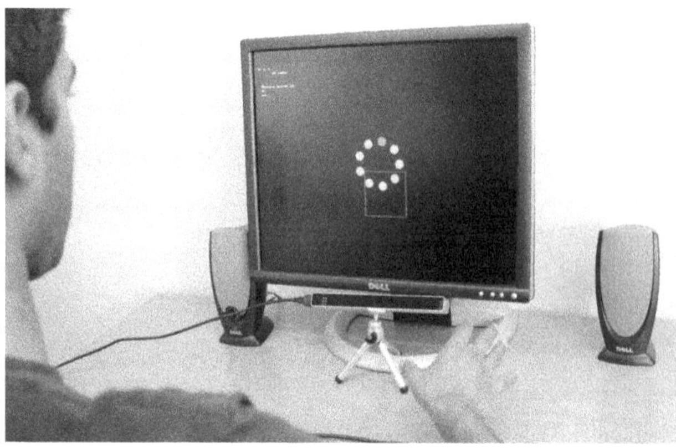

Figure 8. Gaze+gesture pointing technique. The blue square indicates the approximate gaze position.

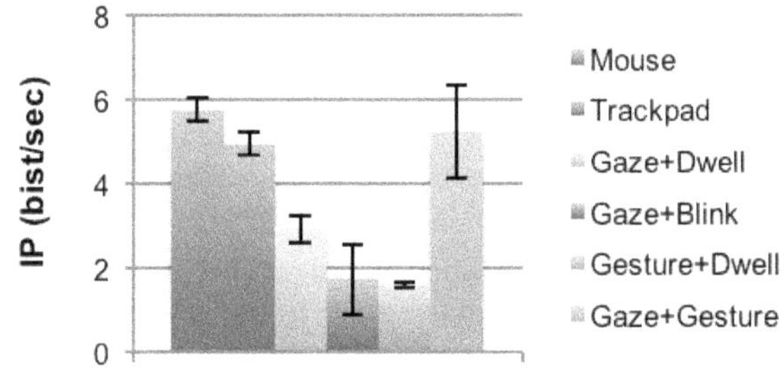

Figure 9. Index of Performance by input method. Error bars represent standard error.

sented nine circular targets in a multidirectional targeting task yielding nine movement times (trials) per block (Figure 8). Target width corresponded to target diameter while target distance corresponded to arrangement diameter. The order of the blocks was randomized within each input method. The target was denoted in red, while all others were grey. If users were unable to select the target within five seconds, the trial was skipped and logged as a time-out.

With each new input method, users were given a brief explanation and were allowed to practice for no more than five minutes. Users were permitted to rest after each block if they wished. The total number of trials generated was 19 participants x 6 input methods x 3 widths x 4 distances x 9 trials = 12,312, including time-outs.

6. RESULTS

We assessed both the Fitts-derived index of performance (IP) as well as the number of timed-out trials to evaluate the scalability of the techniques to small targets.

6.1 Performance

Figure 9 shows the mean IP across the six input methods. Repeated measures analysis of variance showed a significant main effect for difference between the mean of input methods ($F_{5,108} = 9.31$, $p < .0001$). From greatest to least, the mean indices of performance in bits/sec were: mouse, 5.77; gaze+gesture, 5.23; trackpad, 4.95; gaze+dwell, 2.91; gaze+blink, 1.72; and gesture+dwell, 1.57.

We then performed a Tukey HSD test to identify significant differences. The results show that there is no significant performance difference between the gaze+gesture, mouse, and trackpad conditions, which is a positive result given that we included the latter two as gold standards. However, these three methods all significantly outperform gaze+blink and gesture+dwell ($p < 0.05$). Only mouse and trackpad significantly outperform gaze+dwell.

6.2 Scalability to Small Targets

We hypothesized that supplementing gaze targeting with a low-CD-gain gesture suffix would enable users to more readily access smaller targets. To assess this, we look not at IP, but at the percentage of trials with timeouts at different size targets (i.e., the trials in which the user was not able to click the target within five seconds). As expected, the error rate increases as target size decreases (although neither the mouse nor trackpad conditions had any timeouts, and are thus not shown in Figure 10). The timeout rate is comparable across input methods with targets of size 3.0 and 4.5cm. With 1.5cm targets, methods relying on gaze alone (gaze+dwell and gaze+blink) dramatically increase in error. However, those relying on gesture (gesture+dwell and gaze+gesture) have a softer slope, with gaze+gesture performing best.

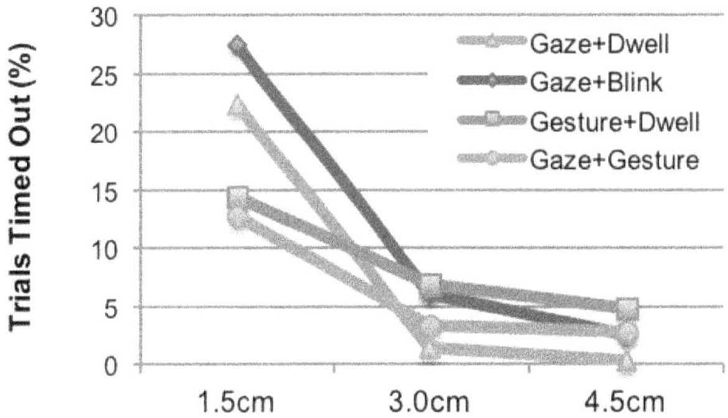

Figure 10. Percentage of timed-out trials by target size.

7. CONCLUSION

We have presented a set of interaction techniques combining gaze and free-space gesture to support common digital activities. We used a taxonomic breakdown to guide our development, organized along two basic interactive dimensions: whether the size of a desired object is above or below the eye tracker's accuracy threshold and whether the subsequent operation involves a discrete hand pose or continuous manipulation. For interactions with objects smaller than the eye tracker threshold, we proposed a synergistic gaze plus fine grain hand manipulation technique. We found that this technique was robust to sensing inaccuracies in commodity hardware, suggesting our approach could be used on low cost, off-the-shelf components. We compare the aforementioned precision pointing method against five baseline techniques; results suggest the technique could enhance systems using gaze or gesture alone.

Today, end-user gaze-augmented systems are rare. However, the increasing prevalence of high-resolution front-facing cameras on laptops, phones and tablets (especially the 2014 introduction of the face-tracking Amazon Fire Phone, which features four, front-facing, high speed infrared cameras) hints that gaze tracking could become ubiquitous on consumer devices in the future. Moreover, researchers continue to make progress on calibration-free eye trackers [32, 46], which would make it possible to create practical walk-up or pick-up and use gesture-augmented systems. Combined with other input modalities, powerful new interaction paradigms are possible. We believe that our example scenarios and interaction techniques underscore this opportunity, pointing the way towards more expressive and efficient free-space interactions.

8. REFERENCES

[1] Bérard, F., Ip, J., Benovoy, M., El-Shimy, D., Blum, J.R. and Cooperstock, J.R. Did "Minority Report" Get It Wrong? Superiority of the Mouse over 3D Input Devices in a 3D Placement Task. In *Proc. INTERACT '09*, 400-414.

[2] Bolt, R.A. Put-That-There: Voice and Gesture at the Graphics Interface. In *Proc. SIGGRAPH '80*, 262-270.

[3] Card, S.K., English, W.K. and Burr, B.J. 1978. Evaluation of mouse, rate-controlled isometric joystick, step keys, and text keys for text selection on a CRT. *Ergonomics* 21(8), 601-613.

[4] Chen, L. Incorporating gesture and gaze into multimodal models of human-to-human communication. In *Proc. NAACL-DocConsortium '06*, 211-214.

[5] Chi, C.F. and Lin, C.L. 1997. Speed and accuracy of eye-gaze pointing. *Percept. Mot. Skills*, 85(2), 705-718.

[6] Cockburn. A., Quinn, P., Gutwin, C., Ramos, G. and Looser, J. 2011. Air pointing: Design and evaluation of spatial target acquisition with and without visual feedback. *Int. J. Human-Computer Studies*, 69, 401-414.

[7] Connolly, K.J. 1998. Psychobiology of the Hand. Cambridge University Press.

[8] Erol, A., Bebis, G., Nicolescu, M., Boyle, R., and Twombly, X. 2007. Vision-based hand pose estimation: A review. *Comput. Vis. Image Und.*, 108(1), 52-73.

[9] The EyeTribe. Eye Tribe Tracker. `http://theeyetribe.com`

[10] Grauman, K., Betke, M., Lombardi, J., Gips, J. and Bradski, J.R. 2003. Communication via eye blinks and eyebrow raises: Video-based human-computer interfaces. *Univers. Access. Inform. Soc.* 2(4), 359-373.

[11] Hales, J., Rozado, D. and Mardanbegi, D. Interacting with objects in the environment by gaze and hand gestures. In *Proc. PETMEI '13*, 1-9.

[12] Hardenberg, C. and Bérard, F. Bare-Hand Human-Computer Interaction. In *Proc. PUI '01*, 1-8.

[13] Hutchinson, T. E., White, K. P. Jr., Martin, W. N., Reichert, K. C. and Frey, L. A. 1989. Human-computer interaction using eye-gaze input. *IEEE Trans. Syst., Man, Cybern.* 19(6), 1527-1534.

[14] ISO/DIS 9241-9. 1998. Ergonomic Requirements for Office Work with Visual Display Terminals, Non-keyboard Input Device Requirements.

[15] Jacob, R. J. K. What you look at is what you get: eye movement-based interaction techniques. In *Proc. CHI '90*, 11-18.

[16] Jones, B., Sodhi, R., Forsyth, D., Bailey, B., and Maciocci, G. Around device interaction for multiscale navigation. In *Proc. MobileHCI '12*, 83-92.

[17] Kim, H-J., Kim, H., Chae, S., Seo, J. and Han, T-D. AR pen and hand gestures: a new tool for pen drawings. In *CHI EA '13*, 943-948.

[18] Kratz, S., Rohs, M., Guse, D., Müller, J., Bailly, G. and Nischt, M. PalmSpace: continuous around-device gestures vs. multitouch for 3D rotation tasks on mobile devices. In *Proc. AVI '12,* 181-188.

[19] Kumar, M., Paepcke, A. and Winograd, T. EyePoint: Practical Pointing and Selection Using Gaze and Keyboard. In *Proc. CHI '07*, 421-430.

[20] Leap Motion, Inc. `https://www.leapmotion.com`

[21] MacKenzie, C. L., and Iberall, T. 1994. The Grasping Hand. Advances in Psychology, Vol. 104. Elsevier Science B.V. Amsterdam, The Netherlands.

[22] MacKenzie, I. S. 2012. Evaluating eye tracking systems for computer input. Gaze interaction and applications of eye tracking: Advances in assistive technologies, 205-225.

[23] Mateo, J.C., Agustin, J.S. and Hansen, J.P. Gaze Beats Mouse: Hands-free Selection by Combining Gaze and EMG. In *CHI EA '08*, 3039-3044.

[24] Microsoft Corp. Kinect. `http://www.xbox.com/en-US/kinect`

[25] Miniotas, D. Application of Fitts' law to eye gaze interaction. In *CHI EA '00*, 339-340.

[26] Morimoto, C. H. and Mimica, M. R. M. 2005. Eye gaze tracking techniques for interactive applications. *Comput. Vis. Image Underst.* 98(1), 4-24.

[27] Nevalainen, S. and Sajaniemi, J. Comparison of Three Eye Tracking Devices in Psychology of Programming Research. In *Proc. PPIG '04,* 151-158.

[28] Pfeuffer, K., Alexander, J., Chong, M.K. and Gellersen, H. Gaze-touch: Combining Gaze with Multi-touch for Interaction on the Same Surface. In *Proc. UIST '14.*

[29] Pouke, M., Karhu, A., Hickey, S., Arhippainen, L. Gaze tracking and non-touch gesture based interaction method for mobile 3D virtual spaces. In *Proc. OzCHI '12*, 505-512.

[30] Schiffman, H.R. 2001. Sensation and Perception: An Integrated Approach. New York: John Wiley & Sons, Inc. p. 70.

[31] Schwaller, M. and Lalanne, D. Pointing in the Air: Measuring the Effect of Hand Selection Strategies on Performance and Effort. In *SouthCHI '13*, 732-747.

[32] Shih, S. W., Wu, Y. T., & Liu, J. A calibration-free gaze tracking technique. In *Proc. ICPR '00*, 201-204.

[33] Sibert, L.E. and Jacob, R.J. Evaluation of Eye Gaze Interaction. In *Proc. CHI '00*, 281-288.

[34] Slaney, M., Rajan, R., Stolcke, A. and Parthasarathy, P. Gaze-enhanced speech recognition. In *Proc. ICASSP '14,* 3236-3240.

[35] Špakov, O., Isokoski, P. and Majaranta, P. Look and Lean: Accurate Head-Assisted Eye Pointing. In *Proc. ETRA '14*, 35-42.

[36] Starner, T., Auxier, J., Ashbrook, D. and Gandy, M. The Gesture Pendant: A Self-illuminating, Wearable, Infrared Computer Vision System for Home Automation Control and Medical Monitoring. In *Proc. ISWC '00*, 87-94.

[37] Stellmach, S., and Dachselt, R. Look & touch: gaze-supported target acquisition. In *Proc. CHI '12*, 2981-2990.

[38] Stellmach, S. and Dachselt, R. Still looking: investigating seamless gaze-supported selection, positioning, and manipulation of distant targets. In *Proc. CHI '13*, 285-294.

[39] Ware, C. and Mikaelian, H.H. An evaluation of an eye tracker as a device for computer input. In *Proc. CHI '87*, 183-188.

[40] Wigdor, D. and Wixon, D. 2011. Brave NUI World: Designing Natural User Interfaces for Touch and Gesture. Morgan Kaufmann, 97-104.

[41] Wilson, A. and Cutrell, E. FlowMouse: a computer vision-based pointing and gesture input device. In *Proc. INTERACT '05*, 565-578.

[42] Wilson, F. 1998. The Hand: How Its Use Shapes the Brain, Language, and Human Culture. Pantheon Books, New York.

[43] Yoo, B., et al. 3D user interface combining gaze and hand gestures for large-scale display. In *CHI EA '10*, 3709-3714.

[44] Zhai, S., Morimoto, C. and Ihde, S. Manual and gaze input cascaded (MAGIC) pointing. In *Proc. CHI '99*, 246-253.

[45] Zhang, X., Chen, X., Wang, W., Yang, J., Lantz, V. and Wang, K. Hand gesture recognition and virtual game control based on 3D accelerometer and EMG sensors. In *Proc. IUI '09*, 401-406.

[46] Zhu, Z., & Ji, Q. 2004. Eye and gaze tracking for interactive graphic display. *Mach. Vis. Appl.*, *15*(3), 139-148.

[47] Zimmerman, T., Lanier, J., Blanchard, C., Bryson, S. and Harvill, Y. A hand gesture interface device. In *Proc. CHI '87*, 189-192.

Digital Flavor: Towards Digitally Simulating Virtual Flavors

Nimesha Ranasinghe[1], Gajan Suthokumar[2], Kuan-Yi Lee[3], Ellen Yi-Luen Do[4]
Keio-NUS CUTE Center
Interactive and Digital Media Institute
National University of Singapore
nimesha82@gmail.com[1], {gajan004[2], kuanyi22[3]}@gmail.com, ellendo@acm.org[4]

ABSTRACT

Flavor is often a pleasurable sensory perception we experience daily while eating and drinking. However, the sensation of flavor is rarely considered in the age of digital communication mainly due to the unavailability of flavors as a digitally controllable media. This paper introduces a digital instrument (Digital Flavor Synthesizing device), which actuates taste (electrical and thermal stimulation) and smell sensations (controlled scent emitting) together to simulate different flavors digitally. A preliminary user experiment is conducted to study the effectiveness of this method with predefined five different flavor stimuli. Experimental results show that the users were effectively able to identify different flavors such as minty, spicy, and lemony. Moreover, we outline several challenges ahead along with future possibilities of this technology. In summary, our work demonstrates a novel controllable instrument for flavor simulation, which will be valuable in multimodal interactive systems for rendering virtual flavors digitally.

Categories and Subject Descriptors

H.5.1 [**Information Interfaces and Presentation (I.7)**]: Multimedia Information Systems - Artificial, augmented, and virtual realities; H.5.m. [**Information Interfaces and Presentation (e.g. HCI)**]: Miscellaneous

General Terms

Experimentation, Measurement

Keywords

Flavor, Artificial flavor, Smell, Taste, Multimodal interaction, User interfaces, Virtual reality

1. INTRODUCTION

The sensation of flavor is mostly referred to the stimulus experienced in the mouth (or tongue) when consuming food or drinks. Thus, flavor is one of the most apparent factors that contributes to successful food choice in humans. However, it is a complex multisensory experience mainly recognized as a combination of taste (gustation) and smell (olfaction) sensations [1, 10]. In addition to the senses of taste and smell, the senses of vision, audition, and tactition (somatosensory) are also involved in flavor perception [3].

Important contributions of taste and smell senses (including the interactions between these two senses) for flavor perception is highlighted in several experimental studies [5, 33]. They have shown that people frequently get confused between the taste of food or beverages with the sensations of smell and vice versa. For example, when the participants were asked to explain the odor of vanilla, they consistently reported it as smelling 'sweet,' where sweet is one of the primary taste sensations, which is a sensory function directly associated with the human tongue. Taste is typically the five sensations (sour, salty, sweet, bitter, and umami), whereas flavor is infinite and cognitive. This example highlights the significance of both taste and smell sensations to perception of flavors.

Today, the importance of electronic media is enormous as it is closely associated with our daily interactions. However, these interactions are still dependent on limited senses or channels [9]. Few research works had paid attention to simulate the sensation of flavor in digital form. Furthermore, the experience of flavor is often richly layered with emotions and memories [12, 13], and the mutual enjoyment of food is a common means of bonding between people [35]. However, currently, it has been difficult to share flavors digitally other than verbal and pictorial descriptions of those sensations due to three main issues: 1) there has not been a standard methodology to utilize flavors as a digitally controllable media, 2) lack of understanding of the sensation itself and how the brain perceives it, and 3) cross sensory perception of flavor and contributions from different senses. Thus, this paper introduces Digital Flavor, a new form of digital technology to simulate sensations of flavors digitally in humans.

The Digital Flavor technology combines the simulation of the taste and smell sensations (shown in Figure 1). To deliver artificial flavors, we developed a digital control system, the Digital Flavor Synthesizer, which digitally synthesizes taste and smell sensations. It has two main modules for simulating the sensations of taste and smell. The taste simulation technology is developed on existing research that has discovered the possibility of generating certain taste sensations by applying controlled electrical pulses and heating and

ICMI '15, November 9–13, 2015, Seattle, WA, USA.
© 2015 ACM. ISBN 978-1-4503-3912-4/15/11 ...$15.00.
DOI: http://dx.doi.org/10.1145/2818346.2820761.

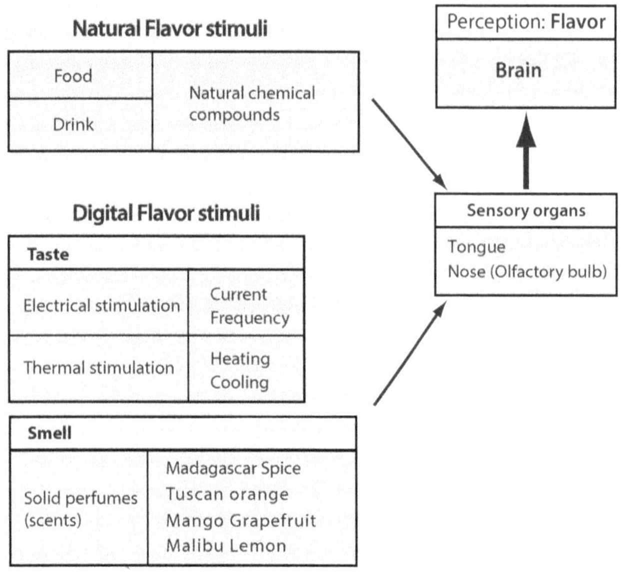

Figure 1: Correspondence between natural flavor stimuli and digital flavor stimuli to actuate specific flavors on humans

cooling the human tongue [6, 21, 25, 28]. The system has two silver electrodes to actuate the user's tongue to simulate taste sensations. Furthermore, a smell emitting module is developed to incorporate distinct scents using solid perfumes through a controlled heating mechanism.

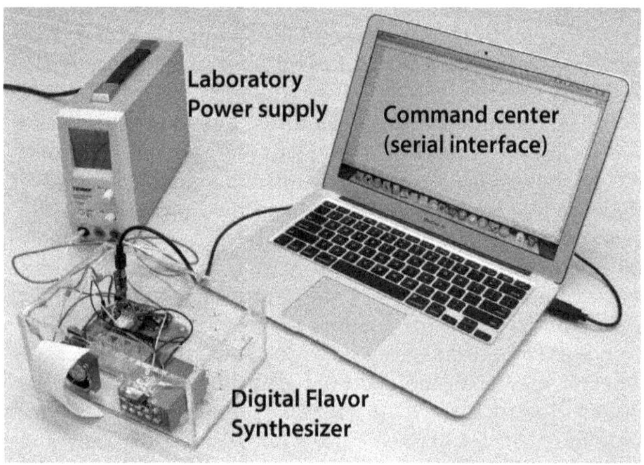

Figure 2: Setup of the Digital Flavor Synthesizer with the control-command computer and DC power supply

The laboratory setup of the Digital Flavor Synthesizer is shown in Figure 2. The system has several submodules for electrical stimulation, thermal stimulation, smell emitting, and a wearable tongue interface (which consists of a pair of silver electrodes). The electrical stimulation submodule sends weak and controlled electrical pulses (by manipulating the frequency and current of the electrical stimuli) to silver electrodes. Additionally, temperature changes are achieved on silver electrodes using a Peltier semiconductor element[1], which is able to heat and cool rapidly. A heat sink is used to provide an efficient temperature control. In addition, the smell emitting submodule has four small compartments to store four different scents in the form of solid perfumes. Each of these compartments has a resister based heating mechanism to emit smells. Additionally, the computer is connected to the Digital Flavor Synthesizer as a command center to manipulate different stimuli through a serial interface. As shown in Figure 3, when using the device, artificial flavors are delivered as a combination of digital stimulated taste sensations and different scents.

[1]http://www.peltier-info.com/

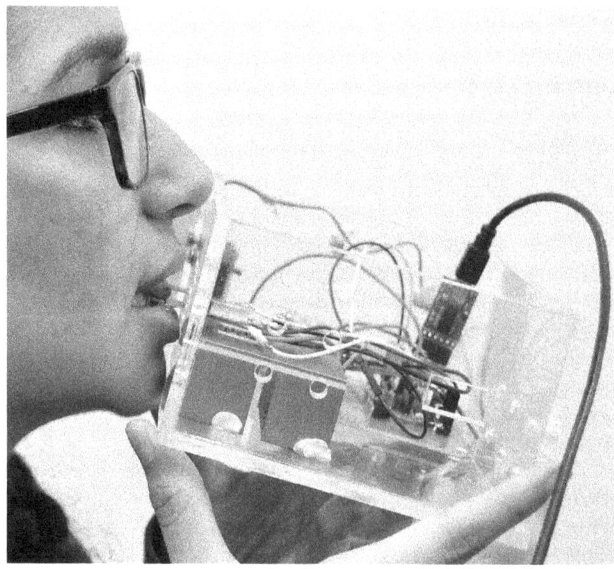

Figure 3: A participant is using the Digital Flavor synthesizing device. Her tip of the tongue is contacting the two silver electrodes, while smell emitting module directs the corresponding scent using a small fan

A preliminary user experiment was conducted with untrained participants on several pre-defined flavor (smell and taste) combinations. The primary motivation of this experiment was to study the effects of overlaying different smells on artificially simulated taste sensations. Thus, we hypothesize that the artificial taste sensations (perceived through electrical and thermal stimulation on the tongue) can be enhanced as flavor sensations by overlaying different scents. As studied in [21, 25, 28], sour taste is reported as the most prevailing sensation through electrical stimulation on the human tongue. In addition, users also reported spicy (when the temperature is increased) and minty (when the temperature is decreased) sensations through thermal stimulation on the tongue. Thus, we selected these three as main perceptions through tongue (sour, spicy, and minty) to further experiment with different combinations of smells (solid perfumes[2]: Tuscan Orange, Brazilian Mango, Malibu Lemon, and Madagascar Spice).

A summary of different formulated artificial flavor stimuli is described below with the corresponding properties of thermal and electrical stimulation. We examine sour taste (which is the only primary taste sensation used in this study)

[2]http://www.pacificaperfume.com/beauty/perfume/solid-perfumes

with three different smell sensations to further explore the variations in perceiving different flavors due to the differences in smell sensations only. The rationale behind selecting these stimuli is to simulate real fruits or drinks. For example, when we explain the flavor of an orange, we usually divide the perception as sour taste and orange smell.

1. **Sour** (magnitude of current: 180μA, Frequency: 800Hz) AND **Orange**
2. **Sour** (magnitude of current: 180μA, Frequency: 800Hz) AND **Mango**
3. **Sour** (magnitude of current: 180μA, Frequency: 800Hz) AND **Lemon**
4. **Spicy** (magnitude of current: 20μA, Frequency: 400Hz, Temperature: 36°C) AND **Spice (spicy clove)**
5. **Minty** (magnitude of current: 20μA, Frequency: 400Hz, Temperature: 18°C) AND **Lemon**

The initial results clearly show that artificial taste sensations can be extended by overlaying different smells. For each stimulus, more than 60% agreed that the perceived sensations are richer than the taste sensations. Moreover, in stimulus 1 (sour + orange), 2 (sour + mango), and 3 (sour + lemon) participants were able to recognize different flavors although the same taste sensation was incorporated.

The rest of the paper is organized as follows. In the following section, we first review related work of Digital Flavor Simulation. Then we describe the system components and implementation of the Digital Taste Synthesizer. In the next two subsequent sections, we describe the findings of initial user experiments and current limitations of our system. Before concluding the paper, we present a detailed discussion of future challenges along with application possibilities of the digital flavor technology.

2. RELATED WORK

The last few years have seen an active growth of research attention in the study of two important human senses, the taste and smell, both in medical (neuroscience) and engineering (taste and smell simulation) domains. In this section, we discuss related research focusing mainly on taste and smell simulation technologies.

There have been a few attempts to develop an integrated and comprehensive approach to simulate all five basic human senses. Sensorama is one of the earliest machines developed for multisensory interactions (immersion) including the sense of smell [11]. It is a mechanical device which considered as the cinema of the future. It also has a significant recognition in the history of virtual reality and interactive computer graphics technologies.

In recent years, a virtual reality helmet, "Virtual cocoon," is developed by British scientists to simulate all five human senses [7]. The helmet releases chemicals in order to stimulate both smell and taste senses, while hearing, sight, and touch senses are stimulated digitally. However, the system is considerably larger in size since it uses several arrays of chemical to stimulate smell and taste senses, hence the system is not portable.

Another example of using chemicals to actuate the sense of taste is TasteScreen [19]. The system, which attaches to the top of the user's computer screen, holds 20 different chemical flavoring cartridges to mix and spray toward the display. Then the user is able to taste the dispensed taste by licking the computer screen. However, this approach is questionable in two aspects. Firstly, the use of a computer screen as the delivery method for chemicals may not be easy to interact. Secondly, the suggested user behaviors may not be feasible since most users may find licking their screens distasteful.

In recent research, not only the smell simulation technologies but also smell based interactions, and its future possibilities are envisioned. "Smelling Screen" describes a new olfactory display system that can be embedded into a display/screen. The system has four fans in four corners along with liquid-state smell sources. When required, the system emits the odors, and the directions can be manipulated by controlling the airflow, which creates a virtual odor experience for the viewers [18].

Furthermore, Narumi et al. introduces several studies based on cross-sensory interactions of visual, taste, and smell. In "Augmented Reality Flavors", Narumi et al. describes a system that overlays visual and olfactory information on existing cookies. The cookies have edible AR markers printed on top of them, where the system identifies them and overlays appropriate visual and olfactory information. The experimental results show that the users perceive different tastes of cookies based on virtual cross-sensory information overlaid [22, 23].

In "Opportunities for Odor", Obrist et al. investigates the experiences of smell and emotions that connect to them from a future design perspective. They collected total of 439 smell stories and categorized them into ten primary groups including smell based memory, smell based detection, smell based social interactions, smell based mood and behavior. Later, several implications were developed based on these categories to provide guidance for smell enhanced technology designs [24]. Some of these implications are smell-enhanced storytelling, reminders with smell, sharing smells with family members, and smells combined with everyday objects and experiences.

Alternatively, two related research works, which are useful for this research, are conducted by Nakamura et al. [21] and Ranasinghe et al. [28].

Nakamura et al. demonstrated the use of electricity for augmented gustation in [21]. They apply electric current through isotonic drinks (which contains electrolytes) and food (juicy vegetables, fruits, and cheese) to change the taste perception of those drinks and food. In this study, they are mainly concerned with the level of voltage and augmented sensations of food items. However, this technology concerns only on altering the taste sensations.

Additionally, Ranasinghe et al. presents Digital Taste Interface to simulate primary taste sensations based on electrical and thermal stimulation of the human tongue in [25, 26, 28]. Based on their experimental results, sour, salty, bitter, sweet (minor), spicy and minty sensations are simulated through electrical and thermal stimulation on the human tongue. However, their results are mostly limited to the primary taste sensations and not focusing on complex sensations, i.e. flavors.

In this work, we combined artificial taste simulation technology (based on electrical and thermal stimulation on the human tongue) and a smell emitting mechanism (by heating solid perfumes) into a single piece of technology and developed an interactive platform to synthesize flavors digitally. The primary motivation of the Digital Flavor technology is to create virtual flavors where people can enjoy digitally, however, not necessarily to augment chemical flavors or existing flavors with the technology. Thus, one of the advantageous of Digital Flavor technology is its ability to create and experiment with new flavors virtually by digitally blending distinct taste and smell sensations. In the future, simulation of flavors will be interested in food and beverage industry to develop experimental flavors and evaluate their acceptance with the people. Furthermore, in our system users do not want to ingest any chemical substances through their mouth to create virtual flavors.

Specific contributions of this Digital Flavor Synthesis are:

- Novel use of artificial taste sensations and smells together to formulate digital flavor experiences
- Digital controllability and repeatability of the generation of flavor sensations
- Introducing a method to implement virtual flavor experiences or interactions in human-computer interactive systems

3. SYSTEM DESCRIPTION

This section presents technical details of the Digital Flavor Synthesizer and specific technical measurements. As explained, there are four different submodules in the system: electrical stimulation submodule, thermal stimulation submodule, smell emitting submodule, and wearable tongue interface. To control these submodules, an Arduino Pro Mini[3] is used as the master controller module. The Digital Flavor Synthesizer system is displayed in Figure 4.

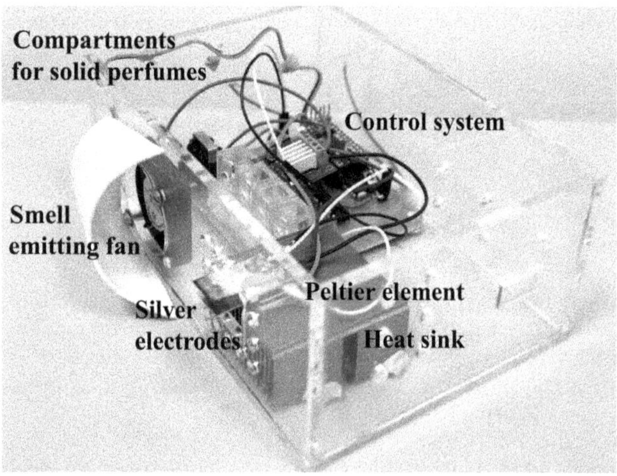

Figure 4: The implementation of Digital Flavor Synthesizer with main components.

3.1 Electrical stimulation submodule

The electrical stimulation submodule consists of a digital potentiometer (POT) and a constant-current source. The output voltage of the digital potentiometer is configured through the wiper position of digital POT. The output voltage controlled by the digital POT becomes the input for the constant-current source. To control the frequency, a Pulse-Width Modulation (PWM) based technique is developed.

The constant-current source is required since the impedance of the tongue has slight variations from person to person due to the differences in types and density of papillae on the tongue surface [15]. It is implemented using an operational amplifier (op-amp), a resister, and a NPN transistor to maintain constant current regardless of minor changes of the resistance. The electrical stimulation submodule provides square wave pulses to the silver electrodes with diverse current from 20μA to 200μA and frequency from 100Hz to 1200Hz. The output current of the electrical stimulation submodule is connected to two silver electrodes in the tongue interface.

3.2 Thermal stimulation submodule

A Peltier semiconductor element [16] is used for effective temperature control on the tongue. To drive the Peltier module, a Pololu motor driver[4] is used. A basic proportional-integral-derivative (PID) controller is implemented to drive the peltier module for the desired temperature. The direction, forward (heating) and reverse (cooling) is manually controlled by the user through the computer attached. The system is calibrated to work between 15°C and 40°C for the user experiments. The PID controller is configured to use three performance settings: optimum, medium, and slow. For example, in slow mode it draws less current, hence the system works extended period of time before the thermal shutdown occurs. For the experiments, we used medium settings to operate the system for a relatively extended period without effecting the thermal shutdown.

3.3 Smell emitting submodule

The smell emitting submodule is based on a simple, controllable heating mechanism using three resistors per each compartment filled with solid perfume paste. Each compartment has three parallel resistors valued at 15Ω connected through individual N-Channel Mosfets[5]. When the temperature is more than 40°C, the solid perfumes start to melt, thus emitting the corresponding scent. The intensity of the smell sensation can be managed using the PWM technique. The laboratory DC power-supply provides required power to operate the heating mechanism. Since the smell emitting module does not require accurate temperature control, the heating module is implemented using resistors. It has two main benefits, low power operation and fast heating. Main components of this module are illustrated in Figure 5.

We used solid perfume and temperature-based smell-diffusing mechanism mainly due to simplicity of the system. Using solid perfume is easier than using liquid based scents: both in terms of prototyping as well as cleaning and using the system. However, eventually we used an airflow mechanism to deliver scents by attaching a fan as shown in Figure 5.

3.4 Wearable tongue interface

The wearable tongue interface is developed with a Peltier element, two silver electrodes, and a heat sink. These components are arranged as a sandwich in different layers as shown in Figure 6. Two silver electrodes (95%) each with

[3]http://arduino.cc/en/Main/ArduinoBoardProMini

[4]http://www.pololu.com/

[5]IRFD014PBF

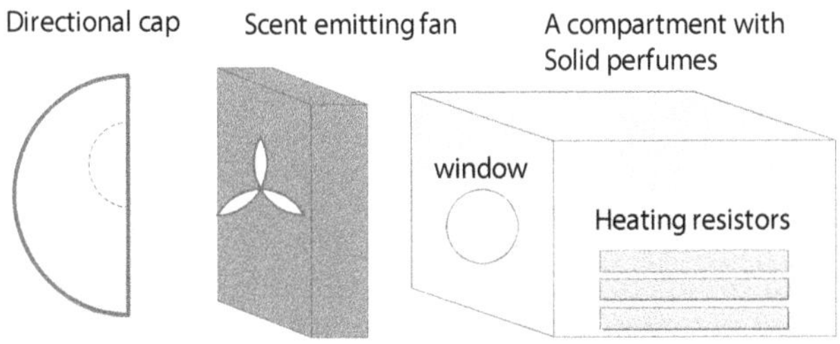

Figure 5: Different components used in scent emitting process including the heating resistors, extracting fan, and the directional cap used to blow scents towards users nose.

the dimensions of 40mm x 15mm x 0.2mm is used to connect the tongue interface with the users' tongue. These dimensions are selected to fit into the users' tongue comfortably and effortlessly. Silver is selected due to its high thermal and electrical conductivity [29, 20] and the non-toxic behavior with human tissues [17].

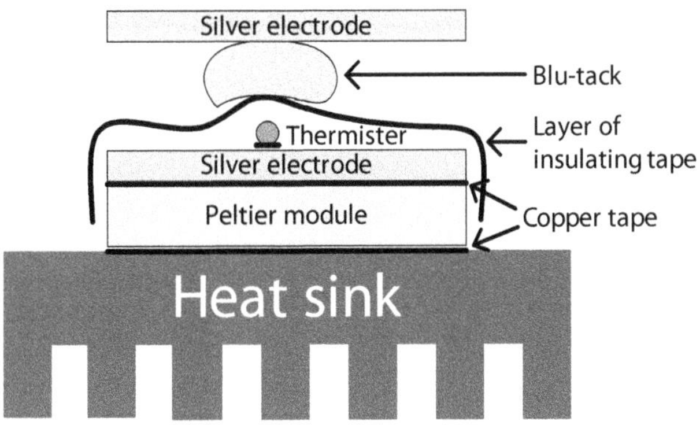

Figure 6: The integrated version of tongue interface for taste simulation. A sample of blu-tack (http://www.blutack.com) is used to control the distance between silver electrodes.

4. PRELIMINARY USER EXPERIMENT

To determine the effectiveness of artificial flavors, we conducted a user experiment with the Digital Flavor Synthesizer. For taste simulation, the tip of the tongue is contacted with two silver electrodes [2, 4, 28]. At the same time, depending on the settings, the smell emitting submodule emits scents towards users' nose.

4.0.1 Participants

Twenty four (24) participants (19 male and 5 female), aged between 20-40, were recruited for this experiment. Participants were randomly chosen and had no training before being tested. All participants were in good health (without known problems like cold, fever, or runny nose, etc.) and reported no taste or smell problems. They were explicitly informed not to smoke, nor to consume spiced meals, alcoholic beverages, strong tea or coffee one hour prior to the testing period as they may affect the results. After each experiment,

Trial	Taste stimuli	Flavor stimuli
1	Sour	Sour + Orange
2	Sour	Sour + Mango
3	Sour	Sour + Lemon
4	Spicy	Spicy + Spice (clove)
5	Minty	Minty + Lemon

Table 1: Different stimuli were presented to capture distinct flavor experiences.

participants were asked to describe their experience and any pertinent information related to their experience.

4.0.2 Apparatus

The experiments were conducted in a quiet private meeting room inside the laboratory. As shown in Figure 2, a notebook computer (control center), Digital Flavor Synthesizer, and a DC power supply were used during the experiments. Participants use the anterior ("tip") of the tongue to interact with silver electrodes. Before each experiment, both electrodes were rinsed using tap water, then sterilized using 70% isopropyl alcohol swabs, followed by deionized water [8].

4.0.3 Experimental setup

As mentioned, the experiment focused on studying the effects of flavor experiences when different smells are overlaid on artificially simulated taste sensations. Participants were presented with different stimuli in random order (first taste only then flavor stimulus) as stated in Table 1. Furthermore, participants rinsed their mouth with deionized water and smelled plain water between each stimuli and relaxed five minutes to prevent bias and counter balancing. We did not undertake any calibration to the system for individual participants and used the pre-configured stimuli as mentioned. Furthermore, in few occasions, we had to manually arrange the silver electrode on the participant's tongue for proper placement. We also continuously monitored the position of the electrodes on tongue during both experiments. This was essential for better and standard results.

One of the difficult challenges was to obtain accurate feedback from the participants' during the experiments. We prepared an information sheet to obtain their feedback on different stimuli (taste vs. flavor) by rating each stimulus in five-point Likert scales. It was prepared by considering three factors: 1) level of perception, 2) participant's likeliness or preference, and 3) comparison with a corresponding natural sensation, to determine the quality of different stimuli and experience.

Results suggested that during all five trials artificial flavor stimuli have stronger and richer perceptions than the artificial taste only stimuli. The normalized and averaged results are displayed in Figure 7. In addition, individual percentages of improvements are stated in Table 2.

Among all of the trials, minty has shown the highest improvement by integrating with the smell of lemon. During interviews after the experiments, many participants explained that they sensed 'minty + lemon' flavor similar to a cool menthol refreshing sensation. In addition, participants identified the spicy flavor as a hot and spicy burning sensation on their tongue. Several users also mentioned that flavor stimuli makes the sensations clearer and easier to dis-

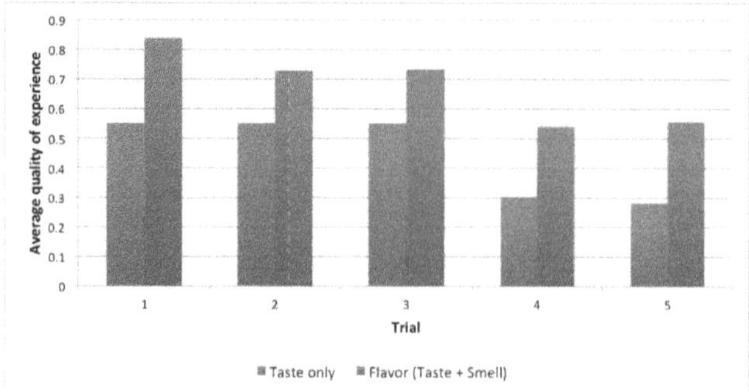

Figure 7: Average qualities reported for different stimuli (taste only and both smell and taste together - flavor) combinations

Trial	Improvement %
1	70.83
2	66.66
3	62.50
4	75.00
5	83.33

Table 2: Percentages of improvements reported from digital flavor experience over the taste only experience.

tinguish between them. Some of the users' comments are as follows: "overall it was a good experience and the flavors can be uniquely identified", "unique in its own special way, it enhances the taste sensations", "the sensation come even after my tongue removed from the machine due to the smells", "don't have any motivation to suck the metal chips", and "wish I could have more flavors such as curry or wasabi".

Most importantly, we noticed improvements of perceptions when using matching pairs of taste and smell sensations, for instance in trial 4 (combinations of spicy or hotness on the tongue and smell of spices). Similar to the matching combinations, user preferences are also highlighted in our results, particularly in trial 5. Many participants highlighted that even when they consume beverages in their daily lives, they would prefer minty lemony flavor over minty only.

5. LIMITATIONS AND FUTURE WORK

The Digital Flavor Synthesizer was specifically designed and developed to simulate different flavors on human beings. Hence, both accuracy and safety issues were considered during the design process. After the first few experiments conducted on human participants, it was noted that the system works in a stable manner and was comfortable for the user during the experiments.

Most participants found the experience as pleasant and surprising. However, one of the participants indicated that she did not like the flavors generated through the device, though she was surprised by the different sensations this instrument could simulate. In addition, several participants stated that some sensations were hard to identify and describe verbally. For instance, few participants commented that, "it's like a combined taste... sour and sweet together".

Moreover, on several occasions elicited flavors were found to be subjective (noteworthily between trials 1 and 3). We believe this occurred due to the similarity of citrus scents used in these trials (orange and lemon scents) and individual differences in perceiving them. However, we have not considered subjective differences during the experiments conducted (to record standard results), thus, our experimental findings do not reflect individual differences. Additionally, some participants stated that the smell of solid perfume felt a little artificial. Although we did not study this in detail, we suspect that the lack of visual information may contribute to this effect (either as real fruits: oranges & lemon or different colors: orange & yellow, as opposed to real world interactions with pieces of fruits or beverages).

As a possible solution, we suggest calibrating the stimuli (intensity of the scent and magnitude of current) according to users' perceptions in the future experiments to overcome this notable limitation. In addition, additional information through the visual channel should greatly improve the simulated perception as explained in [30]. These phenomena are usually observed in chemical (or natural) perception of flavors as well [36].

Additionally, it is important to conduct further studies on different electrode placements on the tongue for electrical and thermal stimulation. We selected the tip of the tongue for this experiment due to two main reasons: 1) easy to access and monitor the placement of electrodes for all the participants, and 2) the tip of the tongue identifies varieties of sensations (even for chemical stimulation of taste sensations), though the threshold of sensitivity can be slightly different [14].

We also observed the intriguing and interesting phenomenon of the cross sensory interactions as explained in [31]. Therefore, in future studies, other sensory information such as visual and auditory should also be incorporated into the technology as they all affect the perception of flavor. Also, further studies should conduct to learn how various intensity levels from different sensory channels are contributing to simulate more flavors.

Furthermore, as our focus was to simulate flavors without food or drinks, in this work we focused only on orthonasal stimulation of scents. However, in the real world, we perceive odor molecules of food and beverages (when we eat or drink) through retronasal stimulation, which commonly known as the "mouth smell" [32]. Therefore, it is also essential to focus future studies to understand the differences between orthonasal and retronasal stimulations of flavors.

5.1 Challenges ahead

Despite the significant progress on taste and smell simulation methodologies in recent years, much research works remains to be conducted before taste and smell sensors become integral part of virtual interactions. Apart from the fundamental difficulties, designing interfaces for these two senses (i.e. taste and smell) has wider challenges. We discuss few of them below:

- The primary difficulty of designing digital appliances for the sense of smell is the challenge of accessing the olfactory bulb or the nasal cavity externally, whereas, in the sense of taste it is easier to stimulate the tongue directly using external interfaces. Scientists have been discussing two viable methods for simulating smells using non-chemical means, 1) using non-contactable stimuli such as Infrared, Ultrasound, and the like or 2) using direct brain stimulation as explained in [27].

- Salivation and excess drainage in the nasal cavity are two of other related issues due to the nature of these senses. Wearable interfaces, especially for the sense of taste, has to compensate such situations to function properly. In addition, opening the mouth during stimulations might cause the tongue to dry, thus, affecting the functionality of the interface.

- Another notable challenge is the comfort level of the end users of such interfaces. For instance, wearable interfaces in mouth and nose, are not comfortable for the users. Moreover, users would get tired easily after holding the devices while using. One of the possibilities is to adopt a more user friendly interface design, for example in the form of a spoon, fork, straw, lollipop, and the like. Nevertheless, research works should conduct to learn more about the user acceptance of in-mouth or interfaces that are used very close to the users' mouth or face.

6. APPLICATIONS AND OPPORTUNITIES IN THE FUTURE

Applications of flavor simulation technologies are interdisciplinary, and extend not only towards multimodal interactions but also to several other disciplines such as medicine, food and flavor technologies, mixed reality, gaming, and entertainment. For example, an interesting application area would be to enhance remote co-dining and co-cooking experience (thereby improve existing work such as [34]). In one scenario, we envision a simple consumer technology that enables lonely elderly individuals to cook and taste meals collaboratively with their children from remote locations.

Furthermore, flavor (taste and smell) communication and messaging (Ex: Flavor Messaging System) will expand the interaction space in the digital world that will result in mindful interactions similar to the real world interactions. We will then be able to share and experience flavors digitally through social networks rather than sharing pictorial and text descriptions.

Furthermore, related to food and flavoring technologies, artificial taste and smell sensations can also be used as digital food ingredients in the future. For instance, with such technologies, in the near future people may eat plain porridge with virtual salt or sour ingredients; may drink water where a flavor simulating system can add different virtual soft drink flavors. These possibilities will also help in the medical domain for heart and diabetic patients, who are under restricted diets of sodium and sugar.

In addition, these research work might also have important implications for theoritical concepts such as the future of Internet with multisensory interactions by integrating the taste and smell senses into the existing web architecture [37].

Moreover, as an example of a medical application, diabetic patients would be able to use a similar digital instrument to stimulate sweet sensations without harming their actual blood sugar levels.

In gaming or virtual environment, users may taste as though they are in a natural environment by incorporating the proposed device into their gaming systems. For example, suppose the player is in a virtual kitchen; through the Digital Flavor Synthesizing method, the user can taste different virtual dishes prepared in the kitchen.

Moreover, we are keen to explore new opportunities of the Digital Flavor Synthesizer in the domains of ubiquitous and wearable technologies, mainly to utilize this technology in our everyday interactions. In the future, it is probable to embed this technology into eating-utensils, kitchenware, drink-ware, and the like. Conversely, the applications may also be reached customized tools such as personal grooming devices and mobile phone accessories.

7. CONCLUSION

In conclusion, a method for digitally synthesizing artificial flavors is presented in this paper. The technology is based on stimulating various combinations of taste and smell sensations using electrical stimulation, thermal stimulation, and solid perfumes. Five different trials with the distinct taste vs flavor combinations were examined during the user experiment. More importantly, this study has highlighted that the range of virtual taste perceptions can be improved by incorporating other sensation modalities into the electronic taste experiences.

The key contribution of this paper is the introduction of the sensation of flavor as a digitally controllable media. In the future, this methodology may develop new multisensory interaction technologies such as communicating flavors remotely and new possibilities such as selecting the spiciness of the food when ordering online or to verify the flavor of the food even before ordering them.

Furthermore, being an exploratory study, this work deserves several further experimental evaluations in different directions. One disadvantage of the current study is that we conduct the experiments in a controlled environment. To address this drawback, future research could investigate contributions from other modalities such as vision, texture, and audition by conducting experiments in different and natural settings in a dining room or a cafe. There is much work to be done before taste and smell interfaces can revolutionize the domain of digital interactions. However, we believe that this research on digital flavor simulation will enable cross-disciplinary, novel, and innovative application possibilities in the future.

8. ACKNOWLEDGMENTS

This research is supported by the Singapore National Research Foundation under its International Research Center Keio-NUS CUTE Center @ Singapore Funding Initiative and administered by the IDM Program Office.

9. REFERENCES

[1] M. Auvray and C. Spence. The multisensory perception of flavor. *Consciousness and cognition*, 17(3):1016–1031, 2008.

[2] J. Aviv, C. Hecht, H. Weinberg, J. Dalton, M. Urken, et al. Surface sensibility of the floor of the mouth and tongue in healthy controls and in radiated patients. *Otolaryngology–head and neck surgery: official journal of American Academy of Otolaryngology-Head and Neck Surgery*, 107(3):418, 1992.

[3] N. Bakalar. Sensory science: partners in flavour. *Nature*, 486(7403):S4–S5, 2012.

[4] R. Brown and D. McNeill. The" tip of the tongue" phenomenon. *Journal of verbal learning and verbal behavior*, 5(4):325–337, 1966.

[5] K. J. Burdach, J. H. Kroeze, and E. Köster. Nasal, retronasal, and gustatory perception: an experimental comparison. *Perception & psychophysics*, 36(3):205–208, 1984.

[6] A. Cruz and B. Green. Thermal stimulation of taste. *Nature*, 403(6772):889–892, 2000.

[7] D. Derbyshire. Revealed: The headset that will mimic all five senses and make the virtual world as convincing as real life, March 2009.

[8] R. Dobrin. Liquid cleaner-disinfectant composition for use in wiping down dental operatories, Aug. 7 1984. US Patent 4,464,293.

[9] T. H. Eriksen. *Tyranny of the moment: Fast and slow time in the information age*. Pluto Press, 2001.

[10] S. Firestein. How the olfactory system makes sense of scents. *Nature*, 413(6852):211–218, 2001.

[11] M. L. Heilig. Sensorama simulator, Aug. 28 1962. US Patent 3,050,870.

[12] R. S. Herz. Are odors the best cues to memory? a cross-modal comparison of associative memory stimulia. *Annals of the New York Academy of Sciences*, 855(1):670–674, 1998.

[13] R. S. Herz and G. C. Cupchik. The emotional distinctiveness of odor-evoked memories. *Chemical Senses*, 20(5):517–528, 1995.

[14] C. Kobayashi, L. Kennedy, and B. Halpern. Experience-induced changes in taste identification of monosodium glutamate (msg) are reversible. *Chemical senses*, 31(4):301–306, 2006.

[15] I. Lackovic and Z. Stare. Low-frequency dielectric properties of the oral mucosa. In *13th International Conference on Electrical Bioimpedance and the 8th Conference on Electrical Impedance Tomography*, pages 154–157. Springer, 2007.

[16] N. Maekawa, K. Shimoda, T. Komatsu, S. Murase, H. Okada, and H. Inoue. Peltier module, Nov. 24 1998. US Patent 5,841,064.

[17] G. Martinez-Castanon, N. Nino-Martinez, F. Martinez-Gutierrez, J. Martinez-Mendoza, and F. Ruiz. Synthesis and antibacterial activity of silver nanoparticles with different sizes. *Journal of Nanoparticle Research*, 10(8):1343–1348, 2008.

[18] H. Matsukura, T. Yoneda, and H. Ishida. Smelling screen: Development and evaluation of an olfactory display system for presenting a virtual odor source. *Visualization and Computer Graphics, IEEE Transactions on*, 19(4):606–615, 2013.

[19] D. Maynes-Aminzade. Edible bits: Seamless interfaces between people, data and food. *ACM CHI 2005 Extended Abstracts*, pages 2207–2210, 2005.

[20] N. Mott. The electrical conductivity of transition metals. *Proceedings of the Royal Society of London. Series A, Mathematical and Physical Sciences*, 153(880):699–717, 1936.

[21] H. Nakamura and H. Miyashita. Augmented gustation using electricity. In *Proceedings of the 2nd Augmented Human International Conference*, page 34. ACM, 2011.

[22] T. Narumi, M. Miyaura, T. Tanikawa, and M. Hirose. Simplification of olfactory stimuli in pseudo-gustatory displays. *IEEE transactions on visualization and computer graphics*, 20(4):504–512, 2014.

[23] T. Narumi, S. Nishizaka, T. Kajinami, T. Tanikawa, and M. Hirose. Augmented reality flavors: gustatory display based on edible marker and cross-modal interaction. In *Proceedings of the SIGCHI Conference on Human Factors in Computing Systems*, pages 93–102. ACM, 2011.

[24] M. Obrist, A. N. Tuch, and K. Hornbaek. Opportunities for odor: experiences with smell and implications for technology. In *Proceedings of the 32nd annual ACM conference on Human factors in computing systems*, pages 2843–2852. ACM, 2014.

[25] N. Ranasinghe, A. Cheok, R. Nakatsu, and E. Y.-L. Do. Simulating the sensation of taste for immersive experiences. In *Proceedings of the 2013 ACM international workshop on Immersive media experiences*, pages 29–34. ACM, 2013.

[26] N. Ranasinghe, A. D. Cheok, and R. Nakatsu. Taste/ip: the sensation of taste for digital communication. In *Proceedings of the 14th ACM international conference on Multimodal interaction*, pages 409–416. ACM, 2012.

[27] N. Ranasinghe, K. Karunanayaka, A. D. Cheok, O. N. N. Fernando, H. Nii, and P. Gopalakrishnakone. Digital taste and smell communication. In *Proceedings of the 6th International Conference on Body Area Networks*, pages 78–84. ICST, 2011.

[28] N. Ranasinghe, R. Nakatsu, H. Nii, and P. Gopalakrishnakone. Tongue mounted interface for digitally actuating the sense of taste. In *Wearable Computers (ISWC), 2012 16th International Symposium on*, pages 80–87. IEEE, 2012.

[29] J. Shackelford and W. Alexander. *CRC materials science and engineering handbook*. CRC, 2001.

[30] M. U. Shankar, C. A. Levitan, J. Prescott, and C. Spence. The influence of color and label information on flavor perception. *Chemosensory Perception*, 2(2):53–58, 2009.

[31] J. Simner, C. Cuskley, and S. Kirby. What sound does that taste? cross-modal mappings across gustation and audition. *Perception*, 39(4):553, 2010.

[32] C. Spence. Multisensory flavour perception. *Current Biology*, 23(9):R365–R369, 2013.

[33] R. J. Stevenson and R. A. Boakes. Sweet and sour smells: learned synesthesia between the senses of taste and smell. *The handbook of multisensory processes*, pages 69–83, 2004.

[34] J. Wei, A. D. Cheok, and R. Nakatsu. Let's have dinner together: evaluate the mediated co-dining experience. In *Proceedings of the 14th ACM international conference on Multimodal interaction*, pages 225–228. ACM, 2012.

[35] L. Wright, M. Hickson, and G. Frost. Eating together is important: using a dining room in an acute elderly medical ward increases energy intake. *Journal of human nutrition and dietetics*, 19(1):23–26, 2006.

[36] M. Zampini, E. Wantling, N. Phillips, and C. Spence. Multisensory flavor perception: Assessing the influence of fruit acids and color cues on the perception of fruit-flavored beverages. *Food quality and preference*, 19(3):335–343, 2008.

[37] H. Zhuge. Future interconnection environment. *Computer*, 38(4):27–33, 2005.

Different Strokes and Different Folks: Economical Dynamic Surface Sensing and Affect-Related Touch Recognition

Xi Laura Cang, Paul Bucci, Andrew Strang, Jeff Allen, Karon MacLean, H. Y. Sean Liu
Department of Computer Science
University of British Columbia
Vancouver, BC, Canada
{cang, pbucci, agstrang, jephalun, maclean, hliu02}@cs.ubc.ca

ABSTRACT

Social touch is an essential non-verbal channel whose great interactive potential can be realized by the ability to recognize gestures performed on inviting surfaces. To assess impact on recognition performance of sensor motion, substrate and coverings, we collected gesture data from a low-cost multitouch fabric pressure-location sensor while varying these factors. For six gestures most relevant in a haptic social robot context plus a no-touch control, we conducted two studies, with the sensor (1) stationary, varying *substrate* and *cover* (n=10); and (2) attached to a robot under a fur covering, *flexing* or *stationary* (n=16).

For a stationary sensor, a random forest model achieved 90.0% recognition accuracy (chance 14.2%) when trained on all data, but as high as 94.6% (mean 89.1%) when trained on the same individual. A curved, flexing surface achieved 79.4% overall but averaged 85.7% when trained and tested on the same individual. These results suggest that under realistic conditions, recognition with this type of flexible sensor is sufficient for many applications of interactive social touch. We further found evidence that users exhibit an idiosyncratic 'touch signature', with potential to identify the toucher. Both findings enable varied contexts of affective or functional touch communication, from physically interactive robots to any touch-sensitive object.

Categories and Subject Descriptors

H.5.2 [**INFORMATION INTERFACES AND PRESENTATION**]: User Interfaces—*Haptic I/O*; I.5.2 [**PATTERN RECOGNITION**]: Design Methodology—*Classifier design and evaluation, Feature evaluation and selection*; I.5.4 [**PATTERN RECOGNITION**]: Applications—*Signal Processing*

General Terms

Gesture, Touch and Haptics; Affective Computing and Interaction; Human-Robot Interaction; Non-verbal behaviors

Keywords

Haptics, tangible interaction, social touch, affective touch, flexible touch sensor, pressure-location sensing, recognition techniques

ICMI 2015, November 9–13, 2015, Seattle, WA, USA.

ACM 978-1-4503-3912-4/15/11 ...$15.00.
DOI: http://dx.doi.org/10.1145/2818346.2820756.

1. INTRODUCTION

Words can sometimes be inefficient for communicating instructions or affective content. In many contexts, touch may be the best modality for conveying directive and emotion: imagine how informing someone to get out of the way quickly and clearly with one simple touch. To harness this communication channel, social robots working in tandem with humans must recognize the same haptic language that we use, of which gestures and affect are key components.

We focus on exploring the range of touch gestures detectable by a custom-built flexible fabric pressure sensor and evaluating the added noise from curvature, motion and material cover. Using common machine learning techniques, we highlight salient features of touch for recognizing both the type of gesture being performed, and the person performing the gesture—both the 'touch' and the 'toucher'.

Reliable gesture recognition is an important step towards further research in the field of affective touch. A strong foundation of research on gesture may allow us to detect the toucher's emotional state [14]. Until recently, this kind of research was difficult, as touch sensors were not easily deformable nor cheap in both price and computational resources. Our 10×10 sensor has 100 fingerpad-scale taxels recording pressure and 2-D location data, and we use a random forest classification method to approximate in situ recognition rates.

We first collected touch data for a set of six validated touch gestures [32] plus one control on a stationary sensor under a variety of substrate stiffnesses and coverings. We then mounted the same sensor on an actuated robot skeleton and collected similar data while varying the sensor's covering and motion (Fig. 1). Recognition rates were within 80–95% for all conditions we tested (chance 14.2%), a level of accuracy which will suffice for many purposes and is enough to merit empirical comparison to human recognition ability in future work. At the same time, we found individuals' touch signatures were idiosyncratic enough to permit identification of toucher within this sample, at an accuracy rate similar to that of the gestures themselves.

1.1 Questions and Contributions

We wished to learn:

Q1: How accurate is our flexible fabric sensor in predicting gesture and differentiating between users?;

Q2: How does sensor performance hold up under deformation due to curvature and motion, such as that produced by a zoomorphic social robot?; and

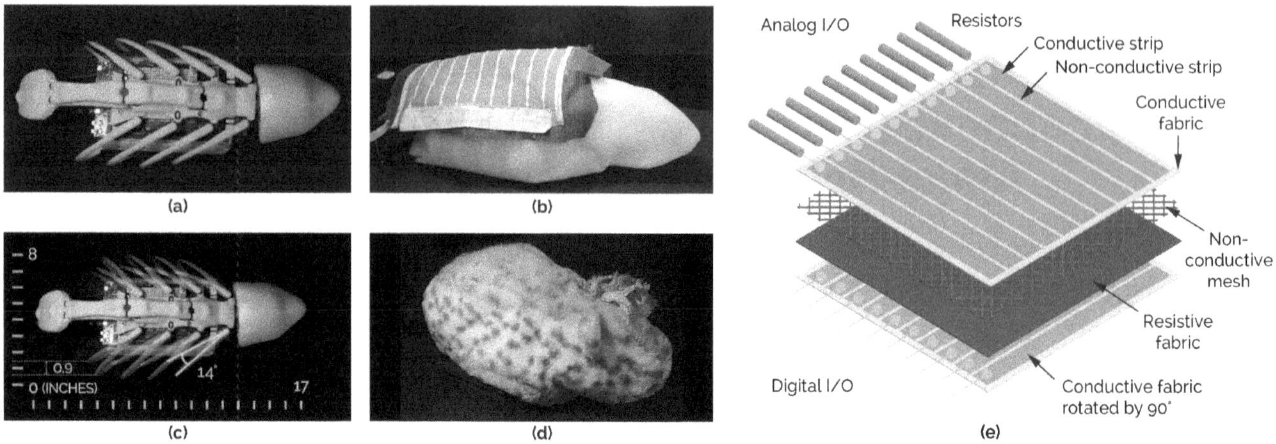

Figure 1: (a) Top view of the CuddleBot skeleton. (b) Touch sensor, pinned to foam substrate wrapped around the skeleton and corresponding to a *No touch* × *No motion* × *No cover* condition. (c) Full range of breathing motion used. (d) The fully-covered robot; a covering of nearly identical material was used in the study to facilitate quick condition changes. (e) The fabric pressure sensor constructed out of EeonTex conductive fabric <www.eeonyx.com>, wired to an Arduino microprocessor.

Q3: Is real-time gesture recognition computationally viable?

With 20-fold cross validation on random forest models, we contribute initial results of:

- deployable accuracy in gesture recognition (6 gestures + control): 91.4% on a firm, flat surface, 90.3% on a foam, curved surface, and 88.4% on a foam, curved, moving surface;
- differentiating toucher at 88.8% accuracy (n=26);
- factors underlying recognition performance;
- feasibility of real-time gesture recognition.

We also make our data and analysis publicly available[1].

Our study compares gesture recognition performance across a variety of conditions that approach real-time dynamic gesture recognition. Toucher recognition accuracy shows promise for incorporating personalized responses to an individual touch signature.

1.2 Applications

Accurate gesture recognition on a fabric touch sensor opens up gesture-based controls on any electronic device. For example, patients with limited speech could use a smart blanket with gesture recognition capabilities for comfort or health-reporting purposes. In the context of social robots, a sensor that can wrap around any irregular form could be used as a touch-sensitive skin. Outside of explicit gesture recognition, pressure-sensitive hospital sheets could alert caregivers of bedsore risk.

In a behavioural education context, a soft touch-sensing playmate capable of recognizing touch signatures may use this data to interpret and influence emotional state [14]. Such a robot could aid students testing on the autism spectrum by responding to anxious or agitated strokes with slow, soothing, regulated breathing—a behaviour shown to have calming benefits [23].

1.3 Detailed Requirements

Our sensing requirements are dictated by a zoomorphic robot, affectionately dubbed the CuddleBot, that invites touch with a soft furry body. Since a user will expect to interact with the CuddleBot via touch, having a full-body sensor that deforms with robot motion is required.

[1] All collected data and select analysis can be found at <www.cs.ubc.ca/labs/spin/data>

Movement and elasticity: The sensor must be highly flexible, somewhat elastic, and perform well while mounted on non-rigid and/or actuated surfaces.

Pressure range: Based on a preliminary survey of these touch pressures, we determined that our sensor needed to register touches between 0.005 and 1 kg. This range is appropriate for light tickles to heavy pats.

Multitouch: Multitouch capability allows us to compute varying pressure over an area, differentiating touches like *constant* and *pat* from *tickle* and *scratch*.

Resolution and computational cost: Taxel resolution, sampling rate, and computational cost must be balanced to achieve usable recognition accuracy. For real-time, our computational cost is dominated by sensor polling and grows with the number of taxels per grid edge. Our recognition tasks and feature selection explicitly analyze the differences between frames. In this case, accuracy plateaus with fingerpad-scale taxels, when sampled fast enough to capture voluntary movement (peaking at 10Hz [25]). We must be able to recognize changes in pressure and localized hand motions up to this frequency.

Single-fingerpad resolution ($\approx$2 taxels per inch) could capture small fluctuations; however, our gestures (not including our control *no touch*) either involve the flat or palm of hand (*constant*, *pat*, *rub*, *stroke*), or tend towards quickly crossing many taxels (*tickle*, *scratch*). This suggests that using statistical features that emphasized the changes from frame to frame could be used to achieve reasonable classification rates even at $\approx$1 inch taxels [7].

2. RELATED WORK

We situate our work in the context of social robotics and affect-encoding social touch. Gestural touch has been identified as a key component of human-robot cooperation [2]. However, the semantics of that touch is conveyed through nuance. For example, the same gesture could halt, contribute or modify another person's behaviour [2] depending on the emotional content inferred from pressure dynamics [14].

2.1 Social & Affective Touch Communication

In collaboration with human workers, robots employed in a laboratory or workshop setting presupposes a lexicon of social touch for operational interactions [8]. To ensure safe and effective communication, Gleeson et al identify the requirements of both a comprehensive gestural dictionary and lightweight sensing technology. The intimate nature of collaborative robotic household help emphasizes the importance of affect detection for social robots in this context [20, 1].

Previous work revealed correlations between gestural social touch and emotional communication [11, 14]. Humans recognize the affect encoded in gestural touch [12, 11], suggesting that machine recognition of emotional state can be achieved with sufficient sensing technology and clever feature extraction.

Much of the current work on social touch recognition uses a sensor worn on a static human or robotic arm [14, 26, 15, 16]. The collected data and signal processing procedures may not account for the added deformation noise of a soft-tissue zoomorphic robotic form in motion.

The use of animals [6] and interactive robots in animal form (such as Sony's pet-dog AIBO [3, 28], the seal-shaped PARO [31, 13, 18, 24]) suggest potential benefits in therapeutic use. Other touchable social robots include the teddy bear-like Huggable [27]; and Probo [22], which does not have a recognizable animal analogue. However, while real pets respond to complex touch commands anywhere on the body, this has been difficult to achieve without a generalized touch-sensitive skin.

In trying to establish zoomorphic robots as an emotional agent [7, 32], touch sensing strategies have included fur-level conductive threads, extensive biometric data, gyroscopes and accelerometers, to name a few. While this cavalcade of sensing produces encouraging results for social gesture classification [7, 32], it is far from the light-weight system required for automatic, real-time recognition.

An unexpected result emerging from social touch recognition is the demonstrably higher accuracy results for within-subject classification over between-subject [7, 15]. Leveraging this result may allow us to use touch behaviours to identify individuals and thus, recognize the nuances of an individual's "touch signature" to better predict touch gestures and, eventually, basic emotional content.

2.2 Flexible Pressure-Location Sensors

Real-time classification of social touch gestures on a flexing, noisy surface requires that we have manageable signal processing while retaining the ability to represent pressure and location.

Here we examine the suitability of existing sensing technology and recognize their influence on our custom build. We do not present our sensor as a contribution.

While many highly accurate pressure-location sensors exist, such as those developed for robot grippers used in dexterous manipulation [21, 30], these tend to be insufficiently flexible, overkill in terms of resolution, and considerably too expensive for the objectives outlined here.

Other work has used Force-Sensing Resistors (FSRs) affixed to a hard shell [32]. This reduces the need to calibrate for sensor drift over continued use, however, the trade-off non-aesthetic tactility, and difficulty in detecting touches between sensors—limiting rendered motion [2, 4].

Stretch sensors designed for medical purposes by Vista Medical[2] is the foremost inspiration for our custom sensor. However, Vista's sensors recognized only pressure without localization and did not have multitouch capability.

Several multitouch, flexible fabric sensors are available [16]. However, flexibility alone does not afford a full range of motion; it must be able to stretch and deform to approximate animal skin.

[2]Stretchable sensors can be purchased commercially from Vista Medical <www.vista-medical.com/subsite/stretch.php>

The design and sensing capabilities described by Flagg et al [7] informed many of our requirements and suggested that the bulk of the recognition accuracy could be achieved by the "below surface" sensor alone. However, Flagg's study did not consider the full design space of a robot in motion including a non-sensing fur and a variety of configurations. To evaluate how much information is compromised under these conditions, we applied a variety of realistic use noise sources to the sensor, both directly and indirectly.

3. STUDIES

We hypothesized that:

H1: *gesture recognition rates will decrease with noise-creating factors*—allowing us to rank these factors' impact on recognition performance, and their interactions therein.

H2: *variability in gesture execution will be higher between subjects than within subjects*—giving rise to the potential of differentiating individuals based on personal touch signatures.

3.1 Apparatus

We constructed a sensor by layering two squares of conductive EeonTex[3] Zebra fabric, aligned at 90 degrees, with a plastic standoff mesh separator and a sheet of EeonTex SLPA 20kΩ resistive fabric. Resistance value across a given taxel drops when pressure is applied, compressing the mesh separator so the conductive layers more closely approach each other. A circuit is constructed using an Arduino Mega microprocessor. Each fabric stripe is connected to a single I/O pin: the top layer is connected to analog input pins, and the bottom layer is connected to digital output pins (Fig. 1(e)).

The sensor is polled by sequentially sending a voltage through the bottom layer's digital pins. The analog pins read current; resistance (and hence current) varies with pressure.

Preliminary testing of our sensor using stationary weights showed that under ideal conditions, we were able to achieve a touch weight range of 0.005–1kg using 1kΩ resistors. Under the most severe conditions, lighter touches were lost in the dense fur; at the heavier end, touches were equalized by the yielding foam substrate. For Study 1, the curved-foam substrate with thick fur cover was the most obscuring condition; for Study 2, this was the cover condition with bot in motion.

Dynamic range is modulated through choice of resistor value. We found that values greater than 1kΩ allowed our sensor to register greater forces, but lost resolution; conversely, lower values gave greater granularity in recognizing very fine touches, but were too vulnerable to saturation at commonly applied force levels. The same sensor and microprocessor set were used in all studies described here.

3.2 Methods

Our two studies assessed how realistic conditions impacted sensor data and hence recognition accuracy; gestures and data collection procedures were unchanged.

3.2.1 Gestures and Sampling

We selected gestures from Yohanan et al's touch dictionary [32], choosing items most appropriate for human-animal interactions [7]. The sensor was placed on a table in front of a seated participant, a reference sheet with very general definitions for six selected gestures and one control was provided (Table 1). Participants were instructed to interpret each gesture as they saw fit; no further performance clarifications were provided.

[3]Sensor fabric purchased from <www.eeonyx.com>

Table 1: Touch gesture instructions as provided to participants.

Gesture	Suggested Definition
no touch	no contact with the sensor (control)
constant	touch contact without movement
pat	quick & gentle touches with the flat of the hand
rub	moving the hand to and fro with firm pressure
scratch	rubbing with the fingertips
stroke	moving hand repeatedly
tickle	touching with light finger movements

A frame consisted of pressure data from all 100 taxels in the 10×10 grid. We collected 10 seconds of continuous hand touch data at 54 frames per second for each combination of gesture and condition, randomizing gestures and conditions wherever possible.

3.2.2 Study 1: Cover and Substrate on Static Robot

We first measured gesture recognition for the static (unmoving) case, to assess impact of the sensor's substrate stiffness, curvature and covering thickness in absence of movement noise. This produced a factorial design of $4 \times 3 \times 7$ ($cover \times substrate \times gesture$), using gestures listed in Table 1.

$Cover$: The fabric's pile or density varied from no cover (participant touched sensor directly) to a very long, thick synthetic fur. Minky (a short furry fabric generally used for baby blankets), and a longer-furred fabric comprised intermediate variations.

$Substrate$: The material underneath the sensor consisted of a firm, flat surface (sensor affixed by velcro to a table); a spongy foam, flat surface; and a spongy foam, curved surface. In cases with foam, the sensor was pinned directly to the foam substrate.

To minimize sensor reading disturbances due to transitions (i.e., unwrapping and replacing the sensor on/off the robot body), we blocked our design on the $cover \times substrate$ conditions. Condition order was randomly generated for every participant, and gesture order was further randomized over each condition set. All participants completed all twelve masking conditions, with each generating 48 2s sample windows per gesture. A study session took approximately 50 minutes to complete. 10 volunteers (4 female, 6 male) were compensated $10 for their time.

3.2.3 Study 2: Stationary vs Moving Robot

Our second study focused on the impact of the robot's breathing movement. We varied $cover \times motion \times gesture$, for a $2 \times 2 \times 7$ factorial design. Factors consisted of $cover$ = {cover, no cover}, $motion$ = {breathing, not breathing}, and $gesture$ = {set of seven gestures}. Each participant performed each condition combination twice in a randomly generated order.

In the breathing condition, the sensor was attached to the CuddleBot, a cat-sized robot designed for therapeutic use. Fig. 1(a-b) shows the naked skeleton and the sensor pinned to the foam intermediary. The robot's 'breathing' motion was created by extending and contracting the paired rib assemblies in a $14°$ arc from the spine at 0.5Hz (Fig. 1(c)). We draped and pinned fabric over the sensor, approximating a full fur jacket for condition randomization while limiting sensor disruption (Fig. 1(d)),

Each session began by asking the participant to interact freely with the covered, moving robot for 1 minute to reduce novelty. Each condition was then presented twice, in random order, for a total of $((2 \times 2 \times 7) + 1) = 57$ trials. 16 participants (10 female, 6 male) were compensated $5 for the 30 minute session, each providing 32 2s samples of each gesture for every condition.

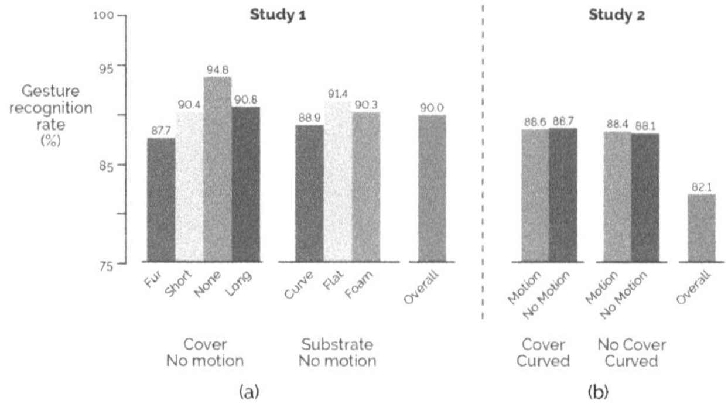

Figure 2: Mean gesture prediction accuracy rates with added pressure noise when (a) varying $substrate$ or $cover$ in Study 1 and (b) varying $motion$ and $cover$ on the same curved structure as in Study 2. Each bar represents an average accuracy rate over 10 trials; error bars are omitted as Δ across trials $< 0.001\%$ in each case.

3.3 Analysis and Results

We discarded the first and last second of each 10s gesture capture and divided the remaining 8s into four 2s windows. The 2s window (at 54Hz) was chosen to allow each gesture some periodicity; all gestures fit completely within 1s (Flagg [7]). Given the challenge of determining gesture boundaries in a realistic, real-time setting when a motion is steadily repeated, a 2s window allows capture of *at least* 1 complete gesture cycle.

To account for translatory gestures, we also calculated a centroid (average geometric centre) weighted by the pressure reading for each frame. Centroids were defined by row C_x (Eq. 1) and column position C_y (Eq. 1 with *i* and *j* indices reversed):

$$C_x = \frac{\sum_{i=1}^{10} \sum_{j=1}^{10} i * pressure(i,j)}{\sum_{i=1}^{10} \sum_{j=1}^{10} pressure(i,j)} \qquad (1)$$

We calculated weighted *pressure* by summing readings across each row, multiplying by index, and dividing by the unweighted frame sum (the sum of the full frame sensor reading). Repeated for each column, this provided a tuple of frame sum and centroid per frame.

As a "baseline" for both studies, we sampled sensor frames in the absence of gestures. In Study 1, each of the 12 (4 $cover \times$ 3 $substrate$) condition sets contributed 4320 frames; in Study 2, each of the 4 (2 $motion \times 2$ $cover$) condition sets contributed 6912 frames. To establish the effect of noise under each condition, we ran MANOVA over three frame-level dependent variables: pressure, C_x-coordinate, and C_y-coordinate. In all cases except one[4], all three variables showed significant differences at the $p < 0.001$ level. This indicates that the sensor is sensitive to changes in these conditions.

The data fails the Shapiro-Wilks test of normality; however, visual inspections of residual Q-Q plots did not reveal any systematic patterns. Together with our large sample size (n>4000 frames / condition), we proceeded with the normality assumption, alert to risk of inflated Type I error.

The six gestures (omitting no-touch data) were then compared with each other under the conditions of each study. MANOVA over the same three metrics (pressure, C_x, C_y) showed that gesture and participant combinations were statistically significant ($p < 0.001$). Differences in participant touch were detectable at frame level.

[4]For Study 2, the condition of *with-cover*$\times$*with-motion* under *no touch* did not show statistically significant differences in C_x data.

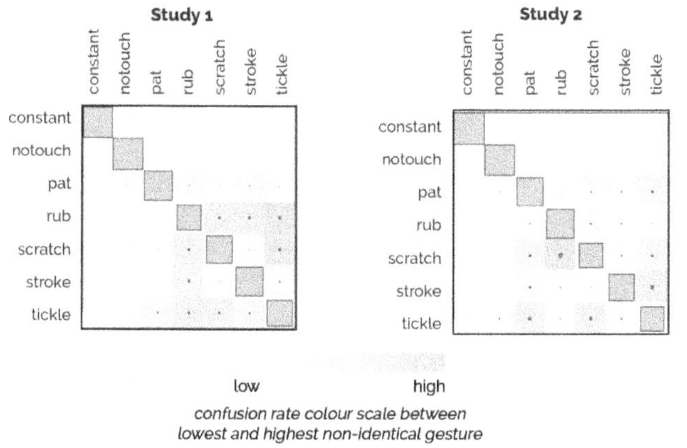

Figure 3: A modified Hinton confusion matrix for gesture classification. Horizontal (row) gestures are classified as the vertical (column) gesture. Saturation in non-diagonal squares represents number of misclassifications.

We calculated seven features across these three dimensions (frame value, C_x, C_y) for each 2s window for a total of 21 features. For each dimension, features are {maximum, minimum, mean, median, variance across all frames, total variance within the 2s window, area under the curve}. Condition variables ($curvature$, fur) or ($cover$, $motion$) make up the other features. $Participant$ labels were included for $gesture$ predictions and vice versa.

Each capture produced four 2s windows, providing repetition for training. Pairwise comparisons of all within- and between- capture windows generated two binomial distributions for statistically significant pairs using two-sample Kolmogorov-Smirnov (KS) tests. Permutation testing [9] using the KS test statistic did not detect a statistically significant difference ($p = 0.214$) between the distributions. This is consistent with our observations of participants varying touch behaviour both between and within captures.

We used Weka, an open-source machine learning application to classify gestures [10]. Flagg's comparison of random forest and a number of other algorithms showed that random forest performed best in gesture recognition of this kind [7]. We ran k-fold Cross Validation (CV) on Study 1 participant data for k = {5, 10, 20, 100} and found less than 1% improvement between 20- and 100-folds. While this CV technique does ensure that any one instance is included in the test or training set and not both, it cannot promise subject-independent classification. Running Leave-One-Out classification yielded slightly improved results but we were cautious to the inflated bias [17]. All reported classification performance is therefore based on the slightly conservative 20-fold cross validation of random forest models. Accuracy is defined as the percentage of data instances that are correctly classified.

3.3.1 Gesture Classification by Condition

H1: Gesture recognition rates will decrease with increase in noise-creating factors—*accepted*.

Comparing classification under Study 1 conditions (static surface), we found highest recognition accuracy with no cover on the firm, flat substrate case. Lowest performers were dense fur and curved, foam substrate. In Study 2 (dynamic surface, heavy versus no cover), conditioning across each of surface and motion factors had minor effect recognition rates (all $\approx$88%).

With models trained on individual, Study 1 showed little change in gesture prediction rate compared to all-data models. Study 2 individually-trained results are more similar to other studies, which also report training on single-condition data [7, 16, 19, 29].

Cover-substrate-motion: Fig. 2 shows overall gesture recognition accuracy by study and condition set.

We assessed relative noise levels by calculating effect sizes of significant conditions. Cohen's d reveals a large effect ($|d| \geq 0.8$ [5]) with the introduction of curvature (vs *no substrate*) and fur and short minky (vs *no cover*) in Study 1. Large effects ($|d| \geq 0.8$ [5]) from Study 2 were from introducing the cover (regardless of motion), and from the combination of having motion and cover. Interestingly enough, adding motion by itself produced a very low effect ($d \leq 0.08$). Further investigation into the interaction between cover and motion on pressure readings included Tukey's HSD of adjusted p-values to clarify the significance of stratified factors. While all other combinations remained significant at $p < 0.05$, the case of varying motion in the presence of a cover was alone insignificant at $p.adj = 0.7$.

A confusion matrix (Fig. 3) indicates how gestures were misclassified. In both studies, the most-misclassified was *tickle*.

Participant: We classified gestures with models trained by participant. In Study 1, mean accuracy was 89.1% (max=94.6%)[5]. Models trained on all Study 1 data were accurate at 90.0%, i.e. within 1% of the mean accuracy of the individual-trained models. This indicated that training on participants did not improve recognition when data was not conditioned on noise-creating factors.

For Study 2 (fewer noise factors) we found a greater effect for models trained on participants (mean=86.5%, max=97.3%)[6]. Training across all data gave 82.1% accuracy.

The $motion \times cover$ condition had an overall 79.4% recognition rate. Training on the subset of data with the most challenging conditions (in-motion, with-cover) still produced a higher recognition rate when using individual-trained models (mean=85.7%, min=73.7%, max=95.1%).

We compared mean pressure of gesture behaviours by individual versus that of the entire pool (i.e. how P1 performed $scratch$ versus how all participants performed $scratch$). All incidences were significant at $p < 0.05$ (Cohen's d effect sizes reported in Fig. 4).

3.3.2 Toucher Recognition

H2: Variability in gesture execution will be higher between subjects than within subjects—*partially accepted*, for the case of data compared within the same noise conditions.

The ability to recognize toucher may have great impact on reading emotional state. We compared performance in participant classification for models trained across the entire dataset, with those trained on the 6 meaningful gestures of our $gesture$ set (omitting *no touch*). We also look at accuracy rates on data collected in the most realistic condition (in-motion, with-cover).

Recognition rate by study: We compare recognition rate by study and gesture in Fig. 5. Study 1 achieves an overall accuracy rate of 78.5% (chance 10%), but for models trained by gesture, a mean of 87.9%. The highest contributing gesture is *constant* at 92.7%, followed by *pat* at 88.9%.

Using all Study 2 data, participant recognition was 80.3%. Training by gesture again showed recognition improvement; *constant* was best at 93.8%, followed by *pat* at 89.8% (mean, all 6 gestures: 85.4%).

Conditioning on only the *in-motion, with cover* factor, referred to in Fig. 5 as Study 2b, average recognition rates of participants

[5] Study 1 gesture recognition accuracy by participant: P1-93.0%, P2-83.8%, P3-85.0%, P4-92.6%, P5-93.2%, P6-88.0%, P7-94.6%, P8-91.7%, P9-86.0%, P10-83.4%

[6] Study 2 gesture recognition accuracy by participant: P1-90.2%, P2-86.6%, P3-86.6%, P4-91.1%, P5-81.3%, P6-86.1%, P7-84.8%, P8-79.5%, P9-95.5%, P10-79.5%, P11-90.2%, P12-93.8%, P13-97.3%, P14-83.0%, P15-79.5%, P16-79.5%

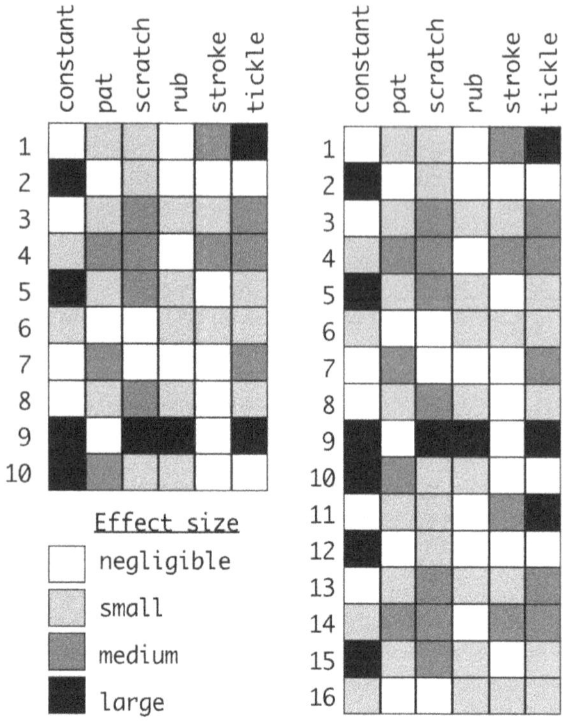

Figure 4: Cohen's d effect sizes of participant by gesture for each study.

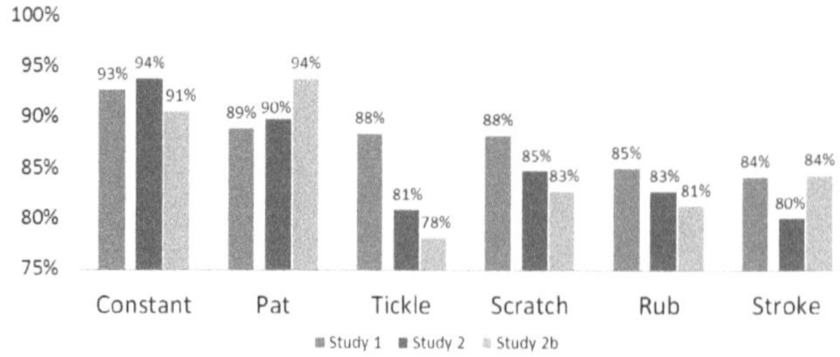

Figure 5: Mean subject recognition rates by gesture and study over 10 trials; error bars omitted as Δ across trials $< 0.01\%$ in each case. Study 2b refers to the 'in-motion, with cover' condition.

are 89.8%. Further splitting data to additionally train models by gesture does not provide additional improvement in mean performance (85.2%); this time *pat* is the highest performer (93.8%) and *constant* a close second (90.6%).

We again refer to effect sizes (Fig. 4) to consider the role of pressure in participant recognition; individuals making different gestures exhibit considerable variation in pressure patterns.

4. DISCUSSION

We discuss our findings in direct response to questions posed in Section 1.1.

Q1a: Potential accuracy of sensor in gesture recognition

Unsurprisingly, we found the highest recognition rate (94.8%) for the case of no covering and a flat, stiff, stationary surface (Study 1); these are the least demanding conditions and the ones we expected to perform the best.

In evaluating the degree to which noise factors degraded performance, we expected the noisiest conditions to be in Study 2: moving, curved, springy surface under a heavy fur cover. This achieved 88.6% recognition rate of our 6 gestures and 'no touch', among the lowest we observed. However, at just under 90%, this value is still usably high. Further work is required to assess the impact of nonuniform motion, as well as unknown gesture segmentation boundaries in lesser controlled conditions.

Q1b: Potential accuracy of sensor in user differentiation

Our studies show that the ability to pick a particular 'toucher' out of a known group varies by gesture. A priori knowledge of a condition also improves prediction accuracy, jumping from 80.3% trained over all data to 89.8% when trained on *in-motion*, *with-cover*, the noisiest condition. To see how this may change over the various gestures, we refer to Fig. 5 which ranks *constant* and *pat* as most identifiable. Fig. 4, which compares the effect size of pressure reading by participant and gesture, reveals that there are many large effects for *constant* gesture. This focus on pressure suggests that there may be revealing variations in individual 'heaviness of hand'.

Q2a: Impact on accuracy due to cover, substrate and motion

Over our two studies, we examined variations in cover thickness, substrate stiffness and curvature, and motion. Summarized in Fig. 2, we now discuss the impact of these factors individually.

Cover: The effect of a cover on classification performance is significant; more so than the underlying motion (as noted by Section 3.3.1). Fig. 2 further illustrates this. Regardless of whether we partition our data by *cover* on/off or *motion* present/absent, we achieve gesture recognition of at least 88.1%, 6% higher than training overall (82.1%).

The pressure applied over a denser, heavier fur cover may muffle some of the lighter touches and degrade transmission of touch pressure and/or location, thus confusing some gestures.

Another possible explanation could be from added familiarity that the cover affords. For example, according to one subject, *"When it had the fur on, I had a more pleasant experience...Without the fur, I found it difficult to touch it." (S7)* This opinion was expressed in some form by 10 of 16 Study 2 participants. More research is needed to determine if the fur invited more naturalistic touching.

Substrate: Compared to a flat, hard surface, a flat foam substrate decreased recognition accuracy by about 1% (Fig. 2a). It had slightly less impact than curvature or, comparing to Study 2, than motion. Given the sensor's piezoresistive construction, we anticipated the effect of firmly compliant backing to be small; this finding confirms that a somewhat springy underlying surface (helpful for conveying the sense of an animal body as well as a pleasant tactility) is feasible under a large-body touch sensor.

Motion: The relatively small effect size of motion in raw frame data is unexpected. However, in the context of Tukey's HSD results (with a cover, the motion effect is insignificant), we gain some further insight into just how small the effect of regular periodic motion is, and we confidently rank motion noise behind that of a cover.

This is very promising for the larger premise of reliable touch sensing on a flexing surface.

Interaction of motion and cover: There is a large effect size for the interaction between *cover* and *motion*, which is absent in recognition performance conditioned on added noise factors (Fig. 2). This consistent improvement over training on all data (overall at 82.1%) suggests that these large effect sizes of noise interference have little effect on recognition as long as we train and test on the same condition.

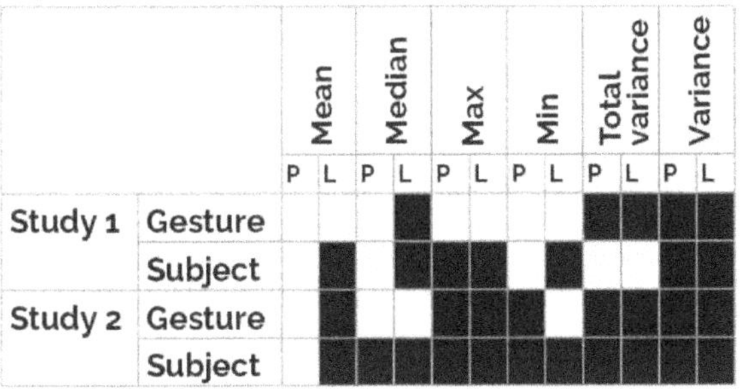

Figure 6: Top features as selected by Weka for each study. Classification tasks are Gesture and Subject, by Location (C_x,C_y) and Pressure features. Features selected at under 25% frequency in 20-fold cross validation are omitted.

Q2b: Gesture Recognizability:
Gesture confusion patterns reveal a considerable range of misclassification (the more saturated cells in Fig. 3). In Study 1, the most commonly misclassified gesture is rub as $tickle$; in Study 2 $scratch$ is most misclassified as rub. Both pairs are commonly executed as quick back-and-forth motions. This may be related to relative gesture pressure by individual: gestures like $constant$, generally more stationary, are predicted consistently and also indicate a larger effect size by pressure (Fig. 4). Quick motions being lost in the heavier covering may also contribute to these errors.

Q3a: Feature Utility
Making computational economy is the key to real-time recognition. Prioritized feature selection allows us to focus on high-performing dimensions. To help understand relative feature utility in our recognition tasks, we used Weka's Attribute Evaluator function to find the highest-weighted features for the random forest model (Fig. 6).

The feature set with the greatest ability to differentiate *gestures* related to pressure variance; meanwhile, location variance facilitated *toucher* recognition. People's touch signatures may vary more in physical location range, but, a gesture may be better characterized using pressure when *toucher* is known (Fig. 4).

These results suggest that using a subset of the features described here could increase computational efficiency, depending on the priority of recognition task needed and the variance exhibited by an actual data pool. Meanwhile, evaluating the performance of a reduced feature set is difficult due to the lack of a benchmark for comparing accuracy rates [15].

Q3b: Computational viability of real-time gesture recognition
The conditions evaluated here approached realism in some respects, specifically that of sensor covering, substrate, and underlying motion. Our post-hoc analysis indicated that a modern microprocessor could keep up with both sampling and recognition.

Our setup fell short of realism in at least one important factor: people are unlikely to perform distinct, discrete gestures with well-defined boundaries. A different computational architecture will be required to handle this problem (a topic of ongoing work). However at present, computational load is dominated by sampling rather than recognition, an overhead cost that will not necessarily change with real-time use (unless more selective sampling can be employed based on observed patterns of touching). It is thus quite likely that a more capable recognition engine will also be feasible with comparable computational resources. In situ real-time recognition may be better approximated by speaker-independent Leave-One-Out (LOO) sliding window. Our work uses k-fold CV as the more conservative accuracy rate (as compared to LOO), as we do expect a calibration process in which speaker behaviour is learned. Until we optimize, the best window size is unknown.

5. CONCLUSIONS

The results described here represent an initial feasibility assessment of the impact of flexing surfaces on gesture recognition performance. We found recognition rates from 80–95% for optimal to noisy conditions when distinguishing between social touch gestures relevant to interacting with a small touch-centric robotic entity. We further found an ability to distinguish individual toucher at a rate of 78.5% and 80.3% in Study 1 and Study 2 respectively. In the noisiest case (also the most realistic), training by condition increased participant recognition accuracy to 89.8%. The next step is evaluating more comprehensive sets of movement conditions.

The implication of a sensing system able to detect both individuality touch and toucher is considerable. For example, a sensor able to differentiate between users could provide a personalized set of experiences or controls.

Further, identifying the touch brings us closer to differentiating affective intent [14]; identifying toucher may allow us to qualify their touch behaviour. A sensor loaded with a personal touch profile could determine how far an individual deviates from that profile on a given day, and infer emotional status. To build such a profile, it will be important to establish the dimensions of a touch signature.

6. FUTURE WORK

We foresee many ways in which to extend this work.

More extensive movement conditions: The present study employed steady periodic motion of an underlying surface for a flexible sensor. A more general, and potentially challenging, environment will include irregular and unexpected motions.

Continuous gestures: The single-gesture samples of this study removed the need to segment data in pre-processing. In future, an algorithm will not know of gesture boundaries or length a priori, and will need to handle the case of seamlessly transitioning gestures.

One approach is to run several sampling windows of different length to search for varying touch activations at the cost of increased computational load. Future work needs to explore this and other architecture to determine a strategy to optimize for computational efficiency.

Pragmatic gestures: In this study, participants were instructed to perform a particular named touch gesture, but not with communicative intent or emotion context. The semantics of a "natural" touch will be dependent on context of situation and the user's own state; to determine communicative intent, it may be necessary to observe other factors as well.

Our participants often varied in how they interpreted a given gesture, both between participants, and individually between and within conditions. For the latter, we suspect users may have performed more authentic gestures on the moving, fur-covered robot than when it was flat, stationary and/or uncovered. We also observed differing touch behaviour from the beginning through the end of one capture, but our sensing mechanisms are unable to distinguish these cases.

Gesture stabilization and system interactivity: Finally, with more efficient algorithms deployable in realistic conditions, we plan a longitudinal study of long-term interactions in natural settings to investigate how individual gestures change over time as a toucher learns to interact with the sensing system.

7. ACKNOWLEDGMENTS

We would like to thank the Natural Sciences and Engineering Research Council of Canada (NSERC), SurfNet and the UBC SURE program for providing partial support of this work. We also thank Michael Phan-Ba for engineering the firmware and robot control, Philippe Kruchten for his mentorship, and finally, Oliver Schneider for the excellent title.

8. REFERENCES

[1] J. Allen and K. E. MacLean. Personal space invaders: Exploring robot-initated touch-based gestures for collaborative robotics. In *Proc ACM/IEEE Int'l Conf on Human-Robot Interaction - Extended Abstracts*, pages 185–186, 2015.

[2] B. D. Argall and A. G. Billard. A survey of tactile human–robot interactions. *Robotics and Autonomous Systems*, 58(10):1159–1176, 2010.

[3] M. R. Banks, L. M. Willoughby, and W. A. Banks. Animal-assisted therapy and loneliness in nursing homes: use of robotic versus living dogs. *J American Medical Directors Assoc*, 9(3):173–177, 2008.

[4] J. Chang, K. MacLean, and S. Yohanan. Gesture recognition in the haptic creature. In *Eurohaptics*, pages 385–391, 2010.

[5] J. Cohen. A power primer. *Psychological bulletin*, 112(1):155, 1992.

[6] K. M. Cole, A. Gawlinski, N. Steers, and J. Kotlerman. Animal-assisted therapy in patients hospitalized with heart failure. *American J of Critical Care*, 16(6):575–585, 2007.

[7] A. Flagg and K. MacLean. Affective touch gesture recognition for a furry zoomorphic machine. In *Proc Intl Conf on Tangible, Embedded and Embodied Interaction*, pages 25–32, 2013.

[8] B. Gleeson, K. MacLean, A. Haddadi, E. Croft, and J. Alcazar. Gestures for industry: intuitive human-robot communication from human observation. In *Proc. ACM/IEEE Int'l Conf on Human-robot interaction*, pages 349–356, 2013.

[9] P. Good. *Permutation tests: a practical guide to resampling methods for testing hypotheses*. Springer Science & Business Media, 2013.

[10] M. Hall, E. Frank, G. Holmes, B. Pfahringer, P. Reutemann, and I. H. Witten. The weka data mining software: an update. *ACM SIGKDD Explorations Newsletter*, 11(1):10–18, 2009.

[11] M. J. Hertenstein, R. Holmes, M. McCullough, and D. Keltner. The communication of emotion via touch. *Emotion*, 9(4):566, 2009.

[12] M. J. Hertenstein, D. Keltner, B. App, B. A. Bulleit, and A. R. Jaskolka. Touch communicates distinct emotions. *Emotion*, 6(3):528, 2006.

[13] K. Inoue, K. Wada, and R. Uehara. How effective is robot therapy?: Paro and people with dementia. In *Intl Fed for Medical and Biological Engineering*, pages 784–787, 2012.

[14] H. Y. Joung and E. Y.-L. Do. Tactile hand gesture recognition through haptic feedback for affective online communication. In *Universal Access in Human-Computer Interaction*, pages 555–563. Springer, 2011.

[15] M. M. Jung. Towards social touch intelligence: developing a robust system for automatic touch recognition. In *Proc Intl Conf on Multimodal Interaction*, pages 344–348, 2014.

[16] M. M. Jung, R. Poppe, M. Poel, and D. K. Heylen. Touching the void–introducing cost: Corpus of social touch. In *Proc Intl Conf on Multimodal Interaction*, pages 120–127, 2014.

[17] R. Kohavi et al. A study of cross-validation and bootstrap for accuracy estimation and model selection. In *Ijcai*, volume 14, pages 1137–1145, 1995.

[18] P. Marti, A. Pollini, A. Rullo, and T. Shibata. Engaging with artificial pets. In *Proc. Annual Conf European Assoc Cognitive Ergonomics*, pages 99–106, 2005.

[19] K. Nakajima, Y. Itoh, Y. Hayashi, K. Ikeda, K. Fujita, and T. Onoye. Emoballoon. In *Advances in Computer Entertainment*, pages 182–197. Springer, 2013.

[20] P. Rani, C. Liu, N. Sarkar, and E. Vanman. An empirical study of machine learning techniques for affect recognition in human–robot interaction. *Pattern Analysis and Applications*, 9(1):58–69, 2006.

[21] B. Robins, K. Dautenhahn, F. Amirabdollahian, F. Mastrogiovanni, and G. Cannata. Developing skin-based technologies for interactive robots-challenges in design, development and the possible integration in therapeutic environments. In *IEEE ROMAN*, pages xxii–xxiii, 2011.

[22] J. Saldien, K. Goris, S. Yilmazyildiz, W. Verhelst, and D. Lefeber. On the design of the huggable robot probo. *J. Physical Agents*, 2(2):3–12, 2008.

[23] Y. Sefidgar, K. MacLean, S. Yohanan, H. Van der Loos, E. Croft, et al. Design and evaluation of a touch-centered calming interaction with a social robot *in press*.

[24] T. Shibata and K. Wada. Robot therapy: a new approach for mental healthcare of the elderly-a mini-review. *Gerontology*, 57(4):378–386, 2010.

[25] K. B. Shimoga. Finger force and touch feedback issues in dexterous telemanipulation. In *Proc Intelligent Robotic Systems for Space Exploration*, pages 159–178, 1992.

[26] D. Silvera-Tawil, D. Rye, and M. Velonaki. Interpretation of social touch on an artificial arm covered with an eit-based sensitive skin. *Intl J of Social Robotics*, 6(4):489–505, 2014.

[27] W. D. Stiehl, J. Lieberman, C. Breazeal, L. Basel, L. Lalla, and M. Wolf. Design of a therapeutic robotic companion for relational, affective touch. In *ROMAN Workshop on Robot & Human Interactive Communication*, pages 408–415, 2005.

[28] T. Tamura, S. Yonemitsu, A. Itoh, D. Oikawa, A. Kawakami, Y. Higashi, T. Fujimooto, and K. Nakajima. Is an entertainment robot useful in the care of elderly people with severe dementia? *J Gerontology Series A: Biological Sciences and Medical Sciences*, 59(1):M83–M85, 2004.

[29] D. S. Tawil, D. Rye, and M. Velonaki. Touch modality interpretation for an eit-based sensitive skin. In *IEEE Conf on Robotics and Automation (ICRA)*, pages 3770–3776, 2011.

[30] J. Ulmen and M. Cutkosky. A robust, low-cost and low-noise artificial skin for human-friendly robots. In *Proc. IEEE Robotics and Automation (ICRA)*, pages 4836–4841, 2010.

[31] K. Wada, Y. Ikeda, K. Inoue, and R. Uehara. Development and preliminary evaluation of a caregiver's manual for robot therapy using the therapeutic seal robot paro. In *ROMAN*, pages 533–538, 2010.

[32] S. Yohanan and K. E. MacLean. The role of affective touch in human-robot interaction: Human intent and expectations in touching the haptic creature. *International Journal of Social Robotics*, 4(2):163–180, 2012.

MPHA: A Personal Hearing Doctor Based on Mobile Devices

Yuhao Wu
Research Group of Human Computer Speech Interaction
Tsinghua University, Beijing, China, 100084
yh-wu14@mails.tsinghua.edu.cn

Jia Jia
Research Group of Human Computer Speech Interaction
Tsinghua University, Beijing, China, 100084
jjia@mail.tsinghua.edu.cn

WaiKim Leung
Research Group of Human Computer Speech Interaction
Tsinghua University, Beijing, China, 100084
william.tsinghua2014@gmail.com

Yejun Liu
Research Group of Human Computer Speech Interaction
Tsinghua University, Beijing, China, 100084
onlyeye@live.cn

Lianhong Cai
Research Group of Human Computer Speech Interaction
Tsinghua University, Beijing, China, 100084
clh-dcs@mail.tsinghua.edu.cn

ABSTRACT

As more and more people inquire to know their hearing level condition, audiometry is becoming increasingly important. However, traditional audiometric method requires the involvement of audiometers, which are very expensive and time consuming. In this paper, we present mobile personal hearing assessment (MPHA), a novel interactive mode for testing hearing level based on mobile devices. MPHA, 1) provides a general method to calibrate sound intensity for mobile devices to guarantee the reliability and validity of the audiometry system; 2) designs an audiometric correction algorithm for the real noisy audiometric environment. The experimental results show that MPHA is reliable and valid compared with conventional audiometric assessment.

Categories and Subject Descriptors

H.5.2. [**Information Interfaces and Presentation**]: User Interfaces - Graphical user interfaces

Keywords

Multimodal interaction; Mobile device; Assessment; Audiometry; Hearing level; Health care.

1. INTRODUCTION

Hearing plays an important role in our daily life. Auditory sense influences not only the ability of listening, but also the ability of speaking and reading [21]. There is no doubt that hearing health has a strong relationship with our daily communication. So it is quite necessary to pay more attention to our hearing health condition.

Traditional hearing level assessment must be proceeded in hospital department of ear-nose-throat (E.N.T.), or hearing rehabilitation centers [10, 11]. The equipment (audiometer and soundproof room) is so expensive that not every E.N.T. holds qualification to evaluate people's hearing condition, resulting in medical resources lack for hearing health. Since it is always overcrowded in those medical institutes, people feel inconvenient to have an audiometry assessment regularly. Usually, we don't realize our hearing health condition until some serious problems on our listening come up, and have missed the best treatment period [21, 1].

To resolve the issues above, we propose a novel interactive mode to assess audiometry on mobile devices called mobile personal hearing assessment (MPHA). During the procedure of audiometric accessment using MPHA, no assistant people is needed. MPHA generates a series of accurate test tones and play them to users directly. Users judge whether they can hear the sound and feed back to MPHA. After the test, MPHA will show the results of hearing level healthy to the users.

Experiments results show that with an available interactive distance(30 ± 5 cm) and angle(30° to 90°), the MPHA can generate accurate sound signals compared with audiometers. Moreover, MPHA is proved to be reliable in both quiet and daily noisy(35dB) environment, and the errors are within the smallest unit(5dB) in audiometry.

The main contributions of the paper are:

- We present an automatic and reliable interactive mode to audiometry based on mobile devices. It is a good alternative for the pre-screening phase of hearing diagnosis, which is cost effective and convenient compared with the doctor-to-patient mode used in conventional hospitals.
- We propose a general method to calibrate sound intensity for mobile devices. It provides accurate test sounds, which guarantees the reliability and validity of the audiometry system.

ICMI 2015, November 9–13, 2015, Seattle, WA, USA.
 ISBN 978-1-4503-3912-4/15/11 ...$15.00.
DOI: http://dx.doi.org/10.1145/2818346.2820753.

- For the real audiometric environment with noises, we design an audiometric correction algorithm. Our implementation enables people to check his hearing level in working environment.

The rest of the paper is organized as follows. We first give an overview of related work in Section 2. Then in Section 3, we present our preliminary survey of 100 people, inquiring about their attitude towards hearing condition evaluation. The design and implementation of MPHA is described in Section 4 and five experimental results are reported in Section 5. We present the application scenarios of MPHA in Section 6 and conclude our work in Section 7.

2. BACKGROUND AND MOTIVATION

In clinical audiology, pure tone audiometry is a widely adopted method to test people's hearing sensitivity [21, 10, 1]. Pure tone audiometry is used to find out people's auditory threshold (i.e. the lowest sound people can hear) at different frequencies, and check hearing condition at each frequency level. The results of pure tone audiometry are basis of diagnosis and follow-up treatment [21, 10] and our work of hearing level assessment is based on the pure tone audiology.

Up to now, audiometry is proceeded in soundproof room, and it involves the participation of an audiometer, a subject, and a doctor each time. The subject and the hearing doctor both sit in the soundproof room. The doctor operates the audiometer to play a sound signal to the subject, then the subject feeds back hearing information to the doctor. The doctor decides what to do next according to subject's feedback [11, 9]. For traditional audiology assessment, there are some problems to overcome. First, the equipment and human resources are very expensive, and therefore small hospitals such as infirmary and community hospitals are not able to provide hearing health care. Second, the process is inconvenient and time-consuming, so people usually are not willing to check hearing conditioin regularly. Inspired by these findings, MPHA is designed to facilitate hearing health condition assessment.

3. PRELIMINARY STUDY

Before our research, we conducted a survey about people's attitude towards hearing assessment [20]. We invited 100 participants to answer a questionnaire (60 males and 40 females) involving teachers, managers, IT developers, and university students majoring in computer science, chemistry, physics, art and mathematics. [20, 18].

Questions in the questionnaire were divided into three parts [16]. The first part was about their knowledge of audiometry diseases and diseases potentially lead to hearing impairment. The second part inquired their habits of using ears and self-evaluation of hearing condition. The last part gathered information about whether they needed a convenient method, with which they can have self-assessment regularly, or take a test before going to hospital.

In part 1 of our study, only 3 of 20 kinds of audiometry diseases were known by participants (tinnitus 90%; otitis media 79%; and congenital deafness 71%). Only 29% of the participants had never been attacked by diseases could bring about hearing impair, while the others had got a number of problems such as hypertension (32%), chicken pox (29%) and diabetes (21%).

In part 2, only 12% of our participants never wear headset, while the others all wore headset as shown in Figure 1(a), 46% of them wore headset 2 or 3 days every week. And more than three quarters (76%) had to work in the noisy environment, as depicted in Figure 1(b).

Half of the participants had felt their hearing level decreased (51%), and a quarter of them paid no attention to their hearing condition at all as shown in Figure 1(c). On the other hand, only 17% of all the participants had ever checked their hearing health. For the reason why they didn't go to hospital, 68% of them chose the inconvenience.

In the final part, we asked them whether they needed an application for a private hearing condition assessment. The results illustrated in Figure 1(d) show that 81% of the participants chose yes, and no one opposed this accesssment.

From the results in our preliminary study, we can get conclusion as follow:

- People know little about audiometry.
- Many people don't have a good habit of using ears or silent enough working environment.
- Nearly half of them don't have a good hearing heath condition while many of them don't even realize.
- The majority need an application with which they can take a self-check for their hearing condition.

4. MOBILE PERSONAL HEARING ASSESSMENT (MPHA)

MPHA provides a convenient and reliable audiometry [12, 5]. Moreover, it provides a novel interacting mode based on mobile devices . In order for the validity, international standard [10, 11, 9] is fully taken into consideration during the design of MPHA, as detailed belows. For the convenience of users, we implement the MPHA on the iPad [14].

4.1 Application Design

According to the ISO 8253-2 [11], the MPHA we design is composed of three parts: the test signals generation, the assessment procedure and the hearing condition release[22].

In part 1, MPHA generates accurate test sound signals chosen by the users themselves and the parameter model [11, 22]. In part 2, MPHA plays one signal to subject, and collects user's feedback. Then, MPHA chooses the signal of the next round according to its algorithm [10, 22, 6]. The next frequency and sound intensity should be based on information collected from the users, as the requirements of ISO 6189 [9]. During the interactive process, the MPHA computes the user's hearing level according to [9].

4.2 Target Devices

MPHA requires a stable sound card of the mobile devices. The sound card of iPad has a wide range of frequency response, covering from 30Hz to 9kHz [14]. The frequency response range required by the MPHA is 250Hz to 8kHz [10, 11, 9]. In this work, we choose the iPad as our experimental devices.

4.3 The interactive mode of MPHA

MPHA is implemented on iPad. Sound signals are pure tone signals of 6 frequencies (250Hz, 500Hz, 1000Hz, 2000Hz,

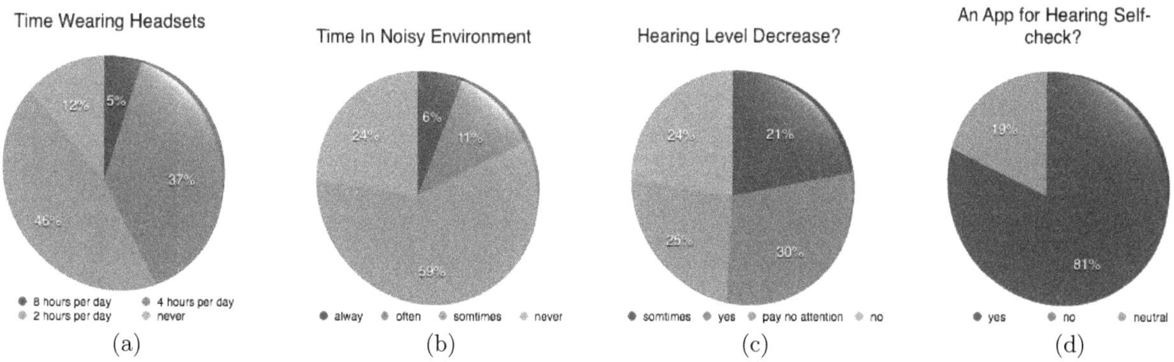

Figure 1: Results of preliminary study.

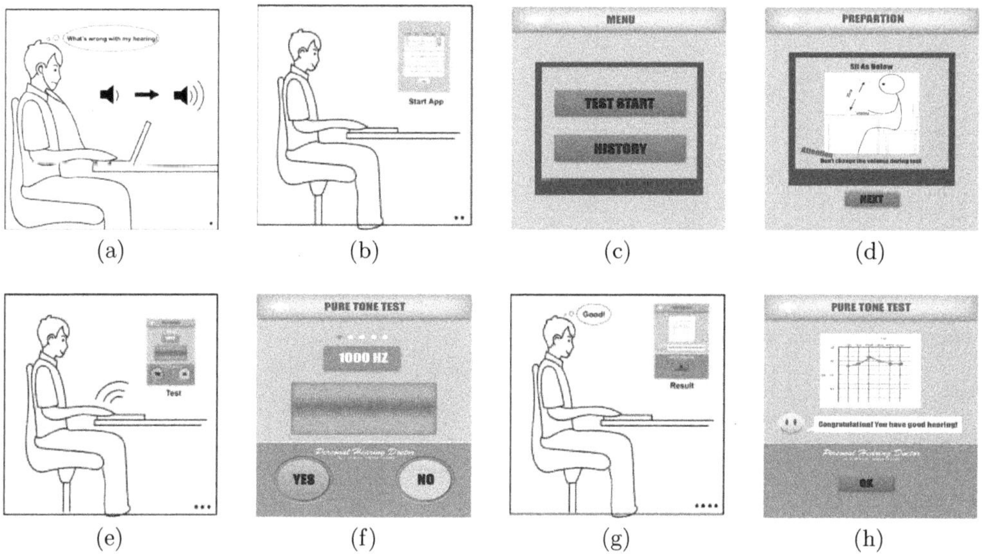

Figure 2: The interface of mobile personal hearing assessment (MPHA).

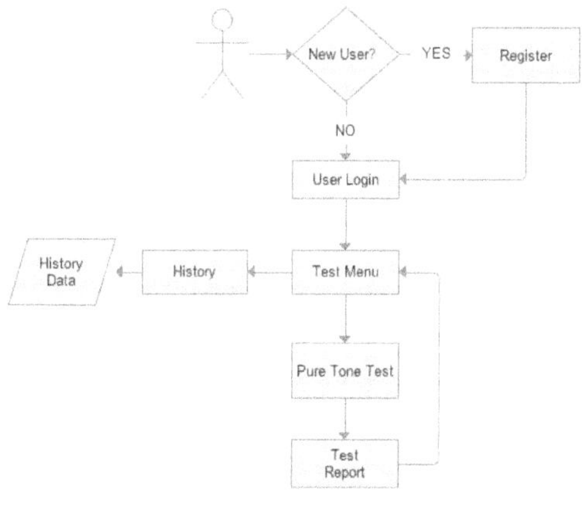

Figure 3: The entrance of MPHA.

4000Hz, 8000Hz) [10, 11, 3]. Sound intensity covers from -10dB SPL to 75dB SPL. The flow path and interactive interface of MPHA is shown in Figure 2, Figure 3, and Figure 4, described as followed.

Step 1, when user wants to have a self-check about his hearing level, user should be seated as shown in Figure 2(a). In this step, the user will see a login page. The user needs to register and login for his/her first access to use MPHA. After login, he/she can choose taking a new test or looking up the test history. The flow is shown in Figure 3 and interface is illustrated in Figure 2(c). If the user chooses to look up the history data, he can track the condition of his hearing health, as shown in Figure 2(h).

Step 2, if the user chooses to have a new self-check, MPHA will do the following two things before assessment. First, it tells the right sitting posture like Figure 2(d). Second, it tests the environment noise. If the background is too noisy, MPHA will suggest not testing right now. The MPHA records the background noise and then comes to the hearing level assessment, with the interface shown in Figure 2(f). In this step, MPHA generates a sound signal and plays it to the user. There are two buttons (Yes and No) on this page. User should click Yes when has heard the sound, or No otherwise. The logic flow of this step is shown in Figure 4.

Step 3, MPHA releases hearing level report when completing pure tone test[7, 8], as Figure 2(h). In the report, the

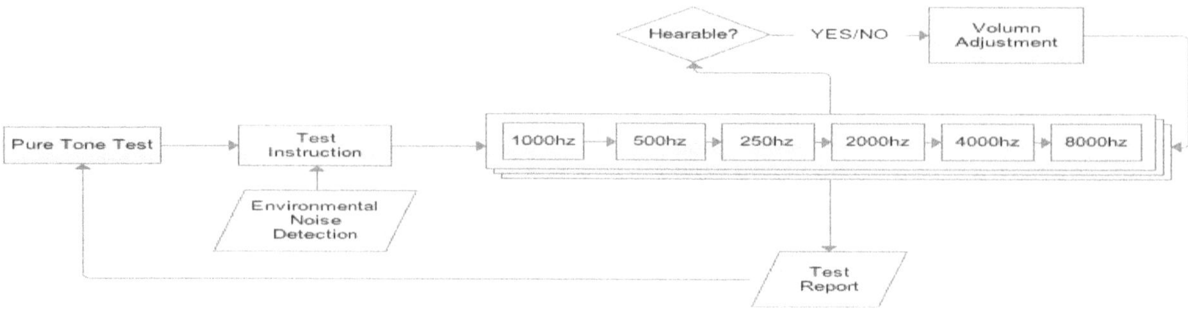

Figure 4: The flow chart of pure tone test.

interactive

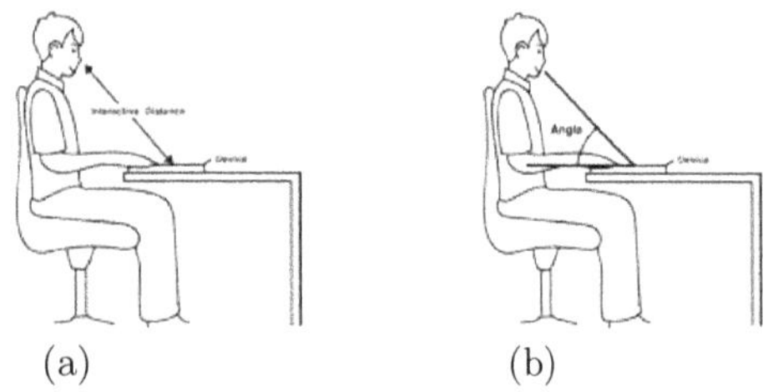

Figure 5: Interactive distance and angle of MPHA.

user can find his/her hearing threshold at the six frequencies, and whether his/her hearing status healthy or impaired.

5. EVALUATION

This section consists of five experiments to evaluate both accuracy and adaptability of MPHA [15]. All the experiments are running on an iPad2 with iOS 8.

Experiment 5.1 shows the available interactive distance of the MPHA. Experiment 5.2 shows the available angle of the MPHA. Experiment 5.3 compares the audiometry results of the MPHA with the traditional audiometer. Experiment 5.4 compares the results of two testing environment: the soundproof room and the regular working office. Experiment 5.5 further compares the hearing level condition of one person on different times of one day.

5.1 Interactive Distance

The interactive distance is defined as the distance between the center of the iPad and ears, shown in Figure 5(a). We measure the difference of sound signals intensity and analyze the variation with the distance increases.

5.1.1 Platform

The experiment is set up in a soundproof room, excluding interference from other acoustic sources. Sound sources are pure tone signals, of which the frequencies are covered from 250Hz to 8kHz, and the amplitude are covered from 10 to 20000. We use a sound level meter with the model of Bruel Kjaer 2250 to collect the sound signals and analyze the intensity, as simulation of subjects-ears.

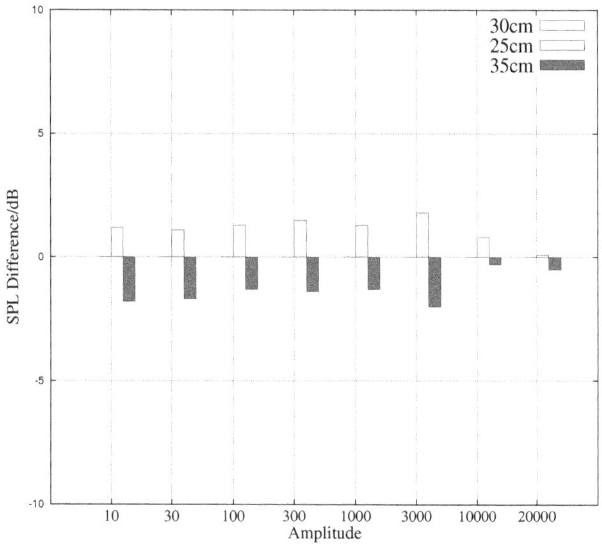

Figure 6: Comparison of sound signal intensity at different interactive distances.

5.1.2 Content

During this experiment, the iPad device is placed on a table with a fixed position. For each pure tone signal, we put the sound level meter with its fixed position above the iPad device. The dB SPL value is recorded according to the sound level meter, after the signal is played. Three different distances (i.e. 25cm, 30cm, 35cm) are tested, imitating the interactive distance between users and the iPad device. Each record is repeated three times for accuracy.

5.1.3 Quantitative Results

The comparison of sound signal intensity with different interactive distances is depicted in Figure 6. The results shows that average signal intensity of 25cm is higher than that of 30cm by 1.2dB SPL, and average signal intensity of 35cm is lower than that of 30cm by 1.3dB SPL.

In audiometry, the smallest unit of measurement is 5dB SPL [21, 10]. As a result, there is no substantial variation of sound signal intensity beyond the range of 25cm $\sim$ 35cm. Meanwhile, we have designed and implemented the compensation algorithm in our previous work for this difference caused by interactive distance [22, 7, 8]. To summarize, available interactive distance of MPHA is 30 $\pm 5cm$.

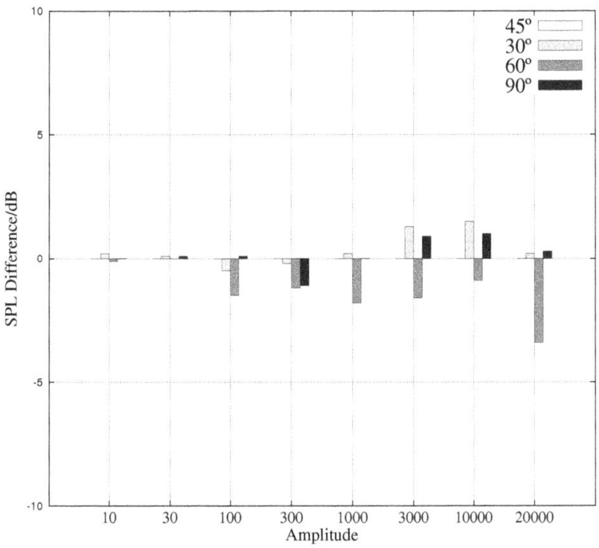

Figure 7: Comparison of sound signal intensity at different interactive angles.

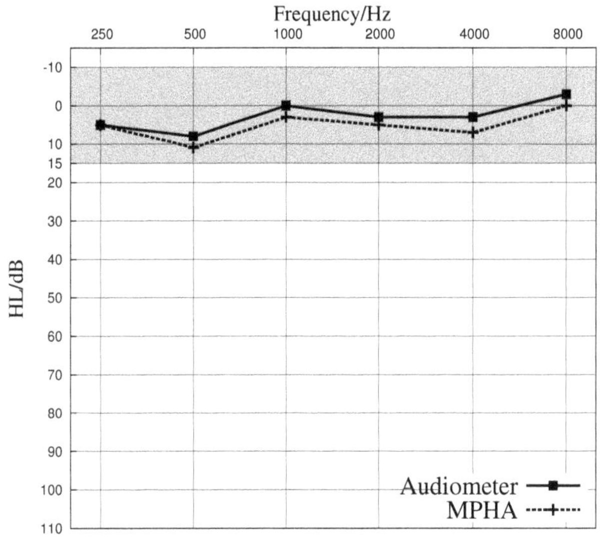

Figure 8: The auditory curve of MPHA and audiometer in a soundproof room.

5.2 Interactive Angle

The interactive angle is defined as the angle of subjects-ears to the iPad device as shown in Figure 5(b). With different angles testes, we analyzed its impact on sound signal intensity. The platform of this experiment is the same with that of Section 5.1.

5.2.1 Content

Similar to the test in Section 5.1, for each pure tone signal, we put the sound level meter with its fixed position above the iPad device. Then we vary the angel between 30° to 90° , imitating the interactive angel of users. The dB SPL value is recorded after the number remains unchanged on the sound level meter display.

5.2.2 Quantitative Results

The comparison of sound signal intensity with different interactive angles is shown in Figure 7. The results shows that average signal intensity at 30°, 60° and 90° is higher than that at 45° by 0.6dB SPL, 1.4dB SPL and 0.2dB SPL respectively. In our previous work, we have also designed and implemented a compensation algorithm for this difference caused by interactive angel [22, 7, 8]. As a result, the avaliable range of interactive angle for MPHA is between 30° and 90°.

5.3 Comparison with Audiometer

In clinical audiology, audiometer is the standard tool to measure hearing level. To prove the reliability of the MPHA, we make a comparison with the traditional audiometer.

5.3.1 Platform & Participants

This experiment is conducted in a soundproof room with an area of 10 square meters. The iPad device and the audiometer is the same with that in Section 5.1. Thirty university students majoring in computer science, art, mathematics, and physics (20 males and 10 females; 20 - 25 years old) have participated in this experiment.

5.3.2 Content

The participants are asked to take a hearing level test with the MPHA first, and then take a traditional test involving the audiometer and a doctor. With the MPHA, participants can freely complete the procedure by themselves. However, they have to feed back relevant information constantly to the audiometry doctor in the second test. Both methods are repeated three times for each participant.

5.3.3 Quantitative Results

Figure 8 shows that the difference between the two methods is 0dB, 1dB, 3dB, 2dB, 3dB, 3dB at the six frequencies respectively. None of these values is higher than 5dB, which is the smallest unit in audiometry. Moreover, the trend of these two curves is nearly the same. It proves the accuracy and validity of the MPHA.

It worth to be noted that the MPHA has greatly improved the efficiency of audiometry. The time of the whole precedure is measured and we find that with MPHA, the average time spent on each participant is 120s, while the number is up to 300 for the traditional method.

5.4 MPHA in Office

Since the soundproof room is scarce in daily life and it may potentially limit the wide usage of the MPHA, we compare the results of the hearing condition of these participants in a soundproof room and then in a working office.

5.4.1 Platform & Participants

This experiment is conducted in a regular working office with an area of about 30 square meters. The background noise is 35dB. Participants are the same with that in Section 5.3.

5.4.2 Content

The participants are asked to take a hearing level test with MPHA. To prove its robustness, the same test is repeated in the soundproof room and the working office.

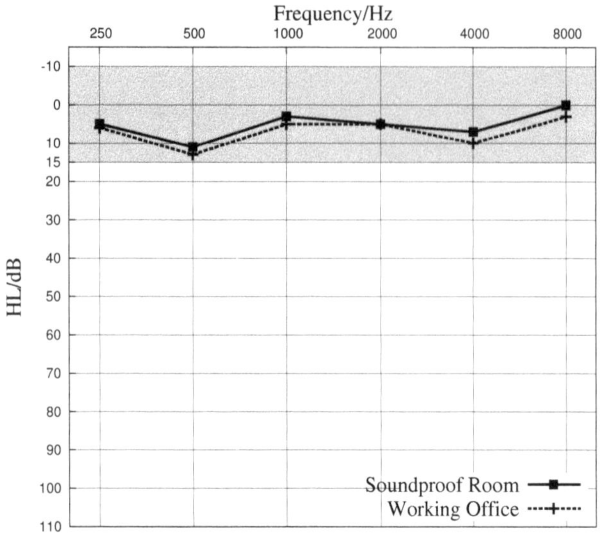

Figure 9: The auditory curve of MPHA in a soundproof room and a working office.

5.4.3 Quantitative Results

We compare the results in this experiment with the data in Section 5.3, as shown in Figure 9. We can see that the difference between the two kinds of environment is 1dB, 2dB, 2dB, 0dB, 3dB, 3dB at the six frequencies respectively. These two auditory curves indicate that MPHA has good reliability even for the noisy environment.

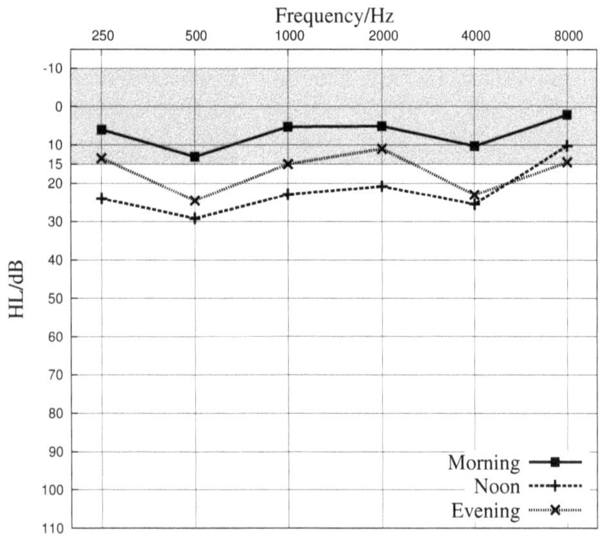

Figure 10: The auditory curve of MPHA in a day.

5.5 Morning, Noon and Evening in a Day

In this experiment, different times of one day is taken into consideration for the hearing test with MPHA. The platform and participants are the same with Section 5.5. The hearing condition at 9:00, 15:00 and 20:00 are recorded and analyzed.

5.5.1 Quantitative Results

The results are depicted in Figure 10. We can see that people's hearing level is best in the morning, and then evening but the worst at noon. Our hearing level is actually influenced by a number of things, and we should pay more attention to our hearing health.

5.6 Summary of Experimental Results

Overall, the participants have a nice experience with the MPHA. Through the five experiments, we can come to the following 4 conclusion:

- In the interactive distance and angle tasks (Section 5.1 and 5.2), MPHA showed great accuracy compared with traditional audiometry.
- In the comparison between MPHA and audiometer in soundproof room (Section 5.3), MPHA gets nearly the same results(auditory curve) with the audiometer. But the MPHA takes less time.
- In the noisy environment test(Section 5.4), MPHA generate the acceptable results compared with ideal quiet environment(soundproof room).
- In the one-day task (Section 5.5) for track recording, we find people' hearing level is actually greatly relevant to the time. Additionally, MPHA is able to tell our hearing health status in real time.

Before each experiment started, we asked the participants when they wanted a hearing test as the traditional way [18, 16, 17, 4]. 22 of the 30 participants chose NO. However, after the experiment, the nice experience with the MPHA impressed them, and 26 of them chose YES with the MPHA. As mentioned in the introduction, people are willing to pay more attention to their health condition if the procedure is not that complicated. We believe the MPHA will become popular [13, 2, 19].

6. POTENTIAL APPLICATION SCENARIOS

From the experimental results, we present possible application and extensions for future implementation of MPHA.

- **Hearing Condition Self-Check**
  Self-check of hearing condition is one of the main focus of the MPHA. As shown in the experimental results, MPHA can be used in quiet environment as well as working offices. In particular, hearing condition test in the traditional way with audiometer is very time-consuming. A mobile device with MPHA provides a effective interaction model for hearing condition self-check.
- **Recovery Record for Hearing Impaired Persons**
  For hearing impaired people, they may not able to have access to regular hearing check. After they have weared the hearing aids for a period of time, it is likely that their hearing level condition have changed. It means the hearing aids are not fully suitable for their ears any more, and the follow-up treatment should be adjusted. The MPHA facilitates the access of people's hearing condition, favouring the recovery process.

- **Pre-Screening in Hearing Rehabilitation Center**
  Even though there are many hearing rehabilitation centers, their audiometric equipment is usually expensive and energy-consuming. Additionally, the assessment procedure with traditional audiometric method needs the involvement of professional audiometry doctors. From the description in Section 4.3, MPHA can be used freely by the users themselves, which greatly improves the efficiency. Even for the hearing rehabilitation centers, the MPHA can be applied to alleviate the overcrowded environment.

Our MPHA technique is a sound-signal-based implementation for the current testing scenario, the accuracy of the pure tones generated has not been calibrated strictly for a large numbers of mobile devices. The sound volume generated by different mobile devices is actually different, so the application/interface should be calibrated.

The implementation of MPHA is dependant on sound card of devices to some extent. In this work, the highest sound intensity of the mobile device used(iPad) is 75dB. As a result, our MPHA cannot be correctly used in too noisy environment. For instance, the noise intensity of aircraft cockpit can reach higher than 80dB, currently MPHA can't work in such a environment. Generating high intensity signals on mobile devices is a part of the future work.

Finally, whether non-semantics sound is acceptable is still under investigation, especially for the tests in the working environment. However, we believe that the MPHA has shown the potential of popularity because of the concise access to people's hearing condition.

7. CONCLUSION

We present a novel interactive mode called MPHA, which evaluates people's hearing level on mobile devices. MPHA can generate accurate sound signals for audiometry, interact with users in a convenient way, and figure out users' hearing level reliably. The experimental results show that MPHA has proved its reliability and validity in quiet and noisy environment. Compared with conventional audiometry, MPHA is more efficient and cost effective. The concise audiometric assessment provided by MPHA can be further applied to a number of mobile devices, which helps people better understand their hearing health.

8. ACKNOWLEDGMENTS

The author would like to thank the anonymous reviewer for their valuable comments. This study was supported by funding from the National Natural Science Foundation of China(61370023).

9. REFERENCES

[1] M. Dayou. Modern acoustics theory foundation, 2004.

[2] P. Dragicevic, F. Chevalier, and S. Huot. Running an hci experiment in multiple parallel universes. In *CHI'14 Extended Abstracts on Human Factors in Computing Systems*, pages 607–618. ACM, 2014.

[3] GB-3240. Preferred frequencies for the acoustical measurement, 1982.

[4] J. Heikkinen, E. Mäkinen, J. Lylykangas, T. Pakkanen, K. Väänänen-Vainio-Mattila, and R. Raisamo. Mobile devices as infotainment user interfaces in the car: contextual study and design implications. In *Proceedings of the 15th international conference on Human-computer interaction with mobile devices and services*, pages 137–146. ACM, 2013.

[5] L. Hickson, B. S. Thy, M. Aud, and B. Murdoch. Longitudinal study of speech perception, speech, and language for children with hearing loss in an auditory-verbal therapy program. *Volta*, 109(2-3):61–85, 2009.

[6] ISO. Acoustics-audiometric test methods-part 3: Speech audiometry. 1996.

[7] ISO-389.5. Acoustics–reference zero for the calibration of audiometric equipment– part 5:reference equivalent threshold sound pressure levels for pure tones in the frequency range 8 khz to 16 khz, 2006.

[8] ISO-389.7. Acoustics–reference zero for the calibration of audiometric equipment– part 7:reference threshold of hearing under free-field and diffuse-field listening conditions, 2005.

[9] ISO-6189. Acoustics–pure tone air conduction threshold audiometry for hearing conservation purposes, 1983.

[10] ISO-8253-1. Acoustics-audiometric test methods-part 1: Basic pure tone air and bone conduction threshold audiometry. *Geneva: International Organization for Standardization*, 1989.

[11] ISO-8253-2. Acoustics-audiometric test methods. sound field audiometry with pure tone and narrowband test signals, 1992.

[12] P. Liu, K.-W. Yuen, W.-K. Leung, and H. M. Meng. menunciate: Development of a computer-aided pronunciation training system on a cross-platform framework for mobile, speech-enabled application development. In *ISCSLP*, pages 170–173, 2012.

[13] M. Lohse, R. Rothuis, J. Gallego-Pérez, D. E. Karreman, and V. Evers. Robot gestures make difficult tasks easier: the impact of gestures on perceived workload and task performance. In *Proceedings of the 32nd annual ACM conference on Human factors in computing systems*, pages 1459–1466. ACM, 2014.

[14] T. Lund. Audio for mobile tv, ipad and ipod. In *Proc. NAB BE Conference*, 2013.

[15] Y. Pan, D. Jiang, L. Yao, M. Picheny, and Y. Qin. Effects of automated transcription quality on non-native speakers' comprehension in real-time computer-mediated communication. In *Proceedings of the SIGCHI Conference on Human Factors in Computing Systems*, pages 1725–1734. ACM, 2010.

[16] M. Pielot and R. d. Oliveira. Peripheral vibro-tactile displays. In *Proceedings of the 15th international conference on Human-computer interaction with mobile devices and services*, pages 1–10. ACM, 2013.

[17] D. Raptis, N. Tselios, J. Kjeldskov, and M. B. Skov. Does size matter?: investigating the impact of mobile phone screen size on users' perceived usability, effectiveness and efficiency. In *Proceedings of the 15th international conference on Human-computer interaction with mobile devices and services*, pages 127–136. ACM, 2013.

[18] D. Sakamoto, T. Komatsu, and T. Igarashi. Voice augmented manipulation: using paralinguistic information to manipulate mobile devices. In *Proceedings of the 15th international conference on Human-computer interaction with mobile devices and services*, pages 69–78. ACM, 2013.

[19] A. Sauppé and B. Mutlu. Design patterns for exploring and prototyping human-robot interactions. In *Proceedings of the 32nd annual ACM conference on Human factors in computing systems*, pages 1439–1448. ACM, 2014.

[20] D. Spelmezan, C. Appert, O. Chapuis, and E. Pietriga. Side pressure for bidirectional navigation on small devices. In *Proceedings of the 15th international conference on Human-computer interaction with mobile devices and services*, pages 11–20. ACM, 2013.

[21] B. Stach. *Clinical audiology: an introduction*. Cengage Learning, 2008.

[22] Y. Wu, J. Jia, X. Zhang, and L. Cai. Algorithm of pure tone audiometry based on multiple judgment. In *Chinese Spoken Language Processing (ISCSLP), 2014 9th International Symposium on*, pages 398–398. IEEE, 2014.

Towards Attentive, Bi-directional MOOC Learning on Mobile Phones

Xiang Xiao[1,2] and Jingtao Wang[1,2]
[1]Department of Computer Science
[2]Learning Research and Development Center (LRDC)
University of Pittsburgh
210 S. Bouquet Street
Pittsburgh, PA 15260, USA
{xiangxiao, jingtaow}@cs.pitt.edu

ABSTRACT
AttentiveLearner is a mobile learning system optimized for consuming lecture videos in Massive Open Online Courses (MOOCs) and flipped classrooms. AttentiveLearner converts the built-in camera of mobile devices into both a tangible video control channel and an implicit heart rate sensing channel by analyzing the learner's fingertip transparency changes in real time. In this paper, we report disciplined research efforts in making AttentiveLearner truly practical in real-world use. Through two 18-participant user studies and follow-up analyses, we found that 1) the tangible video control interface is intuitive to use and efficient to operate; 2) heart rate signals implicitly captured by AttentiveLearner can be used to infer both the learner's interests and perceived confusion levels towards the corresponding learning topics; 3) AttentiveLearner can achieve significantly higher accuracy by predicting *extreme personal learning events* and *aggregated learning events*.

Categories and Subject Descriptors
H5.2 [**Information interfaces and presentation**]: User Interfaces. – *Graphical user interfaces, theory and methods.*

General Terms
Design; Experimentation; Human Factors.

Keywords
MOOC; Heart Rate; Intelligent Tutoring Systems; Physiological Signals; Affective Computing, Mobile Interfaces

1. INTRODUCTION
Massive Open Online Courses (MOOCs) are experiencing rapid growth. MOOC providers such as Coursera, edX, Udacity, and Khan Academy, have offered more than 2,400 courses to over 16 million learners by late 2014 [21]. Although polarized opinions still persist, many experts believe that MOOCs and flipped courses, when properly designed and executed, could serve as an excellent complement to traditional education by delivering high quality education on a large scale at a lower cost [4]. In current MOOCs, the courses are mostly organized as sequences of pre-recorded lecture videos, split into 3-15 minute pieces for better engagement [6]. Such small video clips are also easy to consume on mobile devices during learners' fragmented time.

ICMI '15, November 09-13, 2015, Seattle, WA, USA

ISBN 978-1-4503-3912-4/15/11…$15.00
DOI: http://dx.doi.org/10.1145/2818346.2820754

Despite the great potential, current MOOCs still face major challenges such as low completion rates (10% in [4], 7% in [17]), more frequent distractions [18], separation of learning, discussion and assessment activities [15], and most importantly, lack of direct, immediate feedback channels from students to instructors [5]. For example, teachers no longer have access to important cues in traditional classrooms, such as facial expressions, raised hands, or oral questions to infer student engagement. Although questionnaires, post-lecture reflections [5], and browser log analysis (including both activities in learning sessions [6] and follow-up discussion forums [2]) can be used to infer the quality of learning, such post-hoc analysis techniques are usually coarse-grained, highly delayed, and indirect measurements of the actual learning process.

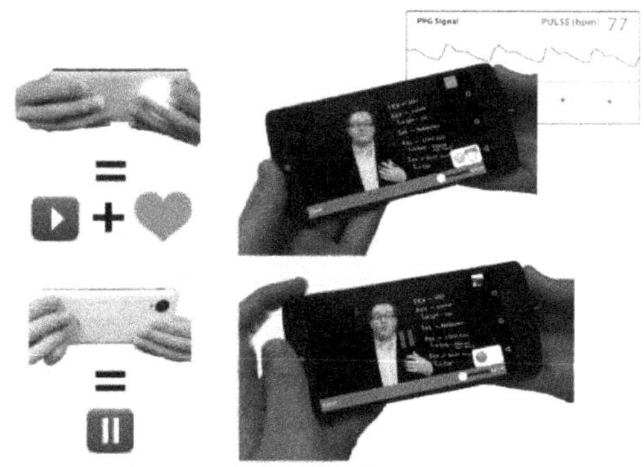

Figure 1. AttentiveLearner uses the back camera as both a tangible video control channel and an implicit heart rate sensing channel in MOOC learning

To explore the opportunities of collecting and using fine-grained, real-time feedback on learners' actual cognitive states in learning, we propose AttentiveLearner (Figure 1), a mobile learning system that captures learners' physiological states in MOOC learning through implicit heart rate sensing on unmodified mobile phones. AttentiveLearner uses on-lens finger gestures for video control (i.e. covering and holding the back camera lens to play a lecture video, uncovering the lens to pause the video) and monitors learners' heart rates implicitly based on the fingertip transparency change captured by the back camera. This work builds on and extends findings by Pham et al [18]. While Phuong and Wang [18] focused on demonstrating the *feasibility* of predicting Mind Wandering (MW) events by analyzing learners' heart rates implicitly captured by mobile cameras, we directly address fundamental challenges in making AttentiveLearner practical in real-world use via systematic, disciplined research. For example, is the tangible video control interface of AttentiveLearner responsive and accurate enough to use when compared with traditional touchscreen widgets? Is this interface easy to learn and comfortable to use through extended learning sessions? Can we infer learners' fine-grained interest/boredom and confusion states via the noisy physiological signals captured by unmodified mobile phones?

This paper offers three major contributions:

1. We present the design and evaluation of the tangible video control interface in AttentiveLearner through two 18-particpant studies.
2. We show that heart rate signals, implicitly recorded by the built-in camera of mobile phones, can be used to infer learners' interests and perceived confusion levels during watching the corresponding lecture videos.
3. AttentiveLearner can achieve significantly higher accuracy by predicting *extreme personal learning* events and *aggregated learning events*.

2. RELATED WORK

2.1 Technologies for Improving MOOCs

The passive, asynchronous, distributed viewing experiences of MOOCs present unique challenges to quality education. Researchers have explored various techniques to 1) improve the interactivity of MOOC videos [10][11][15][16]; 2) enhance student-student interactions [13] and student-instructor feedback [5][10] in MOOCs; and 3) conduct post-hoc video/log analyses [2][6][12].

Kim et al. [11] designed a learner activity augmented timeline to facilitate video navigation. The timeline visualizes learner interaction peaks based on historical interactions and enables non-linear scrubbing through friction. L.IVE by Monserrat et al. [15] provides in-situ learning, discussion, and assessment via an interactive overlay directly on top of the lecture video. RIMES [10] supports interactive, multimedia responses (handwriting, audio, and video) in lecture videos. Glassman and colleagues [5] invented the Muddy Card technique to allow students to indicate confusing concepts (muddy points) on the corresponding lecture slide. Such end-of-lecture reflections are helpful to both students and teachers.

Guo et al. [6] discovered that shorter videos and Khan-style videos are more engaging through a large-scale correlation analysis of activity logs in edX. Kim et al. [12] went one step further by applying temporal pattern analysis techniques on video play activities. Interesting findings include students tended to selectively pick parts of the video to watch, and 61% of the interaction peaks involved a visual transition that proceeds or after the peak [12].

Although server-side activity logs are easy to collect and can reveal insightful information, mouse clicks and keystrokes are relatively sparse in a single learning session. More importantly, they reveal learners' *actions* rather than actual *cognitive states* in learning. In comparison, AttentiveLearner explores the continual collection and use of spontaneous heart rate signals in MOOC learning. Such physiological signals correlate directly with learners' physiological states and cognitive states [19] and can complement today's log analysis techniques.

2.2 Using Physiological Signals in Education

Researchers have explored the use of various physiological signals, such as heart rates [8][9][18], galvanic skin responses (GSR) [23], facial expressions [3][23], and Electroencephalography (EEG) [22], to infer learners' cognitive and affective states (e.g. boredom, confusion, frustration) in learning.

AutoTutor [3][8] is a pioneer in detecting and adapting to learners' affects from multi-channel physiological signals in an intelligent tutoring system. The authors used supervised machine learning algorithms to achieve satisfactory performance on affect classification (Kappa = 0.35 for predicting valence and Kappa = 0.23 for predicting arousal).

Szafir et al [22] demonstrated the feasibility of using a wireless EEG headset to predict learners' attention and support adaptive review for topics with low-attention levels.

To predict students' affective states, the Wayang intelligent tutor [23] used four types of sensor data: facial expressions, seat pressure, mouse pressure and GSR. Empirical studies showed that the animated affect-aware agents improved average learning gains by 12% after only two classes and had benefits such as improving learners' self-concept and making them more engaged.

Jraidi et. al. [9] proposed a hierarchical probabilistic framework for detecting learners' experiences and emotional responses in an intelligent learning system. The framework took into account three types of modality measurements (physiology, behavior, and performance) as the diagnostic component of a dynamic Bayesian network.

One common problem with most of today's systems [3][8][9][22][23] is the requirement of dedicated sensors, such as chest bands and EEG headsets for signal collection. The cost, availability, and portability of such equipment have prevented the wide adoption of such systems beyond lab settings. In comparison, AttentiveLearner uses the built-in camera to detect heart rates and infer learners' cognitive states, thus eliminating the requirement of dedicated physiological sensors.

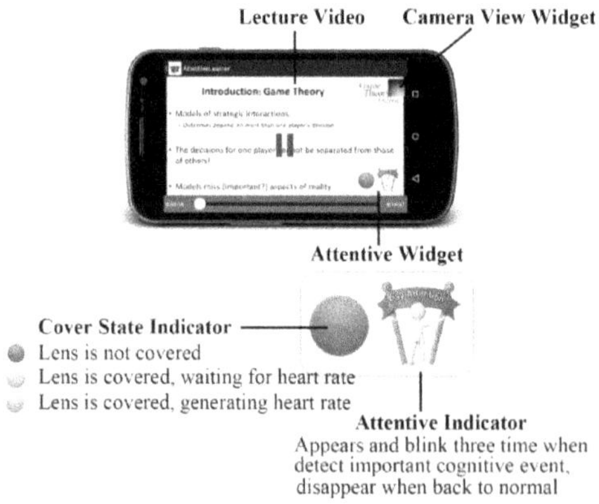

Figure 2. The video play interface of AttentiveLearner

In [18], Pham and Wang showed that it is feasible to predict learners' mind wandering (MW) states via heart rates extracted from noisy image frames via mobile cameras in mobile MOOC learning. Our research builds on Pham and colleagues' work by addressing critical usability issues to make AttentiveLearner more practical. Our research shows that AttentiveLearner is able to predict learners' cognitive states such as interest/boredom and confusion. Furthermore, the prediction accuracy can be significantly improved by focusing on *extreme personal learning events* and *aggregated learning events*.

3. DESIGN OF ATTENTIVELEARNER

Similar to existing MOOC mobile clients by Coursera, edX, and Udacity, AttentiveLearner allows learners to browse, stream, and watch lecture videos on their mobile phones. Figure 2 shows the primary interface of AttentiveLearner. AttentiveLearner runs on both smartphones and tablet devices. There are four unique components in AttentiveLearner: 1) a tangible video control channel, 2) an implicit heart rate sensing module, 3) an on-screen AttentiveWidget, and 4) cognitive state detection algorithms.

3.1 Tangible Video Control

As illustrated in Figure 1, a learner plays the instructional video by covering and holding the camera lens with her fingertip, pausing the video by uncovering the lens. Such a (seemingly strange) tangible video control mechanism has three advantages when compared with traditional touch screen widgets: 1) the edge/bezel of the camera optical assembly can provide natural tactile feedback to the learner' finger; 2) the "cover-and-hold-to-play" mechanism allows the learner to naturally pause the video during "unintentional interruptions"; 3) this approach enables the implicit extraction of heart rates via commodity-camera-based photoplethysmography (PPG) [7] in MOOC learning.

We extended the *Static LensGesture* detection algorithm in [24] to detect the lens-covering actions in AttentiveLearner. There are two major differences between usage scenarios of LensGesture in [24] and those in AttentiveLearner. First, the flashlight of the mobile camera is on by default in AttentiveLearner to improve heart rate measurements in low illumination conditions[1]; second, the original *Static LensGesture* algorithm [24] only determines the coverage of camera lens without differentiating whether the coverage was by a finger or inorganic surfaces (e.g., putting the phone on a desk).

Figure 3. Samples images. First row: lens is not covered. Second row: lens is covered. Third row: lens partially covered (first two images) or blocked by surface (last two images).

To enhance the lens covering detection algorithm based on AttentiveLearner's unique requirements, we collected 483 representative test images in 4 (lens fully covered by finger, lens partially covered by finger, lens blocked by opaque surface, lens uncovered) x 2 (flashlight on, flashlight off) x 4 (indoor high illumination, indoor low illumination, outdoor direct sunshine, and outdoor in the shade) conditions from 10 subjects. All the subjects were graduate students in a local university, recruited through school mailing lists. Figure 3 shows some sample images collected.

Figure 4 shows scatter plots of global mean vs. global standard deviation of all test images when the flashlight was on (left) and off (right) respectively. We found that when the flashlight was turned on, the full-covering-by-fingertip samples (inside the black rectangle) are more aggregated than when the flashlight was off. We also observed turning on the flashlight can significantly reduce the variations caused by environmental illumination (Figure 3's left second row vs. Figure 3's right second row).

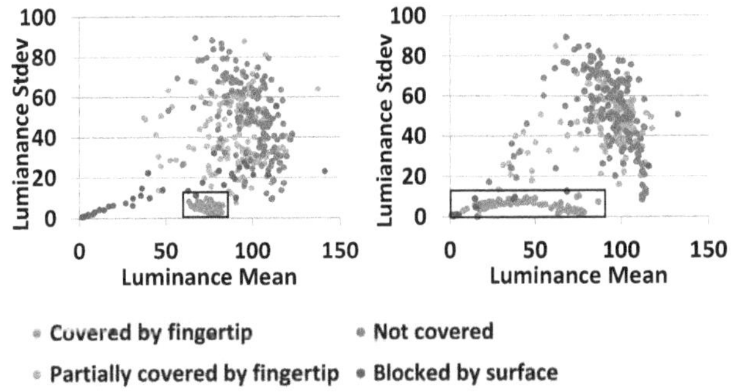

Figure 4. Global mean vs. standard deviation of pixels in sample images (no-covering: blue dot, full-covering-by-fingertip: red dot, partial-covering-by-fingertip: green dot, blocked-by-surface: purple dot). Left: samples when the flashlight was on. Right: samples when the flashlight was off.

3.2 Accuracy

We achieved an accuracy of 99.59% when using $60 \leq$ mean ≤ 90, stdev ≤ 15 as the decision boundaries for detecting lens-covering gestures. The only two misclassifications were false positives when the mobile phone was on a red semi-transparent plastic surface (of a plastic flying disc). AttentiveLearner can reject such false positives by incorporating output from the heart rate sensing module, since non-body parts cannot generate periodic transparency changes expected by the PPG detection algorithm.

3.3 Speed

We quantitatively studied the responsiveness of the AttentiveLearner tangible video control channel (described in Section 3.1) and a traditional touchscreen widget. We ran an 18-participant (7 females) study to measure the response time of both interfaces. In the experiment, in response to a randomly appearing visual stimulus (a 200dp x 200dp "Play" icon in the center of the screen), participants were instructed to play the video by either touching the on-screen "Play" button (traditional, widget interface) or by covering the camera lens (the AttentiveLearner tangible video control channel) as fast as possible. Each participant completed 20 trials in each condition and the order of conditions was counterbalanced. The participants could choose their preferred hands to complete all the tasks. We used a Nexus 5 smartphone with a 5 inch, 1080 x 1920 pixel display for the experiment.

We collected 360 successful inputs from the traditional interface and 359 successful inputs from the tangible video control interface (the only invalid input happened when the subject covered the lens before the "Play" icon appeared). The average response time of the traditional interface was 462.6ms (σ = 109.3); the average response time of the tangible video control interface was 625.9ms (σ = 171.1). Although the tangible

[1] The flashlight in AttentiveLearner can be turned off if the environmental illumination is sufficient.

interface in AttentiveLearner was 160ms slower, it is acceptable for interactive tasks such as playing and pausing a video. We attribute the current delay to two reasons. First, there is a 30ms latency caused by the 30fps camera frame sampling rate and follow-up image processing. Second, the new tangible video control channel was less familiar to the participants. We expect that the users' response time will decrease when high frame rate cameras become popular and the learners have more practice with the tangible interface.

3.4 Usability

Three major usability concerns arise when we use lens-covering gestures for video playback. First, is it comfortable and natural to cover and hold the camera lens during video watching? Second, will the camera lens get scratched or damaged due to such lens-covering gestures? Third, will AttentiveLearner drain the battery of a smartphone quickly?

To answer the first question, we reviewed representative smartphones on the market. We found that the touchscreens of most phones were 4 to 5.7 inches and the back cameras were located in the upper region of the device. When holding the mobile phone in landscape mode, index or middle fingers of the same hand can naturally reach and cover the lens under normal grip in both one-handed and two-handed holding postures. Figure 5 shows various lens-covering postures we observed during our user study in section 4. Despite the various fingers and postures used, our algorithm can detect lens-covering actions accurately. The only problematic posture we found was to cover the lens with a whole palm. In this situation, the collected heart rate signals were weak and unreliable. We also collected the users' subjective preference on the tangible video control channel in an 18-subject MOOC learning study to be detailed in the next section. Results showed that participants could comfortably use AttentiveLearner to watch lecture videos without pausing for at least 8 minutes. Eight minutes is longer than the recommended 6-min duration of MOOC videos [6]. For longer video clips, the learners can pause the video by uncovering the lens at any time.

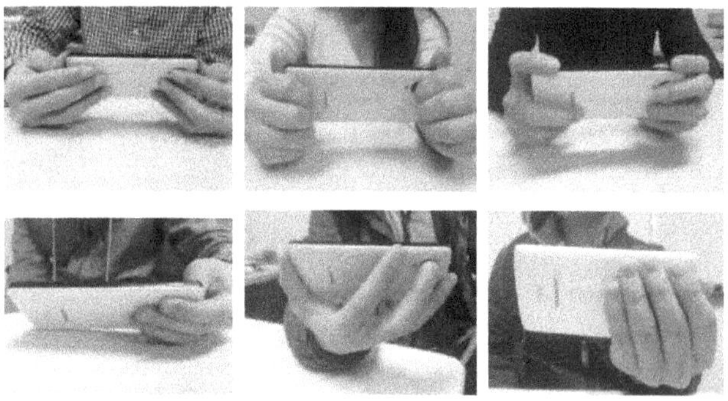

Figure 5. Users cover the lens using various hand postures (back camera is in the top right corner).

According to [24], the optical assembly of smartphone cameras is made of strong materials, such as crystal glass, cyclic olefin copolymer, or sapphire. These materials withstand the friction caused by fingertip touch. As a result, extended use of the lens-covering gesture in AttentiveLearner won't damage the camera lens.

For question 3, we ran three mini-experiments to test the impact of AttentiveLearner on battery life. We used a Nexus 5 smartphone running Android 5.0.1 for the mini-experiments. We compared the battery life with both the built-in video player in Android and AttentiveLearner. We tested battery life with 50% backlight of the screen.

Table 1. Battery life in video playback

Condition	Duration
Built-in video player	6 hours 19 minutes
AttentiveLearner, flashlight off	3 hours 57 minutes
AttentiveLearner, flashlight on	2 hours 31 minutes

As shown in Table 1, AttentiveLearner can run 2.5 hours after a full charge, which is a 60% playtime reduction when compared with the built-in video player. The playtime can be significantly improved considering that 1) Nexus 5 has a below average battery life when compared with existing smartphones on the market; 2) Hardware-accelerated video decoding was used by the built-in video player but not AttentiveLearner in the experiment. Implementing hardware-accelerated decoding could significantly improve the battery life of AttentiveLearner. Last but not least, considering that the average time spent in lecture videos is 2 to 3 hours *per week* for devoted certificate earners [20] and people usually charge their smart phones daily, we believe that the 2.5 hour battery life is enough to support most learners in MOOCs or flipped courses

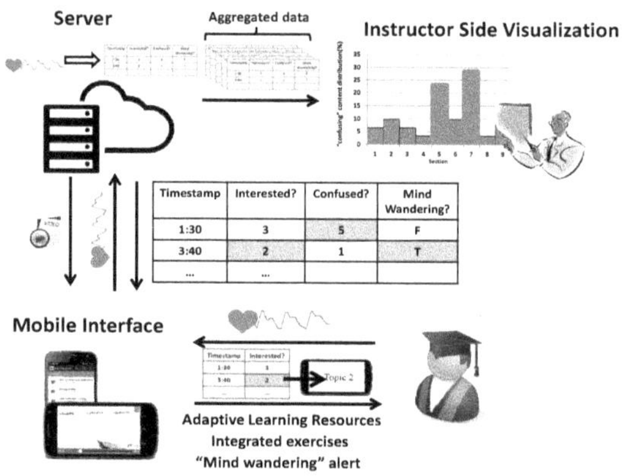

Figure 6. The infrastructure of AttentiveLearner

3.5 Infrastructure

AttentiveLearner captures each learner's heart rate implicitly during learning via commodity-camera-based photoplethysmography (PPG) [7][18]. AttentiveLearner uses LivePulse[2] [7] to get raw PPG waveform and heart rate signals.

Given the possibility to monitor learners' physiological signals in learning continuously and *implicitly*, and the feasibility to infer learners' cognitive, affective states and attention [14][18][19] from physiological signals, intelligent learning and analytics systems in the future may take advantage of this new form of feedback and enable attentive and bi-directional learning on unmodified mobile phones (Figure 6).

AttentiveLearner can benefit learners by providing personalized learning materials and instructional paradigms. For example, when a learner is not interested in a topic, AttentiveLearner may

[2] LivePulse [7] is a heuristic based peaks/valleys counting algorithm.

switch to a different learning resource or use integrated exercises [5][15] to engage the learner. AttentiveLearner can also use visual and tactile feedback to remind learners when they are "mind wandering". Such interactions have the potential to make the MOOC learning process more *attentive and personalized.*

AttentiveLearner can benefit instructors via fine-grained, aggregated visualization of learners' physiological, cognitive, and affective states synchronized with the learning materials. An instructor can identify and reflect upon areas needing improvement within the curriculum. For example, which parts of a lecture are more confusing to students? Did my joke "wake up" the students? Or, were students bored by the end of the lecture? We believe this fine-grained, continual, implicit feedback channel through learners' physiological signals can serve as a valuable complement to existing technologies such as log analysis [2][6], questionnaires, and post-lecture reflections [5]. Such information can help instructors to identify both struggling students and lecture materials that need improvements, hence enabling *bi-directional* communication between learners and instructors.

4. USER STUDY

We conducted a lab-based study to better understand AttentiveLearner. We had two major goals for the study. First, we were interested in evaluating the usability of AttentiveLearner during actual MOOC learning sessions. Second, we would like to investigate the feasibility of using heart rate signals collected by AttentiveLearner to predict learners' cognitive states.

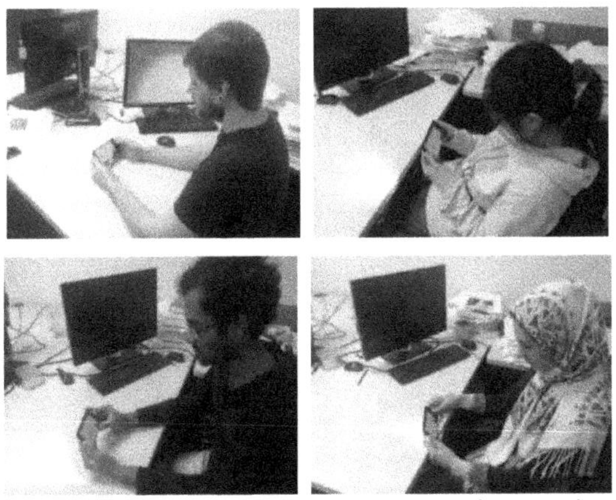

Figure 7. Some participants in our experiment using AttentiveLearner to learn video lectures.

4.1 Experiment Design

The study was consisted of three parts:

Overview. We first gave participants a brief introduction to the AttentiveLearner project and then collected background information. We demonstrated the AttentiveLearner mobile app to the participants and answered their questions.

MOOC Learning. Participants studied the introductory chapter of a MOOC course (Game Theory) with AttentiveLearner. The chapter ("Informal Analysis and Definitions") had four video lectures named "Introduction to Game Theory and the Predator Prey Example", "Normal Form Definitions", "Dominance", and "Nash Equilibrium". The durations of the four lectures were *14m47s*, *16m54s*, *8m48s*, and *8m24s* respectively. The duration of the whole chapter was *48m53s*.

For each of the four video lecture clips, participants first watched the video using AttentiveLearner in landscape mode. Participants could pause the video at any time. Immediately after finishing each video lecture, participants were instructed to rate the interest levels and confusion levels of each topic in the lecture on a 5-point Likert scale. There were 7, 9, 5, and 7 topics in the four video lectures respectively. Participants could take a short break between two video lectures.

Qualitative Feedback. Each participant completed a closing questionnaire after finishing the lesson.

4.2 Participants and Apparatus

Eighteen subjects (7 females) participated in our study (Figure 7). The average participant age was 24.9 ($\sigma = 2.2$) ranging from 22 to 30. All participants were undergraduate or graduate students from a local university. Ten out of the 18 participants also participated in the usability study reported in section 3.3. All participants had little or no knowledge of Game Theory. Among the 18 participants, 8 took MOOC courses prior to the study. Only 2 subjects actually finished a MOOC course, suggesting a low completion rate in MOOC learning. Three subjects had experiences in using mobile MOOC learning apps.

Our experiment was completed on a Nexus 5 smartphone with a 4.95 inch, 1920 x 1080 pixel display, 2.26 GHz quad core Krait 400 processor, running Android 5.0.1. It has an 8 mega-pixel back camera with an LED flash.

5. RESULTS

5.1 Subjective Feedback

Participants reported favorable experiences with AttentiveLearner, giving an average rating of 4.11 ($\sigma = 0.68$) on the overall experience of AttentiveLearner on a five-point Likert scale (1-very unsatisfied, 5-very satisfied).

Regarding the tangible video control interface, participants gave an average rating of 4.33 ($\sigma = 0.59$) on intuitiveness, and an average rating of 4.11 ($\sigma = 0.83$) on responsiveness. All participants agreed that it was comfortable to cover-and-hold the lens while watching the video.

Fifteen subjects commented that they would continue to use AttentiveLearner to take MOOC courses in the future. When asked about what they like about AttentiveLearner, participants were most impressed by the flexibility of the video control channel:

'The lens-covering control is interesting. It is an easy and intuitive way to play/pause video.'

'I like the auto-pause feature. You just put the device aside and it automatically stops.'

'A user can play/pause the video easily with one hand. No need to touch the screen which normally needs two hands.'

Some participants also believed the video control channel made them pay more attention to the video:

'It can help me focus on the lesson; you need to hold the mobile phone while listening to the instructors'

'Because I'd like to keep covering the lens, I am paying attention to the video all the time.'

5.2 PPG Signals

Interruptions: Although we encouraged participants to pause the video when needed, we only observed a total of 17 user-initiated pauses (i.e. interruptions) from 7 subjects. The main reason for interruptions was finger or eye fatigue. However, two participants reported that they paused the video to take a closer look at the slides and digest the topic.

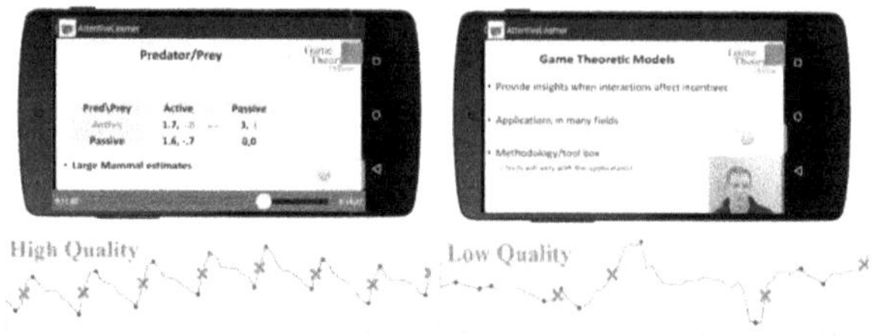

Figure 8. Top: Screenshots of AttentiveLearner in the experiment. Bottom: PPG signal at the time of the screenshot. Left: high quality PPG, right: low quality PPG.

Interestingly, we found that 14 of the interruptions (82.3%) occurred after 8 minutes of video play; 12 of them (70.5%) occurred after 10 minutes of video play. This suggests that participants usually felt fatigue and needed a rest when they used AttentiveLearner to watch a video nonstop for more than 8 minutes.

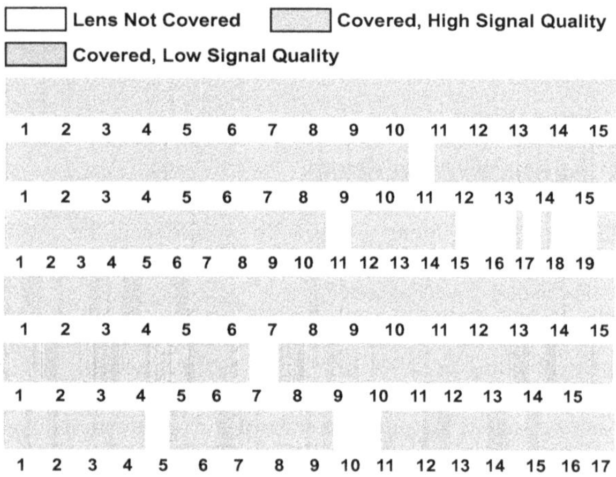

Figure 9. PPG signals of six participants during watching the first video clip.

Signal Quality: We analyzed the quality of PPG signals by investigating the RR-intervals (the cardiac interval between two heart beats) in a 5-second moving window. We used the heuristics that a window contains high quality PPG signal if at least 80% of RR-intervals in that window are within a given range (+/- 25% from the median). Figure 8 shows two sample sequences of PPG signals (left: high quality; right: low quality) and the corresponding screenshot of AttentiveLearner. In 88.9% of the 72 video sessions (18 subjects x 4 videos), more than 80% of the signals were in high quality. This suggests that AttentiveLearner can collect high quality PPG signals reliably from learners' fingertips during video watching.

Figure 9 shows quality illustrations of PPG signals collected in six learning sessions. The white areas were interruptions in the signal (video pauses). The pink areas were high quality PPG signals and the cyan areas were low quality signals. The percentage of high quality signals for the six video sessions in Figure 9 were 97.74%, 95.70%, 96.76%, 84.71%, 81.22%, and 74.90% respectively from top to bottom. We observed that the low quality signals were scattered across the whole video session and that each low quality signal sequence usually had short durations (less than 30 seconds). Therefore, we can still extract high quality PPG signals from major portions of the learning sessions even if the video session contained low-quality signals (sessions 4 – 6 in Figure 9).

5.3 Heart Rate as Fine-grained Feedback

We also explored the feasibility of using PPG signals collected in our experiment to predict learners' cognitive states. Specifically, we were interested in learners' two cognitive states: interest/boredom and confusion in learning.

We used participants' self-reported ratings on learning topics as the gold standard. We collected a total of 522 user ratings (29 topics * 18 subjects) in our study. We excluded sessions with the same rating for all topics, implying that the participant reported the same feeling throughout the session. The whole dataset contained 428 samples of interest/boredom predictions (23.83% of the topics were rated boring/uninteresting, rating ≤ 2) and 490 samples of confusion predictions (19.8% were rated confusing, rating ≥ 4).

For each video session, we used the LivePulse algorithm [7] to extract RR-intervals and heart rates from the corresponding PPG signals. We applied the following heuristics to eliminate outliers in RR-intervals:

- Discard RR-intervals corresponding to heart rates beyond 40 ~ 140 bpm;
- Discard RR-intervals corresponding to heart rates differ more than 20 bpm from the median over the video session;
- Discard RR-intervals corresponding to heart rates differ more than 10 bpm from the previous RR-interval.

We extracted 14 dimensions of features from raw PPG signals of each learning topic. The durations of a topic ranged between 33s to 2m46s (average: 1m41s). Among these features, 7 dimensions were *global features* extracted from the PPG signals of the entire topic section. The 7 global features were these: 1) Mean-HR (average heart rate); 2) SD-HR (standard deviation of the heart rate); 3) AVNN (average RR-intervals); 4) SDNN (standard deviation of the RR-intervals); 5) pNN50 (percentage of adjacent RR-intervals with a difference longer than 50ms); 6) rMSSD (Square root of the mean of the squares of difference between adjacent RR-intervals); 7) MAD (median absolute deviation of all RR-intervals). These features were common short-term time domain heart rate and HRV features. The other 7 dimensions (e.g., Local Mean-HR) were *local features* extracted by averaging the same features in multiple fix-sized, non-overlapping local windows within the topic section (Figure 10). If the last local window overlapped with the beginning of the next topic, only signals that had fallen within the current topic were used. We also normalized the features in each video session for each participant.

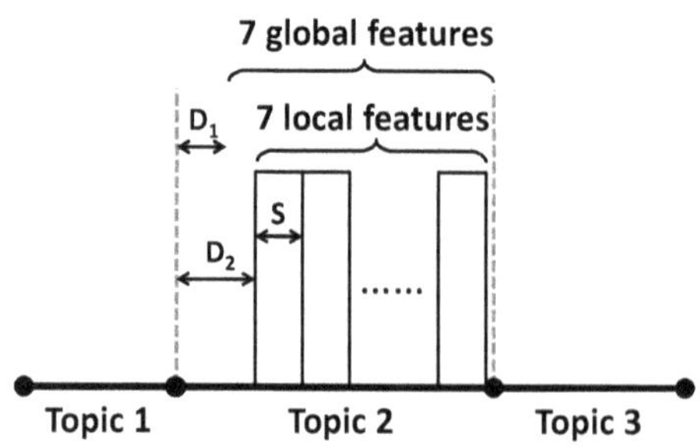

Figure 10. Extracting local and global features from PPG signals captured within a topic

We tested five supervised machine learning algorithms to predict learners' interest/boredom and confusion states. The algorithms were *k*-nearest neighbors (kNN), Naïve Bayes (NB), Decision Tree (DT), support vector machine with linear kernel (LinearSVM), and support vector machine with radial basis function kernel (RBFSVM). We used WEKA to train and optimize the classifiers.

We used the leave-one-subject-out method to evaluate performance of the models. Therefore, all results reported were *user-independent*. We calculated and reported Cohen's Kappa because the distributions of class labels were skewed so reporting accuracies alone would be insufficient. The optimal parameters of a classifier were chosen according to the best average Kappa over all subjects. We tried 5 different delays D_1 for extracting the global features (0s, 5s, 10s, 15s, 20s) × 5 different delays D_2 for the first window (0s, 5s, 10s, 15s, 20s) × 12 window sizes S (10s, 15s, 20s … 60s) for extracting local features (Figure 10).

Table 2. Performance of the classifiers for boredom prediction and confusion prediction

Prediction of the boring topics in a video session				
Model	**Accuracy**	**Precision**	**Recall**	**Kappa**
kNN	77.29%	**0.504**	0.325	0.258
NB	69.37%	0.376	0.373	0.162
DT	**78.56%**	0.523	0.180	0.191
LinearSVM	67.71%	0.397	**0.538**	0.237
RBFSVM	73.58%	0.462	0.499	**0.297**
Prediction of the confusing topics in a video session				
kNN	77.17%	0.396	0.316	0.211
NB	77.99%	0.358	0.164	0.116
DT	**81.96%**	0.523	0.208	0.224
LinearSVM	75.74%	0.402	**0.366**	0.223
RBFSVM	77.69%	**0.516**	0.353	**0.269**

Table 2 lists the best performance (in Kappa) achieved by each classifier. The RBF-kernel SVM has best overall Kappa (0.297 and 0.269) for predicting both boring and confusing topics. We found that the local window size had a significant impact on the classifier performance (Figure 11). A window size of 50 seconds had the best performance for predicting perceived boredom and a smaller window (30 seconds) led to the best performance for predicting confusing topics.

The performance of our classifiers is comparable with existing systems that rely on dedicated physiological sensors to detect human affect (e.g., Hussain et. al. [8] developed user dependent models with Kappa scores of 0.35 and 0.23 for detecting three-level valence and arousal). It is worth highlighting that our performance was achieved on today's mobile phones without any hardware modifications. We also only used the heart rate signals and did not use any contextual features used by some other studies. The Kappa scores indicate that AttentiveLearner is capable of identifying the perceived boring and confusing parts of a video in a user-independent fashion.

Considering that our classifiers were binary and were used to predict two cognitive states (interest/boredom and confusion), it is not clear whether the current approach is sensitive enough to differentiate fine-grained cognitive states with similar physiological arousal levels (e.g., happy vs. interested). We plan to run follow-up studies to test the feasibility of discriminating multiple, fine-grained cognitive states. New features (e.g., lecture contents, facial expressions) might be necessary to improve the prediction performance in the future.

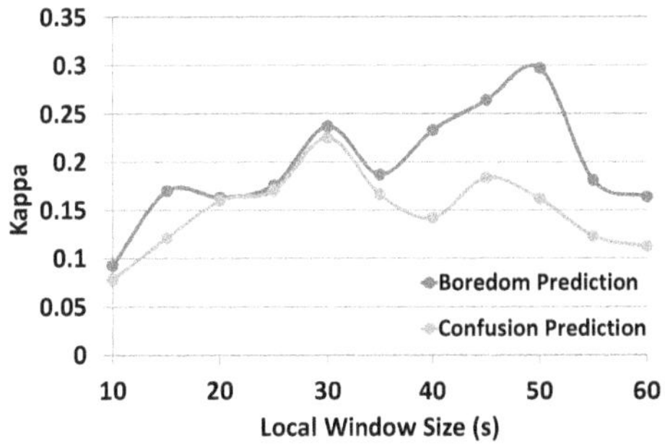

Figure 11. Classifiers' Kappa by local window size

5.4 Extreme Events and Aggregated Events

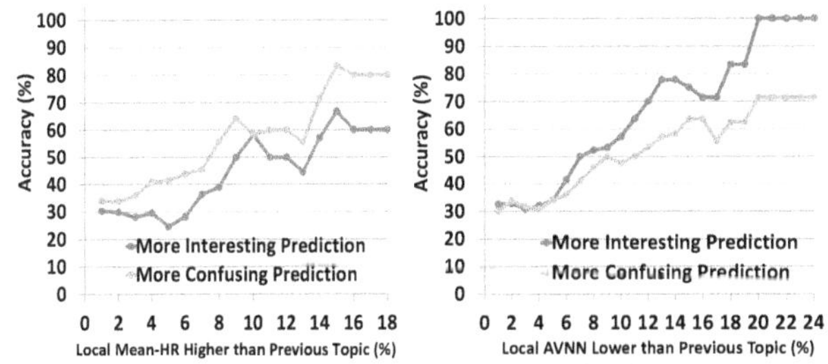

Figure 12. Predication accuracy when using local mean-HR (left) and local AVNN (right) as markers of "extreme personal learning events"

We found predicting *extreme personal learning events* and *aggregated learning events* can significantly improve the classification accuracies. We define *extreme personal learning events* as a small fraction of events from a learner that are drastically different from other events based on a specific marker. We define *aggregated learning events* as the aggregated responses of all learners towards a learning topic.

Figure 12 shows the use of local mean-HR feature (left) and local AVNN feature (right) as markers of "*extreme personal learning events*" and the corresponding prediction accuracies on relative interest/boredom and confusion. We can predict with 60% accuracy in relative confusion by restricting predictions to events where the local mean-HR was at least 11% higher than the previous topic. We can predict with 83.3% accuracy by restricting predictions to events where the local mean-HR was at least 15% higher than the previous topic (Figure 12 left). Similarly, the local AVNN can also be used as an effective marker for predicting relative interest/boredom and confusion (Figure 12 right). In our experiments, local mean-HR was a better marker for predicting relative confusion (Figure 12 left) and local AVNN was a better marker for predicting relative interest/boredom (Figure 12 right).

We also found that PPG signals from a group of learners can be aggregated for more accurate prediction of cognitive states. Such aggregated events are informative to instructors because they convey the overall feedback from students on a specific learning topic. For example, Figure 13 shows the aggregated histogram of "confusing" topic from both reported results (left) and predicted results (right) for the second lecture ("Normal Form Definitions"). It is clear that our aggregated prediction is consistent with participants' ratings. In both histograms, the 7th topic has more confusion than any other topic, implying that this topic is challenging during learning. After investigating the corresponding lecture video, we found that the 7th topic contains an in-depth analysis of the "Team Games" concept. Such insights captured from learners' physiological signals can help teachers refine instructional content for the future.

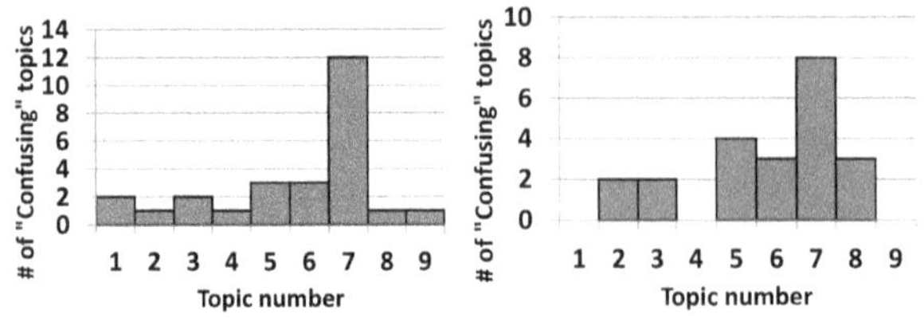

Figure 13. Histograms of "Confusing" topics of video clip 2. Left: reported results. Right: predicted results.

6. CONCLUSIONS AND FUTURE WORK

We presented AttentiveLearner, a mobile learning system optimized for consuming lecture videos in Massive Open Online Courses (MOOCs) and flipped classrooms. We explained in detail the design, usability and feasibility of AttentiveLearner as a rich, fined-grained feedback channel from students to teachers. Through two 18-participant user studies and follow-up analyses, we found the tangible video control interface in AttentiveLearner to be intuitive to learn, and accurate and responsive to use. We also showed that heart rate signals implicitly captured by AttentiveLearner can be used to predict both learners' interests and perceived confusion levels towards the corresponding learning topics. AttentiveLearner can achieve significantly higher accuracy by predicting *extreme personal learning events* and *aggregated learning events*.

We have four specific goals in the near future. First, we plan to conduct large-scale, longitudinal studies in learners' everyday environments. We shall make AttentiveLearner freely available for public use at http://www.attentivelearner.com in this process. Second, the current studies were completed in a lab. Learners are likely to study in more interrupted, fragmented sessions in highly diversified environments (e.g., standing, sitting, public transit). One important issue is to exclude confounding effects of the environments on physiological signals. We shall investigate how to infer reliable cognitive state information from noisy, highly interrupted physiological signals. Third, security and privacy issues arise when learners' physiological signals are transmitted, stored, and visualized on the server-side. We are working with researchers in privacy to explore security algorithms and policies to provide rich feedback without disclosing unnecessary privacy from learners. Fourth, we plan to explore how different techniques of learning analytics (e.g. log analysis, post-lecture feedback, and AttentiveLearner) can be integrated to provide informative feedback to both instructors and students.

7. ACKNOWLEDGEMENTS

We thank Reed Armstrong, Guy Gadola, Michael Lipschultz, Nils Murrugarra Llerena, and Phuong Pham for their help and suggestions. We also thank the anonymous reviewers for the constructive feedback.

This research is in-part supported by an RDF from the Learning Research and Development Center (LRDC) at the University of Pittsburgh.

8. REFERENCES

[1] Bixler, R. and D'Mello, S. Toward fully automated person-independent detection of mind wandering. In Proc. UMAP 2014

[2] Coetzee, D., Fox, A., Hearst, M., Hartmann, B., Chatrooms in MOOCs: All talk and no action? In Proc. ACM LAS 2014.

[3] D'Mello, S., Picard, R. W., and Graesser, A. Toward an affect-sensitive AutoTutor. IEEE Intelligent Systems, (4) 2007.

[4] Fowler, G., An early report card on massive open online courses. The Wall Street Journal, October 8, 2013.

[5] Glassman, E. L., Kim, J., Monroy-Hernández, A. and Morris, M. R. Mudslide: A spatially anchored census of student confusion for online lecture videos. In Proc. CHI 2015, pp1555-1564.

[6] Guo, P. J., Kim, J., and Rubin, R. How video production affects student engagement: An empirical study of MOOC videos. In Proc. ACM LAS 2014, pp41–50.

[7] Han, T., Xiao, X., Shi, L., Canny, J., and Wang, J. Balancing accuracy and fun: designing camera based mobile games for implicit heart rate monitoring. In Proc. CHI 2015, pp847-856.

[8] Hussain, M. S., AlZoubi, O., Calvo, R. A., and D'Mello, S. K. Affect detection from multichannel physiology during learning sessions with AutoTutor. In Proc. AIED 2011, pp131-138.

[9] Jraidi, I., Chaouachi, M., and Frasson, C. A dynamic multimodal approach for assessing learners' interaction experience. In Proc. ACM ICMI 2013, pp271-278.

[10] Kim, J., Glassman, E. L., Monroy-Hernández, A. and Morris, M. R. RIMES: embedding interactive multimedia exercises in lecture videos. In Proc. CHI 2015, pp1535-1544.

[11] Kim, J., Guo, P. J., Cai, C. J., Li, S. W. D., Gajos, K. Z., and Miller, R. C. Data-driven interaction techniques for improving navigation of educational videos. In Proc. ACM UIST, pp563-572.

[12] Kim, J., Guo, P. J., Seaton, D. T., Mitros, P., Gajos, K. Z., and Miller, R. C. Understanding in-video dropouts and interaction peaks in online lecture videos. In Proc. ACM LAS 2014.

[13] Lee, Y. C., Lin, W. C., Cherng, F. Y., Wang, H. C., Sung, C. Y., and King, J. T. Using time-anchored peer comments to enhance social interaction in online educational videos. In Proc. CHI 2015.

[14] Mark, G., Wang, Y., and Niiya, M. Stress and multitasking in everyday college life: an empirical study of online activity. In Proc. CHI 2014, pp41-50.

[15] Monserrat, T. J. K. P., Li, Y., Zhao, S., and Cao, X, L. IVE: an integrated interactive video-based learning environment. In Proc. CHI 2014, pp3399-3402.

[16] Monserrat, T. J. K. P., Zhao, S., McGee, K., and Pandey, A. V., Notevideo: Facilitating navigation of blackboard-style lecture videos. In Proc. CHI 2013, pp1139-1148.

[17] Parr, C., Not Staying the Course, Times Higher Education, May 10, 2013.

[18] Pham, P., and Wang, J. AttentiveLearner: improving mobile MOOC learning via implicit heart rate tracking. In Proc. AIED 2015, pp367-376.

[19] Picard, R. Affective computing. MIT Press, 2000.

[20] Seaton, D. T., Bergner, Y., Chuang, I., Mitros, P., and Pritchard, D. E. Who does what in a massive open online course? Comm. of the ACM, 57(4) 2014, pp58-65.

[21] Shah, D., MOOCs in 2014: Breaking Down the Numbers, edSurge 2014.

[22] Szafir, D., and Mutlu, B. Artful: Adaptive review technology for flipped learning. In Proc. CHI 2013, pp1001–1010.

[23] Woolf, B., Burleson, W., Arroyo, I., Dragon, T., Cooper, D., and Picard, R. Affect-aware tutors' recognising and responding to student affect. Int. J. Learn. Technol. 4, ¾, Oct. 2009, pp129–164.

[24] Xiao, X., Han, T., and Wang, J. LensGesture: augmenting mobile interactions with back-of-device finger gestures. In Proc. ACM ICMI 2013, pp287-294

An Experiment on the Feasibility of Spatial Acquisition Using a Moving Auditory Cue for Pedestrian Navigation

Yeseul Park
Seoul National University
1 Gwanak-ro, Gwanak-Gu,
Seoul 151-744, Korea
+82-2-880-7044
yspark@hcil.snu.ac.kr

Kyle Koh
Seoul National University
1 Gwanak-ro, Gwanak-Gu,
Seoul 151-744, Korea
+82-2-880-7044
kyle@hcil.snu.ac.kr

Heonjin Park
Seoul National University
1 Gwanak-ro, Gwanak-Gu,
Seoul 151-744, Korea
+82-2-880-7044
hounjini@hcil.snu.ac.kr

Jinwook Seo
Seoul National University
1 Gwanak-ro, Gwanak-Gu,
Seoul 151-744, Korea
+82-2-880-7044
jseo@snu.ac.kr

ABSTRACT
We conducted a feasibility study on the use of a moving auditory cue for spatial acquisition for pedestrian navigation by comparing its performance with a static auditory cue, the use of which has been investigated in previous studies. To investigate the performance of human sound azimuthal localization, we designed and conducted a controlled experiment with 15 participants and found that performance was statistically significantly more accurate with an auditory source moving from the opposite direction over users' heads to the target direction than with a static sound. Based on this finding, we designed a bimodal pedestrian navigation system using both visual and auditory feedback. We evaluated the system by conducting a field study with four users and received overall positive feedback.

Categories and Subject Descriptors
H.5.2 [Information Interfaces and Presentation]: User Interfaces—auditory feedback, evaluation/methodology

General Terms
Measurement, Design, Experimentation, Human Factors.

Keywords
sound localization; spatial audio

1. INTRODUCTION
There have been several efforts to develop efficient navigation systems for pedestrians, such as route planners showing the shortest path to a destination. Spatial knowledge acquisition based on landmarks [10] such as traffic signs and wayfinding based on turn-by-turn instructions commonly used in car navigation cannot be directly applied because of fundamental differences in modalities and goals between drivers and pedestrians [7]. For example, while cars move on designated roads, pedestrians can more freely walk through parks and grass fields and can take shortcuts not accessible by car.

While visual stimuli can deliver the most accurate data with more information bandwidth than is possible with other sensory stimuli, they are not without their limitations. Exploring strange surroundings using a traditional pictorial map could prove a cognitive overload for users. People navigating to a destination need to recognize their orientation and position within the area as well as to predict changes in spatial relationships between themselves and environments upon a change in the direction of movement. Safety is another important issue to consider. A pedestrian concentrating on a map and walking on roadways always carries a risk of accident due to a lack of attention to his or her surroundings. To alleviate these issues, many pedestrian navigation systems suggest alternative solutions to lighten the cognitive burden through the use of additional sensory channels like auditory or haptic signals: [8], [9].

This study suggests a spatial acquisition method with moving auditory cues. The feasibility of the method was evaluated in a psychoacoustic experiment to compare human sound azimuthal localization performance between stationary and moving auditory cues. After confirming the feasibility, we designed a bimodal navigational system involving both visual and auditory feedback for pedestrians. Through a field study using the system, we have confirmed that moving auditory cues can help pedestrians navigate in a safe and engaging way.

2. DESIGN RATIONALE
There have been many attempts to use auditory cues for pedestrian navigation. Liljedahl et al. used a sound source moving from center to left or right of the pedestrian to indicate upcoming turns [3], while Fujimoto and Turk used a sound that swept from the center to the target direction [2]. Unlike [2] and [3], in which the sound moved from the center to a target position, in our prototype method, it moved from the 180° opposite direction towards the target position (Figure 1). We speculated that such movement would result in more accurate detection of direction because of 1) greater changes in intensity of the sound in each channel than in [2] and [3] and 2) the additional sound from one more (exact opposite) direction, which gave more azimuthal information than would have been possible with just one sound.

Also, we constantly updated the position of the sound relative to users' head movements using a compass. Although the front–back confusion is common in simulated surround sound using a stereo channel, even a small change in the directional movement of the sound could be detected [6] and help compensate for the error [12]. It was reasonable to assume that users do not hold their heads perfectly straight all the time while navigating through the street or even sitting in an office environment [5]. By introducing the

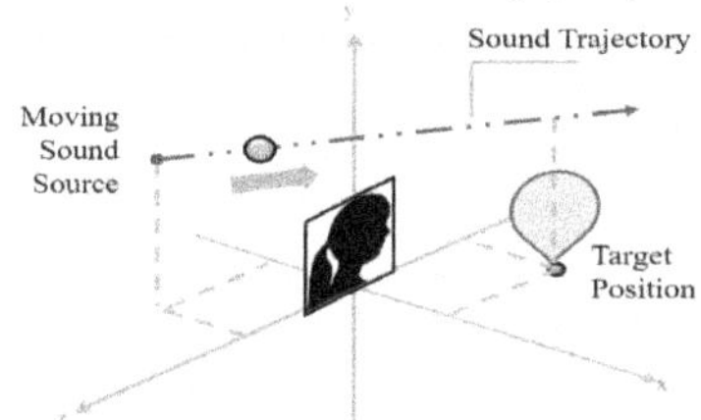

Figure 1. The sound moves from the opposite side to a target position, passing above the user's head with HRTF.

ICMI '15, November 09 - 13, 2015, Seattle, WA, USA

ACM 978-1-4503-3912-4/15/11…$15.00
DOI: http://dx.doi.org/10.1145/2818346.2820779

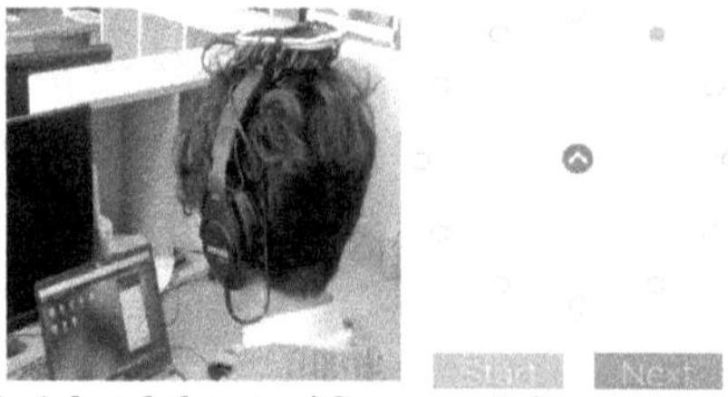

Figure 2. A headphone with a smartphone mounted on top (Left) and the user interface for responding (Right).

constant directional update to the sound, we were able to achieve 360° of spatial acquisition.

However, we did not choose music as an auditory stimulus, as in [2], since the test results would have heavily depended on the melody, tempo, or type of music, making it difficult to compare performance. Also, human speech might draw too much attention from users, introducing safety hazards [13]. Instead, we used a repeated chime. The stimulus was generated as a non-individualized head-related transfer function (HRTF) using OpenAL (for Open Audio Library) on an Android application. The chime was repeated at a pace of 75 BPM while it took 20 seconds for it to move from the opposite side to the destination.

Although the primary goal of navigation systems is to direct users to their target destinations, they do not always provide the shortest or most efficient route. Brown et al.'s ethnographic study on designing a new navigation system for city tourists found that they usually use a map to locate or orient themselves as heading in a "roughly correct" direction and enjoy exploring an unfamiliar city [1]. Based on this idea, we did not design our navigation system solely focusing on achieving maximum accuracy in spatial acquisition. Instead of providing turn-by-turn navigation, our method was designed to help "wanderers" explore the city and reach their destinations within an acceptable timeframe. For our field study, which involved using a navigation system with both visual and auditory cues, we tested users' ability to reach roughly guided locations as wanderers without getting lost.

3. EXPERIMENT WITH A MOVING CUE

To evaluate the feasibility of the moving auditory cue, we designed a controlled user study.

3.1 Procedure

Fifteen adults (*age = 19 to 33, M = 25.88*) participated in the experiment as paid volunteers. All had normal hearing with no history of hearing problems of any kind. No subject had any previous experience with psychoacoustic experiments.

The experiment was carried out in a quiet classroom. A participant sat in a turning chair and wore headphones with a smartphone attached on top (Figure 2). The experiment consisted of two sessions, one for the stationary sound and one for the moving sound. Each session comprised 20 tests. The test was designed as a within-subject comparison, and the order of the sessions was counterbalanced to prevent learning effects. The participants were allowed to review instructions and conduct trial tests until they felt comfortable with the procedure. The orientation sensor was calibrated before every test.

Each participant was asked to try to figure out the azimuthal location of the sound. While participants' heads were locked to a chinrest in most previous psychoacoustic experiments, we allowed head movement as part of natural behavior, although answers had to be given in relation to the straightforward direction. There was no noticeable latency for head tracking. Once the direction was determined, participants recorded their answers by selecting one of the twelve buttons on the computer screen. The reaction time and judged location were recorded. The azimuthal direction of the sound source was distributed from 0° to 330° at intervals of 30° and was randomly picked.

In this experiment, the relationship between intended and responded azimuthal locations was measured only on the horizontal plane, rather than in 3D, to keep things simple.

3.2 Results

Based on the azimuthal localization responses of all participants shown in Figure 3, the accuracy of sound localization using the moving sound was on par with or significantly better than with the static sound (except at 120°). The moving sound performed slightly worse than the stationary sound at 150°, as well, although the difference was not significant. We wonder if this could be generalized to argue that the sound starting at the front and fading toward the back does not provide a more accurate azimuthal cue than does the stationary sound, although a more elaborate study is required in the future. Also, we currently do not know the cause of the especially high error rates at 60° and 150° for the stationary sound, although we speculate that it is because they are close to "nice" angles like 90° and 180°.

The Shapiro-Wilk normality test shows that the data for each type do not come from a normally distributed population ($p < .0001$). The Wilcoxon signed rank test shows that the difference in the absolute error angles between the static sound (*avg. rank of 85.09*, $\mu = 14.13°$ $\sigma = 23.31$) and the moving sound (*avg. rank of 83.44*, $\mu = 21.7°$ $\sigma = 29.75$) was significant ($Z = -3.63, p < .001$). It should be noted that the result could vary under different experimental setup factors, such as the use of headphones or a loudspeaker, whether head movement is allowed, the interval angle (30° for us), and the type of answers requested (discrete and forced choice vs. free answers). The RMS errors for the moving and stationary sounds were 27.28° ($\sigma = 11.35$) and 37.75° ($\sigma = 11.54$), respectively.

Overall, the front–back confusion error rates for the static sound and the moving sound among all participants were 7% and 2.67%, respectively. In particular, front–back confusion was most prominent for the two participants (P8 and P10) responsible for 76.2% of the entire confusion for the static sound. Their confusion rate dropped by 75% when they used the moving sound, implying that the moving sound not only helped improve the determination of azimuthal localization but also decreased front–back confusion, especially for those who suffered from significant front–back confusion.

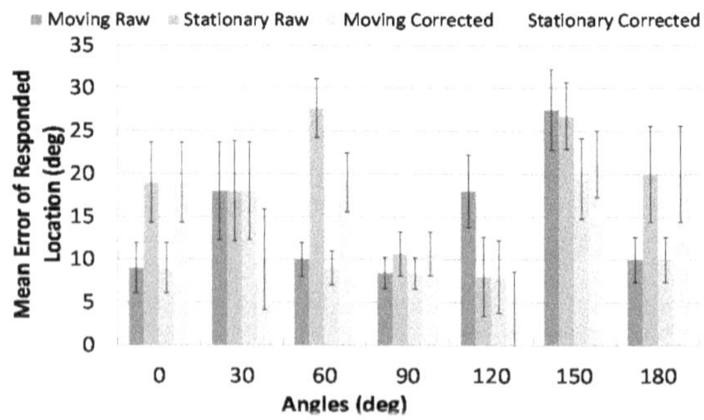

Figure 3. Mean error (in degree) for each azimuthal location. The results from the same angle from both sides were merged (i.e., ±30°, ±60°, ±90°, ±120°, and ±150°). The blue bars show the original errors, while the green bars show responses after front–back confusion is compensated.

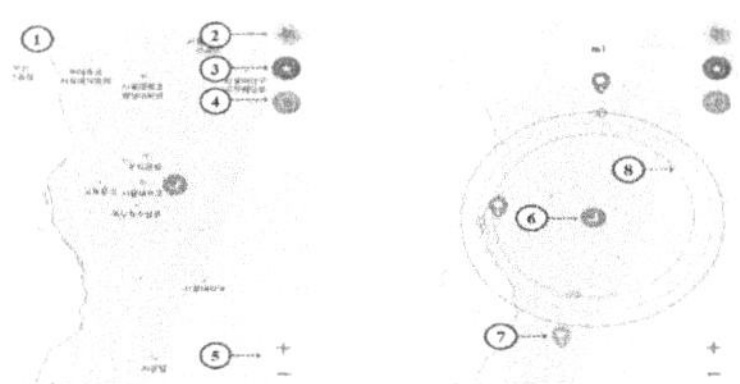

Figure 4. Screenshots of the mobile app used for the study.

The Wilcoxon signed rank test shows that the difference in the absolute error angles between the static sound (*avg. rank of 147.67,* $\mu = 16.21s$ $\sigma = 8.21$) and the moving sound (*avg. rank of 169.51,* $\mu = 18.30s$ $\sigma = 8.89$) was significant ($Z = -3.74$, $p < .001$). The result conforms to previous research findings (i.e. participants tend to delay their judgment for the moving sound until the sound has passed above their heads.) It remains to be seen how long the cycle must be in order to provide such an improvement, although it was certainly the case for 20 seconds.

In conclusion, we were able to confirm the feasibility of a moving auditory cue for sound localization on the horizontal plane as a more accurate method than a stationary sound.

4. FIELD STUDY

Encouraged by the results above, we built a bimodal navigation system for pedestrians using visual and moving auditory feedback. The system comprised five components: a map, a user state marker, a destination marker, an orientation guide as a visual cue of orientation, and an auditory cue using spatial sound with HRTF (Figure 4). The visual/auditory design would allow users to refer to the display as needed, which would be beneficial for "wanderers."

Users tend to zoom in on (Fig. 4–6, 8) a map when trying to orient and locate themselves. Because the action results in the destination markers (Fig. 4–7) being pushed outside the screen, the macroscopic orientation of a destination was indicated in this study via consistently sized circles (Fig. 4–8) around a user state marker (Fig. 4–6), making it harder to find the "rough" route without the help of a route planner. The orientation guide (Fig. 4–3) always showed the azimuthal direction of the final destination regardless of map scale, allowing users to see a big picture of the path to be taken.

An auditory cue informed users of the orientation of the destination. When a user tapped a target marker, the tinkling sound moved from the opposite side to an origin, then to the destination.

4.1 Implementation

The prototype was built on a Samsung Galaxy S III smartphone with SHURE SHR440 stereo headphones. The phone measured current location and orientation using its GPS, an orientation sensor. Spatial information was provided to users via both visual and auditory feedback. In the field study, to test a more realistic scenario, we did not use headphones with a smartphone attached on top, as we had in the experiment in the previous section, because readily available headphones do not usually come with a compass built in. Instead, we relied on the orientation of the smartphone. Heller et al.'s study, which reports that the head-yaw stays within a 10° angle to both sides, except for some delays between the head-turn and the body/device-turn [3], inspired us to make this decision. We also told participants to keep the device as straightforward from the head as possible.

4.2 Evaluation

Since there is no consensus on criteria for the quantitative evaluation of multimodal navigation systems, it is difficult to quantitatively analyze the performance of the system. Also, users' walking speeds and innate senses of spatial knowledge acquisition differ. Thus, we took a qualitative approach. The test was conducted to shed light on questions such as the following:

- Is this system really helpful in finding destinations?
- How can users control this system to find a way to the destination?

4.3 Design of the User Test

The test took place on a university campus. Four subjects (three of whom were female) aged 25 to 33 without any problems with sight, hearing, or mobility participated in the test. All participants had previous experience using smartphone navigation and had never been to the campus before.

All participants took part in adequate training sessions before the main test. In the main test, they were asked to navigate their way to three predesignated destinations marked on the map. While they were performing their tasks, they were asked to "think aloud" about their feelings and experience. The experimenter accompanied participants for safety and to record data. Post-test interviews were conducted after the main test collected users' subjective impressions of this system.

4.4 Observations

All participants successfully reached all three destinations without any significant disorientation. The mean time to complete the task was 25 min. and 30 sec. However, as mentioned above, completion time is not very meaningful because of individual differences and preferences among participants. We also did not observe any functional anomalies, like fatigue, among the participants within that time. The traces and the behavioral patterns gave us more valuable insights.

There were two main types of usage patterns for the moving auditory cue. Some participants showed a usage pattern of following the auditory cues throughout the whole test to find the destinations. They played the sound as they started the test and then kept the cue playing until they reached their destinations. A noticeable observation of this type of user is that they relied on the sound especially when they felt lost.

"I can get to a destination by following only the sound. It was easier to follow the movement of the sound than I thought" (P1).

"I lost my orientation when I got confused in the forked road, like just now. I will just follow the sound" (P3).

One participant also showed a usage pattern of not relying on the auditory cues so much. This participant used only the visual map to get closer to the target and used the auditory cues to find an accurate target position when nearing the destination.

"I prefer to wander to find the target when I am lost rather than to stop and look at the map standing up. It makes me more confused to find my position and orientation in the map. However, the sound cue is less confusing than the visual map" (P2).

4.5 Insights from the Interviews

In post-test interviews, the participants gave positive scores to the auditory cues and the orientation guide in a satisfactory survey with nine-point Likert-scale questions.

4.5.1 The Auditory Cue as a Moving Sound

Users gave positive feedback overall on the auditory cues (avg. 7.5 out of 9). No participants had previously used navigation with auditory cues. They felt a bit confused at first, but shortly got used to this system.

"I think that a novice needs to get used to the sound cue. I was confused at first, because the sound was moving. But now I feel I could get to my destination by simply following it" (P4).

"I like the moving sound because I can recognize the direction of moving easily. Even when I had some difficulties, I was able to figure it out as soon as it moved to the direction towards the destination from the opposite side" (P1).

Some users reported weak auditory cues. Three users had difficulty figuring out whether the sound was moving forward or backward. However, the constant update on the movement of sound relative to the device helped them reorient themselves.

"I could easily figure out whether the sound was moving to the left or right. But it was quite hard to distinguish front and back. So I had to turn my head around to find the direction" (P3).

Although OpenAL provided a binaural effect using HRTF, the difference was subtle to make substantial changes to the results.

4.5.2 The Orientation Guide

This feature also earned positive feedback but was less favored by users than the auditory cues (avg. 6.25 out of 9). The main attraction was that the orientation guide was always visible regardless of map scale, so users could establish the relationship between their orientation and the destination whenever they turned around. Most users, however, thought that the orientation guide was not a key feature but a supplemental cue.

"This orientation ring surely gives me the rough information of the orientation of the destination even when I zoom in to the map. But if I want to listen to the auditory cue of the destination, I have to find the marker to tap it anyway" (P3).

4.6 Discussion

Overall, the main two features helped pedestrians use the system and the moving auditory feedback played a significant role in navigating with satisfactory results. However, there are remaining issues, such as front–back confusion, which were somewhat improved but far from completely resolved. Perhaps additional cues, such as changes in tone, can be applied. The following comment shows both the pros and cons of this system.

"I think that I could take a roundabout way to the destination by just following the sound, particularly when I reach a fork. So I think I have to check the map sometimes even if I am satisfied with this system. But it is quite convenient that there is no need to concentrate on the map throughout the wandering" (P1).

The experiment comes with a few limitations. Although we have allowed the users free head movement while the sound is playing, with continuous updates to the direction to which the auditory cue moves, there was still a front–back confusion. Also, the field study conducted with headphones introduced a safety issue due to users being insulated from ambient sound. It remains to be seen whether devices like bone conduction headphones can provide enough auditory cues without sacrificing accuracy.

5. CONCLUSION

We explored the feasibility of using a moving auditory cue generated by HRTF for spatial acquisition for pedestrian navigation. From a controlled experiment, we found that users can more accurately determine the direction of a moving sound than a static sound. Also, a field study with a navigation system with such a capability revealed that pedestrians can be guided to their destinations without the need to constantly look at a map.

6. ACKNOWLEDGMENTS

This work was supported by the National Research Foundation of Korea (NRF) grant funded by the Korea government (MEST) (No. NRF-2014R1A2A2A03006998) and Samsung Electronics. Jinwook Seo is the corresponding author.

7. REFERENCES

[1] Brown, B., & Laurier, E. 2005. Designing electronic maps: an ethnographic approach. *In Map-based Mobile Services* (pp. 241-257). Springer Berlin Heidelberg.

[2] Fujimoto, E., & Turk, M. 2014. Non-Visual Navigation Using Combined Audio Music and Haptic Cues. *In Proc. of the 16th Int. Conf. on Multimodal Interaction* (pp. 411-418). ACM.

[3] Heller, F., Krämer, A., & Borchers, J. 2014. Simplifying orientation measurement for mobile audio augmented reality applications. *In Proc. of the 32nd annual ACM conf. on Human factors in computing systems* (pp. 615-624).

[4] Liljedahl, M., Lindberg, S., Delsing, K., Polojärvi, M., Saloranta, T., & Alakärppä, I. 2012. Testing two tools for multimodal navigation. *Advances in Human-Computer Interaction*, 2012, 15.

[5] Minnaar, P., Olesen, S. K., Christensen, F., & Moller, H. 2001. The importance of head movements for binaural room synthesis. *In Proc. of Int. Conf. on Auditory Display*, (Espoo, Finland, 2001 July), pp. 21–25.

[6] Perrott, D. R., & Musicant, A. D. 1977. Minimum auditory movement angle: Binaural localization of moving sound sources. *The Journal of the Acoustical Society of America*, 62(6), 1463-1466.

[7] Pielot, M., & Boll, S. 2010. "In Fifty Metres Turn Left": Why Turn-by-turn Instructions Fail Pedestrians. *In Proc. of HaptiMap, Workshop at MobileHCI*. ACM, New York (pp. 26-28).

[8] Pielot, M., Poppinga, B., & Boll, S. 2010. PocketNavigator: vibro-tactile waypoint navigation for everyday mobile devices. *In Proc. of the 12th Int. Conf. on Human Computer Interaction with Mobile Devices and Services* (pp. 423-426). ACM.

[9] Rieser, J. 2008. Theory and issues in research on blindness and brain plasticity. *Blindness and brain plasticity in navigation and object perception*, 3-12.

[10] Siegel, A. W., & White, S. H. 1975. The development of spatial representations of large-scale environments. *Advances in child development and behavior*, 10, 9.

[11] Strachan, S., Eslambolchilar, P., Murray-Smith, R., Hughes, S., & O'Modhrain, S. 2005. GpsTunes: controlling navigation via audio feedback. *In Proc. of the 7th Int. Conf. on Human Computer Interaction with Mobile Devices & Services* (pp. 275-278). ACM.

[12] Wightman, F. L., & Kistler, D. J. 1999. Resolution of front–back ambiguity in spatial hearing by listener and source movement. *The Journal of the Acoustical Society of America*, 105(5), 2841-2853.

[13] Wilson, J., Walker, B. N., Lindsay, J., Cambias, C., & Dellaert, F. (2007, October). Swan: System for wearable audio navigation. *In Wearable Computers, 2007 11th IEEE Int. Symp. on* (pp. 91-98). IEEE.

A Wearable Multimodal Interface for Exploring Urban Points of Interest

Antti Jylhä †, Yi-Ta Hsieh †, Valeria Orso ‡, Salvatore Andolina †, Luciano Gamberini ‡, Giulio Jacucci †§
†Helsinki Institute for Information Technology HIIT, Department of Computer Science, University of Helsinki, Finland
first.last@helsinki.fi
§Helsinki Institute for Information Technology HIIT, Aalto University, Finland
‡Human Inspired Technology Research Centre HIT, Department of General Psychology, University of Padova, Italy
first.last@unipd.it

ABSTRACT

Locating points of interest (POIs) in cities is typically facilitated by visual aids such as paper maps, brochures, and mobile applications. However, these techniques require visual attention, which ideally should be on the surroundings. Non-visual techniques for navigating towards specific POIs typically lack support for free exploration of the city or more detailed guidance. To overcome these issues, we propose a multimodal, wearable system for alerting the user of nearby recommended POIs. The system, built around a tactile glove, provides audio-tactile cues when a new POI is in the vicinity, and more detailed information and guidance if the user expresses interest in this POI. We evaluated the system in a field study, comparing it to a visual baseline application. The encouraging results show that the glove-based system helps keep the attention on the surroundings and that its performance is on the same level as that of the baseline.

Categories and Subject Descriptors

H.5.2 [**Information Interfaces and Presentation**]: User Interfaces

Keywords

Wearable computing; multimodal interaction; cultural heritage; tactile feedback; auditory icons

1. INTRODUCTION

Traditionally, exploration of points of interest (POIs) in cities has relied on printed materials such as maps and guide books. The smartphone era is effectively rendering these techniques obsolete, with a plethora of available interactive maps and tourist guide applications. Techniques range from visual augmented reality (e.g., [36], [29], [14]) to mixed reality approaches for displaying content on 2D maps(e.g., [23], [2]). More complex interaction techniques have also been developed for mobile 3D maps (e.g., [24], [25], [18]). In addition, location-aware mobile applications, such as Foursquare[1], are redefining the way tourists explore new places.

However, hand-held visual interfaces may suffer from issues such as screen reflections interfering with content visibility [16, 37] and require visual attention on the device, which results in sharing cognitive resources between the device and the environment [6, 26]. This may disconnect the user from the surroundings and hamper the user experience [3]. A remedy for these issues can be provided by head-mounted displays or non-visual interfaces.

Several approaches have been proposed making use of the auditory and/or haptic modalities to enhance the user experience, to enable the use of the system in situations when visual attention cannot be on the device, and to cater also for visual disabilities. However, the vast majority of these systems have been designed for navigating a defined route or finding a specific place, thus limiting their use for truly exploring the city, which is also a relevant mode of sightseeing [5, 12]. This leads to our primary research question: how to design a non-visual interaction technique that supports exploratory, serendipitous discovery of POIs (see Fig. 1 for a conceptual illustration of the setting.).

Figure 1: Conceptual illustration of exploring urban points of interest. Instead of visual markers, our system uses audio-tactile feedback to notify the user of POIs in the vicinity and to guide the pointing hand of the user to locate the POIs.

ICMI 2015, November 9–13, 2015, Seattle, WA, USA.
 ISBN 978-1-4503-3912-4/15/11 ...$15.00.
DOI: http://dx.doi.org/10.1145/2818346.2820763.

[1]https://foursquare.com

We present a novel location-aware, wearable audio-tactile system with an exploratory approach to find POIs. The interaction technique is designed for free exploration, without the need for pre-defined itineraries or direct contact with a mobile device. The system, based on a sensor-equipped tactile glove, gives audio-tactile cues indicating the *category* of a POI when the user is approaching it. If the user shows explicit interest in the POI, the system can guide the attention of the user towards the POI by audio-tactile feedback. Tour guide-like spoken descriptions give more information. Our main hypothesis, which is assessed through a comparison study, is that the user experience of the proposed system outperforms a visual mobile application. Based on the findings, we discuss the implications for the design of non-visual POI exploration. We contribute to the field of multimodal interaction with a novel non-visual technique for exploring POIs in cities, its evaluation in a field study, and implications for the design of non-visual tour guides.

2. BACKGROUND

In this section, we cover the related work on mobile and wearable tactile and auditory guidance systems.

2.1 Vibrotactile Guidance

Deploying vibrotactile feedback for guidance has been studied with both mobile devices and wearables. In outdoor contexts, the predominant use cases have been waypoint navigation and target finding, for which proposed solutions include, e.g., belts [7] [34] [4], shoes [8], and mobile applications such as PocketNavigator [27], Tactile Compass [28], NaviRadar [31], and the Time Machine [33, 21]. These examples, however, tend to assume that the user is navigating towards a defined destination and lack support for exploration. Mobile device-based target scanning techniques by Ahmaniemi and Lantz [1] and Robinson et al. [30] differ in the sense that they do not guide the user towards a specific destination, but instead enable scanning targets by pointing with a mobile device. The laboratory-based findings of the latter study [30] suggest that while people tend to slightly slow down their walking pace when looking for targets based on haptic feedback, they are still able to find the targets while maintaining awareness of their surroundings.

Other form factors of wearable tactile guidance for pointing, such as gloves, have mainly been applied in indoor settings (e.g., [32], [19]), in which hand movements can be tracked visually, e.g., with depth cameras. While these feedback techniques can be efficient in guiding the pointing hand, the requirement for visual tracking fits poorly in outdoor contexts. This can be overcome by integrated sensors [13] that track the hand orientation.

Hornecker et al. [12] presented a serendipitous tour guide mobile application making use of vibrotactile cues. In their approach, the system is initialized by the places and attractions the user wishes to see. They utilize proximity model-based vibrotactile cues, when the user is approaching a relevant place. They also experimented with generic notification sounds, but found them not to be useful in pilot tests.

Our design makes use of both proximity-based vibrotactile notifications and more refined vibrotactile guidance for pointing at the recommended target. Our technique does not assume the user has any pre-defined destination, enabling true exploration of the city, while still being able to provide fine-grained guidance on demand to a specific POI.

2.2 Auditory Guidance and Recommendations

In addition to haptics, audio has been used in many ways in tour guide applications and related systems. The use of sound in these systems can be categorized to guidance cues [11, 20, 15], notifications [15], contextual sounds [22, 33, 21], and spoken information content [21].

Directional guidance sounds are most often seen in navigation systems. Among the first was AudioGPS [11], which utilized spatial panning and Geiger counter metaphor for guiding the navigation. A related approach was deployed by Kostiainen et al. [15] in an audio-based mobile journey planner. The application used stereo panning cues to guide the person on the move, e.g., when riding a bicycle, to inform whether they deviated from the correct route. The application also made use of various notification sounds, e.g., to indicate that the person should exit the bus at the next stop. A different guidance scheme was used by Liljedahl and Lindberg [20], who developed a target scanning application with auditory proximity cues to relevant places in the direction where the mobile device was pointing.

The Lund Time Machine [33, 21] mobile application makes use of ambient sounds related to the history of a location to contextualize the user to the setting. The application uses by default vibration bursts for feedback when scanning the environment with the device, but also offers the possibility to use sound or speech for guidance.

As an example of a technique for serendipitous discovery, McGookin et al. [22] developed Audio Bubbles, an application that uses virtual geolocated spheres as auditory "homing beacons". When a person enters an audio bubble, they start hearing a sound that relates to the POI in the center of the bubble. The approach empowers the traveler to choose which audio bubbles they want to attend to. In a somewhat similar fashion, Vazquez-Alvarez et al. [35] studied the use of earcons and spatial audio in an augmented reality "sound garden." The system was tuned for presenting information on multiple targets at the same time, making use of source separation enabled by the spatial audio. Their results indicate that two simultaneous sound sources are distinguishable, but with three or more the task becomes difficult.

Ankolekar et al. [3] compared different cues for serendipitous discovery of POIs. The cues were musicons (music snippets related to a POI), auditory icons (sound samples related to the category of the POI [9]), speech (name and address of the POI), visual (name, address, category, and picture of the POI), and non-visual cues combined. The results indicate that ambiguous cues such as musicons and auditory icons result in a weaker confidence in identifying the POI, but give a greater sense of autonomy to the user. Speech cues were the fastest for identifying the POIs, while auditory icons were deemed more challenging to identify.

In summary, previous solutions for tactile or auditory guidance in cities typically do not support free exploration and serendipitous discovery of POIs. While a few counter-examples exist, they tend to either lack more fine-grained guidance, do not provide more detailed information on the POI, or present the user with potentially too many alternatives at a time. In addition, many systems require carrying a mobile device in hand and rely on visual feedback. Our system not only supports serendipity in discovering the POIs but also emphasizes users' autonomy to choose which recommended POIs they are interested in.

3. DESIGN

Our system supports exploring POIs in cities through two functional steps in the interaction technique:

1. Serendipitous discovery of POIs is supported by location-aware, contextual audio-tactile cues, which deliver the information of the category of a nearby POI. The user has the option to skip or pursue the recommended POI.
2. Locating the POI is supported by audio-tactile guidance that guides user's pointing hand to point at the direction of the POI in question.

The interaction technique has been designed to be paired with a backend, which takes into account the preferences and POI history of the user to filter and personalize the content. In this paper we focus on the interaction technique.

3.1 Tactile Glove

The system is based on a tactile glove (see Fig. 2), which is equipped with vibrotactile actuators and a set of sensors, and an Android mobile device. The glove has been constructed of thin elastic fabric — to make it adaptable to different hand sizes — and several electronic components. Two Arduino microcontrollers (Arduino Pro Mini) process the sensor signals and commands, and control the vibrotactile feedback. For sensing hand orientation, the glove is equipped with a 9-axis Inertial Measurement Unit (IMU, InvenSense MPU-9150), which consists of a gyroscope, an accelerometer, and a compass. Flexible bend sensors (Spectra Symbol flex sensor) are deployed on three fingers (thumb, index, and middle finger). A set of three vibrotactile actuators (Precision Microdrives 10mm shaftless vibration motor) is mounted for providing notification cues and directional guidance on the thumb, index, and middle fingers. The glove communicates wirelessly over Bluetooth with an Android mobile phone running the application software. The glove has been built for right-handed interactions.

A glove has been chosen as the form factor of our system for several reasons. Firstly, a glove allows natural hand gestures, which enables an embodied experience in interacting with the environment. Point-by-finger interaction naturally fits our tourism context, and information associated with a specific POI could be accessed via hand gestures projected on the POI itself. Moreover, fingers are more sensitive for tactile stimuli than, for example, the forearm [17].

3.2 Proximity-Based Cues and Contextual Information

The core idea of the interaction technique is to allow the user to freely walk around in the city and discover POIs. This is achieved by proximity-based audio-tactile notifications. The user's location is tracked by the GPS sensor on the mobile device. Each POI is associated with a proximity radius which is determined by its physical size and visibility. For example, a prominent palace has a larger radius than an ordinary shop. Considering using the real environment as the genuine visual cue of our non-visual system, the visibility of the POI also affects its proximity radius. If the POI is only visible after passing a corner, the radius is reduced to the distance between the corner and the POI. When the user crosses a proximity radius of a specific POI, the actuators on the glove vibrate to notify that a POI is nearby. Simultaneously, a contextual auditory icon is played through headphones to indicate the category of this POI. In the current setup, we have defined five categories of POIs: architecture, shop, cafe, restaurant, and religious. An archetypal auditory icon was designed for each category. The sound material for the icons is summarized in Table 1, and was carefully chosen to yield designs that are easily distinguishable from each other and from typical environmental sounds. The duration of each auditory icon is approximately 2.5 seconds.

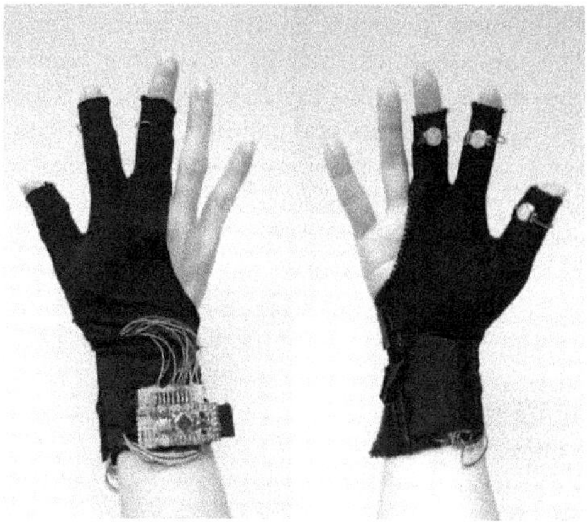

Figure 2: The tactile glove showing both sides.

Table 1: Description of the auditory icons designed for the system. The icons were formed as overlaid collages of multiple archetypal sound recordings related to the category.

POI Category	Sound Material
Architecture	Hammering, sawing
Shop	Old cashier machine, coins dropped on metal tray
Cafe	Espresso machine steam, grinding beans, pouring liquid, spoon hitting a coffee cup, sipping coffee
Restaurant	Knives and forks hitting each other and a plate
Religious	Church bells, Gregorian chanting

The audio-tactile notification lasts for 15 seconds, with the auditory icons playing back repeatedly, accompanied by vibration bursts (100 ms activation with 400 ms silence) on the glove. During this period, the user can make a selection gesture by bending the index finger. Alternatively if they are not interested, they can reject the recommendation by bending the thumb or ignore the cue until it fades out. Selection gesture results in hearing the spoken name of the POI, followed by a brief (max 10 seconds) spoken description of the POI. This spoken introduction is meant for giving the user more autonomy over choosing interesting POIs, and they can skip the POI if they find it uninteresting.

3.3 Guidance for Pointing at the Target

When the user has listened to the initial description, they start getting directional guidance to spot the POI. The assumption is that the POI is in view of the user. The rationale behind this step is that there may be several POIs of one category in close proximity to each other. For example, it is common to have multiple restaurants or cafes side by side, and finding the correct one may require effort.

The directional guidance on the glove assumes that the user starts pointing with their glove-wearing hand with the palm facing down, browsing the environment to find the POI. The pointing interaction was chosen, because pointing at landmarks is a common phenomenon among tourists. Based on the sensor readings of the IMU on the glove and the GPS locations of both the user and the POI, the system computes the angular difference between the pointing direction and the actual direction of the POI. This information is then applied to the directional audio-tactile cues. When the user is very close to the POI, poor GPS accuracy might result in inaccurate guidance. To compensate for potential locally sub-optimal accuracy of the GPS, if the user is estimated to be within 10 m of the POI, the system stops giving guidance and simply plays back a spoken audio piece: "You are now in front of" followed by the name of the POI.

The vibrotactile guidance follows the metaphor of pulling the hand towards the vibrations. If the user is pointing too much to the right, they will feel continuous vibrotactile bursts (100 ms activation with 400 ms silence) on their thumb, indicating they need to point more to the left. Conversely, the guidance cue is presented on the middle finger to guide pointing to the right. When the user is pointing at the target, all three actuators vibrate with a faster rate (100 ms activation and 200 ms silence). The spatial left/right mapping for the tactile cue was chosen because it gives an immediate indication of the direction, which would be lacking in an intensity-based hot/cold metaphor approach.

The angular width of the target ranges from 23 to 45 degrees depending on the physical size of the POI, the current distance, and the run-time GPS accuracy. The minimal angular width was derived from a pilot study, in which users repeatedly pointed with the glove at four marked dots in different directions. The sensor readings were sampled, and the mean deviation was set as the minimal target size.

The audio guidance works together with the vibrations to enhance the perception of the directional cue. An amplitude-and-phase-modulated wideband tone, with the fundamental frequency of approximately 200 Hz, is played through the headphones with stereo panning, guiding pointing to left and right with the same metaphor as with the vibrations. The pulsation frequency of the modulated sound is much faster than that of the vibration bursts, in order to minimize possible negative cross-modal rhythm perception effects that could result if the two cues have a similar pulsation tempo but are slightly out of sync. When the user is pointing at the correct target, they hear the spoken name of that target and feel the vibrotactile on-target cue.

Once the user is pointing at the correct target and makes a selection gesture, they hear a longer spoken description of the POI. This description may include, e.g., facts related to the history of a building, or the cuisine of a restaurant. The user can continue the exploration when the spoken description is finished, or make a rejection gesture to terminate.

4. EVALUATION

We evaluated the interaction technique in a guided, task-based experiment. In this section, we present the venue, method, procedure, and materials used in the evaluation.

4.1 Study Setting

The experiment was conducted in the center of a mid-sized city, in a touristic area with a lot of applicable POIs. We chose 13 POIs from an area of roughly 0.12 km sq, and two extra POIs for training purposes outside the main area (See Fig.3). The POIs included, e.g., a church, two cafes, two shops, a statue, and facades and towers of old buildings.

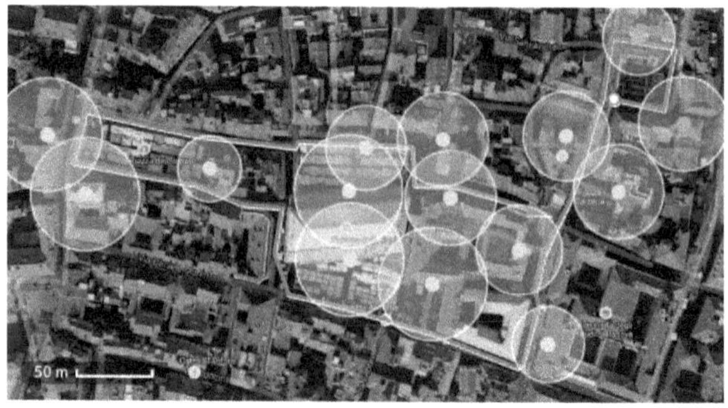

Figure 3: A map showing the locations of POIs and their associated proximity radius. The red line indicates the route users took in the study. The two targets in the top right corner were used for training.

For each POI, we prepared tour guide-like content related to the POI in both written and spoken format. The content included the name of the POI, a short introduction (roughly 10 seconds) to the POI, and a longer (approximately 30 seconds) description. Each content was also associated with the corresponding auditory icon representing the category of the POI. To ensure that all the contents were equally accessible to all participants and to avoid them going outside the GPS coverage, we defined a route to be followed within the area.

4.2 Experiment Design

The evaluation followed between-subjects design with two conditions. The primary condition involved using the proposed glove-based interaction technique for exploring the POIs. As a baseline condition, we implemented a mobile application manifesting relevant features competitive with commercial products available on the latest market. Figure 4 depicts users in both conditions.

4.2.1 Baseline Application

The baseline (Fig. 5) mimics the behavior of popular mobile apps for city exploration. Two main features presented here are push notification of recommended POI, as in Foursquare[2], and showing direction with compass, as in Tripadvisor City Guides[3].

When a new POI is nearby, the app triggers a vibration and shows a notification suggesting to check out the POI (Fig. 5a). Users can decide to either discard the notification or to see more info about the POI (Fig. 5b), including picture, textual, and audio description. Similarly to our main system, the baseline also provides directional guidance to spot the POI, but using visual feedback as opposed to tactile feedback with an arrow pointing towards the POI (Fig. 5c).

4.3 Participants

Overall twelve people (five women) volunteered for the experimental trials, half of whom were assigned to the baseline group (three women), whilst the other half (two women)

[2]https://foursquare.com
[3]http://www.tripadvisor.com/apps

Figure 4: Participants operating the baseline application (left) and the tactile glove (right).

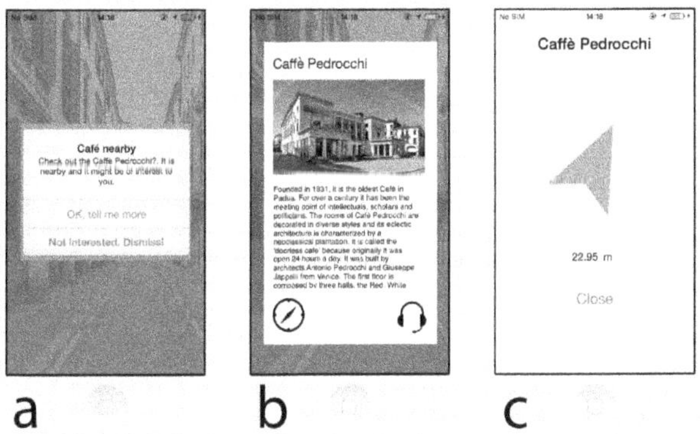

Figure 5: Baseline. a) A new POI nearby triggers visual and tactile (vibration) notification. b) Main view with image and description of the poi; directions and audio description are accessible from here. c) Directions View

used the tactile glove. They were all right-handed and had normal or corrected-to-normal vision. All participants were tourists recruited in the field and all of them reported to have none or very limited knowledge of the city. The mean age of the total sample was 34 years ($SD = 17.9$); the baseline group had an average age of 34.66 years ($SD = 17.97$) and the experimental group 30.66 years ($SD = 19.49$).

4.4 Apparatus

The participants of the proposed interaction technique wore the tactile glove in their right hand. Participants carried a neck pouch with an Android device (Samsung Galaxy S3) inside. The phone was used to run an application with the experiment logic, communicating wirelessly with the glove. Audio feedback was presented through an over-ear headset connected to the phone. Although an in-ear headset would have ensured better acoustic insulation, an over-ear headset was preferred due to hygienic reasons and to not disconnect the subject from the environment.

The participants of the baseline condition used an iPhone 5, with the baseline application pre-installed, and the same headphones as the other participants.

4.5 Procedure

Participants first gave informed consent to participate in the study and then filled in a short background questionnaire. Next, the experimenter explained how the device, either the tactile glove or the baseline application, depending on the experimental assignment, worked. When the user confirmed that the system functioning was clear, she received the device and the training phase began. This stage had the aim of familiarizing the user with the device and the interaction modalities involved. The training consisted of a guided exploration of a small square, on which there were two POIs that the participant had to explore. Participants were free to repeat the training phase if needed. When the user reported as ready, the experimental trial started. During the trial, the participant was instructed to follow the experimenter along the pre-defined route (approximately 800 meters in length). During the experimental session, the participant was asked to avoid any interaction with the experimenter, with the exception of reporting which building or monument they perceived to be attending. Participants using the iPhone were free to hold it in their hand or keep it in their pocket. When the participant reached the end of the route, she was asked to fill in a short questionnaire and to answer a brief semi-structured interview.

4.6 Data Collection

The measures recorded during the test include observations, questionnaires, and logged data. The entire trial was video-recorded to allow off-line analysis of the users' behavior. Furthermore, during the testing session, the correct identification of each POI was recorded online by the experimenter, who explicitly asked the participant to indicate the location to which the guidance referred.

In addition to a post-test interview, two questionnaires were administered. One was filled before the experimental session and aimed at collecting background information regarding participants' age, origin, level of knowledge of the city, and how participants were used to sightseeing a city as tourists. The questionnaire completed after the trial explored users' impressions of the user experience. The survey explored participants' general feeling of naturalness and pleasantness in using the devices (3 items) and their impressions regarding the feedback (5 items). Finally 3 items explored the fear of appearing strange in the eyes of other people while using the device. Participants using the tactile glove were asked to complete a longer version of the questionnaire, in which they were also asked to evaluate the audio signals they received (5 items) and the physical sensations they had while wearing the tactile glove (5 items). Participants were asked to mark their level of agreement with each statement on a 5-point Likert scale. The final phase consisted of a brief semi-structured interview, in which participants were asked about their general impression of their use of the devices, what they found easy or difficult, what they liked, what they thought of the audio and vibrotactile signals and if they felt confident of the indications they received.

Both systems logged timestamped data that contained users' behavior including time spent in each stage, decisions of accepting/rejecting the notification, and distance to the POI, as well as environmental data like GPS accuracy.

5. RESULTS

In the evaluation we focused on the validation of the interaction technique and user experience. In terms of efficiency, the result shows that our non-visual interface performs as well as its visual counterpart. Positive user experience was

Table 2: Time spent on different stages in the interaction. Response time: the duration between getting and accepting the recommendation. Finding time: the time spent on finding the POI with guidance. Mean time in bold and standard deviation in parentheses.

Stage	Glove	Baseline
Response Time (s)	**5.9** (4.23)	**3.58** (2.04)
Finding Time (s)	**11.1** (14.25)	**13.48** (20.66)

achieved with both conditions. However, glove users were able to focus their attention on the environment, while baseline users paid much less attention on their surroundings. In this section, we present the results in detail.

5.1 Reacting to the Cues

Users' interactions with the devices were logged by the system. The time required to respond to the notification and to find the POIs are reported in Table 2. In general, the response time of the glove condition is longer than the baseline, yet the difference is not significant according to a Mann-Whitney test (U= 8.00 p=.109). This can be explained, at last in part, by the fact that all participants in the baseline condition chose to hold the iPhone in their hand. Apart from the vibrotactile cue, which was the same in both conditions, the baseline application showed immediately explicit information regarding the POI on the screen, while the glove interface required the user to listen to the playback of auditory icons before making a selection and accessing introductory information of the POI. On-site observation also contributed to explain the difference. While glove users tended to slow down smoothly after the notification, baseline users tended to abruptly stop to interact with the phone. Regarding the time needed to find a POI, users in the glove condition were faster compared to those in the baseline group. Again, the difference was not significant according to a Mann-Whitney test (U= 12 p= .96).

Since participants were free to accept or reject the notification, four glove users and two baseline users actively rejected or passively ignored some of the notifications. We also observed that not all POIs were successfully recommended to users due to poor GPS coverage in some conditions. The recorded accuracy of GPS was typically good, ranging from 5 m to 30 m with an average of 12.37 m. With a single user at two POIs the accuracy dropped to 50 m and 100 m.

5.2 Identifying the POIs

An index of POI identification accuracy was computed for each participant, consisting of the percentage of the number of correct POI identifications with respect to the total number of POIs delivered by the system. Given the limited sample size, a Mann-Whitney test was run to compare the POI identification accuracy in the two conditions. The analysis revealed no significant difference between the conditions (U=18.00 p=1), with an average success rate of 89.24% (SD= 10.6) for the group exploring the city center with the baseline application and an average success rate of 88.35% (SD= 11.62) for the group wearing the tactile glove. This finding suggests that the tactile glove is able to guide the user to locate a POI with the same accuracy as a more familiar application that provides an extra visual clue, a picture, for identifying the target.

5.3 General User Experience

Referring to the opinions that emerged from the Likert-scale questionnaires, no significant difference in user experience was found. In particular, both groups showed a positive attitude toward the applications: both the glove and the baseline were considered unobtrusive (baseline M = 2; glove M = 1.6), natural (baseline M = 3.83; glove M = 3.83) , pleasant to use (baseline M = 4; glove M = 4.16), and not interfering with the main task (baseline M = 2.16; glove M = 1.6). Vibration signals were well received in both conditions, being evaluated as attention getting (baseline M = 4; glove M = 4.16), accurate (baseline M = 3.83; glove M = 4), and easy to interpret (baseline M = 4.16; glove M = 4). Furthermore, participants considered them pleasant (baseline M = 4; glove M = 3.6) and not disturbing (baseline M = 1.16; glove M = 1.3). Interestingly, participants in both conditions showed only low concern of looking strange to other people (baseline M = 2.16; glove M = 2.6), even if the proposed technique is all but common. It is worth noticing that participants of both groups did not feel hampered by the device they were employing to explore the city (baseline M = 2.16; glove M = 2.3).

All the participants appreciated the intuitiveness and ease of use of both the tactile glove and the baseline application. Some participants in the tactile glove condition commented spontaneously after the trial "I enjoyed it!" One user commented "I liked it! It really works, it was very precise." Regarding the feeling of wearing the glove, users found the glove light-weight (M = 4.66, SD = 0.51), comfortable (M = 4, SD = 0.63), and well-suited to their hand (M = 4.33, SD = 0.51). Finally, the tactile glove was not found bulky (M = 2, SD = 0.63) or rigid (M = 1.83, SD = 0.4), nor to limit the movements of the hand (M = 2.16, SD = 0.75).

5.4 Attention on the Surroundings

In general, participants praised the alerts coming only in the proximity of a certain POI, instead of having to pay attention to a paper map or a guide during the entire walk. Two participants in the baseline group explicitly said they felt detached from the environment, as they were focusing their attention on the application: "I was certainly thinking of the smartphone and not looking so much at the city." On the other hand, in the group of the tactile glove users, the feeling of being disengaged from the surroundings occurred only for one respondent, with one user reporting an opposite feeling "I felt like I was in a museum."

When the exploration was led by the baseline application, participants seemed to divide their attention between the surroundings and the screen of the smartphone. Based on the video analysis, from the notification until finding the POI, they spent on average 70.27% (SD=13.25) of the time looking at the screen (including, of course, the time to read the textual content). Participants tended to periodically check the screen of the phone while walking from a certain POI to the following one. When they received the notification of a POI in the proximity, they tended to stop abruptly and to focus their gaze on the screen. Even if they explicitly followed the directional cues provided by the baseline application to identify the POI, they usually then checked by comparing what they were seeing in front of them and the picture displayed on the screen. The screen seemed to grab participants' gaze even when they were listening to the audio description.

Video analysis shows that glove users seemed to be having a walk around the city. When they got a notification of approaching a POI, they slowed down smoothly and simply concentrated on the vibrations. When the audio description was playing, they looked at the POI or took quick glances around. Interestingly, even when they showed some uncertainties in interpreting the tactile guidance, none of the participants ever looked down at the glove. Overall, the glove did not appear as an external device put onto the user's body, but rather seemed well integrated with the flow of actions. Users operated it with the same naturalness as if they were making a movement with their hand.

6. DISCUSSION

In previous studies, non-visual interfaces have not been considered as efficient as their visual counterparts (e.g., [3]). Our evaluation surprisingly indicates that the performance of the presented non-visual solution is not significantly different from the visual baseline application for locating the POIs. This might be explained by two considerations.

First, the users of the baseline application need to divide their attention between the visual guidance and the real surroundings, repeatedly switching their gaze between the screen and the environment, while the glove-based solution gives people the chance to keep their visual attention on the surroundings. Potentially, extending the arm to a "pointing posture" while holding the phone would better align the gaze, the screen, and the target, but this does not seem like an intuitive way of interacting with the smartphone. None of the participants applied this strategy.

Second, while there is no visual feedback from the glove-based system, the surroundings themselves can provide strong visual cues to accompany the audio-tactile guidance. The combined information of the auditory icon, the spoken name of the target, and the short spoken description provide the user with relevant information to be able to distinguish the POI visually from others. When facilitated by the audio-tactile feedback and the possibility of not having to look at the device, the proposed solution is actually slightly faster in the guidance step than the visual baseline.

However, efficiency is not always the highest priority [3]. In our case, achieving a more immersed experience where users' attention is on the real surroundings is a key consideration. In addition to the non-visual directional guidance, this immersion is in part also supported by the auditory icons, which augment the surroundings with contextual information. It should be noted that interpreting the auditory icons might not require much cognitive load but a certain time duration is necessary to be spent on listening to decode the information.

Regarding user experience, there were no significant differences in questionnaire responses. The lack of differences is actually encouraging, for example, in terms of social acceptability of operating the glove in the wild, since it was not considered significantly more obtrusive than operating the smartphone.

The glove proved to be a good form factor for "browsing" the city on the go. While other wearables such as shoes [8] or belts [7] could be used for guidance as well, the glove provides a nice integrated package for versatile interactions both as an input device using onboard sensors and as an output device via the tactile feedback. Furthermore, these interactions make use of a standard practice in tourism, i.e., pointing at things in the surroundings.

6.1 Limitations

In this study, we used GPS for positioning. While it performs generally well in open areas outdoors, the positioning may be inaccurate in certain places such as in very narrow streets. For these situations, the positioning accuracy should be taken into account when notifying the user about new content in proximity. Clearly, if the interaction technique would be adapted for indoor use, for example in museums, a different positioning technique would be required, involving perhaps the reading of fiducial markers ([10]) or other specific approach tuned for those situations.

Since the non-visual interface provides no visual reference, in some situations the user might be unsure whether she is pointing at the correct POI. On a related note, in this study the system relied on manually determining the visibility of the POIs along the given path. We are currently working on determining POI visibility on the system side.

We did not encode any directional information in the auditory content, unlike some previous systems (e.g., [35]). We did not want to impose multiple directional guidance schemes on the user at this stage, but are considering pursuing this in the future. Another essential future development will be to integrate the interaction technique with a recommendation engine backend to personalize the content. Now that we have confirmed that the interaction technique itself works, in future studies we will work towards an integrated, multimodal system for exploring new places.

7. CONCLUSION

We proposed a novel interaction technique for exploring POIs in cities. The technique, based on audio-tactile feedback and a tactile glove, was evaluated in a field study and was shown to be as successful as a visual baseline application for locating and identifying the POIs. Interestingly, there were no major differences in questionnaire-based user experience between the two techniques, but observations and interviews revealed that the proposed technique let the user focus more attention on the surroundings than on the device compared to the baseline. Also, while the glove represents an unfamiliar technique and relies on pointing with the hand to operate, the results indicate that it was not considered to be more obtrusive to use than the baseline application, suggesting that its social acceptability does not pose significant problems compared to more standard mobile applications. In the future, we will integrate the interaction technique with a backend, which will personalize the POI content according to user preferences.

8. ACKNOWLEDGMENTS

The research leading to these results has received funding from the European Union Seventh Framework Programme (FP7/2007-2013) under grant agreement n°601139.

9. REFERENCES

[1] T. T. Ahmaniemi and V. T. Lantz. Augmented reality target finding based on tactile cues. In *Proc. ICMI-MLMI*, pages 335–342, 2009.

[2] S. Andolina, D. Pirrone, G. Russo, S. Sorce, and A. Gentile. Exploitation of mobile access to

context-based information in cultural heritage fruition. In *Proc. BWCCA '12*, pages 322–328, 2012.

[3] A. Ankolekar, T. Sandholm, and L. Yu. Play it by ear: a case for serendipitous discovery of places with musicons. In *Proc. CHI*, pages 2959–2968, 2013.

[4] A. Asif, W. Heuten, and S. Boll. Exploring distance encodings with a tactile display to convey turn by turn information in automobiles. In *Proc. NordiCHI*, pages 32–41, 2010.

[5] B. Brown and M. Chalmers. Tourism and mobile technology. In *ECSCW 2003*, pages 335–354, 2003.

[6] L. Chittaro. Distinctive aspects of mobile interaction and their implications for the design of multimodal interfaces. *J. Multimodal User Interfaces*, 3(3):157–165, 2010.

[7] J. B. F. V. Erp, H. A. H. C. V. Veen, C. Jansen, and T. Dobbins. Waypoint navigation with a vibrotactile waist belt. *ACM Trans. Appl. Percept.*, 2(2):106–117, Apr. 2005.

[8] M. Frey. CabBoots: Shoes with Integrated Guidance System. In *Proc. TEI '07*, pages 245–246, 2007.

[9] W. W. Gaver. Auditory icons: Using sound in computer interfaces. *Human-Computer Interaction*, 2(2):167–177, 1986.

[10] A. Gentile, S. Andolina, A. Massara, D. Pirrone, G. Russo, A. Santangelo, E. Trumello, and S. Sorce. A multichannel information system to build and deliver rich user-experiences in exhibits and museums. In *Proc. BWCCA '11*, pages 57–64, 2011.

[11] S. Holland, D. R. Morse, and H. Gedenryd. AudioGPS: Spatial audio navigation with a minimal attention interface. *Personal and Ubiquit. Comput.*, 6(4):253–259, 2002.

[12] E. Hornecker, S. Swindells, and M. Dunlop. A mobile guide for serendipitous exploration of cities. In *Proc. MobileHCI*, pages 557–562, 2011.

[13] Y.-T. Hsieh, A. Jylhä, and G. Jacucci. Pointing and selecting with tactile glove in 3d environment. In *Proc. Symbiotic 2014*, pages 133–137, 2014.

[14] H. Jo, S. Hwang, H. Park, and J. Hee Ryu. Aroundplot: Focus+Context Interface for Off-Screen Objects in 3D Environments. *Computers & Graphics*, 35(4):841–853, 2011.

[15] J. Kostiainen, C. Erkut, and F. B. Piella. Design of an audio-based mobile journey planner application. In *Proc. Academic MindTrek Conf.*, pages 107–113, 2011.

[16] E. Kruijff, J. E. Swan II, and S. Feiner. Perceptual issues in augmented reality revisited. In *Proc. ISMAR*, pages 3–12, 2010.

[17] S. J. Lederman. Skin and touch. *Encyclopedia of Human Biology*, 7:51–63, 1991.

[18] V. Lehtinen, A. Nurminen, and A. Oulasvirta. Integrating spatial sensing to an interactive mobile 3D map. In *Proc. 3DUI*, pages 11–14, March 2012.

[19] V. Lehtinen, A. Oulasvirta, A. Salovaara, and P. Nurmi. Dynamic tactile guidance for visual search tasks. In *Proc. UIST*, pages 445–452, 2012.

[20] M. Liljedahl and S. Lindberg. Sound parameters for expressing geographic distance in a mobile navigation application. In *Proc. Audio Mostly*, pages 1–7, 2011.

[21] C. Magnusson, K. Rassmus-Gröhn, and D. Szymczak. Exploring history: a mobile inclusive virtual tourist guide. In *Proc. NordiCHI*, pages 69–78, 2014.

[22] D. Mcgookin, S. Brewster, and P. Priego. Audio bubbles: Employing non-speech audio to support tourist wayfinding. In *Proc. HAID*, pages 41–50. 2009.

[23] A. Mulloni, A. Dünser, and D. Schmalstieg. Zooming interfaces for augmented reality browsers. In *Proc. MobileHCI*, pages 161–170, 2010.

[24] A. Nurminen. m-LOMA - a mobile 3D city map. In *Proc. Web3D '06*, pages 7–18, 2006.

[25] A. Oulasvirta, S. Estlander, and A. Nurminen. Embodied interaction with a 3D versus 2D mobile map. *Personal and Ubiquit. Comput.*, 13(4):303–320, 2008.

[26] A. Oulasvirta, S. Tamminen, V. Roto, and J. Kuorelahti. Interaction in 4-second bursts: the fragmented nature of attentional resources in mobile HCI. In *Proc. CHI*, pages 919–928, 2005.

[27] M. Pielot, B. Poppinga, and S. Boll. PocketNavigator: vibro-tactile waypoint navigation for everyday mobile devices. In *Proc. MobileHCI*, pages 423–426, 2010.

[28] M. Pielot, B. Poppinga, W. Heuten, and S. Boll. A tactile compass for eyes-free pedestrian navigation. In P. Campos, N. Graham, J. Jorge, N. Nunes, P. Palanque, and M. Winckler, editors, *Proc. INTERACT*, volume 6947 of *Lecture Notes in Computer Science*, pages 640–656. 2011.

[29] M. Rantanen, A. Oulasvirta, J. Blom, S. Tiitta, and M. Mäntylä. InfoRadar: Group and Public Messaging in the Mobile Context. In *Proc. NordiCHI*, pages 131–140, 2004.

[30] S. Robinson, P. Eslambolchilar, and M. Jones. Evaluating haptics for information discovery while walking. In *Proc. British HCI*, pages 93–102, 2009.

[31] S. Rümelin, E. Rukzio, and R. Hardy. NaviRadar: a novel tactile information display for pedestrian navigation. In *Proc. UIST*, pages 293–302, 2011.

[32] R. Scheibe, M. Moehring, and B. Froehlich. Tactile feedback at the finger tips for improved direct interaction in immersive environments. In *Proc. 3DUI*, pages 1–7, 2007.

[33] D. Szymczak, K. Rassmus-Gröhn, C. Magnusson, and P.-O. Hedvall. A real-world study of an audio-tactile tourist guide. In *Proc. MobileHCI*, pages 335–344, 2012.

[34] K. Tsukada and M. Yasumura. Activebelt: Belt-type wearable tactile display for directional navigation. In N. Davies, E. Mynatt, and I. Siio, editors, *Proc. UbiComp*, volume 3205 of *Lecture Notes in Computer Science*, pages 384–399. 2004.

[35] Y. Vazquez-Alvarez, I. Oakley, and S. A. Brewster. Auditory display design for exploration in mobile audio-augmented reality. *Personal and Ubiquit. Comput.*, 16(8):987–999, 2012.

[36] D. Wagner and D. Schmalstieg. First steps towards handheld augmented reality. In *Proc. ISWC*, pages 127–135, 2003.

[37] S. Wei, G. Ren, and E. O'Neill. Haptic and audio displays for augmented reality tourism applications. In *Proc. HAPTICS*, pages 485–488, 2014.

ECA Control using a Single Affective User Dimension

Fred Charles
Teesside University
School of Computing
Middlesbrough, UK
f.charles@tees.ac.uk

Florian Pecune
CNRS - LTCI
Telecom ParisTech
Paris, France
pecune@enst.fr

Gabor Aranyi
Teesside University
School of Computing
Middlesbrough, UK
g.aranyi@tees.ac.uk

Catherine Pelachaud*
CNRS - LTCI
Telecom ParisTech
Paris, France
pelachaud@enst.fr

Marc Cavazza*
Teesside University
School of Computing
Middlesbrough, UK
m.o.cavazza@tees.ac.uk

ABSTRACT

User interaction with Embodied Conversational Agents (ECA) should involve a significant affective component to achieve realism in communication. This aspect has been studied through different frameworks describing the relationship between user and ECA, for instance alignment, rapport and empathy. We conducted an experiment to explore how an ECA's non-verbal expression can be controlled to respond to a single affective dimension generated by users as input. Our system is based on the mapping of a high-level affective dimension, approach/avoidance, onto a new ECA control mechanism in which Action Units (AU) are activated through a neural network. Since 'approach' has been associated to prefrontal cortex activation, we use a measure of prefrontal cortex left-asymmetry through fNIRS as a single input signal representing the user's attitude towards the ECA. We carried out the experiment with 10 subjects, who have been instructed to express a positive mental attitude towards the ECA. In return, the ECA facial expression would reflect the perceived attitude under a neurofeedback paradigm. Our results suggest that users are able to successfully interact with the ECA and perceive its response as consistent and realistic, both in terms of ECA responsiveness and in terms of relevance of facial expressions. From a system perspective, the empirical calibration of the network supports a progressive recruitment of various AUs, which provides a principled description of the ECA response and its intensity. Our findings suggest that complex ECA facial expressions can be successfully aligned with one high-level affective dimension. Furthermore, this use of a single dimension as input could support experiments in the fine-tuning of AU activation or their personalization to user preferred modalities.

*corresponding authors

ICMI 2015, November 9–13, 2015, Seattle, WA, USA.

DOI: http://dx.doi.org/10.1145/2818346.2820730.

Categories and Subject Descriptors

H.5.1 [**Multimedia Information Systems**]: Artificial, Augmented, and Virtual Realities; H.5.2 [**Information Interfaces and Presentation**]: User Interfaces

Keywords

Embodied Conversational Agent; Brain-Computer Interface; Functional Near-Infrared Spectroscopy (fNIRS)

1. INTRODUCTION AND RATIONALE

One important research direction to improve ECA use in user interfaces is to study the fundamental properties of the ECA-user relationship. These have been described through various concepts such as *empathy* and *alignment*. For instance, ECA are able to induce *empathy* in a human user, which usually translates into exploring appropriate ways for the agent to reveal its internal state. Furthermore, *alignment* aims at mapping between the recognition of facial expressions, in terms of emotion recognition, of the user and the elicitation of the emotional response from the virtual agent through the generation of appropriate facial expressions.

Here, we investigate the potential of using a single high-level emotional dimension as an input to control a virtual agent's response. We aim at using a Brain-Computer Interface (BCI) in a Neurofeedback (NF) setting to provide the user with compelling multimodal visual feedback using complex generation of appropriate facial expressions in response to their (perceived) disposition towards the virtual agent.

In this paper, the ECA is designed to provide alignment between the users' positive thoughts, collected via fNIRS-based BCI input signals, and the generation of perceived internal emotions of a virtual agent through the display of appropriate facial expressions. In the next sections, we provide an overview of the related works in virtual agents, and their ability to generate emotions, as well as a detailed description of the virtual agent configuration and the experimental setup we have designed. Finally, we present the results of our experiments.

2. PREVIOUS AND RELATED WORK

To enhance human-agent interaction, several studies have reported the importance of an agent's ability to display emo-

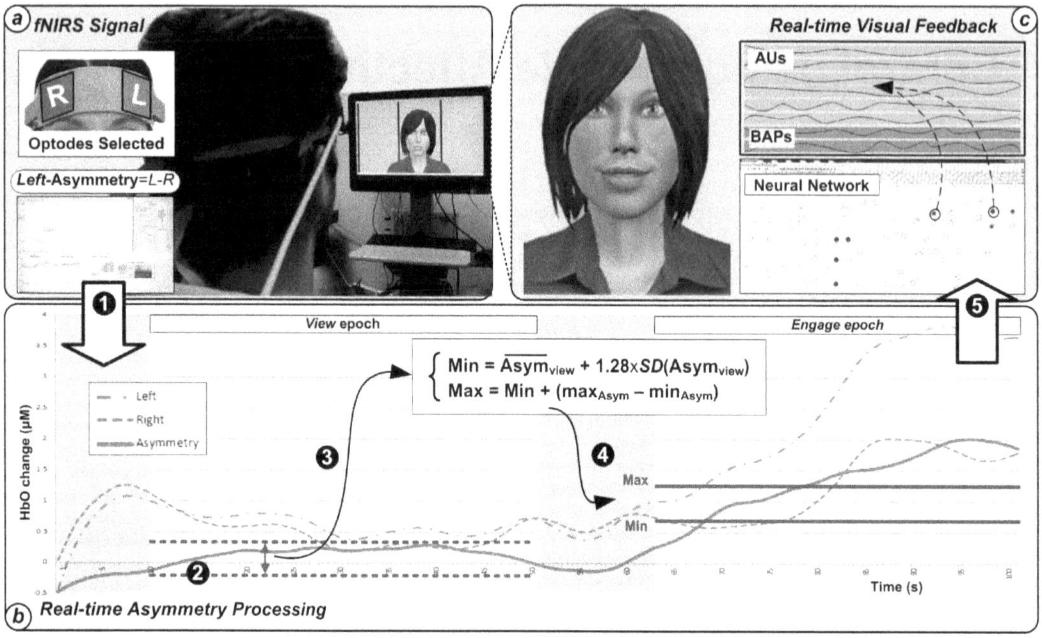

Figure 1: System Overview. Brain signals are collected through fNIRS system ⓐ, where left-most and right-most channels are processed to generate a left-asymmetry score ①. During the *View* epoch ②, the left-asymmetry values are used to define the *Min* and *Max* bounds ③ to be used during the *Engage* epoch where the real-time left-asymmetry scores ④ are normalized before being used as single input ⑤ to the virtual agent's facial expressions (AUs) and body parameters (BAPs) under the neural network's control ⓒ.

tions [5, 25, 26]. However, the appropriateness of the displayed emotions is paramount. Expressing an emotion that is inappropriate in the context of the interaction will damage the interaction more than not showing any emotion at all [25]. Moreover, *empathic* virtual agents have a greater impact on users' perception than agents that are fully impulsive and express their felt emotions without consideration of their interlocutors' emotions nor the social context of the interaction [5, 25]. Previous research has investigated both empathic agents supporting the user in learning situations [26] and agents that elicit empathy from users. The use of physiological signals has been experimented in both contexts [16, 26]. Gilroy et al. [16] have described the use of EEG prefrontal asymmetry to capture empathy towards a virtual agent during an interactive narrative, but have not explored the agent's expressions, instead using a simplified feedback mechanism based only on color saturation.

Agents display their emotional states through their verbal and non-verbal behaviors. While earlier models focused on the six prototypical expressions of emotion, latest models allow modeling a large variety of facial expressions as a combination of the expressions of emotions [1] as sequences of multimodal signals [22], or even as a blend of expressions [23]. Models may rely on pure combinatorial approaches where the expression of an emotion is the result of an algebraic combination of other expressions [1] of regions on the face [7, 23]; other models have relied on corpora annotation [22] where videos are carefully annotated to extract multimodal signals expressing emotions. Others have applied a perceptual approach [15, 17] where human users are asked to create expressions of the virtual agents for given emotions. Yet other approaches have implemented the dynamic evolution of facial expression of emotion following Scherer's appraisal model [2, 11].

Additionally, an important research topic in relation to the idea of 'alignment' between human users and virtual agents is 'rapport' defined in [18] as the feeling of being 'in-sync' with a conversational partner. They also report that virtual agents can create rapport during interactions with human users by generating proper verbal, and non-verbal behaviors. This provides a setting whereby we assume that generated non-verbal behaviors (i.e., facial expressions) are the reflection of the human user which thus creates a relationship between the user's input signals and the resulting visual feedback generated by the virtual agent. Lately, Cassell and colleagues [32] have taken into account the expressed and perceived mental state of each participant of a dyad to model 'rapport'. Their model reasons about the beliefs and intentions of one participant and how it perceives its interlocutor's state of mind.

In the next sections, we present the overall system design, introducing how user disposition towards the agent can be captured by a fNIRS-based BCI and mapped onto control parameters for the ECA.

3. SYSTEM OVERVIEW

We designed a software platform to experiment with ECA control from a single affective dimension, which is captured through an fNIRS BCI (see Figure 1). From the user's perspective, the ECA behaves as an autonomous agent, responding to what it perceives as the user's mental disposition towards itself. The ECA possesses a range of spontaneous and expressive behaviors, ranging from idle animations, with (neutral) spontaneous motion and postural changes, to affective expression of graded intensity. Users are instructed to express positive feelings towards the agent in order to capture its interest. This should in turn result in the ECA responding to the user with an expression matching the perceived interest in both valence and intensity. Users' attitudes are captured through their levels of Pre-Frontal Cortex (PFC) asymmetry, using fNIRS to measure differences in activity in *left* versus *right* PFC (Figure 1(a)). This is based on extensive work relating the approach/withdrawal affective dimension to PFC asymmetry, measured through EEG [12] as well as MRI [33]. We have adopted fNIRS because of its lesser sensitivity to artefacts compared to EEG and the fact that it is well-suited to capture activity in the PFC, in particular its dorsolateral region [13]. Furthermore, experience gained when studying PFC asymmetry through fMRI [9] could provide guidance to design fNIRS experiments. From the ECA perspective, the main challenge is to design an appropriate control process that would interpret and respond appropriately to the level of approach expressed mentally by the user. The system uses a network-like control representation to relate a single input to an array of Action Units (AU) and Body Action Parameters (BAP) that provide low-level control for the ECA's animation (Figure 1(c)).

An overview of the operation of the system is as follows. The system captures PFC asymmetry in real-time and produces a matching ECA response. The PFC asymmetry baseline, which is subject-dependent, is acquired through an epoch during which subjects watch the ECA (displaying a neutral attitude) while carrying out a simple mental counting task (Figure 1(b)). During active engagement by subjects, PFC asymmetry is measured and its increase over the baseline is interpreted as the intensity of the approach towards the ECA. Finally, the value is passed to the control network, which will generate matching ECA behavior, interrupting idle behavior and producing appropriate facial expressions.

In the next sections, we describe in more detail the various components of the system, as well as the techniques for data acquisition and calibration, which have been used to map BCI data onto the ECA controller.

3.1 Affective BCI Input

Previous uses of fNIRS in affective research [21, 31] have investigated emotional responses (to music or video clips) rather than the active expression of emotions as an input modality. Here, we used fNIRS as an active, affective BCI based on fNIRS (see [8] for a general description of fNIRS).

For the purpose of providing real-time NF, we used measurements of changes in oxygenated hemoglobin (HbO) concentration[1], because it is commonly associated with neural activity [28]. We used an fNIR400 Optical Brain Imaging Station by Biopac Systems, with a 16-channel sensor with fixed 2.5cm source-detector separation (Figure 1(a). Raw data and oxygenation values were collected with a 2Hz sampling rate using software provided by the device manufacturer (COBI Studio and FnirSoft v3.5), and was sent to a bespoke remote client experimental software over TCP/IP (using FnirSoft DAQ Tools). To characterize left PFC asymmetry for real-time feedback, we derived a metric of inter-hemispheric difference in HbO change by averaging HbO values over the four leftmost and four rightmost channels (located over the left and right dorsolateral prefrontal cortex, respectively), then subtracting average *Right* from average *Left* [13].

The resulting asymmetry metric (henceforth called *left-asymmetry*) reflects the inter-hemispheric difference in HbO change in micromolar units (μM/L) which defines the single affective dimension as continuous input signal to control the ECA.

[1]As opposed to deoxygenated or total hemoglobin (HbR and HbT, respectively).

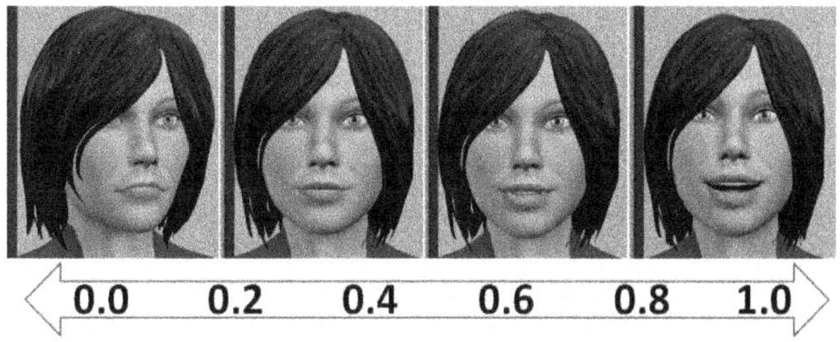

Figure 2: Evolution of the agent's behaviors according to the user's level of engagement.

3.2 Virtual Agent Control Mechanism

Our virtual agent [6] is a synthetic computer animated character designed to autonomously interact with humans in various activities. The agent relies on procedural models involving upper body modalities: facial expression (eyebrow, eyelid, cheek, lip and jaw), gaze, head and upper torso motions. The facial expressions of the virtual agent are defined using FACS, Facial Action Coding System [14], where face movements are decomposed into several Action Units (AUs). For instance, a raise of inner eyebrows corresponds to AU1, while a jaw dropping corresponds to AU26. Each AU is represented by a value varying from 0 (no activation) to 1 (maximum activation). For the body animation, our agent follows the MPEG-4 standard which defines several Body Animation Parameters (BAPs). Each BAP represents the rotation angle of one body joint on one axis.

The ECA responds by aligning its nonverbal behavior to the user's detected empathy level. The detected empathy level is computed over one single affective dimension, ranging from zero to one. As just explained, a very low value of the affective dimension corresponds to a user with very low level of empathy; while a very high value corresponds to a user with very high level of empathy. To achieve agent's behavior alignment with user's detected empathy level, we mapped user's low level of empathy with agent's disengagement and user's high level of empathy with agent's full engagement. Thus, as user's positive thoughts increases, the agent gives more positive feedbacks as sign of its engagement level. For intermediate levels of engagement, the agent displays different variation of positive expressions. The design of the agent's nonverbal behavior, mapped to AUs/BAPs, is drawn from literature [19] and is validated from consensus of a small number of participants.

We consider four different levels of empathy (see Figure 2). If the user's detected level of empathy is minimal (i.e. ≤ 0.2), the agent looks disengaged mirroring to the user his detected mental state. In this case, the agent does not direct its gaze towards the user; it tilts its head and its body, and it displays boredom through a lip pout. Then, whilst the user's detected level of empathy remains below average (i.e.

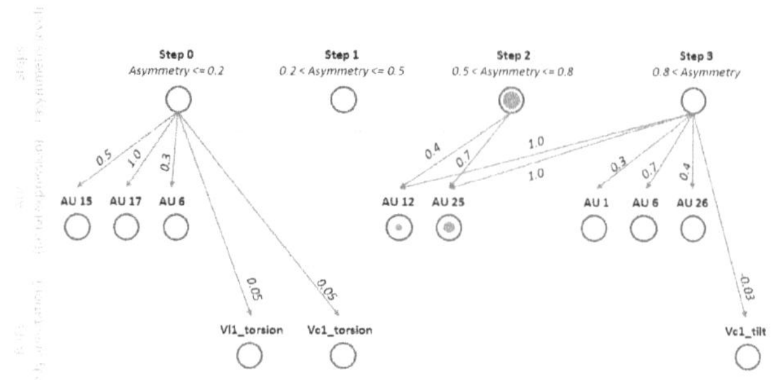

Figure 3: Example of network mapping asymmetry levels to AUs and BAPs. Here the transition step based on the user's perceived level of empathy leads to the activation of AU12 (Lip Corner Puller) and AU25 (Lips Part).

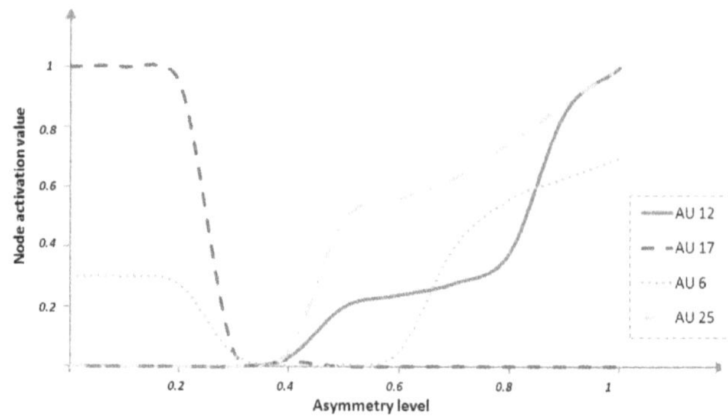

Figure 4: Activation patterns of AUs defined in the network according to the changes in the user's asymmetry levels.

≤0.5), the agent shows a neutral facial expression with its gaze and body oriented towards the user. When the user's detected level of empathy reaches above average (>0.5 but ≤0.8) the agent shows a more positive attitude, expressing happiness. It keeps its head and its gaze directed at the user, and it displays a smile. Finally, once the user's detected level of empathy reaches near maximum (i.e., >0.8), the agent displays a real delight to interact with the user. Its smile widens, crow's feet appear around the eyes as the cheeks are raised and its head slightly tilts backwards.

To provide continuous feedbacks to the user, the agent varies its behavior in real-time. Thus, in order to modify the generated animation in real-time, we developed a graphical tool allowing us to map any kind of input (here, the user's perceived level of empathy mapped from the left-asymmetry value) into animation parameters for our agent (AUs and BAPs). We created a graph where the nodes are the inputs and outputs and the arcs represent the links between the input nodes and the output ones. Like in neural networks, nodes have their own activation values, while arcs have their own weights.

In the graph shown in Figure 3, each of the transition step is represented by an input node whose value ranges from 0 (no activation) to 1 (maximum activation). Depending on the user's perceived level of empathy, a particular node is activated. On the output side, every AU and BAP is also represented by its own node. The values of a node for each AU vary from 0 (no activation) to 1 (maximum activation). So for example, if the node AU12 (Lip Corner Puller) is fully activated (its value is 1), the agent will smile with the greatest intensity. For the BAPs, nodes values range from -1 to 1. These values are then transformed into radian angles to be interpreted by our animation system, as specified by the MPEG-4 norm. For instance, if the value of the node vc1 tilt (cerebral vertebra along the neck) is set to -1, the agent's head will be tilted backwards with an angle of $-\pi$.

Finally, arcs are drawn to connect inputs (left-asymmetry level nodes) to the outputs (AUs and BAPs nodes). For each level of empathy, we define a combination of AUs and BAPs conveying the associated behavior. It corresponds to defining 4 different nonverbal behaviors to be displayed by the virtual agent in response to user's level of left-asymmetry. For instance, to express disengagement (reflecting a low level of left-asymmetry), AU6 (Cheek Raiser), AU15 (Lip Corner Depressor) and AU17 (Chin Raiser) are activated, as well as BAPs vc1 tilt (cerebral vertebra along the neck) and vl1 tilt (lumber vertebra of the trunk). This expression corresponds to a pout with the agent not gazing at the participant. Thus, five arcs are connecting the input node Step0 to the five corresponding output nodes. The weight of each arc connecting level p with p+1 is set by calibrating AUs and BAPs with their extreme values of step p, in order to obtain a smooth animation during the transition phase between step p and step p+1, allowing the agent to display believable behavior.

Each arc has its own weight, representing how much the input node will influence the output one. Weights vary from -1 (negative influence) to 1 (positive influence). The output nodes activation value is computed based on McCulloch and Pitts activation function [20]. The final output activation value is a weighted sum of the inputs where w_{ij} represents the weights of the links and a_i represents the activation values of the input nodes. θ_j represents the initial activation value of the output node.

$$a_j = \sum_{i}^{n} w_{ij} * a_i + \theta_j$$

For instance, if the input node Step0 is fully activated and connected to the output node AU62 (Eyes turn right) by an arc whose weight is 0.3, the agent will slightly look to its right. Therefore, whenever one input node is activated, the corresponding AUs and BAPs are activated. To ensure smooth transitions between the different behaviors associated to each step, we interpolate the animations. When the user's perceived level of empathy generates a change from

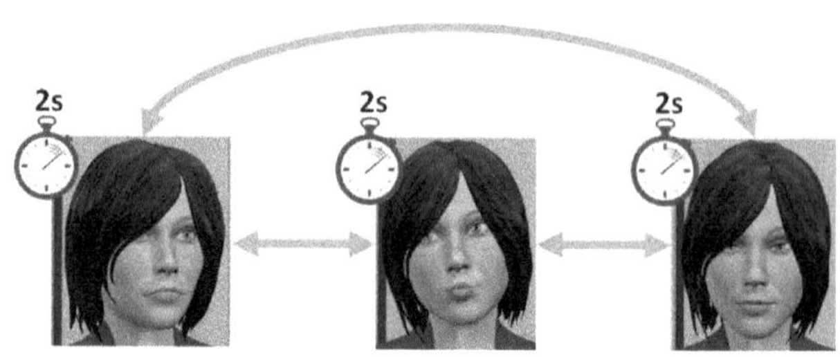

Figure 5: Example of variations of 'idle' behaviors (randomly generated every 2s).

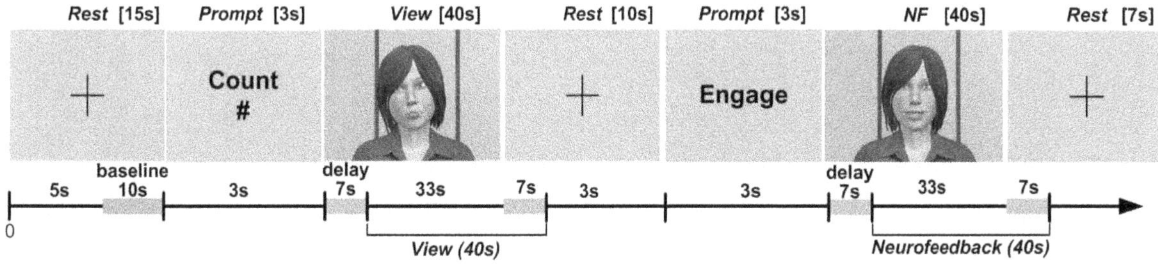

Figure 6: Protocol design, including setting the baseline of the fNIRS system, as well as windowing the data collection during the *View* and *Engage* epochs to account for the delay in hemodynamic response.

one step to another, the corresponding input nodes are not directly activated or inhibited, but instead, the activation and inhibition of these nodes follow an exponential function illustrated in Figure 4.

Furthermore, to avoid the agent displaying repetitively the same facial expression, we introduce alternative combinations of AUs and BAPs for each step. When communicating, different behaviors can be used while conveying similar meanings [24]. The new expressions defined for each step are built as variations of behaviors. Variations can be a change of AU or BAP intensity, a change of AUs (e.g. a change between AU25 (Lips Part) and AU26 (Jaw Drop)), etc. The variation of expressions ensures the agent not to display repetitive behaviors but also not to freeze if remaining in a same step for a long duration. Without such a variation, the agent would display a unique expression that would remain static and thus would appear uncanny. Moreover, it also allows giving continuous feedback to the user about his level of engagement, thus whilst the user is perceived to maintain a level of empathy, a particular, though constantly relevant, behavior should be generated. Hence, we introduce a timer that triggers the display of one of the variants of the behavior of the corresponding level. Empirically, we defined the timer to be 2s for which the user maintains a particular level of left-asymmetry (see Figure 5). This mechanism preserves the naturalness of facial expressions as the agent displays continuously expressive and dynamic behavior.

3.3 Experimental Task

For the design of our BCI experiment to investigate ECA control from a single affective dimension, we followed the recommendation of Solovey et al. [30] for the use of fNIRS in HCI settings. The experimental task consisted in completing 8 identical blocks (preceded by a practice block which was not analyzed). The structure of the blocks is presented in Figure 6. Each block included three epochs: *Rest*, *View*, and *Engage*.

During *Rest* epochs, subjects were instructed to look at a crosshair located in the center of a gray screen to try to clear their head of thoughts and relax. During *View* epochs, subjects were instructed to keep looking at the agent while carrying out a simple mental counting task (counting backwards from 500 by increments of a given integer). This task was included to control for unwanted mental processes (see [29]). During *Engage* epochs, subjects were instructed to engage with the ECA through positive thinking, and to 'cheer her up' with their thoughts. We were deliberately vague with support instructions in order to allow subjects to develop their own cognitive strategies. After completing each block, subjects were asked to describe their strategies in general terms.

During *Engage* epochs, subjects received real-time feedback of their left-asymmetry. To ensure consistent mapping of individual variations in left-asymmetry onto the feedback signal, we used the range of variation of HbO asymmetry during the *View* epoch in each block to determine the mapping of the level of engagement from the user to the visual feedback signal (i.e., ECA's variations in facial expressions - see Figure 1(3)). This was calculated by the experimental software during the last 3s of the *Rest* epoch between the *View* and *Engage* epochs.

We defined the minimum point for mapping *Min* as the mean of left-asymmetry values during the *View* epoch plus 1.28 times their standard deviation. In normally distributed asymmetry scores, this threshold would result in no feedback for 90% of the spontaneous asymmetry variations during the reference (*View*) epoch[2]. To determine the maximum *Max* point for mapping, we increased the threshold asymmetry value for feedback *Min* by the variation range of asymmetry values during the *View* epoch. Asymmetry values within the range [*Min*;*Max*] during the *Engage* epoch were mapped linearly onto the ECA's facial expression, with the same 2Hz frequency as the acquisition of asymmetry values.

Ten subjects participated in the experiment (5 female, Mean age=43.89 years, SD=8.15, Range=[31; 53]). Subjects were right-handed and had no history of psychiatric conditions. They provided written consent prior to participation and received an online retailer voucher equivalent to $30 as compensation. The study was approved by a research ethics committee at the authors' institution. Subjects were sat in a comfortable chair to minimize movement artifacts, approximately 47" (120cm) away from a 24" flat monitor that displayed the virtual agent. The room was quiet (but not soundproof) and dimly lit. The fNIRS probe positioned on their forehead was also covered with non-transparent fabric to prevent ambient light from reaching the sensors. Subjects were instructed to refrain from moving their limbs, frowning and talking while they carried out the experimental tasks.

To attenuate noise for post-hoc analyses (resulting from minor head movements, heartbeat and respiration), we applied sliding-window motion artifact rejection and raw data were low-pass filtered using a finite impulse response filter with order 20 and 0.1Hz cut-off frequency [4]. Additionally, we applied first order linear detrending on data from each channel [3]. HbO for each channel was calculated with re-

[2]Note that this approach to determining NF threshold for left-asymmetry is consistent with the original one of Rosenfeld et al. [27].

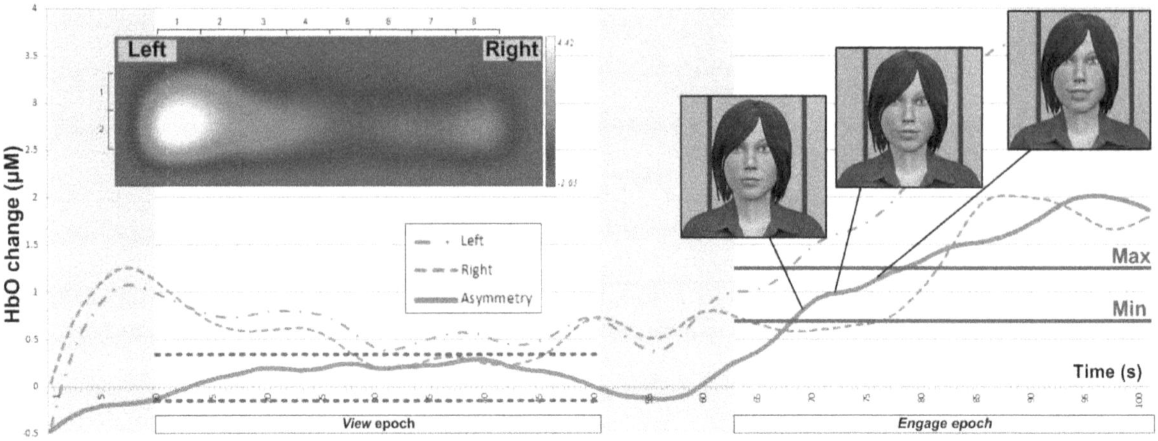

Figure 7: Example of a successful block where the asymmetry values in the *Engage* epoch are significantly greater than the ones in the *View* epoch, mapped onto the changes in the ECA's facial expressions. The topographic view (top-left) shows the 16 optodes' activation with a significant increase of left oxygenation during the *Engage* epoch.

spect to the baseline measured at the end of each rest period at the start of each data-collection block [4].

We extracted HbO values on each channel for *View* and *Engage* epochs within each block, using time synchronization markers. To accommodate for the approximately 7s delay in the hemodynamic response [8], we excluded the first 14 data points (corresponding to 7s sampled at 2Hz) of each epoch on each channel, and included 14 data points after the completion of the epoch (see Figure 10; also see [29] for a similar approach).

4. RESULTS

Out of the 80 blocks collected from the 10 subjects, 16 blocks were excluded due to minor malfunctions, excessive movement, and reported discontinuation of the tasks during the block. This left 64 valid blocks for analysis.

We defined block success as a statistically significant increase in average left-asymmetry during the *Engage* epoch compared to the *View* epoch within the same block[3]. To determine success, we used an independent t-test with a bootstrapping resampling method (1000 samples, 95% confidence intervals) on asymmetry scores in consecutive *View* and *Engage* epochs. Based on this criterion, 37 blocks were successful (58% of blocks).

On a subject basis, we judged a subject to have been successful in the NF task if at least 50% of their valid blocks were successful (consistent with previous literature [9]). According to this criterion, 70% of subjects achieved neurofeedback success. Median success ratio (i.e., the proportion of successful blocks per subject) was 50%. Each subject completed at least one block successfully, and one subject completed all of the blocks successfully.

[3]We elected to compare *View* and *Engage* epochs to determine block success, as opposed to simply comparing asymmetry during *Engage* against the baseline, because the visual stimulus during these epochs was very similar (and conceptually the same), and subjects' cognitive activity was controlled with explicit instructions (i.e., count during *View* and expressing positive thoughts during *Engage*).

The majority of excluded blocks were due to subjects abandoning the counting task due to its high subjective difficulty. Since *View* and *Engage* epochs were comparable in terms of the presented visual stimulus and adequately matched for task difficulty, the observed differences in the left-asymmetry signal within blocks can be attributed to switching from the neutral task to the control task during which the user's level of engagement with the ECA through positive thinking.

We calculated the effect-size measure r to characterize the substantive significance of increase in asymmetry scores between successive *View* and *Engage* epochs within successful blocks. The smallest r effect-size that could be detected was .34 (medium)[4], which can be interpreted as approximately 11.5% of variance explained in asymmetry values by the *Engage* task. This indicates that our experimental setup was sensitive in detecting increase in left-asymmetry during *Engage* epochs. The median r in successful blocks was .82

[4]We use Cohen's [10] conventions for interpreting the magnitude of the effect-size measure r.

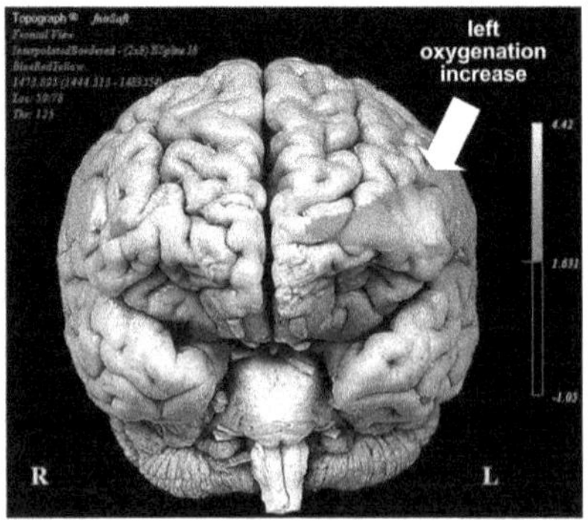

Figure 8: Topographic image of asymmetric dorsolateral prefrontal oxygenation increase during a successful NF epoch, overlaid on a brain surface image (generated using fNIRSoft by Biopac Systems).

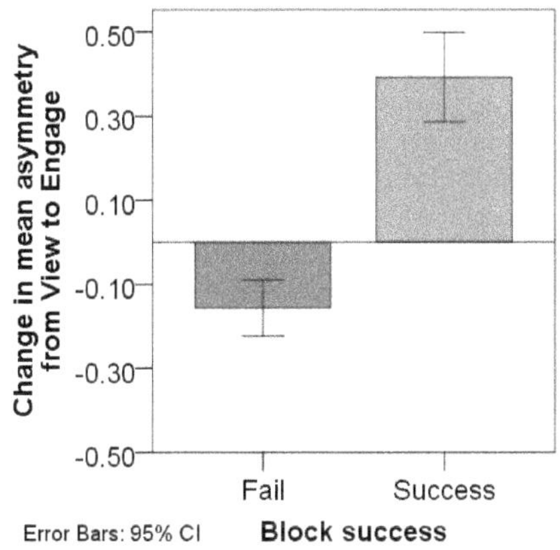

Figure 9: Change in mean asymmetry in successive *View* and *Engage* epochs, within successful and non-successful blocks. Note that non-successful blocks are characterized by a slight decrease in left-asymmetry during *Engage*, while successful blocks are characterized by a marked increase in left-asymmetry.

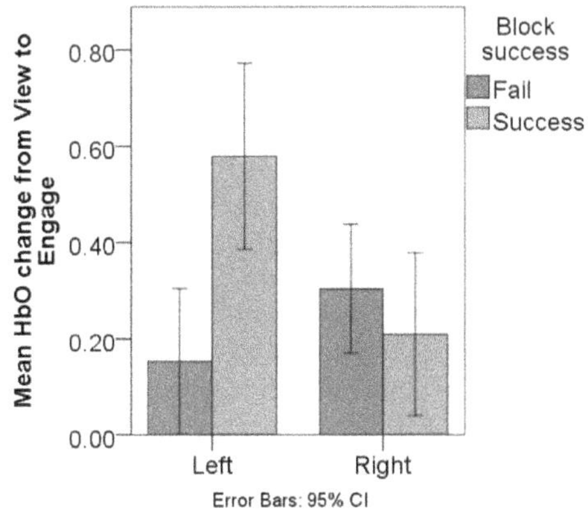

Figure 10: Differences in oxygenation increase from *View* to *Engage* epochs within successful and non-successful blocks, separately for the left and right sides. Note the marked increase in left-side oxygenation in successful blocks, while right-side oxygenation changes are at a similar level in the successful and non successful blocks.

(large) with the interquartile range [.55; .87], which indicates that successful blocks were characterized with a marked increase in left-asymmetry during the *Engage* epoch, clearly distinguishable from the *View* epoch.

Figure 7 demonstrates how HbO changes on both sides contributed to the increase in asymmetry from *View* to *Engage* epochs. Left-side oxygenation was statistically significantly larger in successful blocks (M = 0.58, SD = 0.58) than in non-successful ones (M = 0.15, SD = 0.38), t(62) = 3.33, $p < .001$, r = .39 (medium). Conversely, right-side oxygenation did not differ significantly between non-successful blocks (M = 0.30, SD = 0.34) and successful ones (M = 0.21, SD = 0.51), t(62) = 0.40, p = .375, ns. These findings indicate that change in left-asymmetry in successful blocks was predominantly due to increase in left-side oxygenation during the *Engage* task, which is consistent with previous literature (see Figure 8).

Changes in left-asymmetry oxygenation between successive *View* and *Engage* epochs are presented in Figure 9, separately for successful and non-successful blocks. Non-successful blocks were characterized with a slight decrease in left-asymmetry during *Engage* (M = -0.16, SD = 0.17), while successful blocks were characterized with a marked and comparably large increase in left-asymmetry (M = 0.39, SD = 0.32).

Immediately after completing a block, subjects described their cognitive strategy to engage with the agent. Although the sample size of 37 successful blocks does not allow for a detailed content analysis, subjects' comments on their strategies suggest that thinking about personal positive memories was most conducive in capturing the ECA's attention, clearly illustrated on Figure 7 where as left-asymmetry increases during *Engage* epoch.

5. CONCLUSIONS

We have presented a novel experimental framework, which attempts to relate previous conceptualizations of the relationship between a user and an ECA to a single affective dimension. The expression of *approach* by users, captured through variations of their PFC asymmetry, could constitute an empirical basis to capture user disposition towards an ECA, in a more specific way than previously described concepts of engagement, empathy, alignment or rapport, which all refer to wider frameworks. What we have shown specifically is that, while approach was measured on the *user* side, on the *ECA* side it could be used to generate appropriate responsive behavior through the coordination of expressive parameters such as AUs and BAPs. These findings indicate that users were able to express a mental disposition to engage through the use of positive thoughts, which resulted in an appropriate response from the ECA congruent to their affective state. Although these early results are encouraging, further work should be dedicated to exploring the closed-loop aspects of these experiments, in particular the effects of ECA backchannel on users' attitudes.

6. REFERENCES

[1] I. Albrecht, M. Schröder, J. Haber, and H. Seidel. Mixed feelings: expression of non-basic emotions in a muscle-based talking head. *Special issue of Journal of Virtual Reality on Language, Speech & Gesture*, 8(4):201–212, 2005.

[2] R. Amini and C. Lisetti. HapFACS: An open source API/software to generate FACS-based expressions for ECAs animation and for corpus generation. In *Affective Computing and Intelligent Interaction (ACII)*, pages 270–275, 2013.

[3] H. Ayaz. *Functional near infrared spectroscopy based brain computer interface*. PhD thesis, School of Biomedical Engineering Science, 2010.

[4] H. Ayaz, M. Izzetoglu, P. A. Shewokis, and B. Onaral. Sliding-window motion artifact rejection for functional near-infrared spectroscopy. In *Engineering in Medicine and Biology Society (EMBC)*, pages 6567–6570, 2010.

[5] R. Beale and C. Creed. Affective interaction: How emotional agents affect users. *International Journal of Human-Computer Studies*, 67(9):755–776, 2009.

[6] E. Bevacqua, K. Prepin, R. Niewiadomski, E. de Sevin, and C. Pelachaud. Greta: Towards an interactive conversational virtual companion. *Artificial Companions in Society: perspectives on the Present and Future*, pages 143–156, 2010.

[7] T. D. Bui, D. Heylen, M. Poel, and A. Nijholt. Generation of facial expressions from emotion using a fuzzy rule based system. In D. C. M. Stumptner and M. Brooks, editors, *Australian Joint Conference on Artificial Intelligence*, pages 83–94, 2001.

[8] S. C. Bunce, M. Izzetoglu, K. Izzetoglu, B. Onaral, and K. Pourrezaei. Functional near-infrared spectroscopy. *Engineering in Medicine and Biology Society (EMBC)*, 25(4):54–62, 2006.

[9] M. Cavazza, G. Aranyi, F. Charles, J. Porteous, S. Gilroy, G. Jackont, I. Klovatch, G. Raz, N. J. Keynan, A. Cohen, et al. Frontal alpha asymmetry neurofeedback for brain-computer interfaces. In *Brain-Computer Interface Conference*, 2014.

[10] J. Cohen. *Statistical power analysis for the behavioral sciences*. Lawrence Erlbaum Associates, 1988.

[11] M. Courgeon, C. Clavel, and J. Martin. Modeling facial signs of appraisal during interaction: impact on users' perception and behavior. In *International Conference on Autonomous Agents and Multi-Agent Systems (AAMAS)*, pages 765–772, 2014.

[12] R. J. Davidson, P. Ekman, C. D. Saron, J. A. Senulis, and W. V. Friesen. Approach-withdrawal and cerebral asymmetry: Emotional expression and brain physiology: I. *Journal of Personality and Social Psychology*, 58(2):330–341, 1990.

[13] H. Doi, S. Nishitani, and K. Shinohara. NIRS as a tool for assaying emotional function in the prefrontal cortex. *Frontiers in Human Neuroscience*, 7, 2013.

[14] P. Ekman, W. V. Friesen, and J. C. Hager. *Facial Action Coding System: A Technique for the Measurement of Facial Movement*. Consulting Psychologists Press, Palo Alto, CA, 2002.

[15] S. A. Etemad, A. Arya, A. Parush, and S. DiPaola. Perceptual validity in animation of human motion. *Computer Animation and Virtual Worlds*, 2015.

[16] S. W. Gilroy, J. Porteous, F. Charles, M. Cavazza, E. Soreq, G. Raz, L. Ikar, A. Or-Borichov, U. Ben-Arie, I. Klovatch, et al. A brain-computer interface to a plan-based narrative. In *International Joint Conference on Artificial Intelligence (IJCAI)*, pages 1997–2005, 2013.

[17] K. Grammer and E. Oberzaucher. The reconstruction of facial expressions in embodied systems. *ZiF: Mitteilungen*, 2, 2006.

[18] L. Huang, L.-P. Morency, and J. Gratch. Virtual rapport 2.0. In *Intelligent Virtual Agents (IVA)*, pages 68–79, 2011.

[19] E. Krumhuber, A. S. Manstead, D. Cosker, D. Marshall, and P. L. Rosin. Effects of dynamic attributes of smiles in human and synthetic faces: A simulated job interview setting. *Journal of Nonverbal Behavior*, 33(1):1–15, 2009.

[20] W. S. McCulloch and W. Pitts. A logical calculus of the ideas immanent in nervous activity. *The Bulletin of Mathematical Biophysics*, 5(4):115–133, 1943.

[21] S. Moghimi, A. Kushki, S. Power, A. M. Guerguerian, and T. Chau. Automatic detection of a prefrontal cortical response to emotionally rated music using multi-channel near-infrared spectroscopy. *Journal of Neural Engineering*, 9(2), 2012.

[22] R. Niewiadomski, S. J. Hyniewska, and C. Pelachaud. Constraint-based model for synthesis of multimodal sequential expressions of emotions. *IEEE Transactions on Affective Computing*, 2(3):134–146, 2011.

[23] R. Niewiadomski and C. Pelachaud. Model of facial expressions management for an embodied conversational agent. In *Affective Computing and Intelligent Interaction (ACII)*, pages 12–23. 2007.

[24] M. Ochs and C. Pelachaud. Socially aware virtual characters: the social signal of smiles. *IEEE Signal Processing Magazine*, 30(2):128–132, 2013.

[25] M. Ochs, C. Pelachaud, and D. Sadek. An empathic virtual dialog agent to improve human-machine interaction. In *International Joint Conference on Autonomous Agents and Multi-Agent Systems (AAMAS)*, pages 89–96, 2008.

[26] H. Prendinger and M. Ishizuka. The empathic companion: A character-based interface that addresses users' affective states. *International Journal of Applied Artificial Intelligence*, 19(3):297–285, 2005.

[27] J. P. Rosenfeld, G. Cha, T. Blair, and I. H. Gotlib. Operant (biofeedback) control of left-right frontal alpha power differences: Potential neurotherapy for affective disorders. *Biofeedback and Self-Regulation*, 20(3):241–258, 1995.

[28] A. C. Ruocco, A. H. Rodrigo, J. Lam, S. I. Di Domenico, B. Graves, and H. Ayaz. A problem-solving task specialized for functional neuroimaging: validation of the scarborough adaptation of the tower of london (s-tol) using near-infrared spectroscopy. *Frontiers in Human Neuroscience*, 8, 2014.

[29] P. Sarkheil, A. Zilverstand, N. Kilian-Hütten, F. Schneider, R. Goebel, and K. Mathiak. fMRI feedback enhances emotion regulation as evidenced by a reduced amygdala response. *Behavioural Brain Research*, 281:326–332, 2015.

[30] E. T. Solovey, A. Girouard, K. Chauncey, L. M. Hirshfield, A. Sassaroli, F. Zheng, S. Fantini, and R. J. Jacob. Using fNIRS brain sensing in realistic HCI settings: experiments and guidelines. In *the 22nd annual ACM symposium on User Interface Software and Technology (UIST)*, pages 157–166, 2009.

[31] K. Tai and T. Chau. Single-trial classification of NIRS signals during emotional induction tasks: towards a corporeal machine interface. *Journal of NeuroEngineering and Rehabilitation*, 6(1):1–14, 2009.

[32] R. Zhao, A. Papangelis, and J. Cassell. Towards a dyadic computational model of rapport management for human-virtual agent interaction. In *Intelligent Virtual Agents (IVA)*, pages 514–527, 2014.

[33] V. Zotev, R. Phillips, H. Yuan, M. Misaki, and J. Bodurka. Self-regulation of human brain activity using simultaneous real-time fMRI and EEG neurofeedback. *NeuroImage*, 85:985–995, 2014.

Multimodal Interaction with a Bifocal View on Mobile Devices

Sebastien Pelurson[1,2] and Laurence Nigay[1]

[1]Univ. Grenoble Alpes, LIG, CNRS
F-38000 Grenoble, France
{Sébastien.Pelurson, Laurence.Nigay}@imag.fr

[2]Motwin Company
F-38240 Meylan, France
Sebastien.Pelurson@motwin.com

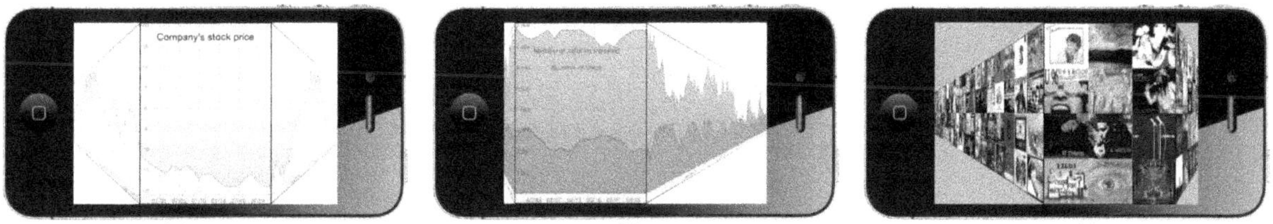

(a) (b) (c)

Figure 1. Implemented bifocal display on iPhone 4. Three examples of applications: (a) Financial market: Stock prices. (b) Health&Well-being: Comparison of the numbers of steps and calories ingested. (c) Music library: Album covers.

ABSTRACT

On a mobile device, the intuitive Focus+Context layout of a detailed view (focus) and perspective/distorted panels on either side (context) is particularly suitable for maximizing the utilization of the limited available display area. Interacting with such a bifocal view requires both fast access to data in the context view and high precision interaction with data in the detailed focus view. We introduce combined modalities that solve this problem by combining the well-known flick-drag gesture-based precise modality with modalities for fast access to data in the context view. The modalities for fast access to data in the context view include direct touch in the context view as well as navigation based on drag gestures, on tilting the device, on side-pressure inputs or by spatially moving the device (dynamic peephole). Results of a comparison experiment of the combined modalities show that the performance can be analyzed according to a 3-phase model of the task: a focus-targeting phase, a transition phase (modality switch) and a cursor-pointing phase. Moreover modalities of the focus-targeting phase based on a discrete mode of navigation control (direct access, pressure sensors as discrete navigation controller) require a long transition phase: this is mainly due to disorientation induced by the loss of control in movements. This effect is significantly more pronounced than the articulatory time for changing the position of the fingers between the two modalities ("homing" time).

Categories and Subject Descriptors

H.5.2 [**Information interfaces and presentation (e.g., HCI)**]: User Interfaces.

General Terms

Design, Human Factors.

Keywords

Mobile devices; Bifocal view; Multimodal interaction.

ICMI 2015, November 9–13, 2015, Seattle, WA, USA.
© 2015 ACM. ISBN 978-1-4503-3912-4/15/11…$15.00.
DOI: http://dx.doi.org/10.1145/2818346.2820731

1. INTRODUCTION

As mobile technology increasingly becomes a very common mode of access to information and services, one challenge is be able to manage large information spaces on mobile devices. Interactive visualization on mobile devices addresses the problem of large information spaces and small displays. Although mobile displays increase in size and resolution (e.g., iPhone 6 Plus, 5.5", 1920 x 1080 pixels), information spaces are increasing more rapidly.

Several studies have focused on the interactive visualization of spatial and tabular information structures on mobile devices and in particular mobile maps [19, 23, 29]. We note that nowadays 1D and temporal information structures are increasingly managed on mobile devices, including financial data and more recently health and wellness data (number of steps, calories ingested, etc.). Figure 1 includes three examples of applications. Addressing this challenge we focus on the interactive visualization of 1D/temporal information structure on mobile devices.

Facing a large information space, zooming interfaces display the data at one level of detail at a given time and the user must navigate between the levels of data by zooming because of the display space limitation. As an alternative to pan&zoom navigation, the Overview+Detail and Focus+Context interfaces simultaneously display the data at multiple levels of detail. Overview+Detail interfaces simultaneously display two spatially separate views, each view containing data at a given level of detail. Overview+Detail interfaces on mobile devices are explored by Burigat&Chittaro [7]. Avoiding the mental effort to relate the two separate views, Focus+Context interfaces integrate the detailed view (focus) within the context view that displays the rest of the data with less detail. This paper focuses on bifocal display on mobile devices, one type of Focus+Context interfaces with two levels of detail as illustrated in Figure 1.

The paper introduces input modalities for interacting with a bifocal visualization on mobile devices. The addressed problem is to provide both a fast access to data in the context view and high precision interaction with data in the detailed focus view as described by Appert et al. [2]. Our design approach relies on the combination of modalities. Designed combined modalities are made of one modality for fast access to data in the context view and one modality for precise interaction in the detailed focus view. The results of an experimental evaluation of several designed combined modalities show that the performance can be analyzed according to a 3-phase model of the task: a focus-targeting phase (interaction in the context view), a transition phase (modality switch) and a cursor-pointing phase (interaction in the focus view). The performance of the observed navigation strategy is mainly based on the time of the focus-targeting phase and the time of the transition phase. Furthermore modalities based on a discrete mode of navigation control (direct access, pressure sensors as discrete navigation controller) require a long transition phase for switching to the precise modality. Due to the disorientation induced by the loss of full continuous control over the movements, this effect is significantly more pronounced than the articulatory time for changing the position of the fingers between the two modalities.

2. IMPLEMENTED BIFOCAL VIEW

Several Focus+Context techniques have been designed and empirically evaluated on a desktop PC such as the one described by Kincaid [18]. But such experimental results no longer hold on mobile devices because here specific constraints are present including the small size of the screen and instability due to mobility as described by Chittaro [9]. For instance Jakobsen&Hornbæk [16] compared of a Focus+Context technique on three different sizes of display and revealed the inferiority of a small display both in terms of task completion time and subjective assessments of effort. Moreover Gutwin [13], found that navigating on a small screen is slower than on a normal screen.

On mobile devices, Focus+Context techniques have been designed [8, 11, 29], exploring different types of information structures and application domains, including web browsers, scatterplots and maps. For instance the fisheye calendar DateLens presented by Bederson & al. [5] was found superior to an existing calendar. Moreover, although Jakobsen&Hornbæk [16] showed poor performance for a Focus+Context technique, the experimental comparison of different visualization techniques (Pan&Zoom, Overview+Detail, Focus+Context) in [8, 13] showed the viability of a Focus+Context technique for a 2D information structure, highlighting the value of the navigational context on mobile devices. We therefore chose one type of Focus+Context techniques that we study for 1D information structure: a bifocal display in a one-dimensional form (Figure 1).

The Focus+Context technique described by Huot&Lecolinet [14] is dedicated to 1D linear data more suitable for periodic data or for data without much detail. Indeed, most of the screen space is used by the context, so the focus area is small. As opposed to Huot&Lecolinet [14] and based on the requirements of our studied application domains (Figure 1), we designed and implemented a bifocal display with a large detailed view and two distorted sideviews (Figure 1). The display then manages two distinct levels of detail.. While preserving spatial continuity, the drawback is the perceivable discontinuity at the boundaries between the detailed view and the distorted views as described by Leung&Apperley [20]. Providing a smooth transition between the detailed view and the distorted sideviews, the Perspective Wall presented by Mackinlay et al. [22] is a generalization of the bifocal display that implements a non-constant demagnification function. Our goal was to evaluate the input modalities so we implemented a constant demagnification. Nevertheless from the Perspective Wall we reused the intuitive 3D perspective that enables us to display more information in the context area as described by Mackinlay et al. [22]. In the implemented bifocal display, the context is therefore bent perspectively as done by Mackinlay et al. [22] (Figure 1). The user defines the ratio of detail and context by resizing the focus, as done by Mackinlay et al. [22]. We implemented this functionality on the mobile phone with a resizing pinch gesture performed in the focus area. As with the Document Lens of Robertson&Mackinlay [25] and in order to maximize the utilization of the available display area (avoiding the waste of screen real estate, as with the Perspective Wall, when the detailed view, fixed at the center, is at the edges of the information space), the detailed view is not fixed at the center and is moved by users in order to explore the dataset. In the following sections we focus on the input modalities for moving the detailed focus view (i.e., navigation in the context view) and for precise interaction in the detailed focus view.

3. RELATED WORK: NAVIGATION MODALITIES

We restrict our review of related work to navigation modalities on mobile devices. Indeed the main elementary task for a Focus+Context visualization technique is to move the focus area in order to obtain the details of data belonging to the context area.

The first modality is the flick-drag scrolling. It is the traditional input modality commonly used today on mobile devices. For a large information space, the flick-drag scrolling modality can be fastidious and long as explained by Spindler et al. [28]. Moreover cumulative gain across flick gestures (as described by Quinn et al. [24] for iOS) can lead to a very fast scrolling speed that may imply a complete loss of control of the movements.

On the one hand to reduce clutching to cover long distances, the Flick-and-Brake technique of Baglioni et al. [4] is based on flick scrolling but allows the user to control speed deceleration by pressing a finger on screen. Without touching the screen, the motion continues.

On the other hand, several other modalities have been explored and are based on different sensors embedded on the mobile device. The goal of these modalities is to improve the efficiency of navigation but also to avoid finger gestures that cause occlusion of the displayed dataset while navigating and require users to perform switches between navigation mode and edit mode as explained by Spelmezan et al. [27].

- The technique described by Kratz et al. [19] extends the SDAZ technique developed by Igarashi&Hinckley [15] for mobile map navigation using tilt as an input modality. The authors compared it to a standard multitouch modality. The results show that the tilt modality performed at least as well as the multitouch modality. For one-dimensional navigation tasks, the tilt scrolling is compared to the flick scrolling by Fitchett&Cockburn [10]. The results show that tilt scrolling outperforms flick scrolling in a stationary situation. Nevertheless the focus was on reading and analysis tasks. Such tasks involve slow scrolling in short distance navigation tasks. Complementary to this study, we focus on the interaction task only as done by Appert&Fekete [3], without considering the perception task. In addition we consider a large information structure involving long distance tilt navigation tasks.
- SidePress by Spelmezan et al. [27] provides users with navigation capabilities based on pressure sensors located on the side of the mobile device. A comparison with the drag-flick modality shows that the pressure-based modality can be more efficient than finger gesture-based modality. In our study, we consider modalities based on two continuous

pressure sensors located on the top side of the mobile phone used in landscape mode.

- Two studies explore another modality based on the spatial manipulation of the mobile device. Pahud et al. [23] and Spindler et al. [28] compare the spatial manipulation with the standard Pinch-Drag-Flick technique (touch modality). In [23] results show that the spatial manipulation performs as well as the standard modality, whereas Spindler et al. [28] showed that spatial manipulation outperforms the standard modality. All these studies are based on a spatial information structure. In our study on one-dimensional navigation tasks we consider a spatial manipulation-based input modality.

4. DESIGN OF COMBINED MODALITIES

The design of modalities for interacting with a bifocal view on mobile devices is driven by the need for both a fast access to data in the context view and high precision interaction with data in the detailed focus view. To do so and as explained by Appert et al. [2], there are two ways to interact with the bifocal view: either in *focus* space or in *context* space. Interaction at focus scale allows accurate navigation but is slow on long distances. On the contrary, interaction at context scale allows fast navigation but is not accurate because of the magnification factor: a movement of one pixel at context scale corresponds to a movement of *mf* pixels at focus scale, where *mf* is the magnification factor.

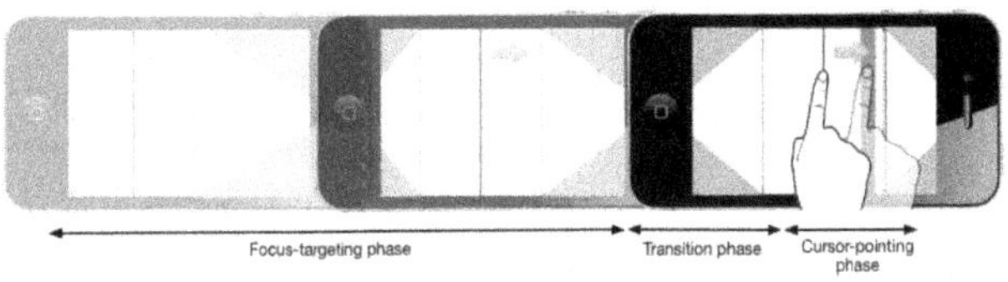

Figure 2. Selection task modeled as three phases.

For bifocal views, we therefore discard the modalities that rely on interacting solely in *focus* space (e.g., standard flick-drag) or that rely on interacting solely in *context* space. And we adopt a multimodal approach to solve the problem. We combine two modalities: the first one controlling the position of the focus area in *context* space to move quickly the cursor near the point of interest, and the second one controlling the position in *focus* space to move accurately the point of interest in the middle of the focus area. We investigate the complementary use (sequential/concomitant use) of these two modalities as described by the multimodal model of Serrano&Nigay [26]. To do so, we model the task as three phases (Figure 2): the fast navigation phase (named focus-targeting phase hereafter as Appert et al. [2], also named motion by Gutwin [12]), the accurate navigation phase (named cursor-pointing hereafter as Appert et al. [2], also named acquisition by Gutwin [12]), and also the modality switch (named transition phase hereafter).

We fix the modality used for the cursor-pointing phase. It relies on the accurate flick-drag modality provided by the iOS SDK. It is well integrated in iOS devices and therefore is a well-established standard for navigation. This modality is active only in the focus area. We made this choice to reinforce the interaction metaphor: when interacting in the focus area, users move the dataset rather than the focus area. Therefore, data remains under the user finger. In return, the focus area appears moving in the opposite direction than the one of the performed gesture as explained by Gutwin [12]. But the small length of the movements performed during this phase minimizes this issue: indeed the focus area movements are almost not perceptible. This modality is used as the precise modality during the cursor-pointing phase for all the combined modalities. We explore the combination of this well-known precise modality with 6 modalities for the focus-targeting phase. The design rationale is based on the type of navigation, with 2 modalities per type, as shown in Table 1.

Table 1. Six modalities for the focus-targeting phase

	Discrete	Continuous
Sequential	DiscretePress, FastDrag	ContinuousPress, Tilt
Non-sequential	DirectTouch, Peephole	

4.1 FastDrag and DirectTouch

FastDrag and DirectTouch are two modalities based on touch interaction. FastDrag is based on drag gestures in *context* space. Thus, a displacement of 1 pixel on screen causes a displacement of the focus area of 1 pixel in *context* space, and therefore a displacement of *mf* pixels in *focus* space (*mf* being the magnification factor). This minimizes clutching caused by scrolling a large dataset. The two modalities FastDrag and flick-drag are based on drag gestures. We distinguish them by the number of fingers on screen: one finger dragging in the focus area performs scrolling in *focus* space (cursor-pointing phase), two fingers dragging anywhere on screen performs scrolling in *context* space (focus-targeting phase). Thus, users can easily switch from a modality to another. The direction of scrolling is the same for both modalities: drag one or two fingers to the left moves data to the left, and therefore the focus area to the right.

DirectTouch enables direct jump to a new position. The user selects a point (by a touch gesture) anywhere in the context area to move it in the focus area. This allows a very fast non-sequential navigation and avoids clutching.. When selecting a point, an animation is triggered helping the user to keep her/his spatial orientation. Because of the magnification factor between *focus* space and *context* space, and the perspective effect of the bifocal view, the modality is not precise. Since the DirectTouch modality is based on touch click, the transition to the flick-drag modality is very fast.

4.2 Tilt

The promising results of Tilt presented by Fitchett&Cockburn [10] motivated us to implement a Tilt modality. This allows users to tilt the device around the vertical axis of the plane defined by the device. Tilting the device on the left (respectively right) moves the focus area to the left (respectively right). The more the device is tilted, the faster the scrolling speed is in *context* space. Our implementation uses accelerometers and gyroscopes of the device. We applied the angle/speed conversion described by MacKenzie [21] using the tilt magnitude with the following equation:

$$tiltMagn = Math.sqrt(pitch * pitch + yaw * yaw)$$

We defined the speed as *tiltMagn* * *gain*, with *gain* equal to 75, as the results of MacKenzie [21] reveals that a tilt gain in range [50, 100] is optimal. This allows users to attain scrolling speeds of between -4500 and 4500 pixels per second with an angle between -60° and 60° around the initial position. This initial position is defined by the device position at the application launch. At any time the users can recalibrate this position by doing a double tap on screen. As done by Fitchett&Cockburn [10], we defined a "safe" area in which no scrolling is performed ([-6.5°, 6.5°] around the initial position). This stable region allows avoiding of undesired scrolling due to tremors or modality switch. Users have therefore to place the device back into this safe area to stop scrolling.

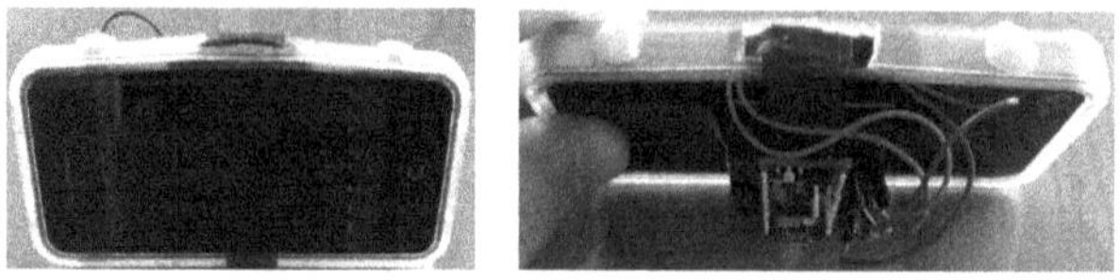

Figure 3. Pressure sensors prototype.

4.3 ContinuousPress and DiscretePress

ContinuousPress and DiscretePress are two modalities based on pressure sensors. Despite the fact that we wanted to use device built-in sensors, we believe that these kind of sensors will be integrated in smartphones in a very near future (i.e. Apple 3D Touch technology), and good results were obtained by Spelmezan et al. [27] with these kind of sensors. We built a prototype using an Arduino Micro board and two pressure sensors Interlink Elektroniks FSR 400 as shown in Figure 3. Sensors were fixed under a phone shell. We added small pieces of fabric onto the phone shell to allow users to sense where to put their fingers without looking at the position. The Arduino board is fixed on the back of the phone. The left (respectively right) sensor moves the focus area to the left (respectively right). As the other modalities for the focus-targeting phase, the scrolling performs on *context* space.

With DiscretePress, sensors are used to perform discrete navigation. Then users navigate by clicking on sensors. As described by Spelmezan et al. [27], two levels of pressure trigger two different events: *light-click* and *strong-click*. *light-click* is triggered after a click with a minimum pressure of 0.5N and a maximum pressure of 2N. It performs a displacement of 80 pixels. *Strong-click* is triggered after a click with a minimum pressure of 2N. It performs a displacement of 800 pixels. *Strong-click* allows users to jump quickly toward the target and *light-click* allows them to be more precise in jumping near the target.

ContinuousPress uses pressure sensors to perform continuous navigation. The stronger the users press a sensor, the faster the scrolling speed is. The navigation remains active until the sensor is released. As we did not have an operational amplifier component to linearize pressure inputs (as done by Spelmezan et al. [27]), we defined 3 ranges of pressure with 3 different speed gains to simulate a linearization: 3 under 0.5N, 4 between 0.5N and 2.5N, and 6 over 2.5N. These factors are applied to values returned by the Arduino board that are numbers between 0 and 1023 (0 = no pressure, 1023 = max pressure). This allows having a scrolling speed similar to that of the Tilt modality.

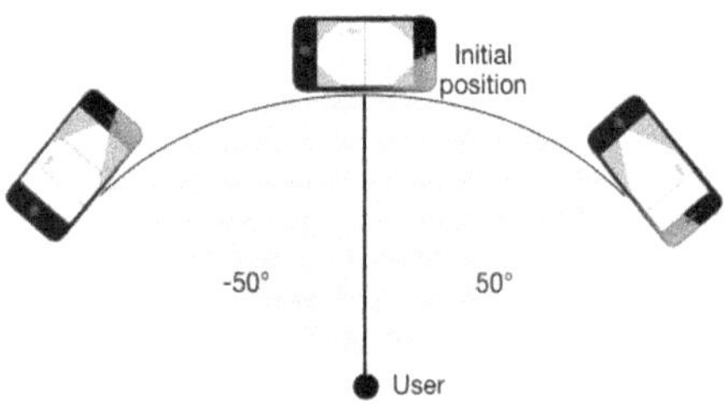

Figure 4. Peephole: a spatial-input-based modality.

4.4 Peephole

This modality uses spatial manipulation in order to map a physical position of the device to a virtual position in the dataset. This avoids interacting on the screen and therefore avoids clutching and occlusion problems. Three different mapping functions are presented by Pahud et al. [23]: a fixed planar mapping, a fixed spherical mapping and a dynamic mapping. We chose a spherical mapping (Figure 4). The spherical mapping is described by Pahud et al. [23] as difficult to use when spatial manipulation allows the users to zoom when moving the device closer to the body: this is not our case. Moreover a spherical mapping allows us to implement the modality without an accurate external positioning system (e.g., Optitrack): indeed we used the built-in compass to detect solely rotation around the user (using angle relative to the North). Finally users tend to sweep their arm in broad arcs when panning, as explained by Pahud et al. [23], so the spherical mapping seems to be a suitable mapping.

At the application launch, the current angle is retrieved and mapped to the middle of the dataset (because this is the initial position of the focus area). We restricted the movement amplitude in the range of [-50°, 50°] around the initial position (Figure 4). This allows the user to navigate in the entire dataset without making a large body rotation. This modality is activated on-demand, as described by Spindler et al. [28]. Activation is based on the right pressure sensor to avoid the occlusion problem with a finger on screen. The modality is active while the sensor is pressed; it is disabled when the sensor is released. This on-demand activation allows users switching from a relative to absolute mode and provides a stable position when the spatial navigation is disabled. In order to use spatial manipulation, users have to describe a rotation with their arms to the desired position and then press the sensor to move the focus area to the corresponding position.

5. EXPERIMENT

We conducted an exploratory controlled experiment to compare the performance of the six combined modalities described above. Participants were asked to perform pointing tasks with the implemented bifocal view. Our goal was to compare, for each combined modality the execution time for: the entire task, the focus-targeting phase, the cursor-pointing phase, and the transition between modalities. We therefore wanted to study each phase of the task depending on the combined modality.

5.1 Participants

We conducted an experiment with eighteen unpaid volunteers, 15 males and 3 females, aged 25 to 42 year-old (average 30.55, median 29), 14 were non-academic engineers in computer science, and 4 academic researchers in computer science. All of them were regular users of tactile mobile devices but had no experience with modalities except for flick-drag. The experiment was divided into six blocks, one per combined modalities.

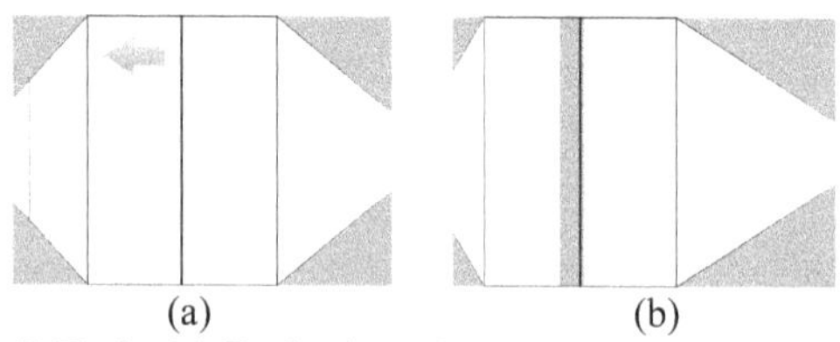

(a) (b)

Figure 5. Task: (a) Beginning of the task: The arrow indicates the direction to the target. (b) End of the task: The cursor is within the target.

5.2 Method

Apparatus. We conducted the experiment on an iPhone 4 (960x640 pixels in landscape mode). The program was fully iOS coded, except a C program that gets pressure sensors values and sends them to the phone using WiFi.

Display. As explained before, in bifocal visualizations, we distinguish the focus space from the context space that are represented on screen at two different scales, respectively in the focus view and the context view (i.e., the two perspective sideviews). First in order to match with the implemented transformation function described by Leung&Apperley [20] that defines how the original context space is mapped to the two perspective sideviews, the focus view and the context view had the same size on screen. Hence the focus view and the context view (divided into two areas on screen) were 480 screen-pixels wide on iPhone 4. Second by assuming one value of the dataset per pixel, the size of the dataset is expressed in pixels, namely value-pixels. The selected size of *focus* space was 57 600 value-pixels, for enabling long distances to targets. Applying the value used in the Perspective Wall implementation of Mackinlay et al. [22], the size of *context* space was therefore 4800 value-pixels wide. We then had a factor (*mf*) equal to 12. We note that those parameters match with concrete application cases: for instance the visualization of a 10 year stock chart with a one-month period displayed in the focus: 480 pixels * 10 years * 12 months = 57600 pixels.

Task. We used the experimental protocol and task described by Appert et al. [2] for navigation of large datasets. Participants had to select targets in the context view. The cursor was displayed at the center of the focus view (Figure 5). Therefore the participants had to move the focus view to bring the cursor on the target and maintain it for 1 second. After that, a new target appeared. The cursor was presented as a 6 pixel wide black line (Figure 5) in order to be clearly visible on the screen. The target was presented as a 60 pixel wide red area (10 times larger than the cursor) in the focus view (Figure 5-a). So its size in the context view was $\frac{60}{mf}$, where *mf* is the magnification factor between *focus* space and *context* space. Then, the target is a 5 pixel wide in the context view (*mf* being equal to 12). The target size has been chosen to be easily selected because the concrete task is to move interesting data points into the focus view in order to obtain their details (i.e., the concrete task is not an accurate pointing task). We therefore do not want the difficulty of the task to be the accuracy of the selection during the cursor-pointing phase. Finally the target became green when the cursor is on it (Figure 5-b). Because of the perspective effect and the magnification factor, the target in the context view was not clearly visible. First a green arrow displayed at the top of the focus view indicated the direction of the target to minimize desert fog effects described by Jul&Furnas [17] (Figure 5-a). Second, the target was surrounded by a blue rectangle in the context view to be always perceptible. This avoids the stage of searching the target, which can be found by chance. We therefore focus only on navigation performance. The order of appearance of the targets forced participants to perform the task in left and right directions.

In our experiment while the magnification factor is defined by the bifocal visualization, we fixed the target size and varied the difficulty of the tasks by considering 4 distances for the target: D1=4800 pixels, D2=9600 pixels, D3=19200 pixels and D4=38400 pixels. Those distances are expressed in *focus* space (respectively 400, 800, 1600 and 3200 pixels in *context* space).

Procedure. We grouped trials into six blocks, one per combined modalities. After a brief demonstration of the combined modality, participants performed six training tasks before starting a block. They could ask any question during this step. The presentation order of the combined modalities was counterbalanced using a Latin square. For each block (i.e., each combined modality), participants had to perform 6 trials per distance. Therefore, they had to perform 24 (6 trials x 4 distances) tasks per combined modality and 144 selection tasks in total. The participants also answered a System Usability Scale (SUS) [6] on the combined modality they just experienced before starting the next one in order to collect the participant's subjective point of view on the modality s/he just experimented. The participants were instructed to be as fast and as accurate as possible. Finally, the participants were asked to rank the three combined modalities they preferred in order of preference and to explain their choices. The entire experiment lasted approximately 35 minutes.

5.3 Hypothesis

Based on the design rationale of the combined modalities, we formulate two hypotheses:

H1: Combined modalities providing direct access (DirectTouch and Peephole) will be faster during the focus-targeting phase than the modalities requiring navigation. The two modalities DirectTouch and Peephole are very inaccurate because of the magnification factor; therefore we also expect that the cursor-pointing phase will be longer because of the large remaining distance to be performed to reach the target.

H2: Combined modalities using the same modalities for the focus-targeting phase and the cursor-pointing phase (FastDrag, DirectTouch) will have a shorter transition time by reducing "homing" time.

5.4 Results and Discussion

5.4.1 Performance: execution time

For each task, we logged events (tactile screen, pressure sensors and embedded sensors) triggered by the participants. A post analysis of the generated log files allows us to measure accurately which phase is performed and for how long.
We check the normality of our data using the Shapiro-Wilk test. It reveals a deviation from the normal distribution, even with a transformation (log, square root). We then use the non-parametric Kruskal-Wallis test in order to test the significance of each factor (modality and distance) effect on each dependent variable (execution time for each phase). Focus-targeting execution time
The Kruskal-Wallis test reveals a significant effect for combined modalities on focus-targeting execution time ($p < 0.001$). A post-hoc test using Dunn with Bonferroni correction shows that there are significant differences between all pairs of combined modalities except between ContinuousPress and DiscretePress ($p = 0.1779$), between ContinuousPress and FastDrag ($p = 0.8912$) and between DiscretePress and FastDrag ($p = 0.2867$).

As expected (H1), DirectTouch is clearly the fastest modality (Figure 6-a), because it provides a direct access. However, for the Peephole modality, which also enables direct access to an area of the context by moving the device, the result is different. So H1 is not verified for Peephole. It is explained by the fact that participants used this combined modality in a continuous way for navigation. Therefore the participants spent more time than expected. This observed usage of the Peephole modality is in contradiction with our design rationale of providing a direct access by positioning the device according to a virtual 1D space in front of the user. Two reasons may explain this observed usage of the modality. First the interaction metaphor of moving the device that provides a window on a virtual information space (namely Lens-in-Hand metaphor by Pahud et al. [23]) is maybe stronger with a 2D virtual space as in [23, 28]. Moreover this Lens-in-Hand interaction metaphor is maybe perceived in opposition to the graphical metaphor of displaying the complete information space (focus and context) on the mobile device screen. For the rest of the analysis we consider that the Peephole modality is a continuous navigation modality as the Tilt modality for instance.

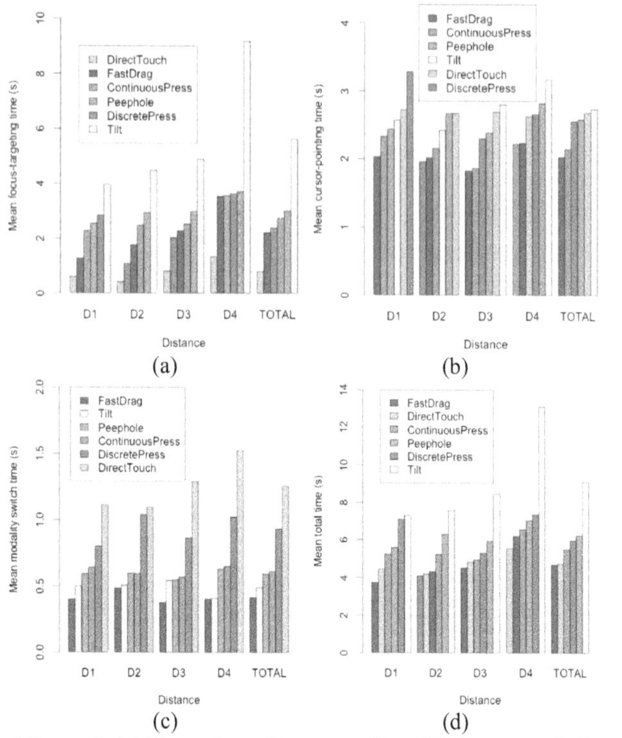

Figure 6. (a) Focus-targeting mean time (b) Cursor-pointing mean time (c) Transition mean time (d) Total mean time.

Execution time is much slower for Tilt. First we observed for the Tilt modality only that the participants accidently came back to the focus-targeting phase (i.e. tilt scrolling) after the cursor-pointing phase (i.e. touch gesture). Although we defined a "safe" area for the tilt ([-6.5°, 6.5°] around the initial position) in which no scrolling is performed, touch interaction provoked tilting the device outside the "safe" area and activated undesired scrolling. This observation explains that the focus-targeting execution time for Tilt was very long. Another explanation is the way participants used the combined modalities. Indeed we observed an unexpected navigation strategy. Rather than quickly moving the focus view not too far from the target to then switch to the precise modality, participants spent time trying to get the target displayed in the focus view. This strategy is perhaps encouraged by the fact that the precise modality implies finger touch gestures in the focus view only. Based on this strategy, the participants wasted time trying to be precise. So the execution time during this phase is related to the accuracy of the modality. This is confirmed by the good performance of the FastDrag modality, which is a precise one. Moreover clutching with FastDrag was minimized, making the modality even faster. With ContinuousPress, a light short press on one pressure sensor performs a very short navigation step and therefore enables the participants to be precise. Regarding Peephole, the on-demand activation with a press on the pressure sensor improves the accuracy. Participants have to simply release the sensor to stop the navigation. Whereas with Tilt, they have to come back to the static position and then anticipate the movement or navigate slower. This is why performance is better with Peephole than Tilt.

Finally, as shown in Figure 6-a, the execution time increases as the distance increases for all combined modalities, except for DiscretePress and DirectTouch. First DiscretePress is slower on the shortest distance. We explain this result by the difficulty for some participants to distinguish the two levels of pressure (confirmed by the user preference). Therefore they performed unwanted long movements. Second, despite that the DirectTouch provides a direct access, it is nevertheless dependent on the distance because of the perspective effect. Indeed the further the target is, the less visible it is and therefore easy to select. Therefore the task could require few more clicks, explaining why the execution time is slower for D4.

5.4.1.1 Cursor-pointing execution time

The Kruskal-Wallis test reveals a significant effect for combined modalities on cursor-pointing execution time ($p < 0.001$). The post-hoc test shows that there is no significant difference between ContinuousPress and DiscretePress ($p = 0.07909$), between ContinuousPress and FastDrag ($p = 0.4561$), between DirectTouch and Peephole ($p = 0.1267$), between DirectTouch and Tilt ($p = 0.5413$), and between Peephole and Tilt ($p = 0.5516$).

As expected, this phase is not dependent on the distance factor (Figure 6-b). Actually, the performance of this phase is dependent on the results of the focus-targeting phase, as explained by Appert et al. [2]. FastDrag is the fastest modality for this phase. This is due to the fact that this combined modality provides a better degree of control during the focus-targeting phase, so allows participants to position the target very close to the cursor. In the same way and as explained above, with the ContinuousPress, a light short press on the pressure sensor performs a very short navigation step, enabling the participants to be precise. Increasing the accuracy during the focus-targeting phase decreases the time of the cursor-pointing phase.

Nevertheless, since participants used the same navigation strategy for all combined modalities by trying to be precise during the focus-targeting phase, it is not surprising to observe small execution time variation between the modalities during this phase. So H1 is not verified: there is no significant difference between DirectTouch, Peephole and Tilt. We calculated the standard deviation for each phase on the entire dataset. We obtain 4.2 for the focus-targeting phase, 0.7 for the transition phase and 1.7 for the cursor-pointing phase. By computing the ratio with the mean time of each phase (2.45 seconds for the focus-targeting phase, 0.71 for the transition phase and 2.82 seconds for the cursor-pointing phase), the cursor-pointing phase has the smallest one (1.71 for the focus-targeting phase, 0.98 for the transition phase and 0.49 for the cursor-pointing phase). This means that the cursor-pointing phase variability is less important than for the two other phases, and that the total execution time with this navigation strategy is mainly influenced by the focus-targeting time and the transition time.

5.4.1.2 Transition time

The Kruskal-Wallis test reveals a significant effect for combined modalities on transition time ($p < 0.001$). The post-hoc test shows that there are significant differences between all pairs of combined modalities except between ContinuousPress and Peephole ($p = 0.6315$).

As expected, the transition time is not dependent on the distance of the target. FastDrag has the shortest transition phase (Figure 6-c), confirming H2 for this modality (no "homing" time). Since Tilt does not have to be activated, the transition can be anticipated, making it very fast: simply tilting the device for fast navigation and touching the screen for precise navigation. ContinuousPress and Peephole have a longer transition phase with similar transition times. For both modalities, we observed that several participants do not feel comfortable interacting on screen with the thumb. Therefore they have to remove their forefingers from the pressure sensors to perform the cursor-pointing phase, increasing the transition time.

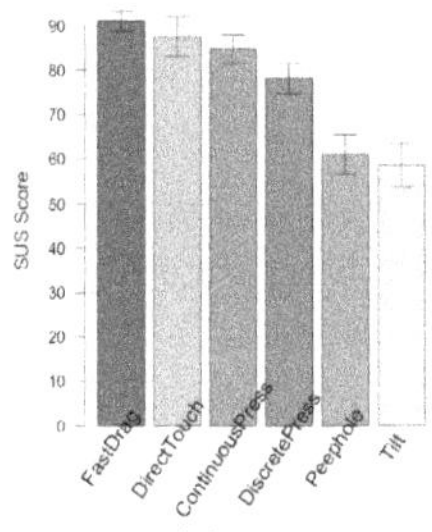

(a)

Technique	#1	#2	#3	Score
DirectTouch	13	3	0	93
FastDrag	1	9	7	79
ContinuousPress	4	5	4	65
DiscretePress	0	0	4	16
Tilt	0	1	2	13
Peephole	0	0	1	4

(b)

Figure 7. (a) Mean SUS score with 95% confidence intervals (b) Preference ranking scores and the number of times the combined modalities were ranked 1st, 2nd or 3rd.

Finally Figure 6-c shows that DirectTouch and DiscretePress have a much longer transition phase. H2 is therefore not verified for DirectTouch. These two modalities involve a discrete mode of navigation control. This implies disorientation due to the loss of control of the movements, even though an animation was provided. The long transition is mainly due to this disorientation effect. This result shows that the articulatory switch (present for Tilt, Peephole, ContinuousPress and DiscretePress modalities) is less important than the disorientation issue caused by the loss of control of the movements with the two modalities DirectTouch and DiscretePress.

5.4.1.3 Total execution time

The Kruskal-Wallis test reveals a significant effect for combined modalities on total execution time ($p < 0.001$). The post-hoc test shows that there are significant differences between all pairs of combined modalities except between FastDrag and ContinuousPress ($p = 0.0734$) and between FastDrag and DirectTouch ($p = 0.2193$). The total execution times confirm the 3-phase modeling of the task. Figure 6-d shows that the three fastest combined modalities are DirectTouch, FastDrag and ContinuousPress. Despite that DirectTouch is very fast during the focus-targeting phase, the difference with the other modalities is seriously reduced for the total execution time, due to the long transition phase.Near-constant times observed during the cursor-pointing phase, show that this phase has little influence on the total execution time. We explained it by the navigation strategy adopted by the participants, trying to obtain the target displayed in the focus view before switching to the cursor-moving phase. With this strategy, the two main factors are the focus-targeting phase and the transition phase. Regarding the dependency between execution time and distance, tendencies are quite similar as those in the focus-pointing phase, reinforcing the fact that the total execution time strongly depends on the focus-targeting time and the transition time.

5.4.2 User Preference

User preferences reflect the performance results. In Figure 7, the modalities are ordered from left to right with decreasing order of mean SUS score. SUS questionnaire shows that participants ranked the FastDrag combined modality as the most usable one.

The preference ranking (Figure 7) is similar to the mean SUS score. The three preferred combined modalities have also been described as the most usable in the SUS questionnaire. We computed the ranking score (S) of a combined modality using the formula $S = 6*1^{st} + 5*2^{nd} + 4*3^{rd}$, where 1st, 2nd and 3rd were its ranking at the corresponding place. We checked that with lower coefficients (respectively 3, 2, 1), the results remained similar.

Participants found the DirectTouch modality very easy to use: "After 1 or 2 clicks I know that I am close enough to switch to the precise modality". Only few participants reported the disorientation issue noted in the performance analysis. We think that the impression of ease and efficiency provided by this known modality compensated this problem.

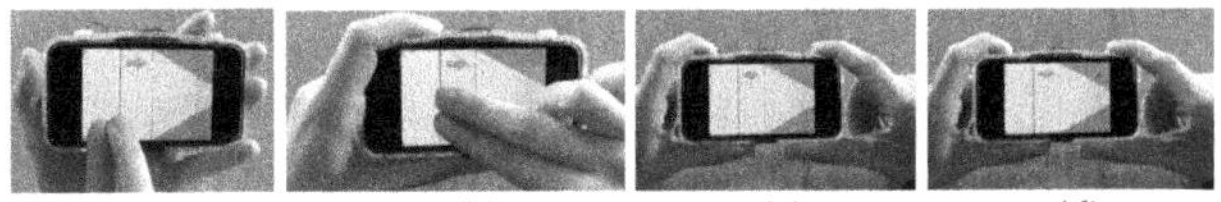

(a) (b) (c) (d)

Figure 8. FastDrag (a) from bottom of the screen: limited occlusion (b) from the side of the screen: large occlusion. DiscretePress (c) Thumbs under the device: light-click and strong-click difficult to distinguish (d) Thumbs on the screen: strong-click hard to perform.

The FastDrag has been appreciated because it is a well-known modality. Even if clutching was minimized (movements in *context* space implying 4 or 5 drag gestures to reach very far targets), several participants reported the clutching issue. Moreover some participants also mentioned the occlusion problem. Depending on how the participants were holding the device, the fingers may occlude a large part of the screen (Figure 8).

Participants explained the bad scores for Tilt, DiscretePress and Peephole. For these combined modalities, several participants told us that they were too complicated for the simple task to be performed. Few of them said that in a real context usage, this perceived difficulty could prevent them to stay focused on the dataset.

- Tilt has been perceived as too sensitive. First in our implementation, we wanted to allow fast navigation without a large tilt angle and thus without reducing the screen visibility. However, some participants told us that the screen visibility while navigating was an issue. Second as explained above, participants tried to be as precise with this modality as with other modalities (e.g., FastDrag or DiscretePress) that allow more precise movements. Finally, we occasionally observed undesired tilt scrolling when the participants were performing touch gestures on screen.
- The DiscretePress modality has two problems according to participants. First and unlike DirectTouch, participants clearly expressed that there was a disorientation issue. They were not able to anticipate the position of the cursor after pressing a pressure sensor. This issue could be minimized and even disappear after a longer learning period. Secondly, depending on how participants were holding the device, they found it difficult to differentiate the light-click event from the strong-click event, or to trigger a strong-click event (Figure 8). Some participants suggested having a calibration step to allow them to choose their preferred levels of pressure.
- For the Peephole modality, almost all participants reported that the physical movements were too constraining and physically tiring. Moreover some participants explicitly mentioned the issue of the social acceptability of this spatial-input-based modality. Despite the fact that the Peephole modality is more commonly used with concave visualizations, and that bifocal view is a convex visualization, participants did not comment on this issue. Instead, they clearly identified the two metaphors: moving a lens on a ribbon (Peephole modality) and scrolling the ribbon (other modalities).

6. SUMMARY AND FUTURE WORK

With a bifocal view, tasks like moving an interesting data point into the focus area becomes difficult because of the large difference of scales between the context view and the focus view. Thus, interacting with a bifocal view requires both a fast access to data in the context view and high precision interaction with data in the detailed focus view. To address this issue, we have investigated a multimodal approach combining one modality for fast access to data with a precise modality for interacting in the focus view. We compared the combination of the well-known flick-drag technique (precise interaction in *focus* space) with six different modalities (fast access in *context* space). There are two main findings from the experimental study that can be used in designing combined modalities: (1) A task is decomposed into three distinct phases: a focus-targeting phase, a transition phase and a cursor-pointing phase. The observed navigation strategy is expressed by this 3-phase modeling of the entire task. (2) The articulatory switch between modalities less affects performance than the disorientation effect of some modalities caused by the loss of movement control.

As future work, the good performance and subjective preferences of the combined continuous modality based on pressure sensors incite us to further investigate this modality: fine-tuning the pressure-dependent control, study an automatic calibration phase according to how the user holds the device and study the position of the sensors to minimize the transition time between modalities.

Moreover we focus on interaction tasks only and more realistic reading or analysis tasks must be considered in further studies. To do so we plan to study the efficiency of the combined modalities for different types of tasks. Based on the taxonomy of Andrienko [1], we would like to consider synoptic tasks requiring us to explore the entire set of data: for instance find the maximum price of a company's stock. Another type of task can be the direct comparison between two distant data points. A general purpose combined modality for interacting with the bifocal view would ideally be efficient for all types of tasks.

7. REFERENCES

[1] Andrienko, N., Andrienko, G. *Exploratory Analysis of Spatial and Temporal Data: A Systematic Approach*. Springer, 2005.

[2] Appert, C., Chapuis, O., Pietriga, E. High-Precision Magnication Lenses. *In Proc. of CHI 2010*. ACM, 273-282.

[3] Appert, C., Fekete, J-D. OrthoZoom scroller: 1D multi-scale navigation. *In Proc. of CHI 2006*. ACM, 21-30.

[4] Baglioni, M., Malacria, S., Lecolinet, E., Guiard, Y. Flick-and-Brake: Finger Control over Inertial/Sustained Scroll Motion. *In Proc. of CHI EA 2011*. ACM, 2281-2286.

[5] Bederson, B. B., Clamage, A., Czerwinski, M. P., Robertson, G. G. (2004). DateLens: A Fisheye Calendar Interface for PDAs. *ACM TOCHI*, 11, 1 (2004), 90-119.

[6] Brooke, J. SUS: A Quick and Dirty Usability Scale. *In Usability Evaluation in Industry*, (1996). Taylor&Francis, 189-194.

[7] Burigat, S., Chittaro, L. On the effectiveness of Overview+Detail visualization on mobile devices. *Springer Journal PUC*, 17, 2 (2013), 371-385.

[8] Büring, T., Gerken, J., Reiterer, H. User Interaction with Scatterplots on Small Screens - A Comparative Evaluation of Geometric-Semantic Zoom and Fisheye Distortion. *IEEE TVCG*, 12, 5 (2006), 829-836.

[9] Chittaro, L. Visualizing Information on Mobile Devices. *IEEE Computer*, 39, 3 (2006), 40-45.

[10] Fitchett, S. Cockburn, A. Evaluating reading and analysis tasks on mobile devices: a case study of tilt and flick scrolling. *In Proc. of OZCHI 2009*. ACM, 225-232.

[11] Ganhör, R. Athmos: Focus+Context for Browsing in Mobile Thumbnail Collections. *In Proc. of ICMR 2014*. ACM, 65-72.

[12] Gutwin, C. Improving focus targeting in interactive fisheye views. *In Proc. of CHI 2002*. ACM, 267–274.

[13] Gutwin, C., Fedak, C. Interacting with big interfaces on small screens: a comparison of fisheye, zoom, and panning techniques. *In Proc. of GI 2004*. CHCCS, 145-152.

[14] Huot, S., Lecolinet, E. Focus+context visualization techniques for displaying large lists with multiple points of interest on small tactile screens. *In Proc. of INTERACT 2007*. Springer, 219-233.

[15] Igarashi, T., Hinckley, K. Speed-dependent automatic zooming for browsing large documents. *In Proc. of UIST 2000*. ACM, 139-148.

[16] Jakobsen R. M., Hornbæk K. Sizing up visualizations: effects of display size in focus+context, overview+detail, and zooming interfaces. *In Proc. of CHI 2011*. ACM, 1451-1460.

[17] Jul, S., Furnas, W. Critical zones in desert fog: aids to mutiscale navigation. *In Proc. of UIST 1998*. ACM, 97-106.

[18] Kincaid, R. SignalLens: Focus+Context Applied to Electronic Time Series. *IEEE TVCG*, 16, 6 (2010), 900-907.

[19] Kratz, K., Brodien, I., Rohs, M. Semi-automatic zooming for mobile map navigation. *In Proc. of MobileHCI 2010*. ACM, 63-72.

[20] Leung Y.K, Apperley M.D. A review and taxonomy of distortion-oriented presentation techniques. *ACM TOCHI*, 1, 2 (1994), 126-160.

[21] MacKenzie, I.S., Teather, R.R. FittsTilt: The application of Fitts' law to tilt-based interaction. *In Proc. of* NordiCHI 2012. ACM, 568-577.

[22] Mackinlay, J.D., Robertson, G.G., Card, S.K. The perspective wall: detail and context smoothly integrated. *In Proc. of CHI 1991*. ACM, 173-176.

[23] Pahud, M., Hinckley, K., Iqbal, S., Sellen, A., Buxton, B. Toward compound navigation tasks on mobiles via spatial manipulation. *In Proc. of MobileHCI 2013*. ACM, 113-122.

[24] Quinn, P., Malacria, S., Cockburn, A. Touch Scrolling Transfer Functions. *In Proc of UIST 2013*. ACM, 61-70.

[25] Robertson, G.G., Mackinlay, J.D. The document lens. *In Proc. of UIST 1993*. ACM, 101-108.

[26] Serrano, M., Nigay, L. Temporal Aspects of CARE-based Multimodal Fusion. *Proc. of ICMI 2009*. ACM. 177-184

[27] Spelmezan, D., Appert, C., Chapuis, O., Pietriga, E. Side Pressure for Bidirectional Navigation on Small Devices. *In Proc. of MobileHCI 2013*. ACM, 11-20.

[28] Spindler, M., Schuessler, M., Martsch, M., Dachselt, R. Pinch-drag-flick vs. spatial input: rethinking zoom & pan on mobile displays. *In Proc. of CHI 2014*. ACM, 1113-1122.

[29] Wang, Y-S., Chi, M-T. Focus+Context Metro Maps. *IEEE TVCG*, 17, 12 (2011), 2528-2535.

NaLMC - a Database on Non-acted and Acted Emotional Sequences in HCI

Kim Hartmann
Institute for Information Technology and Communications
Otto von Guericke University
Magdeburg, Germany
kim.hartmann@ovgu.de

Julia Krüger
University Clinic for Psychosomatic Medicine and Psychotherapy
Otto von Guericke University
Magdeburg, Germany
julia.krueger@med.ovgu.de

Jörg Frommer
University Clinic for Psychosomatic Medicine and Psychotherapy
Otto von Guericke University
Magdeburg, Germany
joerg.frommer@med.ovgu.de

Andreas Wendemuth
Institute for Information Technology and Communications
Otto von Guericke University
Magdeburg, Germany
andreas.wendemuth@ovgu.de

ABSTRACT

We report on the investigation on acted and non-acted emotional speech and the resulting Non-/acted LAST MINUTE corpus (NaLMC) database. The database consists of newly recorded acted emotional speech samples which were designed to allow the direct comparison of acted and non-acted emotional speech. The non-acted samples are taken from the LAST MINUTE corpus (LMC) [1]. Furthermore, emotional labels were added to selected passages of the LMC and a self-rating of the LMC recordings was performed. Although the main objective of the NaLMC database is to allow the comparative analysis of acted and non-acted emotional speech, both audio and video signals were recorded to allow multimodal investigations.

Categories and Subject Descriptors

H.1.2 [**User/Machine Systems**]: Human information processing; H.4 [**Information Systems Applications**]: Miscellaneous

Keywords

Human-computer interaction; Emotion recognition; Database design

1. INTRODUCTION

Within the past years, investigations on emotional speech have gained much attention by the human-computer interaction (HCI) research community. One of the leading research questions is how emotions in natural interactions can be detected automatically through vocal cues.

To investigate the characteristics of emotional speech, researchers refer to databases of recorded emotional material. This material is commonly divided into three groups:
1) acted emotional speech,
2) induced emotional speech or
3) non-acted spontaneous emotional speech.

The LAST MINUTE corpus (LMC) [1] is a corpus of non-acted spontaneous emotional speech. Within the LMC, emotional reactions were evoked through a "Wizard of Oz" set-up (cf. section 2) which allowed the recording of natural, spontaneous emotional human-computer interaction within a controlled environment.

Databases containing acted emotional speech have been preferred in the past to meet the recording requirements necessary for scientific investigations on emotional speech. This procedure allowed the acquisition of emotional samples of similar recording quality, as well as the certain assignment of emotional labels. However, acted material is often claimed to be unrealistic and not applicable to real-life scenarios. A number of difficulties are associated with the deriving of ground-truths primarily from acted emotional speech databases, cf. [2, 3]. Currently, a paradigm shift from acted to non-acted investigations is being discussed.

It is widely assumed that spontaneous non-acted and acted emotional speech may be distinguishable and hence have different acoustic profiles. An acoustic profile refers to the specific feature configuration presented during an audio sample. Emotion recognition research uses these specific feature configurations together with machine learning methods to identify the presented emotion.

It has been difficult to investigate the differences between acted and non-acted emotional speech due to a lack of available datasets. An investigation on this topic was performed by [4], who compare induced and acted emotions.

In order to investigate the differences between acted and non-acted emotional speech samples, a database is needed

ICMI 2015, November 9–13, 2015, Seattle, WA, USA.
© 2015 ACM. ISBN 978-1-4503-3912-4/15/11...$15.00
DOI: http://dx.doi.org/10.1145/2818346.2820772.

that contains both types of samples from the same speakers. In order to minimise influences, a set containing the same phrases both acted and non-acted is to be preferred. These considerations led to the construction of the NaLMC database, a database of emotional speech that allows the comparison of acted and non-acted speech samples.

The NaLMC database was constructed as an add-on to the LMC recordings, where the LMC provided the non-acted speech samples. A post hoc study with a subset of LMC participants was conducted in order to collect matching acted emotional speech to the existing non-acted LMC samples. In the following, the post hoc study and the resulting NaLMC database are described.

2. THE LAST MINUTE CORPUS

The LMC [1] provides multimodal data of naturalistic HCI collected during a widely standardized Wizard of Oz experiment. Therein, participants interacted with a simulated speech-based dialogue system. The system asked the participants for personal information and recent emotional experiences ("personalisation module"). Afterwards, the participants had to solve a mundane planning task ("last minute module") considering different constraints during the solution process (so-called barriers). The participants were asked to imagine that it is summer and they had to pack a suitcase for a spontaneous holiday trip with the help of a computer system. The participants were given 12 different categories to choose items from (e.g. sandals from the category "footwear", anorak from "Jackets and coats") and were not given all details about the trip destination. The task had to be completed within 15 minutes. During the packing process three standardized barriers occurred to obtain emotional utterances.

The LAST MINUTE corpus comprises data from 130 participants, who are balanced with regard to gender, age (young (y): 18-28 years and elderly (e): above 60 years) and educational level ("educated group" with German high school diploma and "less educated" group with a lower qualification). The multimodal recordings gathered during the Wizard of Oz experiment comprise video and audio records as well as psycho-biological data.

3. THE NALMC STUDY

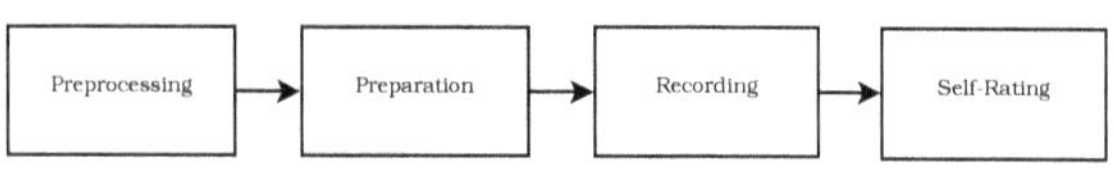

Figure 1: Overview of the NaLMC investigation phases

The post-hoc LMC investigation "Non-/acted Last Minute Corpus" (NaLMC) was performed at Otto von Guericke University Magdeburg, Germany. The investigation was structured into four phases (preprocessing, preparation, recording and self-rating) which were carried out throughout the year 2014, cf. fig. 1. Each phase had different goals contributing to the research aim of investigating feature specific differences in acted and non-acted spontaneous emotional speech.

3.1 Preprocessing Phase

Within the preprocessing phase appropriate participants for the NaLMC investigation were selected from the LMC.

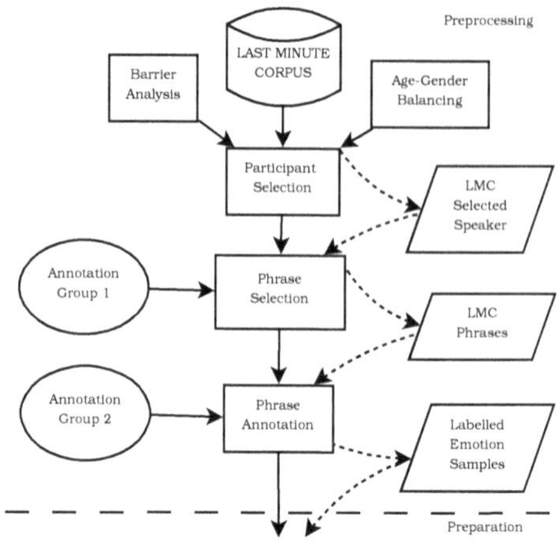

Figure 2: Overview NaLMC preprocessing phase

Furthermore, emotional sequences in the LMC audio records were identified and labelled. Fig. 2 provides a brief overview of the stages of the preprocessing phase, data dependencies and involved entities.

The participant selection was based on the results of the LMC barrier analysis, quality of the available audio material and availability of the participants. A balanced group with respect to age/gender was desired.

Following the participant selection, the phrase selection phase was initiated. Within this phase the LMC audio recordings of possible participants were annotated manually in two stages. Within the first stage ("Phrase Selection") emotional passages fulfilling the NaLMC phrase conditions were selected. These selected passages were labelled in the second stage ("Labelling"). The two stages were performed by two different annotation groups.

LMC passages to be marked as relevant for the NaLMC ("NaLMC phrase conditions") had to contain emotional utterances, have a minimal duration of 1 second and a maximal duration of 60 seconds. The passages must contain phrases and should not contain discourse particles ("ehm", "eh", "mh" and so on, [5]) or interferences with the speech signal (coughing, stumbling, wizard talking). Additionally, the lexical content should be as neutral as possible. These restrictions were made to obtain phrases that could be repeated easily to display different emotions by the NaLMC participants. Examples of such LMC passages are "Ein Paar Socken einpacken" ("Pack one pair of socks"), "Weiter bitte" ("Please continue") or even short statements as "Ja"/"Nein" ("Yes"/"No").

The identification of emotional passages in the LMC recordings was performed by the annotation group 1 consisting of four female annotators. The labels were binary ("emotional"/"no label"). The LMC datasets were distributed among the annotators in such a way that each dataset was annotated by at least two annotators.

The emotional phrases obtained by annotation group 1 were further evaluated to obtain an emotional label by annotation group 2 (16 annotators). Only passages labelled as "emotional" by at least two annotators of group 1 were selected for further processing. The selected passages were distributed equally among the annotation group 2.

The annotators were asked to label the audio samples using the ikannotate tool ([6, 7]). The tool offered two annotation schemes. A first approximation of the emotion per-

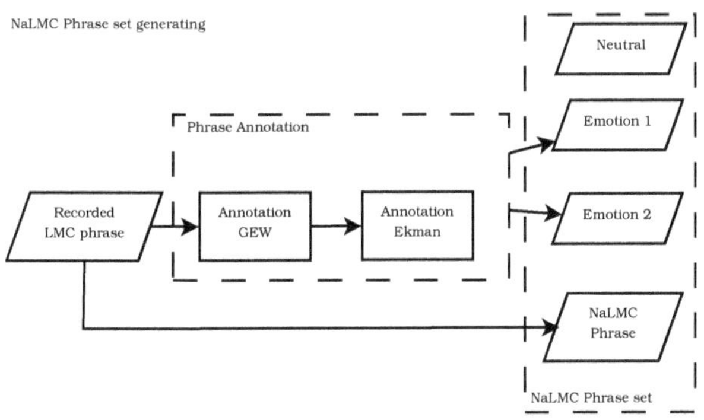

Figure 3: NaLMC phrase sets consist of LMC phrases and emotion labels determined through the annotation process.

ceived was determined with Ekman's basic emotion categories (anger, disgust, fear, joy, sadness, and surprise) ([8]).

The second annotation was performed using the Geneva Emotion Wheel (GEW), cf. [9].

3.2 Preparation Phase

The preprocessing phase identified, selected and labelled LMC recordings of spontaneous, non-acted emotional speech. The goal of the preparation phase is to prepare the selected phrases and labels to allow the investigation of similarities and differences between acted and non-acted emotional speech. The preparation phase connects the preprocessing phase with the recording phase.

Each emotional speech signal carries information on the acoustic, prosodic and lexical level. In order to minimise the effects of lexical variations on emotional speech, the NaLMC investigation decided to invite the speakers of each emotionally labelled phrase to present exactly the identified phrase(s) in different emotional colours. Hence, a phrase set was designed for each speaker, containing textual phrases the participant spoke during the LMC recordings and emotional labels associated with these phrases. The associated emotional labels were determined through the annotation process during the preprocessing phase, cf. fig. 3.

All phrases recorded in the NaLMC recording phase were asked to be acted in two different emotions (plus "neutral"). The emotions were selected based on the annotation results.

3.3 Recording Phase

The participants were informed that the experiment consisted of two parts: One part in which the participants will be given phrases and asked to present these in certain emotions and the second part where the participants will be given auditive samples of emotional speech and asked to determine the emotions presented.

At this stage, the participant was not informed that the audio samples given in part two were taken from his/her LMC recordings. Generally, the participants were not aware of the connection between the current recordings of acted emotional speech and the previous LMC recordings.

The participants were given the opportunity to test the recording situation prior to the real recordings. Recordings of these test phrases exist for the majority of participants but have not been processed further. Help was given if demanded by the participants according to an instruction manual developed prior to the recording phase. A transcript of the instructions provided is available from the corresponding authors. The instructions were designed to not give any concrete descriptions of emotional speech.

The participants were situated in a living-room styled room outside of the laboratory. The instructor and at least one further person monitored the recordings from the laboratory. Structured protocols of the recordings exist.

When the participant had finished all phrase sets the instructor returned to the room. The participant was asked for feedback on the task and questioned whether he/she would like to repeat any of the phrases. If any abnormalities occurred during the recording (grammatical restructuring of phrases, technical abnormalities, high noise exposure) the participant was asked to repeat the affected phrases.

3.4 Self-rating

The self-rating phase is initiated through the termination of the recording phase and the task is introduced by extending the previously given information. Until this part of the experiment, the participants were not aware of the connection between the NaLMC and the LMC recordings.

The participants were enlightened regarding the aim and design of the previously performed recordings and were told that the audio data provided for the self-rating phase was obtained from their own LMC recordings. Special emphasis was laid on the fact that the given self-rating audio files were not taken from the recorded acted emotional speech samples. The participants were given the option to refuse the self-rating, which none of the participants did.

The self-rating is performed by the NaLMC participants with the GEW scheme [9] using the ikannotate-tool [6]. The participants were recorded during the self-rating and were given the option to provide additional vocal explanations of the self-rating.

4. THE NALMC DATABASE

During the NaLMC study, audio and video data was collected. Additionally, a screenrecorder was installed. All recordings of the NaLMC were performed with the same hardware set-up and environment conditions.

The audio material was recorded through two directional microphones (Sennheiser ME66) and one wireless headset (t-bone earmic 500). All three audio signals were recorded monaural at 44100 Hz, 16 Bit resolution.

Video material was obtained using one HD camera (Pike F145C), 1388x1038 px at 25 fps, and two stereo cameras (Bumblebee2 BB2-03S2C), 1280x480 px at 25 fps.

The room was observed using a webcam. During the recording the investigator used a wireless headset (t-bone earmic 500) to communicate with the participant.

In a post-processing step the NaLMC phrases were labelled manually according to the phrases spoken and the number of repetitions. Each phrase was stored separately as .wav-file following the naming scheme: `abbrevation_#`, where `#` stands for the number of repetition.

Additionally, a continuous audio- and video-signal of both the recording and self-rating phase exist. The results obtained through the annotation tool during the self-rating phase are stored per participant and trial. The phrase sets are also stored per participant as PDF files.

An overview of the number of participants and recorded material is given in table 1. Overall 21 participants took part in the NaLMC recordings. One participant from the groups "female" and "young" withdrew her declaration of consent due to private reasons. The material of this participant is not available but listed for the sake of completeness.

	Recorded	Available
Number of participants	21	20
Distribution of gender (m/f)	10/11	10/10
Distribution of age (o/y)	12/9	12/8
Number of files	484	459
Recording length (minutes)	2205*	2100*
Modalities	A/V/Scr	A/V/Scr

Table 1: Overview of the NaLMC database prior to the post-processing of the recorded material. The recorded audio/video signals are counted as one file per device. Abbrevations: A - Audio, V - Video, Scr - Screenrecorder. *Approximated length in min.

A total of 2834 phrases have been recorded within the NaLMC investigation. For the majority of phrases, more than one attempt exists per participant. From the preprocessing phase a total of 240 labelled LMC phrases exist, using both Ekman's basic emotion and the GEW annotation scheme. The NaLMC participants produced 39 text files containing the self-rating of the participants' LMC phrases.

An overview of the available documentation material is given in table 2. The listed documentation contains both material used for the set-up and design of the NaLMC recording environment as well as documentation material from the recordings. The latter is participant specific while e.g. the technical set-up was uniform throughout the recordings.

	Initial	Available
Technical set-up	1	1
Room/Technical check-list	21	20
Recording protocol	21	20
Health questionnaire	21	20
Instructor manual	1	1
Self-rating sheet*	1	1
Declaration of consent	21	20

Table 2: Available NaLMC documentation material. *Sheet with official GEW term translations [10].

4.1 Availability

The NaLMC database is available upon written request to the corresponding author. Separate requests for the preprocessed LMC sequences are to be made according to the specifications made in [1].

5. CONCLUSION AND OUTLOOK

The described investigation and the resulting database "Non-/acted LAST MINUTE corpus" (NaLMC) allow a direct comparison of acted and non-acted emotional sequences. Due to the design of the NaLMC study, the newly recorded material is unlikely to contain any technical side-effects not present in the LMC recordings. Lexical differences have been eliminated due to the use of transcripts of the previously recorded spontaneous, non-acted LMC phrases. Hence, variances observed in the NaLMC recordings are unlikely to be due to lexical or technical effects, but may rather be strongly related to potential differences in acted and non-acted spontaneous emotional reactions.

This construction is unique in the HCI community and allows further investigations on open research questions from the area of emotion detection and assessment. The NaLMC database especially provides material that will assist researchers investigating the differences of acted and non-acted emotion expressions in HCI.

Acknowledgments

We would like to thank our colleagues Ralph Heinemann and Michael Tornow for their technical support throughout the investigation. This research was supported by the German National Academic Foundation and the Transregional Collaborative Research Centre SFB/TRR 62 "Companion-Technology for Cognitive Technical Systems" funded by the German Research Foundation (DFG).

6. REFERENCES

[1] D. Rösner, J. Frommer, R. Friesen, M. Haase, J. Lange, and M. Otto. LAST MINUTE: a multimodal corpus of speech-based user-companion interactions. In *LREC*, pages 2559–2566, 2012.

[2] Klaus R. Scherer. Vocal communication of emotion: A review of research paradigms. *Speech Communication*, 40:227–256, 2003.

[3] Nick Campbell. Databases of emotional speech. *ISCA Workshop on Speech and Emotions, Newcastle, North Ireland*, pages 34–38, 2000.

[4] Klaus R. Scherer. Vocal markers of emotion: Comparing induction and acting elicitation. *Computer Speech and Language*, 27:40–58, 2013.

[5] Francis Quek, David McNeill, Robert Bryll, Susan Duncan, Xin-Feng Ma, Cemil Kirbas, Karl E. McCullough, and Rashid Ansari. Multimodal human discourse: gesture and speech, 2002.

[6] Ronald Böck, Ingo Siegert, Matthias Haase, Julia Lange, and Andreas Wendemuth. ikannotate - a tool for labelling, transcription, and annotation of emotionally coloured speech. In Sidney D'Mello, Arthur Graesser, Björn Schuller, and Jean-Claude Martin, editors, *Affective Computing and Intelligent Interaction.*, volume 6974 of *Lecture Notes in Computer Science*, pages 25–34. Springer Berlin, Heidelberg, 2011.

[7] Ronald Böck, Ingo Siegert, Bogdan Vlasenko, Andreas Wendemuth, Matthias Haase, and Julia Lange. A processing tool for emotionally coloured speech. In *Proceedings of the 2011 IEEE International Conference on Multimedia & Expo*, Barcelona, Spain, July 11-15 2011. IEEE.

[8] Disa A Sauter, Frank Eisner, Paul Ekman, and Sophie K Scott. Cross-cultural recognition of basic emotions through nonverbal emotional vocalizations. *Proceedings of the National Academy of Sciences of the United States of America*, 107:2408–2412, 2010.

[9] Klaus R. Scherer. What are emotions? And how can they be measured? *Social Science Information*, 44(4):695–729, 2005.

[10] K. R. Scherer, editor. *Facets of emotion: Recent research*, chapter Appendix F. Hillsdale, NJ: Erlbaum, 1988. ISBN: 978-0805801422.

Exploiting Multimodal Affect and Semantics to Identify Politically Persuasive Web Videos

Behjat Siddiquie
behjat.siddiquie@sri.com
SRI International

Dave Chisholm
davec@cs.columbia.edu
Columbia University

Ajay Divakaran
ajay.divakaran@sri.com
SRI International

ABSTRACT

We introduce the task of automatically classifying politically persuasive web videos and propose a highly effective multi-modal approach for this task. We extract audio, visual, and textual features that attempt to capture affect and semantics in the audio-visual content and sentiment in the viewers' comments. We demonstrate that each of the feature modalities can be used to classify politically persuasive content, and that fusing them leads to the best performance. We also perform experiments to examine human accuracy and inter-coder reliability for this task and show that our best automatic classifier slightly outperforms average human performance. Finally we show that politically persuasive videos generate more strongly negative viewer comments than non-persuasive videos and analyze how affective content can be used to predict viewer reactions.

Categories and Subject Descriptors

H.3.3 [[**Information Search and Retrieval**]: Search process; I.2.10 [**Vision and Scene Understanding**]: Video analysis

General Terms

Algorithms; Design; Experimentation

Keywords

Video Classification; Affect Recognition; Audio Concepts; Video Concepts; Sentiment Analysis; Multimodal Fusion

1. INTRODUCTION

In the last few years social media has rapidly emerged as an effective means to disseminate information to a large and geographically diverse audience. Its low barrier of entry allows not just well funded organizations but also individuals to share and propagate their opinions and viewpoints. Multimedia content in particular can both express and evoke strong emotional responses, and there is reason to believe that audio-visual content can affect viewers more strongly than text based content [16]. Viewer reactions are also visible in the form of comments, and so in this way social media allows content creators and uploaders to spread a strong, compelling message and observe its impact.

For these reasons, multimedia content on social networks is particularly suitable to propagate political views, and it is used for public influence, political persuasion and even radicalization [10]. It is thus a potent tool to influence and attract new followers, and there is great interest in many sectors in detecting and assessing politically charged or otherwise persuasive social media content.

In this paper, we propose a solution to detect such politically persuasive videos posted on social media and also develop methods to predict and analyze the sentiment of comment responses. In order to analyze the audio-visual content present in the videos we focus on robust extraction of the semantic and affective information. For the audio domain we detect several grades of speech arousal and related semantic categories such as crowd reaction and music. For the visual domain, we detect visual sentiment and semantic content. Finally we analyze the sentiment of comments associated with a video to determine viewer reaction. Our classification results indicate that politically persuasive videos posted online can be reliably detected based on extracted affective and semantic information. Furthermore, we show that politically persuasive videos often generate more negative reactions among viewers and the overall sentiment of reactions can be predicted with a reasonable degree of success solely from audio-visual features. Figure 1 shows an overview of our approach.

There are two **key contributions** of our work:

- We demonstrate that affective and semantic information extracted from the audio, visual and textual content associated with a video can be used to predict whether the video is of a politically persuasive nature.
- We further show that politically persuasive videos generate more negative reactions in comments, that affective content can indicate how viewers may react, and that viewer reaction to semantically similar videos varies with respect to the videos' affective content.

We would like to emphasize that the goal of our work is to demonstrate the utility of multi-modal affective features to reliably identify politically persuasive media content, rather than to develop sophisticated or novel content understanding techniques. In particular, we show that an approach leveraging these affective and semantic features can generally classify such videos as well or better than humans. We

ICMI 2015, November 9–13, 2015, Seattle, WA, USA.
© 2015 ACM. ISBN 978-1-4503-3912-4/15/11 ...$15.00.
DOI: http://dx.doi.org/10.1145/2818346.2820732.

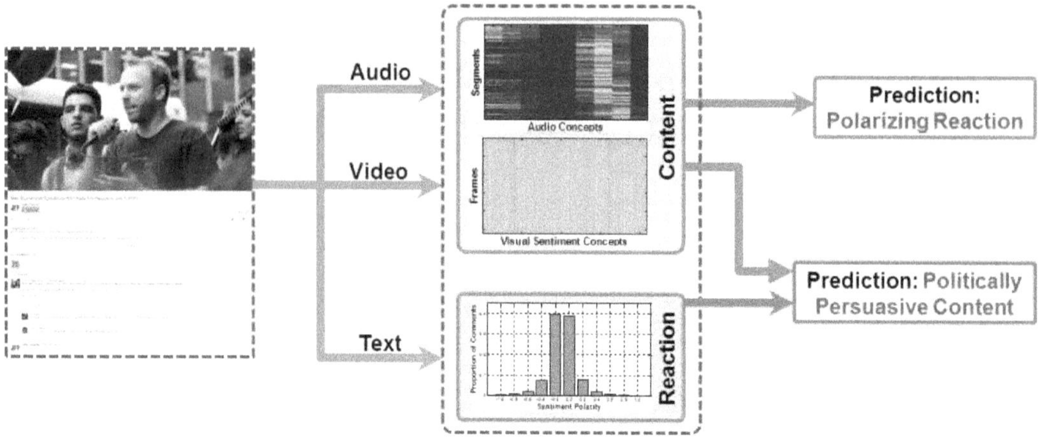

Figure 1: Audio and visual concept scores and features are computed from the audio-visual data of a web video. These scores are used to predict whether the video is politically persuasive and whether the comments in response will be highly polarized. In addition, the actual comments are also used to predict whether a video is politically persuasive, and all three modalities are fused for the best prediction results. In this example our system correctly predicts the video is both politically persuasive and likely to have polarized comments based solely on audio-visual content. (*https://www.youtube.com/watch?v=gDpcsx2CL9E*)

believe that our work opens up an exciting new area of research with a number of interesting applications.

2. RELATED WORK

There has been some recent work on detecting persuasion. Park et al. collected and annotated a corpus of movie review videos in [31]. From this data, they demonstrated that the verbal and non-verbal behavior of the presenter is predictive of how persuasive they are as well as predictive of the cooperative nature of a dyadic interaction. Our work differs from this in three key ways. First and foremost, while that prior work attempts to predict whether a particular sample will persuade a viewer (e.g. "is this persuasive") we attempt to classify whether a video contains a particular type of persuasive content (e.g. "does this video contain fiery political rhetoric"). Secondly, we rely not only on the affective characteristics of a speaker, but also on the affective characteristics of viewers' reactions as well as semantic content unrelated to a main speaker (e.g. crowd reaction, background music). Finally, we analyze a corpus that is collected from a variety of unscripted situations recorded both indoors and outdoors and whose audio-visual quality ranges from good to poor, whereas the corpus in [31] consists of data captured in controlled environments.

Detection of radical online content is a growing research area due to the interest shown in it by law enforcement agencies; Correa presented a survey of such work in [10]. This detection is typically done in two ways: by analysis of the network structure or by analysis of the content itself. Reid et al. presented an network based approach in [32] that capitalized on the notion that websites that promote the same ideology tend to be interconnected by hyperlinks. Most approaches that analyze content, such as the one presented by Abbasi in [1], tend to focus on the textual and linguistic content of websites rather than audio-visual content of videos. To the best of our knowledge, Fu et al. presented the only published work on detecting extremist videos in [14], and their approach used the meta-data associated with the video rather than the actual audio-visual content. In contrast to these works, our approach is independent of any network structure and exploits the audio-visual content itself as well as comments in reaction to it. Moreover, our target class of politically persuasive videos is broader than Fu et al.'s class of extremist videos.

There has been some work on sentiment analysis of visual content. This includes analysis of image aesthetics [20], analysis of image interestingness and memorability [17] and analysis of image affect and emotion [28]. There has also been work on detecting visual sentiment expressed through human behavior - *e.g.* facial expressions [37] - as well as work on detecting image style [22]. We rely directly on two prior works for visual content analysis. First, we use Jia et al.'s CAFFE implementation from [18] which was trained on concepts presented as part of ImageNet in [12]. Second, we also use the Visual Sentiment Ontology presented in [5], which consists of a large-scale ontology of semantic concepts correlated with strong sentiments.

Detecting affect from human speech has grown in importance because of its applications in enabling realistic human interactions [27, 33]. However, most of the work in this area has been demonstrated on datasets collected in controlled environments with little noise. Similarly detecting semantic concepts in audio has long been an important problem in the audio processing community due to its applications in video retrieval [26, 6, 7]. Our audio concept detection, based on [9] combines the best of both these approaches.

Sentiment analysis and opinion mining from text have long been active research topics with varied applications such as analyzing product reviews, improving question answering systems, and mining political opinions. This area is well covered by Pang and Lee's survey in [30]. Recent work, such as Socher et al.'s approach in [35], has improved the accuracy of text based sentiment analysis significantly. There has also been recent work focusing exclusively on text in social media settings, such as Mohammad et al.'s sentiment analysis of Twitter data in [29]. We employ both of these recent approaches to analyze and gauge user reactions and opinions to videos in the form of comments.

There has also been work on combining information from multiple modalities to better detect affect [21, 3]. The key advantage of multimodal affect detection is that different modalities contain complementary information and therefore fusing the information from them can lead to performance improvements in detecting affect. We also adopt a multimodal fusion approach to detect persuasive videos, and fuse not only modalities based on audio-visual content (e.g. speech characteristics, crowd response, visual semantics) but also on viewer response (e.g. sentiment of user comments).

3. DATASET AND CLASSIFICATION TASK

For our experiments we use the *Rallying a Crowd* (RAC) dataset, introduced in [9]. The RAC dataset consists of 230 videos from YouTube comprising over 27 hours of content. The dataset contains 132 positive and 98 negative examples of politically persuasive videos. Positive videos contain a speaker vehemently rallying/persuading a crowd for political causes. Negative videos also contain speakers and crowds but lack political themes. Qualitatively, positive examples are often events such as political rallies or protests. Negative examples contain semantically similar content - e.g. speakers addressing crowds - but lack the highly affected, politically persuasive nature of the positive examples, and are often events such as presentations or entertainment events.

Thus the classification task for these videos is neither one of determining speaker valence nor whether a viewer is actually persuaded, but instead is a binary classification problem of determining whether politically charged videos can be distinguished from videos with ostensibly similar audio-visual content but lacking political content and vehemence. The videos in the dataset were recorded under a wide variety of conditions (e.g. outdoor vs. indoor, near vs. far) with various levels of post-production (e.g. professional quality clips vs. unedited amateur footage) and include samples with multiple languages and settings.

3.1 Annotation and Human Accuracy

To quantify the difficulty of classifying politically charged content and validate it as a legitimate identifiable class we had four human annotators perform binary labeling of positive and negative RAC videos. This also allows us to compare the performance of our automatic approach to human performance. Ground truth was established by using particular search terms and establish a consensus decision for each video among all the authors. We had four annotators first view a "control" portion of the RAC dataset consisting of 52 positive and 40 negative videos to form an opinion of what constituted politically persuasive content. Each annotator then chose a binary label for each of the remaining 80 positive and 58 negative videos. These 138 videos were the same portion used in the binary classification experiments for automatic classifiers as detailed below.

The four annotators had accuracies of 71.0%, 74.6%, 75.4% and 100.0% ($p < 0.001$ for each) and improvements over chance (I_{oc}) of 31.0%, 39.6%, 41.5% and 100%. I_{oc} represents how many fewer errors an annotator is expected to have versus a chance annotation and is defined as $(A_o - A_e)/(1 - A_e)$, where A_e is expected accuracy by chance. We attribute the perfect performance of the the fourth annotator to the extra diligence and time this annotator took compared to the others, and feel it supports the validity of the ground truth. An inter-coder agreement coefficient of 0.524, indicating "moderate agreement", was measured among all annotators using Fleiss's kappa [13, 24]. Inter-coder agreement between all possible pairs of annotators was also measured using Scott's pi and varied from 0.396 ("fair agreement") to 0.658 ("substantial agreement") [34, 24]. We feel the overall classification success, improvements over chance and annotator agreement validate the class of "politically persuasive" videos as coherent and classifiable.

4. EXPERIMENTS

4.1 Experimental Setup

The same setup involving 138 videos (80 positive, 58 negative) was used for each automatic classification experiment. In order to ensure that any results were not influenced by the larger size of the positive class and to ensure that a random classifier would have a classification accuracy of 50%, we randomly sample 58 positive videos from the group of 80 to create a set of 116 videos with an equal number of positive and negative samples. We then classify these 116 videos using 10-fold cross-validation. This random sampling was performed 25 times for each of the modalities listed below, and final results displayed represent the mean and standard deviation of the accuracy over 25 such randomized runs of 10-fold cross validation. For each modality, an RBF SVM classifier was used to perform the final binary classification task. Details on preprocessing and extraction for each modality follow.

4.2 Classification via Audio Analysis

We first investigated the use of the audio content in the videos to distinguish between persuasive and non-persuasive videos. Politically persuasive videos are often characterized by animated speakers, charged content, crowd response and occasional music. Hence, detecting these audio categories would enable us to identify persuasive videos. In order to do so, we use the audio concept detection approach of [9], which we briefly describe in Section 4.2.1.

4.2.1 Audio Concept Detection

Following the work of [9], we detect the following audio concepts: *Crowd*, *Music + Crowd*, *Music*, *Music + Speech*, *Crowd + Speech*, *Calm Speech*, *Slightly Agitated Speech*, *Agitated Speech*, *Very Agitated Speech*. To do so, we first extract a low level feature vector (either prosody, MFCC, or spectrogram based) for each frame of audio using a sliding window approach. Since a single concept label will very rarely apply to an entire audio track, we apply an algorithm based on the unsupervised Simple Linear Iterative Clustering (SLIC) algorithm for image segmentation [2]. The algorithm was adapted for audio and temporally segments the track into a set of homogenous segments likely to contain a single concept. The approach has been shown to work well for semantic concepts on the CCV dataset [19] as well as for affective concepts on the RAC dataset. The low level features for each segment are then encoded into a bag-of-words representation and used to train a non-linear SVM for concept detection. Note that these concept detectors are trained and tested on a disjoint "control" portion the RAC dataset comprised of 52 positive and 40 negative samples. No video was used to create both the concept detectors and the classifiers.

4.2.2 Binary Classifier Setup

Given a set of n videos $\mathcal{V} = \{V_1, V_2, V_3, \ldots, V_n\}$ and their corresponding binary labels $\{y_1, y_2, y_3, \ldots, y_n\}$ that indicate whether the video contains persuasive content, we trained a politically persuasive versus non-persuasive classifier as follows. For each video V_i, we segment the audio and then compute the concept scores as described above. We denote the audio concept scores for video V_i as O_i, where i denotes the video index. The dimensionality of an audio concept score O_i is $T \times C$, where T is the number of segments (dependent on the length of the video and segmentation behavior) and C is the number of audio concepts (fixed at 9). We quantize O_i by linearly resizing it to $T_{fixed} \times C$, where $T_{fixed} = 100$, to obtain $\bar{O}_i$. Now corresponding to each video V_i we have a fixed dimensional feature $\bar{O}_i$. We train an RBF SVM on this data for classification.

This process was performed separately for each of the three low level features (prosody, MFCC, or spectrogram) and the results for each are shown below. Additionally, the three feature types were combined using a Multiple Kernel Learning (MKL) approach [4]. The process was also repeated for using three different temporal scales for the SLIC segmentation algorithm, but very little performance difference was observed between them. The results shown below correspond to a medium scale segmentation.

4.2.3 Results

Following the experimental setup detailed in 4.1, we achieve the results shown below in Table 1. The results indicate that using audio features one can perform reasonably well at detecting persuasive content, and that the spectrogram feature performed best among the possible low level feature types.

Audio Concept Features	Classification Accuracy
Prosody	77.82 ± 12.79
MFCC	73.64 ± 12.17
Spectrogram	81.03 ± 11.93
All Features (MKL)	78.65 ± 11.76

Table 1: SVM classification performance using the audio concept detection features. The margins represent the standard deviations across 25 randomized runs.

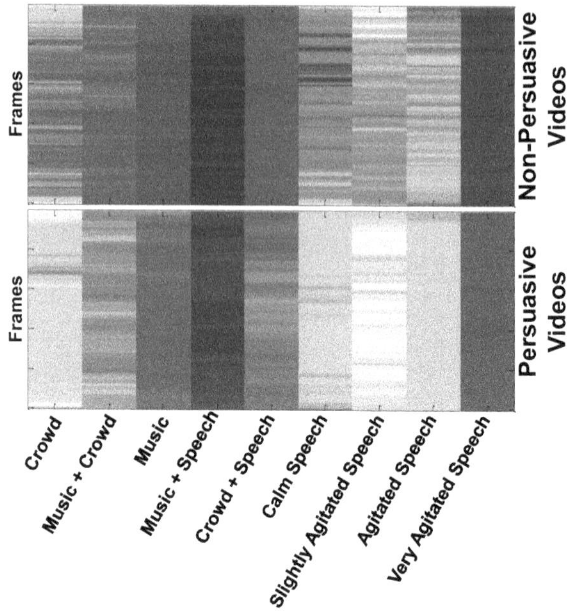

Figure 2: Mean concept detection scores for positive and negative videos. Notice that positive videos tend to have a higher scores for *crowd* and *agitated speech*, while negative videos have higher scores for *calm speech* and *slightly agitated speech*. (Best viewed in color - red/yellow indicate higher scores and blue indicates lower scores.)

4.2.4 Analysis of Results

In order to better understand what the classifiers were learning for distinguishing between the persuasive and non-persuasive videos, we looked at the mean features $\bar{O}_i$ from the persuasive and non-persuasive videos (Figure 2). The figures show that persuasive videos contain a stronger response for *crowd* and *agitated speech*. On the other hand, non-persuasive videos contain a stronger response for *calm speech* and *slightly agitated speech*. Considering the charged content and oratory of many of the persuasive videos, this matched our intuition of how the content would be distributed. Finally, we believe that the concept scores computed from the spectrogram features lead to the best results because they detect the relevant concepts such as *crowd* and *agitated speech* more accurately compared to other features leading to superior results on the classification task.

4.3 Video Analysis

In this subsection, we investigate the use of concepts based on visual content that could be used to differentiate between persuasive and non-persuasive videos. Persuasive videos from the RAC dataset often contain rousing visuals ranging from cheering crowds and heroic figures to images of graphic violence. Overall, the visuals are more striking and extreme than the non-persuasive content, and hence visual features may be useful to identify persuasive content. We primarily focus on deep learning based features that identify semantic concepts and sentiment. Recently deep learning models such as Convolutional Neural Networks (CNNs) have become extremely popular for learning image representations [23]. CNNs, loosely inspired by human vision, are variants of multilayer perceptrons consisting of multiple convolutional and pooling layers followed by fully connected layers [25]. In our work, we implemented a standard network [23] using the popular open source framework CAFFE [18] to extract visual features. We trained two different networks using different datasets. The first network was trained on the ImageNet dataset [12] and the second was trained on the Visual Sentiment Ontology dataset [5]. We next describe each of these processes along with the obtained experimental results.

4.3.1 ImageNet Concepts

In this case, we want to evaluate whether the presence or absence of certain semantic concepts in the video indicates the presence of persuasive content. In order to estimate the presence or absence of concepts in an image we use the CNN trained on the ILSVRC-2012 dataset which is a subset of ImageNet, consisting of around 1.2 million images labeled with 1000 different classes ranging from elephant to space shuttle to stethoscope. The network was trained to maximize the multinomial logistic regression objective for these classes over the training data. We use this 1000 dimensional output as a feature indicating the presence or absence of each class. We also use the outputs of intermediate network layers - which represent more abstract visual features than the final concept outputs and can often provide high classification performance - as features. These three features are referred to as "prob", "fc7" and "fc8" respectively. We extract each of these features from every 30th frame (1 sec.) of the video. As in case of the audio data we now have a vector of dimension F x D (where F is the number of frames sampled) and D is the dimensionality (1000 in case of the prob and 4096 in case of "fc7" and "fc8"). Since F varies based on the length of the video, we linearly resize our feature vector to $F_{fixed} \times D$, where $F_{fixed} = 100$, much like was done for audio in section 4.2.2. Each of the three features were provided individually to an RBF SVM based classifier, and all features were also combined by concatenation. We follow the same experimental protocol as in the earlier experiments described in section 4.2.3. The results are shown in Table 2.

Features	Classification Accuracy
prob	68.52 ± 3.62
fc8	67.61 ± 3.97
fc7	69.62 ± 4.48
All Features	71.81 ± 5.37

Table 2: Classification performance using different features extracted from the CNN network trained on ILSVRC-2012 dataset [12] for recognizing object categories. "prob" refers to the final concept output scores, whereas "fc7" and "fc8" are scores for features from intermediate layers of the CNN.

Classification using each of the features significantly outperforms chance ($p < 0.001$ for each), indicating that visual information is indeed useful for detecting persuasive content. We can also see that the features from the "fc7" layer - which contain more abstract, learned features - outperform the features from the "fc8" and "prob" layers indicating the utility of these over the more specific final concepts. Finally, we can also see that combining the features from all of the layers results in a modest improvement in the performance.

4.3.2 *Visual Sentiment Ontology Concepts*

In this case, we want to evaluate whether the presence or absence of certain visual sentiment concepts in a video can provide information on whether the video contains persuasive content. In order to evaluate this we use the Visual Sentiment Ontology dataset [5] which consists of approximately 930k images. This dataset was collected by searching Flickr for Adjective-Noun-Pairs (ANPs) such as "beautiful flower" or "disgusting food". The advantage of using these ANPs is that they relate particular images of sentiment neutral nouns (e.g "flower") to a strong sentiment by adding an adjective (e.g. "beautiful flower"). Thus the concepts capture both semantic and sentiment information. We used the latest version of Visual Sentiment Ontology DeepSentiBank [8] which consists of CNN based concept detectors for 2089 ANPs. These concept detectors are trained using the same deep learning network [23] described above. As in the earlier case, we use the final "prob" outputs as well as the intermediate layer outputs "fc7" and "fc8" as inputs to our classifier. The results are shown in table 3. Here again we can see that the intermediate layers "fc7" and "fc8" perform better than the final outputs ("prob"). The performance of the SentiBank concepts is slightly better than the performance of the ImageNet concepts, which could be due to use of sentiment in the concepts, or just due to the higher number of concepts present in the SentiBank dataset. Finally, we also looked at combining the features from the ImageNet concepts and the SentiBank concepts, but this did not lead to any meaningful increase in performance.

Features	Classification Accuracy
prob	68.46 ± 3.61
fc8	72.40 ± 2.76
fc7	73.95 ± 2.95
All Features	73.13 ± 3.01

Table 3: Classification performance using different features extracted from the CNN network trained on the Visual Sentiment Ontology dataset [5] for recognizing visual sentiment.

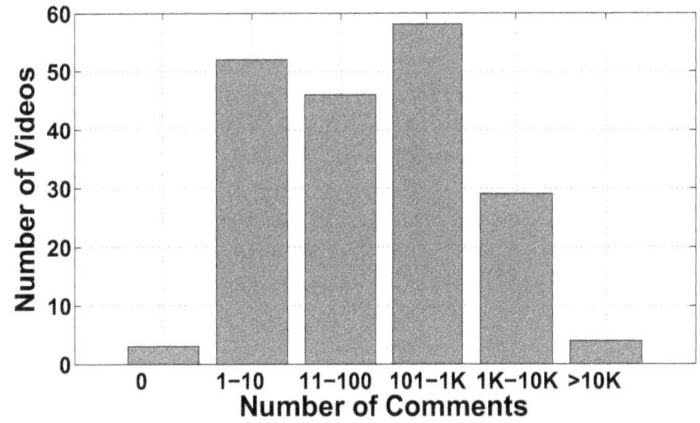

Figure 3: The distribution of the number of comments across the videos in the dataset.

4.3.3 *Analysis of Results*

Ideally, highly scored concepts in positive videos could be used to explain why a video was classified as politically persuasive. In practice we noted a mix of accurate and relevant concepts (e.g. "bad guy" in a violent video) along with concepts that seemed irrelevant. Moreover, we noted that the classification was more accurate using intermediate features than the high level concepts. Thus while the visual concepts are effective for classification, in order to explain classification, a more specific set of visual concepts would need to be used, or detection would need to be improved.

4.4 Text Analysis

We also investigated the use of text associated with the videos, in particular viewer comments. Videos uploaded to YouTube and other video-sharing sites often generate a large number of comments posted by viewers across the world, and many of these comments contain reactions of people to the videos. Intuitively comments generated in response to politically persuasive videos should be of a more polarized nature while other videos generate comments of a more neutral or positive nature. Therefore, exploiting the sentiments contained within these contents should provide us with additional information as to whether the video contains politically persuasive content.

Given a YouTube video we extract all of the associated comments using the YouTube API. The number of comments for to each video varies greatly (Figure 3). Since our videos comprise a geographically diverse range of topics and speakers, many of the comments to some of these videos are in languages other than English. As a pre-processing step we automatically filter out non-English text. In order to do so we use a simple approach of counting the proportion of the words in each comment that are present in a dictionary learnt from a standard English text corpus [36]. Despite its simplicity, we empirically found that this approach worked well for filtering out non-English text in YouTube comments, regardless of the character set of the comments or any spelling or compositional errors. To then detect the sentiment of each comment, we experimented with two different approaches as described below.

SATSVM: We refer to the approach in [29] as Sentiment Analysis of Tweets using SVMs (SATSVM). SATSVM has been specifically developed for social media data such as tweets and so it is appropriate for our data. The approach relies on extracting a number of features from each comment and training an SVM to classify the comment as having a positive or negative sentiment. We implement a simplified version of this approach and instead of using the binary SVM outputs, we use the SVM decision scores which roughly indicate the degree of positivity or negativity in the sentiment.

DeepCompositionalModel: We refer to the sentiment detection approach presented in [35] as the DeepCompositionalModel. It uses a Recursive Neural Tensor Network to build a representation of sentences based on their structure and computes sentiment by accounting for how the constituent words compose with each other. Unlike SATSVM, the DeepCompositionalModel splits each comment into its sentences and assigns a separate sentiment score to each sentence. Its output is a 5 dimensional probability vector indicating the probability of the sentence being *Strongly Negative*, *Negative*, *Neutral*, *Positive* or *Strongly Positive*.

4.4.1 Detecting Persuasion based on Sentiment

Given a video V_i and the set of associated comments $\mathcal{C}_i$ consisting of N individual comments $\{c_{i1}, c_{i2}, c_{i3}, \ldots c_{iN}\}$, we run SATSVM on each element of $\mathcal{C}_i$ to get a set of N scores $\{x_{i1}, x_{i2}, x_{i3}, \ldots x_{iN}\}$ normalized within the range $[-1,\ 1]$. We then quantize these scores by binning them into a histogram consisting of eleven equally spaced bins. Using this technique, each video V_i can be represented by a fixed dimensional histogram H_i. We train a RBF SVM using these histogram features for classifiying videos into persuasive versus non-persuasive. The classification results are shown in Table 4.

Similarly, when using the DeepCompositionalModel, we extract the sentiment for each comment $\{c_{i1}, c_{i2}, c_{i3}, \ldots c_{iN}\}$ obtaining $\mathcal{X}_i = \{\mathbf{x}_{i1}, \mathbf{x}_{i2}, \mathbf{x}_{i3}, \ldots \mathbf{x}_{iM}\}$, where $M (> N)$ is the total number of sentences. (Each comment is split into one or more sentences.) Each $\mathbf{x}_{ij}$ is a 5 dimensional probability vector as described above. Each video V_i is now represented by a set of these features $\mathcal{X}_i$. We train an SVM using a pyramid match kernel [15], which has been shown to be very effective for learning with sets of features, for classifying these videos. The results are shown in Table 4. From the results we can see that both SATSVM and DeepCompositionalModel perform similarly and are significantly better than random ($p < 0.001$ for each).

Approach	Classification Accuracy
SATSVM	69.52 ± 4.31
DeepCompositionalModel	69.94 ± 3.98

Table 4: Performance using sentiment features extracted from SATSVM [29] and DeepCompositionalModel [35].

4.4.2 Analysis of Results

We now try and analyze some of the results in an attempt to understand how sentiment analysis helps in detecting persuasive videos. To analyze the results from SATSVM, we looked at the mean normalized histogram of the positive as well as the negative videos. The histograms in Fig. 4 show that politically persuasive videos contain a higher proportion of negative comments than the non-persuasive videos.

We plot similar histograms for the sentiment detection results obtained from DeepCompositionalModel (Fig. 5). Here we can see that persuasive videos have a larger proportion of negative comments compared to non-persuasive videos. Therefore we can see that while the two sentiment extraction approaches result in different distributions, they tend to support the hypothesis that persuasive videos lead to more negative and fewer positive comments when compared to non-persuasive videos and we can use this to help automatically distinguish between politically persuasive and non-persuasive videos.

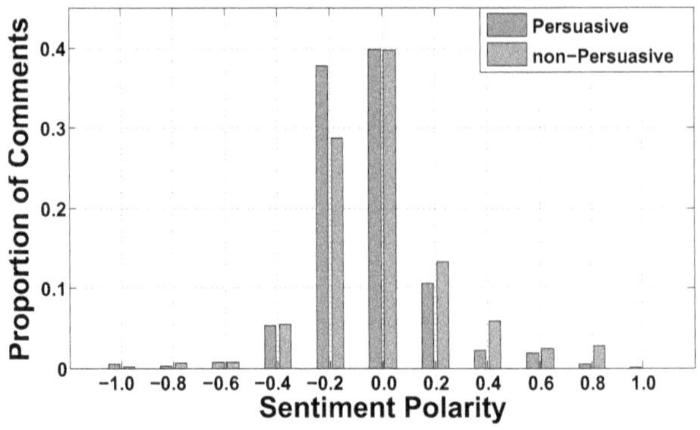

Figure 4: Mean sentiment histograms for the politically persuasive and non-persuasive videos based on SATSVM [29]. Persuasive videos tend to have a higher proportion of negative comments (bin '-0.2').

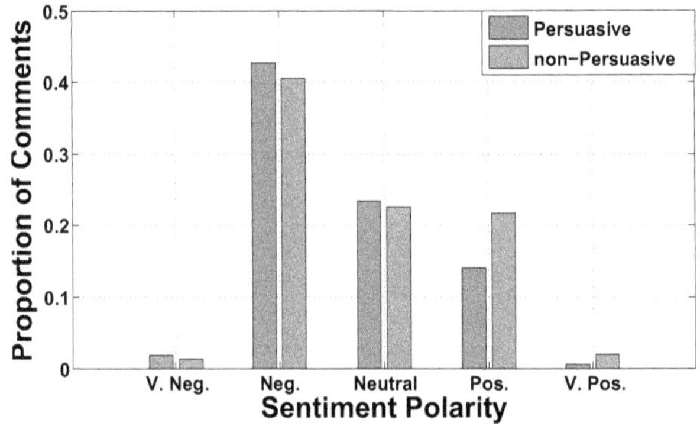

Figure 5: Mean sentiment histograms for the politically persuasive and non-persuasive videos based on the DeepCompositionalModel [35]. Persuasive videos tend to have a lower proportion of positive comments (bin 'Pos.').

4.5 Multimodal Fusion

We next looked at fusing the information from the audio, visual and text modalities. We believe that these modalities contain complementary information and therefore fusing them should boost the overall classification performance. For fusion we considered three different fusion strategies - *Early Fusion*, *Simple Late Fusion* and *Learning based Late Fusion*. For the purpose of fusion, we use the spectrogram features for audio (Table 1), the "fc7" features from the sentiment ontology for video (Table 3) and the SATSVM features for text (Table 4). In case of *Early Fusion* we simply concatenate the features from all of the modalities and train a RBF SVM for classification. In *Simple Late Fusion*, we add up the decision scores obtained from each modality to arrive at a composite decision score to perform classification. For *Learning based Late Fusion*, we train a logistic regression based fusion that combines the decision scores from each modality in a weighted manner. The results are shown in Table 5 and they demonstrate that fusion tends to improve classification results over the individual modalities and late fusion is more effective than early fusion. Furthermore, *Learning based Late Fusion* leads to further performance gains over *Simple Late Fusion*.

Modality	Classification Accuracy
Audio	81.03 ± 11.93
Video	73.13 ± 3.01
Text	69.52 ± 2.31
Early Fusion	81.37 ± 1.47
Simple Late Fusion	83.32 ± 3.40
Learning based Late Fusion	**85.09 ± 1.83**

Table 5: Classification performance on the RAC dataset using different fusion techniques.

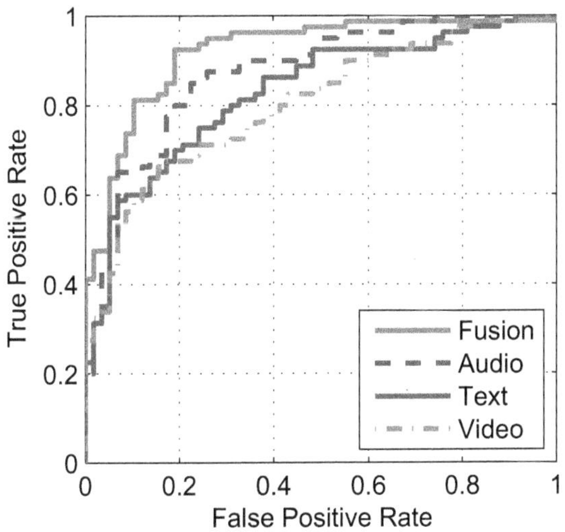

Figure 6: ROC curves for each modality.

Modality	AUC	*p*-Value	I_{oc}
Audio	0.873	$p = 0.02$	62.1%
Video	0.801	$p < 0.01$	46.3%
Text	0.828	$p = 0.03$	39.0%
Fusion	0.919	(n/a)	70.2%

Table 6: AUC values, *p*-values for the difference versus fusion AUC, and improvement-over-chance statistics

4.5.1 *Significance of Multimodal Approach*

In order to further compare the performance of different modalities and establish the significance of a multimodal approach over individual modalities, ROC curves and corresponding statistics were computed for each modality as well as learning based late fusion. The ROC curves for each modality are shown in Figure 6 and were derived from the mean rankings of samples over multiple randomized experiments as noted in Section 4.1. For each ROC curve the area under the curve (AUC) was computed, and for each possible pair of ROC curves the *p*-value was computed for the difference between them. Since our AUCs values are computed on the same underlying set of samples, we chose the method of [11] to compute *p*-values, as it accounts for the correlated nature of data generated from pairs of tests performed on the same samples. A significance threshold of 95% ($p < 0.05$) for this null-hypothesis test was chosen to determine if a performance gain was significant. Using this criteria, the performance gain of the learning based late fusion approach over every individual modality was significant; the corresponding *p*-values are shown in Figure 6. However, the performance differences between individual modalities all failed to meet this threshold. These statistics strongly suggest that fusion of multiple modalities leads to a statistically significant improvement in results.

Additionally, the I_{oc} statistic (as defined in 3.1) for typical performance of each modality was computed. We note that for this statistic, the fusion approach outperformed 3 of the 4 human annotators.

4.6 Predicting Viewer Response

Finally, we investigated the prediction of viewer response to a video. Our goal here is to see whether given a video's audio-visual content, can we predict the sentiment polarity of the comments posted in response to it. In order to do so, we first clustered the test videos based on their sentiment histograms H_i (subsection 4.4), computed using SATSVM [29], in an unsupervised manner. We set the number of clusters to two, partitioning the set of test videos into two clusters that roughly correspond to videos that generated a positive response and videos that generated a negative response. Also note that while these clusters roughly map to the persuasive and non-persuasive classes, the correspondence is not exact. We treat this as a supervised classification problem, using the cluster indices as the class labels, which correspond to videos generating a positive and negative response. As features, we use the spectrogram features for audio (Table 1) and the "fc7" features from the sentiment ontology for video (Table 3). We train non-linear SVMs for classification based on unimodal features and a logistic-regression based late-fusion for multimodal fusion. The results are shown in Table 7. The results show that we can predict the viewer response in advance based on just the extracted audio-visual content with a reasonable degree of accuracy (random accuracy is 50%). Furthermore, fusing the audio and visual modalities leads to an increase in performance.

Modality	Classification Accuracy
Audio	61.97 ± 7.26
Video	61.67 ± 8.83
Learning based Late Fusion	**64.69 ± 4.63**

Table 7: Classification performance for predicting the viewer response on the RAC dataset.

5. CONCLUSION

We have demonstrated that affective and semantic audio and visual concepts as well as sentiment measures on viewer comments are effective at predicting whether a video contains politically persuasive content. Notably, the best automatic classification approach generally outperforms human annotators. Individually, audio concepts are the best predictors, while a fusion of these modalities produces the best results, indicating that each contains some complementary information to the others. Both visual and audio features are also predictive of negatively polarized comments, allowing us to potentially predict the viewer response to a video before comments are left. There are several possible areas for future work. For instance, an attempt to try to identify new videos with politically charged content as they are posted could be based on this approach, or a similarly tailored approach could be applied to other specific types of content besides politically persuasive videos.[1]

[1]This material is based upon work sponsored by the Defense Advanced Projects Agency under the U.S. Army Research Office Contract Number W911NF-12-C-0028, through IBM

6. REFERENCES

[1] A. Abbasi. Affect intensity analysis of dark web forums. *Intelligence and Security Informatics, IEEE*, 2007.

[2] R. Achanta, A. Shaji, K. Smith, A. Lucchi, P. Fua, and S. Susstrunk. Slic superpixels compared to state-of-the-art superpixel methods. In *IEEE PAMI*, 2012.

[3] M. R. Amer, B. Siddiquie, S. Khan, A. Divakaran, and H. Sawhney. Multimodal fusion using dynamic hybrid models. *WACV*, 2014.

[4] F. R. Bach, G. R. G. Lanckriet, and M. I. Jordan. Multiple kernel learning, conic duality, and the smo algorithm. *ICML*, 2004.

[5] D. Borth, R. Ji, T. Chen, T. Breuel, and S.-F. Chang. Large-scale visual sentiment ontology and detectors using adjective noun pairs. In *ACM MM*, 2013.

[6] S.-F. Chang, D. Ellis, W. Jiang, K. Lee, A. Yanagawa, A. C. Loui, and J. Luo. Large-scale multimodal semantic concept detection for consumer video. *ACM MIR*, 2007.

[7] S. Chaudhuri, M. Harvilla, and B. Raj. Unsupervised learning of acoustic unit descriptors for audio content representation and classification. In *INTERSPEECH*, 2011.

[8] T. Chen, D. Borth, T. Darrell, and S. Chang. Deepsentibank: Visual sentiment concept classification with deep convolutional neural networks. *arXiv*, 2014.

[9] D. Chisholm, B. Siddiquie, A. Divakaran, and E. Shriberg. Audio-based affect detection in web videos. In *ICME*, 2015.

[10] D. Correa. Solutions to detect and analyze online radicalization.

[11] E. DeLong, D. DeLong, and D. Clarke-Pearson. Comparing the areas under two or more correlated receiver operating characteristic curves: A nonparametric approach. *Biometrics*, pages 837–845, 1988.

[12] J. Deng, W. Dong, R. Socher, L.-J. Li, K. Li, and L. Fei-Fei. Imagenet: A large-scale hierarchical image database. In *CVPR*, 2009.

[13] J. Fleiss. Measuring nominal scale agreement among many raters. *Psychological Bulletin, 76*, pages 378–382, 1971.

[14] T. Fu, C.-N. Huang, and H. Chen. Identification of extremist videos in online video sharing sites. *Intelligence and Security Informatics, IEEE*, 2009.

[15] K. Grauman and T. Darrell. The pyramid match kernel: Efficient learning with sets of features. *JMLR*, 2007.

[16] J. Hinojosa, L. Carretie, M. Valcarel, C. Mendez-Bertolo, and M. Pozo. Electrophysiological differences in the processing of affective information in words and pictures. *Cognitive, Affective, and Behavioral Neuroscience*, 9 2009.

[17] P. Isola, J. Xiao, A. Torralba, and A. Oliva. What makes an image memorable? *CVPR*, 2011.

Corporation subcontract 4914004308. Any opinions, findings and conclusions or recommendations expressed in this material are those of the author(s) and do not necessarily reflect the position or policy of the U.S. Army Research Office, DARPA, DoD and IBM Corporation and no official endorsement should be inferred.

[18] Y. Jia, E. Shelhamer, J. Donahue, S. Karayev, J. Long, R. Girshick, S. Guadarrama, and T. Darrell. Caffe: Convolutional architecture for fast feature embedding. *arXiv*, 2014.

[19] Y.-G. Jiang, G. Ye, S.-F. Chang, D. Ellis, and A. C. Loui. Consumer video understanding: A benchmark database and an evaluation of human and machine performance. *ICMR*, 2011.

[20] D. Joshi, R. Datta, E. Fedorovskaya, Q. Luong, J. Wang, J. Li, and J. Luo. Aesthetics and emotions in images. *Signal Processing Magazine*, 2011.

[21] A. Kapoor and R. W. Picard. Multimodal affect recognition in learning environments. *MULTIMEDIA*, 2005.

[22] S. Karayev and et al. Recognizing image style. In *BMVC*, 2014.

[23] A. Krizhevsky, I. Sutskever, and G. Hinton. Imagenet classification with deep convolutional neural networks. In *NIPS*, 2012.

[24] J. Landis and G. Koch. The measurement of observer agreement for categorical data. *Biometrics. 33, 1*, pages 159–174, 1977.

[25] Y. LeCun and Y. Bengio. Convolutional networks for images, speech, and time series. In *The handbook of brain theory and neural networks*, 1995.

[26] K. Lee and D. P. W. Ellis. Audio-based semantic concept classification for consumer video. *IEEE TASLP*, 2010.

[27] D. Littman and K. Forbes. Recognizing emotions from student speech in tutoring dialogues. *ASRU*, 2003.

[28] J. Machajdik and A. Hanbury. Affective image classification using features inspired by psychology and art theory. *ACMMM*, 2010.

[29] S. Mohammad, S. Kiritchenko, and X. Zhu. Nrc-canada: Building the state-of-the-art in sentiment analysis of tweets. *SemEval*, 2013.

[30] B. Pang and L. Lee. Opinion mining and sentiment analysis. *Foundations and trends in information retrieval*, 2008.

[31] S. Park, H. S. Shim, M. Chatterjee, K. Sagae, and L.-P. Morency. Computational analysis of persuasiveness in social multimedia: A novel dataset and multimodal prediction approach. *ICMI*, 2014.

[32] E. Reid, J. Qin, Y. Zhou, G. Lai, M. Sageman, G. Weimann, and H. Chen. Collecting and analyzing the presence of terrorists on the web: A case study of jihad websites. *Intelligence and Security Informatics*, 2005.

[33] B. Schuller and et. al. Avec 2011 -the first international audio visual emotion challenge. *ACII*, 2011.

[34] W. Scott. Reliability of content analysis: The case of nominal scale coding. *Public Opinion Quarterly, 19*, pages 321–325, 1955.

[35] R. Socher, A. Perelygin, J. Y. Wu, J. Chuang, C. D. Manning, A. Y. Ng, and C. Potts. Recursive deep models for semantic compositionality over a sentiment treebank. *EMNLP*, 2013.

[36] E. Stamatatos, N. Fakotakis, and G. Kokkinakis. Text genre detection using common word frequencies. In *18th Conference on Computational Linguistics*, 2000.

[37] Y.-L. Tian, T. Kanade, and J. F. Cohn. Facial expression analysis. *Handbook of face recognition*, 2005.

Toward Better Understanding of Engagement in Multiparty Spoken Interaction with Children

Samer Al Moubayed, Jill Fain Lehman

Disney Research
Pittsburgh, PA, USA
{samer, jill.lehman}@disneyresearch.com

ABSTRACT

A system's ability to understand and model a human's engagement during an interactive task is important for both adapting its behavior to the moment and achieving a coherent interaction over time. Standard practice for creating such a capability requires uncovering and modeling the multimodal cues that predict engagement in a given task environment. The first step in this methodology is to have human coders produce "gold standard" judgments of sample behavior. In this paper we report results from applying this first step to the complex and varied behavior of children playing a fast-paced, speech-controlled, side-scrolling game called *Mole Madness*. We introduce a concrete metric for engagement—willingness to continue the interaction—that leads to better inter-coder judgments for children playing in pairs, explore how coders perceive the relative contribution of audio and visual cues, and describe engagement trends and patterns in our population. We also examine how the measures change when the same children play *Mole Madness* with a robot instead of a peer. We conclude by discussing the implications of the differences within and across play conditions for the automatic estimation of engagement and the extension of our autonomous robot player into a "buddy" that can individualize interaction for each player and game.

Categories and Subject Descriptors

H.5.2 [**Information Interfaces and Presentation**]: User Interfaces – Natural Language; D.2.2 [**Software Engineering**] Design Tools and Techniques – State diagrams; D.2.11 [**Software Engineering**] Software Architectures – Languages

General Terms

Design, Human Factors.

Keywords

Multi-party interaction, child-computer interaction, group task engagement, dialogue systems, spoken interaction, child-robot interaction.

ICMI '15, November 09 - 13, 2015, Seattle, WA, USA

ACM 978-1-4503-3912-4/15/11…$15.00
DOI: http://dx.doi.org/10.1145/2818346.2820733

1. INTRODUCTION

Researchers in interaction all begin from a fundamental assumption: to interact one must first engage and to continue to interact one must stay engaged. Working from this assumption we tend to instantiate a methodology that, in the abstract, follows the same plan: gather interaction data, post-process and/or code the data with respect to engagement to create a "gold standard," find the observable or "sense-able" features in the environment that best predict the engagement states we want to distinguish, and use models based on those features to modify the agent's behavior in the interaction. What the commonality of this description tends to ignore is that what each of us means by engagement is a function of how we want to use the feature in both sensing and acting. For some the term is closely related to "attention" or "joint attention," is measured with respect to observable phenomena over short durations, and effects only immediate actions in the agent. This is a rich viewpoint; many researchers who work on conversation analysis and dialog systems have contributed to our understanding of this kind of engagement and identified observable cues such as facial expressions (Sidner et al. 2005), gaze (Nakano & Ishii, 2010), and gesture and posture (Sanghvi et al. 2011) that can be used by an agent to make effective changes in its behavior. Bohus & Horvitz (2009) focus in further on a single critical instance of this kind of engagement—the signals surrounding the moment when users in open spaces show the intention to interact.

The short-duration view of engagement is not unique to researchers in dialog interaction. Leite, for example, uses engagement as a binary feature to code the behavior of groups of children watching and listening to robots acting out a social scenario (Leite et al. 2015). Her goal in the work is to give the robots the ability to sense when children are disengaged. So, although she derives the feature for every 500 msec time slice, she does not consider engagement as something different from disengagement's opposite. That is precisely the change in viewpoint we present in this work—engagement as a continuous, multi-valued phenomena that is expected to wax and wane over an interaction. We see children as more or less engaged in our activities rather than engaged or disengaged, and expect that there are patterns of engagement over time that

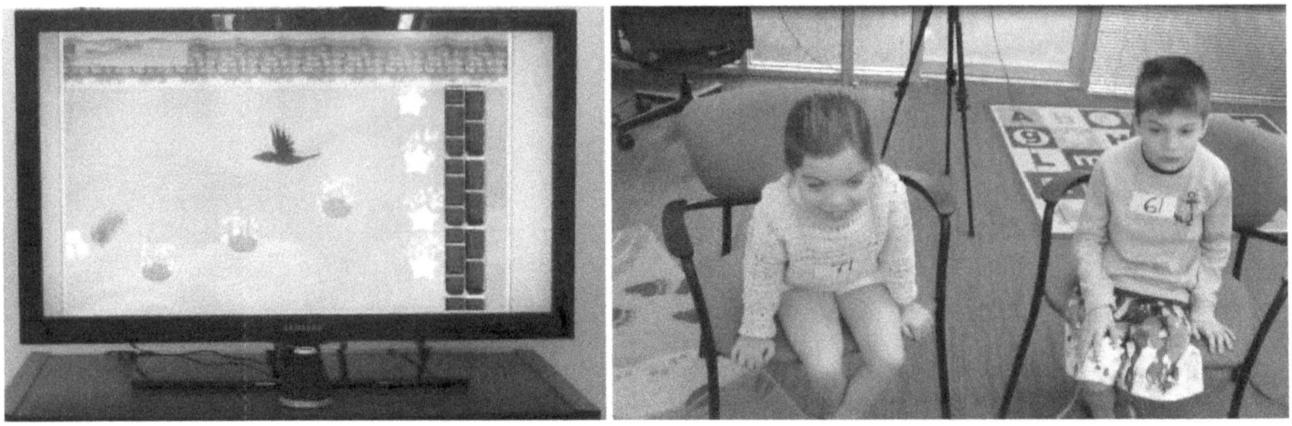

Figure 1. A snapshot of interaction with *Mole Madness*. Left: the game as it appears on a 40" flat screen. Right: Frontal view of two children playing the game.

correspond to successful interactions and patterns that do not. Such a view is clearly related to engagement in the short-term; we also expect that patterns of engagement in the large can be built by sensing different kinds of instances of engagement in the small.

The work reported here is a description of the first two steps of the canonical process toward our goal: gathering interaction data and coding it with respect to patterns of engagement. We describe our interactive game, *Mole Madness*, and the procedure we used to collect data from pairs of children playing together and one-on-one with a non-adaptive robot. We then turn to the coding phase, where we found that the large-scale view of engagement we want to model has unexpected implications and so discuss our eventual decisions and rationales in detail. Having settled on a coding, we examine the patterns of engagement it reveals, primarily with respect to the child-child data we intend to use to build our models, but briefly with respect to the child-robot interactions as well. We conclude with a discussion of the variability in the children's behavior and the challenges it creates for building a robot "buddy" that can adaptively provide a positive experience for each child.

2. *MOLE MADNESS*: A SPEECH-CONTROLLED GAME

Mole Madness is a two-dimensional side-scroller similar to video games like Super Mario Bros®. Each of two players controls an aspect of the mole's movement through its environment using a simple verbal command: *go* for horizontal and *jump* for vertical. Without speech, the mole simply falls to the ground and spins in place.

A close-up of the mole's world, and two children playing the game, can be seen in Figure 1. The environment contains typical kinds of objects for this style of game: walls arranged as barriers to go over or between, items that result in point gain (cabbages, carrots) and point loss (cactuses, birds, rocks), and the occasional special object (star) that acts as a boost to change the mole's normal physics. In addition to providing a familiar and fun experience for the players, the environment is designed to elicit specific patterns of speech. There are flat stretches to evoke isolated consecutive *gos*, steep walls to produce isolated consecutive *jumps*, and crevasses to get through and items to avoid that require coordinated and overlapping sequences of commands. A score bar on the screen updates as the mole touches the various kinds of objects. Although players are not given any specific goal other than to move the mole through the level, players typically adopt maximizing speed and/or points as a goal.

When children play together, task commands (*go*, *jump*) naturally occur in a broader conversational context that includes both non-task utterances directed to the mole ("watch out," "faster") and utterances directed to the other player ("wait, don't say jump yet," "look a star," "he's funny"). For the most part this side-talk is not conversational, in the sense that it rarely requires a verbal response (Lehman & Al Moubayed, 2015). Thus, in robot-child games, the robot periodically generates but does not respond to these kinds of utterances.

With respect to nonverbal behavior, the fast pace and visual processing demands of the game tend to reduce some kinds of expressiveness. Eye and head movements typically seen in face-to-face conversation (such as looking at the person being addressed, looking away to hold the floor, etc. (Abele, 1986)) are impractical when visual attention must remain on the screen. Similarly, facial expressions and body movements that might be interpreted as indicating interest, engagement, and excitement, can be absent in some children who become quite still with intense focus.

From this perspective, and in tasks similar to *Mole Madness*, the perception of small-scale engagement and the sense-able features that signal it might be significantly different from what can be learned from human-human conversation and require an analysis of data that is specific to this type of interaction context.

Figure 2. Snapshots of 6 different video file segments (simultaneous pairs from each of three different games).

3. DATA COLLECTION

In a multi-study data collection, children took part in four activities over the course of a one-hour period, spending approximately ten minutes per interaction with five-minute breaks. *Mole Madness* comprised two of the activities: children played once in pairs, and again, individually with a robot as co-player. All children's families were compensated for their time. Participation took place on four consecutive weekends, at the families' convenience during summer vacation.

Population. Twenty-eight children, ages 5 to 10 (50% female), played in pairs and one-on-one with Sammy J (a back-projected robot head developed by Furhat Robotics, Al Moubayed et al. 2012). Due to hardware failure, the results discussed in this paper are for the 26 children for whom we have complete data sets (child1-child2, child1-Sammy, and child2-Sammy): 12 females and 14 males with a mean age of 8.3 years (SD = 1.2 years).

Children who are unfamiliar with each other or are of substantively different ages can have very different play styles and patterns of engagement than pairs who are familiar and/or developmentally close. Because we are interested in understanding the dynamics of children playing together and how that can guide behavior when each child plays with a robot who should act like a "buddy," we tried to eliminate these most obvious sources of variability across pairs. Thus as a recruiting strategy, the initial family contacted in each pair was asked to bring both their own child and a friend or sibling who was close in age. All thirteen player pairs were either friends or siblings, with a mean age difference of 7.5 months. Eleven of the thirteen pairs were single sex.

Procedure for child-child games. Children were seated in front of, and in an equilateral triangle with respect to, a 40" flat screen where the game was displayed. The basic principles of the game were explained by a confederate. They were told to interact with the game using their voices, and that the mole could be controlled by the words *go* and *jump*. Each child was assigned an initial role arbitrarily, and at a point in the middle of the game, the pair was asked to switch roles/use the other word. They were also told to use the word *next* when the mole reached the target flag and disappeared into his hole at the end of a level in order to bring the mole back out on a new level. The children were not told to avoid speaking to each other or addressing the mole using other words.

Children were unaware that a trained wizard, located in another room, was using a game controller to remotely control the mole's movements in response to their *gos*, *jumps*, and *nexts*. A wizard was used in order to avoid any discrepancies in the quality of the game or the interaction that would stem from problems in recognizing overlapping speech. With only auditory access to the room where the game was played, the wizard had no ability to anticipate the children's speech, and no feedback on the results of his actions or the status of the game play.

The data collection took place in a child-friendly room with minimal hardware intrusion (Figures 1 and 2). Interactions were audio-visually recorded using two high definition cameras, and two stereo microphones. One camera and a stereo microphone were placed on top of the screen capturing a frontal view of the game players (Figure 1-right, Figure 2), and the other capturing a back view with the screen and the game (Figure 1-left). All events from the wizard and from the game were automatically time-logged along with the audiovisual recordings.

Procedure for child-Sammy games. The robot was placed in the right child's position of the same triangular arrangement, and the procedure was identical to the child-child case with two exceptions. First, no wizard was needed because Sammy is able to play autonomously using output from the game and a small microcone array as its only sensory input (details of the dialog design and structure of the system architecture can be found in (Al Moubayed & Lehman, 2015). The second difference was that Sammy always played in the *go* role throughout the activity.

4. DATA PREPARATION

Data recordings comprised fourteen different child-child games, and 28 child-robot interactions. On average, child pairs played for 354 seconds (SD = 65 seconds). Child-Sammy games tended to be shorter (mean=270 seconds, SD=49 seconds).

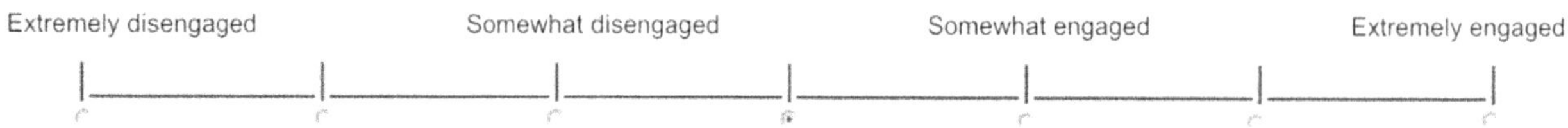

Figure 3. A 7-point scale with four degrees of engagement labeled and separated by non-labeled points.

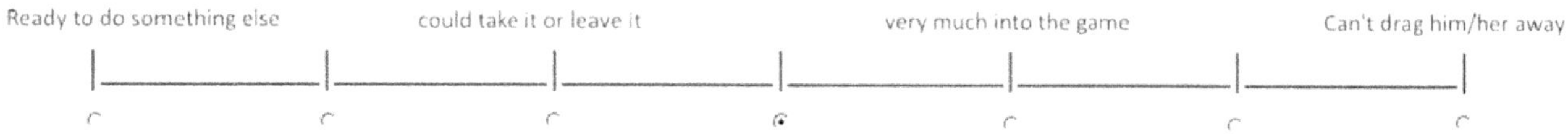

Figure 4. A proxy engagement scale coders used to indicate the "willingness to continue the interaction" based on the segment.

All data streams (audio, video, and logs) were manually synchronized. The recordings were then segmented into game levels, level transitions, and "off-task," the latter defined as any talk or interaction with the confederate. Such events occurred, for example, when a level ended and the children had to be reminded to use the word *next* to continue, or during play when a child turned to the confederate to ask questions or request help. Because we are interested in understanding and modeling engagement in the game, level transitions and off-task segments were removed from further analysis.

5. THE PERCEPTION OF ENGAGEMENT

The work reported here has two primary goals: (1) to characterize the patterns of engagement we see in children playing together and (2) to provide the data from which we will try to determine detectable multimodal features that predict different levels of engagement. To those ends we use human coders to produce judgments and labeling of our audio-video recording.

To prepare the data for coding, full recordings of game play were split into audio-video and video-only ten second segments showing either the child on the left or the child on the right. Separation of left and right players was done so that judgments would be based on the individual child's behavior without the co-player's behavior for comparison. Figure 2 shows examples from three games. Video-only segments were created both to understand the relative contribution of audio cues to the perception of engagement and because audio from the unseen player could not be erased from the audio-video versions.

Child-child sessions produced 822 segments under each of the audio-video and video-only conditions. Coders labeled all video-only segments in random order first, followed by all randomly ordered audio-visual segments. Video-only segments were coded first to isolate any bias in comparing silent segments (due to the intentional removal of the audio track) to files where the verbal contribution of the player was minimal. Coders used a tailor-made annotation tool that allowed efficient progression through the segments and easy use of the engagement scale. Three female coders who have experience with children received training on the tool and were instructed to take a break every 15 minutes to avoid decreased attention over time.

Following standard practice, our coders were initially given a small calibration subset of the data (a 99 segment mixture of video-only and audio-video data randomly distributed across sessions) and asked to rate engagement using a 7-point scale that ranged from "extremely disengaged" to "extremely engaged" with four specified labels and three intermediate points (see Figure 3). The unlabeled values in the scale allow coders flexibility in judging the behavior as lying between the meanings of the labeled points. Annotation values for the calibration set resulted in an inter-rater agreement (Krippendorff's *alpha*) value of a 0.39. Repeated experiments using the same files (with a gap of 24 hours), also showed low test-retest reliability for each annotator.

Low inter-rater and within-rater agreement indicates that whatever observable features our coders were focusing on, they weren't focusing on the same features, weren't focusing on them consistently and/or weren't mapping them consistently to scalar values. To counter this problem we needed a proxy for engagement that they could use more consistently. The kind of engagement we are interested in—something that isn't binary but has an intensity that changes over time—is a subjective experience that we want to render predictable through observable features. Our coders may experience this kind of engagement themselves, but they do not regularly judge it, as "engagement" per se, in others. What they do regularly anticipate and judge is the willingness of a child to be moved between activities. Thus we created the scale shown in Figure 4 and asked coders to re-evaluate each segment based on how willing they thought the child they had watched in the segment would be to continue with the current activity or move to another.

There are three points to be made about the proxy scale. First, although this measure might differ in quality from what engagement is (as an internal subjective experience), it seeks to measure a consequence of engagement in this kind of interaction. Second, it asks for a situated judgment that our coders have experience making with the population and which is relevant in its own right to the issue of creating an enjoyable experience through an adaptable co-player. Third, because it is situated and it does take advantage of our coders' backgrounds, it is not an all-purpose proxy for modeling long-term, variable-intensity engagement. We believe that attempts to model engagement-in-the-large in some other types of task might also find low agreement among coders who use a scale that relies on the word "engagement"; but we also believe that a proxy solution will work better only in so far as the new scale makes sense for the interaction, population and coders involved.

To compare the power of the "willingness" scale to the original, the same 99 files were presented to the three coders using the same tool. The newly coded data achieved an inter-rater agreement (Krippendorff's *alpha*) of 0.59. The increase in overall agreement was coupled with an increase in similarity between coders' distributions over the scale. The Minkowski distances between distributions for each pair of coders were 0.25, 0.29 and 0.49 with the "engagement" scale, but 0.11, 0.17 and 0.06 with "willingness."

Given these improvements, the entire data set was then coded by all three coders using the "willingness" scale, video-only first, as previously described. Krippendorf's *alpha* for the complete data set was 0.58, comparable to the training set. While this value indicates better agreement than we would expect to get from the "engagement" scale, and compares favorably with inter-rater agreement for engagement measures reported by Oertel (2010) ($k = 0.56$, 10-point scale, 30 raters) and Leite ($k = 0.41$, binary scale, two raters), it is not considered statistically strong. Some of the variability between coders no doubt comes from real differences in how they view the behavior in relation to the labeled portions of the scale. But a closer analysis shows that the reliability statistic may be reflecting primarily differences in degree rather than kind. The unlabeled intermediate points on both scales are implicitly defined as "about halfway between the two labeled values." For the "willingness" scale 90% of all segments had pair-wise coder values that were within one point of each. In other words, for the majority of segments coders were disagreeing about the degree to which the same category applied. For the "engagement" scale this was true of only 26% of the subsample.

6. RESULTS AND ANALYSIS

Despite the overall improvement in reliability that came from using a proxy for engagement, a conservative view would argue that there remains some degree of consistent difference across coders. In analyzing the results we could eliminate those differences by using a mean or median value for each segment, essentially creating an average coder. Elsewhere it has been argued that the idea of a single correct truth for human annotations in semantic interpretation tasks obscures our ability to get at the nature of the inherent subjectivity in such judgments and the range of reasonable interpretations for complex phenomena (Aroyo & Welty, 2015). With respect to our data, we note that by better situating the scale in the coders' own experiences we may have invited some systematic individual differences in the judgments if each coder based her decisions on the observable features that she has found valuable in redirecting the children she knows. We do not know at this stage how well we will be able to predict a coder's data with the features we are able to sense, nor how much overlap there will be in the features that best predict in each case. It is possible that the differences in the data produce no differences in the sense-able feature sets at all, in which case an average coder model would make sense. But it is also possible that one coder's decisions can be more accurately modeled given current sensors; if that's true we may choose to model a particular way of measuring long-term engagement even though it gives rise to some judgments with which the average coder would not agree. Given this possibility, we choose to preserve the individual differences at this point in the process. To continue here, then, we discuss general results that hold across coders but choose a representative coder, Coder 2, to present the children's patterns from a single coherent view.

6.1 Audio-video versus video-only trends

Recall that each coder judged every segment both with and without audio. Every coder gave an average score across all segments that was higher in the case of audio-visual cues. In particular, Coder 2's values remained unchanged for 57% of the child-child segments, increased for 29% of segments when sound was present, and decreased in 14% of cases. The absolute percent of changed versus unchanged values differed for the other two coders, but the relative split of twice as many increasing as decreasing when there was change, held. Almost all children (at least 25/28 for each coder) received some bump in their mean engagement score from audio, although some children clearly benefited more than others. Further, how much of a bump an individual child received depended on coder, reinforcing the idea that individual coders cared differentially about the presence or absence of specific audio and visual cues.

6.2 Engagement trends

Considered in pairs, we found no correlation between the average engagement level of one child and the average engagement level of the second for any coder. In turning to a more finely grained view, Figure 5 shows the engagement plots for both children in each of the child-child games, using Coder 2's audio-visual values. The plots also show a linear fit for the data of each child.

The graphs show large variability in levels of engagement and in engagement patterns, both within and across games, despite the fact that all pairs of children were familiar with each other, were of similar age, typically the same gender, and played the same game. Four patterns occur to different degrees. The top row of Figure 5 groups players who maintain similar engagement values over time, with both enjoying an increasing trend over the course of the game. The middle two rows show players that also maintain a similar pattern of engagement, but because their values hold steady. The bottom row shows the last two patterns, defined by players who start and/or end at different engagement levels. The two pairs at the left have one child converge toward the other as the game unfolds, while the two pairs on the right show players that diverge over the course of the game. If the values do reflect something meaningful about the children's internal state, then clearly the emotional arcs experienced by our participants are not all positive. Equally clearly, some interactions were more successful than others, at least in the

Figure 5. Plots of the engagement trends (engagement over time) for each of the 14 different *Mole Madness* games. Each plot shows the audio-visual data for Coder 2 and a linear fit for a pair of children that played the game together. The plots are arranged in order of similarity and convergence showing large variability across children and games. Two games show divergence in the engagement of the children (the last two plots), while the remainder show a pair with steady or increasing engagement, or one child converging toward the child with the higher engagement.

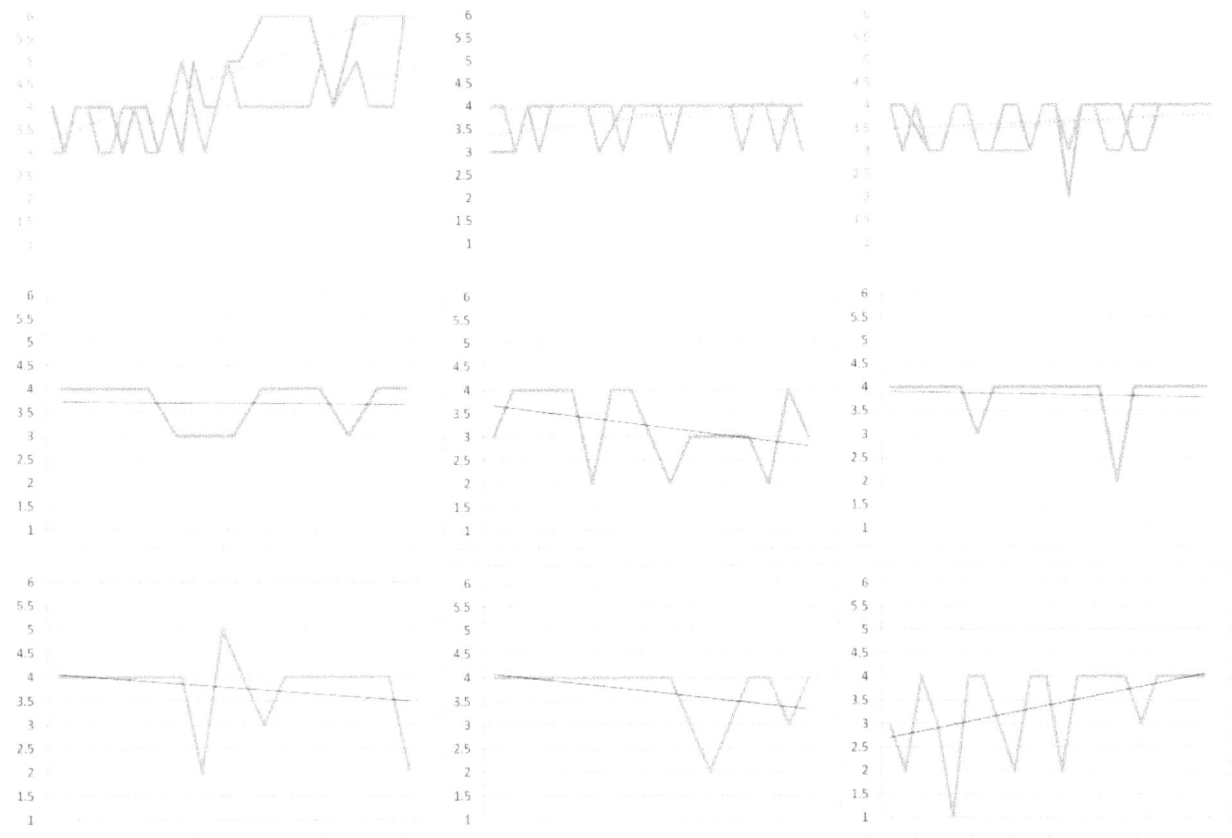

Figure 6. Three examples of trends across peer conditions. Top row is the engagement of two children playing *Mole Madness* together. Lower two rows are the engagement trends of the same children when each played separately with Sammy.

sense that both players enjoyed a high or increasing desire to remain engaged in the experience over time.

The variability we see implies that there is no "average" player and no "canonical" interaction with respect to engagement—the game and co-player afford a range of experiences. A robot peer that cannot detect and track changing levels of engagement and flexibly adapt its behavior to coordinate with them, is unlikely to produce an optimal experience for each child.

7. CHILD-SAMMY INTERACTION

As mentioned, each child also played *Mole Madness* with an autonomous but non-adaptive robot, Sammy J, in the *go* role. In this section we briefly explore the coders' perceptions of the children's willingness to continue to engage with the robot as co-player. Again, we use Coder 2 as our specific representative when one is needed.

The mean engagement score over all segments was lower for the child-Sammy sessions for all coders, although the difference for Coder 2 was negligible (3.78 to 3.75). As in the child-child games, audio-visual scores tended to be higher than video-only judgments for all coders. Coder 2's remained unchanged for 50% of segments, increased for 35% and decreased for 15%. And as before, most children benefited although some children benefited more than others, and which children did depended on the coder. For any given coder, there was no correlation between those who benefited from audio in the child-child condition and those who benefited with Sammy. We conjecture that there may have been individual differences in aspects of the child's vocalizations with friend versus robot, and intend to explore that possibility in future work.

We also examined the engagement trends of children in the child-robot condition. Although space precludes a complete side-by-side comparison, Figure 6 shows examples for six children when playing with Sammy, repeating the child-child graph for each pair. Despite the cumulative statistic being nearly identical, for many of the children, the game felt quite different. For children with flat or decreasing engagement, the ability of the system to detect the situation as it changes (or fails to change) and adapt its behavior to influence the long-term pattern seems critical to an emotionally successful interaction.

8. DISCUSSION AND FUTURE WORK

The work presented in this paper constitutes only a first step towards understanding how to detect, model and influence engagement in interactive spoken games with children. We treat engagement as a variable quantity that can rise and fall gradually over the course of an interaction, rather than as a single description of the interaction as a whole, or a binary moment-to-moment correlate of attention. We described our method and decision process in arriving at a more useful way to elicit engagement judgments via a proxy scale that both situates the coder's task in more concrete language and allows us to characterize the rise and fall of the measure over time. Although the "willingness" scale offered better inter-rater reliability among coders, and was comparable to what some other researchers have found, standard statistical measures were not high enough to conclude that all values meant exactly the same thing. We did find that most of the differences between coders corresponded to differences in degree rather than kind, but we do not know whether the differences in judgments ultimately correspond to substantively different mixtures of sense-able features in the environment. A clear next step to this work is to build models based on audio and visual features that predict the different levels of engagement, both to see whether the coders' differences matter in practice and to give Sammy the ability to see what the coders see.

A closer examination of one coder's data revealed variability of engagement level within a game as well as variability in overall patterns across different players as a function of both time and co-player. We have begun the work of exploring whether linguistic entrainment and other types of acoustic coordination are more or less present in what seem to be the desirable patterns and trends. Indeed, for the subset of this data for which we have high quality audio without dropout (eight pairs), we have found that some verbal and acoustic features demonstrate significantly more synchrony when the children are in a high engagement state (Chaspari et al, 2015). To respond in kind, Sammy's repertoire of behavior will need to be extended to produce comparable signals. When added to the ability to sense what path the child is on, such adaptive behaviors can be used to reinforce or change that movement in peer-like ways. The patterns of behavior in the current data, both child-child and child-robot, present a backdrop against which we can measure Sammy's growth toward producing more satisfying interactions for all children.

9. ACKNOWLEDGMENTS.

We would like to thank Preben Wik for advice on designing the personality of the robot character, Jon Lew for help in game design and programming, and Peijin Zhang for help in data collection and preparation.

REFERENCES

[1] Al Moubayed, S., Beskow, J., Skantze, G., and Granström, B. 2012. *Furhat: A Back-projected Human-like Robot Head for Multiparty Human-Machine Interaction*. In Esposito, A., et al. (Eds.), Cognitive Behavioural Systems. Lecture Notes in Computer Science, pp 114-130.

[2] Al Moubayed, S. and Lehman, J F. 2015. *Design and Architecture of a Robot-Child Speech-Controlled Game*. In Proceedings of the Tenth Annual ACM/IEEE International Conference on Human-Robot Interaction HRI2015, Portland, OR, USA.

[3] Aroyo, L. and Welty, C. 2015. Truth Is a Lie: Crowd Truth and the Seven Myths of Human Annotation, *AI Magazine*, AAAI Press, Volume 36, Number 1, pages 15-24.

[4] Bohus, D. and Horvitz, E. 2009. *Learning to Predict Engagement with a Spoken Dialog System in Open-World Settings*, in Proceedings of SIGdial'09, London, UK.

[5] Chaspari, T., Al Moubayed, S., and Lehman, J. 2015. *Exploring Children's Verbal and Acoustic Synchrony: Towards Promoting Engagement in Speech-Controlled Robot-Companion Games*. In Proceedings of the First International Workshop on Modeling Interpersonal Synchrhony, ICMI.

[6] Gatica-Perez, D. 2009. Automatic nonverbal analysis of social interaction in small groups: A review, *Image Vis. Comput.*, vol. 27, no. 12, pp. 1775–1787, November.

[7] Lehman, J. and Al Moubayed, S. 2015. *Mole Madness – a Multi-Child, Fast-Paced, Speech-Controlled Game*. AAAI Symposium on Turn-taking and Coordination in Human-Machine Interaction. Stanford, CA

[8] Leite, I., Mccoy, M., Ullman, D., Salomons, N., Scassellati, B., and Haven, N. 2015. *Comparing Models of Disengagement in Individual and Group Interactions*. In 10th ACM/IEEE International Conference on Human Robot Interaction Conference (2015).

[9] Nakano, Y and Ishii, R. 2010. *Estimating user's engagement from eye-gaze behaviors in human-agent conversations*. In Proc. of the 15th International Conf. on Intelligent User Interfaces, IUI '10, pages 139{148. New York, NY, USA, 2010. ACM.

[10] Oertel, C. 2010. Identification of Cues for the Automatic Detection of Hotspots, *Master's Thesis*, Bielefeld University.

[11] Rich, C., Ponsler, B., Holroyd, A. and Sidner, C. 2010. *Recognizing engagement in human-robot interaction*. In Proc. of the 5th ACM/IEEE International Conf. on Human-Robot Interaction, pages 375{382. IEEE.

[12] Sanghvi, J., Castellano, G., Leite, I. Pereira, A., McOwan, P., and Paiva, A. 2011. *Automatic analysis of affective postures and body motion to detect engagement with a game companion*. In Proc. of the 6th International Conf. on Human-robot Interaction, pages 305{312, New York, NY, USA, 2011. ACM.

[13] Sidner, C., Lee, C., Kidd, C., Lesh, N. and Rich, C. 2005. Explorations in engagement for humans and robots. *Artificial Intelligence*, 166(1):140{164, 2005.

[14] Yu, Z., Papangelis, A. and Rudnicky, A. 21015. *TickTock: Engagement Awareness in a non-Goal-Oriented Multimodal Dialogue Systems*. In Proceedings of the AAAI 2015 Spring Symposium on Turn-taking and Coordination in Human-Machine Interaction. Stanford, USA, 2015.

Gestimator - Shape and Stroke Similarity Based Gesture Recognition

Yina Ye, Petteri Nurmi
Helsinki Institute for Information Technology HIIT
Department of Computer Science, PO Box 68, FI-00014, University of Helsinki, Finland
yina.ye.yyn@gmail.com
petteri.nurmi@cs.helsinki.fi

ABSTRACT

Template-based approaches are currently the most popular gesture recognition solution for interactive systems as they provide accurate and runtime efficient performance in a wide range of applications. The basic idea in these approaches is to measure similarity between a user gesture and a set of pre-recorded templates, and to determine the appropriate gesture type using a nearest neighbor classifier. While simple and elegant, this approach performs well only when the gestures are relatively simple and unambiguous. In increasingly many scenarios, such as authentication, interactive learning, and health care applications, the gestures of interest are complex, consist of multiple sub-strokes, and closely resemble other gestures. Merely considering the shape of the gesture is not sufficient for these scenarios, and robust identification of the constituent sequence of sub-strokes is also required. The present paper contributes by introducing Gestimator, a novel gesture recognizer that combines shape and stroke-based similarity into a sequential classification framework for robust gesture recognition. Experiments carried out using three datasets demonstrate significant performance gains compared to current state-of-the-art techniques. The performance improvements are highest for complex gestures, but consistent improvements are achieved even for simple and widely studied gesture types.

Categories and Subject Descriptors

I.5.2 [**Pattern Recognition**]: Design Methodology: Feature evaluation and selection; I.5.4 [**Pattern Recognition**]: Applications: Signal processing; H.4.m [**Information Systems**]: Information Systems Applications: Miscellaneous

General Terms

Algorithms, Experimentation

Keywords

Gesture Recognition; Segmentation; Pattern Matching

ICMI 2015, November 9–13, 2015, Seattle, WA, USA.
© 2015 ACM. ISBN 978-1-4503-3912-4/15/11 ...$15.00.
DOI: http://dx.doi.org/10.1145/2818346.2820734 .

1. INTRODUCTION

Popularity of touch screen devices combined with increased availability of low-cost gesture tracking technologies, such as consumer-grade depth cameras and accelerometer equipped wearable devices, has resulted in a surge of gesture-based interfaces. Examples of platforms for gesture-based interfaces include gaming consoles [15], mobile devices [1, 9], and smart watches [10]. At the same time, highly accurate and easy to implement gesture recognizers have become available [3, 14, 23], providing increasingly opportunities for developing and prototyping gesture-based interfaces.

Template-based algorithms are currently the most popular gesture recognition approach for interactive systems as they provide several advantages over their counterparts. Firstly, they are computationally efficient, which is particularly important for emerging gesture recognition solutions operating on resource constrained devices, such as smartwatches, smartphones, or other wearable devices [1, 2, 9]. Secondly, template-based recognizers have been shown to provide robust and accurate recognition rates (typically over 90%) even with small amounts of training data [3, 14]. Thirdly, template-based algorithms are intuitive to understand and easy to implement, making it possible to develop and deploy them without expertise in machine learning techniques.

The basic idea in template-based gesture recognizers is to measure similarity between a user's gesture and previously seen gestures, or templates. The user's gesture can then be classified as the type of gesture with highest overall similarity. While simple and elegant, this approach performs well only when gestures are simple and unambiguous. This problem is illustrated in Figure 1 which shows two motion trajectories, one corresponding to the character '{' and the other to '['. When only the similarity of the entire trajectory is considered, these gestures can be easily mistaken, resulting in a wrong interpretation. The issue is further exacerbated by the fact that visual (dis)similarity does not directly translate into gesture (dis)similarity due to the design of gesture recognizers. In fact, as will be later shown, even relatively dissimilar gestures such as a triangle and a circle can be misinterpreted by contemporary gesture recognizers, making it difficult for designers to determine gesture sets that only include unambiguous gestures. At the same, novel domains for gesture interaction are emerging where gestures are inherently complex and ambiguous. Examples of these domains include authentication [17], interactive learning [24], interactive performances [8], and health care [5]. Providing an easy to implement, accurate, and run-time efficient gesture recognition algorithm that can cope with complex and ambiguous gestures currently remains an open challenge.

The present paper contributes by developing *Gestimator* as a novel stroke-based gesture recognizer. The key intuition in Gestimator is to segment gestures into strokes and to match gestures by comparing the similarity of their constituent strokes. Segmenting gestures into strokes helps to resolve ambiguity in the recognition phase, improving overall gesture recognition performance. This is illustrated on the right-hand side of Figure 1 which shows how the strokes of '{' and '[' help to distinguish the two gestures. Segmenting gestures into constituents, however, is far from straightforward as noise and variations in the gesture trajectories, resulting from variations in how users perform gestures, make it difficult to produce a consistent and unique segmentation for a gesture. To overcome these issues, Gestimator builds on a novel adaptive segmentation and matching framework that adapts to the noise level of each gesture and that provides consistent and accurate recognition performance even in the presence of segmentation differences for a specific gesture.

We demonstrate the effectiveness of Gestimator through extensive benchmark experiments carried out using three gesture datasets: a set of unistroke command gestures [23], the Execution Difficulty Set (EDS1) of Vatavu et al. [20], and a dataset consisting of mid-air gestures from a device pairing scenario [2]. As part of the experiments we compare Gestimator against three state-of-the-art gesture recognition techniques: the $1 recognizer [23], Protractor [14], and a DTW-based recognizer [13]. Results of the experiments demonstrate significant performance improvements for all datasets considered in the experiments. The improvements are largest for complex gestures, but consistent improvements are achieved even for simple and widely studied gesture types. As part of the experiments, we also demonstrate that Gestimator results in robust and consistent segmentation performance and that the runtime performance of Gestimator is comparable to state-of-the-art template-based gesture recognizers.

The contributions of the paper are summarized as follows:

1. We develop Gestimator, a novel stroke-based gesture recognizer.
2. We develop a novel adaptive and sequential segment and match framework for comparing gestures based on the combined similarity of their overall shape and the similarity of their constituent strokes.
3. We carry out extensive empirical evaluation of Gestimator, demonstrating that it improves gesture recognition performance compared to popular state-of-the-art gesture recognizers while at the same time preserving runtime efficiency and simplicity of implementation.

2. RELATED WORK

Gesture recognition algorithms can be categorized into two main classes. *Parametric* approaches extract different features from the user's gesture and treat recognition as a classification task. A prominent example is Rubine [16], which uses 13 features extracted from the user's gesture as input to a linear discriminant classifier. Vuurpilj and Schomaker [21] extract features related to relative position, orientation, and curvature. Willems et al. [22] introduce a set of 48 different gesture features. Generally parametric approaches can use any (supervised) classification technique, with Support Vector Machines and Hidden Markov models being popular choices; see, e.g., [11, 22]. The main limitations of parametric approaches are their need for large amounts of training data, and the difficulty of integrating them into user interfaces.

The alternative is to use a *template-based* recognizer which determines the type of gesture by comparing user's input against previously seen gestures, or templates. An early example of template-based recognizers is the SHARK2 [13] system for tablet computers, which uses dynamic time warping (DTW) to compare the similarity of gestures. Another example is the $1 recognizer [23], which uses Euclidean distance to compare gestures. The $1 recognizer also incorporates various preprocessing steps, such as scaling, subsampling, and alignment of gesture orientations, to provide robust performance against minor changes in gesture directions and variations in gesture tracking technology. The 1¢ recognizer [7] is a variation of the $1 recognizer that uses distances from the gesture centroid instead of the original points for recognition. Instead of using Euclidean distance, Protractor [14] compares gestures using minimal angular distance. Kratz and Rohs propose a close-formed quaternion representation for reorienting gestures in order to extend the Protractor algorithm to support 3D gestures. Anthony and Wobbrock [3] propose the $N recognizer, which extends the $1 recognizer to support multi-stroke gestures. Vatavu [18] explores the effect of sampling rate on the performance of template-based recognizers, demonstrating that even small sampling rates tend to result in highly accurate performance. The $P recognizer is another extension of the $1 recognizer, which ignores the ordering of points within gestures during the recognition process [19].

To summarize, previous research on template-based gesture recognition has predominantly targeted development of recognizers that are easy to implement and integrate as part of gesture interfaces. These recognizers are well suited for scenarios where the user gestures are relatively simple, e.g., commands for scrolling, rotating or zooming, and do not contain ambiguity. Our work provides a novel simple-to-implement template-based recognizer that extends the scope of template-based recognition techniques to support scenarios where the gestures are complex, contain ambiguity, and significant amount of user variation.

3. GESTIMATOR: STROKE-BASED GESTURE RECOGNITION

We have developed Gestimator as a novel gesture recognizer that simultaneously compares the similarity of the entire gesture and its constituent sub-strokes. The key technical contributions of Gestimator are (i) an adaptive segmentation algorithm that breaks down the user's gesture into constituents; and (ii) a sequential matching formulation that calculates the similarity of two gestures by comparing its constituent sub-strokes. As our experiments demonstrate, the combination of these contributions provides consistent improvements in gesture recognition accuracy, in particular for complex and ambiguous gestures.

Figure 1 shows an overview of the different processing phases in Gestimator. First, in a *preprocessing* phase, noise is removed from the user's gesture and the gesture data is transformed into a scale and position invariant form. The main source of noise we consider is jitter resulting from sub-

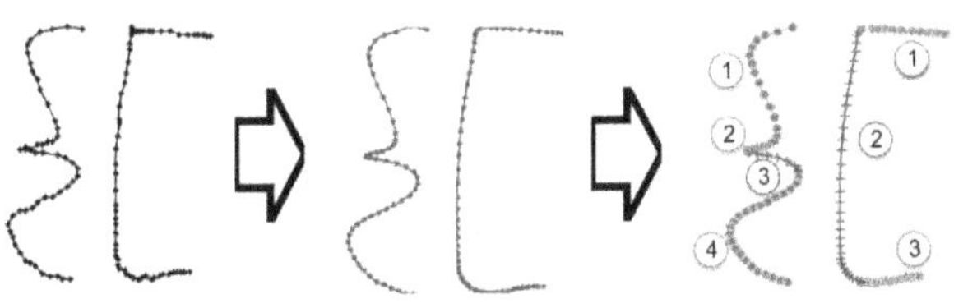

Figure 1: Overview of the gesture recognition pipeline in Gestimator. The raw gesture input (left) is first smoothed and cleaned (middle), after which it is segmented into constituent strokes (right). The gesture recognition phase sequentially compares the strokes in a gesture against previously seen templates to determine appropriate gesture type.

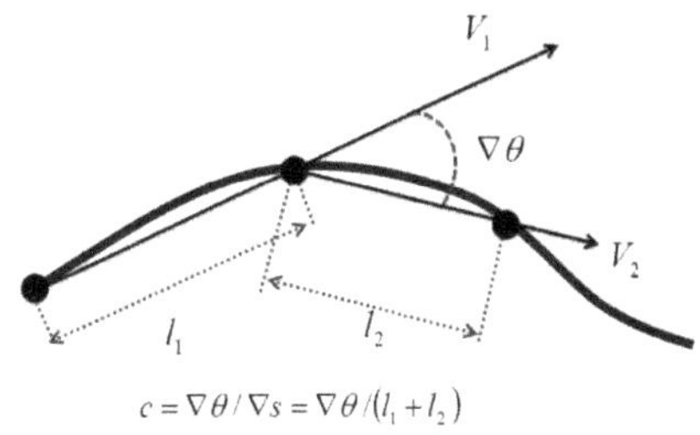

Figure 2: The curvature of a gesture is defined as the ratio of change over a given distance.

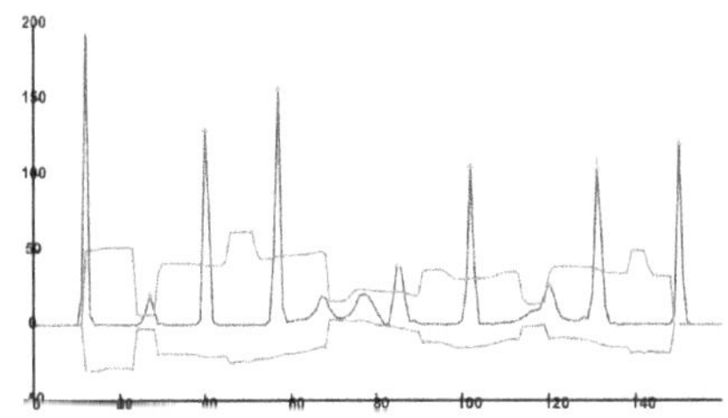

Figure 3: Curvature plot for a gesture together with the confidence bound used for segmentation and the associated peaks corresponding to segment points.

tle hand movements and inaccuracies in the gesture data. Next, the preprocessed gesture is *segmented* into constituent sub-strokes using an adaptive algorithm that identifies peaks in the curvature of the gesture data. Finally, *gesture matching* determines the type of the gesture by comparing the segmented gesture against previously seen gesture trajectories. The matching is performed using a novel sequential matching algorithm that allows local mismatches in the constituent sub-strokes, enabling the matching to operate accurately against different segmentations of the same gesture. In the following we describe the different phases of Gestimator in detail.

3.1 Preprocessing

Gestimator operates on multi dimensional measurements containing timestamped position vectors. In the experiments we consider motion gestures captured from a touch-screen and mid-air gestures captured using a Kinect[1]. We first perform jitter removal by applying a centered moving average filter on the measurements. Jitter results from inaccuracies in the gesture tracking and from subtle, unconscious hand movements. The latter is particularly prominent with in-air gestures, where the hand performing the gesture never is completely stationary. Performing noise removal is essential for ensuring consistent segmentation performance as otherwise small errors in the gesture trajectory can result in additional strokes being detected.

After noise removal, we perform start and end point removal on the gesture data. In our experiments we have observed that users often start and end gestures by having a short stationary period during which subtle hand movements cause changes in the gesture trajectory. These periods can degrade the performance of the segmentation phase unless they are dealt with appropriately. We perform start and end point removal using a density-based clustering algorithm that iteratively merges the first (resp. last) points in the trajectory until a consistent movement trajectory is identified. All points in the detected clusters are removed as noise; see left-hand side of Fig. 1 for illustration. After noise removal, in line with current best practices [14, 23], we normalize the gesture by unit scaling and centering it, thus achieving scale invariance. Rotation invariance can be achieved by normalizing the orientation of the gesture [14, 23]. In our experiments only scale invariance is considered.

[1]We consider gestures to be multi-stroke whenever they can be seen to contain multiple constituents. In the case of handwriting or touch-screen gestures, constituents can be identified from touch or pen motions. However, in the context of mid-air gestures clear boundaries seldom can be identified.

3.2 Stroke Segmentation

Gestimator builds on the novel idea of comparing gestures as sequences of sub-strokes. Segmenting the gesture enables resolving ambiguity by focusing on differences in smaller subsequences of the gesture instead of comparing the entire gesture. To ensure best possible recognition performance, a robust and accurate method for segmenting the gesture into constituent strokes is required. In particular, the segmentation should be consistent across different repetitions of the same gesture and able to identify the most distinguishable parts of the gesture. To preserve the main benefits of template-based recognizers, we also need to ensure the segmentation is sufficiently lightweight to remain runtime efficient even on resource constrained devices.

To accomplish these goals, Gestimator considers an adaptive segmentation algorithm that identifies peaks in the *curvature* of the gesture (see Fig. 2 for a definition). Curvature is well suited for segmentation as it provides a unified measure for changes in the speed and direction. Changes in speed have been widely used to segment sketches into constituents [6], whereas changes in orientation are a staple of line simplification methods, used, e.g., in computer graphics and trajectory monitoring [4, 12]. In practice, however, gestures tend to contain significant variation, e.g., some users simplify gestures in order to perform them more smoothly whereas others consistently monitor their speed to perform the gesture shape as accurately as possible. As we demonstrate in the experiments, using curvature enables robust segmentation across these variations.

Our approach for segmenting gestures into strokes is summarized in Algorithm 1. We first construct a curvature vector V from the preprocessed gesture and apply a sliding win-

Algorithm 1 Segmentation Algorithm

1: A sliding window stroke segmentation method:
2: *Inputs: V vector of input gesture curvature, α_w window length to total length ratio.*
3: Outputs: T vector containing the segmentation indexes of the gesture.
4: **procedure** T = StrokeSegment(V, α_w)
5: $\quad l_w \leftarrow \lfloor$ Length(V^*) $\times \alpha_w \rfloor$
6: $\quad P \leftarrow \emptyset$
7: $\quad$ **for** $i = 1 : \lfloor l_w \rfloor$: Length(V) **do**
8: $\qquad l^* \leftarrow$ getWindow(i)
9: $\qquad I \leftarrow$ DetectSegmentPoint(l^*)
10: $\qquad P := P \bigcup I$
11: $\quad$ **end for**
12: $\quad$ **for** i = Length(V) : $\lfloor l_w \rfloor$: 1 **do**
13: $\qquad l^* \leftarrow$ getWindow(i)
14: $\qquad I \leftarrow$ DetectSegmentPoint(l^*)
15: $\qquad P := P \bigcup I$
16: $\quad$ **end for**
17: $\quad$ **return** T
18: **end procedure**

dow based peak detection on V. To ensure the segmentation can cope with gestures of different length, we determine the size of the sliding window adaptively based on the overall length of the gesture (line 5). For each window, we apply a peak detection method (lines 9 and 14) that identifies points where the curvature changes significantly. Specifically, our peak detection method first constructs a 95% confidence interval for the curvature values within a window. Successive points that fall outside the confidence interval form a so-called *peak area* and the maximal value within each peak area is then chosen as a segmentation point; see Figure 3 for an illustration. To ensure all relevant segment points can be detected, we apply the peak detection in both forward (lines 7 - 11) and backward directions (lines 12 - 16). Once the segment points are detected, we represent the gesture as a sequence of its constituents. Formally, we denote the segmented gesture using $a =< a_1, \ldots, a_k >$ where k is the number of sub-strokes in the gesture.

3.3 Gesture Matching

Gestimator recognizes gestures by comparing the sequence of sub-strokes in a gesture against the sub-strokes of previously seen templates. The general principle is that the higher the similarity between each sub-stroke, the more likely the gesture corresponds to the given template. A challenge with this scheme, however, is that variations in the way gestures are performed can cause two segmentations of the same gesture to differ from each other, e.g., a square can be segmented into three sub-strokes when one of the turns is performed as a round corner. To ensure high recognition performance in the presence of segmentation differences, we consider an accumulative matching framework where subsequent strokes can be merged if they produce higher similarity than the individual strokes alone would.

The intuition behind the accumulative matching framework considered in Gestimator is illustrated in Figure 4. Given two gestures $a =< a_1, \ldots, a_k >$ and $b =< b_1, \ldots, b_l >$, we represent them as binary trees and progressively traverse the corresponding trees by comparing different combinations of strokes. Specifically, each node in the tree correspond to

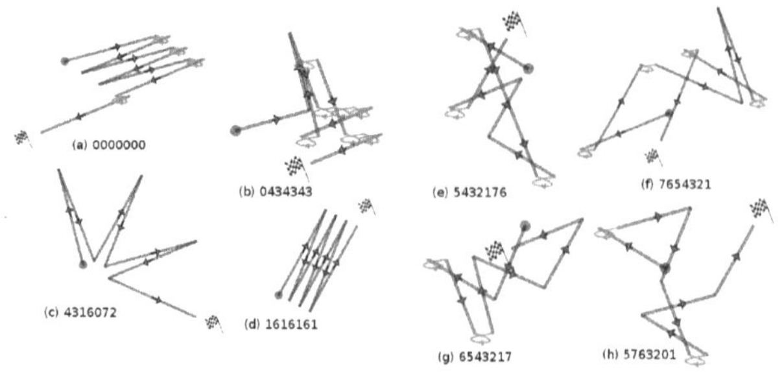

Figure 5: The gesture types in the **Authentication** dataset. The green circle indicates the start of the gesture, and the checkered flag represents the end. Arrows indicate direction of motion. The red swirl gestures are used to reverse the direction of next stroke to constrain the overall gesture within a hand reachable region.

one stroke of the corresponding gesture. The left child of a node corresponds to the case where the subsequent stroke is compared independently of the current stroke, whereas the right child correspond to an accumulative comparison where the two strokes are merged. At each node, the child with higher similarity is chosen. We use DTW as the similarity measure for the strokes since it enables an elastic comparison that accounts for different execution speeds and lengths of the strokes. Note that, as the comparison is performed separately for each stroke, DTW cannot use overall similarity to compensate for intermediate gaps, which is the main problem of current DTW-based recognizers [13]. To ensure efficient runtime performance, we consider a simple traversal heuristic that only considers the subtree specified by the most recent stroke. Consequently, we only need to perform three comparisons at each level of the binary tree, resulting in linear runtime complexity. In practice, the runtime of the matching phase in Gestimator is comparable to that of using a DTW-based recognizer.

4. EXPERIMENTAL SETUP

We demonstrate the effectiveness of Gestimator through rigorous and extensive benchmark evaluations carried out using three datasets. As part of the evaluation, we compare Gestimator against three popular state-of-the-art gesture recognizers: the $1 recognizer [23], Protractor [14], and a DTW-based recognizer [13]. The preprocessing phases and parameters of the baseline algorithms were chosen according to the original articles, and we verified our results by comparing them against the original publications. The datasets we consider were chosen to contain gestures of different complexity and ambiguity, ranging from simple unistroke command gestures to complex multi-stroke authentication gestures. The datasets considered in our evaluation are summarized as follows:

1. **Unistroke** is a dataset of pen-based unistroke gestures[2], collected by Wobbrock et al. [3] from 10 participants. For each participant, the dataset contains 10 repetitions of 16 different command gestures performed with 3 different execution speed levels: fast, medium and slow. The Unistroke dataset has been

[2]Available from: `http://depts.washington.edu/aimgroup/proj/dollar/`.

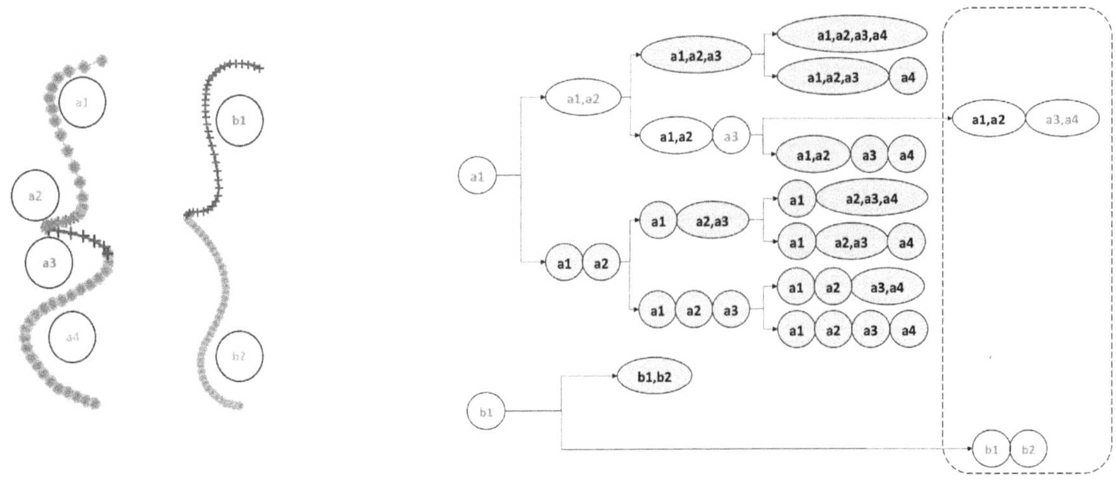

Figure 4: Illustration of the accumulative gesture matching process. The constituents of gestures $a =< a_1, a_2, a_3, a_4 >$ and $b =< b_1, b_2 >$ are progressively compared by traversing the corresponding binary trees and assessing the similarity of the constituents. The highest similarity is obtained for the combination $(a_1, a_2), (a_3, a_4)$ and b_1, b_2.

widely used to evaluate template-based recognizers and we included it to provide a baseline for comparison for the performance of Gestimator.

2. **Execution Difficulty Set #1 (*EDS1*)** is a dataset of pen stroke gestures[3] collected by Vatavu et al. [20]. The dataset contains 20 repetitions of 18 gesture types by 14 participants.
3. **Authentication** consists of continuous mid-air gestures recorded using a Kinect[4]. The gestures are generated automatically and consist of 7 straight line segments and additional swirl strokes, which are used to ensure the gestures remain confined to a sufficiently small region. The dataset contains measurements from 13 participants who performed 8 different gestures for 6 times; see Fig. 5 for the gesture types. As can be observed, the gesture patterns are complex and contain ambiguity, enabling us to assess the performance of Gestimator in a complex usage scenario of practical interest. More details about the application scenario and the experimental setup are given in [2].

#Training:	1	2	3	4	5	Avg.
			Unistroke			
DTW	5.24	2.61	1.92	1.43	1.19	2.48
$1	6.26	3.18	2.06	1.72	1.36	2.91
Protractor	3.61	1.60	1.22	1.00	0.76	1.64
Gestimator	2.36	1.27	0.94	0.84	0.73	1.23
			EDS1			
DTW	4.52	2.50	0.95	0.75	0.79	1.90
$1	5.02	2.29	1.39	1.13	0.84	2.13
Protractor	5.50	2.46	1.54	0.96	0.92	2.28
Gestimator	3.18	0.83	0.42	0.19	0.13	0.94
			Authentication			
DTW	8.44	3.80	2.91	2.73	0.99	3.77
$1	10.87	5.35	3.92	3.42	0.90	4.89
Protractor	17.91	9.23	6.87	5.87	1.82	8.34
Gestimator	8.82	3.55	2.04	1.89	0.68	3.39

Table 1: Recognition error of Gestimator and the baseline algorithms as a function of amount of training data.

5. RESULTS

To assess the performance of Gestimator, we have used the datasets described in the previous section to carry out an extensive and rigorous set of benchmark experiments. In our evaluation we consider the performance of Gestimator both in user-dependent (i.e., personalized) and user-independent gesture recognition, and compare Gestimator against state-of-the-art baselines. We also separately consider the performance of Gestimator in the presence of ambiguous gestures, and evaluate the accuracy and consistency of the stroke segmentation algorithm.

5.1 User-Dependent Recognition

We first consider the recognition performance of Gestimator in user-dependent testing, i.e., in a personalized scenario where training samples from the end user are available. We perform our evaluation by considering a cross-validation scheme that is analogous to the one used by Wobbrock et al. [23] to evaluate the $1 recognizer. Specifically, we test each user separately, taking k randomly sampled repetitions of each gesture as training data and using the remaining samples as test data. In the experiment k was varied from 1 to 5 and the experiment was carried out 100 times for each level of k, i.e., for a given user and gesture we performed 500 recognition tests.

The results of the evaluation are summarized in Table 1. From the results we can observe that all algorithms generally achieve high recognition accuracy on the simpler pen gestures, but their performance decreases on the authentication gestures. Gestimator has best overall performance, with an average recognition error of 1.85%. Compared to the baselines, Gestimator is able to consistently outperform

[3] Available from `http://www.eed.usv.ro/~vatavu/index.php?menuItem=pengestures2011`.

[4] Available for research purposes from `universe.hiit.fi/gesture`

them, particularly on the EDS1 and authentication datasets, which contain complex and ambiguous gesture pairs. We analyzed statistical significance of the performance differences by conducting McNemar's tests with Yates' correction on the on the confusion matrices of the recognizers. The results of the significance analysis showed the performance differences between Gestimator and the baseline methods to be statistically significant for all datasets ($p < .001$).

One of the main benefits of template-based recognizers is that they are capable of achieving high recognition rates with very small amounts of training data. From the results in Table 1 we can observe this to be the case also for Gestimator, which outperforms the baselines with a single exception. On the authentication dataset Gestimator performs slightly worse than DTW when only a single training sample is available. However, the difference between the algorithms is not statistically significant and both algorithms perform an order of magnitude better the other two baselines. From the results we can also observe that, on the simpler pen-based gesture datasets, the performance difference between Gestimator and the baseline techniques is highest when only one or two training samples per gesture are available.

We also assessed the runtime performance of the different algorithms as part of the experiment. Protractor has the fastest overall performance, reaching an average matching time of 28ms. The next best is $1 (mean 37ms) followed by DTW (mean 52ms). The matching time of Gestimator is expectedly slowest (mean 86 ms), especially since it builds on DTW. While slower than that of other techniques, it remains more than feasible for most practical applications of gesture recognition. Overall the results thus demonstrate that Gestimator is capable of providing significant improvements in the robustness and accuracy of gesture recognition in a diverse set of scenarios. Moreover, these improvements are reached even when very small amounts of training data are available. These improvements are obtained with a small decrease in runtime performance. However, overall the results suggest that Gestimator is the best suited algorihtm, unless the gestures are very simple and sufficient amounts of training data are available.

5.2 User-Independent Recognition

We next consider the generalization performance of Gestimator in a user independent gesture recognition scenario. We carry out the evaluation by randomly choosing one user as test subject. To train the different algorithms, we construct a training dataset by randomly choosing p other users. For each training user, we randomly choose k different repetitions of each gesture type. The randomization is performed 100 times for each different value of p and k.

The results of this evaluation are summarized in Table 2. Generally the performance of all algorithms suffers in the user-independent case, with particularly Protractor resulting in significant performance degradation. When training from only one or two test users is available, Gestimator loses against the DTW recognizer. However, when data from three or more users is available, Gestimator already starts to consistently outperform the other algorithms. The decrease in performance is likely to be caused by the fact that Gestimator assumes gestures are performed in the same order, whereas there are some variations in the order people perform gestures. As illustrated in the previous section, Gestimator only requires very limited amount of data from each different type of user, thus demonstrating generally a good generalization performance.

Table 2: Error rates (percentage) of user independent testing

# Training	1	2	3	4	5
			Unistroke		
DTW	13.19	8.22	5.86	4.99	3.96
$1	14.27	8.79	6.79	5.52	4.72
Protractor	16.46	9.96	7.54	6.38	4.83
Gestimator	14.11	8.06	4.41	3.26	2.57
			EDS1		
DTW	2.35	0.53	0.20	0.19	0.17
$1	3.33	1.06	0.56	0.25	0.13
Protractor	10.37	4.80	2.96	2.25	1.73
Gestimator	8.15	2.41	0.27	0.00	0.00
			Authentication		
DTW	7.42	6.23	5.25	5.53	4.59
$1	24.86	12.71	10.11	6.33	6.50
Protractor	28.66	20.27	12.86	11.98	11.71
Gestimator	16.56	6.75	4.62	3.40	3.06

5.3 Gesture Ambiguity

One of the main design goals for Gestimator has been to improve recognition rates in the presence of ambiguous gestures. We demonstrate this is the case by carrying out an evaluation where we consider all gesture with error rate of 2.5% or higher with any of the algorithms considered in the evaluation. The results of this evaluation are summarized in Table 3. From the table, we can observe that ambiguity is highly algorithm dependent, with different pairs being problematic for different recognizers. Besides the example of detecting '{' and '[' being generally difficult, also somewhat surprising pairs such as triangle vs. rectangle and circle vs. 6 cause difficulties to recognizers that rely on overall shape similarity. The results also show that ambiguity can depend on the characteristics of the dataset as the gesture pair rectangle vs. circle is more difficult for all recognizers in the EDS1 dataset than in the Unistroke dataset.

For the majority of the ambiguous gesture pairs (21/35), we can observe that Gestimator outperforms the baseline algorithms, and even in the remaining cases Gestimator is usually within 1% error of the best performing algorithm. Only two exceptions can be observed, both of which are on the authentication dataset (0434343 vs. 0000000 and 6543217 vs. 5432176; see Fig. 5). The reason for errors in these gesture pairs is that the pairs have many matching strokes, despite having different overall similarity. As we have used an elastic similarity measure, the mismatching strokes are not always sufficient for separating the gesture pairs. This issue can be mitigated by adjusting the similarity measure to assign higher gap penalty for mismatches between stroke pairs. However, even for these highly complex gesture pairs the recognition rate of Gestimator is high, achiving smaller than 3.5% error rate.

5.4 Segmentation Performance

The performance of Gestimator depends on the accuracy of the stroke segmentation algorithm described in Sec. 3.2.

Unistroke		DTW	$1	Prot.	Gest.
check	v	3.09	2.67	**1.56**	1.67
circle	rectangle	5.60	5.24	1.82	**0.85**
circle	triangle	2.69	3.13	**0.05**	1.73
{	[	3.29	4.67	3.36	**1.34**
?	caret	2.55	3.44	**0.51**	0.82
?	]	2.00	3.02	**1.13**	1.33
rectangle	circle	0.07	0.22	3.36	**0.07**
triangle	circle	3.47	4.56	1.75	**1.72**
triangle	rectangle	4.29	6.18	0.87	**0.75**
v	check	3.07	2.00	**1.91**	2.69
EDS1		DTW	$1	Prot.	Gest.
8	reversed-pi	1.14	2.83	1.97	**0.08**
8	strike-through	4.00	3.07	2.30	**0.00**
8	turn-90	0.86	3.43	2.49	**0.00**
circle	6	6.00	5.34	4.96	**0.00**
circle	rectangle	4.29	3.99	4.89	**0.80**
rectangle	circle	0.86	**0.31**	2.46	1.12
steep-hill	sail-boat	0.43	2.73	2.87	**0.00**
triangle	6	3.29	2.80	2.80	**0.00**
triangle	circle	2.86	2.53	3.66	**0.37**
Authentication		DTW	$1	Prot.	Gest.
0000000	0434343	**1.92**	3.52	2.91	2.06
0000000	1616161	2.69	1.20	**1.02**	1.13
0000000	4316072	0.93	2.18	3.89	**0.88**
0434343	0000000	1.78	**0.78**	0.98	3.49
0434343	4316072	1.38	2.55	2.98	**0.15**
1616161	4316072	1.55	4.63	7.12	**0.56**
4316072	1616161	1.52	3.05	3.38	**1.47**
4316072	6543217	0.15	0.11	4.50	**0.13**
5432176	5763201	3.63	**2.34**	2.36	3.11
5432176	6543217	3.57	3.51	3.76	**2.24**
5763201	0000000	0.14	1.23	3.81	**0.14**
5763201	4316072	0.38	1.78	4.86	**0.35**
6543217	5432176	3.20	**1.57**	2.46	3.33

Table 3: Error rates of different algorithms for gesture pairs with the highest error rates.

Specifically, accurate segmentation ensures consistent subsequences of the original gesture are being compared during the matching phase. Accurate segmentation also translates into faster runtime performance by reducing the number of look-ahead steps in the matching phase. As the next step of evaluation we demonstrate that Gestimator is capable of segmenting gestures accurately and consistently.

We assess segmentation accuracy by comparing the number of strokes resulting from the gesture segmentation against the actual number of strokes in a gesture. Ground truth for the Unistroke and EDS1 datasets was obtained through majority voting on the results of five independent annotators. Inter-rater reliability was assessed using Cohen's kappa and found to be substantial ($\kappa > .7, p < .001$). For the authentication dataset, the number of strokes was predetermined by the encoding scheme used to generate the gestures. Segmentation consistency was measured by calculating the variance and range of the number of strokes for each repetition of the same gesture.

Figure 6 shows the cumulative distribution plot of the segmentation errors for the different datasets. The low-

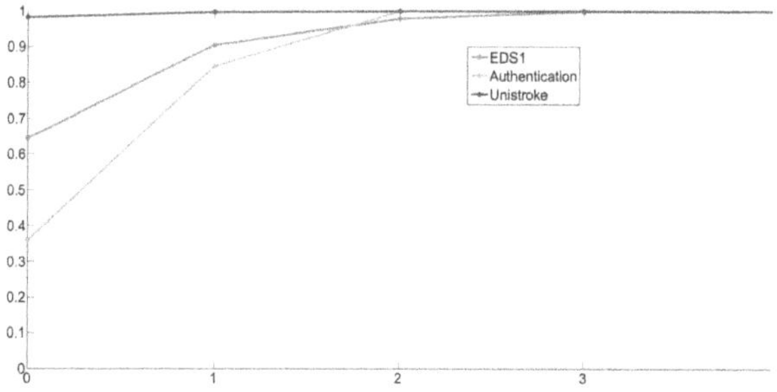

Figure 6: Cumulative probability distribution plot for segmentation error. The values on the x-axis correspond to the error in number of strokes, whereas the y-axis shows the cumulative probability.

Dataset	Variance	Range
Unistroke	0.43	0 - 2
EDS1	0.41	0 - 2
Authentication	1.48	0 - 4

Table 4: Summary of the results for evaluation of segmentation consistency.

est performance is obtained for the authentication dataset where 97.8% of the gestures being segmented with at most 2 additional strokes. The main reason for errors in the authentication dataset are the circular swirl motions, which sometimes are segmented into multiple segments. For the other two datasets segmentation accuracy is much higher. On the Unistroke dataset 98.2% of the gestures result in accurate segmentation. On the EDS1 dataset 90.5% of the gestures are segmented with an error of at most a single stroke. The results for segmentation consistency, summarized in Table 4, closely mirror the results of segmentation error. On the Unistroke and EDS1 datasets the average variance of the number of strokes for the same gesture is below 0.5, suggesting that most gestures are segmented with at most a single stroke difference. On the authentication dataset the number of strokes varies bit more, with an average difference of 1.5 strokes and a maximum error of 4 strokes. Analogously to the segmentation error results, most of these differences are due to variations in the way users perform swirl motions. To summarize, overall the results demonstrate that Gestimator has accurate segmentation performance and is capable of providing consistent segmentation across different users and across variations in user performance.

6. SUMMARY AND CONCLUSION

We have contributed by presenting Gestimator, a novel template-based gesture recognizer that compares gestures by considering the similarity of stroke sequences in them. The main technical contributions of our work have been an algorithm for segmenting gestures into strokes, and an algorithm for assessing the similarity of stroke sequences, taking into account possible errors in segmentation. Experiments carried out using three datasets demonstrate significant performance gains compared to existing state-of-the-art techniques. The results also demonstrate that Gestimator is capable of accurately and consistently segmenting gestures into strokes, and that it has good generalization performance against different sources of variation in gesture trajectories.

The results also demonstrate that the performance gains of Gestimator are particularly significant for gesture pairs that contain ambiguity or a high level of complexity.

7. ACKNOWLEDGMENTS

The work has been partially funded by DIGILE D2I SHOK programme. The work only reflects the authors' views.

8. REFERENCES

[1] S. Agrawal, I. Constandache, S. Gaonkar, R. R. Choudhury, K. Caves, and F. DeRuyter. Using mobile phones to write in air. In *Proceedings of the 9th International Conference on Mobile Systems, Applications, and Services (MobiSys 2011)*, 2011.

[2] I. Ahmed, Y. Ye, S. Bhattacharya, N. Asokan, G. Jacucci, P. Nurmi, and S. Tarkoma. Checksum Gestures: Continuous Gestures as an Out-of-Band Channel for Secure Pairing. In *Proceedings of The 2015 ACM International Joint Conference on Pervasive and Ubiquitous Computing (UbiComp)*, 2015.

[3] L. Anthony and J. O. Wobbrock. A lightweight multistroke recognizer for user interface prototypes. In *Graphics Interface*, 2010.

[4] J. Brault and R. Plamondon. Segmenting handwritten signatures at their perceptually important points. *Pattern Analysis and Machine Intelligence*, 15:953 – 957, 1993.

[5] M. Fan, D. Gravem, D. M. Cooper, and D. J. Patterson. Augmenting gesture recognition with erlang-cox models to identify neurological disorders in premature babies. In *Proceedings of the 2012 ACM Conference on Ubiquitous Computing (UbiComp)*, 2012.

[6] J. Herold and T. F. SpeedSeg: A technique for segmenting pen strokes using pen speed. *Computers and Graphics*, 35:250 – 264, 2011.

[7] J. Herold and T. F. Stahovich. The One Cent Recognizer: A Fast, Accurate, and Easy-to-Implement Handwritten Gesture Recognition Technique. In *Proceedings of the Symposium on Sketch Based Interfaces and Modeling (SBM)*, pages 39–46. Eurographics Association, 2012.

[8] H.-S. Ip, K. Law, and B. Kwong. Cyber Composer: Hand Gesture-Driven Intelligent Music Composition and Generation. In *Proceedings of the 11th International Multimedia Modelling Conference (MMM)*, 2005.

[9] W. Kienzle and K. Hinckley. Writing handwritten messages on a small touchscreen. In *Proceedings of the 15th International Conference on Human-Computer Interaction with Mobile Devices and Services*, 2013.

[10] J. Kim, J. He, K. Lyons, and T. Starner. The Gesture Watch: A Wireless Contact-free Gesture based Wrist Interface. In *Proceedings of the 11th IEEE International Symposium on Wearable Computers (ISWC)*, 2007.

[11] J.-B. Kim, K.-H. Park, W.-C. Bang, and Z. Bien. Continuous gesture recognition system for Korean sign language based on fuzzy logic and hidden Markov model. In *Proceedings of the 2002 IEEE International Conference on Fuzzy Systems*, pages 1574–1579. IEEE, 2002.

[12] M. B. Kjærgaard, S. Bhattacharya, H. Blunck, and P. Nurmi. Energy-efficient trajectory tracking for mobile devices. In *Proceedings of the 9th International Conference on Mobile Systems, Applications and Services (MobiSys)*, 2011.

[13] P. O. Kristensson and S. Zhai. SHARK^2: a large vocabulary shorthand writing system for pen-based computers. In *Proceedings of the 17th Annual ACM Symposium on User Interface Software and Technology (UIST)*, 2004.

[14] Y. Li. Protractor: A Fast and Accurate Gesture Recognizer. In *Proceedings of the SIGCHI Conference on Human Factors in Computing Systems (CHI)*, 2010.

[15] M. Raptis, D. Kirovski, and H. Hoppe. Real-Time Classification of Dance Gesturesfrom Skeleton Animation. In *Proceedings of the 2011 Eurographics/ACM SIGGRAPH Symposium on Computer Animation*, 2011.

[16] D. Rubine. Specifying gestures by example. In *Proceedings of the 18th Annual Conference on Computer Graphics and Interactive Techniques (SIGGRAPH)*, 1991.

[17] M. Sherman, G. Clark, Y. Yang, S. Sugrim, A. Modig, J. Lindqvist, A. Oulasvirta, and T. Roos. User-generated free-form gestures for authentication: Security and memorability. In *The 12th International Conference on Mobile Systems, Applications, and Services (MobiSys)*, 2014.

[18] R.-D. Vatavu. The effect of sampling rate on the performance of template-based gesture recognizers. In *Proceedings of the 13th International Conference on Multimodal Interfaces (ICMI)*, 2011.

[19] R.-D. Vatavu, L. Anthony, and J. O. Wobbrock. Gestures as point clouds: a $P recognizer for user interface prototypes. In *Proceedings of the International Conference on Multimodal Interaction (ICMI)*, 2012.

[20] R.-D. Vatavu, D. Vogel, G. Casiez, and L. Grisoni. Estimating the perceived difficulty of pen gestures. In *Human-Computer Interaction–INTERACT 2011*, pages 89–106. Springer, 2011.

[21] L. Vuurpijl and L. Schomaker. Finding structure in diversity: a hierarchical clustering method for the categorization of allographs in handwriting. In *Proceedings of the 4th International Conference Document Analysis and Recognition (ICDAR)*, 1997.

[22] D. Willems, R. Niels, M. van Gerven, and L. Vuurpijl. Iconic and multi-stroke gesture recognition. *Pattern Recognition*, 12:3303–3312, 2009.

[23] J. O. Wobbrock, A. D. Wilson, and Y. Li. Gestures without libraries, toolkits or training: a $1 recognizer for user interface prototypes. In *Proceedings of the 20th Annual ACM Symposium on User Interface Software and Technology (UIST)*, pages 159–168. ACM, 2007.

[24] Z. Zafrulla, H. Brashear, T. Starner, H. Hamilton, and P. Presti. American sign language recognition with the kinect. In *Proceedings of the 13th International Conference on Multimodal Interfaces (ICMI)*, 2011.

Classification of Children's Social Dominance in Group Interactions with Robots

Sarah Strohkorb
Yale University
51 Prospect Street
New Haven, CT 06521 USA
sarah.strohkorb@yale.edu

Iolanda Leite
Yale University
51 Prospect Street
New Haven, CT 06521 USA
iolanda.leite@yale.edu

Natalie Warren
Yale University
51 Prospect Street
New Haven, CT 06521 USA
natalie.warren@yale.edu

Brian Scassellati
Yale University
51 Prospect Street
New Haven, CT 06521 USA
brian.scassellati@yale.edu

ABSTRACT

As social robots become more widespread in educational environments, their ability to understand group dynamics and engage multiple children in social interactions is crucial. Social dominance is a highly influential factor in social interactions, expressed through both verbal and nonverbal behaviors. In this paper, we present a method for determining whether a participant is high or low in social dominance in a group interaction with children and robots. We investigated the correlation between many verbal and nonverbal behavioral features with social dominance levels collected through teacher surveys. We additionally implemented Logistic Regression and Support Vector Machines models with classification accuracies of 81% and 89%, respectively, showing that using a small subset of nonverbal behavioral features, these models can successfully classify children's social dominance level. Our approach for classifying social dominance is novel not only for its application to children, but also for achieving high classification accuracies using a reduced set of nonverbal features that, in future work, can be automatically extracted with current sensing technology.

Categories and Subject Descriptors

I.2.6 [**Artificial Intelligence**]: Learning

Keywords

Social dominance; children; classification; groups; human-robot interaction.

ICMI 2015, November 9–13, 2015, Seattle, WA, USA.
 ISBN 978-1-4503-3912-4/15/11 ...$15.00.
DOI: http://dx.doi.org/10.1145/XXX.2818346.2820735.

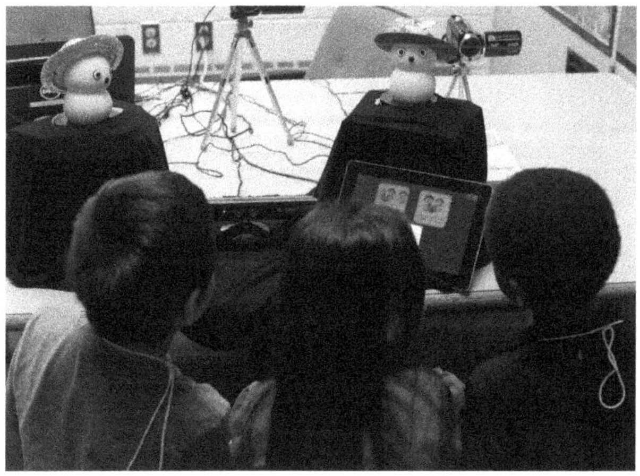

Figure 1: Interactive narrative scenario with social robots Leo and Berry (Robot 1 and Robot 2, respectively) used for data collection.

1. INTRODUCTION

Social robots are becoming increasingly common tools in education [19, 26]. As they are deployed in unstructured real-world environments such as museums and schools, their ability to interact with groups of users (children in particular) acquires a fundamental importance. In addition to evident decreases in cost, time, and space, research suggests that interactions between groups of children and robots share some of the positive outcomes of traditional learning experiences in groups [17]. However, the dynamics of group social interactions introduce additional challenges that are nonexistent in typical one-on-one human-robot interactions. For example, some children might dominate the interaction, giving other group members fewer opportunities to contribute. If robots could detect such situations, they could mediate the interaction so that all children can benefit from the group learning experience.

One of the most important constructs in group dynamics is the notion of social dominance, defined as "a relational, behavioral and interacting state that reflects the actual achievement of influence or control over another via communicative actions" [5]. Social dominance literature suggests that high dominant individuals benefit from social attention that low dominant ones do not [10], which can potentially impact the performance of low dominant children in group learning environments. Since it plays such an important role in interpersonal group relationships, social dominance has been conceptualized and studied from many different perspectives, from evolutionary theories [9] to psychological approaches [22]. Across disciplines, most authors agree that social dominance differs from the related concepts of power and status in that dominance is a means of achieving these through creating expressive, relationally-based strategies or actions [5].

The communicative nature of social dominance offers an opportunity for machines to automatically recognize dominant behaviors in social interactions. In fact, several efforts have been successful at automatically classifying dominance levels in adults based on their behavior [12, 13, 14]. While there have also been attempts at understanding the most common behaviors in dominant children [15, 24], none of these works focused on automatic classification using those behaviors.

In this paper, we provide a first investigation on the automatic classification of children's dominance level (high vs. low) using verbal and nonverbal behavioral features. The motivation for addressing automatic classification of social dominance in groups of children, given similar efforts in adults, is twofold. First, theory suggests that dominant behaviors in children are more related to evolutionary approaches of resource acquisition and conflict. As stated by Hawley [9], social dominance in children is "grounded in the differential ability to acquire resources in the social group, regardless of the means by which this is done." Second, previous research on automatic analysis of social behavior in groups of children shows that adult rules do not necessarily apply to children [16]. If dominant behaviors in children differ from adult behaviors, one cannot expect that the adult computational models will generalize well when applied to children.

This work is situated within a project whose overarching goal is to use socially assistive robots to help children build their emotional intelligence skills through interactive role-playing. The effective acquisition of emotional skills is crucial for children's social development [3, 21, 27], but it requires constant practice in diverse social situations. One way for developing these skills is by active learning techniques such as role-playing scenarios. However, in emotionally charged domains (e.g., bullying prevention), having children take an active part in the role-play may cause undesirable consequences, but observing the interaction might adequately serve as a learning experience. Here, robots offer an inexpensive alternative to human actors because they can display controlled behavior across interventions while having more social presence than virtual characters on a screen [18, 20].

To investigate whether high and low dominant children can be automatically classified using verbal and nonverbal behaviors, we started by collecting a data corpus of 21 children (ages 6 to 8 years) interacting with social robots in the context of interactive educational narratives described above. Our ground truth was based on teacher evaluations of each student using an Interpersonal Dominance Scale [5]. After analyzing and annotating the videos in our data corpus, a set of verbal and nonverbal features were extracted and used as the input of two machine learning binary classifiers (Logistic Regression and Support Vector Machines). Our results suggest that high/low children's dominance level can be successfully classified with accuracy values of 81% and 89% for the Logistic Regression and Support Vector Machines methods, respectively. The fact that most of the relevant features in our model can be extracted automatically with current state-of-the-art perception systems strengthens the contribution of our approach, given the possibility of applying the obtained models in real-time to groups of children interacting with robots.

2. RELATED WORK

This section describes previous research on social dominance in both adults and children. We give special attention to works that investigate which verbal and nonverbal behaviors are relevant for characterizing dominance across the lifespan.

2.1 Social Dominance in Adults

Most of the work on automatic classification of social dominance has been conducted with adult participants. The Augmented Multi-Party Interaction (AMI) corpus is a main source of interaction data for many researchers interested in computational modeling of this construct [12, 13, 14]. The AMI corpus consists of videos of meetings of 4-5 people with prescribed individual roles working towards a common goal. While this corpus has contributed significantly to advances in social dominance research in adults, for the reasons enumerated earlier it is not expected that the outcomes of this research can generalize well to groups of children.

Previous work has identified a set of multimodal features relevant for the automatic classification of social dominance in adults, including verbal cues like speech energy [13, 14] and interruptions [8, 14, 25, 28], visual cues like eye gaze [12, 23] and looking at another while talking [8], as well as kinesic cues like body posture [8] and gestures [8, 13]. In particular, there is a good deal of evidence that speaking time is a very strong cue for dominance in adults [14, 25]. Jayagopi et al. [13] obtained a high classification accuracy using an unsupervised model with only a total speaking length feature. The total number of speaking turns (with short utterances removed) performed equally well in an unsupervised model, and a combination of audio features showed over 90% accuracy in a supervised model [13]. Gaze and looking-time measures have also been used in many adult social dominance studies. The Visual Dominance Ratio introduced by Dovidio and Ellyson [7] and the amount of time others look at the participant in question have proven especially significant in this domain [8, 12].

2.2 Social Dominance in Children

The smaller body of work investigating cues to social dominance in children is different from work with adults in several important ways. First, children undergo a shift in the ways they manifest dominance around the age of five. Younger children tend to display dominance in terms of aggression and resource-directness, but this gives way to more prosocial behaviors as they age [9]. Hawley's work examining dominance expression supports this claim, showing that on average, socially dominant children ages 4-7 exhibited prosocial behavior twice as often as they exhibited coercive behaviors, while non-socially dominant children engaged in both behaviors equally [10]. This explains why there are many studies exploring the link between aggression and social dominance in young children, but not in older children or adults. In research on dominance levels of 6- to 8-year-old children, it is reasonable to analyze features both found in adults and younger children, in order to capture dominance-cueing behaviors on both sides of this developmental shift.

Many of the dominance cues observed in younger children are actively social or agonistic in nature – for example, peer visual regard [24], hostility and aggression [10], and reactions to initiated agonism [29]. A few studies have investigated the connection between dominance and resource utilization ratios, comparing time children spent engaged in an enjoyable individual activity (watching a movie on a viewing machine that must be hand-cranked by someone other than the viewer), to time spent helping others enjoy the activity [15]. Pellegrini et al. [24] studied naturalistic social interactions focusing on aggressive bouts. These methods yielded extremely interesting results, but were extremely time-intensive and focused on the idea of resource utilization rather than general social dominance. A main limitation of these studies is that, with the notable exception of peer visual regard, many of these cues are highly domain-specific. That is, the cues are only present or are only relevant within the specific social groups and environments set up by the researchers. Another limitation is that some of these cues, such as hostility, are potentially as hard to capture automatically as the notion of social dominance itself.

2.3 Our Approach

In light of the limitations of prior research in this area, our work attempts to establish reliable cues to social dominance in children which, like the features explored in adults, can be easily extracted over a short stretch of typical group interactions. The included features not only directly correspond to intuitive ideas of dominance, but also show high potential for good results in computational modeling. The use of machine learning models, which to our knowledge have not yet been applied to children's data in this domain, provides an opportunity to accurately classify dominance behaviors at an age where children's manifestations of dominance are radically shifting.

3. INTERACTIVE NARRATIVES FOR EMOTIONAL LITERACY

Previous research has shown that emotional intelligence skills are crucial for guiding decision-making, attention, and behavioral responses, and are necessary for children to engage in the social world [3, 21]. The case study used in this work includes two MyKeepon Robots (see Figure 1) that play out an interactive story about inclusion. One of the robots, Leo (hereafter referred to as Robot 2), is new at school. At specific moments in the narrative, children can influence the storyline by choosing from a set of actions that Berry (hereafter referred to as Robot 1) can take to make Leo feel included. Children can pick among the story options using a tablet. In other words, they can tell Berry what to do and see the impact of the selected actions on the course of the story. The robots can display different animations during the interaction, such as speaking, idling (while they are waiting for children's choices or listening to the other robot) or bouncing (moving up and down and to the sides). Pre-recorded adult utterances, with modified pitch signal to make them more childlike, were used for the robots' voices.

In the data collection experiment reported in this paper, the only perception the robots had from the environment was the children's story choice input from the tablet. However, our ultimate goal is to endow the robots with social awareness mechanisms that will likely improve the interaction and learning experience. One such mechanism is an automatic system for classifying children's dominance levels in this setting. With this knowledge about the group, the robots could prevent socially dominant children from controlling the interaction and prompt less dominant children to intervene more often.

4. DATA COLLECTION

We collected a corpus of video and audio data of groups of children interacting with robots using the interactive narrative scenario presented in the previous section.

4.1 Participants

Our data corpus consists of 21 children (13 female, 8 male), with ages between 6 and 8 years old ($M = 7.53$, $SD = 0.51$), interacting in small groups of 3 (7 groups in total) with two social robots. One group had females only and all the other groups were gender balanced (at least one male or female). Participants were first and second graders from an elementary school in the East Coast region of the United States. Each group contained students from the same class and our participant pool included 5 different classes. The data collection took place in a small meeting room of the elementary school.

Ethnicity, as reported by guardians, was 17.5% African American, 17.5% Caucasian, 25% Hispanic; 27.5% reported more than one ethnicity, and 12.5% did not report. The annual income reported by guardians was as follows: 30% in \$0-\$20,000, 42.5% in \$20,000-\$50,000, and 10% in the \$50,000-\$100,000 range; 17.5% did not report.

4.2 Procedure

One experimenter was present in the small meeting room for the entire data collection session. The experimenter started by introducing the participants to the two robots, Berry (Robot 1) and Leo (Robot 2), and explaining that the robots would play out a story, and then when the story stopped, they could decide what action Berry would take next from the options that appeared on the tablet. Participants were told that they would have to choose the next story option as a group, and then one of them would select their choice on the tablet.

The interactive story about inclusion used in this data collection contained an introductory scene and three different options that participants could then freely explore. The interaction ended when participants explored all three story options. The average interaction time, from the moment when participants selected the first story option until the robots played all the possible scenes, was 4 minutes 36 seconds ($SD = 39$ seconds).

4.3 Interaction Data

Three HD cameras were used to record the interaction. Each camera captured mainly the upper body posture and face of one participant. Log files containing the content of the robots' actions (speech and nonverbal behaviors) and the story choices made by the children were generated. The logs contained timestamps to allow future synchronization with the remaining data.

A coding scheme including verbal and nonverbal behaviors was developed based on the social dominance literature reported in section 2. Using the videos collected during the interactions, five annotators coded the start and end times of specified participant behaviors defined in the coding scheme. The verbal behaviors included **utterance type** – *making a demand*, *making a suggestion or prompt*, *helping others*, *thinking aloud*, *insulting* or *other* for all the talking behaviors that did not fit in the earlier categories, **utterance addressee** – *to colleagues*, *to robots*, *to experimenter*, or *thinking aloud*, and **interruptions** – *successful* or *unsuccessful*. The nonverbal behaviors defined in the coding scheme were **gaze** – *looking at the robots*, *looking at other participants*, *looking elsewhere* and *unclear*, **gestures** – *intrusive* (e.g., gestures that take others' space), *illustrative* gestures while talking and *adaptors* (e.g., nervous habits, or fidgeting), and the presence of **physical coercion**. Annotations were done using the ELAN annotation tool [4]. To avoid issues with intra-coder reliability, each coding category was coded by only one annotator.

4.4 Social Dominance Ground Truth

Our ground truth values for social dominance were based on teacher evaluations of participants collected during an individual interview with each teacher. We adapted the Interpersonal Dominance Scale developed by Burgoon [5], which has been previously used in HCI research [2, 11]. Out of the 32 items comprising Burgoon's original Interpersonal Dominance Scale, we selected the ones that seemed more relevant to group interactions between children, ending up with 11 items. We asked the teachers, for each study participant in his/her class, how often this child (1) takes charge of conversations, (2) talks more than listens, (3) influences others, (4) is very expressive during interactions, (5) wins arguments against his/her peers, (6) is concerned with what others think of him/her, (7) is successful at persuading others, (8) exhibits "bossy" behaviors, (9) wants to be in charge, (10) is the main focus of attention and (11) has influence in choosing group activities. Teachers were asked to rate each one of these assertions on a scale of 1 to 5, 1 meaning "almost never" and 5 meaning "almost always."

Our social dominance scale had excellent internal consistency (Chronbach's $\alpha = 0.96$). We averaged the teacher scores on all 11 scale items to obtain an absolute dominance score for each participant between the range of 1.0 and 5.0 ($M = 2.86, SD = 1.27$). The least dominant child had an average score of 1.27, while the most dominant was scored 4.73. The distribution of the scores is shown in Figure 2.

5. FEATURE EXTRACTION & ANALYSIS

From the annotations described in section 4.3, we extracted a set of domain-independent verbal, nonverbal and combined (verbal and nonverbal) features for further analysis. In addition to these, gender was also included as a feature given the controversial results as to whether or not it has an effect on children's dominance [9, 15].

The feature analysis described here and the generated models reported in the next section rely on hand-annotated data. This deliberate choice was made because we wanted to distinguish the adequacy of our feature set to classify social dominance from the adequacy of particular feature detectors. However, our future goal is to replace the human-annotated features with autonomous perception systems, such that we can run a real-time implementation of the developed models in our robots.

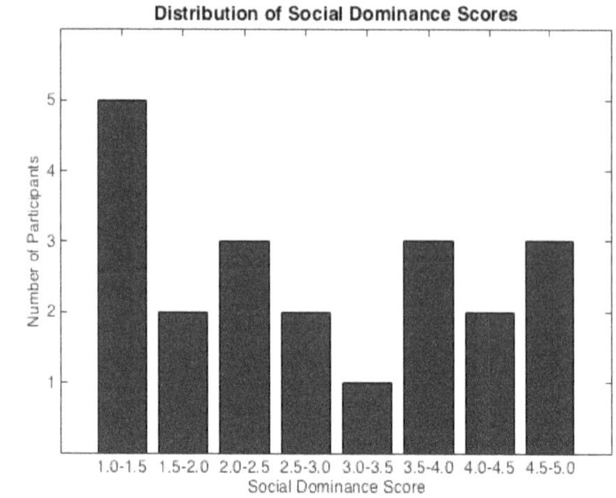

Figure 2: The distribution of the social dominance scores as evaluated by the teachers of the participants ($M = 2.86, SD = 1.27$).

5.1 Verbal Behaviors

We examined the following verbal behaviors that characterize participants' utterances: total talking time, interruptions, utterance addressee and utterance type. The extracted features from all these behaviors represent the total duration that each participant expressed that behavior, normalized by the length of the interaction.

Total talking time. We recorded the total talking time of each participant during the interaction.

Interruptions. This feature encodes the total time a participant spends interrupting other participants. An interruption is defined as any time a participant starts to talk while another participant is already talking. Interruptions are noted as either successful or unsuccessful. A successful interruption is marked for participant A when they start talking while participant B is talking and participant B stops talking before participant A does.

Utterance Addressee. We recorded the total time a participant's vocalization is directed to one of the following audiences: (1) to colleagues, (2) to robots, (3) to experimenter, or (4) thinking aloud. Utterance addressee is used to compute some of the combined features described later on (looking while talking and looking while listening).

Utterance Type. The subject of each utterance is recorded in order to evaluate the use of prosocial vs. coercive behaviors. We recorded the total time a participant's utterances fall into one of the following categories: (1) making a demand, (2) making a suggestion or prompt, (3) helping (demonstrate, guide, or help), (4) thinking aloud, (5) insulting, (6) other.

(a) Illustrative Gesture (b) Physical Coercion

Figure 3: Examples of some of our nonverbal behavior features: illustrative gestures and physical coercion.

5.2 Nonverbal Behaviors

We also investigated the following nonverbal behavior features: gestures, physical coercion, and gaze. These features represent the total time each participant exhibits these behaviors and are normalized by the duration of the interaction. Some of these nonverbal features (illustrative gestures and physical coercion) are shown in selected participants in Figure 3.

Gestures. We recorded the total time each a participant expressed either illustrative, intrusive, or adaptor gestures. An illustrative gesture is displayed with the goal of making a point or accentuate what the participant is saying. A intrusive gesture invades the other children's social space, such as pointing somewhere in an aggressive manner. An adaptor gesture is a nervous habit like playing with hair, clothes or putting fingers in the mouth.

Physical Coercion. We recorded the total time participant expressed physical coercion (shoving, grabbing, intentionally bumping into, etc.).

Gaze. We recorded the time each participant looks at one of the following specified targets in the scenario: (1) looking at Robot 1, (2) looking at Robot 2, (3) looking at left participant, (4) looking at middle participant, (5) looking at right participant, (6) looking elsewhere, (7) unclear. This feature is used to calculate some of the combined features of the next subsection (looking while talking and looking while listening) as well as the 'looked at' feature. The 'looked at' feature represents the total time each participant is looked at by their peers (derived from the features looking at left/middle/right participant).

5.3 Verbal/Nonverbal Combined Behaviors

Research has shown that individuals with high social dominance spend more time looking at the person they are talking to while talking, and less time looking at others while listening to them compared to individuals lower in social dominance [7, 8, 12]. Using a combination of the 'utterance addressee' and 'gaze' features, we derived the following features:

Looking while listening to colleagues. The total time that a participant looks at their colleagues while their colleagues are talking. This feature is normalized by the total time their peers are talking during the interaction.

Looking while listening to robots. The total time that a participant looks at the robots while they are talking. This feature is normalized by the duration of the interaction because the robots talk for an equivalent amount of time in each interaction.

Looking while talking to colleagues. The total time that a participant looks at their colleagues when they are talking to them. This feature is normalized by the total time the participant talks during the interaction.

Looking while talking to robots. The total time that a participant looks at the robots when they are talking to them. This feature is also normalized by the total time the participant talks during the interaction.

5.4 Individual Differences

In addition to the verbal, nonverbal, and combined verbal/nonverbal behaviors, we also noted each participant's gender: either male (1) or female (0).

5.5 Feature Correlation Analysis

We calculated the Pearson correlation coefficients (ρ) between children's social dominance scores and all the features we just described. In our feature set, two features were significantly correlated: 'looked at' ($\rho = -0.587$, $p \leq 0.01$) and 'looking at Robot 1' ($\rho = -0.449$, $p \leq 0.05$). Additionally, a visual analysis of all scatter plots revealed marginally significant trends in other features as well, particularly in the ones with higher absolute correlation coefficients. The marginal significance in these features might have been due to the limited duration of the interaction or the moderate number of participants in our data.

From the literature, we would expect that there would be a positive, not negative, correlation between the amount of time a participant is looked at and their social dominance rank [12]. Our observed negative correlation could be due to the changes in the interaction dynamics and the presence of the robots, who are talking for most of the interaction. It is possible that the most dominant agent in the interaction is one of the robots – potentially Robot 1 (Berry), who does most of the talking. Thus, the way that the robots potentially affect the group dynamics could account for this negative correlation.

It is also interesting to observe that the amount of time that a participant looks at Robot 1 (Berry), the robot whose actions the children are choosing, has a negative correlation with the social dominance rank. It is plausible that Robot 1 is the most dominant agent in the interaction, and would be looked at less by the high dominant participants. Previous literature reported in section 2 supports this idea, showing that individuals with high social dominance spend less time looking at others while listening to them compared to individuals lower in social dominance [7, 8, 12].

6. SOCIAL DOMINANCE CLASSIFICATION

This section describes the experimental procedure followed to automatically classify social dominance based on a selected set of features. We discuss the accuracy of the obtained data-driven models and their ability to classify social dominance in small groups of children.

6.1 High/Low Classification Labels

Considering the number of participants in our data set, we opted for binary classification, grouping participants in either *high* or *low* social dominance categories. Using the social dominance scores collected from the teachers (ranging from 1 to 5), each child was labelled as high in dominance if their total score was greater than or equal to 3.0, and low dominance otherwise. Of the 21 participants, 9 participants (6 females and 3 males) were classified as high ($M = 4.16, SD = 0.50$) and 12 participants (7 females and 5 males) were classified as low ($M = 1.88, SD = 0.58$) in social dominance.

6.2 Models of Social Dominance

For classification, we chose to pursue Logistic Regression [30] because this classification method does not require the features to be independent from each other, and Support Vector Machines (SVMs) [6] due to their effectiveness in dealing with a large set of features without overfitting.

We selected the 4 behavioral features with the highest Pearson correlation (ρ) absolute value for training our models. This final set of behavioral features and their corresponding absolute Pearson correlation values are shown in Table 1.

Behavior Feature	**Abs(ρ)**
Looked at	0.587
Looking at Robot 1	0.449
Physical coercion	0.388
Illustrative gestures	0.369

Table 1: The top 4 ranked behavior features based on the absolute value of the Pearson correlation value (ρ) of each feature with the respective ground truth.

To evaluate the performance of these models, we used a Leave-Pair-Out Cross Validation (LPOCV) procedure [1]. LPOCV has low-variance in both high and low dimensional feature space for small sample sizes, which makes it a good approach for our data. For each iteration, 2 participants were 'left out' as a test set and the remaining 19 participants constituted the training set. The model was then trained and evaluated using the chosen training and test sets. This process was repeated for all $\binom{21}{2} = 210$ combinations of participants. After all combinations were tried, the mean Accuracy and F1 Score were calculated. The Logistic Regression and SVM models used a C value (error penalty) of $1,000$ and the SVM model used a RBF (Radial Basis Function) Kernel.

We were able to achieve an accuracy of 0.890 and F1 Score of 0.871 with our SVM model an an accuracy of 0.807 and F1 Score of 0.764 with our Logistic Regression model. These results allow us to conclude that from a selection of behavioral features, it is possible to accurately predict high/low social dominance in children in group interactions.

7. DISCUSSION

Beyond the mean accuracy measures of the models, we also investigated the individuals that accounted for the majority of the model testing error. The chart in Figure 4 shows the number of misclassifications for each participant. Both the SVM and Logistic Regression models worked very well for most participants, but misclassified the same 2 or 3 participants in the majority of the cross-validation cycles. With the LPOCV (leave-pair-out cross validation) process, each participant is tested 20 times. Examining Figure 4, participants 6 and 13, with social dominance scores of 3.91 and 2.18, are misclassified every time they are tested by both the SVM and Logistic Regression models, accounting for most of the model testing error. From this analysis of where the misclassifications occur, our models seem to very accurately classify the majority of individuals, but there are a few individuals that the models consistently fail to classify correctly.

It is possible that our model misclassified a few participants consistently because we have not captured dimensions in our features that explain the behavior of these participants. These participants could have behaved differently because they had a complex social relationship with the other peers or they behaved in a different manner due to the presence of a very high or low dominant colleague. There are many possibilities because the dynamics of social interactions are so complex and difficult to quantify. In the future, it would be interesting to investigate these factors in a larger data corpus to better understand the main limitations of our models. It would also be interesting to see how additional features encoding friendship relations, physical size, and personality traits among the group members would contribute increase the accuracy of the models.

Contrasting to previous work in adults where verbal behavior plays a major role in the automatic classification of social dominance, the most discriminative features for classifying dominance in groups of children with our model were all nonverbal. Although these results are in line with previous research on children's dominance behavior, one should be careful about generalizing this finding beyond this particular learning domain [10, 24]. The absence of discriminative verbal features could have been due to the fact that, in our dataset, the percentage of talking time during the interaction is low and very similar for all children.

With regards to our classification of participants as either 'high' or 'low' in social dominance, this division might not not necessarily be the only or best labeling scheme. For our population size of 21 participants, we opted for a binary labeling criterion. Depending on the context and application of social dominance classification, a multiclass classification

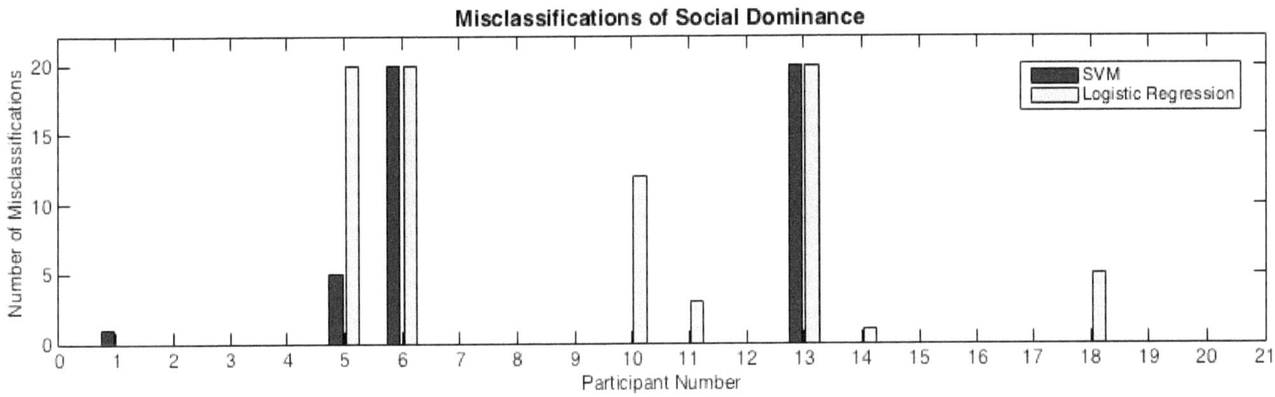

Figure 4: Number of misclassifications per participant in both SVM (dark blue) and Logistic Regression models (light blue). With the LPOCV (leave-par-out cross validation) process, each participant has 20 predictions. So the participants that has 20 misclassifications were misclassified every time they were tested. From this bar graph, it is clear that a few participants are responsible for the majority of our prediction errors.

criterion could be more appropriate. Based on our results, predicting the social dominance level automatically based on a set of behavioral features works for a high/low labeling and could work for other labelings as well.

8. CONCLUSION

The use of robots in educational settings is very promising because robots can provide children with much-needed individual attention. As robots enter real-world environments, they need to gain the necessary skills for interacting with groups of children, so they can provide teachers and students with more possibilities for personalized instruction.

In this paper, we investigated data-driven models to automatically classify social dominance levels of children (high vs. low) while interacting with robots in small groups. We trained Logistic Regression and SVM models with different feature sizes using multimodal data. Our Logistic Regression model had a mean accuracy of 0.807 and a F1 Score of 0.764, while our Support Vector Machines model had a mean accuracy of 0.890 and a F1 Score of 0.871. These results were obtained using hand-annotated nonverbal and verbal features. In the future, these features could feasibly be automated with the use of audio processing and visual perception tools, and be used in a real-time implementation. Such a classifier would allow a robot to be in a better position to mediate a group learning task.

Our results show that using a fairly reduced subset of nonverbal behaviors (eye gaze, physical coercion and illustrative gestures), we can automatically classify children's social dominance levels in this child-robot interaction domain. Moreover, the models seem robust independent of the dominance level of the other group elements. Further research is needed to ensure that similar results also apply when predicting social dominance in children using other group sizes, age groups and interaction contexts. Nevertheless, these findings are promising not only for human-robot interaction, but also for other types of interactive technology involving groups of children.

9. ACKNOWLEDGMENTS

This work is supported by NSF grant 1139078.

10. REFERENCES

[1] A. Airola, T. Pahikkala, W. Waegeman, B. De Baets, and T. Salakoski. A comparison of AUC estimators in small-sample studies. In *Proceedings of the 3rd International workshop on Machine Learning in Systems Biology*, pages 15–23, 2009.

[2] J. P. Birnholtz, T. Grossman, C. Mak, and R. Balakrishnan. An exploratory study of input configuration and group process in a negotiation task using a large display. In *Proceedings of the SIGCHI Conference on Human Factors in Computing Systems*, pages 91–100. ACM, 2007.

[3] M. A. Brackett, S. E. Rivers, and P. Salovey. Emotional intelligence: Implications for personal, social, academic, and workplace success. *Social and Personality Psychology Compass*, 5(1):88–103, 2011.

[4] H. Brugman, A. Russel, and X. Nijmegen. Annotating multi-media/multi-modal resources with elan. In *LREC*, 2004.

[5] J. K. Burgoon, M. L. Johnson, and P. T. Koch. The nature and measurement of interpersonal dominance. *Communications Monographs*, 65(4):308–335, 1998.

[6] C. Cortes and V. Vapnik. Support-vector networks. *Machine Learning*, 20(3):273–297, 1995.

[7] J. F. Dovidio and S. L. Ellyson. Decoding visual dominance: Attributions of power based on relative percentages of looking while speaking and looking while listening. *Social Psychology Quarterly*, 45(2):106–113, 1982.

[8] N. E. Dunbar and J. K. Burgoon. Perceptions of power and interactional dominance in interpersonal relationships. *Journal of Social and Personal Relationships*, 22(2):207–233, 2005.

[9] P. H. Hawley. The ontogenesis of social dominance: A strategy-based evolutionary perspective. *Developmental Review*, 19(1):97–132, 1999.

[10] P. H. Hawley. Social dominance and prosocial and coercive strategies of resource control in preschoolers. *International Journal of Behavioral Development*, 26(2):167–176, 2002.

[11] W. Huang, J. S. Olson, and G. M. Olson. Camera angle affects dominance in video-mediated

communication. In *CHI '02 Extended Abstracts on Human Factors in Computing Systems*, pages 716–717. ACM, 2002.
[12] H. Hung, D. B. Jayagopi, S. Ba, J.-M. Odobez, and D. Gatica-Perez. Investigating automatic dominance estimation in groups from visual attention and speaking activity. In *Proceedings of the 10th International Conference on Multimodal Interfaces*, pages 233–236. ACM, 2008.
[13] D. B. Jayagopi, H. Hung, C. Yeo, and D. Gatica-Perez. Modeling dominance in group conversations using nonverbal activity cues. *IEEE Transactions on Audio, Speech, and Language Processing*, 17(3):501–513, 2009.
[14] C. Jie and P. Peng. Recognize the most dominant person in multi-party meetings using nontraditional features. In *2010 IEEE International Conference on Intelligent Computing and Intelligent Systems (ICIS)*, volume 1, pages 312–316. IEEE, 2010.
[15] P. J. La Freniere and W. R. Charlesworth. Effects of friendship and dominance status on preschooler's resource utilization in a cooperative/competitive situation. *International Journal of Behavioral Development*, 10(3):345–358, 1987.
[16] I. Leite, H. Hajishirzi, S. Andrist, and J. Lehman. Managing chaos: Models of turn-taking in character-multichild interactions. In *Proceedings of the 15th International Conference on Multimodal Interaction*, ICMI '13, pages 43–50. ACM, 2013.
[17] I. Leite, M. McCoy, M. Lohani, D. Ullman, N. Salomons, C. Stokes, S. Rivers, and B. Scassellati. Emotional storytelling in the classroom: Individual versus group interaction between children and robots. In *Proceedings of the 10th Annual ACM/IEEE International Conference on Human-Robot Interaction*, HRI '15. ACM, 2015 (to appear).
[18] I. Leite, A. Pereira, C. Martinho, and A. Paiva. Are emotional robots more fun to play with? In *The 17th IEEE International Symposium on Robot and Human Interactive Communication (RO-MAN 2008)*, pages 77–82. IEEE, 2008.
[19] D. Leyzberg, S. Spaulding, and B. Scassellati. Personalizing robot tutors to individuals' learning differences. In *Proceedings of the 2014 ACM/IEEE International Conference on Human-Robot Interaction*, HRI '14, pages 423–430. ACM, 2014.
[20] D. Leyzberg, S. Spaulding, M. Toneva, and B. Scassellati. The physical presence of a robot tutor increases cognitive learning gains. In *Proceedings of the 34th Annual Conference of the Cognitive Science Society. Austin, TX: Cognitive Science Society*, 2012.
[21] P. N. Lopes, P. Salovey, S. Coté, and M. Beers. Emotion regulation abilities and the quality of social interaction. *Emotion*, 5(1):113–118, 2005.
[22] H. A. Murray. *Explorations in Personality*. Oxford University Press, 1938.
[23] Y. Nakano and Y. Fukuhara. Estimating conversational dominance in multiparty interaction. In *Proceedings of the 14th ACM International Conference on Multimodal Interaction*, ICMI '12, pages 77–84, New York, NY, USA, 2012. ACM.
[24] A. D. Pellegrini, C. J. Roseth, S. Mliner, C. M. Bohn, M. Van Ryzin, N. Vance, C. L. Cheatham, and A. Tarullo. Social dominance in preschool classrooms. *Journal of Comparative Psychology*, 121(1):54–64, 2007.
[25] R. Rienks and D. Heylen. Dominance detection in meetings using easily obtainable features. In *Machine Learning for Multimodal Interaction*, pages 76–86. Springer, 2006.
[26] M. Saerbeck, T. Schut, C. Bartneck, and M. D. Janse. Expressive robots in education: varying the degree of social supportive behavior of a robotic tutor. In *Proceedings of the SIGCHI Conference on Human Factors in Computing Systems*, pages 1613–1622. ACM, 2010.
[27] P. Salovey and J. D. Mayer. Emotional intelligence. *Imagination, cognition and personality*, 9:185–211, 1989.
[28] L. Smith-Lovin and C. Brody. Interruptions in group discussions: The effects of gender and group composition. *American Sociological Review*, 54(3):424–435, 1989.
[29] F. Strayer and J. Strayer. An ethological analysis of social agonism and dominance relations among preschool children. *Child Development*, 47(4):980–989, 1976.
[30] H. Yu, F. Huang, and C. Lin. Dual coordinate descent methods for logistic regression and maximum entropy models. *Machine Learning*, 85(1-2):41–75, 2011.

Spectators' Synchronization Detection based on Manifold Representation of Physiological Signals: Application to Movie Highlights Detection

Michal Muszynski
Computer Vision and Multimedia Laboratory
University of Geneva
Switzerland
michal.muszynski@unige.ch

Theodoros Kostoulas
Computer Vision and Multimedia Laboratory & Swiss Center for Affective Sciences
University of Geneva
Switzerland
theodoros.kostoulas@unige.ch

Guillaume Chanel
Swiss Center for Affective Sciences & Computer Vision and Multimedia Laboratory
University of Geneva
Switzerland
guillaume.chanel@unige.ch

Patrizia Lombardo
Department of Modern French & Swiss Center for Affective Sciences
University of Geneva
Switzerland
patrizia.lombardo@unige.ch

Thierry Pun
Computer Vision and Multimedia Laboratory & Swiss Center for Affective Sciences
University of Geneva
Switzerland
thierry.pun@unige.ch

ABSTRACT

Detection of highlights in movies is a challenge for the affective understanding and implicit tagging of films. Under the hypothesis that synchronization of the reaction of spectators indicates such highlights, we define a synchronization measure between spectators that is capable of extracting movie highlights. The intuitive idea of our approach is to define (a) a parameterization of one spectator's physiological data on a manifold; (b) the synchronization measure between spectators as the Kolmogorov-Smirnov distance between local shape distributions of the underlying manifolds. We evaluate our approach using data collected in an experiment where the electro-dermal activity of spectators was recorded during the entire projection of a movie in a cinema. We compare our methodology with baseline synchronization measures, such as correlation, Spearman's rank correlation, mutual information, Kolmogorov-Smirnov distance. Results indicate that the proposed approach allows to accurately distinguish highlight from non-highlight scenes.

Categories and Subject Descriptors

I.5.4 [**Pattern Recognition**]: Applications—*signal processing*; I.5.2 [**Pattern Recognition**]: Design Methodology—*pattern analysis*

ICMI 2015, November 9–13, 2015, Seattle, WA, USA.

DOI: http://dx.doi.org/10.1145/2818346.2820773.

Keywords

Synchronization; Physiological Signals; Affective Computing; Time Delay Embedding; Manifold Learning; Dimensionality Reduction; Diffusion Maps; Highlights Detection

1. INTRODUCTION

Detection and recognition of highlights in movies are difficult tasks due to the large variability of actions, scenes and sequences that strongly depend on the film genre. Adopting a supervised approach to highlights detection needs a large number of manually annotated samples [13]. Moreover, the movie annotation process is very tedious in itself and often biased by personal preferences of the annotators.

In the last decade, researchers have attempted to match physiological responses to the affective state of viewers and the appearance of highlights in films [4]. Measuring physiological responses to the movie content can provide insight into the viewers' aesthetic experiences, and can help better understand emotions elicited from the particular scenes [13].

In the field of affective computing, much research on emotion recognition in response to multimedia content has been carried out using EEG signals, peripheral physiological signals and facial expressions [9], [11]. In the area of highlights detection, various models have involved physiological measurements of a single viewer when watching of media, such as movies [7], music excerpts [14], and sport events [6]. Another approach to highlights detection which was based on the analysis of several spectators' physiological signals has been proposed in [4]. The authors used a physiological index of social interaction to determine general highlights of videos. That method allowed the detection of highlights that are relevant to the majority of viewers. Those experiments allow the evaluation of the feedback of one spectator, but they cannot take into account interactions among a group of viewers.

Strong interactions among viewers can occur while watching spectacular types of highlights e.g. special effects. Furthermore, viewers can feel strong empathy with the movie characters, and have similar reactions to a certain movie content e.g. dramatic events. In these cases, we expect that similar physiological reactions of viewers are evoked. Under these assumptions, we propose that a level of physiological synchronization can be considered as a reliable indicator of highlights appearance in movies. Using multiple viewers' physiological recordings allows us to alleviate the impact of their personal preferences. Contrarily to methods which rely on emotion assessment, the proposed approach can be applied directly on multi-person physiological signals, and does not require the tedious annotation of movies (however, the expert's annotation is used only to evaluate the method in our study).

Many different synchronization measures have been employed lately to process physiological signals. One such possible synchronization measure is for instance the Pearson correlation coefficient (Spearman's rank correlation coefficient) that is able to quantify linear correlations between pairs of signals. Another approach to synchronization originates from information theory. Signals can be regarded as a collection of random variables which represents the evolution of a system over time. In this context, a basic similarity measure is mutual information or Kolmogorov - Smirnov distance that can be used as a similarity measure between distributions of signals.

In the area of emotion recognition, feature vectors of images and videos have been modeled recently as points lying on some Riemannian manifold to retrieve intrinsic structure of data [10]. This approach cannot be used to investigate a family of manifolds as is the case for highlights detection where processing of several viewers' physiological signals takes place.

2. TIME DELAY EMBEDDING AND DIFFUSION MAPS

Time-delay coordinate embedding has been used in the analysis of dynamical systems [12]. This method embeds a scalar time series into an m-dimensional space to reconstruct the trajectory of a system. For each time series $\{x_i\}, i = 1,2,3,...,n$ a representation of the delay-coordinate embedding can be expressed as the following vector X_i which consists of m components

$$X_i = [x_i, x_{i+j}, x_{i+2j}, .., x_{i+(m-1)j}], \tag{1}$$

where j is the index delay and m is the embedding dimension.

We assume that the high-dimensional representation of physiological signals X_i is controlled by a low-dimensional process that corresponds to a physiological response to the stimulus. Applying diffusion maps to time-delay coordinate embedding, we provide a new low dimensional parameterization that still captures physiological activity. When diffusion maps are used [5], an affinity metric $K(x_i, x_j)$ is defined between pairs of physiological samples x_i and x_j based on their representation in time-delay coordinate X_i and X_j, respectively. Then, we consider only a collection $\mathcal{M}$ of k samples x_i to define the following kernel

$$K(x_i, x_j) = e^{\frac{-||X_i - X_j||}{\epsilon}}, \tag{2}$$

where ϵ is the scale parameter of the affinity metric and $k < n$. Now, note that $i, j = 1,2,3,...,k$. We can look at the collection $\mathcal{M}$ as nodes of an undirected symmetric graph, where two nodes x_i and x_j are connected by an edge with the affinity weight $K(x_i, x_j)$. We pursue the construction of a Markov chain on the graph nodes by normalizing the kernel $K(\cdot,\cdot)$. Let K be the kernel matrix, and let $P = D^{-1}K$ be the corresponding transition matrix, where D is a diagonal matrix with elements $D_{ii} = \sum_{j=1}^{k} K(x_i, x_j)$. In sequence, we can calculate P_t analogues to P. Now, $P(x_i, x_j)$ is the probability of transition in a single step from node x_i to node x_j. Similarly, we define $P_t(x_i, x_j)$ as the transition probability in t steps from node x_i to node x_j. The idea is that the transition probability between two nodes can reflect the local geometry of the data. This leads us to a definition of the diffusion distance $D_t(x_i, x_j)$ between pairs of samples, expressed by [5]:

$$D_t(x_i, x_j) = \sqrt{\sum_{l=1}^{k} (P(x_i, x_l) - P(x_j, x_l))^2 w(x_l)}, \tag{3}$$

where $w(x_l)$ is a normalization weight. Intuitively, two points are similar when many short paths with large weights connect them. It is proven that the diffusion distance $D_t(x_i, x_j)$ can be computed using the eigenvalues $\{\lambda_i\}$, that tend to 0 and have a modulus strictly less than 1, and the corresponding eigenvectors $\{\varphi_i\}$ of the transition matrix P [5]. Let $\Phi_t(x_i)$ for some $t \geq 0$ be the diffusion maps of time series samples $\{x_i\}, i = 1,2,3,...,k$ into Euclidean space $\mathbb{R}^s$ that is defined by

$$\Phi_t(x_i) = [\lambda_1^{2t}\varphi_1(x_i), ..., \lambda_s^{2t}\varphi_s(x_i)], \tag{4}$$

where $s \in \{1,2,...,k-1\}$ is the new space dimensionality.

It has been shown that the diffusion distance between samples x_i and x_j equals the Euclidean distance in the diffusion maps space that is expressed as follows [5]

$$D_t(x_i, x_j) = ||\Phi_t(x_i) - \Phi_t(x_j)||. \tag{5}$$

3. LOCAL SHAPE DISTRIBUTION OF MANIFOLD REPRESENTATION

In this paragraph we present a geometric framework which computes the amount of synchronization between a pair of physiological signals. The concept is to measure the similarity between local shapes of reconstructed signal manifolds. Firstly, in order to capture the unique local geometric properties of a signal manifold, we introduce the local shape cumulative distribution function $F^{\sigma}_{x_i}(\delta)$ of pairwise diffusion distances for each sample x_i and its delay samples $x_i, x_{i+1}, ..., x_{i+\sigma}$ denoted by

$$F^{\sigma}_{x_i}(\delta) = \int 1_{\tilde{D}_t(x_i, x_{i+q}) \leq \delta} d\mu, \tag{6}$$

where $q \in \{1, \sigma\}$, μ is a counting measure and $1_{\tilde{D}_t(x_i, x_{i+q})}$ is an indicator function with respect to a delay sample on manifolds. $\tilde{D}_t(\cdot,\cdot)$ is the cosine distance in the diffusion maps space that can be derived from the Euclidean dot product.

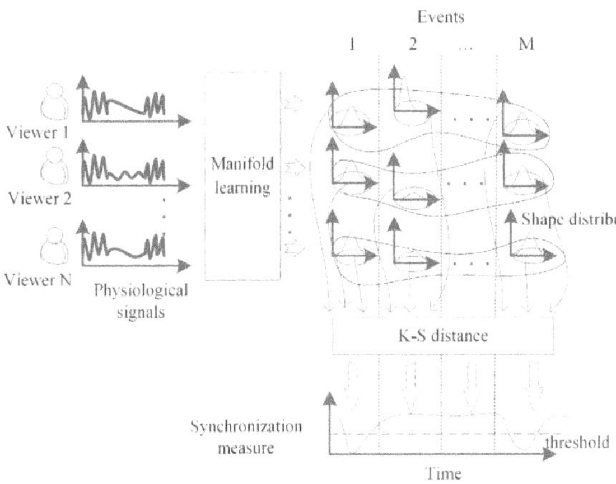

Figure 1: Overview of the proposed approach to highlights detection. In this fictitious example, all viewers 1,2,...,N are synchronized for event 1 and M in the movie since the manifolds are similar. This is not the case for event 2.

In our case, it is advantageous to use normalized the local shape distribution

$$\mathcal{F}_{x_i}^{\sigma}(\delta) = \frac{F_{x_i}^{\sigma}(\delta)}{F_{x_i}^{\sigma}(\infty)}. \tag{7}$$

For two time series $\{x_i\}$ and $\{y_i\}$, the synchronization measure is reduced to computing the Kolmogorov - Smirnov distance between two local shape distributions of their manifold representations for each time step i that is shown in Figure 1., and expressed as follows

$$S_{\sigma}(x_i, y_i) = \max_{\delta} |\mathcal{F}_{x_i}^{\sigma}(\delta) - \mathcal{F}_{y_i}^{\sigma}(\delta)|. \tag{8}$$

If two signals are the same $S_{\sigma}(x_i, y_i)$ is equal to 0. When the number of signals is more than 2, the overall synchronization can be obtained by averaging synchronization values of all possible non-overlapping pairs of signals.

4. EXPERIMENTS AND DISCUSSION

The synchronization measure was applied to physiological signals recorded during the watching of the movie (Taxi Driver, 1976) in a real cinema (Grütli cinema, Geneva) where viewers were wearing electro-dermal activity sensors. Our goal is to test if physiological signals synchrony can be used to detect the movie highlights defined by a cinema critic. In the present study, we utilize 12 skin conductance signals out of 30 recorded signals, and their sampling frequency is 10 Hz [8]. These signals are segmented in overlapping windows with time step and window length equal 0.5s and 5s, respectively. For diffusion map we set up s equals 3 based on values of eigenvalues of the transition matrix P, and for estimation of the local shape distribution we use 50 nearest samples ($\sigma = 50$) in time.

Annotation of the movie content was performed offline by an experienced movie critic, who annotated the movie based on the following five types of highlights [1], [2]. The so-called "Form-highlights" are:
- *H1*: Spectacular (technical choice, special effects);
- *H2*: Subtle (use of camera, lighting, music).

The so-called "Content-highlights" are:
- *H3*: Character development (characters' emotions and responses to dramatic events);
- *H4*: Dialogue (motivation of actions and tensions among characters);
- *H5*: Theme development (unusual close up, urban theme).

We apply our synchronization measure to determine scenes containing one particular type of highlights among (*H1*, *H2*, *H3*, *H4*, *H5*), as opposed to scenes without highlight. If the overall measure of the synchronization among all spectators (the average Kolmogorov-Smirnov distance between two local shape distributions) at time step i is lower than a threshold we assign this sample to a highlight scene.

We compare our methodology (*shape distribution dist.*) with baseline synchronization measures such as *correlation*, Spearman's rank correlation (*Spearman's correlation*), *mutual information* and Kolmogorov-Smirnov distance (*K-S distance*) that are applied to each signal window. The receiver operating characteristic (ROC) curves and the areas under the ROC curves (AUC) are depicted in Figure 2. and Table 1., respectively.

Table 1: Area under curve (AUC) for each highlight type ($H1$, $H2$, $H3$, $H4$, $H5$), and each different synchronization measure

Measure \ Highlights	*H1*	*H2*	*H3*	*H4*	*H5*
correlation	0.43	0.50	0.47	0.43	0.40
Spearman's correlation	0.48	0.50	0.48	0.42	0.41
mutual information	0.68	0.56	**0.58**	0.46	0.46
K-S distance	0.46	0.55	0.33	0.32	0.29
shape distribution dist.	**0.71**	**0.58**	0.48	**0.57**	**0.60**

The proposed methodology (*shape distribution dist.*) has significantly the highest performance for highlights *H1* which corresponds to AUC equal to 0.71 (Bradley test [3], $\alpha = 0.05$). This can be justified by the nature of the corresponding events, where it is expected to elicit strong physiological reactions from the spectators. In this case, our approach is capable of effectively discovering the similarity of skin conductance peaks because of its ability to explore the intrinsic structure of the data. On the other hand, the rest of the methods fail to detect synchronization among the spectators, and thus are not useful for the identification of movie highlights, for the given movie.

For detection of highlights *H2*, *H3*, our methodology and *mutual information* obtain significantly the best performance, respectively (Bradley test [3], $\alpha = 0.05$). The area under the ROC curve is equal to 0.58 in these cases. These results can be explained by a lack of strong synchronized reactions among all viewers to subtle contents of the movie, and character development that takes place. For highlight *H3*, this is also supported by the result of the *K-S distance* method, where we observe that the pairs of spectators are significantly low synchronized (Bradley test [3], $\alpha = 0.05$). It appears that possible single responses to these type of events cannot be well identified because of averaging synchronization over all pairs of spectators.

Furthermore, our method has significantly the highest performance (Bradley test [3], $\alpha = 0.05$) for detection of highlights *H4* and *H5* in the comparison with the baseline methods. The area under the ROC curve is equal to 0.57 and 0.60, respectively.

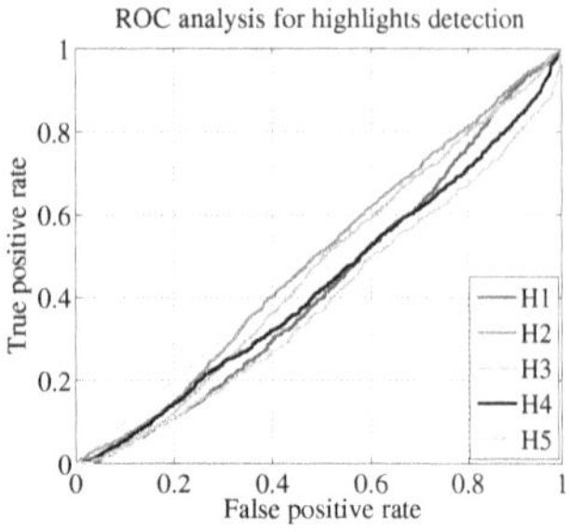

(a) *correlation*

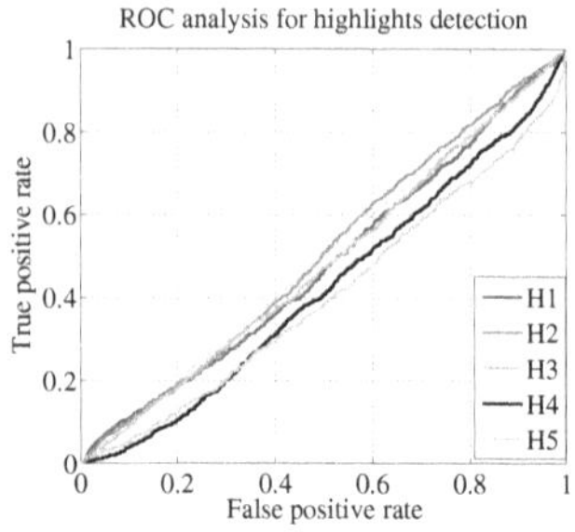

(b) *Spearman's correlation*

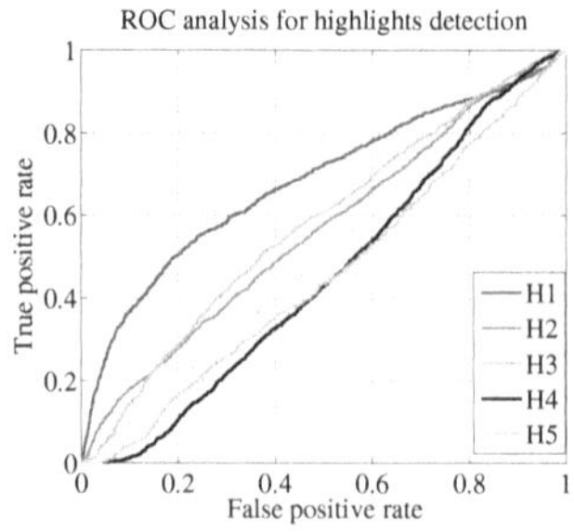

(c) *mutual information*

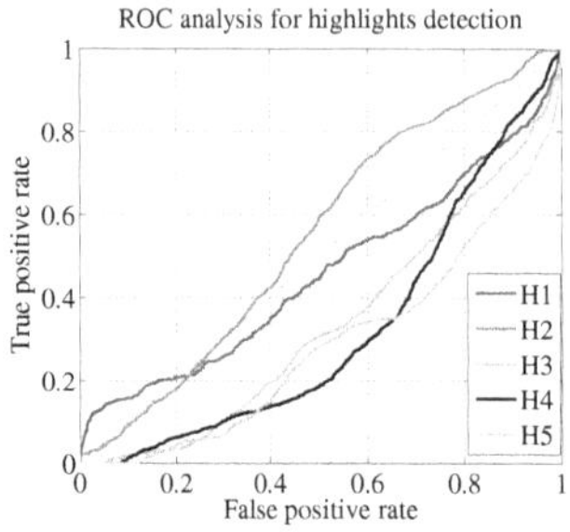

(d) *K-S distance*

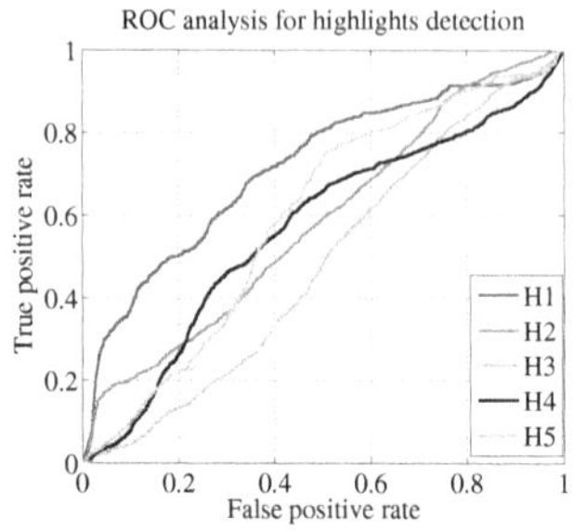

(e) *shape distribution dist.*

Figure 2: ROC analysis for each highlight class detection (*H1*, *H2*, *H3*, *H4*, *H5*). Pink line corresponds to random detection.

5. CONCLUSIONS

In this work we propose a synchronization measure which is based on comparing local shapes of the manifold representation of signals. The comparison of the local shape distributions of diffusion distances on the manifolds is relatively invariant to scale (normalization in eq. 7) and topological changes of the signals. The results that we obtain on data recorded in a cinema indicate the ability of our methodology to identify some types of highlights in the movie based on synchronization of viewers' skin conductance signals.

6. ACKNOWLEDGMENTS

This work is supported by the grant from the Swiss National Science Foundation.

7. REFERENCES

[1] A. Bazin. *What is cinema?* University of California Press, 2004.

[2] D. Bordwell, K. Thompson, and J. Ashton. *Film art: an introduction.* McGraw-Hill New York, 1997.

[3] A. Bradley. The use of the area under the roc curve in the evaluation of machine learning algorithms. *Pattern recognition*, 30(7):1145–1159, 1997.

[4] C. Chênes, G. Chanel, M. Soleymani, and T. Pun. Highlight detection in movie scenes through inter-users, physiological linkage. In *Social Media Retrieval*, pages 217–237, 2013.

[5] R. R. Coifman and S. Lafon. Diffusion maps. *Applied and computational harmonic analysis*, 21(1):5–30, 2006.

[6] A. Jaimes, T. Echigo, M. Teraguchi, and F. Satoh. Learning personalized video highlights from detailed mpeg-7 metadata. In *Image Processing. 2002. Proceedings. 2002 International Conference on*, pages 133–136. IEEE, 2002.

[7] H. Joho, J. Staiano, N. Sebe, and J. M. Jose. Looking at the viewer: analysing facial activity to detect personal highlights of multimedia contents. *Multimedia Tools and Applications*, 51(2):505–523, 2011.

[8] T. Kostoulas, G. Chanel, M. Muszynski, P. Lombardo, and T. Pun. Identifying aesthetic highlights in movies from clustering of physiological and behavioral signals. In *Quality of Multimedia Experience (QoMEX), 2015 Seventh International Workshop on*, May 2015.

[9] E. Kroupi, J.-M. Vesin, and T. Ebrahimi. Phase-amplitude coupling between eeg and eda while experiencing multimedia content. In *Affective Computing and Intelligent Interaction (ACII), 2013 Humaine Association Conference on*, pages 865–870. IEEE, 2013.

[10] M. Liu, R. Wang, S. Li, S. Shan, Z. Huang, and X. Chen. Combining multiple kernel methods on riemannian manifold for emotion recognition in the wild. In *Proceedings of the 16th International Conference on Multimodal Interaction*, pages 494–501. ACM, 2014.

[11] M. Soleymani, S. Asghari-Esfeden, M. Pantic, and Y. Fu. Continuous emotion detection using eeg signals and facial expressions. In *Multimedia and Expo (ICME), 2014 IEEE International Conference on*, pages 1–6. IEEE, 2014.

[12] F. Takens. Detecting strange attractors in turbulence. *Dynamical Systems and Turbulence, Lecture Notes in Mathematics*, 898:366–381, 1981.

[13] H. L. Wang and L.-F. Cheong. Affective understanding in film. *IEEE Transactions on Circuits and Systems for Video Technology*, 16(6):689–704, June 2006.

[14] J.-C. Wang, Y.-H. Yang, H.-M. Wang, and S.-K. Jeng. Modeling the affective content of music with a gaussian mixture model. *Affective Computing, IEEE Transactions on*, 6(1):56–68, 2015.

Implicit User-centric Personality Recognition based on Physiological Responses to Emotional Videos

Julia Wache[1], Ramanathan Subramanian[2], Mojtaba Khomami Abadi[1], Radu-Laurentiu Vieriu[1], Nicu Sebe[1], Stefan Winkler[1]
[1]Department of Information Engineering and Computer Science (DISI), University of Trento, Italy
[2]Advanced Digital Sciences Center (ADSC), University of Illinois at Urbana-Champaign, Singapore
Julia.Wache@unitn.it, Subramanian.R@adsc.com.sg,
mojtaba.khomamiabadi@unitn.it, vieriu@disi.unitn.it, sebe@disi.unitn.it,
Stefan.Winkler@adsc.com.sg

ABSTRACT

We present a novel framework for recognizing personality traits based on users' physiological responses to affective movie clips. Extending studies that have correlated explicit/implicit affective user responses with Extraversion and Neuroticism traits, we perform single-trial recognition of the **big-five** traits from Electrocardiogram (ECG), Galvanic Skin Response (GSR), Electroencephalogram (EEG) and facial emotional responses compiled from 36 users using off-the-shelf sensors. Firstly, we examine relationships among personality scales and (explicit) affective user ratings acquired in the context of prior observations. Secondly, we isolate physiological correlates of personality traits. Finally, unimodal and multimodal personality recognition results are presented. Personality differences are better revealed while analyzing responses to emotionally homogeneous (*e.g.*, high valence, high arousal) clips, and significantly above-chance recognition is achieved for all five traits.

Categories and Subject Descriptors

H.1.2 [**User/Machine Systems**]: Human information processing; I.5.2 [**Pattern Recognition Design Methodology**]: Pattern analysis

General Terms

Measurement; Algorithms; Verification; Human Factors

Keywords

Personality recognition; Affective physiological responses

1. INTRODUCTION

The need to recognize the affective state of users for effective human-computer interaction has been widely acknowledged. Nevertheless, affect is a highly subjective phenomenon influenced by a number of contextual and psychological factors including *personality*. The relationship between individuals' personality traits and emotional responses has been actively studied by social psychologists ever since a correlation between the two was proposed in Eysenck's personality model [10]. Eysenck posited that (i) Extraversion, the personality dimension that describes a person as being either talkative or reserved, is accompanied by low cortical arousal– *i.e.*, extraverts require more external stimulation than introverts, and ii) Neurotics, characterized by negative feelings such as depression and anxiety, become very easily upset or nervous due to minor stressors, while emotionally stable persons remain composed under pressure.

Many affective studies have attempted to validate and extend Eyesenk's personality theory. Some have employed explicit user feedback in the form of affective ratings [13, 22], while others have measured implicit user responses such as Electroencephalogram (EEG) activity [27] and heart rate [9] for their analyses. However, few works have investigated affective correlations with traits other than Extraversion and Neuroticism. On the other hand, social psychology studies have primarily examined personality correlates with non-verbal social behavioral cues (see [30] for a comprehensive review), but have not attempted personality trait characterization based on emotional responses.

This paper examines the influence of personality differences on users' affective behavior as understanding the personality–affect relationship is crucial for effective emotional interaction. We try to understand the relation between emotions and personality as well as recognize it directly from the physiological signals. More specifically, we characterize both user-expressed emotions and personality traits, via heart rate, skin conductance, EEG response and facial activity patterns observed while viewing affective movie clips. We designed a study with movie clips as movies are inherently intended to evoke emotions, and movie genres such as *thriller*, *comedy* or *horror* are expressly defined by the emotions they evoke. Also, we used commercial sensors for measuring physiological responses to ensure that our study is repeatable, ecologically valid and scalable for large-scale personality recognition.

First, we study relationships between users' valence and arousal ratings provided for 36 emotional clips, and their personality scores. We then examine physiological correlates of affective and personality measures. Finally, single-trial recognition results for the five personality dimensions

ICMI '15, November 09-13, 2015, Seattle, WA, USA.
© 2015 ACM ISBN 978-1-4503-3912-4/15/11:.$15.00.
DOI: http://dx.doi.org/10.1145/2818346.2820736.

are presented. Personality recognition is attempted considering implicit user responses, the physiological signals, for (a) all movie clips, and (b) emotionally similar clips corresponding to a particular quadrant in the valence-arousal (VA) plane (*e.g.*, high valence, high arousal clips). Significantly above-chance recognition is achieved for all five traits in (b) as compared to only three in (a), implying that personality differences are better revealed on comparing affective responses to emotionally homogeneous stimuli.

Contributions. This work makes the following research contributions: (i) Personality traits have traditionally been assessed via the use of questionnaires, or by analyzing social behavior. Differently, we recognize the big-five traits by examining affective physiological responses (to our knowledge, the only other work to this end is [1]); (ii) We employ physiological signals recorded using commercial and portable sensors for recognition, which affirms the repeatability and scalability of this study; (iii) We demonstrate that personality differences are better revealed on comparing user responses to emotionally similar videos (or more generally, under similar emotion conditions).

2. RELATED WORK

This section reviews related work on (a) multimodal affect recognition, (b) personality recognition and (c) examining the personality–affect relationship.

2.1 Multimodal affect recognition

As emotions are conveyed by content creators using multiple means (audio, video), and expressed by humans in a number of ways (facial expressions, speech and phsyiological responses), many affect recognition (AR) methods employ a multimodal framework. Content-based AR works utilize audio, video and audio–visual cues (see [32] for a review). Recent AR methodologies have focused on the user and leveraged the use of physiological sensors (*e.g.*, EEG, ECG, GSR) for efficient emotion representation. Emotions induced by music clips are recognized via heart rate, muscle movements, skin conductivity and respiration changes in [14]. Lisetti and Nasoz [18] use affective clips and mathematical equations to elicit emotions, and use GSR, heart rate and temperature signals to recognize them. Koelstra *et al.* [15] analyze blood volume pressure, respiration rate, skin temperature and Electrooculogram (EOG) patterns for recognizing the level of valence and arousal induced by music videos. Implicit user-centered AR from visual, speech, physiological and eye-gaze patterns is discussed in [25]. Abadi *et al.* [3] study Magnetoencephalogram (MEG), Electromyogram (EMG), EOG and ECG responses from users for music and movie clips, and observe that movie clips are better for emotion elicitation and AR.

2.2 Personality recognition

The big-five or the five-factor model [8] describes human personality in terms of five dimensions – Extraversion (*sociable* vs *reserved*), Neuroticism or the degree of emotional stability (*nervous* vs *confident*), Agreeableness (*compassionate* vs *dispassionate*), Conscientiousness (*dutiful* vs *easy-going*) and Openness (*curious/creative* vs *cautious/conservative*). A comprehensive survey of personality computing approaches is presented in [30]. The traditional means to measure personality dimensions are questionnaires or self-reports [20]. Argamon *et al.* [4] pioneered automated personality recognition using lexical cues from informal texts for recognizing Extraversion (*Ex*) and Neuroticism (*Neu*). Olguin *et al.* [23] show that non-verbal behavioral measures acquired using a sociometric badge such as the amount of speech and physical activity, number of social interactions and physical proximity to other objects is highly correlated with personality. Much work has since employed non-verbal social behavioral cues for personality recognition including [17], where *Ex* is recognized using speech and social attention cues in round-table meetings, and [28, 31] which estimate *Ex* and *Neu* from proxemic and attention cues in party settings. Among works that attempt to recognize the big-five traits, Mairesse *et al.* [19] use acoustic and lexical features, while Srivastava *et al.* [26] automatically complete personality questionnaires for 50 movie characters utilizing lexical, audio and visual behavioral cues. Similar cues are used in [5] for trait recognition from self-presentation videos.

2.3 Personality-Affect relationship

The relationship between personality traits and emotional responses has been extensively studied in social psychology, but hardly in a computational setting. Eysenck's seminal personality theory [10] posits that extraverts require more external stimulation than introverts, and that neurotics are aroused more easily. Many psychology studies have since examined the personality–affect relationship by studying explicit or implicit user responses. Personality effects on brain activation related to valence and arousal is investigated in [13]. Based on functional magnetic resonance imaging (fMRI) responses, this study concludes that *Neu* level correlates negatively with valence, and positively with arousal. In an EEG-based study relating personality and arousability [27], a negative correlation is observed between *Ex* and arousal, while positive correlation between *Neu* and arousal is noted for negative stimuli. The impact of personality traits on affective user ratings is studied using path analysis in [29]. Feedback scores from 133 students are analyzed in [22] to conclude that neurotics experience positive emotions similar to emotionally stable counterparts in pleasant situations even though they may experience negative emotions more strongly. Event-related potentials (ERPs) and heart rate changes are studied in [9] to confirm a positive correlation between *Neu* and arousal for negative stimuli, while signal-detection is used in [11] to conclude that extraverts are generally less aroused than introverts.

Examining the above studies, it is evident that hardly any of them have ventured beyond the *Ex* and *Neu* traits. The only work to recognize the big-five traits from affective responses is that of Abadi *et al.* [1], and our work is closest to theirs in this respect. Nevertheless, we consider user responses to a larger stimulus set (36 clips vs 16 in [1]), and show superior personality recognition by comparing affective user responses to emotionally similar clips.

3. METHODOLOGY

An overview of our personality recognition framework is presented in Fig. 1 (left). To study the personality–affect relationship, we performed a study where users' physiological responses were recorded as they viewed 36 affective movie clips used in [2]. Explicit feedback in the form of *arousal*, *valence*, *liking*, *engagement* and *familiarity* ratings was obtained after they viewed each movie clip but only arousal and valence ratings are analysed in this study. Users' per-

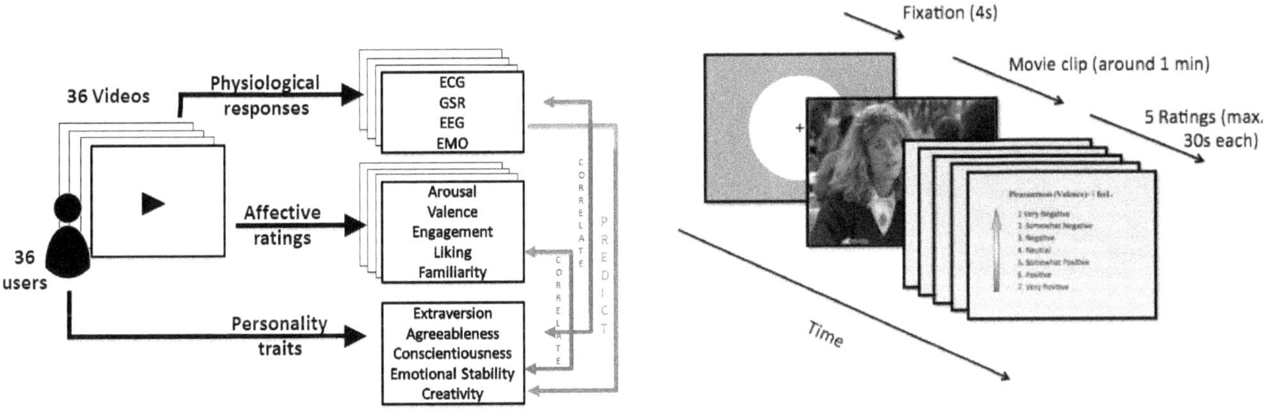

Figure 1: (left) User study overview. (right) Timeline for each trial.

sonality measures for the big-five dimensions were compiled using a big-five marker scale (BFMS) questionnaire [24].

3.1 Materials and methods

Subjects: 36 university students (mean age = 29.2, 12 female) of various nationalities participated in our study. All subjects were fluent in English and were habitual Hollywood movie watchers.

Materials: One PC with two monitors was used for the experiment. One monitor was used for video clip presentation at 1024×768 pixel resolution with 60 Hz screen refresh rate, and was placed roughly one meter in front of the user. The other monitor allowed the experimenter to check the recorded sensor data. Following informed consent, physiological sensors were positioned on the user's body as shown in Fig. 2(a). The GSR sensor was tied to the left wrist, and two electrodes were fixed to the index and middle finger phalanges. Two measuring electrodes for ECG were placed at each arm crook, with the reference electrode placed at the left foot. A single dry-electrode EEG device was placed on the head like a normal headset, with the EEG sensor touching the forehead and the reference electrode clipped to the left ear. EEG data samples were logged using the `Lucid Scribe` software, and all sensor data were recorded via bluetooth. Also, a webcam was used to record facial activity. Synchronized data recording, pre-processing and analyses were performed using MATLAB Psychtoolbox[1].

Protocol: Each user performed the experiment in a session lasting about 90 minutes. Viewing of each movie clip is denoted as a trial. After two practice trials involving clips that were not part of the actual study, users watched movie clips randomly shown in two blocks of 18 trials, with a short break in-between to avoid fatigue. In each trial (Fig. 1(right)), a fixation cross was displayed for four seconds followed by clip presentation. On viewing each clip, users provided their affective ratings within a time limit of 30 seconds as described below. Participants also completed a personality questionnaire after the experiment.

Stimuli: We adopted the 36 movie clips used in [2] for our study. These clips are between 51–127 sec long (μ =80, σ =20), and are shown to be uniformly distributed (9 clips per quadrant) over the VA plane.

[1]http://psychtoolbox.org/

Affective ratings: For each movie clip, we compiled valence (V) and arousal (A) ratings reflecting the user's first impression. A 7-point scale was used with a -3 (*very negative*) to 3 (*very positive*) scale for V, and a 0 (*very boring*) to 6 (*very exciting*) scale for A. Ratings concerning *engagement*, *liking* and *familiarity* were also acquired, but are not analyzed in this work. Mean user VA ratings for the 36 clips are plotted in Fig. 2(b), and are color coded based on the associated categories from the ground-truth ratings from [2]. Ratings form a C-shape in the VA plane, similar to prior affective studies [2,15].

Personality scores: Participants also completed the big-five marker scale (BFMS) questionnaire [24] which has been used in many personality recognition works [17,28,31]. Personality measure distributions along the five traits are shown in Fig. 2(c).

3.2 Physiological feature extraction

We extracted affective physiological features corresponding to each trial over the final 50 seconds of stimulus presentation, owing to two reasons: (1) The clips used in [3] are not emotionally homogeneous, but are more emotional towards the end. (2) Some employed features (see Table 1) are nonlinear functions of the input signal length, and fixed time-intervals needed to be considered as the movie clips were of varying lengths. A brief description of the different physiological signals analyzed in this work are as follows.

Galvanic Skin Response (GSR). GSR measures transpiration rate of the skin. When two electrodes are positioned on the middle and index fingers' phalanges and a small current is sent through the body, resistance to current flow changes with the skin transpiration rate. Most of the GSR information is contained in low-frequency components, and the signal is recorded at 100 Hz sampling frequency with a commercial and portable bluetooth sensor. Following [14,15,25], we extracted 31 GSR features listed in Table 1.

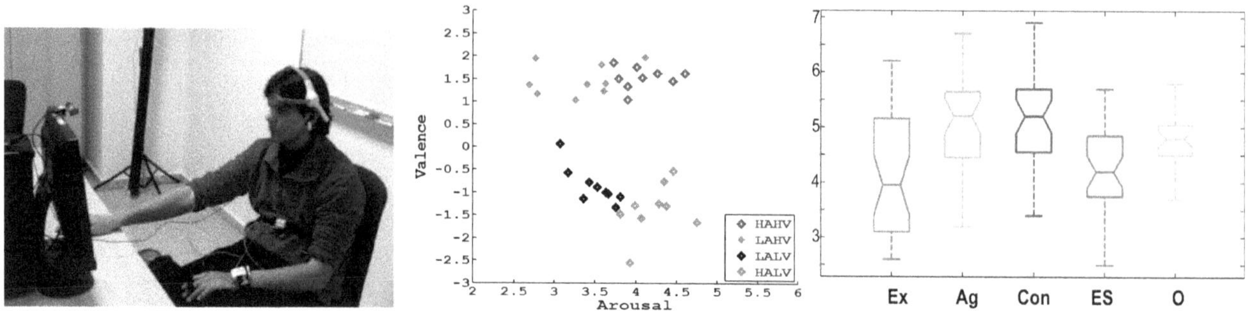

(a) (b) (c)

Figure 2: (a) Participant with sensors (EEG, ECG and GSR visible) during the experiment, (b) Mean Valence-Arousal (VA) ratings for the 36 movie clips used in our study and (c) Box-plots showing distribution for 36 users of the big-five personality trait scores Extroversion (Ex), Agreeableness (Ag), Conscientiousness (Con), Emotional Stability (ES) and Openness (O).

Table 1: Extracted features for each modality (feature dimension stated in parenthesis). *Statistics* denote mean, standard deviation (std), skewness, kurtosis of the raw feature over time, and % of times the feature value is above/below mean±std.

Modality	Extracted features
ECG (32)	Ten low frequency ([0-2.4] Hz) power spectral densities (PSDs), four very slow response (VSR [0-0.04] Hz) PSDs, IBI, HR and HRV statistics.
GSR (31)	Mean skin resistance and mean of derivative, mean differential for negative values only (mean decrease rate during decay time), proportion of negative derivative samples, number of local minima in the GSR signal, average rising time of the GSR signal, spectral power in the [0-2.4] Hz band, zero crossing rate of skin conductance slow response (SCSR) [0-0.2] Hz, zero crossing rate of skin conductance very slow response (SCVSR) [0-0.08] Hz, mean SCSR and SCVSR peak magnitude
Frontal EEG (88)	Average of first derivative, proportion of negative differential samples, mean number of peaks, mean derivative of the inverse channel signal, average number of peaks in the inverse signal, statistics over each of the 8 signal channels provided by the Neurosky software
EMO (72)	Statistics concerning horizontal and vertical movement of 12 motion units (MUs) specified in [12].

Electroencephalography (EEG). EEG measures small changes in the skull's electrical field produced by brain activities, and information is encoded in the EEG signal amplitude as well as in certain frequency components. We used a commercial, single dry-electrode EEG sensor[2], which records eight information channels sampled at 32 Hz. The recorded information includes frontal lobe activity, level of facial activation, eye-blink rate and strength, which are relevant emotional responses.

Electrocardiogram (ECG). Heart rate characteristics have been routinely used for user-centered emotion recognition. We performed R-peak detection on the ECG signal to compute users' inter-beat intervals (IBI), heart rate (HR), and the heart rate variability (HRV). We also extracted power spectral density (PSD) in low frequency bands as in [14,25].

Facial landmark trajectories (EMO). A facial feature tracker [12] was used to compute displacements of 12 interest points or motion units (MU) in each video frame. We calculated 6 statistical measures for each landmark to obtain a total of 72 features (Table 1).

4. PERSONALITY SCORES VS RATINGS

We now examine relationships among user valence (V) and arousal (A) ratings and their personality trait scores in the context of previous hypotheses put forth in literature. To this end, we (i) computed correlations between users' personality scales and VA ratings for each movie clip, and determined significant correlations according to Fisher's method (Table 2), and ii) dichotomized personality measures based on the median score to determine *high/low* trait groups (*e.g.*, extraverts and introverts), and studied the affective ratings of each group.

Table 2: Mean correlations between personality scales and user VA ratings for all movie clips. * denotes significant correlations (p<0.01) obtained using Fisher's method.

	Ex	Ag	Con	ES	Open
Arousal	-0.15*	-0.05	-0.04	0.07	-0.08*
Valence	0.22*	0.16	-0.06	0.08	0.15

4.1 H1: Extraversion vs Arousal and Valence

The correlation between Extraversion and arousal has been investigated in many studies– EEG measurements in [27], signal detection analysis in [11], and fMRI [13] have shown lower arousal in extraverts as compared to introverts, consistent with Eyesenck's personality theory. Also, Extraversion has been found to correlate with positive valence in a number of works [7].

Correlation analyses presented in Table 2 confirm a slight but significant negative correlation between *Ex* and A as noted in the literature. Likewise, a significant positive correlation is noted between *Ex* and V mirroring prior findings. Therefore, our data corroborates previous observations connecting Extraversion and affective behavior.

[2]www.neurosky.com

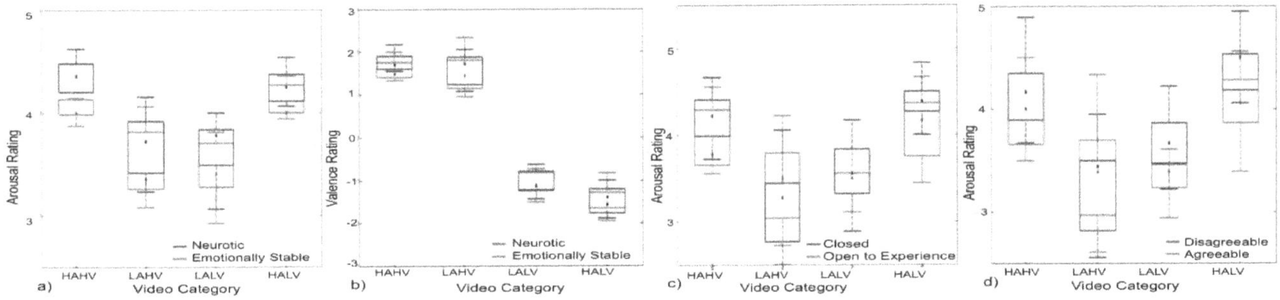

Figure 3: Quadrant-wise comparisons of A,V ratings for Neurotics vs emotionally stable subjects are shown in (a,b). Arousal rating comparisons for (c) Open vs Closed, and (d) Agreeable vs Disagreeable subjects.

4.2 H2: Neuroticism vs Arousal

The relationship between Neuroticism and A has been extensively studied and commented on– a positive correlation between *Neu* and A is revealed through fMRI responses [13], and EEG analysis [27] reinforces this observation especially for negative valence stimuli. [22] further remarks that neurotics experience negative emotions stronger than emotionally stable persons.

As no significant correlation is observed between *Neu* scores and A ratings in Table 2, we used t-tests to compare mean A ratings provided by the neurotic and emotionally stable (*ES*) groups upon dichotomization of the *Neu* scale by thresholding at the median score (which was midway between the extremes, resulting in equal-sized groups). To examine if our data suggested a positive correlation between *Neu* and A, we performed a left-tailed t-test comparing the A ratings of the *ES* and neurotic groups– the test revealed a significant difference in A ratings for high arousal clips ($t(34) = -1.8058, p = 0.0399$), and a marginally significant difference for low arousal clips ($t(34) = -1.4041, p = 0.0847$).

Quadrant-wise distributions of A ratings for the *ES* and neurotic groups are presented in Fig. 3(a). Quadrant-wise comparisons show that neurotics generally experience higher arousal than *ES* subjects. Left-tailed t-tests confirm that neurotics provided significantly higher A ratings for HAHV ($t(16) = -2.5828, p < 0.0100$) clips, and marginally higher A ratings for LALV ($t(16) = -1.6077, p = 0.0637$) and HALV ($t(16) = -1.3859, p = 0.0924$) stimuli. No difference was however observed for LAHV clips ($t(16) = -0.9946$, n.s.). In general, our analyses support the observation that Neuroticism is associated with higher arousal.

4.3 H3: Neuroticism vs Valence

Differing observations have been made regarding the relationship between Neuroticism and valence. A negative correlation between *Neu* and positive valence is observed in [13], while a positive relationship between the two for low arousal stimuli is noted in [29]. [22] remarks that the *Neu*-V relation is moderated by situation– while neurotics may feel less positive in unpleasant situations, they experience positive emotions as strongly as *ES* subjects in pleasant conditions.

Again, as no significant correlation between *Neu* and V is noted in Table 2, we focus on V ratings of the neurotic and *ES* groups. Very similar V ratings are noted for high/low valence clips. Quadrant-wise V rating comparisons (Fig. 3(b)) reveal that neurotics feel slightly more positive than *ES* subjects on viewing HAHV clips but the difference is not significant ($t(16) = -1.489, p = 0.1558$) clips. Overall, our analyses do not reveal any definitive relationship between *Neu* and valence.

4.4 H4: Openness vs Arousal and Valence

Among the few works to study Openness, [29] notes a positive correlation between Openness and valence under low arousal conditions, which is attributed to the intelligence and sensitivity of creative individuals[3], enabling them to better appreciate subtly emotional stimuli.

To examine this hypothesis, we used right-tailed t-tests comparing V, A ratings of the groups *open* and *closed* to experience upon dichotomization. Very similar valence ratings are noted for the *open* and *closed* groups. Quadrant-based comparisons reveal that open individuals experienced only slightly higher valence while viewing LAHV clips ($t(16) = 1.4706, p = 0.0804$).

Note the significant and slightly negative correlation between Openness and A from Table 2. Focusing on A ratings of the *open* vs *closed* groups, marginally different A ratings ($t(34) = -1.5767, p = 0.0621$) are noted for high arousal stimuli. For fine-grained analysis, we again used left-tailed t-tests for quadrant based comparisons (Fig. 3(c)), which reveal that *closed* individuals experienced significantly higher arousal for HALV clips ($t(16) = -1.9834, p = 0.0324$), and slightly higher arousal for HAHV clips ($t(16) = -1.5402, p = 0.0715$). In summary, we observe a negative relationship between Openness and arousal, and a slightly positive relationship between Openness and valence as noted in [29].

4.5 Agreeableness and Conscientiousness

Comparison of arousal ratings of the *agreeable* and *disagreeable* groups (Fig. 3(d)) revealed that *agreeable* individuals are generally less aroused by LV videos ($t(34) = -2.1859, p = 0.0358$). Quadrant-based analyses also show that *disagreeable* individuals felt more aroused by HALV ($t(16) = -2.5493, p = 0.0214$) and marginally more aroused for LALV ($t(16) = -2.0976, p = 0.0522$) clips. Conscientiousness scale differences did not significantly influence the VA ratings in any manner.

5. PERSONALITY RECOGNITION FROM PHYSIOLOGICAL SIGNALS

In Sec. 4, a direct correlation with affective ratings is only noted for the Extraversion and Openness personality traits. For the other traits, the influence of personality differences

[3]Creativity strongly correlates with Openness [21].

Table 3: Physiological correlates of emotion and personality. R° denotes the number of significant feature correlates, while R^2 is the coefficient of determination for the regression model with the significant correlates as predictors. Bold values denote linear regression models with a significant R^2 statistic.

		Arousal		Valence		Extra.		Agreeable		Conscient		Em. Stab.		Open	
Video Set	Feature	R^o	R^2	R^o	R^2	R^o	R^2	R^o	R^2	R^o	R^2	R^o	R^2	R^o	R^2
All	**ECG**			1	**0.17**	2	0.51					1	0.49	1	0.35
	GSR														
	EMO													1	**0.28**
	EEG	1	0.45	1	0.27	2	0.66	2	0.64	2	**0.68**	2	0.54	2	0.49
HAHV	**ECG**					1	0.46					1	0.45		
	GSR														
	EMO			1	0.59							3	0.75	3	0.77
	EEG			1	0.49	2	0.54							1	0.50
LAHV	**ECG**			1	**0.15**	3	0.55			1	0.44	1	0.46	1	0.42
	GSR														
	EMO	1	**0.20**			1	0.30	1	0.29					2	**0.51**
	EEG	1	0.54											1	0.56
LALV	**ECG**	1	0.41			2	0.55					1	0.44	1	0.42
	GSR														
	EMO			1	0.22	2	0.61	1	0.40					2	0.45
	EEG			1	0.40	1	0.57			3	0.63	1	0.58		
HALV	**ECG**											2	0.57		
	GSR														
	EMO													1	**0.13**
	EEG			1	**0.59**	3	**0.69**			2	0.53			1	0.39

Table 4: Personality recognition performance considering affective responses to a) all, and b) emotionally homogeneous stimuli. Maximum F1-scores with unimodal and multimodal methods are shown in bold.

		Extravert		Agreeable		Conscient		Em. Stab		Open	
Videos	Method	acc	F1	acc	F1	acc	F1	acc	F1	acc	F1
	ECG	0.45	0.43	0.42	**0.37**	0.45	**0.31**	0.52	**0.50**	0.55	0.54
	GSR	0.15	0.14	0.42	0.34	0.39	0.28	0.24	0.20	0.91	**0.91**
All	EMO	0.61	**0.59**	0.42	0.34	0.12	0.11	0.42	0.37	0.27	0.26
	$\mathbf{W}^{t}_{est}$	0.61	**0.60**	0.42	**0.39**	0.45	**0.31**	0.64	**0.63**	0.91	**0.91**
	ECG	0.69	**0.69**	0.75	0.75	0.19	0.18	0.63	**0.63**	0.06	0.06
	GSR	0.59	0.59	0.78	0.78	0.25	0.25	0.31	0.29	0.78	**0.78**
HAHV	EMO	0.31	0.31	0.84	**0.84**	0.41	**0.41**	0.47	0.44	0.22	0.21
	EEG	0.09	0.09	0.72	0.72	0.34	0.34	0.41	0.39	0.53	0.53
	$\mathbf{W}^{t}_{est}$	0.78	**0.78**	0.84	**0.84**	0.56	**0.56**	0.69	**0.69**	0.78	**0.78**
	ECG	0.45	0.45	0.76	**0.76**	0.34	0.26	0.45	0.41	0.55	0.55
	GSR	0.72	**0.72**	0.72	0.72	0.55	0.55	0.21	0.19	0.69	**0.69**
HALV	EMO	0.38	0.34	0.38	0.37	0.38	0.34	0.52	**0.51**	0.62	0.62
	EEG	0.34	0.32	0.24	0.23	0.69	**0.69**	0.31	0.29	0.62	0.61
	$\mathbf{W}^{t}_{est}$	0.72	**0.72**	0.79	**0.79**	0.76	**0.76**	0.55	**0.54**	0.69	**0.69**
	ECG	0.45	0.39	0.32	0.31	0.42	0.34	0.55	0.45	0.58	0.56
	GSR	0.32	0.27	0.45	0.44	0.42	0.34	0.42	0.30	0.77	**0.77**
LAHV	EMO	0.65	**0.63**	0.26	0.23	0.65	**0.64**	0.65	**0.63**	0.29	0.25
	EEG	0.32	0.30	0.65	**0.63**	0.65	0.62	0.52	0.52	0.68	0.67
	$\mathbf{W}^{t}_{est}$	0.68	**0.67**	0.68	**0.67**	0.65	**0.64**	0.74	**0.74**	0.81	**0.81**
	ECG	0.50	**0.49**	0.20	0.20	0.13	0.13	0.37	0.27	0.30	0.29
	GSR	0.27	0.26	0.23	0.23	0.33	**0.33**	0.60	0.57	0.63	**0.63**
LALV	EMO	0.43	0.43	0.47	**0.46**	0.27	0.27	0.30	0.26	0.17	0.16
	EEG	0.33	0.33	0.00	0.00	0.10	0.10	0.67	**0.66**	0.37	0.35
	$\mathbf{W}^{t}_{est}$	0.57	**0.54**	0.53	**0.53**	0.33	**0.33**	0.70	**0.69**	0.63	**0.63**

on users' affective behavior is only revealed via quadrant-wise comparisons, where affective ratings of the *high* and *low* trait groups for emotionally similar (or homogeneous) stimuli are examined. While affective ratings represent an explicit reflection of one's emotional state, it would be reasonable to expect affective physiological responses, to also reveal personality differences as they implicitly convey the same information. We therefore examined correlations between physiological features, affective ratings and personality traits (Table 3), and attempted personality recognition (Table 4) considering responses to (a) all, and (b) emotionally similar clips.

5.1 Correlation analyses

We attempted to discover physiological correlates of emotional and big-five personality attributes via partial Pearson correlations. Given the large number of extracted physiological features (Table 1) as compared to the population size for this study, we first performed a principal component analysis (PCA) on features to avoid overfitting, and retained those components that explained 99% of the variance. Table 3 presents correlations between these principal components, and users' affective ratings and personality scales. For each of the modalities, we determined components that significantly correlated with the personality scales for the five dimensions (R° denotes number of significant correlates). For affective dimensions, we determined significant correlates considering mean V,A ratings provided by all users for the 36 clips. We also trained regression models with the significantly correlating components as predictors of the dependent emotion/personality variable, and the squared correlations of these models (R^2) are also tabulated.

Considering correlations with arousal and valence, while only few correlates are observed possibly owing to the nature of the sensors used in this study, more correlates are observed for V than for A overall. At least one significant correlate is noted for all modalities except GSR. EEG is the modality found to correlate most with A, with one correlate observed for all and LAHV movie clips. EEG also has the most number of correlates with V (one significant correlate per video set), but this is unsurprising as a number of works have successfully recognized V with commercial-grade sensors [6]. For V, one ECG correlate is noted for all and LAHV videos, and one Emo correlate for HAHV and LALV videos. Prior studies [3, 15] have also noted that these modalities correlate better with V than A.

Focusing on personality dimensions, a larger number of physiological correlates are observed as compared to emotional attributes. Least number of correlates are noted for Agreeableness, while most correlates are noted for Extraversion. The EEG modality corresponds the maximum number of correlates, while no correlates are observed for GSR. In general, a larger number of physiological correlates are noted for emotionally similar videos for all traits except Agreeableness. Also, models with a higher R^2 statistic are noted for similar clips, implying that physiology–based linear models can more effectively predict personality traits while comparing user responses under similar affective conditions.

5.2 Recognition results

Recognition accuracies and F1-scores achieved using the above-computed physiological features for the five personality dimensions are presented in Table 4. Linear SVMs and leave-one-user-out cross-validation were used, and the late multimodal fusion technique proposed in [16] was used to improve on the unimodal results. Multimodal results are denoted using W^t_{est} where the test sample label is computed as $\sum_{i=1}^{4} \alpha_i^* t_i p_i$. Here, i indexes the four modalities used in this work, p_i's denote posterior SVM probabilities, $\{\alpha_i^*\}$ are the optimal weights maximizing the F1-score on the training set and $t_i = \alpha_i F_i / \sum_{i=1}^{4} \alpha_i F_i$, where F_i denotes the F1-score obtained on the training set with the ith modality.

Upon dichotomizing the personality scores based on the median, an inexact split (19 vs 17) was obtained only for the Conscientiousness and Openness traits. Therefore, baseline accuracy/F1-score for these two traits is 0.53, while being 0.5 for the others. Considering affective responses to all videos, greater-than-chance recognition is achieved only for three traits (excepting Agreeableness and Conscientiousness). When physiological responses to emotionally similar videos are considered, the best unimodal F1-scores for all personality traits are above-chance with the exception of facial activity features for Conscientiousness. These results confirm that personality differences between users with high and low traits are better revealed on comparing their affective responses to emotionally similar clips. Consistently high recognition performance is achieved for the Openness trait, and also for Agreeableness considering homogeneous videos. Conscientiousness is the most difficult trait to recognize using the considered physiological features, and generally low recognition performance is also noted for Neuroticism. Focusing on the sensing modalities, GSR consistently produces the best performance for Openness while ECG performs best for Agreeableness in three out of five conditions.

6. DISCUSSION & CONCLUSION

We performed personality trait recognition from emotional user responses recorded using commercial sensors. This paper represents one of the first works to extend Eyesenck's observations relating personality traits and emotional behavior in a computational setting. Also, the use of commercial sensors ensures that the study is ecologically valid and scalable. Analyzing relationships between users' affective ratings and personality traits, Extraversion is found to be positively correlated with valence and negatively correlated with arousal. Also, quadrant-based analysis reveals that Neuroticism is associated with higher arousal, in line with prior observations.

We then computed physiological correlates of personality, and physiological features are found to correlate better with personality trait scales when user responses to emotionally homogeneous videos are considered. Also, considerably better-than-chance recognition is achieved for all personality traits considering homogeneous clips (excepting Conscientiousness considering LALV clips). These results confirm that personality differences are better revealed when emotional responses to similar clips are considered, in line with the statistical analyses. Best recognition results are obtained for Openness and Agreeableness, while worst performance is noted for Conscientiousness.

It is pertinent to point out some limitations of our analyses and study in general. Weak linear correlations are noted between emotional and personality attributes in Table 2, and only few physiological correlates of emotion and personality are observed in Table 3, implying that the personality–affect relationship may not be best captured via linear correlations. Nevertheless, some patterns do emerge from the presented analyses. Maximum number of physiological correlates are noted for Openness, and the best recognition performance is also achieved for this trait. Also, some correlation was noted between emotional attributes and personality traits with the exception of Conscientiousness in Section 4, and least recognition performance is obtained for this trait. Overall, promising personality trait recognition is achieved with the proposed framework employing inexpensive, portable and commercial sensors. Finally, we will also make the compiled data publicly available for furthering related research.

7. ACKNOWLEDGEMENTS

This research was funded by the HCCS research grant from Singapore's Agency for Science, Technology and Research (A*STAR), the FP7 European Project xLiMe and SensAura Tech.

8. REFERENCES

[1] M. K. Abadi, J. A. M. Correa, J. Wache, H. Yang, I. Patras, and N. Sebe. Inference of Personality Traits and Affect Schedule by Analysis of Spontaneous Reactions to Affective Videos. In *FG*, 2015.

[2] M. K. Abadi, S. M. Kia, R. Subramanian, P. Avesani, and N. Sebe. User-centric Affective Video Tagging from MEG and Peripheral Physiological Responses. In *ACII*, 2013.

[3] M. K. Abadi, R. Subramanian, S. Kia, P. Avesani, I. Patras, and N. Sebe. DECAF: MEG-based Multimodal Database for Decoding Affective Physiological Responses. *IEEE Trans. Affective Computing*, 2015.

[4] S. Argamon, S. Dhawle, M. Koppel, and Pennbaker. Lexical predictors of personality type. In *Interface and the Classification Society of North America*, 2005.

[5] L. M. Batrinca, N. Mana, B. Lepri, F. Pianesi, and N. Sebe. Please, tell me about yourself: Automatic Personality Assessment Using Short Self-Presentations. In *ICMI*, 2011.

[6] L. Brown, B. Grundlehner, and J. Penders. Towards wireless emotional valence detection from EEG. In *EMBS*, pages 2188–2191, 2011.

[7] P. T. Costa and R. R. McCrae. Influence of Extraversion and Neuroticism on Subjective Well-Being: Happy and Unhappy People. *Journal of Personality and Social Psychology*, 38(4):668, 1980.

[8] P. T. J. Costa and R. R. McCrae. *NEO-PI-R Professional Manual: Revised NEO Personality and NEO Five-Factor Inventory (NEO-FFI)*, volume 4. Psychological Assessment Resources, 1992.

[9] V. De Pascalis, E. Strippoli, P. Riccardi, and F. Vergari. Personality, Event-Related Potential (ERP) and Heart Rate (HR) in Emotional Word Processing. *Pers. Individ. Dif.*, 36:873–891, 2004.

[10] H. J. Eysenck. *Dimensions of Personality*, volume 5. Transaction Publishers, 1950.

[11] S. Gupta and J. Nicholson. Simple visual reaction time, personality strength of the nervous system: theory approach. *Pers. Individ. Dif.*, 6(4):461–469, 1985.

[12] H. Joho, J. Staiano, N. Sebe, and J. M. Jose. Looking at the viewer: analysing facial activity to detect personal highlights of multimedia contents. *Multimedia Tools Appl.*, 51(2):505–523, 2011.

[13] E. G. Kehoe, J. M. Toomey, J. H. Balsters, and A. L. W. Bokde. Personality modulates the effects of emotional arousal and valence on brain activation. *Soc. Cogn. Affect. Neurosci.*, 7:858–70, 2012.

[14] J. Kim and E. Andre. Emotion recognition based on physiological changes in music listening. *IEEE TPAMI*, 30(12):2067–2083, 2008.

[15] S. Koelstra, C. Mühl, M. Soleymani, J.-S. Lee, A. Yazdan, T. Ebrahimi, T. Pun, A. Nijholt, and I. Patras. DEAP: A Database for Emotion Analysis Using Physiological Signals. *IEEE Trans. Affective Computing*, 3(1):18–31, 2012.

[16] S. Koelstra and I. Patras. Fusion of facial expressions and EEG for implicit affective tagging. *Image and Vision Computing*, 31(2):164–174, 2013.

[17] B. Lepri, R. Subramanian, K. Kalimeri, J. Staiano, F. Pianesi, and N. Sebe. Connecting meeting behavior with extraversion - a systematic study. *IEEE Trans. Affective Computing*, 3(4):443–455, 2012.

[18] C. L. Lisetti and F. Nasoz. Using noninvasive wearable computers to recognize human emotions from physiological signals. *EURASIP J. Adv. Sig. Proc.*, 2004(11):1672–1687, 2004.

[19] F. Mairesse, M. A. Walker, M. R. Mehl, and R. K. Moore. Using linguistic cues for the automatic recognition of personality in conversation and text. *Journal of Artificial Intelligence Research*, 30:457–500, 2007.

[20] R. R. McCrae and P. T. Costa. A contemplated revision of the neo five-factor inventory. *Pers. Individ. Dif.*, 36(3):587–596, 2004.

[21] I. Mervielde, F. De Fruyt, and S. Jarmuz. Linking openness and intellect in childhood and adulthood. *Parental descriptions of child personality: Developmental antecedents of the Big Five*, pages 105–126, 1998.

[22] W. Ng. Clarifying the relation between neuroticism and positive emotions. *Pers. Individ. Dif.*, 47(1):69–72, 2009.

[23] D. Olguin, B. Waber, T. Kim, A. Mohan, K. Ara, and A. Pentland. Sensible organizations: Technology and methodology for automatically measuring organizational behavior. *IEEE Trans. Systems, Man, and Cybernetics*, 39(1):43–55, 2009.

[24] M. Perugini and L. Di Blas. Analyzing Personality-Related Adjectives from an Eticemic Perspective: the Big Five Marker Scale (BFMS) and the Italian AB5C Taxonomy. *Big Five Assessment*, pages 281–304, 2002.

[25] M. Soleymani, J. Lichtenauer, T. Pun, and M. Pantic. A multimodal database for affect recognition and implicit tagging. *IEEE Trans. Affective Computing*, 3:42–55, 2012.

[26] R. Srivastava, J. Feng, S. Roy, S. Yan, and T. Sim. Don't Ask Me What I'm Like, Just Watch and Listen. In *ACMMM*, 2012.

[27] G. Stenberg. Personality and the EEG: Arousal and emotional arousability. *Pers. Individ. Dif.*, 13:1097–1113, 1992.

[28] R. Subramanian, Y. Yan, J. Staiano, O. Lanz, and N. Sebe. On the relationship between head pose, social attention and personality prediction for unstructured and dynamic group interactions. In *ICMI*, 2013.

[29] S. Tok, M. Koyuncu, S. Dural, and F. Catikkas. Evaluation of International Affective Picture System (IAPS) ratings in an athlete population and its relations to personality. *Pers. Individ. Dif.*, 49(5):461–466, 2010.

[30] A. Vinciarelli and G. Mohammadi. A survey of personality computing. *IEEE Trans. Affective Computing*, (3):273–291, 2014.

[31] G. Zen, B. Lepri, E. Ricci, and O. Lanz. Space speaks: towards socially and personality aware visual surveillance. In *ACMMPVA*, pages 37–42, 2010.

[32] Z. Zeng, M. Pantic, G. I. Roisman, and T. S. Huang. A survey of affect recognition methods: audio, visual, and spontaneous expressions. *IEEE TPAMI*, 31(1):39–58, 2009.

Detecting Mastication - A Wearable Approach

Abdelkareem Bedri
College of Computing
Georgia Tech
abedri6@gatech.edu

Apoorva Verlekar
College of Computing
Georgia Tech
ayp3@gatech.edu

Edison Thomaz
College of Computing
Georgia Tech
ethomaz@gatech.edu

Valerie Avva
College of Computing
Georgia Tech
vavva3@gatech.edu

Thad Starner
College of Computing
Georgia Tech
thad@gatech.edu

ABSTRACT

We explore using the Outer Ear Interface (OEI) to recognize eating activities. OEI contains a 3D gyroscope and a set of proximity sensors encapsulated in an off-the-shelf earpiece to monitor jaw movement by measuring ear canal deformation. In a laboratory setting with 20 participants, OEI could distinguish eating from other activities, such as walking, talking, and silently reading, with over 90% accuracy (user independent). In a second study, six subjects wore the system for 6 hours each while performing their normal daily activities. OEI correctly classified five minute segments of time as eating or non-eating with 93% accuracy (user dependent).

Categories and Subject Descriptors

H.5.2 [**Information Interfaces and Presentation (e.g. HCI)**]: User Interfaces

General Terms

Human Factors, Experimentation, Design

Keywords

ear; eating; food intake monitoring; wearable computer

1. INTRODUCTION

In trying to map the relationship between diet and disease [14] researchers have relied on self-report methods to answer questions about what, how and when people eat. Food frequency questionnaires and 24-hour recalls are the most typical instruments employed in this context [5, 14]; they are widely used by health experts and serve as the foundation for nutritional surveillance systems [3].

ICMI '15, November 09-13, 2015, Seattle, WA, USA
©2015 ACM. ISBN 978-1-4503-3912-4/15/11 $15.00
DOI: http://dx.doi.org/10.1145/2818346.2820767

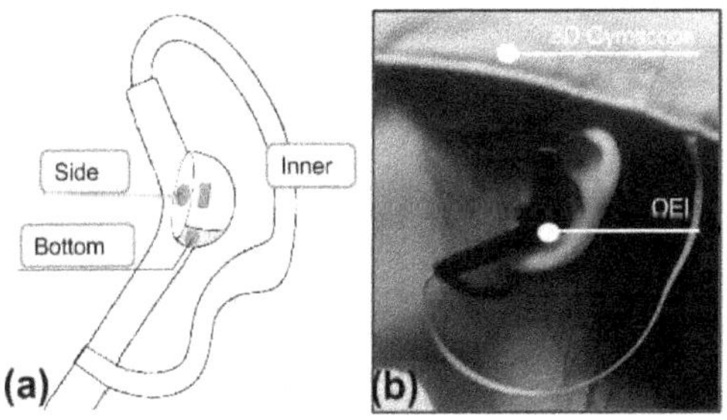

Figure 1: OEI system: a) The proximity sensors on the earpiece. b) User wearing OEI

However, self-report survey tools suffer from biases and are dependent on one's ability to recollect events and activities [8, 9, 10]. This problem has motivated research towards systems that can automatically and objectively track eating both in laboratory and real-world settings [1, 12, 13].

One option is to capture images or video of the user's day continuously and then search for episodes of eating. However, the review of the data would be onerous. A wearable system that could detect eating could help health researchers (or the wearer) find the appropriate episodes in video quickly. Other journaling options include triggering capture only during suspected eating events or querying the user as to what they are eating. Beyond dietary monitoring, an eating detection system might also prompt the user to take medication or perform a necessary procedure (e.g., insulin injection) at appropriate times.

We explore the use of the Outer Ear Interface (OEI) to detect mastication automatically, distinguishing eating activities from non-eating ones. OEI is packaged in an off-the-shelf consumer earbud that mounts outside the ear canal. The system monitors jaw movement by using proximity sensors to measure the deformation it causes in the ear canal and uses a gyro to prevent errors due to body motion.

Contributions of this paper include

- The design of a system that distinguishes eating activities from non-eating activities.
- An evaluation of the system in a laboratory setting where activity sessions were divided into 5-minute segments and labelled as eating or not-eating.
- An evaluation in real-world settings encompassing six one-hour long sessions with six participants.

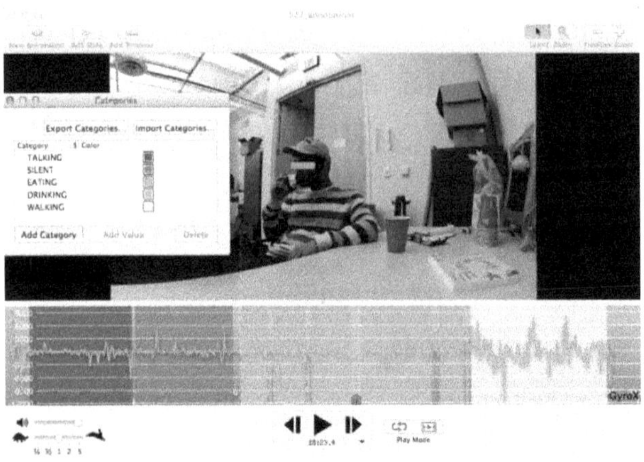

Figure 2: Annotating video using ChronoViz.

2. RELATED WORK

Over the last 20 years, wearable and ubiquitous computing researchers have proposed a variety of methods for automating food tracking and recognition. Acoustic and inertial sensing have been the most commonly used modalities.

Several food intake monitoring systems have been designed for neck placement, such as Bodyscope and Bodybeat [11, 15]. Kalantarian et al. demonstrated distinguishing solids and liquids with an F-measure of 85% and 86% with a sensor located in the neck region. Fontana et al. detected food intake with 89.8% precision, 89.9% recall, and 89.8% accuracy [6] fusing data from a jaw motion sensor, a hand gesture sensor and an accelerometer.

Laboratory studies by Amft et al. [2] with four participants suggests that the placement of a microphone inside the ear canal can distinguish between speech and eating foods (except for very soft foods like rice) at around 99% accuracy and can distinguish between four types of foods with 80% to 100% accuracy. However, wearing a microphone in the ear canal can be obtrusive to the user.

In a previous paper on OEI [4], we report frame level accuracy for detecting eating, talking, walking and silence in a lab setting. Here, we expand upon that analysis, focusing on eating, and move toward real-world practicality of the method with an in-the-wild experiment.

3. SYSTEM DESCRIPTION

The current version of the OEI system (Figure 1) contains three infrared proximity sensors placed in an off-the-shelf sport earpiece and a 3D gyroscope placed in a hat. The sport earpiece has an adjustable loop that goes around the pinna to stabilize the unit, and the three proximity sensors are placed orthogonally with respect to each other to cover a wider area of the ear canal. Due to the wide variety of ear shapes, fitting the sensors properly is difficult; having the three proximity sensors provides redundancy. When a user walks, the earpiece may slightly shift in an out along with the body motion. This movement causes the proximity sensors to generate signals similar to those obtained during mastication. The gyroscope data helps combat this problem (see Section 7). The sensors are sampled at 100 Hz, and the data is logged on an SD card.

4. DATA COLLECTION AND LABELING

Our first experiment was conducted in a laboratory setting. We invited participants to wear the system for about half an hour and asked them to perform a fixed set of activities, including eating, drinking, walking, reading aloud and being silent. The second experiment was an in-the-wild study where we asked participants to wear the system for six hours and perform their normal daily activities. We had different participants in both sets of experiments.

4.1 Laboratory Experiment

In the laboratory study, we had a total of 23 participants with ages varying from 18 to 41, a mean of 24 and a standard deviation of 4.83. We had to discard data from three participants due to errors in data collection.

We designed the study to be easily replicated to ensure uniformity across subjects. Each subject began with 5 minutes of reading aloud from a book, followed by 5 minutes of silently reading or browsing the Internet. Next were 10 to 15 minutes of eating and drinking. Participants were encouraged to behave as they would in normal eating environments. However, the range of food types they could eat was restricted to M&Ms, apples, and bananas. They could also drink from a glass of water. Afterwards, an experimenter walked for five minutes with the participant to a crowded street and down a flight of stairs to test the system's robustness to the user's movement. On average, about 45% of the recorded time was spent in eating activities. Sessions were video recorded for later annotation of ground truth except for when the user left the lab for walking.

We used ChronoViz [7] for annotating the video footage obtained in the laboratory study (Figure 2). The annotation was done by two authors and then verified by a third. Only a few boundary errors were found in the verification step. To synchronize the video footage with the data recorded by OEI on ChronoViz, we used a simple head gesture (move head sidewise from left to right 4 or 5 times) which was distinct in the video as well as in the gyroscope data.

4.2 Wild Experiment

We conducted an in-the-wild study to test the system in more realistic conditions. Participants in this study used the system for six hours each during their daily activities. They were asked to keep a record of any activities that exceeded 15 minutes and to indicate whether they were eating-related activities. This duration can be sufficient for real time applications in the health field, such as reminding a patient to take medication with food. For food intake activities, participants had to specify when start and end to within one minute. We used these labels as ground truth. We obtained data from a total of 6 participants (4 females). One of the authors visually checked regions marked by the participants as eating activity to verify that the gyro and proximity data looked appropriate. Another author reviewed these annotations. A few boundary errors were found and corrected. Of the total time recorded by the participants, 11.2% of the time was spent in eating activities.

5. FEATURE SELECTION

We selected five features to use from the sensor data. The first feature is obtained by dimensionality reduction using Principal Component Analysis (PCA). We performed PCA on the three proximity sensors and selected the first component. Proximity data were smoothed (with an averaging window size of 5 samples), and we took the first derivative of the values to remove signal offset before the dimensionality reduction step. PCA helps recover the jaw movement from the OEI without being affected by the heterogeneity of the user's ear shape.

The second feature reflects the energy in the jaw movement signal, which can be a major difference between speech and mastication gestures. Energy is computed using the RMS value of a sliding window of 50 samples across the values of the first feature. The last three features are the raw gyroscope data from axis X, Y and Z. These features can help detect body motion like walking, which may result in shaking or shifting the OEI sensor causing it to produce signals similar to the ones caused by jaw movement.

In a previous work [4] we used an energy feature computed by averaging the energy in the band between 1.2 Hz to 4.6 Hz. Generating this feature requires short time FFT calculation, which is computationally expensive when compared with RMS. To assess the validity of using the RMS feature we ran a frame level evaluation (frame size 5 seconds) using user independent HMM models built from the same data set [4] and obtained a slightly higher accuracy (83.7 % using FFT feature to 84.3 % with RMS feature).

6. EATING EVENT RECOGNITION

Our goal is to evaluate OEI's capability to recognize eating events when they happen. In food logging, users or health researchers split the time period they are monitoring into smaller time segments, and report in which segments food intake occurs. We follow a similar approach here.

6.1 Training and Testing

Hidden Markov models (HMMs) were trained of eating and null classes using frames of 5 seconds with 50% overlap, extracted from labeled intervals. To recognize eating segments in the recorded data, we performed a sequence of steps. First, we extracted 5 second frames from the entire recorded period using a sliding window that advanced by one second. After computing the features on each frame we test their accuracy against the trained models and classify results as an *Eating* or *Non_eating* frame. A binary vector is then generated from recognition results to be compared with ground truth labels.

Before the final comparison the binary recognition vector is filtered using two stages. Using a predefined window size of 15 seconds, the first stage looks for periods where continuous eating is recognized. Unless a period is larger or equal to the window size it will be considered as *Non_eating*. The second stage smooths the results of the first stage using an averaging window of 150 seconds.

Comparison between ground truth and predicted results are made by segmenting the recorded period into same size non-overlapping intervals. Intervals are marked as eating if any eating activity was labeled or predicted in that interval. We use Precision $= TP/(TP+FP)$, Recall $= TP/(TP+FN)$ and Accuracy (percentage of correctly labelled segments) $= (TP+TN)/(Number\_of\_segments)$ as metrics.

7. LABORATORY EXPERIMENT RESULTS

Using the data collected from 20 participants for a period of half an hour in the lab environment, we trained HMM models for eating as the main class and talking, walking and silence as three null classes. Although drinking events were annotated, they were not used in training steps due to insufficient data. We empirically selected a 10-state, left-right topology for talking and silence classes, and an eight-state left-right topology with additional transitions between $(4 \rightarrow 1)$ and $(7 \rightarrow 5)$ for eating and walking classes.

Table 1 shows the mean and the standard deviation of the precision, recall and accuracy percentages by evaluating the system in intervals of 1 minute, 3 minutes and 5 minutes, tested on leave-one-user-out, user independent models.

Table 1: User independent laboratory results

Window Size	Precision %	Recall %	Correct %
1 minute	88.2(± 12.1)	86.1 (± 20.7)	88.5(± 10.4)
3 minutes	89.6(± 15.2)	90.2 (± 16.2)	87.8 (± 12.9)
5 minutes	92.6(± 13.5)	93.3 (± 14.5)	90.4 (± 12.9)

Table 2: User dependent in-the-wild results

ID	False+/hour	Precision %	Recall %	Correct %
S1	0.7	58.3	100	93.1
S2	0.4	57.1	80	94.6
S3	0.4	66.7	100	95.9
S4	0.4	76.9	100	96.1
S5	1.6	52.2	92.2	83.6
S6	0.6	70	100	93.8
Avr	0.68(±0.5)	63.5(±9.2)	95.4 (±8)	92.9 (±4.7)

As expected, the gyro was important in distinguishing eating and other classes. Evaluating the eating classifier in a window of 15 seconds without the incorporating inertia features resulted in a significant drop in accuracy (86.7% → 70.5%), precision (86.3% → 63.2%)and recall (76.5% → 50.4%). 67% of false positives and 80.1% of false negatives were due to walking activities.

8. IN-THE-WILD RESULTS

We trained two HMM models, one each for *Eating* and *Non_eating*. A left-right topology of eight states with no skip states was used for both models. We used leave-one-user-out cross validation training for user independent testing. For user dependent testing, we randomly reserved 33% of each user's session as an independent test set and used the rest for training.

In Tables 2 and 3 we list user dependent and user independent test results. We provide the average false positive per hour rate as an additional metric for evaluation. The

Table 3: User independent in-the-wild results

ID	False+/hr	Precision %	Recall %	Correct %
S1	1.1	42.9	85.7	87.5
S2	3	16	80	70.3
S3	2.7	24	100	75.3
S4	1.4	47.4	90	85.7
S5	0.6	73.3	84.6	91.8
S6	1.6	46.7	100	83.3
Ave	1.7 (±0.9)	41.7(±20.2)	90.1(±8.3)	82.3 (±8)

time interval window for both tables is five minutes (72 total segments per participant).

9. DISCUSSION

In order to discover food allergies and understand eating behaviors and disorders, health researchers and clinicians conduct laboratory experiments and diary studies. To help encourage patient compliance with reminders based on eating detection, the OEI project strives to create a semi-automatic food journaling device that is unobtrusive and appears similar to current consumer electronics devices on the market. Given the current OEI hardware, one can imagine the proximity sensors and gyro integrated into a popular Bluetooth headset, like the LG Tone Pro or Jawbone. In this sense, OEI is less obtrusive than the devices described by Fontana et al.[6], Rahman et al. [11, 15], and Yatani and Truong[15]. When a potential eating session is detected, a connected smartphone app might ask the user to confirm that they are eating and prompt the wearer to journal the food either by speaking it or typing it on their phone. For such applications, precision and recall for eating detection can significantly improve by adapting the classifier to a specific patient. This goal can be achieved by customizing preexisting user-independent models with correctly classified samples from the current user. For in-lab studies, one could imagine integrating the OEI with a camera pendant, like the Narrative Clip or Looxcie, that constantly images the user's hands and automatically marks segments with a high probability of being an eating event.

In both proposed uses, the recognition system must have a high recall rate and not have so many false positives to annoy the wearer or overwhelm the health researcher. In that regard, the results here are encouraging. The user independent, leave-one-out laboratory study shows recall, precision, and accuracy rates above 90% (a baseline system that would mark everything as *Non_eating* would be 55% accurate).

The in-the-wild results are also encouraging, with a recall rate of over 90%. While the accuracy was poorer than baseline (82% versus 89% for a system that always returns *Non_eating*), the result is understandable given the bias towards the null classes. Assuming the current precision results, a health researcher using a camera pendant would only need to review 1/4 of the continuously captured imagery, and the wearer of an eating journal reminder system would be interrupted falsely 1.7 times per hour. These numbers are higher than desired but may reflect a lack of training data. To investigate, we created a user dependent (and session dependent) model by using two thirds of the data frames extracted from each in-the-wild session to train models for each user and tested the model on the remainder of the 6 hours of data obtained from the same user in the same session. False positives per hour were reduced to 0.68, and the precision improved to 63.5%, suggesting that more data would indeed help improve rates. Looking at the false positives, we noticed a considerable amount of talking (e.g. having a phone call, on a meeting and cooking with a friend), which suggests that creating a null class for talking and adding a microphone might further improve the results.

10. CONCLUSION AND FUTURE WORK

We evaluated the OEI system for detecting eating events both in-the-wild and in the laboratory. We focused development towards making a non-intrusive, everyday-wear system which could help patients remember to take medicine with food or help clinicians sift through "lifelogs" to find eating events. The results are promising and suggest that larger amounts of in-the-wild training and additional sensors may help improve system performance. Going further, perhaps combining OEI's proximity sensors with Amft's microphone-based type-of-food detector [2] might overcome previous limitations with soft foods and lead to a system that identifies more food types.

11. REFERENCES

[1] O. Amft. A wearable earpad sensor for chewing monitoring. *Sensors, 2010 IEEE*, pages 222–227, 2010.

[2] O. Amft, M. Stäger, P. Lukowicz, and G. Tröster. Analysis of chewing sounds for dietary monitoring. In *UbiComp*. Springer-Verlag, Sept. 2005.

[3] E. Archer, G. A. Hand, and S. N. Blair. Validity of U.S. Nutritional Surveillance: National Health and Nutrition Examination Survey Caloric Energy Intake Data, 1971–2010. *PLoS ONE*, 8(10):76632, Oct. 2013.

[4] A. Bedri, A. Verlekar, E. Thomaz, V. Avva, and T. Starner. A wearable system for detecting eating activities with proximity sensors in the outer ear. In *ISWC*, pages 91–92. ACM, 2015.

[5] Z. Z. Falomir, M. M. Arregui, F. F. Madueño, D. D. Corella, and O. O. Coltell. Automation of Food Questionnaires in Medical Studies: A state-of-the-art review and future prospects. *Computers in Biology and Medicine*, 42(10):964–974, Oct. 2012.

[6] J. M. Fontana, M. Farooq, and E. Sazonov. Automatic Ingestion Monitor: A Novel Wearable Device for Monitoring of Ingestive Behavior. *IEEE Transactions on Biomedical Engineering*, 61(6):1772–1779, 2014.

[7] A. Fouse, N. Weibel, E. Hutchins, and J. D. Hollan. Chronoviz: a system for supporting navigation of time-coded data. In *CHI*, pages 299–304. ACM, 2011.

[8] D. R. Jacobs. Challenges in research in nutritional epidemiology. *Nutritional Health*, pages 29–42, 2012.

[9] K. B. Michels. A renaissance for measurement error. *International journal of epidemiology*, 30(3):421–422, June 2001.

[10] K. B. Michels. Nutritional epidemiology–past, present, future. *International journal of epidemiology*, 32(4):486–488, Aug. 2003.

[11] T. Rahman, A. T. Adams, M. Zhang, E. Cherry, B. Zhou, H. Peng, and T. Choudhury. BodyBeat: a mobile system for sensing non-speech body sounds. *MobiSys*, pages 2–13, 2014.

[12] E. S. Sazonov and J. M. Fontana. A Sensor System for Automatic Detection of Food Intake Through Non-Invasive Monitoring of Chewing. *IEEE Sensors Journal*, 12(5):1340–1348, Apr. 2012.

[13] E. Thomaz, C. Zhang, I. Essa, and G. D. Abowd. Inferring Meal Eating Activities in Real World Settings from Ambient Sounds. In *IUI*, pages 427–431, New York, USA, 2015. ACM Press.

[14] W. Willett. *Nutritional Epidemiology*. Oxford University Press, Oct. 2012.

[15] K. Yatani and K. N. Truong. BodyScope: a wearable acoustic sensor for activity recognition. *UbiComp*, pages 341–350, 2012.

Exploring Behavior Representation for Learning Analytics

Marcelo Worsley
Rossier School of Education
& Institute for Creative Technologies
University of Southern California
Los Angeles, CA, USA
worsley@usc.edu

Stefan Scherer
Institute for Creative Technologies
University of Southern California
Playa Vista, CA, USA
scherer@ict.usc.edu

Louis-Philippe Morency
School of Computer Science
Carnegie Mellon University
Pittsburgh, PA, USA
morency@cs.cmu.edu

Paulo Blikstein
Graduate School of Education
Stanford University
Stanford, CA, USA
paulob@stanford.edu

ABSTRACT

Multimodal analysis has long been an integral part of studying learning. Historically multimodal analyses of learning have been extremely laborious and time intensive. However, researchers have recently been exploring ways to use multimodal computational analysis in the service of studying how people learn in complex learning environments. In an effort to advance this research agenda, we present a comparative analysis of four different data segmentation techniques. In particular, we propose affect- and pose-based data segmentation, as alternatives to human-based segmentation, and fixed-window segmentation. In a study of ten dyads working on an open-ended engineering design task, we find that affect- and pose-based segmentation are more effective, than traditional approaches, for drawing correlations between learning-relevant constructs, and multimodal behaviors. We also find that pose-based segmentation outperforms the two more traditional segmentation strategies for predicting student success on the hands-on task. In this paper we discuss the algorithms used, our results, and the implications that this work may have in non-education-related contexts.

Categories and Subject Descriptors

H.5.m [**Information Interfaces and Presentation**]: Miscellaneous

J.4 [**Computer Applications**]: Social and Behavioral Sciences

General Terms

Algorithms, Human Factors, Experimentation, Performance.

Keywords

Learning Sciences, Interaction Analysis, Modeling

1. INTRODUCTION

Multimodal learning analytics [3,22,28] is still a nascent field. Over the past few years there has been increasing interest and participation in this research domain [11,12,18]. As researchers move towards integrating multimodal human perception with education research, there are a host of important questions that need to be explored.

As in all studies that leverage multimodal data, there is the question of how to appropriately represent the student's behaviors. This entails selecting a set of modalities which reliably capture behaviors that correlate with the dependent variable. As an additional question, there are a host of constructs - success, persistence, learning, motivation – that may all be of interest for a given learning analytics study. Once the dependent variable and the modalities have been selected, the researcher must then wrestle with how to utilize the data to map between user behavior and the dependent variable. One element of mapping between data and a learning construct is closely linked to how the data is segmented. Comparing different segmentation methods is a primary contribution of this paper.

In multimodal learning analytics research, and multimodal interaction research more generally, researchers often use one of two approaches for segmenting data. Some rely on human-annotation to properly denote an appropriate segment of interaction. This approach is extremely laborious, but has the advantage of incorporating elements of human perception that can enable detection of hard to identify interactions of verbal and non-verbal cues. Another advantage is that human-based segmentation can handle variable length segments. Our prior research in multimodal learning analytics [24,25] and that of many others, was based on human segmentation. At the other end of the spectrum is fixed-, or sliding-, window segmentation. Researchers select the window size that garners the best results, or that was established by prior research, to automatically segment the data. This approach has the advantage of being far less laborious, but assumes that the appropriate unit of analysis is fixed in length, and is tied to a certain amount of time. In this paper we propose two approaches that look to simultaneously harness the affordances of human-based segmentation and fixed-window segmentation. In particular, we compare affect-based segmentation, and pose-based segmentation to more traditional models of human-based segmentation and fixed-window segmentation, for modeling student behavior and learning. These different approaches will be compared to see how well they can be used to model and predict student behaviors as it relates to three constructs: success, experimental condition and learning. (Each of these constructs

ICMI '15, November 09-13, 2015, Seattle, WA, USA
© 2015 ACM. ISBN 978-1-4503-3912-4/15/11...$15.00
DOI: http://dx.doi.org/10.1145/2818346.2820737

will be described in more details in the methods section.) (Note: some researchers simplify the process of human-based segmentation by incorporating ways that allow the data to be collected on a per problem, per task or per session basis, for example. This often times provides a representation that is too coarse, but can offer a middle ground between human annotation and automated techniques).

Our hypothesis is that affect- and pose-based segmentation will offer a means for providing a semantically relevant, automated approach for understanding and predicting learning-relevant constructs that is as good as, or better than, human-based segmentation and/or fixed-window segmentation.

In what follows we briefly present our theoretical framework and pertinent prior literature; describe the experiment from which the data was derived; delineate the basic algorithm used to analyze the data; summarize important results; and discuss the implications of this work.

2. PRIOR LITERATURE

2.1 Theoretical Framework

The current analyses are influenced by prior literature on Interaction Analysis [13], Embodied Cognition [16], Epistemological Framing [20,23] and Cognitive Disequilibrium [8].

In particular, Interaction Analysis

> "investigates human activities, such as talk, nonverbal interaction, and the use of artifacts and technologies, identifying routine practices and problems and the resources for their solution. [13] "

The emphasis on how individuals interact with one another and with the resources at their disposal is of central interest to the current analyses. Furthermore, interaction analysis takes a situated perspective, in which a given behavior can only be understood in the context of the surrounding actions. As such, one way for framing the current analyses is towards determining an appropriate means for identifying a unit of analysis that can be used to develop meaningful segments of interactions. Additionally, Interaction Analysis is firmly rooted in human-based ethnographic video analysis. Accordingly the current effort aims to create automated approaches for conducting rich interaction analysis.

Given the apparent ties to Interaction Analysis, the connection to Embodied Cognition [16] should be apparent. However, invoking embodied cognition goes one step further by actively suggesting that there is a dependence on the body in order to fully engage in the process of cognition. The multimodal behavioral representations that we construct may serve as a window into better understanding the connections between body and mind. More specifically, the multimodal behavior representation may provide a glimpse into the behaviors that foster meaningful insights during a given task, and those that seem to detract from learning.

The current work is also informed by the theory of Epistemological Frames. [20,23] describe the connection between multimodal behavior and epistemology. Moreover, their work suggests that a student's body position, gaze, speech, and gesticulations can provide a lens into how a students is approaching a given task. It can also reflect the student's understanding of how they think they are expected to approach a given task. As an example of this, [23] identified four epistemological frames that could be used to model how students are approaching group work with their peers. Each of those epistemology frames could be reliably coded using multimodal data. Given that these multimodal markers can be a good indicator of student epistemology it would follow that identifying these moments in the context of learning could provide a useful way for denoting different "phases" of an activity, and subsequently, be useful for data segmentation.

Finally, this study is informed by work on Cognitive Disequilibrium which suggests that students experience learning when they enter into states of confusion [8]. Furthermore, the researchers have found that cognitive disequilibrium and feelings of frustration are mirrored in individual body movements as "fractal scaling" or pink noise [7]. If affective states represent such an important aspect of learning, and cognitive disequilibrium can be evidenced in body movement, it seems appropriate to explore the possibility of using facial expressions, a proxy for affective state, as a means for providing semantically relevant segments.

2.2 Multimodal Segmentation

There are certainly instances of prior research that utilize multimodal data to automatically segment data. Several examples exist within the television domain where researchers wish to utilize audio/visual data to automatically detect commercials, or naturally segment news broadcasts [5,10]. Other researchers have used multimodal data to conduct better segmentation of spoken text [6,19]. However, we know of no prior research that looks to use changes in facial expression and/or changes in body pose to automatically segment multimodal process data, especially when used in the context of trying to better understand and predict constructs related to student learning and cognition.

3. METHODS

To provide the reader with additional context, we briefly describe the research participants and the task that they completed before entering into a discussion of the analyses and results.

The task was motivated by prior work in Constructionism[17]. Students were given common household materials: one paper plate, 4 ft. of garden wire, four drinking straws and five wooden Popsicle sticks. The objective was to use the materials provided to create a structure that could support a weight of approximately half a pound. Participants were also asked to support the weight as high off the table as possible.

Our population of students consisted of twelve 9th- through 12th-grade students and eight undergraduate students. Pairs of students were randomly assigned to either use example- or principle-based reasoning, after controlling for prior education experience. Thus, each condition had six high school students and four undergraduate students. In the example-based condition, students generated three example structures from their home, community or school in order to motivate their design. In the principle-based condition, students identified three engineering principles that conferred strength and stability to a ladder, an igloo and a bridge, before embarking on the building task.

The data capture environment included: a Kinect sensor – for capturing audio, gesture and video; a high resolution web camera - to record how students moved the different materials; and an electro-dermal activation sensor – for measuring stress and/or arousal. All sensor data was synchronized through the data collection software, and also verified by a research assistant.

3.1 Activity Sequence

The overall flow of activities that students completed included: a pre-test; an intervention, i.e. one of the two conditions; a preliminary design drawing; a hands-on building activity; post-test; and reflection (Figure 1).

Figure 1. Overall study design

3.2 Learning-Related Constructs

As previously noted, our analysis was conducted against three different learning-related constructs: success, learning and experimental condition.

Success. Success is based on the performance of each pair's structure. Structures that are able to support the weight for more than thirty seconds, are coded as being successful. Structures that are unable to support the weight for more than thirty seconds are coded as being unsuccessful.

Learning. Learning is based on learning gains from pre-test to post-test. The pre- and post-tests asked students to identify important concepts in engineering design. Students who experienced positive learning gains were identified as having learned. Students who did not experience positive learning gains were said to have not learned.

Experimental Condition. As previously noted, students participated in one of two interventions. The first intervention, example-based reasoning, involved the students working together to come up with a design based on a real-world object from their home, community or school. The second intervention, principle-based reasoning, involved the students working together to come up with a design based on engineering principles. From prior work, we've observed that students in the principle-based reasoning condition are more successful and experience higher learning gains [26]. We've also observed that students use a better engineering design process when employing principle-based reasoning strategies. Hence, even though there is a correlation between experimental condition, success and learning, we are independently interested in identifying the multimodal behaviors associated with the two experimental conditions.

3.3 Data

The analyses included in this paper are drawn from the following multimodal data.

Audio data. Data was derived from a combination of audio channels from an overheard web camera, and from the Xbox Kinect sensor. Custom software was developed based on the Carnegie Mellon University (CMU) Sphinx Speech Recognition Toolkit [14]. Specifically, the source code was modified to leverage the program's voice activity detection feature. Voice activity detection is an automated means for determining when voice-based audio is being generated. Several speech recognition software solutions contain some variant of voice activity detection. The custom software provided voice detection start and stop times for all of the audio channels. Audio was considered to be present if either of the audio sources detected a voice, within a given second of time. Thus the final format of this data is a binary representation. Every second of the activity is labeled with a zero or one, for the absence or presence of audio at that time stamp. Because the audio channel captured sound from both participants this piece of data is the same for each person in a dyad.

Hand/wrist movement. Hand/wrist movement data was generated from the Xbox Kinect sensor. A custom built application was used to store three dimensional data for twelve upper body joints. The application uses native features available from the Kinect for Windows SDK, specifically, the ability to conduct skeletal tracking in the seated position. The custom application stores the data at 10 Hz. From the file generated, we utilize only the left and right wrist, hand and elbow data points. For each successive pair of data points we compute the angular displacement for the vectors that connect: left wrist and left hand; left wrist and left elbow, right wrist and right hand; right wrist and right elbow. The eventual angular displacement that is recorded is an average of the four angular displacements. Using angle as the means for comparison reduces biases introduced by participants having different sized bodies and limbs. Accordingly, for each tenth of a second in time we have stored the angular hand/wrist displacement. Finally, the cumulative angular displacement for each second of time is stored for each participant.

Electro-dermal Activation (EDA). Electro-dermal activation (also referred to as galvanic skin response and/or skin conductance) readings were captured at 8 Hz. Processing electro-dermal activation data involved controlling for individual differences in variance, as well as individual differences in stress response. In practice, this was achieved by collecting baseline data as students completed the task of counting down by 7.We will refer to this as the "math" stress test. As additional baseline data, students also completed a Stroop test, and had their electro-dermal activation recorded during non-task related activities. As before, each data point was time-stamped with the local date and time. Each data point was then transformed into an index value by subtracting the mean from the "math" stress test, and then dividing by the standard deviation of the "math" stress test data for that student. When we compared electro-dermal activation index values across the different activities, there were no statistically significant differences between experimental conditions for the baseline data, the Stroop test, or the math test. However, across the intervention, design phase and the building activity, differences were statistically significant. This provided validation that this normalization was effective. Electro-dermal activation index for each second of time was determined by taking the average electro-dermal activation index for a given second in time.

Facial Expression: Facial expression was extracted from frontal images using FACET SDK [15]. The facial expressions included: joy, anger, sadness, surprise, fear, contempt, disgust, confusion, and frustration. Evidence values for each of the facial expressions were used as an indicator for the presence and/or absence of each facial expression. Data points were recorded and stored at 1-second increments. All facial expressions were used for affect-based segmentation, while only confusion was used when quantifying multimodal behaviors. This will be described in more detail in the following sections.

Head Pose: Head pose estimation was determined from frontal images using a custom Constrained Local Neural Fields [2] application. The software provided pitch, roll and yaw at 1-second increments. Because participants have oppositely signed yaw values when they are looking at each other (they were seated side by side), the yaw values were transformed so that positive yaw corresponds to looking toward their partner and negative yaw corresponds to looking away from their partner. Finally, pitch and yaw are stored separately in the resultant vector.

3.4 Algorithm

The approach follows our previous work [25,27] on analyzing design strategies and success in hands-on engineering tasks. Here we significantly extend that work by incorporating different data segmentation strategies. A visualization of the general algorithm is provided in Figure 2 and Figure 3. A summary of each step is included below.

Time-stamp. The first step of extracting process data is to ensure that all data is properly time-stamped. This provides a means for synchronizing across the different modalities and results in a 7-dimensional matrix for each student. The dimensions of this matrix are time, confusion evidence, pitch, yaw (in terms of looking away from or towards one's partner), electro-dermal activation index, hand/wrist displacement and audio.

Segment. The time-stamped data is then segmented. We will refer to these segments as "data segments." Segmentation was adopted to help smooth the data, and provide units of analysis that are meaningful given the learning constructs of interest.

For this study we compare four different segmentation strategies: human-based, pose-based, affect-based and fixed-window.

Human-based segmentation creates a new segment every time a pair's structure is tested. This approach is based on interpreting testing as an instance in which at least one person in the pair is eliciting feedback that will update the students on the current stability of their structure. Testing usually takes the form of a team member placing the weight on the structure. Under this segmentation strategy dyads had the same number of "data segments." Finally, this approach is informed by traditional Interaction Analysis techniques [13] and our prior work [24,25,27].

Pose-based segmentation creates a new segment every time a given student changes the direction of their head pose. In more precise terms, a new segment was defined as a change in the sign of the pitch and/or yaw. A minimum pose duration of 8 seconds is imposed, though this limit is seldom utilized. Recall that this approach is motivated, in part, by Epistemological Framing [20,23].

Affect-based segmentation creates a new segment every time there is a change in the most evident facial expression. Once again, a minimum segment duration of 8 seconds is imposed. A primary motivation for this segmentation strategy is research on the importance and manifestations of cognitive disequilibrium [7,9]

Fixed-window segmentation creates a new segment at every second of time. In conducting our analysis, we tested varying fixed-window sizes (e.g. 4, 8, 10 and 30 seconds) but found that 1 second windows worked the best. Because the data is preprocessed to be grouped on a per second basis, fixed-window segmentation requires no additional processing at this step.

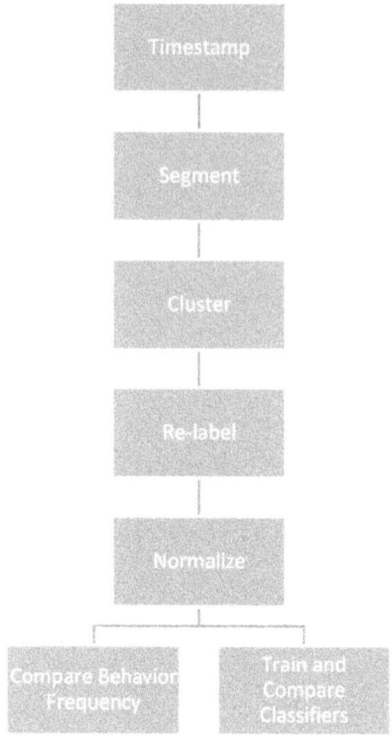

Figure 2. General algorithm

As a whole, the segmentation process serves to smooth the data. Instead of having to take into account each of the spikes and troughs that may emerge from any of the data streams, segmentation allows us to look at broader trends. Noise reduction is also achieved during the forthcoming clustering step.

Segmentation always resulted in a single value for each data stream. For the audio data the value is the speech fraction. For the hand/wrist movement data, the value is the average total angular displacement during that "data segment." For electro-dermal activation, the value is the average index value during that particular "data segment." Similarly, for head pose estimation, and confusion evidence, the values indicate the average pitch, yaw, and confusion evidence.

Cluster. After the segmentation step, there are hundreds to thousands of unique "data segments." Some of these will be very similar to one another, only differing by an infinitesimal amount, while others will vary quite extensively from one another. The goal of clustering is to identify natural groupings among the various "data segments" and ultimately provide a common set of states, or behaviors, by which to compare students. However, before proceeding with clustering, we first do data standardization. Namely, we adjust each value, such that all of the data in a given column has a mean of zero and a standard deviation of one. This process eliminates bias in clustering, by ensuring that each column contributes equally to the distance metric, which in the case was Euclidean distance. After standardizing the data, we used K-Means clustering, with a Euclidean distance metric, to group the data points into a set of four clusters that place each "data segment" with the other "data segments" that it is most similar to. Four clusters was used based on our prior experience with this dataset. Specifically, in

[27] we found through human observation that four clusters provided the most meaningful semantic meaning.

Several iterations were completed to avoid local maxima. Once each "data segment" has been grouped with similar "data segments," each cluster, or group, can be described based on the cluster centroid value. These values provide the basis for determining common behavioral practices in later sections.

Note: We tried variable sized clusters, allowing for each segmentation strategy to use the number of clusters that conferred the greatest predictive accuracy. However, there was very little difference in the results. Hence, we used the same number of clusters for each segmentation strategy, as to reduce algorithmic variation, and simplify the analysis.

Re-label. All "data segments" that are put into the same cluster are given the same name and value. Accordingly, each student's sequence of "data segments" is represented as a list of clusters.

Normalize. In the normalization step, each student's data is reduced to a four dimensional vector that features the frequency that cluster was used by that student (L-1 normalization).

Compare Behavior Frequency. After L-1 normalization, the next step is to compare behavior frequency data across the three metrics of interest: success, experimental condition; and learning. The comparisons are based on two-tailed t-tests along each of the individual clusters for a given segmentation strategy.

Train and Compare Classifiers. The frequency values are used to train classifiers for predicting the three metrics of interest: success, experimental condition; and learning. In this study we trained a support vector machine, with a linear kernel. Sixteen fold leave-one out training and testing was completed to determine the effectiveness of each approach. Comparisons were based on F-score from the test data, as compared to a majority class classifier.

4. RESULTS

4.1 Correlations between cluster frequency and learning constructs

We begin our presentation of the results with a discussion of the cluster frequencies, paying particular attention to how well each cluster correlated with success, learning and experimental condition (Tables 1 – 4). We report Pearson correlation values, and p-values based on two-tailed t-tests, with 15 degrees of freedom. Specifically, for each construct we compute the level of correlation and the probability that successful students used a given cluster (multimodal behavior) with greater frequency than unsuccessful students, for example. In each table "*", "**" and "***" correspond to $p < 0.05$, 0.01 ad 0.001, respectively.

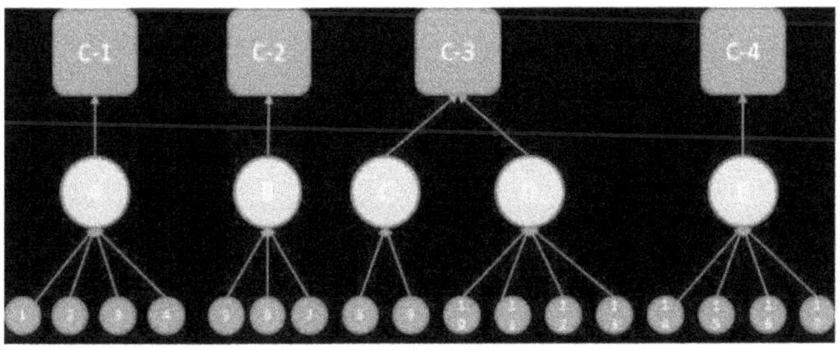

Figure 3. Pictorial representation of the data algorithm. Numbers 1 through 17 represent different seconds in time. A through E represent "data segments" that are defined based on the individual timestamps associated with them. C-1, C-2, C-3, C-4 represent multimodal behavior clusters. The clusters are based on using K-means to group "data segments".

Table 1. Pearson r values and p-values for cluster usage by construct for fixed window segmentation

	Fixed Window		
Cluster	Success	Condition	Learning
1	0.50*	0.44*	0.62*
2	0.48*	0.44	0.29
3	0.22	0.11	0.25
4	0.34	0.11*	0.46

Table 2. Pearson r values and p-values for cluster usage by construct for affect-based segmentation

	Affect		
Cluster	Success	Condition	Learning
1	0.50*	0.46*	0.67*
2	0.49	0.45	0.41
3	0.35	0.32*	0.44
4	0.25	0.12	0.25

Table 3. Pearson r values and p-values for cluster usage by construct for pose-based segmentation

	Pose		
Cluster	Success	Condition	Learning
1	0.44*	0.55*	0.90***
2	0.38	0.48*	0.56*
3	0.19	0.25	0.25
4	0.19	0.25	0.25

Table 4. Pearson r values and p-values for cluster usage by construct for human-based segmentation

	Human		
Cluster	Success	Condition	Learning
1	0.42*	0.37	0.35
2	0.47	0.25	0.25
3	0.52	0.29	0.22
4	0.48	0.32	0.25

Substantively, we see that cluster 1 from affect-, pose- and fixed-window based segmentation, significantly correlate with success, learning and experimental condition (see Table 1, Table 2 and Table 3) all with relatively large effect sizes (between 0.44 and 0.90). Additionally, cluster 2 from fixed-window segmentation (Table 1), cluster 3 from affect-based segmentation (Table 2) segmentation, and cluster 1 from human-based segmentation all correlate with success (Table 4). We also see that cluster 2 from pose-based segmentation correlates with experimental condition and learning (Table 3).

Looking at the Pearson r values we see that across learning constructs, affect- and/or pose-based segmentation are typically of equal or greater correlation than fixed-window and human-based segmentation. This is especially true for experimental condition and learning.

In summary, then, affect-, pose- and fixed-window-based segmentation result in cluster centroids that offer greater correlation with the three learning constructs of interest, than human-based segmentation. Furthermore, we see the pose-based segmentation provided the greatest number of significant correlations among the cluster centroids and learning constructs, all with relatively large effect sizes.

4.2 Cluster Interpretation

Now that we have seen that the clusters have significance for drawing correlations between multimodal behaviors and the three learning constructs, we now turn to briefly analyzing the behaviors associated with the clusters.

To simplify the interpretation of each cluster centroid, and facilitate comparison, we transformed the cluster centroid values into relative values along each dimension, as follows:

High: cluster centroid value more than a half of the standard deviation above the mean.

Medium: cluster centroid value more than a tenth of a standard deviation above the mean, but less than half of a standard deviation above the mean.

Low: cluster centroid value less than a tenth of a standard deviation above the mean (includes values that are less than the mean).

Head pose estimation was transformed into a single value that describes overall gaze. A prefix of "u" denotes looking up, while a prefix of "d" denotes down. "p" refers to looking toward their partner, while "a" denotes looking away from their partner.

Table 5 describes cluster 1 for each segmentation technique. Recall that cluster 1 usage frequency generally correlated with success, learning and experimental condition.

Table 5. Characteristics for Cluster 1 from each approach. In the Pose dimension, "d" denotes down, "u" denotes up, "p" denotes towards their partner, "a" denotes away from their partner

	Confusion	*Pose*	*EDA*	*Gesture*	*Audio*
Fixed Window	medium	d p	low	medium	high
Affect	medium	d p	low	medium	high
Pose	medium	u p	high	medium	medium
Human	medium	u p	low	medium	high

From Table 5, we see that cluster 1 from fixed window segmentation and affect-based segmentation constitute a very similar multimodal behavior that is typified by actively engaging the task while looking in the direction of one's partner. Engagement is observed by the high audio, and medium gesticulation values. In fact, all of the cluster 1's share above average hand/wrist movement, and above average audio, suggesting that the participants are engaged. This is in contrast to a cluster that may be typified by low gesticulation and low audio. Deviating away from a behavior that is characterized by active engagement, appears to be associated with less successful designs, lower learning gains, and example-based reasoning. This result mirrors what was observed in our prior work [27].

To summarize, then, our comparison across the four different approaches, in terms of correlations between multimodal behaviors to the three learning-related constructs, shows that affect- and pose-based segmentation appear to be equally as effective as fixed-window segmentation, and superior to human-based segmentation. Part of this correlation appears to be couched in detecting "engaged" behavior. Additionally, pose-based segmentation stands out as a particularly good strategy for examining these correlations. In the next section we examine if this is also true for making predictions about success, learning and experimental condition.

4.3 Predictive power of segmentation approach

An SVM classifier with a linear kernel was trained using the cluster centroid frequencies for each student, and each approach. Precision and recall were computed for each class, against ground truth. Those values were then used to compute the average F-score as a point of comparison across the four different approaches. Results are summarized in Table 6.

Table 6. Average F-score by learning construct and segmentation approach (baseline denotes a majority class single assignment classifier). Bold denotes high performer.

Approach	*Condition*	*Learning*	*Success*
Pose	**0.73**	0.26	**0.62**
Fixed Window	0.68	0.54	0.56
Affect	0.68	0.11	0.55
Human	0.52	**0.64**	**0.62**
Baseline	0.33	0.45	0.38

From Table 6, we see that for predicting each student's experimental condition, pose-based segmentation results in the highest average F-score, clearly outperforming the majority class classify, human-based segmentation and fixed-window segmentation. Additionally, pose-based segmentation matched human-based segmentation for predicting success. However, as it relates to "learning," human-based segmentation and fixed-window segmentation significantly outperformed affect- and pose-based segmentation. Furthermore, affect- and pose-based segmentation failed to outperform the majority class classifier for "learning."

5. DISCUSSION

The current analyses were motivated by a desire to identify data segmentation strategies that could provide comparable results to those achieved using human-based segmentation and fixed-window segmentation. More specifically, we hypothesized that affect- and pose-based segmentation would be as effective, or more effective, than human-based and fixed-window segmentation, for correlating and predicting the learning-related constructs: success, learning and experimental condition.

The correlation analysis made salient the relative effectiveness of affect- and pose-based segmentation for drawing connections between multimodal behaviors and all three of the learning constructs. In particular, the analysis revealed that fixed-window, affect-based, and pose-based segmentation, all produced at least one cluster that constituted a multimodal state of "active engagement." Students who performed better, learned more and came from the principle-based reasoning condition were more likely to evidence this multimodal state of "active engagement." In this way, the affect- and pose-based segmentation strategies proved to be just as effective as the fixed-window segmentation strategy. Additionally, pose-based segmentation outperformed fixed-window segmentation in that it had a second cluster centroid that correlated with experimental condition and learning. As such, the hypothesis that affect- and pose-based segmentation can be equally as effective for correlating among multimodal behaviors and learning-related constructs appears to be confirmed.

On the topic of predicting each of the learning-related constructs, the results were slightly different. The classifier built using the pose-based segmentation approach was the best for predicting both success and experimental condition. And while affect-based segmentation was generally the worst for all three of the learning constructs, it did outperform both human-based annotation and the majority class classifier for predicting experimental condition. However, whereas pose- and affect- based segmentation demonstrate great promise for predicting success and experimental condition, they were both extremely ineffective for predicting learning. As such, it may be that learning, as a construct, is harder to predict than success and experimental condition. Put differently, the link between multimodal behaviors and learning, may not be as easily represented, because learning is a process that often involves cognitive processes that do not map as easily onto multimodal behaviors.

As we consider the reasons for why affect- and pose-based segmentation were effective in this study, we first return to the idea of variable length "data segments." One of our conjectures for the utility of human-based segmentation is that it results in variable length segments, as opposed to fixed length segments. Having variable length segments seems to more closely mirror our human experiences, as a lot of how humans learn and operate, is situational [4]. Accordingly, it may be that affect- and pose-based segmentation are benefiting from improvements related to variable length segments.

Another area for consideration, is the level of granularity across the four approaches (Table 7). When we examine the total number of segments for each approach, we see that human-based segmentation has the fewest, affect-based has the second fewest, pose-based has the second most, and fixed-window segmentation has the most. This puts affect- and pose- based segmentation near the middle of the spectrum and may help in providing enough granularity that correlations can be accurately observed. At the same time, being at the middle of the spectrum may also provide enough aggregation that there is somewhat of a semantic meaning to segments, beyond an aggregation of otherwise disconnected moment-by-moment actions. In our ongoing research we intend to investigate this further.

Table 7. Number of segments by segmentation approach

Approach	*Number of Segments*
Human	236
Affect	768
Pose	5995
Fixed Window	24569

Finally, prior work on levels of abstraction may offer some insights here as different constructs are evidenced over markedly different time scales [1] and at different levels of abstraction [21]. [1] describes learning as happening on the order of days and months, whereas something like success, or epistemology can more easily be inferred through more fine-grained data. [21] makes a similar point that moving across different levels of abstraction can be quite challenging, may require larger data sets and novel approaches for dealing with uncertainty.

6. FUTURE WORK

In future work we plan to examine the efficacy of affect- and pose-based segmentation on a larger data set. As part of this study, we will be curious to look a more fine grain differences in pose and affect that we could not reliably examine with the current data set, due to its relatively small sample size. For example, the current affect-based segments were based on changes in facial expression evidence. With a larger dataset a may be possible to pay more attention to actions units, and/or look at a larger array of possible poses. With a larger dataset, we would also explore modeling how certain multimodal behaviors may actually be useful for predicting the subsequent pose, and vice versa. Additionally, because pose-based segmentation appeared to be particularly promising, future analyses will study dyadic pose-based interactions, and more in-depth differentiation of poses.

7. CONCLUSION

Our primary objective for this paper was to explore the possibility of using affect- and posed-based segmentation as an alternative to human-based segmentation and fixed-window segmentation. We correctly hypothesized that affect- and pose-based segmentation would be on par with the two more traditional techniques for studying correlations between multimodal behaviors and three constructs related to a given learning experience: success, learning and experimental condition. Pose- and affect-based segmentation both performed extremely well for defining correlations between multimodal behavior and the three constructs. Moreover, pose-based segmentation stood out as extremely relevant for this study. Similarly, on the prediction task, pose-based segmentation, proved to be a top performer for predicting success and experimental condition, easily outperforming the majority class baseline and the two traditional forms of data segmentation. However, affect- and pose-based segmentation performed quite poorly for predicting learning, significantly lagging behind human-based segmentation, which proved to be the best for this particular construct. Nonetheless, along nearly all of the dimensions of comparison affect- and pose-based segmentation performed quite well, suggesting that they may present a viable means for automatically segmenting process data in a way that results in variable length segments, and that maintains semantic meaning. Finally, while this process was presented in the context of student learning, it may have useful implications in other domains for which variable length segments are common.

8. ACKNOWLEDGEMENTS

A portion of this research was made possible through the financial support of the University of Southern California's Provost's Signature Fellowships and the Stanford University Vice Provost of Graduate Education.

9. REFERENCES

1. John Anderson. 2002. Spanning seven orders of magnitude: a challenge for cognitive modeling. *Cognitive Science* 26, 1, 85–112. http://doi.org/10.1207/s15516709cog2601_3
2. Tadas Baltrušaitis, Peter Robinson, and Louis Philippe Morency. 2013. Constrained local neural fields for robust facial landmark detection in the wild. *Proceedings of the*

IEEE International Conference on Computer Vision, 354–361. http://doi.org/10.1109/ICCVW.2013.54
3. Paulo Blikstein and Marcelo Worsley. in press. Multimodal Learning Analytics: a methodological framework for research in constructivist learning. *Journal of Learning Analytics*.
4. JD Bransford, AL Brown, and RR Cocking. 2000. How people learn. Retrieved July 15, 2014 from http://www.csun.edu/~SB4310/How People Learn.pdf
5. Mattia Broilo, Eric Zavesky, Andrea Basso, and Francesco G B De Natale. 2010. Unsupervised Event Segmentation of News Content with Multimodal Cues. *Proceedings of the 3rd International Workshop on Automated Information Extraction in Media Production*, ACM, 39–44. http://doi.org/10.1145/1877850.1877862
6. Lei Chen. 2006. Incorporating Gesture and Gaze into Multimodal Models of Human-to-human Communication. *Proceedings of the 2006 Conference of the North American Chapter of the Association for Computational Linguistics on Human Language Technology: Companion Volume: Doctoral Consortium*, Association for Computational Linguistics, 211–214. http://doi.org/10.3115/1225797.1225798
7. S D'Mello, Rick Dale, and Art Graesser. 2012. Disequilibrium in the mind, disharmony in the body. *Cognition & emotion*, 1–28. Retrieved May 06, 2014 from http://www.tandfonline.com/doi/abs/10.1080/02699931.2011.575767
8. Sidney D'Mello and Art Graesser. 2012. Dynamics of affective states during complex learning. *Learning and Instruction* 22, 2, 145–157. http://doi.org/10.1016/j.learninstruc.2011.10.001
9. SK D'Mello, B Lehman, and Natalie Person. 2010. Monitoring affect states during effortful problem solving activities. ... *Journal of Artificial Intelligence in* .... Retrieved May 19, 2014 from http://iospress.metapress.com/index/V9200K51R3820T58.pdf
10. Ling-Yu Duan, Jinqiao Wang, Yantao Zheng, Jesse S Jin, Hanqing Lu, and Changsheng Xu. 2006. Segmentation, Categorization, and Identification of Commercial Clips from TV Streams Using Multimodal Analysis. *Proceedings of the 14th Annual ACM International Conference on Multimedia*, ACM, 201–210. http://doi.org/10.1145/1180639.1180697
11. Joseph F Grafsgaard. 2014. Multimodal Analysis and Modeling of Nonverbal Behaviors During Tutoring. *Proceedings of the 16th International Conference on Multimodal Interaction*, ACM, 404–408. http://doi.org/10.1145/2663204.2667611
12. Larry Johnson, Samantha Adams, Malcolm Cummins, Victoria Estrada, Alex Freeman, and Holly Ludgate. 2013. The NMC horizon report: 2013 higher education edition.
13. Brigitte Jordan and Austin Henderson. 1995. Interaction Analysis: Foundations and Practice. *The Journal of the Learning Sciences* 4, 1, pp. 39–103. Retrieved from http://www.jstor.org/stable/1466849
14. Kai Fu Lee, Hsiao Wuen Hon, and Raj Reddy. 1990. Overview of the SPHINX speech recognition system. *IEEE Transactions on Acoustics, Speech, and Signal Processing* 38, 35–45. http://doi.org/10.1109/29.45616
15. Gwen Littlewort, Jacob Whitehill, Tingfan Wu, et al. 2011. The computer expression recognition toolbox (CERT). *2011 IEEE International Conference on Automatic Face and Gesture Recognition and Workshops, FG 2011*, 298–305. http://doi.org/10.1109/FG.2011.5771414
16. RE Núñez, LD Edwards, and JF Matos. 1999. Embodied cognition as grounding for situatedness and context in mathematics education. *Educational Studies in Mathematics*, 39, 45–65. Retrieved March 17, 2014 from http://link.springer.com/article/10.1023/A:1003759711966
17. Seymour Papert. 1980. *Mindstorms: Children, computers, and powerful ideas*. Basic Books, Inc.
18. Roy Pea. 2014. THE LEARNING ANALYTICS Workgroup A Report on Building the Field of Learning Analytics.
19. Francis Quek, David McNeill, Robert Bryll, et al. 2002. Multimodal Human Discourse: Gesture and Speech. *ACM Trans. Comput.-Hum. Interact.* 9, 3, 171–193. http://doi.org/10.1145/568513.568514
20. Rosemary S. Russ, Victor R. Lee, and Bruce L. Sherin. 2012. Framing in cognitive clinical interviews about intuitive science knowledge: Dynamic student understandings of the discourse interaction. *Science Education* 96, 4, 573–599. http://doi.org/10.1002/sce.21014
21. Stefan Scherer, Michael Glodek, Georg Layher, et al. 2012. A generic framework for the inference of user states in human computer interaction. *Journal on Multimodal User Interfaces* 6, 3-4, 117–141.
22. Stefan Scherer, Marcelo Worsley, and Louis-Philippe Morency. 2012. 1st international workshop on multimodal learning analytics. *ICMI*, 609–610.
23. Rachel E. Scherr and David Hammer. 2009. Student Behavior and Epistemological Framing: Examples from Collaborative Active-Learning Activities in Physics. *Cognition and Instruction* 27, 2, 147–174. http://doi.org/10.1080/07370000902797379
24. Marcelo Worsley and Paulo Blikstein. 2013. Towards the Development of Multimodal Action Based Assessment. *Proceedings of the Third International Conference on Learning Analytics and Knowledge*, ACM, 94–101. http://doi.org/10.1145/2460296.2460315
25. Marcelo Worsley and Paulo Blikstein. 2014. Analyzing Engineering Design through the Lens of Computation. *Journal of Learning Analytics* 1, 2, 151–186.
26. Marcelo Worsley and Paulo Blikstein. 2014. Assessing the Makers: The Impact of Principle-Based Reasoning on Hands-on, Project-Based Learning. *Proceedings of the 2014 International Conference of the Learning Sciences (ICLS)* 3, 1147–1151.
27. Marcelo Worsley and Paulo Blikstein. 2015. Leveraging Multimodal Learning Analytics to Differentiate Student Learning Strategies. *Proceedings of the Fifth International Conference on Learning Analytics And Knowledge*, ACM, 360–367. http://doi.org/10.1145/2723576.2723624
28. Marcelo Worsley. 2012. Multimodal learning analytics: enabling the future of learning through multimodal data analysis and interfaces. *Proceedings of the 14th ACM international conference on Multimodal interaction*, 353–356.

Multimodal Human Activity Recognition for Industrial Manufacturing Processes in Robotic Workcells

Alina Roitberg
Technische Universität München
Boltzmannstr. 3
85748 Garching
roitberg@in.tum.de

Nikhil Somani
fortiss GmbH
Guerickestr. 25
80805 München
somani@fortiss.org

Alexander Perzylo
fortiss GmbH
Guerickestr. 25
80805 München
perzylo@fortiss.org

Markus Rickert
fortiss GmbH
Guerickestr. 25
80805 München
rickert@fortiss.org

Alois Knoll
Technische Universität München
Boltzmannstr. 3
85748 Garching
knoll@in.tum.de

ABSTRACT

We present an approach for monitoring and interpreting human activities based on a novel multimodal vision-based interface, aiming at improving the efficiency of human-robot interaction (HRI) in industrial environments.

Multi-modality is an important concept in this design, where we combine inputs from several state-of-the-art sensors to provide a variety of information, e.g. skeleton and fingertip poses.

Based on typical industrial workflows, we derived multiple levels of human activity labels, including large-scale activities (e.g. assembly) and simpler sub-activities (e.g. hand gestures), creating a duration- and complexity-based hierarchy. We train supervised generative classifiers for each activity level and combine the output of this stage with a trained Hierarchical Hidden Markov Model (HHMM), which models not only the temporal aspects between the activities on the same level, but also the hierarchical relationships between the levels.

Categories and Subject Descriptors

I.5.2 [**Design Methodology**]: Classifier design and evaluation, Pattern analysis

General Terms

Theory, Design, Experimentation

Keywords

Human activity recognition; Hierarchical Hidden Markov Model; Industrial robotics; Cognitive robotics

ICMI 2015, November 9–13, 2015, Seattle, WA, USA.

ACM 978-1-4503-3912-4/15/11 ...$15.00.
DOI: http://dx.doi.org/10.1145/2818346.2820738.

1. INTRODUCTION

Vision-based human activity recognition has a strong potential to improve the quality of human-robot-interaction, e.g., for communication, dynamic task adaptation, or safety. A lot of work has been done recently with a focus on recognizing activities based on human skeleton tracking. Industrial scenarios are typically more constrained and require higher precision, especially for manipulation centric scenarios where hand movement is a key element.

Different uses of human activity recognition may require different levels of granularity. While the hand movement might be important in manipulation tasks, the position of the human in the working area might be sufficient for other tasks. In order to handle these different requirements, we propose a multi layer representation of activities (Fig. 1), from coarse identification to fine grained detection.

Industrial usage requires a higher level of robustness. Different sensors suffer from their individual limitations. In addition, certain sensors are optimized for specific use cases, e.g., hand-, head-, or skeleton tracking (Fig. 2). Therefore, a combination of multiple different sensors is required to provide adequate information to the system and to ensure robust communication between the human and the robot.

We designed a set of typical industrial workflows and derived four levels of human activities, ranging from large-scale activities (e.g., assembly) to simple hand gestures, which span a duration- and complexity-based hierarchy. A major contribution of this work is the machine learning based approach for multi-level recognition of human activities with respect to the defined semantics of this activity hierarchy.

The evaluation of this system was conducted on a data set containing 98 recordings of six different people, four different interaction scenarios and 38 activity types, using manual frame-wise ground-truth labeling and 4-fold cross validation. We systematically compare and discuss different generative classifiers for the first recognition stage, the impact of dimensionality reduction and the effects of combining data from multiple sensors compared to using only one sensor. The best recognition results were achieved using multiple input modalities, and recognizing the human activity by combining a SVM with radial-basis-function kernel with a HHMM. The average recognition accuracy varied between 81 % and

98 % for different levels of abstraction, which is especially significant since it was evaluated across multiple different people. A video showcasing results from the activity recognition framework can be found online.[1]

2. RELATED WORK

Human activity recognition is a well-studied area, hitherto mostly focused on 2D video data [13, 17]. Over the past few years the methods for obtaining high-quality 3D data have drastically improved due to the emergence of new affordable RGB-D sensors such as Microsoft Kinect or Asus Xtion. This progress strongly influenced the activity recognition research, with a large fraction of recent works based on 3D skeleton data captured by these devices [11, 12]. In our work, we also use the Kinect v2 and Leap Motion sensors, which are not yet popular for human activity recognition.

Various machine learning methods have been used for human activity recognition, with a systematic overview of the existing approaches provided in [1, 13]. In general, the ways of addressing this problem can be divided in two categories. In the first category, each feature vector carries all the information used for prediction and is directly classified without considering the temporal aspect. Such discriminative algorithms are widely used for activity recognition, with SVM and KNN being the most prominent approaches [2, 4, 12, 19]. In contrast, generative models such as Hidden Markov Models (HMM) also handle the temporal relationships between different classes of activities. Yamato et al. [18] were the first to use discrete HMMs for human activity recognition. In recent years, discriminative and generative approaches were often combined (e.g. SVM-HMM) [9, 6]. Fine et. al [3] extended HMM to a Hierarchical Hidden Markov Model (HHMM), which is capable of modeling parent-child relationships between the states and has also been used for human activity recognition [10].

The Cornell Activity Dataset (CAD) [16] includes 12 activities from five different domestic environments, e.g., cooking or brushing teeth. Sung et al. [16] proposed to decompose complex activities into sub-activities and to use a maximum entropy Markov model for recognition. With this method the authors reached precision and recall values of 67.9 % and 55.5 % respectively, with leave-one-person-out cross validation. Koppula et al. [7] reported significantly improved recognition results (precision 80.8 %, recall 71.4 %) by using structured support vector machines on the same dataset. Since no public datasets are available for the scenario of human-robot cooperation in an industrial context, we used a database that we recorded ourselves.

Hand gestures as an intuitive way of communication during industrial assembly tasks have been recently discussed by Gleeson et al. [5]. The results of the user study conducted in this work has shown the high potential of body gestures as an efficient way of interaction, although the interpretation of the gestures by a user unfamiliar with the definitions is highly context sensitive. These findings demonstrate the importance of realizing HRI systems based on body gestures, which is also the focus of our work. Despite the findings of Gleeson et al., research on human activity recognition addressing industrial environments has been sparse so far.

The work most similar to ours is that of Lenz et al. [8], where the authors automatically recognized the activities of humans who were sitting in front of a work table and collaborating with an industrial robot. They tracked the positions of the humans' hands using 3D occupancy grids and used a composite HMM for the recognition of hand gestures and workflow analysis.

[1] `https://www.youtube.com/watch?v=ggb6nU0EcjE`

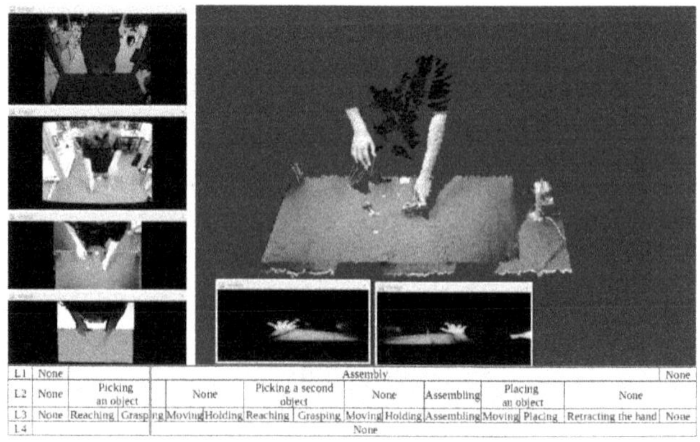

Figure 1: HRI workcell used for human activity recognition in industrial assembly scenarios. Data from the Asus Xtion Pro sensor is processed into a 3D point cloud and further extended with the finger tip positions obtained by Leap Motion sensors (red arrows). The timeline bar on the bottom shows the suggested multilevel annotation of human activities.

In our previous work, we used skeleton information provided by a Microsoft Kinect sensor with a combination of Random Forests and HMM for the recognition of simple human activities in industrial contexts [15]. In this work, we exploit multiple and more advanced modalities to recognize an extended set of more complex industrial activities with different levels of granularity. Similar to the previous work, a discriminative classifier is combined with a temporal model. However, the key component of the proposed recognition framework, i.e. its hierarchical modeling with HHMM, is a new aspect.

3. MULTIMODAL INTERFACE DESIGN

We specifically target production processes in robotic workcells. While typical domestic activities (e.g. jumping, waving) are well represented using the body skeleton, industrial systems have to accurately handle activities centered around the hands. Thus, industrial HRI-interfaces additionally require accurate articulated hand tracking. Further challenges of such systems are complex and occluded environments, and visibility limitations caused by compact sizes of workcells.

3.1 System Setup

We propose a new multimodal HRI-system, that is integrated in a typical industrial workcell and equipped with three different kinds of sensors (Fig. 2). A Microsoft Kinect v2 RGB-D sensor is mounted in front of the person, facing diagonally from above. The Kinect v2 is used to detect and track the human skeleton. An Asus Xtion Pro is placed on the metal cage facing straight down towards the table, and is intended for detecting objects on the table. For precise tracking of the hand skeleton, the Leap Motion Sensor is used. It is capable of calculating the position, orientation,

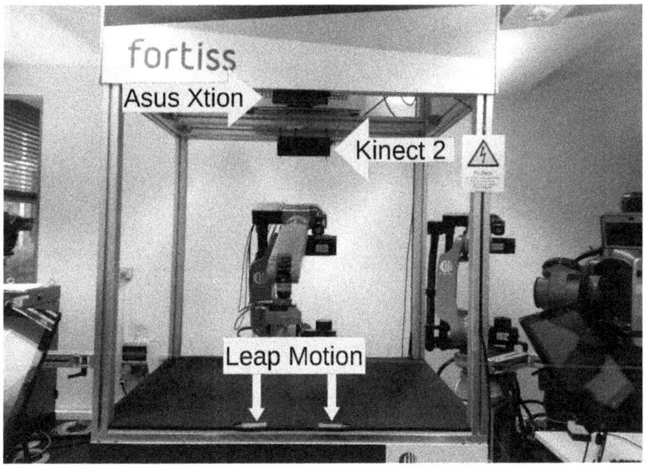

Property	Kinect v2	Asus Xtion PRO	LeapMotion
Hardware basics	Infrared (IR) light source, RGB and IR-cameras, microphone	Infrared (IR) light source, RGB and IR-cameras, microphone	Three IR LEDs , two IR cameras
Raw image data and resolution	RGB: 1920×1080 Depth: 512x424	RGB: 1280x1024 Depth: 640x480	Both IR cameras: 640x240
Data frequency	30 FPS (15-20 in our system)	30 FPS	20 to 200 (around 90 in our system)
Input for the proposed HRI system	Skeleton tracking with Kinect SDK v2: pose of 25 skeletal joints	Intended be used for object tracking from RGB-D pointclouds	Hand skeleton tracking with Leap Motion SDK: pose and velocity of hands and fingers
Data example	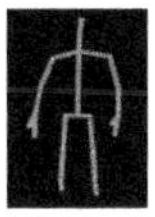	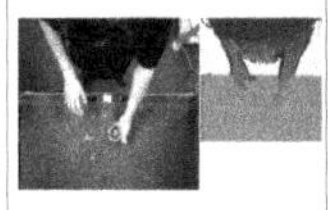	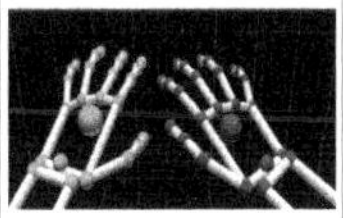

Figure 2: Overview of the input modalities and their integration in the industrial environment. The workcell was equipped with three different types of sensors to capture human activities. A Kinect 2 sensor is frontally facing the worker. An Asus Xtion Pro sensor monitors the work table (for future object tracking). Leap Motion sensors are integrated into the tabletop.

direction and velocity of the finger tips with sub-millimeter accuracy. Due to the small size, accurate hand tracking can only be achieved within a very limited range. Hence, we have integrated two Leap Motion sensors inside the tabletop facing towards the expected working area of each hand.

3.2 Sensor Data Synchronization

When combining data from sensors produced by different manufacturers, data fusion quickly becomes a problem. Besides, the skeleton tracking software Kinect SDK v2 is restricted to Windows 8.1 only and multiple Leap Motion sensors cannot be connected to the same machine due to the lack of driver support.

We implemented a communication and control framework which unifies the sensor data over multiple machines and operating systems using the Robot Operating System (ROS) and ZeroC ICE. The master server manages the entire input as ROS messages, which can be easily saved and replayed as ROS BAG files. Limitations of the network bandwidth as well as the high resolution of the streamed videos occasionally lead to the loss of Kinect v2 data, which is subsequently corrected with a Kalman filter. The framework (Fig. 3) synchronizes the data at 30 frames per second and keeps track of the different coordinate systems using the ROS-TF library and manually calculated calibration data.

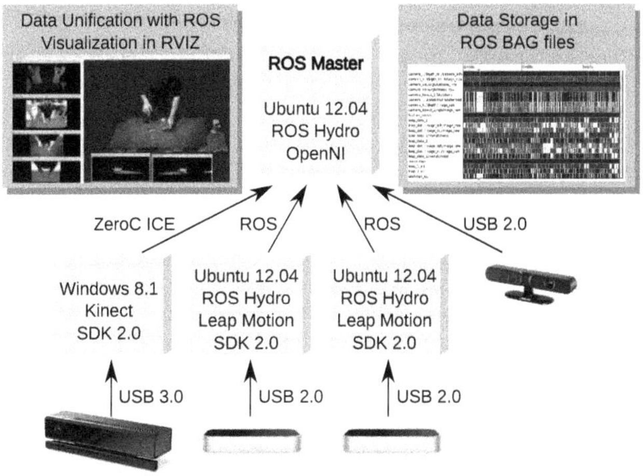

Figure 3: System overview: communication and control of multiple sensors.

4. HUMAN ACTIVITY RECOGNITION

The pipeline for human activity recognition consists of several steps. In an offline stage, the scenarios and target activities at different levels are defined. This is followed by the design of the multimodal sensor setup and calibration. During runtime, the sensor data is processed to generate feature vectors that are used by the machine learning framework to estimate the activity labels.

4.1 Scenarios and Activities

We defined four different interaction scenarios for human-robot cooperation that are typically seen in industrial manufacturing processes. In the first scenario, a worker is fixing a screw on a work piece by hand and tightening it further using a tool. The second and third scenarios aim at the specification of welding tasks, by defining start and end points (second scenario) or a trajectory (third scenario) on a piece of metal using a predefined set of hand gestures. After the gesture based command is given, the welding task is assumed to be performed and the worker bends and takes a closer look at the result (Fig. 4). The fourth scenario is another assembly task with a different set of objects.

We analyzed the scenarios and derived a four-level hierarchy of activities (Fig. 5). The structure of the hierarchy is based on complexity, duration (which is highly correlated) and generalization. The activity of Level n (L_n) is linked by a set of grammar rules to sub-activities from L_{n+1}. In some cases, activities from L_n are generalizations of sub-activities from L_{n+1}, for example, the FIXING activity from L_2 is a generalization of FIXING WITH TOOL and FIXING WITH HANDS from L_3. While the set of activities for each

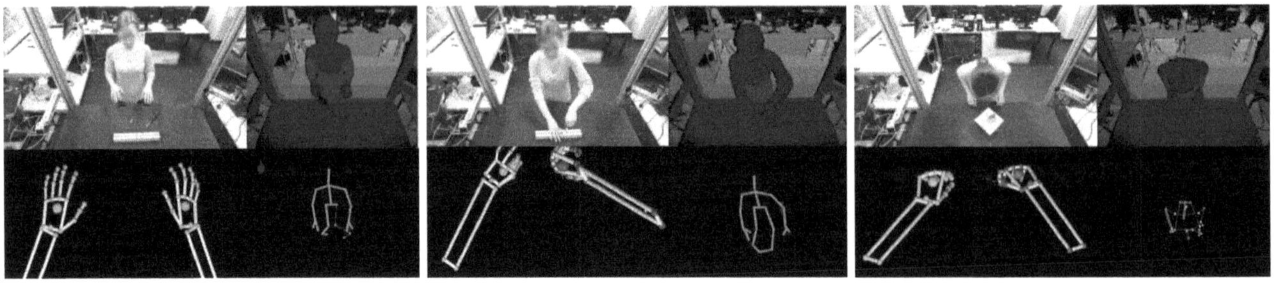

(a) None (b) Fixing (c) Leaning forward to check result

Figure 4: Visualization of multimodal input to the HRI interface. For each of the three exemplary activities, it depicts the RGB and Depth images (top left and top right) from a Kinect v2 sensor, the derived body skeleton (bottom right), and the hand skeletons (bottom left) detected by two Leap Motion sensors.

level was derived manually by observing the recordings, the exact semantics of the hierarchy was implicitly learned by the proposed classification algorithm.

4.2 Feature Calculation and Preprocessing

In this section, we describe our preprocessing framework for constructing feature representations from the sensor input. The inputs to our machine learning framework are poses of 25 skeleton joints calculated with the Kinect SDK v2 at a frequency of 15-20 FPS along with poses, velocities and directions of the hands and fingertips calculated with the Leap Motion SDK at approx. 90 FPS.

To estimate the current state of activity, meaningful features have to be carefully selected. Since the worker's legs are completely covered by the work table, skeleton information about the lower body joints has very low confidence and is hence ignored. We also calculate a set of position, orientation and motion features, that are suited for our application. Each position feature contains the 3D coordinates (X, Y, Z) transformed in the coordinate system of the body (skeleton joints) or the hand (finger tips). Orientation features are either angles with a single value (α) or 3D rotations represented as Euler angles $(roll, pitch, yaw)$.

Due to the dynamic nature of human activities, motion features carry significant information about human behaviour. Thus, we capture the change of feature values within certain time segments, i.e., the delta value as well as the variance within a segment.

Kinect v2 features. We use the positions of the hands, wrists and elbows and their motion information in the segment of the last 0.5 s. We put strong emphasis on the motion of the skeletal angles of the upper body joints as well as the orientation of the hip-, shoulder- and spine-line. Since the Kinect SDK does not provide any velocity information, we calculate the motion information in the last 0.5 s, 1 s as well as the motion history in the frame segments of 0.5 s to 1 s and 1 s to 2 s.

Leap Features. We use the positions of the fingertips and the hands, their orientations as Euler angles and their velocities, as provided by the Leap Motion SDK.

We use the same set of features for the training of L_1 to 3. Since L_4 consists of hand gestures intentionally performed with the right hand, we dismiss a set of features obviously linked to the left body part. After the selection, the feature set for L_1, L_2 and L_3 consist of 162 Kinect v2 features and 96 Leap Motion features, while the set for L_4 contains 146 Kinect v2 features and 45 Leap Features.

Since our feature vectors are derived from multiple sources observing overlapping parts of the same scene, they have a high number of redundant dimensions that also differ in their representative power for our application. Dimensions with low information content often result in noisy training data that adversely affects the classification results. Furthermore, high dimensionality requires higher computational power, which is also an important aspect since we aim for the development of a live interaction interface. We therefore use Principal Component Analysis (PCA) for dimensionality reduction.

4.3 Classification

Inferring human activity from skeleton information is a complex task with various facets. On the one hand, a single data frame with wisely selected pose features already provides a significant amount of information and can be categorized with a discriminative classifier, such as SVM or Random Forests. On the other hand, transitions between different activities have a strong causal and temporal aspect which can be modeled with generative methods as a part of the recognition approach, e.g., MOVING AN OBJECT requires GRASPING AN OBJECT as its predecessor. Furthermore, multiple abstraction levels for activities imply additional causal relationships inside the hierarchy. Integrating these dependencies in the recognition framework is crucial for two reasons. Firstly, knowing current activity states of the other levels would provide additional information for classification. Secondly, a strict hierarchical model ensures consistency of the classification output, e.g., L_3 activity SELECTING TRAJECTORY and L_2 activity ASSEMBLING, can not occur simultaneously.

4.3.1 Hidden Markov Models

An excellent way to model such sequential processes are Hidden Markov Models (HMM), which are widely used in speech and video recognition. First introduced by Rabiner, a discrete HMM is given by an alphabet of n possible hidden states and a set of m possible observations [14]. Assuming there are n hidden states and m possible emissions, a HMM can be specified as a triplet (π, A, B) where A is a $n \times n$ transition matrix containing transition probabilities between the states, B is the $n \times m$ emission matrix with $B(i, j)$ showing the probability of a hidden state i producing a visible emission j and π the initial probability vector of hidden states.

Algorithm 1 Training of a discriminative classifier

1: **Input:** $X = [X_1, ..., X_n]$ - a set of n feature vectors with m features; start and end of each recording segment is marked in X. $S^1 = [S^1_1, ...S^1_n]$ - annotation set containing ground-truth states of activities, with s possible states.

2: **Output:** C^1 - a discriminative classifier. Y^1 - a sequence of predicted states constructed by classifying X with C^1. Y^1 is later used as input for the second phase.

3: Randomization: from the given training data X, randomly select a subset ($\alpha = 75\,\%$) of samples (feature vectors) $X_{.75}$ and the corresponding annotation $S^1_{.75}$. This step is done to avoid over-fitting in the second training phase.

4: We use $X_{.75}$ and $S^1_{.75}$ for the training of a supervised classifier C^1 (e.g. SVM).

5: We use C^1 to categorize the whole initial training data set X (where $1-\alpha$ is the percentage not used for training of C^1), which results in the predicted sequence Y^1 with n samples.
Note: the notation a^b_c uses both, subscript c and superscript b as indices. The superscript does not represent the exponent of the variable. In most cases, the variable superscript b depicts a level in the activity hierarchy, while the subscript c is a simple enumeration index.

The classification problem is equivalent to the estimation of the most likely sequence of hidden states that took place with a previously trained model (π, A, B) and an observed sequence of emissions X. This problem can be solved with the Viterbi Algorithm with a run-time complexity of $O(n^2T)$, where n is the number of hidden states and T the length of the sequence.

For our activity recognition approach, we propose a strictly hierarchical two-stage machine learning framework, which combines discriminative and generative classification methods. The lowest level L_1 is not subordinate to any other levels and is processed independently from them. Consequently, the hierarchical aspect is not present at this stage and we use a discriminative classifier with a HMM for this stage (Algorithms 1 and 2). The other three activity levels are modeled using a Hierarchical Hidden Markov Model (HHMM).

4.3.2 Hierarchical HMMs

Given n levels of states (activities), the recognition algorithm is intended to produce n state predictions for each data frame, while taking into account the semantics of the learned hierarchy. In the previous section, we described our classification approach on the lowest level of the hierarchy, which is independent from the other levels, by combining a discriminative classifier with a HMM. In this section we describe the classification approach for all levels present in the hierarchy.

Using a hierarchical model is highly significant for preserving consistency between different levels, since the proposed structure of activities follows certain semantic rules. Fig. 5 shows the conditional probabilities of activities from the neighboring levels of abstraction. In other words, it is the probability $P(a_n|a_{n-1})$ of an activity a_n from a subordinate level L_n occurring simultaneously with an activity a_{n-1} from a higher level of abstraction L_{n-1}. The conditional probability of 1 means that the subordinate activity is a specialization of a higher activity, while a value of 0 (a missing edge in Fig. 5) shows that those two activities (from different levels) never occur simultaneously in the database.

The Hierarchical Hidden Markov Model (HHMM) is an extension of HMM, that is capable of handling a topology of states based on parent-child relationships between multiple levels[3]. A HHMM consists of a set of simple HMMs with separate model parameters (π, A, B). The essence of a HHMM is a strict hierarchical order of the levels $L_1, ..., L_n$, where every possible state of the L_{k-1} itself contains an HMM for the classification of L_k. The algorithm for training a HHMM is presented in Algorithm 3.

Algorithm 2 Training of a HMM

1: **Input:** Y^1 - a sequence of predicted states from the first phase of training. $S^1 = [S^1_1, ...S^1_n]$ - annotation set containing ground-truth states of activities, with s possible states.

2: **Output of both phases:** $(C^1, (\pi, A, B)^1)$, a trained model for activity recognition on level 1, where C^1 is a discriminative classifier used in the first phase and $(\pi, A, B)^1)$ is the HMM of the second phase.

3: Calculate the transition matrix A ($s \times s$) by calculating the transition probabilities for each pair of possible states from the annotation sequence S^1.

4: Calculate the emission matrix E ($s \times s$) by calculating the probabilities for possible combination of states (given by S^1) and emissions (given by Y^1). The predictions of C^1 are used as observed emissions. The set of possible states and emissions is equivalent in our case.

5: Calculate the vector of initial state probabilities, π. π is calculated by counting the frequencies for each possible state of being the first state in a sub-segment.

Algorithm 3 Training approach with HHMM for Level K

1: **Input:** $X = [X_1, ..., X_n]$ - a set of n feature vectors with m features; start and end of each recording segment are marked in X. $S^k = [S^k_1, ...S^k_n]$ - annotation set containing n ground-truth states of activities for the current level K, with s^k possible states and s^k_i referring to the i-th possible state in the state set of level K. $S^{k-1} = [S^{k-1}_1, ...S^{k-1}_n]$ - annotation set containing n ground-truth states of activities for previous level $K-1$, with s^{k-1} possible states.

2: **Output:** The training of a higher level of a HHMM results in s^{k-1} separate trained classification models $(C^k_{s^{k-1}_i}, (\pi, A, B)^k_{s^{k-1}_i})$, where s^{k-1}_i is the state of the previous level, to which our model belongs.

3: Sorting the training data (X, S^k) by the state of previous level $K-1$: we divide the training data into s^{k-1}, where each sub-set corresponds to a possible state of previous level $K-1$. This results in a set of feature vectors and corresponding annotation of level K for every state of level $K-1$: $T = [(X^1, S^{k,1}), ..., (X^{s^{k-1}}, S^{k,s^{k-1}})]$.

4: Training of multiple models: For every possible state $s^{k-1}_i, i \subset [1, s^{k-1}]$, we train a classification model $(C^k_{s^{k-1}_i}, (\pi, A, B)^k_{s^{k-1}_i})$ with the same training approach used for the lowest activity level, as described in before.

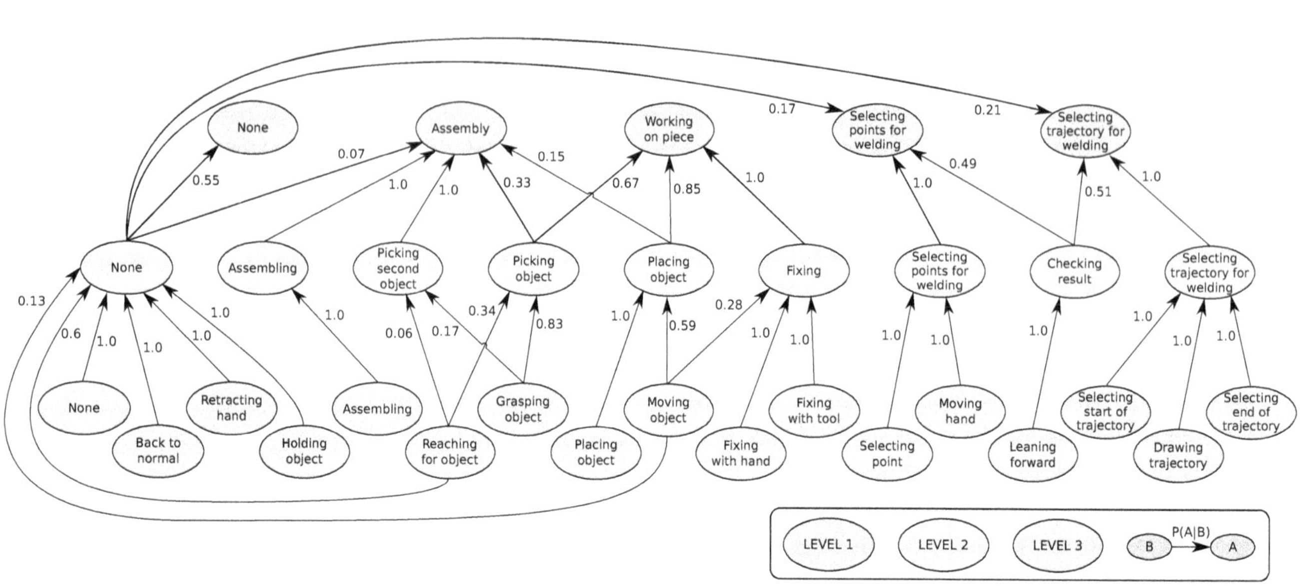

Figure 5: Conditional probabilities of the activities from levels L_1 to L_3 calculated from the collected database.

5. EVALUATION

The framework was evaluated on a database containing 98 recordings of four interaction scenarios with six different people. Video and skeleton data was recorded as ROS BAG files with manual frame-wise annotation added to it as a post-processing step. Please note that the data collected from the Asus Xtion sensor was not yet used for the activity recognition, but will be integrated in the system for object detection. The whole data set contains 33032 data frames after synchronization.

5.1 Methodology

Our approach was evaluated using 4-fold cross validation, where the data set was randomly divided into four equal subsets containing approx. 25 recordings each. It was ensured that each scenario was equally represented in each data set, while no such regularity was made as it came to different users. This was made intentionally, since recognition of unknown people is important for the practical usage of our system and the possibility of a person being present only in the test set or training set is a reasonable approximation.

Since each frame was annotated manually, accuracy of the ground-truth labeling itself should be taken into account. Due to the high frequency (30 Hz), slight annotation glitches during activity transitions are inevitable. The impact of this error is strongly dependent on the activity duration. For short dynamic activities, e.g., PUTTING THE THUMB DOWN, that start and end within a fraction of a second, false classification of a few frames at the beginning and the end can lead to a strong decline in accuracy.

For practical use, it is important that an activity is detected in its essential phase. To address this issue, we evaluate our system by counting correctly classified **activity sequences**, in contrast to correctly classified frames. We define a single activity sequence as the segment of frames during which the ground-truth activity label has not changed.

5.1.1 Metrics

The following notation is being used for the evaluation: $[A_1, ..., A_n]$ represent possible activity labels; A_i^{corr} is the number of correctly classified instances of class A_i; A_i^{total} is the true total number of instances of class A_i; A_i^{pred} is the number of instances classified as class A_i.

$$Avg.Accuracy = \frac{\sum_{i=1}^{n} \frac{A_i^{corr}}{A_i^{total}}}{n} \quad (1)$$

$$P = \frac{A_i^{corr}}{A_i^{pred}}, R = \frac{A_i^{corr}}{A_i^{total}}, F1 = 2 \times \frac{P \times R}{P + R} \quad (2)$$

In order to avoid a bias towards overrepresented classes, we use the average accuracy over all possible activity classes as the evaluation metric for the comparison of different classifiers (Fig. 6). In Table 1 we present a detailed evaluation of the recognition framework for each activity individually and evaluate the performance when using single sensor and multi sensor input. We calculate the Precision (P), Recall (R) and F1-score (2), with the F1-score being the key metric for single sensor and multi sensor comparisons.

5.2 Recognition and Prediction Results

We have tested several widely used classification algorithms for the first phase of the training and achieved best recognition results with a RBF-SVM estimator (98 %, 92 %, 81 %, 81 %), closely followed by linear SVM. Good classification results were also achieved by using Random Forests or K-Nearest-Neighbors with 20 neighbors (KNN-20), while KNN-200 and Gaussian Naive Bayes performed poorly. Detailed evaluation results are shown in Fig. 6.

Table 1 shows classification results for each activity individually and compares different subsets of features (*Leap*, *Kinect v2* and *Kinect v2 + Leap*), while Figure 7 shows the confusion matrices for every activity level with the best feature set (*Kinect v2 + Leap* for L_1, L_2, L_3 and *Leap* for L_4).

The lowest level $L1$ consists of a small number of large-scale activities and had the best recognition results, with 99 % of the sequences classified correctly when using *Kinect v2 + Leap* features. The confusion between the activities SELECTING POINTS FOR WELDING and SELECTING TRAJEC-

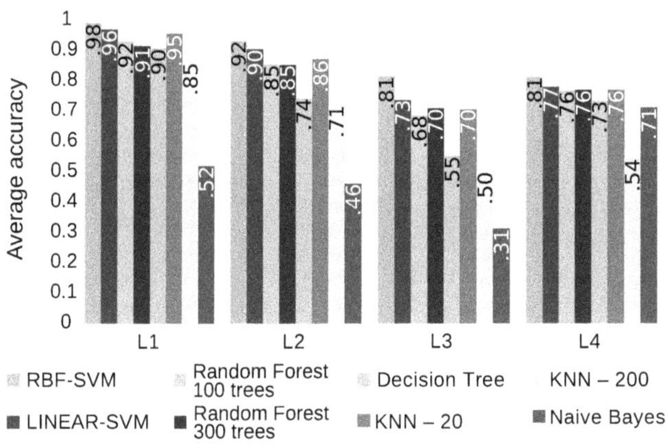

Figure 6: **Average classification accuracy of different discriminative classification methods considered for the first phase of training. Best results were achieved with RBF-SVM for all levels.**

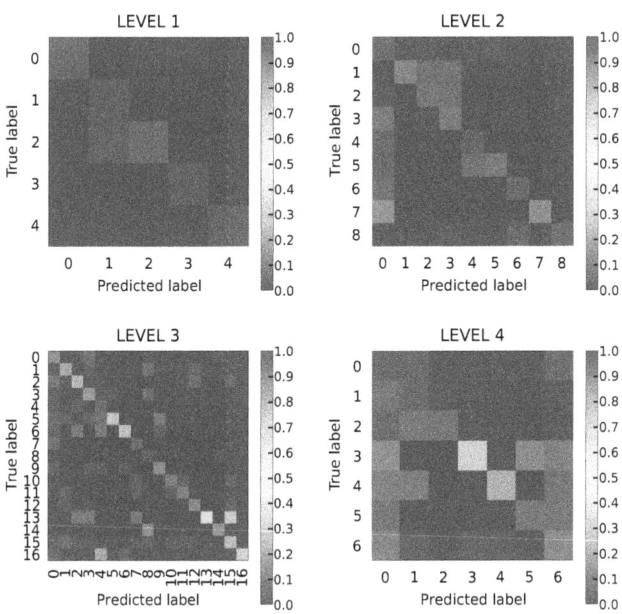

Figure 7: Confusion matrices for each level of activities with the best recognition approach (RBF-SVM + HHMM). Correspondence of the IDs to the actual activity names can be found in Table 1

TORY FOR WELDING is to be expected, since the scenarios differ only in the way of specifying the trajectory.

L_2 represents decomposition of L_1 in more specific sub-activities. The best results were achieved when combining both sensors (avg. F1=0.93), except for the activities SELECTING POINTS FOR WELDING and SELECTING TRAJECTORY FOR WELDING, where best results were achieved when using *Leap* features only. This is because these scenarios contain predefined hand gestures, for which precise finger tracking is crucial, while rough body pose is insignificant. Hence, these activities are the two most poorly recognized labels when using *Kinect v2* data only. On the other hand, the activity CHECKING THE RESULT, where the human leans forward and takes a closer look at the workpiece, relies on the body pose only and can not be recognized with *Leap* data only (R=28 %). When using both sensors or *Kinect v2* only, the situation drastically improves (R=85 %). Combining both sensors still provides the best average recognition results.

		Kinect 2 + Leap			Leap only			Kinect 2 only		
		R	P	F1	R	P	F1	R	P	F1
ID	LEVEL 1									
0	None	0.98	1.00	**0.99**	0.91	0.98	0.94	0.87	0.99	0.92
1	Selecting points for welding	1.00	0.96	**0.98**	0.96	1.00	**0.98**	0.79	0.79	0.79
2	Selecting trajectory for welding	0.96	1.00	**0.98**	0.93	1.00	0.96	0.75	0.99	0.85
3	Working on a piece	1.00	1.00	**1.00**	1.00	1.00	**1.00**	1.00	1.00	**1.00**
4	Assembly	1.00	1.00	**1.00**	0.94	0.94	0.94	0.88	0.88	0.88
	Average	0.99	0.99	**0.99**	0.95	0.98	0.96	0.86	0.93	0.89
	LEVEL 2									
0	None	0.94	0.95	**0.94**	0.91	0.98	**0.94**	0.83	0.84	0.83
1	Picking a second object	0.88	1.00	**0.93**	0.75	0.80	0.77	0.81	0.93	0.87
2	Picking an object	0.90	0.98	**0.94**	0.83	0.95	0.89	0.68	0.94	0.79
3	Placing an object	0.89	1.00	**0.94**	0.79	0.99	0.88	0.75	0.98	0.85
4	Selecting points for welding	0.96	0.92	0.94	1.00	0.96	**0.98**	0.50	0.74	0.60
5	Selecting trajectory for welding	0.89	1.00	0.94	0.93	1.00	**0.96**	0.61	0.98	0.75
6	Assembling	0.94	0.79	**0.86**	0.94	0.71	0.81	0.50	0.73	0.59
7	Checking the result	0.85	1.00	**0.92**	0.28	0.76	0.41	0.85	0.85	0.85
8	Fixing	0.95	0.96	**0.95**	0.91	0.93	0.92	0.98	0.86	0.92
	Average	0.91	0.96	**0.93**	0.82	0.90	0.84	0.72	0.87	0.78
	LEVEL 3									
0	None	0.89	0.90	**0.90**	0.85	0.86	0.85	0.78	0.65	0.71
1	Placing an object	0.71	0.96	**0.81**	0.67	0.90	0.77	0.74	0.91	**0.81**
2	Reaching for an object	0.69	0.88	0.77	0.68	0.96	**0.80**	0.43	0.91	0.59
3	Retracting the hand	0.67	0.93	0.78	0.77	0.95	**0.85**	0.60	0.92	0.72
4	Selecting a point	0.88	0.95	**0.91**	0.94	0.88	**0.91**	0.50	0.75	0.60
5	Selecting the trajectory end	0.69	1.00	0.82	0.71	1.00	**0.83**	0.11	0.98	0.19
6	Selecting the trajectory start	0.64	1.00	0.78	0.79	1.00	**0.88**	0.34	0.98	0.51
7	Assembling	0.89	0.88	**0.89**	0.94	0.56	0.70	0.56	0.38	0.45
8	Back to normal	0.88	0.50	0.64	0.33	0.60	0.42	0.80	0.56	**0.66**
9	Drawing the trajectory	0.84	0.88	0.86	0.89	0.93	**0.91**	0.50	0.29	0.30
10	Fixing with a tool	0.89	0.88	**0.88**	0.96	0.75	0.84	0.96	0.59	0.73
11	Fixing with hands	0.84	0.89	**0.86**	0.79	0.67	0.72	0.82	0.72	0.77
12	Grasping an object	0.79	0.78	**0.79**	0.80	0.79	**0.79**	0.64	0.65	0.65
13	Holding an object	0.19	0.57	0.29	0.20	0.50	0.29	0.40	0.33	**0.36**
14	Leaning forward	0.73	0.96	**0.83**	0.35	0.57	0.43	0.85	0.81	0.83
15	Moving an object	0.64	0.87	0.74	0.76	0.82	**0.79**	0.57	0.86	0.68
16	Moving the hand	0.54	0.80	0.65	0.71	0.85	**0.77**	0.13	0.75	0.21
	Average	0.73	0.86	**0.78**	0.71	0.80	0.74	0.57	0.71	0.58
	LEVEL 4 (Gestures)									
0	None	0.95	0.58	0.72	0.93	0.70	**0.80**	0.98	0.23	0.37
1	Pointing	0.82	0.82	0.82	0.92	0.89	**0.90**	0.15	0.48	0.23
2	Thumb double-click	0.71	0.83	0.76	0.88	1.00	**0.93**	0.10	0.42	0.17
3	Two fingers: putting thumb down	0.30	1.00	0.46	0.63	0.95	**0.76**	0.00	nan	nan
4	Two fingers: releasing the thumb	0.42	1.00	0.59	0.74	0.96	**0.84**	0.06	1.00	0.12
5	Two fingers: thumb down	0.83	0.91	0.87	0.87	0.99	**0.93**	0.20	0.97	0.33
6	Two fingers: thumb up	0.75	0.99	0.86	0.84	0.99	**0.91**	0.28	0.98	0.44
7	Average	0.68	0.88	0.73	0.83	0.93	**0.87**	0.25	0.68	0.28

Table 1: Single sensor and multi sensor recognition results: Precision (P), Recall (R) and F1-score for each type of activity. Using multiple sensors shows the best average recognition results for L_1, L_2 and L_3. L_4 contains hand gestures, with the best classification results therefore obtained with the Leap Motion features only.

L_3 has 17 sub-activities, with the best recognition results achieved with the combination of sensors (avg. F1=0.78). Since we aimed at a very precise set of sub-activities, the frequency of occurrence in the data set may vary.

In contrast to the other levels, best recognition results for L_4 were obtained by using Leap features only (F1=0.87). The activities at this level contain both very short dynamic gestures that last for fractions of a second (e.g. putting the thumb up or releasing it back down) and static gestures, which usually last longer. Short dynamic gestures were harder to classify, with PUTTING THE THUMB DOWN showing the lowest classification result (F1=0.76), while all static gestures have reached an F1 score over 0.9.

6. CONCLUSION

The contributions of this paper are two-fold. Firstly, we designed a multimodal interface integrated in a robotic workcell for HRI, tailored to recognize human activities and gestures. In spite of the diverse data sources and the complex communication framework, the system is easy to maintain and extend due to its compatibility with ROS. Secondly, we proposed a two-stages machine learning approach for the classification of human activities on multiple levels of abstraction. We use PCA for dimensionality reduction and combine a RBF-SVM estimator with a HHMM. The comparison of the recognition results using single and multiple sensors shows that multi-modality is crucial for our application. While the Leap Motion sensor offers the key data for the recognition of hand-centered activities, the Kinect v2 sensor provides better information about large-scale body movements, such as LEANING FORWARD. All in all, fusing multiple sensors is highly beneficial as it comes to recognizing both, hand-centered and body-centered movements. However, if the set of activities is limited to a certain type of movements, it might be useful to select the best data source and hence avoid unnecessary noise. The hand tracking provided by the Leap Motion sensor is therefore more significant for industrial manufacturing processes, than the body skeleton obtained with the Kinect v2 sensor. Besides higher success rates during the activity recognition, a combination of multiple data sources improves the system reliability by enlarging the observable area and adding input redundancy. Hence, a failure of one sensor can be compensated by another one. In the live system, it would be recommended to use three trained models, one for a combined feature set and one for each feature set originated from one of the sensors only. The system could use the combined model as long as all of the devices are providing reliable data, and switch to a single-sensor mode in case of a sensor drop out.

Acknowledgements

The research leading to these results has received funding from the European Union Seventh Framework Programme (FP7/2007-2013) under grant agreement no. 287787 in the project SMErobotics.

7. REFERENCES

[1] J. K. Aggarwal and M. S. Ryoo. Human activity analysis: A review. *ACM Computing Surveys (CSUR)*, 43(3):16, 2011.

[2] O. Boiman, E. Shechtman, and M. Irani. In defense of nearest-neighbor based image classification. In *Computer Vision and Pattern Recognition(CVPR) IEEE Conference on*, pages 1–8. IEEE, 2008.

[3] S. Fine, Y. Singer, and N. Tishby. The hierarchical hidden markov model: Analysis and applications. *Machine learning*, 32(1):41–62, 1998.

[4] L. Gan and F. Chen. Human action recognition using apj3d and random forests. *Journal of Software*, 8(9):2238–2245, 2013.

[5] B. Gleeson, K. MacLean, A. Haddadi, E. Croft, and J. Alcazar. Gestures for industry: Intuitive human-robot communication from human observation. In *Proceedings of the 8th ACM/IEEE International Conference on Human-robot Interaction*, HRI, pages 349–356. IEEE Press, 2013.

[6] V. Kellokumpu, M. Pietikäinen, and J. Heikkilä. Human activity recognition using sequences of postures. In *IAPR Conference on Machine Vision Applications*, pages 570–573, 2005.

[7] H. S. Koppula, R. Gupta, and A. Saxena. Learning human activities and object affordances from rgb-d videos. *The International Journal of Robotics Research*, 32(8):951–970, 2013.

[8] C. Lenz, A. Sotzek, T. Röder, H. Radrich, A. Knoll, M. Huber, and S. Glasauer. Human workflow analysis using 3D occupancy grid hand tracking in a human-robot collaboration scenario. In *IROS*, pages 3375–3380. IEEE, 2011.

[9] B. Liang and L. Zheng. Multi-modal gesture recognition using skeletal joints and motion trail model. In *Computer Vision-ECCV Workshops*, pages 623–638. Springer, 2014.

[10] N. T. Nguyen, D. Q. Phung, S. Venkatesh, and H. Bui. Learning and detecting activities from movement trajectories using the hierarchical hidden markov model. In *Computer Vision and Pattern Recognition (CVPR), IEEE Computer Society Conference on*, volume 2, pages 955–960. IEEE, 2005.

[11] F. Ofli, R. Chaudhry, G. Kurillo, R. Vidal, and R. Bajcsy. Sequence of the most informative joints (smij): A new representation for human skeletal action recognition. *Journal of Visual Communication and Image Representation*, 25(1):24–38, 2014.

[12] G. T. Papadopoulos, A. Axenopoulos, and P. Daras. Real-time skeleton-tracking-based human action recognition using kinect data. In *MultiMedia Modeling*, pages 473–483. Springer, 2014.

[13] R. Poppe. A survey on vision-based human action recognition. *Image and vision computing*, 28(6):976–990, 2010.

[14] L. R. Rabiner and B. H. Juang. An introduction to hidden markov models. *ASSP Magazine*, pages 4–16, Jan. 1986.

[15] A. Roitberg, A. Perzylo, N. Somani, M. Giuliani, M. Rickert, and A. Knoll. Human activity recognition in the context of industrial human-robot interaction. In *Asia-Pacific Signal and Information Processing Association, 2014 Annual Summit and Conference (APSIPA)*, pages 1–10. IEEE, 2014.

[16] J. Sung, C. Ponce, B. Selman, and A. Saxena. Unstructured human activity detection from RGBD images. In *IEEE International Conference on Robotics and Automation (ICRA)*, 2012.

[17] P. Turaga, R. Chellappa, V. S. Subrahmanian, and O. Udrea. Machine recognition of human activities: A survey. *Circuits and Systems for Video Technology, IEEE Transactions on*, 18(11):1473–1488, 2008.

[18] J. Yamato, J. Ohya, and K. Ishii. Recognizing human action in time-sequential images using hidden markov model. In *CVPR*, pages 379–385, 1992.

[19] Y. Zhu, W. Chen, and G. Guo. Fusing spatiotemporal features and joints for 3d action recognition. In *Computer Vision and Pattern Recognition Workshops (CVPRW), IEEE Conference on*, pages 486–491. IEEE, 2013.

Accuracy vs. Availability Heuristic in Multimodal Affect Detection in the Wild

Nigel Bosch[1], Huili Chen[1], Ryan Baker[2], Valerie Shute[3], & Sidney D'Mello[1]
[1]University of Notre Dame, Notre Dame, IN 46556, USA
[2]Teachers College, Columbia University, New York, NY 10027, USA
[3]Florida State University, Tallahassee, FL 32306-4453, USA
pbosch1@nd.edu, hchen6@nd.edu, baker2@tc.columbia.edu, vshute@fsu.edu, sdmello@nd.edu

ABSTRACT

This paper discusses multimodal affect detection from a fusion of facial expressions and interaction features derived from students' interactions with an educational game in the noisy real-world context of a computer-enabled classroom. Log data of students' interactions with the game and face videos from 133 students were recorded in a computer-enabled classroom over a two day period. Human observers live annotated learning-centered affective states such as engagement, confusion, and frustration. The face-only detectors were more accurate than interaction-only detectors. Multimodal affect detectors did not show any substantial improvement in accuracy over the face-only detectors. However, the face-only detectors were only applicable to 65% of the cases due to face registration errors caused by excessive movement, occlusion, poor lighting, and other factors. Multimodal fusion techniques were able to improve the applicability of detectors to 98% of cases without sacrificing classification accuracy. Balancing the accuracy vs. applicability tradeoff appears to be an important feature of multimodal affect detection.

Categories and Subject Descriptors

H.1.2 [**Models and Principles**]: User/Machine Systems – *human factors*.

General Terms

Measurement, Performance, Experimentation, Human Factors.

Author Keywords

Missing data; Affect; Affect detection; Facial expressions; Interaction.

1. INTRODUCTION

Affect sensitivity has been shown to have considerable promise for improving learning in computerized educational environments [22]. There are many ways in which an interface can leverage knowledge of students' affective states to improve learning. For example, bored and disengaged students may be directed to new learning tasks to help them re-engage, while students who are frequently frustrated due to excessively difficult tasks might be presented with material more appropriate for their knowledge and skills.

ICMI '15, November 09-13, 2015, Seattle, WA, USA
© 2015 ACM. ISBN 978-1-4503-3912-4/15/11…$15.00
DOI: http://dx.doi.org/10.1145/2818346.2820739

Affect sensitivity requires affect detection. Consequently, there have been many proposed methods for affect detection [25,33], of which multimodal affect detection is of interest here. D'Mello and Kory [25] recently provided a review and meta-analysis of 90 multimodal affect detection system. Their review revealed that two of the most common modalities for affect detection were facial features and audio features, which were used in 76.7% (face) and 82.2% (audio) of surveyed studies. Thus, audiovisual affect detection is clearly the most prominent multimodal fusion approach. Taking a somewhat different approach, the current paper presents affect detection results from a fusion of facial and interaction features (e.g., clicks, response times).

1.1 Related Work

Face-based affect detection has been well studied in a variety of learning contexts in recent years. A variety of computer vision techniques have been used for affect detection, such as texture, shape, and motion features extracted from faces. The full scope of work is beyond this paper, but recent review articles cover face-based affect detection in some detail [8,25,33].

Interaction log-based affect detection are less common, but have been increasingly studied over the last decade [3–5,24,28,29]. Unlike physical sensor-based detectors, which rely upon the nonverbal responses, these detectors infer affective states from students' interactions with computerized learning systems. We expect these features to be useful for affect detection because a student's affect could alter how they interact with the learning environment. For example, a bored student might not interact very frequently, or might aimlessly repeat an action. An engaged student might be more likely to try various strategies in the game and succeed more. The fact that interaction-based affect detectors rely on logs of student actions makes it possible for them to be deployed at no extra cost to a school that is using the learning system. Their unobtrusive and cost-efficient nature also makes it feasible to apply interaction-based detectors at scale, leading to a growing field of research regarding discovery with models [6].

Multimodal combinations of face- and interaction- features are few and far between. In one of the first studies, Kapoor et al. [17] used multimodal techniques with face- and posture- based features collected from naturalistic data to develop a detector of student interest. Facial features, such as detected head nods, shakes, and smiles, were combined with posture features gathered from a pressure-sensitive chair and interaction log features from the learning environment. The best unimodal detector (posture-based) classified high interest vs. low interest vs. taking a break, and had 82% accuracy (chance being 52%). The best multimodal detector combining all channels had 87% accuracy, demonstrating a modest improvement over the best unimodal detector. Further, Kapoor et al. [16] used facial features, a pressure-sensing chair, a pressure-sensitive mouse, a skin conductance sensor, and interaction log data to predict frustration. They were able to predict when a user would self-report frustration with 79% accuracy (chance being 58%).

D'Mello et al. [23] developed a multimodal affect detection system that discriminated between naturally occurring affective states in a learning environment. They used conversational cues, gross body language, and facial features as inputs for classification. Using fixed affect labels (every 20 seconds), mean Cohen's kappa improved from .220 (best individual modality model) to .288 in the best multimodal models. Using spontaneous affect labels (labeled at any point at the coder's discretion), mean kappa improved from .374 (unimodal) to .391 (multimodal). These results also demonstrated a small advantage for multimodal affect detection in terms of accuracy. However, facial features were manually annotated in this paper, an approach which is not feasible for large datasets or real-time interventions in a learning environment.

More recently, Grafsgaard et al. [12] developed multimodal affect detectors that utilized both facial features and student interaction features (as well as tutor-student dialog) in computer-mediated human-human tutoring sessions. They predicted engagement, frustration, and learning (all self-reported by the students) using linear regression with leave-one-student-out cross validation. A combination of facial features and interaction features predicted engagement (R^2 = .112) and frustration (R^2 = .134) more accurately than unimodal features (best R^2 = .048 and -.010 respectively for engagement and frustration). Adding tutor-student dialogue features improved results even further, R^2 = .282 and R^2 = .520 for engagement and frustration, respectively. This shows that a fusion of features can outperform individual modalities. However, affect detection was done at a course-grained level across an entire learning session, which limits its applicability to drive real-time interventions.

While the previous studies were conducted in somewhat controlled settings, Arroyo et al. [2] tracked emotions of high school and college mathematics students in computer-enabled classrooms. They used self-reports (for ground truth) and several modalities (interaction data from log-files, facial features, posture, skin conductance, and mouse movements). Their best models explained 67% of the variance (R^2) for self-reported confidence, 52% for frustration, 69% for excitement, and 29% for interest. Average R^2 was .1 higher for multimodal models with all modalities combined compared to the single modality (interaction-only) models reported. Although this research suggests that it might be possible to perform automated affect detection in classroom, this conclusion should be interpreted with a modicum of caution. This is because the model was not validated with a separate testing set (i.e. no cross validation was performed), and the size of the data set was very small (20-36 instances depending on model) due to missing data. These issues raise concerns of overfitting, but also serve to illustrate how much missing data occurs in classroom data collection.

1.2 Current Study: Novelty and Contributions

The current study expands on previous research by building a multimodal face- and interaction-based affect detector for a game-based learning environment called Physics Playground [31]. Previous research on these data has demonstrated the possibility of building both face-only and interaction-only detectors individually ([7,15]). Integrating these modalities also provides some unique challenges. Facial expressions are often brief (such as a delighted smile after succeeding in a task), whereas interaction events tend to unfold over a longer period of time (e.g., number of mouse clicks may be zero unless aggregated over a longer period of time).

Multimodal approaches have been shown to produce "modest" improvements in affect detection accuracy, according to a recent meta-analysis of 90 studies [25]. The meta-analysis showed that median improvement of multimodal approaches over the best single modality was 6.60%. The meta-analysis also revealed that multimodal classification of natural affect has shown an average of only one third of the benefit of multimodal classification than observed with acted affect. The present focus is also on classifying naturalistic affect displays rather than acted or posed affect. Thus, we do not expect large gains in classification accuracy from multimodal fusion.

However, there is more to consider than mere accuracy when evaluating multimodal affect detectors in the wild. Our multimodal affect detector is designed to operate in computer-enabled classrooms, a context that is rife with noisy and missing data, thereby providing additional challenges for multimodal affect detection. One key limitation of unimodal affect detection is the inability to operate when data are missing, a limitation that affects nearly every modality commonly used for affect detection. Heart rate, skin conductance, electroencephalogram, and other modalities measured via bodily contact sensors can be unavailable do to noise in the data or lack of contact caused by movement. Facial features can be unavailable when the person's face is occluded by hand-to-face gestures, when the person falls outside the camera's field of view, or when rapid motion causes detection errors. Environmental factors such as lighting can also cause face registration errors. Similarly, interaction features can be unavailable when a person is not frequently interacting with an interface, due to disengagement or non-interactive tasks such as reading or video watching.

This missing data problem was particularly prevalent in the present context where data was collected in the wild, specifically in a computer-enabled classroom environment with up to 30 students at a time playing an educational physics game. Students talked to one another, laughed, moved around, and gestured, as is expected in a game-based learning environment and in naturalistic contexts. Face data was frequently unavailable due to face registration failures caused by excessive movements or occlusions, while interaction data was not be present when the student was passively processing information rather than actively interacting. To address this issue, this paper considers both accuracy and availability while developing a unique multimodal combination of face + interaction data in the noisy real-world context of computer-enabled classrooms.

2. METHOD

2.1 Data Collection

The sample consisted of 137 8th and 9th grade students (57 male, 80 female) who were enrolled in a public school in a medium-sized city in the Southeastern U.S. They were tested in groups of about 20 students per class period for a total of four periods on four different days (55 minutes per period). Students in the 8th and 9th grades were selected because of the alignment of the learning content and the state standards (relating to Newtonian Physics) at those grade levels.

2.1.1 *Learning Environment (Physics Playground)*

Physics Playground (PP) [31] is a two-dimensional game that requires the player to apply principles of Newtonian Physics in an attempt to guide a green ball to a red balloon in many challenging configurations (key goal). The player can nudge the ball to the left and right (if the surface is flat) but the primary way to move the ball is by drawing/creating simple machines (which are called "agents of force and motion" in the game) on the screen that "come to life" once the object is drawn (example in Figure 1). Thus, the problems in PP require the player to draw/create four different agents (which are simple machine-like objects): inclined plane/ramps, pendulums, levers, and springboards. All solutions are drawn with colored lines using the mouse. Everything in the game obeys the basic laws of physics relating to gravity and Newton's three laws of motion.

The game includes seven playgrounds (each one containing 10–11 problems, for a total of 74 problems) that progressively get more difficult. The difficulty of a problem is based on a number of factors including the relative location of ball to balloon, obstacles, the number of agents required to solve the problem, and the novelty of the problem. The game is nonlinear in that students have complete choice in selecting playgrounds and levels. Progress in the game is represented by silver and gold trophies, which are displayed in the top left part of the screen. While a silver trophy is obtained for any solution to a problem, students earn a gold trophy if a solution is under a certain number of objects (the threshold varies by problem, but is typically < 3). PP maintains detailed log files that record the problem, student actions and when they occurred, system responses, trophies awarded, and so on.

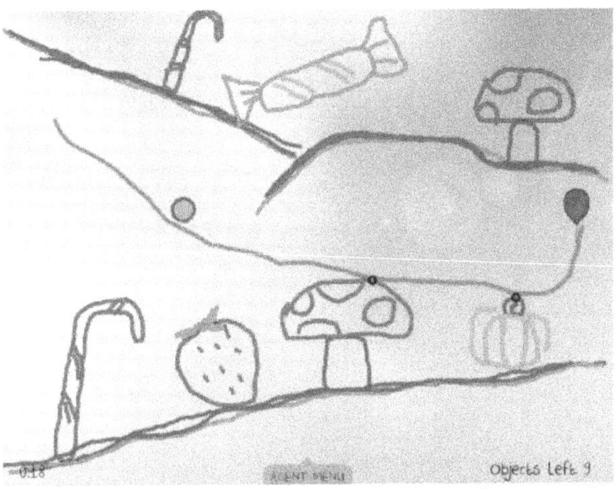

Figure 1. Ramp solution for a simple Physics Playground problem.

2.1.2 *Procedure*

The study took place in one of the school's computer-enabled classrooms, which was equipped with 30 desktop computers. Each computer was equipped with a monitor, mouse, keyboard, and headphones. Inexpensive webcams ($30) were affixed at the top of the monitor of each computer. At the beginning of each session, the data collection software displayed an interface that allowed students to position their faces in the center of the camera's view by adjusting the camera angle up or down. This process was guided by on-screen instructions and verbal instructions given by the experimenters, who were also available to answer any additional questions and to troubleshoot any problems.

We administered a qualitative physics pretest during the first day and a posttest at the end of the fourth day (both online). In this study we considered data from the second and third days (roughly two hours total) when students were only playing the game and not being tested.

Students' affective states were "live" (real-time) annotated during their interactions with PP using the Baker-Rodrigo Observation Method Protocol (BROMP) [27]. In BROMP, trained observers perform live affect annotations (real-time observations made while students played PP) by observing students one at a time using a round-robin technique (observing one student until visible affect is detected or 20 seconds have elapsed and moving on to the next student). Observers use side glances to make a holistic judgment of the students' affect based on facial expressions, speech, body posture, gestures, and student interaction with the computer program (e.g., whether a student is progressing or struggling). Observers record students in a pre-determined order to maintain a representative sampling of students' affect, rather than focusing on the most interesting (but not most prevalent) things occurring in the classroom. Every BROMP observer was trained and tested on the protocol and achieved sufficient agreement (kappa ≥ .6) with a certified BROMP observer before coding the data.

The coding process was implemented using the HART application for Android devices [27], which enforces the protocol while facilitating data collection. Observation-codes recorded in HART were synchronized with the videos recorded on the individual computers using Internet time servers. Observers averaged 3.2 observations per minute (approximately 19 seconds per observation). Observers moved on to the next student when they were confident in their rating so that timestamps coincide with affective manifestations.

It should be noted that there are many possible affect annotation schemes, each with their strengths and weaknesses, as recently reviewed in [30]. BROMP was selected for this study because it has been shown to achieve adequate reliability (among over 70 coders in over a dozen studies with a variety of learning environments [26]) in annotating affective states of a large number of students occurring in the "heat of the moment" and without interrupting or biasing students by asking them to self-report affect.

The affective states of interest were boredom, confusion, delight, engaged concentration, and frustration. This list of states was selected based on previous research [21] and from observing students during the first day of data collection (these data were not used in the current detectors). BROMP-coded observations of these states served as the ground truth labels for affect detection.

2.1.3 *Instances of Affect Observed*

Data from the two main days of game-play were collated and jointly analyzed in this study. We obtained 1,838 observations of affective states across the two days of data used in this study. Recording errors eliminated 44 face-based instances from consideration due to occasional computer crashes and performance issues. The most common affective state observed was engaged concentration (77.6%), followed by frustrated (13.5%), bored (4.3%), delighted (2.3%), and confused (2.3%).

2.2 Feature Engineering

We computed features from video recordings of students' faces as they played the game (facial features) and features obtained from logs of their interactions in the learning environment (interaction features). These features were then used to develop affect detectors for each individual modality as well as for feature- and decision-level multimodal fusion models.

2.2.1 Facial Features

We used FACET for facial feature extraction. FACET is a commercialized version of the Computer Expression Recognition Toolbox (CERT) computer vision software [19]. Like CERT, FACET provides likelihood estimates for the presence of 19 Action Units (AUs) as well as head pose (orientation) and position information detected from video. Data from FACET was temporally aligned with affect observations in small windows. We tested five different window sizes (3, 6, 9, or 12 seconds). Features were created by aggregating (using maximum, median, standard deviation) values obtained from FACET (AUs, orientation, and position of the face) in a window of time leading up to each observation. For example, for a six-second window we created three features from the AU4 channel (brow lower). Those features were the maximum, median, and standard deviation of AU4 likelihood within the six seconds leading up to an affect observation. In all there were 78 facial features for each window.

We also used features computed from gross body movement estimated in the videos ([7]). Body movement was calculated by measuring the proportion of pixels in each video frame that differed from a continuously updated estimate of the background image generated from the four previous frames. Previous work has shown that features derived using this technique correlate with relevant affective states including boredom, confusion, and frustration [20]. We created three body movement features using the maximum, median, and standard deviation of the proportion of "motion" pixels within the window of time leading up to an observation, similar to the method used to create FACET features. In all, there were 3 body movement features, thereby yielding a total of 81 video-based features.

Facial features were only available for 65% of the instances due to face-registration errors. The unregisterable instances were treated as missing data and were addressed during multimodal fusion.

2.2.2 Interaction Features

Interaction features capture key aspects of students' actions as they played Physics Playground. The basic set of features considered the number of specific objects drawn as well as actions and events occurring during gameplay. Some examples include the number of springboard structures created in a level, the number of freeform objects drawn in a level, the time between start to end of a level, the number of gold trophies obtained in a level, and the number of stacking events (cheating behavior) in a level. In addition, time-based features focused on the amount of time elapsed between specific student actions, such as starting and pausing a level, as well as the time it took for a variety of events to occur within each level. In all, there were 113 interaction features.

Features were aggregated within a 20 second window leading up to each affect observation. A larger window size was required for interaction features than facial features because interaction events occur less frequently. Windows of all sizes for both facial and interaction features were synchronized to end at the same point in time. Differing window sizes thus did not affect the number of instances or alignment of instances between face and interaction modalities.

Occasional missing values were present at certain points in the dataset when a particular interaction was not logged. For example, a feature specifying the amount of time between the student beginning a level and his/her first restart of the level would contain a missing value if the student manages to complete a level without having to restart it. Zero imputations were performed where the missing values were replaced by the value 0. However, if all interaction features were missing for a particular instance, values were not replaced with 0. These instances occurred infrequently in situations where students did not interact with the game at all or when they were not interacting with a level, as was the case when selecting a new level or watching instructional videos on how to play the game. In all, interaction data was available for 94% of the instances compared to 65% for facial features.

2.2.3 Feature Selection

Tolerance analysis was used to eliminate features with high multicollinearity (variance inflation factor > 5) within each modality [1]. Feature selection was used to obtain a sparser and potentially more diagnostic set of features for classification. A common feature selection technique RELIEF-F [18] was run on the *training* data in order to rank features. A proportion of the highest ranked features were then used in the detectors (proportions of .1, .2, .3, .4, .5, and .75 were tested).

2.3 Supervised Learning

We built detectors using 14 different classifiers including support vector machines, C4.5 trees, Bayesian classifiers, and others in the Waikato Environment for Knowledge Analysis (WEKA), a machine learning tool [13]. A large number of classifiers were considered since we are unaware of the best approach for this type of data.

A two-class approach was used for each affective state, where that affective state was discriminated from all others. For example, engaged concentration was discriminated from all frustrated, bored, delighted, and confused instances combined (referred to as "all other"). Building individual detectors for each state allows the parameters (e.g., window size, features used) to be optimized for that particular affective state

The affective distributions lead to large class imbalances (e.g. .04 vs. .96 class priors in the bored vs. all other classification). Two different sampling techniques were used (on training data only) to compensate for class imbalance. These included downsampling (removal of random instances from the majority class) and synthetic oversampling (with SMOTE; [9]) to create equal class sizes. SMOTE creates synthetic training data by interpolating feature values between an instance and randomly chosen nearest neighbors. The distributions in the testing data were not changed, to preserve the validity of the results.

Detectors were cross-validated at the student level using leave-one-student-out cross validation. A detector was trained on data from all but one holdout student, then tested on data from the holdout student. Feature selection was performed using nested cross-validation on training data only (see below). Ten iterations of feature selection were run on the training data, using data from a randomly chosen 67% of students within the training set for each iteration. The entire cross-validation process was repeated for every student to produce student-independent predictions for every instance. This helps detectors generalize to new students since training and testing data sets are student-independent.

2.4 Multimodal Fusion

Basic feature-level fusion and decision-level fusion techniques were used in the present paper. Feature level fusion involved combining features from both modalities into a single dataset and then building a detector. The disadvantage of this simplistic approach is that the data must be present in every modality for training and testing. Decision-level fusion, on the other hand, involved creating a detector separately with each modality, thus exploiting all the training data available for that modality. Individual detector outputs were then combined by training an additional classifier on the outputs of the individual classifiers to form a final classification. Both approaches used leave-one-student-out cross validation.

3. RESULTS

The results are organized with respect to three aspects of multimodal classification. First, how does multimodal accuracy compare to unimodal accuracy; second, does a multimodal approach improve detector availability; and third, what are the benefits of a more sophisticated multimodal approach compared to a simplistic one.

The Area Under the ROC Curve (AUC) was used to measure classification accuracy. AUC measures the tradeoff between the true positive and false positive rates of a detector. AUC ranges from 0 (completely incorrect classification) to 1 (perfect classification), while an AUC of .5 represents chance-level classification. AUC is a recommended accuracy metric when dealing with imbalanced data [14], which is the case in the current study (e.g., boredom comprised only 4.23% of data).

3.1 Fusion with Nonmissing Data only

The applicability of the feature-level fusion detector was limited because a significant number of instances were missing either one modality or the other. To make a fair comparison with identical instances, training and testing datasets contained only instances when both face and interaction data were valid. Table 1 shows a comparison of classification accuracy of the face-only, interaction-only, feature-level fusion, and decision-level fusion detectors on identical instances. The number of instances (N) varies between affective states because the window sizes varied. On average, 1,124 instances out of 1,838 total instances were used in these analyses, so a considerable amount of data were being unused.

The results indicated that the multimodal detectors yielded similar accuracies compared to the best unimodal detectors for boredom, delight, engagement, and frustration. Detection accuracy for confusion was higher for the feature-level fusion detector compared to the unimodal detectors.

Table 1. AUC comparison of modalities and fusion methods using identical instances.

	Face	Interaction	Feature-Level Fusion	Decision-Level Fusion	N
Boredom	**.594**	.546	.520	**.598**	1229
Confusion	.573	**.600**	**.663**	.596	1229
Delight	**.869**	.662	.848	**.865**	943
Engagement	**.670**	.505	.669	**.673**	1153
Frustration	**.627**	.556	**.634**	.623	1064
Mean	**.667**	.574	.667	**.671**	

Note: Bold indicates best unimodal and multimodal models.

3.2 Fusion with All Available Data

The comparison in Section 3.1 shows that the feature-level and decision-level fusion approaches are at least comparable to the best individual modalities, but did not offer a large benefit in terms of accuracy with the minor exception of confusion. This finding was not unexpected, given the null to modest multimodal improvements typically obtained for naturalistic affective expressions [25]. In the Introduction, we argued that there may be additional benefits to multimodal affect detection beyond accuracy. Here, we consider the potential of multimodal affect detection as a means to improve availability (i.e., handling of missing data).

The analyses preceded as follows. Multimodal detectors were built to operate on as many instances as possible by predicting affect for every instance as long as it contained either face or interaction data (or both). Decision-level fusion was used because it affords training individual base detectors for each modality. Each base detector can then provide a prediction (decision) for an instance if data are available for that modality. The decisions from each modality's detector can then be combined. This procedure maximizes the use of training data because the detector for each modality can be trained using all of the data from that modality. It also maximizes the availability of the detector by making a prediction whenever any of the individual modalities has available data.

There are many possible methods of combining the decisions of individual modalities to provide an overall prediction for an instance. We built three types of decision-level fusion detectors. The first type used the face-only detector whenever possible and the interaction-only detector only when face data were unavailable (face-biased). The second type was the complement, using interaction-only detection whenever possible and using the face-only detector as a backup (interaction-biased). The third type used a classifier to make decisions with the output of each of the individual modalities as input features, thereby essentially learning how to weigh each modality (learned-bias). When a channel was not available, its prediction was taken to be 0.5 (even odds for a two-way classification problem). We also experimented with 0 and 1 replacement, but found 0.5 to produce better results, which is expected since it is unlikely to bias the classifier's decision significantly. Table 2 contains an overview of the modalities used for each of the fusion methods. The AUC accuracy of these three detection-schemes after averaging across the affective states is shown in Figure 2, where we note a small advantage of the learned-bias detector compared to the face-biased and interaction-biased detectors.

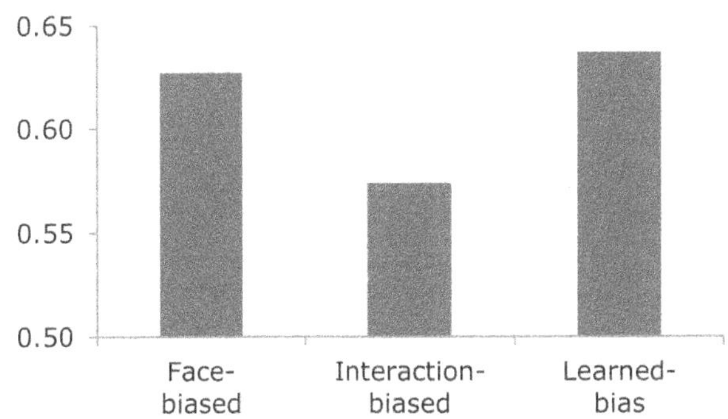

Figure 2. Comparison of decision-level fusion methods.

3.3 Accuracy vs. Availability

Section 3.1 indicated that the face-only model yielded the best accuracy when only considering cases with nonmissing instances. This lead to large data loss (high accuracy and low availability). In Section 3.2, using the interaction-biased weighting scheme yielded the best results while using all available instances. Here, we attempt to reconcile these two results.

Table 2. Modality used in multimodal fusion methods.

Available		Modality Used For Decision			
Face	**Interaction**	**Feature-level**	**Face-biased**	**Interaction-biased**	**Learned-bias**
Yes	Yes	Both	Face	Interaction	Both
Yes	No	None	Face	Face	Face
No	Yes	None	Interaction	Interaction	Interaction

Figure 3 displays and compares the available percentage of total instances and the accuracy of individual modalities versus the learned-bias multimodal detectors. We note that the proportion of total instances available for classification increased notably with the use of decision-level multimodal fusion. Thus, availability was dramatically improved over the face-only detector with little reduction in classification accuracy. Availability also marginally improved over the interaction-only detector, but accuracy was dramatically improved in this case.

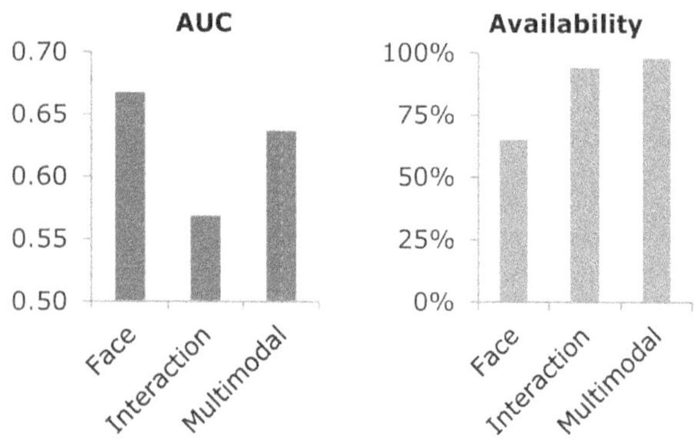

Figure 3. Comparison of accuracy versus availability for unimodal and multimodal detection.

3.4 Analysis of Learned-bias Multimodal Detector

Figure 3 showed that using multimodal fusion increased the percentage of situations in which the detectors could be applied to nearly 100% of the cases. However, the average multimodal detector accuracy was slightly lower than the face-only detectors. Thus, further analysis of the accuracy of this combined detector is needed to more clearly understand why accuracy was diminished. We examined the accuracy of the learned-bias detector in different situations (face data available vs. missing) to determine why this was the case.

There was an average of 595 instances where interaction data were available but face data were missing. In this situation the learned-bias detectors had an average accuracy of AUC = .583. In contrast, the average accuracy when the face data were present was AUC = .694. Thus, the detectors performed better when the face was present, which could be expected since the face generally outperformed the interaction-only detectors. It might be reasoned from this that most of the learned-bias detectors' predictive power stems from the face modality. However, the learned-bias detectors were more slightly accurate than simply using the face-only detector whenever possible (see Figure 2). It appears that the learned-bias detector made productive use of the information contained in the less accurate interaction modality even when the more accurate face modality was available. Thus, there was some improvement to be gained through a weighted fusion rather than simply using the face-only detector when available and reverting to the interaction-only detector otherwise. Table 3 shows the details of how individual modalities were weighted in the learned-bias detectors for the best classifiers (from those listed in section 2.3).

Table 3. Details of learned-bias detectors.

Affect	AUC	Classifier	Face Weight	Interaction Weight
Boredom	.590	Logistic Regression	0.415	0.157
Confusion	.585	Logistic Regression	1.20	20.7
Delight	.775	Logistic Regression	0.043	0.137
Engagement	.621	Updateable Naïve Bayes	NA	NA
Frustration	.614	Logistic Regression	0.314	0.064

Note: Weights denote odds ratios in logistic regression. No weights were available from the Updateable Naïve Bayes classifier.

As can be seen in Table 3, the confusion detectors are heavily biased toward using the interaction modality. That finding is consistent with Table 1, which showed that confusion was the one modality where interaction-only detectors out-performed face-only detectors, despite using instances where the face data was available. Surprisingly, the delight classifier also weighted interaction more highly than face, though not to the same extent. One possible reason for that finding is that the face data were so frequently missing for delight (48.7% missing) due to the short, 3-second window size. Thus the learned-bias detector learned to rely more heavily on the interaction detector instead.

4. GENERAL DISCUSSION

We explored multimodal affect detection in a classroom environment where students interacted with a game-based learning environment called Physics Playground [31]. Specifically, we focus on the use of multimodal approaches to affect detection as a means of improving the accuracy and availability of detectors in this noisy environment where missing data are prevalent. We employed face-only and interaction-only affect detection methods as two modalities with a tradeoff between accuracy and availability (applicability to a large number of situations and instances). In this section we review our main findings, point out limitations and opportunities for future work, and discuss implications for affect-sensitive learning environments.

4.1 Main Findings

We investigated multimodal classification of affect in several ways. First, we compared multimodal detectors with unimodal detectors. We did not expect large improvements based on previous research [25]. Indeed we found no major improvement in average accuracy with multimodal classification, but established that accuracy was at least not diminished. Face-only affect detection was more accurate but there were a larger number of missing instances, while interaction-only detection was applicable to a larger number of instances but was less accurate. Thus, our primary goal was to improve the availability of detectors without significantly reducing accuracy. We used decision-level fusion to develop detectors that worked for 98% of the instances in our data—a notable improvement over the 65% availability of the face modality. Accuracy of these multimodal detectors was close to that of the face-only detectors. Thus, we appear to have struck an appropriate balance between accuracy and availability in this context.

We further investigated the accuracy of the improved detectors in two ways. First, we examined accuracy in situations where the face (most frequently missing modality) was missing versus those where it was not. We found that accuracy was notably better when face data were available, but that the accuracy of learned-bias multimodal detectors improved through the use of interaction data even when face data were available. This finding is significant because it shows there was benefit to the interaction modality despite its lower accuracy. A deeper analysis of the logistic regression weights of individual modalities in the final decision-level fusion detectors revealed that the interaction modality was indeed influencing the final classification decision (Table 3).

4.2 Limitations and Future Work

Some limitations of this study should be noted. First, additional modalities such as acoustic features might have proven useful, but were not collected. Future work should address this by considering other common affect detection modalities and determining which are suitable for use given the constraints of having multiple students in a computer-enabled classroom. Second, though the students in this study varied widely across some demographic variables, they were all approximately the same age and in the same location. A further study testing detectors on data with more variability in age and geographic distribution would be useful for determining the level to which results might generalize to different group of students. Third, the observation method used (BROMP) requires observers to be in the room, which could influence students displays of affect akin to a Hawthorne effect [10]. These limitations could be addressed by an additional study comparing the incidence of affective states experienced by students with different demographics using a variety of different sensors and affect annotation methodologies.

4.3 Implications for Affect-Sensitive Interfaces

Our results were particularly relevant to affect detection efforts in intelligent learning interfaces for computer-enabled classrooms. For example, the detectors we developed will be used to improve intelligent instructional strategies towards developing an affect-sensitive version of Physics Playground. Separate strategies will be used for each affective state and off-task behavior. For example, when the detectors determine that a student is engaged or delighted, Physics Playground may not intervene at all. Confusion and frustration offer intervention opportunities in the form of hints or revisiting introductory material related to the concepts in the current level. If the student has recently been frustrated and unable to complete levels, an easier level might be suggested. Conversely, a more difficult level might be appropriate if the student has not been challenged by recently completed levels. Boredom might be addressed by suggesting that the student attempt a new level or by calibrating difficulty.

4.4 Concluding Remarks

Affect interventions require real-time affect detection, and this work has extended the amount of cases where an affect detector can operate while maintaining accuracy. In particular, face-only affect detection systems seem likely to suffer from considerable missing data. Interaction-only detectors suffered less from missing data, but accuracy was significantly worse than for face-only detectors in this context. Our multimodal fusion solution offered 98% availability in the wild with better accuracy than the interaction-only method and equivalent to face-only detection. The next step is to embed our multimodal affect detection into intelligent, adaptive educational interfaces for use in computer-enabled classrooms.

5. ACKNOWLEDGMENTS

This research was supported by the National Science Foundation (NSF) (DRL 1235958) and the Bill & Melinda Gates Foundation. Any opinions, findings and conclusions, or recommendations expressed in this paper are those of the authors and do not necessarily reflect the views of the NSF or the Bill & Melinda Gates Foundation.

6. REFERENCES

1. Paul D. Allison. 1999. *Multiple regression: A primer*. Pine Forge Press.
2. Ivon Arroyo, David G. Cooper, Winslow Burleson, Beverly Park Woolf, Kasia Muldner, and Robert Christopherson. 2009. Emotion sensors go to school. *Proceedings of the 14th International Conference on Artificial Intelligence in Education*, IOS Press, 17–24.
3. Ryan Baker, Sujith M. Gowda, Michael Wixon, et al. 2012. Towards sensor-free affect detection in cognitive tutor algebra. *Proceedings of the 5th International Conference on Educational Data Mining*, 126–133.
4. Ryan Baker and Jaclyn Ocumpaugh. 2015. Interaction-based affect detection in educational software. In *The Oxford Handbook of Affective Computing*, Rafael Calvo, Sidney D'Mello, J. Gratch and A. Kappas (eds.). New York: Oxford University Press, 233–245.
5. Ryan Baker, Jaclyn Ocumpaugh, Sujith M. Gowda, Amy M. Kamarainen, and Shari J. Metcalf. 2014. Extending log-based affect detection to a multi-user virtual environment for science. *22nd Conference on User Modeling, Adaptation and Personalization (UMAP 2014)*, Springer, 290–300.
6. Ryan Baker and Kalina Yacef. 2009. The state of educational data mining in 2009: A review and future visions. *Journal of Educational Data Mining* 1, 1: 3–16.
7. Nigel Bosch, Sidney D'Mello, Ryan Baker, et al. 2015. Automatic detection of learning-centered affective states in the wild. *Proceedings of the 2015 International Conference on Intelligent User Interfaces (IUI 2015)*, New York, NY: ACM, 379–388.
8. R.A. Calvo and Sidney D'Mello. 2010. Affect detection: An interdisciplinary review of models, methods, and their applications. *IEEE Transactions on Affective Computing* 1, 1: 18–37.
9. N. V. Chawla, K. W. Bowyer, L. O. Hall, and W. P. Kegelmeyer. 2011. SMOTE: synthetic minority over-sampling technique. *Journal of Artificial Intelligence Research* 16: 321–357.
10. Desmond L. Cook. 1962. The Hawthorne effect in educational research. *Phi Delta Kappan*: 116–122.
11. Joseph F. Grafsgaard, Joseph B. Wiggins, Kristy Elizabeth Boyer, Eric N. Wiebe, and James C. Lester. 2013.

Automatically recognizing facial expression: Predicting engagement and frustration. *Proceedings of the 6th International Conference on Educational Data Mining.*
12. Joseph F. Grafsgaard, Joseph B. Wiggins, Alexandria Katarina Vail, Kristy Elizabeth Boyer, Eric N. Wiebe, and James C. Lester. 2014. The additive value of multimodal features for predicting engagement, frustration, and learning during tutoring. *Proceedings of the 16th International Conference on Multimodal Interaction*, ACM, 42–49.
13. G. Holmes, A. Donkin, and I.H. Witten. 1994. WEKA: a machine learning workbench. *Proceedings of the Second Australian and New Zealand Conference on Intelligent Information Systems*, 357–361.
14. L.A Jeni, J.F. Cohn, and F. de la Torre. 2013. Facing imbalanced data–Recommendations for the use of performance metrics. *2013 Humaine Association Conference on Affective Computing and Intelligent Interaction (ACII)*, 245–251.
15. Shiming Kai, Luc Paquette, Ryan Baker, et al. 2015. Comparison of face-based and interaction-based affect detectors in physics playground. *Proceedings of the 8th International Conference on Educational Data Mining (EDM 2015)*, International Educational Data Mining Society, 77–84.
16. Ashish Kapoor, Winslow Burleson, and Rosalind W. Picard. 2007. Automatic prediction of frustration. *International Journal of Human-Computer Studies* 65, 8: 724–736.
17. Ashish Kapoor and Rosalind W. Picard. 2005. Multimodal affect recognition in learning environments. *Proceedings of the 13th Annual ACM International Conference on Multimedia*, ACM, 677–682.
18. Igor Kononenko. 1994. Estimating attributes: Analysis and extensions of RELIEF. In *Machine Learning: ECML-94*, Francesco Bergadano and Luc De Raedt (eds.). Springer, Berlin Heidelberg, 171–182.
19. Gwen Littlewort, J. Whitehill, Tingfan Wu, et al. 2011. The computer expression recognition toolbox (CERT). *2011 IEEE International Conference on Automatic Face Gesture Recognition and Workshops (FG 2011)*, 298–305.
20. Sidney D'Mello. 2011. Dynamical emotions: Bodily dynamics of affect during problem solving. *Proceedings of the 33rd Annual Conference of the Cognitive Science Society.*
21. Sidney D'Mello. 2013. A selective meta-analysis on the relative incidence of discrete affective states during learning with technology. *Journal of Educational Psychology* 105, 4: 1082–1099.
22. Sidney D'Mello, Nathan Blanchard, Ryan Baker, Jaclyn Ocumpaugh, and Keith Brawner. 2014. I feel your pain: A selective review of affect-sensitive instructional strategies. In *Design Recommendations for Intelligent Tutoring Systems - Volume 2: Instructional Management*, Robert Sottilare, Art Graesser, Xiangen Hu and Benjamin Goldberg (eds.). 35–48.
23. Sidney D'Mello and Art Graesser. 2010. Multimodal semi-automated affect detection from conversational cues, gross body language, and facial features. *User Modeling and User-Adapted Interaction* 20, 2: 147–187.
24. Sidney D'Mello, Tanner Jackson, Scotty Craig, et al. 2008. AutoTutor detects and responds to learners affective and cognitive states. *Workshop on Emotional and Cognitive Issues at the International Conference on Intelligent Tutoring Systems.*
25. Sidney D'Mello and Jacqueline Kory. 2015. A review and meta-analysis of multimodal affect detection systems. *ACM Computing Surveys* 47, 3: 43:1–43:36.
26. Jaclyn Ocumpaugh, Ryan Baker, Amy Kamarainen, and Shari Metcalf. 2014. Modifying field observation methods on the fly: Creative metanarrative and disgust in an environmental MUVE. *Proceedings of the 4th International Workshop on Personalization Approaches in Learning Environments (PALE), held in conjunction with the 22nd International Conference on User Modeling, Adaptation, and Personalization (UMAP 2014)*, 49–54.
27. Jaclyn Ocumpaugh, Ryan Baker, and Ma Mercedes T. Rodrigo. 2012. *Baker-Rodrigo observation method protocol (BROMP) 1.0. Training manual version 1.0.* Technical Report. New York, NY: EdLab. Manila, Philippines: Ateneo Laboratory for the Learning Sciences.
28. Luc Paquette, Ryan S.J.d. Baker, Michael Sao Pedro, et al. 2014. Sensor-Free Affect Detection for a Simulation-Based Science Inquiry Learning Environment. *Proceedings of the 12th International Conference on Intelligent Tutoring Systems, ITS 2014*, 1–10.
29. Zachary a. Pardos, Ryan S.J.d. Baker, Maria O. C. Z. San Pedro, Sujith M. Gowda, and Supreeth M. Gowda. 2014. Affective states and state tests: Investigating how affect and engagement during the school year predict end of year learning outcomes. *Journal of Learning Analytics* 1, 1: 107–128.
30. Kaśka Porayska-Pomsta, Manolis Mavrikis, Sidney D'Mello, Cristina Conati, and Ryan Baker. 2013. Knowledge elicitation methods for affect modelling in education. *International Journal of Artificial Intelligence in Education* 22, 3: 107–140.
31. Valerie Shute and Matthew Ventura. 2013. *Measuring and supporting learning in games: Stealth assessment*. The MIT Press, Cambridge, MA.
32. J. Whitehill, Z. Serpell, Yi-Ching Lin, A Foster, and J.R. Movellan. 2014. The faces of engagement: Automatic recognition of student engagement from facial expressions. *IEEE Transactions on Affective Computing* 5, 1: 86–98.
33. Z. Zeng, M. Pantic, G.I. Roisman, and T.S. Huang. 2009. A survey of affect recognition methods: Audio, visual, and spontaneous expressions. *IEEE Transactions on Pattern Analysis and Machine Intelligence* 31, 1: 39–58.

Dynamic Active Learning Based on Agreement and Applied to Emotion Recognition in Spoken Interactions

Yue Zhang
Department of Computing
Imperial College London
London, U.K.
yue.zhang1@imperial.ac.uk

Eduardo Coutinho
Department of Computing
Imperial College London
London, U.K.
e.coutinho@imperial.ac.uk

Zixing Zhang
Chair of Complex & Intelligent Systems
University of Passau
Passau, Germany
Zixing.Zhang@uni-passau.de

Caijiao Quan
Machine Intelligence & Signal Processing group, MMK
Technische Universität München
Munich, Germany

Björn Schuller
Department of Computing
Imperial College London
London, U.K.
bjoern.schuller@imperial.ac.uk

ABSTRACT

In this contribution, we propose a novel method for Active Learning (AL) - *Dynamic Active Learning (DAL)* - which targets the reduction of the costly human labelling work necessary for modelling subjective tasks such as emotion recognition in spoken interactions. The method implements an adaptive query strategy that minimises the amount of human labelling work by deciding for each instance whether it should automatically be labelled by machine or manually by human, as well as how many human annotators are required. Extensive experiments on standardised test-beds show that DAL significantly improves the efficiency of conventional AL. In particular, DAL achieves the same classification accuracy obtained with AL with up to 79.17 % less human annotation effort.

Categories and Subject Descriptors

H.4 [**Information Systems Applications**]: Affective Computing and Human-Machine-Interaction

General Terms

Algorithm, Experimentation

Keywords

Active Learning; Adaptive Query Strategy; Speech Emotion Recognition; Acoustics

ICMI 2015, November 9–13, 2015, Seattle, WA, USA.
© 2015 ACM. ISBN 978-1-4503-3912-4/15/11 ...$15.00.
DOI: http://dx.doi.org/10.1145/2818346.2820774.

1. INTRODUCTION

In recent years, research on recognition of human emotion from natural speech has received increasing attention due to its manifold applications in human-machine communication, human-robot communication, and multimedia retrieval. In this light, one of the major barriers is the scarcity of annotated realistic speech data, which are of paramount importance for subjective tasks [15, 14], but are time-consuming and expensive to obtain. To overcome this limitation, a plethora of approaches in machine learning have been proposed for the exploitation of unlabelled data, which is nowadays pervasive in digital format and relatively easy and inexpensive to acquire (e. g., from public resources such as social media). Among others, the most prevailing approaches are Semi-Supervised Learning (SSL) [18], Active Learning (AL) [9] and various combinations thereof [12, 19]. AL algorithms aim at improving a model's performance by 'actively' choosing the 'most informative' instances from a large pool of unlabelled data, and passing them to human oracles for labelling. There are various measures by which the informativeness of unlabelled samples can be accessed (commonly referred to as *query strategies* [9]). One of the easiest methods is to determine the uncertainty of the predictions on unlabelled data based on a previously trained model (uncertainty sampling), and then query an annotator for labelling the instances with the least certain classification [17]. Other query strategies evaluating the informativeness of unlabelled instances include the query-by-committee method, which compares multiple competing models for the same task [4]; the expected-error-reduction method, which aims to measure how much its generalization error is likely to be reduced [6]; the expected-model-change-based method, which selects those instances that have a greater impact on the current model [10]; and the diversity-density-related method, which aims to maximise the learning benefits of relevance feedback on retrieving documents [13]. One major drawback regarding these conventional AL algorithms is that a fixed number of human annotators is set for all instances to be labelled (hereinafter referred to as 'Static' AL or SAL). As a consequence of this constraint, SAL still requires a considerable amount of human labelling work and thus can be impractical in many cases. This fact motivates us to propose a novel avenue of research for AL algorithms – Dynamic Active Learning (DAL) – that shifts the perspective from standard majority voting procedures to an agreement based annotation strategy. The core underlying principle is simple – instead of requesting all available annotators and then forming the majority of their votes, we adapt the number of annotators for each instance to a certain task-specific agreement level (i. e., a certain number of votes for a common category, e. g., class label). In this way, the DAL approach leads to the same gold standard as with majority voting while omitting dispensable annotations, thus dramatically reducing the annotation effort.

The rest of this paper is organised as follows: In Section 2, we describe in detail the DAL algorithm. Then, we introduce the database and the feature set used to evaluate the DAL algorithm in Sections 3 and 4, respectively. The experimental settings and results are presented in Sections 5.1 and 5.2. Finally, in Section 6 we discuss our findings and impulses for future work.

2. METHODOLOGY

A common and straightforward decision rule in SAL is majority voting among multiple raters, who are considered equally reliable. It is evident that querying a fixed number of annotators for each instance as being implemented in SAL is a rather ineffective method. The DAL approach aims to avoid this disadvantage by following the intuitive assumption that in the context of subjective tasks, the higher the inter-rater agreement is, the more established the resulting gold-standard label is.

2.1 SVM and Prediction Uncertainty

Similar to conventional AL, the dynamic active learner actively selects the data from which it learns by considering the prediction uncertainty of the trained classifier in terms of confidence values. For this purpose, we apply Support Vector Machines (SVMs) that construct decision hyperplanes to separate instances of different classes, while maximising the functional margin. For each instance, the output distances to the decision boundaries are then transformed into probability values through a parametric method of logistic regression [5]. For the selection of the instances to be annotated at each iteration, we use a medium certainty query strategy, which has the potential advantage of avoiding the selection of noisy instances, as shown in [16].

2.2 Agreement Levels

Given the number n of annotators who are available for labelling a specific database, we define the *agreement level* as the minimum number of raters agreeing on one common category. Accordingly, $j \in \{1, ..., \lfloor\frac{n+1}{2}\rfloor\}$, with $j, n \in \mathbb{N}$, agreement levels can be selected. For the upper limit of the interval, the floor is considered with regard to even numbers of annotators. Specifically, $n' \in \{j, ..., 2j-1\}, n' \in \mathbb{N}$ raters might be needed until a certain agreement level j is achieved. The SAL performance that is achieved through majority voting among all n raters is defined as the baseline of our experiments.

2.3 Algorithms and Data Structure

For the applied algorithm, we define the following notations: $\mathcal{L} = ([\mathbf{x}_1, y_1], \ldots, [\mathbf{x}_l, y_l]), i = 1, 2, ..., l$, denotes a small set of labelled training data, where $\mathbf{x}_i$ is a d-dimensional feature vector, and y_i is the assigned emotion-related label. Additionally, a large pool of unlabelled data $\mathcal{U} = (\mathbf{x}'_1, \ldots, \mathbf{x}'_u), k = 1, 2, ...u$, exists where $u \gg l$ and $\mathbf{x}'_k$ is a d-dimensional feature vector. The number of votes for a specific class label y' that is manually assigned to an example instance $\mathbf{x}' \in \mathcal{N}_a$ is named v'. Figure 1 shows the pseudo-code description of the DAL algorithm. The learning process starts by training a model on the labelled data $\mathcal{L}$ and subsequently using this model to classify all instances of the unlabelled data pool $\mathcal{U}$. According to the medium certainty query strategy, a subset $\mathcal{N}_a \subset \mathcal{U}$ is selected and submitted to human annotation. The sequential process is repeated until a certain number of instances are annotated. The main improvement compared to the SAL method is presented in the fifth item. The stopping criterion for manual labelling of each instance is fulfilled when the predefined agreement level for a specific task has been achieved.

Algorithm: *Dynamic Active Learning (DAL)*
Repeat:

1. (Optional) Upsample the training set $\mathcal{L}$ to obtain even class distribution $\mathcal{L}_D$
2. Use $\mathcal{L}/\mathcal{L}_D$ to train a classifier $\mathcal{H}$, and then classify the unlabelled data set $\mathcal{U}$
3. Rank the data based on the prediction confidence values C and store them in a queue
4. Select a subset $\mathcal{N}_a$ with medium certainty
5. **For** each instance $\mathbf{x}'$ in $\mathcal{N}_a$
   (a) Randomise the query order of raters
   (b) Submit $\mathbf{x}'$ to the first j raters
   (c) If $v' = j$; **STOP**
   else **repeat**: select one rater for annotation
   until agreement level j is achieved
   (d) Assign y' to $\mathbf{x}'$
6. Remove $\mathcal{N}_a$ from the unlabelled set $\mathcal{U}$, $\mathcal{U} = \mathcal{U} \setminus \mathcal{N}_a$
7. Add $\mathcal{N}_a$ to the labelled set $\mathcal{L}$, $\mathcal{L} = \mathcal{L} \cup \mathcal{N}_a$

Figure 1: Pseudocode description of the DAL algorithm based on the medium certainty strategy for a predefined agreement level j.

3. DATABASE

In our experiments, we use the FAU Aibo Emotion Corpus (AEC) [11] of the INTERSPEECH 2009 Emotion Challenge (IS09 EC) [8, 7]. The database contains spontaneous and emotionally coloured speech of children interacting with Sony's pet robot Aibo. The recordings were taken from 51 children (age 10-13, about 9.2 hours of speech without pauses) at two different schools, referred to as 'MONT' and 'OHM'. For binary classification, the emotional states are categorised into the classes **NEG**(agative) and **IDL**(e). The frequencies for the two-class problem are given in Table 1.

Table 1: **Distribution of speakers and instances per partition of the FAU AEC dataset. M: male; F: female; NEG: negative emotions; IDL: neutral and positive emotions.**

	# speakers		# instances per class		
FAU AEC	M	F	NEG	IDL	Σ
Pool	13	13	3 358	6 601	9 959
Validation	8	17	2 465	5 792	8 257
Σ	21	30	5 823	12 393	18 216

4. SELECTED ACOUSTIC FEATURES

The acoustic features used in our experiments are adopted from the baseline feature set of IS09 EC. This is created with the openSMILE framework [2, 1] by applying statistical functionals to frame-wise low-level-descriptors (LLDs). To each of the 16 LLDs, the delta coefficients are computed. Finally, the 12 functionals are applied on a per-chunk level. As result of the 'brute-forcing' method, the total feature vector per chunk contains $16 \times 2 \times 12 = 384$ attributes.

5. EXPERIMENTS AND RESULTS

In the following, we investigate the performance of the DAL algorithm by evaluating the classification accuracy in relation to the number of human annotations. The optimised results are compared with the SAL baseline performance.

5.1 Experimental Setup

For transparency and reproducibility, we used open-source classifier implementations of SVMs from the WEKA data mining toolkit [3]. As classifiers, we chose linear kernel SVMs trained with a complexity parameter C constant of 0.05 and with Sequential Minimal Optimization (SMO), as they are robust against over-fitting in high dimensional feature spaces. For initial training of the model, 200 instances were randomly selected from the training data, whereas the remaining instances were used as the unlabelled data pool. At each learning iteration, we selected a subset $\mathcal{N}_a$ comprising 200 instances to be submitted to manual annotation. The learning process stopped after 4 800 instances had been manually annotated, where the total number of human annotations differs in each experimental scenario. The training process was repeated 20 times with randomly generated initializations. As evaluation measure, we considered the unweighted average recall (UAR).

5.2 Discussion of Results

Table 2: **Relative cost reduction (CR) measured by the number of human annotations and comparing DAL on agreement levels $j = 1, 2, 3$ with the SAL baseline at UAR_{max}**

	UAR_{max}	CR (%)
SAL	68.79	–
j=3	68.79	25.58
j=2	68.84	54.83
j=1	68.38	79.17

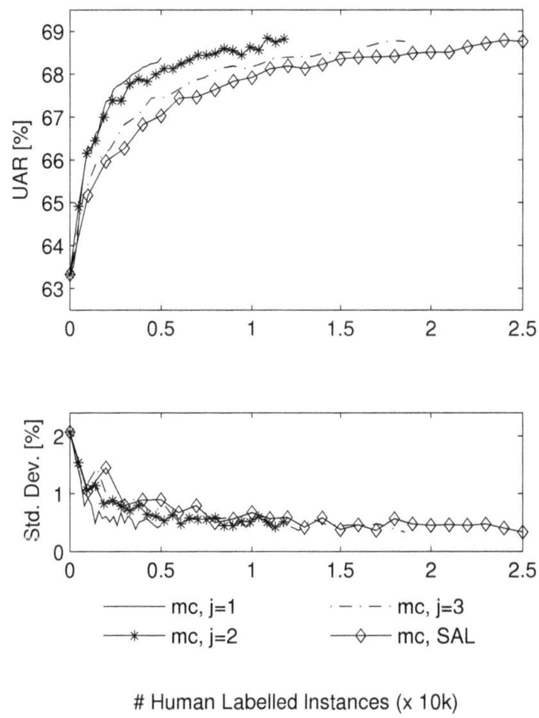

Figure 2: **Dynamic Active Learning (DAL) vs Static Active Learning (SAL): the performance measures show the UAR values averaged across 20 runs of the algorithm and the respective standard deviations vs the number of human annotations.**

Figure 2 shows the characteristic curve progression of AL: the sequential addition of human-labelled instances to the initial training set leads to continuous improvements in the performance of the classifier. More importantly, it can be clearly seen that all DAL curves corresponding to the different agreement levels are above the SAL baseline. This marked 'shrinking' effect demonstrates a dramatic cost reduction in the sense that less human annotations are required to achieve the same classification accuracy. In order to substantiate our findings, we compare the costs measured by the number of human annotations at the highest UAR (UAR_{max}) achieved by each method. According to Table 2, the relative cost reduction (CR) increases with lower agreement levels. Finally, the analysis of standard deviation shows that the stability of the model is enhanced during the learning process.

6. CONCLUSIONS AND FUTURE WORK

In this paper, we introduced a novel approach for Dynamic Active Learning that allows significant reduction of the costly human labelling work by adapting the number of human annotators for each instance to a predefined agreement level. In particular, our results demonstrate that the DAL method leads to the same performance of the trained model, but requires up to 79.17 % less human annotations with the medium certainty (*mc*)query strategy. For future research, we will investigate the robustness of the DAL method by conducting experiments with multiple corpora, different feature sets, and varying amount of initial training instances.

7. ACKNOWLEDGMENTS

The research leading to these results has received funding from the European Union's Framework Programme for Research and Innovation HORIZON 2020 under the Grant No. 645378 (ARIA-VALUSPA) and the European Union's Seventh Framework Programme under the ERC Starting Grant No. 338164 (iHEARu).

8. REFERENCES

[1] F. Eyben, F. Weninger, F. Groß, and B. Schuller. Recent developments in opensmile, the munich open-source multimedia feature extractor. In *Proc. of ACM MM*, pages 835–838, Barcelona, Spain, 2013.

[2] F. Eyben, M. Wöllmer, and B. Schuller. openSMILE – the Munich versatile and fast open-source audio feature extractor. In *Proc. of ACM MM*, pages 1459–1462, Florence, Italy, 2010.

[3] M. Hall, E. Frank, G. Holmes, B. Pfahringer, P. Reutemann, and I. H. Witten. The WEKA data mining software: an update. *ACM SIGKDD Explorations Newsletter*, 11(1):10–18, 2009.

[4] R. Liere and P. Tadepalli. Active learning with committees for text categorization. In *Proc. of AAAI/IAAI*, pages 591–596, Providence, RI, 1997.

[5] J. Platt. Probabilistic outputs for support vector machines and comparisons to regularized likelihood methods. In A. Smola, P. Bartlett, B. Schölkopf, and D. Schuurmans, editors, *Advances in large margin classifiers*, pages 61–74. MIT Press, Cambridge, MA, 1999.

[6] N. Roy and A. McCallum. Toward optimal active learning through sampling estimation of error reduction. In *Proc. of ICML*, pages 441–448, Williamstown, MA, 2001.

[7] B. Schuller. The computational paralinguistics challenge. *IEEE Signal Processing Magazine*, 29(4):97–101, 2012.

[8] B. Schuller, S. Steidl, and A. Batliner. The INTERSPEECH 2009 emotion challenge. In *Proc. of INTERSPEECH*, pages 312–315, Brighton, UK, 2009.

[9] B. Settles. Active learning literature survey. Technical report, Department of Computer Sciences, University of Wisconsin–Madison, Wisconsin, WI, 2009.

[10] B. Settles and M. Craven. An analysis of active learning strategies for sequence labeling tasks. In *Proc. of Empirical Methods in Natural Language Processing (EMNLP)*, pages 1070–1079, Honolulu, HY, 2008.

[11] S. Steidl. *Automatic Classification of Emotion-Related User States in Spontaneous Children's Speech*. Logos Verlag, Berlin, 2009.

[12] G. Tur, D. Hakkani-Tür, and R. E. Schapire. Combining active and semi-supervised learning for spoken language understanding. *Speech Communication*, 45(2):171–186, 2005.

[13] Z. Xu, R. Akella, and Y. Zhang. Incorporating diversity and density in active learning for relevance feedback. In *Proc. of European Conference on Information Retrieval (ECIR)*, pages 246–257, Rome, Italy, 2007.

[14] Y. Zhang, E. Coutinho, Z. Zhang, M. Adam, and B. Schuller. On Rater Reliability and Correlation Based Dynamic Active Learning. In *Proc. 6th biannual Conference on Affective Computing and Intelligent Interaction (ACII 2015)*, Xi'an, P. R. China, 2015. AAAC, IEEE. 7 pages.

[15] Y. Zhang, E. Coutinho, Z. Zhang, C. Quan, and B. Schuller. Agreement-based Dynamic Active Learning with Least and Medium Certainty Query Strategy. In *Proc. Advances in Active Learning : Bridging Theory and Practice Workshop held in conjunction with the 32nd International Conference on Machine Learning, ICML 2015*, Lille, France, 2015. International Machine Learning Society, IMLS. 5 pages.

[16] Z. Zhang and B. Schuller. Active learning by sparse instance tracking and classifier confidence in acoustic emotion recognition. In *Proc. of INTERSPEECH*, Portland, OR, 2012. 4 pages.

[17] J. Zhu, H. Wang, B. K. Tsou, and M. Ma. Active learning with sampling by uncertainty and density for data annotations. *IEEE Transactions on Audio, Speech, and Language Processing*, 18(6):1323 –1331, 2010.

[18] X. Zhu. Semi-supervised learning literature survey. Technical Report TR 1530, Department of Computer Sciences, University of Wisconsin at Madison, Madison, WI, 2006.

[19] X. Zhu, J. Lafferty, and Z. Ghahramani. Combining active learning and semi-supervised learning using Gaussian fields and harmonic functions. In *ICML 2003 workshop on the continuum from labeled to unlabeled data in machine learning and data mining*, pages 58–65, Washington DC, 2003.

Sharing Touch Interfaces: Proximity-Sensitive Touch Targets for Tablet-Mediated Collaboration

Ilhan Aslan[1,2], Thomas Meneweger[1], Verena Fuchsberger[1], and Manfred Tscheligi[1]
[1]Christian-Doppler-Laboratory "Contextual Interfaces", Center for HCI, Universtiy of Salzburg, Austria
[2]Human-Centered Multimedia Lab, University of Augsburg, Germany
[1]firstname.lastname@sbg.ac.at, [2]aslan@hcm-lab.de

ABSTRACT

During conversational practices, such as a tablet-mediated sales conversation between a salesperson and a customer, tablets are often used by two users who prefer specific bodily formations in order to easily face each other and the surface of the touchscreen. In a series of studies, we investigated bodily formations that are preferred during tablet-mediated sales conversations, and explored the effect of these formations on performance in acquiring touch targets (e.g., buttons) on a tablet device. We found that bodily formations cause decreased viewing angles to the shared screen, which results in a decreased performance in target acquisition. In order to address this issue, a multi-modal design consideration is presented, which combines mid-air finger movement and touch into a unified input modality, allowing the design of proximity sensitive touch targets. We conclude that the proposed embodied interaction design not only has potential to improve targeting performance, but also adapts the "agency" of touch targets for multi-user settings.

Keywords

touch interface design; target acquisition; sharing interfaces; situated constraints

Categories and Subject Descriptors

H.5.2. [**Information Interfaces and Presentation**]: User Interfaces - Interaction styles;

1. INTRODUCTION

For more than a decade, touch as an input modality has shaped the design of screen-based interfaces on mobile devices (e.g., tablets), including the visual design of buttons, sliders, etc. Since mobile devices are used in varying contexts, related work (e.g., [13, 15, 28] investigated target acquisition, as a key factor, which defines the performance of a touch interface in a specific context of use. In studies investigating target acquisition, typically the position of actual touch in relation to the position of the target that was aimed for is used to inform future designs, such as making suggestions on beneficial sizes and positions for touch targets. In this paper, we investigate target acquisition, focussing on social context (i.e., tablet-mediated sales conversations between two persons). Thus, our aim is an informed design consideration for touch targets on mobile devices, which improves target acquisition during device-mediated conversational practices and multi-user interaction.

To do this, the following research questions are addressed:

- RQ1: Are there situated constraints affecting target acquisition during a tablet-mediated conversational practice (i.e., a sales conversation)?
- RQ2: How can we address situated constraints through interaction design, including multi-modal solutions?

In the following section, we first describe the background of our work. Then results from our inquiries in tablet mediated sales are presented, including two focus groups and a subsequent lab study. Afterwards, (negative) effects on target acquisition due to decreased viewing angles to the shared screen in preferred bodily formations are addressed. Therefore, several design considerations for touch targets are discussed resulting in the implementation of one multi-modal solution, in which touch targets adapt to the proximity of a finger mid-air before touch (e.g., moving towards the finger).

Based on a workshop with experts and the prototype system, we conclude that in addition to a potential for improving targeting performance, the multi-modal solution augments a touch target's agency by providing them the means to signify "its" intention (e.g., wanting to be touched) and act on it. We also discuss how unification of touch and mid-air modalities could transform the landscape of screen-based interface design for future touch interfaces.

2. BACKGROUND

In the retail area, counter free stores are a recent trend (e.g., in Apple stores), where desktop computers are replaced by mobile touch-based interfaces. These mobile interfaces assist and mediate during daily sales conversations, which are as social practices associated with embodied processes; e.g., specific body postures and bodily formations taken by conversing co-located persons. In the following, we describe related work in target acquisition, which mainly focusses on single user scenarios. Then methods to improve performance in target acquisition are summarized, which have been proposed to improve targeting when interaction is somehow con-

ICMI 2015, November 9–13, 2015, Seattle, WA, USA.

DOI: http://dx.doi.org/10.1145/2818346.2820740.

strained by the context. Afterwards we return to the particular social context of tablet mediated conversations and summarize related research in (touch-based) interaction in the presence of co-located persons.

2.1 Target Acquisition and Fitts's Law

Related work in target acquisition has, for example investigated how touch targets are acquired by a user in a seated posture [15], how they are acquired on a mobile device during walking [28], and how target location on the screen of a mobile influences target acquisition during general everyday usage [13]. Results inform the design of touch targets, for example that expanding touch targets counter-balances the negative effect in target acquisition during walking [28], or that by separating the virtual touch area and the graphical area of the touch target errors due to behavioral patterns (e.g., how users systematically miss the center of a button) can be addressed (e.g., [13]).

Essentially, acquiring target objects on touch screens involves aimed movements. Thus, a variety of designs exist that aim to improve target acquisition, referring to Fitts's law [9]. Fitts's law provides a model for aimed movements that predicts the time of successful movements by referring to a trade-off between speed and accuracy [25]. It states that when the interaction setting is fix (e.g., the same pointing "device" is used in repeated aimed movements) the difference in movement time dependents only in "distance to the target" and "size of the target". A formula is provided that explains in detail how an aimed successful movement takes more time when the target is further away and how it takes less time when a target's size is expanded and vice versa. However, when touch targets represent real world objects additional semantic measures may also influence targeting performance [3].

2.2 Adaptive (Touch) Targets

As a consequence to the speed-accuracy trade-off researchers have studied compromises by proposing a multitude of methods to increase target sizes. For example, Albinson and Zhai [1] propose techniques for manually zooming in areas on the screen in order to perform subsequent pointing of a finer scale. Similar techniques to improve accuracy in acquiring small targets on touch screens have been proposed by Roudaut et al. [27]. However, these kinds of manually zooming techniques often require additional interactions, concluding in lower performance (i.e., task completion times).

Another way to improve performance is to use multi-modal solutions, allowing automatic target expansion techniques (e.g., [7, 24, 29]), which use additional sensors to compute context information (e.g., proximity to targets) and alter target sizes automatically, depending (solely) on the context information without requiring additional interactions. McGuffin and Balakrishnan [24] have studied the relation between Fitts's law (which is based on static targets sizes) and expanding targets. In their studies targets (i.e., widgets on the screen) expanded depending on the proximity of a mouse pointer. They have shown that Fitts's law is applicable to expanding targets and that movement time depends (solely) on the final target width [24].

Yang et al. [29] have studied how expanding targets could be used to allow touch-based interaction with laptop user interfaces (i.e., how UI components could be transitioned based on off-screen movement of user's index finger for touch-based use). They implemented *TouchCuts* and *TouchZoom* as expansion techniques for single and multiple targets and showed that selection times could be reduced with expanding targets and touch-based input in comparison to a mouse. Many of the earlier work (e.g., [24, 29]) took mouse-based interfaces with small targets and aimed to optimize them for touch-based interaction through target expansion techniques.

In comparison, Chen et al. [7] have recently studied mid-air movements of fingers before, after, and in-between touch events in one-handed touch based interaction. They have explored how touch and mid-air movement could be in general interwoven in order to create a unified input modality for mobiles, which already have interfaces designed for touch-based interaction.

Device interaction taking place with co-present people (e.g., [5, 30]), and especially group interaction with touch interfaces such as tabletops (e.g., [17, 18, 22]) has already been in the focus of research. However, as far as we know, research has not yet investigated group interaction on mobile devices, addressing situated constraints for target acquisition and the design of touch targets for collaborative settings and small sized mobile screens. Similar to related work in adaptive targets, we do not restrict ourselves to capabilities of touch screens but also consider additional design options, which result when for instance touch is combined with mid-air finger movement into a unified input modality.

2.3 Tablet-mediated Conversations

The way people spatially arrange themselves during face to face communications is described by Kendon as F-formation [19]. F-formations have been utilized in related work to analyze how users arrange themselves around tabletops and discuss potentials of technology to transform space [23] in order to constrain or encourage shared activities. What is suggested is, that in the presence of a mobile device with a surface for presenting relevant information and mediating the conversation, spatial arrangements are "disrupted". Similar to a third person the mobile with its surface influence how two conversing people spatially rearrange themselves in the presence of a third person.

Marshall et al. [23] argues that there is a need for analyzing face-to-face settings, since ubiquitous technology (e.g., mobile technology) is more and more introduced in these social settings with a potential to transform particular physical spaces and extend conversational practices [23]. This is also true for co-located sales conversations. For example, one could argue that the introduction of mobile devices as an assistant for sales persons causes the space in shops to change (e.g., counters are becoming obsolete since the sales process can be completed with the help of a mobile device).

Furthermore, the use of mobile devices during sales conversations, as we report in this paper, encourages specific F-formations between a sales person and a customer. While related results indicate that contextual factors, such as walking speed [20] influence target acquisition, the effect of specific F-formations taken during tablet mediated (sales) conversations remains unclear so far.

3. STUDY OF SITUATED CONSTRAINTS

We have argued that target acquisition can be influenced by context of use, such as bodily formations that are preferred during a tablet mediated conversation between two persons sharing the same touch screen. In order to identify such preferred bodily formations in a realistic and exemplified situation we conducted two focus groups, exploring how (professional) sales persons and (their) customers envision bodily formations during a tablet-mediated sales conversation. Afterwards, a lab study was performed to collect quantitative touch data and investigate the effect of bodily formations on target acquisition.

3.1 Focus Groups

3.1.1 Participants and Procedure

In the first focus group five experienced sales persons participated. They were employed in the telecommunications sector and thus have expert knowledge with and daily exposure to mobile devices. The sales persons were between 21 and 28 years of age and four of them were male and one female. For the second focus group we recruited six participants who reported to have recently bought items from a telecommunication shop. We recruited three male and three female customers, that were between 18 and 53 years old.

The focus groups were video recorded after the participants gave their informed consent. Two researchers, one moderating and another one taking notes, facilitated the focus groups. Both focus groups started with an open discussion regarding the relevant postures and F-formations coming along with a tablet-mediated sales-conversation. For this discussion up to one hour was reserved.

In both groups, participants were asked to discuss typical scenarios of sales situations where a tablet device could be used to assist during conversations. To support the participants anticipation of these future tablet-mediated sales situations we provided a tablet device (first generation iPad). Participants were asked to describe and demonstrate the situations (e.g., role play). During the focus group with customers the participants were additionally asked to discuss their view on using a tablet during a sales situation and how they evaluate the postures, as identified in the prior focus group with sales persons.

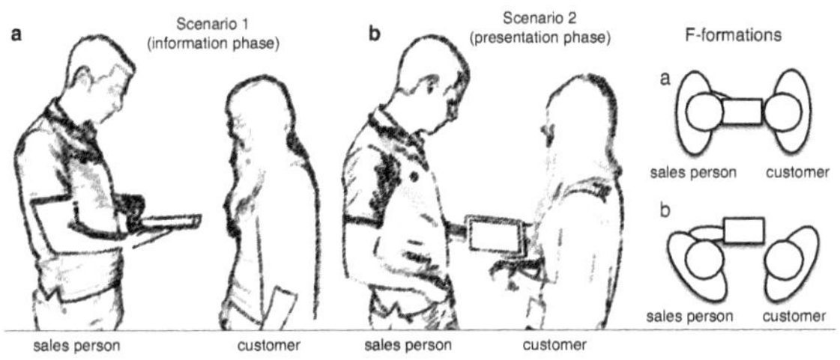

Figure 1: Resulting body postures during tablet mediated sales conversations and associated F-formations: a) Face to face b) L-arrangement

3.1.2 Findings

Figure 1 presents the two key bodily formations, which were identified with sales persons. Also presented on the right side of Figure 1 are the corresponding *tablet mediated F-formations*. No additional formations were required by the customers group. They reported that both formations are conceivable and acceptable for them as well. The two formations are tightly connected to two phases in a currently performed sales process: the information phase and the presentation phase, which we briefly describe in the following:

(a) Opposite each other during the information phase: The initial phase of a sales process is the information phase, the so-called needs analysis, where the salesperson talks to the customer and aims to identify her/his wishes and needs. The sales persons ask questions, aiming to detect for which purpose the customer wants the product. During this phase of the sales conversation, the salesperson positions himself right in front of the customer (see Figure 1a).

(b) Besides each other during the presentation phase: Based on the needs analysis the salesperson picks the products he/she will present to the customer. During this presentation phase the salesperson positions herself/himself beside the customer in an open position. As this F-formation provides a more comfortable and personal atmosphere, the salespersons take up this posture for making an offer or presenting a product (see Figure 1b).

3.2 Lab Study

Having identified the key bodily formations we next conducted a lab study with participants of both focus groups. Our aim was to explore the effect of these bodily formation on performance in target acquisition. Therefore, participants were asked to perform a target acquisition task repeatedly on an iPad device. For the study we used 10 participants. One participant from the customers group was excluded from the lab study, since we only chose to use right handed participants to reduce bias. The lab study was performed with one participant at a time. All participants completed the lab study within 10 minutes or less.

3.2.1 Study and Procedure

We asked participants to conduct the same target acquisition task in three different scenarios. Two of these scenarios represented the bodily formations, which we identified in the focus groups. The third scenario was a single user setting, which we used as a baseline for comparisons. Since the study was performed with one participant at a time a researcher took the part of the conversing partner to prototype the experience and simulate the social context [6]. With the salespersons the researcher positioned her/himself like a customer who needs to be able to interact with the display. In the study with customers the researcher held the mobile device the way a sales person would hold it.

In all three scenarios participants were asked to tap a cross line that was presented at the center of the iPad screen repeatedly and rapidly but also as precise as possible. We chose a cross line since similar tasks with cross lines have been proposed in related research (e.g., [15]). The order of the scenarios in which participants were asked to perform the trials were randomized in order to reduce any bias. In each setting participants repeated the task for exactly one minute, allowing us to collect data from 33 to 50 touches from each participant and each scenario.

3.2.2 Data Analysis

From each participant and each trial we collected data representing x and y coordinates of touch. We computed two measures explaining touch accuracy that we refer to as *x-offset* and *offset distance*. The range for *x-offset* was measured in pixel and from negative to positive values; i.e., a touch event that occurred left from the center of the cross

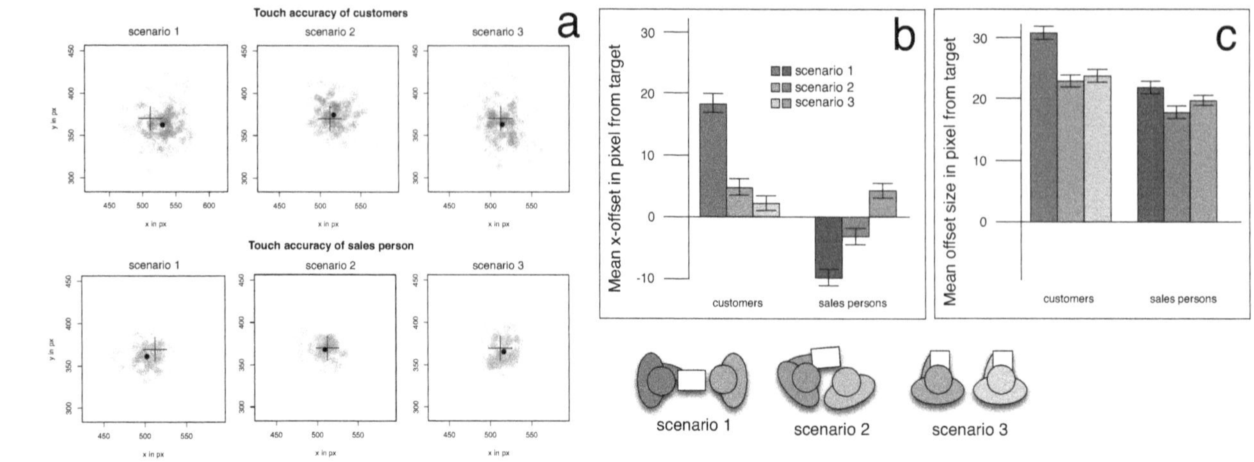

Figure 2: a) Overview of touch accuracy during the target acquisition task separated in 3 different scenarios and two groups of participants (i.e., customers and sales persons). Cross line represents the center of the target and the black dot the mean touch position during target acquisition over all participants. b) Overview of x-offset (negative values refer to trials where touch occurred left from the target and positive values refer to trials where touch occurred right from the target) and c) offset size (i.e., distance from the target independent from the exact position of touch). Error bars denote standard error of the mean.

line would result in a negative *x-offset* value and vice versa. Thus *x-offset* provided directional information. In contrast *offset distance* resulted always in positive values; i.e., how far away (in pixel) the touch event occurred from the center of the target object (i.e., the crossline).

Offset distance was chosen as a measure of general accuracy, showing any differences between sales person and customers. We expected a difference since the device is held by sales persons and therefore they should be able to target an object on the screen more accurately (using both hands for the task) than customers, who have to interact with the device while the device is being held by a sales person. We chose *x-offset* as an additional measure, since we expected to observe a directional effect; e.g., that participants standing on the left side of the tablet would touch the target object on the left side.

3.2.3 Results

Figure 2a shows that there seems to be a difference between customers' and sales persons' target acquisition behavior for scenarios one and two, which are the multi-user scenarios. In contrast, in scenario three, which is the baseline scenario (i.e., single user setting) the data shows no visible difference. The difference in the data for scenarios one and two is even more visible in Figure 2b, which shows mean values for *x-offset*. Participants indeed seem to be influenced by the spatial arrangement associated with bodily formations and viewing angles to the screen.

To study the significance of our observations we conducted subsequent statistical analyses. Since repeated measurements were collected from individuals a repeated measures ANOVA was computed, and to obtain the required balanced data set for this type of analysis, we used from each participant the first 33 trials for the statistical analysis (33 was the minimum number of trials done by any of the participants). Thus, 990 measures were used overall for the analyses collected from 10 participants in 3 different scenarios and 33 repetitions.

The repeated measures ANOVA showed that the type of participant (i.e., sales person or customer) had a main effect on *x-offset*; $F(1, 9) = 7.5$, $p<0.03$. Furthermore, we observed a highly significant interaction between type of participant and scenario $F(2, 8) = 26.3$, $p<0.001$. The interaction relates to how in scenario 1 the difference between customers and sales person is high and decreases for scenario 2 and even further decreases for scenario 3 (see Figure 2b).

The ANOVA for *offset size* as the independent variable showed that scenario had a main effect on *offset size*; $F(1, 9) = 5.0$, $p<0.02$. Worth mentioning is that type of user had no significant effect $F(1, 9) = 4.3$, $p=0.07$ on *offset size*. We conducted three post hoc comparisons using pairwise t-tests with adjusted p-values and identified that a significant difference between scenario 1 (M=26px, SD=15px) and scenario 2 (M=20px, SD=14px); $p<0.001$ and a significant difference between scenario 1 (M=26px, SD=15px) and scenario 3 (M=21px, SD=13px); $p<0.001$. No significant difference was found between scenario 2 (M=20px, SD=14px) and scenario 3 (M=21px, SD=13px);$p=0.2$.

3.2.4 Summary

The statistics we have computed (especially the highly significant interaction between type of participant and scenario, which is observable in Figure 2b) indeed support our main assumptions that scenario (bodily formation during multi-user settings) would have a significant effect on target acquisition. Only our additional assumption that because sales persons hold the device that they would achieve better accuracy (as measured with *offset size*) was rejected with a p-value of 0.07.

When participants had to perform the acquisition tasks in a multi-user setting we observed a great influence on touch accuracy; i.e., on offset size and even more on the directional (i.e., horizontal) offset which is explained by the measure *x-offset*. The offset we observed seems to depend on the viewing and approaching angle of the user and thus relative position of the user to the device.

A user standing left from the device tends to produce an offset left from the target and vice versa. Thus, two users sharing a tablet but targeting the same object on the screen have in mean 28px difference in touch accuracy. Since we used a first generation iPad with a pixel density of 132 pixel per inch, the mean difference of 28px is equal to 5mm. Consequently, the point that users actually touch while target the same target differs by 5 mm. In addition if the viewing and reaching angle to the device is wide, sharing also causes a significant increase in offset size in general, meaning that these situations are more error prone.

3.3 Design Considerations

In sum, our studies highlighted a significant difference in target acquisition between customers and sales persons depending on how they face each other and the shared tablet device. The derived problem statement entails that designing an interface for both user groups would result in very large target sizes.

The data we have collected and analyzed inspires several design options to deal with contrasting user groups and the dilemma of deciding whom the design should address (i.e, salespersons or customers). Instead of designing only for one user our aim is to have an implicit way of recognizing which user is interacting with the touch surface and adapting the virtual or physical position of the target. Common to the design considerations is a notion of embodiment (e.g., [8, 16]), which refers to broadly speaking making use of natural skills in humans based on how they interact in a physical and social world (e.g., making use of hand and finger ergonomics as well as behavioral patterns during conversations and sharing). Hereby our goal is to use automatic or adaptive methods, which do not overload the touch interaction, such as requiring users to perform additional interactions on the touch screen, such as "touch and hold" ([21]).

3.3.1 After-Touch Adaptation

Current operating systems and software development kits (SDKs) only use the position of touch for interaction. However, there are other dimensions such as finger pitch and yaw (e.g., [26]), or shear force (e.g., [14]), which could be used to address the design problem. They can only be sensed after a touch occurs. Nevertheless, these dimensions can be used to adapt positions of virtual touch targets, allowing an improved touch sensing in settings where small sized touch screens are shared. Finger jaw and pitch could be used to calculate the intended touch position of users taking into account that the user is not facing the touch screen directly. Similar to finger jaw and pitch, shear force could be used to identify the positions of virtual touch targets; however, current touch screens can not sense shear forces without for example additional device covers augmented with sensing technology (e.g., [14]). Depending on the shared situations further exploration would be needed to identify exact values of finger pitch and yaw, and to exactly calculate positions of virtual touch targets. While making use of additional dimensions in touch is a promising idea to address identified constraints in touch targeting there are also limitations. The main limitations is that any adaptation is only possible after a touch occurs. Therefore concrete designs, which follow this idea have potential to improve touch accuracy but not necessarily task completion times.

Another after-touch strategy is related to the device's position itself. There is some flexibility of how the mobile device is exactly held; i.e., the viewing angle of the person who is interacting with the device. Usually the angle is a little more towards the person who is interacting with the device. Consequently the device is being moved from an angle, which suits one person to an angle which suits the other person and vice versa. Using acceleration sensors embedded in the tablet device little movements of the device could be utilized to automatically identify who is interacting with the interface. Consequently, positions of virtual touch targets could be changed, whenever the device is moved in a certain way.

3.3.2 Pre-Touch Adaptations

A slightly different approach is to adapt targets before a touch occurs. Hereby, the proximity (and direction) of an approaching hand (belonging to either the salesperson or the customer) could be sensed to adapt the interface to a person. In addition to being able to identify the user (e.g., differentiate between a sales person and a customer) a main benefit of this approach is that consequent adaptations could not only improve target acquisition in constraint situations but also influence targeting time.

For example, single targets could receive situated priority depending on the probability that a user intends to hit the target. Single targets (or virtual targets) could be expanded or moved towards the approaching finger while other targets would receive low situated priority and could shrink or move away. Yang et al. [29] have demonstrated that through finger proximity sensing it is possible to make an otherwise touch unfriendly interface usable. They have explored interaction techniques (e.g., touch-zoom and touch-cut) to improve touch-based interaction with small targets by expanding targets using finger proximity. Proximity sensing has been used for different modalities in the past mainly to improve targeting time (e.g., [11]).

Furthermore, proximity is a physical measure, which plays an important role in sense making in human-environment interaction, including human-human interaction. A paradigmatic example is proxemics [12] a research area in the social sciences dealing with interpersonal distance, it's subjective meaning (e.g., due to culture) and how people interpret and use it in everyday interpersonal interactions. Thus, there is great potential of proximity-sensitive target adaptation strategies for the aforementioned tablet mediated social contexts, including the identified bodily formations. In order to study this potential, we implemented a prototype and explored different proximity-sensitive target adaptation strategies, which we describe in the following section in detail.

4. PROXIMITY-SENSITIVE TOUCH TARGET BEHAVIOUR

For a detailed study of proximity-sensitive touch target behavior, we developed a prototype system and implemented a set of different target behaviors (e.g., combinations of moving and expanding targets). Based on results in related work on the performance of expanding targets (e.g., [24, 29]), and our own very recent results on exploring expanding touch targets in cars [2], there is no doubt that expanding targets can improve performance in acquiring touch targets. Thus, we decided to focus on exploring the design space and future potentials of proximity sensitive touch targets designed for collaborative settings and conducted a workshop with HCI experts, utilizing the prototype system to foster experiences and discussions.

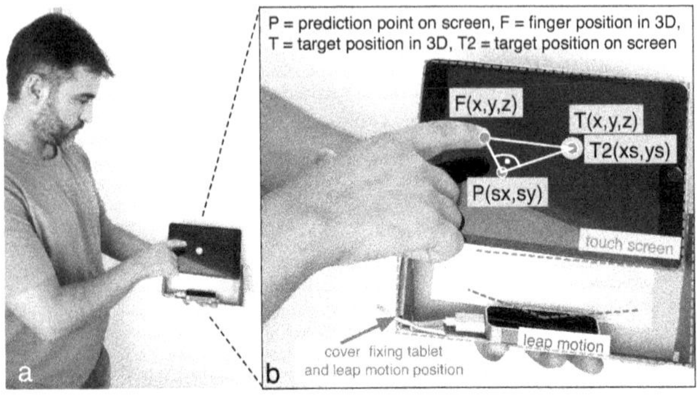

Figure 3: a) Overview of the prototype b) Highlighted measures, which are used to adapt touch targets to finger proximity.

4.1 Prototype

In order to augment touch targets with the capability of sensing a user's finger proximity a tablet device was combined with a leap motion controller (see Figure 3).

4.1.1 Hardware Setup and Software

The hardware of the prototype system consists of an iPad mini, a leap motion controller, and a carton cover that fixes the positions of the leap motion and the iPad screen. In addition, the leap motion controller is connected via USB cable with a notebook. The leap motion controller sends data, such as the 3D position of the index finger (based on the leap motion coordinate system) to a web server on the notebook. Over a web socket connection the iPad mini has access to the leap motion data based on the official leap motion javascript SDK and HTML. Thus, synchronization of leap motion data, touch events, and touch target animation on the screen happens on the iPad mini in Javascript. The iPad mini has access to the finger positions in real time and adapts the graphical interfaces (e.g., appearance of a touch target) according to the 3D position of the user's (index) finger mid-air.

4.1.2 Synchronization of 3D and 2D interaction space

In order to map 2D screen positions (in pixel) and the finger position in 3D, a user needs to perform a preliminary configuration task. During the configuration task three targets are presented at different corners of the touch screen. When the user touches targets, each target memorizes its position in 3D and expands thereafter depending on the user's finger proximity to the center of the touch target (FPCT). This provides user feedback and once the user is happy with the expansion behavior of all three touch targets the calibration can be finished. Then the three 3D positions are used to span a 2D plan (corresponding to the relative iPad screen position to the leap motion sensor) on the leap motion coordinate system and to project the 3d finger position of the user on the 2D screen of the iPad (which we refer to as the *Prediction Point (PP)*).

4.1.3 Touch Target Behaviors

In our implementations the PP is only used to adapt touch target movement. The FPCT is used to expand a target and to decide if the target needs to be moved towards the PP. Based on the position of the PP and proximity information (i.e., FPCT and proximity to the PP), we implemented five proximity sensitive touch target behaviors, intending to explore the design space of proximity sensitive touch targets in tablet-mediated collaboration settings:

1. *Expanding Touch Targets:* In the first implementation a targets initial size (100px) expands depending solely on FPCT (within the range up to 4cm) to a maximum size of (200px) in a linear fashion.
2. *Moving Touch Targets:* In the second implementation the target moves towards the PP if the FPCT is less than 4cm.
3. *Expanding and Moving Touch Targets:* This third implementation is a combination of the first and the second implementation.
4. *Vertically Constrained Moving Touch Targets:* The 4th and the 5th implementation are version of the second and third with the target movement constrained vertically, resulting in target movement towards the PP only horizontally (i.e., the target moves only to the left or to the right but not up or down).

4.2 Workshop with Experts

Workshop participants were five HCI experts with different backgrounds from computer science, design, social sciences, and psychology. One researcher facilitated the workshop and a second researcher took notes. Initially, the facilitator provided a brief overview of the findings and results of the previously conducted focus groups and lab study. Then the participants were introduced to the prototype and had the possibility to get hands on experience with the prototype and explore the five implementations for themselves. After that, the facilitator guided a semi-structured discussion. The discussion aimed at identifying limitations, potentials, and general attitudes of the participants regarding the interaction design. To ease the discussion, it was structured into (i) collecting feedback on potentials and weaknesses associated with the prototype system and experiences with the five exemplary target behaviors, (ii) discussing possibilities for future touch target behaviors, (iii) an open discussion on how the multi-modal design changes the perception of screen and touch-based interaction in collaboration settings. The workshop data was analyzed according to the basics of a thematic analysis approach [4]. Following this approach, the collected data was thematically structured in order to reveal the prevalent thematic issues raised by the experts.

4.3 Workshop Results and Discussion

The main insights gained from the workshop are centered around target behavior and a feeling of connectedness, and the agency associated with touch targets, which will be discussed hereafter.

4.3.1 Touch Target Behavior and Connectedness

Considering the prototype system and the provided exemplary target behaviors, the experts argued that the expanding targets implementation worked best and felt most sophisticated. The experts argued when targets moved (i.e., changed their positions) that it felt like the target was trying to escape even when the target was moving on the 2D screen towards the approaching finger. This experience was less dominant in the implementation where vertical movements were constrained.

On the other hand, experts agreed that a target moving towards the finger was perceived as an invitation to touch it. They argued that in tablet mediated situations, such as during sales conversations, persons tend to point to the screen and a target recognizing the pointing action and slightly moving towards the finger position could motivate the user to dare to touch the target. It was argued that instead of targets moving, in future targets could alternatively shake, rotate themselves towards the approaching finger, change their form or semantically transition their imagery. Especially when targets include text or imagery, a target rotating towards a user could be perceived as a target facing the user and thereby inviting the user even more.

The experts were in general agreement that especially with the expanding targets implementation a feeling of connectedness between the touch target and the user was established. They argued that this was a potentially powerful experience worth exploring. In this regard, experts argued that designers could use the connectedness to design for specific user experiences, such as fun or trust.

Consequently, experts agreed that the main challenge in designing future target behaviors would be in matching target behavior and what is being communicated (e.g., signifying interaction possibilities).

4.3.2 Proximity-Sensitivity and Agency

In the beginning of the workshop, participants were in the process of "mentally" grasping how proximity-sensitive touch targets were different from regular touch targets. In the later discussions many of the comments made included greater implications and how a completely new (and larger) design space was being spanned by the combination of touch and mid-air input modalities. For example, one expert with a background in Psychology stated that with the combined interaction modality touch targets felt if they were expanding to the space above the screen, reaching out to the user. A concluding group discussion revealed, similar to persons having interpersonal space (around their bodies) that proximity-sensitive touch targets had their "personal" space. One expert stated that she could imagine a decrease of a collocated person's presence due to the "strong" connectedness between a digital target and the user during mediated interaction with the tablet. We believe that this feeling of connectedness is associated with the "real time" sensormotoric coupling supported by our implementations of proximity-sensitive targets, in which targets (seem to) enact a user's intention (represented in their finger movement).

An interesting outcome of the workshop was how agency which is associated with the mediating tablet itself changes with proximity-sensitive touch targets. While with uni-modal touch screens the agency is associated with the tablet as a whole, in the multi-modal solution the agency of the tablet moves towards the background (of consciousness) and agency is associated with each proximity sensitive target on the screen in different ways (since each target has potentially different intentions). For example, the experts in the workshop discussed how the capability of proximity-sensitive targets to differentiate between users (e.g., between a sales person and customers) could be utilized to implement different behaviors, such as more inviting and persuasive behavior towards customers than towards sales persons.

A question on for whom target behavior should be designed resulted in a discussion of who the user is in a collaborative setting and who owns the device. For example, in the sales situation, if the tablet is owned by the sales person the target behavior should be designed to support the sales person's intentions. According to Alfred Gell [10], the agency of art (or artifacts in more general) is associate with a person who's agency is mediate, which is typically the artist, the designer, or some times even a patron. Similarly, human-computer interfaces are often designed as "physical" mediators for a person's agency. In tablet-mediated sales conversations the tablet serves as the physical mediator of the sales person's agency. With proximity-sensitive touch targets an additional level of agency emerges and becomes associated with the content. In sum, the mediation quality of tablets is increased, offering a broader spectrum of design possibilities for collaborative settings.

In sum, the workshop shed light on the diverse potential of proximity-sensitive touch targets and how they can be used through design to mediate intentions in collaborative settings (e.g., as persuasive interfaces). In our future work, we aim to continue our exploration of this design space and improve our understanding of how spatial user interaction is embedded in social practices.

5. CONCLUSION

Our aim was to address two research questions. First, to explore situated constraints on target acquisition on touch screens in a social context (i.e., tablet mediated sales conversations). With regard to this research question, results from a series of studies have been presented. In two focus groups, two bodily formations during tablet mediated sales conversations have been identified. A subsequent lab study showed that identified bodily formations caused (due to decreased viewing/interaction angles to the touch screen) a spatially systematic decrease of touch accuracy.

The second research question that we aimed to study was how situated constraints could be addressed through (multi-modal) interaction design. We discussed possible design considerations to improve touch accuracy, focussing on adaptation strategies before and after the actual touch event. We argued that before touch adaptation strategies for touch targets showed most potential to improve touch-based interaction during tablet mediated interaction. Consequently, a multi-modal system combining mid-air movement and touch was presented. Five proximity-sensitive adaptation strategies were implemented as examples with the purpose to provide hands-on experiences and facilitate discussion in an expert worksop. The concluding workshop with experts provided insights beyond our initial research questions associated with the design space spanned by the multi-modal solution.

6. ACKNOWLEDGMENTS

The financial support by the Austrian Federal Ministry of Science, Research and Economy and the National Foundation for Research, Technology and Development is gratefully acknowledged (Christian Doppler Laboratory for "Contextual Interfaces"), as is the Austrian project "ASSIST 4.0" funded by the Austrian Research Promotion Agency (FFG).

7. REFERENCES

[1] P.-A. Albinsson and S. Zhai. High precision touch screen interaction. In *Proc. of CHI '03*, pages 105–112, New York, NY, USA, 2003.

[2] I. Aslan, A. Krischkowsky, A. Meschtscherjakov, M. Wuchse, and M. Tscheligi. A leap for touch: proximity sensitive touch targets in cars. In *Proc. of AutomotiveUI'15*, pages 39–46. ACM, 2015.

[3] I. Aslan, M. Murer, V. Fuchsberger, A. Fugard, and M. Tscheligi. Drag and drop the apple: The semantic weight of words and images in touch-based interaction. In *Proc. of TEI '13*, pages 159–166, New York, NY, USA, 2013. ACM.

[4] V. Braun and V. Clarke. Using thematic analysis in psychology. *Qualitative research in psychology*, 3(2):77–101, 2006.

[5] B. Brown, M. McGregor, and E. Laurier. iphone in vivo: Video analysis of mobile device use. In *Proc. of CHI '13*, pages 1031–1040, New York, NY, USA, 2013. ACM.

[6] M. Buchenau and J. F. Suri. Experience prototyping. In *Proceedings of the 3rd Conference on Designing Interactive Systems: Processes, Practices, Methods, and Techniques*, DIS '00, pages 424–433, New York, NY, USA, 2000. ACM.

[7] X. A. Chen, J. Schwarz, C. Harrison, J. Mankoff, and S. E. Hudson. Air+touch: Interweaving touch & in-air gestures. In *Proc of UIST '14*, pages 519–525, New York, NY, USA, 2014. ACM.

[8] P. Dourish. *Where the Action is: The Foundations of Embodied Interaction.* A Bradford book. Bradford Books, 2004.

[9] P. M. Fitts. The information capacity of the human motor system in controlling the amplitude of movement. 1954. *J Exp Psychol Gen*, 121(3):262–269, Sept. 1992.

[10] A. Gell. Art and agency. *An anthropological theory*, pages 19–34, 1998.

[11] T. Grossman and R. Balakrishnan. The bubble cursor: Enhancing target acquisition by dynamic resizing of the cursor's activation area. In *Proc. of CHI '05*, pages 281–290, New York, NY, USA, 2005.

[12] E. T. Hall and E. T. Hall. *The hidden dimension*, volume 1990. Anchor Books New York, 1969.

[13] N. Henze, E. Rukzio, and S. Boll. 100,000,000 taps: analysis and improvement of touch performance in the large. MobileHCI '11, pages 133–142, New York, NY, USA, 2011. ACM.

[14] S. Heo and G. Lee. Force gestures: Augmented touch screen gestures using normal and tangential force. In *CHI '11 Extended Abstracts on Human Factors in Computing Systems*, pages 1909–1914, New York, NY, USA, 2011. ACM.

[15] C. Holz and P. Baudisch. Understanding touch. CHI '11, pages 2501–2510, New York, NY, USA, 2011.

[16] E. Hornecker and J. Buur. Getting a grip on tangible interaction: A framework on physical space and social interaction. In *Proc. of CHI '06*, pages 437–446, New York, NY, USA, 2006. ACM.

[17] E. Hornecker, P. Marshall, N. S. Dalton, and Y. Rogers. Collaboration and interference: Awareness with mice or touch input. In *Proc. of CSCW '08*, pages 167–176, New York, NY, USA, 2008. ACM.

[18] I. Jamil, K. O'Hara, M. Perry, A. Karnik, and S. Subramanian. The effects of interaction techniques on talk patterns in collaborative peer learning around interactive tables. In *Proc. of CHI '11*, CHI '11, pages 3043–3052, New York, NY, USA, 2011.

[19] A. Kendon. *Conducting Interaction: Patterns of Behavior in Focused Encounters (Studies in Interactional Sociolinguistics).* Cambridge University Press, Nov. 1990.

[20] J. B. Lehtovirta, A. Oulasvirta, and S. Brewster. The effects of walking speed on target acquisition on a touchscreen interface. In *Proc.of MobileHCI '11*, MobileHCI '11, pages 143–146, New York, NY, USA, 2011. ACM.

[21] Y. Li, K. Hinckley, Z. Guan, and J. A. Landay. Experimental analysis of mode switching techniques in pen-based user interfaces. In *Proc. of CHI '05*, pages 461–470, New York, NY, USA, 2005. ACM.

[22] P. Marshall, R. Morris, Y. Rogers, S. Kreitmayer, and M. Davies. Rethinking 'multi-user': An in-the-wild study of how groups approach a walk-up-and-use tabletop interface. In *Proc. of CHI '11*, CHI '11, pages 3033–3042, New York, NY, USA, 2011. ACM.

[23] P. Marshall, Y. Rogers, and N. Pantidi. Using f-formations to analyse spatial patterns of interaction in physical environments. CSCW '11, pages 445–454, New York, NY, USA, 2011.

[24] M. McGuffin and R. Balakrishnan. Acquisition of expanding targets. In *Proceedings of the SIGCHI Conference on Human Factors in Computing Systems*, CHI '02, pages 57–64, New York, NY, USA, 2002.

[25] D. E. Meyer, R. A. Abrams, S. Kornblum, C. E. Wright, and J. Keith Smith. Optimality in human motor performance: ideal control of rapid aimed movements. *Psychological review*, 95(3), 1988.

[26] S. Rogers, J. Williamson, C. Stewart, and R. Murray-Smith. Anglepose: Robust, precise capacitive touch tracking via 3d orientation estimation. In *In Proc. of CHI'11*, pages 2575–2584, New York, NY, USA, 2011. ACM.

[27] A. Roudaut, S. Huot, and E. Lecolinet. Taptap and magstick: Improving one-handed target acquisition on small touch-screens. In *Proc. of AVI'08*, pages 146–153, New York, NY, USA, 2008. ACM.

[28] B. Schildbach and E. Rukzio. Investigating selection and reading performance on a mobile phone while walking. In Proc. MobileHCI '10, pages 93–102, New York, NY, USA, 2010. ACM.

[29] X.-D. Yang, T. Grossman, P. Irani, and G. Fitzmaurice. Touchcuts and touchzoom: Enhanced target selection for touch displays using finger proximity sensing. In *Proc. of CHI '11*, pages 2585–2594, New York, NY, USA, 2011. ACM.

[30] N. Yuill and Y. Rogers. Mechanisms for collaboration: A design and evaluation framework for multi-user interfaces. *ACM Trans. Comput.-Hum. Interact.*, 19(1):1:1–1:25, May 2012.

Analyzing Multimodality of Video for User Engagement Assessment

Fahim A. Salim
ADAPT Centre
Trinity College Dublin
Ireland
salimf@tcd.ie

Fasih Haider
SCSS,Trinity College Dublin
Ireland
haiderf@scss.tcd.ie

Owen Conlan
ADAPT Centre
Trinity College Dublin
Ireland
owen.conlan@scss.tcd.ie

Saturnino Luz
IPHSI, University of Edinburgh
UK
S.Luz@ed.ac.uk

Nick Campbell
SCSS,Trinity College Dublin
Ireland
nick@tcd.ie

ABSTRACT

These days, several hours of new video content is uploaded to the internet every second. It is simply impossible for anyone to see every piece of video which could be engaging or even useful to them. Therefore it is desirable to identify videos that might be regarded as engaging automatically, for a variety of applications such as recommendation and personalized video segmentation etc. This paper explores how multimodal characteristics of video, such as prosodic, visual and paralinguistic features, can help in assessing user engagement with videos. The approach proposed in this paper achieved good accuracy (maximum F score of 96.93%) through a novel combination of features extracted directly from video recordings, demonstrating the potential of this method in identifying engaging content.

Categories and Subject Descriptors

H.4 [**Information Systems Applications**]: Multimedia Information Systems; D.2.8 [**Computing methodologies**]: Multimodal Analysis—*Signal Processing, Artificial intelligence*

General Terms

User Engagement

Keywords

Personalization, Multimodality, Video Analysis, Paralinguistic

1. INTRODUCTION

In terms of multimodality, videos are one of the most versatile form of content we consume on a regular basis. Over 6 billion hours of video are watched each month on YouTube[1]. The set of videos available on this platform is very diverse, with one hundred hours of new video being added every minute[1]. Each kind of video engages users differently, or to put it in a different way, users watch different types of videos for different reasons, i.e. engagement with content is context dependent [2].

This raises the question of clearly defining the meaning of user engagement within this context and equally important of how to quantify it. According to [17] user engagement is based on six factors. Specifically for videos [9] and [13] analyse user engagement by measuring for how long a user watched a video. Questionnaires are also a very common method for analysing engagement factors in video artifacts as in [4] and [14] . As it can be seen there is not much agreement in measuring engagement since it is highly context dependent. Therefore we view engagement as the elaborate feedback system described in detail in section 3.1. Given the amount of content available, it would be beneficial from an application point of view if we could automatically differentiate engaging videos from non-engaging ones for a particular consumer.

We believe that it is possible to extract quantifiable multimodal features from a video presentation automatically and correlate these with user engagement criterion for a variety of interesting applications. Whether to predict if a video is engaging or not to a user, or to identify video segments of interest, it is valuable to build a model so as to automatically address these questions. Additionally extracting and indexing those features and their correlation to engagement could help content adaptability and contextualizing search.

This paper proposes a novel multimodal user engagement assessment approach. We extracted multimodal features from TED videos and use them to identify their relationship with user engagement. We believe that this experiment will be a useful building block for our envisioned system to provide personalized and contextually aware recomposed video slices [18].

2. STATE OF THE ART

The most closely related research we could find in the literature is that conducted by Wernicke [21]. He performed

ICMI '2015 Seattle, Washington USA
© 2015 ACM. ISBN 978-1-4503-3912-4/15/11 ...$15.00.
DOI: http://dx.doi.org/10.1145/2818346.2820775.

[1]https://www.youtube.com/yt/press/statistics.html

statistical analysis on TED talks to propose a metric for creating an optimal TED talk based on user ratings. A major difference between this study and the current one is that, the TED user ratings on which the former study is based were considerably simpler. In other words, the viewer could simply 'like' or 'unlike' a particular TED talk and not the comprehensive rating system we have described in section 3.1.

Creating recommender systems for users based on their viewing habits and commenting patterns also attracts a lot of interest. For example, in [20], the authors use heterogeneous data from different sources to create a better recommender system based on user video preferences. In [6], the authors attempt to predict user movie preferences by clustering movie subtitles, low level visual features and ratings given by users. In [1], an attempt is made to file videos into different categories based on their features.

We ultimately aim to produce a mathematical model that will support our goal of personalized and contextually aware video slices. The video summarization literature is worth investigating to this end. Although we are not creating video summaries in this study, the process of creating a video summary involves similar steps to those we needed for this study. The work presented here also involves extracting multimodal features from videos and correlating them with user ratings to see if we can find any signal to predict engagement. A significant amount of research is currently being performed within the field of video summarization. It would not be farfetched to say that in video summarization, importance is usually attributed to visual feature [4] and [8]. However multimodal features are also receiving considerable attention due to the added value they bring in terms of identifying important chunks. An example of comprehensive multimodal feature extraction is the work of Evangelopoulos et Al. [11], who take advantage of all three visual, audio and linguistic modalities to create video summaries. Other interesting examples of multimodal feature extraction are [10] and [14].

Extracting all these multimodal features and properly indexing them would make videos more searchable and also helps in correlating the video with user feedback thereby user engagement.

3. EXPERIMENTATION

3.1 TED Talks and User Feedback

"TED is a non-profit organization devoted to spreading ideas, usually in the form of short, powerful talks (18 minutes or less)". The TED website, instead of asking users to simply give like or dislike feedback, asks viewers to describe the video in terms of particular words. Among the 14 rating words provided to users, we can identify 9 as being positive words, 4 as being negative, and 1 as neutral. A user can choose up to 3 words to rate a video (table 1).

By giving these choices to users, the TED website provides elaborate feedback on a given video. This makes our problem more interesting. Instead of crisp binary feedback to learn from, we have fuzzy description of what viewers thought about a particular video. The rating system for user feedback thus provides a more nuanced characterisation of user engagement with the video presentation. Since the ratings consist of voluntarily information given by the users, in terms of semantically positive and negative words, it provides good basis for analysis of the relevant factors of engagement [17] for TED talks.

Table 1: Average number of user ratings per each rating criteria for 1340 Ted videos across different topics.

Rating	Avg. (Count)	Avg.(%)
Beautiful	120	6.67
Confusing	15	1.17
Courageous	122	6.08
Fascinating	234	12.64
Funny	106	4.73
Informative	246	15.24
Ingenious	134	7.64
Inspiring	384	18.16
Jaw-dropping	118	5.45
Longwinded	28	2.23
Obnoxious	23	1.62
OK	65	4.88
Persuasive	188	9.70
Unconvincing	51	3.73

3.2 Analysis of User Rating

The TED website reports what percentage of viewers rated the video as saying "Inspiring" or "Longwinded" etc. But we cannot simply rely on ratings given to an individual video because it may not give the whole story. As seen in Table 1, ratings tend to be overwhelmingly positive. Both count and percentage, positive criterion tend to score much higher than negative or neutral ones. Even the highest scoring negative ratings "Unconvincing" has average count and percentage 51 and 3.73 less than the lowest scoring positive rating "Funny" with average score of 106 and 4.34.

If only the ratings of an individual video are considered then it would seem like all the videos only positively engage the viewers. Since we did not see a video to which a negative rating word got the highest count by the viewers. So to deduct which video is found to be "Obnoxious" or "Longwinded" by viewers, some kind of normalization is required.

In order to do that we used the following definitions for our purpose for a video to be considered "Beautiful" or "Persuasive" etc. it must have a rating count more than average rating count for that particular rating word. With this, TED talks were categorized as "Beautiful and not Beautiful", "Inspiring and not Inspiring", "Persuasive and not Persuasive" etc. giving two classes for classification for each of the 14 rating words.

TED talks provide topic tags with each video. For example, a TED talk could have topic tags like "Culture, poverty, history and photography". These topics tags are quite diverse i.e. out of the 1340 videos we have used, there were a total of 321 unique tags found many of them only appearing once while a single video had up to 10 different topic tags.

We allowed for more variation than a simple yes/no categorization of video ratings by introducing concept of "very strong", "strong", "simple" or "not" for each rating word. A video is considered "very strongly beautiful" if its "Beautiful" count is more than average for the majority of tags it contains, "strongly beautiful" if only for the minority of tags and "simply beautiful" if only more than the global average.

This way we got four classes for classification for each of the 14 ratings words.

3.3 Features Extraction

For visual features, we use HAAR cascades [15], from the OpenCV library [5], to detect whether the speaker is on the screen or not. For this study we looked at for how many seconds there was a close up shot of the speaker and when there was a distant shot and when the speaker was not on the screen. For non-visual features we looked at number of laughter and applauses and laughter applause ratio within TED talks. Since TED talks come with subtitles, getting this information was a simple process and was obtained with a simple python script. For all extracted features, we also measured whether for each video, the value of each feature was greater or less than the average value for that feature. E.g if the number of close up face seconds for a given video was greater than the average number of close up face seconds, we assigned the value 1 to the feature "Above average close up shots" and 0 otherwise. We did the same for other features thereby doubling the number of visual and paralinguistic features to 12 for the experimentation.

For prosodic features, we used the openSMILE toolkit [12]. This extraction was performed on the audio files extracted from TED talks videos using FFMPEG [3]. The extracted audio files have a sampling frequency of 44.1 KHz with a resolution of 16 bits. Prosodic features have been shown to correlate to structure in dialogue interaction and evidence of participant status and engagement levels [7, 16]. We hypothesize that these features might also occur in monologues such as TED talks. Therefore, in this study, we choose the prosody feature set of ComParE challenge used in The INTERSPEECH 2013 computational paralinguistics challenge [19] (6373 features in total).

The ComParE feature set includes the Energy, Spectral, Mel-Frequency Cepstral Coefficients (MFCCs), and Voicing related Low-Level Descriptors (LLDs). A few LLDs including logarithmic harmonic-to-noise ratio (HNR), Voice quality features (harmonic to noise ratio), Viterbi smoothing for F0, Spectral harmonicity and Psychoacoustic spectral sharpness.

3.4 Classification Method

We first normalize our feature set using z-score normalization technique and then scale them in the range of [0 1]. To reduce the high dimensionality of features we employ PCA (Principle Component Analysis) over the feature set to reduce the number of dimensions to number of instances. After that we map our data to the reduced dimensions. From the statistical significance ($\boldsymbol{p}$) of the transformed feature set with the rating (yes or no), we select the transformed features with $\boldsymbol{p}$ value less than 0.5.

We employed MATLAB[2] (Statistics and Machine Learning Toolbox) to perform classification and apply the discriminant analysis method with 10-fold cross validation. The classification method works by assuming that the feature sets of the classes to be discerned are drawn from different Gaussian distributions and adopting a pseudo-linear discriminant analysis (i.e. using the pseudo-inverse of the covariance matrix.)

[2]http://uk.mathworks.com/products/matlab/

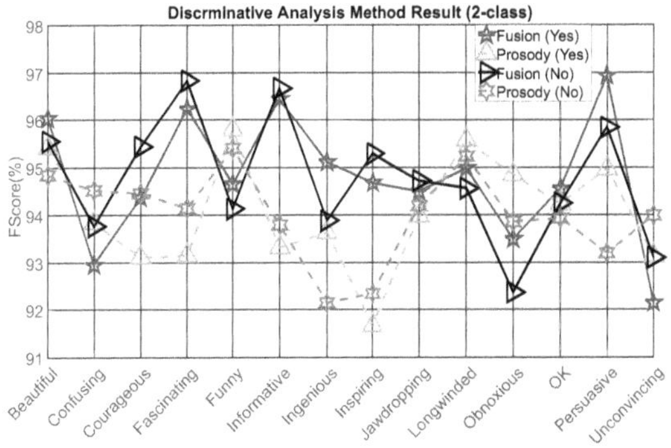

Figure 1: Classifier results (F Score) for 2-class problem, comparison of Fusion and Prosody features.

4. RESULTS AND DISCUSSION

In addition of automatically assessing user engagement in videos, we also investigate the value within different modalities of video for application purposes. Therefore we performed experiments comparing prosodic features alone and prosodic features combined with visual and paralinguistic features to see if there is any difference in classification results.

We performed classification as both a 2-class and 4-class problem mentioned in section 3.2, and assessed the results using the F score statistic (with the β parameter set to 1). In this setting, the F score is equivalent to the harmonic mean of the precision and recall scores. For two-class "Yes" and "No" classification, we were able to obtain F-scores as high as 96.93% (Fig.1). Although the highest F-score was achieved with the fusion of prosodic and other features, it was not the case that fusion improved the score in all cases. The number of cases where fusion increased the F-score are equal to the cases where prosodic features alone resulted in a higher score(see Fig.1 for details).

We were also able to achieve good results using 4 classes (Fig.2). Again the highest F-score 83.14% was achieved with the combination of multimodal features. Although in some cases the F-score actually dropped with the combination of features compared to prosodic features alone, but in majority of cases the combination did achieve improvement in F-score (see Fig.2 for details).

These results are widely applicable. The resulting model would become a component of a personalized video recommender system. It can also enhance contextual search queries since extracted features for the study together with their timestamps in the video can be indexed to support segmentation and add value to any other metadata of the video collection. This multimodal metadata and engagement correlation, combined with other extracted metadata would help a personalization engine in converting a video form a single artifact into a personalized and context aware information retrieval source.

For further investigation, in addition to including more visual features to the fold we will also combine linguistic features in our assessment of user engagement with video content. We will apply the presented approach to convert a video artifact into more query-able multimodal content source. This will be feed into a model to create multimodal

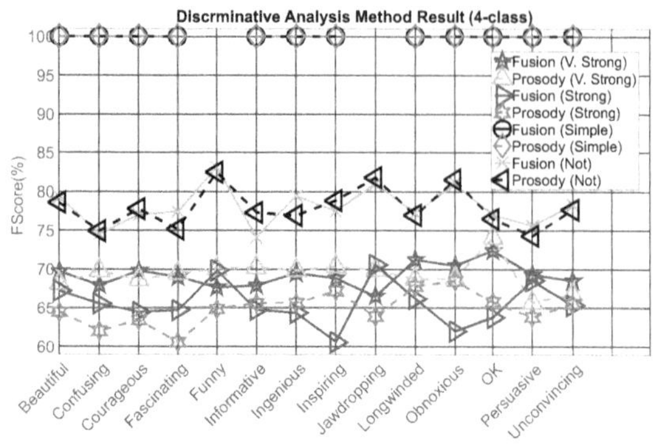

Figure 2: Classifier results (F Score) for 4-class problem, comparison of Fusion and Prosody features.

segments in a personalized and contextually aware manner, although different features, e.g. semantic extraction from the audio track, will most likely prove more valuable in the recomposition.

5. ACKNOWLEDGEMENT

This research is supported by Science Foundation Ireland through the CNGL Programme (Grant 12/CE/I2267) in the ADAPT Centre (www.adaptcentre.ie) at School of Computer Science and Statistics, Trinity College Dublin and FP7-METALOGUE project under Grant No. 611073.

6. REFERENCES

[1] A. Anwar, G. I. Salama, and M. B. Abdelhalim. Video Classification And Retrieval Using Arabic Closed Caption. In *ICIT 2013 The 6th International Conference on Information Technology VIDEO*, 2013.

[2] S. Attfield, B. Piwowarski, and G. Kazai. Towards a science of user engagement (Position Paper). In *WSDM Workshop on User Modelling for Web Applications*, Hong Kong, 2011.

[3] F. Bellard, M. Niedermayer, et al. Ffmpeg. *ht tp://ffmpeg. org*, 2012.

[4] S. Benini, P. Migliorati, and R. Leonardi. Statistical Skimming of Feature Films. *International Journal of Digital Multimedia Broadcasting*, 2010:1–11, 2010.

[5] G. Bradski. The OpenCV Library. *Dr. DobbâĂŹs Journal of Software Tools*, 2000.

[6] D. Brezeale and D. J. Cook. Learning video preferences using visual features and closed captions. *IEEE Multimedia*, 16(3):39–47, 2009.

[7] N. Campbell. Multimodal processing of discourse information; the effect of synchrony. In *2008 Second International Symposium on Universal Communication*, pages 12–15. IEEE, 2008.

[8] F. Chen, C. De Vleeschouwer, and A. Cavallaro. Resource allocation for personalized video summarization. *IEEE Transactions on Multimedia*, 16(2):455–469, 2014.

[9] F. Dobrian, A. Awan, D. Joseph, A. Ganjam, J. Zhan, V. Sel, I. Stoica, and H. Zhang. Understanding the Impact of Video Quality on User Engagement. In *Communications of the ACM*, pages 91–99, 2013.

[10] A. Dong and H. Li. Ontology-Driven Annotation and Access of Presentation Video Data. *Estudios de Economía Aplicada*, 2008.

[11] G. Evangelopoulos, A. Zlatintsi, A. Potamianos, P. Maragos, K. Rapantzikos, G. Skoumas, and Y. Avrithis. Multimodal saliency and fusion for movie summarization based on aural, visual, and textual attention. *IEEE Transactions on Multimedia*, 15(7):1553–1568, 2013.

[12] F. Eyben, F. Weninger, F. Groß, and B. Schuller. Recent developments in opensmile, the munich open-source multimedia feature extractor. In *Proceedings of the 21st ACM international conference on Multimedia*, pages 835–838. ACM, 2013.

[13] P. J. Guo, J. Kim, and R. Rubin. How Video Production Affects Student Engagement : An Empirical Study of MOOC Videos. In *L@S 2014 - Proceedings of the 1st ACM Conference on Learning at Scale*, pages 41–50, 2014.

[14] M. Haesen, J. Meskens, K. Luyten, K. Coninx, J. H. Becker, T. Tuytelaars, G.-J. Poulisse, P. T. Pham, and M.-F. Moens. Finding a needle in a haystack: an interactive video archive explorer for professional video searchers. *Multimedia Tools and Applications*, 63(2):331–356, May 2011.

[15] R. Lienhart, A. Kuranov, and V. Pisarevsky. Empirical analysis of detection cascades of boosted classifiers for rapid object detection. In *Proceedings of the 25th DAGM Pattern Recognition Symposium*, pages 297–304, 2003.

[16] S. Luz. The non-verbal structure of patient case discussions in multidisciplinary medical team meetings. *ACM Transactions on Information Systems*, 30(3):17:1–17:24, 2012.

[17] H. L. O'Brien and E. G. Toms. Examining the generalizability of the User Engagement Scale (UES) in exploratory search. *Information Processing and Management*, 49(5):1092–1107, 2013.

[18] F. A. Salim. From artifact to content source: Using multimodality in video to support personalized recomposition. In *User Modeling, Adaptation and Personalization 2015*. UMAP, 2015.

[19] B. Schuller, S. Steidl, A. Batliner, A. Vinciarelli, K. Scherer, F. Ringeval, M. Chetouani, F. Weninger, F. Eyben, E. Marchi, et al. The interspeech 2013 computational paralinguistics challenge: social signals, conflict, emotion, autism. 2013.

[20] S. Tan, J. Bu, X. Qin, C. Chen, and D. Cai. Cross domain recommendation based on multi-type media fusion. *Neurocomputing*, 127:124–134, Mar. 2014.

[21] S. Wernicke. Lies, damned lies and statistics (about tedtalks). http://go.ted.com/bDrm, 2010.

Adjacent Vehicle Collision Warning System using Image Sensor and Inertial Measurement Unit

Asif Iqbal
Department of Electrical Engineering
SeRViCE Lab
University of Texas at Dallas,
800 W Campbell Rd,
Richardson TX 75080, USA
axi122230@utdallas.edu

Carlos Busso
Department of Electrical Engineering
Multimodal Signal Processing (MSP) Laboratory
University of Texas at Dallas,
800 W Campbell Rd,
Richardson TX 75080, USA
cxb093000@utdallas.edu

Nicholas R. Gans
Department of Electrical Engineering
SeRViCE Lab
University of Texas at Dallas,
800 W Campbell Rd,
Richardson TX 75080, USA
nrg092000@utdallas.edu

ABSTRACT

Advanced driver assistance systems are the newest addition to vehicular technology. Such systems use a wide array of sensors to provide a superior driving experience. Vehicle safety and driver alert are important parts of these system. This paper proposes a driver alert system to prevent and mitigate adjacent vehicle collisions by proving warning information of on-road vehicles and possible collisions. A dynamic Bayesian network (DBN) is utilized to fuse multiple sensors to provide driver awareness. It detects oncoming adjacent vehicles and gathers ego vehicle motion characteristics using an on-board camera and inertial measurement unit (IMU). A histogram of oriented gradient feature based classifier is used to detect any adjacent vehicles. Vehicles front-rear end and side faces were considered in training the classifier. Ego vehicles heading, speed and acceleration are captured from the IMU and feed into the DBN. The network parameters were learned from data via expectation maximization(EM) algorithm. The DBN is designed to provide two type of warning to the driver, a cautionary warning and a brake alert for possible collision with other vehicles. Experiments were completed on multiple public databases, demonstrating successful warnings and brake alerts in most situations.

Categories and Subject Descriptors

I.4.8 [**Image Processing and Computer Vision**]: Scene Analysis—*Object recognition, Sensor fusion*

Keywords

Driver Assistance System; dynamic Bayesian network; Expectation Maximization; inertial measurement unit; vehicle detection

ICMI 2015, November 9–13, 2015, Seattle, WA, USA.

ACM 978-1-4503-3912-4/15/11 ...$15.00.
DOI: http://dx.doi.org/10.1145/2818346.2820741.

1. INTRODUCTION

Advanced driver assistance systems (ADAS) are an active research area in recent years. Various algorithms have been developed to aid drivers on-road to keep them alert for possible collisions and assist them in driving safely by proving superior guidance. Safe and accurate ADAS systems are crucial due to the frequency of collisions caused by distracted drivers. Statistics shows that approximately 60% of rear-end collisions can be avoided if the driver had additional warning [1]. According to the U.S. Census Bureau, there were approximately 10.8 million motor vehicle accidents in 2009 alone, and 35,900 deaths were reported from road accidents [2]. Among those, about 40% of the deaths were caused by motor vehicle crashes. Drivers' delay to recognize or estimate possible collisions is a major cause of these accidents. Even a half second prior warning can significantly reduce the amount and severity of accidents. These observations point to the need of a system that can alert and warn the driver appropriately.

With the advent of inexpensive vision sensors, accurate inertial measurement units (IMUs), lidar, and radar scanners, robust driver assistance systems and fully autonomous vehicles have become a goal for near future. Collision avoidance is an important area in driver assistance as well as in autonomous driving. Detecting nearby vehicles and providing appropriate warning to the drivers remains a challenging research area [3]. Many researchers have been working in the area of driver alert and awareness; therefore, multiple systems have been proposed to detect and track vehicles on-road and monitor the driver's behavior [4]. Some researchers have tried to monitor the driving behavior and facial reaction [5] , while others have tried to identify different objects such as pedestrians and traffic signs and provide driver awareness based on the vehicle's state [6]. Some researchers have focused in solving simple tasks, such as predicting turning behavior and lane change collision avoidance. Using only one sensor modality, such an awareness system can be ineffective. Almost all the proposed methods have used multiple modalities to achieve robust performance.

This paper proposes an on-road adjacent vehicle collision warning system. The method incorporates a multi-vehicle detection system based on a histogram of oriented gradient (HOG) features trained with AdaBoosted classifier and on-board vehicle IMU measurement unit. A dynamic Bayesian network integrates all the measurements to provide correct warnings to driver. The proposed method is tested on real driving databases with varying road and weather conditions.

The rest of the paper is constructed as follows. A background study of the related area is discussed in Section 2. Section 3 explains the proposed method, including the introduction of the DBN model, extraction of IMU data, vehicle detection module and parametrization of the DBN model using EM. Section 4 describes the experimental results and limitations of the model. Section 5 discusses future direction of our research work.

2. RELATED WORK

The start of 21st century has seen automakers introduce several safety features like adaptive cruise control (ACC), dual-stage front air bags, and antilock brakes. Automakers are currently pursuing research to introduce other advanced features like collision warning and avoidance systems. Several researchers have implemented methods using various modalities to raise awareness and provide warnings to driver. Research topics include monitoring driver's behavior through face detection, eye tracking, drowsiness and fatigue detection and several other driver monitoring methods. Other researchers focused on searching the surrounding environment for any possible collision or abnormal driving by nearby vehicles. Both of these research are crucial for developing safety warning system for vehicles.

Sun et al. [7] proposed a context-awareness model for smart cars. The model accurately captured several elements of contextual information such as turn left and right, drive constantly and lane change. A petri net model is introduced for context awareness, with transition probabilities for different situations. Rakotonirainy [8] described a real-time contextual aware system, capturing information, from the surrounding that is then later reasoned with Bayesian network. The network can predict the future states of the vehicle based on both reliable and unreliable information but was unable to give information about current condition of the driver. Lee et al. [9], developed a system to map captured images to global co-ordinates to monitor driving behavior. Using a hidden Markov Model (HMM), they were able to deduce four driving forms. Tsu-Tian et al. [10] demonstrated a multi-sensor fused system to create a collision maneuver warning system on a embedded platform. Matthias et al. [11] proposed a dynamic Bayesian network to model a situation-aware driver assistance system. Their approach laid an architecture to fuse information from inter-vehicle and intra infrastructure-to-vehicle network connectivity. Mitrovic [12] proposed a method using a HMM to accurately recognize driving events such as turns, curve and turns on roundabout. Eren et al. [13] proposed to determine driving behavior using only a smart-phone. They used mobile sensor data with Bayes classification to determine risky or safe driving pattern.

The integration of sensors in the context of collision avoidance with vehicles, has multiple methods. The sensors can be categorized as, active or passive. Active sensors include sonar, radar, ladar/lidar, accelerometers and global positioning system (GPS), and passive sesnors include infrared and vision camera. Kalman filter, Bayesian network, sequential Monte Carlo and their variants are some of the methods to fuse these sensors. Using a vision sensor, the detection may be performed using a single camera or multiple camera setup. Sivaraman and Trivedi [14,15] and Mukhtar et al. [6], provided a comprehensive idea on the state of the vehicle detection, collison avoidance and behavior analysis framework. HOG [16], Gabor [17,18] and Haar-like features [19] are well represented in visual-based model whereas, optical flow [20], 3D point clustering and stixel are approaches in motion-based method. Shadow, symmetry and edge features are also used as vehicle cues. Li et al. [21] provided a system for rear-end vehicle collision avoidance using mobile device sensors. It monitors the driver's reaction to detected vehicles taillights and provides warning or passive safety. The detection of vehicles can be divided into two parts, visual and motion based. van Leeuwen and Groen [22] presented a method to detect midrange, distant and passing vehicles without any knowledge of distance of the road. The passing vehicles were detected using temporal difference and projected motion.

3. FRAMEWORK

The goal of this project is to provide warning to the driver about adjacent vehicles on-road and provide brake alert to driver in case of probable collision. The first step is to capture the IMU data and process the data to obtain velocity, heading and acceleration. The second step is to detect nearby vehicles on-road using a HOG feature based AdaBoosted classifier. Finally, all the processed data is fused in a dynamic Bayesian network to issue the probabilities of warning and brake alert. The information used to build the DBN model are:

- Vehicle heading
- Vehicle speed
- Vehicle acceleration
- Detected vehicle's position with respect to the ego vehicle - Left, Middle or, Right

The IMU data is processed to acquire the heading, speed and acceleration of the ego-vehicle, and nearby vehicles are detected using a image classifier. Warnings are issued based on heading, speed, and detected vehicle's position; brake alert is issued based on speed, acceleration and current warning status.

3.1 Driver Alert System

The driver alert system provides warnings to the driver based on the position of detected vehicles in the image frame and the ego-vehicle's motion characteristics. The captured data from the IMU and camera can provide multitude of possible combinations to derive warnings. In addition to the available data, the different states may be unobserved. The information may be incomplete due to sensor error or, failure to meet input threshold. An accurate and efficient driver alert system requires fusion of different type of contexts, observable and unobservable. A dynamic Bayesian network (DBN) was implemented to provide warnings. DBN is a directed acyclic graph that represents the conditional independence between a set of nodes. It can handle incomplete and uncertain states with probabilistic inference upon receiving evidences. It consists of a set of nodes that represent the states and a set of directed edges representing the independence or dependence between variables. It can be

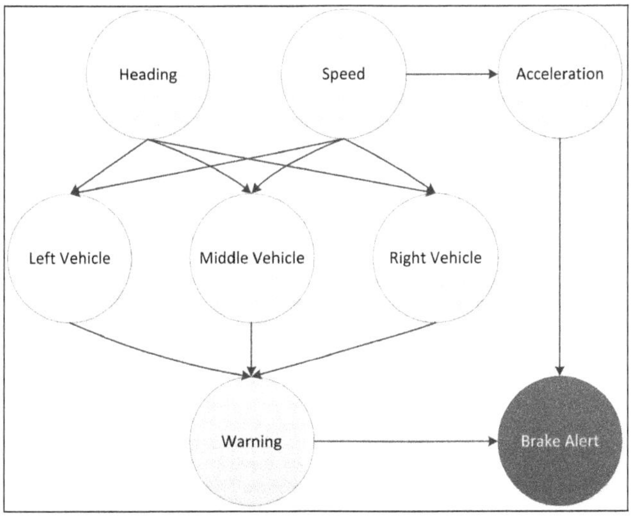

Figure 1: The dynamic Bayesian network model

represented as a set of static Bayesian networks with simple temporal features [23] [24]. Figure 1 represents the proposed model.

The vehicle alert system has two possible nodes, warning and brake alert. Warning situation includes existence of nearby vehicles and high speed driving. Brake alert is for situations of a possible collisions with nearby vehicles due to high speed or abnormal acceleration. The various situations considered in the system can be summarized below:

- Vehicles coming from a blind spot or passing vehicles pose a bigger threat than vehicles that are in front. The driver's focus is mostly towards the forward road and existing front vehicles. The passing and side vehicles are out of the driver's view. So, warnings about the vehicles existing in the sideways can help the driver.
- If the vehicle's heading is towards the existing vehicles and its acceleration is higher than usual, then there is a possible collision with the vehicle. In this situation it is necessary to issue a brake alert to driver.
- The brake alert may be removed if the driver decreases its acceleration or the existing vehicle goes out of the possible collision distance.
- If the vehicle is heading and speeding towards the existing vehicles, then a warning is issued to the driver.

The decision to provide the warning is based on the IMU data, (heading, speed and acceleration), and adjacent vehicle position, (left, middle and right) with respect to the ego vehicle. The proposed model is shown in Figure.1. The nodes and their corresponding states are listed below:

- Heading - Leftward, Straight and Rightward
- Speed - Low and High
- Acceleration - Decreasing and Increasing
- Detected position of vehicle with respect to driver. The corresponding nodes are,
  - Left - False and True.
  - Middle (in-front of the vehicle) - False and True.
  - Right - False and True.
- Warning - False and True.
- Brake Alert - False and True.

A further description of the nodes and their different states will be provided in the following sections.

3.2 IMU Data processing

IMUs are commonly used to navigate aircraft, including unmanned aerial vehicles (UAVs) and spacecraft, satellites and landers. It is a self-contained system that generally consists of three accelerometers and three gyroscopes that provide three acceleration and three angular velocity components. It may be used to determine both position and orientation of an object by integrating acceleration and angular velocity from IMU measurements. The accuracy and reliability of IMUs have enabled it to be widely used in navigation and maneuvering application.This section describes the process of acquiring the three inputs: heading, speed and orientation.

The gyroscope of an IMU provides information about the angular velocity of the ego-vehicle. These signals can be processed to estimate the current orientation of the vehicle [25], such as three angle measurements, pitch, yaw and roll. The yaw angle is used to determine the current heading of the ego vehicle. Knowing the direction of movement with respect to other vehicles' position helps dictate warning to drivers. Vehicle heading are categorized in three directions as described earlier: Straight, which indicates no change of driving direction; leftward or rightward, which may indicate vehicles intention of lane change or taking left or right turn. While vehicles can go reverse, it is not considered here as typical highway and street driving. The yaw_t is the yaw in radian units at time instant t, and ranges between $-pi$ to $+pi$. A zero value means heading is towards east, positive value indicates angle in the counter clockwise direction. The current value is compared with average of the past values to calculate the change in direction. A value between -1 to $+1$ indicates a forward direction and a value greater than 2 indicate a leftward and less than -2 for rightward direction. The following condition was used in calculating the direction,

$$Heading = \begin{cases} Left, & \text{if } yaw_t > 2 \\ Straight, & \text{if } |yaw_t| < 1 \\ Right, & \text{if } yaw_t < -2 \end{cases} \quad (1)$$

where,

$$yaw_t = yaw_t - \frac{1}{3}\sum_{i=1}^{3}(yaw_{t-i}).$$

If the conditions are not met in any of the three cases, the evidence from input is not provided to the DBN model.

Speed limits vary with respect to the location such as residential, business, city and freeways. Current focus is on residential and city roads, so in our proposed method we wanted to distinguish between driving in a residential and city roads. We looked at the data for several states in the USA and other countries, and we found out that residential area speed limit ranges from 10-30 mph, and in urban city roads, the speed ranges from 35 to 55 mph. The following equation is based on these assumptions and categorizes the vehicle speed as either low or high speed.

$$Speed = \begin{cases} Low, & \text{if } {v_t^f}^2 + {v_t^l}^2 \leq 625; \\ High, & \text{if } {v_t^f}^2 + {v_t^l}^2 \geq 1225. \end{cases} \quad (2)$$

Here, *speed* is regarded low if it is less than 25 mph and high if it is greater than 35 mph. Generally, an IMU does not provide vehicle speed data, but it can be estimated [26]. The captured data from the IMU unit were, v_t^f-forward velocity, and v_t^l-leftward velocity; both measurements are parallel to earth-surface, at time t. The units are in miles per hour.

Vehicle acceleration is another measurement that provides information of possible collision if the ego vehicle moving faster towards an adjacent vehicle. Acceleration, coupled with the heading and speed provides the DBN the required data to issue warnings in an appropriate manner. We obtain the average difference between acceleration rather than the instantaneous difference. The IMU unit provides acceleration in three axis directions. In this case, two data classifications were considered for calculating the acceleration, forward acceleration, a^f, and leftward acceleration, a^l (negative if rightward). The acceleration units used was $(m \backslash s^2)$. Increasing acceleration indicates the buildup of speed possibly due to driver's intent or downhill road. Decreasing acceleration indicates the slowing in case of braking or uphill road. This helps DBN decide the outcome of possible warnings.

$$Acceleration = \begin{cases} Decreasing, & \text{if } a_t^f < -1 \vee a_t^l < -1 \\ Increasing, & \text{if } \left|a_t^f\right| > 0.8 \vee \left|a_t^l\right| > 0.8 \end{cases} \quad (3)$$

where,

$$a_t^f = \tfrac{1}{3} \sum_{i=0}^{2} a_{t-i}^f - \tfrac{1}{4} \sum_{i=1}^{4} a_{t-i}^f$$
$$a_t^l = \tfrac{1}{3} \sum_{i=0}^{2} a_{t-i}^l - \tfrac{1}{4} \sum_{i=1}^{4} a_{t-i}^l.$$

The process to give evidence from the IMU to the DBN nodes are described here. If the conditions are not met in any of the cases, evidence from the input is not provided to the DBN model.

3.3 Vehicle Detection

Vehicle detection using vision has become an integrated part of ADAS systems. Recent image-based classification algorithms are efficient and popular in real-time applications [15]. The detection module recognizes vehicles from the front and side view of the ego-vehicle. Vehicles look different from these view points, so the training of the classifier includes both front-rear end and side views of a vehicle.

A HOG feature based AdaBoosted classifier was used in detecting vehicles on-road. HOG features are previously used in vehicle detection studies [15]. It was developed by Dalal and Triggs [16], and is a image descriptor defined from a set of gradient orientation histograms extracted over a patch in the image. The patch is a small region of image, and over each patch the intensity gradients or edge direction are computed. A histogram of the edge orientation is collected to form the feature vector.

The training database included images from several public databases and Craigslist vehicle images. There were approximately 2000 positive and 5000 negative images collected for training. We included 80% image data for training and 20% for testing purposes. Figure. 2 shows several output of the vehicle detection module is shown.

Figure 2: Results of on-road vehicle detection

Figure 3: Vehicle position

After detecting vehicles, the position of vehicles in the image frame is determined by extracting regions for left, middle and right vehicles. These regions are created based on the heading information provided by yaw estimation to locate the position of the detected vehicles with respect to the ego vehicle. The image is divided in three parts, evenly based on the width of the image frame. The center part is used as the heading or middle region for the vehicle, if the heading angle (yaw) is zero. It is shifted toward the left or right according to the heading angle of the ego vehicle. The position of the detected vehicles is decided by the heading region. If the bounding box of the detected vehicle is inside the heading region, then the vehicle is in the middle position. If it's position is to the left of the heading region then the vehicle is in the left position. Similar rules are defined for the right region. The vehicle's position with respect to the ego-vehicle will provide information to the DBN to process collision probabilities. In Figure. 3 shows the three regions where the green region is the region for middle vehicle.

3.4 Network Parameterization

The network parameterization step finds the probabilities of the root nodes and conditional probabilities of the child nodes of the network. All of the nodes in the network and their possible states have been specified. Acquiring the correct probability for each node is important for the network performance. A DBN model can be parameterized in several ways and primarily Maximum Likelihood Estimate (MLE) and expectation–maximization are used for parameter learning of the Bayesian network. In Bayesian estimation, the goal is to compute a full posterior over the parameters. The MLE or Maximum A Posteriori (MAP) method provides a point estimate that maximizes the likelihood function. If the data of the model is partially observed as in models with hidden variables, then the EM algorithm can be used to learn the parameters.

The EM algorithm was used to obtain the parameters for the DBN. The EM algorithm iteratively determines the MLE of the model that describes the distribution of a given incomplete data set. Before EM, partially observed parameters of the model were provided. It was difficult to obtain such data for collision warning system. Therefore, information from published work in this area and other related studies related to it were adapted to the system to parameterize the network properly [27–29]. The training data included both random parameters and observed cases obtained from the literature study. These observed parameters were based on the real world conditions and their corresponding warning probabilities.

In EM, the E-step is performed first, and involves the determination of the complete data log-likelihood constrained by the incomplete or partially observed data. The M-step is then performed for the estimated completed data log-likelihood. The maximized estimations are used in the repeated EM steps until a predefined convergence or constraints are met. Bayes net toolbox for Matlab [30] was used to design the network and perform EM operations. Multiple runs were completed with randomized initial points, and the best performance were achieved by the probability table shown in Figure. 4. Now, the trained DBN model can be used to issue warning and brake alert based on the evidences received from the IMU and vehicle detection. Since the IMU and camera have different sampling rate, the IMU data closest to the image frame time was chosen as the corresponding data.

4. EXPERIMENT AND RESULTS

Our experiment was completed on several public databases that included both camera and IMU data. A significant amount of vehicle images were used for HOG classifier training. The performance of the vehicle detector was evaluated on several public databases including the TME Motorway Dataset [31], Lisa Vehicle Detection Dataset [3] and KITTI database [32], the Málaga Stereo and Laser Urban Data Set [33]. We have considered both front, back and side faces of vehicles in our database. Moreover, we have considered only personal vehicles such as sedans and SUVs in our design of the classifier. For this reason, large trucks and heavy duty vehicles are mostly unrecognized in the images. In future work, we intend to cover all major classes of vehicles. Both the DBN and vehicle detection performance are discussed here.

Database	Front vehicle	Side vehicle
KITTI	78.6	81.7
Lisa Vehicle Detection	73.1	78.3
Málaga Stereo and Laser Urban Data Set	76.5	80.6
TME Motorway Dataset	77.3	79.1

Table 1: Average precision of Vehicle detection

4.1 Vehicle Detection Performance

Vehicle detection is the major component in the DBN for providing warning. Without an robust and accurate system, it will fail to provide appropriate warnings. The HOG feature based classifier has shown effective performance in pedestrian detection [16]. The evaluation procedure involved gathering different road and weather condition scenarios. The database included roads with no vehicle and sometimes very few vehicles on-road. Therefore, we captured several 3 to 5 minute segments from the database where there are 2-5 vehicles present. A total of 14 segments from the mentioned database were acquired. The classifier training procedure were performed using Matlab libraries. Performance measurement was done using average precision (AP) metric.

The average precision of vehicle detection is shown in Table 1. Both front and side vehicle detection perfomance is included in the table. Our performance shows that our classifier was able to detect on average, more than 75% of vehicles on-road. The performance can be improved by reducing the false positives. This can achieved by adding motion information to verify detected vehicles.

4.2 DBN Performance

The DBN was evaluated under various situations to determine whether it provides the appropriate warning and brake alert on time. The performance of the system required gathering ground truth from the database and creating corresponding warning and brake alert. The databases had vehicle location and size labeled, but unfortunately the selected databases provided no ground truth for any sort of safety or warning system. So out of the evaluated videos, a small set was annotated and used as ground truth. It had labeled vehicle location provided by the corresponding database. The heading, speed and acceleration were gathered from the IMU, and situations such as high speed, high acceleration, stationary vehicle label in each frame were added. There were in total 30 minutes of video (45000 frames), labeled manually based on several possible required warning and crash situation. The warning and brake alert performance result were estimated using failure rate criteria. This simple criteria can be explained by the failure rate over time duration t given by,

$$\lambda(t) = \frac{f(t)}{R(t)}$$

where $f(t)$ is the number of failures to provide corresponding warning or alert over the time duration t, and $R(t)$ is the total occurrence of warning or alert over the time duration t.

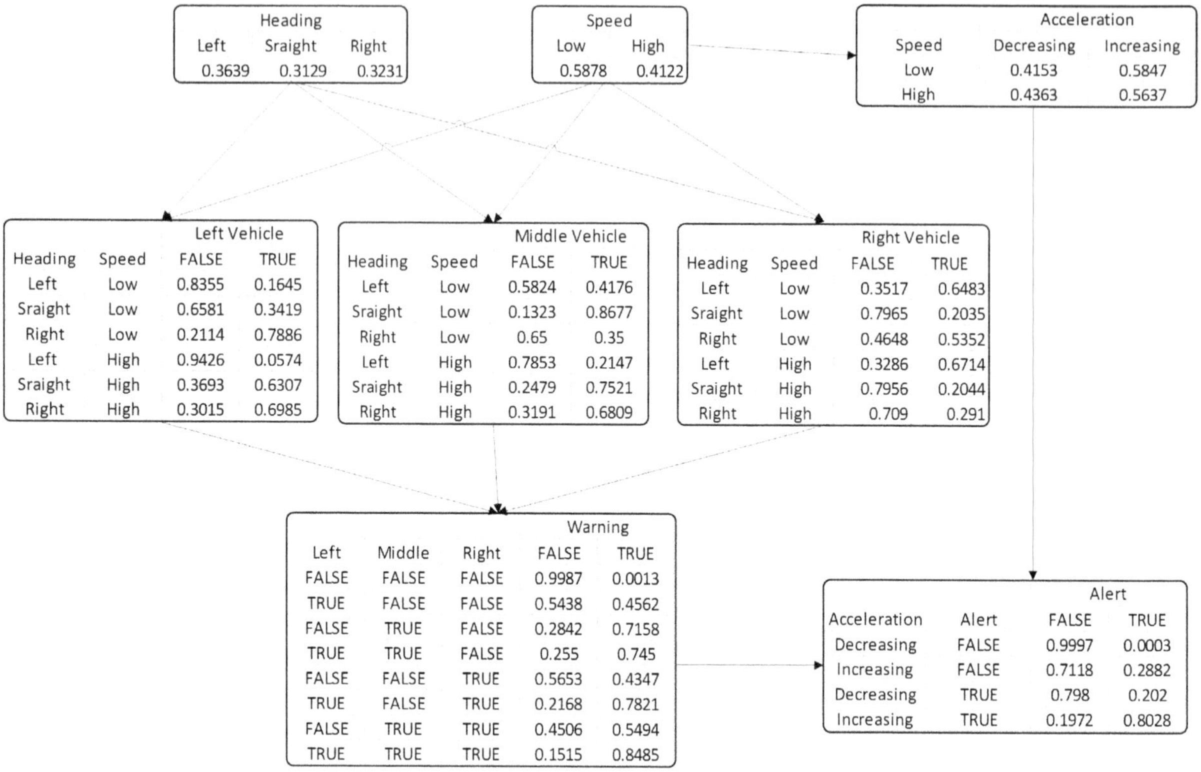

Figure 4: The priors and conditional probabilities for the DBN model

Several cases were considered and examined in the test condition. Cases such as vehicle heading, speed, acceleration and detected vehicle's position were included. The results can be seen in the Table 2. Separate failure rates for warning and alert were calculated. Hidden states means IMU data generated unobserved conditions in the DBN. Warning are issued when there is an adjacent vehicle and the speed is high towards the vehicles. If the vehicles accelerates further towards the vehicle, a brake alert is provided. In the Figure. 5 several warning and alert cases are shown with the corresponding results from the DBN. The results show our system performs well in detecting vehicles and issuing warnings to the driver with low failure rate. Although the brake alert had higher failure rates than the warning, it can be improved by providing more information about surrounding vehicles, such as distance to the detected vehicle and minimum distance from ego-vehicles to prevent collisions and relative speed measurements.

Cases				Failure Rate	
Heading	Speed	Acceleration	Vehicles detected	Warning	Brake Alert
Straight	Low	Hidden	Yes	5%	N/A
Straight	Low	Increasing	Yes	3%	22%
Straight	High	Increasing	No	6%	N/A
Straight	Hidden	Decreasing	Yes	5%	13%
Right	High	Hidden	Yes	8%	26%
Right	Low	Increasing	Yes	4%	17%
Left	Low	Increasing	Yes	3%	17%
Left	High	Increasing	No	4%	N/A
Left	High	Decreasing	Yes	9%	19%

Table 2: Performance of the Vehicle Alert System. N/A in brake cases means no brake is needed in those situation and Hidden means the values were unobserved in DBN.

5. CONCLUSION

This study introduces a framework to alert drivers about surrounding vehicles and current driving behavior. The final output of the system is estimated by a dynamic Bayesian network that requires an IMU sensor and a camera. The system detected nearby vehicles, and ego vehicle's speed, heading and acceleration. The network was able to provide suitable warning to the driver of adjacent vehicles and alert the driver in the case of potential collision. Experiment results showed a good performance in generating these warnings. Warning were issued with a very low failure rate and alert were generated in 80% of test cases.

Future work will improve performance using additional sensor modalities, such as radar and lidar sensors. Vehicle-to-vehicle communication could also provide information about nearby vehicle speed and turning intention. This would require a more sophisticated DBN setup. Sensor reliability and uncertainty were also an issue in the design. These parameters can be incorporated in the future designs. One key issue is the lack of suitable open training data for collision avoidance. Expectation Maximization could be improved with a more complete training data for the Bayesian network. Another avenue of future work will focus on gathering such data. Vehicle detection performance can be improved using a convolutional neural network (CNN). This work could also be extended to include detection of pedestrians and traffic signs. ADAS will be an active research area for the coming years. This work in vehicle safety can mitigate life-threating crashes.

No Warning, as no vehicles and low speed

Warning Issued, as adjacent vehicles detected

Warning issued, as adjacent vehicles created a possible collision

Warning issued, a high acceleration was found in an right turn.

Both Warning & Brake Alert are issued, as high acceleration with adjacent vehicles created a possible collision situation

Both Warning & Brake Alert are issued, a high acceleration was found in an abrupt left turn.

Figure 5: Several results of the DBN alert system

6. REFERENCES

[1] H. Cheng, *Autonomous Intelligent Vehicles: Theory, Algorithms, and Implementation.* Springer Science & Business Media, 2011.

[2] U. C. Bureau, "Transportation: Motor vehicle accidents and fatalities."

[3] S. Sivaraman and M. M. Trivedi, "A general active-learning framework for on-road vehicle recognition and tracking," *Intelligent Transportation Systems, IEEE Transactions on*, vol. 11, no. 2, pp. 267–276, 2010.

[4] N. Li and C. Busso, "Predicting perceived visual and cognitive distractions of drivers with multimodal features," *IEEE Transactions on Intelligent Transportation Systems*, vol. 16, no. 1, pp. 51–65, February 2015.

[5] N. Li, J. Jain, and C. Busso, "Modeling of driver behavior in real world scenarios using multiple noninvasive sensors," *IEEE Transactions on Multimedia*, vol. 15, no. 5, pp. 1213–1225, August 2013.

[6] A. Mukhtar, L. Xia, and T. Tang, "Vehicle detection techniques for collision avoidance systems: A review," *Intelligent Transportation Systems, IEEE Transactions on*, vol. PP, no. 99, pp. 1–21, 2015.

[7] J. Sun, Y. Zhang, and K. He, "Providing context-awareness in the smart car environment," in *Computer and Information Technology (CIT), 2010 IEEE 10th International Conference on*, June 2010, pp. 13–19.

[8] A. Rakotonirainy, "Design of context-aware systems for vehicle using complex systems paradigms," 2005.

[9] J.-D. Lee, J.-D. Li, L.-C. Liu, and C.-M. Chen, "A novel driving pattern recognition and status monitoring system," in *Advances in Image and Video Technology.* Springer, 2006, pp. 504–512.

[10] T.-T. Lee, H.-H. Chiang, J.-W. Perng, J.-J. Jiang, and B.-F. Wu, "Multi-sensor information integration on dsp platform for vehicle navigation safety and driving aid," in *Networking, Sensing and Control, 2009. ICNSC '09. International Conference on*, March 2009, pp. 653–658.

[11] M. Rockl, P. Robertson, K. Frank, and T. Strang, "An architecture for situation-aware driver assistance systems," in *Vehicular Technology Conference, 2007. VTC2007-Spring. IEEE 65th*, April 2007, pp. 2555–2559.

[12] D. Mitrovic, "Reliable method for driving events recognition," *Intelligent Transportation Systems, IEEE Transactions on*, vol. 6, no. 2, pp. 198–205, June 2005.

[13] H. Eren, S. Makinist, E. Akin, and A. Yilmaz, "Estimating driving behavior by a smartphone," in *Intelligent Vehicles Symposium (IV), 2012 IEEE.* IEEE, 2012, pp. 234–239.

[14] S. Sivaraman and M. Trivedi, "Active learning for on-road vehicle detection: a comparative study," *Machine Vision and Applications*, vol. 25, no. 3, pp. 599–611, 2014. [Online]. Available: http://dx.doi.org/10.1007/s00138-011-0388-y

[15] S. Sivaraman and M. M. Trivedi, "Looking at vehicles on the road: A survey of vision-based vehicle detection, tracking, and behavior analysis," *Intelligent Transportation Systems, IEEE Transactions on*, vol. 14, no. 4, pp. 1773–1795, 2013.

[16] N. Dalal and B. Triggs, "Histograms of oriented gradients for human detection," in *Computer Vision and Pattern Recognition, 2005. CVPR 2005. IEEE Computer Society Conference on*, vol. 1. IEEE, 2005, pp. 886–893.

[17] S. E. Grigorescu, N. Petkov, and P. Kruizinga, "Comparison of texture features based on gabor filters," *Image Processing, IEEE Transactions on*, vol. 11, no. 10, pp. 1160–1167, 2002.

[18] L. Shen and L. Bai, "Adaboost gabor feature selection for classification," in *Proc. of Image and Vision Computing NewZealand*. Citeseer, 2004, pp. 77–83.

[19] P. Viola and M. Jones, "Rapid object detection using a boosted cascade of simple features," in *Computer Vision and Pattern Recognition, 2001. CVPR 2001. Proceedings of the 2001 IEEE Computer Society Conference on*, vol. 1. IEEE, 2001, pp. I–511.

[20] J. J. Gibson, "The perception of the visual world." 1950.

[21] N. Li, A. Sathyanarayana, C. Busso, and J. H. Hansen, "Rear-end collision prevention using mobile devices."

[22] M. van Leeuwen and F. Groen, "Vehicle detection with a mobile camera: spotting midrange, distant, and passing cars," *Robotics Automation Magazine, IEEE*, vol. 12, no. 1, pp. 37–43, March 2005.

[23] F. Jensen and T. Nielsen, *Bayesian networks and decision graphs*. New York, NY, USA: Springer Verlag, November 2010.

[24] S. Al-Sultan, A. H. Al-Bayatti, and H. Zedan, "Context-aware driver behavior detection system in intelligent transportation systems," *Vehicular Technology, IEEE Transactions on*, vol. 62, no. 9, pp. 4264–4275, 2013.

[25] S. O. Madgwick, "An efficient orientation filter for inertial and inertial/magnetic sensor arrays," *Report x-io and University of Bristol (UK)*, 2010.

[26] B. Barshan and H. F. Durrant-Whyte, "Inertial navigation systems for mobile robots," *Robotics and Automation, IEEE Transactions on*, vol. 11, no. 3, pp. 328–342, 1995.

[27] T. Imamura, H. Yamashita, Z. Zhang, M. Rizal bin Othman, and T. Miyake, "A study of classification for driver conditions using driving behaviors," in *Systems, Man and Cybernetics, 2008. SMC 2008. IEEE International Conference on*. IEEE, 2008, pp. 1506–1511.

[28] N. Oliver and A. P. Pentland, "Driver behavior recognition and prediction in a smartcar," pp. 280–290, 2000.

[29] T. Bar, D. Nienhuser, R. Kohlhaas, and J. Zollner, "Probabilistic driving style determination by means of a situation based analysis of the vehicle data," in *Intelligent Transportation Systems (ITSC), 2011 14th International IEEE Conference on*, Oct 2011, pp. 1698–1703.

[30] K. P. Murphy, "The bayes net toolbox for matlab," *Computing Science and Statistics*, vol. 33, p. 2001, 2001.

[31] C. Caraffi, T. Vojir, J. Trefny, J. Sochman, and J. Matas, "A system for real-time detection and tracking of vehicles from a single car-mounted camera," in *ITS Conference*, Sep. 2012, pp. 975–982.

[32] A. Geiger, P. Lenz, and R. Urtasun, "Are we ready for autonomous driving? the kitti vision benchmark suite," in *Computer Vision and Pattern Recognition (CVPR), 2012 IEEE Conference on*. IEEE, 2012, pp. 3354–3361.

[33] J.-L. Blanco-Claraco, F.-Á. Moreno-Dueñas, and J. González-Jiménez, "The málaga urban dataset: High-rate stereo and lidar in a realistic urban scenario," *The International Journal of Robotics Research*, vol. 33, no. 2, pp. 207–214, 2014.

Automatic Detection of Mind Wandering During Reading Using Gaze and Physiology

Robert Bixler[1], Nathaniel Blanchard[1], Luke Garrison[1], Sidney D'Mello[1,2]

[1]Department of Computer Science and Engineering
[2]Department of Psychology
University of Notre Dame, Notre Dame, IN, 46556, USA
{rbixler, nblancha, lgarrison, sdmello}@nd.edu

ABSTRACT

Mind wandering (MW) entails an involuntary shift in attention from task-related thoughts to task-unrelated thoughts, and has been shown to have detrimental effects on performance in a number of contexts. This paper proposes an automated multimodal detector of MW using eye gaze and physiology (skin conductance and skin temperature) and aspects of the context (e.g., time on task, task difficulty). Data in the form of eye gaze and physiological signals were collected as 178 participants read four instructional texts from a computer interface. Participants periodically provided self-reports of MW in response to pseudorandom auditory probes during reading. Supervised machine learning models trained on features extracted from participants' gaze fixations, physiological signals, and contextual cues were used to detect pages where participants provided positive responses of MW to the auditory probes. Two methods of combining gaze and physiology features were explored. Feature level fusion entailed building a single model by combining feature vectors from individual modalities. Decision level fusion entailed building individual models for each modality and adjudicating amongst individual decisions. Feature level fusion resulted in an 11% improvement in classification accuracy over the best unimodal model, but there was no comparable improvement for decision level fusion. This was reflected by a small improvement in both precision and recall. An analysis of the features indicated that MW was associated with fewer and longer fixations and saccades, and a higher more deterministic skin temperature. Possible applications of the detector are discussed.

Categories and Subject Descriptors

H.5.m [Information Interfaces and Presentation]: Miscellaneous

General Terms

Human Factors

Keywords

Mind wandering; gaze tracking; user modeling; affect detection

1. INTRODUCTION

Mind wandering (MW) is a ubiquitous phenomenon that is characterized by an involuntary shift in attention away from the task at hand toward task-unrelated thoughts. Studies have shown that MW occurs frequently [17, 18, 29, 36] and that it is negatively correlated with performance across a variety of tasks requiring conscious control (see meta-analysis [25]). For example, MW is associated with increased error rates during signal detection tasks [33], lower recall during memory tasks [35], and poor comprehension during reading tasks [10, 31]. Based on this research, it is evident that performance on tasks that require attentional focus can be hindered by MW. This suggests that there is an opportunity to improve task performance by attempting to reduce MW and correct its negative effects. Automatic detection of MW is a fundamental step needed towards creating a system capable of responding to MW. As reviewed below, prior work has mainly focused on unimodal MW detection. This paper explores the potential benefits of multimodal MW detection by fusing eye gaze data and physiology data along with contextual cues during computerized reading.

ICMI '15, November 09-13, 2015, Seattle, WA, USA
© 2015 ACM. ISBN 978-1-4503-3912-4/15/11…$15.00
DOI: http://dx.doi.org/10.1145/2818346.2820742

1.1 Related Work

MW detection is most closely related to the field of attentional state estimation. Attentional state estimation has been explored in a variety of domains and with a variety of end-goals. For example, attention has been used to evaluate adaptive hints in an educational game [22] and to optimize the position of news items on a screen [23]. Attentional state estimators have been developed for several tasks such as identifying object saliency during video viewing [42], and for monitoring driver fatigue and distraction [8]. These studies mainly focus on unimodal detection of attention using eye gaze, though the studies on driver fatigue also use driving performance measures such as steering wheel motion.

Some studies combine multiple modalities for attention detection. For example, Stiefelhagen *et. al* [37] attempted to detect the focus of attention of individuals in an office space based on gaze and sound. They found that accuracy increased to 75.9% when combining both modalities, compared to an accuracy of 73.9% when using gaze alone. Similarly, Sun *et. al* [38], focused on detecting attention using keystroke dynamics and facial expression. They logged keystrokes and mouse movements while recording participants' faces as they completed three tasks related to conducting research, such as searching for and reading academic papers. Combining features from these modalities resulted in an attention detection accuracy of 77.8%, which reflects a negligible improvement compared to the best unimodal model with an accuracy of 76.8%.

This work focuses on MW detection and shares similarities and differences from previous work on attentional state estimation. Although both attentional state estimation and MW detection entail identifying aspects of a user's attention, MW detection is concerned with detecting more covert forms of involuntary attentional lapses. MW can be considered to be a form of looking without seeing – gaze might be focused on relevant parts of the interface (e.g., an image on a multimedia presentation), but attention is focused on completely unrelated thoughts (e.g., what to have for dinner).

There have recently been a number of studies that have attempted to create MW detectors using a variety of modalities, including acoustic prosodic information [9], eye gaze [4], physiology [5, 24], reading time [11], and interaction patterns [20]. A subset of these are briefly reviewed below.

Drummond and Litman [9] were the first to build a MW detector using acoustic-prosodic information. Participants were instructed to read and summarize a biology paragraph aloud while indicating at set intervals their degree of "zoning out" on a 7 point Likert scale. Responses of 1-3 were taken to reflect "low zone outs" while responses of 4-7 corresponded to "high zone outs." Their model was able to discriminate between "low" versus "high" zone outs with an accuracy of 64%, which reflects a 22% improvement over chance. However, it is unclear if their model generalizes to new users as the authors did not use user-independent cross validation.

Eye gaze has shown considerable promise for MW detection due to decades of information showing support for a link between external information and eye movements during reading [16, 26]. For example, compared to normal reading, MW during reading is associated with longer fixation durations [27], a higher frequency of subsequent fixations on the same word [39], a higher frequency of blinks [36], and larger pupil diameters [12, 32]. Capitalizing on these relationships, Bixler *et. al* [4], used eye gaze features to detect MW while students read instructional texts with a computer interface. Their models attained an above chance classification accuracy of 28% using user-independent cross validation.

Physiology might also be a suitable modality for MW detection due to the relationship between physiological arousal from the sympathetic nervous system and attentional states [1]. In particular, a relationship between MW and skin conductance has previously been documented [33]. Blanchard *et. al* [5] leveraged this information to detect MW using galvanic skin response and skin temperature collected with the Affectiva Q sensor. The authors were able to achieve an above-chance classification accuracy of 22% in a manner that generalized to new users.

1.2 Current Study: Novelty and Contribution

The current study builds on our previous work on MW detection from eye gaze [4] and physiology [5] by considering a combination of modalities along with the inclusion of contextual cues. To the best of our knowledge, this represents the first multimodal MW detector and one of the few attempts to combine eye gaze, physiology, and contextual factors. This particularly unique combination of modalities poses interesting challenges (discussed below) since the three channels operate at rather different time scales.

The multimodal MW detector was developed in the context of computerized reading, which is a critical component of many real-world tasks. By focusing on a more general activity such as reading, we aim for the detector to be applied more broadly. There is also a particularly strong negative correlation between MW and reading comprehension [10, 29, 34], suggesting the need for automated methods to detect and eventually address MW during reading.

Our approach entails simultaneously collecting eye gaze data via an eye tracker and physiology data via a wearable sensor while participants read instructional texts on a computer screen. MW was tracked using auditory thought probes (discussed further below). Features are extracted from the eye gaze signal, physiology signal, and contextual cues from the reading interface. Supervised machine learning models used these features to detect the presence or absence of MW (from thought probes). We adopted rather simple modality fusion approaches in this early stage of research. Feature level fusion entailed creating one model after fusing features from the individual modalities. Decision level fusion entailed training a separate model for each modality and combining their decisions. We constructed and validate our models in a user-independent fashion that involves no user overlap across training and testing sets.

A challenge when combining gaze and physiology data pertained to how much data should be used to compute features. It is desirable to detect MW using the least amount of data possible so it can be detected sooner. Eye gaze is a modality that quickly reflects stimuli-related changes, while physiological signals like skin temperature and skin conductance take longer to respond [33]. Although smaller amounts of data might work when using eye gaze to detect MW, the same amount of data might not adequately capture changes in the physiological signal. The previous related studies built MW detectors using between 3-30 seconds of data, so it was important to investigate how the amount of data monitored affected detection accuracy. It could also be the case that a different amount of data are optimal for unimodal versus multimodal detection. Hence, we built a variety of single and multimodal models using different window sizes and combinations of window sizes.

2. DATA COLLECTION

2.1 Participants

The entire dataset consisted of 178 undergraduate students that participated for course credit. Of these, 93 participants were from a medium-sized private Midwestern university while 85 were from a large public university in the South. The average age of participants was 20 years (SD = 3.6). Demographics included 62.7% female, 49% Caucasian, 34% African American, 6% Hispanic, and 4% "Other." There was no physiology data available for the large public university in the South. As a result, we focused on data from the medium-sized private Midwestern university.

2.2 Texts and Experimental Manipulations

Participants read four different texts on research methods topics (experimenter bias, replication, causality, and dependent variables) adapted from a set of texts used in the educational game *Operation ARA!* [15]. On average the texts contained 1,500 words (*SD* = 10) and were split across 30-36 pages with approximately 60 words per page. Each page was presented on a computer screen with size 36 Courier New font.

There were two within-subject experimental manipulations: difficulty and value. The difficulty manipulation consisted of presenting either an easy or a difficult version of each text. A text was made more difficult by replacing words and sentences with more complex alternatives while retaining semantics, length, and content. The value manipulation involved designating each text as either a *high-value* text or a *low-value* text. Participants were informed that a post-test followed the reading, and questions from *high-value* texts would be worth three times as much as questions from *low-value* texts.

Each participant read four texts on four topics in four experimental conditions (easy-low value; easy-high value; difficult-low value; difficult-high value). The order of the four texts, experimental conditions, and assignment of condition to text was counterbalanced across participants using a Graeco-Latin Square design. The difficulty and value manipulations were part of a larger research study [19] and are only used here as contextual features when building the MW detectors.

2.3 Mind Wandering Probes

Nine pseudorandom pages in each text were identified as *probe pages*. An auditory thought probe (i.e., a beep) was triggered on probe pages at a randomly chosen time interval 4 to 12 seconds after the page appeared. These probes were considered to be *within-page probes*. An *end-of-page probe* was triggered if the page was a probe page and the participant attempted to advance to the next page before the within-page probe was triggered. Participants were instructed to indicate if they were MW or not by pressing keys marked "yes" or "no," respectively. MW was defined to participants as follows: "At some point during reading, you may realize that you have no idea what you just read. Not only were you not thinking about the text, you were thinking about something else altogether." Thought probes are a standard and validated method for collecting online MW reports [21, 34]. Although misreports are possible, alternatives for tracking MW such as EEG or fMRI have yet to be sufficiently validated and are not practical in many real world applications due to their cost.

2.4 Procedure

All procedures were approved by the ethics board of both Universities prior to data collection. After signing an informed consent, participants were asked to be seated in front of either a Tobii TX 300 or Tobii T60 eye tracker depending on the university (both were in binocular mode). The Tobii eye trackers are remote eye trackers, so participants could read freely without any restrictions on head movement. In addition, an Affectiva Q sensor was strapped to the inside of the participant's non-dominate wrist, a standard placement to measure skin conductance.

Participants completed a multiple choice pretest on their knowledge of the research methods topics followed by a 60-second standard eye tracking calibration procedure. Participants were then instructed how to respond to the MW probes based on the definition discussed above and instructions from previous studies [10]. Next, they then read four texts for an average reading time of 32.4 minutes (*SD* = 9.09) on a page-by-page basis, using the space bar to navigate forward. Participants then completed a post-test and were fully debriefed.

2.5 Instances of Mind Wandering

There were a total of 6,408 probes with responses from the 178 participants. However, there were two factors that reduced the final number of instances. First, there was only physiology data for participants from one of the two schools, which reduced the number of instances to 3,361. Second, within-page and end-of-page probes capture different types of MW, so separate models had to be built for each type of probe. This resulted in 2,556 instances for within-page probes and 805 instances for end-of-page probes. End-of-page models are not analyzed further because of the relatively low number of instances. Of the remaining 2,556 within-page probes, participants responded "yes" 663 times, resulting in a MW rate of 26%.

3. SUPERVISED CLASSIFICATION

The goal was to build supervised machine learning models from short windows of data prior to each MW report. We began by detecting eye movements from the raw gaze signal and computing features based on the eye movements within each window. We then processed the physiological signal by filtering measurements compromised by abrupt movements based on accelerometer readings from the Affectiva Q [5]. A variety of operations were applied to the datasets, such as resampling the training set to correct class imbalance through downsampling the majority class or oversampling the minority class, and removing outliers. Our models were evaluated with a leave-one-participant-out cross-validation method, where data for each participant was classified using a model built from the data from the other participants.

3.1 Feature Engineering

3.1.1 Gaze Features

The first step was to convert the raw gaze data into eye movements. Gaze fixations (points where gaze was maintained on the same location) and saccades (eye movements between fixations) were estimated from raw gaze data using a fixation filter algorithm from the Open Gaze And Mouse Analyzer (OGAMA), an open source gaze analyzer [40]. Next, the time series of gaze fixations was segmented into windows of varying length (4, 6, and 8 seconds), each ending with a MW probe. The windows ended immediately before the auditory probe was triggered in order to avoid confounds associated with motor activities in preparation for the key press in response to the probe.

The window sizes of 4, 6, and 8 seconds were selected based on the constraints of the experimental design in that probes occurred between 4 to 12 seconds into the onset of a page. Windows shorter than four seconds were not considered because they likely did not contain sufficient data to compute gaze features. Window sizes above 8 were not considered because there were too few pages where the probe occurred past the 8 second mark to build meaningful models. Furthermore, windows that contained less than five fixations were also eliminated due to insufficient data for the computation of gaze features.

Two sets of gaze features were computed: 46 global gaze features and 23 local gaze features, yielding 69 gaze features overall. The features are listed below but the reader is directed to [3] for detailed descriptions of the gaze features.

Global gaze features were independent of the words being read and consisted of two categories. Eye behavior measurements captured descriptive statistics of five properties of eye gaze: *fixation duration, saccade duration, saccade distance, saccade angle*, and *pupil diameter*. For each of these five behavior measurements, we computed the minimum, maximum, mean, median, standard deviation, skew, kurtosis, and range, thereby yielding 40 features. Additional global features included *number of saccades*, proportion of *horizontal saccades*, *blink count, blink time, fixation dispersion*, and *fixation duration/saccade duration ratio*.

Unlike global features, *local gaze features* were sensitive to the words being read. The first set of local features captured information pertaining to different fixation types. These included *first pass fixations, regression fixations, single fixations, gaze fixations,* and *non-word fixations* [4]. Specific local features included the mean and standard deviation of the durations of each fixation type and the proportion of each fixation type compared to the total number of fixations. This resulted in 15 local features. The number of *end-of-clause* fixations was also used as a feature, based on the well documented sentence wrap-up effect [41], which suggests that fixations at the end of clauses should result in longer processing times.

Four additional local features captured the extent to which well-known relationships between characteristics of words (in each window) and gaze fixations were observed. These included Pearson correlations between fixation durations and *length*, *hypernym depth*, *global frequency* [2], and *synset size* of a word. These features exploit known relationships during normal reading, such as a positive correlation between word length and fixation duration, which are expected to break down due to the perceptual decoupling associated with MW [28].

Three final local features captured relationships between the movements of the eye across the screen with respect to the position of the words on the screen. These included the proportion of *cross line saccades*, *words skipped*, and the *reading time ratio*.

3.1.2 Physiology Features

Physiology features were calculated from skin conductance (SC) and skin temperature (ST) signals collected with an Affectiva Q sensor attached to participants' wrists. In all, 89 physiology features were calculated. Similar to the gaze data, features were calculated from a specific period of time prior to each probe. However, physiology data is not as sensitive to changing screens (when participants advance to the next page), so it was feasible to compute larger windows that extended beyond page boundaries. Window sizes were chosen based on results from a previous study [5], and included both short (i.e., 3 and 6 seconds) and long (i.e., 20, and 30 seconds) windows.

The physiology data were preprocessed in several ways. First, both SC and ST signals were z-score standardized at the participant level to mitigate individual differences in physiological responses. Second, a low pass 0.3 Hz filter was applied to the SC data in order to reduce noise. Finally, abrupt movements were detected using the accelerometer data (also collected by the sensor) and were removed because they can introduce noise in the physiological signals.

The same 43 features were calculated from the SC signal and the ST signal, resulting in 86 features. Signal processing techniques were employed to create different transformations of each signal and the mean, standard deviation, maximum, ratio of peaks to signal length, and ratio of valleys to signal length of the different versions were computed and used as features. The different transformations included the *standardized signal*, an approximation of the *derivation of the signal* (D1) obtained by taking the difference between the data points of the original signal, the *second derivative* (D2) obtained by taking the difference between the data points of D1, the *phase* component and the *magnitude* component of the signal computed with a Fourier transform; the spectral density of the original signal obtained using *Welch*'s method; the *autocorrelation* of the original signal; and the *magnitude squared coherence*. Finally, the slope and y-intercept of the slope *coefficient* of the linear trend line were also calculated. Additional details on the features can be found in [5].

3.1.3 Context Features

Context features were considered to be secondary to gaze and physiological features because they mainly captured situational rather than individualized aspects of the reading task. Context features included *session time*, *text time*, *session page number*, *text page number*, *average page time, previous page time,* ratio of the *previous page time* to the *average page time, current difficulty, current value, previous difficulty* and *previous value*. In all, there were 11 context features that are fully described in [4].

3.2 Model Building

Supervised classifiers were built using the aforementioned features to discriminate positive instances of MW (responding "yes" to a MW probe) from negative instances (responding "no" to a MW probe) of MW. Thirteen supervised machine learning algorithms from Weka [13] were used, including Bayesian models, decision tables, lazy learners, logistic regression, and support vector machines. Models were built from datasets with a number of varying parameters in order to identify the most accurate models as well as to explore how different factors affect classification accuracy.

The first parameter varied was the window size used. For gaze data, windows were 4, 6, or 8 seconds before each MW probe. A wider range of window sizes was available for physiology data, so window sizes of 3, 6, 20, and 30 were used. The same window sizes were used for both ST and SC data.

Second, *feature selection* was applied to the *training set only* in order to remove collinear features (e.g., number of fixations and number of saccades) and to identify the most diagnostic features. Features that were strongly correlated with other features but weakly correlated with MW reports were ranked using correlation-based feature selection (CFS) [14]. The top 20%, 30%, 40%, 50%, 60%, 70%, or 80% of features ranked by CFS were included; the specific percentage was another parameter that was varied.

Third, outlier treatment was performed in order to remove the destabilizing effect of outliers on our models. Outlier treatment consisted of replacing values greater/lower than 3 standard deviations above/below the mean with the corresponding value +3 or -3 standard deviations above/below the mean. Datasets were constructed either with outliers treated or with outliers retained.

Fourth, the *training* data was resampled to maintain an even class distribution ("no" MW responses accounted for 74% of all responses), as an uneven class distribution can have adverse effects on classification accuracy. Downsampling consisted of removing instances from the most common MW response (i.e., "no" responses) at random until there were an equal number of "yes" and "no" responses in the training set. Oversampling consisted of using the SMOTE (Synthetic Minority Over-sampling Technique) algorithm [6] as implemented in Weka to oversample the minority class by generating synthetic surrogates. Importantly, the sampling methods were only applied to the training data, but not the testing data.

Finally, we varied the features used and the method of fusing modalities. Unimodal models included gaze and context features or physiology and context features. Context features were combined with gaze and physiology features rather than included alone because previous research indicated that are mainly complementary features that improve accuracy rather than stand on their own [4, 5]. As the inclusion of the context features was consistent across models, any multimodal improvement could be attributed to the fusion of the physiology and gaze features. We also tested two standard methods of fusing the modalities as discussed below.

3.3 Multimodal Fusion

Two approaches were used for multimodal fusion. For feature level fusion, gaze and physiology features were calculated separately. The first step was to combine the feature vectors corresponding to the same probe. If either gaze features or physiology features were missing for a given probe the entire instance was removed. For feature level fusion, it was deemed important that each modality be equally represented in the set of features. Therefore, an equal number of features was selected from each modality. For example, suppose there were 32 features after collinear features were removed. If feature selection was set to select 50% of the features, then eight features from one modality and eight features from the other would be selected, resulting in a total of 16 features.

Decision level fusion consisted of building two unimodal models and combining the results to reach a final conclusion. The unimodal models provided a confidence (ranging from 0 to 1) for each instance being classified as MW. The confidence values for each model were averaged. If the average confidence was above 0.5, the instance was classified as a positive instance of MW, otherwise it was classified as a negative instance of MW. In the case where there was confidence from only one modality due to missing data, the final decision was based on the modality with available data only.

3.4 Validation

A leave-one-participant-out validation method was used to ensure that data from each participant was exclusive to either the training or testing set. Using this method, data from one participant were held aside for the testing set while data from the remaining participants were used to train the model. Furthermore, a nested cross validation was performed on the training set in order to optimize feature selection. Specifically, data from a random 66% of the participants in the training set were used to perform feature selection. Feature selection was repeated five times in order to remove the variance caused by a random selection of participants. The feature rankings were averaged over these five iterations, and a certain percentage (ranging from 20%-80% - see above) of the highest ranked features were included in the model. Sampling was performed after feature selection and was repeated five times.

Model performance was evaluated using the kappa value [7], Which corrects for random guessing in the presence of uneven class distribution, as is the case for our data. The kappa value is calculated using the formula K = (Observed Accuracy - Expected Accuracy) / (1 - Expected Accuracy), where Observed Accuracy is equivalent to recognition rate and Expected Accuracy is computed from the marginal class distributions. Kappa values of 0, 1, > 0, and < 0 indicate chance, perfect, above chance, and below chance agreement, respectively.

4. RESULTS

4.1 Feature Level Fusion

We built a feature level fusion model for each variation of the parameters as described above and selected the best performing feature level fusion model based on two criteria. We first identified models with a precision greater than .5. From those models, we chose the one with the highest kappa value. We then compared these models to two unimodal models (gaze-context, physiology-context) chosen in the same manner. The unimodal models were built using only the instances that contained data from both modalities so that the same instances were used to build both the unimodal models and the feature level fusion models. The best feature level fusion models and the corresponding unimodal models for each combination of window sizes are shown in Table 1.

Table 1. Results for feature level fusion models

Window Size		**N**	**Kappa**			**% Better**
G+C	*P+C*		*G+C*	*P+C*	*F*	
4	3	1483	.07	.09	.11	22%
4	6	1485	.11	.12	.12	0%
4	20	1491	.10	.11	.15	36%
4	30	1490	.12	.11	.11	-8%
6	3	1057	.11	.11	.17	55%
6	6	1064	.14	.12	.15	7%
6	20	1063	.11	.09	.09	-18%
6	30	1054	.11	.09	.12	9%
8	3	655	.14	.16	.16	0%
8	6	659	.13	.11	.15	15%
8	20	659	.14	.10	.13	-7%
8	30	652	**.15**	**.15**	**.19**	27%
Mean			**.12**	**.11**	**.14**	**11%**

Note: G = gaze; P = physiology; C = context;
F = feature level fusion

For each window size combination, we calculated the percent improvement of the feature level fusion model over the best unimodal model. In three cases the gaze-context model performed best; this occurred for window sizes of 4 and 30, 6 and 20, and 8 and 20 for gaze and physiology respectively. However, in every other case the feature level fusion model performed either better than or equivalent to either unimodal models alone. On average, there was an 11% improvement in multimodal classification accuracy compared to accuracy of the best unimodal model. The overall best model was a feature level fusion model with a kappa of .19, reflecting a 27% improvement over the best unimodal model (kappa of 0.15).

A previous study [4] found that gaze window size had an effect on classification accuracy. In order to investigate this effect for our feature level fusion models, we averaged the best models of each gaze and physiology window size (Table 2). We note that as the gaze window size increases, so too does the accuracy of the unimodal models and the feature level fusion models. This is likely due to more available information for the larger window sizes. However, the improvement due to feature level fusion remained consistent among all window sizes. The physiology window size did not have a noticeable effect on the overall accuracy of the models, though the greatest improvement was seen with a physiology window size of 3.

We then analyzed the effect of feature level fusion by comparing the precision and recall between the best feature level fusion model and the two unimodal models with the same window size. The gaze model had a precision of .607 and a recall of .327 while the physiology model had a precision of .503 and a recall of .336. The feature level fusion model improved both the number of instances of MW that were correctly classified, with a precision of .613, as well as increased the number of instances classified as MW, with a recall of .351. Therefore, feature level fusion resulted in a subtle but definitive improvement.

Table 2. Results for feature level fusion models aggregated across window sizes

Window Size		Avg N	Kappa			% Better
			G + C	*P + C*	*F*	
G	4	1487	.10	.11	.12	14%
	6	1060	.12	.11	.13	13%
	8	656	.14	.13	.16	13%
P	3	1065	.11	.12	.15	22%
	6	1069	.13	.12	.14	11%
	20	1071	.11	.10	.12	6%
	30	1065	.13	.11	.14	11%

Note: G = gaze; P = physiology; C = context; F = feature level fusion

4.2 Decision Level Fusion

The results for decision level fusion are shown in Table 3. The decision level models and unimodal models were chosen using the same selection criteria as was used for selecting the feature level fusion models. Of note is that the unimodal models in this comparison contained a larger number of instances than the unimodal models in the feature level fusion comparison. This is because any instances without data from both modalities were removed when building the feature level fusion models. However, each unimodal model within the decision level model fusion used all the available instances regardless of the other modality.

In contrast to the feature level fusion models, only three decision level models resulted in a positive improvement (window sizes of 4 and 6, 8 and 3, and 8 and 30 for gaze and physiology respectively). Every other decision level model resulted in a lower kappa value than the best associated unimodal model. On average, decision level fusion had a negative effect on classification accuracy, and will not be analyzed further.

Table 3. Results for best decision level models

Window Size		N		Kappa			% Better
G+C	*P+C*	*G+C*	*P+C*	*G+C*	*P+C*	*D*	
4	3	2020	1995	.06	.13	.10	-21%
4	6	2020	2006	.06	.10	.13	29%
4	20	2020	2011	.06	.13	.12	-7%
4	30	2020	2013	.06	.11	.10	-10%
6	3	1464	1995	.09	.13	.11	-17%
6	6	1464	2006	.09	.10	.10	0%
6	20	1464	2011	.09	.13	.10	-25%
6	30	1464	2013	.09	.11	.10	-8%
8	3	906	1995	**.10**	**.13**	**.14**	6%
8	6	906	2006	.10	.1	.10	-2%
8	20	906	2011	.10	.13	.11	-14%
8	30	906	2013	.10	.11	.12	11%
Mean				**.08**	**.12**	**.11**	**-5%**

Note: G = gaze; P = physiology; C = context; D = decision level fusion

4.3 Feature Analysis

We also investigated how the features varied between positive ("yes" responses to a MW probe) and negative ("no" responses to a MW probe) instances of MW in order to obtain a better understanding of how eye gaze and physiology differ during MW compared to normal reading. The mean values of each feature for "yes" and "no" MW responses were analyzed using a paired samples *t*-test. We chose to analyze the dataset associated with the best performing feature level fusion model shown in Table 1 above. It was necessary that there to be at least one "yes" response and one "no" response from each participant in order to perform a paired samples *t*-test. As a result, only 39 participants with both types of responses in this dataset were included in the analysis. The features that were significantly different (two tailed $p < .05$) between "yes" and "no" MW responses are included in Table 4.

There are several conclusions that can be drawn from Table 4. Saccades were greater in duration and fewer in number (implying fewer fixations as well) during MW compared to normal reading. In addition, there were fewer horizontal saccades during MW. Fixations were also greater in duration, evidenced by a greater mean, median, standard deviation, and maximum overall fixation duration. This is also supported by a greater mean duration for single fixations, first pass fixations, and gaze fixations, and a greater standard deviation for first pass fixations. A greater fixation duration during MW is corroborated by previous research [27]. Thus, with respect to eye gaze, MW was associated with fewer, but longer fixations along with longer and more irregular saccades (since saccades during reading should largely be horizontal). There were also differences in ST, such as a greater number of peaks in the autocorrelation of the ST signal, fewer peaks and valleys in the frequency of the ST signal, and a greater mean ST during MW. These results suggest that the ST was higher and more consistent during MW.

Table 4. Mean value of features for Yes and No responses to MW probes for the best performing feature level fusion model

Feature	Mean Yes	Mean No
Number of Saccades	51.79	58.89
Fixation Duration Mean	242.89	226.64
Fixation Duration Median	216.98	205.64
Fixation Duration SD	110.58	89.93
Fixation Duration Max	574.66	504.59
Single Fixation Duration Mean	249.78	222.34
First Pass Fixation Duration Mean	239.48	225.94
First Pass Fixation Duration SD	96.62	81.90
Gaze Fixation Duration Mean	240.55	222.90
Saccade Duration Median	26.65	20.33
Horizontal Saccade Proportion	.96	.98
Temp Autocorrelation Peak Ratio	.21	-.10
Temp Frequency Valley Ratio	-.22	.10
Temp Frequency Peak Ratio	-.21	.10
Temp Standardized Signal Mean	.10	-.17

Note: SD = standard deviation; degrees of freedom = 38; all differences are significant at $p < .05$

5. DISCUSSION

The paper focused on building the first multimodal MW detector using eye-gaze, physiology, and context features. In the remainder of this section, we discuss our main findings, consider applications of the MW detector, and discuss limitations and avenues for future work.

5.1 Main Findings

Our results highlight a number of important findings for building MW detectors. Most importantly, we developed the first MW detector built using both gaze and physiological data. Our results show that there is an average improvement in kappa value of 11% when using feature level fusion compared to unimodal detectors alone. In contrast, decision level fusion resulted in a small 5% drop in accuracy when compared to unimodal detection. Feature level fusion also resulted in a small improvement in both precision and recall compared to unimodal classification. We also found that larger gaze window sizes resulted in higher kappa values overall, which is consistent with previous research [3]. This is likely because smaller gaze windows provide less evidence to distinguish MW from normal reading, resulting in lower accuracy. It is also possible that the difference in window sizes is partially due to the methodology of the study. The instances with a gaze window of 8 seconds are a subset of those with a gaze window of 4 seconds. It could be the case that reports that occur before 8 seconds are more difficult to classify than those that occur later. In contrast to gaze window sizes, there was not a clear difference in accuracy across different physiology window sizes, suggesting that the choice of physiology window size matters less. Further research with larger gaze window sizes and with different tasks would be useful towards determining an ideal gaze window size, and if it is consistent across tasks. Finally, we analyzed how features differed between positive and negative instances of MW. Our findings were largely similar to previous findings, in that MW was associated with fewer fixations of greater duration [27] and a deviation from normal reading patterns exhibited by greater saccade durations and fewer horizontal saccades [3]. We also discovered that skin temperature followed more deterministic patterns and was higher during MW compared to normal reading.

5.2 Applications

The primary application of a MW detector is inclusion in an interface with the intent of improving productivity. MW has been shown to negatively affect text comprehension [25], so any interface that includes text comprehension could be improved by dynamically responding to MW. One example of an intervention is to recommend to re-read or self-explain a passage when MW is detected. Interventions should not disrupt the participant if MW is detected incorrectly and should be used sparingly so participants are not overwhelmed. In addition to reading, it is possible that MW detection and intervention could also be attempted across a wider array of tasks and contexts. For example, outside of learning contexts, a MW detector could be employed in situations requiring vigilance such as driving or operation of a control room. More research is needed to understand the need for and potential of automatic MW detection systems in different domains.

5.3 Limitations and Future Work

There are some limitations to the current study. The data was collected in a lab environment and participants were limited to undergraduates located in the United States. This limits our claims of generalizability to individuals from different populations. In addition, physiological data was available for only half of the participants. This ended up resulting in a smaller amount of data available to build models. This is one potential cause of the lower unimodal kappa values in relation to previous MW detectors [4, 5]. With this in mind, a second study with data from both modalities and from both schools is warranted. Another limitation is that an expensive, high quality eye tracker was used for data collection, which limits the scalability of using eye gaze as a modality for MW detection. However, this could be addressed by the decreasing cost of consumer-grade eye tracking technology, such as Eye Tribe and Tobii EyeX, or with promising alternatives that use webcams for gaze tracking [30]. It is also possible that participants did not provide accurate or honest self-caught reports. This is a clear limitation although it should be noted that both the probe-caught and self-caught methods have been validated in a number of studies [33, 34] and there is no clear alternative for tracking a highly internal state like MW. Alternatives such as EEG and fMRI can be costly, and their efficacy is equivocal. Another limitation is our moderate classification results, with the best user-independent kappa of .19. There are several reasons for the moderate accuracy. MW is a subtle and highly internal state and little is known about the onset and duration of MW. Further, we did not optimize our model for individual users or optimize the classification algorithm parameters, which would ostensibly improve performance but also run the risk of overfitting.

5.4 Concluding Remarks

In summary, this study demonstrated the possibility of a MW detector that uses both eye movements and physiology data along with contextual cues. We combined these modalities through feature level fusion and decision level fusion. Feature level fusion resulted in an average improvement of 11% while there was no improvement for decision level fusion. Importantly, our approach used an unobtrusive remote eye tracker and wrist-attached physiological sensor, thereby allowing for unrestricted head and body movement. The next step involves integrating the detector into an adaptive system in order to trigger interventions that attempt to reorient attentional focus when MW is detected.

Acknowledgment. This research was supported by the National Science Foundation (DRL 1235958). Any opinions, findings and conclusions, or recommendations expressed are those of the authors and do not necessarily reflect the views of NSF.

References

[1] Andreassi, J.L. 2013. *Psychophysiology Human Behavior & Physiological Response.* Psychology Press.

[2] Baayen, R.H. et al. 1995. The CELEX Lexical Database (Release 2).

[3] Bixler, R. and D'Mello, S. 2015. Automatic Gaze-Based Detection of Mind Wandering with Metacognitive Awareness. *User Modeling, Adaptation, and Personalization.* Springer. 31-43

[4] Bixler, R. and D'Mello, S. 2014. Toward Fully Automated Person-Independent Detection of Mind Wandering. *User Modeling, Adaptation, and Personalization.* Springer. 37–48.

[5] Blanchard, N. et al. 2014. Automated Physiological-Based Detection of Mind Wandering During Learning. *Intelligent Tutoring Systems*, 55–60.

[6] Chawla, N.V. et al. 2002. SMOTE: Synthetic Minority Over-Sampling Technique. *Journal of Artificial Intelligence Research.* 16, 1, 321–357.

[7] Cohen, J. 1960. A Coefficient of Agreement for Nominal Scales. *Educational and Psychological Measurement.* 20, 1, 37–46.

[8] Dong, Y. et al. 2011. Driver Inattention Monitoring System for Intelligent Vehicles: A Review. *IEEE Transactions on Intelligent Transportation Systems.* 12, 2, 596–614.

[9] Drummond, J. and Litman, D. 2010. In the Zone: Towards Detecting Student Zoning Out Using Supervised Machine Learning. *Intelligent Tutoring Systems*, 306–308.

[10] Feng, S. et al. 2013. Mind Wandering While Reading Easy and Difficult Texts. *Psychonomic Bulletin & Review*. 20, 3, 586–592.

[11] Franklin, M.S. et al. 2011. Catching The Mind in Flight: Using Behavioral Indices to Detect Mindless Reading in Real Time. *Psychonomic Bulletin & Review*. 18, 5, 992–997.

[12] Franklin, M.S. et al. 2013. Window to the Wandering Mind: Pupillometry of Spontaneous Thought While Reading. *The Quarterly Journal of Experimental Psychology*. 66, 12, 2289–2294.

[13] Hall, M. et al. 2009. The WEKA Data Mining Software: an Update. *ACM SIGKDD Explorations Newsletter*. 11, 1, 10–18.

[14] Hall, M.A. 1999. *Correlation-Based Feature Selection for Machine Learning*. Department of Computer Science, The University of Waikato, Hamilton, New Zealand.

[15] Halpern, D.F. et al. 2012. Operation ARA: A Computerized Learning Game that Teaches Critical Thinking and Scientific Reasoning. *Thinking Skills and Creativity*. 7, 2, 93–100.

[16] Just, M.A. and Carpenter, P.A. 1980. A Theory of Reading: From Eye Fixations to Comprehension. *Psychological Review*. 87, 4, 329.

[17] Kane, M.J. et al. 2007. For Whom the Mind Wanders, and When An Experience-Sampling Study of Working Memory and Executive Control in Daily Life. *Psychological Science*. 18, 7, 614–621.

[18] Killingsworth, M.A. and Gilbert, D.T. 2010. A Wandering Mind is an Unhappy Mind. *Science*. 330, 6006, 932–932.

[19] Mills, C. et al. 2015. The Influence of Consequence Value and Text Difficulty on Affect, Attention, and Learning While Reading Instructional Texts. *Learning and Instruction*. 40, 9–20.

[20] Mills, C. and D'Mello, S. In Press. Toward a Real-time (Day) Dreamcatcher: Detecting Mind Wandering Episodes During Online Reading. *Proceedings of the 8th International Conference on Educational Data Mining*.

[21] Mooneyham, B.W. and Schooler, J.W. 2013. The Costs and Benefits of Mind-Wandering: A Review. *Canadian Journal of Experimental Psychology/Revue Canadienne de Psychologie Expérimentale*. 67, 1, 11–18.

[22] Muir, M. and Conati, C. 2012. An Analysis of Attention to Student – Adaptive Hints in an Educational Game. *Intelligent Tutoring Systems*. S.A. Cerri et al., eds. Springer Berlin Heidelberg. 112–122.

[23] Navalpakkam, V. et al. 2012. Attention and Selection in Online Choice Tasks. *User Modeling, Adaptation, and Personalization*. J. Masthoff et al., eds. Springer Berlin Heidelberg. 200–211.

[24] Pham, P. and Wang, J. 2015. AttentiveLearner: Improving Mobile MOOC Learning via Implicit Heart Rate Tracking. *Artificial Intelligence in Education*. C. Conati et al., eds. Springer International Publishing. 367–376.

[25] Randall, J.G. et al. 2014. Mind-Wandering, Cognition, and Performance: A Theory-Driven Meta-Analysis of Attention Regulation. *Psychological Bulletin*. 140, 6, 1411–1431.

[26] Rayner, K. 1998. Eye Movements in Reading and Information Processing: 20 Years of Research. *Psychological bulletin*. 124, 3, 372.

[27] Reichle, E.D. et al. 2010. Eye Movements During Mindless Reading. *Psychological Science*. 21, 9, 1300–1310.

[28] Schooler, J.W. et al. 2011. Meta-Awareness, Perceptual Decoupling and the Wandering Mind. *Trends in Cognitive Sciences*. 15, 7, 319–326.

[29] Schooler, J.W. et al. 2004. Zoning Out While Reading: Evidence for Dissociations Between Experience and Metaconsciousness. *Thinking and Seeing: Visual Metacognition in Adults and Children*. D.T. Levin, ed. MIT Press. 203–226.

[30] Sewell, W. and Komogortsev, O. 2010. Real-Time Eye Gaze Tracking with an Unmodified Commodity Webcam Employing a Neural Network. *CHI'10 Extended Abstracts on Human Factors in Computing Systems*, 3739–3744.

[31] Smallwood, J. et al. 2007. Counting the Cost of an Absent Mind: Mind Wandering as an Underrecognized Influence on Educational Performance. *Psychonomic Bulletin & Review*. 14, 2, 230–236.

[32] Smallwood, J. et al. 2011. Pupillometric Evidence for the Decoupling of Attention from Perceptual Input During Offline Thought. *PLoS ONE*. 6, 3.

[33] Smallwood, J. et al. 2004. Subjective Experience and the Attentional Lapse: Task Engagement and Disengagement During Sustained Attention. *Consciousness and Cognition*. 13, 4, 657–690.

[34] Smallwood, J. et al. 2008. When Attention Matters: The Curious Incident of the Wandering Mind. *Memory & Cognition*. 36, 6, 1144–1150.

[35] Smallwood, J. and Schooler, J.W. 2006. The Restless Mind. *Psychological Bulletin*. 132, 6, 946–958.

[36] Smilek, D. et al. 2010. Out of Mind, Out of Sight: Eye Blinking as Indicator and Embodiment of Mind Wandering. *Psychological Science*. 21, 6, 786–789.

[37] Stiefelhagen, R. et al. 2001. Estimating Focus of Attention Based on Gaze and Sound. *Proceedings of the 2001 workshop on Perceptive user interfaces*, 1–9.

[38] Sun, H.J. et al. 2014. Nonintrusive Multimodal Attention Detection. *ACHI 2014, The Seventh International Conference on Advances in Computer-Human Interactions*, 192–199.

[39] Uzzaman, S. and Joordens, S. 2011. The Eyes Know What You are Thinking: Eye Movements as an Objective Measure of Mind Wandering. *Consciousness and Cognition*. 20, 4, 1882–1886.

[40] Voßkühler, A. et al. 2008. OGAMA (Open Gaze and Mouse Analyzer): Open-Source Software Designed to Analyze Eye and Mouse Movements in Slideshow Study Designs. *Behavior Research Methods*. 40, 4, 1150–1162.

[41] Warren, T. et al. 2009. Investigating the Causes of Wrap-Up Effects: Evidence from Eye Movements and E–Z Reader. *Cognition*. 111, 1, 132–137.

[42] Yonetani, R. et al. 2012. Multi-Mode Saliency Dynamics Model for Analyzing Gaze and Attention. *Proceedings of the Symposium on Eye Tracking Research and Applications*, 115–122.

Multimodal Detection of Depression in Clinical Interviews

Hamdi Dibeklioğlu[1,*], Zakia Hammal[2,*], Ying Yang[3], and Jeffrey F. Cohn[2,4]
[1]Pattern Recognition and Bioinformatics Group, Delft University of Technology, Delft, The Netherlands
[2]Robotics Institute, Carnegie Mellon University, Pittsburgh, PA, USA
[3]Center for Cognitive Brain Imaging, Carnegie Mellon University, Pittsburgh, PA, USA
[4]Department of Psychology, University of Pittsburgh, Pittsburgh, PA, USA
h.dibeklioglu@tudelft.nl, zakia_hammal@yahoo.fr, yingyang02@gmail.com, jeffcohn@cs.cmu.edu

ABSTRACT

Current methods for depression assessment depend almost entirely on clinical interview or self-report ratings. Such measures lack systematic and efficient ways of incorporating behavioral observations that are strong indicators of psychological disorder. We compared a clinical interview of depression severity with automatic measurement in 48 participants undergoing treatment for depression. Interviews were obtained at 7-week intervals on up to four occasions. Following standard cut-offs, participants at each session were classified as remitted, intermediate, or depressed. Logistic regression classifiers using leave-one-out validation were compared for facial movement dynamics, head movement dynamics, and vocal prosody individually and in combination. Accuracy (remitted versus depressed) for facial movement dynamics was higher than that for head movement dynamics; and each was substantially higher than that for vocal prosody. Accuracy for all three modalities together reached 88.93%, exceeding that for any single modality or pair of modalities. These findings suggest that automatic detection of depression from behavioral indicators is feasible and that multimodal measures afford most powerful detection.

Categories and Subject Descriptors

I.5.4 [**Pattern Recognition**]: Applications; J.4 [**Social and Behavioral Sciences**]: Psychology

Keywords

Depression; Facial Movement; Head Movement; Vocal Prosody

1. INTRODUCTION

Depression is one of the most common and recurrent psychological disorders and a leading cause of disease burden [23]. The World Health Organization predicts that depression will become the leading cause of disease burden within the next 15 years [21]. Reliable assessment is critical to understand mechanisms, discover and implement more effective treatment, and ameliorate this trend.

*These authors contributed equally.

ICMI 2015, November 9–13, 2015, Seattle, WA, USA.
© 2015 ACM. ISBN 978-1-4503-3912-4/15/11 ...$15.00.
DOI: http://dx.doi.org/10.1145/2818346.2820776.

Many symptoms of depression are observable. They profoundly influence the behavior of affected individuals and the reactions of their family members and others. DSM-5 [4] describes a range of audiovisual indicators. These include facial expression and demeanor, inability to sit still, pacing, hand-wringing and other signs of psychomotor agitation, slowed speech and body movements, reduced interpersonal responsiveness, and decreased vocal intensity and inflection in psychomotor retardation. Yet, screening and diagnosis of depression fail to exploit these signs and symptoms. They rely instead almost entirely on patients' verbal reports. Recent advances in automatic analysis of face, voice, and body movement could play a vital role in the clinical science of depression, screening efforts, treatment, and community intervention.

Automatic assessment of depression from behavioral cues is of increasingly interest to both psychologists and computer scientists. The latter use signal processing, computer vision, and pattern recognition methodologies. From the computer-science perspective, efforts have sought to identify depression from vocal utterances [10], facial expression [9, 25], head movements/pose [1, 20, 25], body movements [20], and gaze [2]. While most research is limited to a single modality, there is increasing interest in multimodal approaches to depression detection [22, 26]. Multimodal assessment raises several issues. One is whether one or another modality is more informative? Ekman [13] claimed that facial expression is less revealing than body and was equivocal about face relative to voice. Alternatively, one could imagine that high redundancy across channels would render modest any potential gain of a multimodal approach. Comparative studies are needed to explore these questions. Two is choice of context. Audio/Visual Emotion Challenge (AVEC) explored multimodal expression during an individual task, for which audience effects would likely be absent. Research by Fridlund and others [16] suggests that when other people are present, signal strength of nonverbal behavior increases. Nonverbal reactions to and from others present additional sources of information. Three, feature selection and approaches to fusion are critical. Several studies are relevant to these issues.

We investigated the discriminative power of three modalities – facial movement dynamics, head movement dynamics, and vocal prosody– individually and in combination. Instead of using a large number of descriptors, or selecting informative features individually, an optimum feature set was obtained by maximizing the combined mutual information. In contrast to previous work, we focused on both individual and interpersonal behavior. Informed by the psychology literature, we anticipated that interpersonal context would provide powerful detection of depression. To capture aspects of psychomotor retardation and agitation, we include dynamic measures of expressive behavior. Additionally, in contrast to previous work, all participants met DSM criteria for major depression as determined by diagnostic interview, and symptom severity and recovery were ground-truth using state-of-the-art depression severity interviews. Diagnostic criteria are important because many non-depressive disorders are confusable with depression. By using diagnostic criteria, we were able to rule out participants that may have had PTSD or other related disorder.

2. MATERIALS

2.1 Participants

Fifty-seven depressed participants (34 women, 23 men) were recruited from a clinical trial for treatment of depression. They ranged in age from 19 to 65 years (μ=39.65) and were Euro- or African-American (46 and 11, respectively). At the time of study intake, all met DSM-IV [3] criteria for Major Depressive Disorder [14]. Although not a focus of this report, participants were randomized to either anti-depressant treatment with a selective serotonin re-uptake inhibitor or Interpersonal Psychotherapy. Both treatments are empirically validated for treatment of depression [18]. Data from 48 participants were available for analysis. Participant loss was due to change in original diagnosis, severe suicidal ideation, and methodological reasons (e.g., missing audio/video).

2.2 Observational Procedures

Symptom severity was evaluated on four occasions at 1, 7, 13, and 21 weeks by ten female clinical interviewers. Interviewers were not assigned to specific participants, and they varied in the number of interviews they conducted. Four interviewers were responsible for the bulk of the interviews. Interviews were conducted using the Hamilton Rating Scale for Depression (HRSD), which is a criterion measure of depression severity [17]. Interviewers were expert in the HRSD and reliability was maintained above 0.90. HRSD scores >14 are considered to indicate moderate to severe depression; scores <8 indicate return to normal [15]. These cut-off scores were used to define depression and remission status. Sessions with scores between 7 and 15 were removed from analyses.

Video was obtained from a VGA camera positioned about 15° from frontal view. Audio from participants and interviewers was digitized at 48 kHz and later down-sampled to 16 kHz for speech processing. Missing data occurred from missed appointments and technical problems. To be included for analysis, we required a minimum of 20 speaker turns of 3 seconds minimum duration and at least 50 seconds of vocalization in total. The final sample was 95 sessions from 48 participants; 58 depressed and 37 remitted.

3. METHODS

Since depression can impact a wide range of behavior, we propose a multimodal assessment from facial movement, head movement, and vocal prosody.

3.1 Tracking of Landmarks and Head Pose

To track and align facial shape and head pose, we used a person-independent approach (ZFace) [19], which accomplishes 3D registration from 2D video without requiring person-specific training (for details, see [19]). Forty-nine facial landmarks (fiducial points on the regions of eyebrows, eyes, nose, and mouth), and the three degrees of rigid head movements (i.e., pitch, yaw, and roll) were tracked.

3.1.1 *Facial Movement Dynamics*

Previous research has found that facial movement dynamics are discriminative for facial expressions [8, 12]. We investigated the reliability of depression severity assessment from facial movement dynamics. To control for variation due to rigid head movement, fiducial points were normalized by removing translation, rotation, and scale. The movement of the normalized 98 time series (49 fiducial points $\times$ x and y coordinates) was then smoothed by the 4253H-twice method [27]. For a compact representation, principal component analysis was used to reduce the 98 time series to 15 time series components $\mathcal{D}_i$, where $i = \{1, 2, 3, \ldots, 15\}$. These 15 components accounted for 95% of the variance; they are referred to as amplitude of facial movement. The velocity ($\mathcal{V}_i = \frac{d\mathcal{D}_i}{dt}$) and acceleration ($\mathcal{A}_i = \frac{d^2\mathcal{D}_i}{dt^2}$) of change in the extracted 15 time series were computed as the derivatives of the corresponding amplitude. Based on previous research [11], each time series is divided into increasing ($^+$) and decreasing ($^-$) segments for dynamic feature extraction. Twenty one features were then used to measure the dynamics of facial displacement, velocity, and acceleration, respectively, as described in Table 1. By concatenating the features extracted from the 15 time series components, 315-dimensional (21 features $\times$ 15 time series components) dynamic features were obtained.

Table 1: Twenty one dynamic features for facial fiducial points and head pitch, yaw, and roll.

Feature	Definition
Maximum Ampl.:	$\max(\mathcal{D})$
Mean Amplitude:	$\left[\frac{\sum\mathcal{D}}{\eta(\mathcal{D})}, \frac{\sum\mathcal{D}^+}{\eta(\mathcal{D}^+)}, \frac{\sum\mathcal{D}^-}{\eta(\mathcal{D}^-)} \right]$
STD of Amplitude:	$\mathrm{std}(\mathcal{D})$
Maximum Speed:	$\left[\max(\lvert\mathcal{V}\rvert), \max(\lvert\mathcal{V}^+\rvert), \max(\lvert\mathcal{V}^-\rvert) \right]$
Mean Speed:	$\left[\frac{\sum\mathcal{V}}{\eta(\mathcal{V})}, \frac{\sum\mathcal{V}^+}{\eta(\mathcal{V}^+)}, \frac{\sum\mathcal{V}^-}{\eta(\mathcal{V}^-)} \right]$
STD of Speed:	$\mathrm{std}(\mathcal{V})$
Maximum Accel.:	$\left[\max(\lvert\mathcal{A}\rvert), \max(\lvert\mathcal{A}^+\rvert), \max(\lvert\mathcal{A}^-\rvert) \right]$
Mean Accel.:	$\left[\frac{\sum\mathcal{A}}{\eta(\mathcal{A})}, \frac{\sum\mathcal{A}^+}{\eta(\mathcal{A}^+)}, \frac{\sum\mathcal{A}^-}{\eta(\mathcal{A}^-)} \right]$
STD of Accel.:	$\mathrm{std}(\mathcal{A})$
$^+/^-$ Frequency:	$\left[\frac{\tau^+}{\eta(\mathcal{A}^+)}, \frac{\tau^-}{\eta(\mathcal{A}^-)} \right]$

3.1.2 *Head Movement Dynamics*

Head angles in the horizontal, vertical, and lateral directions were used to measure head movement. These directions correspond to head nods (i.e. pitch), head turns (i.e. yaw), and lateral head inclinations (i.e. roll). Similarly to fiducial points, head angles were first smoothed using the 4253H-twice method [27]. The three normalized time series of pitch, yaw, and roll were then used to measure head movement amplitudes. Head movement velocity and acceleration for pitch, yaw, and roll were computed as the derivative of the amplitude and velocity, respectively. Twenty one features were then used to measure the magnitude of variation of the amplitude, velocity, and acceleration of head movement (see Table 1). By concatenating the features extracted from the 3 time series components, 63-dimensional (21 features $\times$ 3 time series components) dynamic features were extracted.

3.2 Vocal Prosody

Previous research has shown that switching pause duration and vocal fundamental frequency (f_0) are discriminative features for depression severity assessment [9, 28]. We used both features for depression assessment.

Since audio was recorded in a clinical office setting rather than laboratory setting, some acoustic noise was unavoidable. An intermediate level of 40% noise reduction was used to achieve the desired signal-to-noise ratio without distorting the original signal. Each pair of recordings was transcribed manually using Transcriber software [6], force-aligned using CMU Sphinx III [7], and post-processed using Praat [5]. Because session recordings exceeded the memory limits of Sphinx, it was necessary to segment recordings prior to forced alignment. We segmented recordings at transcription boundaries; that is, whenever a change in speaker occurred, resulting in speaker-specific segments. Forced alignment produced a matrix of four columns: speaker (which encoded both individual and simultaneous speech), start time, stop time, and utterance (see [28] for details). The forced alignment timings were used to identify speaker-turns and speaker diarization for the subsequent automatic feature extraction.

3.2.1 *Switching Pause Duration*

Switching pause, or latency to speak, is defined as the pause duration between the end of one speaker's utterance and the start of an utterance by the other. Switching pauses were identified from the matrix output of Sphinx. So that back channel utterances would not confound switching pauses, overlapping voiced frames were excluded. Switching-pauses were aggregated to yield mean duration and coefficient of variation (CV) for both participants and interviewers. The CV is the ratio of standard deviation to the mean. It reflects the variability of switching pauses when the effect of mean differences in duration is removed. In order to characterize the participants latency to speak, mean, variance, and variation coefficient of switching pause durations were computed.

3.2.2 *Fundamental Frequency (f_0)*

For each participant's utterance, f_0 was computed automatically using the autocorrelation function in Praat [5] with a window shift of 10 ms. Since microphones were not calibrated for intensity, intensity measures were not considered. To measure dynamic changes in f_0, mean amplitude, variation coefficient of amplitude, mean speed, and mean acceleration of f_0 were extracted.

3.3 Feature Selection and Classification

Min-Redundancy Max-Relevance (mRMR) algorithm [24] was used to select the most relevant features based on mutual information. Let S_{m-1} be the set of selected $m-1$ features, then the mth feature can be selected from the set $\{F - S_{m-1}\}$ as:

$$\max_{f_j \in F - S_{m-1}} \left[I(f_j, c) - \frac{1}{m-1} \sum_{f_i \in S_{m-1}} I(f_j, f_i) \right], \quad (1)$$

where I is the mutual information function and c is the target class. F and S denote the original feature set, and the selected sub set of features, respectively. Eq. 1 is used to determine which feature is selected at each iteration of the algorithm. The size of the selected feature set is determined based on the validation error.

Due to notable overlap in the feature space, density-based models would be an efficient choice for distinguishing between depression and remission. Logistic regression classifiers using leave-one participant-out cross-validation were employed for depression assessment from facial movement dynamics, head movement dynamics, and vocal prosody.

4. RESULTS

We seek to discriminate depression (HRSD <8) and remission (HRSD >14) using facial movement dynamics, head movement dynamics, and vocal prosody, separately and in combination. We use a two-level leave-one participant-out cross-validation scheme:

Table 2: Accuracy (%) of using the different modalities.

	Modality	Remission	Depression	Mean
Current Study	Facial Movement Dynamics	78.38	84.49	81.44
	Head Movement Dynamics	72.97	86.21	79.59
	Vocal Prosody	75.68	63.79	69.73
Previous Studies	Facial Movements [9]	75.68	81.03	78.35
	Head Mov. GMM [1]	74.97	65.07	70.02
	Head Mov. Functionals [1]	83.71	74.16	78.94
	Vocal Prosody [28]	56.76	79.31	68.03

Table 3: Accuracy (%) of different feature selection methods.

	Modality	Feature Selection		
		none	t-test based	mRMR
Current Study	Facial Movement Dynamics	71.83	73.56	**81.44**
	Head Movement Dynamics	72.09	68.03	**79.59**
	Vocal Prosody	**69.73**	68.52	**69.73**
Previous Studies	Facial Movements [9]	71.34	71.71	**78.35**
	Head Mov. GMM [1]	58.67	68.97	**70.02**
	Head Mov. Functionals [1]	70.97	77.89	**78.94**
	Vocal Prosody [28]	68.03	**68.52**	68.03

Each time a test fold is separated, a leave-one participant-out cross-validation is used to train the system, and parameters are optimized without using the test partition. Minimum classification error on a separate validation set is used to determine the most discriminative set of features. For the fusions, whole set of features are fused into one low-abstraction vector and feature selection is applied afterwards to optimize the informativeness of the feature combinations.

4.1 Assessment of Modalities

Accuracy differed between modalities ($F_{2,282} = 3.16$, p=0.04). Both facial movement dynamics and head movement dynamics performed better than vocal prosody for depression status (p=0.02, t =2.24, df=94 and p=0.03, t=2.24, df=94, respectively). No difference was found between facial movement dynamics and head movement dynamics (p=0.83, t=2.20, df=94). Overall, visual information performed better for depression status than vocal prosody.

To further assess the quality of the feature sets, we compared the obtained results with recently proposed methods using facial movement [9], head movement [1], and prosodic features [28] for depression detection. For a fair comparison, we evaluated all methods using the same feature selection algorithm (i.e., mRMR), and the same classification procedure (i.e., logistic regression).

As shown in Table 2, the proposed features outperformed their counterparts for each modality. The accuracy of the proposed facial movement dynamics is approximately 3% higher than that of facial movement features in [9]. Proposed head movement dynamics performed better than representing head movements by Gaussian Mixture Model (GMM) parameters or functionals as in [1]. A small increase (1.7%) was obtained with the proposed prosodic features compared to their counterpart in [28].

4.2 Assessment of Feature Selection

To evaluate the reliability and effectiveness of mRMR feature selection, we compare mRMR results to the t-test threshold based feature selection method proposed in [1], and without any feature selection step (see Table 3). Because the number of samples per class was unbalanced, average accuracies for remission and depression are reported instead of total correct classification rate.

Feature selection using mRMR performed better for all but voice features in [28]. The t-test based method provided a 0.5% accuracy improvement over the use of raw features. This finding may be explained by the carefully defined feature sets with a limited dimen-

Table 4: Accuracy (%) of fusing different modalities.

Modality	Remission	Depression	Mean
Face + Head	81.08	89.66	85.37
Face + Voice	78.38	87.93	83.15
Head + Voice	83.78	81.03	82.41
Head + Face + Voice	**86.49**	**91.38**	**88.93**

Note: Face and Head refer to the facial movement dynamics and head movement dynamics, respectively (see Table 1 and Section 3.1). Voice refers to the prosodic features (see Section 3.2).

sionality (4 vocal features in [28], 7 vocal features in the current study). Overall, the results suggest the value of maximizing the combined mutual information of individual features.

4.3 Multimodal Fusion

Because individual features may provide additional discrimination power, we concatenated features of different modalities prior to feature selection. As shown in Table 4, the combination of facial and head movement dynamics performed best, followed by facial movement dynamics and vocal prosody. Fusing of all modalities gave best result. Interestingly, correct classification patterns for each fusion combination were very different.

5. CONCLUSIONS

We proposed an automatic, multimodal assessment of depression using facial, postural, and vocal behavioral measures in participants undergoing treatment for depression. We systematically investigated the discriminative power of facial movement dynamics, head movement dynamics, and vocal prosody, individually and in combination. Face and head movement dynamics outperformed vocal prosody. Best performances were obtained when all modalities were combined.

Acknowledgements

Supported in part by NIH award 51435 to U. Pittsburgh.

6. REFERENCES

[1] S. Alghowinem, R. Goecke, M. Wagner, G. Parker, and M. Breakspear. Head pose and movement analysis as an indicator of depression. ACII, pages 283–288, 2013.

[2] S. Alghowinem, R. Goecke, M. Wagner, G. Parker, and M. Breakspear. Eye movement analysis for depression detection. ICIP, pages 4220–4224, 2013.

[3] American Psychiatric Association. *Diagnostic and statistical manual of mental disorders*. Washington, DC, 1994.

[4] American Psychiatric Association. *Diagnostic and statistical manual of mental disorders*. Washington, DC, 2013.

[5] P. Boersma and D. Weenink. Praat, a system for doing phonetics by computer. *Glot International* 5(9/10):341-345, 2001.

[6] K. Boudahmane, M. Manta, F. Antoine, S. Galliano, and C. Barras. TranscriberAG, 2011.

[7] CMU Sphinx: Open source toolkit for speech recognition. http://cmusphinx.sourceforge.net/.

[8] J.F. Cohn and K.L. Schmidt. The timing of facial motion in posed and spontaneous smiles. *Int. Journal of Wavelets, Multires. and Information Processing*, 2(2):121–132, 2004.

[9] J.F. Cohn, T.S. Kruez, I. Matthews, Y. Yang, M.H. Nguyen, M.T. Padilla, F. Zhou, and F. De la Torre. Detecting depression from facial actions and vocal prosody. ACII, 2009.

[10] N. Cummins, S. Scherer, J. Krajewskid, S. Schniederd, J. Eppsa, and T.F. Quatierif. A review of depression and suicide risk assessment using speech analysis. *Speech Communication*, 71:10–49, 2015.

[11] H. Dibeklioğlu, A.A. Salah, and T. Gevers, Are you really smiling at me? Spontaneous versus posed enjoyment smiles. ECCV, pages 525–538, 2012.

[12] H. Dibeklioğlu, A.A. Salah, and T. Gevers. Recognition of genuine smiles. *IEEE Transactions on Multimedia*, 17(3):279–294, 2015.

[13] P. Ekman. *Telling lies*. New York, NY: Norton, 2009.

[14] M.B. First, R.L. Spitzer, M. Gibbon, and J. B.W. Williams. *Structured clinical interview for DSM-IV axis I disorders: Patient Edition* (SCID-I/P, version 2.0). Biometrics Research Department, New York State Psychiatric Institute, New York, 1995.

[15] J.C. Fournier, R.J. DeRubeis, S.D. Hollon, S. Dimidjian, J.D. Amsterdam, R.C. Shelton, and J. Fawcett. Antidepressant drug effects and depression severity: A patient-level meta-analysis. *JAMA*, 303(1):47–53, 2010.

[16] A.J. Fridlund. The behavioral ecology and sociality of human faces. In M.S. Clark (Ed.), *Emotion*, pages 90–121, Sage Publications, 1992.

[17] M. Hamilton. A rating scale for depression. *Journal of Neurology and Neurosurgery*, 23:56–61, 1960.

[18] S.D. Hollon, M.E. Thase, and J.C. Markowitz. Treatment and prevention of depression. *Psychological Science in the Public Interest*, 3(2):38–77, 2002.

[19] L.A. Jeni, J.F. Cohn, T. Kanade. Dense 3D face alignment from 2D videos in real-time. AFGR, 2015.

[20] J. Joshi, R. Goecke, M. Breakspear, and G. Parker. Can body expressions contribute to automatic depression analysis? AFGR, 2013.

[21] J.P. Lepine, and M. Briley. The increasing burden of depression. *Neuropsychiatric Disease and Treatment*, 7(Suppl 1):3, 2011.

[22] G.M. Lucas, J. Gratch, S. Scherer, J. Boberg, and G. Stratou. Towards an affective interface for assessment of psychological distress. ACII, 2015.

[23] C.D. Mathers, D. Loncar. Projections of global mortality and burden of disease from 2002 to 2030. *PLoS Medicine*, 3(11) e442, 2006.

[24] H. Peng, F. Long, and C. Ding. Feature selection based on mutual information criteria of max-dependency, max-relevance, and min-redundancy. *IEEE Transactions on PAMI*, 27(8):1226–1238, 2005.

[25] G. Stratou, S. Scherer, J. Gratch, and L.-P. Morency. Automatic nonverbal behavior indicators of depression and PTSD: Exploring gender differences. ACII, pages 147–152, 2013.

[26] M.F. Valstar, B. Schuller, K. Smith, F. Eyben, B. Jiang, S. Bilakhia, S.Schnieder, R. Cowie, and M. Pantic. Int. Workshop on AVEC, pages 3–10, 2013.

[27] P.F. Velleman. Definition and comparison of robust nonlinear data smoothing algorithms. *J. Amer. Statist. Assoc.*, 75(371):609–615, 1980.

[28] Y. Yang, C. Fairbairn, and J.F. Cohn. Detecting depression severity from vocal prosody. *IEEE Transactions on Affective Computing*, 4(2):142-150, 2013.

Spoken Interruptions Signal Productive Problem Solving and Domain Expertise in Mathematics

Sharon Oviatt
Incaa Designs
137 Fisher King Lane
Deer Harbor, WA. USA 98243
oviatt@incaadesigns.org

Kevin Hang
University New South Wales
Australia
Kevin.hang07@gmail.com

Jianlong Zhou & Fang Chen
National ICT, Australia
Jianlong.Zhou@nicta.com
Fang.Chen@nicta.com.au

ABSTRACT
Prevailing social norms prohibit interrupting another person when they are speaking. In this research, simultaneous speech was investigated in groups of students as they jointly solved math problems and peer tutored one another. Analyses were based on the Math Data Corpus, which includes ground-truth performance coding and speech transcriptions. Simultaneous speech was elevated 120-143% during the most productive phase of problem solving, compared with matched intervals. It also was elevated 18-37% in students who were domain experts, compared with non-experts. Qualitative analyses revealed that experts differed from non-experts in the function of their interruptions. Analysis of these functional asymmetries produced nine key behaviors that were used to identify the dominant math expert in a group with 95-100% accuracy in three minutes. This research demonstrates that overlapped speech is a marker of group problem-solving progress and domain expertise. It provides valuable information for the emerging field of learning analytics.

Categories and Subject Descriptors
H5.2 Information interfaces and presentation: User interfaces—user-centered design, voice I/O, input devices and strategies, evaluation/methodology.

General Terms
Experimentation, Human factors, Performance, Design

Author Keywords
Collaborative problem solving; domain expertise; Math Data Corpus; simultaneous speech; interruption; dynamic group processes; multimodal learning analytics

1. INTRODUCTION
Prevailing social norms for interpersonal dialogue characterize speech interruptions as a violation of one-speaker-at-a-time turn-taking rules [18]. Conversation analysts have described overlapped speech as "problematic for the participants, and for the organization of interaction" [19]. They explain how participants "deal with such simultaneous talk," using what they describe as an "overlap resolution device" [19]. In fact, an interrupting person often is stigmatized as inconsiderate or even domineering. To avoid being interrupted, social protocol recommends that you talk faster, louder, and avoid looking directly at your interlocutor. Cautionary advice adds that when you pause, even to take a breath, you are giving another person the opportunity to interrupt. Instead, you should "power through" your utterance to get the job done. If interrupted nonetheless, you should challenge your partner with, "Can I finish?"

1.1 Related literature on simultaneous speech
Contrary to prescriptive conversation analysis ideas, social psychologists and speech researchers have acknowledged that speech interruptions actually are a frequently occurring and natural conversational behavior [7; 17]. For example, Shriberg et al [21] examined speech overlaps in different multi-party meeting and telephone corpora, and found that all corpora had high overall rates of overlapped speech. These rates ranged from 8.8% to 17% of spoken words when backchannels were included, and 5.6% to 14.1% when excluded.

Nonetheless, the basic function of simultaneous speech remains poorly understood, and almost no research has investigated its relation to task performance. Krauss and Chiu [7] critiqued research in this area for neglecting to analyze the relation of simultaneous speech to domain expertise: "A factor that is seldom taken into account in studies of [speech] interactional style is the speaker's familiarity or expertise with respect to the discussion topic." —Krauss & Chiu, p. 53

1.2 Engagement and emotional involvement
Other research indicates that speech overlaps are not necessarily indicative of attempts by a speaker to dominate [6]. In some cases, they have been associated with positive group performance dynamics [2; 4; 7]. Krauss and Chiu [7] stated that high interruption rates can result from high engagement, rather than a desire to dominate. In a similar vein, Cetin & Shriberg [2] found that speech overlaps are 50% higher during "hot spots," or periods of time when participants experience increased affective involvement during meetings. In another recent study, Dong and colleagues [4] were interested in simultaneous speech as an index of increased involvement and group "intensity." They found that higher–performing groups had an elevated incidence of overlapped speech when playing a game of twenty questions, compared with lower-performing ones. During modeling of four-person group brainstorming sessions, the number of simultaneous speakers was the best linear predictor (R^2 >.33-.35) of the total number of ideas and also the number of unique correct ideas that were produced, compared with other metrics investigated [4].

1.3 Activity theory
From an Activity theory viewpoint [10; 22], elevated speech activity serves to mediate and refine thought. Therefore, heightened simultaneous speech during multi-person conversation should be associated with improved performance, not simply heightened engagement. In particular, it should be elevated during

ICMI'15, November 09-13, 2015, Seattle, WA, USA

ACM 978-1-4503-3912-4/15/11…$15.00.
DOI: http://dx.doi.org/10.1145/2818346.2820743

the most productive phase of problem solving, when insights about solutions are most actively generated, discussed, and refined. In addition, domain experts would be expected to participate more frequently in overlapped speech events, since they are more capable of contributing insights needed to solve problems. In summary, a central novel conjecture of this research is that *simultaneous speech reflects increased conceptual activity during group problem-solving dynamics, not simply greater engagement.*

1.4 Multimodal learning analytics

If simultaneous speech does reflect heightened conceptual activity and performance, then it potentially could provide a valuable predictive index of domain expertise and learning. It may be especially valuable since past work has shown that it is not sparse data. Within learning analytics, multimodal learning analytics (MMLA) is an emerging area that analyzes natural communication modalities, such as speech, writing, gestures, facial expressions, physical activity patterns, and their combination [11; 20; 23]. It aims to identify domain expertise and learning rapidly, reliably, and objectively, and also to identify learning-oriented precursors. Unlike most current educational data mining and learning analytics work, MMLA is not limited to click-stream analysis based on keyboard interfaces. Analysis of natural communication modalities can be applied to both interpersonal and computer-mediated learning activities [14]. MMLA techniques also can collect and analyze multimodal input on cell phones and other mobile interfaces, which are the dominant and fastest growing educational platform worldwide. Most cell phones now have multimodal interfaces that support combined input using speech, touch, gestures, virtual keyboard, sensors, and pen [11; 13]. To evaluate performance and learning when using these devices, new MMLA techniques will be required rather than simple click-stream analysis.

Related literature on prediction of domain expertise and learning has studied speech signal features and lexical content quite extensively. Experts are known to have a lower rate of speech disfluencies, and to express more domain specific technical terms, lexical certainly, and positive affect. Their linguistic expressions are also more concise (i.e., lower ratio words to concepts) and reflect stronger meta-cognitive skills [3; 5; 8; 16; 23; 24]. In addition, experts' speech is delivered faster and with altered peak slope [5; 20]. The present research focuses on the temporal dynamics of speech activity in groups, with a special interest in simultaneous speech as a potential marker of domain expertise and phases of more productive problem solving.

1.5 Research objectives

To investigate this topic, simultaneous speech was examined in small groups of high school students as they jointly solved math problems and peer tutored one another. Analyses were based on the well structured Math Data Corpus, which is described in section 2 and related papers [12; 15]. This resource includes twelve time-synchronized multimodal data streams that were collected during group interactions while students solved math problems varying in difficulty (i.e., easy, moderate, hard, very hard). These data resources include detailed speech transcriptions, with the start and end time of each individual's utterance so overlapping speech could be assessed. They also include coding of problem phases, and ground-truth coding of students' problem-solving accuracy. Performance coding provides basic information on which problems during a session were solved correctly, and which student in each group was the dominant domain expert in math. Judgments regarding expertise status were based on a cumulative expertise rating described in the methods section.

In this research, specific hypotheses that were investigated include that domain experts would be identifiable by their involvement in:

- More total incidents of overlapped speech
- Longer durations of overlapped speech
- More frequent interruptions of other students

Prior research based on the Math Data Corpus has shown that experts and non-experts did not differ significantly in total speech (Scherer et al., 2012). In fact, experts spoke fewer words when explaining answers (Oviatt et al., in press), which is consistent with the research described in 1.4 documenting that domain experts are more concise. Therefore, any differences in experts' speech overlaps could not be attributed to simply talking more.

These same indices of overlapped speech also were hypothesized to be higher during "moment-of-insight" problem phases (MOI), compared with matched intervals during problem solving. The MOI phase begins when a student first proposes a problem solution orally that the group subsequently submits as their answer, and it ends when the answer is actually submitted. It represents a productive period when insights about solutions are being formulated and refined.

An additional aim of this research was to assess the function of interruptions qualitatively, and asymmetries between experts and non-experts in the purpose of their interrupting contributions. Information from these analyses then was used to create a set of distinguishing features for a composite index of predictive expertise, with the aim of rapidly and reliably distinguishing students who are domain experts from non-experts.

2. METHOD

2.1 Student participants

Participants included 18 high school students, 9 female and 9 male, who ranged in age from 15 to 17 years old. All had recently completed Introductory Geometry at a local high school. They represented a range of geometry skills from low to high performers. For the basis of student performance ratings, see Lunsford et al. [9]. Participants were paid volunteers and native English speakers. During the data collection, small groups of three students jointly solved problems and mentored one another. Each student group was matched on gender and approximate geometry skill level (low to high) to facilitate reciprocal interactions.

2.2 Math tasks

During each session, students engaged in authentic problem solving and peer tutoring as they worked on 16 geometry and algebra problems, four apiece representing easy, moderate, hard, and very hard difficulty levels. Figure 1 illustrates that these math problems were presented as word problems. They varied along dimensions known to make them more challenging (for details, see [9]).

2.3 Data collection procedure

Each of the six student groups met for two sessions, during which students could view the math problems one at a time on a tabletop computer screen. The sessions were facilitated by a system that presented the problems with accompanying visuals, terms, and equations related to solving the problems, as well as worked examples and solutions. This system was controlled by a simulation environment [1], which could deliver feedback multimodally. One student in the group was designated as the

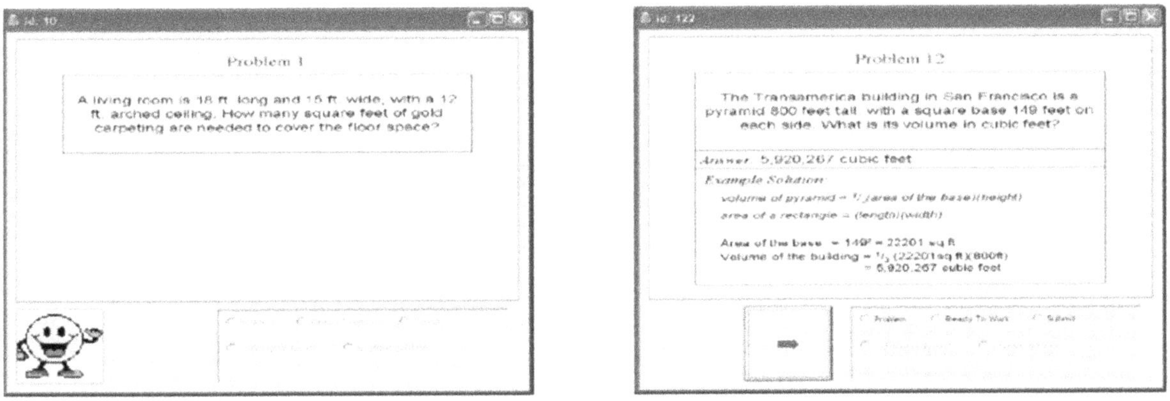

(a) Interface displaying an easy math problem.

(b) Interface displaying a very hard math problem, answer, and example solution.

Figure 1. Computer displaying easy math problem (left), and very hard one (right) along with its answer and worked solution.

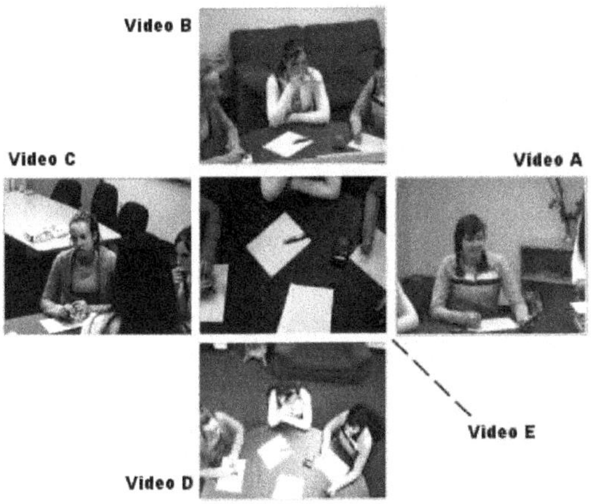

Figure 2. Synchronized views from all five cameras at same moment in time during data collection. Videos A, B and C show close-up views of individual students, video D a wide-angle view, and video E top-down view of tabletop artifacts.

leader for a given session, and this designated leader switched on the group's second session to a different student. This resulted in a total of 12 sessions involving 12 different leaders.

Each group was instructed to exchange information and expertise as they worked on solving the problems so that everyone understood the solution and could explain it if asked. To ensure that all students participated fully, they were told that during the session each participant would be randomly asked to explain one or more of the group's math solutions. The group leader was told that he or she was responsible for coordinating the group's activity and interacting with the computer system. The leader was instructed that he or she could request the system to: (1) display the problem, (2) provide definitions of math terms, (3) provide formulas, (4) turn off, to avoid distracting students while working, (5) collect the group's answer, (6) show the correct solution after the group's answer was submitted, and (7) provide a sample solution for how to solve the problem.

During each math problem, there was a predictable series of problem-solving phases. First students asked for a new problem, and they spent time reading and clarifying its meaning. During this preparatory phase, they often diagrammed the problem, and asked the system to display related information about terms and equations. Next they moved into a phase of actively working on the problem by writing relevant formulas, completing calculations, and discussing their ideas with one another. A "moment-of-insight" (MOI) phase began when one student initially proposed the solution that the group subsequently adopted and submitted as their answer. During this especially productive phase, the group discussed, refined, and submitted their solution, which then ended the MOI phase. Afterwards, students asked the system to see the correct answer so they could verify their solution. They sometimes also asked to see a worked example, especially if their answer was incorrect, in order to ensure that everyone understood how to solve the problem. During the final phase, the system often randomly called upon one student to explain how they calculated the group's solution before the group leader moved on to the next problem.

All students were allowed to use a calculator, digital pen, and large sheets of digital paper to draw diagrams, make calculations, etc. while working on each problem. Following orientation and instructions, each group was given three sample math problems to solve in order to orient them with the problems, computer, and materials. Each group session lasted about 60 to 90 minutes.

2.4 Multimodal data collection

For each group session, twelve data streams were collected involving multimodal input from video cameras, digital pens, and close-talking microphones. Figure 2 illustrates high-resolution data collected from five camera views. Digital audio recordings were collected of each participant's speech using close-talking microphones. A fourth combined audio recording was collected using an omni-directional microphone hung above the table. Each participant's writing was collected using Nokia digital pens and large sheets of Anoto digital paper. The pens provided the unique identification of each student, even when they wrote on another student's paper. Technical details of multimodal data collection are described elsewhere [15].

For the present research, detailed speech transcriptions were used based on the close-talking audio recordings from each individual student in the group. These transcriptions included the start and end time of each student utterance, its verbatim lexical content, the problem and problem phase being worked on, and which student contributed the utterance. Verbatim lexical transcription included disfluencies, confirmations, and subvocalized or whispered speech for which the content could be interpreted.

The verbatim speech transcriptions involved a 3-pass process by three professionals. A fourth expert conducted reliability checks on 20% of the final-pass transcripts, including checking for utterance content & start/end times of utterances within problem boundaries. Utterance start/end times were coded for each student individually, with the coder blind to whether other students were speaking at the same time. Software later automatically identified overlapped speech regions during a group's interaction. This process resulted in inter-rater reliabilities averaging 95% for coding the lexical content of verbatim speech and speech start and end times to the nearest one second[1]. Detailed transcription & inter-rater reliability conventions are described elsewhere [15]. Readers also can download the dataset, and conduct their own analyses as part of a series of data-driven grand challenge workshops on multimodal learning analytics (for details, see [15]).

2.5 Data coding & performance metrics

2.5.1 Segmentation of problem phases

Data were segmented into the start and end of the 16 problem-solving episodes. During each problem, the start and end of the "moment of insight" (MOI) interval also was identified. This MOI phase began when a student first proposed a solution orally, which the group later submited as their answer. It ended when the answer was actually submitted. In this research, 192 matched pairs of MOI versus non-MOI problem intervals were compared based on the same session, students, problems solved, and interaction time in seconds.

2.5.2 Ground-truth cumulative expertise rating

Each math problem had a canonical correct answer, based on objective criteria. An expert math teacher prepared scoring templates, and two coders scored all problems that each group worked on for correctness to ensure a 100% match. The student who orally initiated a problem solution that later was adopted and submitted by the group was scored for every problem, as well as whether their solution was correct or not. To assess domain expertise, each student's cumulative problem-solving performance was calculated across the two sessions. Whenever a student was the oral initiator of a group solution, the following numeric values were assigned: total number of easy problems solved versus missed (+1 or -1 pt.), moderate problems (+2 or -2 pts.), hard problems (+3 or -3 pt.), and very hard problems (+4 or -4 pt.). Based on totals, the dominant expert in each student group was identified. See [15] for details of ground-truth performance coding for the Math Data Corpus[2].

2.5.3 Total incidents of overlapped speech

The total number of times that two or more students overlapped by one second or longer in spoken utterances involving articulated speech was coded throughout the sessions. The students and problem phases involved in each incident of overlapped speech were recorded and totaled for a given session.

2.5.4 Total duration of overlapped speech

The total duration of each incident of speech overlap was coded, and totaled for each student and problem phase during a session.

2.5.5 Total number of interruptions

Each student involved in an incident of overlapped speech was coded as either the interrupted or interrupting person. The second student to speak during each incident was considered to have interrupted the first speaker. The total number of interruptions was coded by student expertise and problem phase.

2.5.6 Function of interruptions

A sample of 100 overlapped speech incidents was coded to determine the function of interrupting contributions. Half of this sample involved the dominant expert as the interrupting person, and the other half a non-expert. As a result, a sample was constructed with matched pairs based on a given problem-solving session, including the student group, math problems solved, and total interaction time. The purpose of this qualitative analysis was to uncover reasons why expert versus non-expert students differed in interruption rates, and to determine what role their interruption served with respect to advancing group problem solving.

2.5.7 Predictive index of expertise

Another goal of the functional analysis was to uncover new behavioral markers for distinguishing domain experts from non-experts. These features then potentially could be combined into a more reliable predictive index of expertise than any single marker, and they also could support more continuous prediction over time. Nine key behavioral features ultimately were identified and combined (see results section), including the following markers of expertise. Each of these behaviors received a +1 coding for expertise status per instance during the first three minutes of a group's interaction:

- Total number of interruptions
- Lexical content involving technical terms (e.g., rhombus, Pythagorean theorem)
- Utterances involving problem-solving strategies and actions (e.g., "we need to check our answer"; "now multiply by 4 cuz it's a rhombus")
- Utterances involving procedural steps and actions required during problem solving (e.g., "Submit our answer"; "Get the next problem")
- Lexical content involving disagreement (e.g., "no, wait"; "it shouldn't be…")
- Lexical content involving criticism (e.g., "you're messing up"; "you did it wrong")

In addition, each of these behaviors received a -1 coding for expertise status per instance during the first three minutes of a group's interaction:

- Asking a question about problem content (e.g., "How did you get 39?")
- Conceding or apologizing for an error (e.g., "woops, my mistake"; "I'm sorry, I forgot")

For confidence terms, positive instances indicating a high degree of confidence were coded +1, whereas the use of terms indicating a lack of confidence were coded -1 during the first three minutes of a group's interaction:

- Positive ("That's simple"), versus negative ("math makes me nervous") confidence terms

This index combined authoritative and meta-regulatory behaviors indicated by experts, along with expressions of uncertainty and acknowledgment of an expert's authoritative status by the non-experts. Analyses then evaluated a matched pair of expert/non-expert students from each group on their average index, which controlled for these students' leadership role, problem difficulty level, and total interaction time. Inter-rater reliabilities conducted on 20% of this coded data resulted in a match of 90% or above for each of the nine coded behaviors.

3. RESULTS

Data were available for analysis on 18 students during 12 group sessions, 192 problem-solving episodes (each with an MOI

---

[1] Results reported in this paper replicated when speech overlaps averaging 3 seconds or longer were analyzed.

[2] Cumulative expertise ratings based on written data were highly correlated with ones based on speech, or 86%.

phase), and 1,435 incidents of overlapped speech between two or more students.

3.1 Frequency of overlapped speech

Incidents of overlapped speech were a very frequent occurrence during these problem-solving sessions. They ranged in duration from one to sixteen seconds, and occurred at an average rate of once every 20 seconds. The rate of overlaps per minute from session 1 to 2 averaged 2.78 and 2.76, with no significant change.

3.2 Overlapped speech & moment-of-insight phase

Figure 3 illustrates the typical progression through problem-solving phases. The MOI phase was a relatively brief interval, but during this time the frequency of speech overlaps increased sharply among group members, compared with other phases. Table 1 summarizes the percentage change in both the frequency and duration of overlapped speech for matched time intervals before versus during the MOI phase for all sessions. It shows that the frequency of overlapped speech averaged a substantial 120% higher during the MOI interval. Among the twelve student sessions, all increased during the MOI phase, with increases ranging from +58% to +274%. In addition, the duration of overlaps averaged 143% higher during the MOI period. Once again, all twelve student sessions increased, with the percentage change ranging from +61% to +228%.

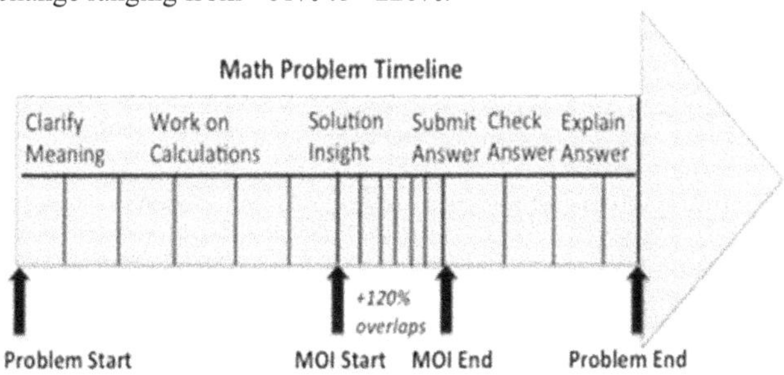

Figure 3. Typical math problem timeline with sharp increase in overlapped speech during moment-of-insight (MOI) phase.

3.3. Overlapped speech and domain expertise

Figures 4-6 illustrate the average total number of speech overlaps, average total duration of speech overlaps, and average total number of interruptions per session by students who were domain experts versus non-experts, including when members of each group were or were not serving as the group leader. Matching was performed on leadership role because previous reports have shown that the group leader speaks more than non-leaders (Scherer et al., 2012). Compared with non-experts, matched expert students were consistently elevated across all metrics involving speech overlaps.

When experts were matched with non-experts on leadership status and problem-solving session (i.e., time spent, math problems solved), statistical comparisons confirmed that experts were involved in significantly more frequent speech overlaps, paired $t = 3.76$, $p < .01$, one-tailed. They also were involved in a significantly longer duration of speech overlaps, paired $t = 3.236$, $p < .016$, one-tailed. In fact, in 100% of the matched pairs the expert students were involved in more frequent and longer speech overlaps than were non-experts. Overall, expert students were involved in 18.7% more speech overlaps, and the duration of these overlaps was 18.4% longer. During incidents of overlapped speech, experts also were the interrupting person 37.2% more often than non-experts, paired $t = 2.12$, $p < .05$, one-tailed.

Table 1. Average percentage increase in overlapped speech during matched MOI- versus non-MOI phases for all sessions

Student Group & Session	Percentage Change in Number of Overlaps	Percentage Change in Duration of Overlaps
G1D1	+84%	+163%
G1D2	+58%	+91%
G2D1	+74%	+84%
G2D2	+177%	+172%
G3D1	+111%	+146%
G3D2	+127%	+105%
G4D1	+82%	+61%
G4D2	+274%	+228%
G5D1	+197%	+227%
G5D2	+90%	+73%
G6D1	+94%	+184%
G6D2	+78%	+186%
Grand Mean	**+120%**	**+143%**

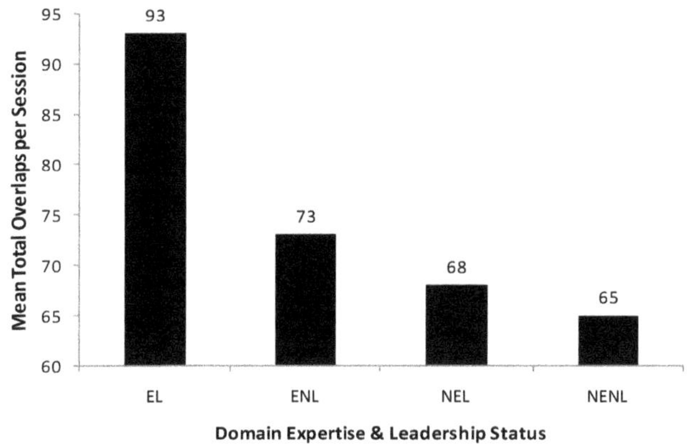

Figure 4. Average total number of speech overlaps per session for experts serving as leader or not (EL, ENL) and non-experts serving as leader or not (NEL, NENL)

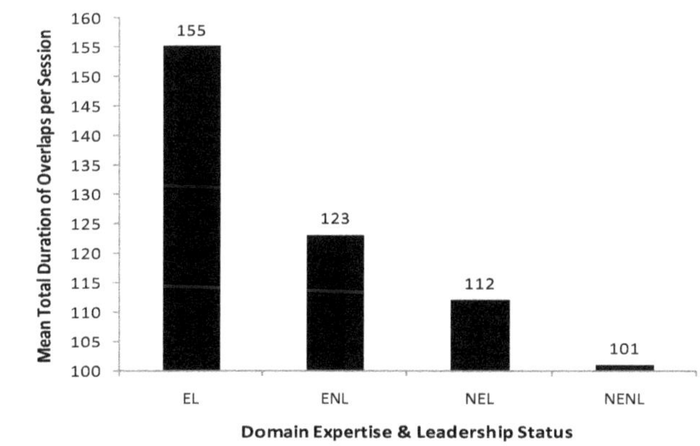

Figure 5. Average total duration of speech overlaps in seconds per session for experts serving as leader or not (EL, ENL) and non-experts serving as leader or not (NEL, NENL)

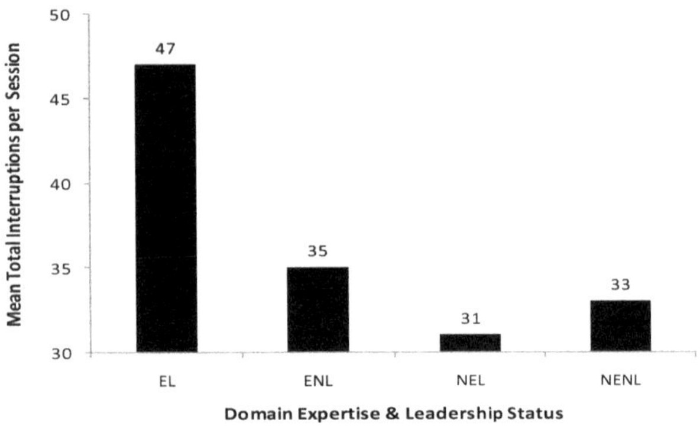

Figure 6. Average total number of interruptions per session by experts serving as leader or not (EL, ENL) and non-experts serving as leader or not (NEL, NENL)

3.4 Function of interruptions

Since domain experts interrupted substantially more frequently than non-experts during simultaneous speech events, qualitative coding was performed on the function of their interruptive contributions, compared with those by non-experts. Comparison of expert versus non-expert interruptions was based on matched pairs involving the same problem-solving session, including the same group, math problems, and time spent solving problems. This qualitative analysis was conducted to identify why expert students had higher interruption rates, and what role interruptions may play in supporting effective group problem solving.

Table 2 illustrates that interruptions by domain experts were most distinct in functioning to either (1) direct others on performing the next required problem-solving or procedural action, and (2) disagree and correct others on previous problem-solving content or a problem-solving procedure. In this regard, experts' interruptions played a direct meta-regulatory role within the group to keep the problem-solving process on track. The nature of their interruptions presumed knowledge about problem content, signaled an authoritative role, and assumed responsibility for regulating the problem-solving process for the whole group.

In contrast, less frequent interruptions by non-experts were most distinct in functioning to (1) ask questions about problem content or an answer, and (2) concede an error, apologize for making an error, or agree with an expert's correction of their error. These distinctive interruptions by non-experts explicitly signaled a lack of knowledge about problem content. In contrast with typical expert interruptions, they concede a lack of knowledge and solicit information and guidance from the expert.

3.5 Overlapped speech and group performance level

A median-split on the highest- versus lowest-performing student groups did not reveal any significant difference in the rate of simultaneous speech. The highest-performing student groups solved 94% of the math problems correctly, and their rate of simultaneous speech averaged 2.73 per minute. The lowest-performing groups averaged 68% problems correct, and 2.81 overlaps per minute.

Table 2. Function of interruptions typical of expert (E), non-expert (NE), or both, with transcript examples

Most Typical of Expert Interrupting Non-expert:

1. *Directs others on problem-solving or procedural action*

Example of problem-solving action:

NE: "Hello, 3 squared, 4 squared, 5 squared ok, cuz that's a zero at the end so it's the same"

E: "We always have to check our answer"

Example of procedural action:

NE: "Hold on, 4 feet in diameter, oh I'm sorry guys"

E: "Just click ready to work!"

2. *Disagrees or corrects others on problem-solving action*

Example of correcting problem-solving action:

NE: "well, 25 feet weighs 12 pounds, so we'll just divide."

E: "divide? you mean multiply, right?"

Example of correcting problem-solving strategy:

NE: "by doing that Pythagor// yeah, just use pythagorean theorem?"

E: "No, you don't need to do that, cuz you just have to find the area of one triangle and then multiply it by 4 because it's a rhombus"

Most Typical of Non-expert Interrupting Expert:

3. *Asks question about problem content or answer*

Example:

E: "Yeah, just write 113 or whatever"

NE: "What is our answer?"

4. *Apologizes for or agrees to expert's correction of error*

Example of apologizing for error:

E: "Vin is like bringing our score down"

NE: "I'm sorry Bruce."

Example of conceding error:

E: "no, 3 feet"

NE: "oh, I forgot the mower is 3 feet wide, not one foot wide"

Typical of Both:

5. *Contributes relevant information or answer to problem*

Example:

NE: "ok, 9-5-5-7"

E: "feet squared"

6. *Answers question or confirms information by others*

Example:

NE: "Do we need to go into that many decimals?"

E: "Yes, I don't like rounding stuff."

Example:

E: "and one triangle is one half base times height. So 3.5 times 6."

NE: "Base times height, ok"

3.6 Overlapped speech and problem difficulty

There was no significant change in average frequency of overlapped speech between easy and very hard problems.

3.7 Predictive index of expertise

Based on a combined index of expertise, which was composed of nine behavioral markers that each distinguished expert from non-expert behavior, the dominant expert in a group of three students could be identified 100% of the time within three minutes during easy, moderate, and hard problems. Across all problem difficulty levels, including very hard ones, the dominant expert could be identified accurately 95% of the time. These comparisons involved matched pairs of expert versus non-expert students within each student group, with leadership role, problem difficulty level, and interaction time all controlled.

Table 3 summarizes the average predictive index of expertise based on two problems for these non-expert/expert pairs, and the percentage change in this index for expert students. The data for each group are shown separately for easy, moderate, hard, and very hard problems. As shown in the table, the predictive index of expertise averaged +113% higher for experts on easy problems, +144% higher on moderate ones, +88% higher on hard, and +101% higher on very hard problems. Separate analyses all confirmed that these differences were statistically reliable and replicated over the easy, moderate, hard, and very hard problem levels, paired t = 5.25, $p < .003$ (one-tailed), paired t = 2.66, $p < .028$ (one-tailed), and paired t = 2.48, $p < .034$ (one-tailed), and paired t = 2.12, $p < .05$ (one-tailed) respectively.

Student Group	Percent Change for Experts, Easy	Percent Change for Experts, Moderate	Percent Change for Experts, Hard	Percent Change for Experts, VeryHard
Group 1	+500% (1,6)	+14% (7,8)	+240% (5,17)	+350% (8,36)
Group 3	+40% (5,7)	+233% (6,20)	+39% (23,32)	-30% (27,19)
Group 4	+400% (2,10)	+40% (5,9)	+500% (6,36)	+35% (17,23)
Group 5	+88% (8,15)	+500% (4,24)	+36% (22,30)	+300% (7,28)
Group 6	+63% (8,13)	+70% (10,17)	+8% (12,13)	+162%
Average	**+113%**	**+144%**	**+88%**	**+101%**

Table 3. Average predictive index of expertise for matched non-expert/expert pairs, including percentage change for experts, on problems varying in difficulty

4. DISCUSSION

Contrary to language theorists who have asserted that overlapped speech is a "violation of one-speaker-at-a-time turn-taking rules" [18], this research demonstrates that it is associated with domain expertise and highly productive phases during group problem-solving interactions. Simultaneous speech was elevated by a substantial 120-143% across a variety of related metrics during the most productive phase of problem solving, when solution insights were being proposed and refined. In addition, domain experts were involved in significantly more and longer incidents of overlapped speech than non-experts, and they interrupted non-experts 37% more often than non-experts interrupted them. Since experts did not speak more than non-experts, these overlapped speech behaviors were not a by-product of simply talking more.

Furthermore, a qualitative analysis of the function of interrupting contributions exposed major distinctions between experts and non-experts in content. Specifically, experts' interruptions were distinct in directing non-experts in the group on what procedural or problem-solving action to perform next. They also more often disagreed with or corrected non-experts on past problem-solving procedures or content. In these respects, expert behavior was *authoritative* and played a *meta-regulatory* role. In contrast, non-experts' interruptions often functioned to ask questions about the problem content, and to concede an error or apologize for making one. These characteristic behaviors expressed uncertainty. They also acknowledged the expert's more authoritative status.

Based on insights gained from the functional asymmetries evident between experts and non-experts in their speech interruptions, a predictive index of expertise was formulated based on nine distinguishing behavioral features. This index accurately predicted which student in a group of three was the dominant math expert 100% of the time within the first three minutes of interaction during easy to hard problems, and 95% of the time across all difficulty levels including very hard problems. This compares with a chance rate of 33%.

In addition to directly assessing interruptions, this index tracked *authoritative behaviors* by experts, such as their use of technical terms and confidence terms. It also tracked *meta-cognitive behaviors,* such as the language experts used to regulate the group's problem-solving strategy, content, and procedural steps. This included frequent disagreement and correction of others during problem solving, and criticism of others when they made errors. In addition, the index incorporated markers that typified non-expert behavior, including *expressing uncertainty* by asking questions about problem content, and voicing a lack of confidence about their ability or problem solving actions. It also included behaviors that *acknowledged the more authoritative status* of experts by conceding or apologizing for errors.

During the student problem-solving interactions observed, interrupting speech contributions played a positive role in facilitating group interactions and overall performance. In fact, interruptions were central and critical for the success of group problem solving. Their urgency may have led to timing them to literally cut off another person's misguided problem-solving actions. Overlapped speech in these cases could serve to more effectively attract others' attention to particularly important or contrary new information, and to more closely and effectively guide others' physical actions. In these respects, the simultaneous speech observed was a collaborative activity that supported the group's goal of achieving correct math problem solutions. From an Activity theory perspective, it should be viewed as a type of activity that dovetailed with the group's physical activity patterns to contribute to a sequence of productive problem-solving steps with a correct outcome. These functions of interrupting speech go well beyond simply reflecting increased engagement or emotional involvement.

From the viewpoint of learning analytics, analysis of simultaneous speech patterns during group problem-solving activities provided a fertile avenue for uncovering behaviors characteristic of experts versus non-experts. Speech signals and the lexical content they carry are a rich part of natural multimodal communication, and they provide an opportune window on human performance and learning. One aim of this work is to contribute to the growing body of research on multimodal learning analytics. Using new data resources like the Math Data Corpus, early results on this topic have begun to identify individual unimodal behaviors in speech, writing, vision, text, and other modes that are predictive of domain expertise, correct problem solving, and learning. The present research has focused on group dynamics, rather than individual student behaviors, as a level of analysis required to understand collaborative learning. It also combines multiple behavioral markers of expertise into a more reliable, rapid, and continuous index for predicting the presence or absence of math domain expertise in student groups.

These findings contribute to the development of learning analytics techniques based on natural rich communication modalities, which are increasingly available on many mobile devices. Future work will be needed to test the generality of these findings on larger datasets, in other content domains, and during situated classroom interactions. In the future, the present results based on speech should be combined with features identified in modalities like writing and vision to achieve improved prediction for learning analytics applications.

5. ACKNOWLEDGMENTS

This research was supported by National ICT Australia in Sydney, and Incaa Designs in the U.S. (http://www.incaadesigns.org/). Additional support was provided by the Faculty of Engineering at the University of New South Wales for a research exchange at UNSW by the first author as part of their Eminent Visiting Scholars program. Thanks also to Kate Thompson and the Center for Computer-Supported Collaborative Learning (CoCo) at the University of Sydney for their major contribution to speech transcription.

6. REFERENCES

[1] Arthur, A., Lunsford, R., Wesson, M. & Oviatt, S.L. (2006) Prototyping novel collaborative multimodal systems: Simulation, data collection and analysis tools for the next decade, *Eighth International Conference on Multimodal Interfaces (ICMI'06),* ACM: New York, 209-226.

[2] Cetin, O. & Shriberg, L. (2006) Overlap in meetings: ASR effects and analysis by dialog factors, speakers, and collection site, *Machine Learning and Multimodal Interaction, Lecture Notes in Computer Science, Springer, vol. 4299,* 212-224.

[3] Chi, M.T.H., Glaser, R., and Rees, E. (1982). Expertise in problem solving. In R.J. Sternberg (Ed.), *Advances in the psychology of human intelligence,* (Vol. 1). Hillsdale, NJ: Erlbaum.

[4] Dong, W., Kim, T. & Pentland, A. (2009) A Quantitative Analysis of Collective Creativity in Playing 20-Questions Games, *ACM Creativity & Cognition*, Berkeley, CA, October 27-30, 2009.

[5] Dral, J., Heylen, D. & op den Akker, R. (2008) Detecting uncertainty in spoken dialogues: An explorative research to the automatic detection of a speakers' uncertainty by using prosodic markers, *Sentiment analysis: emotion, metaphor, ontology and terminology*, Marrakech, Morocco, 72-78.

[6] Ferguson, N. (1977) Simultaneous speech, interruptions, and dominance, *British Journal of Social and Clinical Psychology*, 16, 295-302.

[7] Krauss, R. & Chiu, C.-Y. (1997) Language and social behavior, in D. Gilbert, S. Fiske & G. Lindsey (eds.) *Handbook of social psychology*, 4th edition, vol. 2, Boston: McGraw-Hill, 41-88.

[8] Liscombe, J., Hirschberg, J. & Vendetti, J. (2005) Detecting certainness in spoken tutorial dialogs, *Proc. of Interspeech Europeech*, Lisbon, Portugal.

[9] Lunsford, R., Oviatt, S. L. & Arthur, A. (2006) Toward open-microphone engagement for multiparty interactions, *Eighth International Conference on Multimodal Interfaces (ICMI'06),* ACM: New York, 273-280.

[10] Luria, A. (1961) *The Role of Speech in the Regulation of Normal and Abnormal Behavior*, Liveright: NY.

[11] Oviatt, S.L. (2012) Multimodal interfaces, The *Human-Computer Interaction Handbook: Fundamentals, Evolving Technologies and Emerging Applications (3rd ed.)*, (ed. by J. Jacko), LEA: Mahwah, NJ, chap. 18, 405-430.

[12] Oviatt, S.L. (2013a) Problem solving, domain expertise and learning: Ground-truth performance results for math data corpus, *Second Intl. Grand Challenge Workshop on Multimodal Learning Analytics*, December 2013.

[13] Oviatt, S.L. (2013b) *The Design of Future Educational Interfaces*, Routledge Press.

[14] Oviatt, S., Cohen, A. & Weibel, N. (2013) Multimodal learning analytics: Description of math data corpus for ICMI grand challenge workshop, *Second International Workshop on Multimodal Learning Analytics*, Sydney Australia, Dec. 2013.

[15] Oviatt, S., Cohen, A. & Weibel, N., Hang, K. & Thompson, K. (2014) Multimodal learning analytics data resources: Description of math data corpus and coded documents, *Third Intl. Workshop on Multimodal Learning Analytics*, Istanbul Turkey (for version with full appendices, see: http://mla.ucsd.edu/data/MMLA_Math_Data_Corpus.pdf

[16] Oviatt, S.L., Hang, K., Zhou, J., Yu, K. & Chen, F. (in press) Dynamic handwriting signal features predict domain expertise.

[17] Purandare, A. & Litman, D. (2008) Content-learning correlations in spoken tutoring dialogs at word, turn, and discourse levels, *Proc. of the 21st Intl. FLAIRS Conference*, Coconut Grove, FL.

[18] Roger, D. Bull, P. & Smith, S. (1988) The development of a comprehensive system for classifying interruptions, *Journal of Language and Social Psychology*, 7, 27-34.

[19] Sacks, H., Schegloff, E.A. & Jefferson, G. (1974) A simplest systematics for the organization of turn-taking for conversation, *Language*, 50(4), 696-735.

[20] Schegloff, E.A. (2000) Overlapping talk and the organization of turn-taking for conversation, *Language in Society*, 29:1, 1-63.

[21] Scherer, S., Weibel, N., Oviatt, S. & Morency, L.P. (2012) Multimodal prediction of expertise and leadership in learning groups, *Proc. of the First International Workshop on Multimodal Learning Analytics*, ACM: N.Y.

[22] Shriberg, L., Stolcke, A. & Baron, D. (2001) Observations on Overlap: Findings and implications for automatic processing of multi-party conversation, *Proc. of Eurospeech.*

[23] Vygotsky, L. (1962) *Thought and Language*, MIT Press, Cambridge MA. (Transl. by Hanfmann & Vakar from 1934 original).

[24] Worsley, M. & Blikstein, P. (2010) Toward the development of learning analytics: Student speech as an automatic and natural form of assessment, *AERA Conference.*

[25] Zimmerman, B. (2006) Development and adaptation of expertise: The role of self-regulatory processes and beliefs, *The Cambridge Handbook of Expertise and Expert Performance* (ed. by K. Ericsson, N. Charness, P. Feltovich & R. Hoffman), Cambridge University Press: New York, 705-722.

Active Haptic Feedback for Touch Enabled TV Remote

Anton Treskunov
Samsung Research America
Mountain View, CA, USA
treskunov@acm.org

Mike Darnell
Samsung Research America
Mountain View, CA, USA
mike.darnell@samsung.com

Rongrong Wang
Samsung Research America
Mountain View, CA, USA
rongrong.w@samsung.com

ABSTRACT

Recently a number of TV manufacturers introduced TV remotes with a touchpad which is used for indirect control of TV UI. Users can navigate the UI by moving a finger across the touch pad. However, due to the latency in visual feedback, there is a disconnection between the finger movement on the touchpad and the visual perception in the TV UI, which often causes overshooting. In this paper, we investigate how haptic feedback affects the user experience of the touchpad-based TV remote. We described two haptic prototypes built on the smartphone and Samsung 2013 TV remote respectively. We conducted two user studies with two prototypes to evaluate how the user preference and the user performance been affected. The results show that there is overwhelming support of haptic feedback in terms of subjective user preference, though we didn't find significant difference in performance between with and without haptic feedback conditions.

Categories and Subject Descriptors

H.5.2 [**User Interfaces**]: Haptic I/O

General Terms

Interaction, Feedback

Keywords

Haptic; Touch; User Study; TV Remote

1. INTRODUCTION

Grid-based UI is widely adopted in existing Smart TV products, such as Samsung Smart TV, Google TV, Roku etc. A highlight is used to indicate where the currently focused UI element is. For example, Figure 2 shows a grid-based TV with the highlight at the top right corner. The users navigate the UI by moving the highlight with arrow keys on TV remote.

ICMI 2015, November 9–13, 2015, Seattle, WA, USA.

ACM 978-1-4503-3912-4/15/11 ...$15.00.
DOI: http://dx.doi.org/10.1145/2818346.2820768.

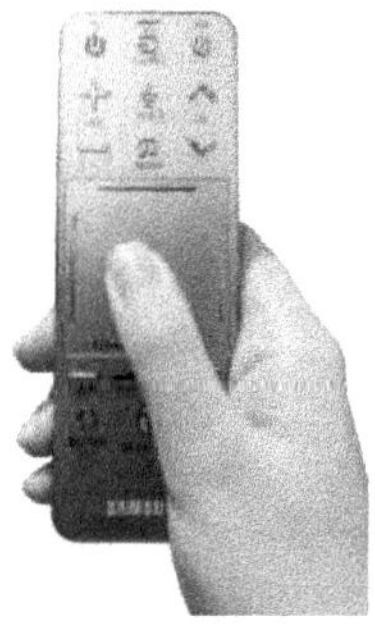

Figure 1: 2013 Samsung Smart Touch Remote.

To keep users attention on the screen, decrease the energy consumption and keep the cost low, TV remote generally don't have a screen. Therefore, interaction with TV UI via the remote is indirect and relies on various types of feedback, such as visual, auditory and tactile.

Recently a number of TV and set top box (STB) manufacturers introduced touchpad based TV remotes. Notable examples are the Samsung 2012-2013, Sony 2014-2015, Sharp 2015 and Dish 2015. With such remotes, sliding a finger across the surface of touchpad moves a highlight by one or several steps in grid-based UI. Indirect interaction with a TV screen via handheld touch surface causes a sensory disconnect leading to navigational errors. The most typical such error is overshooting, meaning that the finger moved too far and the highlight switched to the item passed the desired one. We theorize that the main cause of this is a significant feedback delay, meaning that by the time visual information is processed by brain, finger may have already moved too far.

In this paper we investigate the effects of adding active haptic feedback to touchpad based remote. In particular, we are interested in whether this additional haptic feedback can bridge the disconnection and improve the user experience of touchpad-based TV remote. In the following sections we describe our design considerations of haptic feedback, two haptic TV prototypes based on smartphone and Samsung 2013 touchpad based TV remote, and two user studies with 17 participants total evaluating the users' preference and performance with our haptic prototypes.

2. RELATED WORK

It was shown previously that active haptic feedback can

- enhance user experience, providing enjoyment and increased feel of engagement. Levesque et al [6] explored the design possibilities and outcomes using a large area textile pattern display. They found that variable friction demonstrated a positive impact on the enjoyment, engagement and sense of realism of touch interfaces.
- increase the sense of realism by restoring mechanical feel. Some researchers investigated new technologies to render mechanical haptic feedback in a higher level of realism. For example, Bau et al [1] presented a electrovibration–enabled touch surface, which provides a wide range of tactile feedback sensations to fingers moving across. Their experiments are promising for designing realistic and effective tactile feedback.
- measurably increase the performance for targeting tasks. Burke et al [2] conducted a meta-analysis comparing visual-auditory and visual-tactile feedback on user performance. In general, additional modality added to visual feedback improves performance overall. But visual-tactile feedback is more effective when multiple tasks are being performed and workload conditions are high. Richter et al [10] reported similar results obtained in multitasking situations such as the interaction with touch-based in-vehicle systems. Their preliminary quantitative study shows significantly reduced error rates as well as input time in with-haptic feedback condition.
- decrease the reliance on vision. Pasquero and Hayward [8] evaluated the use of tactile feedback in navigating a long list in mobile UI. They used a hand-held device which tightly coupled the touch input and haptic feedback. Their results showed 28% decrease of reliance on vision when tactile feedback was enabled.

Inspired by these previous research, we investigate whether additional haptic feedback on TV remote can have similar effects to improve user experience of TV UI.

3. DESIGN OF HAPTICS

Providing haptic feedback to TV UI is not a trivial task. Three types of design decisions should be made. First of all, we need to identify what type of hardware solutions is appropriate to augment TV remote with haptic modality. Secondly, we need to identify the TV interaction scenarios which is appropriate to use haptic feedbacks. Thirdly, we need to understand how haptic modality work with other modalities, such as visual and auditory.

Haptic Hardware. For the first design question, we considered several types of haptic actuators. Some haptic actuators change the physical shape of interaction surface [11]; some induce haptic sensation by electrostatic vibration [1]. The most widely used and commercially available haptic actuators are based on mechanical vibration of the interaction surface, such as Eccentric Rotating Mass (ERM), Linear Resonant Actuator(LRA), Piezo and Electro-Active Polymer Actuators (EAPs).

We ruled out shape changing actuators as interfering with smooth finger movement over touch surface. We also ruled out electrostatic vibration actuators as requiring high voltage, which is problematic in form factor of handheld remote control. ERM needs a time to spin out motors and therefore have higher latency. For our prototype LRA was chosen as having both low latency and low power consumption. To provide feedback in situations of finger being off touchpad surface we attached haptic device to the back surface of the remote, so it was being felt by a palm.

Haptic Interaction Design. For the second design question, we focus on providing haptic feedback for the most basic TV UI interaction, which is moving highlights up, down, left or right. Because of this simple navigation task, the haptic effect design is also relatively simple. We decided to provide a sharp click haptic effect to a highlight move event. Every time when the user's finger movement on the touch pad triggers the highlight to move one step on the TV UI, a haptic sharp click is also triggered.

Congruency with Other Modalities. For the third design question, we need to understand how haptic modality should be coordinated with other modalities, such as visual and auditory. In other words, would it matter if haptic modality work independently or should it be time-synced with other modalities? According to Lylykangas et. al. [7], a preferred perception of tactile feedback requires careful design and controlling of the timing parameters. Haptic feedback is more sensitive to latency than a visual feedback. Jay, Glencross and Hubbold [5] found that "whilst latency affects visual feedback from 50 msec, it impacts on haptic task performance 25 ms earlier, and causes haptic measures of performance deterioration to rise far more steeply than visual." As cited in [3], in terms of discerning consecutive events tactile sensation is in between visual and sound stimuli, being 5 ms vs 25 ms and 0.1 ms respectively. Based on that number, Poupyrev et al [9] suggested that "minimum required latency of a tactile actuator to be 5 ms". As we mentioned earlier about overshooting issue, indirect interaction with a TV UI via touch on a remote leads to a sensory disconnection. On the one hand, our hypothesis is that overshooting is a result of a feedback latency, thus we should reduce the latency of haptic feedback as much as possible. On the other hand, haptic and visual feedback should act in a time-synced manner. To understand how the latency affect haptic feedback, we decided on two different latency values: 5 ms and 25 ms with latter aiming at keeping haptic and visual feedback in a time-synced manner.

The latency value has a big impact on implementation of TV system. Thus, 5 ms latency would require all processing to happen on the remote itself to avoid communication round-trip delay between the remote and TV, while 25 ms and longer latency could be achieved having much simpler implementation of software on TV host.

4. FIRST PROTOTYPE AND PILOT STUDY

For rapid prototyping we developed a prototype emulating touchpad behavior using smartphones. Specifically, we used QT based Nokia N9 and Android based Samsung Galaxy S3. Both phones have embedded LRA haptic actuators.

A quick pilot study was conducted to assess 8 participants' preference for haptic feedback. In the study, an app on a Nokia N9 smartphone was developed to simulate a remote control directional pad (d-pad).

In the Samsung 2013 SmartHub a user navigates the TV User Interface by flicking and sliding her finger across the

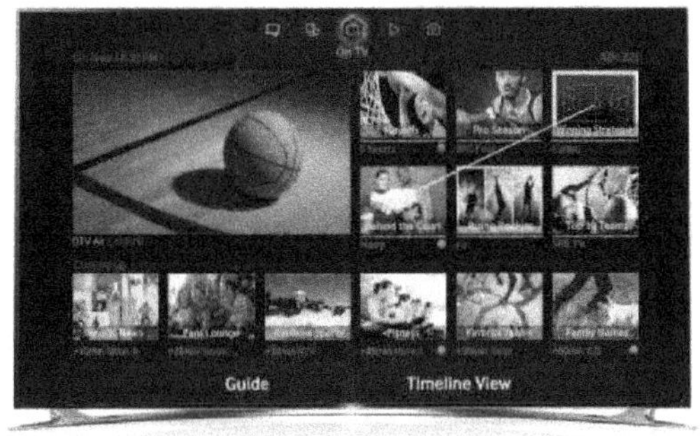

Figure 2: SmartHub, with yellow line indicating highlight move.

touchpad surface. Depending on tracking speed settings each finger movement may result in one or more directional navigation commands. For example, sliding to the right and a bit up may cause a Right-Right-Up sequence to be sent to the TV. This behavior corresponds to pressing the directional buttons on a traditional button based remote causing the highlight to move in the grid based UI, see figure 2.

Participants used the smartphone as a touch pad to navigate through lists of movie and TV show posters on TV and type on an on-screen keyboard. In a counterbalanced order, participants navigated with and without haptic feedback. Afterwards they stated their preference for haptic or no-haptic feedback.

All 8 participants preferred haptic feedback. Here are some quotes from N9 study explaining why participants did prefer haptic.

P1 "I prefer the buzzing, it feels like it makes me make meaningful decisions."

P2 "it almost gives me another sense of knowing I am going in the right direction."

P3 "subconscious thing, reassuring that I am doing a right thing."

P4 "I like the vibration a lot. It lets you know you did something... it lets you know you made one jump or two jumps or something... "

Encouraged by the results of the pilot study, we proceed to evaluate how haptic feedback affects the user performance as well as user preference when navigating the grid-based TV UI.

5. SYSTEM IMPLEMENTATION

To achieve a high fidelity prototype, we used the 2013 Samsung Touch Remote Control as a primary hardware platform, see figure 1. Haptic hardware consisted from LRA actuator and a controller from Texas Instruments implementing Immersion [4] library of haptic effects. Actuator was placed on the bottom back of the device. "Sharp Click" effect of immersion library was tuned to get a crisp rendering effect.

The TV platform was implemented as PC application communicating with remote prototype via Bluetooth connection at 60 Hz. There was no explicit audio feedback and haptic actuators were silent as well.

Haptic activation commands were issued immediately after directional navigation command. Navigation software that converts finger movement on touchpad to navigational commands was implemented in two variants: as a JavaScript code running on the PC — variant B; and as a native code running on TV remote embedded processor — variant A.

Variant B besides being a less complex implementation provided a tighter synchronization between haptic and visual feedback since navigation and UI updating were done on the same machine. However, it relied on Bluetooth channel to convey haptic commands and hence introduced additional communication latency as long as 15 ms.

Variant A was implemented in C++ for ARM processor in TV remote. Thus, on the remote control, end-to-end haptic latency was estimated to be as low as 5 ms vs 25 ms for variant B.

6. USER STUDY

6.1 User Study Design

Each participant was asked to complete 12 practice trials and 108 test trials composed of the factorial combination of 3 tracking speeds (fast, medium, slow) - see section 4, 3 haptic conditions (A: 5ms, B: 25ms, No Haptic) - see section 5 and 12 trial types. The trial types were composed of 3 target sizes (large, medium, small) and 3 movement directions (horizontal only, vertical only, diagonal); plus for small targets only there were both long and short movements. None of the tasks involved scrolling. There were 9 blocks of 12 test trials for each participant. The order of the blocks was counterbalanced using a 9x9 Latin Square.

These factors were designed to represent the domain of TV navigation tasks and to allow a detailed analysis of which tasks might be more affected by the haptic feedback.

The trials were designed to simulate the common tasks of navigating to a known target position on the TV screen. Real life examples included selecting an item from a menu, selecting a TV show in a program guide, and selecting a key on an on-screen keyboard.

Although performance improve over time is an interesting topic, our experiment was not designed to collect enough data to answer such question.

6.1.1 Participants

Nine participants were recruited for this one-hour study. Participants included 5 females (ages: 22, 27, 34, 44 and 55) and 4 males (ages: 27, 31, 38 and 57). Participants sat on a sofa holding the touchpad remote control (figure 1) about 10 feet from a 55 inches Samsung LED TV.

6.1.2 Data Collection

To initiate each trial, the participant clicked the touchpad remote, which presented a grid of cells on the TV screen (see figure 3). One of the cells, the target, had a unique color. The task was to use the touchpad to move the highlight (which always started on the top left cell) to the target cell as quickly and accurately as possible. After selecting the target by highlighting it and clicking the touchpad, the participant could initiate the next trial. Task time, number of cells navigated and accuracy were measured for each trial.

For each block of 9 trials, representing a tracking speed and haptic condition, the participant rated the usability of

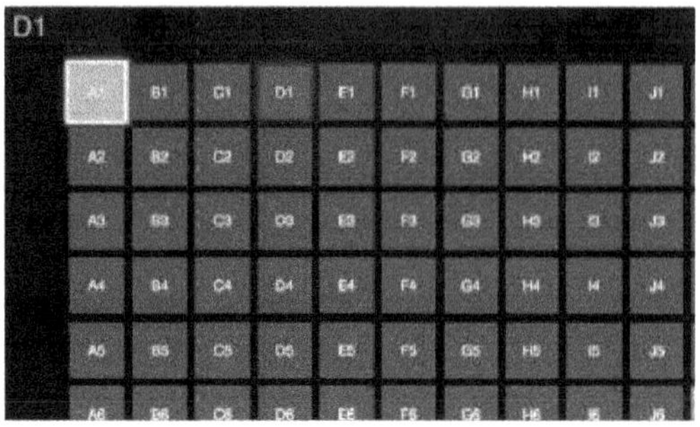

Figure 3: Sample task: Participants used the touchpad remote to move the highlight (blue) to the target cell (green) as quickly and accurately as possible.

the touchpad on a Likert scale ranging from 1 (very unusable) to 7 (very usable).

6.2 Results

The task time, errors, number of cells navigated and user ratings were analyzed with ANOVA for tracking speed and haptic conditions. None of the effects of time, errors or ratings were significant. There was a significant effect of tracking speed on number of cells navigated $F(2,16) = 10.79$; $p < 0.001$. The faster the tracking speed, the more cells were navigated (8.2 cells, 8.6 cells, 9.8 cells, respectively). This is consistent with correlation of people overshooting the target and correcting with greater tracking speeds. After participants completed all the trials they were asked to choose which haptic condition they preferred (A: 5ms, B: 25ms, No Haptic) Although, some participants had difficulty distinguishing between the A: 5ms and B: 25ms conditions, 8 of the 9 participants preferred haptic feedback over no haptic feedback. *Binomial Probability* $p = 0.039$.

6.3 Discussion

Although the experiment did not find a performance effect, participants had a clear preference for haptic feedback. We are especially confident in this conclusion when combined with the results from our earlier study using a Nokia N9 phone to simulate a remote control in which all 8 participants preferred haptic feedback. Our current study doesn't provide the reason behind the overwhelming preference, but plausible explanation could be feeling of responsiveness. We plan to explore this in future work.

The current experiment was powerful enough to detect the effect of tracking speed on user performance, however, an effect of haptic feedback on performance was not found. This would be expected if the haptic effect on performance is relatively small. Future experiments could include more participants and/or trials to increase the power of the statistical tests to measure effects of haptic feedback on performance.

In absence of such measurable effect on performance we think that haptic UX design should focus user *subjective* satisfaction. It means, rather than striving to get the earliest possible feedback emphasize haptic as another feedback modality, make it synchronized with visual stimuli. Future studies are necessary to validate our hypothesis.

7. CONCLUSION

In this work we investigated benefits of adding active feedback to touchpad based TV remote control. Two prototypes were built with approximately 5 and 25 ms latencies. In the conducted user study 8 out 9 participants prefer haptic enabled remote, though we didn't find significant performance difference. Although, performance findings do not confirm prior art conclusion about haptic performance benefits and need to be verified in future work. Despite that, we conclude that adding active haptic feedback significantly improves self reported satisfaction and leads to improved user experience.

8. REFERENCES

[1] O. Bau, I. Poupyrev, A. Israr, and C. Harrison. Teslatouch: Electrovibration for touch surfaces. In *Proc. of UIST '10*, pages 283–292. ACM, 2010.

[2] J. L. Burke, M. S. Prewett, A. A. Gray, L. Yang, F. R. B. Stilson, M. D. Coovert, L. R. Elliot, and E. Redden. Comparing the effects of visual-auditory and visual-tactile feedback on user performance: A meta-analysis. In *Proc. of ICMI '06*, pages 108–117. ACM, 2006.

[3] R. W. Cholewiak and A. A. Collins. Sensory and physiological bases of touch. *The psychology of touch*, pages 23–60, 1991.

[4] Immersion corporation — haptics for the digital user experience. `http://www.test.org/doe/`, June 2009. [Online; accessed 13-May-2015].

[5] C. Jay, M. Glencross, and R. Hubbold. Modeling the effects of delayed haptic and visual feedback in a collaborative virtual environment. *ACM Trans. Comput.-Hum. Interact.*, 14(2), Aug. 2007.

[6] V. Levesque, L. Oram, K. MacLean, A. Cockburn, N. D. Marchuk, D. Johnson, J. E. Colgate, and M. A. Peshkin. Enhancing physicality in touch interaction with programmable friction. In *Proc. of CHI '11*, pages 2481–2490. ACM, 2011.

[7] J. Lylykangas, V. Surakka, K. Salminen, J. Raisamo, P. Laitinen, K. Rönning, and R. Raisamo. Designing tactile feedback for piezo buttons. In *Proc. of CHI '11*, pages 3281–3284. ACM, 2011.

[8] J. Pasquero and V. Hayward. Tactile feedback can assist vision during mobile interactions. In *Proc. of CHI '11*, pages 3277–3280. ACM, 2011.

[9] I. Poupyrev, S. Maruyama, and J. Rekimoto. Ambient touch: Designing tactile interfaces for handheld devices. In *Proc. of UIST '02*, pages 51–60. ACM, 2002.

[10] H. Richter, R. Ecker, C. Deisler, and A. Butz. Haptouch and the 2+1 state model: Potentials of haptic feedback on touch based in-vehicle information systems. In *Proc. of AutomotiveUI '10*, pages 72–79. ACM, 2010.

[11] Tactus techology whitepaper. `http://tactustechnology.com/wp-content/uploads/2014/08/White-Paper-New-Tagged-PDF.pdf`, 2012. [Online; accessed 12-January-2015].

A Visual Analytics Approach to Finding Factors Improving Automatic Speaker Identifications

Pierrick Bruneau
LIST
L-4362 Esch-sur-Alzette
pierrick.bruneau@list.lu

Mickaël Stefas
LIST
L-4362 Esch-sur-Alzette
mickael.stefas@list.lu

Hervé Bredin
LIMSI - CNRS
F-91405 Orsay
herve.bredin@limsi.fr

Johann Poignant
LIMSI - CNRS
F-91405 Orsay
johann.poignant@limsi.fr

Thomas Tamisier
LIST
L-4362 Esch-sur-Alzette
thomas.tamisier@list.lu

Claude Barras
LIMSI - CNRS
F-91405 Orsay
claude.barras@limsi.fr

ABSTRACT

Classification quality criteria such as precision, recall, and F-measure are generally the basis for evaluating contributions in automatic speaker recognition. Specifically, comparisons are carried out mostly via mean values estimated on a set of media. Whilst this approach is relevant to assess improvement w.r.t. the state-of-the-art, or ranking participants in the context of an automatic annotation challenge, it gives little insight to system designers in terms of cues for improving algorithms, hypothesis formulation, and evidence display. This paper presents a design study of a visual and interactive approach to analyze errors made by automatic annotation algorithms. A timeline-based tool emerged from prior steps of this study. A critical review, driven by user interviews, exposes caveats and refines user objectives. The next step of the study is then initiated by sketching designs combining elements of the current prototype to principles newly identified as relevant.

Categories and Subject Descriptors

H.4 [**Information Systems Applications**]: Miscellaneous; D.2.8 [**Software Engineering**]: Metrics—*complexity measures, performance measures*

General Terms

Speaker identification; Visual Analytics

1. INTRODUCTION

Identifying speakers in audio signal, e.g., phone records, radio and TV broadcasts is an active field of research [4]. Speaker recognition systems generally proceed in a succession of steps: the audio signal is first segmented in speech turns, then feeding a clustering algorithm (i.e., diarization step). These clusters are then labelled using supervised speaker models. Obtained clusters are finally relabelled by matching them to a bank of speaker models trained supervisedly (a short review of such systems is given in [4]).

Annotations associate meta-data to segments in media. Such meta-data can be of any type, potentially complex [11]. The scope of this paper is limited to speaker annotations, i.e., meta-data restricted to speaker names, following the pattern *Firstname_LASTNAME*. Each name embodies a class (or equivalently category). Annotations are gathered in tracks characterized by their nature, e.g., reference manually annotated ground truth, or a hypothesis resulting from a given speaker identification algorithm. The difference between a hypothesis and the respective reference track can then be seen as an additional annotation track taking values in 0 and 1, respectively for error and success.

Established evaluation campaigns [6, 8] have supported notable improvements in algorithmic performance. Whilst ranks in evaluations and challenges rely on global error rates, researchers have also devoted efforts to more thorough performance analysis, with a view to understand factors leading to effective recognition. For example, the influence of speaker-specific properties (e.g., speech style) and acoustic conditions has been investigated [7].

Supportive evidence is then generally hard to build, and exploring hypotheses is costly. Interactive tools are expected to alleviate this bottleneck. The purpose of this paper is to consider the performance analysis task with a visual analytics approach. This process aims at harnessing recent progress in performance analysis, with visual and interactive tools enabling fast hypothesis formulation and verification. We address this problem within a design study framework, that iterates capturing requirements, agile implementations and evaluation steps [12].

Initial requirements led to proposing a tool to facilitate the differential analysis of algorithmic results with respect to a reference ground truth [3]. This early contribution is summarized in Section 2 among other related work. The first contribution of this work is to put the prior steps of our design study into perspective. The critical view in Section 3 relies on user interviews and a recent study in performance analysis [4]. From this critical view, sketches for the next step of the design study are proposed in Section 4. A summary of the contribution, along with perspectives for future work, conclude the paper in Section 5.

ICMI 2015, November 9–13, 2015, Seattle, WA, USA.
© 2015 ACM. ISBN 978-1-4503-3912-4/15/11 ...$15.00.
DOI: http://dx.doi.org/10.1145/2818346.2820769.

2. RELATED WORK

The most natural way to visualize annotations for researchers in multimedia processing is to display them as glyphs in tracks of a timeline, marking punctual or time-spanning events. For instance, this view is prevalent in professional video editing software such as Adobe Premiere [1], and in existing tools for scholar media annotations edition and visualization. For example, some tools use this view to facilitate input and inspection of complex multimodal annotations [2, 11]. However these approaches do not concern themselves with difference between annotation tracks, and analyzing their distribution. StoViz [5] uses a timeline in the context of multimodal algorithmic errors for story arcs identification. Segmentation errors were emphasized by a dual use of animation and color-coding.

To our knowledge, the analysis of scholar annotations has not much been considered by the information visualization community. Yet annotations can be seen as categorical data, and models for handling and processing such data are classically based on tables of frequencies, also known as contingency tables [14]. Actually, confusion tables (see Section 4) are specific instances of contingency tables in the context of classifier output. Log-linear models (among which are logistic regression and ANOVA models) are then central tools for analyzing patterns of dependence or independence between variables. Contributions in visual and interactive support to these models [14] strengthen their relevance as building blocks for this paper.

ROC curves are a classical way to visualize classifier quality, but are restricted to binary classification, and lack interaction. Alternatively, Kapoor et al. bring interaction by allowing interactive adaptation of a classifier [10]. Often classifiers have probabilistic outputs translated to classes using thresholds, intuitively interpreted as costs of misclassification. The approach uses a confusion matrix that can be directly modified. Alpha-blended colors indicate the positive or negative influence associated to potential modifications. This principle inspired the interactive equation presented in Section 4. However in this paper misclassification costs are uniform across speakers and the objective is not so much on directly improving a classifier, than on locating speakers and media subject to error, and help hypothesis formulation in an outer step.

Following initial discussions with two users expert in speaker annotation algorithms, a video playback interface has been synchronized with a timeline view [3]. For supporting monomodal speech processing a waveform view could also have been considered. But the additional information regarding speaker identities may be useful for users, and open the way for handling multimodal data and algorithms.

Glyph widths in Figure 1 encode respective time segments, and their colors encode the associated meta-data (i.e., either speaker name or recognition success). For speakers, an automatic categorical color palette is used (see [3] for details), and difference between hypothesis and reference is mapped to a polar color scale to efficiently denote success and error. Figure 1 illustrates these features using data from the REPERE challenge [6].

Total durations for each category can be inspected in summary charts (i.e., pie chart, bar chart or treemap, see Figure 1b). A Focus+Context navigation bar supports rectangular selection, enabling zooming in the medium for local inspection in the displayed focus, while recalling the general distribution of annotations with grey-shaded glyphs (see Figure 1a), and instantly adapting displayed summary views to the visible annotations. Hovering over glyphs in the timeline reveals the meta-data and respective timings. Clicks on timeline glyphs command the playback position, enabling inspections of the associated medium content.

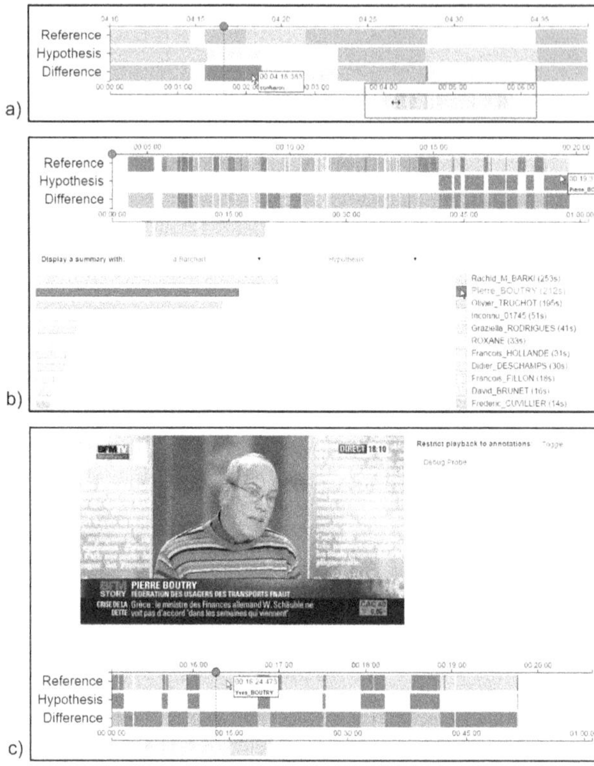

Figure 1: a) Segmentation problems in the hypothesis track are revealed. The red rectangle highlights the context bar at the bottom. The rectangular selection can be moved and its lateral bounds modified interactively, updating the focus accordingly. b) The interactive summary view (here bar chart) highlights associated annotations in the timeline. c) Joint use of the video playback and the timeline helps checking the validity of errors.

Summary views can be used to navigate in the set of speakers, e.g., identifying speakers strongly associated to errors. In the case shown in Figure 1b, it is clear that inferring speaker *Pierre_BOUTRY* is always leading to errors. Using the navigation bar to narrow down the view and seeking in the medium reveals this inference is actually correct, the homonym speaker *Yves_BOUTRY* being mistakenly recorded in the ground truth (see Figure 1c).

3. CRITICAL ANALYSIS

In the context of challenges such as REPERE [6], prior to being ranked, participants have the opportunity to flag mistakes in the reference track: this is the adjudication phase. Confronting users to the software proposed in [3] qualitatively revealed its ability to spot small-scale patterns, and more generally its fit as support to this adjudication activity.

Though the zooming feature may for example emphasize speech turn segmentation problems (see Figure 1a), that were shown as positively correlated with error in speaker diarization and identification [4], discussions established the timeline-based view as rather ineffective when it comes to hypothesizing factors influencing speaker recognition.

The adequate tool must allow to take a wider scope, as actually does a recent batch analysis of annotation errors [4]. For example, the error distribution in supervised speaker identification systems is there shown as highly speaker-specific, i.e., most often a speaker is either always or never correctly recognized [4]. The authors also found this distribution to be even more bimodal when using a manually curated segmentation in speech turns.

Several speaker characteristics have been hypothesized as influential to unsuccessful recognition, either *internal* (i.e., computed from data available in the corpus, e.g., total and average duration of speech turns, pause between speech turns) or *external* (e.g., amount of supplemental data for training respective dictionary speaker models). A post-hoc analysis was then performed by learning a decision tree classifier evaluating the influence of these characteristics on identification performance for the respective speakers. This process defines a hierarchy of importance among explanatory variables and led to conclude on the prevalence of the total duration of speech turns for effective recognition.

This study helped the users identify the true objective that an interactive tool must pursue, i.e., finding characteristics in media and speakers that influence, positively or negatively, their effective recognition. Moreover, considering a collection of annotated media, to date this analysis has been performed on each medium separately. The advantage of using a whole corpus of data holistically has to be explored.

Specifically, media, tracks and speakers would then be seen as independent dimensions. Analyses would then proceed by selections and projections on these axes, with adequate interactive filtering tools. For example, within this framework, the timeline view discussed in Section 2 can be seen as combined projections and selections on the media and tracks axes. Building upon the observations above, the next section describes simulated scenarios of use that serve to introduce new adequate statistical and interactive tools in context.

4. DESIGN SKETCHING

In this section we assume only one hypothesis track is available, originating from the algorithm the user wants to investigate and improve. Reference annotations are then background information that serves to compute quality metrics. We follow definitions in [4] and define $T_i^{\text{reference}}$ and $T_i^{\text{hypothesis}}$ as the total speech duration of speaker i over the corpus, respectively in the reference and the hypothesis tracks. Likewise, T_i^{correct} is the duration of correct identification of speaker i. Precision, recall and F1-measure defined with respect to these quantities are used as metrics of recognition quality in the remainder of the paper.

Instead of imposing the selection of a specific medium before actually visualizing annotations, we propose to initially aggregate over all media, leading to an *overview* of the set of speakers. Speakers can be sorted according to a metric among those mentioned above. The list, potentially large, can be filtered on demand. In Figure 2a, a bar chart is used for this display. The bar length encodes the metric. Behind the scenes category colors are mapped to speakers, but as each bar refers to a distinct speaker, it is not necessary to show them at this stage.

One or more speakers can then be selected before proceeding. When only one speaker is selected, a *unidimensional* analysis is triggered. The distribution of the speaker over media is then displayed, along with a filtered confusion matrix. The respective reference speech durations are mapped to glyph sizes, and the metric is mapped to glyph colors (see Figure 2b). Here the user can estimate the distribution of the speaker across the corpus and see whether the associated error is uniform, and immediately spot dubious media. Clicking on a medium glyph reveals a video playback with an associated timeline. The timeline presented in Section 2 is adapted by filtering displayed annotations to the selected speaker, along with any other mistaken with him.

Confusion durations are normalized and mapped to colors in the respective table. Clicking on a cell here reveals the distribution of media relating the two selected speakers, with similar media glyph mapping as shown in Figure 2b. The process steps are recalled on top of the view. The filters applied at the *overview* level remain valid (Figure 2a). Prior steps of the process can thus be recalled and updated, dynamically affecting subsequent steps.

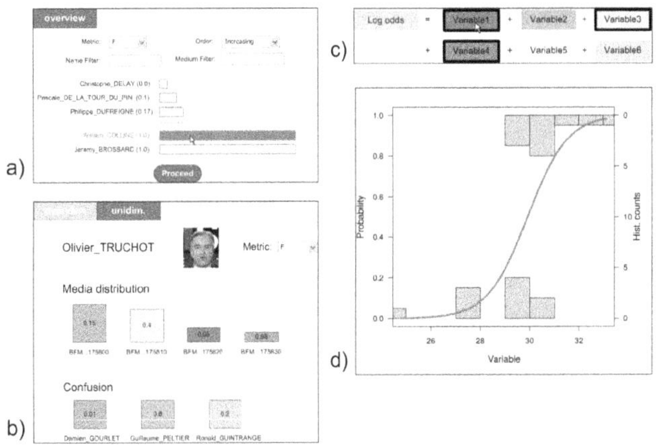

Figure 2: a) Initial overview of the speaker set. b) Unidimensional, single-speaker analysis. Related speakers and media are indicated and mapped with relevant metrics. c) Interactive logit model relating the performance metric with the set of explaining factors. d) Visualization of the logit model. The red curve shows the predicted probabilities, and observed responses are reported in bar charts [13]

From the *overview* step, multiple (potentially all) speakers can be selected. Proceeding from such a state launches a *multidimensional* analysis akin to the post-hoc classification presented in [4]. Figure 2c shows an interactive fitting process, that tentatively predicts the performance metric for speakers using a set of pre-defined explanatory variables (see Section 3) with a logit (i.e logistic regression) model. The latter is generally used for binary classification, whereas performance metrics defined in this paper lie in [0, 1]. As in [4], this situation could be handled by discretizing measures to binary values using a threshold. Yet the logit model grounds upon a probabilistic formalism, the loss function of which can be easily adapted to fuzzy rather than discrete values. Moreover, logit models seamlessly handle categorical and numerical variables.

In this model, no hierarchy of variables is defined, and alternatively finding relevant explaining factors is seen as a model selection procedure. Exhaustive search in the space of models (i.e., subsets of retained explanatory variables) is computationally prohibitive, especially if interactivity is expected. Combining statistics and interactive features has already been proposed as a way to alleviate this problem [9].

We take an interactive top-down approach, by initially including all explanatory variables. The model is represented by an interactive equation (see Figure 2c). The overall goodness-of-fit of the model is mapped to the box on the l.h.s. of the equation. The contribution of each explanatory variable can be tested by comparing outcomes of the models including or omitting it [14]. Stroked bounding boxes indicate selected variables. The strength of the negative impact of removing (respectively the positive impact of adding) variables is mapped to the alpha channel of boxes on the r.h.s.

The user can interactively add or remove explanatory variables. Color mappings are updated according to renewed test results. Assuming N explanatory variables are available, we note that each addition or removal requires the estimation of $N+1$ models and fitting tests. This amount remains small compared to the complete set of $N!$ models: yet in case computations are too long for interactive expectations, a progress bar can be included.

Logit model plots usually link the response probability to a single explanatory variable (see Figure 2d). In the context of the *multidimensional* analysis, this view can be enabled for a selected variable by collapsing all remaining variables to the intercept. The specific contribution of the variable to the current model is thus illustrated. Additional features, such as adding confidence intervals, and empirical sample estimates have also been studied [14].

5. CONCLUSION

The critical analysis in this paper helped identify the relevance of the timeline-based tool for user adjudication, but highlighted its inadequacy for performance analysis as generally coined in the literature. Directions drawn in Section 3, supported by our literature review, led to corpus-level, speaker-centric, novel designs.

Two complementary analysis procedures were described. When focused on a single speaker, it exploits the speaker-specific error distributions, with a view to emphasize dubious media or confusion patterns with other speakers. Alternatively, multiple speaker selections from the overview lead to analyze factors influencing the associated recognition performance. An interactive logistic regression model then supports user investigations.

Perspectives of course include implementing the sketches in Section 4, and carry out thorough qualitative and quantitative evaluations as soon as preliminary user interviews are satisfactory.

For the sake of clarity, segmentation-specific error was not explicitly accounted for in the designs in Section 4. Segmentation-oriented analyses could be derived by designing metrics aggregating those mentioned in Section 4 and alignment measures between reference and hypothesis.

6. ACKNOWLEDGMENTS

This work was done in the context of the CHIST-ERA CAMOMILE project funded by the ANR (Agence Nationale de la Recherche, France) and the FNR (Fonds National de la Recherche, Luxembourg).

7. REFERENCES

[1] Adobe Premiere Pro CC, 2015.

[2] O. Aubert and Y. Prié. Advene: active reading through hypervideo. In *ACM conference on Hypertext and hypermedia*, pages 235–244, 2005.

[3] P. Bruneau, M. Stefas, H. Bredin, A.-P. Ta, T. Tamisier, and C. Barras. A Web-Based Tool for the Visual Analysis of Media Annotations. In *IV 2014*, pages 145–150, 2014.

[4] D. Charlet, J. Poignant, H. Bredin, C. Fredouille, and S. Meignier. What Makes a Speaker Recognizable in TV Broadcast? Going Beyond Speaker Identification Error Rate. In *ERRARE Workshop*, 2015.

[5] P. Ercolessi, H. Bredin, and C. Sénac. StoViz: story visualization of TV series. In *ACM Multimedia*, pages 1329–1330, 2012.

[6] A. Giraudel, M. Carré, V. Mapelli, J. Kahn, O. Galibert, and L. Quintard. The REPERE Corpus: a multimodal corpus for person recognition. In *LREC*, pages 1102–1107, 2012.

[7] C. S. Greenberg, A. Martin, and M. Przybocki. The 2011 best speaker recognition interim assessment. In *Odyssey*, pages 275–282, 2012.

[8] C. S. Greenberg, V. M. Stanford, A. F. Martin, M. Yadagiri, G. R. Doddington, J. J. Godfrey, and J. Hernandez-Cordero. The 2012 NIST speaker recognition evaluation. In *INTERSPEECH*, pages 1971–1975, 2013.

[9] S. Johansson Fernstad, J. Shaw, and J. Johansson. Quality-based guidance for exploratory dimensionality reduction. *Information Visualization*, 12(1):44–64, 2013.

[10] A. Kapoor, B. Lee, D. Tan, and E. Horvitz. Interactive optimization for steering machine classification. In *CHI*, pages 1343–1352, 2010.

[11] M. Kipp. *Anvil: The video annotation research tool.* Oxford University Press, 2011.

[12] M. Sedlmair, M. Meyer, and T. Munzner. Design study methodology: Reflections from the trenches and the stacks. *IEEE TVCG*, 18(12):2431–2440, 2012.

[13] C. J. Stubben and B. G. Milligan. Estimating and analyzing demographic models using the popbio package in R. *J. Stat. Softw.*, 22(11), 2007.

[14] F. W. Young, P. M. Valero-Mora, and M. Friendly. *Visual statistics: seeing data with dynamic interactive graphics.* John Wiley & Sons, 2011.

The Influence of Visual Cues on Passive Tactile Sensations in a Multimodal Immersive Virtual Environment

Nina Rosa
Utrecht University
Utrecht, the Netherlands
n.e.rosa@students.uu.nl

Wolfgang Hürst
Utrecht University
Utrecht, the Netherlands
huerst@uu.nl

Wouter Vos
Elitac B.V.
Amsterdam, the Netherlands
w.vos@elitac.nl

Peter Werkhoven
Utrecht University
Utrecht, the Netherlands
werkhoven@wxs.nl

ABSTRACT

Haptic feedback, such as the sensation of 'being touched', is an essential part of how we experience our environment. Yet, it is often disregarded in current virtual reality (VR) systems. In addition to the technical challenge of creating such tactile experiences there are also human aspects that are not fully understood, especially with respect to how humans integrate multimodal stimuli. In this research, we proved that the visual stimuli in a VR setting can influence how vibrotactile stimuli are perceived. In particular, we identified how visual cues that are associated with the characteristic of weight influence tactile perception, whereas a similar effect could not be achieved for a temperature-related visual cue. Our results have technical implications – for example, suggesting that a rather simple vibration motor may be sufficient to create a complex tactile experience such as perceiving weight – and relevance for practical implementations – for example, indicating that vibration intensities need to be 'exaggerated' to achieve certain effects.

Categories and Subject Descriptors

H.1.2 [**Models and Principles**]: User/Machine Systems; H.5.1 [**Information Interfaces and Presentation**]: Multimedia Information Systems—*Artificial, augmented, and virtual realities*

General Terms

Human Factors

Keywords

Virtual reality; passive touch; multimodal experiences

ICMI 2015, November 9–13, 2015, Seattle, WA, USA.
 ISBN 978-1-4503-3912-4/15/11 ...$15.00.
DOI: http://dx.doi.org/10.1145/2818346.2820744.

1. INTRODUCTION

Virtual reality (VR) set-ups generally aim at creating a high level of realism. Yet, most current systems only support vision and audio, omitting other senses, such as haptic experiences. While adding, for example, the sensation of *passive touch*, (e.g., being touched by a character or object) would likely increase realism, implementing this is very difficult. First, there is the technical challenge: tactile devices are only able to simulate one single property of touch, such as weight or temperature of an object. In addition, it is not straightforward how to integrate the haptic sensation with other senses. Past research studied, for example, how the haptic and visual sense work together, and how they can change the perception of an object's texture [21, 26], hardness [11], temperature [15, 12], and weight [7, 29, 10, 1].

Inspired by these studies, which all used real haptic objects, our general aim is to verify if similar experiences exist in pure virtual environments. In particular, we investigate if visual signals that are commonly associated with the two characteristics *weight* and *temperature* have an influence on vibrotactile perceptions, i.e. tactile feedback created by vibration motors placed on, for example, your arm. In the ideal case, we would expect that the richer and more complex visual stimuli can influence this rather simple tactile perception in a way that creates a better, more realistic VR experience. In this study, we show that this is the case for weight but not temperature, and also identify potential issues concerning general psychophysical experiments and the body transfer illusion.

2. BACKGROUND AND RELATED WORK

2.1 Virtual Reality and Tactile Sensations

Current consumer VR devices generally address the visual and auditory component but lack in modalities associated with tactile, gustatory, and olfactory senses. While there are tools for motion tracking that support kinesthetic senses, we are still far from being able to create a full, realistic tactile VR experience. Good overviews on how to simulate haptic feedback can be found in [27] (addressing classifications and techniques) and chapter 3.3 of [6] (focusing on devices). Newer techniques not covered in these references include, for example, electrovibrations adding tactile feedback to touch screens [16]. Vibrotactile displays, i.e. vibration motors or *tactors* placed on your skin, can be used to create the illusion of touch through vibration. Although these approaches have proven their feasibility, not all are equally applicable. Especially for consumer use, common aims are inexpensiveness and expressiveness, to impose limited cumber upon the user, that the system should be easily scalable and reconfigurable, and that the mapping of input data to stimulus output should be straightforward [17]. The vibrotactile displays used in our work to create the illusion of passive touch satisfy all of these requirements besides the last. The *general aim of our research* is therefore to provide better insight about the integration of such devices in the overall interaction experience and increase knowledge about mutual dependencies between stimuli of different modalities.

2.2 Presence and Passive Experience in VR

According to the model by Steuer [28], presence in VR is a human experience and a consequence of immersive technologies. It has two determining dimensions: vividness with the two contributing factors breadth and depth of included modalities; and interactivity with the three contributing factors speed, range, and mapping. Many studies target increasing interactivity by focusing on improving task performance [2, 22, 4]. Yet, when the goal is to improve experiences that users can take part in passively, vividness becomes a vital part of the system, even more urgent than interactivity. Here, we focus on this less studied aspect by specifying the *sub-goal of our research* as investigating the experience of passive touch under varying visual conditions.

A phenomenon closely related to presence is the body transfer illusion. Such an illusion causes users to perceive part of or an entire artificial body as their own. For this reason, it is believed that it can increase presence in a virtual environment [23]. Factors that enhance this illusion are first person perspective over a fake humanoid body and congruent visuotactile cues [18, 20]. It has been shown that a first person perspective of a life-sized virtual human body is sufficient to generate a body transfer illusion [25]. In our experiments we thus apply this methodology focusing on first person body experiences.

2.3 Multimodal Integration

Research from cognitive science identified important illusions with respect to multimodal integration, including the McGurk effect [19], ventriloquist effect [14], double-flash illusion [24], and the rubber hand illusion [3] (an example of the body transfer illusion). Other illusions that specifically concern the tactile and visual sense are changing surface texture and roughness [21, 26], changing object hardness [11], changing object temperature [15, 12], and changing object weight and collision force [7, 29, 10, 1]. Each of these studies used the actual tactile property to test the effect of adding visual cues. However, simulating all of these properties is not feasible in a VR system, thus a substitution is needed. The *concrete research problem addressed in this paper* is therefore to investigate whether the findings above would still apply when using vibrotactile stimuli in a passive situation rather than an active task such as in [10]. In particular, we are investigating the illusion of weight utilizing visual cues in the form of size [29] and speed [1], which were both shown to work with a contrast effect, rather than an averaging effect (the latter being the most common effect found in multimodality studies [8]). For temperature, we use object color as visual cue, similar to one of the experiments in [12].

3. OBJECTIVE

Resulting from the general aim, sub-goal, and related research problem introduced in the preceding section, we phrase our *research question* as:

> *Is it possible to create the illusion of experiencing different intensities of a certain property (weight or temperature) using a rather simple and unrelated type of touch (vibrations) together with compelling, type-related visuals (speed/size and color, respectively)?*

We address this via an exploratory investigation where the two properties weight and temperature of a 'touching' object are studied. Intensity of each property will be varied: tactile intensity is mapped to a vibration intensity; and visual intensity is controlled by different cues motivated by related work (cf. 2.3), cf. Table 1. The *objective* is therefore to measure the perceived weight and temperature intensity with a range of visual intensities. To do this, we use two psychophysical experiments in the form of a matching task (cf. 4.2). We motivate this methodology by the fact that experience is a qualitative characteristic and thus difficult to verify objectively. Although the used matching task is technically a performance verification, it verifies how humans perceive the intensity of varying multimodal stimuli, thus also allowing us to draw conclusions about their expected experience.

Property	Cue	Levels (low - med - high)		
Temperature	Color	Blue	- Gray	- Red
Weight	Size & Speed	Small & Slow	- Med & Normal	- Large & Fast

Table 1: Tactile properties with corresponding visual cues and intensity levels used in the experiments.

4. EXPERIMENTS

In the following, we outline the general setup and methodology used in our experiments (4.1 and 4.2) before describing the unique characteristics and results of the weight and temperature test (4.3 and 4.4).

4.1 Framework and Material

The same framework is used for the following two experiments. A plain indoor room was created with Unity Pro version 4.6.3f1, and scripts were written in C# using Microsoft Visual Studio 2013. Assets used to create the environment were free downloads from the Unity Asset Store. An Oculus Rift Development Kit 2 is used as head-mounted display (HMD) to create the visual stimuli and VR experience. It has a resolution of 960 × 1080 pixels per eye, and a nominal field of view of 100 degrees. Tactile stimuli are supplied via vibrations through an Elitac tactile display, with one tactor (vibration motor) and a control module attached to the participant's arm using an elastic band with Velcro, cf. Figure 1. This tactile display has 16 intensity levels on a logarithmic vibration power scale corresponding to a linearly perceived intensity scale with fundamental frequency 158±2.4 Hz at maximum vibration strength. The root mean square acceleration at maximum vibration strength is 55.5±9.5 m/s^2. Sennheiser HD201 headphones are used to produce pink noise in the background to mask the sound of the tactor and eliminate all other acoustic influences.

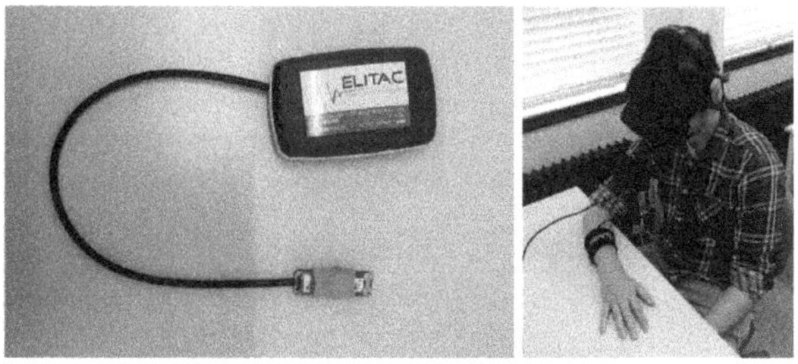

Figure 1: The measurement setup; (left) the Elitac control module and a single tactor, (right) a participant sitting in the correct position wearing the HMD, tactile sleeve and headphones.

4.2 Method and procedure

Before starting any experiment, participants were seated in a neutral room, signed a consent form and filled out a general information form. All subjects volunteered and were not reimbursed for their time. The experimenter gave instructions on how they should be positioned, and aided them while putting on the HMD and tactile display. Participants familiarized themselves with the virtual environment by looking around. In the setup, the avatar was sitting on a chair with the left arm placed on their lap under the table (out of sight), and the right arm on the table such that the lower arm was resting horizontally in front of them. The avatar was a humanoid figure (its gender matched the participant's) placed such that the participant had a first-person perspective; cf. Figure 2. Before each condition, a short training session took place, to make sure the participant understood the procedure and to induce a body transfer illusion. Because of the first person perspective, we can assume that this body transfer illusion occurs for all subjects [25].

Each subject tested two conditions: the control (no indicative visual cues), and either the weight or temperature conditions. The order of the conditions was counterbalanced over all participants. The conditions were made up of trials, each trial consisting of a matching task. A matching task uses a method of adjustment as described in [9] (Ch. 3). In a general matching task, participants are presented with a stimulus that must be adjusted such that it is above or below a certain threshold. In our experiments, a variation was used in which the participant had to adjust the tactile comparison stimulus until it matched (was perceived as equal to) the tactile reference stimulus. The participant's final choice of the matching comparison stimulus was logged. With such a task, we are able to obtain objective measurements about the perception of stimuli.

There were three tactile reference intensity levels (5, 8, 11), three visual intensity levels (0, 1, 2), two starting tactile comparison intensity levels (2 levels lower and 2 levels higher; i.e. 3 and 7 for reference 5), and four repetitions for each starting level, resulting in 72 trials in total. The reference intensity levels were chosen from a practical point of view: the levels are approximately in the center of the allowed range, such that the participants had room for adjustment in both directions. The control condition had no visual intensity levels, thus leading to 24 trials; resulting in a total of 96 trials per participant. A break of about three minutes was taken after every 24 trials (so three breaks in total), where the participant was allowed to take the HMD off. After taking part in the experiment, each participant was verbally asked two questions:

1. Did you have the feeling the virtual arm was your own arm?
2. Did you use the visual weight/temperature of the ball to deduce your answer or did you use the intensity of the sensation on your arm?

While these subjective measures were not the main focus of this study, they can provide additional insight especially when interpreting the relevance of the measured quantitative data. Duration of the experiment for one subject was approximately one hour.

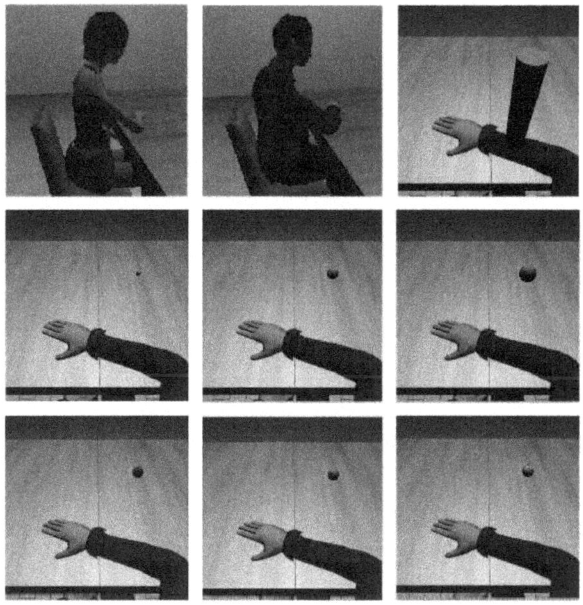

Figure 2: The virtual environment: (top-left) the female avatar, (top-center) the male avatar, (top-right) the occluder for the control condition, (center row) weight visuals where the steps in speed were exponential, (bottom row) temperature visuals.

4.3 Weight Experiment

4.3.1 Participants

Twelve subjects took part in the weight experiment. Ages ranged from 21-27 (average 22.8), eleven male and one female participant, eleven were right-handed, one was mixed-handed. Four had no prior experience with HMDs, seven had taken part in one or a few demonstrations, and one owned an HMD personally. Due to the basic characteristic of the task and related measures, we do not expect that these differences have any influence on the outcome nor did we observe any related indications – neither during the tests nor in the related data analysis. Likewise, we verified visual clarity during the training session in order to reduce any related influence due to colorblindness (two subjects) and prescription glasses (six subjects), and checked that none had any restrictions concerning touch sensations on the skin. Data of an additional thirteenth participant had to be discarded due to a system error that appeared during the test.

4.3.2 Matching Task

Each experiment consisted of the actual weight test, and a pure tactile control condition (without any visual cues). At the beginning of the weight experiment, the participant received the following instructions: 'In this experiment, you will feel a virtual object with a certain weight falling on your right arm. In each round, the object will first be blocked from your view, and the second time you will be able to see it. These two sensations on your arm may feel different. After feeling both, you must indicate whether the second ball felt as heavy as the first, or that the second felt lighter or heavier than the first. The goal is to adjust the tactile sensation such that you experience them the same.'

In each trial, the participant was presented with a reference and a comparison stimulus. The reference stimulus was a tactile-only stimulus, while the comparison stimulus was a combination of a tactile and a visual stimulus: a sphere that was small and slow, medium and normal, or large and fast. For the reference stimulus, an occluder in the form of a cylinder would appear, covering the vertical trajectory the sphere would cover; cf. Figure 2. Then two audio beeps with a 700 ms interval would occur, and after another 700 ms the tactor on the arm was activated at intensity level x for 200 ms so the participant felt a vibration. This was followed by the comparison condition, where the occluder disappeared. After one beep a gray sphere with a certain size appeared in mid-air at eye-level and remained in this position for 700 ms. Then another beep occurred, after which the sphere fell in a vertical trajectory onto the virtual arm with a certain speed. Upon contact, the tactor was activated at intensity y for 200 ms and the sphere disappeared. At this stage the participant replied whether the sensations were the same, or whether the second was lighter or heavier than the first. If they answered that they were the same, the trial was over, and a new reference stimulus was presented. Otherwise, the tactile comparison intensity was adjusted to $y+1$ if the participant answered 'lighter', or to $y-1$ if they said 'heavier'. The reference and comparison stimuli were then presented as before, but now the tactile comparison intensity was at the adjusted level. This presenting and adjusting continued until the participant felt that the sensations matched. Table 2 outlines single trial. All *tactile reference intensity - visual comparison intensity - final tactile comparison intensity* combinations were logged separately for each participant.

Step	Experiment
1	Tactile Reference α Tactile Comparison μ + Visual x
2	Tactile Reference α Tactile Comparison ν + Visual x
⋮	↓ adjust tactile
m	Tactile Reference α Tactile Comparison π + Visual x

Table 2: Outline of a single trial in the weight and temperature conditions. Gray cells indicate the presence of the occluder. Log for this example: $\alpha - x - \pi$

For the control condition, the participant was given no verbal or visual indication of the tactile property of the sphere. Terminology was changed to 'less intense'/'more intense' rather than 'lighter'/'heavier'. Also, the comparison stimulus was identical to the reference stimulus. That is, the spheres were always visually blocked by the occluder. Table 3 outlines a single trial in the control condition. All *tactile reference intensity - final tactile comparison intensity* combinations were logged separately for each participant.

Step	Experiment
1	Tactile Reference α Tactile Comparison μ
2	Tactile Reference α Tactile Comparison ν
⋮	↓ adjust tactile
m	Tactile Reference α Tactile Comparison π

Table 3: Outline of a single trial in the control condition. Gray cells indicate the presence of the occluder. Log for this example: $\alpha - \pi$

4.3.3 Results

First, we discuss the method for handling the results of the weight experiment. Consider one particular participant. The mean of all final tactile comparison intensities (eight values) is determined for every combination of tactile reference intensity and visual comparison intensity. This results in twelve values per participant. These values are then standardized by subtracting 5, 8 or 11, corresponding to the tactile reference intensity. The standardized means are given in Table 4 and are visualized in Figure 3. Normality was tested using Shapiro-Wilk tests; four cases were not normally distributed, namely: *Ref5-Control* ($W(12) = 0.833; p = 0.023$), *Ref5-Visual1* ($W(12) = 0.752; p = 0.003$), *Ref5-Visual2* ($W(12) = 0.643; p < 0.001$), and *Ref8-Visual2* ($W(12) = 0.814; p = 0.014$).

The data was analyzed with a two-way repeated measures ANOVA, with factors visual comparison intensity (three levels) and reference intensity (three levels). Mauchly's Test of Sphericity indicated that the assumption of sphericity had been violated in the reference intensity factor ($\chi^2(2) = 12.530, p = 0.002$), and a Greenhouse-Geisser correction was used for this factor. The analysis gave the following results: there was a significant main effect over reference intensity ($F(1.167, 12.833) = 45.438; p < 0.00001$), a significant main effect over visual intensity ($F(2, 22) = 8.855; p = 0.002$), but the interaction effect was not significant ($F(4, 44) = 0.028; p = 0.998$). Pairwise comparisons with a Bonferroni adjustment showed that each reference intensity differed significantly from the others (all $p < 0.001$), and that visual intensities 0 and 2 ($p = 0.005$) and 1 and 2 ($p = 0.013$) differed significantly. Nine paired t-tests were run between control results and each visual intensity within each reference intensity. These showed that the results of none of the

	Ref5	Ref8	Ref11
Control	0.292	-0.094	-0.385
Visual0	0.177	-0.198	-0.708
Visual1	0.271	-0.073	-0.573
Visual2	0.510	0.167	-0.333

Table 4: Standardized means over all conditions of the weight experiment.

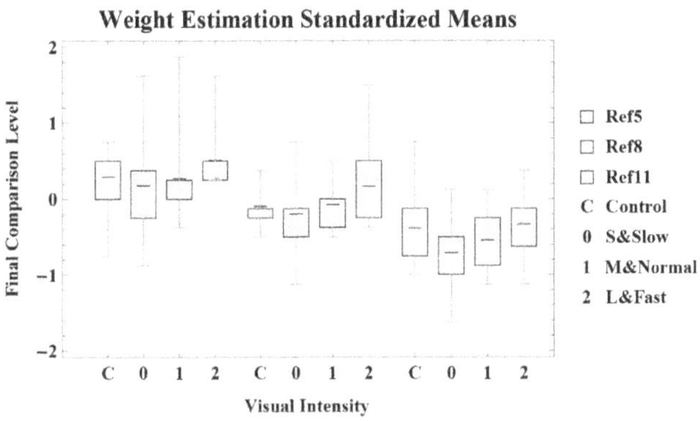

Figure 3: Boxplots of the standardized results of the weight experiment with mean markers. The labels *5, 8, 11* refer to the tactile reference intensity, *C, 0, 1, 2* to the visual intensity.

Question	Answer	Weight	Temperature
1. Virtual arm your own	strong	3	2
	weak	5	2
	none	4	6
2. Visual or tactile	visual	2	0
	tactile	10 (4)	10 (4)

Table 5: Answers to the post-experiment questions by experiment. The number in brackets indicates the number of participants who initially used visual cues.

visual conditions differed significantly from those of the corresponding control.

Qualitative results of the post-experiment questions are summarized in Table 5 in column *Weight*. Three participants answered that they had a strong feeling that the avatar's arm was their own, five had a less strong feeling, and four responded to not feeling any connection at all. Regarding using visual weight or intensity, two participants responded that they used the size and the speed of the spheres, and the other ten used the vibration intensity, of which four stated they tried to use the size and weight, but found it unreliable after a few rounds.

4.4 Temperature Experiment

4.4.1 Participants

Ten participants took part in the temperature experiment – eight male, two female, ages from 22-24 (average 23.2), nine right-handed, one ambidextrous. Four had no prior experience with HMDs, four had taken part in one or a few demonstrations, and two had worked on projects using one. None were colorblind, two wore prescription glasses, and none had any restrictions concerning touch sensations on the skin. Again, we do not see any influences of these parameters on the evaluation results. Data of three additionally tested subjects had to be discarded due to one system error and two premature terminations due to the subjects being unfit as a result of strain on their eyes.

4.4.2 Matching Task

The method used during this experiment is equivalent to that described in Section 4.3.2, now using the terminology

	Ref5	Ref8	Ref11
Control	-0.113	-0.150	-0.463
Visual0	0.075	-0.213	-0.250
Visual1	0.050	-0.338	-0.475
Visual2	-0.188	-0.188	-0.425

Table 6: Standardized means over all conditions of the temperature experiment.

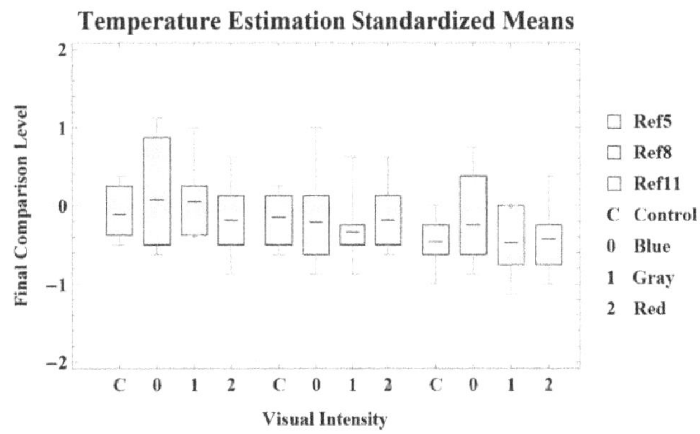

Figure 4: Boxplots of the standardized results of the temperature experiment with mean markers. The labels *5, 8, 11* refer to the tactile reference intensity, *C, 0, 1, 2* to the visual intensity.

'temperature' instead of 'weight', and 'colder'/'warmer' instead of 'lighter'/'heavier'. In addition, all spheres have the same size and falling speed, but different colors: blue, gray and red, which are commonly associated with cold, neutral, and warm temperature, respectively; cf. Figure 2.

4.4.3 Results

The results were standardized as in the previous experiment, see section 4.3.3. The standardized means are given in Table 6 and visualized in Figure 4. Normality was tested using Shapiro-Wilk tests, which showed that three cases were not normally distributed: *Ref5-Control* ($W(10) = 0.843; p = 0.048$), *Ref5-Visual0* ($W(10) = 0.840; p = 0.044$), and *Ref8-Visual1* ($W(10) = 0.810; p = 0.019$).

Mauchly's Test of Sphericity indicated that the sphericity assumption had been violated in the interaction effect ($\chi^2(9) = 18.643; p = 0.032$), so a Greenhouse-Geisser correction was used for this effect. A two-way repeated measures ANOVA showed that there was no significant main effect over reference intensity ($F(2,18) = 2.028; p = 0.161$), no significant main effect over visual intensity ($F(2,18) = 0.946; p = 0.407$) and there was also no significant interaction effect ($F(2.037, 18.332) = 1.817; p = 0.190$).

Although there was no significant main effect over reference intensity in the results of the temperature experiment, the results of both experiments are combined to investigate this effect further. Three independent samples t-tests were run for each reference intensity, which showed that only the results for reference intensity 5 differed significantly between groups ($t(86) = 3.293; p = 0.001$). In the same way, three independent sample t-tests were run for the control results, which showed that again only the results of reference intensity 5 differed significantly between groups ($t(20) = 2.479; p = 0.022$). Normality was tested for each reference intensity with Shapiro-Wilk tests, which showed that reference intensities 5 and 8 were not normal ($W(88) = 0.959; p = 0.007$ and $W(88) = 0.950; p = 0.002$). Sphericity was violated according to Mauchly's Test ($\chi^2(2) = 28.988; p = 0.000001$) so a Huynh-Feldt correction was used. A one-way repeated measured ANOVA with factor reference intensity (three levels) showed that there was a significant main effect ($F(1.578, 137.298) = 58.238; p < 0.0000001$), and pairwise comparisons with Bonferroni correction showed that each comparison was significant ($p < 0.000001$).

Qualitative results of the questions are summarized in column *Temperature* of Table 5. Two participants answered that they had a strong feeling the avatar's arm was their own, two had a less strong feeling, and six responded to not feeling any connection at all. All participants used the vibration intensity to come to an answer, of which four stated they thought they may have been influenced by the color of the sphere.

5. DISCUSSION

The experiment addressed the research question: *Is it possible to create the illusion of experiencing different intensities of a certain property (weight or temperature) using a rather simple and unrelated type of touch (vibrations of different intensities) together with compelling, type-related visuals (speed/size and color, respectively)?* Using a matching task, we speculated that related quantitative measures enable us to identify if people are likely to associate such tactile experiences with these properties and if or how concrete intensity levels have to be set when visual stimuli change. We expected that the richer visual stimuli can be used to change a user's tactile perception – ideally in a way that enables us to simulate more complex tactile experiences.

This conjecture was verified for the weight property, but not for the temperature property. In the weight experiment, the consistent increase in equally perceived tactile intensities when visual intensity was increased means the sensation felt on the skin was estimated 'lighter' when the visual sphere looked heavier, even though the true tactile vibration intensities were held constant. This is consistent with the speed-force illusion [1] and the size-weight illusion [29]. However, after analysis of the post-experiment responses, it was clear that almost all participants eventually used the intensity of the vibrations in order to respond in each trial. This means that the visual cues caused participants to subconsciously generate an expectation which changed not only the intensity of the felt sensation, but possibly also the type. However, consciously no association to weight was made. While we can thus *not* conclude that people will associate such related vibrations with the characteristic of weight, these observations are essential for system design when including tactile feedback into such a VR setting. Roughly speaking, if a visual stimulus suggests a higher weight, but the matching tactile feedback is experienced as less intense, there is a high likelihood that the illusion of weight is not only not apparent but even 'destroyed'. The added modality would then not increase the experience but make it even worse, whereas an adjustment of intensity as suggested by our results will guarantee a 'perceived' match of both modalities.

Although the observed contrast effect is in line with various studies concerning weight, pressure and force [5], the question remains why it occurred here. An assumption was that the visual stimuli would contribute to the perception of weight, which means that when the visual intensity is increased, the tactile intensity must be decreased. However, if these stimuli actually weakened the weight perception rather than contributed, then the tactile intensity must in fact be increased when visual intensity was increased. This is reasonable since the weight estimation of the comparison stimulus is decided indirectly through cognitive processes, while that of the reference stimulus is decided directly through sensory processes. On the other hand, we cannot state that the participants indeed perceived weight; participants may have, for example, estimated transferred energy per unit area of skin contact, i.e. maximum pressure. When assuming constant mass, a larger area of skin contact would lead to a lower level of perceived pressure.

In the temperature experiment, no significant differences were found over visual intensity. The question that arises is why this occurred for the property weight, but not for temperature. The participants could either not associate vibrations with temperature, or color with temperature, or both. An explanation concerning the first scenario is that impact induced by the weight of an object can either be felt through a vibration, or is easier to translate from a vibration than the temperature of an object – a reasoning that can be supported by examining different receptors found in human skin. Mechanoreceptors respond to mechanical pressure and distortion, and there exist different types: Pacinian corpuscles, Meissner corpuscles, Merkel receptors, Ruffini end organs, and receptors in hair follicles. Each one responds to vibrations in a certain frequency range. Since impact and vibration are of the same nature, i.e. they both cause skin distortion, it may be the case that both sensations can be felt, and which is finally chosen is caused by surrounding/congruent factors. In the case of the change in weight, the participants were visually expecting a sense of impact to occur, and not a vibration. Changes in temperature, on the other hand, are sensed through thermoreceptors, causing the perceptual 'gap' between vibration and temperature to be too large to bridge despite the visuals. The second scenario, i.e. that participants could not associate temperature with color, was disproved in a study by Ho et al. [13]. By objective performance measurements, it was shown that humans make a cross-modal correspondence between color and temperature, specifically in the direction color-temperature, and not temperature-color.

An interesting observation can be made when looking at the results with respect to the order of presentation. Because we used a method of adjustment, we had to present the reference stimulus first, followed by the comparison that subjects had to adjust. This is in contrast to references (e.g., [9]) suggesting a counterbalanced representation in order to avoid a shift in results; generally, for psychophysical experiments, it is assumed that the second stimulus is often judged as 'greater' than the true equality. While in our case, 'greater' does not necessarily correspond to a higher vibration intensity, it does however suggest that a shift in one direction may occur. A significant main effect was found over tactile reference intensity in the weight experiment, but not in the temperature experiment. The combined results, however, show this effect as well. This means that low vibrotactile intensities are experienced as weaker than they really are, and high vibrotactile intensities as stronger. Because this shift is not consistently in the same direction, it may indicate an interesting aspect with respect to the design of psychophysical experiments worth investigating in future research.

Another noteworthy aspect appears when examining the post-experiment answers with respect to the so-called rubber hand illusion [3] – a body illusion experiment where subjects 'experience' a rubber hand as being their own due to a visual stimulus on the artificial hand (e.g., being stroked by the object) that is congruent to a real tactile sensation on their (visually hidden) real hand. The results from Table 5 suggest that participants in the weight experiment were able to generate a stronger rubber hand illusion than those in the temperature experiment. This in turn suggests that when visual and haptic information are 'more congruent' then a strong rubber hand illusion occurs, or the other way around, i.e. that when a strong rubber hand illusion occurs then visual and haptic information are 'more congruent'. The findings of [20] are in line with the first suggestion; correct visual perspective together with correlated multisensory information trigger a strong illusion. However, in [18] it was observed that incongruent cues are not experienced as incorrect when the illusion was strong, which is in line with the second suggestion. It is clear that these elements are strongly related, however at this stage it is unclear how.

Two rather curious artifacts worth mentioning are first, that the results from the control condition in the case of tactile reference intensity 5 differed significantly between experiment groups, and not in the case of intensities 8 and 11. However, the control conditions were identical in both experiments and thus this difference should only be caused by chance. Second, from the answers to the post-experiment questions it was clear that the body transfer illusion was not very strong for most participants. This is in contrast to our assumption that a first person view will be sufficient to achieve this (which in turn was based on related research; cf. Section 2.3). Because a first person experience is not essential for the tests presented in the paper, we do not suspect any related impact on our results. The observed effect does however raise an interesting question for future research. Is this lack of body transfer just due to the used setup (e.g. several participants noted that finger movements in the real world were not directly mapped to the virtual world) or does the introduced combination of modalities, i.e., tactile and visuals have an effect as well?

6. CONCLUSION AND FUTURE WORK

The work presented in this paper was motivated by the goal to gain a better understanding of passive touch perception and to investigate if a simple vibration feedback has the potential to improve VR experience when used in combination with richer visual stimuli. In a series of experiments, we have shown that visual cues that give an indication of weight, specifically size and falling speed, can change the perceived intensity of a vibration felt on the skin upon collision. Precisely, the sensation felt on the skin was estimated 'lighter' when the visual ball looked heavier. This means that future VR systems with the goal of creating different weight intensities would need to substantially exaggerate the weight by vibration in order for it to seem realistic for humans. This was not the case when using vibrations to simulate a temperature in combination with color as a visual cue. We conclude that it is not possible to let humans perceive different temperatures through vibrations and accompanying visual color cues; while other temperature-indicating cues may produce other results, our study suggests that such an investigation may not be worthwhile.

The results of this research also identified two more general open problems. The first was of fundamental ground regarding general psychophysical experiments, namely what the consequences are of presenting reference and comparison stimuli successively and in the same order. Specifically, our results suggest that in the case of vibrotactile stimuli, the bias in judgement due to unbalanced presentation is not consistently in one direction as was previously thought. The second problem concerned body transfer illusion, and questioned whether the body transfer illusion was a consequence or a cause of accepting incongruent stimuli as plausible. This is an important practical observation, because both possibilities show that only one is needed in the design of a compelling multimodal experience.

As this study was an exploratory investigation, the successful result for weight simulation opens various opportunities for interesting future research. An initial idea is to broaden the range of acceptable touch; this study was only able to add the concept of weight to this range using visual speed and size, but it is not misplaced to insist that this could happen for other properties. An intriguing question of course is then what kind of accompanying visuals are necessary to accomplish this. Lastly, this study only used two modalities: haptic and visual. It is worth investigating whether audio cues strengthen the effect found in this study and thus have the potential to create even better, more immersive experiences.

7. ACKNOWLEDGMENTS

Our thanks go to Elitac B.V. for supplying the necessary hardware and valuable support during this research.

8. REFERENCES

[1] K. Arai and K. Okajima. Tactile force perception depends on the visual speed of the collision object. *Journal of Vision*, 9(11):19, 2009.

[2] K. W. Arthur, K. S. Booth, and C. Ware. Evaluating 3D task performance for fish tank virtual worlds. *ACM Transactions on Information Systems (TOIS)*, 11(3):239–265, 1993.

[3] M. Botvinick and J. Cohen. Rubber hands 'feel' touch that eyes see. *Nature*, 391:756–756, 1998.

[4] D. Bowman, D. Johnson, and L. Hodges. Testbed evaluation of virtual environment interaction techniques. *Presence*, 10(1):75–95, 2001.

[5] J. B. Brayanov and M. A. Smith. Bayesian and "anti-bayesian" biases in sensory integration for action and perception in the size–weight illusion. *Journal of Neurophysiology*, 103(3):1518–1531, 2010.

[6] G. Burdea and P. Coiffet. *Virtual Reality Technology.* John Wiley & Sons, Inc., Hoboken, New Jersey, second edition, 2003.

[7] R. R. Ellis and S. J. Lederman. The role of haptic versus visual volume cues in the size-weight illusion. *Perception & Psychophysics*, 53(3):315–324, 1993.

[8] M. O. Ernst and M. S. Banks. Humans integrate visual and haptic information in a statistically optimal fashion. *Nature*, 415:429–433, 2002.

[9] G. A. Gescheider. *Psychophysics: the fundamentals.* Lawrence Erlbaum Associated, Inc., 1997.

[10] E. Heineken and F. P. Schulte. Seeing size and feeling weight: The size-weight illusion in natural and virtual reality. *Human Factors: The Journal of the Human Factors and Ergonomics Society*, 49(1):136–144, 2007.

[11] Y. Hirano, A. Kimura, F. Shibata, and H. Tamura. Psychophysical influence of mixed-reality visual stimulation on sense of hardness. In *Virtual Reality Conference (VR), 2011 IEEE*, pages 51–54. IEEE, 2011.

[12] H.-N. Ho, D. Iwai, Y. Yoshikawa, J. Watanabe, and S. Nishida. Combining colour and temperature: A blue object is more likely to be judged as warm than a red object. *Scientific reports*, 4(5527), 2014.

[13] H.-N. Ho, G. H. Van Doorn, T. Kawabe, J. Watanabe, and C. Spence. Colour-temperature correspondences: When reactions to thermal stimuli are influenced by colour. *PloS one*, 9(3):e91854, 2014.

[14] I. P. Howard and W. B. Templeton. *Human spatial orientation.* John Wiley & Sons, 1966.

[15] S. Kanaya, Y. Matsushima, and K. Yokosawa. Does seeing ice really feel cold? visual-thermal interaction under an illusory body-ownership. *PloS one*, 7(11):e47293, 2012.

[16] S.-C. Kim, A. Israr, and I. Poupyrev. Tactile rendering of 3D features on touch surfaces. In *Proceedings of the 26th annual ACM symposium on User interface software and technology*, pages 531–538. ACM, 2013.

[17] R. W. Lindeman, Y. Yanagida, H. Noma, and K. Hosaka. Wearable vibrotactile systems for virtual contact and information display. *Virtual Reality*, 9(2-3):203–213, 2006.

[18] A. Maselli and M. Slater. The building blocks of the full body ownership illusion. *Frontiers in human neuroscience*, 7(83), 2013.

[19] H. McGurk and J. MacDonald. Hearing lips and seeing voices. *Nature*, 264(5588):746–748, 1976.

[20] V. I. Petkova and H. H. Ehrsson. If I were you: perceptual illusion of body swapping. *PloS one*, 3(12):e3832, 2008.

[21] G. L. Poling, J. M. Weisenberger, and T. Kerwin. The role of multisensory feedback in haptic surface perception. In *Proceedings of the 11th Symposium on Haptic Interfaces for Virtual Environment and Teleoperator Systems, 2003. HAPTICS 2003.*, pages 187–194. IEEE, 2003.

[22] P. Richard, G. Burdea, G. Birebent, D. Gomez, N. Langrana, and P. Coiffet. Effect of frame rate and force feedback on virtual objects manipulation. *Presence-Teleoperators and Virtual Environments (MIT Press)*, 15:95–108, 1996.

[23] M. V. Sanchez-Vives and M. Slater. From presence to consciousness through virtual reality. *Nature Reviews Neuroscience*, 6(4):332–339, 2005.

[24] L. Shams, Y. Kamitani, and S. Shimojo. Illusions: What you see is what you hear. *Nature*, 408(6814):788–788, 2000.

[25] M. Slater, B. Spanlang, M. V. Sanchez-Vives, and O. Blanke. First person experience of body transfer in virtual reality. *PloS one*, 5(5):e10564, 2010.

[26] A. Somada, A. Kimura, F. Shibata, H. Tamura, et al. Psychophysical influence on tactual impression by mixed-reality visual stimulation. In *Virtual Reality Conference, 2008. VR'08. IEEE*, pages 265–266. IEEE, 2008.

[27] M. A. Srinivasan and C. Basdogan. Haptics in virtual environments: Taxonomy, research status, and challenges. *Computers & Graphics*, 21(4):393–404, 1997.

[28] J. Steuer. Defining virtual reality: Dimensions determining telepresence. *Journal of communication*, 42(4):73–93, 1992.

[29] J. C. Stevens and L. L. Rubin. Psychophysical scales of apparent heaviness and the size-weight illusion. *Perception & Psychophysics*, 8(4):225–230, 1970.

Detection of Deception in the Mafia Party Game

Sergey Demyanov
s.demyanov@student.unimelb.edu.au

James Bailey
baileyj@unimelb.edu.au

Kotagiri Ramamohanarao
kotagiri@unimelb.edu.au

Christopher Leckie
caleckie@unimelb.edu.au

Department of Computing and Information Systems
The University of Melbourne, Melbourne, VIC, Australia

ABSTRACT

The problem of deception detection is very challenging. Only trained people with specialist knowledge are able to demonstrate an accuracy that is sufficiently higher than random predictions. We present a multi-stage automatic system for extracting features from facial cues and evaluate it on the Mafia game database which we have collected. It is a large database of truthful and deceptive people, recorded in conditions more variable and realistic than many other databases of similar kind. We demonstrate that using the extracted features we are able to correctly classify instances with an average AUC (area under the ROC curve) equal to 0.61, significantly better than random predictions.

Categories and Subject Descriptors

I.2 [**Artificial Intelligence**]: Miscellaneous

Keywords

deception; classification; facial cues; action units; video processing

1. INTRODUCTION

Many organizations such as police, secret services, border security services and insurance companies depend on the recognition of deception and truthfulness of their clients. According to previous research ([22],[2]), the average person detects liars with a probability that is statistically significant, but just slightly above a random chance. However, results of other experiments have demonstrated that when people have a motivation to lie, their deception cues are present via four non-verbal channels: facial expressions, gestures and body language, verbal style and voice characteristics. Using these, trained people can achieve an accuracy of up to 73% ([6], [7]). Moreover, in [12] it is claimed that the analysis of facial expressions considered simultaneously with context could further increase this accuracy up to 90%, considerably higher than human performance. Current technologies allow us to perform such analysis automatically in real-time. Since the face is the richest source of information, detection of facial cues of deception is one of the most important parts of such a deception detection system.

In this article we present a new database of truthful and deceptive people based on the videos of the Mafia party game (also known as Werewolf), and describe a methodology for feature extraction and classification of each person's role. In each game players are assigned to be either truthful or deceptive. At the same time there are no requirements on what the players have to say and how they should behave. A more detailed explanation of the game rules is given in Section 3. This new database contains 6001 labeled episodes from 270 participants with a total duration of 5 hours.

Our goal was to identify the players' roles based on their close-up face recordings. To create features we consider the first N minutes of each game, where N varies from 5 to 35 minutes. We extract features corresponding to the particular movements of facial muscles. Some of them are caused by experienced emotions, and therefore can be the signs of verity or the cues of deception. According to these features we build an automatic classifier of truthful and deceptive people.

First we give an overview of related work (Section 2), present the Mafia database (Section 3) and discuss the methodology of our research (Section 4). In the next key sections we describe the procedure of facial movement detection (Section 5), and explain the details of feature engineering (Section 6). Later we compare the obtained accuracy with the accuracy of a random classifier and demonstrate that the predictions are statistically significant (Section 7.1). Finally we analyze the most predictive features and show that they agree with the theory (Section 7.2). The conclusion (Section 8) finalizes the article. We believe our research can boost interest in the area of deception detection from facial cues.

2. RELATED WORK

The problem of deception detection has attracted considerable interest in recent years. Work in [22] established that the leakage of cues to deception is caused by the increased cognitive load experienced by liars, and therefore cannot be avoided. In [3] the authors analyzed 158 cues including facial expressions, linguistic features, physiological features and others. They discovered that people with

ICMI 2015, November 9–13, 2015, Seattle, WA, USA.

DOI: http://dx.doi.org/10.1145/2818346.2820745

higher cognitive loads are more likely to have less illustrators and body movements, more hesitations, longer pauses in speech, greater pupil dilation and more gaze aversion. Deceptive people can also experience a sudden increase of blood flow in the region of the eyes, which can be detected in thermal images [1]. Moreover, deception is often related with one of the 3 emotions: fear, guilt or delight [23]. The facial expressions of these emotions can also reveal these emotions.

In the experiments by Warren et al. [25], participants watched emotional and unemotional videos and were asked to lie about what they saw. The average classification accuracy for predicting lying was around 50%, however it was 64% for the group lying about emotional videos. This confirms the hypothesis that emotions can cause the non-verbal leakage of the deception cues. Their database is known as YorkDDT. Another database was collected by Frank et al. [9]. They recorded videos for an interrogation scenario with 100 participants of 2.5 minutes each. A multimodal database with 30 participants that includes video, thermal video, speech and physiological data have been collected in [?]. Mihalcea and Burzo [14] obtained 140 videos with truthful and deceptive people using Amazon Mechanical Turk. Zhang et al. [28] developed a system of expression classification based on facial key points and demonstrated its good performance.

A number of attempts have been made to develop an automatic system for deception detection. However, in most of them the features are not related to facial expressions. Several of them are based on linguistic features. For example, Fornaciari and Poesio used stylometric techniques to identify deception in the corpus of hearings collected in Italian courts [8]. Using only the linguistic features, Mihalcea et al. [15] could reach an accuracy $52-73\%$.

Thermal imaging approaches are also popular. Warmelink et al. [24] applied it to identify deception in airports. Their system demonstrated an accuracy higher than 60%. Rajoub et al. performed similar experiments with thermal videos on a set of 492 samples from 25 participants. While they were able to reach a very high level of accuracy of 87% for within-person predictions, the results of inter-person predictions (around 60%) were similar to other experiments. Another attempt to use thermal imaging has been performed by Jain et al. in [10]. They also obtained a classification accuracy for predicting lying of around 62%. In [1] the authors presented a system based on a multimodal approach, combining physiological features such as temperature, heart rate and pulse with linguistic features. The obtained accuracy was shown to be better than random, achieving 70% in some scenarios.

Some attention has also been paid to micro-expressions. The authors of [17] developed the system of micro-expression detection using LBP-TOP features. They evaluated it on the corpus of video clips from [25] and their own database, and obtained quite promising results. Another database of 195 micro-expressions was collected in [27, 26]. The authors also provide the labels of the appearing action units with their timestamps. However, there were no attempts to use these databases and algorithms for deception detection.

3. THE MAFIA GAME DATABASE

We present a new database collected from the Mafia TV show, which contains 5 hours of videos from 270 participants. Unlike others, it was recorded in much more natural conditions than the experiments in other publications. Comparing with other deception detection databases in Table 1, it makes the Mafia database one of the largest. The source videos [1], the episode timestamps and player labels [2] are available online. We hope that it will be interesting for the research community and will boost progress in the area of deception detection.

Table 1: The main parameters of deception detection video databases

database	Participants	Duration, min	Link
Mafia DB	270	300	
Amazon Turk DB	140	315	[14]
RU-FACS-1	100	250	[9]
Multimodal DB	30	75	[1]
YorkDDT	20	23	[25]

The Mafia party game (also known as Werewolf) was invented in 1986 by the students of Moscow State University studying in the Department of Psychology. This is how the game is described in Wikipedia: "[It is] modeling a conflict between an informed minority (the Mafia) and an uninformed majority (the innocents). At the start of the game each player is secretly assigned a role affiliated with one of these teams. The game has two alternating phases: 'night', during which the Mafia may covertly 'murder' an innocent, and 'day', in which surviving players debate the identities of the mafiosi and vote to eliminate a suspect. After elimination the player reveals his role. Play continues until all of the Mafia has been eliminated, or until the Mafia outnumbers the innocents". While the 'day' stage contains long discussions and voting, during the 'night' stage the 'Mafia' members silently show who they want to eliminate, and usually agree on a candidature within about 10-20 seconds.

The Mafia TV show series was shown on the Russian TV channel MuzTV in 2009 and 2010. The game participants were Russian celebrities and TV channel spectators. In total there were 30 series in this period [3]. The length of each of them is about 45 minutes. In each game there were 9 players. Two of them were from the Mafia team, the others were innocent. The role depends on the card the player gets at the beginning of the game. A black card corresponds to Mafia and a red card corresponds to innocents. Depending on the situation, each game had from 2 to 4 rounds of 'day'-'night' pairs.

Since during the 'day' stage the players from the Mafia team pretend to be innocent, we labeled them as deceptive. Others were labeled as truthful. Thus, our database contains 60 deceptive and 210 truthful players, 270 players in total. Note that the label of each player depends only on his role and is not changing within a game regardless of the current player's actions and words. Moreover, note that 'night' stage recordings are very short and do not contain discussions, so we excluded all 'night' appearances from our database.

4. METHODOLOGY

[1]`https://www.youtube.com/user/muzTV/search?query=mafia`

[2]`https://sites.google.com/site/mafiadatabase`

[3]60 more series were shown later. Thus, the database can be increased by 3 times.

All facial expressions are caused by particular combinations of facial muscles. The list of these muscles is known from physiology. Based on this list, the Swedish anatomist Carl-Herman Hjortsjö developed the Facial Action Coding System (FACS), that was later published by Paul Ekman et al. in 1978 and revised in 2002 [5]. This system defines 27 possible **Action Units** (AU) related with particular muscles (9 of them are in the upper part of the face and 17 in the lower part) and 6 basic emotions (fear, sadness, happiness, anger, disgust and surprise) that consist of different action units. The visual appearance of these action units can be found online [4].

Facial expressions can also be classified as *posed*, *spontaneous* or *concealed*. Posed expressions appear deliberately in order to cause a certain impression. In contrast, spontaneous expressions appear unconsciously as a reaction on the ongoing events. Concealed expressions are also spontaneous, but their appearance is suppressed and therefore they have much smaller amplitudes.

In the book "Telling lies" [4], Paul Ekman provides a comprehensive analysis of the nature of deception. Chapter 5 describes the facial cues of deception. Ekman states that posed and spontaneous expressions are caused by different parts of the brain, and therefore have some subtle differences. One of them is that some facial muscles are involved only in spontaneous expressions and they cannot be readily inhibited. These muscles are called *reliable*. For example, only 10 percent of people can pull the corners of their lips down keeping their chin muscle fixed. The characteristic of being hard to suppress was called the inhibition hypothesis. This hypothesis was later confirmed in the experiments of [18].

Since facial expressions are supposed to be related with action units, we used this information to extract features. In order to do this we collected examples of action units and searched for their appearance in the Mafia database. The similarity scores of each player were used as features. We explain the full procedure in detail below. First we describe the algorithm of frame processing, and then provide the details of feature engineering.

5. FRAME PROCESSING

Since the camera shows players from all angles and distances, players wear glasses and gesticulate in front of the face, as well as other difficulties, frame processing is not an easy task. For this purpose we developed a multi-stage automatic procedure which is briefly described in Algorithm 1.

Algorithm 1 Frame processing

1. Face and eyes detection using OpenCV library
2. Initial in-plane rotation using eyes coordinates
3. Facial keypoint feature detection using Luxand FaceSDK
4. Width, height and angle normalization using keypoint features
5. Linear and non-linear image registration
6. Grid displacement computation for a sequence of frames.

5.1 Face detection

As the first element we employed the Viola-Jones algorithm [21] from the OpenCV library to detect faces. This library provides a detector that is already learned, so we could apply it straight away. In our experiments we considered only one face on each episode, so when we met more than one, we chose the one that is closest to the previously detected face. Once the face was detected, we applied the same algorithm for eye detection. The library provides different classifiers for the left and right eyes, so we approximately identified the regions for eyes and applied the classifiers in these regions. If no eyes were detected, we considered it as a false registration. In the case when only one eye was not detected on the current frame, but it was detected on the previous frame, we measured the displacement of the other eye and applied it to the current one. This situation happened quite often for people with glasses, and it allowed to treat such frames with the standard procedure. We used the position of detected eyes for initial in-plane rotation, so that the eyes become horizontally aligned.

5.2 Facial feature detection and normalization

After initial processing we applied the proprietary Luxand FaceSDK[5] software for facial feature detection. For a given face it returns the location of 66 facial points: 11 for each eye, 14 for mouth, etc. If the toolbox could not detect the features, we omitted such a frame. First we employed the obtained features to compute more precise coordinates of the left eye and right eyes (average of all left and right eye features, Fig. ??). These coordinates were used for additional in-plane rotation, so that the eyes are located on the horizontal line.

Second, we used these features to perform width and height normalization. To normalize width we computed the distance between eyes and scaled the image to make this distance equal to 80 px. Similarly we computed the visible nose height (the mean of the difference between y-coordinates of the left and right nose corners and its top), and scaled the image to make it equal to 50 px.

Third, we performed normalization with respect to other two types of rotation. While the in-plane rotation is a linear transformation and it can be easily suppressed using the eye coordinates, the other two out-of-plane types of rotation appear as a non-rigid transformation. In our problem we have only 2 regions of interest: eyes and mouth, so instead of registration of the whole face we cropped these two regions and treated them separately. These regions were considered as vertical cylinders with predefined radius values, so an up-down region rotation appears as a squeeze/stretch of an image in the vertical dimension, and therefore is a linear transformation. The same cylinder model makes it possible to handle a left-right rotation. We estimated the rotation angle using the eyes and nose coordinates obtained earlier, and computed how these cylinders would appear without rotation. In other words, we considered the visible face region as a projection of a cylinder on a rotated axis and computed its projection on the original axis. It leads to a non-linear

[4] `http://www.cs.cmu.edu/~face/facs.htm`

[5] `https://www.luxand.com/facesdk/`

stretching of the part that is closer to the observer and otherwise.

5.3 Image registration

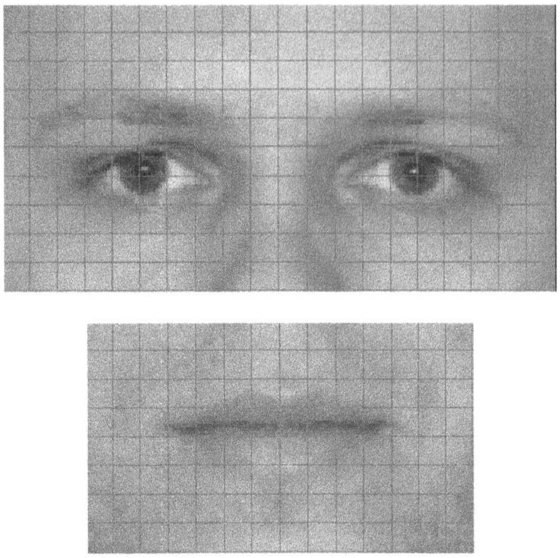

Figure 1: An example of normalized eyes and mouth with the 8×8 uniform grids

After face normalization we perform image registration. It allows allows us to obtain a description of non-linear movements within a face, that are related to action units. This procedure is based on the method of nonrigid registration using free form deformations, described in [19], and used in [11].

The problem is the following: for two similar images we want to find a non-linear transformation that maps one image into the other one. As in [11], we also use a sum of squared distances between pixels as a similarity measure. We model the transformation by the displacement of nodes of the uniform grid in Fig. 1 with the size of a cell 8×8 px. For the displacements p_k of the nodes of the uniform grid x_k, the value for the pixel x is taken from the pixel $T(x)$ of the original image:

$$T(x) = x + \sum_{x_k \in N_x} p_k \beta\left(\frac{x - x_k}{\sigma}\right),$$

Here N_x is the set if 16 nodes around the point x, p_k's are the displacements of these grid nodes, β is the cubic multidimensional b-spline polynomial function and σ is the regular grid spacing (8). To avoid problems with the corner pixels, the regular grid has 2 rows and columns outside the image from each size. Thus, the parameters of the model are the coordinates of the extended uniform grid nodes ($16 \times 26 \times 2 = 832$ variables for the eye region and $14 \times 20 \times \times 2 = 560$ variables for the mouth region). The minimization problem is solved using the L-BFGS algorithm.

Before solving non-rigid registration problem, we first equalize the intensity histograms in order to avoid variations in brightness. Second, we perform affine registration, which also minimizes the SSD measure. It gives us the 3×3 affine transformation matrix, which aligns frames linearly. The non-linear transformation is performed in two steps with different grid spacing. First the SSD measure is minimized only for a half of nodes (i.e., using double spacing), and after it the solution is updated using all nodes.

Because non-rigid registration works well only when the difference between frames is small enough, we applied it only to nearby frames. To obtain the transformation function between two frames on an arbitrary distance, we sequentially applied the grids for frames between them. In other words, if we know all functions T_{i-1}^i for $i = 1 \ldots N$, then the function T_0^N is just their composition, i.e.

$$T_0^N(x) = T_{N-1}^N(\ldots T_1^2(T_0^1(x))\ldots).$$

Here T_{i-1}^i is the function that transforms the points from the frame $i-1$ to the frame i. However, this process is not precise and good results can be obtained only for a sequence of not more than 30 frames. Note that the functions $T(x)$ are defined only for pixels in the image, while the output $T(x)$ may be outside the image. In this case we do not have 16 nodes around this output (that is an input for the next function) and we have to approximate the displacements for these non-existing nodes. This leads to inaccurate results of the points near the border.

6. FEATURE ENGINEERING

Algorithm 1 allows us to compute the displacement of grid nodes in a sequence of consecutive frames. These node displacements give a compact representation of the movements between the first and the last frames. Here we describe the procedure of feature extraction using this information. Its scheme is given in Algorithm 2.

Algorithm 2 Feature extraction

1. Extract all episodes from the Mafia videos using Algorithm 1
2. Choose a collection of AU examples from the MMI database
3. Compute the displacement grids for the onsets and offsets of chosen examples using Algorithm 1
4. Find the subsequences of the episodes that are most similar to the AU examples
5. Compute their similarity scores
6. Aggregate the similarity scores over all episodes of each player (choose the minimum)

6.1 Episode extraction

We processed all source Mafia videos to extract the sequences of neighboring frames that are registered to each other using Algorithm 1. We refer to them as *episodes*. However, within a single episode some frames might be omitted for different reasons. For example, it might happen because the face is occluded by a hand and therefore it is not detectable. Their number should be small enough to have the registered frames be close to each other and large enough to keep the episodes continuous, for example in the situations of people with glasses. In our case the maximum allowed number of consecutive omitted frames in a single episode was 10. It the number was larger, we ended the episode and started a new one. Given that each pair of frames required about 3 seconds for registration, it was the most time consuming part of the total pipeline.

We extracted episodes in the interval from 7 to 42 minutes, when all the game actions were taking place. In total we obtained 6733 episodes in 30 games with an average of 224 episodes per game, 29 per player. The minimum and maximum number of episodes in one game were 175 and 284. The average length of each episode was 77 frames, i.e., about 3 seconds. Each episode was manually viewed and labeled according to the player appearing on it. If the episode was corrupted, contained non-players or players after the game, it was labeled as 0 and was omitted in further calculations. The total number of episodes after elimination is 6001.

6.2 MMI database

The MMI database ([16]) contains a wide range of videos and images representing different emotions. Some of the videos are also labeled according to the Action Units they contain. Additionally they contain the information about AU stage (onset (or start), peak, offset (or finish), neutral) for each frame. We employed this information for feature selection.

Theory suggests [4, 18], that the action units caused by reliable muscles (like AU1) correspond to felt emotions. Depending on the emotion it can be a sign of either truthfulness or deception. Therefore, it was plausible to find the appearance of such action units. For this purpose we employed the same image registration procedure for MMI examples as for the Mafia database. We selected a maximum of 3 examples of non-empty onsets and offsets for each of the 14 most common action units (namely 1, 2, 4, 5, 6, 7, 9, 12, 15, 16, 17, 20, 23 and 24), 79 in total. The indices of video clips with AU examples from the MMI database including the duration of onset and offset stages are presented in the Table 2. The choice of 3 examples provides a balance between the variety of AU representation and the generalization ability of the trained model. AU templates are similar, and the corresponding features are highly correlated. If the number of features was too large, this could result in overfitting behavior by standard classifiers such as the employed logistic regression. The examples were chosen randomly (in fact, in lexicographical order of their numbers) in order to avoid inflation of reported performance due to over tuning of feature selection.

For each example we performed image registration of the frames with the 'onset' and 'offset' labels. Then we used the computed transformation functions to compute the new coordinates of the uniform grid nodes on the last frame of the resulting sequences. For each of these sequences we also computed the cumulative linear transformation by multiplying the transformation matrices for each frame in the sequence. The new coordinates were multiplied on the inverse cumulative transformation matrix in order to suppress head movements. Since different action units appear in different areas of the eyes and mouth, we used only the subset of nodes located in these areas. The list of these nodes for each AU is also provided on the database website. The displacements of these nodes uniquely identify the appeared action unit.

There might be some concerns about the validity of usage of posed AU examples from the MMI database in order to find the spontaneous appearance of AU in the Mafia database. However, our algorithm takes the difference between posed and spontaneous expressions into account. More specifically, that most of the difference lies in the temporal dimension, which is effectively handled in our algorithm by considering all possible pairs of first and last frames to detect action units. Second, our algorithm detects the presence of AUs, rather than their type. AU type is another discriminative factor, which might further boost accuracy, but is more difficult to correctly detect. The employed algorithm is more preferable than approaches like CERT, where the AU appearance scores are based on each frame independent of others. On the other hand, our displacement grids are based on changes in time, thus containing richer information, which is exploitable in our framework.

Table 2: The indices of Action Units from the MMI database, which are used as examples. The numbers of onset and offset frames are provided in the brackets

AU	Examples (onset and offset duration)		
1	1931 (3, 0)	24 (18, 18)	582 (4, 6)
2	144 (3, 9)	145 (10, 13)	1649 (6, 8)
4	1047 (4, 7)	1384 (5, 3)	1823 (6, 13)
5	1 (5, 9)	1275 (6, 11)	144 (3, 9)
6	1074 (5, 5)	1088 (7, 8)	123 (11, 16)
7	1316 (0, 2)	1874 (3, 7)	1973 (5, 6)
9	1384 (5, 5)	1964 (11, 10)	199 (3, 5)
12	123 (17, 37)	124 (28, 39)	125 (12, 19)
15	1077 (7, 3)	1152 (7, 7)	1153 (5, 5)
16	134 (5, 6)	135 (7, 17)	14 (11, 18)
17	1152 (8, 6)	1153 (4, 3)	12 (10, 14)
20	1088 (7, 8)	1812 (13, 4)	1813 (10, 7)
23	382 (8, 4)	611 (12, 12)	
24	1874 (11, 8)	1931 (3, 0)	1973 (4, 6)

6.3 Feature extraction

The next step was to find the appearance of action units in the extracted episodes. Since they might have appeared at any moment, we considered all subsequences of consecutive frames of total length not more than 30. For each of them we computed the displacement of the subset of uniform grid nodes specific for this AU, the same way as we did for MMI examples. Then we computed the Euclidean distance between the displacement vectors of each episode subsequence and each onset and offset of examples of the action units from the MMI database obtained in the previous step.

We assume that within a single episode a particular action unit can appear only once. Given that, we computed the minimum distance among all subsequences and recorded it as a feature for this episode. Thus, for each episode we obtained 79 features (40 onset and 39 offset features). For convenience we recorded them with a negative sign. We will refer to them as the similarity scores.

The next goal was to create features for each player in each game. As before, we used maximum to aggregate the scores over each player episodes. We thus selected the maximum similarity scores over all episodes for a particular player and consider them as features for this player.

While a higher similarity score corresponds to a higher probability of AU appearance, the similarity scores are still quite noisy. In fact, after the visual examination we determined that only the first quartile of their values correspond to the episodes that are similar to the related action unit. Other 3 quartiles seemed to contain random episodes, regardless of the score value. To incorporate this knowledge in the dataset we subtracted the 78% - percentiles (7/9, the percentage of truthful players) and set all the negative values to 0. Therefore, we produced a sparse dataset with no difference in the feature values between non-top values.

7. EXPERIMENTAL RESULTS

During the game some players are eliminated and do not appear in the later stages. This causes an imbalance in the total observation time. Moreover, the eliminated players are more likely to be truthful, because only truthful players are eliminated during the 'night' stage. This might also introduce a bias in the features. In order to validate the obtained results we created a number of datasets, corresponding to the different game duration. We split all 35 minutes on 10 second intervals and considered game durations in the range from 5 to 35 minutes, totally 181 intervals. For each of them we selected only those episodes that completely fall into this interval. Thus, each set of these episodes gives an independent dataset.

7.1 Classification

Since the dataset is highly unbalanced, we used the area under the ROC curve (AUC) as a performance metric instead of classification accuracy. We employed the simple multinomial logistic regression classifier. Before classification we eliminated the players without observed episodes. There are 22 of them for the 5 minute game duration, and only one (player 3 in the game 16) for the 35 minutes. We performed 30-fold cross-validation, every time leaving out the players from a single game. Thus we kept the same proportion of the players in the training and test sets as in the full dataset.

Fig. 2 presents the plots of overall AUC depending on the game duration. It demonstrates a clear increase of performance in the range from 5 to 12 minutes, that corresponds to the increase of the number of considered episodes. This is a natural behavior: once we take more information into account, the predictions become more and more accurate. After that the AUC remains on the same level around 0.61. The maximum duration of 35 minutes gives the $AUC = 0.6391$. It corresponds to the accuracy 70.26%, while the random predictions give the average accuracy 65.35%. Choosing a classification threshold such that the number of predicted positive examples is equal to the one in the training set, we get the same corresponding precision and recall: 0.8082, and so is the F1-score. From Fig. 2 (b,c) we can see that eyes features independently perform better than mouth features, which reach the significance level only after 25 minutes. The reason might be a larger variety of mouth movements, caused by speech. Since it acts as noise, more time is required to collect meaningful statistics. We also evaluated the performance of onset and offset features independently. As expected, the results are worse than when they are combined together. However, onset features appear to be more predictive. Similar results were obtained using a linear SVM classifier with the regularization parameter $C = 1000$.

In order to assess the statistical significance of the results, we computed the critical AUC values. We tested the hypothesis that such AUC values could be obtained for a random distribution of labels. For each dataset, corresponding to a particular game duration, we performed the classification with the randomly permuted labels, 400 permutations. Permutations allowed to preserve the ratio of positive and negative instances. The critical values for the 0.05 significance level are presented by the orange curve in Fig. 2. As we can see from it, the obtained AUC is higher than the critical curve for almost every dataset based on more than 13 minutes. As it follows from the definition of critical values, the probability of this to be random is less than 0.05. It confirms that computed features are indeed the label predictors, containing relevant information.

Figure 2: Plots show the AUC (area under ROC curve) values as a function of game duration for eyes, mouth and all features. The orange line represents the critical values for the 0.05 significance level.

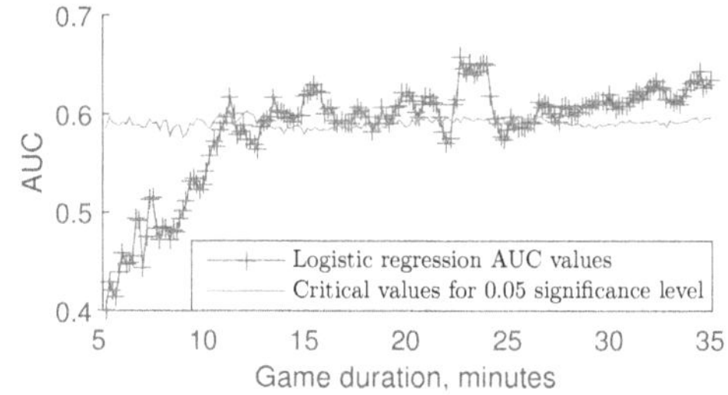

(a) All features

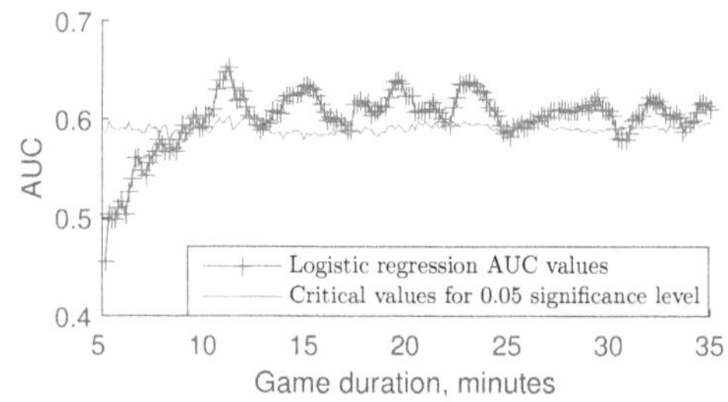

(b) Eyes features

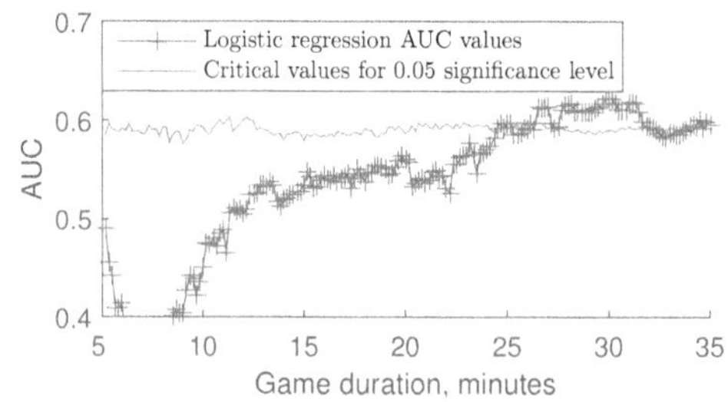

(c) Mouth features

We also computed the mean of AUC for all time intervals $5 - 35$ (0.5849) and time intervals $15 - 35$ (0.6106). Using the same randomization, we computed their p-values: 0.0104 and 0.0026 accordingly. Both of them are much lower than 0.05, indicating a result due to random chance is unlikely.

It is interesting to compare the obtained accuracy with a human baseline. We can compute a rough estimation the following way. Recall that a game consists of repeating 'day'-

'night' phases. While in the 'day' phase players try to eliminate a deceptive player, in the 'night' phase they always lose one truthful player. For a predefined number of players (7 vs 2) there is a limited number of possible outcomes (10). Assuming a random choice of eliminated players in the 'day' phase, we can compute the probability of each of these outcomes. The Mafia team wins in 4 of them, with the total probability equal to $221/315 \approx 70.16\%$. In fact, the Mafia team won in 21 among 30 games, i.e., exactly in 70% of cases. It confirms that people detect deception very close to random, even when they get information from all channels including video, audio and context. The same result was established earlier in psychological research [2].

Figure 3: Top 3 the most significant features

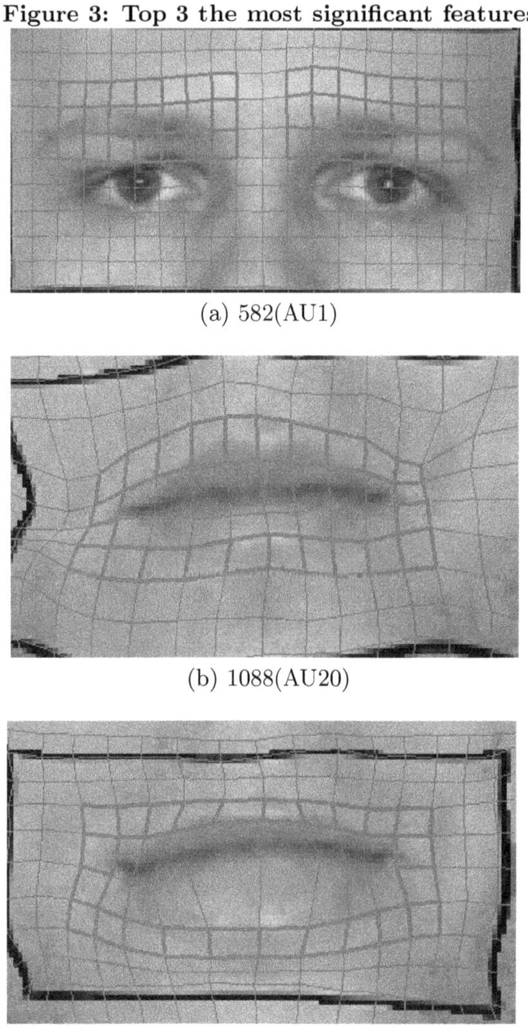

(a) 582(AU1)

(b) 1088(AU20)

(c) 135(AU16)

7.2 Feature analysis

The logistic regression classifier also provides p-values for the obtained coefficients. We used these coefficients to identify the most statistically significant features. The top 3 of them are presented on Fig. 3. Note that all of them are caused by the reliable muscles [13], and therefore are difficult to be simulated. We also computed the corresponding feature coefficients. While their amplitude depends on the similarity scores and does not provide any information, their signs show how the feature influences the final prediction. Positive coefficients increase the probability of truthful people, while negative ones decrease it. Here we use the average of coefficients over all 30 folds and game durations from 15 to 35 minutes, when the datasets are based on a sufficient number of episodes.

The first of the top 3 features is an example of the onset of Action unit 1 (inner brow raiser). It has a positive coefficient, with the p-value 0.030. The second feature represents the offset of the AU20 (lip stretcher). It has a negative coefficient with the p-value 0.037. The third feature is connected with the AU16 (lower lip depressor). It also has a positive coefficient. Its p-value is 0.039.

We can provide a possible explanation of these results. Theory says that deceptive people tend to experience fear, guilt or delight [23]. Opposite to that, sadness has been shown to be a sign of verity [20]. It is known [5] that AU1 and AU16 might be caused by sadness, while AU20 can appear as a result of fear. Therefore, their coefficient signs do not contradict the theory.

We also tested the performance of these 3 most significant features independently. None of them achieved statistically significant classification accuracy, which confirms that only a combination of cues can give a reliable result. This was earlier stated in [23].

8. CONCLUSION

In this article we presented an automatic system of deception detection based on the features extracted from movements of eyebrows, eyes and mouth on videos. We demonstrated that these features contain sufficient information to achieve a classification accuracy significantly higher than random predictions. The list of the most predictive features can be explained according to the results previously established in the psychological literature. We also introduced the new Mafia database of truthful and deceptive people, which was recorded in more natural conditions compared to previous studies. This database contains in total 5 hours of video, which make it one of the largest available. We hope that it will become a benchmark for assessing algorithms for deception detection. The demonstrated performance is not good enough to be used in practice, but it establishes a lower bound for the future.

This research is in its beginning. Future research might improve all parts of the presented system. For example, one might explore developing more accurate methods of action unit detection, extraction of more meaningful features or usage of other modalities such as voice tone and language features. The multimodal approach that combines all types of features seems to be the most promising. Another significant drawback of the algorithm is its speed. The process of image registration takes about 3 seconds per frame, which does not it to be used for real-time predictions. This procedure might be accelerated by using less expensive features or more powerful hardware like a GPU. It would be a big step forward to make the algorithm work in real-time without loss of accuracy. Moreover, one can increase the database by processing all other 60 videos and labeling extracted episodes. That would make the database the largest one. We believe that this research will stimulate interest in the challenging problem of automatic deception detection.

9. REFERENCES

[1] Mohamed Abouelenien, Veronica Pérez-Rosas, Rada Mihalcea, and Mihai Burzo. Deception detection using a multimodal approach. In *Proceedings of the 16th International Conference on Multimodal Interaction*, pages 58–65. ACM, 2014.

[2] Charles F Bond and Bella M DePaulo. Accuracy of deception judgments. *Personality and social psychology Review*, 10(3):214–234, 2006.

[3] Bella M DePaulo, James J Lindsay, Brian E Malone, Laura Muhlenbruck, Kelly Charlton, and Harris Cooper. Cues to deception. *Psychological bulletin*, 129(1):74, 2003.

[4] Paul Ekman. *Telling Lies: Clues to Deceit in the Marketplace, Politics, and Marriage (Revised Edition).* WW Norton & Company, 2009.

[5] Paul Ekman and Wallace V Friesen. *Manual for the facial action coding system.* Consulting Psychologists Press, 1978.

[6] Paul Ekman and Maureen O'Sullivan. Who can catch a liar? *American psychologist*, 46(9):913, 1991.

[7] Paul Ekman, Maureen O'Sullivan, and Mark G Frank. A few can catch a liar. *Psychological Science*, 10(3):263–266, 1999.

[8] Tommaso Fornaciari and Massimo Poesio. Automatic deception detection in italian court cases. *Artificial intelligence and law*, 21(3):303–340, 2013.

[9] M Frank, J Movellan, M Bartlett, and G Littleworth. Ru-facs-1 database. *Machine Perception Laboratory, UC San Diego*, 1, 2012.

[10] Uday Jain, Bozhao Tan, and Qi Li. Concealed knowledge identification using facial thermal imaging. In *Acoustics, Speech and Signal Processing (ICASSP), 2012 IEEE International Conference on*, pages 1677–1680. IEEE, 2012.

[11] Sander Koelstra, Maja Pantic, and Ioannis Patras. A dynamic texture-based approach to recognition of facial actions and their temporal models. *Pattern Analysis and Machine Intelligence, IEEE Transactions on*, 32(11):1940–1954, 2010.

[12] David Matsumoto, Hyi Sung Hwang, Lisa Skinner, and MG Frank. Evaluating truthfulness and detecting deception. *FBI Law Enforcement Bulletin*, 80:1–25, 2011.

[13] Marc Mehu, Marcello Mortillaro, Tanja Bänziger, and Klaus R Scherer. Reliable facial muscle activation enhances recognizability and credibility of emotional expression. *Emotion*, 12(4):701, 2012.

[14] Rada Mihalcea and Mihai Burzo. Towards multimodal deception detection–step 1: building a collection of deceptive videos. In *Proceedings of the 14th ACM international conference on Multimodal interaction*, pages 189–192. ACM, 2012.

[15] Rada Mihalcea, Verónica Pérez-Rosas, and Mihai Burzo. Automatic detection of deceit in verbal communication. In *Proceedings of the 15th ACM on International conference on multimodal interaction*, pages 131–134. ACM, 2013.

[16] Maja Pantic, Michel Valstar, Ron Rademaker, and Ludo Maat. Web-based database for facial expression analysis. In *Multimedia and Expo, 2005. ICME 2005. IEEE International Conference on*, pages 5–pp. IEEE, 2005.

[17] Tomas Pfister, Xiaobai Li, Guoying Zhao, and Matti Pietikainen. Recognising spontaneous facial micro-expressions. In *Computer Vision (ICCV), 2011 IEEE International Conference on*, pages 1449–1456. IEEE, 2011.

[18] Stephen Porter, Leanne ten Brinke, and Brendan Wallace. Secrets and lies: Involuntary leakage in deceptive facial expressions as a function of emotional intensity. *Journal of Nonverbal Behavior*, 36(1):23–37, 2012.

[19] Daniel Rueckert, Luke I Sonoda, Carmel Hayes, Derek LG Hill, Martin O Leach, and David J Hawkes. Nonrigid registration using free-form deformations: application to breast mr images. *Medical Imaging, IEEE Transactions on*, 18(8):712–721, 1999.

[20] Thomas E Slowe and Venu Govindaraju. Automatic deceit indication through reliable facial expressions. In *Automatic Identification Advanced Technologies, 2007 IEEE Workshop on*, pages 87–92. IEEE, 2007.

[21] Paul Viola and Michael Jones. Rapid object detection using a boosted cascade of simple features. In *Computer Vision and Pattern Recognition, 2001. CVPR 2001. Proceedings of the 2001 IEEE Computer Society Conference on*, volume 1, pages I–511. IEEE, 2001.

[22] Aldert Vrij. *Detecting lies and deceit: The psychology of lying and implications for professional practice.* Wiley, 2000.

[23] Aldert Vrij. *Detecting lies and deceit: Pitfalls and opportunities.* John Wiley & Sons, 2008.

[24] Lara Warmelink, Aldert Vrij, Samantha Mann, Sharon Leal, Dave Forrester, and Ronald P Fisher. Thermal imaging as a lie detection tool at airports. *Law and human behavior*, 35(1):40, 2011.

[25] Gemma Warren, Elizabeth Schertler, and Peter Bull. Detecting deception from emotional and unemotional cues. *Journal of Nonverbal Behavior*, 33(1):59–69, 2009.

[26] Wen-Jing Yan, Su-Jing Wang, Yong-Jin Liu, Qi Wu, and Xiaolan Fu. For micro-expression recognition: Database and suggestions. *Neurocomputing*, 136:82–87, 2014.

[27] Wen-Jing Yan, Qi Wu, Yong-Jin Liu, Su-Jing Wang, and Xiaolan Fu. Casme database: a dataset of spontaneous micro-expressions collected from neutralized faces. In *Automatic Face and Gesture Recognition (FG), 2013 10th IEEE International Conference and Workshops on*, pages 1–7. IEEE, 2013.

[28] Zhi Zhang, Vartika Singh, Thomas E Slowe, Sergey Tulyakov, and Venugopal Govindaraju. Real-time automatic deceit detection from involuntary facial expressions. In *Computer Vision and Pattern Recognition, 2007. CVPR'07. IEEE Conference on*, pages 1–6. IEEE, 2007.

Individuality-Preserving Voice Reconstruction for Articulation Disorders Using Text-to-Speech Synthesis

Reina Ueda, Tetsuya Takiguchi, Yasuo Ariki
Graduate School of System Informatics, Kobe University
1-1, Rokkodai, Nada, Kobe, 6578501, Japan
reina_1102@me.cs.scitec.kobe-u.ac.jp, takigu@kobe-u.ac.jp, ariki@kobe-u.ac.jp

ABSTRACT

This paper presents a speech synthesis method for people with articulation disorders. Because the movements of such speakers are limited by their athetoid symptoms, their prosody is often unstable and their speech rate differs from that of a physically unimpaired person, which causes their speech to be less intelligible and, consequently, makes communication with physically unimpaired persons difficult. In order to deal with these problems, this paper describes a Hidden Markov Model (HMM)-based text-to-speech synthesis approach that preserves the individuality of a person with an articulation disorder and aids them in their communication. In our method, a duration model of a physically unimpaired person is used for the HMM synthesis system and an F0 model in the system is trained using the F0 patterns of the physically unimpaired person, with the average F0 being converted to the target F0 in advance. In order to preserve the target speaker's individuality, a spectral model is built from target spectra. Through experimental evaluations, we have confirmed that the proposed method successfully synthesizes intelligible speech while maintaining the target speaker's individuality.

Keywords

articulation disorders, speech synthesis system, hidden Markov Model, assistive Technologies

Categories and Subject Descriptors

H.5.5 [**INFORMATION INTERFACES AND PRESENTATION**]: Sound and Music Computing—*modeling, signal analysis, synthesis, and processing*
; K.4.2 [**COMPUTERS AND SOCIETY**]: Social Issues—*Assistive technologies for persons with disabilities*

1. INTRODUCTION

In this study, we focused on a person with an articulation disorder resulting from the athetoid type of cerebral palsy. Cerebral palsy results from damage to the central nervous system, and the damage causes movement disorders. It is classified into the following types: 1)spastic, 2)athetoid, 3)ataxic, 4)atonic, 5)rigid, and a mixture of these types [2]. In the case of a person with an articulation disorder resulting from the athetoid type of cerebral palsy, his/her movements are sometimes more unstable than usual. That means their utterances (especially their consonants) are often unstable or unclear due to the athetoid symptoms. This is why there is great need for speech synthesis systems to aid them in their communication. An HMM-based speech synthesis system [13] is kind of text-to-speech (TTS) system that can generate any signals from input text data, where the spectrum, F0 and duration are modeled simultaneously in a unified framework. Spectral features are modeled by continuous density HMMs, F0 patterns are modeled by a hidden Markov model based on multi-space probability distribution (MSD-HMM [7]), and state duration densities are modeled by single Gaussian distributions [12].

In the field of assistive technology, Veaux *et al.* [10] used HMM-based speech synthesis to reconstruct the voice of individuals with degenerative speech disorders resulting from Amyotrophic Lateral Sclerosis (ALS). They have proposed a reconstruction method for degenerative speech disorders using an HMM sound synthesis system. In this method, the subject's utterances are used to adapt an average voice model pre-trained on many speakers. Creer *et al.* [3] also adapt the average voice model of multiple speakers to the severe dysarthria data. And Khan *et al.* [1] uses such adaption method to the laryngectomy patient's data. Yamagishi *et al.* [11] proposed a project called "Voice Banking and Reconstruction".

In this paper, we propose an HMM-based speech synthesis method for articulation disorders. Because F0 patterns of articulation disorders are unstable and their duration becomes slow compared to physically unimpaired persons, the output synthesized signals to be indiscernible. To deal with these problems, it is necessary to develop a speech synthesis system in which the output signals are more intelligible and include the patient's individuality. To generate the intelligible voice while preserving the speaker's individuality, our training data include the voice of a physically unimpaired person. Because both the duration and pitch of a person with an articulation disorder are especially different from those of a physically unimpaired person, we use the state duration densities of a physically unimpaired person for the duration model, and the F0 model is trained from F0 patterns of a physically unimpaired person, where the average

ICMI 2015, November 9–13, 2015, Seattle, WA, USA.

DOI: http://dx.doi.org/10.1145/2818346.2820770.

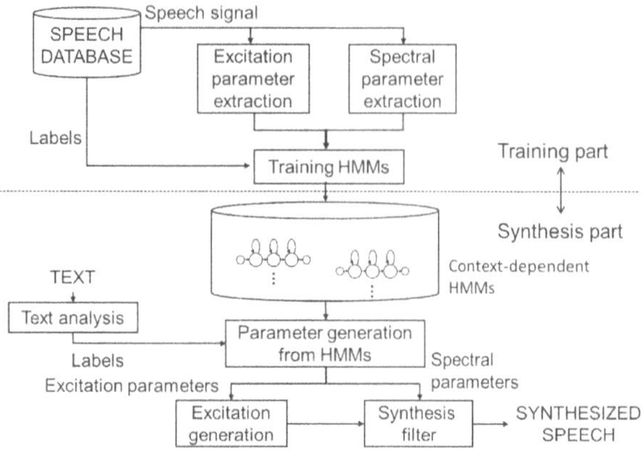

Figure 1: HMM-based speech synthesis system

F0 is converted to F0 of the person with an articulation disorder. To preserve the individuality of the person with an articulation disorder, their spectrum patterns are used for building the spectrum model in the HMM-based speech synthesis.

2. HMM-BASED SOUND SYNTHESIS

2.1 Basic approach

Fig. 1 shows the overview of the basic approach for TTS based on HMMs. This figure shows the training and synthesis parts of the HMM-based TTS system. In the training part, parameters (spectral, F0, and aperiodicity) are extracted as feature vectors. These features are modeled by context-dependent HMMs. Also, by installing the duration model, it is possible to model both each parameter and duration in a unified framework.

In the synthesis part, a context-dependent label sequence is obtained from an input text by text analysis. A sentence HMM is constructed by concatenating context-dependent HMMs according to the context-dependent label sequence. Then, HMM state sequences $q = [q_1, \cdots, q_T]$ are decided from the duration model as follows:

$$\hat{q} = \arg\max_{q} P(q|\lambda) \tag{1}$$

where T, q_t, and λ represent the number of frames, index of the HMM-state of the t-th input frame, and the parameter sets of HMM, respectively. The explicit constraint between static and dynamic features, and signal parameter sets are generated with maximizing HMM likelihood [8] as follows:

$$c = \arg\max_{c} P(\mathbf{W}c|\hat{q}, \lambda) \tag{2}$$

where $c = [c_1{}^{\mathsf{T}}, \cdots, c_t^{\mathsf{T}}, \cdots, c_T^{\mathsf{T}}]^{\mathsf{T}}$ represents signal parameter sequences, $c_t = [c(1), \cdots, c(D)]^{\mathsf{T}}$ represents a signal parameter vector of the t-th frame, and $\mathbf{W}$ represents the matrix constructed from weights which are used for calculating dynamic features [14].

Finally, by using MLSA (Mel-Log Spectrum Approximation) filter [4], speech is synthesized from the generated parameters.

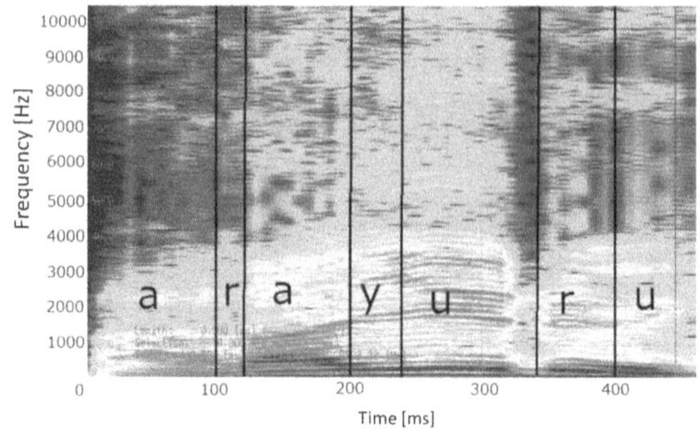

(a) a physically unimpaired person

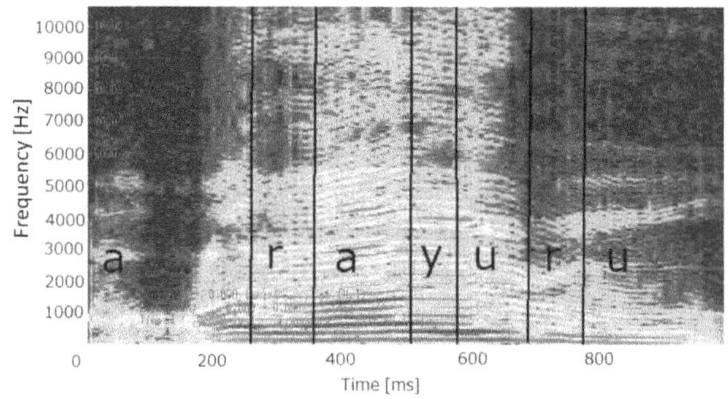

(b) a person with articulation disorders

Figure 2: Examples of spectrogram /a r a y u r u/

2.2 HMM-based speech synthesis for articulation disorders

If each feature parameter in the HMM-based speech synthesis system is trained using acoustic features obtained from a person with an articulation disorder, the synthesized speech becomes indiscernible. Fig. 2 shows the original spectrograms for the word "a ra yu ru" ("all" in English) of a physically unimpaired person and a person with an articulation disorder. The duration of a person with an articulation disorder is longer than that of a physically unimpaired person. This may be one of the reasons behind the unintelligibility. Therefore, in our method, a more intelligible synthesized speech that preserves speaker individuality is generated by using features of both a person with an articulation disorder and a physically unimpaired person. Fig. 3 shows the overview of our proposed method. In this method, the voices of a physically unimpaired person and a person with an articulation disorder are prepared for the training data. First, we extract these two person's speaking voices into three acoustic parameters (F0 contour, spectral envelope, and aperiodicity index (AP)) estimated by using STRAIGHT analysis [6]. For making the F0 feature characteristics close to those of a person with an articulation disorder, both the F0 mean and variance are estimated from training data. Then, the F0 features of a physically unimpaired person are converted to those of a person with an articulation disorder by using the linear transformation as

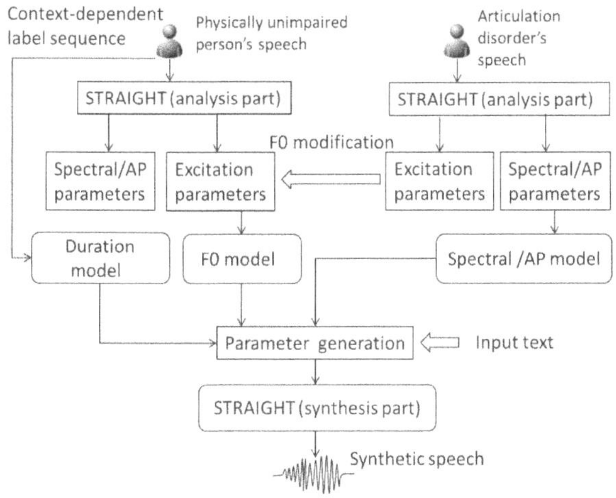

Figure 3: Diagram of HMM-based speech synthesis method for articulation disorders

follows:

$$\hat{x}_t = \frac{\sigma_y}{\sigma_x}(x_t - \mu_x) + \mu_y \qquad (3)$$

where x_t represents a log-scaled F0 of the physically unimpaired person at the frame t, μ_x and σ_x represent the mean and standard deviation of x_t, respectively. μ_y and σ_y represent the mean and standard deviation of a person with an articulation disorder's log-scaled F0, respectively. An F0 model in the HMM-based speech synthesis, which is trained using the F0 features from Eq. (3), generates the F0 sequences so that they include the individuality of a person with an articulation disorder.

The duration model of the physically unimpaired person is used in the HMM-based TTS system, where it is trained using the context-dependent label sequences of the physically unimpaired person because the utterance duration of a person with an articulation disorder is unstable. To preserve the articulation disorder's individuality, the spectral model and the AP model are trained using only spectral and AP sequences of the voice of the person with an articulation disorder. In the synthesis part, after the text to be synthesized is converted to a context-dependent label sequence, parameter sequences are generated from the context label and these models. Parameter sequences are converted to the features (spectral envelope, F0 contour, aperiodicity index), which can be handled in the STRAIGHT. Finally, the output signal is synthesized from these features by using the synthesis part of the STRAIGHT.

3. EXPERIMENTS

3.1 Experimental conditions

We prepared the training data for two men. One is a physically unimpaired person, and the other is a person with an articulation disorder. We used 513 sentences in the ATR Japanese database for a physically unimpaired person, and recorded 429 sentences in the same database uttered by a person with an articulation disorder. (The other 84 sentences were mis-recorded). The speech signals were digitized 16bit/48 kHz. The frame shift was 5 ms. Acoustic and prosodic features were extracted by using STRAIGHT. Mel-cepstrum coefficients (their dynamic, acceleration coefficients) were used as spectral parameters. Log-F0 and 5 band-filtered aperiodicity measures [5] (their dynamic and acceleration coefficients) were used as excitation parameters. Context-dependent phoneme HMMs with five states were used in the speech synthesis system [13].

In order to confirm the effectiveness of our proposed method, we evaluated the aspects of both listening intelligibility and speaker similarity by having subjects listen to voices synthesized under five conditions listed in Table 1.

Table 1: Voices compared in the evaluation tests

Type	Duration Model	F0 Model	AP/Spectral Model
ADM	AD	AD	AD
Ref1	PU	AD	AD
Prop	PU	convPU	AD
Ref2	PU	PU	AD
PUM	PU	PU	PU

ADM: Model of a person with an articulation disorder
Prop: Proposed method
PUM: Model of a physically unimpaired person
AD: Articulation Disordered
PU: Physically Unimpaired
convPU: Creating the model from a physically unimpaired person's parameter sequences which are converted to those of a person with an articulation disorder by Eq. (3)

Ten sentences included in ATR Japanese database were synthesized under those five conditions. A total of 8 Japanese speakers took part in the test using headphones. For the speaker similarity, we performed a MOS (Mean Opinion Score) test [9]. In the MOS test, an opinion score was set to a 5-point scale (5: Identical, 4: Very Similar, 3: Quite Similar, 2: Dissimilar, 1: Very Dissimilar). For the listening intelligibility, a paired comparison test was carried out, where each subject listened to pairs of speech converted by two methods and selected which sample sounded more intelligible.

3.2 Results and discussion

We calculated the average synthesized duration per mora of synthesized signals for 50 sentences. The average duration of ADM is 219.768 $[ms/mora]$ and PUM is 179.69 $[ms/mora]$. As compared to the duration of PUM, that of ADM is quite slower, which leads to the unintelligibility of the synthesized speech.

Fig. 4 shows the results of MOS test on speaker similarity, where the error bars shows a 95% confidence score. As shown in Fig. 4, the synthesized voice from ADM, which trained using only the voice of a person with an articulation disorder, is the most similar to the original voice of the person with an articulation disorder. Also, it is confirmed that the more we use features of a physically unimpaired person for modeling, the more the speaker individuality (of a person with an articulation disorder) will be lost.

Fig. 5 shows the preference score on the listening intelligibility, where the error bar shows a 95% confidence score. As shown in Fig. 5, our proposed method obtained a higher score than Ref1 and ADM. In comparison to Ref2 in regard to intelligibility, there may not be so much influence on intelligibility because only the average F0 is different between our method and Ref2. These results imply that intelligi-

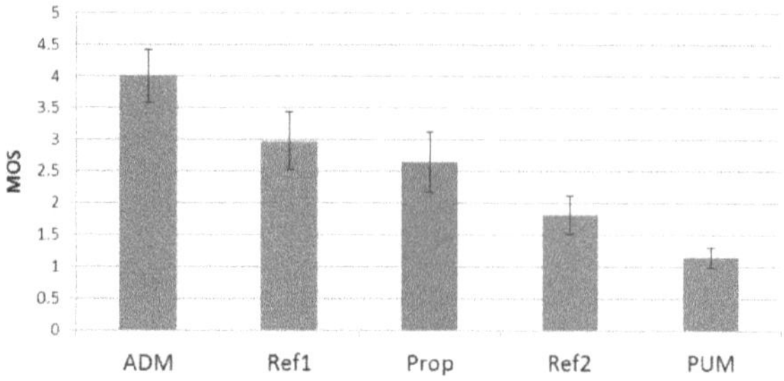

Figure 4: Speaker similarity to the articulation disorder

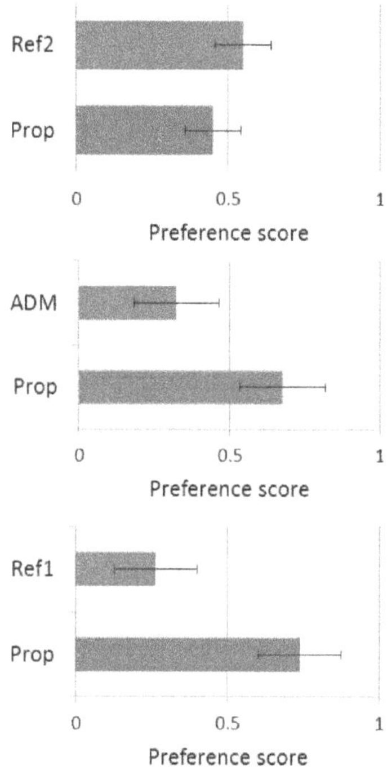

Figure 5: Preference scores for the listening intelligibility

bility can be improved by replacing the duration model of the person with an articulation disorder with the physically unimpaired person's duration model and using the F0 patterns from the physically unimpaired person (with the average F0 being converted to the target (articulation disorder's person) F0 in advance). Therefore, from Figs. 4 and 5, it is confirmed that our proposed method generates synthesized signals that are fairly intelligible and include the individuality of a person with an articulation disorder.

4. CONCLUSION

We proposed a text-to-speech synthesis method based on HMMs for people with articulation disorders. In our method, to generate more intelligible synthesized sounds, the duration model of a physically unimpaired person is used, and the F0 model is trained using F0 features of a physically unimpaired person, where the average F0 is converted to the F0 of the person with an articulation disorder by using the linear transformation. In order to preserve the target individuality, the spectral and AP models are trained using only features of the person with an articulation disorder. The experimental results showed our proposed method greatly improves the listening intelligibility of speech of a person with an articulation disorder. In our future research, we will modify spectral and AP models as well as duration and F0 model to improve the listening intelligibility even more.

5. REFERENCES

[1] Z. Ahmad Khan, P. Green, S. Creer, and S. Cunningham. Reconstructing the voice of an individual following laryngectomy. *Augmentative and Alternative Communication*, 27(1):61–66, 2011.

[2] T. Canale and W. C. Campbell. *Campbell's operative orthopaedics*, volume 12. Technical report, Mosby Year Book, June 2002.

[3] S. Creer, S. Cunningham, P. Green, and J. Yamagishi. Building personalised synthetic voices for individuals with severe speech impairment. *Computer Speech & Language*, 27(6):1178–1193, 2013.

[4] S. Imai, K. Sumita, and C. Furuichi. Mel log spectrum approximation (MLSA) filter for speech synthesis. *Electronics and Communications in Japan (Part I: Communications)*, 66:10–18, 1983.

[5] H. Kawahara, J. Estill, and O. Fujimura. Aperiodicity extraction and control using mixed mode excitation and group delay manipulation for a high quality speech analysis, modification and synthesis system STRAIGHT. In *Proc. of MAVEBA*, pages 59–64, 2001.

[6] H. Kawahara, I. Masuda-Katsuse, and A. D. Cheveigné. Restructuring speech representations using a pitch-adaptive time-frequency smoothing and an instantaneous-frequency-based f0 extraction: Possible role of a repetitive structure in sounds. *Speech communication*, 27:187–207, 1999.

[7] K. Tokuda, T. Masuko, N. Miyazaki, and T. Kobayashi. Hidden Markov models based on multi-space probability distribution for pitch pattern modeling. In *Proc. of ICASSP*, pages 229–232, 1999.

[8] K. Tokuda, T. Yoshimura, T. Masuko, T. Kobayashi, and T. Kitamura. Speech parameter generation algorithms for HMM-based speech synthesis. In *Proc. of ICASSP*, pages 1315–1318, 2000.

[9] I. T. Union. ITU-T Recommendation P.800.1: Mean Opinion Score (MOS) terminology. Technical report, International Telecommunication Union, July 2006.

[10] C. Veaux, J. Yamagishi, and S. King. Using HMM-based speech synthesis to reconstruct the voice of individuals with degenerative speech disorders. In *Proc. of Interspeech*, 2012.

[11] J. Yamagishi, C. Veaux, S. King, and S. Renals. Speech synthesis technologies for individuals with vocal disabilities: Voice banking and reconstruction. *Acoustical Science and Technology*, 33(1):1–5, 2012.

[12] T. Yoshimura, K. Tokuda, T. Masuko, T. Kobayashi, and T. Kitamura. Duration Modeling in HMM-based Speech Synthesis System. In *Proc. of ICSLP*, pages 29–32, 1998.

[13] T. Yoshimura, K. Tokuda, T. Masuko, T. Kobayashi, and T. Kitamura. Simultaneous modeling of spectrum, pitch and duration in HMM-based speech synthesis. In *Proc. of Eurospeech*, pages 2347–2350, 1999.

[14] H. Zen, K. Tokuda, and A. W. Black. Statistical parametric speech synthesis. *Speech Communication*, 51:1039–1064, 2009.

Behavioral and Emotional Spoken Cues Related to Mental States in Human-Robot Social Interaction

Lucile Bechade
LIMSI-CNRS
Université Paris-Saclay
France

Guillaume Dubuisson Duplessis
LIMSI-CNRS
Paris, France

Mohamed Sehili
LIMSI-CNRS
Paris, France

Laurence Devillers
LIMSI-CNRS
Université Paris 4
Paris, France

ABSTRACT

Understanding human behavioral and emotional cues occurring in interaction has become a major research interest due to the emergence of numerous applications such as in social robotics. While there is agreement across different theories that some behavioral signals are involved in communicating information, there is a lack of consensus regarding their specificity, their universality, and whether they convey emotions, affective, cognitive, mental states or all of those. Our goal in this study is to explore the relationship between behavioral and emotional cues extracted from speech (e.g., laughter, speech duration, negative emotions) with different communicative information about the human participant. This study is based on a corpus of audio/video data of humorous interactions between the Nao robot and 37 human participants. Participants filled three questionnaires about their personality, sense of humor and mental states regarding the interaction. This work reveals the existence of many links between behavioral and emotional cues and the mental states reported by human participants through self-report questionnaires. However, we have not found a clear connection between reported mental states and participants profiles.

Categories and Subject Descriptors

H.1.2 [**Information Systems**]: User/Machine Systems—*human factors, human information processing*; I.2.7 [**Computing Methodologies**]: Natural Language Processing—*speech recognition and synthesis*

General Terms

Experimentation, Human Factors

ICMI 2015, November 9–13, 2015, Seattle, WA, USA.
 ISBN 978-1-4503-3912-4/15/11 ...$15.00.
DOI: http://dx.doi.org/10.1145/2818346.2820777.

Keywords

Social robots; Humor; Real-time Emotion Detection; Affective Interaction; Human-Robot Interaction

1. INTRODUCTION

Humans have the essential ability to attribute mental states by observing the behavior of their interlocutor [1]. Indeed, humans communicate a wide range of affective and cognitive mental states which enrich the interaction. If they are not to leave out important communicative information, social robots must be equipped with the ability to infer mental states of their human interlocutor. While there is agreement in the community that some behavioral signals are involved in communication, there is a lack of consensus regarding whether they convey emotions, affective, cognitive, mental states or all of those [12]. A lot of papers relate research about the link between visual cues and mental states [1], notably for emotional cues [13]. To the best of our knowledge, little research has been done with simple cues extracted from the overall dialog such as average of time of answers or speech duration.

This work is part of the JOKER project which aims at building a generic intelligent user interface that provides a multimodal dialog system with social skills including humor and empathy [4]. In this paper, we made the assumption that it is possible to find relationship between raw audio cues extracted from the overall interaction without any knowledge of linguistic content, and the mental states reported by subjects themselves. This work aims at exploring the relationships between audio cues, mental states, and personality traits in order to discover cues and correlations that can be exploited to build useful participant profiles for social Human-Robot Interaction (HRI). This study is a first step using simple and raw spoken cues, mental states reported by participants after interacting with the robot and personality questionnaires (OCEAN [10] and a sense of humor questionnaire [11]).

Section 2 presents work related to the inference of mental states in HRI. Section 3 presents the corpus collection performed with an automatic data collection system on two scenarios. Section 4 is dedicated to the corpus annotation process in terms of audio activity from the human (e.g., emotion, laughter). Behavioral and emotional spoken cues derived from the annotated corpus are listed and defined. Section 5 reveals the existence of many links between behavioral and emotional cues and the mental states reported by human participants. Section 6 concludes this paper and presents perspectives.

2. RELATED WORK

Affect recognition systems have received a wide interest from the affective computing field [13], with a significant focus on the detection of expressions of the six basic emotions from Eckman [6]. However, some works have undertaken the detection of specific mental states. For instance, facial expression recognition methods have been used to detect mental states such as frustration [8] or complex ones such as agreeing, concentrating, disagreeing, interested, thinking, unsure from a video stream of facial expressions and head gestures [7]. Affect expression recognition in audio has been mainly focused on emotion (see, e.g., [5]) as well as some specific application-dependent affective states such as, e.g., certainness in spoken tutorial dialogs [9]. Linguistic cues such as adverbial modifiers have been used in the context of Human-Robot task-based dialog to adapt robot beliefs about other agents based on Gricean maxims, and to convey the robot beliefs and intentions [2].

3. DATA COLLECTION AND CORPUS DESCRIPTION

3.1 Automatic Data Collection System

The automatic data collection system used in this work is a first prototype exploring the paralinguistic aspect of the JOKER project [4]. This system currently takes as input an audio signal. It features a recognition module involving emotion detection, laughter detection and speaker identification from audio signal [4]. It provides paralinguistic cues that are used by the dialog management process to generate a communicative behavior through the Nao robot. A more detailed description of the system can be found in [4]. It has been used in two interaction scenarios that are automatic.

The first scenario is presented to participants as an introduction to expose the robot capabilities and takes the form of an *emotion recognition game* where the system asks the human participant to play some emotion and then told him what it has recognized. Human participants were required to play 4 emotions (joy, anger, sadness and neutral emotion). In the current version, the system asks the user to play a given emotion, and gives a feedback on what it has recognized. To avoid blocking, a maximum number of attempts to play a given emotion was set to 3. In the case where the maximum number of attempts is reached, the system informs the human participant to give up the current emotion, and asks him to play the next one.

The second scenario implements a system-directed social interaction dialog that adapts the telling of riddles and other humorous contributions to some aspect of the user model. In this scenario, the system displays various humor capabilities. It includes the ability to tell different types of riddle (absurd, social, general knowledge) to the human (e.g."– How do you know there are two elephants in your fridge? – You can't close the door."). In addition to riddles, the robot brings about humorous situations by producing unexpected and judicious dialog contributions such as funny short stories, play on words, and laughter.

3.2 Collected Data

The experimentation took place in the cafeteria of the LIMSI-CNRS laboratory with 37 French-speaking participants. Volunteers were 62% male, 38% female, and their ages ranged from 21 to 62 (median: 31.5; mean: 35.1). Participants were seated facing the Nao robot at around one meter from it. Audio data have been acquired thanks to a high-quality AKG Lavalier microphone. Audio tracks of 16kHz have been recorded internally by the system for each interaction. Volunteers first interacted with the robot through the first scenario (emotion recognition game), and then with the second one (humorous interaction). Afterwards, participants were asked to fill several questionnaires (described thereafter). A total of 3h 12min 32sec of audio data has been collected for both scenarios. First scenario accounts for 1h 42min 27sec (average session duration: 2min 46sec; standard deviation: 32sec) while the second scenario accounts for 1h 30min 5sec (average session duration: 2min 26sec; standard deviation: 14sec).

3.3 Questionnaires and Mental States

Participants were asked to fill two personality questionnaires. They fill a sub-version of the OCEAN test [10] for 3 characteristics : Openness, Neuroticism and Extroversion. In addition, participants filled the Sense of Humor Scale (SHS) questionnaire of McGhee [11] to evaluate the impact of individual differences in humor perception. Six dimensions of humor appreciation are assessed in this questionnaire (see in [11]) and a global sense of humor score is rated by the sum of these sub-categories.

Finally, participants filled a self-report questionnaire. This questionnaire is filled once but only relates to the second interaction. It collects the participant evaluation of his state in context. Participants evaluate their own attitudes on a 1 to 5 point-scale (from 1: "Strongly disagree" to 5: "Strongly agree"). The mental states used in the self-report questionnaire are derived from a list defined in [1]. We use the term mental states for states with cognitive and affective components (Baron-Cohen's complex mental states), and emotions for Eckman's basic emotions [6]. The following mental states have been rated by participants: *amused, enthusiastic, self-confident, embarrassed, hurt.* They are divided into two categories: positive mental states which indicate a positive attitude (*amused, enthusiastic, self-confident*) and negative mental states (*embarrassed, hurt*).

4. CORPUS ANNOTATION AND SPOKEN CUES

4.1 Annotation Process

We set up an annotation process dedicated to the labelling of audio segments produced by the human participant while interacting with the robot in the second scenario (social humorous dialog). The annotation scheme for human contribution can be divided into the following dimensions: *speech*, *laughter*, and *other human sound.* The speech dimension is annotated with two classic aspects coming from speech-based emotion detection systems [5]: *emotion labels* (positive/neutral/negative) and *activation behav-*

Table 1: Subset of behavioral and emotional spoken cues computed from an interaction between a human participant and the robot. * Scenario 1, ** Scenario 2.

Behavioral spoken cues	
Audio segment count**	Total number of segments produced by the participant that contain audio activity (speech + non-speech).
Speech segment count**	Total number of segments produced by the participant that contain speech activity (only).
Speech duration**	Accumulated speech duration from the participant in the overall interaction.
Speech reaction time (mean)**	Mean of the durations between the end of the speech produced by the robot and the start of the first speech segment of the human following the robot contribution.
Task completion*	Score measuring the successful recognitions in the emotion recognition game
Emotional spoken cues	
Speech duration NEG**	Accumulated speech duration *expressing a negative emotion* from the participant in the overall interaction.
Speech duration POS**	Accumulated speech duration *expressing a positive emotion* from the participant in the overall interaction.
Laughter count**	Total number of laughter from the participant.

ior (active/passive). Laughter dimension contains a binary annotation labelling the presence or absence in the audio signal of a laughter produced by the human participant. Similarly, the "other human sound" dimension labels the presence or absence of other human audio contributions such as, e.g., filler, onomatopoeia, breathing.

Each human-robot interaction has been annotated by two annotators. Inter-annotator agreement has been measured with the Cohen's kappa score [3]. A moderate agreement has been reached on the labelling of emotion (κ=0.60). The brevity of human speech, namely short utterances in response to Nao contributions, can explain the low score for this inter-annotator agreement. A strong agreement have been reached on other labels (κ>0.70). A golden corpus was constituted by confronting annotated labels from both annotators for each segment. All in all, the golden corpus contains 341 segments annotated on the speech dimension, 103 annotated on the laughter dimension and 105 annotated on the "other human sound" dimension.

4.2 Behavioral and Emotional Spoken Cues

This annotated corpus has been exploited by deriving behavioral and emotional spoken cues for each participant. Table 1 presents a synthesis of several behavioral and emotional spoken cues used in this paper. Behavioral cues consist in enumerations and durations of segments produced by the human which are labeled on at least one of the three dimensions of *speech*, *laughter* and *other human sound*. Emotional spoken cues include *the duration of expressed emotions* (positive, negative, neutral) by the human during the interaction with the robot. They are computed by using the emotion label annotated on the speech dimension. While previous cues have been calculated on scenario 2, we computed a specific *task completion* score from the emotion recognition game (scenario 1). It ranges from 0 (no recognition) to 4 (recognition of the four emotions).

Table 2: Coefficient of linear regression between mental states and spoken cues. ***p-value*<0.01, **p-value*<0.05

37-person sample	amused	enthusiastic	self confident
Speech.count	0.0860	0.2531	0.3855*
Speech.duration	0.2810	0.3274*	0.3369*
Speech.reaction time.mean	-0.2015	-0.31088	-0.3275*

5. RESULTS

5.1 Relation between Reported Mental States and Spoken Cues

We examine first the relationship between the behavioral and emotional spoken cues and the mental states reported by participants in the self-report questionnaires. The primary prediction was that participants in a positive mental state will perform a richer interaction with the robot. We assume that they spoke more and quickly after the robot's contribution, produced more laughter and positive emotions. On the contrary, we assume that participants in a negative mental state interacted less, and then produced less speech, less laughter and more negative emotions.

5.1.1 Positive Mental States : Amused, Enthusiastic, Self-confident

A correlation analysis (Pearson's correlation made using R's implementation) reveals a significant interaction between (i) self-confidence and the number of speech segment (ii) self-confidence and the speech reaction time, and (iii) enthusiasm and the participant speech duration. Results are reported in table 2.

A regression analysis provides us with additional information related to the respective contribution of each of behavioral and emotional cues to the response about mental states reported by participants. The multivariate linear regression analysis to explain the self-confidence mental state regarding the interaction of the speech reaction time, speech duration and the number of speech segment cues shows evidence of correlations ($F(29,7)$= 4.546 and *p-value*=0.0015). We found significant correlation between the cross of the number of audio segment (speech and non-speech), and laughter regarding the amused mental state ($F(33,3)$=2.349 and *p-value*= 0.009).

On the one hand, a person who rated himself as amused tends to laugh more and produce more audio segments. A self-confident person not only speak for a longer period of time, but also produce more speech segments and speak shortly after the robot. On the other hand, we didn't find any significant correlation between speech expressing a positive emotion and the positive mental states.

5.1.2 Negative Mental States : Embarrassed, Hurt

During interaction, the robot can tease participants. We expect this contribution to be perceived negatively by participants, who can express to be *hurt* and *embarrassed* during the interaction.

We first examined Pearson's correlations between the spoken cues and responses to the self-report questionnaire. The only significant correlation that we found is between the hurt mental state and the number of audio segment spoken cue (*c*=-0,4855 and *p-value*=0.0023). A participant who assesses himself as hurt will produce less audible segments.

The multivariate linear regression analysis to explain the hurt mental state regarding the interaction of the duration of speech segment expressing a negative emotion and laughter cues shows evidence of correlations ($F(20,3)$=5.25 and *p-value*=0.0077). A multiple linear regression is made also for the mental state embarrassed. This regression show correlation between a cross of the number of audio segment and the task completion ($F(33,3)$=7.534 and *p-value*=0.0006).

Participants who reported themselves embarrassed have done a poor score on the emotion recognition game and produce less audio segments in interaction. Participants who reported to be hurt by the robot behavior express more negative emotions and less laughter.

5.2 Relation between Mental States and Personality Questionnaires

During the design of the experiment, we expected the personality of participants to impact their interaction with the robot and the expression of their amusement. Our intuition is that the extroversion trait will correlate with the speech duration of participants. Although the mental states reported by participants positively correlates to the examined spoken cues, there is no correlation between these cues and dimensions of personality questionnaires (OCEAN and SHS). Only the extroversion traits correlated significantly and highly with the *self-confident* mental state (c=0.569;*p-value*=0.001).

6. CONCLUSIONS AND FUTURE WORK

This paper has explored ideas related to the inference of mental states reported by participants, in frame of a playful and humorous dialog. While the observed sample is small for definitive conclusions, mental states reported by participants at the end of interaction seem to be related to the participants' behavior. Some simple raw audio cues seem to emerge and to be correlated with the participants representation of their own mental states. The positive mental states are related to a longer speech duration, short reaction time after a robot contribution and laughter. The negative mental states correlate with the lack of laughter, the duration of negative speech and the fact that the participant fails to complete the emotion game. We did not found a clear connection between mental states and participants profiles. One reason may be the short duration of interactions between the human and the robot (< 5min). An interesting prospect lies in the study of interactions on longer periods (or repeated short interaction over time) which could reveal a tangible link.

Future works include further investigations with a larger set of cues such as low-level audio cues (e.g., rhythm, respiration) and visual cues (e.g., smile). We hope to find richer links between these low-level cues and mental states of human participants, which could be fruitfully exploited to build and maintain a rich user profile during Human-Robot interaction.

7. REFERENCES

[1] S. Baron-Cohen, S. Wheelwright, and a. T. Jolliffe. Is there a "language of the eyes"? evidence from normal adults, and adults with autism or asperger syndrome. *Visual Cognition*, 4(3):311–331, Sept. 1997.

[2] G. Briggs and M. Scheutz. Facilitating mental modeling in collaborative human-robot interaction through adverbial cues. In *Proceedings of the SIGDIAL 2011 Conference*, pages 239–247. Association for Computational Linguistics, 2011.

[3] J. Cohen. A coefficient of agreement for nominal scales. *Educational and psychological measurement*, 20(1):37–46, 1960.

[4] L. Devillers, S. Rosset, G. Dubuisson Duplessis, M. A. Sehili, L. Bechade, A. Delaborde, C. Gossart, V. Letard, F. Yang, Y. Yemez, B. B. Turker, M. Sezgin, K. El Haddad, S. Dupont, D. Luzzati, Y. Esteve, G. Emer, and N. Campbell. Multimodal data collection of human-robot humorous interactions in the joker project. In *Affective Computing and Intelligent Interaction (ACII), (accepted)*, 2015.

[5] L. Devillers, L. Vidrascu, and L. Lamel. Challenges in real-life emotion annotation and machine learning based detection. *Neural Networks*, 18(4):407–422, 2005.

[6] P. Eckman. Universal and cultural differences in facial expression of emotion. In *Nebraska symposium on motivation*, volume 19, pages 207–284. University of Nebraska Press Lincoln, 1972.

[7] R. El Kaliouby and P. Robinson. Real-time inference of complex mental states from facial expressions and head gestures. In *Real-time vision for human-computer interaction*, pages 181–200. Springer, 2005.

[8] A. Kapoor, W. Burleson, and R. W. Picard. Automatic prediction of frustration. *International journal of human-computer studies*, 65(8):724–736, 2007.

[9] J. Liscombe, J. B. Hirschberg, and J. J. Venditti. Detecting certainness in spoken tutorial dialogues. 2005.

[10] R. R. McCrae and O. John. An introduction to the five-factor model and its applications. *Journal of Personality*, 60:175–215, 1992.

[11] P. McGhee. *The laughter remedy. Health, healing and the amuse system.* Dubuque, 1996.

[12] M. Pantic, A. Pentland, A. Nijholt, and T. Huang. Human computing and machine understanding of human behavior: A survey. In *Proceedings of the 8th International Conference on Multimodal Interfaces*, ICMI '06, pages 239–248, New York, NY, USA, 2006. ACM.

[13] Z. Zeng, M. Pantic, G. I. Roisman, and T. S. Huang. A survey of affect recognition methods: Audio, visual, and spontaneous expressions. *Pattern Analysis and Machine Intelligence, IEEE Transactions on*, 31(1):39–58, 2009.

Viewpoint Integration for Hand-Based Recognition of Social Interactions from a First-Person View

Sven Bambach[1], David J. Crandall[1], Chen Yu[2]
[1]School of Informatics and Computing
[2]Department of Psychological and Brain Sciences
Indiana University, Bloomington, IN, USA
{sbambach, djcran, chenyu}@indiana.edu

ABSTRACT

Wearable devices are becoming part of everyday life, from first-person cameras (GoPro, Google Glass), to smart watches (Apple Watch), to activity trackers (FitBit). These devices are often equipped with advanced sensors that gather data about the wearer and the environment. These sensors enable new ways of recognizing and analyzing the wearer's everyday personal activities, which could be used for intelligent human-computer interfaces and other applications. We explore one possible application by investigating how egocentric video data collected from head-mounted cameras can be used to recognize social activities between two interacting partners (e.g. playing chess or cards). In particular, we demonstrate that just the positions and poses of hands within the first-person view are highly informative for activity recognition, and present a computer vision approach that detects hands to automatically estimate activities. While hand pose detection is imperfect, we show that combining evidence across first-person views from the two social partners significantly improves activity recognition accuracy. This result highlights how integrating weak but complimentary sources of evidence from social partners engaged in the same task can help to recognize the nature of their interaction.

Categories and Subject Descriptors

H.5 [**Information Interfaces and Presentation**]: Miscellaneous; I.4 [**Image Processing and Computer Vision**]: Segmentation, Applications

General Terms

Human Factors; Experimentation

Keywords

Google Glass; wearable devices; activity recognition; egocentric video; viewpoint integration; hand detection

ICMI 2015, November 9–13, 2015, Seattle, WA, USA.

ACM 978-1-4503-3912-4/15/11 ...$15.00.
DOI: http://dx.doi.org/10.1145/2818346.2820771

1. INTRODUCTION

Thanks to recent advances in technology, wearable devices are becoming increasingly common in our everyday lives. More and more people are wearing these devices, from activity trackers like FitBit that record workouts, to communication devices like the Apple Watch that serve as convenient interfaces to smartphones, to cameras like GoPro Hero and Autographer that let people record egocentric imagery and video, to heads-up display devices like Google Glass that augment the real visual world. Despite their novel form factors, wearable devices are just computers featuring CPUs, network connectivity, and sensors including cameras, microphones, GPS receivers, accelerometers, thermometers, light sensors, and so on. Wearable devices are thus able to sense data from the environment, allowing them to detect and monitor the wearer's activities throughout his or her everyday life [5]. Personal activity recognition in everyday contexts has a wide range of applications for intelligent human-computer interfaces [2, 5, 7, 11, 12].

The aim of the present study is to examine how video data collected from egocentric camera devices like Google Glass can be used to recognize social activities. As the first study to explore this new research direction, we focus on recognizing activities in dyadic interactions in which two social partners perform joint tasks. Using a dataset with four tasks and four actors, we show that egocentric video from a first-person perspective contains particularly informative data that can be used for activity recognition. We present two novel contributions. First, inspired by previous studies on egocentric video [6] that show that one's own hands are almost always present in the first-person view, we develop a new method of activity recognition based on hand detection and segmentation. This omnipresence occurs because the human cognitive system needs real-time visual information to produce visual-guided hand actions [8] and therefore people usually keep their hands in the egocentric view. The advantage of relying on just hands is that we avoid the need to solve much more complicated vision problems, like recognizing all possible objects or environments. Second, we show that integrating synchronous visual information captured from the two views of the social partners can dramatically improve recognition accuracy.

2. HAND INTERACTIONS

We begin by describing several building blocks of our study, including a dataset of first-person video captured from interacting people, and computer vision techniques to automatically detect and segment hands.

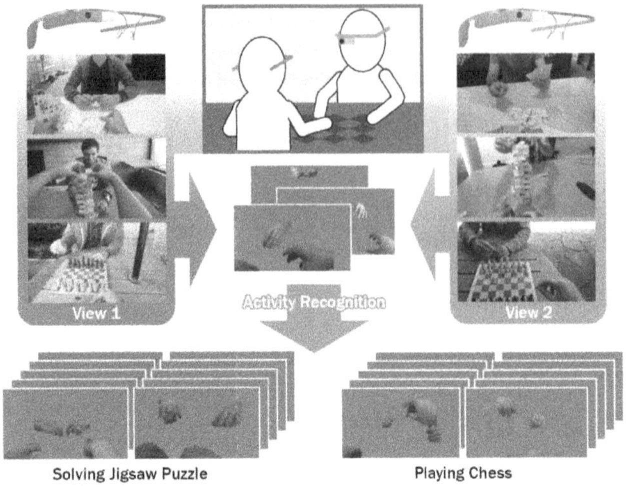

Figure 1: Two actors are engaged in different social interactions, while both wear Google Glass to capture video from each field of view. We present a vision-based framework that extracts hands from each view and jointly estimates the performed activity based on hand pose and position alone.

2.1 Dataset

We collected a dataset of first-person video from interacting subjects [1], using Google Glass to capture video (720p30) from each person's viewpoint, as illustrated in Figure 1. The subjects were asked to perform four different activities: (1) playing cards; (2) playing fast chess; (3) solving a jigsaw puzzle; and (4) playing Jenga (a 3d puzzle game). Sample frames for each activity are shown in Figure 2. To add visual diversity to the dataset, videos were collected in three different locations: a conference room table, an outdoor patio table, and a living room coffee table. We recorded four actors (all male, right-handed students) over several days, ensuring variety in actors' clothing and the surroundings. We systematically collected data from all four actors performing all four activities at all three locations while randomly assigning social pairs, resulting in $4 \times 4 \times 3 = 48$ unique combinations (24 for each viewpoint). Each video is 90 seconds long and synchronized across the two views.

To train and evaluate our computer vision techniques, we manually annotated hand position and shape in a subset of 100 random frames per video, resulting in pixel-level ground truth for 15,053 hands. Figure 2 shows some examples of annotated hands. For both the hand extraction and the activity detection tasks, the dataset was randomly split into a training set of 24 videos (12 pairs), a validation set of 8 videos and a test set of 16 videos such that the four activity classes were evenly distributed in each set.

2.2 Extracting Hands

We used a state-of-the-art computer vision algorithm to automatically extract hands from first-person videos. We briefly describe the approach here; more details, as well as an in-depth quantitative evaluation, are presented elsewhere [1]. The hand extraction process consists of two major steps: detection, which tries to coarsely locate hands in each frame, and segmentation, which estimates the fine-grained pixel-level shape of each hand.

Hand detection. Our hand detector applies convolutional neural networks (CNNs), which are the current state-of-the-art in general object detection [3]. CNNs are designed to solve image-level classification problems. To apply them to object detection, the typical approach is to use a lightweight classifier to generate a large set of image windows that may contain the object of interest (Figure 3a), and then to classify each of them using the more computationally demanding CNN (Figure 3b). In our case, we generate candidate hand regions using color features to identify likely skin regions, while also using the spatial biases inherent in hand positions in first-person videos (e.g. that the camera wearer's hands tend to be lower in the first-person view [6]).

To classify each candidate window, we trained a CNN with the architecture of Krizhevsky et al. [4], using ground-truth hand annotations from the set of training frames. The CNN was trained to perform a five-way classification task, categorizing image regions into background, left or right hand of the camera wearer, and left or right hand of the social partner. The network was trained using stochastic gradient descent until convergence on the validation set. During detection, regions with a sufficiently high classification score are marked as hand candidates, and then a non-maximum suppression step removes duplicate detections caused by overlapping candidates. The result of hand detection is a set of bounding boxes giving the location of up to four hands, corresponding to the two hands of the camera wearer and the two hands of the social partner (see Figure 3b).

Hand segmentation. Given the detected hand bounding box, we next extract finer-grained, pixel-level masks that capture the shape of the hands (Figure 3c). Our approach assumes that most pixels inside a detected hand window correspond with a hand, albeit with a significant number of background pixels caused either by detector error or because of the rectangular bounding boxes. This assumption lets us apply GrabCut, a well-known semi-supervised segmenta-

Figure 2: Sample frames from each activity in our experiments. Colored regions show ground truth hand masks.

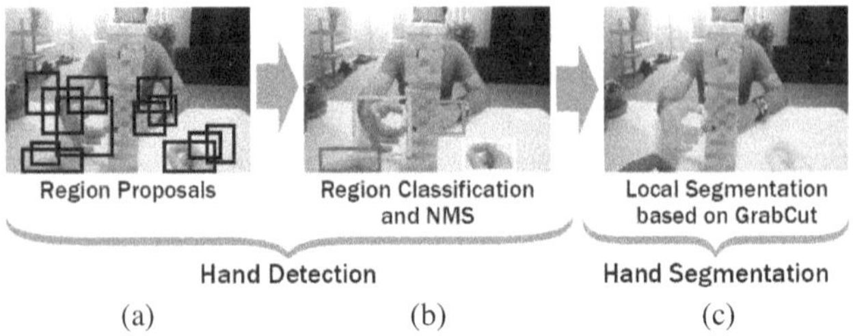

Figure 3: Overview of the hand extraction pipeline, consisting of a detection and a segmentation step.

tion algorithm [9]. Given an approximate foreground mask, GrabCut improves the segmentation by iteratively refining color-based appearance models of the foreground (hand) and the background, and relabeling foreground and background using a Markov Random Field.

While not perfect, this approach produces reasonable results, with a mean average precision (mAP) of 0.74 for detection and a pixel-level intersection-over-union of 0.56 for segmentation on our dataset [1].

3. ACTIVITY RECOGNITION AND VIEWPOINT INTEGRATION

Our main hypothesis is that hand poses by themselves reveal significant evidence about the objects people are interacting with and the activities they are doing. This would imply that automatic activity recognition systems could focus on accurately recognizing one type of object – the hands – instead of having to model and detect the thousands of possible objects and backgrounds that occur in real-world scenarios. While the hand poses in any given video frame may not necessarily be informative, we hypothesize that integrating hand pose evidence across frames and across viewpoints may significantly improve activity recognition results. We investigate (1) how well activities can be recognized in our dataset based on hand pose information alone, and (2) whether the two first-person viewpoints can be complementary with respect to this task.

3.1 Hand-based Activity Recognition

To explore if hand poses can uniquely identify activities, we created masked frames in which all content except hands were replaced by a gray color. Some examples of masked frames are shown in Figures 1 and 4. We trained a CNN with the architecture of [4] on a four-way classification task by feeding it the (rescaled) masked hand frames from the training set, i.e. the inputs to the first network layer were 224×224×3 buffers of normalized RGB pixel values. Each frame was labeled with one of the four activities. In this training phase, we used ground-truth hand segmentations to prevent the classifier from learning any visual bias not related to hands (e.g. portions of other objects that could be visible due to imperfect hand extraction). With 100 annotated frames per video and 24 videos in the training set, this led to a total of 2,400 training images (600 per activity). The network was trained with stochastic gradient descent using a batch size of 256 images until the accuracy on the validation videos converged. As is standard practice, the convolutional layers were initialized with weights from the ImageNet Visual Recognition Challenge [10], which led to convergence after 12 epochs.

To test the performance of the trained CNN, we first applied the hand extraction approach from Section 2 to each frame of all 16 videos in our test dataset, resulting in 16 × 2,700 = 43,200 test frames. Classifying each frame individually gave 53.6% accuracy on the four-way activity problem, nearly twice the random baseline (25.0%). This promising result suggests a strong relationship between hand poses and activities.

3.2 Viewpoint Integration

Of course, our automatic hand extraction is not perfect, and regularly suffers from false negatives (missing hands) and imperfect segmentations (inaccurate hand poses). Even when masks are perfect, they may not be informative: hands may be occluded or not in view at all (see Figure 4). However, even if the hands are occluded or inaccurately extracted in one frame, it is likely that another frame, either from the other person's view or from a nearby moment in time, yields an accurate estimate of the hand pose.

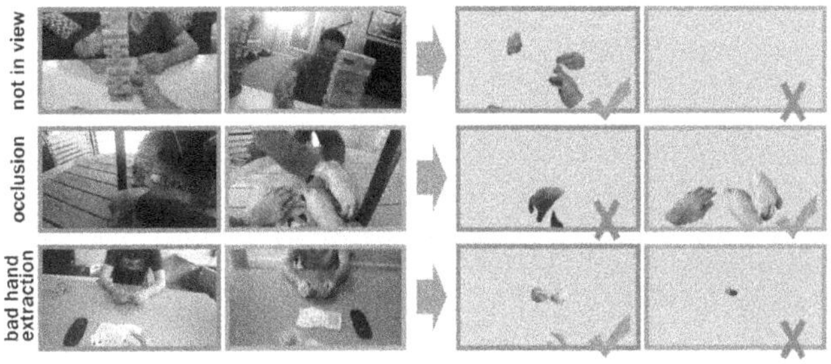

Figure 4: Sample moments where one viewpoint observes much more informative hand poses for activity recognition.

We integrate evidence across frames using a straightforward late fusion method at the decision level. Suppose we have a set $\mathcal{P}$ of actors, each of whom records a sequence of n frames, i.e. $\mathcal{F}_p = (F_p^1, F_p^2, ..., F_p^n)$ for each $p \in \mathcal{P}$. The frames are synchronized so that for any t and pair of actors $p, q \in \mathcal{P}$, F_p^t and F_q^t were captured at the same moment. Without loss of generality, we consider the specific case of two actors, $\mathcal{P} = \{A, B\}$. Suppose that our goal is to jointly estimate the unknown activity label H from a set of possible activities $\mathcal{H}$. By applying the CNN trained in the last section on any given frame F_p^t, we can estimate (using only the evidence in that single frame) the probability that it belongs to any activity $h \in \mathcal{H}$, $P(H = h|F_p^t)$.

Temporal integration. We integrate evidence across the temporal dimension, given the evidence in individual frames across a time window from t_i to t_j in a single view p,

$$\hat{H}_p^{t_i,t_j} = \arg\max_{H\in\mathcal{H}} P(H|F_p^{t_i}, F_p^{t_i+1}, ..., F_p^{t_j}) = \arg\max_{H\in\mathcal{H}} \prod_{k=t_i}^{t_j} P(H|F_p^k),$$

where the latter equation follows from assumptions that frames are conditionally independent given activity, that activities are equally likely *a priori*, and from Bayes' Law. We evaluated this approach by repeatedly testing classification performance on our videos over many different time windows of different lengths (different values of $|t_j - t_i|$). The red line in Figure 5a shows that accuracy increases with the number of frames considered. For instance, when observing 20 seconds of interacting hands from a single viewpoint, the system predicts the interaction with 74% accuracy.

Viewpoint integration. Next we take advantage of the coupled interaction by integrating evidence across viewpoints,

$$\hat{H}^{t_i,t_j} = \arg\max_{H\in\mathcal{H}} \prod_{k=t_i}^{t_j} P(H|F_A^k)P(H|F_B^k),$$

which makes the additional assumption that the viewpoints are independent conditioned on activity. We again test over many different temporal windows of different sizes in our videos, but now using frames from both viewpoints. The re-

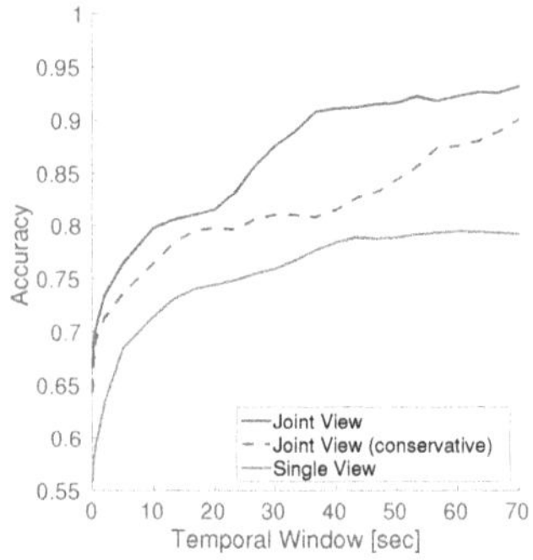

(a)

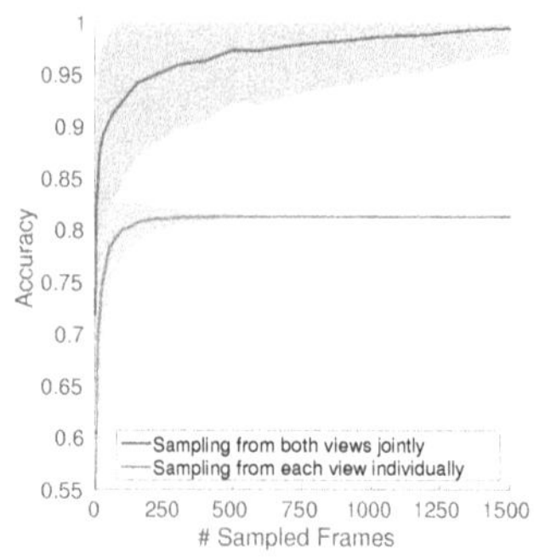

(b)

Figure 5: Comparison of activity recognition accuracy using one (red) and both (blue) viewpoints, using a sliding temporal window (a) and sampling nonadjacent frames (b).

sults are plotted in blue in Figure 5a and clearly outperform the single view approach, showing that the two views are indeed complementary. However, this fusion method has the potentially unfair advantage of seeing twice as many frames as the single view method, so we also show a more conservative line (dashed blue) that considers half the temporal window size (so that for any position on the x-axis, the red line and dashed blue line are seeing the same number of frames). This conservative comparison still outperforms the single view, demonstrating that observing $x/2$ seconds of hand interactions from both viewpoints is more informative than observing x seconds from only one.

Sampling Frames. Adjacent frames are highly correlated, so we hypothesize that it may be better to integrate evidence across wider time periods. A generalization of the above is to use a set $\mathcal{T} \subseteq [1, n]$ of times at which to observe frames,

$$\hat{H}^{\mathcal{T}} = \arg\max_{H \in \mathcal{H}} \prod_{k \in \mathcal{T}} P(H|F_A^k)P(H|F_B^k).$$

We tested this by repeatedly sampling different numbers of frames from each video. The red line in Figure 5b shows accuracy as a function of number of frames ($|\mathcal{T}|$) for single viewpoints (with the shaded area indicating standard deviation over 2,700 sampling iterations). After a high initial variance, accuracy converges to 81.25%, or 13 of 16 videos, at about 500 frames (about 20% of a video). Of the three incorrect videos, two are of chess (where we predict puzzle and cards) and the other is of cards (where we predict Jenga).

Finally, we combine both viewpoints together by sampling sets of corresponding frames from both views. The blue line in Figure 5b shows the results (plotted so that at any position on the x-axis, the red line sees x frames while the blue line sees $x/2$ frames from each viewpoint). Even for a small number of samples, this method dramatically outperforms single view, albeit with a large standard deviation, indicating that some paired samples are much more informative than others. More importantly, as the number of samples increases, the joint view method approaches 100% accuracy. This means that using the complementary information from both viewpoints helps correctly predict the three videos that were not correctly predicted with the single view.

4. CONCLUSION AND FUTURE WORK

We presented a system that can recognize social interactions between two partners who both wear head-mounted cameras (Google Glass) by automatically analyzing each actor's egocentric video stream using state-of-the art computer vision techniques. In particular, we show that the knowledge of hand pose and position alone can provide enough information to distinguish between the four activities present in our data. Further, we demonstrate that the two viewpoints are complementary and that predicting the interaction based on integrating evidence across viewpoints leads to better results than analyzing them individually.

We plan to extend our work in several directions, including testing on a larger set of activities as well as finer-grained actions (such as picking up a card or placing a piece on the chess board). We also plan to investigate more challenging social interactions involving more than two people, as well as integrating other sensor information from Google Glass, such as the accelerometer.

Acknowledgments. This work was supported by the National Science Foundation (CAREER IIS-1253549, CNS-0521433), the National Institutes of Health (R01 HD074601, R21 EY017843), Google, and the IU OVPR through the IUCRG and FRSP programs. It used compute facilities provided by NVidia, the Lilly Endowment through its support of the IU Pervasive Technology Institute, and the Indiana METACyt Initiative. SB was supported by a Paul Purdom Fellowship.

5. REFERENCES

[1] S. Bambach, S. Lee, D. Crandall, and C. Yu. Lending a hand: Detecting hands and recognizing activities in complex egocentric interactions. In *IEEE International Conference on Computer Vision*, 2015.

[2] T. M. T. Do, K. Kalimeri, B. Lepri, F. Pianesi, and D. Gatica-Perez. Inferring social activities with mobile sensor networks. In *ACM International Conference on Multimodal Interaction*, 2013.

[3] R. Girshick, J. Donahue, T. Darrell, and J. Malik. Rich feature hierarchies for accurate object detection and semantic segmentation. In *IEEE Conference on Computer Vision and Pattern Recognition*, 2014.

[4] A. Krizhevsky, I. Sutskever, and G. Hinton. ImageNet classification with deep Convolutional Neural Networks. In *Neural Information Processing Systems*, 2012.

[5] J. R. Kwapisz, G. M. Weiss, and S. A. Moore. Activity recognition using cell phone accelerometers. *ACM SigKDD Explorations Newsletter*, 12(2):74–82, 2011.

[6] S. Lee, S. Bambach, D. Crandall, J. Franchak, and C. Yu. This hand is my hand: A probabilistic approach to hand disambiguation in egocentric video. In *CVPR Workshop on Egocentric Vision*, 2014.

[7] N. Oliver, E. Horvitz, and A. Garg. Layered representations for human activity recognition. In *ACM International Conference on Multimodal Interaction*, 2002.

[8] J. Pelz, M. Hayhoe, and R. Loeber. The coordination of eye, head, and hand movements in a natural task. *Experimental Brain Research*, 139(3):266–277, 2001.

[9] C. Rother, V. Kolmogorov, and A. Blake. Grabcut: Interactive foreground extraction using iterated graph cuts. *ACM Trans. on Graphics*, 23(3):309–314, 2004.

[10] O. Russakovsky, J. Deng, H. Su, et al. ImageNet Large Scale Visual Recognition Challenge. *International Journal of Computer Vision*, 2015.

[11] Y. Song, L. Morency, and R. Davis. Multi-view latent variable discriminative models for action recognition. In *IEEE Conference on Computer Vision and Pattern Recognition*, 2012.

[12] Y. C. Song, H. Kautz, J. Allen, M. Swift, Y. Li, J. Luo, and C. Zhang. A markov logic framework for recognizing complex events from multimodal data. In *ACM International Conference on Multimodal Interaction*, 2013.

A Multimodal System for Real-Time Action Instruction in Motor Skill Learning

Iwan de Kok[1,2,4], Julian Hough[2,4], Felix Hülsmann[1,3,4], Mario Botsch[3,4], David Schlangen[2,4], Stefan Kopp[1,4]
[1]Social Cognitive Systems Group, [2]Dialogue Systems Group, [3]Graphics & Geometry Group, [4]CITEC
Bielefeld University
idekok@techfak.uni-bielefeld.de

ABSTRACT

We present a multimodal coaching system that supports online motor skill learning. In this domain, closed-loop interaction between the movements of the user and the action instructions by the system is an essential requirement. To achieve this, the actions of the user need to be measured and evaluated and the system must be able to give corrective instructions on the ongoing performance. Timely delivery of these instructions, particularly during execution of the motor skill by the user, is thus of the highest importance. Based on the results of an empirical study on motor skill coaching, we analyze the requirements for an interactive coaching system and present an architecture that combines motion analysis, dialogue management, and virtual human animation in a motion tracking and 3D virtual reality hardware setup. In a preliminary study we demonstrate that the current system is capable of delivering the closed-loop interaction that is required in the motor skill learning domain.

Categories and Subject Descriptors

H.5.2 [**Information Interfaces and Presentation**]: User Interfaces—*Natural Language, Virtual Reality*

General Terms

Algorithms, Human Factors

Keywords

Coaching; motor skill learning; multimodal interaction; virtual reality; virtual human

1. INTRODUCTION

Artificial coaching systems that support users doing sport and exercise activities have been around for little over a decade. Most of these have been motivational in nature: some involving long-term motivation Human Robot Interaction [5] and others an artificial fitness instructor who gives instructions and encouragement within the course of a steady-state exercise like cycling [8, 17] or running [3].

There has also been some work in systems that help users improve specific bodily movements, facilitating *motor skill learning*. While this has involved various types of auditory, visual and haptic feedback to optimize the learning gain of the user– see [14] for a review– little attention has been payed to generating *real-time instructions* as the motor skill is being attempted which uses comprehensive motion analysis, nor to the general verbal and gestural generation requirements of multimodal virtual coaching agents who could operate in such a domain with access to this detailed knowledge.

In this paper we address this unique challenge for motor skill coaching by virtual agents, presenting a intelligent coaching space environment capable of analysing a coachee's movement and a virtual coach character that can generate appropriate instructions as the motor skill is performed. The paper is organized as follows: In Section 2 we describe the behavioural and processing requirements of a virtual coach based on our findings from human-human motor skill coaching interactions. In Section 3 we present the hardware and software architecture of our system. Section 4 describes an experiment we carry out addressing different types of instruction giving. The results of the experiment are presented and discussed in Section 5 and we conclude and present an outlook in Section 6.

2. REAL-TIME COACHING BEHAVIOUR IN MOTOR SKILL LEARNING

In the real-world domain of motor skill learning, human coaches exhibit unique online behaviours which present interesting requirements for a virtual coach. In Figure 2 we show a typical interaction found in a corpus study on a human-human coaching scenario wherein a coach trains a coachee to improve their ability at bodyweight squats (those without a weight or barbell)– full details of the study are reported in [6]. Here, we see a coach instructing on the stance width of the squat's preparation phase. In this interaction, the coach first places himself in parallel with the coachee, introducing the element of the skill they should carry out next in (A). He then demonstrates and describes the skill for the coachee in (B) and uses multimodal instructions (deictic gesture and speech) to communicate the desired stance width in (C). In (D), the coach *repairs* the coachee's stance width and instructs her to *adjust* her foot position with 'a bit closer together' until he is satisfied.

While giving feedback after a coachee skill attempt, or

ICMI 2015, November 9–13, 2015, Seattle, WA, USA.

ACM 978-1-4503-3912-4/15/11 ...$15.00.
DOI: http://dx.doi.org/10.1145/2818346.2820746.

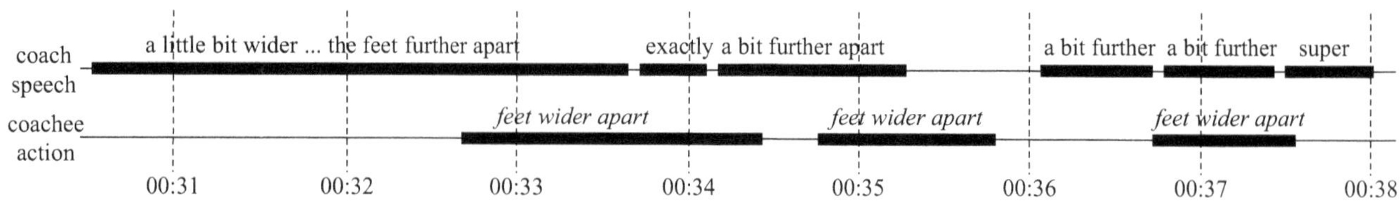

Figure 1: The critical timing of an adjust act by a human coach

even after a series of them, can be an effective strategy for skill improvement – see [14] – we see evidence for the regular need for these kinds of online incremental instructions in our corpus. We tagged each of the coach's utterances for a specialized coaching dialogue act and find that nearly 10% of them consist of these *adjust* acts. These are particularly challenging because of their time-critical nature– see Figure 1 for the temporal representation of a different adjust act where the coach, constantly monitoring the coachee's action, keeps incrementing his contribution with the adjunctive phrase 'a bit further' until the coachee has achieved the desired foot stance. Aside from adjustment cases, the interaction between coach and coachee actions is generally time-critical. We find the mean interval from the end of the instruction to the start of the skill attempt was negative for reactions to instructions for the going down phase of the squat at -0.274s (st.d.=1.204) and even more so for the going up phase at -0.410s (st.d.=0.510), meaning on average coachees were moving well before the end of the utterance. Coachees can take initiative and predict instruction completions easily, just as fine-grained initiative and prediction is common in other situated domains.

We assume the coach is attempting to induce in the coachee a *motor program schema* [13], and evidence as to whether the coachee has learned it or not is observed through their demonstration of the desired outcomes. As a squat has no easily tangible notion of success, particularly for novices, it is crucial that feedback on successful learning be relayed to the coachee to ground the fact it was successful. It is clear that a mixture of offline and online instructions for teaching a motor program schema can be used effectively, and the online instructions provide a particular challenge for a virtual coach.

2.1 Requirements for a virtual motor skill coaching system

Based on the evidence from real coaching interaction, several requirements for a realistic motor skill coaching agent become evident:

- Inherently *multimodal* in both directions– both in the understanding of user's movements and in generation via physical demonstration by the virtual coach. Motor skill acquisition requires detailed monitoring of the user's movements, and also requires demonstration of the skill [4]. The Virtual Agents community takes multimodal generation as a given [10] , however systems involving learning gain for a motor skill largely rely on providing disembodied feedback [14].
- Detailed sports and movement science informed *online movement analysis* in the visual processing pipeline. The goal of the system is to reduce the difference between the observed action and the desired action, so the error analysis should be paramaterised by a user's potential.

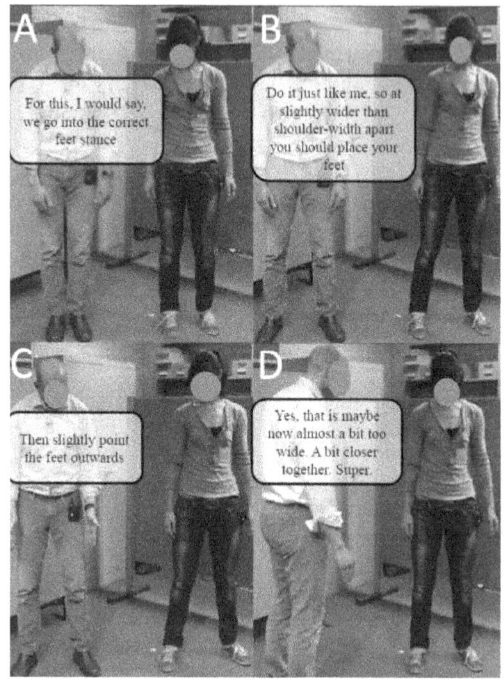

Figure 2: A typical coaching interaction. After the coach introduces a skill phase multimodally in A-C, in D he repairs the coachee's skill attempt and *adjusts* her stance until satisfied.

- Motivational and relevant *feedback generation* to maximise the learning gain and naturalness of the coach.
- Tightly connected *low latency and incremental* processing components from input to output to move towards a *closed-loop system*. Most coaching systems only offer advice and motivation *after* the user's skill attempt, however we require this to be online and during the exercise to simulate a human coach's behaviour as described above. The low latency is in fact vital if the coach is to instruct on and correct a problematic phase of the skill at the relevant time.

It is the last requirement that we focus on in detail in this paper, whilst the others are made possible by our architecture as we will explain. Low latency and incrementality in understanding and generation is key to a motor skill coach, as the closed-loop between perceiving user actions and generating feedback is essential. If there is any latency in an online instruction, this may be interpreted by the coachee as referring to a different part of the movement than intended. Low latency incremental versions of interactive systems have been shown to be preferred to their non-incremental counterparts in simple domains [1, 15], and we use the insight that incremental systems allow fast and responsive behavior [12, 10] as a point of departure for our architecture.

3. INTELLIGENT COACHING SPACE

We now describe the components that make up our intelligent coaching space. The hardware system consists of a CAVE environment and a motion capture system; the software components are composed of a rendering engine, motion analysis and dialogue system– see Figure 3 for an overview.

Here the hardware and render engine (Section 3.1), understanding (Section 3.2) and decision making and realization components of the virtual coach character (Section 3.3) are explained in detail. A more extensive description together with a technical evaluation of latencies of the core system can be found in [20].

3.1 CAVE and Graphics Environment

The virtual coaching space is located inside a two-sided CAVE (L-Shape, 3m x 2.3m for each side) with a resolution of 2100 x 1600 pixels per side.

Our Render Engine runs on a single computer equipped with two NVIDIA Quadro K5000 graphics cards. Rendering runs at approximately 60 fps supporting high quality character rendering, shadows and post-processing and fulfills our low latency requirements.

In the virtual coaching space the user, equipped with passive 3D goggles, is located inside a virtual fitness room, and following the motivation for enhanced learning in [2], they stand in front of a *virtual mirror*. The system maps the user's motion in real time onto an avatar to effect a virtual reflection. The virtual coach is rendered adjacent to the mirror. The virtual world, modulo the coach is capable of providing visual feedback on motor skill performance in two ways: users are able to observe their own movements inside the virtual mirror; and the tint of the mirror adapts depending on the observed performance. In our initial setup, feedback was also provided by a summary of the performance as text overlay inside the virtual world.

In the current setup, in line with our motivation of realistic and interactive virtual coaching, information on motor performance is presented using spoken feedback uttered by the virtual coach. Additionally, the mirror flashes for a short time interval to inform users about the successful recognition of a squat.

3.2 Motion Capture and Analysis

The CAVE is equipped with a 10 camera Prime 13W OptiTrack motion capture system. The Motion Tracker uses information obtained from passive markers attached to a motion capture suit to calculate 20 joint angles / positions of the user. This data is passed on to the Render Engine to display the user in the Virtual Mirror.

3.2.1 Motor Performance Analysis

We represent movements as a sequence of feature vectors. This sequence consist of motor actions (e.g. squats) which are connected by arbitrary transition movements. Motor actions are a sequence of Movement Primitives (MPs). A MP describes a homogeneous part of a more complex movement [21]. The real time analysis system first segments the movement and thus determines which MP the coachee currently performs. Then, it determines the current quality of motor performance. We describe the system in detail in [7].

For each motor action, it is specified which features (e.g. joint angles) are relevant for the definition of the action and its MPs. For the squat, these are mainly the joints of the lower body. Then key-postures for the MPs are defined.

Motion segmentation works via using a state machine: Each motor action and its MPs are represented as states. As soon as a posture similar enough — reaching a given threshold — to the first key posture of the first MP of a motor action is detected, the analyzer switches its state. If the next posture is still valid for the current state it remains there. If the posture belongs to the first key posture of the next MP, it switches its state to the second MP. Otherwise, it assumes that the motor action has been aborted and returns to the idle state. The state of the motion analyzer thus reflects the current motor action and the current MP.

After determining the current action and current MP, the quality of the movement has to be assessed. For our application, a detection of performance errors via just comparing the performed MP to an optimal performance is not sufficient: this would lead to single performance values which just describe the overall deviation to the norm. Indeed, we are interested in providing advice on how to correct the movement. For example, to prevent the user from incorrectly distributing the weight, an appropriate feedback is to instruct the user to move their buttocks back. Thus, we would like to make use of a grounded specification of possible error patterns directly connected to the implications they have for the overall movement, and provide strategies to prevent the error. Hence, we make use of Prototypical Style Patterns (PSPs) described in [7]: A PSP describes movement styles considered as erroneous and is defined by at least one rule. Each rule returns a quantitative error value for the incoming motion. For each motor action – the squat in our case – a list of PSPs is identified. For our feedback system, we define two types of rules:

Type 1 This rule becomes active (returns a value greater zero) as soon as a given condition is violated (e.g. the bending of the neck during a squat performance exceeds a given interval).

Type 2 This rule stays active as long as a given condition is not satisfied (e.g. the user does not go down deep enough during the whole squat).

The following PSPs for non-optimal performances in the motor skill during squats are detected and later connected to verbal feedback:

Not deep enough (Type 2) The goal is to achieve an angle of 100 degrees in the thigh position compared to the user's rest pose. This pattern is active until the user reaches the target joint angle. The return value quantifies the minimal deviation to the 100 degrees, the coachee reached during the squat.

Too much strain on knees (Type 1) One indicator for this error is that the knees are in front of the toes. This error can also be detected via observing the angle of the shin or the ankle. The PSP returns the largest deviation to the allowed posture the coachee performed during the squat.

Neck not straight (Type 1) The angle of the skull-base and the angle at cervical vertebra 7 are important to detect this pattern: If their angle gets too large, the pattern is activated and the largest deviation to the allowed interval of the joints is returned.

All analysis results are transferred to the coaching system (see Section 3.3) in real time at a frequency of around 120

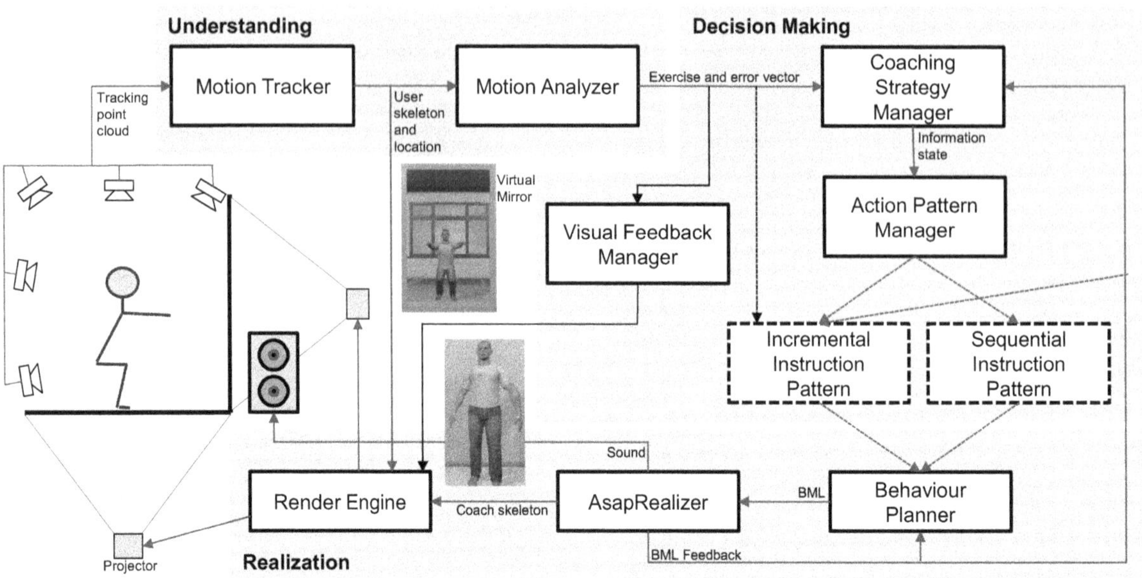

Figure 3: The overall architecture of our intelligent coaching space. On the left the hardware setup is depicted, with wall and floor projection and motion capturing cameras. In our software we have understanding components interpreting the user's actions. Our decision makers comprise both visual feedback (middle part) and a virtual coach and realization components to communicate the decisions back to the user.

Hz, allowing the coach to start planning actions before they need to be realized in accordance with our incremental processing requirement as will be explained. Our approach to the online motor performance analysis allows a fast detection (approx. 1ms for our list of PSPs) and does not need large amounts of annotated training data.

3.2.2 *Pilot Usability Evaluation*

To investigate the usability of the core components in a pilot study, we developed a simple coaching application that offered squat training by exploration: The correct movement was shown to a trainee, who also received additional information such as which parts of the movement are of special importance (e.g. "Make sure to keep your neck straight"). The actual training took place in the above described virtual world, but without the virtual coach. Participants were instructed to perform squats in six sets with a break in between. The mirror showed a red tint until the trainee succeeded in performing a correct squat. To depict the detection of a squat, the mirror flashed yellow. If a PSP was been detected, one keyword for the specific pattern which had been explained to the participant beforehand (e.g."neck") was displayed next to the mirror directly after the performance. After the performance of a correct squat, the mirror changed its color to green. Each set ended as soon as a squat had been performed correctly according to the given rules or as soon as a given time limit had been reached.

Among others, simulator sickness (using the questionnaire by Kennedy et al. [9]) and presence (using a modified version of the Slater, Usoh, Steed questionnaire (SUS) [16]) were measured. 22 participants took part in the experiment, which took 5-6 minutes each. No increase of simulator sickness was reported. The results for presence were at an intermediate level (M = 3.1, SD = 1.5 on a scale from 0 to 6). The relatively low mean may have been due to the fact that this preliminary study used only visual feedback and a very simple virtual environment.

In terms of learning gain, for PSP `not deep enough`, participants were able to reduce the number of necessary squats to produce a correct performance significantly over the sets ($M_{Set1} = 1.8$, $M_{Set2} = 0.6$, $p<0.005$). For all other PSPs, participants did not learn to improve their performance.

These results suggest that the virtual environment is technically sound for measuring error analysis, however the feedback was somewhat static, and not conducive to good interaction or enhancement of skill. In line with our motivation from human coaching set out in Section 2, in our next development phase we introduce our virtual coach character into the coaching space to deliver more natural, human-like instructions during and after the performance of user motor skill attempts. The architecture which enables the virtual coach to deliver these instructions is explained in the following sections.

3.3 Virtual Coach

Our virtual coach aims to bring incremental situated coaching to our intelligent coaching space hitherto described.

The software architecture of the Virtual Coach consists of three main components: The *Coaching Strategy Manager (CSM)* which is responsible for the general structure of the coaching session, *Action Patterns* which generate the behaviour to realize the plans the CSM decides upon, and finally the *Realizer* which transfers the behaviour to the Render Engine. In the following sections these components will be explained in more detail.

3.3.1 *Coaching Strategy Manager*

The Coaching Strategy Manager (CSM) is responsible for making decisions about the overall structure of the interaction. It keeps track of the long term goal of teaching the motor skill and selects the next coaching action that maximizes its utility for achieving it. It is currently implemented as a finite state machine making decisions based on an information state. This information state is updated by processing the incoming user input, in this case the output of the Motion Analyzer, and also feedback from the Realizer which informs the Coaching Strategy Manager on the status of its own behaviour.

The information state keeps track of how many squats have been performed by the user in the current interaction, the errors made during each squat and which phase of the squat the user is currently in.[1] The CSM makes a decision each time a new phase of the squat is detected by the Motion Analyzer or it has completed its previous coaching action.

3.3.2 Action Patterns for Behaviour Generation

For many actions a decision update rate of once every squat phase or every completed coaching action is too infrequent to comply with the incremental system requirements expressed in Section 2. To address this problem we introduce the concept of *Action Patterns.*

Action Patterns are dynamic software modules that can be created, activated and/or stopped at run time. All Action Patterns are their own decision makers within their own expertise that are free to generate behaviour fitting the constraints from earlier decision makers, typically the Coaching Strategy Manager (CSM).

Each Action Pattern can create its own information flow links to all other parts of our system. For instance, the `Incremental Instruction` pattern directly listens to the output of the Motion Analyzer, bypassing the CSM (see Section 4.1.1 for more details). Note that it can still be deactivated by the CSM if it decides on another action.

All Action Patterns are available to the Action Pattern Manager. This manager keeps track of which Action Patterns are currently active and has the power to start and stop them if needed. Action Patterns produce behaviours described in the Behaviour Markup Language (BML) [19].

In the current system each coaching act is implemented as its own Action Pattern. *Greeting*, *Introduction* and *Closing* are lexicon-based Action Patterns where behaviour is hardcoded. The different Action Patterns for *Instruction* are explained in more detail in Section 4.1.

3.3.3 Behaviour Planning and Realization

The BML blocks produced by Action Patterns are collected by the Behaviour Planner. This Behaviour Planner resolves potential conflicts between BML blocks produced by Action Patterns active in parallel, e.g. if two BML blocks want to use a certain body part of the coach at the same time. Currently our system is not rich enough such that many conflicts occur, and we simply delay BML blocks that cause conflicts, however we intend to increase the demand on the behaviour planner in future development in this regard.

The BML blocks are then realized by the AsapRealizer [18]. It transforms the BML blocks into joint rotations and blend shapes which are passed on to the renderer, resulting in animation of the virtual coach character. The coach's speech is synthesized using the CereVoice Engine Text-to-Speech system (voice Nathan).

4. EXPERIMENT

In our corpus analysis we observed two instruction strategies from the coach which differ in timing: coaches giving their instructions either between squats (sequential instructions) or during squats (incremental instructions) depending on the situation. Sequential instructions between squats allow for more elaboration, while incremental instructions allow for precise timing information. In an experiment we explore these instruction types to test whether our architecture can deliver both types successfully and also to gain insight into the user experience of each instruction type both subjectively and in terms of objective learning gain.

4.1 Instructions

Here we address three squat PSPs: `too much strain on knees`, `not deep enough` and `neck not straight` errors (see Section 3.2.1) and the virtual coach addresses these errors using two types of instruction: *incremental* – the instructions are vocalized *during* the squat – and *sequential* – the instructions are vocalized *between* squats. We now briefly detail the interactive effect of these instructions on users and how they are realized in our architecture.

4.1.1 Incremental Instructions

In the incremental instructions setting the virtual coach gives its instructions while the participant is doing the stroke (downward phase) of the squat. The instructions given are short, but occur as soon as the coach becomes aware of the error and has time to produce the instruction. These instructions were generated by an Action Pattern that takes as input the output of the Motion Analyzer at 120 Hz – to detect errors – and the BML feedback from the Realizer – to know when a previous instruction is finished. Instructions were pre-planned [11], meaning that all possible instructions are already submitted to the Realizer in order to pre-process the text-to-speech. They would start playing once an activation signal has been sent to the Realizer.

When no errors occurred the coach would say the following default instructions: "Deeper. Go on. A bit more. A bit more...". It would do so until the PSP `not deep enough` was no longer present. It would then interrupt this sequence by saying "Stop" as soon as possible, interrupting ongoing instructions. If one of the other two errors are detected it would selected that instruction over one of the default instructions, where `too much strain on knees` – instructed by saying "Hips back more" – had priority over `neck not straight` – "Watch your neck", a priority observed in our corpus analysis.

Figure 4 shows an example of the incremental instructions. At time point 1 the squat exercise is first detected by the motion analyzer. At that time `not deep enough` is the only error that is detected, so the action pattern vocalizes an instruction to correct this error, in this case "Deeper". When the coach is finished uttering the instruction and a minimum of 200 ms has passed the next instruction is vocalized (time point 2). At time point 3 the error `neck not straight` is detected. Note that this error is not vocalized until time point 4, after the previous instruction is finished and a minimum amount of silence between instructions has passed. In response to the instruction, the user corrected the neck error (see the adjusted neck angle in skeleton 5), so at time point 5 the coach continues encouraging the coachee to go deeper. At time point 6 the desired deepness of the squat is reached and "Stop" is uttered. Note that this interrupts the ongoing adjust instruction "A bit more".

After each squat the system would ask for another slow

[1]The squat is separated into a preparation phase (assuming the starting position), stroke (going down), strokehold (in the lowest position) and retraction phase (coming up).

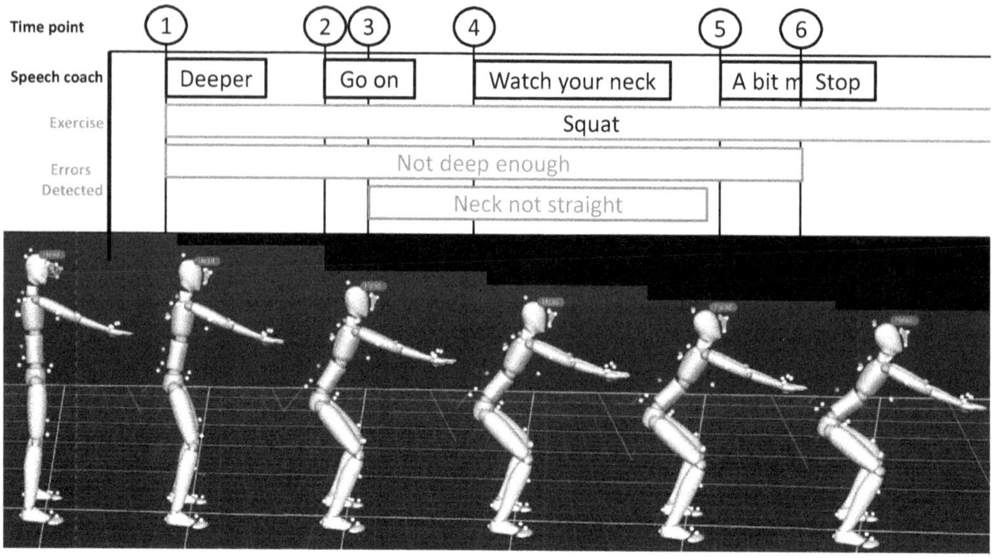

Figure 4: Incremental instructions generated by the virtual coach in response to a user's squat. As soon as a squat is detected (Time point 1) the coach utters instructions to correct the errors detected. Note how the user adjusts the neck angle in response to the instruction "Watch your neck". As soon as the stroke of the squat is completed (Time point 6) the "Stop" instruction interrupts any ongoing instructions.

squat by saying "Okay. Give me another slow one." We ask for a slow squat in this configuration to allow the system to express more instructions. A regular squat only provides enough time to say "Deeper" and "Stop".

4.1.2 Sequential Instructions

In the sequential instructions configuration the virtual coach gives its instructions after the participant completes the entire squat. These instructions were more verbose than the incremental instructions and were generated by an Action Pattern that takes as input from the Coaching Strategy Manager a summary of the squat, indicating which errors occurred in which phases. If errors occurred in the squat the coach would say between squats: "Okay. Give me one more, but this time (keep your neck straight / push your hips back more / go a bit deeper)[2]" or say: "Perfect. Give me one more like that" when no errors occurred.

4.2 Participants and Procedure

Our experiment had 16 participants (9 female, 7 male, age 20-45, mean 26). Participants were recruited through university wide advertisement and were paid 8 Euros or awarded course credit for their time. All but one had done squats before, 7 reported doing squats at least once a week.

After a brief welcome the participants read an explanation of the study and signed a consent form for the data recordings. Then the participant put on the motion capturing suit and tracking markers were attached. When the participants first entered the CAVE a calibration session followed to ensure that all the markers were in place and the tracking was correctly configured. The participants were briefed again about the interactions that would follow.

The participants interacted twice with our virtual coaching system, each time with a different instructions configuration. In each interaction the system would ask for a squat 20 times. The coach gives (*incremental* or *sequential*) instructions on each uneven squat. The even squats are used to measure the performance. Between the two sessions the participants were allowed to take a break as long as they needed. The order of the experimental conditions was balanced between subjects.

After the two interactions with the system a questionnaire (see 4.3) was filled out. In total the experiment lasted between 30 and 45 minutes, depending on calibration time.

4.3 Measures

The questionnaire included items about demographics (gender, age), sport and squat experience (3 items) and 10 items asking to compare the two interactions in terms of several adjectives. These items were 7-point Likert scale items with the low end being instruction DURING squats and the high end instruction AFTER squats. A value of 4 indicates no difference. The 10 adjectival properties used were: helpful, responsive, human-like, friendly, polite, efficient, clear, intelligent, tiring and preferred. This list was inspired by the questionnaire used by Skantze and Hjalmarsson [15]. Finally there was an open feedback field where they could share their thoughts and remarks about the experiment.

We also measured performance of the squats with the motion analysis explained in Section 3.2.1 applied. For each PSP, one overall performance value was obtained, where a smaller value indicates a better performance. This was done for the PSPs `too much strain on knees`, `not deep enough` and `neck not straight`.

5. RESULTS AND DISCUSSION

5.1 Performance

In order to find out whether the instructions of our coaching system resulted in learning gain, for each PSP we investigate whether the error was corrected in subsequent squat or severance of the violation decreased.

[2]All three or only a subset were generated depending on the errors in the squat.

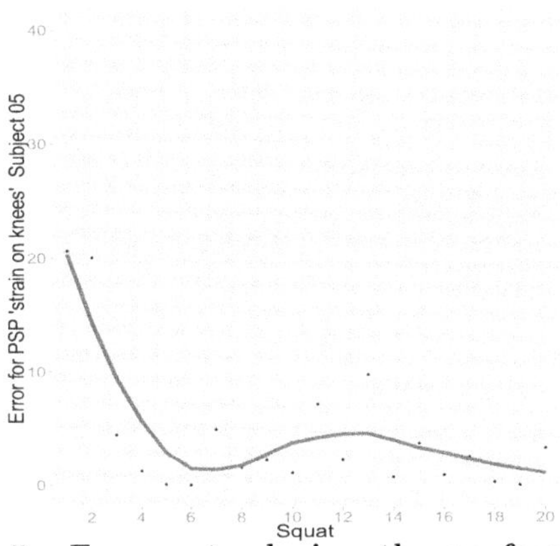

Figure 5: **Error rate during the performance of squats for participant 5.**

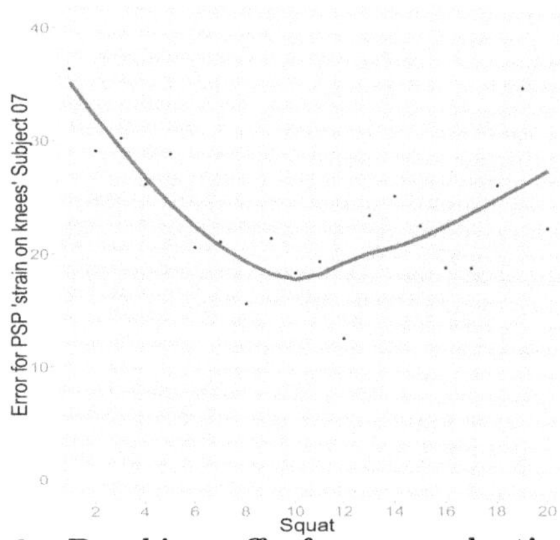

Figure 6: **Breaking off of error reduction during learning, assumed due to exhaustion and lacking quantitative feedback.**

Only three participants performed PSP `not deep enough` during squats (two in the *sequential* instructions condition, one during the *incremental* instructions). All of them were able to correct the error in the subsequent squats. Here, the feedback was quite detailed, combined with a precise instruction ("Go a bit deeper" or a clear "Stop") thus, all were able to fix the error.

`Too much strain on the knees` was performed by many of the participants and most were unable to fix it. For the *incremental* instructions, most participants did not leave the coach enough time for expressing the relevant instruction, forcing the coach to generate "Stop" when the desired angle for the PSP `not deep enough` was reached. For the *sequential* instructions, some participants were able to improve their performance. Figure 5 shows the development of the maximum error value of the squats of one participant who nearly managed to fix PSP `too much strain on the knees` by the end of the session. Some of the participants started reducing the error, but at some point the results became worse again (see Figure 6). Some participants complained that they were not informed about getting better, and thus lost motivation to try and improve.

For `neck not straight` we also observed no learning gain. Participants were aware of the error and tried to fix it (see Figure 4 for on example in the *incremental* instructions configuration). However, the provided instruction was not detailed enough. Since no information was provided on whether the neck was over- or under-stretched, participants where unsure on how to fix the error.

In summary, while promising, the formulation of the instructions should be improved significantly to result in guaranteed learning gain. We need to give more detailed instructions to help users identify their errors and improve their motor program schema.

Another issue was that we tried to address three errors simultaneously. Especially in the *incremental* instructions configuration, this led to incomplete, insufficiently precise instructions given the time constraints of the condition (2-3 seconds for an average squat time).

5.2 Questionnaire

Table 1 presents the results of the questionnaire. The 7-point Likert scale values were condensed to preference for *incremental* (values 1-3), *no difference* (value 4) and *sequential* (values 5-7) (columns 2-4). The mean and standard deviation values are presented in the final column.

	Preference for			
	Incr.	No Diff	Seq.	$\mu(\sigma)$
Helpful	9	3	4	3.38 (1.54)
Responsive	8	3	5	3.31 (1.92)
Humanlike	8	4	4	3.38 (1.70)
Friendly	4	6	6	4.19 (1.62)
Polite	4	6	6	4.38 (1.62)
Efficient	6	4	6	3.75 (1.93)
Clear	8	4	4	3.31 (1.82)
Intelligent	8	7	1	2.94 (1.50)
Tiring	9	3	4	3.43 (2.16)
Preference	7	2	7	3.94 (2.45)

Table 1: Results of the questionnaire.

The *incremental* instructions were found to be significantly more Intelligent ($B(9, 0.5), p < 0.05$). More participants also found that configuration more Helpful, Responsive, Humanlike and Clear. Most also found the *incremental* instructions more Tiring. We attribute this to the fact that the system asked for slower squats. The overall Preference was polarizing, half of them preferred *incremental* instruction, while the other half preferred *sequential* instructions. 9 out of 14 also chose the most extreme value (1 or 7) to express this preference.

6. CONCLUSION AND FUTURE WORK

In this paper we have introduced the challenging domain of motor skill learning through the results of an empirical study and have presented a hard- and software architecture capable of creating the closed-loop interaction that the domain requires.

The system architecture was evaluated by users interacting with two different configurations of the system teaching the motor skill squats. The system gave *incremental* instructions on how to improve during the squat or *sequential* instructions after the squat.

The instructions are not yet accurate or clear enough to result in learning gain for the more complex error patterns. For `not deep enough` both the sequential and incremental instructions were effective in correcting the rare occurrences of the error pattern. For `neck not straight` and `too much` `strain on knees` the incremental instructions provided timing information on when the errors occurred, however without clear directive instructions on how to correct the error pattern, learning proved difficult. This was also the case in the sequential instructions.

Despite the mixed results in terms of learning gain, from a technical viewpoint the interactions were satisfactory, and we fulfill our desiderata of online movement analysis, incrementality and multimodality. The incremental instructions were delivered in a timely manner, such that corrections could be made during skill execution (see neck adjustment between skeleton 4 and 5 in Figure 4), an ability which was a likely factor in leading participants to perceive the incremental instruction setting as more intelligent. In future work we will explore more complex generation strategies, including the effect of our coach demonstrating a skill, to move towards truly interactive multimodal strategies for artificial coaching.

Acknowledgements

This work was supported by the Cluster of Excellence Cognitive Interaction Technology 'CITEC' (EXC 277) at Bielefeld University, funded by the German Research Foundation (DFG).

7. REFERENCES

[1] G. Aist, J. Allen, E. Campana, C. Gomez Gallo, S. Stoness, M. Swift, and M. Tanenhaus. Incremental dialogue system faster than and preferred to its nonincremental counterpart. In *Proceedings of the 29th Annual Conference of the Cognitive Science Society*, 2007.

[2] F. Anderson, T. Grossman, J. Matejka, and G. Fitzmaurice. Youmove: enhancing movement training with an augmented reality mirror. In *Proceedings of the 26th annual ACM symposium on User interface software and technology*, pages 311–320. ACM, 2013.

[3] F. Buttussi, L. Chittaro, and D. Nadalutti. Bringing mobile guides and fitness activities together: a solution based on an embodied virtual trainer. In *MobileHCI*, pages 29–36, 2006.

[4] I. de Kok, J. Hough, C. Frank, D. Schlangen, and S. Kopp. Dialogue structure of coaching sessions. In *Proceedings of the 18th SemDial Workshop on the Semantics and Pragmatics of Dialogue (DialWatt)*, pages 167–169, Edinburgh, September 2014.

[5] J. Fasola and M. J. Mataric. Using socially assistive human–robot interaction to motivate physical exercise for older adults. *Proceedings of the IEEE*, 100(8):2512–2526, 2012.

[6] J. Hough, I. de Kok, D. Schlangen, and S. Kopp. Timing and grounding in motor skill coaching interaction: Consequences for the information state. In *Proceedings of the 19th SemDial Workshop on the Semantics and Pragmatics of Dialogue (goDIAL)*, pages 86–94, Gothenburg, August 2015.

[7] F. Hülsmann, C. Frank, T. Schack, S. Kopp, and M. Botsch. Multi-level analysis of motor actions as a basis for effective coaching in virtual reality. In *International Symposium on Computer Science in Sport*, 2015.

[8] W. IJsselsteijn, Y. de Kort, R. Bonants, J. Westerink, and M. de Jager. Virtual Cycling: Effects of immersion and a virtual coach on motivation and presence in a home fitness application. In *Proceedings Virtual Reality Design and Evaluation Workshop*, pages 22–23, 2004.

[9] R. Kennedy, N. Lane, K. Berbaum, and M. Lilienthal. Simulator Sickness Questionnaire: An enhanced Method for Quantifiying Simulator Sickness. *The International Journal of Aviation Psychology*, 3(3):203–220, 1993.

[10] S. Kopp, H. van Welbergen, R. Yaghoubzadeh, and H. Buschmeier. An architecture for fluid real-time conversational agents: integrating incremental output generation and input processing. *Journal on Multimodal User Interfaces*, 8(1):97–108, 2014.

[11] D. Reidsma, K. Truong, H. van Welbergen, D. Neiberg, S. Pammi, I. de Kok, and B. V. Straalen. Continuous Interaction with a Virtual Human. *Journal on Multimodal User Interfaces*, 4(2):97–118, 2011.

[12] D. Schlangen and G. Skantze. A general, abstract model of incremental dialogue processing. *Dialogue and Discourse*, 2(1):83–111, 2011.

[13] R. A. Schmidt. A schema theory of discrete motor skill learning. *Psychological review*, 82(4):225, 1975.

[14] R. Sigrist, G. Rauter, R. Riener, and P. Wolf. Augmented visual, auditory, haptic, and multimodal feedback in motor learning: A review. *Psychonomic bulletin & review*, 20(1):21–53, 2013.

[15] G. Skantze and A. Hjalmarsson. Towards incremental speech generation in dialogue systems. In *Proceedings of the SIGDIAL 2010 Conference*, pages 1–8, Tokyo, Japan, Sept. 2010.

[16] M. Slater, M. Usoh, and A. Steed. Taking steps: the influence of a walking technique on presence in virtual reality. *ACM Transactions on Computer-Human Interaction*, 2(3):201–219, 1995.

[17] L. Sussenbach, N. Riether, S. Schneider, I. Berger, F. Kummert, I. Lutkebohle, and K. Pitsch. A robot as fitness companion: towards an interactive action-based motivation model. In *Robot and Human Interactive Communication, 2014 RO-MAN: The 23rd IEEE International Symposium on*, pages 286–293, 2014.

[18] H. van Welbergen, R. Yaghoubzadeh, and S. Kopp. AsapRealizer 2.0 : The Next Steps in Fluent Behavior Realization for ECAs. In *Intelligent Virtual Agents*, pages 449–462, 2014.

[19] H. Vilhjalmsson, N. Cantelmo, J. Cassell, N. E. Chafai, M. Kipp, S. Kopp, M. Mancini, S. Marsella, A. N. Marshall, C. Pelachaud, Z. Ruttkay, K. R. Thórisson, H. van Welbergen, and R. J. van der Werf. The behavior markup language: Recent developments and challenges. In *Intelligent Virtual Agents*, pages 99–111, 2007.

[20] T. Waltemate, F. Hülsmann, T. Pfeiffer, S. Kopp, and M. Botsch. Realizing a low-latency virtual reality environment for motor learning. Proceedings of ACM Symposium on Virtual Reality Software and Technology. ACM, 2015.

[21] A. Woch and R. Plamondon. Using the framework of the kinematic theory for the definition of a movement primitive. *Motor Control*, 8:547–557, 2004.

The Application of Word Processor UI paradigms to Audio and Animation Editing

André Milota
418 Beloit Avenue
Kensington CA
510-333-4403. USA
Milota@mindgrip.com

ABSTRACT
This demonstration showcases Quixotic, an audio editor, and Quintessence, an animation editor. Both appropriate many of the interaction techniques found in word processors, and allow users to more quickly create time-variant media. Our different approach to the interface aims to make recorded speech and simple animation into media that can be efficiently used for one-to-one asynchronous communications, quick note taking and documentation, as well as for idea refinement.

Categories and Subject Descriptors
H.5.1 [**Multimedia Information Systems**]
H.4.1 [**Groupware**] H.4.3 [**information systems applications**]

General Terms
Documentation, Design, Human Factors.

Keywords
Audio Editing, Animation, Word Processing

1. INTRODUCTION / MOTIVATION
The most powerful tools employed by humans are those that expand the capability of our intellect. Tools that allow us to save ideas and information using inanimate objects are among some of the most important such mind extenders. Images, text, recorded sound and moving pictures are the most common such tools.

Images and the written word can be very quickly edited using apparatus ranging from pencils and erasers to word processors and paint programs. The alacrity with which we can edit these media allows us to use them to augment our short term memory, collaborate with others, and extend personal longer term recall.

Audio offers a means to ingest information eyes-free - such as when driving. Though it is slower to listen than to read, speaking is roughly 4 to 8 times faster than typing with a full-size keyboard. Text entry on mobile devices is even slower. A major fraction of the world's population is dyslexic, or illiterate for other reasons. The bridge from speech to text provided by ASR, while useful in many circumstances, is generally error-prone, and error repairs can greatly reduce the efficiency gains of speech.

Animation with recorded sound can often be more compelling and explanatory than static text and images. Narrated animations comprising both speech and moving graphics realize the same synergistic modality combinations found in MMUIs and integrated phone and shared whiteboards systems. In these cases, the graphical elements provide an easy way to resolve referenced articles as well as to convey shape and motion.

Time-variant media are difficult to author. Few individuals are capable of thinking, organizing and concisely conveying complex ideas in real time. With today's tools, preparation using scripts and/or story boards or at least notes, is required before recording, and/or much postproduction is needed. This multiple step process, is slow and content changes are hard to make in the later stages.

2. RELATED WORK
A great deal of work has been done on trying to improve the navigation of recorded sound and video, and/or link recordings to scripts, such as in [3] where recognized text is used to label sound recordings. Also, much work has been done in linking images to audio as in [4] or to annotating images and video with audio as in [2]. However, no work we have seen appears to employ a quick acting record button as a primary tool of sound editing.

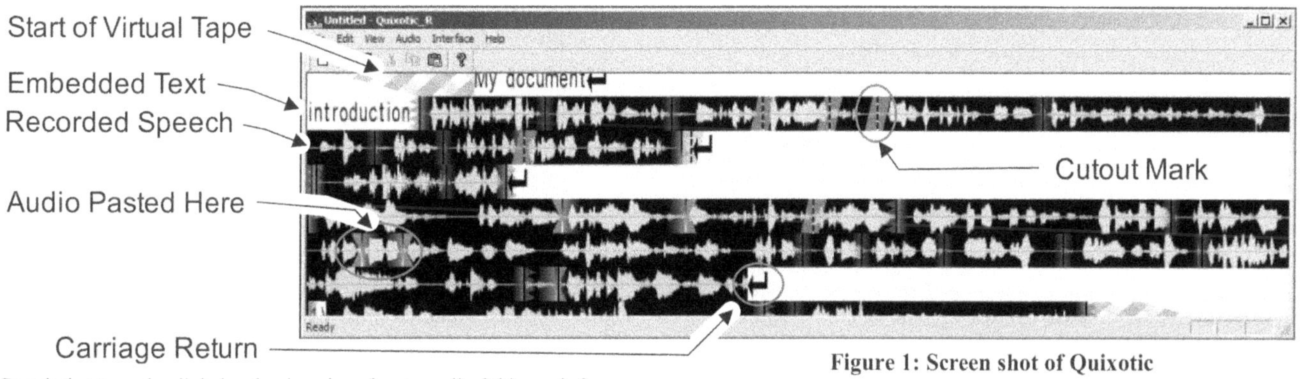

Figure 1: Screen shot of Quixotic

ICMI '15, November 09-13, 2015, Seattle, WA, USA
ACM 978-1-4503-3912-4/15/11.
http://dx.doi.org/10.1145/2818346.2823292

3. QUIXOTIC: A QUICK SOUND EDITOR
Quixotic, our audio recorder/editor, appropriates many of the interactions, mechanisms and metaphors of the typical word processor. The resulting application allows users to wordsmith purely in audio form. The end result is an audio file in which all of the correct words are in the correct order. This is in contrast to

speech recognition interfaces for text editors. Quixotic is also significantly different from existing audio editors in that it enables a more streamlined workflow at the expense of high precision, and omits most traditional sound manipulation tools. Quixotic is optimized for collecting the user's thoughts, with a sequence of very short recording actions interspersed with occasional edit actions, much as how word processors are used. This is in contrast to the longer record/edit cycles of conventional audio production and in marked contrast to video production where different tools are used for recording and editing.

To improve navigation, Quixotic allows users to type text and carriage returns into a window where they are displayed, much like in any simple word processor and can function as a visual outline. However, Quixotic also allows the user to record audio into the same window. Sound recordings are displayed as wave forms which are interspersed with characters. Both the text and audio waveforms wrap around to the next line when they exceed the width of the page. Thus the user is able to view the wave forms in more temporal detail than they would be able to do had the sound been confined to one line. Navigation of the hard to interpret waveforms is further aided by the insertion of *edit marks* which denote where certain edit operations were made. Figure 1 includes various edit marks illustrating where recording stopped, where sound was inserted, cut etc. Additionally, great pains have been taken to display audio waveforms with minimal latency. The current PC interface employs the five function keys on the left hand side of the keyboard, to control the recording and playback of sound. *Play*, *Record* and *Rewind* are set up as Quasimodes - when a key is released the action stops.

Recording and typing will cause sound and text respectively to be inserted into the document rather than overwriting existing content, just as in most word processors. This is dramatically different from many audio editors and animation programs, where adding and removing content and changing the timeline, are separate and sometimes very complex actions. When the user presses *Play*, a cursor moves cross the audio. When it encounters text or other markings it currently skips over them, though text-to-speech may be added at some point to read the text aloud.

4. QUINTESSENCE

Quintessence, our animation editor, is designed for making quick and dirty narrated animations similar in nature to Khan Academy whiteboard videos. Quintessence extends Quixotic with two new elements. 1) It maintains a *presentation window* 2) Key frame objects can be inserted into the list of audio blocks and characters.

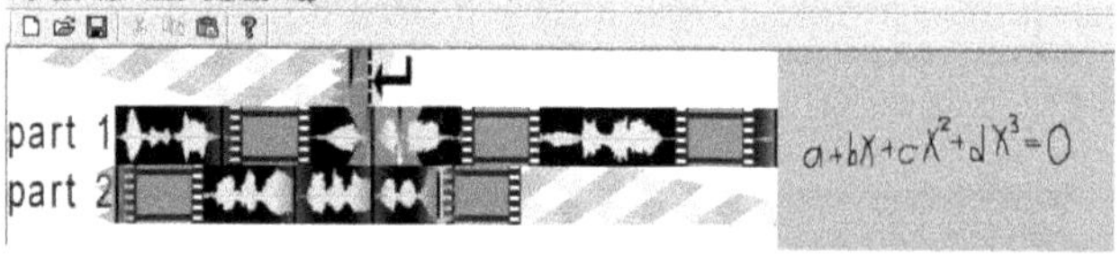

Figure 2. A portion of Quintessence's window, showing part of both the timeline (left) and presentation (right) sub-windows. Key Frames are displayed as film-like icons.

Just as in many other animation programs, when the timeline cursor is placed on a particular key frame or arrives at one during the course of playback, the image stored in the key frame is displayed in the presentation window. Between key frames, various algorithms of the user's choice generate intermediate images (*tweens)*. When the user edits something in the presentation window, the actions taken are recorded into the key frame under the timeline cursor. If the cursor is between key frames, a new key frame will be generated from the current tween.

As with Quixotic, the key to Quintessence is speed through simplicity. Individual objects, while they have a drawing order, do not have independent parallel key frame sequences. Rather, if the amount of audio between two key frames is changed, the rate of change will be adjusted proportionally. We plan to allow sequencing of motions between frames so that multiple strokes made when creating a new key frame will be shown sequentially. To add objects or otherwise make other adjustments across many key frames, such as adding a new background element, the user need only select the desired time range before performing the edit operations. A simple algorithm will then attempt to propagate the changes to all the key frames in the selected range. If necessary, new key frames are placed around the selected region to isolate the changes to just that specified interval.

5. CONCLUSION

By reducing the amount of time required to create sound and animation, these products will enable new uses of these media. We expect Quixotic to be used in conjunction with human transcriptionists, replacing primitive tape recorder emulators. Some individuals may use our product for ideation. Quixotic should also be useful for the writing of dialog, and the creation of casual notes and communications which will remain as audio. This replacement of text with a viable alternative should be very useful for people suffering from dyslexia and similar disabilities, and under some circumstances, provide a solution to the text entry and reading problems encountered on mobile devices. When used with ASR Quixotic allows users to first focus on composition and to perfect wording, before they have to address speech recognition error repair. This approach stands in sharp contrast to that of Kumar [1] who instead reduced the granularity of the talk/correct cycle. Both approaches may have their advantages.

Quintessence could be used for creating multimedia educational presentations. Quintessence should also be very good for creating any form of technical document, ranging from medical records to software documentation, to directions on how a desired task is to be performed; and would support very quick manual translation by any competent dual language speaker. The system could also be modified to track changes by different contributors, contain hypertext links and support collaboration and education with various other mechanisms.

Quixotic and Quintessence consist of about 30,000 lines of C++ written using an object-oriented and aspect-oriented architecture.

REFERENCES

[1] Kumar, A., Paek, P., and Lee, B., "Voice Typing: A New Speech Interaction Model for Dictation on Touchscreen Devices," Proceedings of ACM CHI 2012, May 2012

[2] Lux, M., and Riegler, M., "Voice Annotation of endoscopic videos on mobile devices: a bottom-up approach," MMSys '13 Proceedings of the 4th ACM Multimedia Systems Conference pp. 141-145

[3] Rubin, S., Berthouzoz, F., Mysore, G., Li, W., and Agrawala, M., "Content-Based Tools for Editing Audio Stories," UIST 2013, October 2013. pp. 113-122.

[4] Stifelman, L., Arons, B., and Schmandt, C., "The audio notebook: paper and pen interaction with structured speech," CHI '01 Proceedings of the SIGCHI pp. 182-189

CuddleBits: Friendly, Low-cost Furballs that Respond to Touch

Laura Cang
Dept of Computer Science
University of British Columbia
Vancouver, BC
cang@cs.ubc.ca

Paul Bucci
Dept of Computer Science
University of British Columbia
Vancouver, BC
pbucci@cs.ubc.ca

Karon E. MacLean
Dept of Computer Science
University of British Columbia
Vancouver, BC
maclean@cs.ubc.ca

ABSTRACT

We present a real-time touch gesture recognition system using a low-cost fabric pressure sensor mounted on a small zoomorphic robot, affectionately called the 'CuddleBit'. We explore the relationship between gesture recognition and affect through the lens of human-robot interaction. We demonstrate our real-time gesture recognition system, including both software and hardware, and a haptic display that brings the CuddleBit to life.

Categories and Subject Descriptors

H.5.2 [**User Interfaces**]: Haptic I/O

Keywords

HRI, touch-based gestures, flexible touch sensor

1. INTRODUCTION

The CuddleBit is a small 1-DOF zoomorphic robot that adds to a family of robots collectively called the CuddleBots. There are many CuddleBits, each designed to explore robust yet economical solutions to research in affective human-robot interaction. Each is equipped with a custom flexible full-body fabric pressure sensor that supports touch gesture recognition.

CuddleBits are built to resemble small furry animals, often likened to hamsters or guinea pigs (Fig. 1(c)). Recognizing touch gestures is one of the first steps toward automatic prediction of emotional states[3]. With a real-time touch gesture recognition system, we hope to explore the key features of affective touch and develop a robot that can respond to a diverse set of affective contexts.

2. REQUIREMENTS

As a tool for studying affective touch, the CuddleBit is both required to invite touches with emotional content and

ICMI 2015, November 9–13, 2015, Seattle, WA, USA.
ACM 978-1-4503-3912-4/15/11.
DOI: http://dx.doi.org/10.1145/2818346.2823293.

Figure 1: Three CuddleBits in various sizes and stages of dress. From Left to Right: (a) Large CuddleBit fitted with a fabric touch sensor; (b) Small CuddleBit skeleton; (c) Medium CuddleBit in a faux fur coat.

to encourage continuing interactions through 'believable' responsive behaviours. Our yet-unanswered research questions are:

1. To what extent does touch gesture convey an individual's current affective state?
2. What physical characteristics (e.g., shape, size, fur covering) facilitate a user's sense of appropriate interactivity?
3. What behavioral characteristics (e.g., movements, temporal responsiveness, diversity) facilitate a user's sense of appropriate interactivity?
4. Is a 1-DOF robot platform expressive enough to support exploration of these questions?

In order to elicit naturalistic interactions, a user must imbue the robot with a personality like one might a treasured comfort object. The intent is not to have people believe that the CuddleBit is alive, rather that is a valid receptacle for emotional content. The requirements for this interactive system are two-fold: as an input device, it must be able to recognize touch behaviour; as a display device, it must present appropriate responses to those touches.

3. APPARATUS

To simplify our behaviour design, we intentionally limited our actuation mechanism, following the example of tradi-

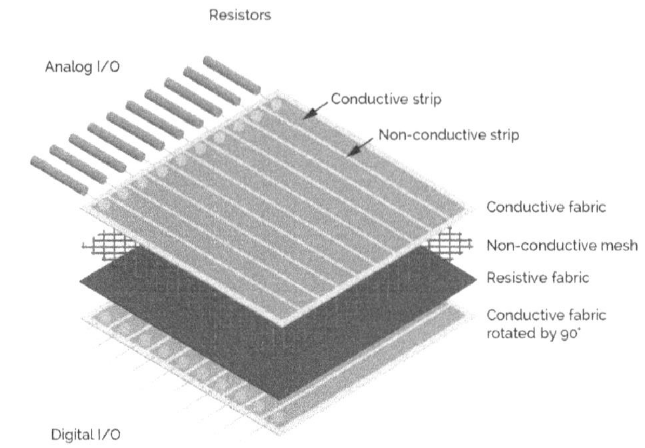

Figure 2: The fabric pressure sensor constructed out of EeonTex conductive fabric (www.eeonyx.com), wired to an Arduino microprocessor.

tional animation techniques[5] and other explorations' attribution of agency to 1-DOF robots[2][4]. The 'skeleton' (Fig. 1(b)) is constructed from flexible plastics to take advantage of the naturalism afforded by deformation and the back-drivability afforded by the material's elasticity. To avoid motor burnout and gear stripping from rough user interactions, the actuation is achieved through a servo motor that drives a pulley.

The touch sensor is constructed from two pieces of conductive piezo-resistive fabric separated by a non-conductive layer and oriented so as to make a 10x10 grid of 1 square-inch taxels (Fig. 2). It is designed to register touches within the range of reasonable social touch, roughly from 50 to 700 grams.

The gesture recognition system works by training a machine learning model on an a series of touch gestures such as 'rub', 'pat', or 'tickle'. Each gesture is recorded continuously and evaluated in 2 second windows. Each window contains roughly one instance of the gesture[1]. The gesture is then classified using a Random Forest model built from training data.

4. APPLICATIONS

A gesture-cognizant, flexible, pressure-sensitive sensor outfitted around a zoomorphic form in motion can be used in a number of scientific applications.

1. As a tool for studying affective touch interaction, the CuddleBit serves as a data collection device for quantitative measurements; with a gesture recognition system, it becomes useful for determining qualitative dimensions of touch semantics. It also serves as a haptic display device to close the interaction loop.

2. As a platform for examining the perceptual range of 1-DOF robot, the CuddleBit allows us to ask:

   (a) which emotions can this robot communicate?

   (b) whether this robot can communicate intention (i.e. does the robot want to be touched?)

   (c) what narratives do people build around the robot?

The above questions will help define the design space of a 1-DOF zoomorphic therapy robot and have direct implications for developing a more complex behavioural system.

5. DEMONSTRATION DESCRIPTION

During a demonstration, visitors will be able to interact with a member of a CuddleBit family as it 'breathes'. We will display the real-time results of the gesture recognition system along with a standalone version of the touch sensor and a touch visualization system. Certain touch gestures will incite behaviours associated with the CuddleBit's personality.

In informal evaluations, we found that supplying a narrative helped users understand how to interact with the CuddleBit. Therefore, our CuddleBit has a 'favourite' touch: it likes to be tickled —but not for too long. If any gesture is recognized consistently over an extended period of time, CuddleBit will shrink away. If it is struck, CuddleBit 'cowers'.

Visitors have an opportunity to experience the CuddleBit as a system where they influence the CuddleBit's behaviour and, hopefully, vice versa. When first approaching the robot, it will be breathing softly. Upon first contact, the CuddleBit will rise to meet the visitor's hand. As the interaction continues, the CuddleBit's body language will convey what the robot wants.

6. DEMONSTRATION REQUIREMENTS

We will require a table accommodating two demonstrators as well as a monitor and accompanying cables to display the visualizations including 2 power strips. One demonstrator will manage the gesture recognition model and the CuddleBits, while the other will manage the standalone sensor. We will bring two laptops, 2–3 touch sensors and CuddleBits.

7. ACKNOWLEDGEMENTS

We would like to thank the Natural Sciences and Engineering Research Council of Canada (NSERC) for providing partial support of this work.

8. REFERENCES

[1] A. Flagg and K. MacLean. Affective touch gesture recognition for a furry zoomorphic machine. In *Proc Intl Conf on Tangible, Embedded and Embodied Interaction*, pages 25–32, 2013.

[2] J. Harris and E. Sharlin. Exploring the affect of abstract motion in social human-robot interaction. In *RO-MAN, 2011 IEEE*, pages 441–448. IEEE, 2011.

[3] H. Y. Joung and E. Y.-L. Do. Tactile hand gesture recognition through haptic feedback for affective online communication. In *Universal Access in Human-Computer Interaction*, pages 555–563. Springer, 2011.

[4] M. Saerbeck and A. J. van Breemen. Design guidelines and tools for creating believable motion for personal robots. In *Robot and Human interactive Communication, 2007. RO-MAN 2007. The 16th IEEE International Symposium on*, pages 386–391. IEEE, 2007.

[5] F. Thomas, O. Johnston, and F. Thomas. *The illusion of life: Disney animation*. Hyperion New York, 1995.

Public Speaking Training with a Multimodal Interactive Virtual Audience Framework - Demonstration

Mathieu Chollet[1], Kalin Stefanov[2], Helmut Prendinger[3] and Stefan Scherer[4]
[1]Japan Society for the Promotion of Science, National Institute of Informatics, Tokyo, Japan
[2]KTH Royal Institute of Technology, Stockholm, Sweden
[3]National Institute of Informatics, Tokyo, Japan
[4]USC Institute for Creative Technologies, Los Angeles, CA, USA
mchollet@enst.fr, kalins@kth.se, scherer@ict.usc.edu, helmut@nii.ac.jp

ABSTRACT

We have developed an interactive virtual audience platform for public speaking training. Users' public speaking behavior is automatically analyzed using multimodal sensors, and ultimodal feedback is produced by virtual characters and generic visual widgets depending on the user's behavior. The flexibility of our system allows to compare different interaction mediums (*e.g.* virtual reality *vs* normal interaction), social situations (*e.g.* one-on-one meetings *vs* large audiences) and trained behaviors (*e.g.* general public speaking performance *vs* specific behaviors).

Categories and Subject Descriptors

H.1.2 [**User/Machine systems**]: [Human information processing];
I.5.4 [**Pattern Recognition Applications**]: Computer Vision, Signal Processing;
K.3.1 [**Computers and Education**]: Computers Uses in Education

Keywords

Virtual audience; public speaking training; automatic behavior recognition

1. INTRODUCTION

Interpersonal skills such as public speaking are essential assets for a large variety of professions and in everyday life. Nonverbal communication (affect, demeanor, posture, eye contact, speech tone and fluency) is a key aspect of successful public speaking and interpersonal communication [5]. Audiences provide indirect feedback during presentations by signaling nonverbally, as they continuously rate and sense the presenter's speaking style, such as nodding and leaning forward in presentations they enjoy, or averting their gaze when they are not interested [3]. Paying attention to these feedback behaviors allows speakers to improve their performance.

ICMI '15 November 09-13, 2015, Seattle, WA, USA

ACM 978-1-4503-3912-4/15/11.
http://dx.doi.org/10.1145/2818346.2823294.

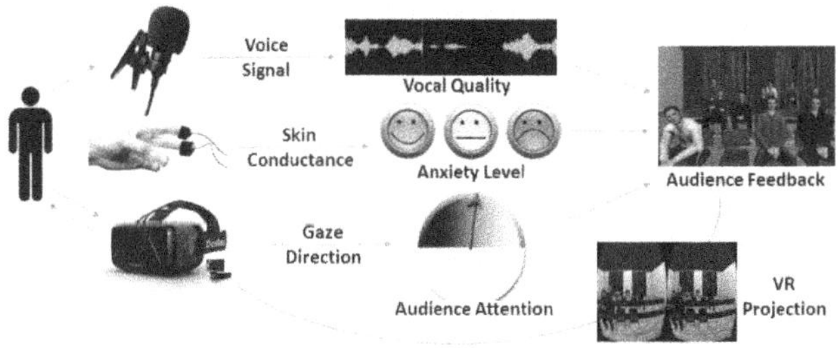

Figure 1: Architecture of our public speaking training system.

However, an actual human audience is not always available or sometimes too intimidating for an anxious speaker. Virtual audiences have already been used successfully in Virtual Reality Therapy (VRT) to mitigate public speaking anxiety [4]. Pushing further, we want to investigate if public speaking performance can be improved using virtual training.

In previous work [1], we built an interactive virtual audience framework for public speaking training which could provide indirect feedback to a user. It relied on a Wizard of Oz to provide input on the user's performance. In this demonstration, we present a fully automatic version of our virtual audience for public speaking training. Multimodal data is obtained from a variety of sensors (e.g. microphone, kinect, physiological sensors), and multimodal feedback is produced by the audience and visual widgets. Additionally, our system was updated to be compatible with a virtual reality headset.

2. SYSTEM ARCHITECTURE

Our public speaking training system consists of two main components: a multimodal signals perception framework, and a virtual environment populated with virtual characters acting as a virtual audience. We use a messaging system allowing for these two components to be distributed over multiple computers.

2.1 Perception framework

Our multimodal signals perception framework integrates signals obtained from a variety of sources. Raw data is analyzed to detect relevant signals or events, such as the oc-

currence of a gesture or the presence or absence of voice. Additionally, these signals can then feed classifiers to provide higher level information, such as the degree of attention the user gives to the audience, or an estimation of the presenter's anxiety. Examples of data sources that have been integrated include:
- *Depth* (*e.g.* Microsoft Kinect): posture, gestures, body activity, ...
- *Audio*: presence or absence of speech, Mel-frequency cepstral coefficients, vocal quality, ...
- *Video* (when not using a virtual reality headset): eyebrow movements, smiles, emotions, ...
- *Physiological*: heart rate, skin conductance, anxiety, ...

Moreover, other inputs or events from the virtual environment can be integrated as perceptual inputs. For instance, the virtual reality headset can provide the head direction of the user and therefore an approximation of his or her gaze direction. Interactions with an integrated slideshow can be used as an indication as whether the presenter is running late or is still on time with the presentation total time.

2.2 Virtual audience

A virtual environment consisting of a presentation room with a slide screen and three layers of chairs has been created within the Unity 3D engine. The layout of the virtual audience (*e.g.* amount of characters, their appearances and their distribution) can be easily customized.

The virtual audience's characters' behavior is driven by the multimodal inputs presented earlier. Each character is assigned a behavior profile, which is a set of rules of the following tuple: $< Descriptor; Signals; Conditions >$. The *Descriptor* refers to the ID of one of the perceptual inputs presented earlier. The *Signals* item represents a behavioral response to be produced by the virtual character when the value of *Descriptor* meets the defined *Conditions*. For instance, in the following example, the character will shake its head when the user has looked at the audience less than half of the time:

$< gaze\_audience,\ < head\ type = "shake" / >,\ in(0, 0.5) >$

Generic visual widgets can also be used to provide direct feedback to the user about his or her performance. For instance, a colored bar can be displayed on top of the screen, directly reflecting the user's performance (*e.g* a full green bar can indicate good performance, whereas a short red bar indicates poor performance), similarly to [2]. Finally, a post-hoc printout of the measured behaviors can be produced to allow the user to reflect on his or her performance.

2.3 Demonstration scenario

For this demonstration, we have designed a public speaking training scenario aimed at training for research conference presentations. Custom slides can be loaded within the virtual environment, allowing a user to train presenting his or her own material. The virtual characters react to the following aspects:

1-*Amount of gaze directed at the audience*: presenters should look at the audience rather than at their slides. Head direction data obtained from the VR headset allows to compute whether the user hasn't looked at the audience for a long time. When that happens, virtual characters signal the user by clearing their throats.

2-*Body activity*: an appropriate amount of gesturing and movement is better while speaking in public. Our perception framework provides a measure of body activity derived from depth data. This measure is used to affect the virtual character's postural behavior: if the user is too active or too passive, the characters lean back in disagreement.

3-*Heart rate*: The user's heart rate or anxiety level can be directly displayed using a visual feedback item (*e.g.* smiling face if the heart rate is in a normal range, sad face if it is elevated).

3. CONCLUSION

We presented a public speaking training system based on an interactive virtual audience framework. Its design is focused on flexibility allowing to easily modify training conditions, audience layouts, trained behaviors and feedback types. In particular, the multiplicity of integrated multimodal sensors allow to detect various types of behaviors, in turn being interpreted into various measures of performance or affect. Multimodal feedback can be produced in realtime according to these behaviors and higher level measures, by virtual characters and generic visual widgets, or after the presentation with a post-hoc printout. Additionally, the system can be used with regular displays or with virtual reality headsets. In future work, we will use this prototype to investigate the efficacy of virtual audiences for the training of public speaking and other related social skills, such as job interviews or conducting meetings. In particular, we will compare and assess which training conditions (e.g. virtual reality *vs* regular interaction) and modalities of feedback (*e.g.* normal audience behavior *vs* exaggerated behavior, such as falling asleep) are the most efficient for improving users' skills.

4. ACKNOWLEDGMENTS

This material is partly supported by the JSPS (Japan Society for the Promotion of Science) and the National Science Foundation under Grant No. IIS-1421330.

5. REFERENCES

[1] M. Chollet, T. Wörtwein, L.-P. Morency, A. Shapiro, and S. Scherer. Exploring feedback strategies to improve public speaking: An interactive virtual audience framework. In *Proceedings of UbiComp'15*, 2015.

[2] I. Damian, C. S. S. Tan, T. Baur, J. Schöning, K. Luyten, and E. André. Augmenting social interactions: Realtime behavioural feedback using social signal processing techniques. In *Proceedings of CHI'15*, pages 565–574. ACM, 2015.

[3] P. D. MacIntyre, K. A. Thivierge, and J. R. MacDonald. The effects of audience interest, responsiveness, and evaluation on public speaking anxiety and related variables. *Communication Research Reports*, 14(2):157–168, 1997.

[4] D.-P. Pertaub, M. Slater, and C. Barker. An experiment on public speaking anxiety in response to three different types of virtual audience. *Presence: Teleoperators and Virtual Environments*, 11(1):68–78, Feb. 2002.

[5] E. Strangert and J. Gustafson. What makes a good speaker? subject ratings, acoustic measurements and perceptual evaluations. In *Interspeech*, page 1688–1691. ISCA, 2008.

A Multimodal System for Public Speaking with Real Time Feedback

Fiona Dermody
Dublin City University
Dublin, Ireland
Fiona.Dermody3@mail.dcu.ie

Alistair Sutherland
Dublin City University
Dublin, Ireland
Alistair.Sutherland@dcu.ie

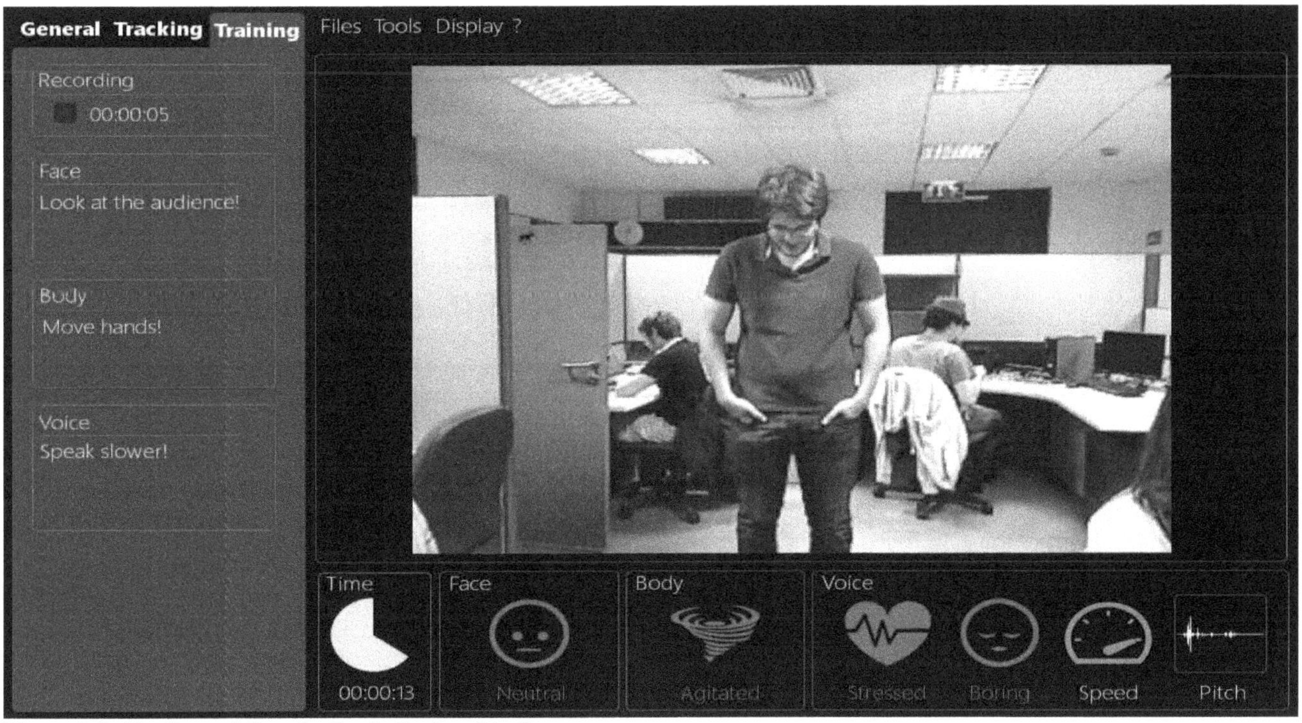

Figure 1: Indicative real time feedback displayed to the user

ABSTRACT

We have developed a multimodal prototype for public speaking with real time feedback using the Microsoft Kinect. Effective speaking involves use of gesture, facial expression, posture, voice as well as the spoken word. These modalities combine to give the appearance of self-confidence in the speaker. This initial prototype detects body pose, facial expressions and voice. Visual and text feedback is displayed in real time to the user using a video panel, icon panel and text feedback panel. The user can also set and view elapsed time during their speaking performance. Real time feedback is displayed on gaze direction, body pose and gesture, vocal tonality, vocal dysfluencies and speaking rate.

ICMI '15, November 09-13, 2015, Seattle, WA, USA
ACM 978-1-4503-3912-4/15/11.
http://dx.doi.org/10.1145/2818346.2823295

Categories and Subject Descriptors

H.5.2. Information interfaces and presentation (e.g., HCI): User Interfaces; Evaluation/methodology; Screen Design; User-centered design;

General Terms

Design, Human Factors.

Keywords

Multimodal Interface; Affective Computing; Human Computer Interaction; Social Signal Processing; Public Speaking.

1. INTRODUCTION

Previous systems such as [1] have provided feedback on all speaking modalities such as voice, gestures and stance but not in real time. We believe that public speaking is a multimodal task that requires a multimodal system with real time feedback [2].

2. OVERVIEW OF PROTOTYPE

An initial prototype has been developed based on the results of a user survey. The prototype can give feedback to the users while they are speaking in real time. The user can select if they want textual feedback or visual feedback or both. We can easily vary the size and color of the textual feedback. The user can also select which combination of speaking modalities they want to receive feedback on. For example, they may elect to receive feedback on their facial expressions only. Alternatively, they may receive feedback on facial expressions, voice and gestures simultaneously. The user can also record their speech and review it afterwards getting more detailed feedback offline. The user can choose to view their speech as live video or as an animated avatar. This enables the user to develop an awareness of how they would appear speaking before an audience. This multimodal interface prototype also contains video tutorials on good speaking practices. It contains example sequences, which the user can imitate and the system gives feedback of the accuracy of their imitation. For example, they could be asked to perform a certain sequence of gestures or they could be asked to vary the pitch of their voice at key moments in the speech. Users will develop the skill of speaking within a certain time limit as the interface has a clock. The clock will give them a visual warning as they approach the end of their allotted timespan.

PROTOTYPE COMPONENTS

2.1 Video Panel

1. The video panel is in the center of the screen and can display the following things
2. A live video of the user performing in front of the Kinect
3. A 3D computer-graphic avatar, which mimics the user's movements. The avatar also has a face which can mimic the user's facial expressions. The limbs of the avatar change color, in order to show whether the Kinect is detecting them or not.
4. A 2D stick man, which tracks the user's movements. This is standard software provided by the Kinect but most users find it difficult to interpret.
5. Recorded videos of the user's performance. The user can use these to review their performance and receive more detailed feedback. The user can pause and rewind the video. They can also review past performances to see how much they have improved.
6. Pre-recorded instructional videos created by a human expert. The user can also view example speeches made by famous orators.
7. The user can select which of the above will be displayed.

2.2 Text Feedback Panel

This sidebar on the left-hand side of the screen contains three textboxes- one for feedback on the face, one for the body and one for the voice. Each box can display several lines of text.

2.3 Icon Feedback Panel

The panel on the bottom of the screen displays feedback in the form of visual icons. There is an icon for the each of face, body and voice. There is also

1. a speedometer, which displays the user's word rate in words per minute. It changes color, if the user is speaking too fast or too slow.
2. a stopwatch, which displays how many minutes and seconds to the end of the allotted time. It changes color to alert the user, when there is, say, one minute left.
3. a pitch-spectrum, which displays the pitch levels of the user's voice

3. TYPES OF FEEDBACK

3.1 Gaze Direction

By detecting the user's gaze direction the system can assess whether the user is engaging different sections of the audience. Gaze direction could also be used to express emotions e.g. looking up could express aspiration, looking down could express humility.

3.2 Body Pose and Gestures

Currently the system can recognize simple body poses such as "hands touching/ hands apart". This allows the system to give feedback on whether the user is making the appropriate gesture at the right time. It will also assess whether the user is moving around on the stage or just standing rigidly in one spot. It will assess whether the user is engaging different sections of the audience by turning the body in different directions. In contrast, the system can also assess whether the user is moving too quickly or is too agitated – perhaps swaying from side to side.

3.3 Vocal Tonality and Dysfluencies

The system can detect monotonous voice. If there is little variation in the pitch of the user's voice, the system will display feedback. It can also detect vocal dysfluencies or 'crutch words' such as 'um' and 'ah'. Speaking rate is also detected as the system can detect the number of words per minute. Feedback on speaking rate is displayed via the speedometer.

4. CONCLUSION

We have developed a multimodal prototype interface to enable a user to develop their skill in public speaking. The initial prototype has been designed using the Microsoft Kinect. It can detect body pose, facial expressions and voice. This multimodal interface will give feedback to the user on their speaking performance in real time.

5. ACKNOWLEDGMENTS

This material is based upon works supported by Dublin City University under the Daniel O'Hare Research Scholarship scheme. This prototype was developed in collaboration with interns from École Polytechnique de l'Université Paris-Sud and l'École Supérieure d'Informatique, Électronique, Automatique (ESIEA) France.

6. REFERENCES

[1] Batrinca, L. *et al*. 2013. Cicero - Towards a Multimodal Virtual Audience Platform for Public Speaking Training. Intelligent Virtual Agents. R. Aylett *et al*., eds. Springer Berlin Heidelberg. 116–128.

[2] Dermody, F. *et al*. 2015. A Multi-Modal System for Public Speaking - Pilot Study on evaluation of real-time feedback. INTERACT 2015, Part IV, LNCS 9299. J. Abascal *et al*., eds. Springer Berlin Heidelberg. 3–5. DOI: 10.1007/978-3-319-22723-8_47.

Model of Personality-Based, Nonverbal Behavior in Affective Virtual Humanoid Character

Maryam Saberi
Simon Fraser University
Vancouver, Canada
msaberi@sfu.ca

Ulysses Bernardet
Simon Fraser University
Vancouver, Canada
ubernard@sfu.ca

Steve DiPaola
Simon Fraser University,
Vancouver, Canada
sdipaola@sfu.ca

ABSTRACT
In this demonstration a human user interacts with a virtual humanoid character in real-time. Our goal is to create a character that is perceived as imbued with a distinct personality while responding dynamically to inputs from the environment [4] [1]. A hybrid model that comprises continuous and discrete components, firstly, drives the logical behavior of the virtual character moving through states of the interaction, and secondly, continuously updates of the emotional expressions of the virtual character depending on feedback from interactions with the environment. A Rock-Paper-Scissors game scenario is used as framework for the interaction scenario and provides an easy-to-learn and engaging demo environment with minimum conversation.

Categories and Subject Descriptors
H.5.1 [**Information Interfaces and Presentation**]: Multimedia Information Systems Animations – *Artificial, augmented, and virtual realities.*

General Terms
Design, Experimentation, Human Factors, Theory

Keywords
Personality-Based behavior; Virtual humanoid character; Turned-based interaction; Hybrid model

1. INTRODUCTION
Characteristics of nonverbal behavior such as the speed of hand movements or frequency of smiling have an important effect on what personality we attribute to a person. Likewise, during human and virtual humanoid character interaction, people attribute personality to virtual characters by relying on clues from their nonverbal behavior [3]. Yet, in many models designed for virtual humanoid characters, nonverbal behavior of the virtual characters are generated for communication purposes and discrete decision making processes while ignoring the importance of personality in the generation of behavior. This leads to virtual humanoid characters with behaviors that are not consistent through time and do not follow human behavioral patterns. Our goal is to develop a psychologically grounded computational model for generating nonverbal behavior to express personality for virtual humanoid characters. An important aspect offered by our model, which is missing from the most affective models, is the possibility of real-time interaction between users and virtual characters [2] [3]. Additionally, the modular structure and model-level access to the components of the model facilitates its further use and extend. Our problem domain is narrowed down to content-free (no speech involved), turn-taking and strategy-based interaction.

ICMI 2015, November 9–13, 2015, Seattle, WA, USA.
ACM 978-1-4503-3912-4/15/11.
DOI: http://dx.doi.org/10.1145/2818346.2823296

2. MODEL ARCHITECTURE
In our model personality traits have a modulatory influence at four levels: 1) Personality parameters affect the generation of non-verbal behavior such as gestures. As a result, low level parameters such as speed of the movements and expressed facial expression are affected by personality. 2) Different personalities affect the level of filtering of emotions. Not all the internal emotions are revealed through facial expressions to users. 3) Different personality parameters affect the coping behavior of the virtual character. For instance, introvert virtual character behaves more passively in coping situations. 4) Personality affects emotional reactions of the virtual character (see Figure 1).

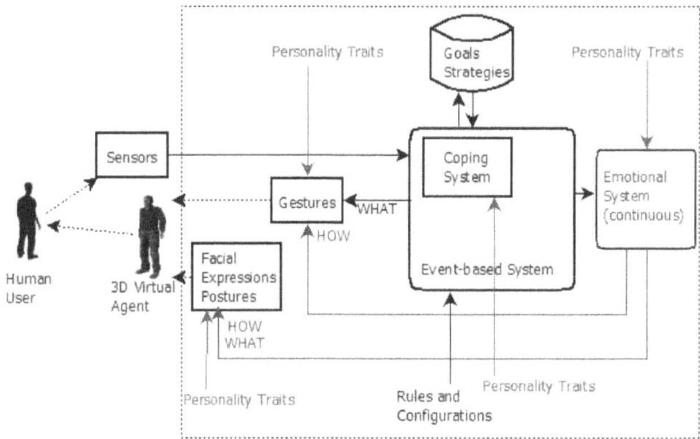

Figure 1: Architecture of the proposed model

The model consists of two main components being an "Emotionally-Continuous" system and an "Event-based" system. In conjunction, the Emotionally-Continuous system and the Event-based system generate the gestures, postures and facial expressions that are expressing personality. The Event-based system is responsible for the logic and flow of the interaction. It determines which gestures should be generated based on rules and configuration parameters defined at the beginning or during the interaction. Opposite to communicative gestures, which are triggered when an environmental event is triggered, emotions are continuously updated based on internal and outside status.

3. DEMO SETUP
Rock-Paper-Scissors game is proposed as a demo scenario with the goal of creating an easy-to-learn and engaging scenario that provides an interactive demonstrator with minimum conversation.

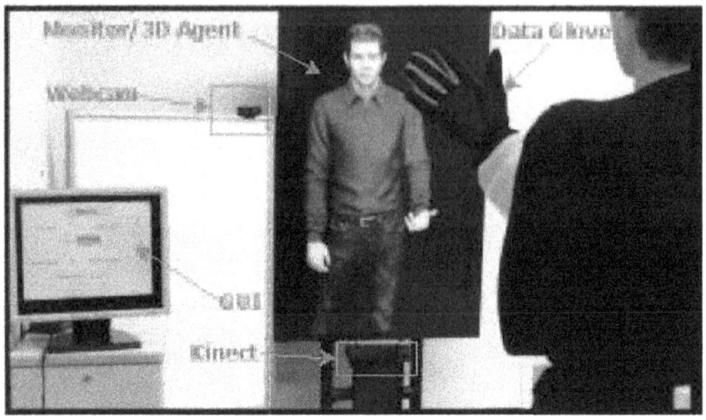

Figure 2: Demonstration of the experiment setup

The demo user stands in front of a monitor displaying a virtual character [5] (see Figure 2). In each game session, 10 rounds of Rock-Paper-Scissors are played between the user and the character. In each round, a graphical user interface (GUI) announces Ready, Go commands to synchronize the game. At the end of the round, it displays who wins the game. The character's hand gestures (rock, paper or scissors) are generated randomly. A data glove sensor is designed to capture the hand gesture of the user. A webcam feeds the facial information of the demo user to SHORE application to detect user's smile [1]. Microsoft Kinect 2.0 feeds the joint information of the user to the system.

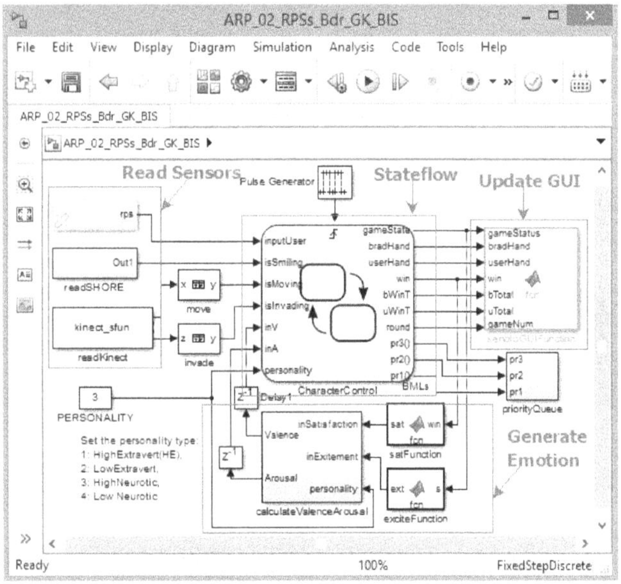

Figure 3: A screenshot of the system (Simulink /Matlab)

Matlab continuously reads the values of sensors, goes though states of interaction, updates the GUI, generate emotional response and sends behavior commands to the behavior realizer (see Figure 3). Using Kinect data, the system locates the user. Additionally, the character's gaze follows the user as she/he moves in the scene and if the user is coming too close or moves too far, the character adjust his personal space by moving forward or backward. Smartbody an academic 3D character animation toolkit is used as our animation rendering system which provides locomotion, gazing and nonverbal behavior in real time under our scripted control via the Behavior Markup Language (BML) [5][6]. Movement + Meaning (m+m) is used as a platform to facilitate acquiring data, managing and rendering movement data (see Figure 4). Key features of the m+m middleware are portability between platforms, low latency and high bandwidth (http://mplusm.ca).

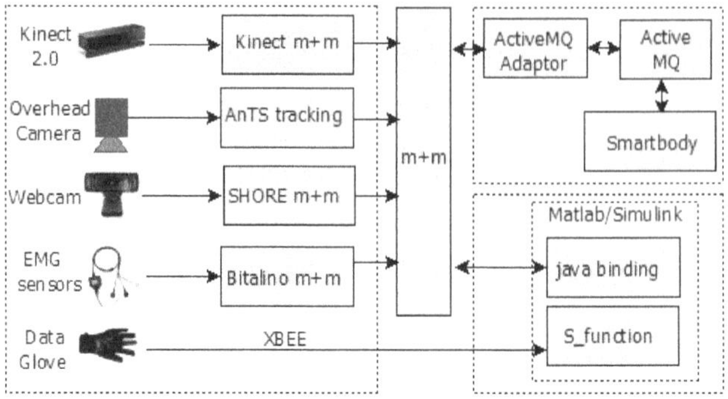

Figure 4: Movement and Meaning (m+m) platform is used to facilitate acquisition, process, and render of movement data.

4. CONCLUSION

We introduce a setup for real-time human and virtual humanoid character interaction. Our goal is to create a character with a distinct personality that responds dynamically to inputs from the environment [4] [1]. Two main components of our proposed model, Emotionally-Continuous system and the Event-based system, in conjunction generate the gestures and facial expressions that express personality. Different aspects of our model can be extended and enriched in future. Using m+m framework, our system has the possibility to feed more channels of inputs from the environment such as noises and light changes. Being responsive to users' gestures and emotions can also enrich the experience.

5. ACKNOWLEDGMENTS

This work is built as a part of and is beneficial for SFU SSHRC / Canarie research projects: Moving Stories and Movement and Meaning research.

6. REFERENCES

[1] Brinkman, Willem-Paul, Joost Broekens, and Dirk Heylen, eds. Intelligent Virtual Agents: 15thInternationalConference, IVA 2015, Delft, The Netherlands, August 26-28, 2015, Proceedings. Vol. 9238. Springer, pages 488-489, 2015.

[2] Lim, Mei Yii, et al. "Creating adaptive affective autonomous NPCs." Autonomous Agents and Multi-Agent Systems 24.2 (2012): 287-311.

[3] McRorie, Margaret, et al. "Evaluation of four designed virtual agent personalities." Affective Computing, IEEE Transactions on 3.3 (2012): 311-322.

[4] Saberi, Maryam, Ulysses Bernardet, and Steve DiPaola. "An Architecture for Personality-based, Nonverbal Behavior in Affective Virtual Humanoid Character." Procedia Computer Science 41 (2014): 204-211.

[5] Thiebaux, Marcus, et al. "Smartbody: Behavior realization for embodied conversational agents." Proceedings of the 7th international joint conference on Autonomous agents and multiagent systems-Volume 1. International Foundation for Autonomous Agents and Multiagent Systems, 2008.

[6] Kopp, Stefan, et al. "Towards a common framework for multimodal generation: The behavior markup language." Intelligent virtual agents. Springer Berlin Heidelberg, 2006.

AttentiveLearner: Adaptive Mobile MOOC Learning via Implicit Cognitive States Inference

Xiang Xiao, Phuong Pham, Jingtao Wang
Computer Science and LRDC, University of Pittsburgh, PA, USA
{xiangxiao, phuongpham, jingtaow}@cs.pitt.edu

ABSTRACT

This demo presents AttentiveLearner, a mobile learning system optimized for consuming lecture videos in Massive Open Online Courses (MOOCs) and flipped classrooms. AttentiveLearner uses on-lens finger gestures for video control and captures learners' physiological states through implicit heart rate tracking on unmodified mobile phones. Through three user studies to date, we found AttentiveLearner easy to learn, and intuitive to use. The heart beat waveforms captured by AttentiveLearner can be used to infer learners' cognitive states and attention. AttentiveLearner may serve as a promising supplemental feedback channel orthogonal to today's learning analytics technologies.

Categories and Subject Descriptors
H5.2 [**Information interfaces and presentation**]: User Interfaces – *Graphical user interfaces, theory and methods.*

General Terms
Design; Experimentation; Human Factors.

Keywords

Mobile Interfaces; Affective Computing; Massive Open Online Courses; MOOC; Heart Rate; Intelligent Tutoring Systems; Physiological Signals.

1. INTRODUCTION
Massive Open Online Courses (MOOCs) are growing rapidly in recent years and provide great opportunities to low-cost knowledge dissemination on a large scale. Despite the great potential, MOOCs today also face major challenges such as low completion rates, more frequent distractions, separation of learning and assessment activities, and the lack of direct, immediate feedback from students to instructors. Different from traditional classrooms, MOOC instructors can no longer rely on facial expressions or in-class behaviors to infer student engagement. Although feedback forms and learner activity logs (e.g. log-in frequency, click-through rates, and video drop-out rates) can be used to predict the quality of learning, such measurements are usually coarse-grained, highly delayed, and indirect measurements of the actual cognitive process in learning.

To explore the possibility of collecting and using fine-grained, real-time feedback from students' actual cognitive states in MOOC learning, we demonstrate AttentiveLearner, a mobile learning system that captures students' physiological signals through implicit heart rate tracking on unmodified mobile phones. AttentiveLearner uses on-lens finger gestures for tangible video control and implicitly monitors learners' heart rates based on the fingertip transparency changes captured by the back camera. We demonstrate the feasibility of inferring learners' cognitive states (e.g., mind wandering events and perceived interest/confusion levels regarding the learning materials) by analyzing the collected heart rate signals. With the low cost inference of learners' cognitive states during MOOC sessions, AttentiveLearner has the potential to enable adaptive tutoring on today's mobile phones (e.g., "mind wandering" alert, personalized learning materials). AttentiveLearner can also benefit instructors by providing fine-grained, aggregated feedback of learners' physiological, and cognitive states synchronized with the learning materials.

2. METHOD
AttentiveLearner allows learners to consume MOOC videos on mobile phones during fragmented time. There are three major components in AttentiveLearner: a tangible video control channel, an implicit heart rate sensing module, and the cognitive state inference algorithms.

2.1 Tangible Video Control
With AttentiveLearner, a learner plays a tutorial video by covering and holding the back camera lens with her fingertip, uncovering the lens to pause the video (**Figure 1**). The lens-covering gesture is detected via a linear classifier on the global mean and standard deviation of all pixels in an incoming image frame [5]. Offline benchmarking on 483 test images achieved an accuracy of 99.59% when detecting lens-covering gestures [5].

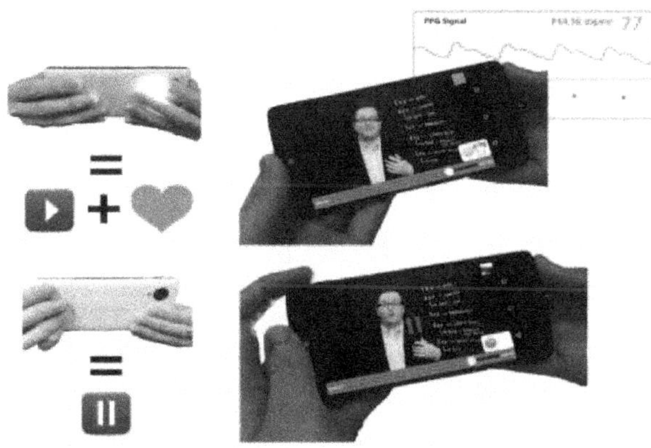

Figure 1. The back camera as both a video play control channel and an implicit heart rate sensing channel in learning

In an 18-participant study on the usability of the tangible video control channel [5], we found this channel was responsive (mean response time = 625.9ms) and easy to use (average = 4.11 on a

ICMI '15, November 09-13, 2015, Seattle, WA, USA
ACM 978-1-4503-3912-4/15/11.
http://dx.doi.org/10.1145/2818346.2823297

five-point Likert scale). We also found participants preferred each video clip to be less than eight minutes in length [5] when using AttentiveLearner.

2.2 Implicit Heart Rate Sensing

AttentiveLearner captures learners' heart rate implicitly during learning via commodity camera based photoplethysmography (PPG). AttentiveLearner uses the PPG waveform extraction algorithm in LivePulse [2] for heart rate measurement. In addition to learners' beat-to-beat instant heart rate, AttentiveLearner also extracts both temporal and frequency domain features from the raw PPG waveforms captured.

2.3 Cognitive States Inference

We also conducted two additional experiments [4][5] to explore the feasibility of using raw PPG waveforms captured by AttentiveLearner to infer learners' attention [4] and cognitive states [5].

In a 24-participant study, Pham and Wang [4] found it was possible to detect learners' mind wandering (MW) events via AttentiveLearner. Both lecture content features and PPG waveform features were extracted from sliding windows (window size = 30s with 5s step) before each prediction moment (**Figure 2a**). We extracted 7 dimension lecture content features including lecture style, duration of current page etc. PPG waveform features include 12 heart rate and heart rate variability (HRV) features, e.g. mean of RR intervals and low frequency of RR intervals (0.04 – 0.15 Hz). The ground truths were obtained by randomly triggering audio beeps (auditory probes) to acquire learners' attention status (MW or not) during each video watching session. The best model (KNN) achieved Kappa=0.22, accuracy=71.2% on MW prediction.

More recently, in an 18-participant study, Xiao and Wang [5] demonstrated the feasibility of predicting learners' interest and confusion levels in MOOC learning via content-agnostic features. 14 time-domain HRV features from PPG signal, including 7 global features (extracted globally from the entire section) and 7 local features (extracted by averaging the same features of multiple local windows within the section), were extracted from the raw PPG waveforms of each topic session (**Figure 2b**). The ground truth labels were obtained via self-reports collected immediately after each learning topic. The best prediction performances were Kappa=0.29, accuracy=73.58% for boredom detection and Kappa=0.27, accuracy=77.69% for confusion detection respectively, using RBF-kernel support vector machines. Furthermore, AttentiveLearner can achieve significantly higher accuracies by predicting *extreme personal learning events* and *aggregated learning events*.

These results were user-independent, achieved on today's mobile phones without hardware modifications. The performances on cognitive states inference were also comparable with state-of-the-art systems using dedicated sensors, such as Blanchard et al. [1] (learner dependent model, kappa=0.22 for MW detection) or Hussain et al. [3] (learner dependent model, kappa=0.31 for arousal classification). In the demo session, we will provide a live demonstration of AttentiveLearner on tangible video control, implicit PPG waveform extraction, and cognitive states prediction.

3. USAGE SCENARIOS

AttentiveLearner improves mobile MOOC learning by enabling attentive and bi-directional learning on unmodified mobile phones. It is worth noting that the lens covering gesture-based control and implicit heart rate measurement can be embedded in different mobile applications and learners can comfortably watch a normal length MOOC video lecture (less than 8 minutes) [5].

From the learners' perspective, AttentiveLearner can enable adaptive and personalized learning by recommending appropriate review materials and exercises based on the learners' attention and interest levels during corresponding learning topics.

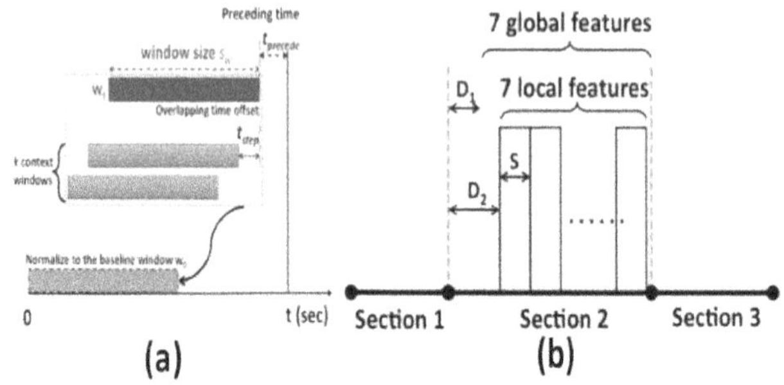

Figure 2. (a) Features from sliding windows before a prediction; (b) features from the entire session and its sliding windows

From the instructors' perspective, AttentiveLearner can provide fine-grained, aggregated visualizations of learners' cognitive states and attention levels synchronized with the lecture contents. Such visualizations can facilitate instructors to identify and reflect upon topics requiring further improvements in the current curriculum. Instructors may also use AttentiveLearner to take "virtual attendance" in flipped classrooms, where around 50% of the students do not watch the required video materials before each lecture according to a recent survey.

4. CONCLUSION

We presented AttentiveLearner, a mobile learning system to monitor learners' cognitive states during mobile MOOC learning via implicit heart rate tracking. The on-lens gesture interface in AttentiveLearner enables both tangible video control and implicit heart rate tracking on today's unmodified smart phones. We hope AttentiveLearner can facilitate and promote the use of physiological signals in large scale learning analytics in MOOCs and flipped classrooms. Additional introductions and demos of AttentiveLearner are available at http://www.attentivelearner.com.

This research is in part supported by an RDF from the Learning Research and Development Center at the University of Pittsburgh.

5. REFERENCES

[1] Blanchard, N., Bixler, R., Joyce, T., D'Mello, S. Automated physiological-based detection of mind wandering during learning. In *Proc. ITS 2014.*

[2] Han, T., Xiao, X., Shi, L., Canny, J., and Wang, J. Balancing accuracy and fun: designing camera based mobile games for implicit heart rate monitoring. In *Proc. CHI 2015.*

[3] Hussain, M. S., AlZoubi, O., Calvo, R. A., and D'Mello, S. K. Affect detection from multichannel physiology during learning sessions with AutoTutor. In Proc. *AIED 2011.*

[4] Pham, P., and Wang, J. AttentiveLearner: improving mobile MOOC learning via implicit heart rate tracking. In *Proc. AIED 2015*, pp367-376.

[5] Xiao, X., and Wang, J. Towards Attentive, Bi-directional MOOC Learning on Mobile Phones. In *Proc. ICMI 2015.*

Interactive Web-based Image Sonification for the Blind

Torsten Wörtwein
uncwt@student.kit.edu

Karin E. Mueller
karin.e.mueller@kit.edu

Boris Schauerte
schauerte@kit.edu

Rainer Stiefelhagen
rainer.stiefelhagen@kit.edu

Karlsruhe Institute of Technology
Vincenz-Prießnitz-Str. 3
76131 Karlsruhe

ABSTRACT

In this demonstration, we show a web-based sonification platform that allows blind users to interactively experience various information using two nowadays widespread technologies: modern web browsers that implement high-level JavaScript APIs and touch-sensitive displays. This way, blind users can easily access information such as, for example, maps or graphs. Our current prototype provides various sonifications that can be switched depending on the image type and user preference. The prototype runs in Chrome and Firefox on PCs, smart phones, and tablets.

Categories and Subject Descriptors

K.4.2 [**Computers And Society**]: Social Issues—*Assistive technologies for persons with disabilities*; I.4.9 [**Image Processing And Computer Vision**]: Applications

General Terms

Human Factors, Experimentation

Keywords

Sonification; Interactive; Blind; Assistive Technology; Web; Mobile; Image Processing

1. INTRODUCTION

The World Health Organisation estimates that 285 million visually impaired people live in the world of which 39 million are blind. The unfortunate fact that the majority of blind people lives in developing countries in combination with the aging global elderly population leads to a huge innovation pressure for affordable and intuitive tools that aid visually impaired people. With the decreasing costs of mobile computing power in the form of tablets and smart phones, computer-based assistive technologies become increasingly affordable and cheaper than traditional means of assistance. For example, blind users commonly access graphical information using tactile graphics printed by a tactile embosser, which cost between US$1,500 and US$150,000. For comparison, Android-powered tablets can be bought for less than US$100 and modern web browsers are free, which makes mobile technologies interesting for cost-effective and easy-to-use assistive systems.

We present our prototype of a web-based image sonification platform, see Fig. 1. We implemented the system based on Javascript and modern Web APIs. This allows our system to operate on desktop PCs as well as mobile devices, with mouse and touchscreen support. We use image processing and computer vision techniques to (pre-)process the image and map the image content to sounds with support for interactive exploration of the image. The exact sonification method depends on the category of the image material and, of course, user preferences. Our system already allows the sonification of various image categories (e.g., maps, graphs, charts, diagrams, and pictures of art) and can easily be extended to support further sonifications (e.g., different means to sonify low-level or task-specific information).

Figure 1: Our web-based user interface. The content of the area within the dotted border is sonified. New images can be loaded by drag-and-drop or a menu. The sonification method and parameters can be selected and changed during runtime by a menu. Our system works on tablets, smart phones, and PCs.

2. SYSTEM

One of our goals is to allow easy access to graphical information for blind users all over the world. For this purpose, we chose to implement our sonification system in Javascript with modern web browsers such as Firefox and Chrome as

ICMI 2015, November 9–13, 2015, Seattle, WA, USA.
ACM 978-1-4503-3912-4/15/11.
DOI: http://dx.doi.org/10.1145/2818346.2823298 .

target platforms. This has several advantages such as: (1.) Users do not have to install special software, since we rely on their readily available web browser. (2.) Although there are technological differences between web browsers themselves and web browsers across platforms such as Android and Windows, the sonification does not depend on the chosen platform, which means that blind users hear the same sounds regardless of whether they use a PC, tablet, or mobile phone. Both aspects also mean that it is less problematic to use our system across different platforms, at work, or on another person's PC or tablet. Furthermore, since our system is a website, it can be accessed from all around the world.

Our implementation relies on the W3C Web Audio API [3], which is encapsulated by the Timbre.js library [1] and allows us to synthesize arbitrary sounds at runtime. Currently, we only synthesize artificial sounds and do not use, for example, musical instruments for sonification. However, the current implementation of the Web Audio API has a major drawback for our application: It does not offer real-time guarantees, which often means that there are noticable delays between the mouse/finger movement and the sonification of the image content at the mouse/finger (cursor) location. In several preliminary studies, we noticed that this significantly irritates users – especially if unaware about the fact – and leads to problems when trying to identify shapes and details with swift finger movements.

Our sonification system follows a pipeline model (image pre-processing, image processing / computer vision, map the information to sound, and sound post-processing), of which all elements are implemented in Javascript and run in the user's browser. First, the input image is pre-processed, which can include blurring (*e.g.*, to reduce noise and abstract the image details) or thresholding as preprocessing step for a distance transformation. Then, the image is processed using image processing and computer vision methods to precompute a map that encodes the auditory signal that we present to the user at a given cursor position. Here, the exact type of image processing depends on the image category (*e.g.*, natural images or graphs) and the user preference (*i.e.*, what does the user want to hear?). For example, we provide the distance transform as a basic sonification for two image categories: (1.) To sonify the distance to the nearest wall when exploring floor maps and (2.) to sonify the distance to the curve of a graph, which makes it simple to follow the curve with the finger. Then, we map image information onto frequencies (*e.g.*, luminance range to a frequency range, or distance to curve to a frequency range with a specified cut-off level) and can combine various sources of information with different combination schemes (*e.g.*, additive mix or overtones). The generated sound is then post-processed, for example, with a Hz to mel transformation [2].

Additionally, we capture click events to allow further user interaction. For example, we implemented a form of "sonar" that sonifies the distance (sampled in a pre-specified number of directions) from the current cursor position to the walls in a floor map. Moreover, we implemented the ability for text-to-speech in the browser and can also provide speech output to the user (*e.g.*, the name of the color at the current cursor position).

3. EXPERIMENTS

We have performed several experiments with various participants (see Fig. 2), including born blind persons. So far, all users had normal hearing and experience with touchscreens. We currently focus our development and thus experiments on three tasks:

Mathematical graphs Allow users to identify the underlying function of a presented graph.

Charts Allow users to interpret the information in charts such as, e.g., bar charts.

Floor maps Allow users to navigate on floor maps, e.g. to find the way through a corridor from one room to another on such a floor map.

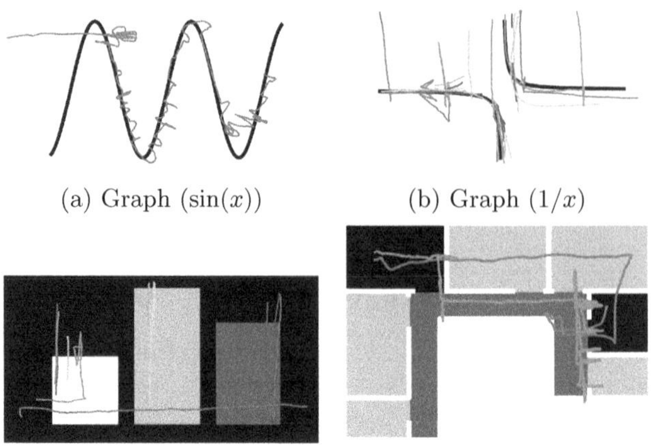

(a) Graph ($\sin(x)$) (b) Graph ($1/x$)

(c) Bar chart (d) Floor map

Figure 2: Examples that illustrate some experimental stimuli and tasks. The colored lines represent the finger movements of one participant.

It is interesting that even untrained users are able to correctly solve such graph identification, chart interpretation, and floor map navigation tasks with very high accuracy (consistently higher than 80%). We asked several users to repeatedly report aspects such as intuitiveness and ease of sound interpretation. Even after few uses, the users rated our system as being highly intuitive to use and the generated sonification as being easy to interpret. These already high ratings increased as the duration with which they used our system.

4. CONCLUSION

We present an interactive sonification platform based on modern web technologies and off-the-shelf hardware, which means that our system is just an URL away from blind users all around the world. In preliminary experiments, we have shown that our system is intuitive to use and allows to accomplish different tasks even with a minimal amount of training.

5. REFERENCES

[1] Mohayonao. Timbre.js. `http://mohayonao.github.io/timbre.js/`, 2015. Online; accessed 21 August 2015.

[2] S. S. Stevens, J. Volkmann, and E. B. Newman. A scale for the measurement of the psychological magnitude pitch. *The Journal of the Acoustical Society of America*, 8(3):185–190, 1937.

[3] W3C. Web Audio API. `http://www.w3.org/TR/webaudio/`, 2015. Online; accessed 21 August 2015.

Nakama: A Companion for Non-verbal Affective Communication

Christian J.A.M. Willemse[1, 2]
[1]University of Twente
P.O. Box 217, 7500 AE, Enschede, The Netherlands
c.j.a.m.willemse@utwente.nl

Gerald M. Munters[1]
g.m.munters@student.utwente.nl

Jan B.F. van Erp[1, 2]
[2]TNO
P.O. Box 23, 3769 ZG, Soesterberg, The Netherlands
jan.vanerp@tno.nl

Dirk K.J. Heylen[1]
d.k.j.heylen@utwente.nl

ABSTRACT

We present "Nakama": A communication device that supports affective communication between a child and its - geographically separated - parent. Nakama consists of a control unit at the parent's end and an actuated teddy bear for the child. The bear contains several communication channels, including social touch, temperature, and vibrotactile heartbeats; all aimed at increasing the sense of presence. The current version of Nakama is suitable for user evaluations in lab settings, with which we aim to gain a more thorough understanding of the opportunities and limitations of these less traditional communication channels.

Categories and Subject Descriptors

H.5.2 [**Information Interfaces and Presentation e.g., HCI**]: User Interfaces—*Haptic I/O, Prototyping*

Keywords

Affective Communication; Mediated Touch; Temperature; Haptics

1. INTRODUCTION

There are several circumstances in which a child is geographically separated from one or both of its parents; for instance due to a divorce, hospitalization, or work-related situations. Because of the absence of the parent, such circumstances may be stressful for the child. In order to provide social support and to create a sense of being together, the absent parent usually utilizes telephone or text messages. These traditional communication media however do not always suffice. That is, they may be too cognitively demanding and/or it may be difficult for the parent to keep the child engaged in the conversation [7]. Moreover, it can be difficult to convey affective feelings by means of only verbal communication. Video conferencing allows one to convey facial expressions in order to emphasize the emotions associated with the spoken words. However, current technologies do oftentimes not facilitate other means of non-verbal affective communication.

The aim of the project was to develop a medium that facilitates affective interaction between child and parent, by utilizing communication channels that address multiple sensory modalities. Moreover, the device should be approachable and engaging for the child. We particularly set out to incorporate several haptic communication channels in the device. This is because these are underrepresented in current communication technologies, despite their potential for affective communication [5].

ICMI '15 November 09-13, 2015, Seattle, WA, USA
ACM 978-1-4503-3912-4/15/11 ...$15.00.
http://dx.doi.org/10.1145/2818346.2823299.

2. NAKAMA

Based on findings from literature as well as from interviews with children, (grand)parents, and researchers in the field of Human-Computer Interaction, we developed *"Nakama"*. Nakama - a Japanese word for "Companion"; derived from the Japanese words *"naka"* ("relationship") and *"ma"* ("space" or "room") - consists of two main components: a control unit which is held by the parent and an output device at the child's side (see Figure 1). The output device has the appearance of an ordinary teddy bear, in order to fit the child's

Figure 1: "Nakama": the bear and control unit.

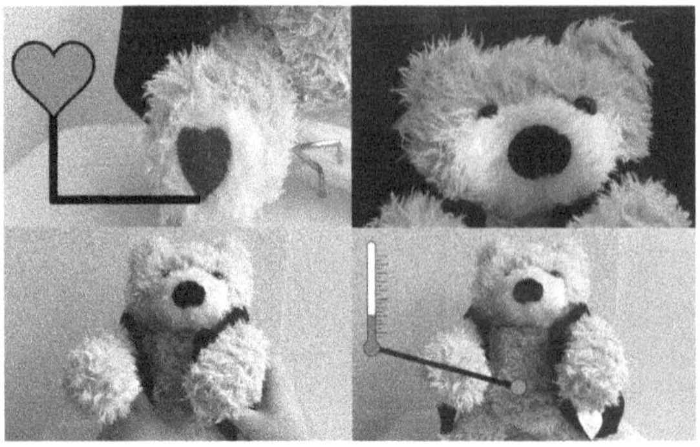

Figure 2: Nakama's communication channels. Clockwise, starting top left: Vibrotactile heartbeat, colors, temperature, and touching and gesturing.

daily surroundings. The output part of Nakama consists of several communication channels that can be controlled by the parent (see Figure 2). Although Nakama can be used as a stand-alone system, the idea is that it is used in conjunction with a videochat function[1].

2.1 Social Touch

In co-located interpersonal interactions, social touches such as a friendly pat on the back or a comforting hug play an important role. Depending on the context and the actual touching action, a touch can have several consequences on a physiological, cognitive, and behavioral level [1]. Moreover, touch is the most important non-verbal communication channel for the conveyance of intimate emotions. Recent research suggests that social responses similar to real-life repsonses can be achieved when the touch is simulated by haptic technology. This applies for touches that are mediated, but may also apply for touches that are initiated by an embodied agent [5]. The importance of affectively touching is also demonstrated by research on so-called robotic companions. "Paro" - a robotic seal that responds to caresses - is for instance applied in elderly care settings, and has proven to decrease feelings of loneliness and physiological stress responses (e.g. [4]). Nakama allows for social touching: The bear is equipped with servo motors in the arms that can be controlled by joysticks on the control unit. When the child is within the arm's reach, the parent can affectively touch the child via Nakama. Moreover, the parent can control the responses of the bear, when the child is touching it.

2.2 Temperature

Another related haptic communication channel consists of a heat pad integrated in the belly of Nakama. When a parent is present and holding the control unit, this presence is detected with a temperature sensor and subsequently conveyed by a temperature increase. The choice for temperature as means of affective communication is based on a recently discovered link between exposure to physical warmth (and coldness) and emotional and behavioral responses associated with temperature. More concrete: When people feel warmth in an object or when the ambient temperature is relatively high, they perceive others as metaphorically warmer people [6], and they feel socially closer to others [2].

[1]See https://youtu.be/3oIu5AyNtEo for a video of Nakama.

2.3 Heartbeats

The third haptic communication channel that is integrated in Nakama is aimed at conveying the parent's heartbeat. A heartrate sensor connected to the control unit is worn by the parent, and the measured heartbeat is displayed to the child by means of a vibrotactile motor in one of the feet of Nakama. Earlier research on heartbeats that are used as an affective communication channel has demonstrated that people, when they hear a heartbeat, attribute emotional meaning to it. Moreover, people perceive hearing another person's heartbeat as being very intimate (e.g., [3]).

2.4 Additional Communication Channels

Besides the haptic communication channels, Nakama utilizes several other means of non-verbal communication. The servo motors in the arms, as well as additional servo motors in the ears of the bear, allow for gesturing (e.g., waving) and wiggling with the ears. Moreover, RGB LEDs are integrated in the cheeks of the bear. Both the color changes and the gestures may be used to play with, to express different moods, or to emphasize other messages. Moreover, a speaker is integrated in the body of Nakama that can play music and pre-recorded messages. All the additional communication channels are controlled via a keypad in the control unit.

3. DISCUSSION

We have developed Nakama, a device that facilitates the conveyance of multimodal messages aimed at supporting affective and engaging child-parent communication. The current version of Nakama is not yet equipped with wireless communication capabilities and can therefore not be applied in practice. The prototype is being used in user studies in the lab; preliminary results indicate that both warmth and heartbeats (when attributed to the parent) can increase the child's sense of being together. We envision several studies aimed at investigating how the child interacts with the bear and the system as a whole, as well as at evaluating the potential social consequences of the communication channels.

4. REFERENCES

[1] T. Field. Touch for socioemotional and physical well-being: A review. *Dev. Rev.*, 30(4):367–383, 2010.

[2] H. IJzerman and G. R. Semin. The thermometer of social relations: Mapping social proximity on temperature. *Psychol. Sci.*, 20(10):1214–1220, 2009.

[3] J. H. Janssen, J. N. Bailenson, W. A. IJsselsteijn, and J. H. D. M. Westerink. Intimate heartbeats: Opportunities for affective communication technology. *IEEE Trans. Affect. Comput.*, 1(2):72–80, 2010.

[4] H. Robinson, B. Macdonald, N. Kerse, and E. Broadbent. The psychosocial effects of a companion robot: A randomized controlled trial. *J. Am. Med. Dir. Assoc.*, 14(9):661–667, 2013.

[5] J. B. F. van Erp and A. Toet. Social touch in human-computer interaction. *Front. Digit. Humanit.*, 2(2), 2015.

[6] L. E. Williams and J. A. Bargh. Experiencing physical warmth promotes interpersonal warmth. *Science*, 322:606–607, 2008.

[7] S. Yarosh, Y. C. Chew, and G. D. Abowd. Supporting parent-child communication in divorced families. *Int. J. Hum. Comput. Stud.*, 67(2):192–203, 2009.

Wir im Kiez

Multimodal App for Mutual Help Among Elderly Neighbours

Sven Schmeier
German Research Center for Artificial Intelligence (DFKI)
Alt-Moabit 91c
10559 Berlin, Germany
sven.schmeier@dfki.de

Aaron Russ
German Research Center for Artificial Intelligence (DFKI)
Alt-Moabit 91c
10559 Berlin, Germany
aaron.russ@dfki.de

Norbert Reithinger
German Research Center for Artificial Intelligence (DFKI)
Alt-Moabit 91c
10559 Berlin, Germany
norbert.reithinger@dfki.de

ABSTRACT

Elderly people often need support in everyday situations – e.g. common daily life activities like taking care of house and garden, or caring for an animal are often not possible without a larger support circle. However, especially in larger western cities, local social networks may not be very tight, friends may have moved away or died, and the traditional support structures found in so-called multi-generational families do not exist anymore. As a result, the quality of life for elderly people suffers crucially. On the other hand, people from the broader neighborhood would often gladly help and respond quickly. With the project *Wir im Kiez* we developed and tested a multimodal social network app equipped with a conversational interface that addresses these issues. In the demonstration, we especially focus on the needs and restrictions of seniors, both in their physical and psychological limitations.

Keywords

mobile multimodal, usability, conversational interface, elderly

1. INTRODUCTION

In the project *Wir im Kiez*, funded by the German ministry of education and research (BMBF), we developed together with the industrial company Cocomore AG[1] a social media platform which brings people in the neighborhood together to help each other in daily activities. It is intended to facilitate a social network which brings people in real life in contact within the local area, keep in touch with friends and family members, or just get informed about the latest local events. The project especially targets elderly people to become part of this community, notably those who lost their marriage partner or friends, who cannot draw on support from family and friends, or who are just feeling lonely for whatever reason. As central issue in the interface design process we had to consider age-related characteristics of the intended user group. With increasing age, typical ailments comprise loss of visual acuity, reduced perception of color-contrasts (e.g. worse for blue and green, better red or yellow), decreased ability to adjust changes in illumination, reduced field of vision, hearing loss especially for high pitched sounds, fine-motor control decline, and also loss of cognitive functions, as for example a decreased short-term memory. These issues play an important role when considering age-related effects in UI design. During the project, feedback from the target group has been collected frequently in usability tests with mock-ups and intermediate system versions. This feedback has been included in the design and realization to ensure that all important aspects and limitations of the target users group were addressed. The UI design is also guided by experiences with previous projects in this area [1]. The application itself is designed for tablet devices. Tests have shown that the target group can handle input via touch especially well compared to input via mouse and keyboard. Feedback mechanisms also play an important role while navigating the application. In Fig.1 we see the home screen of the application; note the large

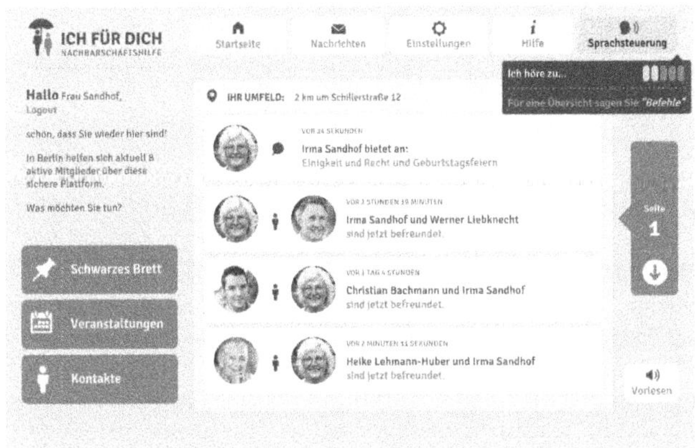

Figure 1: The home screen with active speech control (dt. "Sprachsteuerung"); original size 10.1 in /25.7 cm. ***Demonstrator available as Chrome Extension at*** `https://chrome.google.com/webstore/detail/aeibgffcbkeeipgoeogbehkdickahmdf`

[1] Cocomore AG, Gutleutstr. 30, 60329 Frankfurt am Main, Germany

ICMI 2015, November 9–13, 2015, Seattle, WA, USA.
ACM 978-1-4503-3912-4/15/11.
DOI: http://dx.doi.org/10.1145/2818346.2823300 .

touch targets and the contrast of the chosen colors. In addition to guarantee a barrier-free user experience we added a *conversational interface*. The user can navigate through the interface by using natural language dialogs. A user may talk to the system in the way he/she wants to: no commands need to be learned or recognized.

2. TECHNOLOGY

The multimodal platform is realized using the Mobile Multimodal Interaction and Rendering (MMIR) framework[2], a framework for building lightweight dialog systems on basis of web technologies. Combined with Cordova[3], the framework allows targeting the major mobile platforms. MMIR provides several modules to add speech functionality like Automatic Speech Recognition (ASR) and Text To Speech (TTS) synthesis for different platforms. The Android version uses the Nuance NDEV solution for ASR and TTS, whereas the PC app –in form of an extension for the Chrome browser– utilizes the built-in Web Speech API of Chrome for ASR, and an OpenMARY[4] server for TTS over the web. The content pages are realized as standard web pages that are enriched with our multimodal dialog technology.

When using the conversational interface, i.e. speech control, the recognition results of the ASR are classified according to anchor points of the site map. The classification algorithm that we employ is based on a Rocchio based Machine Learning approach and has been proven to work extremely well on small and unbalanced training data [2]. The algorithm is trained continuously by the users' utterances collected during the use of the system. In case of ambiguities during the categorization, the dialog system will ask questions for clarification (cf. Fig. 2). The dialog system's processing of the event-driven input and application states is realized using State Chart XML (SCXML). It tracks not only the spoken user events, but also the direct tactile user input on the buttons of the page to keep track of the interaction state, to create haptic feedback. In addition to the command-and-control oriented navigation, the dialog system also enables the user to dictate –and correct– text input, e.g. for creating messages and help-offers or -requests.

3. DEMONSTRATION DESCRIPTION

As mentioned before users can interact with system with the modalities GUI/touch and speech. System feedback comprises sounds/earcons and haptics/vibration for confirming interaction. Especially haptic feedback is very important for the targeted user group. Once the conversational modus, i.e. speech control, is activated, the system listens continually for spoken commands, until it is explicitly deactivated again. This modus is prominently indicated by showing a popup-dialog (see upper right in Fig. 1). It contains a 5-bar visual feedback for the microphone input as well as a hint for listing available speech command: the listing can be triggered and used either by voicing the hint, or by touch.

In context of the CARE classification [3], interactions with the dialog system are mainly multimodally *Equivalent*, i.e. an action can be equivalently triggered either by a voice or haptic interaction(s); this allows users to choose their preferred way for controlling the system. Some actions that can

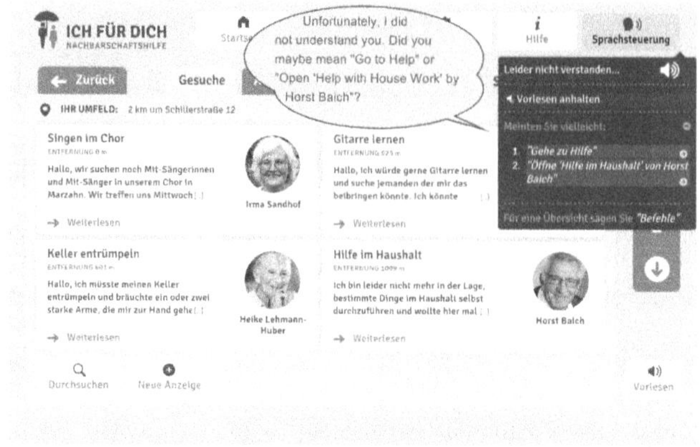

Figure 2: Example for disambiguation: candidates for likely commands are read out via speech synthesis, and also shown in the speech control dialog as *touchable* entries.

be triggered using speech commands may not be available by touch in the current view. In this case, multimodal *Equivalence* is provided by way of the command listing, which can be opened in the command popup-dialog. The currently available commands are listed and can be triggered by touch. Some few actions can only be used in one singular modality (*Assignment*), namely starting the speech control and stopping TTS[5] can only be accomplished using touch. Also user authentication –entering the user name and password– is not possible via speech.

With respect to the targeted user group, the interactions are designed to be simple. This is the main reason, that the dialog system does not provide *Redundant* multimodal interactions: transferring information redundantly in multiple modalities would result in one interaction replacing the other, i.e. *Equivalence* of the interactions. For the same reasons, the system does not provide *Complementarity* multimodal interactions.

4. ACKNOWLEDGMENTS

The work presented in here was funded by the German Ministry of Education and Research in the project *WirImKiez* (16SV6323). The authors would like to thank the Cocomore team and especially Andreas Aue and Nico Beck for their contributions to this work.

5. REFERENCES

[1] M. Haesner, K. Schumacher, A. Steinert, E. Steinhagen-Thiessen, and M. Goevercin, "Evaluating an online cognitive training platform for older adults - user experience and implementation requirements," *Journal of Gerontological Nursing*, 2015.

[2] S. Schmeier, *Exploratory Search on Mobile Devices.* Saarbruecken, Germany: DFKI-LT - Dissertation Series, 2013.

[3] L. Nigay and J. Coutaz, "Multifeature systems: The care properties and their impact on software design," *Intelligence and multimodality in multimedia interfaces*, 1997.

[2] https://github.com/mmig/mmir

[3] https://cordova.apache.org

[4] https://github.com/marytts

[5] Barge-in for speech input is not supported

Interact: Tightly-coupling Multimodal Dialog with an Interactive Virtual Assistant

Ethan Selfridge
Interactions Corporation
25 Broadway, 9th Floor
New York, NY, USA.r
eselfridge@interactions.net

Michael Johnston
Interactions Corporation
25 Broadway, 9th Floor
New York, NY, USA.r
mjohnston@interactions.net

ABSTRACT

Interact is a mobile virtual assistant that uses multimodal dialog to enable an interactive concierge experience over multiple application domains including hotel, restaurants, events, and TV search. Interact demonstrates how multimodal interaction combined with conversational dialog enables a richer and more natural user experience. This demonstration will highlight incremental recognition and understanding, multimodal speech and gesture input, context tracking over multiple simultaneous domains, and the use of multimodal interface techniques to enable disambiguation of errors and online personalization.

Keywords

multimodal agents; incremental recognition; disambiguation

1. INTRODUCTION

Virtual assistants have become commonplace on mobile devices (Siri, Cortana, Google Now, S-voice). The goal of these assistants is to provide the user with a single point of entry, through voice input, to a series of different applications and services available on the device (e.g. messaging, alarms, search). While significant advances have been made in ASR and NLU performance, dialog capabilities are generally limited to basic reference resolution and refinement queries. Furthermore, the dialog is not situated with respect to complex visual displays such as maps (i.e. the assistant can send you to a map, but the dialog itself is not situated within a map display) and multimodal capabilities are limited to visual responses to spoken inputs.

The Interact project explores the application of multimodal interaction and conversational dialog to the virtual assistant paradigm [2, 1]. In Interact, the interaction is situated *across* a series of linked information displays, including dynamic maps, scrollable information views, and calendars. Users are free to use combinations of speech, gesture, touch, and textual input. Another aspect of the work is a focus on enterprise applications where instead of being device or operating system focused, the assistant provides a single point of entry to a range of different services and information sources provided by a business to its customers. For purposes of demonstration, we show examples from the hospitality domain (travel concierge for hotel guests). The central components of the Interact user interface are a dynamic map and information displays used to show the current recognition, system prompts, search results, and active plan elements (Figure 1). Spoken input begins when the user taps a microphone button on the display. As the user speaks, incremental speech recognition results appear. In addition to enabling voice input, the microphone button also activates the map as a drawing canvas, and enables the user to combine speech with drawing in coordinated multimodal commands. For example, a user might say, "sushi in this area" while simultaneously outlining a relevant area on the map. Or a user may say, "hotels along this route". Interact determines the user intent and responds multimodally, by updating the display and using speech synthesis to summarize results, provide feedback, or make requests for clarification and additional information.

2. SAMPLE INTERACTION

Figure 1 provides a sample interaction. The user uses *typed* input to find sushi near their hotel, but Interact does not know the hotel location. Using map navigation, gesture, and touch, the user shows Interact where they are staying, and Interact then searches for sushi. The user asks about TV listings but Interact is not confident in its understanding so it backs off to a web search. The user provides negative

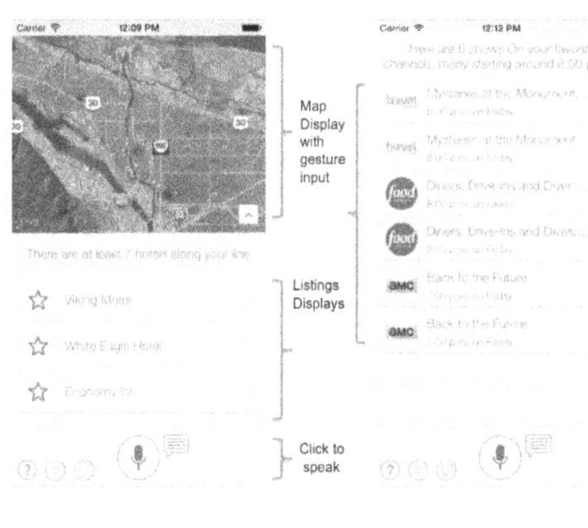

Figure 1: Interact User Interface

ICMI '15, November 09-13, 2015, Seattle, WA, USA
ACM 978-1-4503-3912-4/15/11.
http://dx.doi.org/10.1145/2818346.2823301.

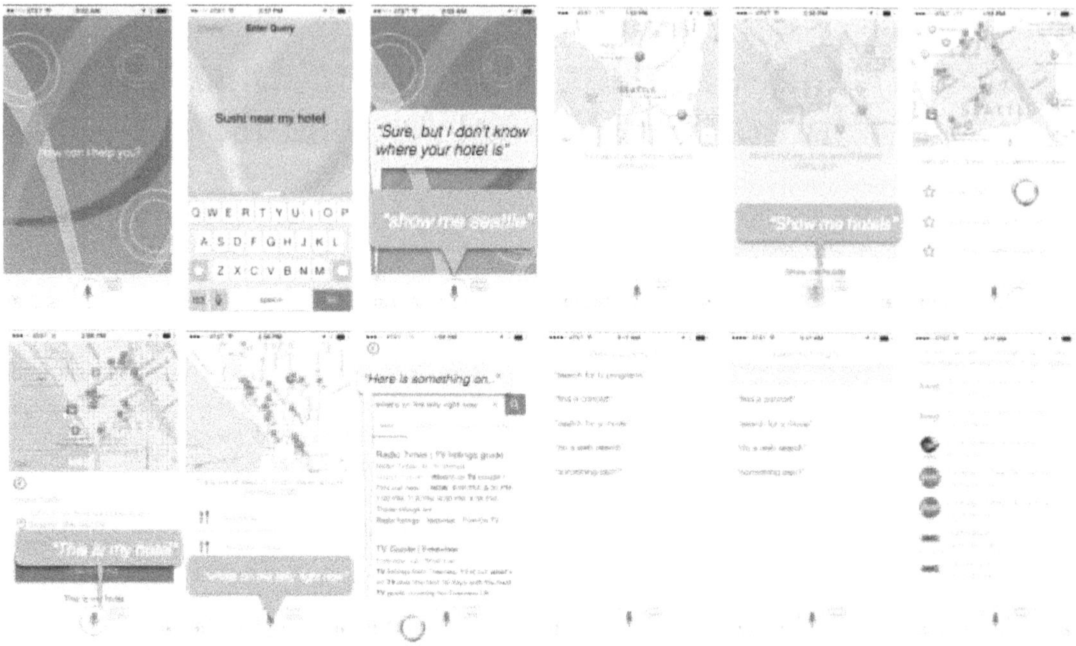

Figure 2: Here is a sample exchange with Interact.

feedback and, using multimodal disambiguation, teaches Interact the proper understanding after which Interact performs the appropriate action.

3. KEY TECHNOLOGY HIGHLIGHTS

In our demonstration, we will showcase three different aspects of Interact: Incremental ASR and NLU, Multi-domain Interaction Management, and Multimodal Disambiguation. The high-level architecture is similar to Johnston et al. [4].

3.1 Incremental Speech Recognition and Understanding

Speech is both recognized and understood as the user is speaking (e.g. [5, 6]. Incremental responses are displayed in the client, operating as an explicit back-channel and giving the user a chance to reject the recognition *in-progress* using the X (on the far right of the Interact UI). Any recognition rejected is not processed by the Interaction Manager, and so does not disrupt the context of the dialogue.

3.2 Multimodal Disambiguation

Interact relies on touch input to overcome ASR and NLU errors following recognition. First, the user always has the option to GO BACK to the last state. This is useful if the user is relying on context to fill in a portion of query, such as refinements ("What about pizza?"), when the error occurs. Second, if speech recognition is correct but Interact does not behave in the expected manner the user can THUMBS DOWN that behavior. Interact then brings up a menu of potential intents that the user can select. In the case where the NLU falls below threshold, Interact will learn the selected intent. In the case where the NLU is ambiguous, user-specific reinforcement learning is applied. And in the case where the NLU is simply wrong, the intent will be folded back into the underlying model.

3.3 Multi-domain Interaction Management

Interact uses a new approach to interaction management we call *Propose-Decide.* This architecture is meant to simplify the burden of creating large-domain virtual agents. Our proposed architecture is not limited by a specific domain depth or modality, provides a simple way to combine rule-based and statistical models [3], and is agnostic to dialogue authoring preference.

Acknowledgements

We would like to thank Antonio Moreno Daniel, Iker Arizmendi, Brant Vasilieff, Hyuckchul Jung, and John Chen, with a special thanks to Jay Wilpon.

4. REFERENCES

[1] P. R. Cohen, M. Johnston, D. McGee, S. Oviatt, J. Pittman, I. Smith, L. Chen, and J. Clow. Quickset: Multimodal interaction for distributed applications. In *ACM Multimedia*, 1997.

[2] P. Ehlen and M. Johnston. Multimodal dialogue in mobile local search. In *ICMI 2012*, 2012.

[3] P. Heeman. Combining reinforcement learning with information-state update rules. In *ACL*, 2007.

[4] M. Johnston, J. Chen, P. Ehlen, H. Jung, J. Lieske, A. Reddy, E. Selfridge, S. Stoyanchev, B. Vasilieff, and J. Wilpon. Mva: The multimodal virtual assistant. In *SIGdial 2014*, 2014.

[5] E. Selfridge, I. Arizmendi, P. Heeman, and J. Williams. Stability and accuracy in incremental speech recognition. In *SIGdial 2011*, 2011.

[6] G. Skantze and D. Schlangen. Incremental dialogue processing in a micro-domain. In *EACL*, 2009.

The UTEP AGENT System

David Novick, Iván Gris, Diego A. Rivera, Adriana Camacho, Alex Rayon, Mario Gutierrez
The University of Texas at El Paso
500 West University Ave.
El Paso, TX 79968 USA
(+1) 915-747-6031
novick@utep.edu, ivangris4@gmail.com,
{darivera2, accamacho2, amrayon2, mgutierrez19}@miners.utep.edu

Categories and Subject Descriptors
H.5.1 [**Information Interfaces and Presentation**]: Multimedia Information Systems – *artificial, augmented, and virtual realities.*

General Terms
Design, Human Factors

Keywords
Embodied Conversational Agents

1. INTRODUCTION
This paper describes a system for embodied conversational agents (ECAs) developed at the University of Texas at El Paso by the Advanced aGent ENgagement Team (AGENT) and one of the applications—Survival on Jungle Island—built with this system. In the Jungle application, the ECA and a human interact with speech and gesture for approximately 40 – 60 minutes in a game composed of 23 scenes. Each scene comprises a collection of speech input, speech output, gesture input, gesture output, scenery, triggers, and decision points.

The UTEP AGENT system, and the applications such as the Jungle game developed with the system, were created to enable research into rapport between ECA and human, with particular emphasis on the effects of paralinguistic behaviors on rapport and on the development of rapport over time. For example, the most recent study conducted using the Jungle game examined whether rapport would increase if the agent asked the human to perform task-related gestures and then perceived these gestures. A current study is examining the effect on rapport of differences in the ECA's speech between extraverted and introverted language.

In developing our system, full automation of the agent was a key consideration. To conduct our research on human-ECA rapport, we needed agents and systems capable of maintaining high levels of engagement with humans, and in some cases over multiple interaction sessions. These sessions can potentially extend to longer periods of time to examine long-term effects of the ECA's behaviors. Indeed, our design had to accommodate the possibility for long-term human-agent interactions extending over several sessions across several weeks. This would have been cumbersome and inefficient if done as Wizard-of-Oz system. Instead, we developed middleware that enabled us to create ECAs through a declarative approach, with XML-style scripting.

ICMI 2015, November 9–13, 2015, Seattle, WA, USA.
ACM 978-1-4503-3912-4/15/11.
DOI: http://dx.doi.org/10.1145/2818346.2823302.

2. SYSTEM ARCHITECTURE
The system's physical implementation uses Unity 4, a Microsoft Kinect, and the Windows Speech SDK, interfaced and networked with each other and synchronized to handle the agent's complex behavior. The system uses the Unity 4 game engine to display the ECA and Unity's Mecanim system to create an extensive array of animations.

The ECAs are built using a three-tiered architecture. At the bottom layer is the Kinect™ sensor, which supports RGB video, audio provided by an array of microphones, and a depth field based on infrared sensor information. The middle layer contains all the logic of the agent's behavior and sensor interpretation, including speech recognition, text-to-speech or audio playback, and gesture recognition. The top layer contains scripts in Unity3D Game Engine, which renders and animates the ECAs and contains the virtual environment (scenery) in which they appear.

The system's software implementation includes over 20 modules, presented in Figure 1. In this paper, we focus on the three most important modules: animations, markup language, and gesture recognition.

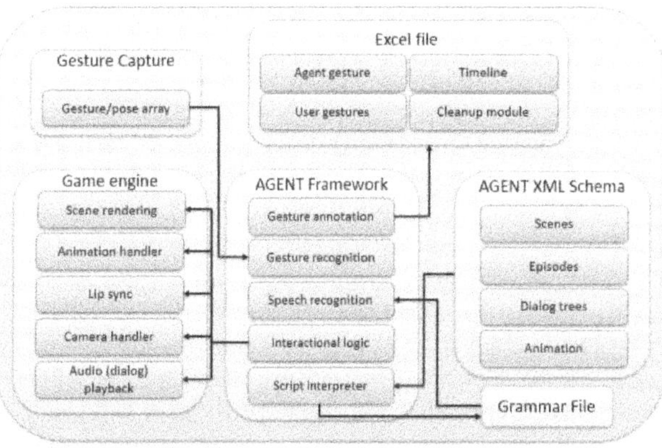

Fig. 1. AGENT system software modules.

2.1 Animations
Animations are played by a state graph that follows author-specified parameters of when an animation should start, end, or blend with another animation. Multiple animations can be blended to obtain a completely different animation in real time and to give the player the impression that the agent never moves in exactly the same way twice. Animations are divided layers that can control different parts of the body, so multiple animations can be played at the same time

and affect different limbs of the agent - for example simultaneously playing a blinking and talking animation on the face only, an explaining animation on the arms, and a walking animation from the hips down. The animation system is described in detail in [1].

2.2 Markup Language

To handle long-term interactions we developed middleware that parses, interprets, and executes XML files that define the scenes [2]. Each virtual environment where the agent can appear is known as a scene. Each scene can contain one or more episodes, which can branch depending on gesture or speech input. Each episode also contains recorded or synthesized dialogs and can contain grammar elements for speech recognition.

2.3 Gesture Recognition

We built a gesture tool using Microsoft's Kinect sensor. The tool itself is built as a standalone Windows application that can be connected to Unity3D, a game engine. In addition, the tool works both, as a way to recognize gestures, or to create gesture libraries that will later be used in the recognition [3]. We also use this tool to automatically log player's behaviors, potentially saving hours of manual coding, and to have our ECAs react to the player's movement in real time, sacrificing accuracy for speed.

3. SURVIVAL AGENT

The latest version of the agent, Adriana, leads the player through a series of activities and conversations while playing a game called Survival on Jungle Island. The system simulates a survival scenario where the player has to collaborate, cooperate, and build a relationship with the ECA to survive. In building the game, we sought to maximize rapport-building opportunities as well as to take advantage of the non-verbal behaviors in a more immersive environment, where both the player and the agent can interact with the same objects in virtual space. The storyline provides the flexibility and decision making without creating a completely open environment where tasks would otherwise be difficult to set up and evaluate.

The scenario comprises 23 scenes plus an introduction, where each scene lasts approximately five to eight minutes depending on the player's choices and interaction speed. Each scene was carefully scripted to enhance an aspect of a rapport-building interaction. The script provided a guideline for the relationship to evolve. The participants covered all scenes with Adriana with an average of 40 minutes of interaction. Although there was an implied one-hour limit to finish the interaction (the sign-in sheets had one hour slots), participants were told to take as much time as necessary. These times ranged between 30 minutes and 55 minutes.

The game starts with a cinematic sequence, which is a non-interactive video that offers some background for the situation. It explains how your ship is sinking in a storm. The few sailors were washed off the deck by a giant wave. The captain is unwilling to abandon his ship but sends you away with the hope that you might survive. This is followed by the first two scenes, which are meant to be instructive for the players without being an obtrusive tutorial that breaks the impression of an immersive reality. During the first scene, the player wakes up on a beach with someone—the agent—looking at the player. The agent introduces herself and asks a few questions, including if the participant is fine, if they can walk, and if they think there are other survivors. These questions help the player get immersed in the interaction. The agent then introduces herself and asks for the player's name. Most open-ended questions are not handled in the system by a language model. Rather, they are treated as wildcards, and the interaction is designed to traverse a dialog path through which any answer to those questions would seem recognized and valid (e.g., "Where are my manners? My name is Adriana. What is your name?" After the player responds, the name is not purposely recognized, and the ECA checks merely for an audio input, to which the agent always replies "Nice to meet you" and then continues the conversation.). These personal questions give the player an impression of seamless recognition and are meant indicate to the player that the agent is processing what it hears. This approach helps avoid command-like answers to questions, where players reply only with single words.

Fig. 2. Survival on Jungle Island.

The purpose of the second scene is to progress the story by providing a plausible explanation why there is a person (the ECA) in the jungle and how she survived thus far. This scene does react appropriately to a player's verbal response. At some point close towards the end of the scene, the ECA asks if they should stay on the same shelter or find a better place. Depending on the player's choice, the story develops.

About half the scenes have versions in which the agent recognizes task-oriented gestures by the player, such as spear-fishing or doing a "high five." In the final scene, the player and the agent are rescued by a helicopter.

4. ACKNOWLEDGMENTS

The authors would like to acknowledge Guillaume Adoneth, David Manuel, Joel Quintana, Anuar Jauregui, Tim Gonzales, Alfonso Peralta, Victoria Bravo, Brynne Blaugrund, Laura Rodriguez, Jaqueline Brixey, Yahaira Reyes, Paola Gallardo, and Nick Farber.

5. REFERENCES

[1] Gris, I., Rivera, D.A., and Novick, D. Animation guidelines for believable embodied conversational agent gestures. In *HCI International 2015*, Los Angeles, CA, August 2015, LNCS 9179, pp 197-205.

[2] Novick, D., Gutierrez, M. Gris, I, and Rivera, D.A. A Mark-Up Language and interpreter for interactive scenes for embodied conversational agents. In *HCI International 2015*, Los Angeles, CA, August 2015, LNCS 9179, pp. 206-215.

[3] Gris, I., Camacho, A., and Novick, D. Full-body gesture recognition for embodied conversational agents: The UTEP AGENT gesture tool. In *Gesture and Speech in Interaction (GESPIN 2015),* Nantes, France, in press.

A Distributed Architecture for Interacting with NAO *

Fabien Badeig, Quentin Pelorson, Soraya Arias, Vincent Drouard
Israel Gebru, Xiaofei Li, Georgios Evangelidis, Radu Horaud
INRIA Grenoble Rhone-Alpes
Montbonnot-Saint-Martin, France
fabien.badeig@inria.fr

One of the main applications of the humanoid robot NAO – a small robot companion – is human-robot interaction (HRI). NAO is particularly well suited for HRI applications because of its design, hardware specifications, programming capabilities, and affordable cost. Indeed, NAO can stand up, walk, wander, dance, play soccer, sit down, recognize and grasp simple objects, detect and identify people, localize sounds, understand some spoken words, engage itself in simple and goal-directed dialogs, and synthesize speech. This is made possible due to the robot's 24 degree-of-freedom articulated structure (body, legs, feet, arms, hands, head, etc.), motors, cameras, microphones, etc., as well as to its on-board computing hardware and embedded software, e.g., robot motion control.

Nevertheless, the current NAO configuration has two drawbacks that restrict the complexity of interactive behaviors that could potentially be implemented. Firstly, the on-board computing resources are inherently limited, which implies that it is difficult to implement sophisticated computer vision and audio signal analysis algorithms required by advanced interactive tasks. Secondly, programming new robot functionalities currently implies the development of embedded software, which is a difficult task in its own right necessitating specialized knowledge. The vast majority of HRI practitioners may not have this kind of expertise and hence they cannot easily and quickly implement their ideas, carry out thorough experimental validations, and design proof-of-concept demonstrators.

We have developed a distributed software architecture that attempts to overcome these two limitations. Broadly speaking, NAO's on-board computing resources are augmented with external computing resources. The latter is a computer platform with its CPUs, GPUs, memory, operating system, libraries, software packages, internet access, etc. This configuration enables easy and fast development in Matlab, C, C++, or Python. Moreover, it allows the user to combine on-board libraries (motion control, face detection, etc.) with external toolboxes, e.g., OpenCv.

An overview of the proposed software architecture is shown on Figure 1. Data coming from NAO (motor positions, images, sampled microphone signals, or data produced by on-board computing modules) are fed into the external computer. Conversely, the latter can control the robot. Currently we have developed three internal-to-external interfaces: *vision*, *audio*, and *locomotion*. The role of these interfaces is twofold: (i) to feed the data into a memory space that is subsequently shared with existing software modules or with modules under development and (ii) to send back to the robot commands that are generated by the external software modules. Although these modules may be developed in a variety of programming languages, special emphasis was put to allow integration with the Matlab programming environment. This allows access to an infinitely large number of libraries and toolboxes. It also allows high-level robot control via Matlab "commands". On-board software modules, e.g., face detection, can be accessed directly from the Matlab environment.

To date, the proposed architecture is demonstrated with five examples of various degrees of complexity:

- *Robot posture control.* This demonstrates that robot actions involving many degrees of freedom can be executed via Matlab commands, e.g., "Stand", "Sit", etc. Matlab programs can easily read the robot-posture data, specify the overall speed of the action, etc. Note that the actuator controller runs on-board and the proposed system allows easy access to this controller, at a high level.
- *Multiple face detection.* This is another on-board software module that can be invoked via the proposed architecture. Note that the robot does not have a display and the developer is not aware of the actual output of vision modules running on-board. This illustrates the integration with C++ modules and libraries.
- *Face detection and robot motion.* This illustrates that several on-board modules can be easily combined together. It involves parallel execution of several modules, possibly written in different programming languages, e.g., a vision module in C++ and a locomotion module in Matlab.
- *Audio-visual localization.* This demonstrates an even more complex interaction. The task is to detect and localize a sound source, to turn the robot's head towards

*This research has received funding from the EU-FP7 STREP project EARS (#609465) and ERC Advanced Grant VHIA (#340113).

ICMI 2015, November 9–13, 2015, Seattle, WA, USA.
ACM 978-1-4503-3912-4/15/11.
DOI: http://dx.doi.org/10.1145/2818346.2823303.

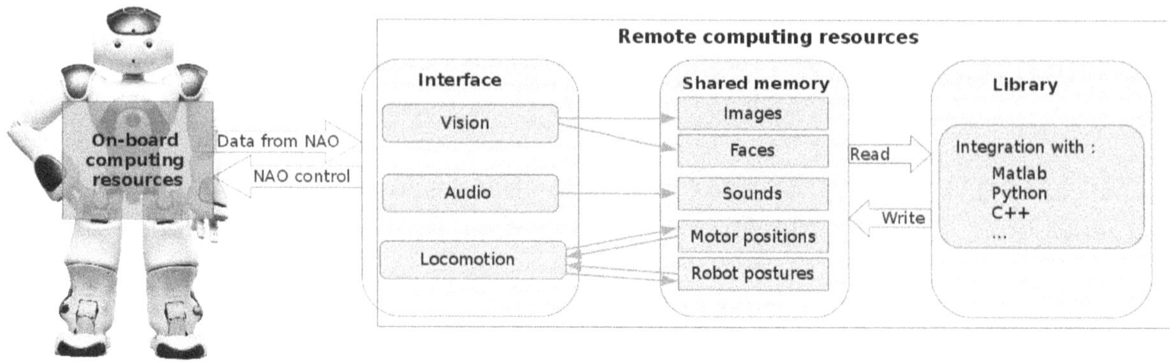

Figure 1: Overview of the proposed distributed architecture that allows fast development of interactive applications using the humanoid robot NAO.

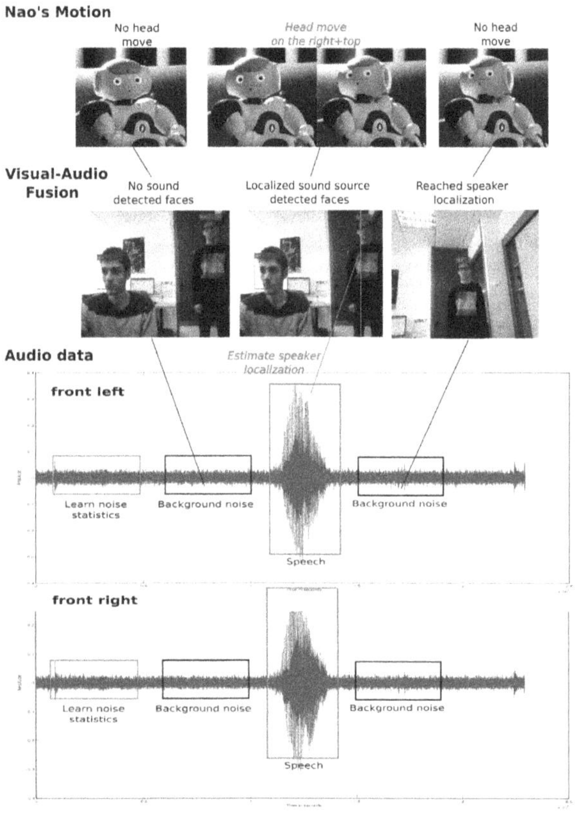

Figure 2: Overview of the audio-visual localization algorithm that involves audio signal processing (voice activity detection, cross-correlation, estimation of time-difference of arrival followed by direction of arrival of the speech signal) computer vision (face detection and localization) and control of the robot's head motions.

the sound direction, to possibly detect a face in this direction and to raise the robot's head towards the perceived human face, Figure 2. The overall integration is done in Matlab, which offers the possibility to develop sound-source localization method, which in turn uses Matlab's signal processing toolbox (voice activity detection, multi-channel cross-correlation, short-time Fourier transform, etc.). The Matlab computer vision toolbox is used for face detection. The control of the robot head is done as above using the robot-posture control module.

Figure 3: The standard NAO head (left) includes two vertically aligned cameras with no common field of view (top camera is heading upwards while bottom camera is heading downwards). Recently, Aldebaran Robotics developed a prototype *stereo head* (right). The wide field of view shared by the cameras enables stereo matching and stereo reconstruction.

- *Stereo reconstruction.* One important feature of HRI is enabling a robot to understand the spatial layout of the observed people. This allows a wide range of possibilities, including the recognition of human actions and gestures, configurations of groups of people, etc. For this purpose we use a stereo head recently developed by Aldebaran Robotics, Figure 3. The on-board image acquisition module allows to transfer synchronized image pairs at 25 FPS at VGA resolution. The camera pair is precisely calibrated using any camera calibration toolbox currently available (computer vision Matlab toolbox, OpenCV, etc.). In this example we used OpenCV stereo matching and reconstruction modules. The visualization of the stereo reconstruction results are done in Matlab. A dense depth map is delivered at 10 FPS.

Software Download

The proposed distributed architecture is compatible with the version 5 of NAO. C++ source modules are downloadable from `https://team.inria.fr/perception/en/naolab/`.

Touch Challenge '15: Recognizing Social Touch Gestures

Merel M. Jung[1], Xi Laura Cang[2], Mannes Poel[1], Karon E. MacLean[2]
[1]University of Twente, P.O. Box 217, 7500 AE, Enschede, The Netherlands
[2]University of British Columbia, 2366 Main Mall, Vancouver, B.C. V6T 1Z4, Canada
m.m.jung@utwente.nl, cang@cs.ubc.ca, m.poel@utwente.nl, maclean@cs.ubc.ca

ABSTRACT

Advances in the field of touch recognition could open up applications for touch-based interaction in areas such as Human-Robot Interaction (HRI). We extended this challenge to the research community working on multimodal interaction with the goal of sparking interest in the touch modality and to promote exploration of the use of data processing techniques from other more mature modalities for touch recognition. Two data sets were made available containing labeled pressure sensor data of social touch gestures that were performed by touching a touch-sensitive surface with the hand. Each set was collected from similar sensor grids, but under conditions reflecting different application orientations: CoST: Corpus of Social Touch and HAART: The Human-Animal Affective Robot Touch gesture set. In this paper we describe the challenge protocol and summarize the results from the touch challenge hosted in conjunction with the 2015 ACM International Conference on Multimodal Interaction (ICMI). The most important outcomes of the challenges were: (1) transferring techniques from other modalities, such as image processing, speech, and human action recognition provided valuable feature sets; (2) gesture classification confusions were similar despite the various data processing methods used.

Categories and Subject Descriptors

H.5.2 [**User Interfaces**]: Haptic I/O; I.5.2 [**PATTERN RECOGNITION**]: Design Methodology—*Classifier design and evaluation, Feature evaluation and selection*; I.5.4 [**PATTERN RECOGNITION**]: Applications—*Signal processing*

General Terms

Performance

Keywords

Social touch; Touch data set; Touch gesture recognition

ICMI 2015, November 9–13, 2015, Seattle, WA, USA.

ACM 978-1-4503-3912-4/15/11 ...$15.00.
DOI: http://dx.doi.org/10.1145/2818346.2829993.

1. INTRODUCTION

Touch is an important non-verbal form of interpersonal social interaction; it is used to communicate emotions and social messages [8]. In order to enable artificial social agents such as robots to understand human touch input there is a need for automatic recognition of different types of touch [14]. Enabling touch-based interaction with robotic animals (e.g., [15, 18]) and humanoid robots (e.g., [6, 13]) is of interest for fields such as Human-Robot Interaction (HRI) [2]. As the recognition of touch behavior has received far less research attention than recognition of behaviors in the visual and auditory modalities (e.g., see [19]), we aimed to spark interest into this relatively new field by organizing a touch challenge.

This challenge focused on the recognition of touch gestures with social meaning that were performed by hand on a pressure-sensitive surface; we call these 'social touch gestures'. Touch data has been collected from subjects performing different sets of touch gestures on different surfaces/embodiments (e.g., [1, 4, 5, 6, 7, 12, 13, 15]). Appropriating methods developed in more mature fields such as speech recognition and video analysis could be beneficial for moving touch recognition forward. By publicizing two distinct touch data sets, we allowed researchers with expertise in other sensory modalities to try out their processing techniques on our touch data.

The remainder of the paper is organized as follows: Section 2 describes the two provided touch data sets; Section 3 highlights the challenge protocol; an overview of the results and discussions of the test set label submissions is in Section 4; and we conclude with high-level findings in Section 5.

2. TOUCH DATA SETS

For the challenge, two data sets were made available containing labeled pressure sensor data of social touch gestures. Table 1 summarizes the data sets' attributes.

2.1 CoST: Corpus of Social Touch

CoST [11, 12, 17] contains 14 touch gestures: grab, hit, massage, pat, pinch, poke, press, rub, scratch, slap, squeeze, stroke, tap, and tickle. These gestures were registered on an 8×8 pressure sensor grid which was wrapped around a mannequin arm. This corpus consists of the data from 31 subjects performing the 14 touch gestures in 3 variations: gentle, normal, and rough. Subjects were restricted neither in the amount of time taken for performing each gesture nor the number of gesture repetitions performed in each capture. The data provided for this challenge consisted of the

Table 1: Data set attributes as provided for the challenge.

Attribute	CoST	HAART
# of touch gestures	14	7
Sensor grid size	8×8	8×8[a]
Sensor sample rate	135 Hz	54 Hz
Sensor values	0–1023	0–1023
Gesture duration	variable	8s[b]
Touch surface	mannequin arm	dependent on condition
Conditions	gentle and normal variations	substrates and covers
# of subjects	31	10
Train/test split	21/10 subjects	7/3 subjects
# of gesture captures	5,203	829

[a]trimmed from collected 10×10 grid, [b]trimmed from collected 10s capture

gentle gesture variation (2,601 captures) and the normal gesture variation (2,602 captures). This data set was provided in both CSV and MATLAB file formats and included segmented gesture captures of varying length, sampled at 135 Hz, and containing pressure values of the 64 channels ranging from 0 to 1023 (i.e. 10 bits). Labels consisted of touch gesture type, gesture variation, and subject number.

2.2 HAART: Human-Animal Affective Robot Touch

HAART [4] contains 7 touch gestures: pat, constant contact without movement (press), rub, scratch, stroke, tickle, and 'no touch'. These gestures were found to be the most often used of those in Yohanan et al's Touch Dictionary [18], gathered to communicate emotion in human-animal interaction. For the HAART data set (collected from 10 subjects), each touch action was performed on a 10×10 pressure sensor [7] for 10 seconds. To assess feature robustness under realistic operating conditions when installed on a robotic animal, each subject contributed gestures with the sensor mounted on all permutations of 3 substrate conditions (firm and flat; foam and flat; foam and curve) and 4 fabric cover conditions (none; short minkee[1]; long minkee; synthetic fur). The resulting data set includes 829 gesture captures (12 conditions × 7 gestures × 10 subjects minus 11 erroneous capture instances). Each capture is 10 seconds of a continuously repeated gesture, sampled at 54 Hz and trimmed to the middle 8s (432 frames); there are generally 10–15 gesture instances per capture. This data set was provided as a CSV file and included the center 8×8 frame (trimmed for consistency with CoST) with pressure values ranging from 0 to 1023. Labels consisted of touch gesture type, condition set, and subject number.

3. CHALLENGE PROTOCOL

The aim of this challenge was to develop relevant features and apply classification methods for recognizing social touch gestures. Gesture classification was independent of the condition (i.e. gesture variant, substrate and cover) for example, 'gentle stroke' and 'normal stroke' were considered to be part of the same class. Participants had the choice of working on one of the data sets or on both. For the train/test sets, subjects were randomly split into 21 train, 10 test subjects for CoST and 7 train, 3 test subjects for HAART. This split ensured that for each of the two data sets, any one subject's touch data belonged to either the training set or the test set.

The training data for both the CoST and HAART data set was made available to the registrants of the challenge. We provided the test data sets without class labels a month after initial publication. Participants were given 2 weeks to process the test data. Any number of test label submissions could be made up to a deadline (see Tables 2 and 3); once this date had passed, we released the true test labels as well as a summary of their results to the challenge participants.

4. TEST LABEL SUBMISSION RESULTS

Results of the test label submissions were reported in the form of a confusion matrix and accuracy was used to measure overall performance (see Tables 2 and 3).

4.1 Data pre-processing

There is not much standardization in the extraction of feature sets for touch data processing. This section discusses the data pre-processing steps that were taken by the challenge participants consisting of data filtering, feature extraction, and feature selection.

The data that was provided for the challenge was previously filtered for erroneous entries and segmented into gesture captures [12]. However, gesture captures of the CoST data set are of variable duration and can contain a single gesture instance or multiple repetitions. This increased the difficulty of automatic segmentation based on pressure differences over time. Ta et al. explored additional techniques for automatic segmentation to further reduce the amount of excess frames [16]. However, these methods for automatic segmentation did not improve classification. The gesture captures from the training set were then manually segmented based on the shape and duration which offered little to negative improvement (see Table 2) suggesting that classifiers are fairly robust to imprecise segmentation.

For the challenge, many interesting features were extracted but we describe only a couple of notable approaches here. In previous literature (e.g., [1, 7, 12, 15]) as well as for this challenge [3, 9, 10, 16] statistics were calculated from the pressure sensor data such as the mean pressure over time. Also, feature extraction methods were borrowed from other domains: speech applications, human action recognition, and image analysis. Ta et al., for example, applied the Sobel operator, an image processing technique used for edge detection [16]. By sharpening the contrast, a second set of

[1]Minkee (or minky) is a chenille-like fabric commonly used for baby blankets and stuffed toys.

Table 2: Results for the CoST data set.

Paper	Classifier	Accuracy
Ta et al. [16]	random forest^a	61.3%
Ta et al. [16]	random forest^b	60.8%
Ta et al. [16]	SVM^b	60.5%
Ta et al. [16]	SVM^a	59.9%
Gaus et al. [9]	random forest	58.7%
Gaus et al. [9]	multiboost	58.2%
Hughes et al. [10]	logistic regression	47.2%
Balli Altugl et al. [3]	random forest	26.0%

^{a}trained on filtered data, ^{b}train on all data

Table 3: Results for the HAART data set.

Paper	Classifier	Accuracy
Ta et al. [16]	random forest	70.9%
Ta et al. [16]	SVM	68.5%
Hughes et al. [10]	logistic regression	67.7%
Gaus et al. [9]	random forest	66.5%
Gaus et al. [9]	multiboost	64.5%
Balli Altugl et al. [3]	random forest	61.0%

data frames was constructed, garnering new values using the same feature extraction procedures. Most features were extracted by feature engineering however, Hughes et al. also included deep autoencoders for automatic feature extraction using dimension reduction, these features were then used to train Hidden Markov Models (HMMs) [10]. The CoST data set was used to determine HMM likelihoods for class membership; these values were included in the feature sets for both CoST and HAART data to examine the viability of applying learned features from one data set to the other.

Feature selection was performed by evaluating the performance of different features or feature sets as a whole on the training set. Relevant features selected using random forest [16] or sequential floating forward search [3] were found to improve the accuracy on the test set. Others compared the accuracies of different feature sets as a whole. Using this approach, the combination of all feature sets yielded the best results [9, 10]. Identifying a small number of highly discriminating features can benefit applications in which computational power is costly, such as on-board real-time touch recognition. Balli Altuglu and Altun [3] showed that a small feature set (number of features < 10) could perform well on the HAART data set.

4.2 Social Touch Classification

Random forest was found to be the most popular classification method [3, 9, 16] and has been used in previous work on touch gesture recognition [1, 7]. Other classification methods that were explored were Support Vector Machines (SVMs) [16], also used by [6, 11, 12], multiboost [9] (a different boosting algorithm was used by [13]), and simple logistic regression [10].

Accuracies reported for the challenge ranged from 26.0%–61.3% for the CoST data set and from 61.0%–70.9% for the HAART data set (see Tables 2 and 3). Previously reported accuracies for the CoST data set were up to 54.0% for the rough gesture variants using leave-one-subject-out cross-validation [12] and up to 64.6% when using 10-fold cross-validation [17]. For the whole CoST data set, classification independent and without knowledge of the gesture variant yielded accuracies up to 52.6% using leave-one-subject-out cross-validation [12]. For the HAART data set, accuracies up to 90.3% were reported using 20-fold cross-validation when subject and condition labels were included as features [4]. However, direct comparisons between the accuracies reported for the challenge [3, 9, 10, 16] and accuracies reported by the authors of CoST [11, 12, 17] and HAART [4] are not meaningful because of the differences in data division and use of condition and/or subject information as labels.

As accuracy rates alone provide little information we looked at the confusion matrices for notable patterns. Frequent confusions between touch gestures for the CoST data set reported by the challenge participants were: 'grab-squeeze', 'hit-pat-slap-tap', 'rub-stroke', and 'scratch-tickle' [3, 9, 10, 16]. The touch gestures were difficult to distinguish across approaches for data pre-processing and classification algorithms. Previous work on the CoST data set, although using different parts and splits of data set, found similar confusions [11, 12, 17]. For the HAART data, rub and tickle were the hardest to correctly classify across challenge participant approaches [3, 9, 10, 16]. Often misclassified was rub as scratch or stroke and tickle as scratch, while the reverse (e.g., misclassification of scratch as rub) was less common. Cang et al. also found that rub and tickle were hardest to classify correctly even while using a extended version of the HAART data set [4]. Compared to the challenge results, their confusion matrices showed more symmetry, indicating there were frequent confusions among certain gesture pairs. Rub was also one of the most difficult to correctly classify for the CoST data set [3, 9, 10, 11, 12, 16, 17].

Based on observations from the recording of the HAART data set, similarities were observed in how subjects performed the touch gestures which may help to explain certain confusions. Scratch and tickle both followed a similar motion trajectory and tended to have fluttery finger movements. Rub and stroke again have analogous motions where the flat of the hand exerts pressure along a roughly linear path. Confusions between touch gestures on the CoST data set could also be explained by gestures showing similarities on characteristics such as duration, contact area, repetition probability, and frequency of direction changes [12].

5. CONCLUSION

The challenge outcomes are encouraging; participants' various approaches open up further avenues for exploring data processing of social touch. Comparing the results from these different approaches also provided us the opportunity to pinpoint the difficulties that need to be addressed to increase the reliability of touch gesture recognition.

Feature extraction from touch data

The challenge provided insights on how techniques for feature extraction that are prominent for other modalities may be applied to touch data. Interestingly enough, many of these techniques were reasonably transferable to touch gesture data without much modification.

Future Work: While we have seen commonalities in feature sets used by challenge participants, developing a standard would help ease the feature engineering process. This challenge has allowed for the field of touch recognition to 'pick up a few tips and tricks' from data processing techniques used for more mature modalities, presenting an opportunity for customizing these methods to meet the particular needs of touch data.

Difficulties in touch gesture recognition
Despite the use of different data pre-processing techniques and classification algorithms, we observed consistent classification confusions between specific gesture pairs. It is yet unclear if these classification difficulties can be resolved by finer-grained feature extraction or if the problem is actually our discretization of touch gestures. For instance, scratch and tickle could be regarded as the same gesture class.

Future Work: We suggest considering the implications of collapsing certain commonly confused gesture pairs: what defines a 'good' gesture set; how many gestures should comprise it; and which ones? There is a lot more to determining touch semantics and intent than performing gesture recognition, that is, the same touch gesture can be used to convey distinct social message in a different contexts. Multimodal cues could add to contextual understanding of touch data.

6. ACKNOWLEDGMENTS

This publication was supported by the Dutch national program COMMIT. The National Sciences and Engineering Research Council of Canada (NSERC) also provided partial support for this work. Finally, we are grateful to the program committee for reviewing the submitted papers and to the challenge participants whose contributions have made this challenge worthwhile.

7. REFERENCES

[1] K. Altun and K. E. MacLean. Recognizing affect in human touch of a robot. *Pattern Recognition Letters*, 2014.

[2] B. D. Argall and A. G. Billard. A survey of tactile human–robot interactions. *Robotics and Autonomous Systems*, 58(10):1159–1176, 2010.

[3] T. Balli Altuglu and K. Altun. Recognizing touch gestures for social human-robot interaction. In *Proceedings of the International Conference on Multimodal Interaction (ICMI), (Seattle, WA)*, in press.

[4] X. L. Cang, P. Bucci, A. Strang, J. Allen, K. E. MacLean, and H. Y. S. Liu. Different strokes and different folks: Economical dynamic surface sensing and affect-related touch recognition. In *Proceedings of the International Conference on Multimodal Interaction (ICMI), (Seattle, WA)*, in press.

[5] J. Chang, K. E. MacLean, and S. Yohanan. Gesture recognition in the haptic creature. In *Proceedings of the International Conference EuroHaptics, (Amsterdam, The Netherlands)*, pages 385–391. 2010.

[6] M. D. Cooney, S. Nishio, and H. Ishiguro. Recognizing affection for a touch-based interaction with a humanoid robot. In *Proceedings of the International Conference on Intelligent Robots and Systems (IROS), (Vilamoura, Portugal)*, pages 1420–1427, 2012.

[7] A. Flagg and K. E. MacLean. Affective touch gesture recognition for a furry zoomorphic machine. In *Proceedings of the International Conference on Tangible, Embedded and Embodied Interaction (TEI), (Barcelona, Spain)*, pages 25–32, 2013.

[8] A. Gallace and C. Spence. The science of interpersonal touch: an overview. *Neuroscience & Biobehavioral Reviews*, 34(2):246–259, 2010.

[9] Y. F. A. Gaus, T. Olugbade, A. Jan, R. Qin, J. Liu, F. Zhang, et al. Social touch gesture recognition using random forest and boosting on distinct feature sets. In *Proceedings of the International Conference on Multimodal Interaction (ICMI), (Seattle, WA)*, in press.

[10] D. Hughes, N. Farrow, H. Profita, and N. Correll. Detecting and identifying tactile gestures using deep autoencoders, geometric moments and gesture level features. In *Proceedings of the International Conference on Multimodal Interaction (ICMI), (Seattle, WA)*, in press.

[11] M. M. Jung. Towards social touch intelligence: developing a robust system for automatic touch recognition. In *Proceedings of the International Conference on Multimodal Interaction (ICMI), (Istanbul, Turkey)*, pages 344–348, 2014.

[12] M. M. Jung, R. Poppe, M. Poel, and D. K. J. Heylen. Touching the void – introducing CoST: Corpus of Social Touch. In *Proceedings of the International Conference on Multimodal Interaction (ICMI), (Istanbul, Turkey)*, pages 120–127. 2014.

[13] D. Silvera-Tawil, D. Rye, and M. Velonaki. Interpretation of the modality of touch on an artificial arm covered with an eit-based sensitive skin. *Robotics Research*, 31(13):1627–1641, 2012.

[14] D. Silvera-Tawil, D. Rye, and M. Velonaki. Artificial skin and tactile sensing for socially interactive robots: A review. *Robotics and Autonomous Systems*, 63:230–243, 2015.

[15] W. D. Stiehl, J. Lieberman, C. Breazeal, L. Basel, L. Lalla, and M. Wolf. Design of a therapeutic robotic companion for relational, affective touch. In *Proceedings of International Workshop on Robot and Human Interactive Communication (ROMAN), (Nashville, TN)*, pages 408–415, 2005.

[16] V.-C. Ta, W. Johal, M. Portaz, E. Castelli, and D. Vaufreydaz. The Grenoble system for the social touch challenge at ICMI 2015. In *Proceedings of the International Conference on Multimodal Interaction (ICMI), (Seattle, WA)*, in press.

[17] S. van Wingerden, T. J. Uebbing, M. M. Jung, and M. Poel. A neural network based approach to social touch classification. In *Proceedings of Workshop on Emotion Representation and Modelling in Human-Computer-Interaction-Systems (ERM4HCI), (Istanbul, Turkey)*, pages 7–12, 2014.

[18] S. Yohanan and K. E. MacLean. The role of affective touch in human-robot interaction: Human intent and expectations in touching the haptic creature. *International Journal of Social Robotics*, 4(2):163–180, 2012.

[19] Z. Zeng, M. Pantic, G. Roisman, and T. S. Huang. A survey of affect recognition methods: Audio, visual, and spontaneous expressions. *Transactions on Pattern Analysis and Machine Intelligence*, 31(1):39–58, 2009.

The Grenoble System for the Social Touch Challenge at ICMI 2015

Viet-Cuong Ta
Prima/LIG, CNRS and International Research Institute MICA HUST-CNRS/UMI 2954-Grenoble INP
Viet-Cuong.Ta@inria.fr

Wafa Johal
MAGMA/LIG, CNRS
University of Grenoble-Alpes
Grenoble, France
Wafa.Johal@imag.fr

Maxime Portaz
Prima/LIG, CNRS
University of Grenoble-Alpes
Inria
Maxime.Portaz@inria.fr

Eric Castelli
International Research Institute MICA HUST-CNRS/UMI 2954-Grenoble INP
Eric.Castelli@mica.edu.vn

Dominique Vaufreydaz
Prima/LIG, CNRS
University of Grenoble-Alpes
Inria
Dominique.Vaufreydaz@inria.fr

ABSTRACT

New technologies and especially robotics is going towards more natural user interfaces. Works have been done in different modality of interaction such as sight (visual computing), and audio (speech and audio recognition) but some other modalities are still less researched. The touch modality is one of the less studied in HRI but could be valuable for naturalistic interaction. However touch signals can vary in semantics. It is therefore necessary to be able to recognize touch gestures in order to make human-robot interaction even more natural. We propose a method to recognize touch gestures. This method was developed on the CoST corpus and then directly applied on the HAART dataset as a participation of the Social Touch Challenge at ICMI 2015. Our touch gesture recognition process is detailed in this article to make it reproducible by other research teams. Besides features set description, we manually filtered the training corpus to produce 2 datasets. For the challenge, we submitted 6 different systems. A Support Vector Machine and a Random Forest classifiers for the HAART dataset. For the CoST dataset, the same classifiers are tested in two conditions: using all or filtered training datasets. As reported by organizers, our systems have the best correct rate in this year's challenge (70.91% on HAART, 61.34% on CoST). Our performances are slightly better that other participants but stay under previous reported state-of-the-art results.

Categories and Subject Descriptors

I.5 [**Pattern Recognition**]: Design Methodology, Implementation; D.2.8 [**Software Engineering**]: Metrics—*performance measures*

ICMI '15 November 09 - 13, 2015, Seattle, WA, USA

ACM 978-1-4503-3912-4/15/11...$15.00
http://dx.doi.org/10.1145/2818346.2830598

Keywords

Multimodal perception, gesture recognition, touch challenge

1. INTRODUCTION

Up to now, research in natural human-robot interaction has mainly focused on visual and audio modalities. However, few studies have given attention to the touch modality of interaction. Some well known robots, such as Aibo (1999), Paro (2001), Nao (2006) or Reeti (2011) are equipped with touch sensors. Some researchers have investigated skin-like sensing, i.e. lot of sensors spread all over the robot body [1, 2, 3]. For a pet robot, with fur, such as Paro, it would be interesting to be equipped with a sensors matrix and to be able to recognize the gestures. For cobots, touching information may increase co-working performance.

Some other approaches tackle squared grid pressure sensors to sense socials gestures from touching information. The CoST [4] and the HAART [5] corpora were recorded in order to study these gestures. This paper focuses on touch gestures recognition and provides new features and recognition systems to enable recognizing up to 14 gestures from the CoST and 7 gestures from the HAART database. The next section develops on the state-of-the art of social touch sensing, and introduces the two dataset we have worked on. We then introduce our recognition method that was presented for participation to the Social Touch Challenge at ICMI2015[1]. Finally, we show our results and discuss them.

2. RELATED WORKS

2.1 Research Context

Touch gestures recognitions is a trending research topic with recent patent such as Google's on grid of touch sensors [6] on flat displays. As recently showed by Cooney et al. [7], touch is one of the main channels of communication of affection in human-robot interaction (HRI). These results suggest more focus of the research in recognizing affective touch gestures and improve human-robot touch communication. In a survey [8], the authors propose to categorize what they call

[1] http://www.utwente.nl/ewi/touch-challenge-2015/

Tactile HRI according to the covers of the sensor and according to king of physical interaction aiming to interfere with the robot's operation (i.e. grab to stop the movement for instance), to be part of the interaction as a way to communicate (i.e. pat to signify satisfaction) or to learn from tactile inputs (i.e. reinforce behaviors by a pat). In this framework, more and more researches focus on recognizing social touch for the robot to react to the user. Sometimes, sensors are spread on a robot to recognize social touch [3].

2.2 Touch Challenge

2.2.1 *The CoST dataset*

The Corpus of Social Touch (CoST) dataset was introduced in [4]. It is a collection of 14 different social gestures performed under three variations: gentle, normal and rough. The data collection has been made via a sensor grid place on a mannequin arm. 31 participants participated to the data acquisition. The collected data consist in an 8x8 grid of pressure intensity at 135 fps. For the first recognition of the 14 gestures of the CoST, authors [4] chose to compute 28 features. They used Gaussian Bayesian and SVM classifiers to constitute the baseline of recognition of gestures form the 8x8 sensors data. The accuracy had an overall maximum of 54% with the Bayesian classifiers. This paper reported also the difficultly to recognize some gestures from others like the gentle gestures. The curvature of the arm on which the sensors are placed could also play a role in the lower recognition rate.

2.2.2 *The HAART dataset*

The aim for recording the HAART corpus [5] was to be able to sense emotion through gestures. Authors collected data from 16 participants at 50fps. They choose 9 gestures for the participants to perform and recorded each gesture for 2 seconds. When trained on all participants the recognition has an accuracy of 86% and when trained on individuals the authors' recognition system reaches 94%. The reader must note that for the challenge, in order to be consistent with the CoST corpus, the 10x10 pressure sensor data has been trimmed to the 8x8 central pressure cells. Thus, for the HAART task, we are not strictly in condition reported by previous researches [2] as they used more pressure cells (100 versus 64).

3. METHODOLOGY

The team involved in the touch challenge for the Grenoble system is multidisciplinary. People have background in several audio and video signal processing (speech recognition, visual tracking, multimodal perception...), Human Robot Interaction and indoor localization. Interest for such a group is to try alternative approaches for the challenge coming from multiple scientific communities.

The first step of our methodology was to decide between HAART and CoST tasks which is the more difficult one. Factually, the CoST corpus has twice more classes. Preliminary simple classification experiments confirmed that the same system performs better on the HAART task. For the challenge, we concentrated our efforts on building the best classification system for the CoST task. Then, we applied recipes directly on the HAART corpus.

Next steps of our methodology are detailed in the following sections. Results using Dynamic Time Warping DTW are reported in 3.3.1. Submitted challenge results using Support Vector Machine and Random Forest are detailed in section 4.

3.1 Looking deeply at the data

Our analysis of the HAART and CoST corpora started with a deep look at the data. Several information where extracted. We computed usual statistics *i.e. min*, *max*, *mean*, *median*, and *standard deviation* of each cell of the pressure sensor for each corpus and for each class. No real differences between *min* and *max* values were noticeable for both corpora. The distribution for each pressure sensor value for CoST gestures is quite uniformly distributed on $[0; 1023]$ (see fig. 1) (99% of values are in the $[0, 770]$ interval). HAART statistics (*mean=7.20*, *median=3*, *std-dev=16.15*) significantly differ from CoST ones (*mean=159.62*, *median=106*, *std-dev=159.37*). Mean and standard deviation from the HAART corpus are lower. 99% of HAART pressure values are in $[0, 75]$. Figure 1 shows some peculiarities of the CoST data. Distribution of pressure values presents a periodic variation $p{=}{\sim}30$: all values do not have the same probability. This result is the same for the 64 sensors. One hypothesis could be that internal quantification algorithm of each pressure sensor is responsible but we cannot conclude definitely. This statistical analysis showed that HAART and CoST corpora have notable disparities.

In order to accurately understand what the gestures are, we used several visual representations (see fig. 2). The 2D visualization represents power of each cell of the 8x8 sensor for a frame. Concatenating then, we built gesture videos. These videos showed that external sensors are less frequently activated. Some visual patterns seem to appear on the 8x8 sensor, humanly recognizable but not for all gestures. We also looked at temporal representation of all training sequences. There are a lot of variations among participants and gestures. For a same touch gesture, intra-participant variations are less important than inter-participant variations. One can find examples of these variations for a simple *roughgrab* on figure 2 and 3 of a previous article about the CoST corpus [4]. We can only make the assumption that even with a specific request, people have different interpretation of a gesture. This hypothesis was consolidated by results presented in previous study on the HAART corpus [5]. Using gestures, the person recognition accuracy was at least equal to 79%. On some gestures (*contact*, *pat*, *tickle*), the accuracy was over 90%.

We learned a lot analyzing data from both corpora. We took benefits from this knowledge to design our classification system.

3.2 Filtering training subsets

An important problem emerged when looking at temporal representations of gestures: bad segmentation for some gestures in the training data. On figure 2, the central example depicted one too long *hit* gesture. The first 320 frames, more than 2.3 seconds[2], do not belong to a *hit* touch and should have been removed. On the *poke* example, the sequence is contrarily too short and does not contain actual information about the gesture.

Armed with this experience, we decided to select data for

[2]The frame rate of the CoST corpus is 135Hz.

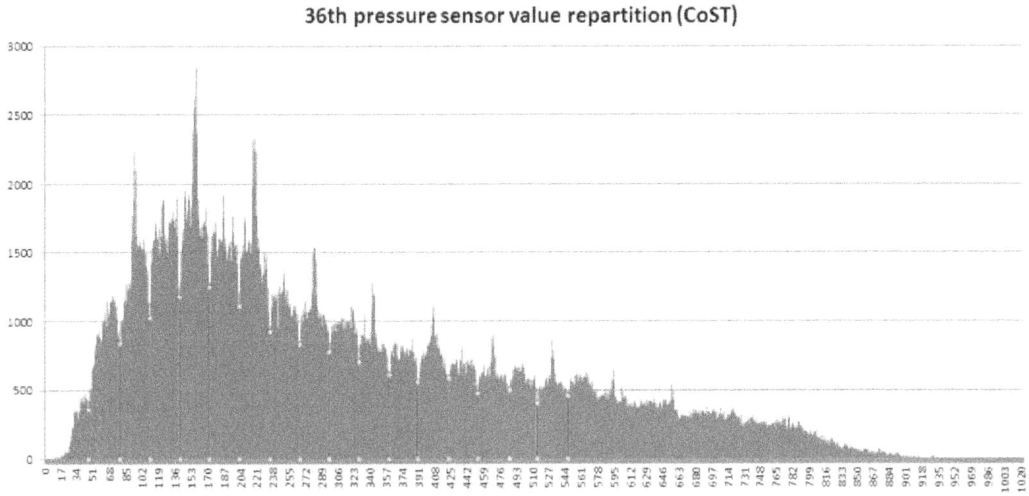

Figure 1: Distribution of pressure values for of the 36th sensor (central) of the CoST corpus. Blue vertical lines highlight periodic variation of the values.

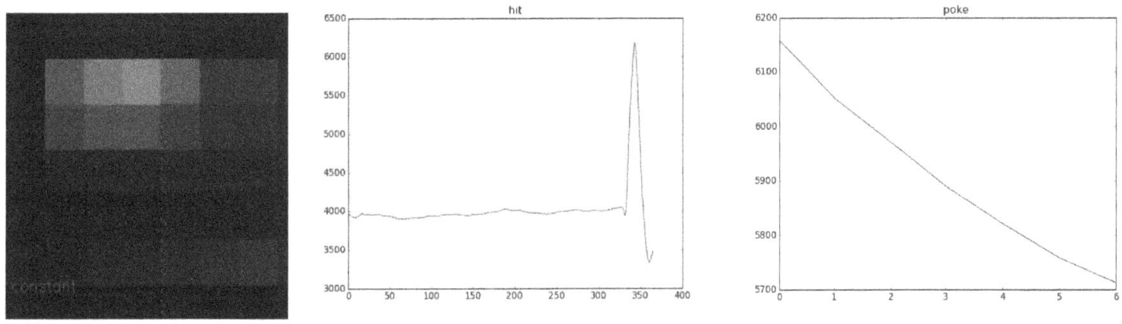

Figure 2: Visualization of data. At left, 2D visualization of a 8x8 sensor for one frame (*constant* example, max value in red). The middle and right figures are temporal representation of respectively *hit* and *poke* examples.

the training of our system in order to increase performance of our classification system. We tried to remove automatically abnormal training sequences. As seen, these gestures were mainly too long or too short sequences. We used statistics on frames, filtering outlier gestures within classes. Several thresholds on length of sequences, median, mean, or maximal pressure values, and selection percentage were unsuccessfully tested. There was no evident automatic filter that significantly increases performance of the classification system at this time.

With the certitude that removing outliers can lead to performance enhancement, we backed down to a manual selection. We did a two pass selection on the data, made by one researcher of our challenge group. The selection criteria were not only based on length of sequences, but also on shapes. For instance, some *pat* gestures looks more like *tap* or *grab*. From the CoST corpus, we removed 164 gestures (~4.5%). We refer to this new training corpus as "filtered" or "clean" later in this article.

As it is a time consuming task, the training selection was only done on the CoST training corpus. The new filtered trained corpus can be retrieve asking to the authors. In section 5, we will see that each classification systems on the CoST corpus, we submitted two results: one on *filtered data* and one on *all training data.*

3.3 Experiments

3.3.1 Dynamic Time Warping experiments

Based on our background in speech processing and on literature in gesture recognition, we tried several Dynamic Time Warping (DTW) approaches. Dynamic Time Warping is used for many time sequence matching problems like speech or gesture recognition [9, 10, 11, 12]. In a similar context to this challenge, DTW have been used for emotion recognition using pressure sensor keyboard [13]. Dynamic Time Warping selects among n models the best candidate, i.e. the model that best matches the input sequence. DTW only needs a feature set and a distance function to process data sequences. Uncountable variants of DTW can be found in literature. Using temporal representation depicted in section 3.1, we implemented several DTW flavors based on models selection or optimization [10], or multidimensionnal DTW (MD-DTW) [14, 12, 15]. MD-DTW does not perform well on the Cost task (~40% of accuracy). Model selection or optimization strategy can elicit better models. As presented in [11], our selection strategy chooses normalized models that minimize intra-class and maximize inter-class distances: 90% of original models are kept. The best score using models selection is ~47%.

None of these global approaches provide more than 50% of accuracy. As we said before, outside pressure cells are less activated than center ones. Not all lines or columns of the

8x8 sensor have the same temporal shape. We did experiments using DTW per lines, per columns and per both axis. A majority vote provides the most detected class, or if there is an ambiguity, the class with the lowest distance score. Finally, we managed to almost equals original results previously reported [4] on the CoST corpus (our best score=52%) using DTW per lines and per columns with model selection.

3.3.2 *Machine learning approach*

As DTW did not perform as expected, we needed to choose among machine learning algorithms. They are many candidates that cannot all be tested. The choice of the underlying classification algorithms has been driven mainly by our expertise and previous results on the corpora. Support Vector Machine (SVM) has demonstrated performance in previous tasks [16]. Random Forest (RF) proved their adequacy on the HAART corpus [5]. The later sections of this article will detail experiments and results using SVM and RF.

4. FEATURES SET

This section details our feature list, the feature selection method and the evaluation of the final feature set.

4.1 Features Extraction

From our research background, previous works [4, 5, 11, 13, 17] and our analysis of the data, we picked a list of features to cater gesture recognition. For easy tracking of the number of features and the way it affects the classification capacity of the model, we divided the features into three groups: *global* features, *channel-based* features, *sequence* of average pressure features.

4.1.1 *Global features (Group 1)*

The 40 features in this group represent overall statistics of the gestures. Some of them are adapted from [4], some came from our deep look at the representation of the gestures (see 3.1):

- Number of frames (i.e. length of the gesture);
- Average pressure on the 64 channels over all frames;
- Maximum value of pressure of all channels over all frames;
- Percentage *no signal* frames. A frame is considered as *no signal* if its average value over all 64 channels is below a threshold t. We set $t=50$ for both datasets;
- Mean pressure over all frames of each column;
- Mean pressure over all frames of each row;
- Variations around a specific value c. *Zero-Crossing Rate* (ZCR) is a time-domain feature still widely used in many speech applications [18]. It is measures variations around the central value (zero in case of speech) of the temporal signal and provides clues information about speech activity. Inspired by this feature and our experiments using DTW, we implemented what can be called *c-crossing*. It considers the 64 channels as 1-dimensional temporal signal by taking the mean value over 64 channels for each frame. This group of feature includes the number of crossing around c, the percentage of the sequence above c, the average length of sequence above c, and the average slope of each crossing. As it was impossible to fixed c for all gestures, we took 5 different values for c: 35th, 50th, 65th, 80th and 95th-percentile of the maximal value.

4.1.2 *Channel-based features (Group 2)*

Channel-based features are extracted on each channel. Basically, they ignore the temporal relationship of consecutive frames and focus on the spatial relationship between different channels. There are a total of 192 features in this group:

- Average pressure of each channel over all frames;
- Average pressure variation of each channel over all frames. First, it takes the absolute difference of each consecutive pair of frames. Then, we add the mean of all the differences through the time per channel;
- Percentage of time when a channel has pressure more than a fixed threshold T: For each channel, we compute the number of times where it reaches above T. It is then divided by the number of frames to get the percentage value. These features reflect the strong active regions of the channels. In our experiments, T is set relatively as the 90-percentile of all the value in the gesture.

4.1.3 *Sequence features (Group 3)*

In this group of features, we want to extract the changes over time of the gestures. These changes should be captured on each individual channel. However, it will drastically increase the size of the feature set. We used the sequence of average pressure over 64-channel for each frame. There are a total of 41 features in this group:

- Fast Fourier transform based features: these features are the results of applying the Fast Fourier operator [19] to the sequence of average pressure. The operator extracts the first 16 highest frequencies values, taking only the real part.
- Discrete cosine transform based features: these features are the results when apply the discrete cosine transform [20] to the sequence of average pressure over 64 channels. We used the discrete cosine transform type 2. The operator extracts the first 25 value. In the case where the length of the gesture is less than 25 frames, the missing values are set to 0. This will set each feature vector have an equal length.

The total set of 273 features is extracted on the original frames. On each individual frame, we applied a Sobel operator to extract local variation of the pressure [21]. We get a new sequence of Sobel frames for each gesture. As this new sequence has the same structure (size, number of channel per frame) of the original one, we can use the same process to extract another 273 features. Our final feature set contains 546 features in total.

4.2 Feature selection

From the process above, there may have noisy, under-correlated or redundant features. For example, the outside channels may contain noise from the extraction process rather than providing valuable information. Hence, we performed feature selection to improve the performance of the system. From 546 feature vector above, we ran a Random Forest model (from the Scikit-learn library [22]), then selecting the 30% highest weighted features with a 3-fold cross-validation on training data (see more details on cross-validation in 4.3.2). The choice of a 3-fold was made to provide a similar relative proportion of the training and test sets in the competition. After this selection step, we got a 164 feature set.

In previous researches in multimodal perception [16], we successfully applied a feature reduction technique from bioinformatics research domain. The Minimum Redundancy Maximum Relevance [23] (MRMR) has the advantage of giving the more relevant features instead of building new features from the observed ones. On our computers, we cannot compute a global selection, but an in-group partial selection. The reduced feature set using MRMR did not improve significantly our results, we kept the previous selection.

4.3 Feature evaluation

As said, the same feature selection scheme can be applied on the CoST and HAART datasets. For time constraint reasons, we choose to rely on only the CoST dataset to estimate the effectiveness of the feature set.

4.3.1 Auto-validation

One preliminary validation was to check whatever we have, among selected features, enough information about the data. The first test was to train a system and to test it against the whole training dataset. This test is not dedicated to check performance but to acknowledge our previous choices and our algorithm implementation. For SVM and RF systems, using the 164 feature set, auto-validation provides 100% of accuracy. With this result, we can go ahead and use our system on the challenge test data.

4.3.2 Cross-validation

Cross-validation is used to validate performance of a system against a corpus. We tried a *k-fold* cross validation on the filtered CoST corpus. In this method, the dataset is partitioned in *k* subsets. One subset is kept for testing and the *k-1* others are used for training the model. This splitting process is repeated *k* times so that each subset is used once for testing against others subsets. Interest of this method resides in two aspects: a clear separation of training and testing parts for evaluation; a validation of all data, subset by subset, to check performance in regards of data distribution within the corpus. As gestures are very user-dependent [5], we implemented a specific *k-fold*. Our folding strategy does not split using gestures and/or variants information but using user ids. Thus, it is impossible to have gestures from the same user both in train and test corpora. Our *3-fold* result is presented on last line of second column of table 1. The best cross-validation score on the CoST task is 69.77%. At this time, it seemed a good improvement from previous results [4, 17].

4.3.3 Contribution of each feature group

To verify the previous score, we ran a Random Forest model with cross validation on the clean training set. We added features group by group to check whether the recognition rate increase or not. After the challenge, with the test data labels, we did the experiment again on the test data. The results are presented in the table 1.

The experiment started with only group 1 as the base features. We kept expanding the size of feature vectors by adding features of group 2, then features of group 3. At last, we tried 164 feature set. By looking at the *k-fold* testing on the training data, each group generates a clear improvement to the starting one. We can conclude that valuable features

Features	Acc. on Train	Acc. on Test
Group 1	58.22%	52.17%
Group 1 + 2	66.56%	56.81%
Group 1 + 2 + 3	66.89%	58.96%
Adding Sobel Frame	68.61%	60.10%
164 features	69.77%	61.34%

Table 1: Incremental feature set performance on the CoST dataset.

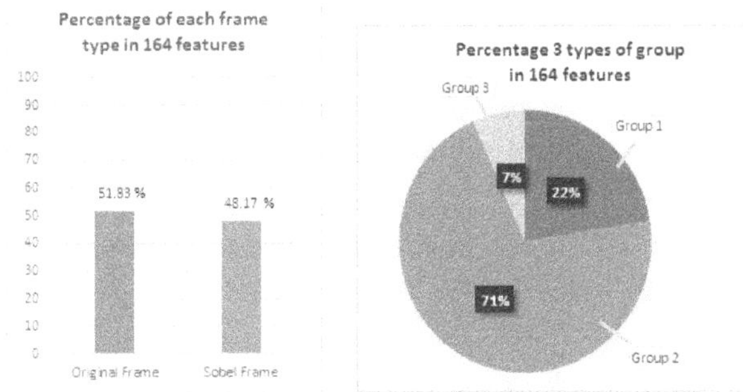

Figure 3: Contribution of each feature group to the final feature set.

are present in all groups. The selection method is useful as it proposes an absolute ~1% accuracy improvement. One can note that there is a high correlation between accuracy in both testing scheme but there is a clear drop of accuracy on testing data.

Additional information can be found on figures 3 and 4. The first one gives additional statistical properties, notably distribution of each feature group, in the 164 feature set. The second provides importance of each channel to classify the gesture types in term of selected channel features. As we expected, the channels around the center contain the highest amount of information.

5. EXPERIMENTAL RESULTS

Random Forest were used for their ability to handle large sets of features and to include irrelevant features. Support Vector Machine (SVM) were used as a baseline for comparison with previous results on classifying gestures on the CoST dataset [4]. SVM used *rbf* kernels and standard parameters from the Scikit-learn library. Results using RF and SVM are depicted in this section. In all tables, RF results have a light gray background.

5.1 Actual results for the challenge

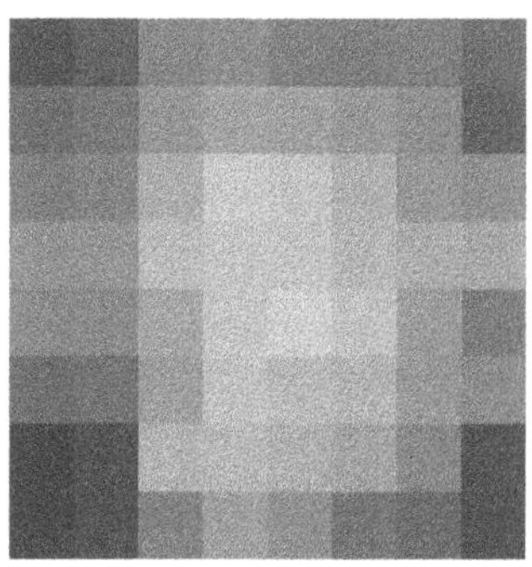

Figure 4: Importance of the 64 channels. The highest one are colored with the brightest color.

After release of the test data, we ran our classification systems on both corpora. For the HAART corpus, we applied directly our SVM and RF systems. For CoST, we used two versions of our systems: one using all training data, one trained on the manually filtered version (see 3.2).

Results on the CoST task for the all flavors of our systems can be found in table 2. At first look, these results confirmed our hypothesis: filtering training data can be of interest. Either for SVM or RF, the classification result is better than using the whole training set. In this table, the best result (61.34%) is a Random Forest system trained on the filtered training set. We cannot definitely conclude that RF is better that SVM. Indeed, feature selection was done using a RF paradigm. This may explain why RF performs better using this final feature set. The matrices (tables 5 and 6) show confusions among our results. There is no outstanding difference in these results between SVM and RF systems, in both training scheme. The list of main confusion groups is (*squeeze*, *grab*), (*tap*, *pat*, *slap*, *hit*), (*rub*, *stroke*) and (*scratch*, *tickle*). For all conditions, the worst performance classification concerns *rub*, *pat*, *scratch* and *squeeze* ($\leq$ 50%). *Rub* is the more difficult gesture to recognize. The best recognize score is for *poke*, followed by *stroke*, *tickle* and *massage*. These results are coherent with previous reported confusion matrices [4] even if the distribution is strictly not the same.

For the HAART task, one can see results in table 3. Again, the RF performs slightly better than SVM. Looking at confusion matrix (see table 4), contrarily to the previous results, there are differences between the SVM and RF classification system. Indeed, even if the global scores are comparable (*SVM=68.52%*, *RF=70.91%*), the inner values for classes notably vary. There is an absolute improvement for the *constant* and the *rub* classes, respectively +34.29% and +30.56% of accuracy. At the same time, the correct rate of some other classes decreases: *pat* −11.11%, *scratch* −25.00% and *tickle* −8.33%. *notouch* and *stoke* remain almost stable. At the writing time of this article, we have no hypothesis to explain these results. We will need more experiments to make assumptions.

5.2 Discussion

Gesture classification does not present the same accuracy for all gestures. Even if auto-validation provides perfect results, it seems that information is missing to fully differentiate the gestures. Our confusion matrices are coherent with the literature. This problem is thus the same for all reported systems. We can place our classification results within the context of the challenge looking at tables 7 and 8. Performances of our classifiers are slightly better than systems proposed by the other participants. Our best scores for both corpora remain below the state-of-the-art results. Nevertheless, the previous results on the HAART corpus [5] are not strictly in the condition of the challenge. The 86% of accuracy is obtained using a 100-fold cross-validation paradigm. Moreover, these results are obtained on a 10x10 pressure sensor. Even if we showed (see figures 2 and 4) that outside channels less contribute to the classification, they are not useless. These facts may explain the huge gap (>15%) between challenge participants and HAART state-of-the-art results. Still, we can compare our system using the available 8x8 pressure data we have and a 100-fold cross-validation. Our score is 76.84%. Difference with state-of-the-art result on the CoST corpus [24] is less important (<5%). Conditions of this result are similar to the challenge condition.

	CoST task	
Training data	manually selected subset	all
SVM	59.91%	60.51%
Random Forest	**61.34%**	60.81%

Table 2: Overall results on the CoST task.

	HAART task
SVM	68.52%
Random Forest	**70.91%**

Table 3: Overall results on the HAART task.

6. CONCLUSION

This paper detailed a method to recognize touch gestures on CoST and HAART corpora. We provide new features and classification system to recognize gestures on a grid touch sensor. Our process was developed on the CoST corpus and then directly applied on the HAART task. For the challenge, we submitted several classifiers. A Support Vector Machine and a Random Forest systems for HAART. For the CoST task, the same classifiers are tested in two conditions: using all training set or our manually filtered one. As reported by organizers, our systems have the best correct rate in this year challenge (70.91% on HAART, 61.34% on CoST). However, our performances are slightly better that other participants and under previous reported state-of-the-art results.

In conclusion, one can say that our statistical analysis of the grid touch sensor and our classification method contribute to social touch classification. Lessons learned and depicted in this article can be combined with information from other participants. This may lead to a next step improvement in social touch recognition domain.

7. REFERENCES

[1] M. D. Cooney, S. Nishio, and H. Ishiguro, "Recognizing affection for a touch-based interaction with a humanoid robot," in *Intelligent Robots and Systems (IROS), 2012 IEEE/RSJ International Conference on*, pp. 1420–1427, IEEE, 2012.

[2] A. Billard, A. Bonfiglio, G. Cannata, P. Cosseddu, T. Dahl, K. Dautenhahn, F. Mastrogiovanni, G. Metta, L. Natale, B. Robins, *et al.*, "The roboskin project: Challenges and results," in *Romansy 19–Robot Design, Dynamics and Control*, pp. 351–358, Springer, 2013.

[3] H. Knight, R. Toscano, W. D. Stiehl, A. Chang, Y. Wang, and C. Breazeal, "Real-time social touch gesture recognition for sensate robots," in *Intelligent Robots and Systems, 2009. IROS 2009. IEEE/RSJ International Conference on*, pp. 3715–3720, IEEE, 2009.

[4] M. M. Jung, "Touching the Void - Introducing CoST : a Corpus of Social Touch," in *Proceedings of the 16th International Conference on Multimodal Interaction*, pp. 1–8, 2014.

	constant		notouch		pat		rub		scratch		stroke		tickle	
constant	**22**	**34**	0	1	0	0	0	0	0	0	0	0	0	0
notouch	1	1	**36**	**35**	0	0	0	0	0	0	0	0	0	0
pat	0	0	0	0	**30**	**26**	0	1	0	0	1	1	0	0
rub	0	0	0	0	0	4	**15**	**28**	2	13	1	4	1	5
scratch	12	0	0	0	1	0	17	3	**27**	**18**	3	0	24	21
stroke	0	0	0	0	5	5	3	3	1	0	**31**	**31**	0	4
tickle	0	0	0	0	0	1	1	1	6	5	0	0	**11**	**6**

Table 4: Confusion matrix for the HAART task. In white, SVM results (correct rate 68.52%). In light gray, Random Forest results (correct rate 70.91%).

	grab	hit	massage	pat	pinch	poke	press	rub	scratch	slap	squeeze	stroke	tap	tickle
grab	**83**	0	4	0	4	0	13	2	0	0	52	0	0	0
hit	0	**71**	0	10	0	0	0	0	0	35	0	0	8	0
massage	0	0	**80**	0	0	0	1	9	6	0	2	0	0	6
pat	0	9	0	**48**	1	0	0	0	0	3	0	0	23	0
pinch	2	1	0	1	**82**	2	7	0	0	0	6	2	0	1
poke	0	8	0	2	14	**107**	8	0	0	0	1	0	5	2
press	0	0	0	2	9	3	**82**	11	0	0	0	1	1	0
rub	1	0	14	0	0	0	1	**47**	17	0	0	11	1	5
scratch	8	0	1	0	0	0	0	7	**50**	0	0	3	0	12
slap	0	14	5	18	1	0	0	0	2	**66**	0	3	17	0
squeeze	26	0	6	0	7	0	7	1	1	0	**58**	0	0	0
stroke	0	0	1	2	0	0	0	32	9	0	0	**94**	0	4
tap	0	17	0	37	2	8	1	0	2	16	0	2	**64**	6
tickle	0	0	9	0	0	0	0	11	33	0	0	4	1	**84**

Table 5: Confusion matrix for the CoST task with SVM using all training data (correct rate 60.51%)

	grab	hit	massage	pat	pinch	poke	press	rub	scratch	slap	squeeze	stroke	tap	tickle
grab	**80**	0	4	0	6	0	14	3	2	0	52	0	0	0
hit	0	**74**	0	13	0	0	0	0	0	41	0	1	13	0
massage	1	0	**91**	0	0	0	1	9	3	0	0	1	0	3
pat	0	6	0	**57**	1	1	0	0	0	2	0	0	23	1
pinch	2	2	0	0	**79**	1	4	0	1	0	8	6	0	2
poke	0	5	0	3	7	**99**	4	0	0	1	1	1	3	0
press	1	0	0	2	13	6	**88**	9	0	0	0	0	2	0
rub	3	0	8	0	0	0	1	**41**	10	0	0	14	0	4
scratch	6	0	7	0	0	0	0	8	**56**	1	0	0	0	15
slap	0	21	0	18	2	0	0	0	0	**64**	0	5	19	0
squeeze	27	0	0	0	12	0	8	1	1	0	**58**	0	0	0
stroke	0	0	1	2	0	0	0	32	11	0	0	**86**	0	4
tap	0	11	0	25	0	13	0	0	0	11	0	1	**60**	3
tickle	0	1	9	0	0	0	0	17	36	0	0	5	0	**88**

Table 6: Confusion matrix for the CoST task with Random Forest using manually selected training data (correct rate 61.34%)

System description	Correct rate
Neural network	35%
Correlation and moments based feature extraction + SVM classification	50%
Random Forests	61%
Decision trees	63%
Multiboost	65%
RandomForest	67%
Ensemble of DNN-HMM, Gaussian HMM and spectral features	68%
Anonymized system (SVM and RF, see table 3)	**from 68.52% to 70.91%**
→*state-of-the-art* [5]	*86%*

Table 7: Results of all other systems for the HAART task as reported by the challenge organizers. In italic, state-of-the-art result from [5]. In bold, our systems. (The system description was provided by the participants).

System description	Correct rate
ConvNet	45%
Neural network	45%
Ensemble of DNN-HMM, Gaussian HMM and spectral features	47%
Correlation and moments based feature extraction + SVM classification	53%
→*state-of-the-art* [4, 24]	*54%*
SVC OneVsRest	54%
Forest Bagging	57%
Multiboost	58%
RandomForest	59%
Anonymized system (SVM and RF, 2 training datasets, see table 2)	**from 59.91% to 61.34%**
→*state-of-the-art* [17]	*64.6%*

Table 8: Results of 8 best other systems for the CoST task as reported by the challenge organizers. In italic, previous state-of-the-art results from [4, 17, 24], In bold, our systems. (The system description was provided by the participants).

[5] A. Flagg and K. MacLean, "Affective touch gesture recognition for a furry zoomorphic machine," in *Proceedings of the 7th International Conference on Tangible, Embedded and Embodied Interaction*, pp. 25–32, ACM, 2013.

[6] W. Hillis, "Bounding box gesture recognition on a touch detecting interactive display," May 18 2010. US Patent 7,719,523.

[7] M. D. Cooney, S. Nishio, and H. Ishiguro, "Importance of Touch for Conveying Affection in a Multimodal Interaction with a Small Humanoid Robot," *International Journal of Humanoid Robotics*, vol. 12, p. 1550002, 2015.

[8] B. D. Argall and A. G. Billard, "A survey of tactile human–robot interactions," *Robotics and Autonomous Systems*, vol. 58, no. 10, pp. 1159–1176, 2010.

[9] W. Abdulla, D. Chow, and G. Sin, "Cross-words reference template for dtw-based speech recognition systems," in *TENCON 2003. Conference on Convergent Technologies for the Asia-Pacific Region*, vol. 4, pp. 1576–1579 Vol.4, Oct 2003.

[10] V. Niennattrakul, D. Srisai, and C. A. Ratanamahatana, "Shape-based template matching for time series data," *Knowledge-Based Systems*, vol. 26, pp. 1–8, 2012.

[11] B. Hartmann and N. Link, "Gesture recognition with inertial sensors and optimized dtw prototypes," in *Systems Man and Cybernetics (SMC), 2010 IEEE International Conference on*, pp. 2102–2109, Oct 2010.

[12] N. Gillian, R. B. Knapp, and S. O?Modhrain, "Recognition of multivariate temporal musical gestures using n-dimensional dynamic time warping," in *Proc of the 11th Int'l conference on New Interfaces for Musical Expression*, 2011.

[13] H.-R. Lv, Z.-L. Lin, W.-J. Yin, and J. Dong, "Emotion recognition based on pressure sensor keyboards," in *Multimedia and Expo, 2008 IEEE International Conference on*, pp. 1089–1092, IEEE, 2008.

[14] G. Ten Holt, M. Reinders, and E. Hendriks, "Multi-dimensional dynamic time warping for gesture recognition," in *Thirteenth annual conference of the Advanced School for Computing and Imaging*, 2007.

[15] S. Uchida and H. Sakoe, "A monotonic and continuous two-dimensional warping based on dynamic programming," in *icpr*, p. 521, IEEE, 1998.

[16] D. Vaufreydaz, W. Johal, and C. Combe, "Starting engagement detection towards a companion robot using multimodal features," *Robotics and Autonomous Systems*, pp. –, 2015.

[17] S. van Wingerden, T. J. Uebbing, M. M. Jung, and M. Poel, "A neural network based approach to social touch classification," in *Proceedings of the 2014 workshop on Emotion Recognition in the Wild Challenge and Workshop*, pp. 7–12, ACM, 2014.

[18] X. Pan, H. Zhao, Y. Zhou, C. Fan, W. Zou, Z. Ren, and X. Chen, "A preliminary study on the feature distribution of deceptive speech signals," *Journal of Fiber Bioengineering and Informatics*, vol. 8, no. 1, pp. 179–193, 2015.

[19] P. Duhamel and M. Vetterli, "Fast fourier transforms: a tutorial review and a state of the art," *Signal processing*, vol. 19, no. 4, pp. 259–299, 1990.

[20] J. Makhoul, "A fast cosine transform in one and two dimensions," *Acoustics, Speech and Signal Processing, IEEE Transactions on*, vol. 28, no. 1, pp. 27–34, 1980.

[21] R. C. Gonzalez and R. E. Woods, "Digital image processing reading," *MA: Addison-Wesley*, 1992.

[22] F. Pedregosa, G. Varoquaux, A. Gramfort, V. Michel, B. Thirion, O. Grisel, M. Blondel, P. Prettenhofer, R. Weiss, V. Dubourg, J. Vanderplas, A. Passos, D. Cournapeau, M. Brucher, M. Perrot, and E. Duchesnay, "Scikit-learn: Machine learning in Python," *Journal of Machine Learning Research*, vol. 12, pp. 2825–2830, 2011.

[23] P. Hanchuan, L. Fuhui, and D. Chris, "Feature Selection Based on Mutual Information : Criteria of Max-Dependency, Max-Relevance and Min-Redundancy," *IEEE Transactions on Pattern Analysis and Machine Intelligence*, vol. 27, no. 8, pp. 1226–1238, 2005.

[24] M. M. Jung, "Towards social touch intelligence: Developing a robust system for automatic touch recognition," in *Proceedings of the 16th International Conference on Multimodal Interaction*, ICMI '14, (New York, NY, USA), pp. 344–348, ACM, 2014.

Social Touch Gesture Recognition using Random Forest and Boosting on Distinct Feature Sets

Yona Falinie A. Gaus
Brunel University London
yonafalinie.abdgaus@brunel.ac.uk

Temitayo Olugbade
UCL Interaction Centre
UCL
temitayo.olugbade.13@ucl.ac.uk

Asim Jan
Brunel University London
asim.jan@brunel.ac.uk

Rui Qin
Brunel University London
rui.qin@brunel.ac.uk

Jingxin Liu
Brunel University London
jingxin.liu@brunel.ac.uk

Fan Zhang
Brunel University London
fan.zhang@brunel.ac.uk

Hongying Meng*
Brunel University London
hongying.meng@brunel.ac.uk

Nadia Bianchi-Berthouze
University College London
nadia.berthouze@ucl.ac.uk

ABSTRACT

Touch is a primary nonverbal communication channel used to communicate emotions or other social messages. Despite its importance, this channel is still very little explored in the affective computing field, as much more focus has been placed on visual and aural channels. In this paper, we investigate the possibility to automatically discriminate between different social touch types. We propose five distinct feature sets for describing touch behaviours captured by a grid of pressure sensors. These features are then combined together by using the Random Forest and Boosting methods for categorizing the touch gesture type. The proposed methods were evaluated on both the HAART (7 gesture types over different surfaces) and the CoST (14 gesture types over the same surface) datasets made available by the Social Touch Gesture Challenge 2015. Well above chance level performances were achieved with a 67% accuracy for the HAART and 59% for the CoST testing datasets respectively.

Categories and Subject Descriptors

H.5 [**Information Interfaces and Presentation**]: User Interfaces; I.2.1 [**Artificial Intelligence**]: Applications and Expert Systems—*Touch*

Keywords

Social Touch, Touch Gesture Recognition, Touch Features

1. INTRODUCTION

Touch is an important channel for affective communication and experience, as such interactive embodied technology should be endowed with the capabilities to interpret it. Despite this growing interest in various disciplines, and clear opportunities for affective-touch aware technology, this affective modality is still very little explored in the affective computing community where the focus has been on other affective modalities ([40] [23] [2]. The Social Touch Gesture Challenge 2015 is timely attempting to stimulate interest and lead to the development of social touch automatic classification systems as the community has done for the other modalities.

Humans communicate emotions and other social messages through touch. We explore and appreciate objects through touch. The emerging understanding of the physiological and neural mechanisms at the basis of affective touch [9],[37] has led to a growing interest in investigating how we communicate or express affect through touch. Studies on multimodal communication, have shown that touch amplify the intensity of an emotion conveyed by the face and through the voice [24]. Burgoon [5] showed that touch itself can convey more complex social feelings such as trust and affection. Hertenstein et al. [17] [16] contributed to this body of work by showing that through touch we do not only communicate the intensity of an emotion, but also its valence and that we are able to discriminate between at least nine discrete emotions from touch behaviour alone. Their work identifies a set of touch gestures and kinematics that are used in social interaction.

Social touch gestures have been investigated in the field of Human-Computer Interaction as a way to build intimacy and facilitate distance relationships. For example, Park et al. [30] have shown that, when given an haptic channel, people develop haptic codes to communicate at distance with their partners. In human-robot interaction, social touch has been shown to increase bond and trust in various therapeutically applications ([32] [33] [19]). In the commercial and design settings, [1] has shown that we use different types of touches not only to understand the characteristics of an object (textile in this case) but also the affective sensations it provokes in us. This is further supported by [31], where it

*Corresponding author.

ICMI '15, November 09-13, 2015, Seattle, WA, USA
© 2015 ACM. ISBN 978-1-4503-3912-4/15/11 ... $15.00.
DOI: http://dx.doi.org/10.1145/2818346.2830599

is shown that, during creative design sessions, designers use affective touch to stimulate their creative processes. They also discuss how designers observe the hands of their customers touching a product to understand what they feel. In more general terms, [20] and [3] discuss the importance and the possibilities that affective touch offers to evaluate the user experience in human-computer interaction contexts.

Initial work towards building systems for the automatic detection of affective touch are summarised in Gao et al. [12]. Through their study, the authors also shows that the kinematics of strokes during a touch-based computer games on smartphone allow the detection of how a player feels obtaining very high performances. However, each of these works focus on one affective/social touch type at the time (e.g., tapping, stroking). Discriminating between different social touch gestures is also very important, as shown by Hertenstein [16]. In addition, for affective and social touch to be ubiquitous, it is important that the ability to classify it is independent of the type and shape of the surface being touched. This capability has become very critical as embedding touch sensors in any type of mobile surface is now achievable at a relatively low cost. Hence, it is mandatory that this channel is investigated beyond the flat surface of touch-based displays. The Social Touch Gesture Challenge 2015 answers to all these needs by providing two touch behaviour datasets: the 'Human-Animal Affective Robot Touch'(HAART) dataset [10] and the 'Corpus of Social Touch' (CoST) [22]. These datasets provide a wide range of type behaviour on surfaces of different shapes and consistencies embedded with pressure sensors. Our paper responds to this challenge by proposing a way to describe the types of touch gestures tracked by the sensors and by proposing an ensemble of machine learning methods to discriminate between the different types of touch behaviour.

The rest of the paper is organized as follows. Section 2 provides an overview of related works. Afterwards, Section 3 illustrates the methodology of our proposed approach including the description of the feature sets and classification methods. Section 4 presents the experimental results on the challenge datasets. The possible influencing factors for different performance indicators are discussed in Section 5 together with future directions.

2. RELATED WORKS

Human-Robot interaction is possibly one of the more active areas where researchers have been investigating how to create touch sensing capabilities. A typical approach is to cover a robot with an artificial skin that simulates human touch sensory system [8] [29] [39] [34] [36]. An indirect way to give robots the capability to sense touch is instead to embed them with sensors that measure temperature, proximity and pressure [38] [18] [28] [42] [7] . Works using these two types of approaches are discussed below.

The earliest work on artificial skin is in 1999 [29], where a robot was covered with gridded pressure-sensitive conductive ink sheets . Five different touch gestures ('pat', 'scratch', 'slap', 'stroke' and 'tickle') were performed on the sensor sheet. Absolute pressure values and temporal difference between pressure values were used as features to discriminate between these different types of touch.

Silvera-Tawil et al [39] developed further the concept of artificial skin by using the principle of electrical impedance tomography (EIT). This innovation enabled to cover larger areas of a robot and allowed to extract information such as location, duration, displacement and intensity of touch. 'Pat', 'push', 'stroke', 'slap' and 'tap' gestures were investigated and the LogitBoost algorithm was used for classification purpose. In a follow-up study, Silvera-Tawil et al [34] successfully implemented an artificial skin to cover the arm of a full-size mannequin. Increasing the number of touch gestures by adding 'pull', 'slap' and 'squeeze', they compared the classification accuracy obtained with the LogitBoost algorithm (71%) with human recognition (90%). Further experiments were shown in [35] by interpreting social touch on the same artificial skin. Up to 90% accuracy were achieved using Logitboost algorithm for both emotions and social messages, similar with human recognition.

The second approach simulates touch perception capabilities by using sensors. This approach has been extensively used in social robotics: Shibata's baby seal Paro [32] [33], SONY's dog, Aibo [11], Stiehl's teddy bear the Huggable [38], Saldien and Goris's elephant-like creature Probo [14] [13], and the latest one is a furry artificial lap-pet called Haptic Creature [6] [42] [10]. Apart from robot-animal like form, other types of interface such as Emoballon [28], TaSSt project [18] can enable remote communication. We cover below some of the more significant differentiating factors in relation to these robots or interfaces.

The Huggable [38] is a robotic companion with the form of a teddy bear, equipped with a combination of temperature, electric field, and QTC force sensors intended to facilitate affective haptic communication between two people. Nine touch gestures ('contact', 'pat', 'pet', 'poke', 'rub', 'scratch', 'slap', 'squeeze' and 'tickle') were performed on an arm of the robot, and features such as change in direction of motion, average sensor value and the number of sensors active among others, were extracted from the sensors.

Probo [14] [13] is an elephant-like social robot equipped with a large variety of sensors. Probo can recognize whether it is being hugged, scratched, or hurt. The robot is used to address anxiety in hospitalized children. Similarly, Paro [32] [33], the famous robot seal, responds to being touched, differentiates between being stroked and hit, and tries to amend its own behaviour accordingly, repeating actions that have been rewarded with stroking, and avoiding actions that have led to being hit.

The Haptic Creature, developed by Yohanan and his colleagues [41] [42], is a furry lap-sized social robot that communicates with the world through touch. By expressing itself through ear stiffness modulations, breathing rate, and purring patterns, the Haptic Creature aims to create a comforting experience through touch-based interactions by sensing and responding to human touch. The first experiments with the Haptic Creature investigated the recognition of four touch gesture types - 'pat', 'stroke', 'slap', 'poke'- by attaching force sensitive resistors all over its body [6]. These four gestures were differentiated with an average of 77% accuracy, depending on the sensor density of where it was touched.

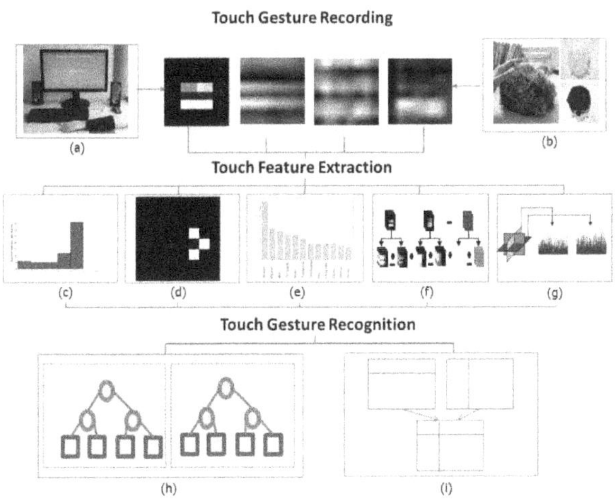

Figure 1: Overview of the proposed social touch gesture recognition system (a) CoST (b) HAART (c) SD (d) BMH (e) MSD (f) SMMHH (g) LBPTOP (h) Random Forest (i) Boosting.

Taking one step further, Yohanan and Maclean [42] examined how humans express their feelings for the Haptic Creature by means of touch gestures. Based on these reports, Yohanan and MacLean compiled a touch dictionary, also called the Yohanan's dictionary. Their findings inspired [10] and [22] to create two datasets containing labelled pressure sensor data of social hand touch gestures: HAART and CoST. The aim of these datasets is to challenge the creation of automatic affective touch classification systems by providing a large variety of touch behaviour types and kinematics as well as surfaces of different shapes and consistencies. We aim to advance the work already carried out on these datasets by proposing new touch features to better capture the characteristics (including shapes and dynamics) of the behaviour and new machine learning approaches to address the complexity of the mapping.

3. METHODOLOGY

This section introduces the two datasets of touch types used in this study, the set of features proposed to describe the touch instances and the methods to classify them. The overall system is shown in Fig 1.

3.1 Touch Gesture Capture

This research is based on the two datasets provided by the Social Touch challenge 2015: HAART and CoST.

3.1.1 HAART dataset

HAART [10] contains 7 touch gestures, performed by 10 subjects on an 8-by-8 grid of pressure sensors, where each sensor is approximately 1 square inch wide. The touch behaviour was recorded at 54 Hz with 64 sensors of data cell per frame. The sensors return integer values ranging between 0 and 972. Each subject performed each gesture under different combinations of substrates and different cover conditions with the sensor lying between the substrate and the surface cover. These are summarized in Table 1.

Table 1: HAART dataset: 7 touch gestures with different substrates and covers.

Substrate	Cover	Gesture
CURVE FOAM NONE	Fur Long None	constant, no touch, pat, rub, tickle, scratch, stroke

Table 2: COST dataset: 14 touch gestures.

1	2	3	4	5	6	7
grab	hit	massage	pat	pinch	poke	press
8	9	10	11	12	13	14
rub	scratch	slap	stroke	squeeze	tap	tickle

3.1.2 CoST dataset

CoST [22] contains 14 types of touch gestures (see Table 2). The touch gestures were performed by 31 subjects on a 8-by-8 grid of pressure sensors wrapped around a mannequin arm. The gestures were recorded with a frame rate of 135 Hz with 64 channels per frame. The values obtained from each channel are integers ranging between 0 and 1023. Each participant performed each gesture 6 times with 3 variations: gentle, normal and rough. More details on the data can be found in [22].

3.2 Touch Feature Extraction

The original recording of the touch sensors provided by the Social Touch Gesture Challenge 2015 needed to be transformed into high-level features, to gain more meaningful descriptions of the touch behaviour. The aim is to develop general features that are as independent as possible of the surface considered and of the kinematics of the gesture type. Parameters tuning is used to optimize their discriminative power to the different recording settings used for the two dataset but not between surfaces within the HAART dataset. Five sets of features are proposed.

3.2.1 Statistical distribution (SD) of pressure surface

We aimed to identify how much surface area (i.e., the number of sensor cells) is either not touched, touched (i.e., we are sure the area is touched and it is not noise) or touched with high pressure. The values used to capture these three conditions are represented in Table 3. For the no-touch and high-pressure conditions, we computed two features for each dataset: one using values computed at gesture level and one using values computed at frame level. For the touched condition, the median pressure value was used as a threshold indicating that the surface had been touched. In the case of the CoST, an analysis of the data, revealed that a pressure value of 100 was also a good threshold for capturing when the surface had been touched.

For each gesture instance and for each pressure value/range (Table 3), we computed the underlying distribution of the number of sensor cells per frames having such value/range. The MATLAB 'histcounts' was used to this purpose. In order to normalize the length of these features within a dataset (given that gestures had different frame numbers), appropriate bin widths and edges (see Table 4) were set to fit all instances. These parameters were estimated using the same Matlab function. An example of resulting feature (repre-

Table 3: Pressure values per datset

	CoST		HAART	
	At frame level	**At gesture instance level**	**At frame level**	**At gesture instance level**
no touch	= min. pressure	= min. pressure	= min. pressure	= min. pressure
touched	–	>= median pressure; >= 100	–	>= median pressure
high pressure	>= (max. pressure - 100)	>= (max. pressure - 100)	= max. pressure	= max. pressure

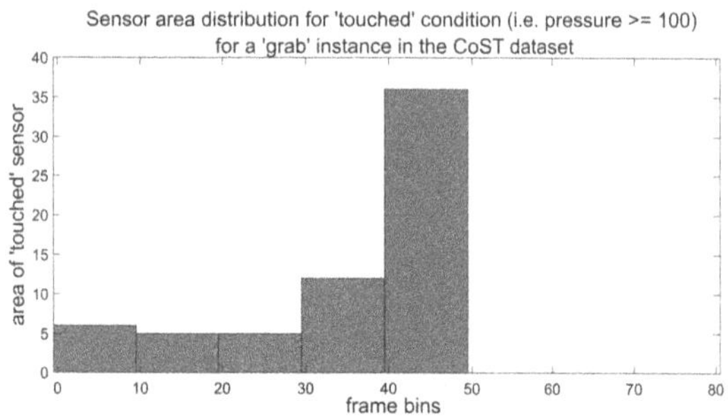

Figure 2: An example of a sensor area distribution feature for the 'touched' condition for a 'grab' instance using the MATLAB function histcounts and the relevant parameters listed in Table 4.

Figure 3: CoST dataset: Binary Motion History images: (from Left): Grab, Pinch, Poke, Rub, Tickle, and Pat.

sented by a histogram) is provided in Fig 2.

Table 4: Parameters computed for the MATLAB function 'histcount'

	CoST		HAART	
	bin width	bin edges leading, trailing	bin width	bin edges leading, trailing
$h_{notouch}$	1	-0.5, 11.5	5	-0.5, 55.5
$h_{touched}$	10	-0.5, 80.5	5	-0.5, 65.5
$h_{highpre.}$	10	-0.5, 100.5	5	-0.5, 55.5

3.2.2 Binary Motion History (BMH)

This set of features aims to capture the 'shape' of a gesture by computing a binary motion history (BMH) for each gesture instance. For each instance, an 8 by 8 matrix representing the sensor grid is created. A cell of the matrix is set to 1 if, throughout the gesture instance, the corresponding sensor cell was touched at least once with high pressure (CoST: pressure >= (maximum − 100); HAART: pressure >= (maximum − 5)), 0 otherwise. Fig. 3 shows examples of BMH for CoST gestures: 'grab', 'pinch', 'poke', 'rub', 'tickle', and 'pat' instances (in order from left to right). These examples illustrate how the BMH features provide an intuitive description of the different shapes from the types of the various gestures.

3.2.3 Motion statistical distribution (MSD)

A third set of features aimed to capture the main trends of the pressure behaviour. Twelve statistic features are extracted from each sensor sequence $F = (f_1, f_2, \cdots, f_L)$ including minimum, maximum, mean, first quartile, median, third quartile, area, total variation, interquartile range, variance, skewness and kurtosis on the changing information for each sensor. 'L' is the number of the frame. 'area' is the sum of all values of each sensor in all frames; 'total variation' is computed as the sum of changes in values for each sensor in all frames. The number of frames for the dataset is fixed as 432 frames, but the number of frames for the CoST dataset varies between instances. The extracted features are based on the whole gesture movement of each sensor independently of the number of frames.

3.2.4 Spatial Multi-scale Motion History Histogram (SMMHH) on touch dynamic

To provide more fine descriptions of the touch dynamics of the recording, the data was also treated as a video. On each frame, 8-by-8 sensors were treated as 8-by-8 pixels. Motion History Histogram (MHH) is a method used for temporal-based motion analysis, detecting pixel movements from a temporal domain and summarizing them as patterns in a spatial domain. This method was first developed for human action recognition by Meng et al.[26] to discriminate between several motion gestures such as walking, boxing, jumping etc. (for further details see [25] and [27]). A variation of the MHH method, called 1-D Motion History Histogram, was suggested by Jan et al. to apply this concept onto a 1-dimensional feature space [21], which looks for binary patterns within the feature vector sequence.

We propose a new variation of the original Motion History Histogram (MHH) algorithm, with two concepts that have been applied to alter the MHH feature. The first concept is the Multi-Scale Motion History Histogram (MMHH) achieved by introducing a new dimension to MHH and by skipping a fixed range of 1 to 5 frames during the motion detection process. By comparing frame n with $n+2:6$ instead of $n+1$, the motion is greatly amplified by the visual differences across the short time range, resulting in capturing motion at different speeds. This gives a more dynamic feature than the original MHH feature, providing a different viewpoint for each gesture as shown in Fig. 4.

The second concept uses the average spatial-pooling on the reshaped data. This allows to extract the motion information from the different scales in a similar way of the convolution neural networks of deep learning.

For the touch challenge, we applied Spatial Pooling three times, producing 4 videos (including the original one) of:

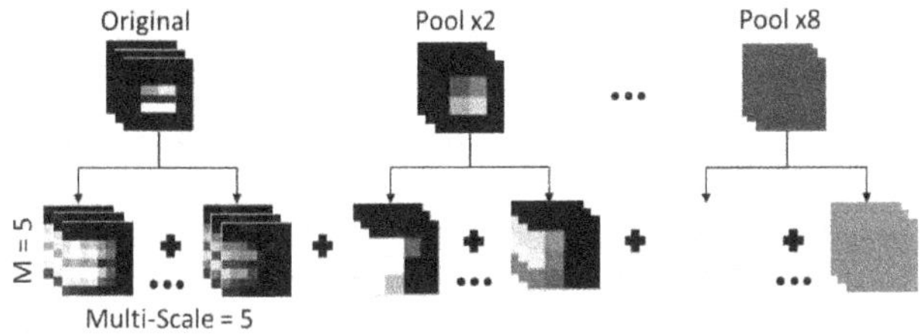

Figure 4: Overview of the Spatial Multi-Scale Motion History Histogram (SMMHH) on Touch Dynamic. Average pooling is applied on the video data and then the Multi-Scale Motion History Histogram is used to capture the motion data across different scales of time.

8x8, 4x4, 2x2 and 1x1 sensors resolutions per gesture. On each of the videos we then extract the Multi-Scale MHH feature with appropriate thresholds. All the features produced are then resized and concatenated together making a feature vector with the dimension of:

$$\sum_{i=1}^{4}(S \times M \times P_i) = 2125 \qquad (1)$$

where i refers to each of the Spatially pooled videos, P_i is the total number of pixels in a frame for each video i, $S = 5$ is the size of the Multi-Scale dimension, which has been set from 2:6 and $M = 5$ is the MHH pattern sequence size [26].

3.2.5 *Local Binary Pattern on Three Orthogonal Planes (LBPTOP) on touch dynamic*

Similar to the SMMHH feature where touch recording data was treated as a video, the popular video dynamic feature LBPTOP [43] is extracted. The aim of the LBPTOP is to capture the distribution of local pressure patterns as the dynamics.

3.3 Touch Gesture Recognition

One of the goals of this challenge was to build an automatic social touch gesture recognition systems. Due to multiple distinct feature sets, ensemble learning methods were chosen in order to combine these features in an optimised way. Within ensemble learning, Random Forest [4] and Boosting methods have been selected for the classification process.

3.3.1 *Random Forest*

The Random Forest (RF) algorithm was selected given its popularity and its generally good performance in solving classification problems. The main idea behind this algorithm is to form a forest by training and combining different kinds of decision trees, and the final classification result is decided through a voting over these trees. The method combines the 'bagging' idea and the random selection of features. Detailed information can be found in [4].

3.3.2 *Boosting Algorithm*

The Boosting algorithm is another ensemble learning method that can convert a weak learner into a strong one. It gives different weights to different features and combines all distinct features together in an optimized way. The boosting implementation algorithm here is called Stage-wise Additive Modelling [15]. The Boosting algorithm was used here in a way similar to Adaboost, but the difference is in how the error rate is computed.The Boosting algorithm gives to erroneously classified data more weight.

4. EXPERIMENTAL RESULTS

The experiments adhered to the Social Touch Gesture Challenge 2015 protocol using the training and testing subsets provided. The models were firstly trained on the training subset and evaluated using a 10 fold cross-validation process. This process was also used for optimizing the parameter set for the feature extraction and for building the models. Once the optimization was completed, the parameters were fixed and the models were tested on the testing subsets by the challenge's organizer (i.e., the labels of the testing datasets were unknown to us). Both HAART and CoST datasets were used.

The Random Forest and the Boosting learning methods were used for the gesture recognition in the testing. For RF, 1000 trees were used. In the Boosting implementation, the Random Forest was used as the weak leaners. 500 iterations were used in all experiments. Both are implemented using Weka software. Accuracy was used as performance measure, that is the percentage of testing samples correctly classified with respect to the true class.

4.1 HAART

In the training subset, only the data from 7 subjects out of 10 subjects were given for a total of 578 gesture instances.

Table 5 shows the experimental results for both the individual feature sets and for the combination of all the feature sets. In the training sets, the average results of 10 fold cross validation were being used as an evaluation purpose to take advantage of all available data. When considering only individual features, MSD, SMMHH and LBPTOP obtained higher recognition rates. However, the combination of all the features led to significant improvement for the training subset, giving 76.7% accuracy on RF and 77.7% for Boosting. Using the combination of features, the networks were trained on all sets of training data and testing on separate sets of testing data. The effect of modelling all training data together decreases accuracy to 66.5% for RF and 64.5% for Boosting. However, despite the drops in recognition accuracy on the testing data, it still shows consistent results across both classifiers.

The confusion matrices, shown respectively in in Table 6 and Table 7, allows us to compare the results of each of the touch gestures. Despite the decreasing accuracy in testing data, both classifiers are still able to model the gestures quite well even if differences apply. Among all the gestures, 'tickle' is the most difficult to classify, showing obvious confusion with scratch, for both classifiers. It is partly because these two gestures are performed in a similar manner, making the discrimination particularly hard on complex surfaces. It should also be noted that the number of instances for 'tickle' is quite small compared to the other gestures. Finally, the choice of

RF as the best reported models are consistent with [10], further showing the power of RF on combined datasets [10]

The results for the HAARTs testing set[1] are illustrated by the confusion matrices for both Random Forest and Boosting classifiers on the combined features presented in Table 6 and Table 7 respectively.

Table 5: HAART dataset: Gesture recognition rates on different feature sets

Data Set	Feature Set	Random Forest	Boosting
Training	SD	36.17%	33.50%
	BMH	22.67%	22.34%
	MSD	54.82%	53.61%
	SMMHH	65.66%	60.84%
	LBPTOP	53.01%	54.82%
	Combined	76.65%	77.67%
Testing[1]	Combined	66.53%	64.54%

Table 6: HAART testing dataset: Confusion matrix for the Random Forest classifier with an average recognition rate of 66.53%

	constant	notouch	pat	rub	scratch	stroke	tickle
constant	**34**	0	0	0	0	0	0
notouch	1	**36**	0	0	1	0	0
pat	0	0	**30**	0	1	0	2
rub	0	0	1	**16**	2	13	0
scratch	0	0	3	17	**26**	3	24
stroke	0	0	1	2	0	**18**	3
tickle	0	0	1	1	6	2	**7**

Table 7: HAART testing dataset: Confusion matrix for the Boosting classifier with an average recognition rate of 64.54%.

	constant	notouch	pat	rub	scratch	stroke	tickle
constant	**34**	1	0	0	0	0	0
notouch	1	**35**	0	0	0	0	0
pat	0	0	**19**	2	2	0	3
rub	0	0	0	**14**	2	4	0
scratch	0	0	6	12	**26**	1	20
stroke	0	0	8	7	2	**30**	9
tickle	0	0	3	1	4	1	**4**

4.2 CoST

Table 8: CoST dataset: Gesture recognition accuracies for different feature sets

Data Set	Feature Set	Random Forest	Boosting
Training	SD	41.24%	41.31%
	BMH	27.55%	28.88%
	MSD	44.82%	44.93%
	SMMHH	52.68%	52.56%
	LBPTOP	45.65%	46.36%
	Combined	64.52%	64.44%
Testing	Combined	58.67%	58.19%

[1]It should be noted that the results were re-calculated by the organizer for our submissions due to a mistake in converting the required format of the labels.

For the CoST dataset, the data from 21 out of 31 subjects were provided for the training, and the remaining were used by the challenge organizers for the testing. There were a total of 3524 and 1679 samples in the training and testing set respectively. The results for both training and testing experiments are shown in Table 8. Similar to HAART, the use of combined features leads to higher accuracy for the training data compared to individual features. It yields 64.5% accuracy in RF and 64.4% in Boosting. In the testing dataset, the classification of 14 gesture classes achieved accuracy of 58.7% using RF and 58.2% using Boosting, which is four percent higher than the one reported in Jung et al [22] (Bayes: 54%; SVM: 53%) for the same database. However, direct comparison is not possible since Jung et al use a leave-one-subject-out cross-validation approach instead of a split training-testing evaluation process as in our case.

The confusion matrices in Table 9 and Table 10 respectively show that 'massage', 'pinch', 'poke', 'press', and 'stroke' are easier to recognize by both classifiers than the other gestures. It can be noted that 'tickle' is better recognized in COST than in HAARTs. This could be due to the fact that in COST the surface is always the same and it is more constant. The most frequent confusion was between the following gestures: 'hit with slap', 'rub with scratch' and 'stroke; squeeze with grab'. These findings resemble those previous reported on this dataset [22].

5. CONCLUSION AND DISCUSSION

In this paper, we investigate how to automatically discriminate between different touch behaviour types that are characteristic of social affective interaction. The HAART and the CoST datasets were used for this investigation. They consist of various types of touch behaviour (e.g., patting, tapping) captured using multiple pressure sensors in a grid setting integrated into different types of substrates. Five sets of high-level features were proposed to provide a rich description of each touch gesture over time. Beyond simple trends captured by statistical features, we proposed features that capture the shape and the dynamic of the touch behaviour at different level of temporal and spatial granularity. These features were inspired by features used in image and video analysis.

Both individual features and combined set of features were evaluated using the training dataset by cross-validations with the ensemble of learning methods Random Forest and Boosting. Within these five sets of features, the video based feature set achieved best performance on both datasets. However, the combination of all features led to better performances possibly by complementing the fine video-based descriptors with more coarse description of the behaviour.

Whilst the results are well beyond chance level, various aspects could be further investigated. 1) The selection of the features and their tuning process (e.g., thresholds) could be optimized to the type of touch surface, i.e., its substrate and its cover. 2) Feature selection could be done on each set of feature in order to maximize its discriminative power. 3)Rather than using a low-level features fusion, models could be built on each set of features separately and then fused at decision level. This would allow a better exploitation of the different nature of the features and touch characteristics

Table 9: CoST testing datset: Confusion matrix for the Randon Forest classifier with a recognition accuracy of 58.7%.

	grab	hit	massage	pat	pinch	poke	press	rub	scratch	slap	squeeze	stroke	tap	tickle
grab	**84**	0	3	0	3	0	13	2	0	0	57	0	0	0
hit	0	**57**	0	19	0	3	0	0	0	27	0	0	22	0
massage	1	0	**88**	0	1	0	1	13	8	0	1	0	0	1
pat	0	0	0	**41**	1	1	0	0	0	0	0	1	18	5
pinch	1	2	4	2	**91**	4	9	0	1	0	8	3	1	5
poke	0	10	0	4	9	**104**	5	0	0	2	1	0	18	4
press	0	0	0	3	6	0	**84**	5	0	0	0	0	3	0
rub	3	0	5	0	0	0	0	**37**	1	0	0	13	0	0
scratch	4	0	12	2	0	0	0	23	**72**	0	0	2	0	29
slap	0	46	0	25	2	0	0	0	0	**87**	0	9	24	0
squeeze	26	0	3	1	7	0	7	4	2	0	**52**	0	0	0
stroke	1	0	3	2	0	0	1	27	10	0	0	**80**	0	2
tap	0	5	0	20	0	8	0	0	1	4	0	0	**34**	0
tickle	0	0	2	1	0	0	0	9	25	0	0	12	0	**74**

Table 10: CoST testing dataset: Confusion matrix for the Boosting classifier with a recognition accuracy of 58.2%.

	grab	hit	massage	pat	pinch	poke	press	rub	scratch	slap	squeeze	stroke	tap	tickle
grab	**93**	0	1	0	4	0	14	2	0	0	73	0	0	0
hit	0	**71**	0	24	1	1	0	0	0	42	0	0	29	0
massage	4	0	**94**	0	1	0	1	20	13	0	1	0	0	9
pat	0	1	0	**52**	2	2	0	0	1	0	0	1	23	6
pinch	0	1	3	3	**83**	4	4	0	1	1	6	1	2	3
poke	0	9	0	3	9	**101**	2	0	0	3	1	0	14	1
press	2	3	0	8	14	2	**92**	6	1	2	2	2	7	0
rub	3	0	5	0	0	0	0	**28**	3	0	0	9	0	2
scratch	2	0	5	1	0	0	0	17	**53**	0	0	1	0	15
slap	0	24	0	13	0	0	0	0	0	**68**	0	5	10	0
squeeze	16	0	4	0	6	0	6	3	1	0	**36**	0	0	0
stroke	0	0	5	2	0	0	1	32	15	0	0	**94**	0	5
tap	0	11	0	14	0	10	0	0	0	3	0	0	**34**	1
tickle	0	0	3	0	0	0	0	12	32	1	0	7	1	**78**

each captures (e.g., its shapes and its dynamics). In particularly, it would be interesting to explore how their different levels of granularity in capturing the spatial (3D) and temporal dynamics of the gestures contribute to the recognition process. Finally, whereas this work has focused on detecting touch types, the next step would be to model their relation with the affective or social message conveyed. This step may require integrating the modelling of types behaviour with more detailed kinemtics [16, 12].

6. REFERENCES

[1] D. Atkinson, P. Orzechowski, B. Petreca, N. Bianchi-Berthouze, P. Watkins, S. Baurley, S. Padilla, and M. Chantler. Tactile perceptions of digital textiles: A design research approach. CHI '13, pages 1669–1678, 2013.

[2] N. Bianchi-Berthouze, L. Berthouze, and T. Kato. Understanding subjectivity: An interactionist view. In *User Modeling*, CISM 407, pages 3–12. Springer Vienna, 1999.

[3] N. Bianchi-Berthouze and A. Tajadura Jimenez. It's not just what we touch but also how we touch it. In *Workshop on Tactile User Experience Evaluation Methods*, CHI'14, 2014.

[4] L. Breiman. Random forests. *Machine Learning*, 45(1):5–32, 2001.

[5] J. Burgoon. Relational message interpretations of touch, conversational distance, and posture. *Journal of Nonverbal Behavior*, 15(4):233–259, 1991.

[6] J. Chang, K. MacLean, and S. Yohanan. Gesture recognition in the haptic creature. EuroHaptics'10, pages 385–391. Springer-Verlag, 2010.

[7] M. D. Cooney, S. Nishio, and H. Ishiguro. Recognizing affection for a touch-based interaction with a humanoid robot. In *IEEE IROS*, pages 1420–1427, 2012.

[8] R. S. Dahiya, G. Metta, M. Valle, and G. Sandini. Tactile sensing-from humans to humanoids. *IEEE Transactions on Robotics*, 26(1):1–20, 2010.

[9] G. K. Essick, F. McGlone, C. Dancer, D. Fabricant, Y. Ragin, N. Phillips, T. Jones, and S. Guest. Quantitative assessment of pleasant touch. *Neuroscience and Biobehavioral Reviews*, 34(2):192 – 203, 2010.

[10] A. Flagg and K. MacLean. Affective touch gesture recognition for a furry zoomorphic machine. *TEI '13*, page 25, 2013.

[11] M. Fujita and H. Kitano. Development of an

Autonomous Quadruped Robot for Robot Entertainment. *Autonomous Robots*, 5:7–20, 1998.
[12] Y. Gao, N. Bianchi-Berthouze, and H. Meng. What does touch tell us about emotions in touchscreen-based gameplay? *ACM Trans. CHI*, 19(4), 2012.
[13] K. Goris, J. Saldien, B. Vanderborght, and D. Lefeber. Mechanical Design of the Huggable Robot Probo. *International Journal of Humanoid Robotics*, 08(03):481–511, 2011.
[14] K. Goris, J. Saldien, I. Vanderniepen, and D. Lefeber. The huggable robot Probo, a multi-disciplinary research platform. In *CCIS*, volume 33, pages 29–41, 2009.
[15] T. Hastie, S. Rosset, J. Zhu, and H. Zou. Multi-class AdaBoost. *Statistics and Its Interface*, 2(3):349–360, 2009.
[16] M. J. Hertenstein, R. Holmes, M. McCullough, and D. Keltner. The communication of emotion via touch. *Emotion*, 9(4):566–573, Aug 2009.
[17] M. J. Hertenstein, D. Keltner, B. App, B. A. Bulleit, and A. R. Jaskolka. Touch communicates distinct emotions. *Emotion*, 6(3):528–533, Aug 2006.
[18] G. Huisman, A. Darriba Frederiks, B. Van Dijk, D. Hevlen, and B. Krose. The TaSSt: Tactile sleeve for social touch. In *HC'13*, pages 211–216, 2013.
[19] S. Hutson, S. Lim, P. Bentley, N. Bianchi-Berthouze, and A. Bowling. Investigating the suitability of social robots for the wellbeing of the elderly. In *ACII'11*, LNCS, Vol. 6974, pages 578–587. 2011.
[20] K. Isbister, K. Höök, M. Sharp, and J. Laaksolahti. The sensual evaluation instrument: Developing an affective evaluation tool. CHI '06, pages 1163–1172, 2006.
[21] A. Jan, H. Meng, Y. F. A. Gaus, F. Zhang, and S. Turabzadeh. Automatic Depression Scale Prediction using Facial Expression Dynamics and Regression. In *AVEC'14*, pages 73–80, 2014.
[22] M. M. Jung, R. Poppe, M. Poel, and D. Heylen. Touching the void - introducing cost: Corpus of social touch. In *ICMI'14*, pages 120–127, 2014.
[23] A. Kleinsmith and N. Bianchi-Berthouze. Affective body expression perception and recognition: A survey. *IEEE Transactions on Affective Computing*, pages 1–20, 2013.
[24] M. L. Knapp and J. A. Hall. *Nonverbal Communication in Human Interaction.* Wadsworth: Cengage Learning, Bosten, USA, 7 edition, 2010.
[25] H. Meng and N. Pears. Descriptive temporal template features for visual motion recognition. *Pattern Recognition Letters*, 30(12):1049–1058, 2009.
[26] H. Meng, N. Pears, and C. Bailey. A human action recognition system for embedded computer vision application. In *CVPR workshop on Embeded Computer Vision*, pages 1–8, 2007.
[27] H. Meng, N. Pears, M. Freeman, and C. Bailey. Motion history histograms for human action recognition. In B. Kisačanin, S. Bhattacharyya, and S. Chai, editors, *Embedded computer vision*, Advances in pattern recognition, pages 139–162. Springer, 2009.
[28] K. Nakajima, Y. Itoh, Y. Hayashi, K. Ikeda, K. Fujita, and T. Onoye. Emoballoon: A balloon-shaped interface recognizing social touch interactions. In *Virtual Reality*, pages 1–4, 2013.
[29] F. Naya, J. Yamato, and K. Shinozawa. Recognizing human touching behaviors using a haptic interface for a pet-robot. In *IEEE ICSMC*, pages 1030–1034 vol.2, 1999.
[30] Y.-W. Park, K.-M. Baek, and T.-J. Nam. The roles of touch during phone conversations: Long-distance couples' use of poke in their homes. CHI '13, pages 1679–1688, 2013.
[31] B. Petreca, N. Bianchi-Berthouze, and B. S. How do designers feel. ACII '15, 2015.
[32] T. Shibata, K. Inoue, and R. Irie. Emotional robot for intelligent system-artificial emotional creature project. *Proceedings 5th IEEE International Workshop on Robot and Human Communication*, 1996.
[33] T. Shibata, T. Mitsui, K. Wada, A. Touda, T. Kumasaka, K. Tagami, and K. Tanie. Mental commit robot and its application to therapy of children. In *IEEE/ASME International Conference on AIM*, pages 1053–1058 vol.2, 2001.
[34] D. Silvera Tawil, D. Rye, and M. Velonaki. Interpretation of the Modality of Touch on an Artificial Arm Covered with an EIT-based Sensitive Skin, 2012.
[35] D. Silvera-Tawil, D. Rye, and M. Velonaki. Interpretation of social touch on an artificial arm covered with an eit-based sensitive skin. *International Journal of Social Robotics*, 6:489–505, 2014.
[36] D. Silvera-Tawil, D. Rye, and M. Velonaki. Artificial skin and tactile sensing for socially interactive robots: A review. *Robotics and Autonomous Systems*, 63:230–243, 2015.
[37] H. Singh, M. Bauer, W. Chowanski, Y. Sui, D. Atkinson, S. Baurley, M. Fry, J. Evans, and N. Bianchi-Berthouze. The brain's response to pleasant touch: an eeg investigation of tactile caressing. *Frontiers in human neuroscience*, 8, 2014.
[38] W. Stiehl, J. Lieberman, and C. Breazeal. Design of a therapeutic robotic companion for relational, affective touch. *Robot and Human*, pages 408–415, 2005.
[39] D. S. Tawil, D. Rye, and M. Velonaki. Touch modality interpretation for an eit-based sensitive skin. In *Proceedings of IEEE ICRA*, pages 3770–3776, 2011.
[40] M. Valstar, B. Schuller, K. Smith, F. Eyben, B. Jiang, S. Bilakhia, S. Schnieder, R. Cowie, and M. Pantic. AVEC 2013: The continuous audio/visual emotion and depression recognition challenge. AVEC '13, pages 3–10, 2013.
[41] S. Yohanan, M. Chan, J. Hopkins, H. Sun, and K. MacLean. Hapticat: Exploration of affective touch. ICMI '05, pages 222–229, 2005.
[42] S. Yohanan and K. E. MacLean. The Role of Affective Touch in Human-Robot Interaction: Human Intent and Expectations in Touching the Haptic Creature. *International Journal of Social Robotics*, 4(2):163–180, 2012.
[43] G. Zhao and M. Pietikainen. Dynamic texture recognition using local binary patterns with an application to facial expressions. *IEEE Trans. PAMI*, 29(6):915–928, June 2007.

Recognizing Touch Gestures for Social Human-Robot Interaction

Tuğçe Ballı Altuğlu
Department of Computer Engineering
Faculty of Engineering and Architecture
Istanbul Kemerburgaz University
Istanbul, Turkey
tugce.balli@kemerburgaz.edu.tr

Kerem Altun
Department of Mechanical Engineering
Faculty of Engineering and Architecture
Istanbul Kemerburgaz University
Istanbul, Turkey
kerem.altun@kemerburgaz.edu.tr

ABSTRACT

In this study, we performed touch gesture recognition on two sets of data provided by "Recognition of Social Touch Gestures Challenge 2015". For the first dataset, dubbed Corpus of Social Touch (CoST), touch is performed on a mannequin arm, whereas for the second dataset (Human-Animal Affective Robot Touch—HAART) touch is performed in a human-pet interaction setting. CoST includes 14 gestures and HAART includes 7 gestures. We used the pressure data, image features, Hurst exponent, Hjorth parameters and autoregressive model coefficients as features, and performed feature selection using sequential forward floating search. We obtained classification results around 60%–70% for the HAART dataset. For the CoST dataset, the results range from 26% to 95% depending on the selection of the training/test sets.

Categories and Subject Descriptors

I.5.2 [**Pattern Recognition**]: Design Methodology—*classifier design and evaluation, feature evaluation and selection*; I.5.4 [**Pattern Recognition**]: Applications—*signal processing*

General Terms

Human-Robot Interaction

Keywords

Gesture recognition; Human-Robot Interaction; Random Forests; Feature Selection; Sequential Floating Forward Search.

1. INTRODUCTION

In recent years there has been an increasing interest on human-robot interaction studies that use touch modality [1][2]. In social human-robot interaction, correct interpretation of touch gestures provides additional information about affective content in touch [3], and can be used together with audio-visual cues [4] to improve affect recognition performance. There are are studies on different machine learning and signal processing methods for increasing the classification accuracy of touch gestures in haptic robots.

In previous studies, robots have been designed that can interpret touch gestures. Some examples of these are PARO [5], Huggable [6], Probo [7], AIBO [8] and Haptic Creature [9]. PARO robot seal can sense if its being stroked or hit through its sensors [5]. Huggable can distinguish between nine touch gestures [6], Probo robot can sense three different touch gestures [7] whereas AIBO robot can sense touch at different locations. Haptic creature has a different characteristic; it can sense human affect along with touch gestures [3]. In another context that investigates human-humanoid robot interaction, the recognition of affective content in touch gestures has been studied [10]. For the interested reader, a comprehensive recent review on touch sensing and interpretation in social robots appears in [2].

In this study, feature extraction, feature selection and classification methods for recognition of touch gestures from two datasets provided by Touch Challenge 2015 have been investigated. Our contributions to Touch Challenge 2015 are twofold. First we have investigated different approaches for converting two dimensional sensor data to one dimensional data. Then we have used one dimensional data to test statistical features, image processing features, autoregressive model parameters and complexity measures for classification of touch gestures. Furthermore we used feature selection to test if using smaller feature subsets would improve the classification accuracy.

2. DATA SETS

Two datasets used in this study were provided by "Recognition of Social Touch Gestures Challenge 2015," organized as part of the 2015 International Conference on Multimodal Interaction.

The first dataset is Corpus of Social Touch (CoST) dataset [11]. CoST data has been recorded on a 8×8 sensor grid wrapped around a mannequin arm. The data consist of pressure value at 8×8 sensor grid sampled at 135 Hz. The data were collected from 31 participants. The participants were asked to perform 14 touch gestures, 6 times, in 3 variations (normal, gentle and rough). This led to a total of 252 gesture instances per participant. Touch gestures were grab, hit, massage, pat, pinch, poke, press, rub, scratch, slap, squeeze, stroke, tap and tickle; taken from Yohanan's

ICMI'15, November 09–13, 2015, Seattle, WA, USA.

ACM 978-1-4503-3912-4/15/11 ...$15.00.
DOI: http://dx.doi.org/10.1145/2818346.2830600 .

touch dictionary [12]. The data released for the challenge includes only the normal and gentle variants.

The second dataset is Human-Animal Affective Robot Touch (HAART) dataset that is a continuation of the study reported in [13]. HAART dataset has been recorded on a 10×10 sensor grid wrapped around a robotic animal model. The data were collected from 10 participants whilst they were performing 7 touch gestures: pat, constant (contact without movement), rub, scratch, stroke, tickle and no touch. The permutations of 3 substrate conditions (firm and flat, foam and flat, foam and curve) and 4 cover conditions (none, short minkee, long minkee and synthetic fur) were used for recording the gestures of each participant. The participants were asked to perform each gesture for 10 seconds where the data were sampled at 54 Hz. The data were trimmed to include middle 8×8 sensor grid and middle 8 seconds. This led to 432 frames for each participant, gesture, substrate and cover condition.

3. DATA PROCESSING

The sensor data were considered as a three dimensional $N \times 8 \times 8$ signal, where 8×8 is sensor data at one time instant (considered as a frame) and N is the length of data. 8×8 data is representative of the pressure applied at each sensor. HAART data set was recorded for a fixed time length of 8 seconds sampled at 54 Hz, thus for each gesture the value of N is $54 \times 8 = 432$. In CoST data set the gestures were not recorded in a fixed time length thus the value of N is variable for each participant and gesture.

For preprocessing of these data sets three dimensional data were converted to one dimensional $1 \times N$ signals. These signals were obtained by calculating:

1. mean pressure of the sensor grid,
2. the x coordinate of the center of pressure in 8×8 sensor grid,
3. the y coordinate of the center of pressure in 8×8 sensor grid,
4. the polar moment of 8×8 sensor grid,
5. the maximum pressure at 8×8 sensor grid,
6. the x coordinate of the maximum pressure at 8×8 sensor grid,
7. the y coordinate of the maximum pressure at 8×8 sensor grid.

Then, each 8×8 frame was converted to a binary image by thresholding with the mean pressure, and MATLAB's *regionprops* function [14] was used to obtain the following $1 \times N$ signals:

1. Area: The number of non-black pixels in the grid
2. Convex Hull: The size of convex polygon that contain non-black pixels in the grid.
3. Solidity: The proportion of the pixels in the convex hull that are also in the region.
4. Major Axis Length: The length of the major axis of the ellipse that has the same normalized second moments as the region.
5. Minor Axis Length: The length of the minor axis of the ellipse that has the same normalized second moments as the region.
6. Eccentricity: The scalar that specifies the eccentricity of the ellipse that has the same second moments as the region.
7. Orientation: The scalar that specifies the angle between the x-axis and the major axis of the ellipse that has the same second-moments as the region.
8. EquivDiameter: The scalar that specifies the diameter of a circle with the same area as the region.
9. EulerNumber: The scalar that specifies the number of objects in the region minus the number of holes in those objects.

4. FEATURE EXTRACTION

A total of 16 $1 \times N$ signals were obtained as described in the previous section. The mean, variance, maximum value, minimum value, median, energy, Hurst exponent, Hjorth complexity (3 features) and autoregressive model coefficients (9 features) were extracted as features from each signal. Therefore a total of 19 features $\times$ 16 signals $=$ 304 features were extracted from both datasets. The first six features were selected based on previous studies as they proved to provide a good characterization of touch sensor signals [3],[13]. The remaining three features are used widely in the processing of EEG signals [15],[16],[17],[18],[19],[20]. Since both EEG signals and touch gestures are recorded from multiple sensors and these features proved to have a good performance in characterization of EEG signals (that have a very complex nature); they were utilized in this study to investigate their efficiency in characterization of touch gesture signals.

We believe the first six features are self-explanatory; the remaining features are explained briefly below.

Hurst Exponent: Hurst exponent measures the self similarity of time series, providing information on the recurrence of similar patterns in time series at different scales. The value of Hurst exponent varies between 0 and 1. $Hurst = 0.5$ indicates that there is no correlation in the time series; $0 < HURST < 0.5$ indicates that time series has long range anti-correlations, that is an increasing value is likely to be followed by a decreasing value and vice versa; $0.5 < HURST < 1$ indicates that there is long range correlations in the time series, that is an increasing value is likely to be followed by an increasing value and vice versa [21].

Hjorth Complexity: Hjorth parameters measure the activity, mobility and the complexity of time series. The activity represents the variance of time series, mobility represents the mean frequency of time series and complexity represents the change in frequency of the signal [15].

Autoregressive Model Parameters: The Autoregressive (AR) model is an infinite impulse response filter. This filter tries to predict a sample y_t in time series by calculating the weighted sum of previous samples, y_{t-1}, y_{t-2}, ...,y_{t-d}, and adding this sum with an error signal (white noise). d represents the order of autoregressive model. In this study the model coefficients were estimated using Burg's method. There are methods for estimating the optimum model order but in this study AR model coefficients were calculated with orders from 2 to 10 [22].

5. FEATURE SELECTION

Feature selection has been used in order to (i) reveal discriminative features, (ii) to improve the classification accuracy by reducing the dimensionality of feature vector, i.e. curse of dimensionality, (iii) to reduce the processing times

Table 1: Touch Challenge 2015 Result of HAART data set

	constant	no-touch	pat	rub	scratch	stroke	tickle
constant	**33**	1	0	0	0	1	0
no-touch	1	**35**	0	0	0	0	0
pat	1	0	**11**	6	5	9	4
rub	1	0	0	**20**	6	8	1
scratch	0	0	0	1	**31**	1	3
stroke	0	0	2	10	1	**22**	1
tickle	0	0	0	1	32	2	**1**

Table 2: HAART data set - confusion matrix with feature selection

	constant	no-touch	pat	rub	scratch	stroke	tickle
constant	**34**	1	0	0	0	0	0
no-touch	0	**36**	0	0	0	0	0
pat	0	0	**28**	3	1	4	0
rub	0	0	2	**18**	10	5	1
scratch	0	0	0	1	**27**	0	8
stroke	0	0	7	4	1	**24**	0
tickle	0	0	0	0	26	0	**10**

Table 3: HAART data set - confusion matrix without feature selection

	constant	no-touch	pat	rub	scratch	stroke	tickle
constant	**34**	1	0	0	0	0	0
no-touch	1	**35**	0	0	0	0	0
pat	0	0	**28**	2	0	6	0
rub	0	0	5	**13**	14	3	1
scratch	0	0	0	0	**25**	0	11
stroke	0	0	2	6	2	**26**	0
tickle	0	0	0	0	26	0	**10**

of feature extraction and classification in a real time setting by extracting smaller number of features (i.e. only discriminative features). In this study, we have applied sequential floating forward search (SFFS) algorithm for feature selection. SFFS algorithm starts off with an empty selected feature set and iteratively the feature that would bring the highest improvement to classification accuracy is added to the selected feature subset (growing phase). If the size of selected feature subset is greater than or equal to three, in each iteration the feature subset is also checked to determine if removal of any feature would bring an improvement to the classification accuracy (pruning phase). If this is the case the corresponding feature is removed from the selected feature subset. This algorithm is iterated until the desired number of features is reached or the classification accuracy reaches a plateau. The number of features selected in this study was set by investigating the convergence of classification accuracy [23].

6. CLASSIFICATION

We used Random Forests (RF) for classification in this study since this algorithm has been previously reported to be successful for touch gesture recognition [3],[13]. Random forests is an ensemble of many decision trees [24]. According to this algorithm 2/3 of the training set is used to grow the trees and the remianing 1/3 is used to test the classification performance of the RF's. In order to grow RF's (i) k training sets are generated from 2/3 of training data using bootstrapping (random samples with replacement) (ii) k decision trees are created based on k training sets (iii) 1/3 of the training set is used optimize the split criterion at each node of generated decision trees - note that a randomly selected feature subset is used for calculation of split criterion at each tree's nodes (iv) the class label of actual test data is determined by majority voting of k trees in the RF. In this study the number of decision trees was set to 50. In our preliminary studies we have confirmed that increasing the number of decision trees up to 1000 would not bring a significant improvement to the classification accuracy.

During feature selection and classification phases subject dependent cross validation was applied. In other words if the number of participants was equal to n, an n-fold cross validation was used where each participant's data was tested once.

7. RESULTS AND DISCUSSION

7.1 HAART Dataset

The labels submitted to Touch Challenge 2015 for HAART dataset were obtained using a smaller subset of signal preprocessing methods described above. For the challenge we have considered only the (i) the pressure at the center of gravity, (ii) x and y location of center of gravity, (iii) the maximum pressure, (iv) the x and y location of maximum pressure, (v) Eccentricity value in 8×8 sensor grid. Thus a total of 7 $1 \times N$ signals were obtained from $8 \times 8 \times N$ sensor data. All features described above were extracted from these 7 signals. In the feature selection phase 7 features were selected among 133 features (7 signals $\times$ 19 features). The selected features were:

Table 4: Touch Challenge 2015 Result of CoST data set

	grab	hit	massage	pat	pinch	poke	press	rub	scratch	slap	squeeze	stroke	tap	tickle
grab	**9**	0	4	0	0	0	4	2	1	0	97	3	0	0
hit	0	**7**	0	23	0	0	0	0	0	68	0	4	15 3	
massage	1	0	**58**	5	1	0	0	2	7	0	17	24	0	5
pat	0	7	0	**37**	0	1	1	0	2	51	0	6	11	4
pinch	0	3	4	26	**10**	1	2	2	6	12	10	27	13	4
poke	0	9	0	30	0	**7**	0	0	0	37	0	5	24	8
press 3	1	1	24	1	0	9	**1**	0	6	42	13	13	6	
rub	1	1	9	9	0	0	0	**14**	5	1	11	63	1	5
scratch	1	3	13	10	0	1	1	9	**14**	4	1	44	2	17
slap	0	7	0	20	0	0	0	0	0	**62**	0	5	25	1
squeeze	9	0	5	1	1	1	0	0	0	2	**99**	1	0	0
stroke	1	4	8	16	5	0	0	12	3	2	3	**59**	3	4
tap	0	11	0	35	0	0	0	0	0	48	0	7	**12**	7
tickle	0	3	9	12	0	1	0	4	25	3	0	20	3	**40**

Table 5: Confusion matrix for Case (iii).

	grab	hit	massage	pat	pinch	poke	press	rub	scratch	slap	squeeze	stroke	tap	tickle
grab	**247**	2	3	0	0	0	0	0	0	0	0	0	0	0
hit	0	**249**	3	0	0	0	0	0	0	0	0	0	0	0
massage	7	0	**240**	0	0	0	0	2	0	0	0	0	0	2
pat	0	0	0	**251**	0	0	0	0	0	0	0	0	0	0
pinch	0	0	0	0	**240**	3	8	0	1	0	0	0	0	0
poke	0	0	0	0	4	**242**	6	0	0	0	0	0	0	0
press	0	0	0	0	6	15	**229**	1	0	0	1	0	0	0
rub	0	0	0	0	3	6	5	**218**	16	1	1	2	0	0
scratch	0	0	0	0	0	0	0	6	**240**	4	1	0	0	1
slap	0	0	1	0	0	0	0	0	2	**249**	0	0	0	0
squeeze	0	0	0	0	1	0	1	0	1	5	**243**	1	0	0
stroke	0	0	0	0	0	0	0	0	0	1	0	**239**	6	5
tap	0	0	0	0	0	0	0	0	0	0	0	5	**242**	5
tickle	0	0	0	0	0	0	0	3	0	0	0	10	5	**233**

1. 10th order AR coefficients of maximum pressure signal,
2. activity measure (hjorth complexity) of maximum pressure data,
3. activity measure (hjorth complexity) of maximum pressure data,
4. Hurst exponent of maximum pressure data,
5. 10th order AR coefficients of X location of centroid data,
6. 2nd order AR coefficients of Y location of centroid data,
7. Hurst exponent of maximum pressure data.

The confusion matrix that was received back from Touch Challenge 2015 is shown in Table 1. The classification acurracy was equal to 60.9%. Here it can be observed that scratch and tickle are the most confused gestures.

The remaining of this subsection explains the studies that have been done after submitting test labels to the Touch Challenge 2015. In this part the pre-processing phase of data analysis was expanded to include mean pressure of the 8×8 grid as well as the remaining image processing methods that are explained in Section 4 (MATLAB regionprops functions).

Table 2 shows the confusion matrix of HAART data set with expanded pre-processing methods. This confusion matrix was obtained by applying feature selection on the training set and classifying the test data with selected features.

In the feature selection phase a total of 8 features were selected, these features were:

1. 10th order AR coefficients of mean pressure signal,
2. mean of maximum pressure signal,
3. 5th order AR coefficients of maximum pressure signal,
4. variance of polar moment signal,
5. 3rd order AR coefficients of Euler number signal,
6. mean of orientation signal,
7. mobility measure (hjorth parameters) of mean pressure signal,
8. energy of maximum pressure signal.

According to the confusion matrix in Table 2 the classification accuracy was equal to 70.5%. These results clearly indicate that image processing methods provide a significant improvement to the classification accuracy. However, scratch and tickle remain as the most confused gestures.

In the growing phase of decision trees in RF's, more discriminative features are selected using Gini index for creating the split criteria. Thus the RF's were also used to classify testing data without feature selection.

The confusion matrix of HAART dataset using 304 features is shown in Table 3. In this case the classification accuracy was 68.1%. In this dataset it is evident that the use of feature selection did not provide a significant improvement to the classification accuracy. However extracting 8

Table 6: Confusion matrix for Case (v).

	grab	hit	massage	pat	pinch	poke	press	rub	scratch	slap	squeeze	stroke	tap	tickle
grab	**83**	0	2	0	1	0	1	1	2	0	25	4	0	1
hit	0	**75**	0	5	1	9	0	0	0	20	0	0	9	1
massage	8	0	**79**	0	2	1	1	6	2	0	4	7	0	10
pat	0	21	0	**51**	0	5	1	0	1	14	0	3	23	1
pinch	1	2	3	0	**76**	10	19	2	0	0	5	2	0	0
poke	0	4	0	1	8	**90**	1	0	0	0	0	0	16	0
press	10	0	0	0	9	1	**80**	4	2	0	12	1	0	1
rub	4	0	11	0	1	0	15	**42**	8	0	0	30	0	9
scratch	1	0	5	2	1	3	1	16	**51**	1	1	11	1	26
slap	0	35	0	3	0	6	0	0	0	**58**	0	0	17	1
squeeze	55	0	5	0	5	0	2	0	0	0	**52**	0	0	0
stroke	0	1	1	2	10	3	1	10	8	1	0	**77**	2	4
tap	0	24	0	23	0	12	3	0	0	16	0	0	**41**	1
tickle	0	0	2	10	2	0	0	4	24	0	0	3	2	**73**

features compared to 304 features would bring a significant improvement in terms of response time in a real time system.

7.2 CoST Dataset

Test labels submitted to Touch Challenge 2015 for CoST data were obtained using the same pre-processing methods as HAART dataset submission. But with this data set only mean, variance, maximum value, minimum value, median value and the energy of signals were extracted as features and feature selection was not done in this feature subspace. Therefore a total of 7 signals $\times$ 6 features = 42 features were extracted from this dataset. The resulting classification accuracy of this data set was 26%.

After submission of test labels to Touch Challenge 2015 a further analysis was done on this dataset. All pre-processing and feature extraction methods explained in the previous sections were used to create the feature vector for this dataset. Additionally, gesture duration feature is also added to the feature set. Then feature selection was performed on the training data using 21 fold cross validation where each participant was used once for testing. In the feature selection phase the mean classification performance from each fold with five features was 87.3%. However when the selected features was tested on test data the classification performance was 7.0%. For a 14 class problem this percentage is equivalent to random generation of class label. Then in the next step same procedure was repeated without feature selection. In that case the classification accuracy was 11.0%. For both cases the classification performance was unexpectedly low.

In order to get a further understanding of this data set and attempt to explain the unexpected difference in performance in training set cross validation and test phases, we ran the following tests using different training and test sets:

(i) The train and test data were combined and a 31 fold (subject dependent) cross validation was performed on the dataset without feature selection. The mean classification accuracy was equal to 79.0%.

(ii) The train and test data were combined and data from 2/3 of randomly selected participants was used for training (without feature selection) the RF's and remaining 1/3 participant's data was used for testing. This was repeated 10 times and the results are averaged. In that case the classification performance was equal to 77.1%.

(iii) In this case we used only training data to train and test the RF's. As there were 21 participants in the training set a 21 fold subject dependent leave one out cross validation was performed on this data set. The mean classification accuracy was equal to 95.4%. The confusion matrix for this case is given in Table 5.

(iv) We used only testing data to train and test the RF's (without feature selection). As there were 10 subjects in the training set 10 fold subject dependent leave one out cross validation was performed. The mean classification accuracy was equal to 46.4%.

(v) Feature selection was performed by using original training data to train RF and original test data to determine the classification accuracy of features. In this case a total of 10 features were selected. The mean classification accuracy was equal to 55.6%. The confusion matrix for this case is given in Table 6. This selected feature set was also used to repeat the tests in (i), (ii), (iii) and (iv) in those cases the classification accuracies were 53.6%, 51.2%, 51.8%, 47.4% respectively.

The list of selected features in Case (v) are as follows:

1. gesture duration,
2. mobility (hjorth complexity) of mean presure data,
3. variance of the polar moment data,
4. 9th order AR coefficients of maximum pressure data,
5. 9th order AR coefficients of mean pressure data,
6. the maximum value in maximum pressure data,
7. activity (hjorth complexity) in x location of maximum pressure data,
8. activity (hjorth complexity) in y location of polar moment data,
9. mean of polar moment data,
10. variance of mean pressure data.

This analysis shows that the gestures performed by participants in the training data are consistent within each other (Case (iii), 95.4%, Table 5). However, training with this set, the test set results drop to about 11%, which is around chance level. This suggests that the test set participants do not follow a similar pattern in performing the gestures. Case (iv) shows that the test set participants are not as consistent as the training set participants within each other either. The large difference in performance for training and test sets could have originated from a problem in the data, or a problem in our implementation of the random forest algorithm, or overfitting in the training set. To check if this is the result of overfitting, we ran Case (ii), where we combined all the participants' data and divided all data into training (2/3) and test (1/3) sets randomly and repeated this procedure 10 times. The average success rate in this case is 77.1%, which is an estimate of the classification performance if the training and test data were permuted while maintaining their sizes. Thus we conclude that our low performance for the organizers' selection of training and test sets did not result from overfitting. In Case (v), we used training and test data as given in the challenge, and selected features using the training set and tested those features using the test set. We believe this is the most realistic scenario and gives the expected gesture classification results (55.6%, Table 6) for a new 32nd test participant. For this case, grab/squeeze, rub/stroke, scratch/tickle and hit/slap are the most confused gestures by our feature set and the algorithm.

8. SUMMARY AND FUTURE WORK

In this study, we used Random Forests to classify touch gestures for two different datasets, obtaining results in the 50%–70% range for different selections of training and test sets. For a training/test set combination that simulates a realistic scenario, the expected correct recognition performance is 55%. For both datasets, scratch and tickle gestures were confused by the algorithm. We applied sequential floating forward search to find the most discriminative features in our feature set and demonstrated that feature selection improves the performance. Image features that are in the original feature set were not selected by the algorithm, suggesting that they are not relevant in gesture recognition. Our future research on touch gesture recognition will focus on finding the most discriminative features. An interesting research track would be to determining the most discriminative features that are physically motivated; i.e., that correspond to physical measurements that can be captured with a sensor. This would be useful for sensor design as well, e.g., touch sensors that capture only the relevant information can be designed. For real human-robot interactions, combining the touch sensor information with other sensing modalities such as cameras or accelerometers equipped on a robot would also improve the recognition performance.

9. REFERENCES

[1] B. D. Argall and A. G. Billard, "A survey of tactile human-robot interactions," *Robotics and Autonomous Systems*, vol. 58, no. 10, pp. 1159–1176, October 2010.

[2] D. Silvera-Tawil, D. Rye, and M. Velonaki, "Artificial skin and tactile sensing for socially interactive robots: a review," *Robotics and Autonomous Systems*, vol. 63, no. 1, pp. 230–243, January 2015.

[3] K. Altun and K. E. MacLean, "Recognizing affect in human touch of a robot," (in press) *Pattern Recognition Letters*, 2014.

[4] Z. Zeng, M. Pantic, G. I. Roisman, and T. S. Huang, "A survey of affect recognition methods: audio, visual, and spontaneous expressions," *IEEE Transactions on Pattern Analysis and Machine Intelligence*, vol. 31, no. 1, pp. 39–58, January 2009.

[5] T. Shibata, K. Inoue, and R. Irie, "Emotional robot for intelligent system—artificial emotional creature project," in *5th IEEE International Workshop on Robot and Human Communication*, 11–14 November 1996, pp. 466–471.

[6] W. D. Stiehl, J. Lieberman, C. Breazeal, L. Basel, L. Lalla, and M. Wolf, "The design of the Huggable: a therapeutic robotic companion for relational, affective touch," in *Proceedings of the AAAI Fall Symposium on Caring Machines: AI in Eldercare*, 2005.

[7] J. Saldien, K. Goris, S. Yılmazyı ldız, W. Verhelst, and D. Lefeber, "On the design of the huggable robot Probo," *Journal of Physical Agents*, vol. 2, no. 2, pp. 3–12, June 2008.

[8] M. Fujita, "AIBO: Toward the era of digital creatures," *International Journal of Robotics Research*, vol. 20, no. 10, pp. 781–794, October 2001.

[9] S. Yohanan and K. E. MacLean, "Design and assessment of the Haptic Creature's affect display," in *HRI '11, Proceedings of the 6th ACM/IEEE International Conference on Human-Robot Interaction*, vol. 1, Lausanne, Switzerland, March 6-9 2011, pp. 473–480.

[10] D. Silvera-Tawil, D. Rye, and M. Velonaki, "Interpretation of social touch on an artificial arm covered with an EIT-based sensitive skin," *International Journal of Social Robotics*, vol. 6, no. 4, pp. 489–505, November 2014.

[11] M. M. Jung, R. Poppe, M. Poel, and D. K. Heylen, "Touching the void – introducing cost: Corpus of social touch," in *Proceedings of the 16th International Conference on Multimodal Interaction*, ser. ICMI '14. New York, NY, USA: ACM, 2014, pp. 120–127. [Online]. Available: http://doi.acm.org/10.1145/2663204.2663242

[12] S. Yohanan and K. E. MacLean, "The role of affective touch in human-robot interaction: human intent and expectations in touching the Haptic Creature," *International Journal of Social Robotics*, vol. 4, no. 2, pp. 163–180, April 2012.

[13] A. Flagg and K. E. MacLean, "Affective touch recognition for a furry therapeutic machine," in *TEI 2013, Proceedings of the International Conference on Tangible, Embedded and Embodied Interaction*, Barcelona, Spain, February 10–13 2013.

[14] *MATLAB Image Processing Toolbox: User's Guide (R2015b)*, The MathWorks, Inc., 2015.

[15] B. Hjorth, "Eeg analysis based on time domain properties," *Electroencephalography and Clinical Neurophysiology*, vol. 29, no. 3, pp. 306–310, 1970.

[16] S. Kumar, A. Kumar, A. Trikha and S. Anand, "Electroencephalogram Based Quantitative Estimation of Pain for Balanced Anaesthesia," *Measurement*, vol. 59, pp. 296–301, 2015.

[17] A.R. Djordjevic, L. Lhotska, V. Gerla, V. Krajca and K. Paul, "Non-linear Analysis of Newborn EEG," *Clinical Neurophysiology*, vol. 126, no. 3, pp. e48–e49, 2015.

[18] S. Datta, A. Khasnobish, A. Konar and D. N. Tibarewala, "Cognitive Activity Classification from

EEG Signals with an Interval Type-2 Fuzzy System," in S. Gupta et al. (eds.), *Advancements of Medical Electronics,* Lecture Notes in Bioengineering, pp. 235–247, 2015.

[19] S. Liang, C. Kuo, Y. Hu, Y. Pan and Y. Wang, "Automatic Stage Scoring of Single-Channel Sleep EEG by Using Multiscale Entropy and Autoregressive Models," *IEEE Transactions on Instrumentation and Measurement,* vol. 61, no. 6, pp. 1649–1657, 2012.

[20] Y. Fang, M. Chen and X. Zheng, "Extracting features from phase space of EEG signals in brain-computer interfaces," *Neurocomputing*, vol. 151, no. 3, pp. 1477–1485, 2015.

[21] H. Hurst, "Long-term storage of reservoirs: an experimental study," *Transactions of the American Society of Civil Engineers*, vol. 116, pp. 770–799, 1951.

[22] M. Steven, *Modern Spectral Estimation: Theory and Application.* Englewood Cliffs, NJ: Prentice Hall, 1988.

[23] P. Pudil, J. Novovicova, and J. Kittler, "Floating search methods in feature selection," *Pattern Recognition Letters*, vol. 15, pp. 1119–1125, 1994.

[24] L. Breimann, "Random forests," *Machine Learning*, vol. 45, pp. 5–32, 2001.

Detecting and Identifying Tactile Gestures using Deep Autoencoders, Geometric Moments and Gesture Level Features

Dana Hughes, Nicholas Farrow, Halley Profita, Nikolaus Correll
Department of Computer Science
University of Colorado–Boulder
Boulder, CO, USA
{dana.hughes, nicholas.farrow, halley.profita, nikolaus.correll}@colorado.edu

ABSTRACT

While several sensing modalities and transduction approaches have been developed for tactile sensing in robotic skins, there has been much less work towards extracting features for or identifying high-level gestures performed on the skin. In this paper, we investigate using deep neural networks with hidden Markov models (DNN-HMMs), geometric moments and gesture level features to identify a set of gestures performed on robotic skins. We demonstrate that these features are useful for identifying gestures, and predict a set of gestures from a 14-class dataset with 56% accuracy, and a 7-class dataset with 71% accuracy.

Categories and Subject Descriptors

H.5.2 [**User Interfaces**]: Haptic I/O; I.5.2 [**Design Methodology**]: Pattern analysis

General Terms

Human Factors, Measurement, Performance

Keywords

Social touch, Gesture recognition

1. INTRODUCTION

The development of large pressure sensitive arrays has led to a recent increase in research into full-body tactile sensing in robotics [5], specifically for tasks such as manipulation, exploration and navigation, and human-robotic interaction. Tactile sensing modalities provides unique means to communicate a variety of information, from guiding robots by physical touch in sensitive environments [4] to expressing emotions and intents through affective touch [14]. In the field of therapeutic robotics, several robotic companions have been developed, including Huggable [26] and the Haptic Creature [30]. Full-body tactile sensitive skins are used in these companions to communicate emotion and intent during interactions.

ICMI '15, November 09-13, 2015, Seattle, WA, USA
© 2015 ACM. ISBN 978-1-4503-3912-4/15/11 ...$15.00.
DOI: http://dx.doi.org/10.1145/2818346.2830601.

While perception of tactile signals is available through a variety of robotic skins, detection and identification of high-level gestures performed during social interactions remain relatively unexplored. Robust gesture recognition has large potential as an application of robotic materials, specifically full-body robotic skins [20, 13]. In addition to classifying gestures from captured data, we are interested in determining if part or all of a classifier model could be incorporated into computing elements in the robotic skin itself. In this paper, we investigate using deep learning, geometric moments, hidden Markov models and gesture-level features to classify a variety of high-level affective gestures. In addition, we report our classification results on two datasets provided for the Recognition of Social Touch Gestures Challenge.

The remainder of the paper is organized in the following manner: Section 2 provides a brief overview of the approaches used to extract features from the datasets, and describes the datasets used in the Recognition of Social Touch Gestures Challenge. Section 3 describes the features extracted from gestures for classification purposes. Section 4 gives the results of the labels generated for the challenge, and compares the individual features used for classification. Section 5 summarizes the results and discusses potential for future improvements.

2. BACKGROUND

Touch has been shown to be capable of communicating distinct emotions between individuals [11]. Affective touch has been explored in several domains, such as with robotic companions [26, 8, 30], touch-screen based games [9] and for wearable devices [14]. Determining the type of touch or recognizing the underlying emotion in a touch is an important aspect of affective touch applications. Several features and classification methods have been explored in the literature. Using touch screen inputs, stroke length, speed, directness and pressure have been used as features to identify four emotions, two valence levels and two arousal levels using discriminant analysis, artificial neural networks and support vector machines [9]. Using a 64 element array of force sensors in a social robot, sensor activity, change in sensor value, touch centroid and direction of motion were extracted and used to classify 8 touches and determine 4 response types [26]. Extracting the average area, average and peak activation, and a movement index from a sensor array on an affective robot, classification of 8 gestures were performed using random forests, neural networks, logistic regression and Bayesian networks [8, 3].

In this paper, we are interested in leveraging recent advances in deep learning to automatically detect features. In addition, we incorporate the temporal aspect of gestures by using hidden Markov models (HMMs), rather than designing features which are time sensitive. HMMs are powerful models for describing sequential data [24], and has been successfully used for identifying sequences, such as in speech recognition [16] and activity recognition [7]. Recently, improvements to such speech models have been made by using deep neural networks (DNN) to generate high-level representations of individual audio frames [25]. Essentially, this type of approach allows for the dimensionality of individual frames to be reduced using a neural network model, and incorporates the temporal aspect of gestures with the HMM models.

The multiple datasets provided demonstrate that, despite similar sensing modalities, the specific goals of gesture recognition can vary between applications. Learning a set of universal gesture features would be optimal, so that transfer learning can be employed to reuse previously learned feature representations [22]. This approach has been demonstrated in computer vision tasks, where features learned in a deep convolutional neural network trained to classify one set of images [18] are leveraged to classify a different set of images [21] by simply replacing the final classification layer.

2.1 Dataset

In this paper, we use the term gesture to refer to the sequence of samples collected from 2D pressure arrays (i.e., frames) while users interact with a tactile-sensitive agent.

This investigation involved developing features for the Recognition of Social Touch Gestures Challenge for ICMI 2015 [1]. This challenge consists of two datasets, both of which were used for this investigation: The Corpus of Social Touch (CoST) gesture set [17], and the Human-Animal Affective Robot Touch (HAART) gesture set [30, 8]. The datasets each consist of a set of gesture captures collected from a number of participants–each capture consists of a sequence of frames, which are the measured pressures on an 8x8 sensor array. We normalized each pressure measurement to values between 0 and 1 as our only preprocessing on the provided data.

The CoST dataset contains 14 touch gestures (grab, hit, massage, pat, pinch, poke, press, rub, scratch, slap squeeze, stroke, tap and tickle), performed by 31 subjects. The pressure sensor array is wrapped around a mannequin arm, and sampled at a rate of 135Hz. Duration of captures ranged from 75 milliseconds to 9.6 seconds. Each capture was performed with three variations (normal, gentle and rough), the normal and gentle variations were used for the challenge. The dataset contains a total of 5203 captures, each subject performing the normal and gentle variation of each gesture 6 times, with 5 instances of captures missing. The dataset was split into a training set from 21 subjects (3524 captures) and a test set from the remaining 10 subjects (1679 captures).

The HAART dataset contains 7 gestures (no touch, constant, pat, rub, scratch, stroke and tickle), performed by 10 subjects. The pressure sensor array was placed over three possible substrates–firm flat back, flat foam and curved foam–and four covers–no cover, dense synthetic fur, long synthetic fibers and short synthetic fibers. The sensor array was sampled at a rate of 54Hz, and captures were trimmed to an 8 second window where the gesture was continuously performed, resulting in each capture consisting of 432 frames. Each participant performed each gesture on each substrate/cover pair. The captures from 7 participants were used as the training set, for a total of 584 captures (missing 4 captures), the captures from the remaining 3 participants were used as the test set (with a missing capture), for a total of 251 captures.

3. APPROACH

To classify gestures, we use two approaches which extract frame-level features for use as observations in a Hidden Markov Model, and an approach which extracts low-level statistics and the fundamental frequency on the gesture capture as a whole. Our first approach utilizes a deep autoencoder to generate a ten dimensional encoding of individual frames. Our second approach calculates a set of geometric moments for each frame. Using either of these frame-level features, we construct a set of Hidden Markov Models, using the features as observations. Finally, we create a feature set by calculating the overall mean and standard deviation of pressures, the fundamental frequency and average center of the gesture. Feature extraction was performed in MATLAB using code we wrote ourselves. We detail each of these approaches below.

3.1 Autoencoder

Deep autoencoders are neural networks designed to be able to transform high-dimensional data into a low-dimensional code, and to recover the original data from the code [12]. By incorporating nonlinearity in the encoding of the data, this approach can encode the data much more efficiently than linear techniques, such as principle components analysis.

To encode individual frames of the gestures, we built an autoencoder using the Caffe framework [15] consisting of four layers of encoding neurons, a code layer, and four layers of decoding neurons, as shown in Figure 1. The encoding layers consist of binary neurons which used a logistic activation function. After normalization, each frame is encoded through a sequence of layers with 200, 100, 50 and 25 binary neurons. This architecture follows a similar approach to that used in [12]: continuous valued inputs are encoded using a larger number of binary units, which are then sequentially halved until the code layer is reached. The code layer consists of linear neurons. The architecture of the decode layers are simply a mirroring of the encoding layers. The autoencoders were trained using Adagrad [6], and were allowed to train for 250,000 epochs.

To determine the optimal size of the code layer, we built autoencoders with code layers consisting of 25, 20, 15, 12, 10, 8 and 5 linear neurons, and calculated the mean L2-error of the reconstructed pixel values. Figure 2 shows the mean reconstruction error of the CoST dataset as a function of epoch for each of the code layer sizes. We used the autoencoder with a code size of 10 neurons–more neurons provide little improvement, and would increase the number of parameters for the HMM models, while fewer neurons show a significant increase in overall reconstruction error.

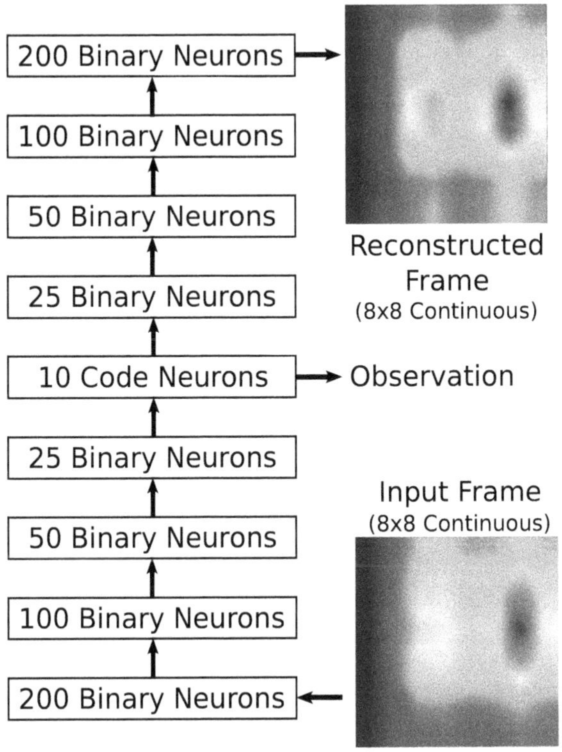

Figure 1: The autoencoder used to encode individual frames of a gesture.

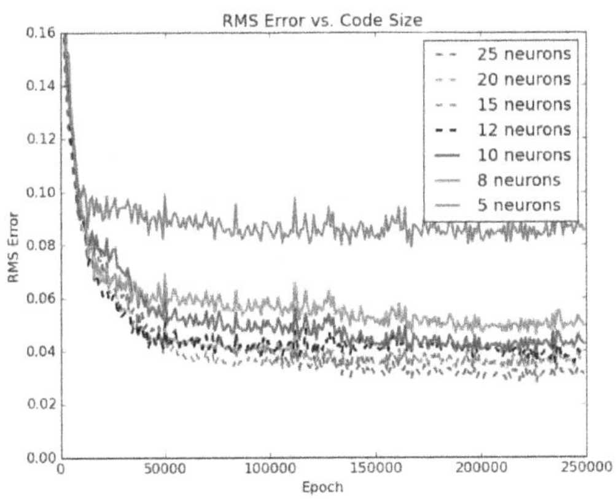

Figure 2: RMS error of reconstructed pixel values for autoencoders with different code sizes.

3.2 Geometric Moments

Geometric moments can be used as an alternative approach to encoding individual frames. Several types of moments have been used for image analysis–images can be described by an arbitrary number of of moments of a particular type, and several types of moments provides invariance to some type of transform in the image (i.e., translation, rotation and/or scaling) [28].

For the purpose of analyzing individual frames of width w pixels and height h pixels using geometric moments, we normalize the moments by the zeroth moment in order to be invariant to the overall intensity of the frame, and moments are calculated about the centroid of the frame (i.e., the first-order moments). The zeroth moment, $\mu_{0,0}$ (i.e., the total "mass" of the frame) and the first-order moments, $\mu_{0,1}$ and $\mu_{1,0}$ (i.e., the "center of mass" of the frame) are given by

$$\begin{aligned} \mu_{0,0} &= \sum_{x=0}^{w}\sum_{y=0}^{h} I(x,y) \\ \mu_{1,0} &= \frac{1}{\mu_{0,0}}\sum_{x=0}^{w}\sum_{y=0}^{h} xI(x,y) \\ \mu_{0,1} &= \frac{1}{\mu_{0,0}}\sum_{x=0}^{w}\sum_{y=0}^{h} yI(x,y) \end{aligned} \tag{1}$$

where $I(x,y)$ is the intensity of the pressure array at position (x,y). Higher-order moments are calculated from the following equation

$$\mu_{i,j} = \frac{1}{\mu_{0,0}}\sum_{x=0}^{w}\sum_{y=0}^{h}(x-\mu_{1,0})^i(y-\mu_{0,1})^j I(x,y) \tag{2}$$

Each frame can be described by a vector of moments. For this investigation, we calculated zeroth, first-, second- and third-order moments for each frame in a capture, resulting an a ten element descriptor of each frame.

3.3 HMM Modeling

Hidden Markov models (HMMs) are stochastic models useful for analyzing a sequence of observations [24]. HMMs consist of a finite number of distinct hidden states, and discrete or continuous observations. At each time step in the sequence, the model changes the hidden state according to some probability distribution, and generates an observation at each state. The hidden states in a sequence form a Markov chain, where the probability of the hidden state at time t, S_t, is dependent only on the hidden state at the previous time step, S_{t-1}. In other words, given a sequence of hidden states, the probability of the next hidden state is simplified to

$$P(S_t|S_0, S_1, S_2, ...) = P(S_t|S_{t-1}) \tag{3}$$

The feature vector calculated from the autoencoder or the geometric moments can be treated as observations at each time step in HMM, as shown in Figure 3. As both of these feature vectors are continuous valued, we treat these as samples from a multivariate Gaussian distribution, the mean and covariance of which is dependent on the current hidden state. Each hidden state in the model, S_i has a mean, μ_1, and covariance matrix, Σ_i, to describe the Gaussian distribution of observations. The probability of an observation, $\mathbf{o}$, given the hidden state is given by

$$P(\mathbf{o}|S_i) = \frac{1}{\sqrt{(2\pi)^{k/2}|\Sigma_i|}} e^{\frac{-1}{2}(\mathbf{o}-\mu_\mathbf{i})^T\Sigma^{-1}(\mathbf{o}-\mu_\mathbf{i})} \tag{4}$$

where k is the dimension of the feature vector (here, 10 for both the autoencoder and geometric moment features).

The probability of a sequence of observations, $o_0, o_1, o_2, ...$, being generated by a given HMM model, λ, can be calculated using the forward algorithm [24]. At each time step, the probability of being in state i is given as $\alpha_t(i)$, and is

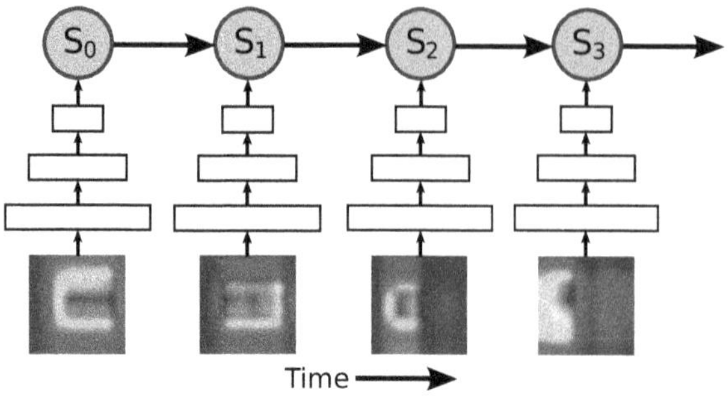

Figure 3: A Hidden Markov Model used to determine the likelihood that a given sequence belongs to a particular class of gestures. Observations are based on encoded versions of individual frames in the gesture.

calculated as the sum of transitioning to state i from all previous states, i.e.,

$$\alpha_t(i) = \sum P(S_i|S_j)\alpha_{t-1}(j) \tag{5}$$

and the probability of observation o_t is the sum of the product of the probability of the observation being generated by each state and the probability of being in the state,

$$\beta_t = \sum P(o_t|S_i)\alpha_t(i) \tag{6}$$

The probability of the sequence of observations is the product of the probability of each observation. The log likelihood of the model generating a sequence is $\sum \beta_t$. We normalize the log likelihood by dividing the probability by the length of the sequence. This is equivalent to determining the geometric mean of the transition / observation probabilities of observing invidivual frames in the sequence given the model.

We used the GaussianHMM implementation in Scikit [23] to generate and train a separate HMM model for each gesture in the CoST dataset, for a total of 28 HMM models (14 using autoencoder features and 14 using geometric moment features). For the autoencoder feature set, we determine the number of states by training a separate HMM for each gesture with a range of hidden states from 2 to 20. We then select the number of states for a specific gesture model by determining which number of states maximize the discrimination ability of the model. In other words, we maximize the difference between the mean log likelihood score of gestures for which a particular model is trained, and the mean log likelihood score of all other gestures. Due to time constraints, we fixed the number of hidden states for the HMMs trained using the geometric moment features to five states for the competition submission. The discriminative ability and the number of hidden states of the HMMs trained on autoencoder features are summarized in Figure 4. For each model, the mean *negative* log likelihood of the gestures being observed by the model is shown. Lower values indicate that a particular gesture class is more likely to have been generated by the particular HMM model. The discriminative ability of the HMMs trained using the geometric moment features are shown in Figure 5.

A maximum likelihood estimate of the label of a capture could be calculated by labeling it with the label of the model with the highest likelihood score. However, as some models provide very high discrimination ability (e.g., the "pat" model is very good at rejecting "grab" and "squeeze" gestures), we later combine the likelihood score using a secondary classifier, as described in Section 4. This also allows for combining the likelihood scores of *both* sets of HMM models, as well as any additional features, such as the gesture level features described in Section 3.4.

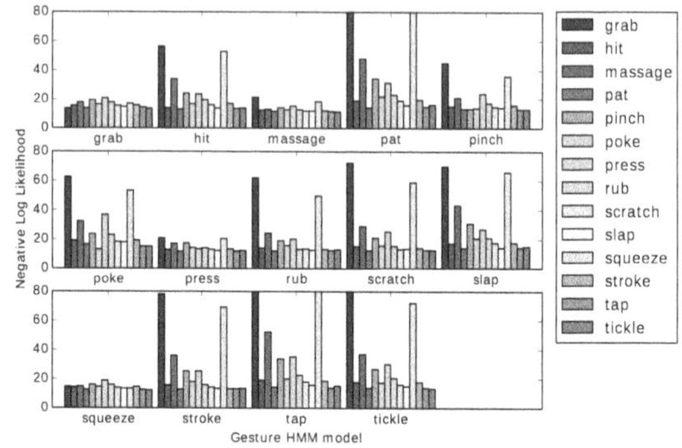

Figure 4: Mean likelihoods of gestures for HMMs generated using autoencoder features. The number of hidden states of each model is given in the parentheses by the model names.

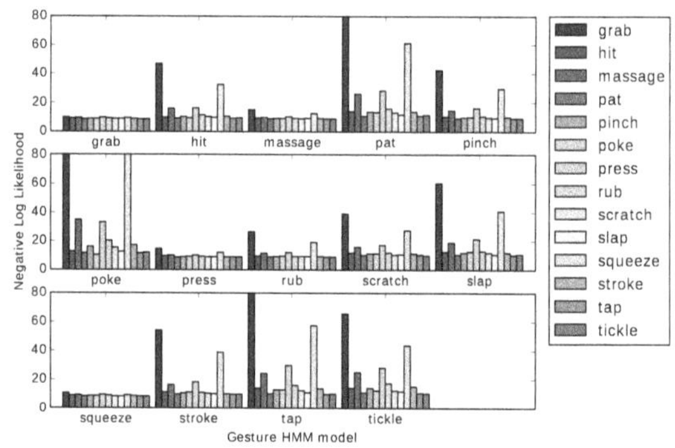

Figure 5: Mean likelihoods of gestures for HMMs generated using geometric moment features.

3.4 Gesture Level Features

The third set of features summarizes the capture as a whole, rather than extracting frame-level features for use with an HMM. These gesture-level features summarize a capture as how much overall pressure is applied during the gesture, how spread out the pressure is, the general position of the gesture and the fundamental frequency of the gesture. We extract a total of seven features from a capture. Given a capture consisting of N frames, two sequences of length N are computed–one consisting of the mean pressure measurement of each frame i in the capture, μ_F^i, and one consisting of the standard deviation of the pressure measurement of each frame, σ_F^i.

The first three features are computed by taking the means

of the mean and standard deviation of the pressure measurements in the frames, and the mean of the standard deviation of the mean pressure measurements. We take the log of the mean and standard deviation of μ_F to assist with classifier training by increasing the relative distance between these features. These first features are calculated by the equations

$$
\begin{aligned}
f_1 &= log\left(\frac{1}{N}\sum \mu_F^i\right) \\
f_2 &= \frac{1}{N}\sum \sigma_F^i \\
f_3 &= log\left(\sqrt{\left(\frac{1}{N}\sum(\mu_F^i - \mu_F)\right)}\right)
\end{aligned}
\tag{7}
$$

where μ_F is the mean of the frame-level pressure means (i.e., the pre-log version of feature 1, e^{f_1}). The motivation behind these features is to discriminate between gestures with consistant contact (e.g., constant) versus sparse contact (e.g., no touch), gestures which are point-like (e.g., tickle) versus spread-out contact (e.g., rub), and gestures which vary in pressure over time (e.g., pats) versus those with constant pressure (e.g., no touch).

The next two features summarize the dominant frequency of the gesture. First, the spectrum of μ_F is calculated using the fast Fourier transform (FFT), $M_F(f) = fft(\mu_F)$. The spectrum is filtered by removing frequencies below 0.625 Hz and above 5 Hz. All gestures, including the rapid ones, contian underlying constant to very slow signal(s) in the spectrum, possibly as an artifact of the data collection procedure as it seemed to be unrelated to the actual gesture. Therefore, to help distinguish the fast gestures from the rest, and to avoid mistakenly labelling all gestures as slow in the frequency domain, we chose a low-end cut-off of 0.625 Hz which elimiated many of the unhelpful low frequency signals that tended to otherwise dominate the spectrum. Occasionally, very high frequencies would also be found in the spectrum, possibly as an artifact of the FFT algorithm itself, and these were removed as well. We chose an upper limit frequency of 5 Hz since physical hand movements - the source of the gestures - more rapid than 5 Hz did not seem plausable, at least not to the authors. After filtering out the high and low frequencies, we then extract the frequency and the amplitude of the dominant frequency in the spectrum

$$
\begin{aligned}
f_4 &= \arg\max_f(M_F(f)) \\
f_5 &= \max(M_F(f))
\end{aligned}
\tag{8}
$$

If the capture consisted of fewer than 64 frames, then μ_F was zero padded to 64 values to ensure sufficient resolution to calculate dominant frequency. These two features are useful for discriminating gestures which are generally consistent (i.e., low-frequency, such as constant) from gestures which are rapidly repeated (i.e., high-frequency, such as rub). The magnitude of the dominant frequency provides a measure of the confidence of this feature.

The final two features calculate the mean center point of the gesture. First, the center point of the gesture in each frame is calculated as the location of the highest pressure,

$$c_x^i, c_y^i = \arg\max_{x,y}(I_i(x,y)) \tag{9}$$

and the final two features is the mean of the center of the gesture

$$
\begin{aligned}
f_6 &= \frac{1}{N}\sum c_x^i \\
f_7 &= \frac{1}{N}\sum c_y^i
\end{aligned}
\tag{10}
$$

These features may be useful for distinguishing gestures which are consistently performed on the same location on a substrate by a user. For instance, a pat may generally be performed on the center of the pressure array, while a tickle may be performed at an off-center point.

4. CLASSIFICATION RESULTS

High-level features are extracted from the dataset using the approaches described above, which are used as input to an arbitrary classifier model, as shown in Figure 6. Features are extracted from each gesture capture, and consist of the following: 14 features from the Autoencoder-HMM models (i.e., likelihood scores from each HMM trained on each gesture in the CoST dataset), 14 features from the Geometric Moment-HMM models (i.e., likelihood scores from each HMM model), and 7 gesture level features. For classification, we used the simple logistic regression model from the Weka, an open source collection of machine learning algorithms [10]. Throughout this section, we refer to the training set as the dataset provided by the challenge to develop models, and the test set as the dataset provided by the challenge after submission of model results. To estimate the performance of our models, we used 10-fold stratefied cross-validation. In 10-fold cross-validation, the training set is partitioned into 10 subsets of approximately equal size and gesture class distribution. The model is trained ten times, leaving one fold out as a test set, and the results are averaged across all ten experiments.

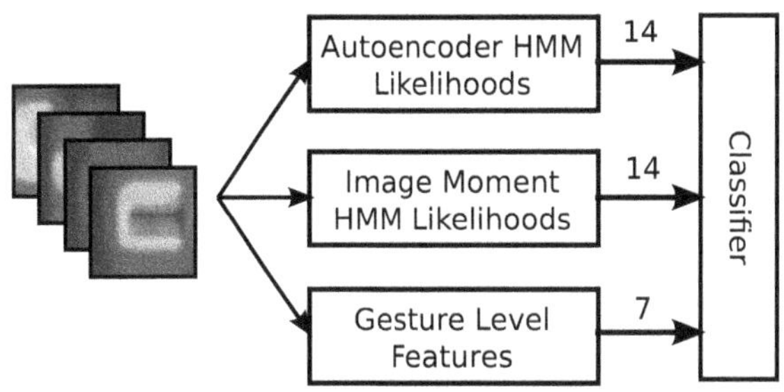

Figure 6: Classification consists of extracting 14 features from the autoencoder HMM models (likelihood of each model), 14 features from the geometric moment HMM models (likelihood of each model), and 7 gesture-level features. These values are used as high-level features for an arbitrary classifier.

HMM models were trained on the CoST and the HAART dataset, and used to classify captures from their respective datasets. In addition, to explore the possibility of transfering learned features from one dataset to another classifier, we also computed the likelihood of gesture captures in the HAART dataset using the HMM models trained on the CoST dataset. The goal of this is to determine if features trained to discriminate the 14 CoST gestures may be used to discriminate HAART gestures without modification, similar to the transfer learning approach shown in [21]. The classification results of the HAART dataset using the CoST HMM models were the ones submitted to the challenge–we trained the HMM models using the HAART dataset after the challenge deadline.

The confusion matrices for the CoST and HAART datasets are shown in Tables 1 and 2, respectively. The confusion matrix for the HAART dataset using the CoST HMM features is shown in Table 3.

Table 2: Confusion Matrix of the HAART test set using HMM models trained on the HAART dataset.

		Classified Label						
		a	b	c	d	e	f	g
Actual Labels	constant (a)	**25**	1	0	6	3	0	0
	no touch (b)	0	**36**	0	0	0	0	0
	pat (c)	0	0	**24**	6	2	3	1
	rub (d)	10	0	3	**12**	3	7	1
	scratch (e)	7	0	4	1	**18**	0	6
	stroke (f)	0	0	0	4	1	**31**	0
	tickle (g)	2	0	0	1	20	0	**13**

Table 3: Confusion Matrix of submitted HAART test set classes using HMM models with CoST features (submitted to challenge).

		Classified Label						
		a	b	c	d	e	f	g
Actual Labels	constant (a)	**33**	1	0	0	0	0	1
	no touch (b)	0	**36**	0	0	0	0	0
	pat (c)	0	0	**23**	6	2	4	1
	rub (d)	0	0	4	**11**	13	7	1
	scratch (e)	1	0	1	1	**28**	1	4
	stroke (f)	0	0	0	4	1	**31**	0
	tickle (g)	0	0	0	3	25	0	**8**

In order to determine the quality of each of the calculated feature sets, we determine the accuracy of the logistic regression classifier using only the autoencoder HMM models (AE-HMM), the geometric moment HMM models (GM-HMM), and gesture-level features (GLF). The accuracies are reported in Tables 4 and 5 for the CoST and HAART datasets, respectively. In addition, the overall accuracy using all features is given, as well as the highest accuracy reported in submissions to the Challenge. The reported accuracy on the training set is the estimated accuracy using 10-fold cross validation. The CoST dataset consists of captures of variable lengths, thus we evaluate the accuracy of the models both with and without the length of the capture in the features. In addition, we calculated the classification accuracy using only capture length. We saw no improvement of accuracy when using other classifiers (e.g., neural networks, SVMs, random forest) over logistic regression, and bagging [2] logistic regressing classifiers showed slight improvement of the overall accuracy.

Table 6 gives the accuracies of classifying the HAART dataset using the CoST HMM models, as well as the classification accuracy using all three feature sets. Compared to the HMM models trained on the HAART dataset, there is over 10-12% reduction in the cross-validation accuracy of

Table 4: Accuracy of the logistic regression classifier for CoST dataset using only the autoencoder HMM models (AE-HMM), geometric moment HMM models (GM-HMM) and gesture level features (GLF).

Features	Training Set	Test Set
with Duration		
AE-HMM	50.57%	40.56%
GM-HMM	39.02%	33.41%
GLF	43.25%	43.30%
without Duration		
AE-HMM	43.16%	33.17%
GM-HMM	28.89%	24.18%
GLF	42.08%	40.80%
Duration Only	19.07%	21.08%
All Features with Duration	56.13%	47.17%
All Features w/o Duration	55.68%	45.38%
All Features with Bagging	56.38%	47.41%
Highest Reported Accuracy	–	61%

Table 5: Accuracy of the logistic regression classifier for HAART dataset using only the autoencoder HMM models (AE-HMM), geometric moment HMM models (GM-HMM) and gesture level features (GLF).

Features	Training Set	Test Set
AE-HMM	46.02%	40.64%
GM-HMM	48.62%	41.83%
GLF	71.80%	66.53%
All Features	73.53%	63.35%
All Features with Bagging	74.57%	62.15%
Highest Reported Accuracy	–	71%

classifying the training set using only one of the HMM models. In addition, there is a slight decrease in the classification accuracy using all the features. Note, however, that the accuracies using the HMM models are still better than using random guessing (approximately 14%). This indicates that while there is some loss of information, transfer learning may still be useful for classifying previously unseen gestures.

Table 6: Accuracy of the logistic regression classifier for HAART dataset using only the autoencoder HMM models (AE-HMM) and geometric moment HMM models (GM-HMM). HMM models used were trained on the CoST dataset.

Features	Training Set	Test Set
AE-HMM	35.81%	44.62%
GM-HMM	36.51%	35.06%
GLF	71.80%	66.53%
All Features	71.11%	67.73%
All Features with Bagging	73.53%	68.92%

5. SUMMARY AND DISCUSSION

We investigate using three different sets of features for classifying a variety of gestures performed on an array of pressure sensors. We extract frame-level features using geometric moments and deep autoencoders, and train hidden Markov models used to calculate likelihood scores for

Table 1: Confusion Matrix of submitted CoST test set classes.

		Classified Label													
		a	b	c	d	e	f	g	h	i	j	k	l	m	n
Actual Labels	grab (a)	**83**	1	4	0	4	0	13	1	0	0	74	0	0	0
	hit (b)	0	**61**	0	19	0	19	0	0	0	36	0	1	19	0
	massage (c)	6	0	**77**	0	1	0	0	7	10	0	7	0	0	10
	pat (d)	0	7	0	**45**	1	1	1	0	2	4	0	3	29	2
	pinch (e)	0	1	2	1	**67**	4	3	0	1	1	5	3	1	5
	poke (f)	0	7	0	1	10	**57**	2	0	1	2	1	0	2	1
	press (g)	13	0	4	0	20	6	**75**	17	10	2	8	4	2	0
	rub (h)	0	0	16	1	2	0	6	**37**	12	0	1	20	1	5
	scratch (i)	3	0	6	2	2	0	1	13	**22**	0	0	4	0	5
	slap (j)	0	33	0	26	1	5	0	0	0	**65**	0	1	29	0
	squeeze (k)	14	0	2	0	3	0	8	4	3	0	**23**	0	0	0
	stroke (l)	1	0	2	5	7	2	11	27	18	0	0	**67**	4	5
	tap (m)	0	8	0	20	0	15	0	0	0	9	0	2	**29**	3
	tickle (n)	0	2	7	0	2	11	0	14	41	1	0	15	4	**84**

each class of gestures in the training set. In addition, we calculate gesture-level features on the full gesture capture. Using these features, we achieved a classification accuracy of 47.17% with the CoST dataset, and 67.73% with the HAART dataset for the challenge. These results are approximately 14% and 3% lower than the most accurate classifiers reported in the Recognition of Social Touch Gestures Challenge, respectively. Training the HMM models on the HAART dataset after the challenge deadline resulted in a classification accuracy of 63.35% on the HAART dataset.

Hidden Markov models are trained on individual gestures to provide a measure of likelihood that a given gesture belongs to a particular class of gestures, based on frame-level features. Individually, models may not provide high levels of discrimination between gesture classes, however, several models produce very low likelihoods for off-model gestures. Consequently, the combination of likelihood scores produce a reasonable feature set for classification. The results from the CoST dataset show that the three feature sets explored here individually produce decent classification accuracies, though much lower than using the combination of these features.

Ideally, we would like to discover features which would be useful for other gesture recognition tasks. To determine if the HMM models may be used in such a manner, a classifier was trained to identify gestures in the HAART dataset using the CoST HMM models as features. While the results were better than random classification, individually, the HMM features were approximately half as accurate as the gesture-level features or the combination of features. This indicates that the quality of the HMM models is highly dependent on the data on which they are trained, and may not be useful for classification tasks with other sensor configurations.

The work presented here could easily be expanded or augmented with variations on the neural network or HMM models. Autoencoders are useful for generating low-dimensional encodings of individual frames, however, there is no mechanism to provide translation invariance of the frame. Convolutional layers would potentially reduce the number of parameters in the neural network, though the size of the sensor array is much smaller than in image recognition tasks, where convolutional neural networks are typically used [18]. In addition, adding sparsity constraints in the autoencoder could also improve encoding of the features [19], as the code layer could be trained such that most units are very near zero for a particular frame.

Hidden Markov models were used in this investigation to handle the temporal aspect of the gestures, treating frame features as samples from a multivariate Gaussian distribution. Sampling the features from a mixture of Gaussians (GMM) allows more complex distributions for HMM states. GMM-HMMs are commonly used for speech recognition tasks [27], and are even useful when features are extracted using deep neural networks [29]. Finally, recurrent neural networks may prove to be a better alternative for modeling the temporal aspects of the gestures.

In addition to classifying gestures, the models explored in this paper may be suitable for larege scale robotic skins with embedded and distributed computing elements, as in [13]. Such skins contain a network inexpensive computing elements collocated with individual or small groups of sensors, such as the pressure array used in the provided datasets. This enables much or all of the task of classifying gestures to be performed within the robotic skin itself, rather than at an external, centralized computer. Such an architecture is more robust to sensor or communication failure, and reduces communication and computation bandwidth to external computers. As memory is limited in the computing elements, efficient classification models are important. Communication bandwidth can be reduced by calculating autoencoder encodings and/or geometric moments of individual frames. If HMM models can also be incorporated, then the robotic skin is capable of performing full detection and identification of gestures, and only requires event-driven communication of gesture and location. We plan on exploring the potential of these models in future work, including the tradeoff between classficiation accuracy and model size.

6. REFERENCES

[1] Recognition of social touch gestures challenge 2015. `http://www.utwente.nl/ewi/touch-challenge-2015/`. Accessed: 2015-08-05.

[2] L. Breiman. Bagging predictors. *Machine Learning*, 24(2):123–140, 1996.

[3] J. Chang, K. MacLean, and S. Yohanan. Gesture recognition in the haptic creature. In *Haptics:*

Generating and Perceiving Tangible Sensations, pages 385–391. Springer, 2010.

[4] T. L. Chen and C. C. Kemp. Lead me by the hand: Evaluation of a direct physical interface for nursing assistant robots. In *Proceedings of the 5th ACM/IEEE international conference on Human-robot interaction*, pages 367–374. IEEE Press, 2010.

[5] R. S. Dahiya, P. Mittendorfer, M. Valle, G. Cheng, and V. J. Lumelsky. Directions toward effective utilization of tactile skin: A review. *IEEE Sensors Journal*, 13(11):4121–4138, 2013.

[6] J. Duchi, E. Hazan, and Y. Singer. Adaptive subgradient methods for online learning and stochastic optimization. *The Journal of Machine Learning Research*, 12:2121–2159, 2011.

[7] T. V. Duong, H. H. Bui, D. Q. Phung, and S. Venkatesh. Activity recognition and abnormality detection with the switching hidden semi-markov model. In *IEEE Computer Society Conference on Computer Vision and Pattern Recognition, 2005*, volume 1, pages 838–845. IEEE, 2005.

[8] A. Flagg and K. MacLean. Affective touch gesture recognition for a furry zoomorphic machine. In *Proceedings of the 7th International Conference on Tangible, Embedded and Embodied Interaction*, pages 25–32. ACM, 2013.

[9] Y. Gao, N. Bianchi-Berthouze, and H. Meng. What does touch tell us about emotions in touchscreen-based gameplay? *ACM Transactions on Computer-Human Interaction*, 19(4):31, 2012.

[10] M. Hall, E. Frank, G. Holmes, B. Pfahringer, P. Reutemann, and I. H. Witten. The weka data mining software: An update. *SIGKDD Explorations*, 11(1), 2009.

[11] M. J. Hertenstein, R. Holmes, M. McCullough, and D. Keltner. The communication of emotion via touch. *Emotion*, 9(4):566–573, 2009.

[12] G. E. Hinton and R. R. Salakhutdinov. Reducing the dimensionality of data with neural networks. *Science*, 313(5786):504–507, 2006.

[13] D. Hughes and N. Correll. Texture recognition and localization in amorphous robotic skin. *Bioinspiration & Biomimetics*, 10(5):055002, 2015.

[14] G. Huisman, A. D. Frederiks, B. V. Dijk, D. Hevlen, and B. Krose. The tasst: Tactile sleeve for social touch. In *World Haptics Conference (WHC), 2013*, pages 211–216. IEEE, 2013.

[15] Y. Jia, E. Shelhamer, J. Donahue, S. Karayev, J. Long, R. Girshick, S. Guadarrama, and T. Darrell. Caffe: Convolutional architecture for fast feature embedding. *arXiv preprint arXiv:1408.5093*, 2014.

[16] H. Jiang. Discriminative training of hmms for automatic speech recognition: A survey. *Computer Speech & Language*, 24(4):589–608, 2010.

[17] M. M. Jung, R. Poppe, M. Poel, and D. K. J. Heylen. Touching the void–introducing cost: Corpus of social touch. In *Proceedings of the 16th International Conference on Multimodal Interaction*, pages 120–127. ACM, 2014.

[18] A. Krizhevsky, I. Sutskever, and G. E. Hinton. Imagenet classification with deep convolutional neural networks. In *Advances in Neural Information Processing Systems*, pages 1097–1105, 2012.

[19] Q. V. Le, M. A. Ranzato, R. Monga, M. Devin, K. Chen, G. S. Corrado, J. Dean, and A. Y. Ng. Building high-level features using large scale unsupervised learning. In *2013 IEEE International Conference on Acoustics, Speech and Signal Processing (ICASSP)*, pages 8595–8598. IEEE, 2013.

[20] M. A. McEvoy and N. Correll. Materials that couple sensing, actuation, computation, and communication. *Science*, 347(6228):1261689, 2015.

[21] M. Oquab, L. Bottou, I. Laptev, and J. Sivic. Learning and transferring mid-level image representations using convolutional neural networks. In *2014 IEEE Conference on Computer Vision and Pattern Recognition (CVPR)*, pages 1717–1724. IEEE, 2014.

[22] S. J. Pan and Q. Yang. A survey on transfer learning. *IEEE Transactions on Knowledge and Data Engineering*, 22(10):1345–1359, 2010.

[23] F. Pedregosa, G. Varoquaux, A. Gramfort, V. Michel, B. Thirion, O. Grisel, M. Blondel, P. Prettenhofer, R. Weiss, V. Dubourg, J. Vanderplas, A. Passos, D. Cournapeau, M. Brucher, M. Perrot, and E. Duchesnay. Scikit-learn: Machine learning in Python. *Journal of Machine Learning Research*, 12:2825–2830, 2011.

[24] L. R. Rabiner. A tutorial on hidden markov models and selected applications in speech recognition. *Proceedings of the IEEE*, 77(2):257–286, 1989.

[25] F. Seide, G. Li, X. Chen, and D. Yu. Feature engineering in context-dependent deep neural networks for conversational speech transcription. In *2011 IEEE Workshop on Automatic Speech Recognition and Understanding (ASRU)*, pages 24–29. IEEE, 2011.

[26] W. D. Stiehl and C. Breazeal. Affective touch for robotic companions. In *Affective Computing and Intelligent Interaction*, pages 747–754. Springer, 2005.

[27] D. Su, X. Wu, and L. Xu. Gmm-hmm acoustic model training by a two level procedure with gaussian components determined by automatic model selection. In *2010 IEEE International Conference on Acoustics Speech and Signal Processing (ICASSP)*, pages 4890–4893. IEEE, 2010.

[28] C.-H. Teh and R. T. Chin. On image analysis by the methods of moments. *IEEE Transactions on Pattern Analysis and Machine Intelligence*, 10(4):496–513, 1988.

[29] Z.-J. Yan, Q. Huo, and J. Xu. A scalable approach to using dnn-derived features in gmm-hmm based acoustic modeling for lvcsr. In *INTERSPEECH*, pages 104–108, 2013.

[30] S. Yohanan and K. E. MacLean. The role of affective touch in human-robot interaction: Human intent and expectations in touching the haptic creature. *International Journal of Social Robotics*, 4(2):163–180, 2012.

Video and Image based Emotion Recognition Challenges in the Wild: EmotiW 2015

Abhinav Dhall
Vision & Sensing Group
University of Canberra
abhinav.dhall@canberra.edu.au

O. V. Ramana Murthy
Vision & Sensing Group
University of Canberra
o.v.ramanamurthy@ieee.org

Roland Goecke
Vision & Sensing Group
University of Canberra/
Australian National University
roland.goecke@ieee.org

Jyoti Joshi
Vision & Sensing Group
University of Canberra
jyoti.joshi@canberra.edu.au

Tom Gedeon
iHCC group
Australian National University
tom.gedeon@anu.edu.au

ABSTRACT

The third Emotion Recognition in the Wild (EmotiW) challenge 2015 consists of an audio-video based emotion and static image based facial expression recognition sub-challenges, which mimics real-world conditions. The two sub-challenges are based on the Acted Facial Expression in the Wild (AFEW) 5.0 and the Static Facial Expression in the Wild (SFEW) 2.0 databases, respectively. The paper describes the data, baseline method, challenge protocol and the challenge results. A total of 12 and 17 teams participated in the video based emotion and image based expression sub-challenges, respectively.

Categories and Subject Descriptors

I.6.3 [**Pattern Recognition**]: Applications; H.2.8 [**Database Applications**]: Image Databases; I.4.m [**IMAGE PROCESSING AND COMPUTER VISION**]: Miscellaneous

Keywords

Audio-video data corpus; Facial expression challenge; Affect analysis in the wild

1. INTRODUCTION

With the advancement in the computational technology and the exponential jump in the amount of data available over the internet, it is useful to develop methods capable of analysing affect in the wild. 'In the wild' here means uncontrolled conditions. Research in automatic affect analysis has been mostly done in controlled environment (such as lab like conditions). In order to improve the current methods for them to perform well in uncontrolled conditions, there is a need of labelled data, which can represent the 'in the wild' settings. The Emotion Recognition in the Wild (EmotiW) challenge aims at providing a platform for researchers to benchmark the performance of their methods on 'in the wild' data. EmotiW 2015 comprises of two sub-challenges – a) Video based emotion Recognition (VReco); b) Static Image based facial expression Recognition (SReco).

There are several challenges in the affect recognition community, which target different challenges in affect recognition. The Facial Expression Recognition challenge and Analysis (FERA) [14] targets facial expression recognition on universal emotion classes on data created by actors in lab conditions. Audio Video Emotion Challenge (AVEC) [11] [12] focusses on depression intensity and continuous affect intensity estimation. On the other hand, EmotiW targets the efforts required towards affect analysis in the wild.

During the first EmotiW challenge [3], which was organised at the ACM International Conference on Multimodal Interaction (ICMI) 2013, Sydney, a total of 27 teams registered for the challenge and 9 teams submitted the test labels. The database for the challenge was AFEW 3.0 [4]. The data was divided into three sets: *Train*, *Val* and *Test*. Ebrahimi et al. [6], proposed a deep learning based emotion recognition method and their system was the challenge winner with classification accuracy of 41.02%. Sikka et al. [13] proposed a multiple kernel learning based technique, which was the runner-up method during EmotiW 2013. From the classification accuracy of the proposed methods in EmotiW 2013, it can be observed that automatic emotion recognition in the wild is not mature enough to work well in uncontrolled settings and there is a lot of scope for future research in this direction. The second EmotiW challenge [2] was organised as part of ACM ICMI 2014, Istanbul, had participation from 9 teams. Mengyi et al. [9]'s method based on manifold learning and convolutional neural networks performed best during EmotiW 2014. Figure 1 compares the classification accuracy of methods proposed in the EmotiW 2014 challenge. The performance of the proposed techniques improved w.r.t. the entries in 2013. However, it is still far away from practical use in real-world conditions. Therefore, we continue with the challenge series. This year for EmotiW 2015 is being organised as part of ACM ICMI 2015, Seattle. A new sub-challenge has been introduced in EmotiW 2015. The static image based facial expression recognition sub-challenge aims to provide a platform for researchers, who

ICMI '15, November 09-13, 2015, Seattle, WA, USA
Copyright 2015 ACM ISBN 978-1-4503-3912-4/15/11 ...$15.00.
DOI: http://dx.doi.org/10.1145/2818346.2829994.

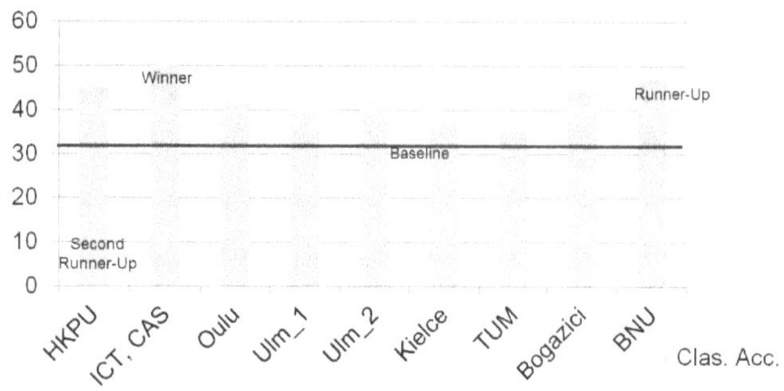

Figure 1: The graph compares the classification accuracy performance of participants in EmotiW 2014 challenge.

Attribute	Description
Length of sequences	300-5400 ms
No. of annotators	3
Expression classes	Anger, Disgust, Fear, Happiness, Neutral, Sadness and Surprise
Total No. of expressions	1645
Video format	AVI
Audio format	WAV

Table 1: Attributes of AFEW 5.0 database.

work on a single image as a sample for facial expression recognition.

2. DATA

EmotiW 2015 has two sub-challenges and there are two datasets as described below:

VReco - For the video based emotion recognition sub-challenge, AFEW 5.0 database is used. AFEW is developed using a semi-automatic process. Subtitle for Deaf & Hearing impaired (SDH) closed captions are parsed for presence of keywords related to emotion such as 'angry', 'cry', 'sad' etc. Short sequences which contain the keyword are selected by the labeller if it contains relevant data. The details of database collection are discussed in [4]. For EmotiW 2015, the database is divided into three sub-sets: *Train* (723 samples), *Val* (383 samples) and *Test* (539 samples). These sets are the extended versions of the EmotiW 2014 [2] sets. The current version of the database, AFEW 5.0 is available at http://cs.anu.edu.au/few contains two labelled sets. sub-challenge task is to classify a sample audio-video clip into one of the seven categories: *Anger*, *Disgust*, *Fear*, *Happiness*, *Neutral*, *Sadness* and *Surprise*. Table 1 discusses the details about the video samples in the database. The labeled training and validation sets were made available early in April and the new, unlabeled test set was made available in July 2015. There are no separate video-only, audio-only, or audio-video challenges. Participants are free to use either modality or both. Results for all methods will be combined into one set in the end. Participants are allowed to use their own features and classification methods. The labels of the testing set are unknown. Participants will need to adhere to the definition of training, validation and testing sets. In their papers, they may report on results obtained on the training and validation sets, but only the results on the testing set will be taken into account for the overall Grand Challenge results.

Low Level Descriptors (LLD)	
Energy/Spectral LLD	PCM Loudness MFCC [0-14] log Mel Frequency Band [0-7] Line Spectral Pairs (LSP) frequency [0-7] F0 F0 Envelope
Voicing related LLD	Voicing Prob. Jitter Local Jitter consecutive frame pairs Shimmer Local

Table 2: Audio feature set - 38 (34 + 4) low-level descriptors.

SReco - SFEW 2.0 forms the basis of the Image based Static Facial Expression Recognition sub-challenge. SFEW is created from AFEW 5.0 using key-frame extraction method. The video clips as discussed above are created using a semi-automatic technique, we added another step to it. Facial points extracted a video sample in VReco are clustered. The frames closest to the cluster centres are chosen as the key-frames. K-means clustering with number of clusters = 6 was used. Similar to AFEW 5.0, SFEW 2.0 has been divided into three sets: Train (880 samples), Val (383 samples) and Test (372 samples). The list of movies used in both VReco and SReco is mentioned in Section 6.

3. BASELINE EXPERIMENTS

3.1 VReco sub-challenge

For computing the baseline results for the VReco sub-challenge, publicly available libraries are used. Pre-trained face models [17] are applied for face detection and initialisation of the Intraface tracking libray [15]. The fiducial points generated by Intraface are used for aligning the face. The face size is set to 128 × 128. Post aligning Local Binary Pattern-Three Orthogonal Planes (LBP-TOP) [16] features are extracted from non-overlapping spatial 4 × 4 blocks. LBP-TOP is a standard texture based feature, which has been extensively used for face-based affect classification [3] [2]. The LBP-TOP feature from each block are concatenated to create one feature vector. Non-linear Chi-square kernel based SVM is learnt for emotion classification (*Anger*, *Disgust*, *Fear*, *Happiness*, *Neutral*, *Sadness* and *Surprise*). The video only baseline system achieves 36.08% and 39.33% classification accuracy for the *Val* and *Test* sets, respectively. Please note that these are unweighed accuracies.

Functionals
Arithmetic Mean
standard deviation
skewness, kurtosis
quartiles, quartile ranges
percentile 1%, 99%
percentile range
Position max./min
up-level time 75/90
linear regression coeff.
linear regression error(quadratic/absolute)

Table 3: Set of functionals applied to LLD.

In this challenge, a set of audio features similar to the features employed in AVEC 2011 [11] motivated from the INTERSPEECH 2010 Paralinguistic challenge (1582 features) [10] are also shared with the participants. The features are extracted using the open-source Emotion and Affect Recognition (openEAR) [7] toolkit backend openSMILE [8]. The feature set consists of 34 energy & spectral related low-level descriptors (LLD) × 21 functionals, 4 voicing related LLD × 19 functionals, 34 delta coefficients of energy & spectral LLD × 21 functionals, 4 delta coefficients of the voicing related LLD × 19 functionals and 2 voiced/unvoiced durational features. Table 2 and 3 describe the details of LLD features and functionals, respectively.

3.2 SReco sub-challenge

The MoPS [17] based face and facial parts detector is applied to SFEW images to compute the baseline for SReco. The fiducial points are aligned using affined warp and the face size is set to 128 × 128. Following our earlier work [1], two feature descriptors are computed. Pyramid of Histogram of Gradients (PHOG) is applied to the aligned face. The parameters are: range = [0-360], pyramid levels = 3 and number of bins = 16. The aligned faces are divided into 4 × 4 non-overlapping blocks and PHOG is computed from each block. The PHOG histograms from each block are further concatenated. Furthermore, Local Phase Quantisation (LPQ) is computed. LPQ is robust to blur and illumination changes and is computed on the aligned face as a whole. PHOG and LPQ are concatenated at feature level and a non-linear SVM is used. The classification accuracy for the *Val* and *Test* set are 35.93% and 39.13%, respectively.

In total 75 teams, registered for the challenge and 22 papers were submitted. 13 papers were accepted for publication with 6 papers accepted as oral presentations and others as posters. Prof. Marian S. Bartlett (University of California San Diego and Emotient Inc) and Prof. Ira Kemelmacher-Shlizerman (University of Washington) will be presenting the keynote talks at the EmotiW event at ICMI, Seattle.

Figure 2 shows a graph, which compares the classification accuracy of the 17 participating teams w.r.t each other and the baseline in SReco sub-challenge. The winning entries are from the teams of KAIST_CNL, NERV and ADSC. Figure 3 shows a graph, which compares the classification accuracy of the 12 participating teams w.r.t each other and the baseline. The winning entries are from the teams of ILC, Bogazici and Poly-Goethe. It is interesting to note that a large number of the proposed methods used deep learning based techniques. The performance of the methods is limited by – a) the amount of labelled data; b) performance limitations of the current state-of-art face and facial parts detectors. Some teams used extra data for training their deep learning pipelines. For the VReco sub-challenge, the facial features should be able to model the temporal dynamics of emotion. Some frames contain multiple subjects, this in itself is one of the problems, which need to be further looked into. Group-level emotion recognition [5] is a new research area and will be worthwhile to explore in future, in order to improve the automatic emotion recognition methods for them to work on multiple people in a scene.

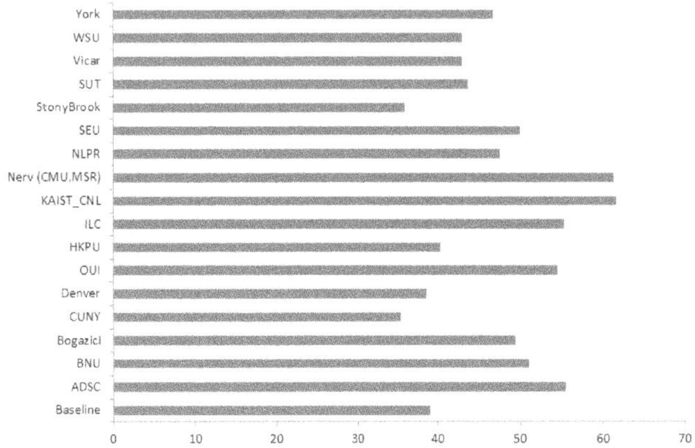

Figure 2: The graph compares the classification accuracy performance of participants in the SReco sub-challenge.

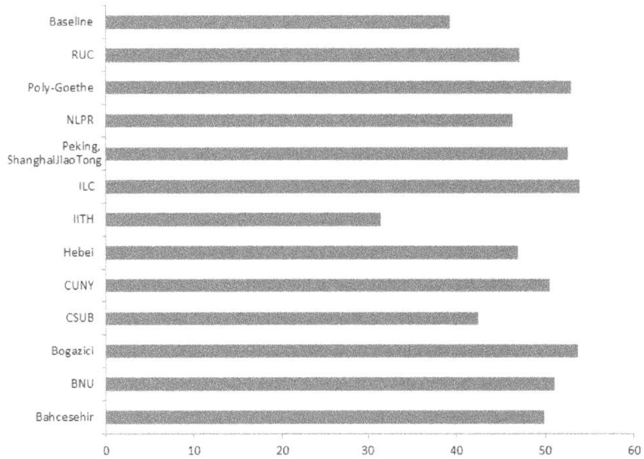

Figure 3: The graph compares the classification accuracy performance of participants in the VReco sub-challenge.

4. CONCLUSION

The third Emotion Recognition in the Wild 2015 challenge provides a platform for researchers to benchmark and compete with their emotion recognition method on the Acted Facial Expressions in the Wild database 5.0 and single image based facial expression recognition methods on the Static Facial Expression in the Wild database 2.0. Emotion recognition in the wild is a challenging problem due to diversity in scenes in the form of head pose, illumination, occlusion and background noise. This year's challenge carry forwards, the platform started by the second EmotiW challenge and adds a new sub-challenge. This paper describes the baselines, data and protocols for the two sub-challenges. The results show that affect analysis in the wild is still an open-problem and there are various sub-problems, which need to be researched upon.

5. ACKNOWLEDGEMENT

We are grateful to the ICMI'15 chairs and EmotiW program committee members. Abhinav Dhall and Roland Goecke are supported by the Australian Research Council Discovery project grant ARCDP130101094.

6. APPENDIX

Movie Names: 21, 50 50, About a boy, A Case of You, After the sunset, Air Heads, American, American History X, And Soon Came the Darkness, Aviator, Black Swan, Bridesmaids, Captivity, Carrie, Change Up, Chernobyl Diaries, Children of Men, Contraband, Crying Game, Cursed, December Boys, Deep Blue Sea, Descendants, Did You Hear About the Morgans?, Dumb and Dumberer: When Harry Met Lloyd, Devil's Due, Elizabeth, Empire of the Sun, Enemy at the Gates, Evil Dead, Eyes Wide Shut, Extremely Loud & Incredibly Close, Feast, Four Weddings and a Funeral, Friends with Benefits, Frost/Nixon, Ghoshtship, Girl with a Pearl Earring, Gone In Sixty Seconds, Grudge, Grudge 2, Grudge 3, Half Light, Hall Pass, Halloween, Halloween Resurrection, Hangover, Harry Potter and the Philosopher's Stone, Harry Potter and the Chamber of Secrets, Harry Potter and the Deathly Hallows Part 1, Harry Potter and the Deathly Hallows Part 2, Harry Potter and the Goblet of Fire, Harry Potter and the Half Blood Prince, Harry Potter and the Order Of Phoenix, Harry Potter and the Prisoners Of Azkaban, Harold & Kumar go to the White Castle, House of Wax, I Am Sam, It's Complicated, I Think I Love My Wife, Jaws 2, Jennifer's Body, Life is Beautiful, Little Manhattan, Messengers, Mama, Mission Impossible 2, Miss March, My Left Foot, Nothing but the Truth, Notting Hill, Not Suitable for Children, One Flew Over the Cuckoo's Nest, Orange and Sunshine, Orphan, Pretty in Pink, Pretty Woman, Pulse, Rapture Palooza, Remember Me, Runaway Bride, Quartet, Romeo Juliet, Saw 3D, Serendipity, Silver Lining Playbook, Solitary Man, Something Borrowed, Step Up 4, Taking Lives, Terms of Endearment, The American, The Aviator, The Caller, The Devil Wears Prada, The Eye, The Fourth Kind, The Girl with Dragon Tattoo, The Hangover, The Haunting, The Haunting of Molly Hartley, The Hills have Eyes 2, The Informant!, The King's Speech, The Last King of Scotland, The Pink Panther 2, The Ring 2, The Shinning, The Social Network, The Terminal, The Theory of Everything, The Town, Valentine Day, Unstoppable, Uninvited, Valkyrie, Vanilla Sky, Woman In Black, Wrong Turn 3, You're Next, You've Got Mail

7. REFERENCES

[1] A. Dhall, A. Asthana, R. Goecke, and T. Gedeon. Emotion recognition using PHOG and LPQ features. In *Proceedings of the IEEE Conference Automatic Faces & Gesture Recognition workshop FERA*, pages 878–883, 2011.

[2] A. Dhall, R. Goecke, J. Joshi, K. Sikka, and T. Gedeon. Emotion recognition in the wild challenge 2014: Baseline, data and protocol. In *Proceedings of the ACM on International Conference on Multimodal Interaction (ICMI)*, 2014.

[3] A. Dhall, R. Goecke, J. Joshi, M. Wagner, and T. Gedeon. Emotion recognition in the wild challenge 2013. In *Proceedings of the ACM on International Conference on Multimodal Interaction (ICMI)*, pages 509–516, 2013.

[4] A. Dhall, R. Goecke, S. Lucey, and T. Gedeon. Collecting large, richly annotated facial-expression databases from movies. *IEEE Multimedia*, 19(3):0034, 2012.

[5] A. Dhall, J. Joshi, I. Radwan, and R. Goecke. Finding Happiest Moments in a Social Context. In *Proceedings of the Asian Conference on Computer Vision (ACCV)*, pages 613–626, 2012.

[6] S. Ebrahimi, C. Pal, X. Bouthillier, P. Froumenty, S. Jean, K. R. Konda, P. Vincent, A. Courville, and Y. Bengio. Combining modality specific deep neural networks for emotion recognition in video. In *Proceedings of the ACM on International Conference on Multimodal Interaction (ICMI)*, pages 543–550, 2013.

[7] F. Eyben, M. Wollmer, and B. Schuller. OpenearâĂŤintroducing the munich open-source emotion and affect recognition toolkit. In *Proceedings of the International Conference on Affective Computing and Intelligent Interaction (ACII)*, pages 1–6, 2009.

[8] F. Eyben, M. Wöllmer, and B. Schuller. Opensmile: the munich versatile and fast open-source audio feature extractor. In *Proceedings of the ACM International Conference on Multimedia (MM)*, pages 1459–1462, 2010.

[9] M. Liu, R. Wang, S. Li, S. Shan, Z. Huang, and X. Chen. Combining multiple kernel methods on riemannian manifold for emotion recognition in the wild. In *Proceedings of the 16th International Conference on Multimodal Interaction*, pages 494–501. ACM, 2014.

[10] B. Schuller, S. Steidl, A. Batliner, F. Burkhardt, L. Devillers, C. A. Müller, and S. S. Narayanan. The interspeech 2010 paralinguistic challenge. In *INTERSPEECH*, pages 2794–2797, 2010.

[11] B. Schuller, M. Valstar, F. Eyben, G. McKeown, R. Cowie, and M. Pantic. Avec 2011–the first international audio/visual emotion challenge. In *Proceedings of the International Conference on Affective Computing and Intelligent Interaction (ACII)*, pages 415–424, 2011.

[12] B. Schuller, M. Valster, F. Eyben, R. Cowie, and M. Pantic. Avec 2012: the continuous audio/visual emotion challenge. In *Proceedings of the ACM on International Conference on Multimodal Interaction (ICMI)*, pages 449–456, 2012.

[13] K. Sikka, K. Dykstra, S. Sathyanarayana, G. Littlewort, and M. Bartlett. Multiple kernel learning for emotion recognition in the wild. In *Proceedings of the ACM on International Conference on Multimodal Interaction (ICMI)*, pages 517–524, 2013.

[14] M. F. Valstar, M. Mehu, B. Jiang, M. Pantic, and K. Scherer. Meta-analysis of the first facial expression recognition challenge. *IEEE Transactions on Systems, Man, and Cybernetics, Part B: Cybernetics*, 42(4):966–979, 2012.

[15] X. Xiong and F. De la Torre. Supervised descent method and its applications to face alignment. In *Proceedings of the IEEE Conference on Computer Vision and Pattern Recognition (CVPR)*, pages 532–539, 2013.

[16] G. Zhao and M. Pietikainen. Dynamic texture recognition using local binary patterns with an application to facial expressions. *IEEE Transaction on Pattern Analysis and Machine Intelligence*, 29(6):915–928, 2007.

[17] X. Zhu and D. Ramanan. Face detection, pose estimation, and landmark localization in the wild. In *Proceedings of the IEEE Conference on Computer Vision and Pattern Recognition (CVPR)*, pages 2879–2886, 2012.

Hierarchical Committee of Deep CNNs with Exponentially-Weighted Decision Fusion for Static Facial Expression Recognition

Bo-Kyeong Kim, Hwaran Lee, Jihyeon Roh, Soo-Young Lee
Department of Electrical Engineering, Korea Advanced Institute of Science and Technology (KAIST)
Daejeon, Republic of Korea
bokyeong1015@gmail.com, {hwaran.lee, rohleejh, sylee}@kaist.ac.kr

ABSTRACT
We present a pattern recognition framework to improve committee machines of deep convolutional neural networks (deep CNNs) and its application to static facial expression recognition in the wild (SFEW). In order to generate enough diversity of decisions, we trained multiple deep CNNs by varying network architectures, input normalization, and weight initialization as well as by adopting several learning strategies to use large external databases. Moreover, with these deep models, we formed hierarchical committees using the validation-accuracy-based exponentially-weighted average (VA-Expo-WA) rule. Through extensive experiments, the great strengths of our committee machines were demonstrated in both structural and decisional ways. On the SFEW2.0 dataset released for the 3rd Emotion Recognition in the Wild (EmotiW) sub-challenge, a test accuracy of 57.3% was obtained from the best single deep CNN, while the single-level committees yielded 58.3% and 60.5% with the simple average rule and with the VA-Expo-WA rule, respectively. Our final submission based on the 3-level hierarchy using the VA-Expo-WA achieved 61.6%, significantly higher than the SFEW baseline of 39.1%.

Categories and Subject Descriptors
I.4.9 [**Image Processing and Computer Vision**]: Applications

Keywords
Hierarchical Committee; Exponentially-Weighted Decision Fusion; Deep Convolutional Neural Network

1. INTRODUCTION
Committee machines (also known as classifier ensembles) generally yield a better performance than a single classifier [1, 2], and thus have extensively applied in various research fields including vision [3, 4], speech [5, 6], text [7], and bio-data [8]. From previous studies on designing a good committee to outperform its individual members, *generating diverse decisions from various individuals* has been shown to be crucial in *providing complementary information about input data* [9, 10].

ICMI '15, November 09-13, 2015, Seattle, WA, USA
© 2015 ACM. ISBN 978-1-4503-3912-4/15/11...$15.00
DOI: http://dx.doi.org/10.1145/2818346.2830590

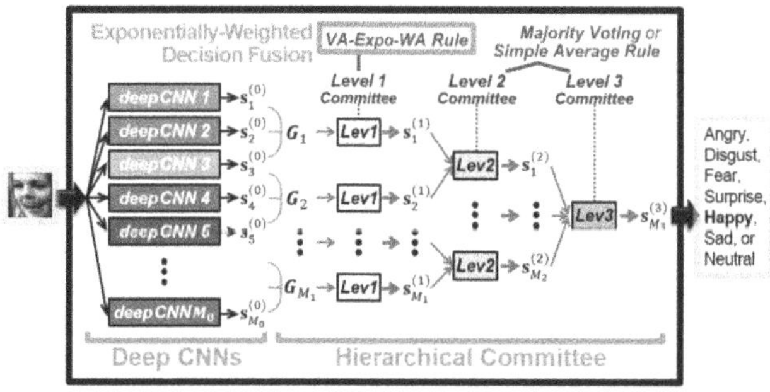

Figure 1. The overall system for facial expression recognition

With recent advances in deep learning and parallel computing, forming a committee of multiple deep neural networks was presented in [11, 12], has attained impressive successes [13-15], and now becomes a widely used approach [16-18]. Particularly, in this paper, we investigate the multi-column deep neural network (MCDNN) [14] for static facial expression recognition in the wild (SFEW). The standard MCDNN is a committee of deep convolutional neural networks (deep CNNs) with a simple averaging decision rule in a single structure level. Since the MCDNN has already proved its superiority in many visual classifications, we expect that its excellence in recognition could also be demonstrated in SFEW.

More importantly, we present 2 simple yet effective ways to improve the MCDNN: '*training more diverse individuals*' and '*forming a better committee in both decisional and structural aspects*'. The former is achieved by designing various network architectures in addition to applying the commonly-used schemes (e.g., different input normalizations and different random weight initialization). Furthermore, we adopt several strategies for using external data in training deep CNNs in order to pursue more diverse decisions and errors. The latter is achieved with a better ensemble rule based on an exponentially-weighted decision fusion. Moreover, we build a hierarchical committee which can make more reliable decisions. As structural levels in the committee become higher, the consensus of multiple sub-groups could be formed and thus enhance the reliability of decisions. The overall proposed system is shown in Figure 1.

Our framework based on the improved committee machines of deep CNNs is tested on the SFEW 2.0 database [19], released for a sub-competition in the 3rd Emotion Recognition in the Wild 2015 (EmotiW2015) challenge. The remainder of this paper describes the proposed approach in detail, experimental results (including our test-label submissions for this SFEW competition), and conclusions.

2. PROPOSED APPROACH

2.1 Deep CNNs as Individual Members

A deep CNN consists of several feature extraction stages (with alternating convolutional and pooling layers), followed by a recognition stage (with fully-connected layers) [15, 20]. Because of its excellent classification ability as well as hierarchical feature development mimicking the human visual system, we selected the deep CNN for the base member of a committee as in a standard MCDNN.

To build diverse deep CNNs in standard MCDNNs, being trained with 'different training data sets' was mainly focused rather than using 'different classifiers'. The effect of 'different training data' was achieved by several preprocessing methods on the original data such as deformation and normalization. For the effect of 'different classifiers', the MCDNNs applied multiple random seeds for weight initialization, but the identical network architectures were used for all individual members. We believed that *various network architectures* also largely contributed to obtaining different classifiers and thus to increasing diversity of decisions in forming a committee. Therefore, we applied various architectures for deep CNNs as well as differently preprocessed data and different weight initialization. Furthermore, we explored several training *strategies for making use of external data* along with the SFEW data in order to pursue more diverse errors. The experimental details about how to build the individual deep CNNs and their recognition accuracies are presented in Section 4.

2.2 Exponentially-Weighted Decision Fusion

When forming a committee, how to combine decisions from individual members has been extensively investigated. In this paper, we first explored 3 widely-used rules for decision fusion [1, 2]: the majority voting, median rule, and simple average rule. Then, we introduced an effective combination rule based on exponential weighting to give more weights on well-performed individuals.

The 'majority voting' directly uses the predicted class labels to select a class with the largest number of votes. On the other hands, instead of using the labels, the 'median rule' and 'simple average rule' use the class-related continuous confidences or scores. In our experiments, the median/simple average rule decided a class with the highest median/average of posterior class probabilities yielded from deep CNNs. For these 3 rules, the individuals have equal rights for participation so that any reliability or importance on each of their decision is not considered.

A straightforward way to regard the importance of members' decisions is to compute a weighted mean of class scores with assigning the weights as validation performances. We denoted it as the 'VA-Simp-WA' rule, short for the validation-accuracy-based simple weighted average. However, when the committee members yield the similar accuracies and thus almost equal weights are used, the VA-Simp-WA does not differ from the 'simple average rule'. Our exponentially-weighted decision fusion has been motivated by considering the aforementioned case. In determining the weights, we adopted *an exponential function which influences on the differences between numbers* (e.g. '3^1-2^1=1' < '3^2-2^2=5'). We expected that *this characteristic of exponent can give more weights on the members with (even slightly) higher accuracies.*

Let us denote our method as the '*VA-Expo-WA*' rule, short for the validation-accuracy-based exponentially-weighted average, and continue our discussion with mathematical notations. Suppose a member model m (=1,...,M) with its validation accuracy of z_m provides a posteriori class probability vector $\mathbf{s}_m$ for an input pattern. Then, the final ensemble of M models' decisions in the VA-Expo-WA becomes

$$\mathbf{s}_{final} = \frac{\sum_{m=1}^{M}(z_m)^q\,\mathbf{s}_m}{\sum_{m=1}^{M}(z_m)^q} = \sum_{m=1}^{M} d_m \mathbf{s}_m \quad (1)$$

where a decision weight d_m reflects the normalized significance of the model m's decision ($0 \leq d_m \leq 1$) and an exponent q is a hyper-parameter to determine how much the qualified members are emphasized ($q>1$) or de-emphasized ($q \leq 1$). Finally, a class with the highest value in exponentially-weighted class probabilities is chosen. Here, the value of q is found by a simple uniform search: scanned over [-50:0.1:150] and selected to provide the maximum performance on validation data after the fusion. The scanning procedure and the corresponding decision weights for the selected q are illustrated in Figure 2. We confirmed that this searching method required little additional computation, while it found a proper q which can improve the generalization on validation data. Note that the VA-Expo-WA rules with q=0 and q=1 are identical to the simple average rule and the VA-Simp-WA, respectively. The superior performance of our VA-Expo-WA rule compared to the commonly-used decision fusion rules are shown in Section 5.

2.3 Hierarchical Committee

The existing literatures using hierarchical architectures of committees aimed to divide a hard problem into the easier ones (based on the divide-and-conquer strategy) with a statistical framework [21, 22] and/or to efficiently combine the outputs of different classifiers trained on heterogeneous features [3, 23]. Meanwhile, we constructed hierarchical committees of deep CNNs with the following procedure according to the 2 expected merits.

1) Organize the M_0 individual members into the 1st level sub-groups, $\{G_1, \ldots, G_{M_1}\}$ having some overlapped members. After that, make a decision for each group according to the 1st level decision fusion rule.
2) Collect all sub-groups' decisions in the lth level, $\{\mathbf{s}_{m_l}^{(l)},\ m_l = 1, \ldots, M_l\}$ where l (= 1, ..., L-1) and m_l are indices for the level and the sub-group, respectively. Then, re-organize them into the (l+1)th level groups, and make a decision for each group according to the (l+1)th level decision fusion rule.
3) Repeat '2)' until reaching to get a final decision at the last L^{th} level.

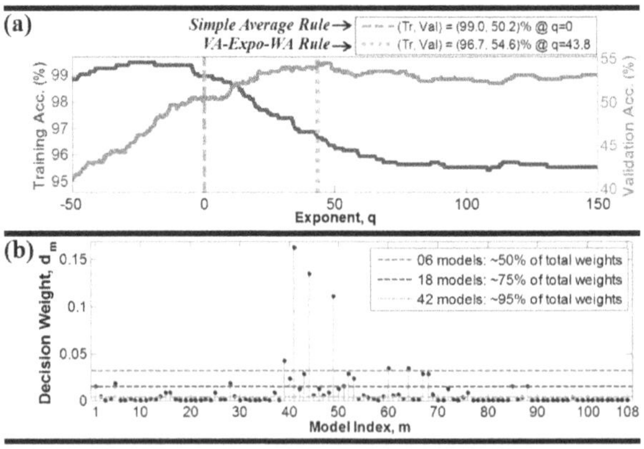

Figure 2. (a) The training and validation accuracies (%) as an exponent '*q*' is scanned in the exponentially-weighted decision fusion and (b) the corresponding decision weights for the selected *q*. This result was obtained when 108 models formed a committee with the VA-Expo-WA rule (see Section 5).

The first merit is that, *more reliable decisions* could come from the *strong consensus of multiple sub-groups* in *higher structural levels*. Second, the *increased diversity of errors* could be obtained by *setting some members to be overlapped in certain sub-groups*. Then, depending on other members in these groups, the *overlapping members differently contribute to the next level decision*. Since the former is quite intuitive, let us explain the latter with a toy example. Suppose a 2-class problem and 5 member classifiers of (a, b, c, d, e) who claim the class label for an input sample as (1, 1, 1, 2, 2), respectively. When they are divided into 2 sub-groups, G_1: {a, b, c} and G_2: {c, d, e}, with an overlapping member 'c' and the majority voting is applied, the 'c' differently contributes to the final decision. More specifically, without grouping, there is no doubt of the selection of class 1 by 3 votes from a, b, and c among 5 members. However, with grouping, both classes get the equal number of mid-level decisions (the class 1 from G_1 and the class 2 from G_2) due to the different impacts of c's claim on both sub-groups, so the final decision depends on the mean class probabilities. We expected that these groups with overlapping members could lead to more various decisions in the low structural levels, finally serving as diverse errors in the last level. See Section 6 for the experimental details and favorable classification results of our hierarchical committees, which outperform the standard single-level committees.

3. FACE REGISTRATION

3.1 SFEW 2.0 Database

The SFEW 2.0 database [19] was created by extracting frames from emotional movie clips in the AFEW data corpus [24]. The task was to assign 7 expression labels (angry, disgust, fear, happy, sad, surprise, and neutral) to these frames in close-to-real world conditions. For the training, validation, and test set, the SFEW database contains 958, 436, and 372 images, respectively.

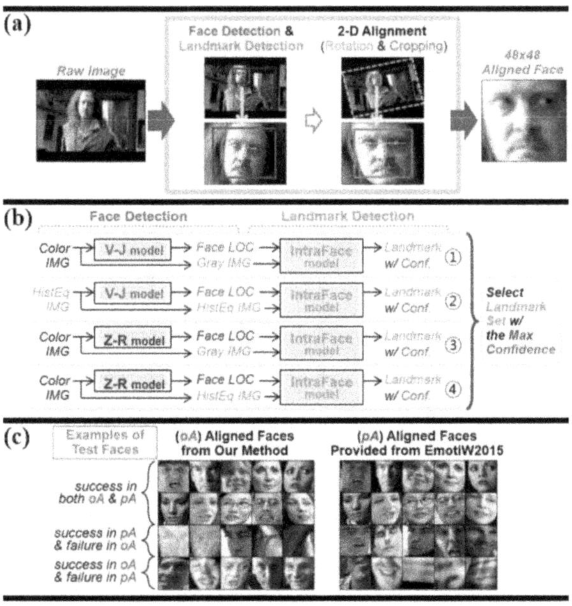

Figure 3. (a) Face registration based on a 2-D alignment, (b) our multi-pipeline-based alignment, and (c) examples of aligned faces for test data. In (b), the terms 'IMG', 'HistEq', 'LOC', and 'Conf' are short for 'image', 'histogram equalized', 'location', and 'confidence', respectively. In (c), faces in the corresponding positions between oA and pA are processed from the same test image.

3.2 Face Registration

For face registration, we conducted a conventional 2-D alignment based on eye locations as illustrated in Figure 3(a). To improve robustness in face/landmark detection, multiple detection pipelines were designed to produce different landmark estimations, and the best estimation among them was finally used for the 2-D alignment. We used the Viola-Jones (V-J) model [25] and the Zhu-Ramanan (Z-R) model [26] for face detection along with the IntraFace model [27] for landmark detection. As shown in Figure 3(b), we considered 4 single pipelines based on the following observations: i) some faces, failed by the V-J, could be detected by the Z-R, and vice versa, ii) depending on face locations from the V-J and Z-R, the landmark estimation of the IntraFace became different, iii) the V-J and IntraFace sometimes yielded complementary outputs when histogram-equalized images were used as input. Among 4 possible landmark sets from those pipelines, the landmark set with the highest confidence provided from the IntraFace was eventually selected for alignment.

In Table 1, we compared the performances between our multi-pipeline-based alignment and single-pipeline-based ones. For each data type, we computed the ratio of successful alignments to the whole number of samples as well as the ratio of cases where only face detection succeeded. Our 4-pipeline-based alignment performed better than the single-pipeline ones, implying that complementary detection results were obtained from 4 single pipelines. Therefore, combining them can lead to the robust face registration in real-world conditions. Note that, for training and validation data, the erroneous and failed alignments were semi-automatically processed by hands for a later usage in training deep models. However, *for testing data*, any human intervention was not applied in the context of *a fully-automatic system*.

Figure 3(c) depicts examples for test faces processed by our alignment method and provided from EmotiW2015. As shown in the 1st and 2nd rows of the figure, the faces processed from our method (oA) were more similarly aligned each other compared to the provided alignments (pA). It could lead to superior accuracies of oA as denoted in Table 2. However, in addition to oA, we also used pA in training deep models for the following reasons: for giving deformation effects (such as translation and rotation) to ours and for providing complementary information when either oA or pA failed (as shown in the 3rd and 4th rows of the figure).

Table 1. Alignment-success rate (%) of our alignments

Alignment Method		Success Rate (%)					
		Alignment (Both Face & Landmark Detection)			**Only Face Detection**		
		Train	Valid	Test	Train	Valid	Test
Single-Pipeline-Based	①	70.5	70.4	73.1	1.4	1.1	2.4
	②	71.6	74.1	77.2	2.6	1.8	3.5
	③	58.6	60.8	57.5	25.5	29.8	30.9
	④	56.6	56.4	53.5	27.5	34.2	34.9
Multi-Pipeline-Based		**81.8**	**83.5**	**90.1**	9.5	6.0	4.0

Table 2. Validation (& testing, if available) accuracy (%) of our alignments (oA) and provided alignments (pA)

Classification Method	oA	pA
{LPQ-pHOG} + rbfSVM: **baseline** [19]	-	36.0 (39.1)
A single deep CNN[a]: ***PREP***iNor – {***CN***NL – ***FC***3072}***R***1	52.5 (57.3)	46.8
A committee of 108 deep CNNs[b] with the VA-Expo-WA rule	54.6 (60.5)	52.2 (56.7)

[a, b] For the detailed information, see Section 4.3 and 5, respectively.

4. DESIGNING AND TRAINING INDIVIDUAL COMMITTEE MEMBERS

In this section, we first described how to design multiple deep CNNs to pursue diverse errors in forming a good committee. Next, for training these models, how to make use of external data along with the SFEW data was presented with other learning details. Finally, classification results of individual models were examined.

4.1 Designing Individual Deep CNNs

With the aim of getting diversity of decisions and errors from individual members, we designed 216 deep CNNs using different input preprocessing methods, random weight initializations, and network architectures. A single deep CNN is denoted as (2) and the detailed explanations for sub-notations are followed.

$$\boldsymbol{PREP}\alpha_1,\alpha_2 - \{\, \boldsymbol{CNN}\beta - \boldsymbol{FC}\gamma \,\}_{\boldsymbol{R}\delta} \qquad (2)$$

$$\text{where}\begin{cases} \boldsymbol{PREP}\alpha_1,\alpha_2\text{: preprocessing type of data,} \\ \quad \alpha_1 = \begin{cases} \text{raw} & \textit{Raw} \\ \text{iNor} & \textit{Illumination Normalization} \\ \text{cEnh} & \textit{Contrast Enhancement} \end{cases} \\ \quad \alpha_2 = \begin{cases} \text{oA} & \textit{Our Aliged Faces} \\ \text{pA} & \textit{Provided Aligned Faces} \end{cases} \\ \boldsymbol{CNN}\beta\text{: size of CNN receptive field,} \\ \quad \beta = \begin{cases} \text{S} & \textit{Small} \\ \text{M} & \textit{Medium} \\ \text{L} & \textit{Large} \end{cases} \\ \boldsymbol{FC}\gamma\text{: number of neurons in a fully-connected hidden layer,} \\ \quad \gamma = \{3072, 2048, 1024, 512\} \\ \boldsymbol{R}\delta\text{: random seed number for weight initialization,} \\ \quad \delta = \{1, 2, 3\} \end{cases}$$

4.1.1 *Preprocessing type of data*

We considered various normalization techniques on differently aligned faces. Each raw image was rescaled from 0 to 1 via a min-max normalization. To reduce illumination variation in images, as used in [28], the isotropic diffusion based normalization [29] from INface toolbox [30] was applied with the default parameter setting. Moreover, to enhance contrast for each image, as used in [14], we applied the histogram equalization implemented in MATLAB. The examples of normalized images are shown in Figure 4(a).

For different input deformations (e.g., translation and rotation), we used the aligned faces provided from EmotiW2015 (pA) as well as our aligned faces (oA), as previously introduced in Section 3.2. Furthermore, some faces erroneously aligned by our method can be compensated by the provided alignments, thus leading to more diverse and complementary information about input data.

4.1.2 *Architectures of deep CNNs*

As the baseline architecture, we referred to Tang's deep CNN [31], the winner model of ICMLW2013's facial expression recognition challenge [32]. It consisted of the 1 input-transform and 3 convolution+pooling stages, followed by fully-connected hidden and output layers. In the input-transform stage for image mirroring and translating, data were augmented by extracting 42x42 patches from the 48x48 faces. The subsequent layers corresponded to a configuration of {***CNN***M - ***FC***3072} in our notation (see Table 3), except for average-pooling in the 2nd and 3rd stages of Tang's model. To get more specific settings, see his implementation at [33].

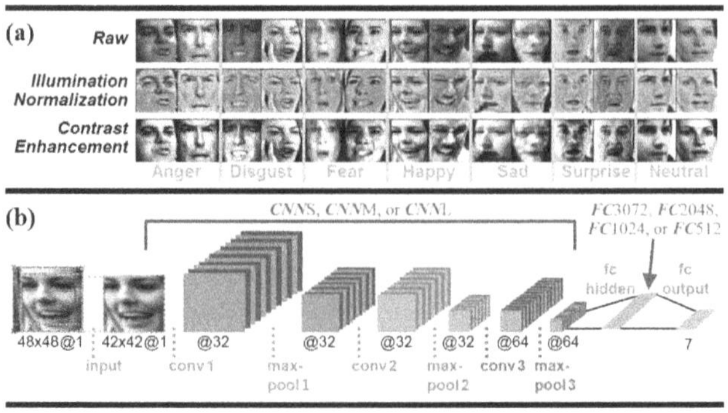

Figure 4. (a) Various normalizations on the aligned validation faces and (b) a deep CNN architecture

Based on Tang's architecture, we designed diverse deep CNNs by changing the sizes of filters for various receptive fields and by changing the number of neurons in a fully-connected hidden layer as denoted in Table 3. The ***CNN***M had a medium-size receptive field (with 5x5, 4x4, and 5x5 filters for each conv layer, respectively), the ***CNN***L had a relatively large receptive field (with 7x7 filters for all conv layers), and the ***CNN***S had a relatively small one (with 3x3 filters for all conv layers). For all ***CNN*** types, the strides and pads were properly set to ensure the same sizes of output maps (5x5 @64) in the max-pool 3 layer. Moreover, for each ***CNN*** type, 4 kinds of fully-connected hidden layer (***FC***) were used. In this ***FC*** layer, the dropout [34] was applied to reduce over-fitting in training deep models. Notice that, from Tang's model, we modified the pooling layers in the 2nd and 3rd stages from average-pooling to max-pooling, since it provided better classification results in our preliminary experiments. For the nonlinearity, Rectified Linear Unit (ReLU) activations were applied for all conv and penultimate layers, and a softmax activation was for the output layer.

Table 3. Configuration of deep CNNs

Layer[a]	***CNN*S**		***CNN*M**		***CNN*L**	
	maps[b]	kernel[c]	maps	kernel	maps	kernel
input	42x42 @1	-	42x42 @1	-	42x42 @1	-
conv 1	42x42 @32	**3x3**, (1,1)	42x42 @32	**5x5**, (1, 2)	42x42 @32	**7x7**, (1, 3)
max -pool 1	21x21 @32	2x2, (2, 0)	21x21 @32	3x3, (2, 1*)	21x21 @32	2x2, (2, 0)
conv 2	19x19 @32	**3x3**, (1, 0)	20x20 @32	**4x4**, (1, 1)	19x19 @32	**7x7**, (1, 2)
max -pool 2	10x10 @32	2x2, (2, 1*)	10x10 @32	3x3, (2, 1*)	10x10 @32	2x2, (2, 1*)
conv 3	10x10 @64	**3x3**, (1, 1)	10x10 @64	**5x5**, (1, 2)	10x10 @64	**7x7**, (1, 3)
max -pool 3	5x5 @64	2x2, (2, 0)	5x5 @64	3x3, (2, 1*)	5x5 @64	2x2, (2, 0)
fc hidden	*FC*3072: 3072 neurons with a dropout probability = 0.8, *FC*2048: 2048 neurons with a dropout probability = 0.5, *FC*1024: 1024 neurons with a dropout probability = 0.5, or *FC*512: 512 neurons with a dropout probability = 0.5					
fc output	7 neurons (one per class)					

[a] conv, max-pool, fc: convolutional, max-pooling, fully-connected.

[b] maps: *the size of output maps @ the number of output maps.*

[c] kernel: *the size of kernels*, (*stride*, *pad*) where '*stride*' refers to spacing size of kernels, '*pad* without an asterisk*' refers to zero-padding to all 4 spatial directions (top, bottom, left and right directions) of input maps, and '*pad* with an asterisk*' refers to zero-padding to the top and left.

4.2 Training Individual Deep CNNs

4.2.1 Usage of external data

The size of SFEW data is quite small to train deep CNNs. Inspired by [28], we also decided to use 2 external databases along with the SFEW data for training models: the Facial Expression Recognition 2013 database (FER-2013 DB) [35] and the Toronto Face Dataset (TFD) [36]. The FER-2013 DB, released for ICMLW2013's sub-challenge [32], was created using the Google image search API. Since realistic facial expressions were collected from the internet, large variations reflecting real-world conditions existed in the FER-2013 DB. From this dataset, 28,698 training faces (after removing 11 non-number-filled images from original training data) and 3,589 private testing faces were used for our experiment. The TFD was constructed by merging together 30 pre-existing face datasets. The faces in TFD were strictly aligned and almost all of them were fully-frontal. From the TFD, 4,178 labelled faces were used. Notice that both datasets contained 48x48 gray-scale faces labelled with the identical 7 expression categories used in the SFEW data.

After determining the external databases to be used, we explored how to use them together with the SFEW data for training models. The following 3 strategies were considered:

i. Random initialization ⇒ In learning, using data as follows:
{FER-2013 DB + TFD} for 'training'
{*SFEW Train* + *SFEW Valid*} for 'validation'

ii. Random initialization ⇒ In learning, using data as follows:
{FER-2013 DB + TFD + *SFEW Train*} for 'training'
{*SFEW Valid*} for 'validation'

iii. Initialization from *a pre-trained model* constructed by using
{FER-2013 DB Train + TFD} for 'training'
{FER-2013 DB Test} for 'validation'
⇒ In learning, using data as follows:
{*SFEW Train*} for 'training'
{*SFEW Valid*} for 'validation'

In [28], the strategies 'i' and 'ii' were discussed to train a deep CNN which yielded per-frame predictions for video-based emotion recognition. In their experiment, the strategy 'i' was finally selected based on a better validation performance. In addition to the 'i' and 'ii', we also investigated one type of *transfer learning* scheme as denoted in the strategy 'iii' [37].

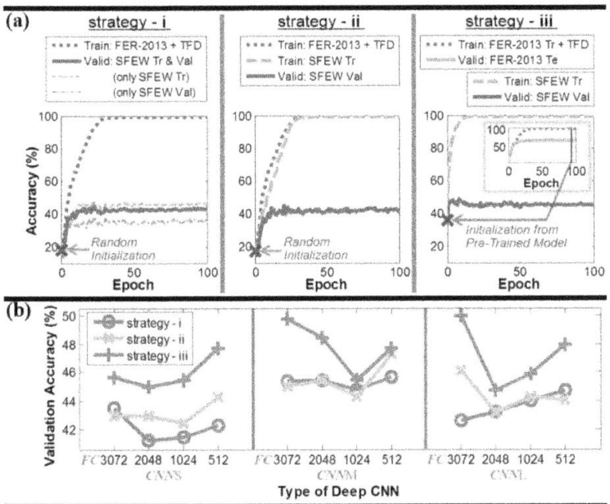

Figure 5. Comparison of 3 strategies for using external data along with SFEW data in training: (a) learning curves from a deep CNN and (b) validation accuracies for 12 deep CNNs

To figure out the most proper usage of external data for this SFEW competition, we evaluated the performances of several models trained differently with the aforementioned 3 strategies. Specifically, the following 12 deep CNNs having various architectures were used:

$$\boldsymbol{PREP}\text{raw,oA} - \{\boldsymbol{CNN}\beta - \boldsymbol{FC}\gamma\}_{\boldsymbol{R}1} \text{ for } \forall\beta, \forall\gamma \tag{3}$$

Figure 5(a) depicts learning curves during training a deep CNN of {*CNN*M - *FC*2048} with 3 strategies. The strategy 'iii' provided superior performances not only at the initial epoch but also at the convergence. Figure 5(b) shows validation accuracies for all examined training strategies and network architectures. Regardless of architectures, the 'iii' outperformed the other two. It indicates that the transfer learning scheme is effective because of representing more similar and suitable feature distributions between training and validation data. Therefore, we eventually decided to use the strategy 'iii'. We first pre-trained 108 deep CNNs using two external data of FER-2013 DB and TFD. Then, 216 models were fine-tuned using the SFEW data: 108 models fine-tuned using oA + 108 using pA. Note that, for the last two submissions, in addition to these 216 models trained with the 'iii', we also incorporated the 24 models with the 'i' and 'ii' to form a committee for a better handling of various facial expressions.

4.2.2 Other training details

We used the MatConvNet toolbox [38] on NVIDIA GeForce GTX 690 GPUs. Each deep CNN was trained using the stochastic gradient descent with a batch size of 200 and momentum of 0.9. Except for the last fully-connected layer with weight decay of 0.002, weight decay of 0.0001 was applied for all other layers. Moreover, the learning rate was equal for all layers, while its value started from 0.004 and became half at every 25 epoch. During total 100 epochs, we selected a model yielding the max validation performance.

To avoid over-fitting, the dropout and data augmentation were applied. A dropout probability of 0.8 was used for deep CNNs with ***FC***3072, while 0.5 was used for ***FC***2048, ***FC***1024, and ***FC***512. The training data were augmented by 10 times, through using 5 crops of size 42x42 (1 from resizing an original 48x48 face and 4 from extracting its 4 corners) and their horizontal flopping. At the test phase, to maintain consistency with the training, 10 patches extracted from each face were fed to the model and the corresponding 10 predictions were averaged to produce a final prediction.

4.3 Classification Performance of Deep CNNs

For 216 deep CNNs trained with the strategy 'iii' (a transfer learning scheme), their classification rates to validation data were reported in Table 4. Our best single model with the highest validation accuracy of 52.5% was ***PREP***iNor,oA – {***CNN***L – ***FC***3072}$_{\boldsymbol{R}1}$. This model became the 1st submission for the SFEW competition, yielding a test accuracy of 57.3%.

We also analyzed general tendencies in performances of deep CNNs. In the aspect of face alignments, the 108 models trained using oA showed a better mean accuracy than those using pA. Furthermore, to examine the trends according to preprocessing types and CNN architectures, we computed the mean accuracy of 36 models for each preprocessing (**per-*PREP* group**) and for each CNN (**per-*CNN* group**). The illumination normalization was superior to other preprocessing types, and the ***CNN***M with the medium size of receptive field performed better than other CNN architectures.

Table 4. Validation accuracy (%) of individual deep CNNs. 108 models (top) trained using our aligned faces and 108 (bottom) using provided alignments from EmotiW2015. The highest accuracy for a given architecture (each column) is written in bold. The asterisk* denotes the single best model.

***Aligned Faces From Our Method* (oA)**		*CNN*S				*CNN*M				*CNN*L				**Mean (Std) of per-*PREP* group**: 36 models / group
		FC 3072	*FC* 2048	*FC* 1024	*FC* 512	*FC* 3072	*FC* 2048	*FC* 1024	*FC* 512	*FC* 3072	*FC* 2048	*FC* 1024	*FC* 512	
PREP raw, oA	***R*1**	45.6	45.0	45.4	47.7	49.8	48.4	45.4	47.7	50.0	44.7	45.9	47.9	*46.9 (1.7)*
	***R*2**	46.3	45.0	46.8	45.0	47.5	48.4	49.1	49.1	47.5	46.1	45.0	46.6	
	***R*3**	45.0	43.6	47.0	45.6	49.1	47.0	47.3	50.0	48.4	45.9	47.3	46.1	
PREP iNor, oA	***R*1**	48.6	**49.5**	**48.6**	49.1	49.1	46.3	**50.9**	50.2	**52.5***	**49.5**	**50.5**	**52.3**	*49.2 (1.6)*
	***R*2**	47.9	46.3	48.4	**50.7**	**52.1**	**49.5**	49.8	50.5	50.2	47.9	48.6	48.2	
	***R*3**	**48.9**	46.3	46.6	49.5	48.6	48.9	47.9	**50.7**	47.5	47.0	**50.5**	50.5	
PREP cEnh, oA	***R*1**	45.9	44.5	45.0	45.9	47.5	45.2	48.2	49.1	42.9	41.3	43.4	43.1	*45.1 (2.4)*
	***R*2**	45.2	44.7	43.8	44.0	49.8	47.5	48.2	49.8	45.2	42.9	39.7	41.3	
	***R*3**	43.4	43.4	46.3	44.7	48.2	44.7	45.9	45.2	45.6	42.2	43.8	45.2	
Mean (Std) of per-*CNN* group: 36 models / group		*46.3 (1.9)*				*48.4 (1.7)*				*46.5 (3.2)*				**Total 108 models** *47.0 (2.5)*

***Aligned Faces Provided From EmotiW2015* (pA)**		*CNN*S				*CNN*M				*CNN*L				**Mean (Std) of per-*PREP* group**: 36 models / group
		FC 3072	*FC* 2048	*FC* 1024	*FC* 512	*FC* 3072	*FC* 2048	*FC* 1024	*FC* 512	*FC* 3072	*FC* 2048	*FC* 1024	*FC* 512	
PREP raw, pA	***R*1**	43.8	43.6	40.8	45.7	48.0	45.2	46.1	45.4	44.5	44.3	45.7	46.8	*44.5 (2.0)*
	***R*2**	43.1	41.9	42.9	40.5	45.9	45.4	46.8	46.4	45.4	43.8	42.9	45.4	
	***R*3**	43.8	39.6	42.9	41.7	47.1	45.7	46.1	44.5	45.0	44.3	45.0	47.3	
PREP iNor, pA	***R*1**	46.4	43.8	**45.4**	42.6	**47.5**	44.7	**48.7**	45.4	46.8	44.0	47.1	45.0	*46.1 (1.9)*
	***R*2**	**47.5**	44.3	43.6	**46.4**	46.8	**46.6**	**48.7**	45.4	47.3	**45.9**	**49.0**	**47.8**	
	***R*3**	46.6	**45.2**	43.6	46.1	46.8	45.7	45.4	**52.2**	**47.8**	45.7	43.3	46.1	
PREP cEnh, pA	***R*1**	44.0	39.1	42.2	41.2	46.4	46.1	46.6	47.8	42.2	42.4	42.2	43.8	*43.5 (2.4)*
	***R*2**	43.8	41.9	44.3	43.6	**47.5**	45.4	44.7	47.8	41.7	42.2	43.6	43.1	
	***R*3**	43.3	40.8	42.4	40.5	46.4	41.0	44.0	46.8	40.3	39.3	41.9	44.3	
Mean (Std) of per-*CNN* group: 36 models / group		*43.3 (2.0)*				*46.3 (1.8)*				*44.5 (2.2)*				**Total 108 models** *44.7 (2.4)*

5. EXPONENTIALLY-WEIGHTED DECISION FUSION

Before moving on examining a hierarchical committee, we demonstrated the superiority of our VA-Expo-WA rule in a conventional single-level committee, by comparing it to the widely-used rules for decision fusion. Here, we formed the 3 committees consisting of 108 models trained using our aligned faces (oA; corresponding to the case of Figure 2), 108 models using provided alignments (pA), and 216 using both alignments of oA and pA. As shown in Table 5, regardless of the committee types, our VA-Expo-WA rule outperformed all other rules. In addition, as we expected, the VA-Simp-WA did not much differ from the simple average rule since individual models produced even and similar validation accuracies as denoted in Table 4.

Table 5. Validation (& testing, if available) accuracy (%) of single-level committees with various decision fusion rules

Decision Fusion Rule	**Single-Level Committee**		
	108 models from oA	**108 models from pA**	**216 models from both**
Majority Voting	51.6	48.2	50.7
Median	50.7	47.3	49.8
Simple Ave. (q=0)	50.2 (58.3)	47.8	49.8
VA-Simp-WA (q=1)	50.7	47.8	49.8
VA-Expo-WA	**54.6 (60.5)**[a]	52.2 (56.7)[b]	**56.4 (60.0)**[c]

[a, b, c] For single-level committees with the VA-Expo-WA rule, the values of exponent q were selected as 43.8, 58.1, and 60.5, respectively.

Meanwhile, it is worth noting that even though the committee of 216 models with the VA-Expo-WA provided the highest classification rate on validation data, its test rate was not the best. The best test accuracy of 60.5% was achieved by the committee of 108 models using oA. It may imply that, at some level yielding a maximum validation performance, adding other models to the committee did not work properly with the VA-Expo-WA. Rather, it seemed to harm the generalization on test data because too many models were participated to improve the final validation accuracy of the committee.

We further investigated the strength of our VA-Expo-WA rule that can reveal the importance or contribution of each individual on a final ensemble. Figure 2(b) shows the decision weights of 108 models using oA, and we computed the threshold above which a certain portion of the total weights was covered. The 6, 18, and 42 models were in charge of about 50%, 75% and 95% of the total, respectively. These information could be used for model selection and pruning.

6. HIERARCHICAL COMMITTEE

To construct hierarchical committees, we organized 216 deep CNNs (obtained with the training strategy 'iii') into 12 sub-groups for the 1st level, having some overlapping members:

G_1: $\boldsymbol{PREP}\text{raw, oA} - \{\, \boldsymbol{CNN}\beta - \boldsymbol{FC}\gamma \,\}_{\boldsymbol{R}\delta}$ for $\forall\beta, \forall\gamma, \forall\delta$
G_2: $\boldsymbol{PREP}\text{iNor, oA} - \{\, \boldsymbol{CNN}\beta - \boldsymbol{FC}\gamma \,\}_{\boldsymbol{R}\delta}$ for $\forall\beta, \forall\gamma, \forall\delta$
G_3: $\boldsymbol{PREP}\text{cEnh, oA} - \{\, \boldsymbol{CNN}\beta - \boldsymbol{FC}\gamma \,\}_{\boldsymbol{R}\delta}$ for $\forall\beta, \forall\gamma, \forall\delta$

G_4: $\boldsymbol{PREP}\text{raw, pA} - \{\, \boldsymbol{CNN}\beta - \boldsymbol{FC}\gamma \,\}_{\boldsymbol{R}\delta}$ for $\forall\beta, \forall\gamma, \forall\delta$
G_5: $\boldsymbol{PREP}\text{iNor, pA} - \{\, \boldsymbol{CNN}\beta - \boldsymbol{FC}\gamma \,\}_{\boldsymbol{R}\delta}$ for $\forall\beta, \forall\gamma, \forall\delta$
G_6: $\boldsymbol{PREP}\text{cEnh, pA} - \{\, \boldsymbol{CNN}\beta - \boldsymbol{FC}\gamma \,\}_{\boldsymbol{R}\delta}$ for $\forall\beta, \forall\gamma, \forall\delta$

G_7: $PREP\alpha_1, \text{oA} - \{\, CNN\text{S} - FC\gamma \,\}_{R\delta}$ for $\forall\alpha_1, \forall\gamma, \forall\delta$
G_8: $PREP\alpha_1, \text{oA} - \{\, CNN\text{M} - FC\gamma \,\}_{R\delta}$ for $\forall\alpha_1, \forall\gamma, \forall\delta$
G_9: $PREP\alpha_1, \text{oA} - \{\, CNN\text{L} - FC\gamma \,\}_{R\delta}$ for $\forall\alpha_1, \forall\gamma, \forall\delta$

G_{10}: $PREP\alpha_1, \text{pA} - \{\, CNN\text{S} - FC\gamma \,\}_{R\delta}$ for $\forall\alpha_1, \forall\gamma, \forall\delta$
G_{11}: $PREP\alpha_1, \text{pA} - \{\, CNN\text{M} - FC\gamma \,\}_{R\delta}$ for $\forall\alpha_1, \forall\gamma, \forall\delta$
G_{12}: $PREP\alpha_1, \text{pA} - \{\, CNN\text{L} - FC\gamma \,\}_{R\delta}$ for $\forall\alpha_1, \forall\gamma, \forall\delta$

Each sub-group consisted of 36 deep CNNs. The 3 **per-*PREP* groups** (***G*₁-*G*₃**) and 3 **per-*CNN* groups** (***G*₇-*G*₉**) were formed from 108 models trained using our aligned faces (oA), and similarly the 3 **per-*PREP*** (***G*₄-*G*₆**) and 3 **per-*CNN*** (***G*₁₀-*G*₁₂**) **groups** were from 108 models using provided alignments (pA).

There were several ways to build the hierarchy in '*structural*' aspects (regarding *the number of hierarchical levels* and *the structure for re-combination of higher-level decisions*) and in '*decisional*' aspects (regarding *the decision fusion rule* for each level). At an earlier phase of experiments, we submitted the predicted test labels obtained from adopting the VA-Expo-WA rule for all structural levels in the hierarchy. From these submissions, we got some unexpected results; validation accuracies were higher than our previous submissions, but testing accuracies dropped. However, we learned an empirical lesson; applying the VA-Expo-WA rule for all levels of a hierarchy may have a negative impact on generalization for test data, since the exponent selection was optimized for the validation performance. Therefore, we decided to use the VA-Expo-WA rule only for the 1st level. For decision fusions in higher levels, the majority voting and simple average rules were used for a better generalization.

We first considered a simple 2-level hierarchical structure as illustrated in Figure 6(a). With a fixed VA-Expo-WA rule of the 1st level, we varied decision fusion rules of the 2nd level as the majority voting or simple average rules. Moreover, as mentioned in Section 4.2.1, for handling more various face expressions and pursuing more diverse errors, we additionally examined 24 models from the training strategies 'i' and 'ii'. These models were also formed into the 1st level groups, having the 12 models each:

g_1: $PREP\text{raw}, \text{oA} - \{\, CNN\beta - FC\gamma \,\}_{R1}$ for $\forall\beta, \forall\gamma$, trained with the ***strategy 'i'***

g_2: $PREP\text{raw}, \text{oA} - \{\, CNN\beta - FC\gamma \,\}_{R1}$ for $\forall\beta, \forall\gamma$, trained with the ***strategy 'ii'***

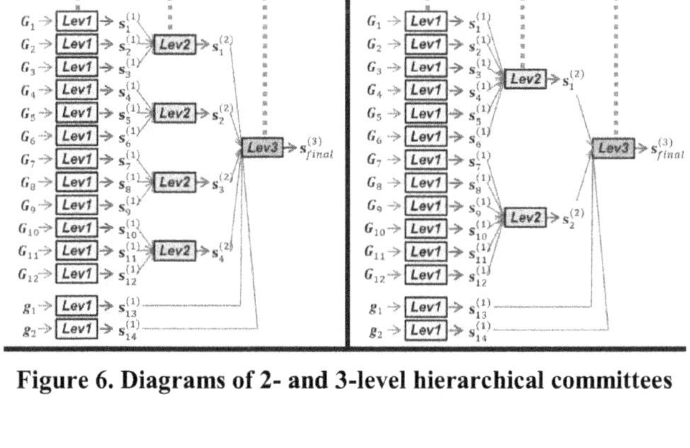

Figure 6. Diagrams of 2- and 3-level hierarchical committees

Table 6. Validation (& testing, if available) accuracy (%) of hierarchical committees with using the VA-Expo-WA rule as the 1st level decision fusion

2-Level Hierarchical Committee	Decision Fusion in the 2nd Level	
	Simple Ave. Rule	Majority Voting
(a)	53.4	56.2
(b)	53.9	56.2 (60.2)
3-Level Hierarchical Committee	**Decision Fusion in the 2nd & 3rd Levels**	
	Simple Ave. Rule & Majority Voting	Majority Voting & Majority Voting
(c)	**53.9 (61.6)**	56.2
(d)	52.5	**52.8 (61.6)**

By adding these 2 groups' decisions to the 1st level, we built another 2-level hierarchy as shown in Figure 6(b). For clarity in the subsequent discussion, we shall to name each hierarchy as each index with a parenthesis in Figure 6. The top part of Table 6 denotes classification performances of the 2-level hierarchies. For both (a) and (b), the majority voting in the 2nd level performed better than the simple average rule. However, the hierarchy (b) with a great validation accuracy of 56.2% did not yield a better test accuracy compared to previous submissions. We suggested the following reason; the added 2 groups, ***g*₁-*g*₂**, to the 1st level were expected to produce more diverse decisions based on different training strategies, but their impacts on the 2nd level were quite small due to competing with 12 decisions from ***G*₁-*G*₁₂**.

Hence, we decided to reduce the influence of decisions from ***G*₁-*G*₁₂** on the final prediction by forming the 3-level hierarchical committee as shown in Figure 6(c) and 6(d). Note that these 3 levels on the side of ***G*₁-*G*₁₂** not only reduced the number of decisions (from 12 in the hierarchy (b) to 4 in the (c) or to 2 in the (d)) but also made compact and reliable decisions passing through multiple levels. Here, 2 types of decision fusions in the 2nd and 3rd levels were considered, as demonstrated in the bottom part of Table 6. Applying majority voting for both 2nd and 3rd levels showed better validation accuracies than using the simple average rule for the 2nd level with the majority voting for the 3rd level. More importantly, in the test performances, these 2 types of 3-level hierarchies did not differ from each other but were superior to the 2-level hierarchies. It indicates that, as forming a hierarchical committee with higher levels, the structural consideration is more important than the decision fusion method to give enough diversity in decisions.

7. CONCLUSION

In this paper, we present a framework based on committee machines of deep CNNs. To generate diverse errors for a better committee, we first constructed multiple deep CNNs as individual committee members. Here, deep models were trained by applying various network architectures, several strategies to use external data, and different input preprocessing and random initialization. With these individuals, we formed hierarchical committees which adopted the valid-accuracy-based exponentially-weighted average. This exponentially-weighted decision fusion was superior to other commonly-used ensemble methods by increasing a generalization capability. Furthermore, the hierarchical structure indeed made more reliable decisions with the consensus of various sub-groups.

Our proposed approach was demonstrated on the SFEW competition data released for the EmotiW 2015 sub-challenge. To sum up our submissions, the test accuracy of the best single deep CNN was 57.3%, while the single-level committees of 108 models trained using our aligned faces yielded 58.3% with the simple average rule and 60.5% with the exponentially-weighted decision fusion. Furthermore, the last two submissions based on 3-level hierarchical committees of total 240 deep CNNs achieved 61.6%, greatly outperforming the SFEW baseline of 39.1%. We believe that the superiority of our committee machines could further be drawn in other pattern recognition problems as well as SFEW.

In our future works, we will design various and good objective functions in training individual deep CNNs in order to get more diverse decisions. Moreover, how to determine the structure of hierarchical committees will be intensively studied in both academic and engineering manners.

8. ACKNOWLEDGMENT

The authors thank Suh-Yeon Dong for her valuable discussions and comments on this work (suhyeon.dong@gmail.com). This work was supported by the Industrial Strategic Technology Development Program (10044009), funded by the Ministry of Knowledge Economy (MKE, Korea).

9. REFERENCES

[1] Kittler, J., *et al.* 1998. On combining classifiers. *IEEE Trans. Pattern Anal. Mach. Intell.*, 20(3), 226-239.

[2] Polikar, R. 2006. Ensemble based systems in decision making. *IEEE Circuits Syst. Mag.*, 6(3), 21-45.

[3] Su, Y., *et al.* 2009. Hierarchical ensemble of global and local classifiers for face recognition. *IEEE Trans. Image Process.*, 18(8), 1885-1896.

[4] Pajares, G., *et al.* 2010. A Hopfield Neural Network for combining classifiers applied to textured images. *Neural Networks,* 23(1), 144-153.

[5] Rodríguez-Liñares, L., *et al.* 2003. On combining classifiers for speaker authentication. *Pattern Recognit.,* 36(2), 347-359.

[6] Wu, C. H., & Liang, W. B. 2011. Emotion recognition of affective speech based on multiple classifiers using acoustic-prosodic information and semantic labels. *IEEE Trans. Affective Comput.,* 2(1), 10-21.

[7] Bell, D., *et al.* 2005, On combining classifier mass functions for text categorization. *IEEE Trans. Knowl. Data Eng.*, 17(10), 1307-1319.

[8] Boulesteix, A. L., *et al.* 2008. Microarray-based classification and clinical predictors: on combined classifiers and additional predictive value. *Bioinformatics*, 24(15), 1698-1706.

[9] Shipp, C. A., & Kuncheva, L. I. 2002. Relationships between combination methods and measures of diversity in combining classifiers. *Inform. Fusion*, 3(2), 135-148.

[10] Aksela, M., & Laaksonen, J. 2006. Using diversity of errors for selecting members of a committee classifier. *Pattern Recognit.*, 39(4), 608-623.

[11] Ciresan, D. C., *et al.* 2010. Deep, big, simple neural nets for handwritten digit recognition. *Neural Comput.*, 22(12), 3207-3220.

[12] Cireşan, D. C., *et al.* 2011. Convolutional neural network committees for handwritten character classification. In *ICDAR 2011*, 1135-1139.

[13] Cireşan, D., *et al.* 2012. Multi-column deep neural network for traffic sign classification. *Neural Networks*, 32, 333-338.

[14] Ciresan, D., *et al.* 2012. Multi-column deep neural networks for image classification. In *CVPR 2012,* 3642-3649.

[15] Krizhevsky, A., *et al.* 2012. Imagenet classification with deep convolutional neural networks. In *NIPS 2012,* 1097-1105.

[16] Agostinelli, F., *et al.* 2013. Adaptive multi-column deep neural networks with application to robust image denoising. In *NIPS 2013,* 1493-1501.

[17] Sun, Y., *et al.* 2014. Deep learning face representation from predicting 10,000 classes. In *CVPR 2014*, 1891-1898.

[18] Wu, D., & Shao, L. 2014. Deep dynamic neural networks for gesture segmentation and recognition. In *ECCV 2014 Workshops*, 552-571.

[19] Dhall, A., *et al.* 2015. Video and Image based Emotion Recognition Challenges in the Wild: EmotiW 2015, In *ICMI 2015*, in press.

[20] LeCun, Y., *et al.* 1998. Gradient-based learning applied to document recognition. *Proceedings of the IEEE*, 86(11), 2278-2324.

[21] Jordan, M. I., & Jacobs, R. A. 1994. Hierarchical mixtures of experts and the EM algorithm. *Neural Comput.*, 6(2), 181-214.

[22] Titsias, M. K., & Likas, A. 2002. Mixture of experts classification using a hierarchical mixture model. *Neural Comput.*, 14(9), 2221-2244.

[23] Liu, M., *et al.* 2012. Hierarchical ensemble of multi-level classifiers for diagnosis of alzheimer's disease. In *MLMI 2012*, LNCS 7588, 27–35.

[24] Dhall, A., *et al.* 2012. Collecting large, richly annotated facial-expression databases from movies. *IEEE Multimedia*, 19(3), 34-41.

[25] Viola, P., & Jones, M. J. 2004. Robust real-time face detection. *Int. J. Comput. Vision*. 57(2), 137-154

[26] Zhu, X., & Ramanan, D. 2012. Face detection, pose estimation, and landmark localization in the wild. In *CVPR 2012*, 2879-2886.

[27] Xiong, X., & De la Torre, F. 2013. Supervised descent method and its applications to face alignment. In *CVPR 2013*, 532-539

[28] Kahou, S. E., *et al.* 2013. Combining modality specific deep neural networks for emotion recognition in video. In *ICMI 2013*, 543-550.

[29] Gross, R., & Brajovic, V. 2003. An image preprocessing algorithm for illumination invariant face recognition. In *AVBPA 2003*, 10-18.

[30] http://luks.fe.uni-lj.si/sl/osebje/vitomir/face_tools/INFace/

[31] Tang, Y. 2013. Deep Learning with Linear Support Vector Machines, In *ICML 2013 Workshop on Representational Learning*, Atlanta, USA.

[32] Goodfellow, I. J., *et al.* 2015. Challenges in representation learning: A report on three machine learning contests, *Neural Networks*, 64, 59-63.

[33] https://code.google.com/p/deep-learning-faces/

[34] Srivastava, N., *et al.* 2014. Dropout: A simple way to prevent neural networks from overfitting. *J. Mach. Learn. Res.*, 15(1), 1929-1958.

[35] http://www.kaggle.com/c/challenges-in-representation-learning-facialexpression-recognition-challenge.

[36] Susskind, J. M., *et al.* 2010. The Toronto face database, *Tech. Rep.*, Department of Computer Science, University of Toronto, Toronto, Canada, TR-2010-001.

[37] Pan, S. J., & Yang, Q. 2010. A survey on transfer learning. *IEEE Trans. Knowl. Data Eng.,* 22(10), 1345-1359.

[38] Vedaldi, A., & Lenc, K. 2014. Matconvnet – convolutional neural networks for matlab. *CoRR.*, abs/1412.4564.

Image based Static Facial Expression Recognition with Multiple Deep Network Learning

Zhiding Yu
Carnegie Mellon University
5000 Forbes Ave
Pittsburgh, PA 15213
yzhiding@andrew.cmu.edu

Cha Zhang
Microsoft Research
One Microsoft Way
Redmond, WA 98052
chazhang@microsoft.com

ABSTRACT

We report our image based static facial expression recognition method for the Emotion Recognition in the Wild Challenge (EmotiW) 2015. We focus on the sub-challenge of the SFEW 2.0 dataset, where one seeks to automatically classify a set of static images into 7 basic emotions. The proposed method contains a face detection module based on the ensemble of three state-of-the-art face detectors, followed by a classification module with the ensemble of multiple deep convolutional neural networks (CNN). Each CNN model is initialized randomly and pre-trained on a larger dataset provided by the Facial Expression Recognition (FER) Challenge 2013. The pre-trained models are then fine-tuned on the training set of SFEW 2.0. To combine multiple CNN models, we present two schemes for learning the ensemble weights of the network responses: by minimizing the log likelihood loss, and by minimizing the hinge loss. Our proposed method generates state-of-the-art result on the FER dataset. It also achieves 55.96% and 61.29% respectively on the validation and test set of SFEW 2.0, surpassing the challenge baseline of 35.96% and 39.13% with significant gains.

Categories and Subject Descriptors

I.5.4 [**Pattern Recognition**]: Applications—*computer vision, signal processing*; I.4.m [**Image Processing and Computer Vision**]: Miscellaneous

Keywords

Facial Expression Recognition; Convolutional Neural Network; Multiple Network Learning; EmotiW 2015 Challenge

1. INTRODUCTION

Automatically perceiving and recognizing human emotions has been one of the key problems in human-computer interaction. Its associated research is inherently a multidisciplinary enterprise involving a wide variety of related fields, including computer vision, speech analysis, linguistics, cognitive psychology, robotics and learning theory, etc [38]. A computer with more powerful emotion recognition intelligence will be able to better understand human and interact more naturally. Many real world applications such as commercial call center and affect-aware game development also benefit from such intelligence.

Possible sources of input for emotion recognition include different types of signals, such as visual signals (image/video), audio, text and bio signals. For vision based emotion recognition, a number of visual cues such as human pose, action and scene context can provide useful information. Nevertheless, facial expression is arguably the most important visual cue for analyzing the underlying human emotions. Despite the continuous research efforts, accurate facial expression recognition under un-controlled environment still remains a significant challenge. Many early facial recognition datasets [23, 36, 3, 14, 27, 4, 24, 35] were collected under "lab-controlled" environments where subjects were asked to artificially generate certain expressions [8]. Such deliberate behavior often results in different visual appearances, audio profiles as well as timing [38], and is therefore by no means a good representation of natural facial expressions [8]. On the other hand, recognizing facial expressions in the wild can be considerably more difficult due to the visually varying and sometimes even ambiguous nature of the problem. Other adverse factors may include poor illumination, low resolution, blur, occlusion, as well as cultural/age differences.

Recent advances in emotion recognition focus on recognizing more spontaneous facial expressions. The Acted Facial Expressions in the Wild (AFEW) dataset [8] and the Static Facial Expressions in the Wild (SFEW) dataset [11] were collected to mimic more spontaneous scenarios and contain 7 basic emotion categories. The video clips of AFEW are extracted from movies, while SFEW is a static subset of AFEW. The idea is that movies, although not truly spontaneous, at least provide facial expressions in a much more natural and versatile way than lab-controlled datasets. This year's Emotion Recognition in the Wild (EmotiW) 2015 Grand Challenge [2] consists two sub-challenges based on AFEW 5.0 and SFEW 2.0 respectively. Both datasets present ever more difficulties than many conventional ones as a result of their more spontaneous characteristics. While a number of hand-crafted features such as Local Binary Patterns on Three Orthogonal Planes (LBP-TOP) [40], Pyramid Histogram of Oriented Gradients (PHOG) [26] and Local Quantized Patterns (LPQ) [5] were proven to work well

ICMI 2015, November 9–13, 2015, Seattle, WA, USA.
 ISBN 978-1-4503-3912-4/15/11 ...$15.00.
DOI: http://dx.doi.org/10.1145/2818346.2830595.

on conventional datasets, they obtain significantly lower performances on these two datasets [8].

Deep convolutional neural network has recently yielded excellent performance in a wide variety of image classification tasks [1, 17, 28, 33, 30]. The careful design of local to global feature learning with convolution, pooling and layered architecture renders very strong visual representation ability, making it a powerful tool for facial expression recognition. In this paper, we focus ourselves on the task of image based static facial expression recognition on SFEW with deep CNNs. Our main contributions can be summarized as follows: 1. We propose a CNN architecture that achieves excellent emotion recognition performance. 2. We propose a data perturbation and voting method that further increases the recognition performance of CNN considerably. 3. We propose two novel constrained optimization frameworks to automatically learn the network ensemble weights by minimizing the loss of ensembled network output responses. Our best submission, achieved with the above methods, reaches 61.29% overall accuracy on the SFEW test set, surpassing the baseline of 39.13% with a significant gain of 21.6%. The proposed framework also achieves the state-of-the-art performance on FER dataset.

2. RELATED WORKS

A number of methods on AFEW were proposed in the past two EmotiW Challenges [10, 9]. Several popular approaches such as multiple kernel learning [29, 7], multiple feature fusion [20] and score-level fusion [32, 21] were reported useful in boosting the recognition performance. Ionescu *et al.* [15] presented a local learning approach to improve bag of words model for image based facial expression recognition. Other works include [19], which proposed a facial expression recognition framework through manifold modeling of videos based on a mid-level representation.

Facial expression and emotion recognition with deep learning methods were reported in [16, 34, 22, 18, 21]. In particular, Tang [34] reported a deep CNN jointly learned with a linear support vector machine (SVM) output. His method achieved the first place on both public (validation) and private data on the FER-2013 Challenge [13]. Liu *et al.* [18] proposed a facial expression recognition framework with 3D-CNN and deformable action parts constraints in order to jointly localizing facial action parts and learning part-based representations for expression recognition. In addition, Liu *et al.* [21] included the pre-trained *Caffe* CNN models to extract image-level features. Finally, the work by Kahou *et al.* [16] is probably the most related to our proposed method. Their method respectively trained a CNN for video and a deep Restricted Boltzmann Machines (RBM) for audio. "Bag of mouth" features are also extracted to further improve the performance. Two large datasets: the Toronto Face Dataset and the Google dataset were combined to train the CNN network. The Google dataset happens to be the very dataset provided to FER-2013 and therefore our method shares part of the training set with [16]. Despite such coincidence, our proposed learning strategy differs from [16] significantly. First, [16] only used the AFEW training data to train the aggregator SVM, while we choose to pre-train our CNN model on external data and fine-tune on the SFEW training data. Fine-tuning proved to be crucial in boosting the classification performance on SFEW, as it increases the accuracy on validation set from 45% to 53%, a significant gain. Second, the ensemble weights of different models in [16] is determined with random search, while our work proposes to automatically learn the ensemble weights through optimizing certain loss functions.

3. FACE DETECTION

The SFEW dataset contains labeled movie frames. While it is possible to directly extract features at frame-level, locating faces benefits the recognition task and the face detector performance is highly correlated with the recognition accuracy. Although the face alignment results provided by EmotiW using Mixtures of Trees (MoT) [11] are accurate under many challenging scenarios, they contain an unignorable amount of missing or false positive faces. Therefore, we ensemble multiple state-of-the-art face detectors to ensure the detection accuracy. Our final face detection module consists of three detectors: the joint cascade detection and alignment (JDA) detector from [6], the Deep-CNN-based (DCNN) detector from [39] and MoT. Before face detection, all input movie frames are resized to 1024×576 pixels in order to restore their original aspect ratio.

JDA is able to return detected faces with very high alignment accuracy and detection precision. As a result we put this detector on the first layer of the detection module. A slight drawback, however, is that JDA's detection recall is unsatisfactory for profile faces. The DCNN-based detector shows excellent detection performance for non-frontal and even profile faces. Under the wild environment of SFEW, it is a very good complement to JDA. For any frame with multiple detections, the largest face is returned. This strategy generally works well except in very occasional cases where the largest face is not intended for emotion recognition. Fig. 1 gives some examples of detection results using both detectors. The first two examples show that JDA gives slightly better localizations than DCNN. The third shows a more difficult case where DCNN complemented JDA. Finally, the last example shows a mistakenly returned face under multiple detections. The left larger face is returned while the right face should be the actual focus.

In rare cases where both JDA and DCNN fail, we include MoT as the last step of the detection hierarchy. An overview diagram of the modules is shown in Fig. 2. Table 1 illustrates the number of correctly detected faces on the SFEW test set using single detectors as well as two cascade combinations. Significantly boosted results are obtained by cascading different detectors. Out of the 372 SFEW test frames, 371 faces are correctly detected by the proposed cascade. Note that "JDA+DCNN" and "JDA+DCNN+MoT" are denoted as "1+2" and "1+2+3" for short.

Table 1: Number of correct detections on SFEW test set using different detectors and cascades.

	JDA	DCNN	MoT	1+2	1+2+3
Det #	333	358	352	363	**371**

4. FACE PREPROCESSING

Face preprocessing proves to be a crucial step for good recognition performance. It helps to remove irrelevant noise and unifies all faces to the same domain. Since we decide to pre-train our deep network model on FER, the detected

Figure 1: Examples of face detections by JDA (red) and DCNN (blue).

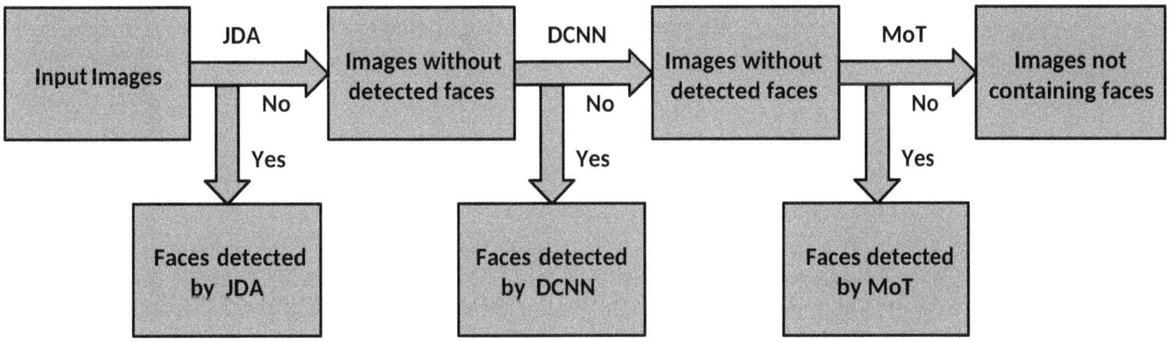

Figure 2: The system diagram of the proposed face detection module on SFEW 2.0.

faces on SFEW are all resized to 48×48 and are transformed to grayscale, which is exactly the same as the FER data.

Both the face images from SFEW and FER datasets are then preprocessed with standard histogram equalization, followed by a linear plane fitting to remove unbalanced illumination. Finally, the image pixel values after plane fitting are normalized to a zero mean and unit variance vector.

5. THE PROPOSED CNN MODEL

We train the deep network models based on our own C++ and Cuda implementation of a 7 hidden layer CNN. The architecture and parameters of our CNN model has been designed to optimize its performance on facial expression recognition tasks. In the rest part of this section we will describe the details of the proposed CNN model.

5.1 The Basic Network Architecture

An overview of the network architecture is shown in Fig. 3. The network contains five convolutional layers, three stochastic pooling layers and three fully connected layers. We adopted stochastic pooling [37] instead of max pooling for its good performance given limited training data. Unlike max pooling which chooses the maximum response, stochastic pooling randomly samples a response based on the probability distribution obtained by normalizing the responses. The fully connected layers contains dropout [31], another mechanism for randomization. These statistical randomness reduces the risk of network overfitting.

The input to the network are the preprocessed 48×48 faces. Both the second and the third stochastic pooling layers include two convolutional layers prior to pooling. The filter step height and width for all convolutional layers are both set to 1. The nonlinear mapping functions for all convolutional layers and fully connected layers are set as rectified linear unit (ReLU) [25]. For stochastic pooling layers, the window sizes are set to 3×3 and the strides are both set to 2. This makes the sizes of response maps reduce to half after each pooling layer.

The last stage of the network includes a softmax layer, followed by a negative log likelihood loss defined as:

$$\mathcal{L} = -\sum_{i=1}^{N} \log P(y_i|\mathbf{x}_i), \tag{1}$$

where N is the total number of training examples. $\mathbf{x}_i$ is the ith training sample, y_i is the label of $\mathbf{x}_i$, and $P(y|\mathbf{x}_i)$ is the network output response on the yth class category given $\mathbf{x}_i$. The network is trained using the adaptive subgradient method [12] with a batch size of 128 examples.

5.2 Generating Randomized Perturbation

While FER contains more than 35000 labeled samples which is considerably larger than SFEW, the classification performance can be further improved if we randomly perturb the input faces with additional transforms. The random perturbation essentially generates additional unseen training samples and therefore makes the network even more robust to deviated and rotated faces.

A similar method is reported in [16] where the authors generate perturbed training data by feeding their network with randomly cropped and flipped 40×40 face images from the original ones. Due to the difficult and wild nature of SFEW, the detected faces may contain a wide variety of different poses, cropped scales and deviations. To cover them as much as possible in training, we consider a much more comprehensive set of perturbations through the following randomized affine image warping:

$$\begin{bmatrix} x' \\ y' \end{bmatrix} = \begin{bmatrix} c & 0 \\ 0 & c \end{bmatrix} \begin{bmatrix} \cos(\theta) & -\sin(\theta) \\ \sin(\theta) & \cos(\theta) \end{bmatrix} \begin{bmatrix} 1 & s_1 \\ s_2 & 1 \end{bmatrix} \begin{bmatrix} x - t_1 \\ y - t_2 \end{bmatrix} \tag{2}$$

where θ is the rotation angle randomly sampled from three different values: $\{-\frac{\pi}{18}, 0, \frac{\pi}{18}\}$. s_1 and s_2 are the skew parameters along x and y directions and are both randomly sampled from $\{-0.1, 0, 0.1\}$. c is a random scale parameter

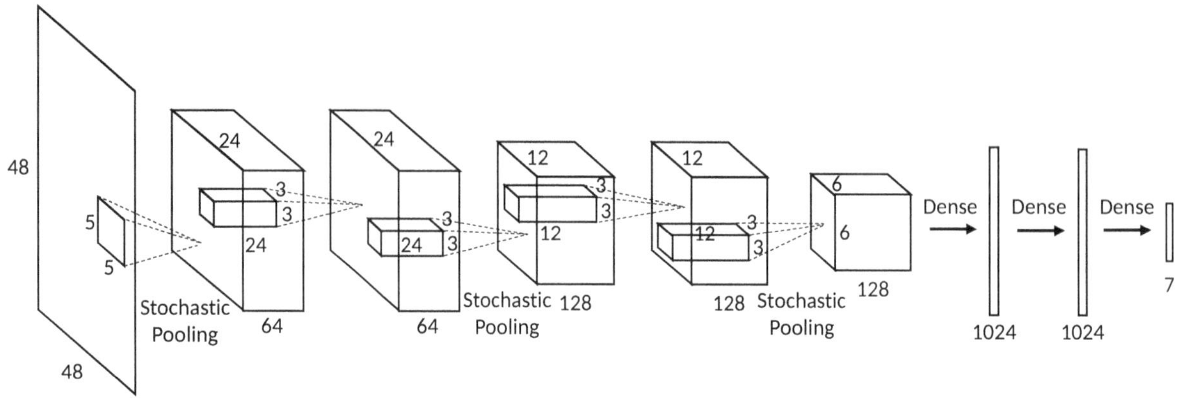

Figure 3: Network architecture of the proposed basic convolutional neural network.

defined as $c = 47/(47 - \delta)$, where δ is a randomly sampled integer on $[0, 4]$. t_1 and t_2 are two translation parameters whose values are sampled from $\{0, \delta\}$ and are coupled with c. In reality one generates the warped image with the following inverse mapping:

$$\begin{bmatrix} x \\ y \end{bmatrix} = \mathbf{A}^{-1} \begin{bmatrix} x' \\ y' \end{bmatrix} + \begin{bmatrix} t_1 \\ t_2 \end{bmatrix}, \tag{3}$$

where $\mathbf{A}$ is the composition of the skew, rotation and scale matrices. The input ($x' \in [0, 47], y' \in [0, 47]$) are the pixel coordinates of the warped image. Eq. (3) simply computes an inverse mapping to find the corresponding (x, y). As the computed mappings mostly contain non-integer coordinates, bilinear interpolation is used to obtain the perturbed image pixel values. For pixels mapped outside the original image, we take pixel value of its mirrored position. Finally, the input training faces are also randomly flipped to further introduce additional robustness. The top row of Fig. 4 gives 6 examples non-perturbed faces while the bottom row shows their corresponding randomly perturbed faces.

Figure 4: Examples of perturbed face with the proposed affine warping strategy.

5.3 Learning and Voting with Perturbation

With the perturbation on training set, the loss function of our network is modified to consider all perturbations:

$$\mathcal{L} = -\sum_{i=1}^{N}\sum_{p=1}^{P} \log P(y_i|\mathbf{x}_i^p), \tag{4}$$

where P is the total number of perturbations. $\mathbf{x}_i^p$ is $\mathbf{x}_i$ with the pth perturbation configuration. In practice, one does not need to truly extend the training set with perturbations. Instead, the 128 samples in each batch are randomly perturbed among the P possible configurations.

An additional crucial improvement in our method is to output the response of each test image as an averaged voting of responses from all the perturbed samples:

$$P(y|\mathbf{X}_i) \triangleq \frac{1}{P}\sum_{p=1}^{P} P(y|\mathbf{x}_i^p), \tag{5}$$

where $\mathbf{X}_i \triangleq \{\mathbf{x}_i^p | p = 1, ..., P\}$. We have considered other voting strategies such as majority voting where the final label prediction is based on counting the predictions of all perturbations. Overall, averaging output response seem to render the best performance. In our experiment, voting often gives a consistent gain of roughly $2 - 3\%$. Conceptually, the test CNN architecture can be illustrated as Fig. 5.

5.4 Network Pre-training on FER

We pre-train our CNN model on the combined FER dataset formed by train, validation and test set. The initial network learning rate is set to 0.005 while the minimum learning rate is set to 0.0001. Each training epoch contains $\lceil N/128 \rceil$ number of mini batches, with the samples randomly selected from the training set and with random perturbation.

The loss and trained network parameters of each epoch are recorded. If there is an increase of training loss with more than 25% or more than 5 consecutive times of loss increase, the learning rate is reduced by half and the previous network with the best loss is reloaded. We found the network hardly overfits due to stochastic pooling and dropout. Thus after all epochs are finished, we select the network from the epoch with the best training accuracy as our final pre-trained model.

5.5 Network Fine-tuning on SFEW

The pre-trained CNN model on FER dataset gives around 45% of accuracy on the SFEW validation set without voting. While both datasets contain the same set of facial expression classes, we noticed that there exist certain level of dataset biases. Domain adaptation, therefore, is necessary for better recognition performance. Our proposed strategy is to fine-tune our network on the SFEW training set.

We adopt the same perturbation and voting strategy, as well as the network learning framework respectively described in Section 5.3 and Section 5.4. To overcome overfitting, we freeze the parameters of all the convolutional layers and only allow the update of parameters at the fully connected layers.

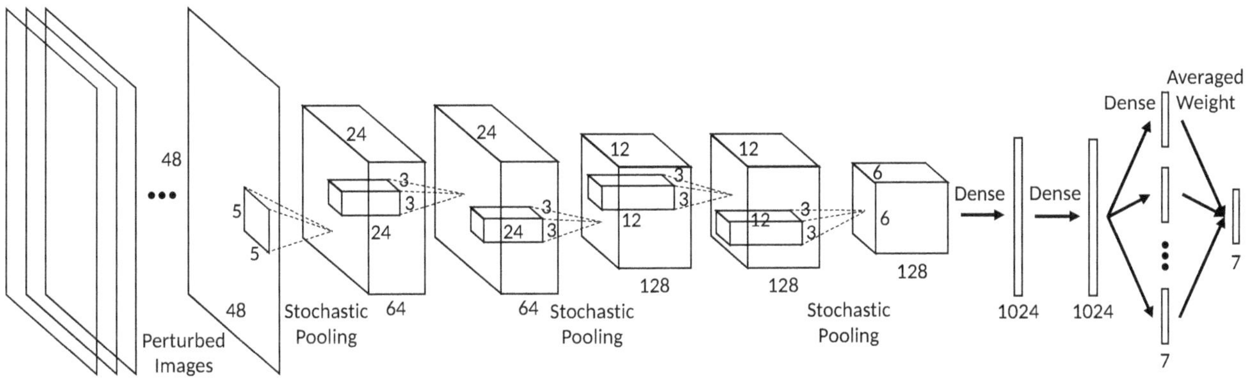

Figure 5: The improved *test* CNN architecture with random perturbations and voting.

We also observe that a slightly larger learning rate helps to reduce the risk of trapping at a local minima and benefits the fine-tuning performance. As a result the initial network learning rate is increased to 0.02.

6. MULTIPLE NETWORK LEARNING

On top of the single CNN model, we present a multiple network learning framework to further enhance the performance. A common way to ensemble multiple networks is to simply average the output responses. We observe that random initialization not only leads to varying network parameters, but also renders diverse network classification abilities for different data. In this case, ensemble with averaged weight is probably sub-optimal as voting is conducted without any discrimination. A better way is to adaptively assign different weights to each network such that the ensembled network responses complement each other.

To learn the ensemble weights $\mathbf{w}$, we independently train multiple differently initialized CNNs and output their training responses. A loss is defined on the weighted ensemble response, with $\mathbf{w}$ optimized to minimize such loss. At testing, the learned $\mathbf{w}$ is also used to compute the ensembled test response. In this paper, we consider the following two optimization frameworks:

6.1 Optimal Ensembled Log Likelihood Loss

The first multiple network learning framework seeks to minimize the following ensembled log likelihood loss:

$$\begin{aligned} \min_{\mathbf{w}} & -\sum_{i=1}^{N} \log \sum_{k=1}^{K} P_k(y_i|\mathbf{X}_i) w_k + \lambda \sum_{k=1}^{K} w_k^2 \\ \text{s.t.} & \sum_{k=1}^{K} w_k = 1 \\ & w_k \geq 0, \forall k \end{aligned} \tag{6}$$

In the objective function, N is the number of training samples, and K is the number of networks. $P_k(y|\mathbf{X}_i)$ is the kth network output response on the yth category given the set of perturbed samples $\mathbf{X}_i$. An l_2 norm regularizer is imposed on the ensemble weights such that the weights are not concentrated on very few networks and the ensemble does not overfit. λ is determined by maximizing the validation accuracy. To maintain a probabilistically meaningful ensembled output response, a convex combination constraint is also imposed on $\mathbf{w}$.

6.2 Optimal Ensembled Hinge Loss

Another considered objective is the following hinge loss:

$$\begin{aligned} \min_{\mathbf{w}} & \sum_{i=1}^{N} \sum_{y \neq y_i} \left[1 - \frac{\sum_{k=1}^{K} (P_k^{i,y_i} - P_k^{i,y}) w_k}{\gamma} \right]_+ + \lambda \sum_{k=1}^{K} w_k^2 \\ \text{s.t.} & \sum_{k=1}^{K} w_k = 1 \\ & w_k \geq 0, \forall k \end{aligned} \tag{7}$$

where $P_k^{i,y} \triangleq P_k(y|\mathbf{X}_i)$. The intuition is that the ensembled output response corresponding to ground truth should be larger than others with a margin γ. With the hinge loss, any case where the response difference is larger than γ will not introduce any penalty. Again, both γ and λ are determined with respect to the accuracy on validation set.

We could have also included the validation loss in our objective to potentially generate better results. However, we decide to strictly adhere to the definition of validation and only use it to determine the fine-tune epoch number.

7. EXPERIMENTAL RESULTS

We conduct a comprehensive set of experiments on both FER and SFEW. The following section reports the performance of our proposed methods on these two datasets.

7.1 Experiment on FER

We first conduct experiment on the FER dataset with single network model. The dataset contains 28709 training images, 3589 validation(public) images and 3589 test(private) images. Fig. 6 shows the training and test accuracies with respect to the number of epochs during training. Note we show the testing accuracy curves of both voting and non-voting (no perturbation at testing) based methods. Clearly, voting with perturbations has a constant gain. The performance of multiple network learning and baselines are shown in Fig. 7, where "Single" refers to the average accuracy of 6 randomly initialized single CNN models (with voting). "Average" refers to averaged ensemble of these networks. The results of FER-2013 Champion are also listed. The proposed multiple network learning is also based on learning with same single CNN models. For the log likelihood loss framework, sub-sampling is conducted 10 times with the sampling rate set to 0.1. λ is set to 280. For the hinge loss framework, γ and λ respectively equals to 0.3 and 7000. The learned network weights are shown in Table 2.

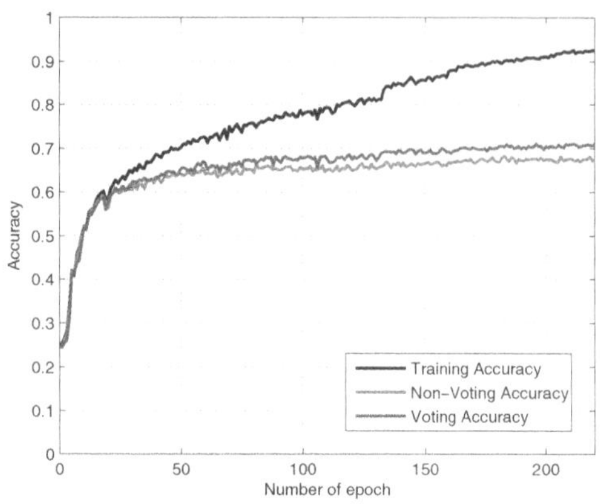

Figure 6: The training and testing accuracy curves on FER dataset.

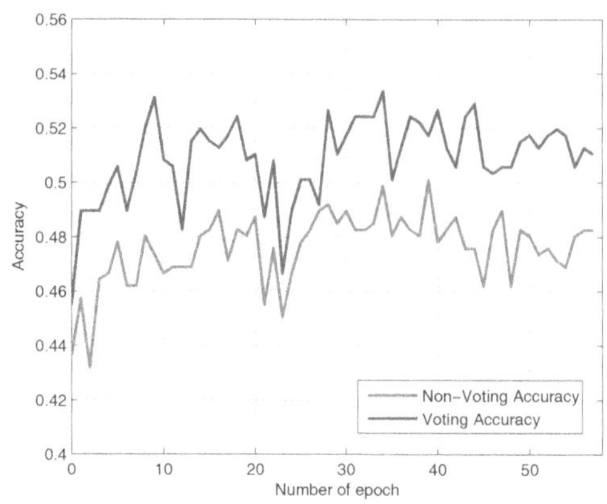

Figure 8: The fine-tuning accuracies of voting and non-voting based methods on SFEW validation set.

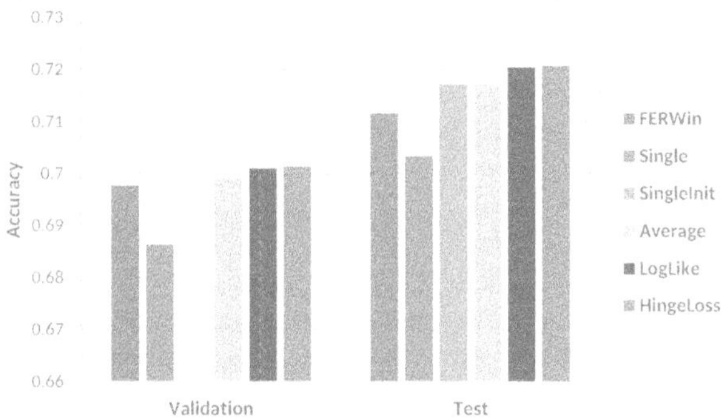

Figure 7: Classification accuracies of different methods on the FER validation and test set.

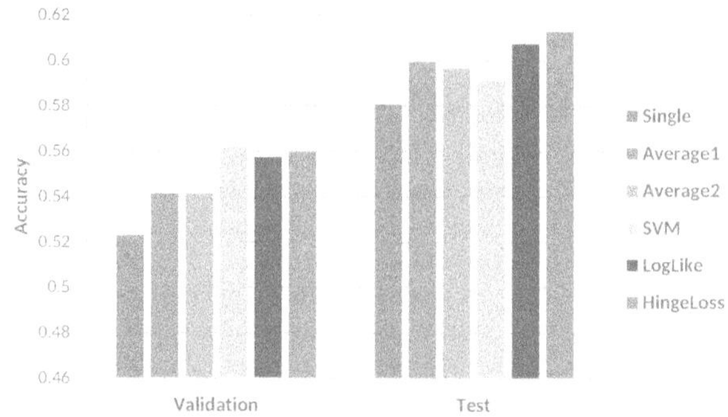

Figure 9: Classification accuracies of different methods on SFEW validation and test set.

Both the proposed ensemble frameworks have surpassed the FER-2013 winner and the average ensemble. Although randomly initialized single model gives slightly worse performance than the champion, we happen to observe that a simple initialization with a previously trained network (without skewing) gives another boost surpassing the champion. Given the observation, we expect that our method can achieve even better results with re-trained networks.

7.2 EmotiW 2015 Results

Fig. 8 shows the fine-tuning accuracy curves of both voting and non-voting based methods on the SFEW validation set. The CNN model is first pre-trained with the combined FER dataset. Again one could see that voting based method constantly outperforms non-voting based method. Finally, We test the proposed multiple network learning on SFEW dataset. Fig. 9 shows both the validation and the test accuracies of our methods and several baselines. In addition, Table 3 shows the corresponding accuracy numbers. In our EmotiW submissions, we mainly experimented with the following baselines: 1. Single CNN model (Single) with random perturbation and voting; 2. Average ensemble with bagging (Average1) where each single CNN model is randomly initialized, pre-trained with randomly sub-sampled FER combined set, and then fine-tuned on SFEW; 3. Average ensemble (Average2) where each single CNN model is trained similar to 2 except without sub-sampling on FER; 4. SVM ensemble (SVM) where each single CNN model is the same as 3 and an SVM is trained and tested on the concatenated network output responses.

Table 2: Learned ensemble weights for each network.

	N#1	N#2	N#3	N#4	N#5	N#6
LL	0.2171	0.2481	0.2943	0	0.1119	0.1286
HL	0.2308	0.2345	0.2805	0	0.1068	0.1473

Table 3: Classification accuracies (%) of different methods on SFEW validation and test set.

Acc	Single	Avg1	Avg2	SVM	LL	HL
Val	52.29	54.13	54.13	**56.19**	55.73	55.96
Test	58.06	59.95	59.67	59.14	60.75	**61.29**

The proposed two ensemble frameworks again achieve the best performance, with respectively 60.75% and 61.29% accuracy on the test set. In the experiment, λ in the log likelihood loss (denoted as "LL") framework is set to 600, while γ and λ in the hinge loss (denoted as "HL") framework are set to 0.1 and 400, all based on validation. Fig. 10 and 11 respectively shows the confusion matrices of both frameworks.

	Angry	Disgust	Fear	Happy	Neutral	Sad	Surprise
Angry	66.24%	1.30%	0.00%	6.49%	9.09%	5.19%	11.69%
Disgust	8.70%	4.35%	4.35%	26.09%	17.39%	8.70%	30.43%
Fear	27.66%	0.00%	4.26%	8.51%	10.64%	21.28%	27.66%
Happy	0.00%	0.00%	0.00%	87.67%	6.85%	1.37%	4.11%
Neutral	5.48%	0.00%	2.74%	2.74%	53.42%	4.11%	31.51%
Sad	22.81%	0.00%	1.75%	7.02%	8.77%	40.35%	19.30%
Surprise	1.16%	0.00%	2.33%	5.81%	17.44%	0.00%	73.26%

(a) Validation set

	Angry	Disgust	Fear	Happy	Neutral	Sad	Surprise
Angry	68.12%	0.00%	1.45%	2.90%	7.25%	5.80%	14.49%
Disgust	5.88%	0.00%	0.00%	23.53%	5.88%	64.71%	0.00%
Fear	21.95%	2.44%	17.07%	2.44%	17.07%	26.83%	12.20%
Happy	2.11%	0.00%	2.11%	83.16%	6.32%	5.26%	1.05%
Neutral	6.90%	0.00%	0.00%	0.00%	72.41%	15.52%	5.17%
Sad	7.27%	1.82%	10.91%	3.64%	18.18%	52.73%	5.45%
Surprise	10.81%	0.00%	18.92%	5.41%	2.70%	2.70%	59.46%

(b) Test set

Figure 10: Confusion matrices of the optimal log likelihood loss ensemble framework on SFEW.

	Angry	Disgust	Fear	Happy	Neutral	Sad	Surprise
Angry	61.04%	0.00%	0.00%	7.79%	10.39%	6.49%	14.29%
Disgust	21.74%	4.35%	4.35%	30.43%	13.04%	4.35%	21.74%
Fear	27.66%	0.00%	6.38%	8.51%	10.64%	19.15%	27.66%
Happy	0.00%	0.00%	0.00%	87.67%	6.85%	1.37%	4.11%
Neutral	5.48%	0.00%	2.74%	1.37%	57.53%	5.48%	27.40%
Sad	21.05%	0.00%	1.75%	7.02%	10.53%	38.60%	21.05%
Surprise	0.00%	0.00%	1.16%	5.81%	17.44%	0.00%	75.59%

(a) Validation set

	Angry	Disgust	Fear	Happy	Neutral	Sad	Surprise
Angry	68.12%	0.00%	1.45%	2.90%	7.25%	7.25%	13.04%
Disgust	5.88%	0.00%	0.00%	23.53%	11.76%	58.82%	0.00%
Fear	21.95%	0.00%	21.95%	2.44%	12.20%	29.27%	12.20%
Happy	2.11%	0.00%	2.11%	83.16%	5.26%	6.32%	1.05%
Neutral	6.90%	0.00%	1.72%	1.72%	68.97%	15.52%	5.17%
Sad	5.45%	1.82%	10.91%	5.45%	16.36%	54.55%	5.45%
Surprise	10.81%	0.00%	13.51%	5.41%	2.70%	5.41%	62.16%

(b) Test set

Figure 11: Confusion matrices of the optimal hinge loss ensemble framework on SFEW.

8. CONCLUSIONS

In this paper, we have proposed a deep convolutional neural network based facial expression recognition method, with multiple improved frameworks to further boost the performance. Our proposed method achieves excellent results on both FER and SFEW dataset, indicating the considerable potential of our facial expression recognition method.

9. REFERENCES

[1] Cuda-convnet Google code home page. https://code.google.com/p/cuda-convnet/.

[2] The Third Emotion Recognition in The Wild (EmotiW) 2015 Grand Challenge. http://cs.anu.edu.au/few/emotiw2015.html.

[3] T. Bänziger and K. R. Scherer. Introducing the geneva multimodal emotion portrayal (gemep) corpus. *Blueprint for affective computing: A sourcebook*, pages 271–294, 2010.

[4] M. S. Bartlett, G. C. Littlewort, M. G. Frank, C. Lainscsek, I. R. Fasel, and J. R. Movellan. Automatic recognition of facial actions in spontaneous expressions. *Journal of multimedia*, 1(6):22–35, 2006.

[5] A. Bosch, A. Zisserman, and X. Munoz. Representing shape with a spatial pyramid kernel. In *Proceedings of the 6th ACM international conference on Image and video retrieval*, pages 401–408. ACM, 2007.

[6] D. Chen, S. Ren, Y. Wei, X. Cao, and J. Sun. Joint cascade face detection and alignment. In *European Conference on Computer Vision (ECCV)*, 2014.

[7] J. Chen, Z. Chen, Z. Chi, and H. Fu. Emotion recognition in the wild with feature fusion and multiple kernel learning. In *Proceedings of the 16th International Conference on Multimodal Interaction*, pages 508–513. ACM, 2014.

[8] A. Dhall et al. Collecting large, richly annotated facial-expression databases from movies. 2012.

[9] A. Dhall, R. Goecke, J. Joshi, K. Sikka, and T. Gedeon. Emotion recognition in the wild challenge 2014: Baseline, data and protocol. In *Proceedings of the 16th International Conference on Multimodal Interaction*, pages 461–466. ACM, 2014.

[10] A. Dhall, R. Goecke, J. Joshi, M. Wagner, and T. Gedeon. Emotion recognition in the wild challenge 2013. In *Proceedings of the 15th ACM on International conference on multimodal interaction*, pages 509–516. ACM, 2013.

[11] A. Dhall, R. Goecke, S. Lucey, and T. Gedeon. Static facial expression analysis in tough conditions: Data, evaluation protocol and benchmark. In *Computer Vision Workshops (ICCV Workshops), 2011 IEEE International Conference on*, pages 2106–2112, 2011.

[12] J. Duchi, E. Hazan, and Y. Singer. Adaptive subgradient methods for online learning and stochastic optimization. *The Journal of Machine Learning Research*, 12:2121–2159, 2011.

[13] I. J. Goodfellow, D. Erhan, P. L. Carrier, A. Courville, M. Mirza, B. Hamner, W. Cukierski, Y. Tang, D. Thaler, D.-H. Lee, et al. Challenges in representation learning: A report on three machine learning contests. In *Neural Information Processing*, pages 117–124. Springer, 2013.

[14] R. Gross, I. Matthews, J. Cohn, T. Kanade, and S. Baker. Multi-pie. *Image and Vision Computing*, 28(5):807–813, 2010.

[15] R. T. Ionescu, M. Popescu, and C. Grozea. Local learning to improve bag of visual words model for facial expression recognition. In *Workshop on Challenges in Representation Learning, ICML*, 2013.

[16] S. E. Kahou, C. Pal, X. Bouthillier, P. Froumenty, Ç. Gülçehre, R. Memisevic, P. Vincent, A. Courville, Y. Bengio, R. C. Ferrari, et al. Combining modality specific deep neural networks for emotion recognition in video. In *Proceedings of the 15th ACM on International conference on multimodal interaction*, pages 543–550. ACM, 2013.

[17] A. Krizhevsky, I. Sutskever, and G. E. Hinton. Imagenet classification with deep convolutional neural networks. In *Advances in neural information processing systems*, pages 1097–1105, 2012.

[18] M. Liu, S. Li, S. Shan, R. Wang, and X. Chen. Deeply learning deformable facial action parts model for dynamic expression analysis. In *Computer Vision–ACCV 2014*, pages 143–157. Springer, 2014.

[19] M. Liu, S. Shan, R. Wang, and X. Chen. Learning expressionlets on spatio-temporal manifold for dynamic facial expression recognition. In *Computer Vision and Pattern Recognition (CVPR), 2014 IEEE Conference on*, pages 1749–1756. IEEE, 2014.

[20] M. Liu, R. Wang, Z. Huang, S. Shan, and X. Chen. Partial least squares regression on grassmannian manifold for emotion recognition. In *Proceedings of the 15th ACM on International conference on multimodal interaction*, pages 525–530. ACM, 2013.

[21] M. Liu, R. Wang, S. Li, S. Shan, Z. Huang, and X. Chen. Combining multiple kernel methods on riemannian manifold for emotion recognition in the wild. In *Proceedings of the 16th International Conference on Multimodal Interaction*, pages 494–501. ACM, 2014.

[22] P. Liu, S. Han, Z. Meng, and Y. Tong. Facial expression recognition via a boosted deep belief network. In *Computer Vision and Pattern Recognition (CVPR), 2014 IEEE Conference on*, pages 1805–1812. IEEE, 2014.

[23] P. Lucey, J. F. Cohn, T. Kanade, J. Saragih, Z. Ambadar, and I. Matthews. The extended cohn-kanade dataset (ck+): A complete dataset for action unit and emotion-specified expression. In *Computer Vision and Pattern Recognition Workshops (CVPRW), 2010 IEEE Computer Society Conference on*, pages 94–101. IEEE, 2010.

[24] G. McKeown, M. F. Valstar, R. Cowie, and M. Pantic. The semaine corpus of emotionally coloured character interactions. In *Multimedia and Expo (ICME), 2010 IEEE International Conference on*, pages 1079–1084. IEEE, 2010.

[25] V. Nair and G. E. Hinton. Rectified linear units improve restricted boltzmann machines. In *Proceedings of the 27th International Conference on Machine Learning (ICML-10)*, pages 807–814, 2010.

[26] V. Ojansivu and J. Heikkilä. Blur insensitive texture classification using local phase quantization. In *Image and signal processing*, pages 236–243. Springer, 2008.

[27] M. Pantic, M. Valstar, R. Rademaker, and L. Maat. Web-based database for facial expression analysis. In *Multimedia and Expo, 2005. ICME 2005. IEEE International Conference on*, pages 5–pp. IEEE, 2005.

[28] O. Russakovsky, J. Deng, H. Su, J. Krause, S. Satheesh, S. Ma, Z. Huang, A. Karpathy, A. Khosla, M. Bernstein, et al. Imagenet large scale visual recognition challenge. *International Journal of Computer Vision*, pages 1–42, 2014.

[29] K. Sikka, K. Dykstra, S. Sathyanarayana, G. Littlewort, and M. Bartlett. Multiple kernel learning for emotion recognition in the wild. In *Proceedings of the 15th ACM on International conference on multimodal interaction*, pages 517–524. ACM, 2013.

[30] K. Simonyan and A. Zisserman. Very deep convolutional networks for large-scale image recognition. *CoRR*, abs/1409.1556, 2014.

[31] N. Srivastava, G. Hinton, A. Krizhevsky, I. Sutskever, and R. Salakhutdinov. Dropout: A simple way to prevent neural networks from overfitting. *The Journal of Machine Learning Research*, 15(1):1929–1958, 2014.

[32] B. Sun, L. Li, T. Zuo, Y. Chen, G. Zhou, and X. Wu. Combining multimodal features with hierarchical classifier fusion for emotion recognition in the wild. In *Proceedings of the 16th International Conference on Multimodal Interaction*, pages 481–486. ACM, 2014.

[33] C. Szegedy, W. Liu, Y. Jia, P. Sermanet, S. Reed, D. Anguelov, D. Erhan, V. Vanhoucke, and A. Rabinovich. Going deeper with convolutions. In *Computer Vision and Pattern Recognition (CVPR), 2015 IEEE Conference on*, 2015.

[34] Y. Tang. Deep learning using linear support vector machines. *arXiv preprint arXiv:1306.0239*, 2013.

[35] A. J. Toole, J. Harms, S. L. Snow, D. R. Hurst, M. R. Pappas, J. H. Ayyad, and H. Abdi. A video database of moving faces and people. *Pattern Analysis and Machine Intelligence, IEEE Transactions on*, 27(5):812–816, 2005.

[36] F. Wallhoff. Facial expressions and emotion database. *Technische Universität München*, 2006.

[37] M. D. Zeiler and R. Fergus. Stochastic pooling for regularization of deep convolutional neural networks. *arXiv preprint arXiv:1301.3557*, 2013.

[38] Z. Zeng, M. Pantic, G. Roisman, T. S. Huang, et al. A survey of affect recognition methods: Audio, visual, and spontaneous expressions. *Pattern Analysis and Machine Intelligence, IEEE Transactions on*, 31(1):39–58, 2009.

[39] C. Zhang and Z. Zhang. Improving multiview face detection with multi-task deep convolutional neural networks. In *Applications of Computer Vision (WACV), 2014 IEEE Winter Conference on*, pages 1036–1041. IEEE, 2014.

[40] G. Zhao and M. Pietikainen. Dynamic texture recognition using local binary patterns with an application to facial expressions. *Pattern Analysis and Machine Intelligence, IEEE Transactions on*, 29(6):915–928, 2007.

[41] X. Zhu and D. Ramanan. Face detection, pose estimation, and landmark localization in the wild. In *Computer Vision and Pattern Recognition (CVPR), 2012 IEEE Conference on*, pages 2879–2886. IEEE, 2012.

Deep Learning for Emotion Recognition on Small Datasets Using Transfer Learning

Hong-Wei Ng, Viet Dung Nguyen, Vassilios Vonikakis, Stefan Winkler
Advanced Digital Sciences Center (ADSC)
University of Illinois at Urbana-Champaign, Singapore
{hongwei.ng, vietdung.n, bbonik, stefan.winkler}@adsc.com.sg

ABSTRACT

This paper presents the techniques employed in our team's submissions to the 2015 Emotion Recognition in the Wild contest, for the sub-challenge of Static Facial Expression Recognition in the Wild. The objective of this sub-challenge is to classify the emotions expressed by the primary human subject in static images extracted from movies. We follow a transfer learning approach for deep Convolutional Neural Network (CNN) architectures. Starting from a network pre-trained on the generic ImageNet dataset, we perform supervised fine-tuning on the network in a two-stage process, first on datasets relevant to facial expressions, followed by the contest's dataset. Experimental results show that this cascading fine-tuning approach achieves better results, compared to a single stage fine-tuning with the combined datasets. Our best submission exhibited an overall accuracy of 48.5% in the validation set and 55.6% in the test set, which compares favorably to the respective 35.96% and 39.13% of the challenge baseline.

Categories and Subject Descriptors

I.5.1 [**Pattern Recognition**]: Models—*Neural nets*

General Terms

Algorithms

Keywords

Emotion Classification, Facial Expression Analysis, Deep Learning Networks

1. INTRODUCTION

Facial expression analysis (also known as emotion estimation, or analysis of facial affect) has attracted significant attention in the computer vision community during the past decade, since it lies in the intersection of many important applications, such as human computer interaction, surveillance, crowd analytics etc.

The majority of existing techniques focus on classifying 7 basic (prototypical) expressions, which have been found to be universal across cultures and subgroups, namely: neutral, happy, surprised, fear, angry, sad, and disgusted [27]. More detailed approaches follow the Facial Action Coding System (FACS), attempting either to classify which Action Units (AU) are activated [24] or to estimate their intensity [18]. Fewer works follow the dimensional approach, according to which facial expressions are treated as regression in the Arousal-Valence space [29]. A very detailed and recent review can be found in [21].

The Emotion Recognition in the Wild (EmotiW) contest, and its Static Facial Expression Recognition in the Wild (SFEW) sub-challenge, follow the categorical approach of the 7 basic expressions. Images are selected from movies, in a semi-automated way, via a system based on subtitles [5, 6]. The challenging characteristics of SFEW are twofold. First, imaging conditions are close to real-life, including low and uneven illumination, low resolution, occlusions, non-frontal head-poses, and motion blur. Second, the size of the dataset is relatively small ($\approx$1K/0.5K/0.3K for training/validation/testing), which makes it difficult to train large-scale models and thus, is prone to overfitting.

In order to overcome these challenges, researchers in the previous EmotiW contests have mainly used *fusion* of multiple features, coupled with different machine learning approaches. In [22], different kernels were learned for LPQ-TOP, audio, gist and SIFT features, and were combined in an SVM classifier. In [14], the optimal fusion of classifiers for HOG, dense SIFT, and deep convolutional features was learned based on a Riemannian manifold. In [23] audio, LPQ-TOP, LBP-TOP, PHOG and SIFT features were used along with a hierarchical classifier fusion method. In [3] HOG-TOP and audio features were fused using multiple kernel learning. In [13] convolutional and audio features were fused using Partial Least Squares and multiple classifiers. Finally, in [11] multiple Deep Convolutional Neural Network (CNN) were introduced for different data modalities (video frames, audio, human actions, mouth analysis), and different combination techniques for these models were explored.

In this paper we follow a *transfer learning* approach for deep CNN architectures, by utilizing a two-stage supervised fine-tuning, in the context of the SFEW sub-challenge. Starting from a generic pre-training of two different deep CNN architectures based on the ImageNet dataset, a first-stage fine-tuning is applied using the FER-2013 facial expression dataset [10], which comprises 28K/32K low resolution images of facial expressions, collected from the Internet using a set of 184 emotion-related keywords. A second-stage fine-tuning then takes place, based only on the *training* part of the EmotiW dataset, adapting the network weights to the characteristics of the SFEW sub-challenge. Both architectures were found to improve their performance through each of the fine-tuning stages,

ICMI'15, November 09-13, 2015, Seattle, WA, USA
© 2015 ACM. ISBN 978-1-4503-3912-4/15/11 ...$15.00.
DOI: http://dx.doi.org/10.1145/2818346.2830593.

while the cascade fine-tuning combination resulted in the submission with the highest performance.

The rest of the paper is organized as follows. Section 2 describes previous works which are related to our study. Section 3 describes in detail the proposed approach. Section 4 discusses the experimental results. Finally, concluding remarks are presented in Section 5.

2. RELATED WORK

Deep Learning-based approaches, particularly those using CNNs, have been very successful at image-related tasks in recent years, due to their ability to extract good representations from data. Judging a person's emotion can sometimes be difficult even for humans, due to subtle differences in expressions between the more nuanced emotions (such as sadness and fear). As a result, efficient features, finely-tuned and optimized for this particular task are of great importance in order for a classifier to make good predictions. It comes as no surprise that CNNs have worked well for emotion classification, as evidenced by their use in a number of state-of-the-art algorithms for this task, as well as winning related competitions [10], particularly previous years' EmotiW challenge [11, 14].

However, due to the small dataset size for the EmotiW 2015 image based static facial expression recognition challenge, it is easy for complex models like CNNs to overfit the data. To work around this problem of training a high-capacity classifier on small datasets, previous works in this area have resorted to using transfer learning across tasks, where the weights of the CNN are initialized with those from a network trained for related tasks before fine-tuning them using the target dataset [8, 9, 17, 26]. This approach has consistently achieved better results, compared to directly training the network on the small dataset, and is the one that we adopt in this paper as well.

3. EXPERIMENTAL SETUP

3.1 Data Preparation

For the EmotiW dataset, all faces were detected with OpenCV's Viola & Jones face detector (frontal and profile) [25]. The Intraface library [4] was used in order to detect 49 facial points. The fit of the alignment model, provided by Intraface, was used to discard false positives faces; any detection with a fit lower than 0.3 was considered a non-face. The average of the 6 points of the eyes (center of the eyes) was used in order to align the image in terms of rotation and scale.

The face bounding box was defined as a ratio of the eye-to-eye distance (e2e): The side boundaries were $0.62 \times$ e2e (counted from the respective eye corner); the upper and lower boundaries were $0.9 \times$ e2e and $1.35 \times$ e2e, respectively. These particular values were selected for three main reasons. First, they result in an approximately square bounding box. This is important, since the DNN training platform requires images to be square. If this condition is not met, images will be stretched, thus affecting their aspect ratio. Second, they ensure that a considerable part of the forehead is included, which exhibits potentially richer visual information for facial expressions, while discarding pixels located below the mouth, with limited visual information. Third, this particular approach resembles the cropping of faces in the FER-2013 dataset, which was used for pre-training, thus increasing the consistency between the two datasets. Finally, all EmotiW images were converted to grayscale, re-sized to 256×256 and normalized using min-max intensity normalization, stretching their intensity values to [0,255]. Fig 1 depicts our cropping method in comparison with the one provided by the organizers.

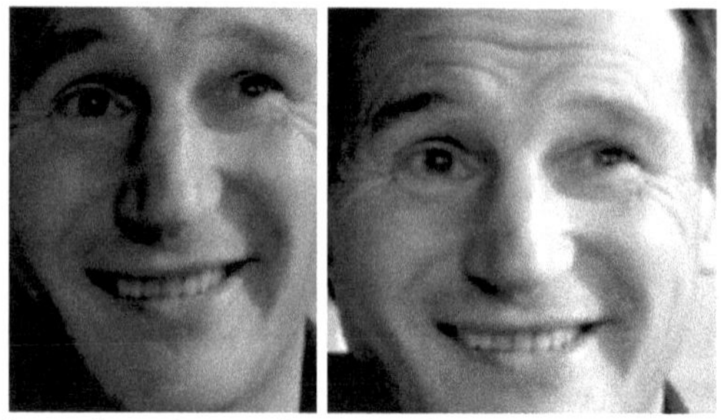

Figure 1: Comparison between our cropping method and the one provided by the organizers.

Regarding the FER-2013 dataset, the small size of its images (48×48 pixels) prevented the reliable detection of facial points. As a result, no alignment was used. Nevertheless, even without aligning these faces, and with their size being much smaller than those in the EmotiW target dataset (48×48 vs. 256×256), we observed a significant performance boost when using them for pre-training (see section 4). Figure 2 depicts a comparison between these two datasets for the 7 classes. Note the similarity in the cropping between the FER-2013 and our EmotiW images.

3.2 Architectures

The success of CNN for face emotion recognition motivated us to base our models on two representative CNN architectures, which we chose because of their nice tradeoffs between speed and accuracy [2]:

1. The ILSVRC-2012 [19] winning entry of [12] (AlexNet).
2. The CNN-M-2048 model from [2] (VGG-CNN-M-2048), which is a variant of the model introduced in [28].

3.3 Dataset and Training

As noted above, it is challenging to train a complex model such as a CNN using only a small amount of training data without overfitting. Our approach to tackling this problem follows recent works [2, 8, 9, 26], which consistently show that supervised fine-tuning with a relatively small dataset on a network pre-trained with a large image dataset of generic objects (e.g., ILSVRC) can lead to significant improvement in performance.

Specifically, we used the the FER-2013 face expression dataset introduced in the ICML 2013 workshop's facial expression recognition challenge [10] as auxiliary data to fine-tune the respective CNNs that were trained using the ILSVRC-2012 data for the architectures mentioned above.

The FER-2013 dataset comprises 3 parts; **a.** The *Original Training Data* (OTD – 28709 images), **b.** the *Public Test Data* (PTD – 3589 images), used when the competition was ongoing to provide feedback on the accuracy of participant's models, and **c.** the *Final Test Data* (FTD – 3589 images), used at the end of the competition to score the final models. We generated 3 variants using these parts of the FER-2013 dataset:

1. **FER28**. This consists of the OTD for training and the PTD for validating our fine-tuned models.
2. **FER32**. This consists of a combination of both the OTD and PTD (28709+3589=32298 total images) for training and the FTD for validating our fine-tuned models.

Figure 2: Comparison between the FER-2013 and EmotiW datasets. Top row: original size of the FER-2013 dataset (48×48 pixels). Middle row: upsampled FER-2013 dataset to 256×256 pixels. Bottom row: EmotiW dataset (256×256 pixels).

3. **FER32 + EmotiW**. This consists of a combination of both the FER32 and the EmotiW training data for training and *only* the EmotiW validation data for validating our fine-tuned models.

We experimented with different schemes for fine-tuning the base pre-trained CNN model using these datasets in combination with the EmotiW training data. These included directly fine-tuning the EmotiW dataset on the CNNs pre-trained on ILSVRC-2012, as well as a "staged" fine-tuning, where we fine-tuned first using data from the FER-2013 dataset before fine-tuning again with the target EmotiW dataset.

The training procedure for our CNNs closely follows that of [12]. They are trained using stochastic gradient descent with hyperparameters (momentum=0.9, weight decay=0.0005, initial learning rate=0.001). Note that since we are fine-tuning CNNs pre-trained on the ILSVRC-2012 dataset [19] using much smaller datasets, we set an initial learning rate of 0.001, which is lower than the typical 0.01 [2, 12], so as not to drastically alter the pre-trained weights. We found that doing so delays the onset of overfitting (as observed from the point where validation loss and training loss start to diverge), allowing the CNN to achieve higher accuracy on the validation data. The learning rate is dropped by a factor of 10 following every 10 epochs of training.

4. RESULTS AND DISCUSSION

The results of our submissions to the EmotiW 2015 SFEW challenge for the validation and test set, as well as some of our experiments that were not submitted, are summarized in Figure 3. The corresponding confusion matrix generated from the predictions of our classifier on the *test* set is shown in Figure 4.

4.1 Effects of Supervised Fine-tuning

Fine-tuning our CNN models using the auxiliary FER-2013 dataset in general led to a 10% increase in accuracy over the baseline method [7] on the test set (the exception being submission 2 with a gain of 7%). A further round of fine-tuning these models using the target EmotiW dataset typically improves the accuracy on the test data by another few percentage points. For our best model (submission 3), this was an overall increase in accuracy of more than 16% over the baseline method (55.6% vs 39.13%) on the test set.

Directly fine-tuning the networks with the EmotiW training data gave an accuracy of 37.8%. While this is slightly worse than that achieved by the baseline method, it is much lower than what we obtained using the auxiliary FER-2013 dataset, which hints at the difficulty of fine-tuning deep neural networks with small datasets, and the importance of using auxiliary data.

However, we note that if we were to train a CNN using data combined from the FER-2013 and EmotiW training set (submission 9), the performance on the test set will only be around 1.5% lower than if we had separated the two datasets and fine-tuned them successively (submission 8). This suggests that the relatively small EmotiW training set (which consists of 921 images) only had a marginal effect in improving performance of a CNN that had already been fine-tuned it on a fairly large dataset such as the FER-2013. We discuss this observation further in the next section.

4.2 Effects of More Labeled Data

Interestingly, even though some of our models were fine-tuned only on the FER-2013, without any data from the target EmotiW dataset, their results on the test set were competitive with those that underwent a second round of fine-tuning on the target dataset. Often the difference in accuracy is within a few percentage points (Figure 3: Submission 1 vs. 3, 6 vs. 8). Furthermore, for our best model that did not use any data from the target EmotiW dataset (Submission 1), its performance on the test set was close to 15% higher than the baseline method. This is surprising because the images in the FER-2013 dataset were thought to be less than ideal as they were not aligned, unlike the target EmotiW dataset, and much smaller in size (48×48 vs 256×256). Yet, models trained using only the FER-2013 dataset were able to give good predictions on the EmotiW dataset. This suggests that the *quantity* rather than quality of the data could be more important for improving the performance of CNN-based face expression classifiers at the early stages of building such classifiers.

The observation that fine-tuning with a low resolution (but larger) dataset has a positive impact on the overall performance is also inline with the latest neuroscientific findings. Mounting evidence suggests that facial expression recognition in humans is *holistic* rather than feature-based, especially in the case of photographs (but not for schematics) [15, 16]. As a result, even people with impaired high frequency vision can distinguish successfully between different expressions, even though they rely only on low frequency visual information [1]. In our case, the lower frequency (but larger) FER-2013 dataset seems to tune the network weights in a way that allows

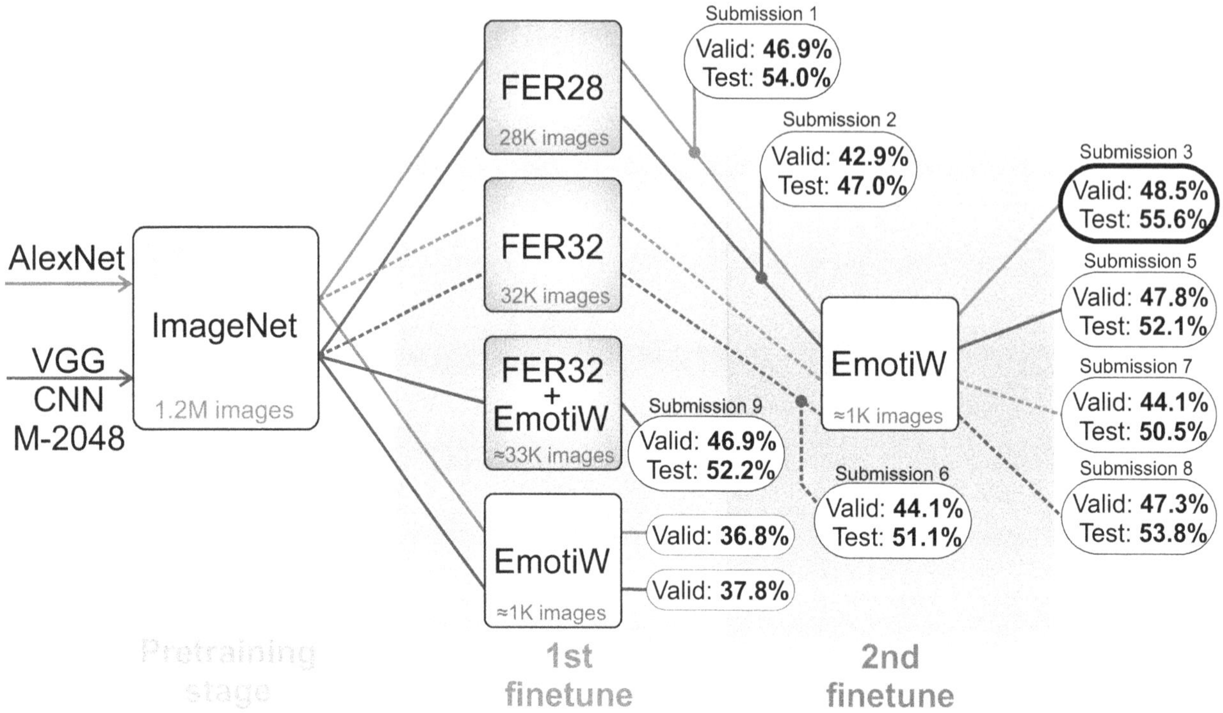

Figure 3: Flowchart of the different fine-tuning combinations used. Our 3rd submission exhibited the best performance.

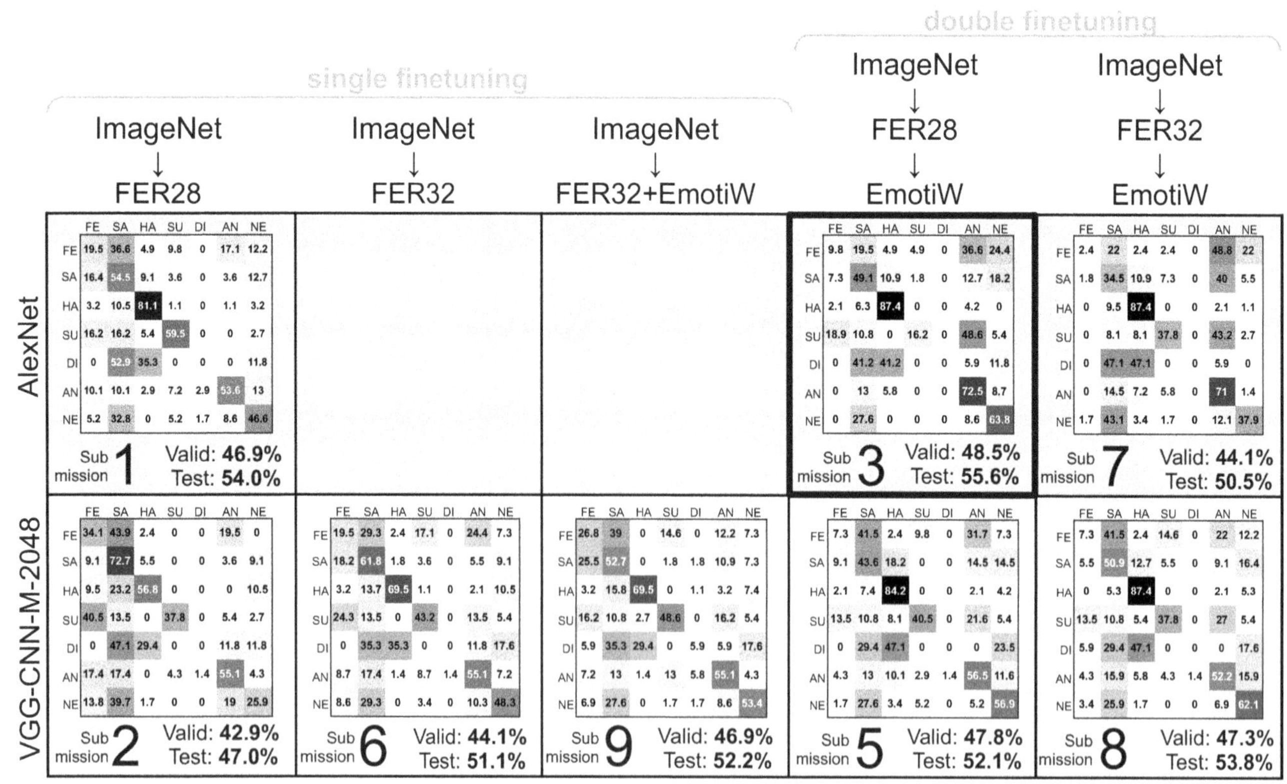

Figure 4: Comparison between the confusion matrices of different models for the EmotiW *test* set. Submission 4 was omitted due to mistakes in training the model. Other omissions were due to lack of time to prepare the models.

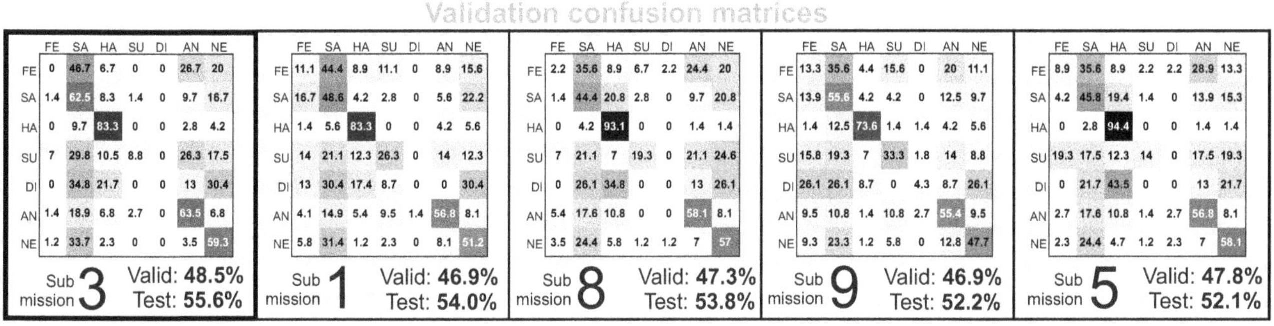

Figure 5: Confusion matrices generated from the EmotiW *validation* set for our 5 best submissions.

a better generalization over data with higher visual frequency, such as the EmotiW dataset.

4.3 Difficulties With Certain Expressions

We observe that some classes appear to be "harder" to train in the sense that, (1) none of our models were able to score highly for them, and (2) our model predictions for those classes tend to fluctuate depending on our training scheme and architecture. This appears to be the case for classes such as "disgust", "fear", "surprise", and "sad". We believe the reasons for this could be twofold. First, these classes tend to have much fewer training samples compared to classes such as "happy", "angry", and "neutral", making it harder to train the CNN to recognize them. Figure 6 depicts the size of the 7 classes on the EmotiW training set, where disgust, fear and surprise are the 3 smallest classes in terms of training samples. Second, these expressions can be very nuanced, making it difficult even for humans to agree on their correct labeling [20].

We suspect that the inherent difficulty in assigning labels to some of the samples may have caused them to be "mislabeled", thereby affecting the models that were trained on them. If this was the case, it would explain why our models (and the organizer's [7]) consistently perform better on the test data than on the validation data. A possible explanation is that samples for the "tricky" cases might (for some reason) be less ambiguous in the test data than they are in the validation data, which would make it less likely that one emotion will be "wrongly" predicted for another, hence causing the accuracy obtained for the test data to be higher than those obtained for the validation data. We arrived at this explanation by comparing the corresponding confusion matrices generated by our top 5 submissions for the EmotiW validation (Figure 5) and test data (Figure 4). Comparing Figures 5 and 4, we observe a general increase in accuracy for the "tricky" classes for all 5 models except that for submission 5, usually at the expense of the "happy" class. Furthermore, we note that "surprise" class, in general, appears to have the largest gain in accuracy (between 7.4% to 33.2% improvement). We also note that this improvement in accuracy from the validation to the test data is also observed in the organizer's baseline paper [7], where their approach improved from an accuracy of 35.96% on the validation data to 39.13% on the test data.

Lastly, we note that all except one of our models were unable to predict a single sample labeled "disgust" correctly. A reason for this could be an imbalance in the training datasets. Indeed, as Figure 6 indicates, "disgust" has the fewest samples in the EmotiW training dataset (comprising 7% of the whole dataset) and in our FER28 and FER32 training datasets (comprising 2% of each of these two datasets). The imbalance in the number of training samples for each class of emotions most likely caused our models to overfit on the emotions with more samples (e.g., "happy") at the expense of this class. Furthermore, the expression of disgust is very subtle, which means that it will be hard for a our CNN models to discover features to robustly distinguish this emotion from other similarly nuanced expressions such as sad, fear and neutral. This can be verified by examining the confusion matrices in Figure 4, which indicates that the "happy" class is often the highest scoring class, and that the classes "disgust", "sad", "fear", "neutral" are often mistaken for each other by our models. The combination of these two factors makes it even harder to train models to predict this emotion accurately. The above observations highlight the difficulty in training CNNs using a small unbalanced dataset with classes that are not visually distinctive.

5. CONCLUSIONS

We have shown that it is possible to obtain a significant improvement in accuracy (up to 16%) over the baseline results for expression classification on the EmotiW dataset using CNNs fine-tuned initially on auxiliary face expression datasets, followed by a final fine-tuning on the target EmotiW dataset. We also showed that, at least for the EmotiW dataset, its small size does not favor it for being used for training CNNs. However, CNNs trained on sufficiently large auxiliary face expression datasets alone can be used to obtain results much better than the baseline, without using any data from the EmotiW dataset. Furthermore, any additional improvement from using the EmotiW dataset, when a sufficiently large face dataset such as FER-2013 is available, whether by adding it to the auxiliary dataset or another round of fine-tuning, is likely to be marginal owing to its small size. This suggests that if we were to exploit deep neural networks such as CNN for face expression recognition to achieve the significant gains seen in other domains, then having bigger datasets is crucial.

Lastly, we also noted the inherent difficulty in assigning correct labels to faces depicting some of the more nuanced emotions, and how that can affect the performance of our models. This suggests that a cost-sensitive performance measure that penalizes a model mistaking samples from one class to another in "similar" classes less harshly might be more appropriate than the binary accuracy measure used for this challenge.

6. ACKNOWLEDGMENTS

This study is supported by the research grant for the Human-Centered Cyber-physical Systems Programme at the Advanced Digital Sciences Center from Singapore's Agency for Science, Technology and Research (A*STAR).

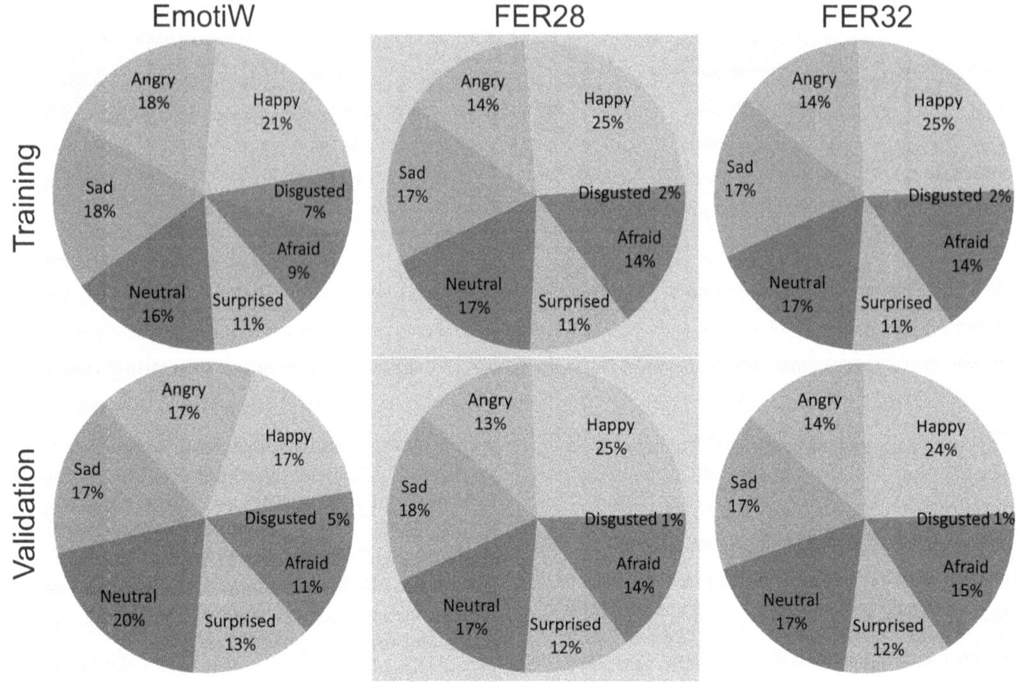

Figure 6: Distributions of the 7 classes on the EmotiW, FER28 and FER32 training and validation sets.

7. REFERENCES

[1] M. Boucart, J.-F. Dinon, P. Despretz, T. Desmettre, K. Hladiuk, and A. Oliva. Recognition of facial emotion in low vision: A flexible usage of facial features. *Visual Neuroscience*, 25(4):603–609, 2008.

[2] K. Chatfield, K. Simonyan, A. Vedaldi, and A. Zisserman. Return of the devil in the details: Delving deep into convolutional nets. In *British Machine Vision Conference*, 2014.

[3] J. Chen, Z. Chen, Z. Chi, and H. Fu. Emotion recognition in the wild with feature fusion and multiple kernel learning. In *Proceedings of the 16th International Conference on Multimodal Interaction*, ICMI '14, pages 508–513, New York, NY, USA, 2014. ACM.

[4] F. De la Torre, W.-S. Chu, X. Xiong, F. Vicente, X. Ding, and J. Cohn. Intraface. In *Automatic Face and Gesture Recognition (FG), 2015 11th IEEE International Conference and Workshops on*, pages 1–8, May 2015.

[5] A. Dhall, R. Goecke, S. Lucey, and T. Gedeon. Static facial expression analysis in tough conditions: Data, evaluation protocol and benchmark. In *Computer Vision Workshops (ICCV Workshops), 2011 IEEE International Conference on*, pages 2106–2112, Nov 2011.

[6] A. Dhall, R. Goecke, S. Lucey, and T. Gedeon. Collecting large, richly annotated facial-expression databases from movies. *MultiMedia, IEEE*, 19(3):34–41, July 2012.

[7] A. Dhall, R. Murthy, R. Goecke, J. Joshi, and T. Gedeon. Video and image based emotion recognition challenges in the wild: Emotiw 2015. In *Proceedings of the 17th International Conference on Multimodal Interaction*, ICMI '15. ACM, 2015.

[8] J. Donahue, Y. Jia, O. Vinyals, J. Hoffman, N. Zhang, E. Tzeng, and T. Darrell. Decaf: A deep convolutional activation feature for generic visual recognition, 2014.

[9] R. Girshick, J. Donahue, T. Darrell, and J. Malik. Rich feature hierarchies for accurate object detection and semantic segmentation. In *Proceedings of the IEEE Conference on Computer Vision and Pattern Recognition (CVPR)*, 2014.

[10] I. J. Goodfellow, D. Erhan, P. L. Carrier, A. Courville, M. Mirza, B. Hamner, W. Cukierski, Y. Tang, D. Thaler, D.-H. Lee, Y. Zhou, C. Ramaiah, F. Feng, R. Li, X. Wang, D. Athanasakis, J. Shawe-Taylor, M. Milakov, J. Park, R. Ionescu, M. Popescu, C. Grozea, J. Bergstra, J. Xie, L. Romaszko, B. Xu, Z. Chuang, and Y. Bengio. Challenges in representation learning: A report on three machine learning contests. *Neural Networks*, 64:59 – 63, 2015. Special Issue on 'Deep Learning of Representations'.

[11] S. E. Kahou, C. Pal, X. Bouthillier, P. Froumenty, c. Gülçehre, R. Memisevic, P. Vincent, A. Courville, Y. Bengio, R. C. Ferrari, M. Mirza, S. Jean, P.-L. Carrier, Y. Dauphin, N. Boulanger-Lewandowski, A. Aggarwal, J. Zumer, P. Lamblin, J.-P. Raymond, G. Desjardins, R. Pascanu, D. Warde-Farley, A. Torabi, A. Sharma, E. Bengio, M. Côté, K. R. Konda, and Z. Wu. Combining modality specific deep neural networks for emotion recognition in video. In *Proceedings of the 15th ACM on International Conference on Multimodal Interaction*, ICMI '13, pages 543–550, New York, NY, USA, 2013. ACM.

[12] A. Krizhevsky, I. Sutskever, and G. E. Hinton. Imagenet classification with deep convolutional neural networks. In F. Pereira, C. Burges, L. Bottou, and K. Weinberger, editors, *Advances in Neural Information Processing Systems 25*, pages 1097–1105. Curran Associates, Inc., 2012.

[13] M. Liu, R. Wang, Z. Huang, S. Shan, and X. Chen. Partial least squares regression on grassmannian manifold for emotion recognition. In *Proceedings of the 15th ACM on International Conference on Multimodal Interaction*, ICMI '13, pages 525–530, New York, NY, USA, 2013. ACM.

[14] M. Liu, R. Wang, S. Li, S. Shan, Z. Huang, and X. Chen. Combining multiple kernel methods on riemannian manifold for emotion recognition in the wild. In *Proceedings of the 16th International Conference on Multimodal Interaction*, ICMI '14, pages 494–501, New York, NY, USA, 2014. ACM.

[15] A. Omigbodun and G. Cottrell. Is facial expression processing holistic? In *Proceedings of the 35th Annual Conference of the Cognitive Science Society*, CogSci 2013. CSS, 2013.

[16] E. R. Prazak and E. D. Burgund. Keeping it real: Recognizing expressions in real compared to schematic faces. *Visual Cognition*, 22(5):737–750, 2014.

[17] R. Raina, A. Battle, H. Lee, B. Packer, and A. Y. Ng. Self-taught learning: Transfer learning from unlabeled data. In *Proceedings of the 24th International Conference on Machine Learning*, ICML '07, pages 759–766, New York, NY, USA, 2007. ACM.

[18] O. Rudovic, V. Pavlovic, and M. Pantic. Context-sensitive dynamic ordinal regression for intensity estimation of facial action units. *Pattern Analysis and Machine Intelligence, IEEE Transactions on*, 37(5):944–958, May 2015.

[19] O. Russakovsky, J. Deng, H. Su, J. Krause, S. Satheesh, S. Ma, Z. Huang, A. Karpathy, A. Khosla, M. Bernstein, A. C. Berg, and L. Fei-Fei. ImageNet large scale visual recognition challenge. *International Journal of Computer Vision (IJCV)*, pages 1–42, April 2015.

[20] J. R. S. Widen and A. Brooks. Anger and disgust: Discrete or overlapping categories? In *Proceedings of the 2004 APS Annual Convention*, 2004.

[21] E. Sariyanidi, H. Gunes, and A. Cavallaro. Automatic analysis of facial affect: A survey of registration, representation, and recognition. *Pattern Analysis and Machine Intelligence, IEEE Transactions on*, 37(6):1113–1133, June 2015.

[22] K. Sikka, K. Dykstra, S. Sathyanarayana, G. Littlewort, and M. Bartlett. Multiple kernel learning for emotion recognition in the wild. In *Proceedings of the 15th ACM on International Conference on Multimodal Interaction*, ICMI '13, pages 517–524, New York, NY, USA, 2013. ACM.

[23] B. Sun, L. Li, T. Zuo, Y. Chen, G. Zhou, and X. Wu. Combining multimodal features with hierarchical classifier fusion for emotion recognition in the wild. In *Proceedings of the 16th International Conference on Multimodal Interaction*, ICMI '14, pages 481–486, New York, NY, USA, 2014. ACM.

[24] Y.-L. Tian, T. Kanade, and J. Cohn. Recognizing action units for facial expression analysis. *Pattern Analysis and Machine Intelligence, IEEE Transactions on*, 23(2):97–115, Feb 2001.

[25] P. A. Viola and M. J. Jones. Robust real-time face detection. *International Journal of Computer Vision*, 57(2):137–154, 2004.

[26] J. Yosinski, J. Clune, Y. Bengio, and H. Lipson. How transferable are features in deep neural networks? In Z. Ghahramani, M. Welling, C. Cortes, N. Lawrence, and K. Weinberger, editors, *Advances in Neural Information Processing Systems 27 (NIPS '14)*, pages 3320–3328. Curran Associates, Inc., 2014.

[27] K. Yu, Z. Wang, L. Zhuo, J. Wang, Z. Chi, and D. Feng. Learning realistic facial expressions from web images. *Pattern Recognition*, 46(8):2144 – 2155, 2013.

[28] M. D. Zeiler and R. Fergus. Visualizing and understanding convolutional networks. *CoRR*, abs/1311.2901, 2013.

[29] L. Zhang, D. Tjondronegoro, and V. Chandran. Representation of facial expression categories in continuous arousal-valence space: Feature and correlation. *Image and Vision Computing*, 32(12):1067 – 1079, 2014.

Capturing AU-Aware Facial Features and Their Latent Relations for Emotion Recognition in the Wild

Anbang Yao
Intel Labs China,
Beijing, 100190, China
anbang.yao@intel.com

Junchao Shao
Intel Labs China,
Beijing, 100190, China
junchao.shao@intel.com

Ningning Ma
Department of Computer Science and Technology, Tsinghua University,
Beijing, 100084, China
mnn15@mails.tsinghua.edu.cn

Yurong Chen
Intel Labs China
Beijing, 100190, China
yurong.chen@intel.com

ABSTRACT

The Emotion Recognition in the Wild (EmotiW) Challenge has been held for three years. Previous winner teams primarily focus on designing specific deep neural networks or fusing diverse hand-crafted and deep convolutional features. They all neglect to explore the significance of the latent relations among changing features resulted from facial muscle motions. In this paper, we study this recognition challenge from the perspective of analyzing the relations among expression-specific facial features in an explicit manner. Our method has three key components. First, we propose a pair-wise learning strategy to automatically seek a set of facial image patches which are important for discriminating two particular emotion categories. We found these learnt local patches are in part consistent with the locations of expression-specific Action Units (AUs), thus the features extracted from such kind of facial patches are named AU-aware facial features. Second, in each pair-wise task, we use an undirected graph structure, which takes learnt facial patches as individual vertices, to encode feature relations between any two learnt facial patches. Finally, a robust emotion representation is constructed by concatenating all task-specific graph-structured facial feature relations sequentially. Extensive experiments on the EmotiW 2015 Challenge testify the efficacy of the proposed approach. Without using additional data, our final submissions achieved competitive results on both sub-challenges including the image based static facial expression recognition (we got 55.38% recognition accuracy outperforming the baseline 39.13% with a margin of 16.25%) and the audio-video based emotion recognition (we got 53.80% recognition accuracy outperforming the baseline 39.33% and the 2014 winner team's final result 50.37% with the margins of 14.47% and 3.43%, respectively).

Categories and Subject Descriptors

I.5.4 [**Pattern Recognition**]: Applications—*computer vision, signal processing*; I.4.m [**Image Processing and Computer Vision**]: Miscellaneous

ICMI '15, November 09-13, 2015, Seattle, WA, USA
© 2015 ACM. ISBN 978-1-4503-3912-4/15/11…$15.00
DOI: http://dx.doi.org/10.1145/2818346.2830585

General Terms

Algorithms, Experimentation

Keywords

Emotion Recognition; Facial Expression Recognition; Action Unit; Facial Feature Relation; EmotiW 2015 Challenge

1. INTRODUCTION

Understanding of human emotions has been of keen interest in the community of psychology, neuroscience, computer vision, pattern recognition, machine learning, and so forth [11]. This is partially due to its significant role in our daily communication, its potential applications as well as its inherent challenges. Having a large volume of well labeled data is the basic prerequisite for advancing the research on automatic emotion recognition. To this end, numerous databases have been collected for comparatively evaluating algorithms [30]. However, most of the widely used databases such as the Cohn-Kanade facial expression database [16, 22], the Man-Machine Interaction facial expression database [23, 25] and the Banse-Scherer vocal affect database [1] are collected in the constrained environments. When collecting such kind of posed data, subjects were asked to perform a series of deliberately expressed emotions in front of the mounted cameras and/or microphones. A main limitation of this state is that the methods having good performance on these posed databases usually fail to generalize well to spontaneously expressed emotions. Starting from 2011, several spontaneous or wild emotion databases [10, 24, 9, 26] have being collected, annotated, and gradually enlarged in size for using in respective competitions held yearly. In this paper, we present our method concerning the submissions for both sub-challenges of the EmotiW 2015 Challenge.[1]

Different from existing dominant databases merely consisting of posed emotion data, all annotated static images and short lived video clips in the EmotiW 2015 Challenge are directly collected from full length movies. A direct consequence is that the data are filled with a wide variety of changes in illumination, subject pose, context scene, subtle affective display and so on, which makes it difficult to achieve high recognition accuracy in both competition tasks. In the previous two years, the winner teams [15, 19] mainly resort to use deep neural networks [17, 13] or design sophisticated

[1] This work was done when Junchao Shao and Ningning Ma were interns at Intel Labs China.

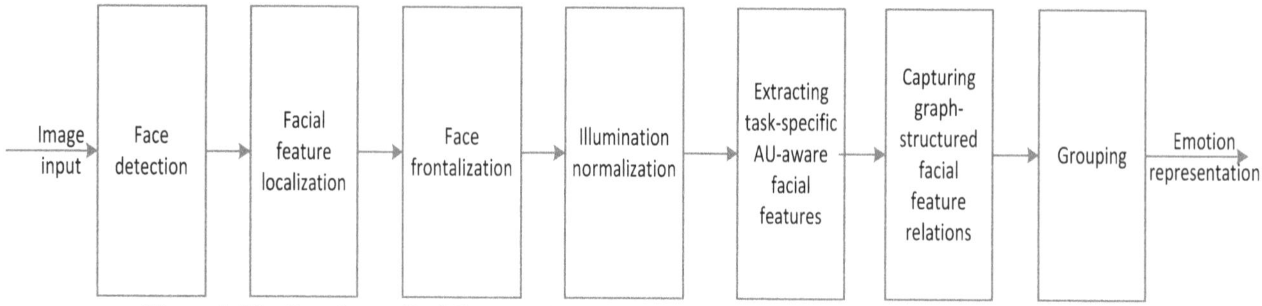

Figure 1. The flowchart of building emotion representation with AU-aware facial feature relations.

method for fusing diverse hand-crafted and deep convolutional features [7, 21, 17]. We also noticed that the accuracy gain from combining audio input into visual input is only ~3% and the performance of audio input alone is relatively poor which implies that visual input plays the key role in the challenge. This motivates us to make a deep study of visual facial expression changes. Existing psychological studies [2, 11] have revealed that facial expressions are the outcomes of human muscle motions, and even a minor change in facial expression is the interaction of the motions of a set of particular muscles. Therefore, we aim to study the problem of classifying emotions spontaneously appeared in the static images and in the dynamic video clips from the perspective of seeking relevant features characterizing expression-specific facial muscle motions and analyzing their latent relations. The contributions of this paper are in four folds:

- A pair-wise learning strategy is introduced to automatically seek a set of discriminative facial patches for classifying two particular emotion categories.
- An undirected graph structure is used to encode inherent task-specific feature relations among learnt facial patches of a respective set.
- A new emotion representation is presented by sequentially concatenating all these task-specific graph-structured facial feature relations.
- Unlike previous teams which usually used outside data to boost the performance of their final models, our models were trained only using given data. Impressively, on both image based static facial expression recognition and audio-video based emotion recognition tasks included in the EmotiW 2015 Challenge, we achieved leading recognition accuracy with large gains compared to the baselines and the 2014 winner team's final result.

We believe that our method provides new insight for handling emotion recognition in the wild. In the following sections, we will describe our detailed method and related experimental results.

2. THE PROPOSED METHOD

Given an image or video frame, Figure 1 shows the flowchart of building respective emotion representation with our proposed AU-aware facial feature relations. Here, we begin with data pre-processing steps (Figure 2 shows illustrative results).

2.1 Data Pre-processing

2.1.1 Face Detection

In our system, face detection is the initial step. We used a self-developed Adaboost based multi-view face detector [27] to locate target faces appeared in the static images or in the first frames of video clips. Although most target faces were successfully detected by our detector, few face instances were missed. For these failed images, we gradually decreased the number of the stages of our face detector until the target faces were finally detected.

2.1.2 Facial Feature Localization

When the faces have been detected and converted to gray-scaled images, the next step is facial feature (i.e., a set of semantic facial landmark points) detection (for static images) or tracking (for video clips). Among many existing methods [6, 3], we used recently proposed Supervised Descent Method (SDM) [29] to detect or track facial features. In tracking scenarios, sometimes it may fail temporally or completely. For temporally failed frames, we directly discarded them. For completely failed video clips, we replaced facial feature tracking by a separate running of face detection and facial feature detection. Based on the detected or tracked facial features, we further cropped out related face regions and rescaled them to a standard size of 156×156 pixels.

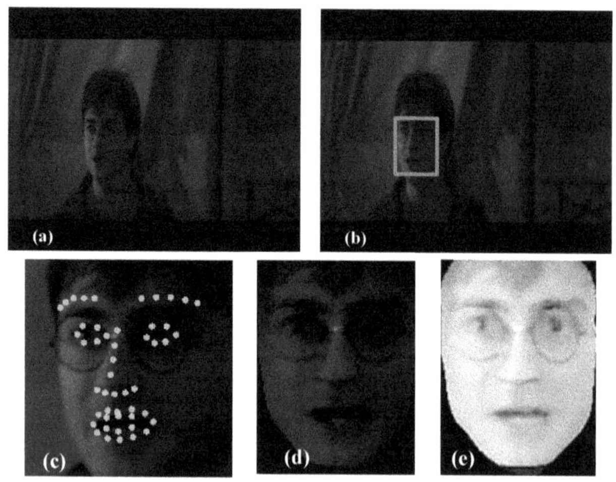

Figure 2. Data pre-processing illustration. (a) Source image; (b) face detection (shown with a red-colored rectangle); (c) facial feature localization (shown with 49 green-colored points) and face cropping; (d) face frontalization; (e) illumination normalization.

2.1.3 Face Frontalization

Once the facial features have been determined, the subsequent step is face registration. Its main goal is to remove the influence of 2D/3D head pose variation, so face images can be geometrically normalized [30]. In our system, we used a straightforward but effective face frontalization method [12] to perform registration. This method first estimates a coarse 3D face surface by directly projecting detected or tracked 2D facial features to a unified 3D facial feature model, and then builds a frontalized face image by back-projecting source image to the reference coordinate system. The frontalized face images were further rescaled into a standard size of 118×156 pixels.

2.1.4 Illumination Normalization

Illumination changes frequently appeared in the EmotiW 2015 datasets. Therefore, the last data pre-processing step in our system is illumination normalization. We implemented a popular Discrete Cosine Transform (DCT) based method [5] to compensate for illumination variations in the logarithm domain. Figure 2 shows typical example results obtained at our pre-processing steps.

2.2 Emotion Representation

Our method is inspired from two factors. First, from previous works [15, 8, 19], we noticed that the performance of the audio modality alone is relatively poor and the gain from combining audio input into visual input is only ~3%. This motivates us to have a deep study of visual facial expression changes. Second, a well-accepted psychological fact is that facial expressions are the outcomes of the motions of different facial muscles. Even a pretty simple facial expression change is observed as a complex blend of the motions of at least several facial muscles. Consequently, we believe that how to effectively detect task-specific active facial features (characterizing facial muscle motions of two particular expression categories) and how to further describe latent relations (interpreting the interactions of facial muscle motions) among active facial features are the most critical two issues for the recognition of spontaneously displayed expressions. In the current research, the detection of Action Units (AUs) [2, 30] is the main stream to describe related facial muscle motions. However, AU detection still remains a very challenging problem. Recently, some efforts have been reported to use AU-aware facial features from multi-task learning [32, 20] and deep Convolutional Neural Networks (CNNs) [18] to address expression recognition task. In [28], the authors used an improved Bayesian Network to model temporal relations among geometric facial features. Our method aims to present a unified framework to jointly learn task-specific AU-aware facial features and encode their latent relations for robust expression recognition.

2.2.1 Learning AU-Aware Facial Patches

Different from [32, 20] in which AU-aware facial features were collectively learnt by multi-task learning, we present a pair-wise learning strategy to discover relevant AU-aware facial features for classifying two particular emotion categories.

Let S be a training dataset consisting of N normalized images (with a size of $w \times h$ pixels) collected from M facial expression categories. Each expression category has n_m training images, and each face image is segmented into $w_p \times h_p$ local patches with an overlapping stride s. We aim to seek an optimal combination of P facial patches for classifying two particular facial expression categories. We call this class-to-class expression classification as pair-wise learning task. With M expression categories, there are totally $M \times (M-1)/2$ above defined tasks. For the task T, let x_k be the feature set to represent the appearances of Q candidate

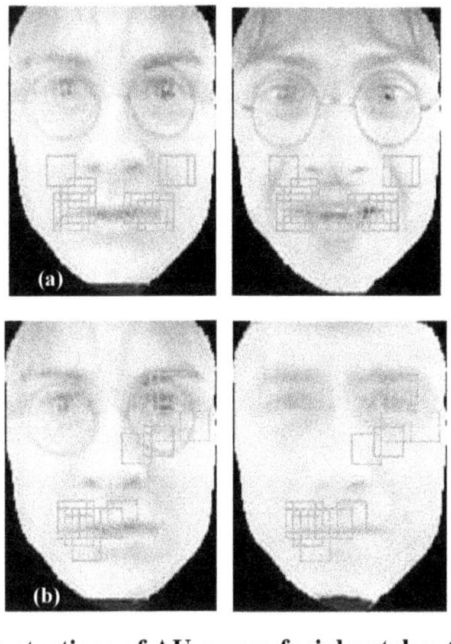

Figure 3. Illustrations of AU-aware facial patches (shown with 16 green-colored rectangles). (a) Samples of Angry-to-Happiness; (b) Samples of Angry-to-Disgust.

local patches of the kth face image from two target expression categories, $y_k \in \{-1,1\}$ be the facial expression label, the objective function in our approach to be minimized can be formulated as

$$\begin{cases} \underset{w,p}{\arg\min} \left(\|w\| + \gamma \sum_{k=1}^{N_T} L\left(w, DoT(p, x_k), y_k\right) \right) \\ Subject\ \ to\ \ \sum_{i=1}^{Q} p_i = P, and\ \ p_i \in \{0,1\} \end{cases}, \qquad (1)$$

where w enforces the weights for feature selection, γ is a positive penalty parameter for regularizing classification error, N_t is the number of the images annotated as two target facial expression categories, and L is defined as a logistic loss function

$$L\left(w, DoT(p, x_k), y_k\right) = \log\left(1 + \exp\left(-y_k w^T DoT(p, x_k)\right)\right), \qquad (2)$$

where operation $DoT(p, x_k)$ indicates P facial patches are finally selected. Note that this optimization problem can be analytically solved by a greedy searching. For simplicity and efficiency, we present a two-stage method to approximate its analytical solution. In each pair-wise learning task, we first compute the recognition rates for all Q individual candidate image patches, and directly choose αP image patches with the highest recognition rates as the refined candidates. Here, $P \le \alpha P << Q$ thus the searching space is largely narrowed down. Then, an alternative solution can be easily obtained by an iterative searching. In the experiments, we found the combination of local image patches obtained from above two-stage method can well approximate real solution in classification accuracy. In this paper, we just used the histograms of basic Local Binary Pattern (LBP) [31] as the testing features to describe the appearance of each facial patch. Figure 3 illustrates discovered AU-aware facial patches regarding two different pair-wise tasks. It can be seen that the local patches discovered by our method are

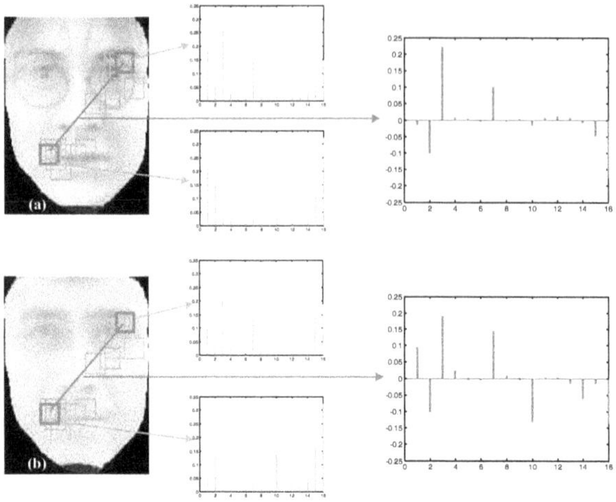

Figure 4. Illustration on computing AU-aware facial feature relations between two local patches determined in Angry-to-Disgust task. In (a) and (b), the left column shows two sample images, the middle column shows LBP histograms extracted from red-colored local patches, and the right column shows respective AU-aware facial feature relations.

mainly located around primary facial components. They are in part consistent with the locations of related expression-specific AUs [2, 30]. Besides, they are visually discriminative.

2.2.2 *Encoding Facial Feature Relations with Graph Structure*

Once respective P facial patches have been discovered for each pair-wise learning task, we then consider the problem of analyzing the latent relations among the features extracted from these facial patches. To this problem, two main issues should be addressed. Regarding each pair-wise task, the first issue is how to measure the feature relation between any two facial patches. Assuming a metric is available, it may be used to estimate the relation between any two facial patches, which may introduces dimensional curse and redundancy. Therefore, the second main issue is how to select and encode feature relations having better discriminations.

Given a face image I, let x_i and x_j be the respective histograms of LBP features extracted from two facial patches determined in the task T, the related feature relation ρ is directly computed as

$$\rho = x_i - x_j . \qquad (3)$$

Here, $x_i, x_j \in \Re^{16}$, and they are the first order statistics of point-wise LBP features. This formed relation metric measures the difference between LBP histograms x_i and x_j. In other words, it is the second order statistics of point-wise LBP features. We found such kind of feature relations is really useful to describe the interactions of facial muscle motions. Figure 4 illustrates the process of computing specific AU-aware facial feature relations.

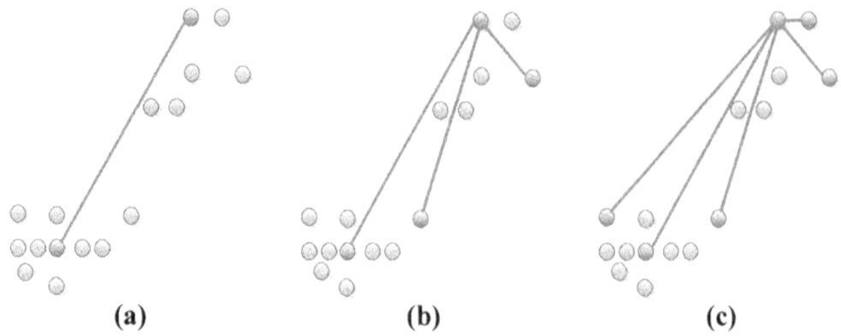

Figure 5. Illustrative graph structures for encoding AU-aware facial feature relations regarding the task of Angry-to-Disgust. A reference vertex (red-colored circle) with (a) one single, (b) three and (c) five connections (red-colored lines). Here, we just draw the connections to one single reference vertex for a better visual effect. The vertices which have connections to the reference vertex are shown as blue-colored circles.

Regarding each pair-wise task, we define an undirected graph structure $G = \{V, E\}$ to encode feature relations among respective facial patches. When constructing a task-specific graph G, the locations of respective P local patches are naturally used as the individual vertices, and the edge connecting any two vertices encodes related feature relation between the respective two local patches of a face image. According to above definition, such kind of task-specific graphs can be either fully connected or highly sparse. Theoretically, there are at most $P-1$ edges to an arbitrary reference vertex. Among $P-1$ candidate edges, $\hat{P}$ edges are finally selected from maximizing mutual information. Figure 5 provides three illustrative examples with $\hat{P} = \{1,3,5\}$.

2.2.3 *Constructing Emotion Representation*

When AU-aware facial patches and a related sparse graph structure are determined in each pair-wise learning task, two novel emotion representations can be built in three-stages. Given a face image, we first extract AU-aware facial features from local patches automatically discovered by each pair-wise learning task. Then we compute related graph-structured facial feature relations regarding each pair-wise learning task. Based on the resulted AU-aware facial features and their relations, two different emotion representations are finally constructed in a similar manner. The more discriminative emotion representation is constructed by concatenating all task-specific graph-structured facial feature relations sequentially, and the other complementary emotion representation is built by directly concatenating all task-specific facial features. Our results on the EmotiW 2015 Challenge fully testify the power of these two emotion representation methods.

3. PERFORMANCE EVALUATION

3.1 The EmotiW 2015 Challenge

The third Emotion Recognition in the Wild Challenge (EmotiW 2015) has two sub-challenges: (1) audio-video based emotion recognition sub-challenge based on the AFEW 5.0 database [10]; (2) image based static facial expression recognition sub-challenge based on the SFEW 2.0 database [10]. The first sub-challenge is a continuation from the challenge of EmotiW 2013&2014 in which the participators are asked to assign one single emotion label from seven possible emotion categories (including Angry, Disgust, Fear, Happiness, Sadness, Surprise and Neutral) to each testing video clip.

Submission No.	Validation (%)	Testing (%)	Method
1	42.43	52.96	Average of 2 linear SVMs trained with AU-aware facial features/relations (face scale: 118×156 pixels)
5	41.97	54.30	Average of 4 linear SVMs trained with AU-aware facial features/relations (two face scales)
6	41.28	53.23	Maximum of 4 linear SVMs trained with AU-aware facial features/relations (two face scales)
9	43.58	**55.38**	Average of 2 SVMs with the RBF kernel trained with AU-aware facial features/relations (face scale: 118×156 pixels)
10	44.04	52.96	Average of 2 linear SVMs & 2 SVMs with the RBF kernel trained with AU-aware facial features/relations (face scale: 118×156 pixels)

Table 1. Our best 5 submissions on the SFEW 2.0 validation and testing sets.

Submission No.	Validation (%)	Testing (%)	Method
1	44.39	44.53	Average of 5 CNN models (two face scales) + 1 Audio model
7	45.39	49.00	Average of 4 linear SVMs trained with AU-aware facial features/relations (two face scales)
8	46.21	51.58	Average of 3 linear SVMs trained with AU-aware facial features/relations (two face scales) + 1 Audio model
9	49.09	53.25	Average of 3 linear SVMs trained with AU-aware facial feature relations (two face scales) + 1 Audio model + 1 CNN model
10	49.09	**53.80**	Average of another 3 linear SVMs trained with AU-aware facial feature relations (two face scales) + 1 Audio model + 1 CNN model

Table 2. Our best 5 submissions on the AFEW 5.0 validation and testing sets.

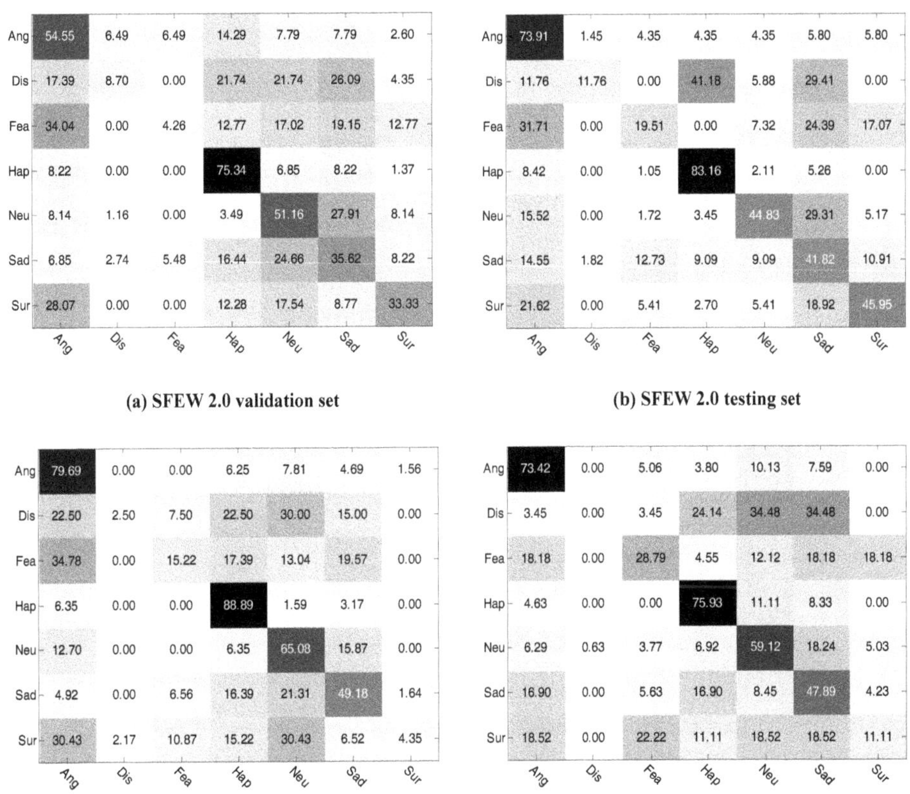

(c) AFEW 5.0 validation set (d) AFEW 5.0 testing set

Figure 6. Confusion matrices of our final submissions. For each validation set, the models were trained with given training data only. For each testing set, the models were trained on the union of given training and validation sets.

In this sub-challenge, there is no constraint on data modality (e.g., video-only, audio-only or audio-video). Compared with the EmotiW 2014 Challenge, the EmotiW 2015 Challenge has more video clips. Specifically, the AFEW 5.0 databased has 1645 video clips which are divided into three parts: 723 for training, 383 for validation and 539 for testing. The second sub-challenge is a new task in which only static images are available and the participators are asked to label each testing image with one single facial expression label from seven possible expression categories (which are same to those in the first sub-challenge). In the SFEW 2.0 database, there are totally 1766 static images which are also divided into three parts: 958 for training, 436 for validation and 372 for testing. Recall that our approach aims to make a deep understanding of visual emotion changes, thus in what follows we begin with our results on the image based static facial expression sub-challenge.

3.2 Facial Expression Recognition on Wild Static Images

3.2.1 Experimental Settings

All face images in the SFEW 2.0 database were normalized into two standard scales: 118×156 pixels and 128×128 pixels. The normalized face images were segmented into $16\times16-pixels$ local patches with an overlapping stride of 8 pixels regardless of their scales. At each face scale, 16 facial patches regarding each related pair-wise learning task were finally determined with our proposed two-stage method. When modeling task-specific graph-structured AU-aware feature relations, the number of the edges connected to each vertex (i.e., facial patch) of a respective graph is 3. For each normalized face image, an AU-aware facial feature relation based representation was computed. To enhance its discrimination, for each face image, we also extracted another representation consisting of sequentially concatenated AU-aware facial features. At the face scale of 118×156 pixels, a linear Support Vector Machine (SVM) and a SVM with Radius Basis Function (RBF) kernel [4] were trained using above two emotion representations independently. At the face scale of 128×128 pixels, 2 linear SVMs were trained. Finally, we trained 6 SVMs using the training set and 6 SVMs using the union of the training and validation sets (with no outside data).

3.2.2 Experimental Results

We take the average or the maximum of the expression scores of any particular combination of trained SVM classifiers to make a final predication on each static face image. Table 1 summarizes the results of our best 5 submissions. It can be seen that a simple combination of our AU-aware facial features and their latent relations demonstrates promising performance on this task, even using linear SVMs as the classifiers. On the validation set, our best recognition accuracy is 44.04% with an improvement of 8.08% compared with the baseline 35.96%. On the testing set, our final recognition accuracy is 55.38% outperforming the baseline 39.13% with a margin of 16.25%. Comparatively, it can be found that a more large accuracy improvement is obtained on the testing set. This is mainly due to the augmentation of the training data by introducing the validation set. Generally, these results fully testify the significance and the effectiveness of our proposed AU-aware facial features and their latent relations. The confusion matrices of our final submissions on the SFEW 2.0 validation and testing sets are shown in Figure 6 (a) and (b), respectively.

3.3 Emotion Recognition on Wild Video Clips

3.3.1 Experimental Settings

On the AFEW 5.0 database, we trained 4 linear SVMs on the training set and 4 linear SVMs using the union of the training and validation sets (with no outside data) under the same parameter settings to those used on the SFEW 2.0 database. To train these SVMs, we only considered the apex frames of the video clips in the training data. Here, we also analyzed the capability of fusing our AU-aware facial features and their latent relations with other popular used features. From the previous works [15, 19], it can be learnt that audio modality can bring ~3% gain in recognition accuracy. So we also trained a SVM with the RBF kernel using audio features extracted with the OpenSmile toolkit. Before extracting audio features, we totally discarded ~20% audio signal at the head and the tail of each clip. On the other side, deep CNNs have been used as the key features in the previous winner teams' solutions [15, 19]. To have a comprehensive comparison, we also trained 5 5-layer CNN models using the Caffe toolkit [14]. These CNN models were trained using the face images with the scale of 118×156 / 128×128 pixels. To these CNN models, the kernels $\{7\times7, 5\times5, 3\times3\}$ used in the 3 convolutional layers are completely same, but the number of output feature channels is $\{\{32,32,32\},\{24,24,24\},\{20,20,20\},\{16,16,16\},\{20,16,16\}\}$. The number of the channels from fully connected layer is 64 or 128. The last layer is a 7-category Softmax classifier. Unlike [15] and [19] in which the authors used outside data to pre-train their CNN models, we just used given data to train our CNN models.

3.3.2 Experimental Results

On the AFEW 5.0 database, we take the average of the emotion scores of any particular combination of trained models to make a final predication on each video clip. On each testing video clip, the emotion scores of a visual feature based model are obtained in two steps. First, it sequentially operates on every frame of each testing video clip. And then the summation of the predicted emotion scores over all frames is used the final emotion scores of this model. The results of our best 5 submissions are summarized in Table 2. Our first six submissions mainly use the combinations of 5 CNN models and one SVM with the RBF kernel trained with audio features. On the validation and the testing sets, the best recognition rates of the CNN dominant combinations are 44.39% and 44.53%, respectively. These results are consistent with those reported in [15] and [19]. Comparatively, a simple combination of our AU-aware facial features and their latent relations shows better performance (45.39% and 49%) just using linear SVMs as the classifiers. By combining them with audio features, we got 51.58% recognition accuracy on the testing set. The performance is further improved by introducing one single CNN model. On the testing set, our final recognition accuracy is 53.8% outperforming the baseline 39.33% and the 2014 winner team's final accuracy 50.37% with the margins of 14.47% and 3.43%, respectively. Comparatively, it can be also noticed that more large accuracy improvements are obtained on the testing set. This is mainly due to the augmentation of the training data by introducing the validation set. The confusion matrices of our final submissions on the AFEW 5.0 validation and testing sets are shown in Figure 6 (c) and (d), respectively.

4. CONCLUSIONS

The EmotiW 2015 Challenge provides a comprehensive dataset collected from full length movies for comparatively evaluating algorithms of recognizing emotions in the wild. In this paper, a new method is proposed to address both tasks included in this challenge. Different from previous works, we aim to analyze spontaneously expressed emotions from the perspective of making a deep exploration of expression-specific AU-aware facial features and their latent relations. In our approach, the AU-aware features characterizing contrasting facial muscle motions regarding two particular emotion categories are first extracted from a set of automatically discovered image patches through a pair-wise learning strategy. To each pair-wise task, we further present an undirected graph structure to capture latent facial feature relations of any pair of image patches. The effectiveness of our emotion representations building from sequentially concatenating all task-specific graph-structured facial features or their latent relations are fully tested in the experiments. We achieved impressively good recognition accuracy in both tasks of the EmotiW 2015 Challenge. The experiments also verify the significance of AU-aware facial features and their latent relations.

5. REFERENCES

[1] R. Banse and K.R. Scherer. Acoustic profiles in vocal emotion expression. *Journal of personality and social psychology*, 70(3):614-636, 1996.

[2] M.S. Bartlett, G. Littlewort, M. Frank, C. Lainscsek, I. Fasel, and J. Movellan. Recognizing facial expression: machine learning and application to spontaneous behavior. In *CVPR*. IEEE, 2005.

[3] X. Cao, Y. Wei, F. Wen, and J. Sun. Face alignment by explicit shape regression. In *CVPR*. IEEE, 2012.

[4] C.C. Chang and C.J. Lin. Libsvm: a library for support vector machines. *ACM Transactions on Intelligent Systems and Technology (TIST)*, 2(3):27, 2011.

[5] W. Chen, M.J. Er, and S. Wu. Illumination compensation and normalization for robust face recognition using discrete cosine transform in logarithm domain. *Systems, Man, and Cybernetics, Part B: Cybernetics, IEEE Transactions on*, 36(2):458-466, 2006.

[6] T.F. Cootes, G.J. Edwards, and C.J. Taylor. Active appearance models. *Pattern Analysis and Machine Intelligence, IEEE Transactions on*, 23(6):681-685, 2001.

[7] N. Dalal and B. Triggs. Histograms of oriented gradients for human detection. In *CVPR*. IEEE, 2005.

[8] A. Dhall, R. Goecke, J. Joshi, K. Sikka, and T. Gedeon. Emotion recognition in the wild challenge 2014: baseline, data and protocol. In *ACM ICMI*. ACM, 2014.

[9] A. Dhall, R. Goecke, S. Lucey, and T. Gedeon. Collecting large, richly annotated facial-expression databases from movies. *IEEE Multimedia*, 2012.

[10] A. Dhall, O.V.R. Murthy, R. Goecke, J. Joshi, and T. Gedeon. Video and image based emotion recognition challenges in the wild: EmotiW 2015. In *ACM ICMI*. ACM, 2015.

[11] P. Ekman and W. Friesen. Facial action coding system: a technique for the measurement of facial movement. *Consulting Psychologists Press Inc.*, San Francisco, CA, 1978.

[12] T. Hassner, S. Harel, E. Paz, and R. Enbar. Effective face frontalization in unconstrained images. In *CVPR*. IEEE, 2015.

[13] G. Hinton, L. Deng, et al. Deep neural networks for acoustic modeling in speech recognition: the shared views of four research groups. *Signal Processing Magazine*, IEEE, 29(6):82-97, 2012.

[14] Y. Jia, E. Shelhamer, et al. Caffe: convolutional architecture for fast feature embedding. In *ACM MM*. ACM, 2014.

[15] S.E. Kahou, C. Pal, et al. Combining modality specific deep neural network models for emotion recognition in video. In *ACM ICMI*. ACM, 2013.

[16] T. Kanade, J. Cohn, and Y. Tian. Comprehensive database for facial expression analysis. In *FG*. IEEE, 2000.

[17] A. Krizhevsky, I. Sutskever, and G. Hinton. Imagenet classification with deep convolutional neural networks. In *NIPS*, 2012.

[18] M. Liu, S. Li, S. Shan, and X. Chen. Au-aware deep networks for facial expression recognition. In *FG*. IEEE, 2013.

[19] M. Liu, R. Wang, S. Li, S. Shan, Z. Huang and X. Chen, Combining multiple kernel methods on Riemannian manifold for emotion recognition in the wild. In *ACM ICMI*. ACM, 2014.

[20] P. Liu, J.T. Zhou, I.W.H. Tsang, Z. Meng, S. Han, and Y. Tong. Feature disentangling machine—a novel approach of feature selection and disentangling in facial expression analysis. In *ECCV*. Springer, 2014.

[21] D. G. Lowe. Distinctive image features from scale-invariant keypoints. *International journal of computer vision*, 60(2):91 -110, 2004.

[22] P. Lucey, J.F. Cohn, T. Kanade, J. Saragih, Z. Ambadar, and I. Matthews. The Extended Cohn-Kanade Dataset (CK+): a complete dataset for action unit and emotion-specified expression. In *CVPR Workshops*. IEEE, 2010.

[23] M. Pantic, M.F. Valstar, R. Rademaker, and L. Maat. Web-based database for facial expression analysis. In *ACM MM*. ACM, 2005.

[24] M. Valstar, B. Jiang, M. Mehu, M. Pantic, and K. Scherer. The first facial expression recognition and analysis challenge. In *FG*. IEEE, 2011.

[25] M. Valstar and M. Pantic. Induced disgust, happiness and surprise: an addition to the MMI facial expression database. In *LREC Workshops*, 2010.

[26] M. Valstar, B. Schuller, K. Smith, F. Eyben, B. Jiang, S. Bilakhia, S. Schnieder, R. Cowie, and M. Pantic. Avec 2013: the continuous audio/visual emotion and depression recognition challenge. In *ACM Workshop on AVEC*. ACM, 2013.

[27] P. Viola and M. Jones. Rapid object detection using a boosted cascade of simple features. In *CVPR*. IEEE, 2001.

[28] Z. Wang, S. Wang, and Q. Ji. Capturing complex spatio-temporal relations among facial muscles for facial expression recognition. In *CVPR*. IEEE, 2013.

[29] X. Xiong and F. de la Torre. Supervised descent method and its applications to face alignment. In *CVPR*. IEEE, 2013.

[30] Z. Zeng, M. Pantic, G. Roisman, and T. S. Huang. A survey of affect recognition methods: audio, visual, and spontaneous expressions. *Pattern Analysis and Machine Intelligence, IEEE Transactions on*, 31(1):39-58, 2009.

[31] G. Zhao and M. Pietikainen. Dynamic texture recognition using local binary patterns with an application to facial expressions. *Pattern Analysis and Machine Intelligence, IEEE Transactions on*, 29(6):915-928, 2007.

[32] L. Zhong, Q. Liu, P. Yang, B. Liu, J. Huang, and D.N. Metaxas. Learning active facial patches for expression analysis. In *CVPR*. IEEE, 2012.

Contrasting and Combining Least Squares Based Learners for Emotion Recognition in the Wild

Heysem Kaya*
Department of Computer Engineering
Boğaziçi University
34342, İstanbul, Turkey
heysem@boun.edu.tr

Furkan Gürpınar
Department of Computational Science and Engineering
Boğaziçi University
34342, İstanbul, Turkey
gurpinarfurkan@gmail.com

Sadaf Afshar
Department of Computational Science and Engineering
Boğaziçi University
34342, İstanbul, Turkey
sa.afshar.sa@gmail.com

Albert Ali Salah
Department of Computer Engineering
Boğaziçi University
34342, İstanbul, Turkey
salah@boun.edu.tr

ABSTRACT

This paper presents our contribution to ACM ICMI 2015 Emotion Recognition in the Wild Challenge (EmotiW 2015). We participate in both static facial expression (SFEW) and audio-visual emotion recognition challenges. In both challenges, we use a set of visual descriptors and their early and late fusion schemes. For AFEW, we also exploit a set of popularly used spatio-temporal modeling alternatives and carry out multi-modal fusion. For classification, we employ two least squares regression based learners that are shown to be fast and accurate on former EmotiW Challenge corpora. Specifically, we use Partial Least Squares Regression (PLS) and Kernel Extreme Learning Machines (ELM), which is closely related to Kernel Regularized Least Squares. We use a General Procrustes Analysis (GPA) based alignment for face registration. By employing different alignments, descriptor types, video modeling strategies and classifiers, we diversify learners to improve the final fusion performance. Test set accuracies reached in both challenges are relatively 25% above the respective baselines.

Categories and Subject Descriptors

I.5.4 [**Computing Methodologies**]: Pattern Recognition-Signal processing; I.4.7 [**Image Processing and Computer Vision**]: Feature Measurement; I.4.8 [**Image Processing and Computer Vision**]: Scene Analysis

*Corresponding author

ICMI '15, November 09 - 13, 2015, Seattle, WA, USA.

ACM 978-1-4503-3912-4/15/11$15.00.
DOI: http://dx.doi.org/10.1145/2818346.2830588.

General Terms

Human-Computer Interaction

Keywords

audio-visual emotion corpus, audio-visual fusion, feature extraction, emotion recognition in the wild, SFEW, AFEW

1. INTRODUCTION

Audio and video based emotion recognition in the wild is challenging, because of noise, large idiosyncratic variance and sensor-related differences. Fixed-protocol challenges in this field provide a unique opportunity to push forward the state-of-the-art and to compare many approaches under very similar conditions. The Emotion Recognition in the Wild (EmotiW) challenge provides out of laboratory data -Acted Facial Expressions in the Wild (AFEW)-, collected from videos that mimic real life [4, 3, 5]. In 2015, the EmotiW campaign introduced a static facial expression challenge based on in-the-wild images collected from videos [6]. In this paper we propose several systems based on combinations of learners for both static and video-based emotion recognition, and report results with the standard challenge protocols.

Our contributions to the EmotiW Challenge are manifold: i) We employ a General Procrustes Analysis (GPA) based alignment method to have improved face registration, ii) we extract and combine a set of visual descriptors such as Scale Invariant Feature Transform (SIFT) [17], Histogram of Oriented Gradients (HOG) [2], Local Phase Quantization (LPQ) [11, 13], Local Binary Patterns (LBP) [18] and its Gabor extension (LGBP), as well as hand-crafted geometric features computed from fitted landmarks of GPA alignment, iii) we use the popular Three Orthogonal Planes (TOP), summarizing functionals (FUN) and Fisher Vector encoding [19] (FV) on low level descriptors for video modeling, iv) we contrast feature and score level fusion strategies using PLS and Kernel ELM classifiers.

The remainder of this paper is organized as follows. In the next section we provide background on the signal processing and machine learning methods used in the study. In Section 3 we briefly introduce the corpora and baseline feature sets. In Sections 4 and 5, we give experimental results for the static and video based challenges, respectively. Finally, Section 6 concludes.

2. BACKGROUND AND METHODOLOGY

Both challenge tasks require detection and registration on facial images. In this section, we provide brief background on the components of our proposed method.

2.1 Facial Registration

Prior to visual feature extraction, we analyzed the set of aligned faces in the challenge dataset subjectively and observed that the images were well-aligned for frontal faces, but the alignment was generally poor in the case of rotations. Moreover, the challenge dataset, which contains face detection annotations that were generated automatically, contains a number of false positives that may effect the subsequent processing adversely. Subsequently, we have decided to i) preprocess the annotated challenge set to remove false positives (purification), ii) to employ an alternative generalized Procrustes analysis (GPA) based alignment on the original images and videos. Procrustes analysis takes a set of landmark points, encoded by geometric coordinates (either in 2D or in 3D), and computes a transformation to align them to a reference face [9].

For the automatically aligned challenge set, we manually remove poorly aligned images from the training set. For the validation set, we use a subspace method to automatically remove false detections. For the test set, all instances are retained.

For the video challenge, the images are resized to 64×64 pixels to cope with the curse of dimensionality. For the static expression recognition challenge, we obtained better results with 128×128 pixel images in our preliminary experiments, therefore used this setting in all our subsequent experiments.

On the validation set, we use principal component analysis (PCA) based data purification as shown to be effective in [16, 25, 15]. The idea is to measure the mean reconstruction error per image $x_i \in \mathbb{R}^D$ with $Err_i = \frac{1}{D}||(x_i - \mu) - W_{pca}^T W_{pca}(x_i - \mu)||$, where $\mu \in \mathbb{R}^D$ is the training set mean vector, and W_{pca} is the reduced PCA projection coefficient matrix learned from the training set. We discard the frames with a high reconstruction error, as these are probably poorly detected or aligned images. In our study, we use the L_1 norm and remove the videos that have less than three valid images from the validation set.

Next, we briefly explain the GPA based alignment method used in the study.

2.1.1 *Generalized Procrustes Analysis*

To obtain a good alignment and face representation, translation, rotation and scale effects should be filtered out. This objective is achieved by constructing a face reference model to which all the faces are aligned. For this we use the procedure that is known as the generalized Procrustes analysis [9]. For this approach, shapes are represented by sets of points, called landmarks. The following iterative approach is applied to obtain a face reference model and at the same time to align all the faces to a unique model:

1. Landmarks of the faces are extracted by a supervised descent based method [29].
2. All the landmarks are centered by subtracting the mean of the landmark coordinates across training samples.
3. An initial approximation of the mean shape, which consists of the centered coordinates of the landmarks, is computed.
4. In order to avoid any shrinking, the landmarks and the mean shape is scale-normalized.
5. All faces are aligned to the current mean shape.
6. The mean shape is re-calculated by using the current set of aligned faces.
7. If the Procrustes distance between the mean shape and the re-calculated mean shape is above a threshold, the mean shape is updated, and the procedure is repeated until convergence.

2.2 Visual Descriptors

We extract SIFT, HOG, LBP, LPQ, and LGBP as visual descriptors in both image and video emotion classification challenges. For LPQ, LBP, and LGBP, the TOP extension is popularly used in video modeling. This extension applies the relevant descriptor on XY, XT and YT planes (where T represents time) independently and concatenates the resulting histograms. Also in our implementation, we divide the video into two equal length volumes over the time axis and extract spatio-temporal TOP features from each volume to further enhance temporal modeling. In the following, we provide brief explanation of LPQ, LBP and LGBP descriptors. We then introduce our hand-crafted geometric features extracted from landmarks provided by Xiong and De La Torre's face detection/tracking method [29].

2.2.1 *Local Phase Quantization*

The LPQ features are computed by taking 2-D Discrete Fourier Transform (DFT) of M-by-M neighborhoods of each pixel in the gray scale image. 2D-DFT is computed at four frequencies $\{[a,0]^T, [0,a]^T, [a,a]^T, [a,-a]^T\}$ with $a = 1/M$, which correspond to four of eight neighboring frequency bins centered at the pixel of interest. The real and imaginary parts of resulting four complex numbers are separately quantized using a threshold of zero, which gives an eight bit string. This string is then converted into an integer value in the range of [0-255]. The pixel based values are finally converted into a histogram of 256 bins. Since this histogram representation does not keep the structural information of facial features, the face is divided into non-overlapping regions and an LPQ histogram is computed per region and concatenated for the final image representation. Here, we use an LPQ version from [11].

2.2.2 *Local Binary Patterns*

After face alignment and conversion to gray scale, LBP computation amounts to finding the sign of difference with respect to a central pixel in a neighborhood, transforming the binary pattern into an integer and finally converting the patterns into a histogram. Uniform LBP clusters 256 patterns into 59 bins, and takes into account occurrence statistics of common patterns [18]. As in LPQ, the face is divided into non overlapping regions and an LBP histogram is computed per region.

2.2.3 *Local Gabor Binary Patterns*

In LGBP, the images are convolved with a set of 2D complex Gabor filters to obtain Gabor-pictures, then LBP is applied to each Gabor-picture (or Gabor-video). A 2D complex Gabor filter is the convolution of a 2D sinusoid (carrier) having phase P, spatial frequencies u_0 and v_0 with a 2D Gaussian kernel (envelope) having amplitude K, orientation ρ, and spatial scales a and b. For simplicity, and in line with [1], we take $a = b = \sigma, u_0 = v_0 = \phi$ and $K = 1$ to obtain:

$$G(x, y) = e^{-\pi\sigma^2((x-x_0)^2_\rho+(y-y_0)^2_\rho)}e^{j(2\pi\phi(x+y)+P)}, \quad (1)$$

where the subscript ρ stands for a clockwise rotation operation around reference point (x_0, y_0) such that:

$$\begin{aligned}(x - x_0)_\rho &= (x - x_0)cos\rho + (y - y_0)sin\rho \\ (y - y_0)_\rho &= -(x - x_0)sin\rho + (y - y_0)cos\rho.\end{aligned} \quad (2)$$

Note that the effect of the phase is canceled out, since only the magnitude response of the filter is used for the descriptor. In this work, we use an open source script for Gabor picture extraction [10] and implement our own LGBP-TOP routine.

2.2.4 *Geometric Features*

Geometric features represent the shape of certain landmarks of the facial image. We used the fitted landmarks provided by the GPA based alignment. The landmark indices are shown in Figure 1.

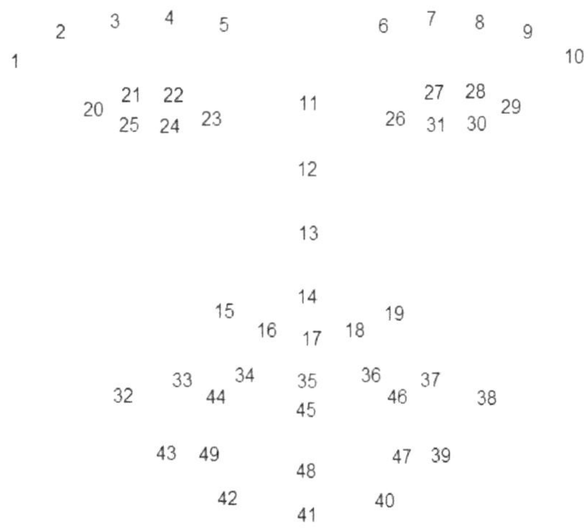

Figure 1: Fiducial points

Detailed explanation of the geometric features extracted from each image (for both challenges) is given in Table 1. As we shall see later on, this small set of hand-crafted geometric features reach the performance of appearance descriptors with much higher dimensionality.

In addition to frame level features, for the video challenge we also included Zero Crossing Rate (ZCR) of z-normalized coordinates of some landmarks over time. These geometric features are especially intended for the improved recognition of the "Disgust" class, whose expression sometimes includes a head oscillation in the yaw axis.

2.3 Video Modeling

In this study, we enhance diversity of learners by incorporating functionals on frame level features and by Fisher vector encoding of low level descriptors.

2.3.1 *Functionals*

In the state-of-the-art acoustic feature extraction pipeline, it is common to use a large set of summarizing functionals over the low level descriptor contours. In video modeling, on the other hand, few functionals such as mean and standard deviation are used. In this work, in addition to mean and standard deviation, we use three functionals based on polynomials, fit to each descriptor contour. The first is curvature, which is the leading coefficient of the second order polynomial. The other two are the slope and offset, computed from the first order polynomial, respectively. Therefore, when we have functional-based encoding, the video feature vector dimensionality is five times the frame-level dimensionality.

2.3.2 *Fisher Vector Encoding*

The Fisher vector (FV) provides a supra-frame encoding of the local descriptors, quantifying the gradient of the parameters of the background model with respect to the data. Given a probability model parametrized with θ, the expected Fisher information matrix $F(\theta)$ is the expectation of the second derivative of the log likelihood with respect to θ:

$$F(\theta) = -E[\frac{\partial^2 \log p(\mathcal{X}|\theta)}{\partial\theta^2}]. \quad (3)$$

The idea in FV in relation to $F(\theta)$ is taking the derivative of the model parameters and normalizing them with respect to the diagonal of $F(\theta)$ [19]. To make the computation feasible, a closed form approximation to the diagonal of $F(\theta)$ is proposed [19]. As a probability density model $p(\theta)$, Gaussian Mixture Models (GMM) with diagonal covariances are used. A K-component GMM is parametrized as $\theta = \{\pi_k, \mu_k, \Sigma_k\}_{k=1}^K$, where the parameters correspond to zeroth (mixture proportion), first (mean), and second order (covariance) statistics, respectively. It has been shown that using the zeroth order statistics is equivalent to the Bag of Words (BoW) model [24], however in FV, they were found to have a negligible effect on performance [19]. Therefore, only gradients of $\{\mu_k, \Sigma_k\}_{k=1}^K$ are used, giving a $2 \times d \times K$ dimensional super vector, where d is the low level descriptor (LLD) dimensionality.

In order to efficiently learn a Background Probability Model (BPM) using GMM with diagonal covariances, we first need to decorrelate the data gathered from all instances. Principal Component Analysis (PCA) is applied on the data for this purpose. To reduce the computational cost, we take LLDs from every second frame to learn PCA and GMM. In our preliminary tests, this sub-sampling did not decrease the performance. Once the parameters of PCA projection and GMM are learned, we use all speech frames from each utterance without sub-sampling to represent them as a FV.

2.4 Model Learning

To learn a classification model, we employ kernel extreme learning machine (ELM) [12] and Partial Least Squares (PLS) regression due to their fast and accurate learning capability.

ELM proposes a multilayer perceptron architecture, but unsupervised, even random generation of the hidden node

Table 1: **Hand-crafted geometric features. LR indicates that the features are averaged over left and right parts of the face. Distance based features are always normalized with the face height. Features 18 through 23 are motivated by [22].**

Feature #	Explanation	Landmarks Involved	Feature Type
1	Eye aspect ratio (LR)	[20:25], [26:31]	Distance
2	Mouth aspect ratio	32, 35, 38, 41	Distance
3	Upper lip angles (LR)	32, 35, 38	Angle
4	Nose tip - mouth corner angles (LR)	17, 32, 38	Angle
5	Lower lip angles (LR)	[32, 42] , [38, 40]	Angle
6	Eyebrow slope (LR)	[1, 5] , [6, 10]	Angle
7,8	Lower eye angles (LR)	[20, 23, 24, 25], [26, 29, 30, 31]	Angle
9	Mouth corner - mouth bottom angles	32, 38, 41	Angle
10	Upper mouth angles (LR)	[32, 34], [36, 38]	Angle
11	Curvature of lower-outer lips (LR)	[32, 43, 42], [38, 39, 40]	Curvature
12	Curvature of lower-inner lips (LR)	[32, 42, 41], [38, 40, 41]	Curvature
13	Bottom lip curvature	[32, 38, 41]	Curvature
14	Mouth opening / mouth width	45, 48, 32, 38	Distance
15	Mouth up/low	35, 41, 45	Distance
16	Eye - middle eyebrow distance (LR)	[3, 20, 23], [8, 26, 29]	Distance
17	Eye - inner eyebrow distance (LR)	[5, 20, 23], [6, 26, 29]	Distance
18	Inner eye - eyebrow center (LR)	[3, 23], [8, 26]	Distance
19	Inner eye - mouth top distance	23, 26, 35	Distance
20	Mouth width	32, 38	Distance
21	Mouth height	35, 41	Distance
22	Upper mouth height	32, 38, 35	Distance
23	Lower mouth height	32, 38, 41	Distance

output matrix $\mathbf{H} \in \mathbb{R}^{N \times h}$, where N and h denote the number of instances and the hidden neurons, respectively. The actual learning takes place in the second layer between $\mathbf{H}$ and the label matrix $\mathbf{T} \in \mathbb{R}^{N \times L}$, where L is the number of classes. $\mathbf{T}$ is composed of continuous annotations in case of regression, therefore is a vector. In the case of L-class classification, $\mathbf{T}$ is represented in one vs. all coding:

$$\mathbf{T}_{t,l} = \begin{cases} +1 & \text{if } y^t = l, \\ -1 & \text{if } y^t \neq l. \end{cases} \tag{4}$$

The second level weights $\beta \in \mathbb{R}^{h \times L}$ are learned by least squares solution to a set of linear equations $\mathbf{H}\beta = \mathbf{T}$. The output weights can be learned via:

$$\beta = \mathbf{H}^{\dagger}\mathbf{T}, \tag{5}$$

where $\mathbf{H}^{\dagger}$ is the Moore-Penrose generalized inverse [20] that gives the minimum L_2 norm solution to $||\mathbf{H}\beta - \mathbf{T}||$, simultaneously minimizing the norm of $||\beta||$. To increase the robustness and generalization capability, the optimization problem of ELM is reformulated using a regularization coefficient on the residual error $||\mathbf{H}\beta - \mathbf{T}||$. The learning rule of this alternative ELM is related to Least Square SVMs (LSSVM) via the following output weight learning formulation:

$$\beta = \mathbf{H}^T(\frac{\mathbf{I}}{C} + \mathbf{H}\mathbf{H}^T)^{-1}\mathbf{T}, \tag{6}$$

where $\mathbf{I}$ is the $N \times N$ identity matrix, and C, which is used to regularize the linear kernel $\mathbf{H}\mathbf{H}^T$, corresponds to the complexity parameter of LSSVM [26]. This formulation is further simplified noting that the hidden layer matrix need not be generated explicitly given a kernel $\mathbf{K}$, which can be seen identical to Kernel Regularized Least Squares [12, 21]:

$$\beta = (\frac{\mathbf{I}}{C} + \mathbf{K})^{-1}\mathbf{T}. \tag{7}$$

PLS regression between two sets of variables $\mathbf{X} \in \mathbb{R}^{N \times d}$ and $\mathbf{Y} \in \mathbb{R}^{N \times p}$ is based on decomposing the matrices as $\mathbf{X} = \mathbf{U}_x\mathbf{V}_x + r_x$, $\mathbf{Y} = \mathbf{U}_y\mathbf{V}_y + r_y$, where $\mathbf{U}$ denotes the latent factors, $\mathbf{V}$ denotes the loadings and r stands for the residuals. The decomposition is done by finding projection weights $\mathbf{W}_x, \mathbf{W}_y$ that jointly maximize the covariance of corresponding columns of $\mathbf{U}_x = \mathbf{X}\mathbf{W}_x$ and $\mathbf{U}_y = \mathbf{Y}\mathbf{W}_y$. For further details of PLS regression, the reader is referred to [28]. PLS is applied to classification in one-versus-all setting between the feature matrix $\mathbf{X}$ and the binary label vector $\mathbf{Y}$, then the class giving the highest regression score is taken as prediction. The number of latent factors is a hyper-parameter to tune via cross-validation.

2.5 Fusion

We contrast two classical fusion schemes, namely early (feature level) and late (decision level) fusion. It has been shown that late fusion gives better results compared to feature level fusion. Furthermore, we apply weighted score fusion for each model and class, where optimal fusion weights are searched over a pool of randomly generated matrices. This scheme is shown to be successful on previous EmotiW Challenge corpora, considering different confusion matrices of each sub-system [14, 15].

We next briefly introduce the Challenge data [5], baseline features and the experimental protocol.

3. CORPORA AND EXPERIMENTAL PROTOCOL

In line with the previous two challenges, EmotiW 2015 presents video clips and images collected from movies representing close-to-real-world conditions [5, 7]. The challenge datasets are partitioned into training, development and test sets. The distribution of instances over partitions based on modality (audio, video) and alignment types is given in Table 2.

Table 2: Instance distribution over partitions, alignment and modality types. GA: Given alignment, GPA: General Procrustes Analysis based alignment

SFEW			
#	Train	Val	Test
Images	958	436	372
GA	891	427	372
GPA	724	343	290
AFEW			
#	Train	Val	Test
Clips	711	383	539
Video-GA	698	369	539
Video-GPA	663	340	455
Audio	707	383	539

The baseline video features consist of Local Binary Patterns from Three Orthogonal Planes (LBP-TOP) compacted via uniform LBP [18]. For SFEW, feature level combination of Pyramid of HOG and LPQ is used in the baseline.

The baseline audio features are extracted via openSMILE tool [8] using INTERSPEECH 2010 Paralinguistic challenge baseline set [23]. We use the baseline acoustic features to model audio modality.

For comparability and reproducibility, we opt to use open-source tools for feature extraction. Particularly, VLFeat library [27] is used for both feature extraction (e.g. LBP, HOG), GMM training, and FV encoding.

In both challenges, we use three preprocessing alternatives: no-normalization (particularly for histogram-type descriptors that are normalized during the process), min-max normalization into [0,1] range, and z-normalization. Here, we report the best results over three alternatives.

The audio and video features are kernelized by means of Linear and Radial Basis Function (RBF) kernels, prior to model learning by classifiers. We optimize the model hyper-parameters on the challenge validation set. These are RBF kernel parameter γ, regularization parameter τ for ELM and number of latent components for PLS. Similarly, the number of PCA eigenvectors p and GMM components K used in the FV encoding are optimized using cross-validation.

The pipeline used in both challenges are very similar, save that we apply spatio-temporal modeling and combine the visual sub-systems with the audio sub-system in AFEW. The experimental results of each challenge are presented in the respective sections.

4. STATIC FACIAL EXPRESSION RECOGNITION CHALLENGE

The pipeline of the proposed multi-level score fusion system used in the SFEW Challenge is given in Figure 2. Since the images detected by different alignment methods do not overlap, we first optimize the fusion weights for each alignment individually then apply a second level fusion, where scores of missing images in an alignment are represented with a zero vector.

We extract 128 dimensional SIFT features from 32-by-32 pixel patches with 16 pixel shifts in both spatial directions. We extract two versions of HOG. One is extracted from the same overlapping patches as SIFT, where each patch is further divided into four non-overlapping sub-regions. This is denoted as HOG-OL. The other HOG version is obtained by dividing the image into 8×8 non-overlapping patches (HOG-NOL). LPQ and LBP are extracted from non-overlapping 6×6 and 8×8 patches, respectively. The validation set performances of extracted visual features from given alignment and GPA based alignment are given in Tables 3 and 4, respectively. On the overall, we observe higher performance of GPA based alignment compared to given aligned images. However, it is important to note that GPA detects face in 343 out of 436 images, whereas given alignment has 427 detected faces. Therefore, the improvement can partially be attributed to clean/less posed images that the GPA aligned systems cast their predictions.

Table 3: Performance of various descriptors extracted from images with challenge alignment (GA).

Descriptor	ELM	PLS	Dimensions
HOG-NOL	36.77	**37.47**	1984
HOG-OL	**39.11**	**39.34**	6076
SIFT	**39.34**	38.64	6272
LBP	36.30	**38.64**	3712
LPQ	34.43	**38.17**	9216

Table 4: Performance of various descriptors extracted from GPA aligned images.

Descriptor	ELM	PLS	Dimensions
GEO	**46.06**	43.44	23
HOG-NOL	46.94	**48.98**	1984
HOG-OL	**48.40**	46.06	6076
SIFT	**46.06**	43.15	6272
LBP	45.48	**46.36**	3712
LPQ	42.86	**43.44**	9216

In terms of feature types, we see that HOG variants give the best performance. SIFT and LBP follow the performance of HOG. An important observation in GPA alignment is that 23 dimensional geometric features have better performance than 9216 dimensional LPQ, and are on-par with 6272 dimensional SIFT features.

We next compare the feature and decision level fusion in pairwise manner. Here, decision fusion is done by simple weighing of score vectors v_1 and v_2 as $\alpha * v_1 + (1-\alpha) * v_2$. The α parameter is searched over [0,1] range with steps of 0.05. The performances of early and late fusion alternatives for GPA aligned visual models are shown in Table 5. We see that: i) simple weighted fusion gives higher performance compared to feature level fusion, and ii) the combination of geometric features with an appearance descriptor (e.g. LBP) reaches the highest performance.

We finally apply multi-level, model- and class-weighted score fusion. Here, we test alternative combinations and observe that LPQ does not contribute to overall performance on the validation set. Therefore, we exclude it from the system. We test HOG-NOL and HOG-OL alternatives and make two test set submissions to see their performances. The fusion system with GPA aligned faces reaches 53.06% accuracy, whereas its given aligned counterpart gives 42.84% on the validation set. The second level fusion of the optimized alignment-specific systems give around 49.5%, where

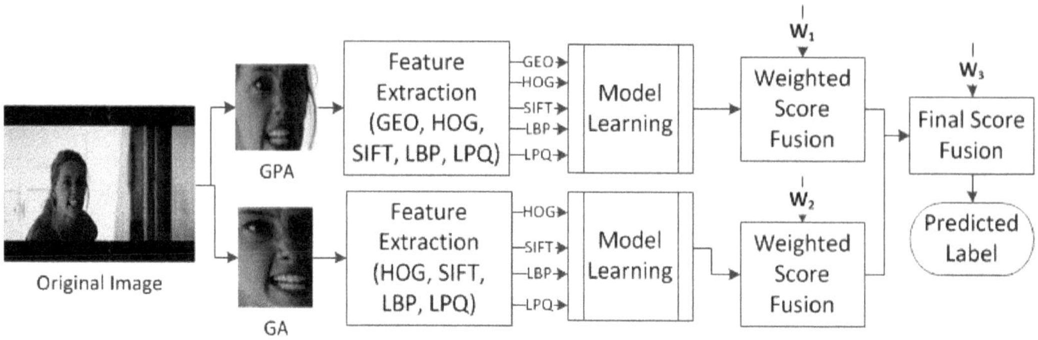

Figure 2: Pipeline of the proposed system for SFEW

Table 5: Comparison of early and late fusion with GPA aligned images.

Feature Level Fusion				
	HOG	SIFT	LBP	LPQ
GEO	**47.81**	46.94	**47.81**	46.94
HOG		45.77	47.23	44.31
SIFT			45.77	45.77
LBP				42.86
Weighted Score Fusion				
	HOG	SIFT	LBP	LPQ
GEO	49.25	48.10	**50.15**	47.23
HOG		49.56	48.40	48.40
SIFT			48.40	46.06
LBP				47.23

we see the GPA based system has higher face miss rate, but improves on the baseline alignment. The best validation set results and corresponding test performances are depicted in Table 6. Note that the validation and test set performances of the submitted systems are very similar, which indicates little effect of overlearning. Our top test set accuracy (49.46%) outperforms the challenge baseline (39.13%) by a large margin. The test set confusion matrix corresponding to the best results is depicted in Figure 3. We see that in the static image based expression recognition, recall of disgust and fear classes fail totally; while recall of happy, angry, neutral and surprise are reasonable.

Table 6: Validation and test set performances of two submitted systems.

GA-Val	GPA-Val	Level 2-Val	Test
42.15	53.06	49.53	49.46
42.84	52.48	49.30	48.92

5. VIDEO BASED EMOTION RECOGNITION CHALLENGE

In addition to frame-level feature extraction, in the AFEW challenge, we carried out video modeling via TOP extension, FV encoding and functionals (FUN). Here, we also benefited from the audio modality to improve the fusion performance. Similar to SFEW, we analyzed the individual and pairwise combined performances of video features. Out of all possible

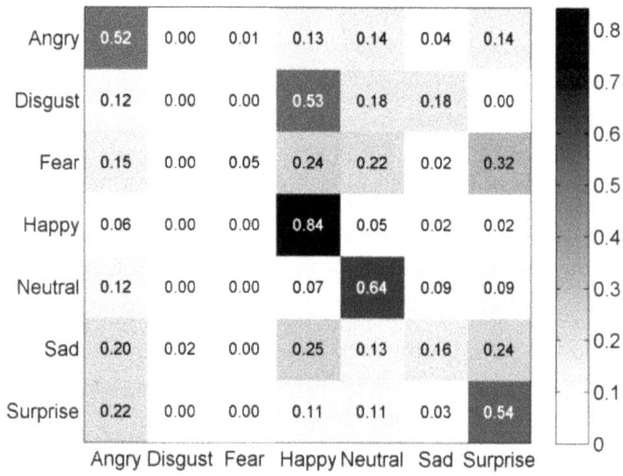

Figure 3: Confusion matrix of the best submission in SFEW.

descriptor-video modeling combinations, we eliminated the alternatives whose best performance is below 40%. A summary of the resulting pruned validation set performances is given in Table 7.

The most remarkable performance is obtained with FV encoded geometric features. This is followed by LGBP-TOP and HOG-FUN. Zero Crossing Rate (ZCR) is applied to z-normalized contours of x coordinate of nose, y coordinate of lower lip, left and right eye heights, vertical distance of left and right eye brows to eye centers. When these six features are combined with GEO-FUN, they gave a considerable boost.

Pairwise feature and decision level fusion resulted in a pattern similar to SFEW. We obtained relatively better results with late fusion and the best results are obtained using combinations of appearance features with FV encoded geometric features. Simple weighted fusion of HOG-FUN with GEO-FV reached a validation set accuracy of 48.24%.

Our first test set submission consisted of weighted fusion of audio, LBP-TOP and LGBP-TOP. This setup is inspired from [15], and is intended to provide us a competitive benchmark. This system reached a test set accuracy of 50.28%. We then combined seven GPA aligned visual models (using GEO-FUN+ZCR and excluding of GEO-FUN) with the

Table 8: Validation and test set accuracies of submitted systems. WF: weighted fusion, FF: feature level fusion.

Submission	System	Val	Test
1	WF (GA: LBP-TOP. LGBP-TOP & Audio)	50.14%	50.28%
2	WF (GPA: 7 Visual sub-sys & Audio)	51.70%	44.71%
3	WF (System 1 & 2)	58.22%	42.64%
4	WF (System 1 & GEO-FV, HOG-FUN)	52.74%	48.61%
5	WF (Audio, GA: LGBP-TOP, LBP-TOP, FF(SIFT-FUN & GEO-FV), LPQ-TOP with PLS)	52.30%	49.17%
6	**WF (Audio, GA: LGBP-TOP, HOG-FUN & SIFT-FV, LBP-TOP, LPQ-TOP with PLS)**	**52.30%**	**53.62%**
7	WF (Audio, GA: LGBP-TOP, HOG-FUN & SIFT-FV, LBP-TOP, LPQ-TOP, GPA: GEO-FV with PLS)	54.47%	52.69%

Table 7: Best validation set performances of two alignment systems.

	Lin		RBF	
Feature	ELM	PLS	ELM	PLS
Audio	**36.59**	**36.29**	35.51	34.73
Visual Features with Given Alignment				
HOG-FUN	39.02	**44.99**	41.46	42.01
SIFT-FUN	40.92	**43.63**	42.28	41.19
LBP-TOP	41.19	41.46	**42.01**	40.65
LGBP-TOP	43.63	43.90	**44.44**	44.17
LPQ-TOP	40.65	41.19	40.65	**42.01**
SIFT-FV	40.11	**41.73**	40.38	40.38
Visual Features with GPA based Alignment				
HOG-FUN	40.59	**43.24**	42.06	40.59
SIFT-FUN	38.53	**42.94**	40.59	39.12
LBP-TOP	41.76	**42.65**	42.06	**42.65**
LGBP-TOP	40.88	**44.12**	40.29	42.06
GEO-FUN	39.12	40.59	**42.65**	40.59
GEO-FUN + ZCR	40.00	40.00	**44.12**	42.06
GEO-FV	42.65	**45.59**	44.12	44.12
SIFT-FV	42.35	41.47	**43.24**	41.76

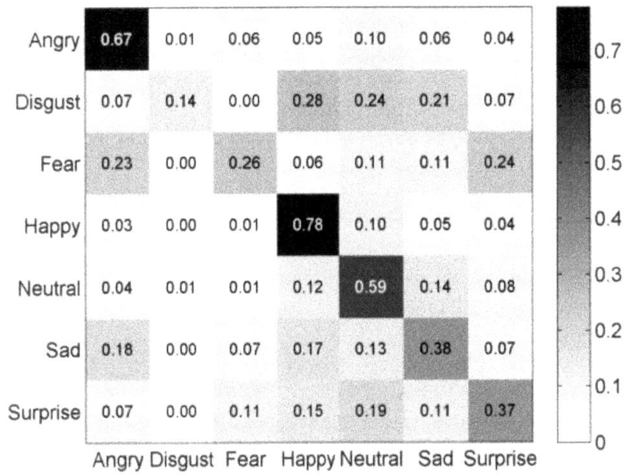

Figure 4: Confusion matrix of the best submission in AFEW.

audio model reaching a validation set accuracy of 51.7%. When this is combined with the first submission system, it reached 58.22% on the validation set. However, their test set performances were 44.71% and 42.64%, respectively. We attributed this dramatic difference to high number of missing test set videos (by GPA alignment) that are represented as zero score vectors during late fusion. During our analyses, we also observed that fusing best scores from PLS and ELM might result in lowered performance due to varying score ranges of these classifiers. For these reasons, we opted to fuse best models from given aligned images with PLS classifier. Our top test set result (53.62%) is obtained using weighted score fusion of audio model with five visual models (see Table 8 and Figure 4 for details). Compared to static expression challenge, the confusion matrix here shows higher recall in disgust and fear classes, which can be attributed to modeling visual dynamics and utilizing audio, respectively.

6. CONCLUSIONS

In this study, we diversify learners using alternative alignment, descriptor type and classifier options. We then use a least squares based classifier and weighted fusion. The multi-level fusion gives good validation set results in both challenges, and generalizes well in SFEW. In AFEW, the best test set results are obtained with single level weighted fusion scheme, although on the validation set better results are be achieved with multi-level version. The reason of the validation-test set performance discrepancy in AFEW is the high number of missing videos when aligned with GPA. Thus, the results on the validation set indicate that if it would be possible to use geometric features from the given alignment, or the number of valid videos in GPA aligned alternative would have been higher, better results could have been reached.

Comparing the confusion matrices of the best test set results, we see that in both challenges, the recall of disgust and fear classes is very low. In SFEW, the recall of these classes fails totally. In audio-only models, it is possible to obtain higher recall for the fear class. Therefore, more effort should be spent to modeling audio modality. On the other hand, disgust can be distinguished with visual cues, especially with dynamics of facial structure. We should note that the class distribution of the challenge data is also responsible from the low recall of this under-sampled class.

In future works, we will focus on the multi-level fusion of various alignments, which have different resolutions. We will also exploit ways for better alternative modeling of audio modality, which is not elaborated thoroughly in this study.

7. REFERENCES

[1] T. R. Almaev and M. F. Valstar. Local Gabor binary patterns from three orthogonal planes for automatic facial expression recognition. In *2013 Humaine Association Conference on Affective Computing and Intelligent Interaction (ACII)*, pages 356–361. IEEE, 2013.

[2] N. Dalal and B. Triggs. Histograms of oriented gradients for human detection. In *IEEE Conference on Computer Vision and Pattern Recognition (CVPR '05)*, volume 1, pages 886–893. IEEE, 2005.

[3] A. Dhall, R. Goecke, J. Joshi, K. Sikka, and T. Gedeon. Emotion recognition in the wild challenge 2014: Baseline, data and protocol. In *Proc. of the 16th ACM Intl. Conf. on Multimodal Interaction (ICMI 2014)*. ACM, 2014.

[4] A. Dhall, R. Goecke, J. Joshi, M. Wagner, and T. Gedeon. Emotion recognition in the wild challenge 2013. In *Proc. of the 15th ACM Intl. Conf. on Multimodal Interaction (ICMI 2013)*, pages 509–516. ACM, 2013.

[5] A. Dhall, R. Goecke, S. Lucey, and T. Gedeon. Collecting large, richly annotated facial-expression databases from movies. *IEEE MultiMedia*, 19(3):34–41, July 2012.

[6] A. Dhall, R. Goecke, L. S, and T. Gedeon. Static facial expression in though conditions: Data, evaluation protocol and benchmark. In *ICCV BEFIT Workshop)*. IEEE, 2011.

[7] A. Dhall, O. V. Ramana Murthy, R. Goecke, J. Joshi, and T. Gedeon. Video and image based emotion recognition challenges in the wild: Emotiw 2015. In *Proc. of the 17th ACM Intl. Conf. on Multimodal Interaction (ICMI 2015)*. ACM, 2015.

[8] F. Eyben, M. Wöllmer, and B. Schuller. Opensmile: the munich versatile and fast open-source audio feature extractor. In *Proc. of the intl. conf. on Multimedia*, pages 1459–1462. ACM, 2010.

[9] J. C. Gower. Generalized procrustes analysis. *Psychometrika*, 40(1):33–51, 1975.

[10] M. Haghighat, S. Zonouz, and M. Abdel-Mottaleb. Identification using encrypted biometrics. In *Computer Analysis of Images and Patterns*, pages 440–448. Springer, 2013.

[11] J. Heikkilä, V. Ojansivu, and E. Rahtu. Improved blur insensitivity for decorrelated local phase quantization. In *20th International Conference on Pattern Recognition (ICPR '10)*, pages 818–821, 2010.

[12] G.-B. Huang, H. Zhou, X. Ding, and R. Zhang. Extreme learning machine for regression and multiclass classification. *Systems, Man, and Cybernetics, Part B: Cybernetics, IEEE Transactions on*, 42(2):513–529, 2012.

[13] B. Jiang, M. Valstar, B. Martinez, and M. Pantic. A dynamic appearance descriptor approach to facial actions temporal modeling. *Cybernetics, IEEE Transactions on*, 44(2):161–174, 2014.

[14] S. E. Kahou, C. Pal, X. Bouthillier, et al. Combining modality specific deep neural networks for emotion recognition in video. In *Proceedings of the 15th ACM on International Conference on Multimodal Interaction*, ICMI '13, pages 543–550, 2013.

[15] H. Kaya and A. A. Salah. Combining modality-specific extreme learning machines for emotion recognition in the wild. *Journal on Multimodal User Interfaces*, 2015.

[16] M. Liu, R. Wang, Z. Huang, S. Shan, and X. Chen. Partial least squares regression on Grassmannian manifold for emotion recognition. In *Proceedings of the 15th ACM on International Conference on Multimodal Interaction*, ICMI '13, pages 525–530, 2013.

[17] D. G. Lowe. Distinctive image features from scale-invariant keypoints. *International Journal of Computer Vision*, 60(2):91–110, 2004.

[18] T. Ojala, M. Pietikainen, and T. Maenpaa. Multiresolution gray-scale and rotation invariant texture classification with local binary patterns. *Pattern Analysis and Machine Intelligence, IEEE Transactions on*, 24(7):971–987, 2002.

[19] F. Perronnin and C. Dance. Fisher kernels on visual vocabularies for image categorization. In *IEEE Conference on Computer Vision and Pattern Recognition*, pages 1–8, Minneapolis, Minnesota, USA, 2007.

[20] C. R. Rao and S. K. Mitra. *Generalized inverse of matrices and its applications*, volume 7. Wiley New York, 1971.

[21] R. Rifkin, G. Yeo, and T. Poggio. Regularized least-squares classification. *NATO Science Series Sub Series III Computer and Systems Sciences*, 190:131–154, 2003.

[22] A. Saeed, A. Al-Hamadi, R. Niese, and M. Elzobi. Effective geometric features for human emotion recognition. In *IEEE 11th International Conference on Signal Processing (ICSP)*, volume 1, pages 623–627, 2012.

[23] B. Schuller, S. Steidl, A. Batliner, F. Burkhardt, L. Devillers, C. A. Müller, and S. S. Narayanan. The interspeech 2010 paralinguistic challenge. In *Proc. INTERSPEECH*, pages 2794–2797, 2010.

[24] J. Sivic and A. Zisserman. Efficient visual search of videos cast as text retrieval. *IEEE Transactions on Pattern Analysis and Machine Intelligence*, 31(4):591–606, 2009.

[25] B. Sun, L. Li, T. Zuo, Y. Chen, G. Zhou, and X. Wu. Combining multimodal features with hierarchical classifier fusion for emotion recognition in the wild. In *Proceedings of the 16th International Conference on Multimodal Interaction*, ICMI '14, pages 481–486, 2014.

[26] J. A. Suykens and J. Vandewalle. Least squares support vector machine classifiers. *Neural processing letters*, 9(3):293–300, 1999.

[27] A. Vedaldi and B. Fulkerson. VLFeat: An open and portable library of computer vision algorithms, 2008.

[28] H. Wold. Partial least squares. In S. Kotz and N. L. Johnson, editors, *Encyclopedia of Statistical Sciences*, pages 581–591. Wiley New York, 1985.

[29] X. Xiong and F. De la Torre. Supervised Descent Method and Its Application to Face Alignment. In *IEEE Conference on Computer Vision and Pattern Recognition (CVPR '13)*, pages 532–539, 2013.

Recurrent Neural Networks for Emotion Recognition in Video

Samira Ebrahimi Kahou
École Polytechnique de Montréal, Canada
samira.ebrahimi-kahou@polymtl.ca

Vincent Michalski
Université de Montréal, Montréal, Canada
vincent.michalski@umontreal.ca

Kishore Konda
Goethe-Universität Frankfurt, Germany
konda.kishorereddy@gmail.com

Roland Memisevic
Université de Montréal, Montréal, Canada
roland.memisevic@umontreal.ca

Christopher Pal
École Polytechnique de Montréal, Canada
christopher.pal@polymtl.ca

ABSTRACT

Deep learning based approaches to facial analysis and video analysis have recently demonstrated high performance on a variety of key tasks such as face recognition, emotion recognition and activity recognition. In the case of video, information often must be aggregated across a variable length sequence of frames to produce a classification result. Prior work using convolutional neural networks (CNNs) for emotion recognition in video has relied on temporal averaging and pooling operations reminiscent of widely used approaches for the spatial aggregation of information. Recurrent neural networks (RNNs) have seen an explosion of recent interest as they yield state-of-the-art performance on a variety of sequence analysis tasks. RNNs provide an attractive framework for propagating information over a sequence using a continuous valued hidden layer representation. In this work we present a complete system for the 2015 Emotion Recognition in the Wild (EmotiW) Challenge. We focus our presentation and experimental analysis on a hybrid CNN-RNN architecture for facial expression analysis that can outperform a previously applied CNN approach using temporal averaging for aggregation.

Categories and Subject Descriptors

I.5 [**Pattern Recognition**]: Models, Applications

Keywords

emotion recognition; deep learning; multimodal learning; model combination; recurrent neural networks

ICMI 2015, November 9–13, 2015, Seattle, WA, USA.
Copyright is held by the owner/author(s). Publication rights licensed to ACM.
ACM 978-1-4503-3912-4/15/11 ...$15.00.
DOI: http://dx.doi.org/10.1145/2818346.2830596 .

1. INTRODUCTION

Human emotion analysis is a challenging machine learning task with a wide range of applications in human-computer interaction, e-learning, health care, advertising and gaming. Emotion analysis is particularly challenging as multiple input modalities, both visual and auditory, play an important role in understanding it. Given a video sequence with a human subject, some of the important cues which help to understand the user's emotion are facial expressions, movements and activities. In some cases speech or high level scene context can also be useful to infer emotion. Most of the time there is a considerable overlap between emotion classes making it a challenging classification task. In this paper we present a deep learning based approach to modeling different input modalities and to combining them in order to infer emotion labels from a given video sequence.

The Emotion recognition in the wild (EmotiW 2015) challenge [9] is an extension of a similar challenge held in 2014 [8]. The task is to predict one of seven emotion labels: angry, disgust, fear, happy, sad, surprise and neutral. The dataset used in the challenge is the Acted Facial Expressions in the Wild (AFEW) 5.0 dataset, which contains short video clips extracted from Hollywood movies. The video clips present emotions with a high degree of variation, e.g. actor identity, age, pose and lighting conditions. The dataset contains 723 videos for training, 383 for validation and 539 test clips.

Traditional approaches to emotion recognition were based on hand-engineered features [17, 28]. With the availability of big datasets, deep learning has emerged as a general approach to machine learning yielding state-of-the-art results in many computer vision and natural language processing tasks [22, 19]. The basic principle of deep learning is to learn hierarchical representations of input data such that the learned representations improve classification performance.

The primary contribution of this work is to model the spatio-temporal evolution of facial expressions of a person in a video using a Recurrent Neural Network (RNN) combined with a Convolutional Neural Network (CNN) in an underlying CNN-RNN architecture. In addition to this, we also employed an Autoencoder based activity recognition pipeline for modelling user activity and a simple Support Vector Machine (SVM) based approach over energy and spectral features for audio. We also present a neural network-based feature level fusion technique to combine different modalities for the final emotion prediction for a short video clip.

Previous work [18, 25] has achieved state-of-the-art results in the emotion recognition challenge using deep learning techniques which includes our work that won the 2013 EmotiW challenge. In contrast to [18, 16], which use an averaging-based aggregation method for visual features in video, here we employ an RNN to model the temporal evolution of facial features in video. We also explore feature-level fusion of our modality-specific models and show that this increases performance.

The remainder of this paper is organized as follows. In Section 2, 3 and 4 we describe each of the models used for different modalities followed by Section 5, which provides details on the fusion methods we applied. Section 6 presents our experimental results and provides a list of our submissions to the challenge. Finally, in Section 7 we draw some conclusions from our experiments.

2. SPATIO-TEMPORAL EVOLUTION OF FACIAL EXPRESSIONS

Modelling the spatio-temporal evolution of visual information plays an important role in understanding the behavior of objects and users in video. Emotion recognition is one of the tasks which involve modelling the behavior of a user. In this work, we use a two step approach to modelling emotion as the spatio-temporal evolution of image structure. In the first step, an CNN is trained to classify static images containing emotions. In the second step, we train an RNN on the higher layer representation of the CNN inferred from individual frames to predict a single emotion for the entire video. RNNs have undergone a resurgence of interest due in part to their impressive performance in handwriting and speech recognition [14, 13]. Much of this interest has been driven by the stability of learning achieved by the use of so-called long short term memory (LSTM) units [15]. RNNs have also proven to be powerful methods for other types of sequential data including video [1, 10] and natural language processing [2, 32]. As such we use an RNN structure for learning a model for video level representation and classification. The higher layer representation from the CNN provides structural information of a given frame and the RNN models the spatio-temporal evolution of the structure over time.

Unlike other work involving video and RNN techniques such as [1, 10], we do not use LSTMs. Here we use IRNNs [24] which are composed of rectified linear units (ReLUs) and employ a special initialization strategy based on scaled variations of the identity matrix. These elements of IRNNs are aimed at providing a much simpler mechanism for dealing with the vanishing and exploding gradient problem compared to the more complex LSTM framework. Recent work has compared IRNNs with LSTMs and found that IRNNs are able to yield comparable results in some tasks, including problems which involve long term dependencies [24].

We provide a detailed explanation of the CNN structure in Section 2.1 and of the RNN in Section 2.2. To compare with the non-sequential approach presented in [16], we also aggregated CNN features to a fixed-length feature vector and trained an SVM. This is described in Section 2.3.

2.1 Frame feature extraction using an CNN

The competition dataset has one emotion label per video which does not correspond to every frame. This introduces a lot of noise if the video labels are used as targets for training an CNN on individual frames. Our visual features are therefore provided by an CNN trained on a combination of two additional emotion datasets of static images. Moreover, using additional data covers a larger variety in age and identity in contrast to the challenge data where the same actor/actress might appear in multiple clips.

2.1.1 *Datasets*

The additional datasets used in the CNN training consists of two large emotion datasets, namely the Toronto Face Database (TFD) [31] with 4,178 images and the Facial Expression Recognition dataset (FER2013) [6] containing 35,887 images, both with seven basic expressions: angry, disgust, fear, happy, sad, surprise and neutral.

2.1.2 *Pre-processing*

To account for varying lighting conditions (in particular, across datasets) we applied histogram equalization. We used the aligned faces provided by the organizers to extract features from the CNN. The alignment involves a combined facial keypoints detection and tracking approach explained in [7]. We shall refer to this dataset as AFEW-faces. Different face detection and/or alignment techniques have been used for FER2013, TFD and AFEW-faces. In order to be able to leverage the additional datasets, we re-aligned all datasets to FER2013 using the following procedure:

1. We detected five facial keypoints for all images in the FER2013, TFD and AFEW-faces training set using the convolutional neural network cascade method in [30].

2. For each dataset we computed the mean shape by averaging the coordinates of keypoints.

3. Datasets have been mapped to FER2013 by using a similarity transformation between mean shapes. By computing one transformation per dataset we let the eyes, nose and mouth be roughly in the same location retaining a slight amount of variation. We added a noisy border for TFD and AFEW-faces as faces were cropped more tightly compared to FER2013.

4. AFEW-faces validation and test sets were mapped using the transformation inferred on the training set.

We also performed dataset normalization with the mean and standard deviation image from the combined FER2013 and TFD (FER+TFD).

2.1.3 *CNN Architecture*

We trained various CNN architectures on FER+TFD without using any challenge data for gradient computations. For early stopping we tried both leaving out 1000 samples of FER+TFD and the challenge data. We observed that the RNN yields slightly better performance when CNN early stopping was done on the challenge data as this avoids overfitting to FER+TFD. Therefore, for our best CNN structure, we trained on all FER+TFD and performed early stopping on AFEW-faces train+validation.

We have explored three main CNN structures:

- a very deep structure with small 3x3 filter size [26, 29],
- a three-layer CNN with 5x5 filters [21, 22] and
- a similar three-layer CNN with 9x9 filter size.

The CNN is trained mainly for feature extraction and we have only used the additional dataset for the training phase. Therefore, we searched for a structure that better generalizes to other datasets. Deep structures are known to learn representations that better generalize to other datasets [29]. However, we observed that the very deep structure quickly over-fitted to FER+TFD, and generalized badly to the challenge dataset. This could be due to the relatively small amount of labeled data available for the emotion recognition task here. For this reason we have tried a shallower network with three layers which appears to have moderately addressed the over-fitting problem. Finally, we increased the filter size from 5 to 9 and reduced the number of filters from 64-64-128 to 32-32-64. For all of the experiments we used data augmentation (horizontal flipping with probability of 0.5 and random cropping), as well as dropout (with rate 0.25).

2.2 Learning Sequences Using an RNN

We use an RNN to aggregate frame features for the following reasons:

- The temporal order of frames is respected in contrast to bag-of-features approaches.
- An RNN has the ability to learn to detect an event, such as the presence of a particular expression, irrespective of the time, at which it occurs in a sequence.
- RNNs naturally deal with a variable number of frames.

RNNs are a type of neural network which transforms a sequence of inputs into a sequence of outputs. At each time-step t, a hidden state $\mathbf{h}_t$ is computed based on the hidden state at time $t-1$ and the input $\mathbf{x}_t$ at time t

$$\mathbf{h}_t = \sigma(\mathbf{W}_{in}\mathbf{x}_t + \mathbf{W}_{rec}\mathbf{h}_{t-1}), \quad (1)$$

where $\mathbf{W}_{in}$ is the input weight matrix, $\mathbf{W}_{rec}$ is the recurrent matrix and σ is the hidden activation function. Each time-step also computes outputs, based on the current hidden state:

$$\mathbf{y}_t = f(\mathbf{W}_{out}\mathbf{h}_t), \quad (2)$$

where $\mathbf{W}_{out}$ is the output weight matrix and f is the output activation function. An example of an RNN in which only the last time-step produces an output is shown in Figure 1.

We use the IRNN, which as discussed above is a simple RNN with rectified linear hidden units (ReLUs) and with a recurrent matrix, that is initialized with scaled variations of the identity matrix [24]. The identity initialization trick ensures good gradient flow at the beginning of training and it allows us to train it on relatively long sequences.

We train the IRNN to classify a video by feeding the features for each frame from the CNN sequentially to the network and using the last time-step softmax output as class prediction. We used Stochastic Gradient Descent (SGD) with a learning rate of 0.005, gradient clipping at 1.0 and a batchsize of 64 sequences. We experimented by using different layers of the CNN as input features and chose the output of the second convolutional layer after max pooling, as this performed best on validation data.

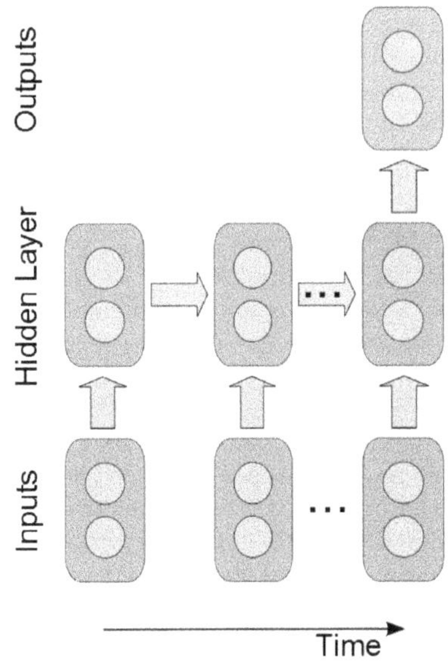

Figure 1: Structure of our recurrent neural network.

2.3 Aggregated CNN Features

As an alternative way of aggregating the frame level structural representations from the CNN, we employed k-average pooling together with an SVM for classification as in [16]. In this approach the per-frame CNN features are averaged into bins to generate a fixed length vector of size k as video representation. Heuristically, we selected $k = 15$ and we used the pre-softmax outputs of the CNN as per-frame features. For videos with a number of frames less than k the frames are locally repeated until sequence length is k.

The vector representations of videos together with corresponding emotion labels are used to train an RBF-kernel SVM. The hyper-parameters of the SVM are set via grid search. As shown in Table 1, the RNN achieves a validation accuracy of 39.6%, which is significantly higher than the aggregated CNN. Simple averaging of the per-frame probabilities yielded a validation accuracy of only 23.7%.

3. AUDIO

Given that the primary focus of this work is on vision based emotion recognition, we simply used the audio features employed in [7] for the audio channel of the video clips. These are based on the approach from [27]. It uses 1582 features extracted with the open-source Emotion and Affect Recognition (openEAR) [12] toolkit which uses openSMILE [11] as backend.

The toolkit encapsulates multiple low level audio feature descriptors (LLDs) and different functionals to apply on them. The feature set consists of 34 energy and spectral related LLDs and 21 functionals, 4 voicing related LLD × 19 functionals, 34 delta coefficients of energy and spectral LLD × 21 functionals, 4 delta coefficients of the voicing related LLD × 19 functionals and 2 voiced/unvoiced durational features.

In this work we used Principal Component Analysis (PCA) based dimensionality reduction as preprocessing on the 1582 dimensional input features and an RBF-kernel SVM for classification. The hyper-parameters for the SVM are set via grid search.

4. ACTIVITY

Spatio-temporal transformations of local image features, or activity, can be an important cue for emotion recognition. A subset of emotions can be represented as changes in facial expressions and in some cases the activity of the entire body of the person. Other approaches, based on vision, described in this work mainly deal with analyzing the emotion in a given video sequence based on static image features and different ways of aggregating them over time. The activity analysis pipeline is the only approach which relies on learning of local spatio-temporal transformations from video.

Our approach for activity analysis is based on the action recognition pipeline from [20, 23] which was also used for emotion recognition previously in [16]. The pipeline mainly consists of three different modules namely, local motion feature extraction, k-means quantization and SVM based classification. A Synchrony Autoencoder (SAE) [20] trained on cropped 3D video blocks of size $16 \times 16 \times 10$ ($space \times space \times time$) is used for local motion feature extraction. Figure 2 shows filters learned by the model on the AFEW 5.0 training set.

5. FUSION

In many discriminative tasks, the fusion of predictions or representations from models trained using different input modalities yields a significant improvement. We use two types of fusion approaches for combining the modality specific models described in previous sections, *feature level* and *decision level* fusion.

5.1 Feature Level

In this approach a combination of intermediate-level representations from the trained models is used as input for training an additional model on the classification task. For feature-level fusion we applied a variant of the regularized feature fusion network from [33]. The feature fusion network is a Multilayer Perceptron (MLP) with separate hidden layers for each modality as shown in Figure 3. The outputs of these layers are concatenated and fed to another hidden layer which is followed by a softmax layer whose number of units is equal to the number of emotion classes. The first layer of the fusion network, consisting of modality specific layers, is regularized to encourage a common representation by sharing similar subsets of hidden units between modalities, while still retaining the discriminative features present in some modalities.

The network is trained with SGD using a learning rate of 0.1 and gradient clipping using clipping threshold 10. The objective function is the categorical cross-entropy between target label and prediction. As input to the fusion network we used aggregated CNN per-frame features, the PCA-whitened audio features and the hidden layer activations of the last time-step of the RNN. We excluded the activity recognition model from the mix, as it tends to overfit its training set. We also explored adding dropout to the hidden layers to prevent over-fitting on the small challenge

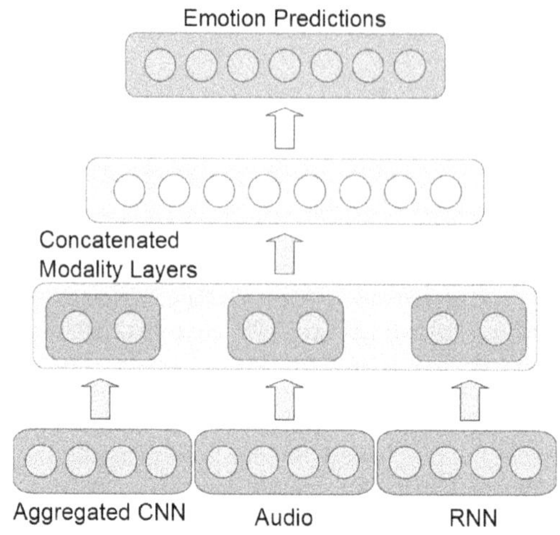

Figure 3: Structure of the feature fusion network.

dataset. The number of hidden layers and their sizes are selected using the validation set. Our best architecture has 100, 10 and 50 units in the aggregated CNN-, the audio- and the RNN-specific hidden layers, respectively. The common hidden layer has 70 units. The search space for determining the optimal size of the modality-specific layers was selected considering the input feature sizes and individual models' performances on the AFEW 5.0 validation set while training on the train set. More details are provided in Section 6.

5.2 Decision Level

For decision-level fusion, i.e. the combination of classifiers, we used a weighted sum of the class probabilities estimated by the modality-specific classifiers and the fusion network. The combined classifier has one weight per modality per class and the resulting score for each class is the weighted sum of all probabilities for the respective class. The combination weights are determined by random search [4], which was also used for model combination in the winning approach for the 2013 EmotiW challenge [18].

Weights are sampled uniformly from $[0.0, 1.0]$ followed by per class re-scaling, so that they sum up to 1. Then the best sampled weights are chosen based on the validation performance. Note that unless noted otherwise, we always use the dataset partition for the random search which was not used for model training, i.e. for models trained on the training set, we perform random search on the validation set and vice versa. After an initial random search with 100,000 iterations, we perform a local random search around the best set of weights found so far. This local random search consists of sampling weights from a Gaussian with mean set to the current best set of weights and standard deviation σ of 0.5. The current best $\tilde{w}$ is updated as soon as a new best is found. After every 100,000 iterations, the σ is decreased by a factor of 0.9 and the local search is stopped when σ is smaller than 0.0001. We also performed uniform local search from $[\tilde{w} - r, \tilde{w} + r]$, where $\tilde{w}$ is the current best set of weights and r is the range in which to search, however it roughly achieved the same performance. We explicitly tried all combinations of subsets of modalities and fusion. Consistently we found that decision level fusion benefited from including all models.

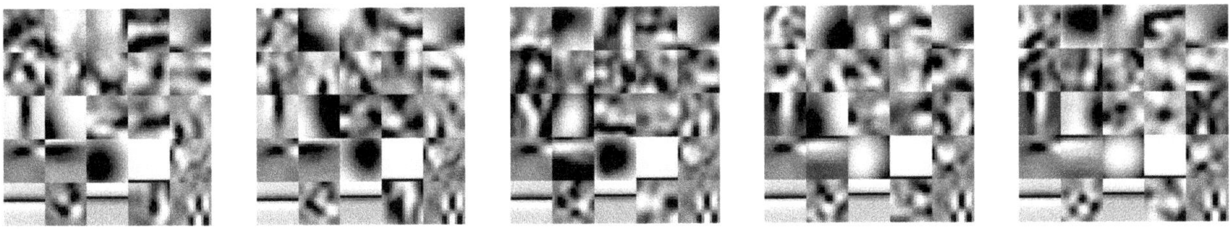

Figure 2: Subset of filters learned by SAE model on the AFEW5 training set. Left to right: Frames 1,3,5,7 and 9.

Table 1: Training and Validation Accuracies for All Modalities (Training on Train partition)

Model	Training	Validation
Activity	0.983	0.266
Audio	0.418	0.332
Aggregated CNN	0.505	0.350
RNN	0.848	**0.396**

6. RESULTS

In this section, we describe our submissions to the EmotiW 2015 challenge. We provide details on per model training strategies and variations of our fusion methods. We also present results and discuss the choices we made in each step.

6.1 Per-model Performance

This work mainly focuses on an RNN approach for visual features. However, given the challenge context we included three further models to achieve competitive performance. Table 1 shows each model's accuracy on the challenge validation set after training on the training set. The corresponding confusion matrices are presented in Figure 4. The matrices show different profiles and strengths for specific emotion classes which is beneficial for combination.

6.2 Feature Level Fusion

As mentioned before, we excluded the activity model from feature level fusion as it tends to over-fit on its training partition. This can be seen in Table 1 where activity has an extremely high discrepancy between training and validation accuracies. The input features to the fusion network are the following:

- The first ten components of the PCA whitened audio features (see Section 3).
- The aggregated CNN features, which are 105-dimensional (7×15 bins) vectors as described in Section 2.3.
- The RNN features, which are the hidden activations of the last time step. These are the only features which have been learned discriminatively on the video level and which therefore contribute strongly to the fusion network. The number of hidden units in the RNN is 200 (see Section 2.2).

For training the fusion network, we tried replacing the sigmoid activation function of the hidden layers with rectified linear units $ReLU(x) = max(0, x)$ and rectified tanh units $RectTanh(x) = max(0, tanh(x))$. While this improved the validation performance by roughly 2%, it did not yield an improvement on the test performance. One observation during training was that the learning curves were oscillating which made the early stopping unreliable. To stabilize the learning, we lowered the learning rate to 0.001 from 0.1 and added momentum of 0.9. Figure 5 compares two learning curves before and after stabilization. The number of epochs in each sub-figure corresponds to the selected learning rate. Our fusion network achieves a validation accuracy of 43.7%, which is higher than any modality-specific classifier.

6.3 Submissions

Our submissions can be divided into two categories: those which use the training set for training and the validation set for early stopping and random search and those for which the training and validation sets were swapped. For both of these categories, we also submitted a version where models were retrained on the full training plus validation set, retaining all hyper-parameters including early stopping epoch number and combination weights. Note that the models that are CNN-based have also been retrained but not the underlying CNN as we used additional static emotion data for training. For all submissions, random search was done on the data partition that was not used for training the underlying models. For example, if models were trained on the training partition, random search was performed on the validation set. Searching on the same partition that the models were trained on was not an option, as random search would assign high weights to the over-fitters, which would result in poor generalization performance.

Table 2 lists our submissions with their training, validation and test accuracies. In the first category we trained modality-specific models and the fusion network on the challenge training data and validation data was used for early stopping. Then for the final predictions we performed random search on the validation set. This achieved a test set accuracy of 44.341%. With the stabilized fusion network the accuracy improved to 48.979%. Retraining the models with the combined training plus validation set, keeping the hyper-parameters of experiment 2, yielded a test accuracy of 50.463%.

In the second category, with swapped training and validation sets, our initial submission achieved a test accuracy of 50.092%. Here the stabilized fusion did not improve the performance, yielding a test accuracy of 47.680%. The retrained version achieved our best result of 52.875%. Note that for each category we picked the best submission for retraining. Random search as the last step in our pipeline has a big influence on the generalization potential of the whole

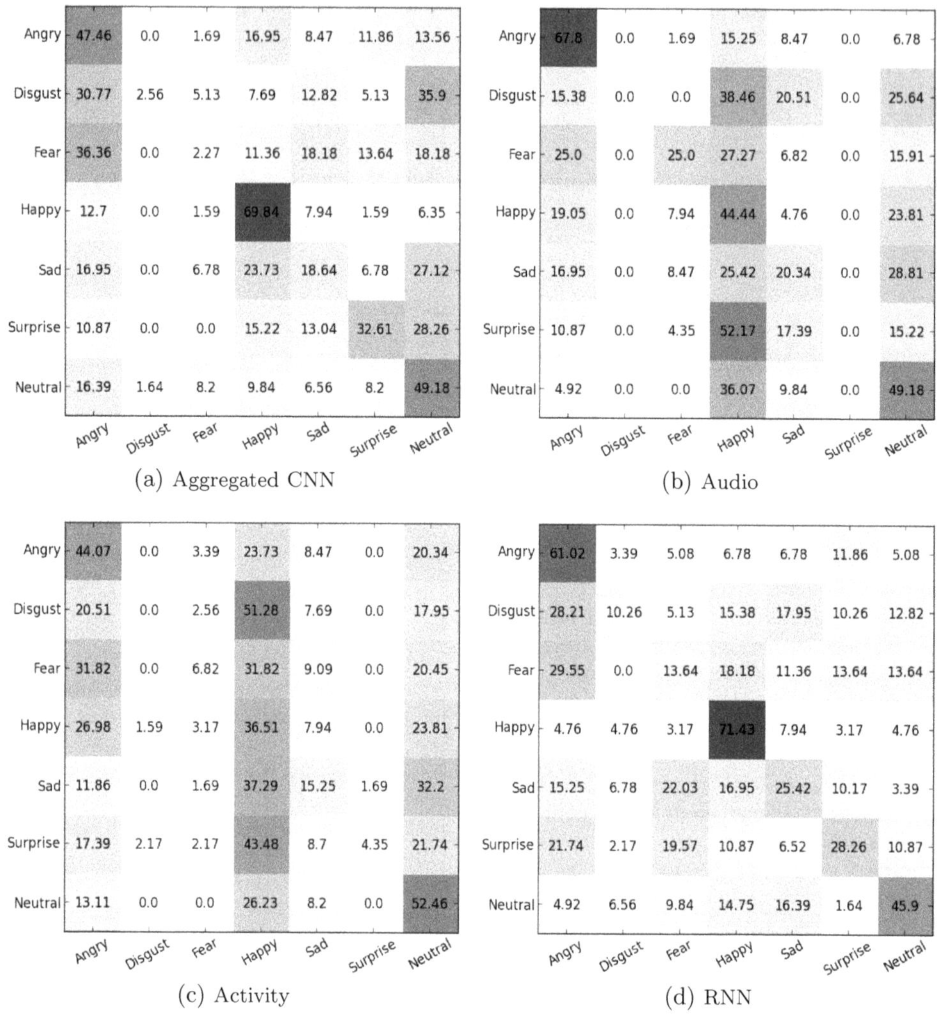

Figure 4: Confusion matrices on the challenge validation set.

Table 2: Our submissions with training, validation and test accuracies (in percent) for the EmotiW 2015 competition (bold font shows the best accuracy)

Sub	Train	Valid	Test	Method
1	86.216	54.716	44.341	Training on Train, Validation on Valid
2	81.997	54.447	48.979	Training on Train, Validation on Valid, stable fusion
3	-	-	50.463	Training on Train+Val, hyperparams from submission 2, stable fusion
4	52.320	71.967	50.092	Training on Val, Validation on Train
5	52.742	68.463	47.680	Training on Val, Validation on Train, stable fusion
6	-	-	**52.875**	Training on Train+Val, hyperparams from submission 4
7	-	-	49.907	Random Search over combinations of submission 3 and 6 on Train+Val

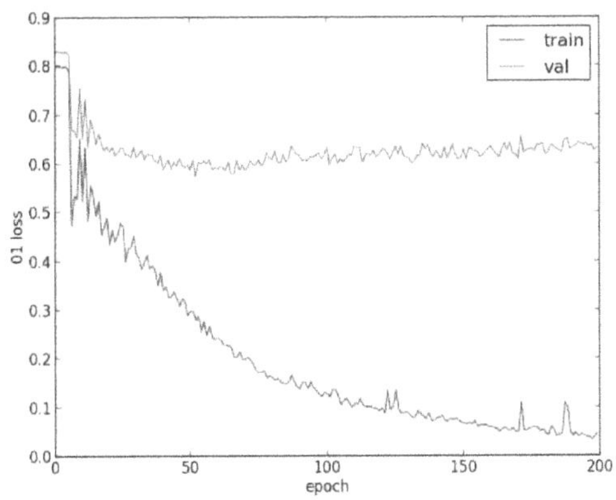

(a)

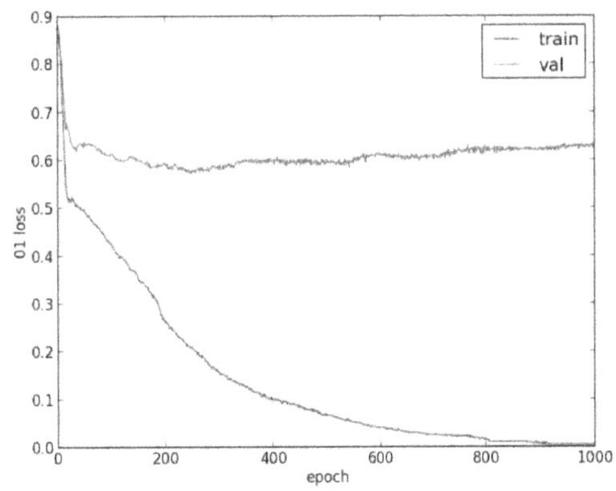

(b)

Figure 5: Comparison of the learning curves (a) before and (b) after stabilization.

model and likely benefits from the larger training set. This explains the higher performance of the swapped partitions.

Our last submission was an attempt to combine our two best submissions that were retrained on the training plus validation set. We combined those two using the same decision-level fusion strategy as before. The inputs to the random search were the probabilities predicted by the two models. A random search on these two models was performed on the full training plus validation set. The resulting test performance was only 49.907%. This might be explained by the fact that the whole data set has been seen which could have led to over-fitting.

7. CONCLUSIONS

We found that the spatio-temporal evolution of facial features is one of the strongest cues for emotion recognition. We presented the application of an RNN for modelling this spatio-temporal evolution via aggregation of facial features to perform emotion recognition in video. Our experiments in Section 2.3 have shown that this approach outperforms all other modalities, the averaging of per-frame vision-based classifications, and also the more sophisticated aggregation method employed by the 2013 challenge winners [18].

Furthermore, we explore two fusion methods, operating on the feature and on the decision level. Our feature-level fusion network combines features from different modalities and achieves a higher validation accuracy than any of the single-modality classifiers. Our experiments show that feature-level and decision-level fusion are complementary, and when combined they achieve a higher classification accuracy. However, care needs to be taken to prevent over-fitting, either by excluding strong over-fitters, as we did with the activity recognition model in the fusion network, or by using different dataset partitions for combination than for model training, as done in the random search.

We found it difficult to draw conclusions from some of our submission results. This might be caused by the large number of ambiguous cases that exist in this domain. We found that a fairly large number of training videos could be argued to show a mixture of two or more basic emotions (such as a mixture of surprise with fear or happy). This suggests that exploring the use of more than a single label for emotion recognition might be a useful direction for future research.

8. ACKNOWLEDGMENTS

The authors would like to thank the developers of Theano [3, 5]. This work was supported by an NSERC Discovery Award and the German BMBF, project 01GQ0841. We also thank the Canadian Foundation for Innovation (CFI) for support under the Leaders program.

9. REFERENCES

[1] M. Baccouche, F. Mamalet, C. Wolf, C. Garcia, and A. Baskurt. Sequential deep learning for human action recognition. In A. Salah and B. Lepri, editors, *Human Behavior Understanding*, volume 7065 of *Lecture Notes in Computer Science*, pages 29–39. Springer Berlin Heidelberg, 2011.

[2] D. Bahdanau, K. Cho, and Y. Bengio. Neural machine translation by jointly learning to align and translate. *CoRR*, abs/1409.0473, 2014.

[3] F. Bastien, P. Lamblin, R. Pascanu, J. Bergstra, I. Goodfellow, A. Bergeron, N. Bouchard, D. Warde-Farley, and Y. Bengio. Theano: new features and speed improvements. *arXiv preprint arXiv:1211.5590*, 2012.

[4] J. Bergstra and Y. Bengio. Random search for hyper-parameter optimization. *The Journal of Machine Learning Research*, 13(1):281–305, 2012.

[5] J. Bergstra, O. Breuleux, F. Bastien, P. Lamblin, R. Pascanu, G. Desjardins, J. Turian, D. Warde-Farley, and Y. Bengio. Theano: a cpu and gpu math expression compiler. In *Proceedings of the Python for scientific computing conference (SciPy)*, volume 4, page 3. Austin, TX, 2010.

[6] P.-L. Carrier, A. Courville, I. J. Goodfellow, M. Mirza, and Y. Bengio. FER-2013 Face Database. Technical report, 1365, Université de Montréal, 2013.

[7] A. Dhall, R. Goecke, J. Joshi, K. Sikka, and T. Gedeon. Emotion recognition in the wild challenge 2014: Baseline, data and protocol. In *Proceedings of*

the 16th International Conference on Multimodal Interaction, ICMI '14, pages 461–466, New York, NY, USA, 2014. ACM.
[8] A. Dhall, R. Goecke, S. Lucey, and T. Gedeon. Collecting large, richly annotated facial-expression databases from movies. *MultiMedia, IEEE*, 19(3):34–41, July 2012.
[9] A. Dhall, O. V. R. Murthy, R. Goecke, J. Joshi, and T. Gedeon. Video and image based emotion recognition challenges in the wild: Emotiw 2015. In *Proceedings of the 17th ACM on International Conference on Multimodal Interaction*, ICMI '15, 2015.
[10] J. Donahue, L. A. Hendricks, S. Guadarrama, M. Rohrbach, S. Venugopalan, K. Saenko, and T. Darrell. Long-term recurrent convolutional networks for visual recognition and description. 2014.
[11] F. Eyben, M. Wöllmer, and B. Schuller. Opensmile: the munich versatile and fast open-source audio feature extractor. In *Proceedings of the international conference on Multimedia*, pages 1459–1462. ACM, 2010.
[12] F. Eyben, M. Wöllmer, and B. Schuller. openear - introducing the munich open-source emotion and affect recognition toolkit. In *ACII*, pages 576–581, 2009.
[13] A. Graves, A.-r. Mohamed, and G. Hinton. Speech recognition with deep recurrent neural networks. In *Acoustics, Speech and Signal Processing (ICASSP), 2013 IEEE International Conference on*, pages 6645–6649. IEEE, 2013.
[14] A. Graves and J. Schmidhuber. Offline handwriting recognition with multidimensional recurrent neural networks. In *Advances in Neural Information Processing Systems*, pages 545–552, 2009.
[15] S. Hochreiter and J. Schmidhuber. Long short-term memory. *Neural computation*, 9(8):1735–1780, 1997.
[16] S. E. Kahou, X. Bouthillier, P. Lamblin, C. Gulcehre, V. Michalski, K. Konda, S. Jean, P. Froumenty, Y. Dauphin, N. Boulanger-Lewandowski, R. Chandias Ferrari, M. Mirza, D. Warde-Farley, A. Courville, P. Vincent, R. Memisevic, C. Pal, and Y. Bengio. Emonets: Multimodal deep learning approaches for emotion recognition in video. *Journal on Multimodal User Interfaces*, pages 1–13, 2015.
[17] S. E. Kahou, P. Froumenty, and C. Pal. Facial expression analysis based on high dimensional binary features. In *ECCV Workshop on Computer Vision with Local Binary Patterns Variants*, Zurich, Switzerland, 2014.
[18] S. E. Kahou, C. Pal, X. Bouthillier, P. Froumenty, C. Gulcehre, R. Memisevic, P. Vincent, A. Courville, Y. Bengio, R. C. Ferrari, M. Mirza, S. Jean, P.-L. Carrier, Y. Dauphin, N. Boulanger-Lewandowski, A. Aggarwal, J. Zumer, P. Lamblin, J.-P. Raymond, G. Desjardins, R. Pascanu, D. Warde-Farley, A. Torabi, A. Sharma, E. Bengio, M. Côté, K. R. Konda, and Z. Wu. Combining modality specific deep neural networks for emotion recognition in video. In *Proceedings of the 15th ACM on International Conference on Multimodal Interaction*, ICMI '13, 2013.
[19] N. Kalchbrenner, E. Grefenstette, and P. Blunsom. A convolutional neural network for modelling sentences. *arXiv:1404.2188*, 2014.
[20] K. R. Konda, R. Memisevic, and V. Michalski. Learning to encode motion using spatio-temporal synchrony. In *Proceedings of ICLR*, April 2014.
[21] A. Krizhevsky. Cuda-convnet Google code home page. `https://code.google.com/p/cuda-convnet/`, Aug. 2012.
[22] A. Krizhevsky, I. Sutskever, and G. E. Hinton. Imagenet classification with deep convolutional neural networks. In *Advances in neural information processing systems*, pages 1097–1105, 2012.
[23] Q. Le, W. Zou, S. Yeung, and A. Ng. Learning hierarchical invariant spatio-temporal features for action recognition with independent subspace analysis. In *CVPR*, 2011.
[24] Q. V. Le, N. Jaitly, and G. E. Hinton. A simple way to initialize recurrent networks of rectified linear units. *arXiv preprint arXiv:1504.00941*, 2015.
[25] M. Liu, R. Wang, S. Li, S. Shan, Z. Huang, and X. Chen. Combining multiple kernel methods on riemannian manifold for emotion recognition in the wild. In *Proceedings of the 16th International Conference on Multimodal Interaction*, ICMI '14, pages 494–501, New York, NY, USA, 2014. ACM.
[26] Nagadomi. Github: kaggle-cifar10-torch7. `https://github.com/nagadomi/kaggle-cifar10-torch7/`, 2014.
[27] B. Schuller, M. Valstar, F. Eyben, G. McKeown, R. Cowie, and M. Pantic. Avec 2011–the first international audio/visual emotion challenge. In *Affective Computing and Intelligent Interaction*, pages 415–424. Springer, 2011.
[28] C. Shan, S. Gong, and P. W. McOwan. Facial expression recognition based on local binary patterns: A comprehensive study. *Image Vision Comput.*, 27(6):803–816, May 2009.
[29] K. Simonyan and A. Zisserman. Very deep convolutional networks for large-scale image recognition. *CoRR*, abs/1409.1556, 2014.
[30] Y. Sun, X. Wang, and X. Tang. Deep convolutional network cascade for facial point detection. In *Proceedings of the 2013 IEEE Conference on Computer Vision and Pattern Recognition*, CVPR '13, pages 3476–3483, Washington, DC, USA, 2013. IEEE Computer Society.
[31] J. Susskind, A. Anderson, and G. Hinton. The toronto face database. Technical report, UTML TR 2010-001, University of Toronto, 2010.
[32] I. Sutskever, O. Vinyals, and Q. V. Le. Sequence to sequence learning with neural networks. In *Advances in neural information processing systems*, pages 3104–3112, 2014.
[33] Z. Wu, X. Wang, Y.-G. Jiang, H. Ye, and X. Xue. Modeling spatial-temporal clues in a hybrid deep learning framework for video classification. *arXiv preprint arXiv:1504.01561*, 2015.

Multiple Models Fusion for Emotion Recognition in the Wild

Jianlong Wu[1], Zhouchen Lin[1,2], Hongbin Zha[1]
[1]Key Laboratory of Machine Perception (MOE), School of EECS, Peking University, Beijing 100871, P. R. China
[2]Cooperative Medianet Innovation Center, Shanghai Jiao Tong University, Shanghai 200240, P. R. China
{jlwu1992, zlin}@pku.edu.cn, zha@cis.pku.edu.cn

ABSTRACT

Emotion recognition in the wild is a very challenging task. In this paper, we propose a multiple models fusion method to automatically recognize the expression in the video clip as part of the third Emotion Recognition in the Wild Challenge (EmotiW 2015). In our method, we first extract dense SIFT, LBP-TOP and audio features from each video clip. For dense SIFT features, we use the bag of features (BoF) model with two different encoding methods (locality-constrained linear coding and group saliency based coding) to further represent it. During the classification process, we use partial least square regression to calculate the regression value of each model. By learning the optimal weight of each model based on the regression value, we fuse these models together. We conduct experiments on the given validation and test datasets, and achieve superior performance. The best recognition accuracy of our fusion method is 52.50% on the test dataset, which is 13.17% higher than the challenge baseline accuracy of 39.33%.

Categories and Subject Descriptors

I.5.4 [**Pattern Recognition**]: Applications; I.4.m [**Image Processing and Computer Vision**]: [Miscellaneous]

Keywords

Emotion Recognition; Multiple Models Fusion; Bag of Features; EmotiW 2015 Challenge

1. INTRODUCTION

Automatic facial expression recognition has become a hot research topic in computer vision because of its significant role in many applications, such as psychological research and human computer interaction (HCI). The primary task of emotion recognition is to classify the given facial images or videos into seven basic expression types, such as angry (AN), disgust (DI), fear (FE), happy (HA), neutral (NE), sad (SA) and surprise (SU). A variety of methods have been proposed towards this problem during the past decade. One may refer to [24] and [33] for a comprehensive survey. However, most existing works focus on expression recognition from static facial images [35, 21, 18]. When it comes to video based emotion recognition or expression recognition in the wild, the recognition results of previous methods are not very satisfactory. Compared with static facial images based emotion recognition, dynamic images based emotion recognition is more complicated.

In recent years, several emotion recognition competitions such as Audio Video Emotion Challenges (AVEC) [25] and Emotion Recognition in the Wild (EmotiW) [4, 6] greatly promoted the development of video based expression recognition. A few methods have been proposed to automatically recognize expression from video clips. For instance, Zhao et al. [34] used LBP-TOP to extract patterns from dynamic facial image sequences. Kahou et al. [11] proposed a deep neural networks based method for emotion recognition. Sikka et al. [22] fused multiple features using multiple kernel learning. Liu et al. [14] represented image set models of video clip with Riemannian kernels. By fusing multiple features through different approach, these methods achieved the state-of-the-art performance.

As these video clips contain rich spatio-temporal information, it is of great importance for video based emotion recognition to combine multiple visual and acoustical features. Feature extraction and classification are two critical processes for recognition. It is vital to select appropriate feature extraction methods and classification combination method. For feature extraction, as LBP-TOP [34] features are robust to variations of grayscale and dense SIFT [16] features are invariant to scale and rotation transformation, we extract both LBP-TOP [34] and dense SIFT [16] features from each video clip. For audio information, we use openSMILE [7] to extract audio features. While the extracted dense SIFT [16] features are redundant and high-dimensional, we adopt bag of features (BoF) [2] model to further represent the SIFT [16] features. According to [32] and [9], both locality and saliency are very essential for image feature encoding. Therefore, we use two corresponding types of encoding methods in BoF to encode features, respectively. During the classification process, compared with feature level and prediction level fusion, score level fusion can better capture the contribution of each model and is more effective. So we first use partial least square regression to calculate the regression value as the score, and then learn the optimal coefficients to fuse these models. Based on above characteristics, in this paper, we construct a multiple

ICMI 2015, November 9–13, 2015, Seattle, WA, USA.
© 2015 ACM. ISBN 978-1-4503-3912-4/15/11 ...$15.00.
DOI: http://dx.doi.org/10.1145/2818346.2830582.

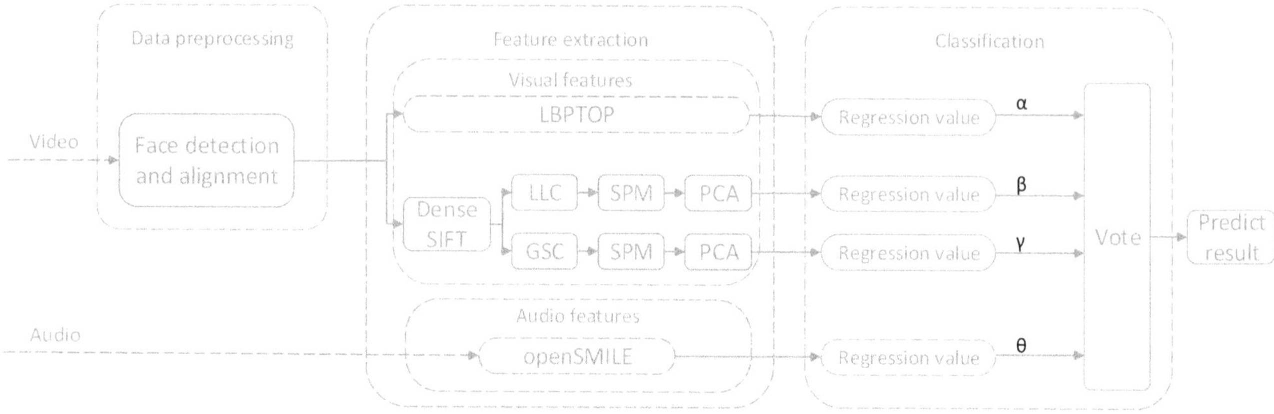

Figure 1: Framework of the proposed multiple models fusion method.

models fusion method for video based emotion recognition in the wild. The proposed method can extract discriminative features for video representation and commendably fuse them for classification.

The rest of this paper is organized as follows. We first introduce the details of BoF model and extracted features in Section 2. Then we present the regression method and our multiple models fusion method in Section 3. In Section 4, we conduct emotion recognition experiments on the given dataset. Finally, Section 5 concludes our paper.

2. VIDEO REPRESENTATION

2.1 Visual Features Extracted with BoF

In this subsection, we first introduce the pipeline of commonly used BoF [2]. Then we present the detailed processes of dense SIFT [16] features extraction and two kinds of encoding methods used in this paper.

2.1.1 The BoF Framework

BoF [2] is one of the most popular and effective image classification frameworks in the recent literature. It is developed from the bag-of-words model in document analysis [10] and has achieved the state-of-the-art performance in many classification tasks, including emotion recognition [23]. As shown in Figure 2, the commonly used BoF framework generally consists of the following three basic modules:

1. **Local features extraction:** In this module, we first divide each input image into many landmark points or dense overlapped patches, and then extract local features such as SIFT [16], HoG [3], and LBP [19] from each block or key point to represent the image. In this paper, we extract SIFT features from dense blocks to represent the facial expression image first.

2. **Descriptors encoding:** Based on the local features of the previous step, we learn a dictionary with the classical K-means [15] clustering algorithm. Each descriptor is encoded into a code vector with codewords in the codebook. By utilizing different encoding methods such as sparse coding [31], saliency coding [8], and LLC [27], we can acquire code vectors with different properties. For a literature survey on encoding methods, one can refer to [12] and [9]. In this paper, we use LLC [27] and GSC [29] to code the descriptors, respectively.

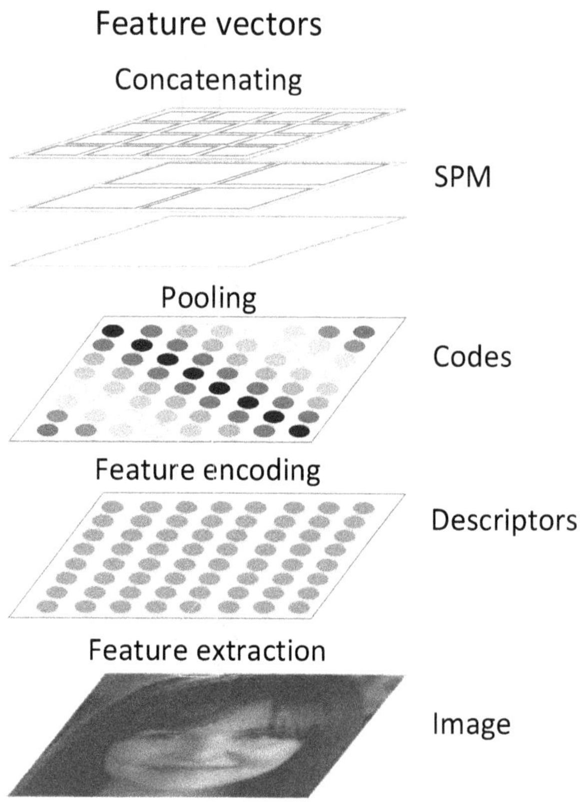

Figure 2: Basic pipeline of the BoF framework.

3. **Spatial pyramid pooling:** In this step, the spatial pyramid matching (SPM) [13] method partitions the image into increasingly finer spatial subregions. Then, pooling process integrates all responses on each codeword in a specific subregion into one value. Max pooling [31] and average pooling [2] are two main pooling methods. We adopt max pooling [31] in this paper. By pooling code vectors in each spatial subregion across different spatial scales, we obtain the local description of every block. The final representation of the image is obtained by concatenating descriptions of all blocks.

2.1.2 Dense SIFT

Scale Invariant Feature Transform (SIFT) [16] is wildly used for feature extraction and image representation. It first detects and selects appropriate keypoints over all scales and image locations, and then computes features in the region around each keypoint. The extracted features are invariant to image scale and rotation. For dense SIFT, we first divide the image into many overlapped grid blocks with a fixed step size, and then compute features on each block. Compared with the original SIFT, dense SIFT does not need to detect keypoints any longer, but the dimension of the extracted features are relatively high. In this case, we adopt BoF [2] for deeper representation.

2.1.3 LLC

Let $X = [x_1, x_2, \cdots, x_N] \in \mathbb{R}^{D\times N}$ be a set of D-dimensional local features extracted from an image. $B = [b_1, b_2, \cdots, b_M] \in \mathbb{R}^{D\times M}$ denotes the codebook with M codewords. Encoded by an encoding algorithm, local features X is converted to N coding vectors $C = [c_1, c_2, \cdots, c_N] \in \mathbb{R}^{M\times N}$.

The core idea of locality-constrained linear coding (LLC) [27] is to reconstruct features with codewords via resolving a least square based optimization problem with locality constraints on the codewords. The objective function of LLC is listed as follows:

$$\begin{aligned}&\arg\min_C \sum_{i=1}^{N}(\|x_i - Bc_i\|^2 + \lambda\|d_i \odot c_i\|^2),\\ &s.t.\ \ \mathbf{1}^T c_i = 1, \forall i,\end{aligned} \tag{1}$$

where $\mathbf{1} \in \mathbb{R}^{M\times 1}$ is a column vector of all ones, $\odot$ denotes the element-wise multiplication and $d_i = \exp(\frac{\text{dist}(x_i,B)}{\sigma}) \in \mathbb{R}^M$ is the locality adaptor. Specifically, $\text{dist}(x_i, B) = [\|x_i - b_1\|_2, \cdots, \|x_i - b_M\|_2]^T$. σ is used for adjusting the weight decay speed. The problem defined in Eq. (1) has a closed-form solution:

$$\begin{aligned}&\hat{c_i} = ((B^T - \mathbf{1}x_i^T)(B^T - \mathbf{1}x_i^T)^T + \lambda \text{diag}^2(d_i))^{-1}\mathbf{1},\\ &c_i = \hat{c_i}/(\mathbf{1}^T\hat{c_i}).\end{aligned} \tag{2}$$

As the solution of LLC only has a few significant values, we can simply use the $K(K < D < M)$ nearest neighbours of x_i in the codebook as the local base $\tilde{B}$ to reconstruct the descriptor x_i, which can speed up the coding process.

2.1.4 GSC

Different from reconstruction based coding method LLC, group saliency coding (GSC) [29] is developed from the saliency based coding [8]. As we use max pooling method to process those encoded features, we believe that saliency is very important for feature coding. We first select K codewords groups for each descriptor x. For each group, GSC [29] calculates the saliency response $\psi^k(x)$, which is then fed back to all the codewords in the group. The final coding result of a feature on each codeword is the maximum response across different group sizes. The computing process of GSC can be formulated as follows:

$$\begin{aligned}&c_i = \max_k\{s_i^k\}, k = 1, 2, \cdots, K,\\ &s_i^k = \begin{cases}\psi^k(x), & \text{if } b_i \in g(x, n_k),\\ 0, & \text{otherwise},\end{cases}\\ &\psi^k(x) = \sum_{j=1}^{K+1-k}(\|x - \tilde{b}_{k+j}\|_2 - \|x - \tilde{b}_k\|_2),\end{aligned} \tag{3}$$

where s_i^k is the coding result for the kth group and $g(x, n_k)$ denotes the n_k closest codewords set of x for the kth group.

2.1.5 Dimension Reduction

After feature extraction of the BoF [2] model, the dimension of extracted feature vectors is very high, especially when the number of spatial pyramids levels is large. High dimensional features will influence both the efficiency and accuracy of classification. In this case, it is necessary to reduce the dimension of features before classification. We use the classical principle component analysis (PCA) [17] for dimension reduction. The core idea of PCA [17] is to maximize the total variance of projection.

2.2 Visual Features Extracted with LBP-TOP

Local Binary Patterns from Three Orthogonal Planes (LBP-TOP) [34], an extension of the widely used LBP [19] operator, is proposed to handle the influence of varying rotation and lighting condition on dynamic textures. This method considers only the co-occurrence statistics of dynamic textures in three directions, concatenating LBP on three orthogonal planes: XY, XT, and YT, where the XY plane provides the spatial texture information, and the XT and YT planes provide information about the spacetime transitions. Features of LBP-TOP [34] are robust to gray-scale and rotations variations. It has been successfully applied to video facial expression recognition while the video can be regarded as a sequence of dynamic facial expression images. We adopt LBP-TOP to extract video features for video based expression recognition.

2.3 Audio Features

Audio information plays an important role in video based emotion recognition [1]. We use the openSMILE toolkit [7], an open-source feature extractor that unites feature extraction algorithms from the speech processing and the Music Information Retrieval communities, to extract audio features. We use 21 energy & spectral related functionals and 19 voicing related functionals to extract corresponding low-level descriptors and delta regression coefficients. By adding 2 voiced/unvoiced durational features, there are 1582 dimensional features in total. For detailed information, please refer to [4].

3. FUSION OF MULTIPLE MODELS

The framework of our proposed method is shown in Figure 1. We first construct four different models to extract features from each facial expression video. For classification, we use the partial least square regression (PLSR) [28] to calculate the regression value of each test sample. Based on the regression value of these four models, we learn the optimal coefficients to fuse them. The final predicted label is the category with the maximum fusion regression value.

Table 1: **Performance comparisons of different methods on both validation and test datasets. BoF^{LLC} stands for the LLC based BoF method and BoF^{GSC} stands for the GSC based BoF method.**

Methods		Accuracy Val	Accuracy Test
Baseline (LBP-TOP)		36.08%	39.33%
Audio	Audio	33.96%	-
Video	BoF^{LLC}	47.44%	-
	BoF^{GSC}	45.82%	-
	LBP-TOP+BoF^{LLC}+BoF^{GSC}	48.52%	-
Audio+ Video	Audio+LBP-TOP+BoF^{LLC}+BoF^{GSC}	49.87%	49.35%
	Audio+LBP-TOP+BoF^{LLC}+BoF^{GSC} (Customized)	-	52.50%

3.1 Partial Least Squares Regression

We adopt the same PLSR manner as that in [14]. For each category, we design an one-vs-all PLSR to calculate the regression value. Let X be feature variables and Y be the 0-1 labels. According to [20], PLSR decomposes these variables into:

$$\begin{aligned} X &= TP^T + E, \\ Y &= UQ^T + F, \end{aligned} \tag{4}$$

where T and U contain the extracted score vectors, P and Q are orthogonal loading matrices, and E and F are residuals. PLSR tries to find the optimal weights w_x and w_y to get the maximum covariance such that:

$$[cov(t, u)]^2 = \max_{|w_x|=|w_y|=1} [cov(Xw_x, Yw_y)]^2. \tag{5}$$

Then we can get the regression coefficients B as:

$$B = X^T U (T^T X X^T U)^{-1} T^T Y. \tag{6}$$

The regression value can be estimated by:

$$V = XB. \tag{7}$$

Following the above process, we can calculate the regression value of test samples for each class.

3.2 Fusion Strategy

For each of these four kinds of feature extraction models (audio, LBP-TOP, LLC based BoF and GSC based BoF), we utilize the PLSR to calculate its corresponding regression value, respectively. Then we adopt the score level fusion method and assign specific weight to each of four previous models:

$$V^{fusion} = \alpha V^{audio} + \beta V^{LBP-TOP} + \gamma V^{LLC} + \theta V^{GSC}, \tag{8}$$

where V represents the regression value. The weight which varies from model to model is relevant to the performance of each model. We learn the optimal weights on the validation dataset.

4. EXPERIMENTS

4.1 Dataset and Parameter Setting

We evaluate the performance of the proposed method on the given AFEW 5.0 dataset [5, 6], which includes 723 train video clips, 383 validation video clips and 539 test video clips. All these video clips are collected from movies that show close-to-real-world conditions. Figure 3 shows example images of seven expressions taken from video clips.

Figure 3: Some example frames of expression videos in the wild.

For each video clip, organizers apply pre-trained face models [36] for face detection and initialization. Then, the intraface tracking library [30] is adopted to align the detected facial images. Each facial image is aligned to size 128×128. LBP-TOP [34] features are extracted from non-overlapping spatial 4×4 blocks [6]. We directly use the aligned facial images as well as the extracted audio and LBP-TOP features provided by organizers. During the process of BoF based feature extraction, we set the parameters as follows. We divide each facial image into overlapped blocks with step 1 and size 16×16. For each block, we use Vlfeat [26] to extract 128-dimensional SIFT features. The dictionary is learned by the K-means [15] clustering algorithm with 1024 centres. Both the nearest neighbours number for LLC [27] and groups number for GSC [29] are set to 5. During the pooling process, we employ the SPM with levels of $[1\times1, 2\times2, 4\times4, 8\times8]$. Under the above settings, dimension of the final BoF representation for each frame is $1024 \times 85 = 87040$. We adopt max pooling to process all the frames of each video to get the video representation. We further use PCA [17] to reduce dimension with principle components ratio 97%. For the fusion process, we set the optimal weights as $\alpha = 0.25$, $\beta = 0.15$, $\gamma = 1.00$ and $\theta = 0.50$, which is learned on the validation dataset.

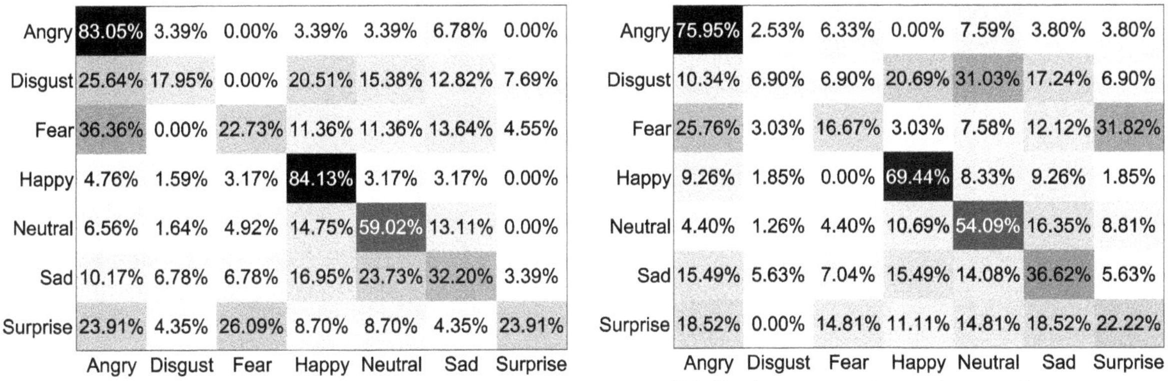

(a) Confusion matrix on the validation dataset

(b) Confusion matrix on the test dataset

Figure 4: Confusion matrices of multiple models fusion method for facial expressions on both validation and test datasets.

4.2 Results

In Table 1, we present the recognition results of our proposed method. Our proposed method achieves competitive results. The baseline recognition rates given by the EmotiW 2015 organizers on validation dataset and test dataset are 36.08% and 39.33%, respectively. We first test the performance of all the single model on the validation dataset. Among these single models, LLC based BoF achieves the best result, with accuracy 47.44%, while the recognition rate of GSC based BoF is 45.82% on the validation dataset. Both BoF models get satisfactory results. For video only emotion recognition, we fuse the regression values of these three video image set based methods (LBP-TOP, LLC based BoF and GSC based BoF), and achieve 48.52% accuracy. Finally, we fuse all the single models with optimal weights. The recognition rate is further improved to 49.87%, which is 13.79% higher than that of the baseline. On the test dataset, our proposed multiple models fusion method achieves 49.35%, which largely surpasses the baseline. For the customized method shown in Table 1, we will explain it in Section 4.3.

Figure 4 shows the confusion matrices of our multiple models fusion method on both validation and test datasets. From these two matrices, we can easily find that angry, happy and neutral expressions are easily to be recognized correctly, while other expressions such as disgust, fear, sad and surprise are more likely to be misclassified.

4.3 Discussion

According to the confusion matrix (computed by the challenge organizers) on the test dataset shown in Figure 4(b), it is difficult to recognize surprise expression, and fear expression samples are easily misclassified to surprise. Few train samples of surprise and high correlation between surprise and fear may account for this phenomenon. We need to note that total sample numbers of fear and surprise expressions on the test dataset are 66 and 26, respectively. By analyzing the statistics in Figure 4(b), we further customize our method slightly. For predicted surprise expression, we use the category with the second largest fusion regression value instead of the largest value as the predicted label. The corresponding recognition result is shown in Figure 5, and the overall recognition accuracy become 52.5%. Comparing the result in Figure 5 with that in Figure 4(b), we can easily see that the improvement of customized method mainly lies in the fact that more than 22% of fear samples, which are misclassified before, are classified correctly this time.

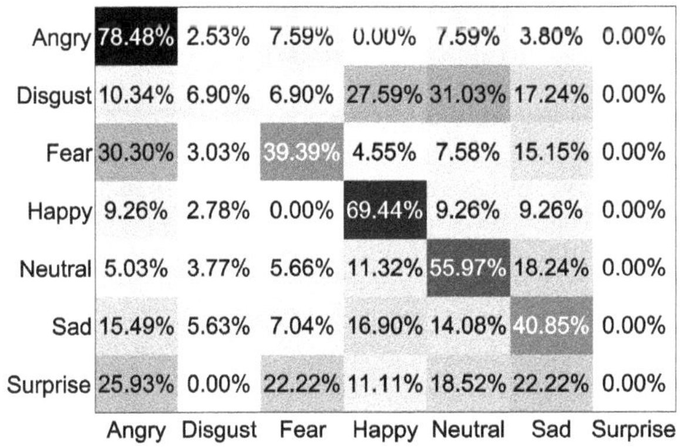

Figure 5: Confusion matrix of customized method on the test dataset.

5. CONCLUSIONS

In this paper, we propose a multiple models fusion method for video based emotion recognition in the wild. We first extract audio features from the video clips. Then dense SIFT and LBP-TOP visual features are extracted from aligned facial image set of each clip. For dense SIFT features, we further use LLC based BoF and GSC based BoF models to represent them. In the classification process, we first use partial least square regression to calculate the regression value of each single model, and then fuse these models together with the optimal coefficients based on the regression values. We validate the performance of our proposed method on the AFEW 5.0 dataset as part of the third Emotion Recognition in the Wild Challenge (EmotiW 2015). Our method achieves excellent performances on both validation and test datasets. As feature extraction and classification are two key processes for video based emotion recognition, in the future, on the one hand, we will further investigate and mine the connection between frames of video clip. On the other hand, we will try to find effective multi-model fusion method for classification.

6. ACKNOWLEDGMENTS

Z. Lin is supported by National Basic Research Program of China (973 Program) (grant no. 2015CB352502), National Natural Science Foundation of China (NSFC) (grant nos. 61272341 and 61231002), and Microsoft Research Asia Collaborative Research Program. H. Zha is supported by 973 Program (grant no. 2011CB302202).

7. REFERENCES

[1] C. Busso, Z. Deng, S. Yildirim, M. Bulut, C. M. Lee, A. Kazemzadeh, S. Lee, U. Neumann, and S. Narayanan. Analysis of emotion recognition using facial expressions, speech and multimodal information. In *Proceedings of the ACM International Conference on Multimodal Interfaces*, pages 205–211, 2004.

[2] G. Csurka, C. Dance, L. Fan, J. Willamowski, and C. Bray. Visual categorization with bags of keypoints. In *Proceedings of European Conference Computer Vision Workshop on Statistical Learning in Computer Vision*, pages 1–2, 2004.

[3] N. Dalal and B. Triggs. Histograms of oriented gradients for human detection. In *Proceedings of the IEEE Conference on Computer Vision and Pattern Recognition (CVPR)*, pages 886–893, 2005.

[4] A. Dhall, R. Goecke, J. Joshi, K. Sikka, and T. Gedeon. Emotion recognition in the wild challenge 2014: Baseline, data and protocol. In *Proceedings of the ACM International Conference on Multimodal Interaction (ICMI)*, pages 461–466, 2014.

[5] A. Dhall, R. Goecke, S. Lucey, and T. Gedeon. Collecting large, richly annotated facial-expression databases from movies. *IEEE Transactions on Multimedia*, 19(3):34–41, 2012.

[6] A. Dhall, O. R. Murthy, R. Goecke, J. Joshi, and T. Gedeon. Video and image based emotion recognition challenges in the wild: Emotiw 2015. In *Proceedings of the ACM International Conference on Multimodal Interaction (ICMI)*, 2015.

[7] F. Eyben, M. Wöllmer, and B. Schuller. Opensmile: The munich versatile and fast open-source audio feature extractor. In *Proceedings of the ACM International Conference on Multimedia (MM)*, pages 1459–1462, 2010.

[8] Y. Huang, K. Huang, Y. Yu, and T. Tan. Salient coding for image classification. In *Proceedings of the IEEE Conference on Computer Vision and Pattern Recognition (CVPR)*, pages 1753–1760, 2011.

[9] Y. Huang, Z. Wu, L. Wang, and T. Tan. Feature coding in image classification: A comprehensive study. *IEEE Transactions on Pattern Analysis and Machine Intelligence*, 36(3):493–506, 2014.

[10] T. Joachims. Text categorization with suport vector machines: Learning with many relevant features. In *Proceedings of the European Conference on Machine Learning (ECML)*. Springer, 1998.

[11] S. E. Kahou, C. Pal, X. Bouthillier, P. Froumenty, c. Gülçehre, R. Memisevic, P. Vincent, A. Courville, and Y. Bengio. Combining modality specific deep neural networks for emotion recognition in video. In *Proceedings of the ACM International Conference on Multimodal Interaction (ICMI)*, pages 543–550, 2013.

[12] A. V. Ken Chatfield, Victor Lempitsky and A. Zisserman. The devil is in the details: an evaluation of recent feature encoding methods. In *Proceedings of the British Machine Vision Conference (BMVC)*, pages 76.1–76.12, 2011.

[13] S. Lazebnik, C. Schmid, and J. Ponce. Beyond bags of features: Spatial pyramid matching for recognizing natural scene categories. In *Proceedings of the IEEE Conference on Computer Vision and Pattern Recognition (CVPR)*, pages 2169–2178, 2006.

[14] M. Liu, R. Wang, S. Li, S. Shan, Z. Huang, and X. Chen. Combining multiple kernel methods on Riemannian manifold for emotion recognition in the wild. In *Proceedings of the ACM International Conference on Multimodal Interaction (ICMI)*, pages 494–501, 2014.

[15] S. Lloyd. Least squares quantization in PCM. *IEEE Transactions on Information Theory*, 28(2):129–137, 1982.

[16] D. G. Lowe. Distinctive image features from scale-invariant keypoints. *International Journal on Computer Vision*, 60(2):91–110, 2004.

[17] B. Moore. Principal component analysis in linear systems: Controllability, observability, and model reduction. *IEEE Transactions on Automatic Control*, 26(1):17–32, 1981.

[18] S. Moore and R. Bowden. Local binary patterns for multi-view facial expression recognition. *Computer Vision and Image Understanding*, 115(4):541–558, 2011.

[19] T. Ojala, M. Pietikainen, and T. Maenpaa. Multiresolution gray-scale and rotation invariant texture classification with local binary patterns. *IEEE Transactions on Pattern Analysis and Machine Intelligence*, 24(7):971–987, 2002.

[20] R. Rosipal and N. Krämer. Overview and recent advances in partial least squares. In *Proceedings of the International Conference on Subspace, Latent Structure and Feature Selection*, pages 34–51. Springer, 2006.

[21] O. Rudovic, M. Pantic, and I. Patras. Coupled Gaussian processes for pose-invariant facial expression recognition. *IEEE Transactions on Pattern Analysis and Machine Intelligence*, 35(6):1357–1369, 2013.

[22] K. Sikka, K. Dykstra, S. Sathyanarayana, G. Littlewort, and M. Bartlett. Multiple kernel learning for emotion recognition in the wild. In *Proceedings of the ACM International Conference on Multimodal Interaction (ICMI)*, pages 517–524, 2013.

[23] K. Sikka, T. Wu, J. Susskind, and M. Bartlett. Exploring bag of words architectures in the facial expression domain. In *Proceedings of European Conference Computer Vision Workshop and Demonstrations*, pages 250–259, 2012.

[24] Y.-L. Tian, T. Kanade, and J. F. Cohn. Facial expression analysis. *Handbook of face recognition*, pages 247–275, 2005.

[25] M. Valstar, B. Schuller, K. Smith, F. Eyben, B. Jiang, S. Bilakhia, S. Schnieder, R. Cowie, and M. Pantic. Avec 2013: The continuous audio/visual emotion and depression recognition challenge. In *Proceedings of the ACM International Workshop on Audio/Visual Emotion Challenge (AVEC)*, pages 3–10, 2013.

[26] A. Vedaldi and B. Fulkerson. Vlfeat: An open and portable library of computer vision algorithms. In *Proceedings of the ACM International Conference on Multimedia (MM)*, pages 1469–1472, 2010.

[27] J. Wang, J. Yang, K. Yu, F. Lv, T. Huang, and Y. Gong. Locality-constrained linear coding for image classification. In *Proceedings of the IEEE Conference on Computer Vision and Pattern Recognition (CVPR)*, pages 3360–3367, 2010.

[28] H. Wold. Partial least squares. *Encyclopedia of statistical sciences*, pages 581–591, 1985.

[29] Z. Wu, Y. Huang, L. Wang, and T. Tan. Group encoding of local features in image classification. In *Proceedings of the IEEE International Conference on Pattern Recognition (ICPR)*, pages 1505–1508, 2012.

[30] X. Xiong and F. de la Torre. Supervised descent method and its applications to face alignment. In *Proceedings of the IEEE Conference on Computer Vision and Pattern Recognition (CVPR)*, pages 532–539, 2013.

[31] J. Yang, K. Yu, Y. Gong, and H. Thomas. Linear spatial pyramid matching using sparse coding for image classification. In *Proceedings of the IEEE Conference on Computer Vision and Pattern Recognition (CVPR)*, pages 1794–1801, 2009.

[32] K. Yu, T. Zhang, and Y. Gong. Nonlinear learning using local coordinate coding. In *Proceedings of the Advances in Neural Information Processing Systems (NIPS)*, pages 2223–2231, 2009.

[33] Z. Zeng, M. Pantic, G. I. Roisman, and T. S. Huang. A survey of affect recognition methods: Audio, visual, and spontaneous expressions. *IEEE Transactions on Pattern Analysis and Machine Intelligence*, 31(1):39–58, 2009.

[34] G. Zhao and M. Pietikainen. Dynamic texture recognition using local binary patterns with an application to facial expressions. *IEEE Transactions on Pattern Analysis and Machine Intelligence*, 29(6):915–928, 2007.

[35] W. Zheng. Multi-view facial expression recognition based on group sparse reduced-rank regression. *IEEE Transactions on Affective Computing*, 5(1):71–85, 2014.

[36] X. Zhu and D. Ramanan. Face detection, pose estimation, and landmark localization in the wild. In *Proceedings of the IEEE Conference on Computer Vision and Pattern Recognition (CVPR)*, pages 2879–2886, 2012.

A Deep Feature based Multi-kernel Learning Approach for Video Emotion Recognition

Wei Li
Dept of Electrical Engineering
CUNY City College
New York, USA
lwei000@citymail.cuny.edu

Farnaz Abtahi
Dept of Computer Science
CUNY Graduate Center
New York, USA
fabtahi@gradcenter.cuny.edu

Zhigang Zhu
Dept of Computer Science
CUNY Graduate Center and
City College. New York, USA
zhu@cs.ccny.cuny.edu

ABSTRACT

In this paper, we describe our proposed approach for participating in the Third Emotion Recognition in the Wild Challenge (EmotiW 2015). We focus on the sub-challenge of Audio-Video Based Emotion Recognition using the AFEW dataset. The AFEW dataset consists of 7 emotion groups corresponding to the 7 basic emotions. Each group includes multiple videos from movie clips with people acting a certain emotion. In our approach, we extract LBP-TOP-based video features, openEAR energy/spectral-based audio features, and CNN (convolutional neural network) based deep image features by fine-tuning a pre-trained model with extra emotion images from the web. For each type of features, we run an SVM grid search to find the best RBF kernel. Then multi-kernel learning is employed to combine the RBF kernels to accomplish the feature fusion and generate a fused RBF kernel. Running multi-class SVM classification, we achieve a 45.23% test accuracy on the AFEW dataset. We then apply a decision optimization method to adjust the label distribution closer to the ground truth, by setting offsets for some of the classifiers' prediction confidence score. By applying this modification, the test accuracy increases to 50.46%, which is a significant improvement comparing to the baseline accuracy 39.33% .

Categories and Subject Descriptors

I.4.9 [**Image Processing and Computer Vision**]: Applications; I.5.4 [**Pattern Recognition**]: Applications

Keywords

Emotion recognition; multimodal features; deep learning; multi kernel learning

1. INTRODUCTION

Emotion recognition, which aims to obtain the type of emotion from captured data, which is either an image or a video clip, has been an interesting research topic for decades. In most existing works, emotions are classified into seven categories: Anger, Disgust, Fear, Happiness, Neutral, Sadness and Surprise. In this paper, we will use the same seven basic emotions. Several emotion datasets are available and many approaches have been applied to these existing datasets [20, 26].The EmotiW challenges in the past few years also followed the same categories of emotions. In the EmotiW 2015 challenge [8, 11], the AFEW5.0 is released by the organizers. The AFEW dataset contains short audio-video clips labeled with the above seven categories in both training and validation datasets. This challenge is a continuation of the EmotiW 2013 and 2014 [9, 10] challenges and the task is to assign an emotion label to the video clips from the unlabeled test dataset that is also provided by the organizers. Comparing to popular datasets, there are no restrictions on the faces in the EmotiW videos. The unconstrained lighting conditions, face poses and image qualities make the emotion recognition much more challenging. As shown in Figure 1, in some of the frames, detecting the face itself is also a challenge.

We propose a multi-feature fusion-based approach to tackle the EmotiW 2015 challenge. The approaches for emotion recognition on common datasets and the methods presented during the previous challenges inspired us to use a combination of engineered and learned features. In our approach, we first extract multimodal features from the images and videos, which include LBP-TOP features from videos, generating audio features from openEAR and extracting two CNN-based features from the fine-tuned model in two levels. Then we build SVM kernels using grid search and fuse the kernels by using Multi-Kernel Learning (MKL). We apply multi-class SVM classification to compute the fused kernel, then optimize the multi-class decision rules to obtain the final result.

The four main ideas proposed in our work are as follows. (1) Hybrid features - two engineered features and two deep-learning features. The two engineered features include LBP-TOP features [29] and openEAR-based audio features [12]. The feature selection rules are defined artificially. We further use CNN-based deep learning to extract learned features from image frames. (2) Multimodal features - video (spatial-temporal), audio (temporal), and image (spatial) deep features. We extract our features from multiple aspects. Since a video contains both temporal and spatial information, we try to take advantage of both. The LBP-TOP features take both individual and consequitive frames into consideration, obtaining both temporal and spatial in-

ICMI 2015, November 9–13, 2015, Seattle, WA, USA.
© 2015 ACM. ISBN 978-1-4503-3912-4/15/11 ...$15.00.
DOI: http://dx.doi.org/10.1145/2818346.2830583

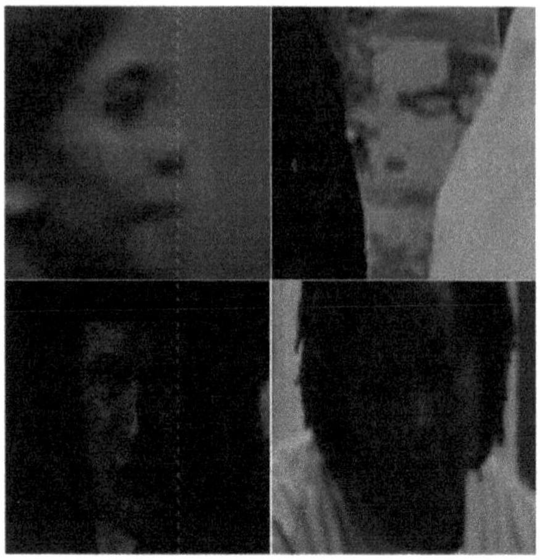

Figure 1: Examples of challenging data.

formation. The audio conveys temporal information in a different modality, and the CNN features contain rich spatial information from the image. (3) The fine-tuning of the pre-trained deep learning model for extracting the two-level deep features. We propose using fine-tuning approach to solve the problem of insufficient images for training a deep CNN structure [13]. We apply our emotion data to train a pertained model for ImageNet [7] and obtain a fine-tuned structure. The fine-tuned model help us extract freatures from two levels of the CNN structure. (4) Multi-class SVM decision optimization to increase the overall emotion classification accuracy. We use multi-class SVM and also dig into the multi-class decision rules and figure out a decision score adjusting method to increase the overall accuracy.

The rest of the paper is organized as follows. In the next section, we review some of the most influential methods of emotion detection which are related to our proposed approach. Section 3 introduces the details of our method. The experiments and the results are explained in Section 4. Finally, the conclusions of our approach are presented in Section 5.

2. RELATED WORK

Most existing facial emotion recognition approaches have focused on recognizing emotions of frontal faces, such as the images in CK+ [20]. Shan, et al [22], proposed a LBP-based feature extractor combined with an SVM for classification. In the method proposed by Xiao, et al [28], comparing to training one model for all emotions, a separate model is trained for each emotion, which improves the performance. Wang, et al [27] modeled facial emotion as a complex activity that consists of temporally overlapping sequence of face events. Then, an Interval Temporal Bayesian Network (ITBN) was used to capture the complex temporal information. Zhao, et al [29] proposed LBP-TOP features to capture the dynamics of the video by transforming the video frames to an x-y-t cube and extracting LBP features from the x-t and y-t planes. The results on the CK+ dataset showed that these features are effective in recognizing emotions in videos.

During recent years, the vision community has been exposed to the wide spread of Deep Learning [25, 24]. Deep learning approaches are also used in emotion detection in many applications. Liu, et al [19] proposed a Boosted Deep Belief Network to perform feature learning, feature selection and classifier construction for emotion recognition. Different DBN models for unsupervised feature learning in audio-visual emotion recognition have been compared in the work done by Kim, et al [15]. Li, et al [17] used CNNs on images collected from the web. To prove the effectiveness of CNNs, they compared their performance on CK+ to the state of the art methods.

Many interesting approaches have been proposed in the EmotiW challenge. Karan, et al [23] extracted multiple channels of features such as Bag of Word (BoW), Histogram of Oriented Gradient (HOG), GIST, etc. To make all these features contribute to the final prediction, Multi-Kernel Learning (MKL) [2] was employed. The results showed that this feature fusion method improves the accuracy. A similar method is proposed by Chen, et al [6]. Liu, et al [18] also suggested a feature fusion approach for the challenge, which used Riemannian manifold to model the video features. Kahou, et al [14] trained a CNN-based on images obtained from the web and then used the class probabilities as deep features. DBNs were used to get valuable features from the audio channel. Afterwards, a random search algorithm [4] was applied, which achieved promising recognition rates.

3. THE PROPOSED APPROACH

The pipeline of our proposed approach includes 4 major parts: the hybrid multimodal features, the fine-tuning of a pre-trained CNN model for extracting deep image features, the multi-kernel learning for feature fusion, and the SVM-based multi-class emotion recognition structure with decision optimization. We will describe each part in the following subsections.

3.1 Hybrid multimodal features

The multimodal features that we utilize include the following three types: LBP-TOP-based video features, openEAR energy/spectral-based audio features, and CNN-based deep image features. The video and audio features convey spatial and temporal information. The learned Deep features focus more on emotion representation in (spatial) images. Our hypothesis is that the combination of both engineered (video and audio features) and learned features (CNNs features) can make the approach more robust.

3.1.1 LBP-TOP video features

Local Binary Pattern (LBP) has been effectively used in many computer vision applications. LBP can be used to describe image appearance by comparing local nearby pixels and generated patterns. A video can be described as a set of consecutive frames. Extracting LBP features from each frame and concatenating the features for the entire video results in lots of redundant information and the temporal characteristics of the video are also lost. Zhao, et al [29] proposed the LBP-TOP (LBP of Three Orthogonal Planes) features. Instead of extracting LBP features from the video frame by frame, we regard the video as a cube with x-y-t coordinates, where the x-y plane represent the spatial image plane and the t axis corresponds to the time. The time axis contains rich temporal information. We extract LBP features on all three planes: x-y, x-t and y-t.

3.1.2 OpenEAR audio features

The speed or strength of the voice during speech can be useful indicators of different emotions. Emotions can be conveyed by voice through changes in pitch, loudness, timbre, speech rate, and pauses which is different from linguistic and semantic information. Study shows that anger and sadness are perceived most easily by using audio information, followed by fear and happiness [3]. To extract audio features, the openEAR tool is used. The tool can provide audio information including energy/spectral low-level features and also voice related features. These features form vectors of length 1583.

3.1.3 CNN-based deep image features

CNN-based deep learning is proved to be effective in image-based classification [16]. CNNs can be used to classify the images directly, or as a feature extractor to generate image features for other classifiers [25]. The CNN features are extracted through different CNN layers. Kahou [14] proposed to use CNN's predicted probabilities for 7 emotions as features, which is obtained from the last layer of the CNN. For videos, features of multiple frames are concatenated to form video features. In our approach, we also extract the probability distribution of the seven emotions from images of a video clip. Since we believe that the penultimate layer features may convey more useful information, we extract features from the penultimate layer as well. To make it simple, we call the probability features CNN-1 and the penultimate features CNN-2. In order to extract deep features from the CNN that are both robust and representative to the facial experession images, in the absence of sufficient number of facial images for training, we propose a unique fine-tuning method by using extra emotion images to update a pre-trained model. We will give more details about the fine-tuning method in the following subsection.

3.2 Fine-tuning a pre-trained model for deep image features

A simple-structured CNN trained on a small dataset is unable to learn the features deeply. Fine-tuning a pre-trained model with extra data can solve this problem. AlexNet is designed for ImageNet classification and shows very good performance [16]. We use AlexNet as our pre-trained model. Then, we need to fine-tune this model by training it on extra emotion images. Li [17] constructed the CIFE dataset by collecting more than 10 thousand instances of the 7 emotion classes. The number of samples of different emotions in the CIFE dataset are: Anger (1785), Disgust (266), Fear (781), Happiness (3636), Neutral (644), Sadness(2485) and Surprise(997). The images are from the web and most of them are not posed. The author reported a 83% recognition rate. This is the dataset we have used in our previous work. Since the number of samples in different classes are not balanced in CIFE, we have added some images to classes with fewer samples (for example Disgust and Fear) to balance the class sizes. After this modification, the number of samples for the 7 emotions become: Anger (1905), Disgust (975), Fear (1381), Happiness (3636), Neutral (2381), Sadness(2485) and Surprise(1993). As our first attempt, we have tried to see if we could use the same three-layer CNN structure as used by Li [17] to extract the learned features. However, with the same structure, the accuracy dropped from 83% to 65% with the balanced dataset. We have also observed the original high performance of 83% in Li's work was due to the unbalanced dataset: the recognition rates for disgust and fear classes were very low, for both the original dataset and the balanced dataset, and hence adding new samples decreased the overall performance. The reason for the low performance is that the three-layer structure is unable to learn the features deeply enough compared to the complicated structure of AlexNet for ImageNet test. Therefore, we choose to utilize the deeper structure of AlexNet as shown in Figure 2.

In the AlexNet structure, there are 5 convolutional layers, 3 fully connected layers, and 60 million parameter in total. Our first guess was that training the AlexNet on our data would results in better classification accuracy. The only problem was the need for larger number of images, as the ImageNet requires millions of images during training. Therefore, we instead propose a CNN fine-tuning method to train a deeper model based on AlexNet. The rationale is that although our task is different from the ImageNet, which focuses on object classification, similar low level filters could be used in emotion recognition. Based on this hypothesis, we can use the AlexNet and utilize our relatively 'small' dataset to update and fine-tune parts of its parameters for adapting it to emotion recognition.

As shown in Figure 2, the parameters of the convolutional layers 1 through 4 are not changed. Our new dataset is used to update the parameters of the convolutional layer 5 and the first fully connect layer, without changing their structures. In the original AlexNet, the number of units of the second fully connected layer and the third layer are 4096 and 1000 respectively. Since the number of classes in our dataset is just 7, we needed to change the structure in these two layers. We reduced the number of neurons in the penultimate layer to 256, and the third fully connected layer to 7. To train and fine-tune the CNN model, we set the learning rate to 0.01 and the training batch size to 256 images. The number of training iterations is chosen to be 800. The classification accuracy by using this model is 78.9% on the balanced CIFE dataset, which shows that the fine-tuning leads to a much better performance than our first attempt of using a three-layer CNN structure.

After the fine-tuning, the model is trained and tested on additional images from the web and then fine-tuned again using the training face images provided for the EmotiW 2015 challenge. By fine-tuning the CNN model, we obtain a model which works well on web images and is hopefully suitable for the challenge faces as well. For utilizing the model, deep image features are extracted from the CNN. Note that the input data that we need to process include videos with different lengths. In order to obtain normalized features, we need to make the number of samples equal in all videos. In our approach, we decided to set the number of samples for all videos to 32, experimentally. Hence, we need to downsample the frames for videos with more than 32 samples and interpolate for those videos with fewer than 32 samples.

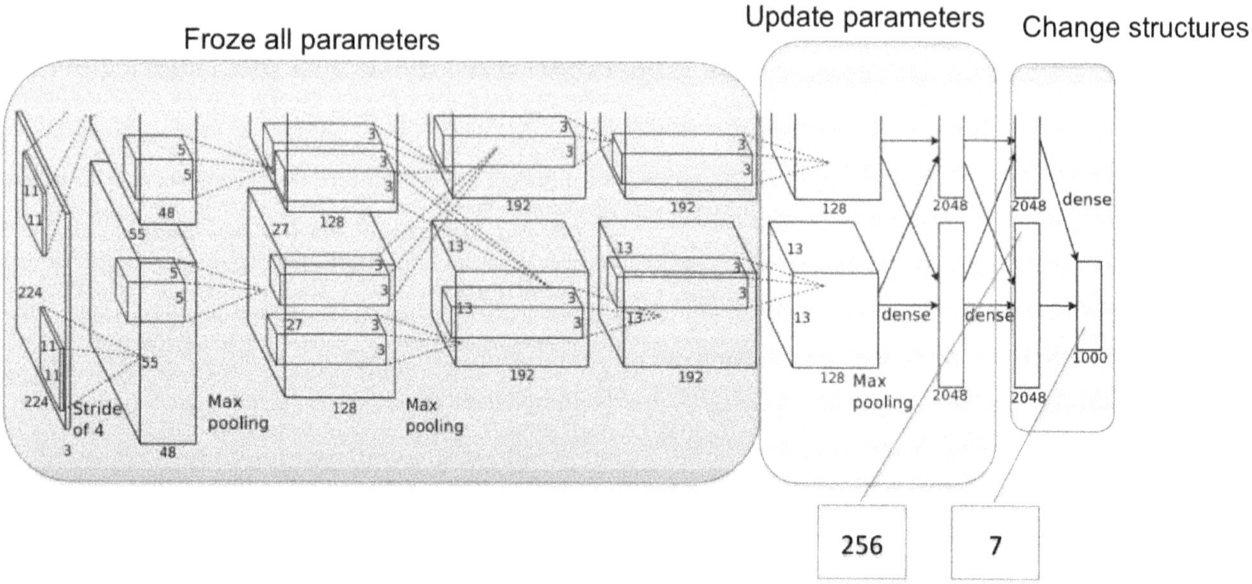

Figure 2: Fine-tuning of the Alexnet

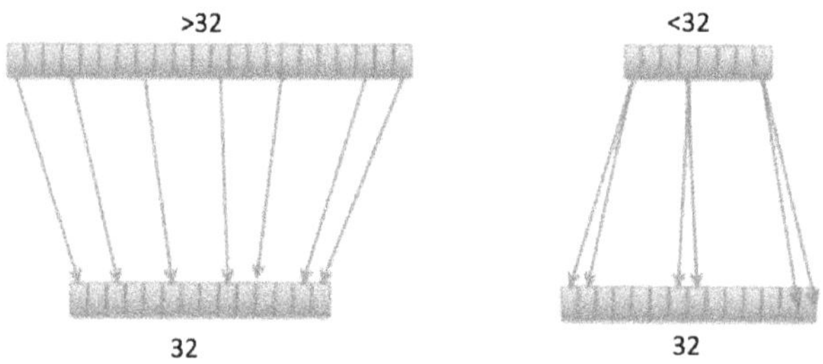

Figure 3: Normalizing the video frames

This process is illustrated in Figure 3. Then we use our fine-tuned CNN model to extract the features from the "normalized" videos. Unlike the work done by Kahou [14] where only the probability vector of the 7 emotions was used, we also extract the penultimate layer features. So we can obtain 2 vectors of lengths 32x7=224 and 32x256=8192, respectively.

3.3 Multiple kernel learning

So far we have explained how we obtain the four types of features we intend to use: LBP-TOP from the videos, openEAR from the audio, and CNN-1 and CNN-2 from the images. Now the next question is how to effectively combine these features to achieve better a emotion recognition rate. Similar to the work done in [23], we decide to use MKL+SVM: multi-kernel learning with SVMs [21, 5, 2]. SVM is a well-known and widely used classifier. The goal of the SVM classifier is to find a hyperplane through the objective function in Equation 1.

$$max[\sum_{i=1}^{N} \boldsymbol{a}_i - \frac{1}{2}\sum_{i=1}^{N}\sum_{j=1}^{N} \boldsymbol{a}_i \boldsymbol{a}_j y_i y_j K(x_i, x_j)] \quad (1)$$

with

$$\sum_{i=1}^{N} \boldsymbol{a}_i y_i = 0, 0 \leq \boldsymbol{a}_i \leq C \quad (2)$$

where x represents the sample and y represents the corresponding label, which is either 1 or -1. C is the penalty factor. K is the SVM kernel, which employs a kernel function (such as RBF in Equation 5 in Section 4) to encode the samples to generate an NxN matrix, where N is the number of samples. The a parameters can be learned by optimization which results in a binary SVM classifier.

The MKL+SVM method is based on SVM, where the only difference is the kernel. The kernel in MKL is a linear combination of SVM kernels as described in Equation 3.

$$K_{mkl}(x_i, x_j) = \sum_{m=1}^{M} \boldsymbol{b}_m K_m(x_i, x_j) \quad (3)$$

with

$$\boldsymbol{b}_m \geq 0, \sum_{m=1}^{m} \boldsymbol{b}_m = 1 \quad (4)$$

where b is the coefficient of the SVM kernels Km $(m=1, ..., M)$. So, each channel of features will generate an SVM kernel, then MKL finds the best coefficients to linearly combine these individual kernels. In this work, the type of the kernels are chosen to be Radius Basic Functions (RBFs).

3.4 SVM-based system structure

SVMs are initially used for binary classification. In our approach, we use multiple binary SVM classifiers to accomplish the classification task of 7 emotions. In many applications,

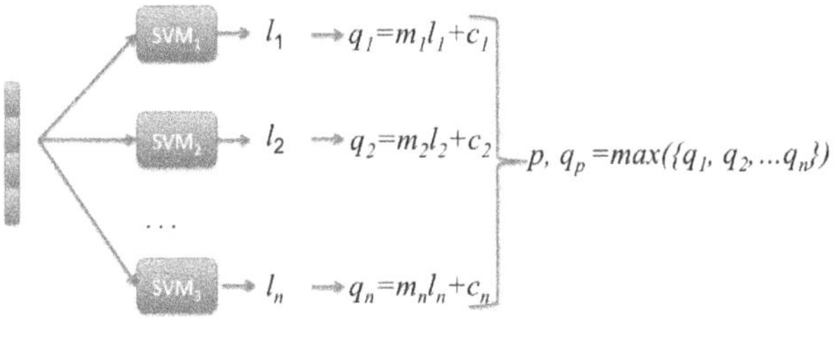

Figure 4: Framework for multi-class SVM prediction

SVM-based multi-class classification is realized by generating and integrating multiple binary SVM models. For an n-class problem, n binary SVM models are trained individually. Then, the confidence (l) of each sample belonging to a specific class is computed by the corresponding SVM. These n confidence values then need to be combined. The easiest and most commonly used way for combining the results is to pick the maximum score and assign the corresponding label to the sample. This may not be the best method to perform multi-class classification, especially when the binary classifiers' accuracies are different due to different number of positive samples used to train them. We propose to solve this problem either by giving a weight (m) to each classifier, or by setting offsets (c) for them, as shown in figure 4, to optimize the recognition results based on the training data. We will explain this method in more details later in section 4.2.

4. EXPERIMENT

In this section, we will discuss the critical components in boosting up the accuracy of emotion recognition with challenging video clips. These components include the construction of the hybrid features from both engineered and learned features, and the optimization of the final classification decisions based on the results of the seven SVM-based classifiers. Then we will discuss our experimental results, emphasizing the role of these two important steps.

4.1 Constructing the features

As discussed earlier, MKL is applied to the RBF kernels. Thus, before using MKL, we need to transform the extracted features to RBF kernels. There are two parameters for the RBF-based SVM that need to be determined: The penalty factor C and the parameter r which appears in the RBF Equation 5.

$$K(x, x') = exp(-r||x - x'||) \quad (5)$$

All SVM classifiers will share the same penalty factor. To make it easy to compute and combine the kernels, we set the penalty factor to the default value 1. For determining r, we perform a grid search for each feature and evaluate the performance of the corresponding SVM on the validation dataset. To achieve the goal of multi-class classification, we use a one-vs-all scheme for each of the emotion classes. This will yield seven classification scores from -1 to 1 for each sample. The scores express the confidence of each classifier in assigning the corresponding class label to that particular sample. For each sample, the class corresponding to the maximum confidence is selected.

Table 1: Comparison of the classification accuracy of different features on each emotion (L-T represents LBP-TOP)

	A	D	F	H	N	Sa	Su	r
L-T	0.75	0	0.04	0.74	0.61	0.17	0.17	0.1
Audio	0.74	0	0.32	0.32	0.52	0.22	0.02	0.1
CNN-1	0.47	0.12	0.15	0.65	0.34	0.32	0.13	0.1
CNN-2	0.58	0.15	0.13	0.67	0.54	0.42	0.23	0.0001

As mentioned before, the best r values for generating the RBF kernels is determined by a grid search. Table 1 shows the r parameter as well as the accuracy for each feature. In this table, we use A, D, F, H, N, Sa, Su to represents Anger, Disgust, Fear, Happiness, Neutral, Sadness and Surprise, respectively. The video features perform very well in recognizing anger, happiness and neutral, but terrible in fear, disgust and sadness. The audio features basically follow the same pattern, but work best in fear. For the deep features, CNN-2 almost outperforms CNN-1 in all classifiers. In the emotions where the video features work best, the CNN-1 does not demonstrate high accuracy, but in emotions like sadness and surprise, the CNN-2 performs much better. The difference in performance could be due to the different focuses of learned and engineered features. The LBP based features represent the facial "texture" well, so for expressions like happy, angry and neutral, the difference in texture is easier for the LBP features to capture and represent. On the other hand, the deep learning features are based on the comparison of different samples and minimizing the loss. So, these features not only capture lower level characteristics like texture, but also some higher level information that differentiate similar emotions. These observations actually draw our attention towards the use of MKL.

we compute coefficients for the kernels by running the MKL algorithm [5]. The coefficients found for video, audio, CNN-1 and CNN-2 features are 0.56, 0.08, 0.0, 0.36. It make sense that the coefficient of CNN-1 is 0 since CNN-2 performs better in most classes. This is also a strong evidence of the effectiveness of extracting CNN-2. Having the coefficients, we can construct the combined kernel and test it on the validation data. By applying the multi-class SVM classification using the fused kernel, we achieve an accuracy of 48.52% on the validation dataset. The confusion matrix of the combined kernel on the validation dataset is shown in Table 2. Compared to the baseline approach that were provided by the organizers, our approach shows a 9% increase in the accuracy. This is the best performance we achieved on the validation data before we use decision optimization; the model also achieves 45.23% accuracy when applied to the test dataset, which is more accurate compared to the 39.33% accuracy of the baseline approach [1].

4.2 Decision optimization

As mentions in Section 3.4, we can use different methods to decide the final classification results in a multi-class SVM. In our initial approach, classification is performed by com-

Table 2: The confusion matrix of the best validation result

	A	D	F	H	N	Sa	Su
A	0.72	0.03	0.05	0.05	0.05	0.05	0.03
D	0.25	0.17	0.05	0.17	0.23	0.05	0.05
F	0.34	0.02	0.13	0.11	0.18	0.02	0.18
H	0.07	0.01	0.03	0.74	0.09	0.01	0.01
N	0.03	0.06	0.01	0.11	0.67	0.06	0.03
Sa	0.13	0.11	0.01	0.08	0.22	0.33	0.08
Su	0.17	0.04	0.08	0.10	0.30	0.02	0.26

Table 3: Test confusion matrix

	A	D	F	H	N	Sa	Su
A	0.73	0.01	0.07	0.02	0.08	0.03	0.02
D	0.07	0.03	0.10	0.20	0.10	0.34	0.14
F	0.36	0.02	0.16	0.07	0.13	0.15	0.10
H	0.11	0.01	0.03	0.56	0.12	0.10	0.06
N	0.12	0.03	0.07	0.09	0.46	0.15	0.06
Sa	0.21	0.01	0.03	0.15	0.04	0.50	0.04
Su	0.18	0.07	0.14	0.07	0.11	0.26	0.15

paring all seven confidence probabilities and selecting the index with the maximum probability value as the final label. A shortcoming of this approach is that some classifiers are weaker as there are unbalanced number of samples across the seven categories in the training dataset. So the output of those classifiers tend to have lower confidence in classification, which may affect the final classification accuracy.

Table 3 shows the sample distribution in the test dataset across the seven classes estimated from the test accuracy for our first submission in Section 4.1, shown in row 1 as "Ground-truth", even though we don't know the ground truth labels. It is obvious that the test dataset is very unbalanced and for some of the emotions, the number of samples are either too low (surprise) or two high (neutral). This leads us to the idea of modifying the decision rule by giving higher scores to under-estimated classes. For instance, we can increase the score for the neutral classifier, as we expect to have more samples classified to that class. This is similar to the use of priors in classification, like reinforcement learning to adjust decision making based on feedback. Now we need to determine the amount of change that we need to apply to the scores.

We assume that if the distribution of the estimated classes is similar to the "ground truth" class distribution, which could be obtained from previous experience, we may have

Table 4: The number of samples for different emotions

	A	D	F	H	N	Sa	Su
Ground truth	79	29	66	108	159	71	27
Before optimization	136	15	40	99	109	102	38
After optimization	114	3	20	97	209	78	18

Table 5: Test confusion matrix after optimization

	A	D	F	H	N	Sa	Su
A	0.69	0	0.13	0.03	0.22	0.05	0
D	0.07	0	0.07	0.21	0.21	0.34	0.10
F	0.32	0.02	0.12	0.07	0.32	0.09	0.06
H	0.08	0	0.09	0.58	0.26	0.03	0.03
N	0.06	0.13	0.19	0.07	0.69	0.11	0.03
Sa	0.15	0	0.03	0.13	0.20	0.48	0.01
Su	0.18	0	0.11	0.04	0.44	0.11	0.11

the chance to obtain higher accuracy by adjusting the decision rules. So in the decision level, we give offsets to some classifiers, that is, we increase the score of those classes that are assumed to be more "popular" due to their higher number of samples. The distribution of the samples to the seven classes estimated by our model before decision optimization is shown in row 2 of Table 3. Based on Table 3 (first 2 rows), we apply this "optimization" to two classes, neutral and happiness. By trying different values for the offsets, we found that increasing the weights by 0.03 and 0.1 will bring the class distribution curve closer to the ground truth. This can be seen in the last row of Table 3. Since we do not know the ground truth, we can not be completely sure that we are using the best pair of offsets. We believe that the values of the offsets can further be optimized. The decision optimization changes our final overall test accuracy to 50.24%, more than 10% improvement over the baseline approach [1]. Our validation accuracy after decision optimization drops to 46.7%. This is understandable since the validation dataset is pretty balanced in the number of samples across the classes. The confusion matrices on the test dataset before and after decision optimization are shown in Table 4 and Table 5, respectively. By comparing the two confusion matrices, we can see that there is an increase in the accuracy of neutral and happy classifiers and a slight drop in the other classifiers. But overall, we have a significant improvement for the test dataset.

4.3 Discussions

By employing the MKL method and decision level optimization, we obtain the accuracy of 50.46%. Compared to the baseline provided by the organizers, the improvement is significant. We have three main contributions in our work:

1. Deep image features are obtained using the AlexNet model. The features generated by AlexNet are very effective in object classification. In order to take advantage of this model, we proposed a fine-tuning method which keeps most of the convolutional filters unchanged, but modifies part of the structure of AlexNet. We apply a fine-tuning training method on a dataset of images obtained from the web, plus the challenge face images to adapt AlexNet to the challenge.

2. Mutli-kernel learning is used to fuse both the engineered and learned features from different channels. These different features (video, audio and images) emphasize on different characteristics. Optimized coefficients of the MKL enables the combined classifier to have the benefit of all individual classifiers and therefore achieves a better overall performance.

3. We utilize a decision optimization method for SVM-based multi-class classification. Instead of treating the confidences of all classifiers equally and assigning the class label corresponding to the highest confidence score, we adjust the decision mechanism by adding extra confidence to the classes that are expected to have more samples classified correctly. This brings the predicted distribution of the classes closer to the ground truth. This may lead to some decrease in the number of predicted samples belonging to some of the classes, but overall, the classification accuracy is improved.

5. CONCLUSION

In this paper, we described the approach that we have proposed and tested to participate in the EmotiW 2015 challenge. Our method combines hybrid and multimodal features for emotion classification, which cover various channels - video (spatial-temporal), audio (temporal) and image (spatial), and include both engineered (LBP-TOP, openEAR), and learned (CNN) features. The CNN features are obtained from our fine-tuned model which is trained on additional images from the web and aligned face images provided by the challenge. Two levels of CNN features are learned. The features are combined using MKL by generating an RBF kernel that is a weighted combination of individual kernels from each classifier. It turned out that the CNN features from the penultimate layer are more effective than the previously used CNN features (probability feature from the last layer). After analyzing the distribution of the classification results, we optimized the multi-class decision rules to make the distribution of the predicted classes similar to the ground truth data. The accuracy of classification after applying this optimization is 50.46% which is significantly higher than the accuracy of the baseline method.

6. ACKOWLEDGEMENT

This work is supported in part by the National Science Foundation (Award # EFRI -1137172), VentureWell (formerly NCIIA, through Award # 10087-12), and a CUNY Graduate Center Enhanced Chancellor Fellowship (to Abtahi).

7. REFERENCES

[1] D. Abhinav, M. O.V. Ramana, G. Roland, J. Jyoti, and G. Tom. Video and image based emotion recognition challenges in the wild: Emotiw 2015. In *ICMI*, 2015.

[2] F. R. Bach, G. R. Lanckriet, and M. I. Jordan. Multiple kernel learning, conic duality, and the smo algorithm. In *Proceedings of the twenty-first international conference on Machine learning*, page 6. ACM, 2004.

[3] J.-A. Bachorowski. Vocal expression and perception of emotion. *Current directions in psychological science*, 8(2):53–57, 1999.

[4] J. Bergstra and Y. Bengio. Random search for hyper-parameter optimization. *The Journal of Machine Learning Research*, 13(1):281–305, 2012.

[5] S. Bucak, R. Jin, and A. K. Jain. Multi-label multiple kernel learning by stochastic approximation: Application to visual object recognition. In *Advances in Neural Information Processing Systems*, pages 325–333, 2010.

[6] J. Chen, Z. Chen, Z. Chi, and H. Fu. Emotion recognition in the wild with feature fusion and multiple kernel learning. In *Proceedings of the 16th International Conference on Multimodal Interaction*, pages 508–513. ACM, 2014.

[7] J. Deng, W. Dong, R. Socher, L.-J. Li, K. Li, and L. Fei-Fei. Imagenet: A large-scale hierarchical image database. In *Computer Vision and Pattern Recognition, 2009. CVPR 2009. IEEE Conference on*, pages 248–255. IEEE, 2009.

[8] A. Dhall et al. Collecting large, richly annotated facial-expression databases from movies. 2012.

[9] A. Dhall, R. Goecke, J. Joshi, K. Sikka, and T. Gedeon. Emotion recognition in the wild challenge 2014: Baseline, data and protocol. In *Proceedings of the 16th International Conference on Multimodal Interaction*, pages 461–466. ACM, 2014.

[10] A. Dhall, R. Goecke, J. Joshi, M. Wagner, and T. Gedeon. Emotion recognition in the wild challenge 2013. In *Proceedings of the 15th ACM on International conference on multimodal interaction*, pages 509–516. ACM, 2013.

[11] A. Dhall, R. Goecke, S. Lucey, and T. Gedeon. Static facial expression analysis in tough conditions: Data, evaluation protocol and benchmark. In *Computer Vision Workshops (ICCV Workshops), 2011 IEEE International Conference on*, pages 2106–2112. IEEE, 2011.

[12] F. Eyben, M. Wöllmer, and B. Schuller. Openear—introducing the munich open-source emotion and affect recognition toolkit. In *Affective Computing and Intelligent Interaction and Workshops, 2009. ACII 2009. 3rd International Conference on*, pages 1–6. IEEE, 2009.

[13] Y. Jia, E. Shelhamer, J. Donahue, S. Karayev, J. Long, R. Girshick, S. Guadarrama, and T. Darrell. Caffe: Convolutional architecture for fast feature embedding. In *Proceedings of the ACM International Conference on Multimedia*, pages 675–678. ACM, 2014.

[14] S. E. Kahou, X. Bouthillier, P. Lamblin, C. Gulcehre, V. Michalski, K. Konda, S. Jean, P. Froumenty, A. Courville, P. Vincent, et al. Emonets: Multimodal deep learning approaches for emotion recognition in video. *arXiv preprint arXiv:1503.01800*, 2015.

[15] Y. Kim, H. Lee, and E. M. Provost. Deep learning for robust feature generation in audiovisual emotion recognition. In *Acoustics, Speech and Signal Processing (ICASSP), 2013 IEEE International Conference on*, pages 3687–3691. IEEE, 2013.

[16] A. Krizhevsky, I. Sutskever, and G. E. Hinton. Imagenet classification with deep convolutional neural networks. In *Advances in neural information processing systems*, pages 1097–1105, 2012.

[17] W. Li, M. Li, Z. Su, and Z. Zhu. A deep-learning approach to facial expression recognition with candid images. In *Machine Vision Applications (MVA), 2015 14th IAPR International Conference on*, pages 279–282. IEEE, 2015.

[18] M. Liu, R. Wang, S. Li, S. Shan, Z. Huang, and X. Chen. Combining multiple kernel methods on riemannian manifold for emotion recognition in the

wild. In *Proceedings of the 16th International Conference on Multimodal Interaction*, pages 494–501. ACM, 2014.

[19] P. Liu, S. Han, Z. Meng, and Y. Tong. Facial expression recognition via a boosted deep belief network. In *Computer Vision and Pattern Recognition (CVPR), 2014 IEEE Conference on*, pages 1805–1812. IEEE, 2014.

[20] P. Lucey, J. F. Cohn, T. Kanade, J. Saragih, Z. Ambadar, and I. Matthews. The extended cohn-kanade dataset (ck+): A complete dataset for action unit and emotion-specified expression. In *Computer Vision and Pattern Recognition Workshops (CVPRW), 2010 IEEE Computer Society Conference on*, pages 94–101. IEEE, 2010.

[21] A. Rakotomamonjy, F. Bach, S. Canu, and Y. Grandvalet. Simplemkl. *Journal of Machine Learning Research*, 9:2491–2521, 2008.

[22] C. Shan, S. Gong, and P. W. McOwan. Facial expression recognition based on local binary patterns: A comprehensive study. *Image and Vision Computing*, 27(6):803–816, 2009.

[23] K. Sikka, K. Dykstra, S. Sathyanarayana, G. Littlewort, and M. Bartlett. Multiple kernel learning for emotion recognition in the wild. In *Proceedings of the 15th ACM on International conference on multimodal interaction*, pages 517–524. ACM, 2013.

[24] Y. Sun, X. Wang, and X. Tang. Deep learning face representation from predicting 10,000 classes. In *Computer Vision and Pattern Recognition (CVPR), 2014 IEEE Conference on*, pages 1891–1898. IEEE, 2014.

[25] Y. Taigman, M. Yang, M. Ranzato, and L. Wolf. Deepface: Closing the gap to human-level performance in face verification. In *Computer Vision and Pattern Recognition (CVPR), 2014 IEEE Conference on*, pages 1701–1708. IEEE, 2014.

[26] M. Valstar and M. Pantic. Induced disgust, happiness and surprise: an addition to the mmi facial expression database. In *Proc. 3rd Intern. Workshop on EMOTION (satellite of LREC): Corpora for Research on Emotion and Affect*, page 65, 2010.

[27] Z. Wang, S. Wang, and Q. Ji. Capturing complex spatio-temporal relations among facial muscles for facial expression recognition. In *Computer Vision and Pattern Recognition (CVPR), 2013 IEEE Conference on*, pages 3422–3429. IEEE, 2013.

[28] R. Xiao, Q. Zhao, D. Zhang, and P. Shi. Facial expression recognition on multiple manifolds. *Pattern Recognition*, 44(1):107–116, 2011.

[29] G. Zhao and M. Pietikainen. Dynamic texture recognition using local binary patterns with an application to facial expressions. *Pattern Analysis and Machine Intelligence, IEEE Transactions on*, 29(6):915–928, 2007.

Transductive Transfer LDA with Riesz-based Volume LBP for Emotion Recognition in The Wild

Yuan Zong[1], Wenming Zheng[1]*, Xiaohua Huang[2,1], Jingwei Yan[1], Tong Zhang[1,3]
[1]Key Laboratory of Child Development and Learning Science of Ministry of Education, Research Center for Learning Science, Southeast University, P. R. China
[2]Center for Machine Vision Research, Department of Computer Science and Engineering, University of Oulu, Finland
[3]School of Information Science and Engineering, Southeast University, P. R. China
{xhzongyuan, wenming_zheng, yanjingwei, tongzhang} @seu.edu.cn
xiaohua.huang@ee.oulu.fi

ABSTRACT

In this paper, we propose the method using Transductive Transfer Linear Discriminant Analysis (TTLDA) and Riesz-based Volume Local Binary Patterns (RVLBP) for image based static facial expression recognition challenge of the Emotion Recognition in the Wild Challenge (EmotiW 2015). The task of this challenge is to assign facial expression labels to frames of some movies containing a face under the real word environment. In our method, we firstly employ a multi-scale image partition scheme to divide each face image into some image blocks and use RVLBP features extracted from each block to describe each facial image. Then, we adopt the TTLDA approach based on RVLBP to cope with the expression recognition task. The experiments on the testing data of SFEW 2.0 database, which is used for image based static facial expression challenge, demonstrate that our method achieves the accuracy of 50%. This result has a 10.87% improvement over the baseline provided by this challenge organizer.

Categories and Subject Descriptors

I.5.4 [**Pattern Recognition**]: Applications; I.4.9 [**Image Processing and Computer Vision**]: Applications

Keywords

Emotion Recognition in The Wild 2015; Facial Expression Recognition; Reisz-based Volume Local Binary Pattern; Transductive Transfer Linear Discriminant Analysis

*Corresponding Author.

ICMI '15, November 09-13, 2015, Seattle, WA, USA
Copyright 2015 ACM ISBN 978-1-4503-3912-4/15/11 ...$15.00.
DOI: http://dx.doi.org/10.1145/2818346.2830584.

1. INTRODUCTION

The research of automatic recognition of human's facial expressions began with the 70s of last century, and has become one of the most attractive research topics in the fields of affective computing, pattern recognition, and human computer interaction [17]. It aims to assign expression labels, such as disgust or surprise, to unseen testing facial images using the model learned based on a set of labeled training samples. Most of facial expression recognition (FER) researches in the past several decades were based on the databases recorded in the controlled lab environment. However, it should be pointed out that in the practical scenarios, extensive complex conditions, e.g. illumination variation, pose change, different ethnics, and many other challenging environments, would significantly degrade the recognition model that may work well for FER task in well-designed environments such as laboratory scenarios. In view of this situation, more attention to FER in the wild would be paid so as to making FER more applicable in real scenarios. But so far FER in the wild is a much more challenging task. Recently, various emotion recognition challenges employing wild databases have been hosted, such as Audio Video Emotion Challenges [15], Emotion Recognition in the Wild [3, 2]. These challenges build a platform for researchers to devote them into this topic and provide a benchmark which is used to evaluate relevant methods developed by researchers.

Now, EmotiW 2015 provides two sub-challenges, i.e., video based emotion recognition and image based static facial expression recognition. In this paper, we will focus on the latter sub-challenge and present an efficient method to deal with it. The task of this sub-challenge is to assign an expression label indicating one of seven common expressions, namely, neutral, happiness, sadness, disgust, fear, anger, and surprise, into each facial image. The database (SFEW 2.0) [5] used for this challenge is divided into three subsets, i.e. training data set, validation data set, and testing data sets. What participants should do is to use features provided by organizers or their own and classification methods to predict labels of testing set. It is notable that the challenge seems to be a traditional machine learning task. However, after observing the facial images, we find that these face images of training, validation and testing sets are selected from different movies, respectively, and these movies are recoded under different conditions. Consequently, this recognition problem should be a typical cross-domain FER since the training image samples and the testing ones are selected from two different video scenarios. To deal with such challenging cross-domain FER problem, we focus our attention on the use of transfer learning approaches [13] to cope with this challenge task. Hence, instead of resorting to the traditional machine learning approaches that simply use the training data set to train a classifier and then use this classifier to infer the expression categories of the testing data set, we investigate the transductive transfer method proposed in our preliminary work in for this purpose. In addition, we will adopt the transductive transfer linear discriminant analysis (TTLDA) model [23] to deal with the domain mismatch problem of the challenge, such that a more reliable model is learned to predict the expression labels of testing samples. In addition, we also employ a new local binary pattern, called Reizs-based volume LBP (RVLBP) [7], rather than the provided features, as the expression features.

The rest of paper is organized as follows. Section 2 describes our proposed method including RVLBP based extraction method and TTLDA model. Section 3 provide the parameter setup of RVLBP and a detailed expression label prediction scheme using TTLDA model and RVLBP features and reports our result on the Val and Test sets. Finally, the paper is concluded in Section 4.

2. PROPOSED METHOD

Generally, static image based facial expression recognition task consists of two key parts, namely facial expression feature extraction part and expression classification part and both parts would significantly affect whether FER system works well. Hence, we will firstly describe a novel features called RVLBP and give a RVLBP feature extraction scheme. Then, we investigate the method of using both TTLDA and RVLBP to cope with the image based static FER challenge of EmotiW 2015.

2.1 Riesz-based Volume Local Binary Pattern

As we know, Felsberg and Sommer proposed to use the Riesz transform for image processing [6]. Until recently, Riesz transform has attracted much interest from researchers in the field for texture classification [20] and face analysis [8, 9, 16]. However, from the intrinsic dimension theorem [18], the 1st-order Riesz transform is designed just for an intrinsic 1D signal, but losing some important complex structures, such as corners. In order to characterize the intrinsic 2D local structures, the higher-order Riesz transforms have been developed for biometric recognition [19] and texture recognition [12]. Recently, a new method based on the higher-order Riesz transform and local binary patterns was proposed to characterize facial expressions, in which they show the promising performance [7]. Therefore, we employ the work of [7], Riesz-based volume local binary pattern (RVLBP), for facial expression representation.

The Riesz transform [14] is a natural generalization of the Hilbert transform. Riesz transform based image analysis has been utilized in numerous fields [8, 9, 12, 19]. Since real images contain a wide range of frequencies, a suitable band-pass filter is needed to filter images. For band-pass filter, a multi-orientation and multi-scale log-Gabor filter are employed, in which the filter is defined in the frequency domain as:

$$G(\omega,\theta) = exp(\frac{log(\frac{\omega}{\omega_0})^2}{2(log(\frac{\sigma_\omega}{\omega_0}))^2})exp(\frac{-(\theta-\theta_0)^2}{2\sigma_\theta^2}), \quad (1)$$

where ω_0 is the center frequency, σ_ω is the width parameter for the frequency, θ_0 is the center orientation, and σ_θ is the width parameter of the orientation.

According to intrinsic dimension [18, 19], he local structure of a 2D image can be characterized by numerous regions of i0D, i1D and i2D structures. Specifically, the 1st-order Riesz transform describes the rotationally invariant analysis of the i1D structure, while the 2nd-order Riesz transform enables i2D image structures such as corners and texture [18]. Therefore, for characterizing the structure of a facial expression image, the 1st-order Riesz image are firstly employed, which are defined as:

$$h_x(\mathbf{Z}) = g(\omega,\theta) * \frac{x}{2\pi|\mathbf{Z}|^3}, \quad (2)$$

$$h_y(\mathbf{Z}) = g(\omega,\theta) * \frac{y}{2\pi|\mathbf{Z}|^3}, \quad (3)$$

and 2nd-order Riesz transforms are secondly used, which are defined as:

$$h_{xx}(\mathbf{Z}) = h_x(\mathbf{Z}) * h_x(\mathbf{Z}), \quad (4)$$

$$h_{yy}(\mathbf{Z}) = h_y(\mathbf{Z}) * h_y(\mathbf{Z}), \quad (5)$$

$$h_{xy}(\mathbf{Z}) = h_x(\mathbf{Z}) * h_y(\mathbf{Z}), \quad (6)$$

where $\mathbf{Z}$ represents coordinates of 2D image, x and y is the direction of Riesz transform, $*$ is a convolution operation.

With log-Gabor filter as defined in Eq.(1), for an image I, a multi-scale and multi-orientation Riesz face $h_x(\mathbf{Z})$ are obtained as

$$R_x = I * [h_x(\mathbf{Z})_1^1, \ \ldots, h_x(\mathbf{Z})_{n_s}^{n_o}]. \quad (7)$$

In order to explore spatial pixel correlation in a Riesz face and the relationship among Riesz faces along frequency and orientation directions, the LBP operator [10] is employed on XY, XZ and YZ of volume-based Riesz faces, respectively. Secondly, we combine the results of these planes to represents faces. For each plane, its histogram is computed as

$$H_j(l) = \sum_{x,y} L(f_j(x,y) = l), l = 0, 1, \ldots, Q_j - 1, \quad (8)$$

where $L(x)$ is a logical function with $L(x) = 1$ if x is true and $L(x) = 0$ otherwise; $f_j(.)$ expresses the LBP codes in the j-th plane ($j = 0 : XY; 1 : XZ; 2 : YZ$), and Q_j is the bin number of the LBP code in the j-th plane. Finally, the histograms H_{XY}, H_{XZ} and H_{YZ} are concatenated into one feature vector H.

For each component R_m ($m = \{x, y, xx, xy, yy\}$), H_m is obtained by using the above-mentioned procedure. These five histograms $H_x, H_y, H_{xx}, H_{xy}, H_{yy}$ are concatenated into one feature vector F for representing the face. This feature vector incorporates the spatial information and the co-occurrence statistics on frequency and orientation domains of Riesz transform, thus is more effective for face representation. The framework of RVLBP is shown in Fig. 1.

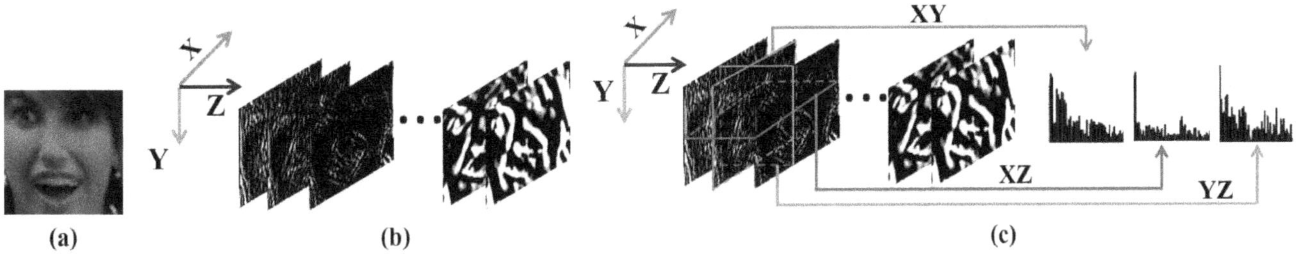

Figure 1: Illustration of Riesz-based volume local binary patterns for R_x: (a) A face image; (b) The 1st-order Riesz face R_x and its volume, where Z represents the axis of scale and orientation of Riesz transform; and (c) feature extraction for the R_x component. [7]

2.2 A Multi-Scale Feature Extraction Scheme

After introducing the features, we propose a multi-scale face image partition scheme to construct more discriminative expression features. In this scheme, we adopt the facial feature extraction strategy proposed in our previous work of [21] by considering different scales of face image divisions instead of simply the single scale image facial feature extraction method. Fig. 2 summarizes the facial image partition scheme. According to this scheme, given a face image, we divide it into non-overlap 1×1, 2×2 , 4×4, and 8×8 image blocks of equal size respectively and we will obtain totally 85 image blocks. Then, we extract 85 RVLBP feature vectors from all the 85 image blocks and denote them by $\{\mathbf{x}_i\}_{i=1}^{85}$, where $\mathbf{x}_i$ denotes the facial feature vector corresponding to the i-th image block. Finally, these RVLBP feature vectors are concatenated into a supervector $\mathbf{x} = [\mathbf{x}_1^T, \mathbf{x}_2^T, \cdots, \mathbf{x}_{85}^T]^T$ to represent the facial image and then is used for the expression recognition task.

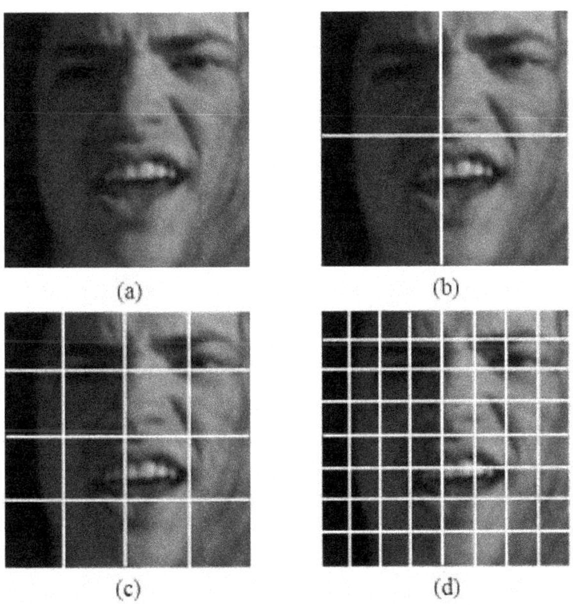

Figure 2: An example of facial image partition scheme, where each face image has the size of 256×256. From (a) to (d), the fice image is divided into 1, 4, 16, and 64 image blocks with the same size respectively

2.3 Transductive Transfer Linear Discriminant Analysis

In our previous work of [23], we have proposed the TTLDA model as a transductive transfer extension of LDA and use it to deal with the cross-pose FER problem. TTLDA reformulate the LDA as a reduced rank regression (RRR) problem based on assumption that the numbers of data samples in each class are approximately equal. In this subsection, we will introduce our TTLDA and describe how it works for feature selection and expression classification in EmotiW 2015.

To begin with, suppose that we have M training image samples and each one is divide them into 85 image blocks as shown in Section 2.2. Let $\mathbf{X}_i = [\mathbf{x}_{1,i}, \mathbf{x}_{2,i}, \cdots, \mathbf{x}_{M,i}]$ be the RVLBP feature matrix corresponding to the ith face image block and thus we can express the training feature matrix as $\mathbf{X} = [\mathbf{X}_1^T, \mathbf{X}_2^T, \cdots, \mathbf{X}_{85}^T]^T$. Let $\mathbf{L} = [\mathbf{l}_1, \mathbf{l}_2, \cdots, \mathbf{l}_M]$ be the corresponding label matrix in which $\mathbf{l}_i = [l_{i,1}, l_{i,2}, \cdots, l_{i,c}]^T$ is a $c\times 1$ vector, where c is the number of expression classes. The value of each entry $l_{i,j}$ takes the value of 0 or 1 according to the following rule:

$$l_{i,j} = \begin{cases} 1, & \text{if } \mathbf{x}_i \text{ belongs to the } i^{th} \text{ expression class;} \\ 0, & \text{otherwise.} \end{cases} \tag{9}$$

Besides, our TTLDA also need some unlabelled testing samples used as auxiliary feature set. Suppose we also have some testing samples and conduct the same RVLBP feature extraction procedure like training sample. Let us denote them as $\mathbf{X}_{au} = [(\mathbf{X}_{au})_1^T, (\mathbf{X}_{au})_2^T, \cdots, (\mathbf{X}_{au})_{85}^T]^T$ where $(\mathbf{X}_{au})_i^T = [(\mathbf{x}_{au})_{1,i}, (\mathbf{x}_{au})_{2,i}, \cdots, (\mathbf{x}_{au})_{M,i}]$. Now, we use TTLDA model (see Eq.(4) in [23]) to build the relationship of these two label matrices and two feature matrices:

$$\min_{\mathbf{L}_{au},\mathbf{A},\mathbf{B}} \|[\mathbf{L}\ \mathbf{L}_{au}] - \mathbf{AB}[\mathbf{X}\ \mathbf{X}_{au}]\|_F^2 \tag{10}$$

where $\mathbf{A}$ and $\mathbf{B}$ are regression coefficient matrix and $\mathbf{L}_{au}$ is label matrix of unknown auxiliary samples. Noting that the goal of our TTLDA is to learn more suitable regression coefficient matrices which can overcome the difference between training and testing samples by means of a transductive way. In dealing with the challenge, for reducing the complexity of model, we will further simplify the TTLDA and reformulate it as a least square regression problem. Let $\mathbf{A}$ be an identity matrix such that $\mathbf{AB} = \mathbf{B}$. Let $\mathbf{B} = \mathbf{C}^T$. Then, Eq.(10) can be rewrite as following:

$$\min_{\mathbf{L}_{au},\mathbf{C}} \|[\mathbf{L}\ \mathbf{L}_{au}] - \mathbf{C}^T[\mathbf{X}\ \mathbf{X}_{au}]\|_F^2 \tag{11}$$

In order to realization of feature block selection, let us next divide $\mathbf{C}$ into 85 parts with the same size such that

$\mathbf{C} = [\mathbf{C}_1^T, \mathbf{C}_2^T, \cdots, \mathbf{C}_{85}^T]^T$ where $\mathbf{C}_i$ is the coefficient matrix and corresponds to feature matrix $[\mathbf{X}_i\ (\mathbf{X}_{au})_i]$. Then, to measure the importance of each feature block, we introduce a weight parameter $\omega_i \in \{0, 1\}$ according to the following rule:

$$\omega_i = \begin{cases} 1, & \text{the feature block is important;} \\ 0, & \text{the feature block is unimportant.} \end{cases} \quad (12)$$

By imposing the weight parameters, the training and auxiliary feature matrix can be rewritten as $\mathbf{X} = [\omega_1 \mathbf{X}_1^T, \omega_2 \mathbf{X}_2^T, \cdots, \omega_{85} \mathbf{X}_{85}^T]^T$ and $\mathbf{X} = [\omega_1 (\mathbf{X}_{au})_1^T, \omega_2 (\mathbf{X}_{au})_2^T, \cdots, \omega_{85} (\mathbf{X}_{au})_{85}^T]^T$, respectively. Thus, we can reformulate Eq.(11) as:

$$\min_{\mathbf{L}_{au}, \mathbf{C}_i, \omega_i \in \{0,1\}} \|[\mathbf{L}\ \mathbf{L}_{au}] - \sum_{i=0}^{85} \omega_i \mathbf{C}_i^T [\mathbf{X}_i\ (\mathbf{X}_{au})_i]\|_F^2 \quad (13)$$

It is clear that ω_i is able to measure the importance of its corresponding feature matrix block. For learning a group of reasonable ω_i's, we impose a regularization term $\sum_{i=0}^{85} \omega_i$ to Eq. 13 and obtain a new objective function as following:

$$\min_{\mathbf{L}_{au}, \mathbf{C}_i, \omega_i \in \{0,1\}} \|[\mathbf{L}\ \mathbf{L}_{au}] - \sum_{i=0}^{85} \omega_i \mathbf{C}_i^T [\mathbf{X}_i\ (\mathbf{X}_{au})_i]\|_F^2 + \lambda \sum_{i=0}^{85} \omega_i \quad (14)$$

where λ is a trade-off parameter.

In this case, we obtain the TTLDA for image based static facial expression recognition which can not only select the important feature blocks based on their contribution to the expression classification but also utilize the distribution information of testing samples:

According to [21] and [23], we obtain that solving the joint optimization problem of (14) can be simplified as solving the following one:

$$\min_{\mathbf{L}_{au}, \tilde{\mathbf{C}}_i} \|[\mathbf{L}\ \mathbf{L}_{au}] - \sum_{i=0}^{85} \tilde{\mathbf{C}}_i^T [\mathbf{X}_i\ (\mathbf{X}_{au})_i]\|_F^2 + \lambda \sum_{i=0}^{85} \|\tilde{\mathbf{C}}_i\|_F \quad (15)$$

The optimization problem of Eq.(15) can be conveniently solved by alternated direction method (ADM) and inexact augmented Lagrangian method (inexact ALM). The detailed solution can be referred to [21] and [22].

After obtaining the learnt TTLDA, we compare the entry values of the estimated label vector to predict the expression label for a testing sample. Specifically, given a testing feature vector $\mathbf{x}_t$, we can estimate its corresponding label vector $\mathbf{l}_t$ by

$$\min_{\mathbf{l}_t} \|\mathbf{l}_t - \sum_{i=0}^{85} \hat{\tilde{\mathbf{C}}}_i^T \mathbf{x}_t\|^2, \ s.t.\ \mathbf{l}_t \succeq 0,\ \mathbf{1}^T \mathbf{l}_t = 1 \quad (16)$$

Then, the expression attribute of the testing sample can be obtained by the following criterion:

$$expression\_label = arg \max_k \{\mathbf{l}_t(k)\} \quad (17)$$

Noting that $\mathbf{l}_t(k)$ in Eq.(17) indicates the kth element of label vector $\mathbf{l}_t$.

3. EXPERIMENTS AND ANALYSIS

3.1 Data Description and Challenge Detail

EmotiW 2015 consists of two sub-challenges. One is video based emotion recognition and the other is image based static facial expression recognition. As we participate in the second challenge, in this section we will briefly describe the database used in this challenge, i.e. the SFEW 2.0 database. This database contains seven basic facial expressions: neutral (NE), happiness (HA), sadness (SA), disgust (DI), fear (FE), anger (AN), and surprise (SU). The data is divided into three sets: Train, Val and Test, respectively containing 958, 436 and 372 images captured from some popular movies. Train and Val sets with facial expression labels are available for researchers, which are used to adjust the parameter and verify the facial expression model, while Test set contains unseen facial images. The goal of this dataset is used to address the challenges in recognizing emotions in real-world conditions including difficult lighting conditions, complex poses and different ethnics. The task of the challenge is to predict the labels of the whole Test set.

Table 1: The recognition accuracies (%) of RVLBP affected by number of scale n_s and orientation n_o on *Val* set.

$n_s \setminus n_o$	4	5	6	7	8
3	33.03	31.19	33.03	34.86	35.09
4	36.01	36.93	37.61	37.39	**38.07**
5	36.24	36.01	37.39	37.16	37.84

3.2 Parameter Selection of RVLBP

For feature extraction, the RVLBP method has two important parameters, *i.e.*, the number of scale n_s and orientation n_o in Eq.(1). We attempt to find out the best parameters for them on Val set. In our experiments, we evaluate the influence of parameters to RVLBP. In this case, we tune the parameters n_s and n_o in range [3 5] and [4 8]. For classification, the support vector machine based on Chi-Square kernel [1] are used. The results are shown in Table 1. As seen from Table 1, we find that the RVLBP obtained the best recognition rate when $n_s = 4$ and $n_o = 8$. In the following experiment, we set n_s and n_o to 4 and 8, respectively.

For comparison, we provide the results of LBP [10] and LPQ [11] in Table 2. From this table, we can find that Local Binary Pattern (LBP) and Local Phase Quantization (LPQ) achieve the recognition rate of 36.47% and 32.80%, respectively. For RVLBP, it achieves the best recognition rate of 38.07%. From this comparison, we can find that RVLBP outperforms to LBP and LPQ.

Furthermore, we conduct the experiments using the RVLBP and SVM with chi-square kernel on Test set, where we employ Train and Val sets to obtain SVM. In this experiment, we only compare the RVLBP with the baseline algorithm provided by organizers, where they used LPQ [11] and Pyramid of Histogram of Gradient (PHOG) as the feature and SVM as the classification. In the Test set, RVLBP obtained the accuracy of 45.70%, while, the baseline algorithm got 39.13%. From this comparison, we can see that the performance is increased by the accuracy of 6.57%. In addition, we provide the confusion matrix for seven facial expression in Fig. 3. From Fig. 3, we can find that RVLBP perform the best on Happy, followed closely by Neutral and Angry, and more distantly by Sad, Fear and Disgust.

3.3 Analysis of TTLDA

In order to make TTLDA work efficiently and obtain a

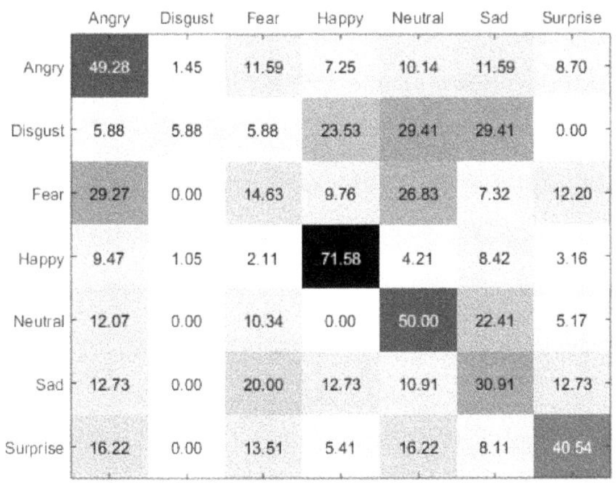

Figure 3: The confusion matrix of classification (%) on Test set by using RVLBP.

Figure 4: The confusion matrix of classification (%) on Test set by TTLDA with multi-scale RVLBP

Table 2: The recognition accuracies (%) tested by numerous methods on the Val and Test set.

Method	Accuracy	
	Val	Test
Baseline(provided by organizers) [5]	35.96	39.13
LBP [10]	36.47	-
LPQ [11]	32.80	-
SVM + RVLBP	38.07	45.70
TTLDA + RVLBP(multi-scale)	-	**50.00**

satisfied challenge result, we use the following strategy to train our TTLDA:

(1) We firstly employ RVLBP for each face image on SFEW 1.0 [4] and SFEW 2.0 databases. For each face image, the feature of each block is normalized by L1 normalization.

(2) In the use of TTLDA, it usually assumes that the numbers of data samples for each class are approximately equal [23]. However, we find that the number of samples for each class are not equal on SFEW 2.0 database. For this reason, we increase the number of some expressions in training data set such that the number of each expression is 200. More specifically, we increase the number of samples of anger, happiness, neutral, and sadness categorizations to 200 by using validation set, while for surprise, and anger to 200 and for disgust to 160 by using SFEW 1.0 database [4].

(3) For the number of auxiliary set, we empirically fixed it at 150 which is nearly 40% of the testing samples. Furthermore, to cover all the testing samples as far as possible and capturing its intrinsic distribution information, experiments for the challenge are conducted 10 trails in which the auxiliary samples are randomly chosen each time. Then, a simple voting strategy is adopted to determine the final expression labels, i.e. for one testing sample, its eventual emotion label is determined by the label which occurs most times. Finally, for parameter of TTLDA λ , we conduct extensive experiments on the Train and Val sets of both two databases and set $\lambda = 5$ eventually.

Talbe 2 depicts the results using TTLDA based on RVLBP on Val and Test Set. It can be seen that our proposed TTLDA with multi-scale RVLBP owns the best recognition accuracy on the Test set reaching 50%. This result exceeds the baseline provided by the organizers (39.13%) [5] with a satisfactory growth of 10.87%.

Fig. 4 shows the confusion matrix of final test results of our TTLDA learned by the balanced training samples. It is clear that angry, happy, neutral, and surprise can be relatively easy to distinguish from other expressions by TTLDA. However, it is still hard to distinguish some difficult expression such as disgust, fear and sad. Especially, no one disgust sample is predicted correctly. We think that except that muscular movements of these expressions are similar to some other expressions, complex conditions are also important factors in real-world environment.

4. CONCLUSION

In this paper, we have proposed an efficient method for image based static facial expression recognition in the wild. In our method, we adopt a multi-scale image segmentation scheme to partition each face image and obtain a series of face image blocks. Then, a type of improved LBP, called RVLBP, of all image blocks are extracted to construct the expression feature vectors. Finally, we present a TTLDA, in which some unlabeled testing samples are introduced to serve as auxiliary feature sets to enhance the discriminative ability of the regression model learned based on the training samples, to address facial expression recognition task. The experimental result evaluated on the static facial expression recognition challenge of EmotiW 2015 shows that our proposed method achieve a significant improvement compared with the baseline provided by the organizers.

5. ACKNOWLEDGE

This work was partly supported by the National Basic Research Program of China under Grant 2015CB351704 and 2011CB302202, the National Natural Science Foundation of China (NSFC) under Grants 61231002 and 61201444, the Natural Science Foundation of Jiangsu Province under Grant BK20130020, the Ph.D. Program Foundation of Ministry Education of China under grant 20120092110054, and the Graduate Research Innovation Project of Jiangsu Province under Grant KYZZ15_0055.

6. REFERENCES

[1] C. Chang and C. Lin. Libsvm: a library for support vector machines. *ACM Transactions on Intelligent Systems and Technology*, 2(27):1–27, 2011.

[2] A. Dhall, R. Goecke, J. Joshi, K. Sikka, and T. Gedeon. Emotion recognition in the wild challenge 2014: Baseline, data and protocol. In *ACM International Conference on Multimodal Interaction*, pages 461–466, 2014.

[3] A. Dhall, R. Goecke, J. Joshi, M. Wagner, and T. Gedeon. Emotion recognition in the wild challenge 2013. In *ACM International Conference on Multimodal Interaction*, pages 371–372, 2013.

[4] A. Dhall, R. Goecke, S. Lucey, and T. Gedeon. Static facial expression analysis in tough conditions: Data, evaluation protocol and benchmark. In *IEEE International Conference on Computer Vision*, pages 2106–2112, 2011.

[5] A. Dhall, O. R. Murthy, R. Goecke, J. Joshi, and T. Gedeon. Video and image based emotion recognition challenges in the wild: Emotiw 2015. In *ACM International Conference on Multimodal Interaction*, 2015.

[6] M. Felsberg and G. Sommer. The monogenic signal. *IEEE Transactions on Signal Processings*, 49(12):3136–3144, 2001.

[7] X. Huang, A. Dhall, G. Zhao, R. Goecke, and M. Pietikäinen. Riesz-based volume local binary pattern and a novel group expression model for group happiness intensity analysis. In *BMVC*, pages 1–13, 2015.

[8] X. Huang, Q. He, X. Hong, G. Zhao, and M. Pietikäinen. Improved spatiotemporal local monogenic binary pattern for emotion recognition in the wild. In *ACM International Conference on Multimodal Interaction*, pages 514–520, 2014.

[9] X. Huang, G. Zhao, W. Zheng, and M. Pietikäinen. Spatiotemporal local monogenic binary patterns for facial expression recognition. *IEEE Signal Processing Letters*, 19(5):243–246, May 2012.

[10] T. Ojala, M. Pietikäinen, and T. Mäenpää. Multiresolution gray-scale and rotation invariant texture classification with local binary pattern. *IEEE Transaction on Pattern Analysis and Machine Intelligence*, 24(7):971–987, 2002.

[11] V. Ojansivu and J. Heikkilä. Blur insensitive texture classification using local phase quantization. In *International Conference on Image and Signal Processing*, pages 236–243, 2008.

[12] J. Pan and Y. Tang. Texture classification based on BIMF Monogenic signals. In *Asian Conference on Computer Vision*, pages 177–187, 2012.

[13] S. Pan and Q. Yang. A survey on transfer learning. *IEEE Transactions on Knowledge and Data Engineering*, 22(10):1345–1359, 2010.

[14] E. Stein and G. Weiss. *Introduction to Fourier analysis on Euclidean spaces.* Princeton University Press, 1971.

[15] M. Valstar, B. Schuller, K. Smith, F. Eyben, B. Jiang, S. Bilakhia, S. Schnieder, R. Cowie, and M. Pantic. Avec 2013: the continuous audio/visual emotion and depression recognition challenge. In *ACM International Workshop on Audio/visual emotion challenge*, pages 3–10, 2013.

[16] M. Yang, L. Zhang, S. Shiu, and D. Zhang. Monogenic binary coding: An efficient local feature extraction approach to face recognition. *IEEE Transactions on Information Forensics and Security*, 7(6):1738–1751, 2012.

[17] Z. Zeng, M. Pantic, G. Roisman, and T. Huang. A survey of affect recognition methods: audio, visual, and spontaneous expressions. *IEEE Transactions on Pattern Analysis and Machine Intelligence*, 31(1):39–58, 2009.

[18] C. Zetzsche and E. Barth. Fundamental limits of linear filters in the visual processing of two dimensional signals. *Vision Research*, 30(7):1111–1117, 1990.

[19] L. Zhang and H. Li. Encoding local image patterns using Riesz transform: With applications to palmpring and finger-knuckle-print recognition. *Image and Vision Computing*, 30(12):1043–1051, 2012.

[20] L. Zhang, D. Zhang, Z. Guo, and D. Zhang. Monogenic-LBP: A new approach for rotation invariant texture classification. In *IEEE International Conference on Image Processing*, pages 2677–2680, 2010.

[21] W. Zheng. Multi-view facial expression recognition based on group sparse reduced-rank regression. *IEEE Transactions on Affective Computing*, 5(1):71–85, 2014.

[22] W. Zheng, M. Xin, X. Wang, and B. Wang. A novel speech emotion recognition method via incomplete sparse least square regression. *IEEE Signal Processing Letters*, 21(5):569–572, 2014.

[23] W. Zheng and X. Zhou. Cross-pose color facial expression recognition using transductive transfer linear discriminant analysis. In *IEEE International Conference on Image Processing*, 2015.

Combining Multimodal Features within a Fusion Network for Emotion Recognition in the Wild

Bo Sun, Liandong Li, Guoyan Zhou, Xuewen Wu, Jun He, Lejun Yu, Dongxue Li, Qinglan Wei
College of Information Science and Technology, Beijing Normal Univ., Beijing, China100875
tosunbo@bnu.edu.cn, bnulee@hotmail.com, zgy@mail.bnu.edu.cn, xuewenwu@hotmail.com, hejun@bnu.edu.cn, yulejun@bnu.edu.cn, li_dx@mail.bnu.edu.cn, qlwei@mail.bnu.edu.cn

ABSTRACT

In this paper, we describe our work in the third Emotion Recognition in the Wild (EmotiW 2015) Challenge. For each video clip, we extract MSDF, LBP-TOP, HOG, LPQ-TOP and acoustic features to recognize the emotions of film characters. For the static facial expression recognition based on video frame, we extract MSDF, DCNN and RCNN features. We train linear SVM classifiers for these kinds of features on the AFEW and SFEW dataset, and we propose a novel fusion network to combine all the extracted features at decision level. The final achievement we gained is 51.02% on the AFEW testing set and 51.08% on the SFEW testing set, which are much better than the baseline recognition rate of 39.33% and 39.13%.

Categories and Subject Descriptors

I.4.m [Image Processing and Computer Vision]: Miscellaneous; I.5.4 [Pattern Recognition]: Applications

General Terms

Algorithms; Performance; Experimentation

Keywords

Emotion Recognition; Fusion Network; Multimodal Features

1. INTRODUCTION

Automatic Emotion recognition in the wild is a very challenging task. Psychologist Mehrabian noted that an emotional state equals "7% of words + 38% of audio message + 55% of facial expressions" [1], so the recognition of facial expression is an important way to analyze the state of human emotions. At the early stage, researchers focused mostly on the emotion analysis from a single static facial image under constrained circumstances [2], resulting in the loss of spatial domain information and not available for practical application scenarios. As human emotions are actually dynamic streaming in real life, the research is turning into recognition through video or image sequences. There are multiple different methods for emotion recognition, which contain different types of feature descriptors, such as Local Binary Pattern (LBP) [3], Local Phase Quantization (LPQ) [4], Histogram of Oriented Gradients (HOG) [5], Scale-invariant feature transform (SIFT) [6], and facial Action Units (AUs) [7] etc. Using a single feature descriptor to recognize emotion is easy to implement, but the result is not satisfactory in most cases.

ICMI 2015, November 9-13, 2015, Seattle, WA, USA.
© 2015 ACM. ISBN 978-1-4503-3912-4/15/11...$15.00.
DOI: http://dx.doi.org/10.1145/2823327.2823332

The third Emotion Recognition in the Wild Challenge and Workshop (EmotiW 2015) Challenge consists of two real-world condition emotion classification sub-challenges: 1) Audio-Video based emotion recognition challenge based on AFEW [8] database; 2) Image based static facial expression recognition challenge based on SFEW [9] database. The tasks are to assign a single emotion label to the video clip or video frame from seven emotions: Anger, Disgust, Fear, Happiness, Sad, Surprise and Neutral. Participants train models and tune parameters on the training and validation set. Then the prediction results of testing set are submitted to the organizers to test the prediction accuracy. Having extracted multimodal features in the audio or temporal-spatial domain from either audio-videos or images, we proposed a novel fusion network to combine the features together.

In this paper, we describe our work in the EmotiW 2015 challenge. The remainder of the paper is organized as: Section 2 gives the proposed method, including acoustic and visual features that we have extracted, classifiers and details of the novel fusion network. Section 3 gives the entire experiments we have done, in which the parameters settings and the recognition rates of the both sub challenges are available. Then the final conclusion is given in Section 4.

2. THE PROPOSED METHOD

2.1 Multimodal Features

Considering an emotion state is efficiently represented with multi-features, we extracted multimodal features in the challenge. Whole pipelines are showed in Figure 1 and 2. For audio-video based sub challenge, we extract MSDF [10], and LBP-TOP as visual features and MFCC, MFB, and PCM [11] as acoustic features. For image based static facial expression recognition, we extract MSDF, DCNN [12] and RCNN [13] features. In addition, LPQ-TOP [4] and HOG [5] features are extracted as comparisons.

2.1.1 Acoustic Descriptors

For acoustic features, we extract several types of low-level descriptors (LLD) through the OpenSMILE toolkit [14] and apply the same filters, functions, and transformations as described in [15] to these descriptors. Then we try concatenating combinations of those descriptors. The compositions of three types of acoustic features we propose are listed in Table I.

Table I. Acoustic features

Acoustic Features	Descriptors
1	MFCC + F0 Envelope
2	MFB + F0 Envelope
3	PCM + delta F0 Envelope + Voicing Prob.

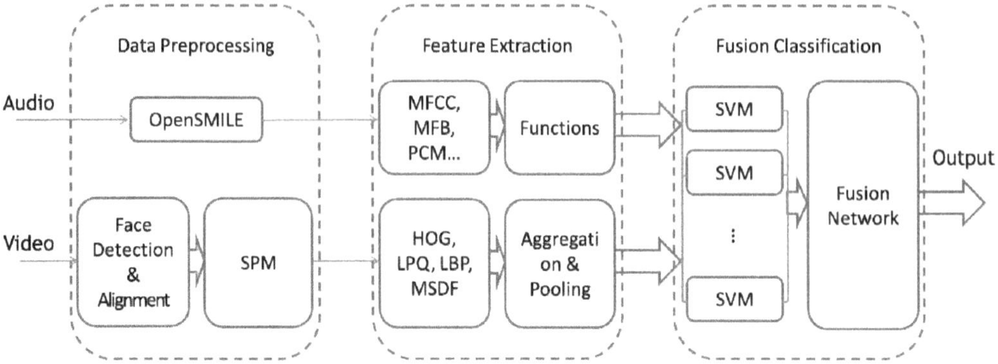

Figure 1. Pipeline of our proposed method for audio-video based emotion recognition

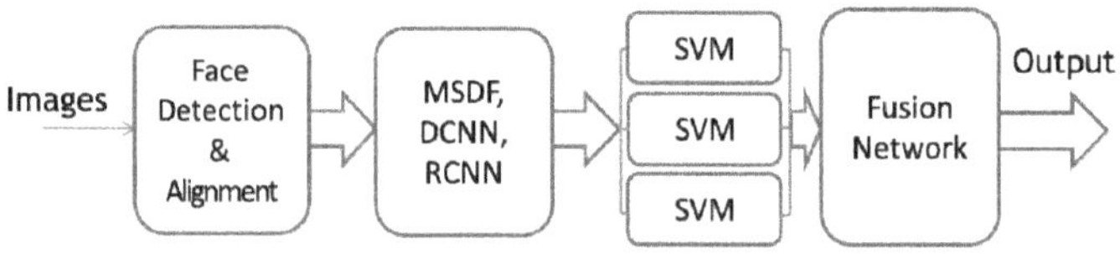

Figure 2. Pipeline of our proposed method for image based static facial expression recognition

2.1.2 SPM LBP-TOP

The Local Binary Patterns from Three Orthogonal Planes (LBP-TOP) [3] method is an efficient representations of dynamic image texture which has been successfully applied to facial expression recognition. It has high recognition accuracy for acted facial expression in lab-controlled environment [3]. We concatenate local binary patterns on three orthogonal planes: XY, XT and YT. We only consider the co-occurrence statistics in these three directions and concatenate them into three histograms. The XY planes histogram provides the spatial texture information, while the XT and YT plane histograms provide information about the space-time transitions.

In our experiments, we try spatial pyramid matching [16] for LBP-TOP descriptors. Experiment results show that spatial pyramid matching can add recognition accuracy by providing more spatial information for final features.

2.1.3 Bag of MSDF

The Bag of Words (BoW) model based on multi-scale dense SIFT features (MSDF) [17] has shown remarkable performance on facial expression recognition [18]. Its recognition ability is still robust even in emotion recognition in the wild. The superiority of this approach lies in the combination of dense SIFT feature extraction, feature encoding using Locality-constrained Linear Coding [19] and spatial information fusion by multi-scale pooling over spatial pyramid [16].

First we extract multi-scale dense SIFT descriptors [20] of some of the image samples. Then all the descriptors are clustered to 800 clustering centers as codewords for encoding. The number 800 is chosen through experiments. Then the whole data sets' dense SIFT descriptors are encoded using the Locality-constrained Linear Coding, which can guarantee the sparse and locality of the coded words. Finally, the coded words are accounted after doing a five layers spatial pyramid matching.

After getting the MSDF BoW features of all image frames of a video clip, max pooling is usually used to aggregating all frame features into one video features. Though still decent performance, it actually loses much detailed temporal information of a video. Based on deep analysis in our experiments, we add temporal information through extracting LBP descriptors or dense SIFT descriptors on the XT and YT planes of a video.

2.1.4 Convolutional Neutral Networks

The Convolutional Neural Network (CNN) [21] is a popular artificial neural network in the community of computer vision. The deep CNN models [22] usually have 5-20 layers of activation functions, convolution computing, and pooling. Every layer can represent some image features that learnt unsupervised. The introducing of convolution and pooling is inspired by the fact that image pixels have locally connection to pixels around them.

We use two kinds of CNN architectures, AlexNet and RCNN. AlexNet [12] is a 9-layers deep model designed for ILSVRC-2012 Challenge [23], using ReLU as activation function. It used data enlarge strategy, normalization and dropout to avoid over-fitting. RCNN [13] (Regions CNN) is a type of deep learning architecture that combines object detection and object recognition. It can detect the object in a scene and then use CNN to classify. These two models are all pre-trained on the ImageNet 2012 dataset.

2.2 Classifier

The features we use are all linearly separable under ideal conditions. So we use linear SVM as basic classifiers. Given a training set of L data points (x_i, y_i), $i = 1, ..., l$, $x_i \in R^n$, $y_i \in \{-1,+1\}$, the support vector classifier solves the following unconstrained optimization problem [24]:

$$\min \frac{1}{2}\theta^T\theta + C\sum_i \xi(\theta;\theta_i, y_i) \quad (1)$$

where C is the penalty parameter and $\xi(\theta; \theta_i, y_i)=\max(1- y_i\theta^T x_i, 0)^2$ is the loss function. For testing data x, SVM predicts it as positive if $\theta^T x>0$, and negative otherwise. Here we use the decision value $\theta^T x$ of SVM Classifier as the input for the next fusion process. As SVM is a binary classifier, we follow one-vs.-rest strategy, which classifies the data points between one category and the rest ones at a time.

2.3 Fusion Network

As different features have different discriminative abilities on specific emotions [25] [26], we propose a novel fusion network as shown in Figure 3 to combine the results of each SVM classifier.

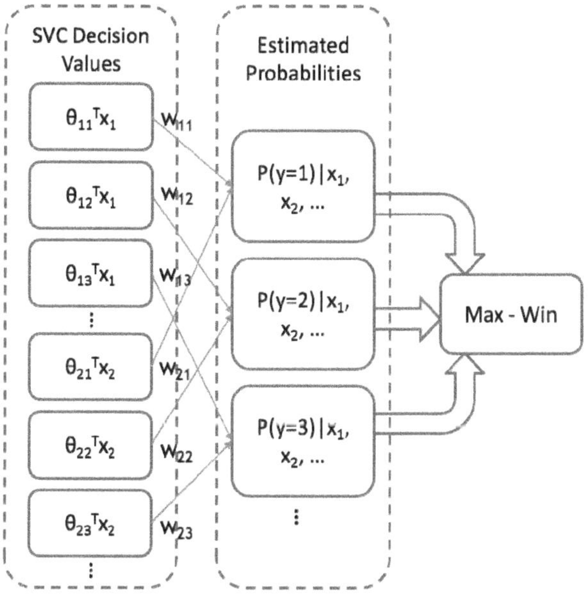

Figure 3. Layers of proposed fusion network

Given m features and n classes, the SVM classifiers generate $m\times n$ decision values, which can be denoted as $a_{(j,k)}=\theta_{jk}^T x_j$, $j=1, \ldots, m$, $k=1, \ldots, n$. Then they are used as input for the fusion network. For input a, we use a hypothesis function $h_w(a)$

$$h_w(a^{(i)}) = \begin{bmatrix} p(y^{(i)}=1 \mid a^{(i)};W) \\ p(y^{(i)}=2 \mid a^{(i)};W) \\ \vdots \\ p(y^{(i)}=n \mid a^{(i)};W) \end{bmatrix} = \frac{1}{\sum_{k=1}^{n} e^{\sum_{j=1}^{m} W_{kj}^T a^{(i)}}} \begin{bmatrix} e^{\sum_{j=1}^{m} W_{j1}^T a_{j1}^{(i)}} \\ e^{\sum_{j=1}^{m} W_{j2}^T a_{j2}^{(i)}} \\ \vdots \\ e^{\sum_{j=1}^{m} W_{jn}^T a_{jn}^{(i)}} \end{bmatrix} \quad (2)$$

to estimate $P(y=k|a)$, which represent the probability of the class label y taking on each of the n different possible values. Here W mean $m\times n$ weights. Thus, the final output is a n dimensional vector, which represent n probabilities. The final prediction is using a max-win strategy to choose the most likely label.

We use a loss function $J(W)$ for optimization. The gradient descent method is applied to get optimized values of W by updating W to $W-\nabla_W J(W)$ at every iteration.

$$J(W) = -\frac{1}{L}\left[\sum_{i=1}^{L}\sum_{k=1}^{m} 1\{y^{(i)}=k\}\log\frac{e^{\sum_{j=1}^{m} W_{jk}^T a_{jk}^{(i)}}}{\sum_{k=1}^{n} e^{\sum_{j=1}^{m} W_{jk}^T a_{jk}^{(i)}}}\right] + \frac{\lambda}{2}\sum_{j=1}^{m}\sum_{k=1}^{n} W_{jk}^2 \quad \ldots(3)$$

$$\nabla_{W_k} J(W) = -\frac{1}{L}\sum_{i=1}^{L}\left[x^{(i)}(1\{y^{(i)}=k\} - p(y^{(i)}=k \mid a^{(i)};W))\right] + \lambda W_k \quad \ldots(4)$$

where λ is the L2-norm parameter, $1\{\cdot\}$ is the indicator function.

In experiments, we also try a simplified version of fusion network, which shared the same W_j between a feature's decision values ($W_{j1} = W_{j2} = W_{j3} = \ldots$).

3. EXPERIMENTS

3.1 Audio-Video Based Emotion Recognition

The emotion recognition challenge contains audio-video short clips labeled using a semi-automatic approach defined in [8]. The task is to assign a single emotion label to the video clip from the six universal emotions (Anger, Disgust, Fear, Happiness, Sad & Surprise) and Neutral. We compare the classification accuracies between several acoustic and visual features on the AFEW dataset. Comparison results and SVM parameters are listed in Table II and III. The SVM classifiers all use linear kernels. Models are trained on training set and parameters are tuned on validation set through a five-fold cross validation in the range from 2^{-3} to 2^{15}.

Table II. Acoustic features classification accuracies on AFEW

Feature	Accuracy	C
Audio	24.07%	4
MFCC*	31.54%	128
MFB*	29.92%	32768
PCM*	31.27%	8

In Table II, the MFCC* represents the concatenated feature of MFCC and F0 Envelope described in 2.1.1, so does for MFB* and PCM*. The audio means the audio baseline feature provided by the EmotiW organizers.

Table III. Visual features classification accuracies on AFEW

Feature	Accuracy	C
Baseline (LBPTOP)	36.08%	N/A
HOG	34.23%	0.125
L4-SPM-LBPTOP	43.67%	1
L5-SPM-LBPTOP	42.32%	1
LPQTOP	42.59%	4
L4-SPM-LPQTOP	44.47%	1
MSDF	46.09%	1
MSDF-TOP	46.45%	1
MSDF-LBP	49.33%	1

From Table III we can see that spatial pyramid matching can add discriminative abilities to naive features. Here the *L4-SPM* means four layers spatial pyramid matching, so does *L5*. We can also see too much layers may cause lower classification accuracy. Comparisons between three types of MSDF features show that temporal information also can improve the classification results.

	AN	DI	FE	HA	NE	SA	SU
AN	0.71	0.01	0.05	0.08	0.09	0.03	0.04
DI	0.07	0.17	0.03	0.24	0.21	0.24	0.03
FE	0.21	0.05	0.24	0.06	0.09	0.12	0.23
HA	0.05	0.05	0.02	0.71	0.06	0.10	0.02
NE	0.04	0.04	0.06	0.11	0.53	0.16	0.05
SA	0.18	0.04	0.04	0.14	0.17	0.38	0.04
SU	0.07	0.04	0.19	0.04	0.11	0.22	0.33

Figure 4. Confusion matrix of our final result on AFEW

Table IV. Fusion results on AFEW of Audio-Video Based Emotion Recognition

Fusion Method	Features	λ	Val	Test
Baseline	LBP-TOP	N/A	36.08%	39.33%
Fusion Network	MFCC*, MSDF-TOP, MSDF-LBP	0.023	50.40%	50.46%
Fusion Network	MFCC*, PCM*, HOG, LBP-TOP, MSDF-TOP, MSDF-LBP	0.01	54.58%	48.98%
Fusion Network	MFCC*, MFB*, PCM*, HOG, LPQ-TOP, MSDF-TOP, MSDF-LBP	0.001	57.41%	N/A
Fusion Network (weight shared)	MFCC*, MFB*, PCM*, MSDF	0.01	49.33%	50.28%
Fusion Network (weight shared)	MFCC*, MFB*, PCM*, MSDF-LBP	0.005	50.67%	50.28%
Fusion Network (weight shared)	MFCC*, MSDF-TOP, MSDF-LBP	0.0001	50.40%	50.83%
Fusion Network (weight shared), Train & Val	MFCC*, MSDF-TOP, MSDF-LBP	0.0001	50.40%	48.24%
Fusion Network (weight shared), Train & Val	MFCC*, HOG, LBP-TOP, MSDF-TOP, MSDF-LBP	0.001	55.05%	**51.02%**

Table V. Fusion results on SFEW of Image Based Static Facial Expression Recognition

Fusion Method	Features	λ	Val	Test
Baseline	PHOG, LPQ	N/A	35.96%	39.13%
Fusion Network	MSDF, DCNN, RCNN	0.03	44.26%	47.31%
MKL	MSDF, DCNN, RCNN	N/A	47.31%	45.97%
Fusion Network	MSDF, DCNN, RCNN	0.01	47.31%	48.12%
Fusion Network	MSDF, DCNN, RCNN	0.0001	48.94%	47.04%
Fusion Network, Train & Val	MSDF, DCNN, RCNN	0.01	47.31%	50.00%
Fusion Network (weight shared)	MSDF, DCNN, RCNN	0.001	46.37%	48.12%
Fusion Network (weight shared), Train & Val	MSDF, DCNN, RCNN	0.001	46.37%	**51.08%**
Fusion Network (weight shared), Train & Val	MSDF, DCNN, RCNN, PHOG	0.001	46.84%	50.00%

Then we use fusion network to combine the classification results of these features. We train fusion network on the validation set. Fusion results are showed in Table IV. Here we can see fusion network have shown promising results on validation set. Though fusion network has better result on the validation set, its prediction result is no better than weight shared fusion on the testing set. Another thing needed to be studied is how to choose the better parameter λ which has significant influence on fusion network's generalization ability. At last, we maintain the parameters C of SVM and learnt weights W of fusion network, and train SVMs on the training and validation set. Result shows that this can further improves the whole recognition result. As submission times are limited, more contrast experiments are done in section 3.2 in the other sub-challenge.

Our best result in this sub-challenge is 51.02%, which fuses MFCC, HOG, LBPTOP, MSDF-TOP and MSDF-LBP through a weight shared fusion network. SVMs are trained on the training and validation set. The confusion matrix of this submission on AFEW dataset is showed in Figure 4. We can see some of the emotions are much more accurately detected than others, maybe that latter emotions are also hard for human to distinguish.

3.2 Image Based Static Facial Expression Recognition

The image based static facial expression recognition contains recognition of frame level facial expression labels. The task is to assign a facial expression label to a frame from SFEW dataset out of the seven emotions. We compare the classification accuracies between several features on the SFEW [9] dataset. Here to make decision values uniform, we took the last pooling layer's output as features that learnt by DCNN (AlexNet) and RCNN, and use linear SVM for classification. Comparison results and the corresponding SVM parameters are listed in Table VI.

Table VI. Image feature classification accuracies on SFEW

Feature	Accuracy	C
Baseline	35.96%	N/A
LPQ	28.08%	64
PHOG	31.79%	256
MSDF	43.33%	1
DCNN	37.00%	0.5
RCNN	43.09%	0.5

From Table VI we can see RCNN can achieve almost the same accuracy with the best handcrafted feature MSDF BoW. Here the CNN models are both pre-trained on ImageNet 2012 dataset [23] and fine-tuned on SFEW set using the implementation of [27].

Then we use fusion network to combine the classification results of these features. Fusion results are showed in Table V. In this sub-challenge, we compare the fusion network with General Multiple Kernel Learning (MKL) [28] which had been used by Sikka et al. in [18]. Results show that our proposed method is better both on validation set and testing set. We also compare the result between SVM learnt on training set alone and SVM learnt on train & validation sets. Contrast experiments results show that our learnt fusion weights are still stable when SVMs are trained on larger data sets. While the original fusion network and the weight shared fusion network achieve the same result on testing set, the enlarged training set result are better when using weight shared network, which means less parameters may be more stable.

Our best result on this sub-challenge is 51.08%, which fuses MSDF, DCNN (AlexNet) and RCNN through a weight shared fusion network. SVMs are trained on training and validation set. The confusion matrix of our best result on SFEW dataset is showed in Figure 5.

	AN	DI	FE	HA	NE	SA	SU
AN	0.67	0.00	0.06	0.03	0.14	0.04	0.06
DI	0.18	0.06	0.00	0.35	0.18	0.18	0.06
FE	0.41	0.00	0.12	0.02	0.12	0.10	0.22
HA	0.09	0.01	0.02	0.74	0.02	0.11	0.01
NE	0.09	0.00	0.05	0.02	0.59	0.17	0.09
SA	0.16	0.00	0.13	0.18	0.02	0.36	0.15
SU	0.30	0.00	0.05	0.08	0.08	0.11	0.38

Figure 5. Confusion matrix of our final result on SFEW

4. CONCLUSIONS

In this paper, we investigate different features for multimodal automatic human emotion recognition in the real world. For each feature, we train individual linear SVM classifier which has different discriminative ability for emotions classification. We propose a novel decision level fusion network to utilize these feature characteristics. The method is evaluated on EmotiW 2015 AFEW and SFEW datasets and gain very promising achievement on the testing sets. In the future, we will try to integrate the feature-level fusion into our fusion network and investigate more types of fusion network models to further improve the recognition performance. And we will conduct more experiments to discuss the performance of gradient descent algorithms in our method.

5. ACKNOWLEDGEMENTS

This work is supported by the Fundamental Research Funds for the Central Universities of China (2014KJJCA15, 2012YBXS10) and the National Education Science Twelfth Five-Year Plan Key Issues of the Ministry of Education (DCA140229).

6. REFERENCES

[1] Mehrabian, A. (1968). Communication without words. *Psychological today,2*, 53-55.

[2] Pantic, M., & Rothkrantz, L. J. M. (2000). Automatic analysis of facial expressions: The state of the art. *Pattern Analysis and Machine Intelligence, IEEE Transactions on*, *22*(12), 1424-1445.

[3] Zhao, G., & Pietikainen, M. (2007). Dynamic texture recognition using local binary patterns with an application to facial expressions. *Pattern Analysis and Machine Intelligence, IEEE Transactions on*, *29*(6), 915-928.

[4] Päivärinta, J., Rahtu, E., & Heikkilä, J. (2011). Volume local phase quantization for blur-insensitive dynamic texture classification. In *Image Analysis* (pp. 360-369). Springer Berlin Heidelberg.

[5] Dalal, N., & Triggs, B. (2005, June). Histograms of oriented gradients for human detection. In *Computer Vision and Pattern Recognition, 2005. CVPR 2005. IEEE Computer Society Conference on* (Vol. 1, pp. 886-893). IEEE.

[6] Lowe, D. G. (1999). Object recognition from local scale-invariant features. In *Computer vision, 1999. The proceedings of the seventh IEEE international conference on* (Vol. 2, pp. 1150-1157). Ieee.

[7] Velusamy, S., Kannan, H., Anand, B., Sharma, A., & Navathe, B. (2011, May). A method to infer emotions from facial action units. In *Acoustics, Speech and Signal Processing (ICASSP), 2011 IEEE International Conference on* (pp. 2028-2031). IEEE.

[8] Dhall, A., Goecke, R., Lucey, S., & Gedeon, T. (2012). Collecting Large, Richly Annotated Facial-Expression Databases from Movies. *MultiMedia, IEEE*, *19*(3), 34-41.

[9] Dhall, A., Goecke, R., Lucey, S., & Gedeon, T. (2011, November). Static facial expression analysis in tough conditions: Data, evaluation protocol and benchmark. In *Computer Vision Workshops (ICCV Workshops), 2011 IEEE International Conference on* (pp. 2106-2112). IEEE.

[10] Sikka, K., Wu, T., Susskind, J., & Bartlett, M. (2012, January). Exploring bag of words architectures in the facial expression domain. In *Computer Vision–ECCV 2012. Workshops and Demonstrations* (pp. 250-259). Springer Berlin Heidelberg.

[11] Schuller, B., Steidl, S., & Batliner, A. (2009, September). The INTERSPEECH 2009 emotion challenge. In *INTERSPEECH* (Vol. 2009, pp. 312-315).

[12] Krizhevsky, A., Sutskever, I., & Hinton, G. E. (2012). Imagenet classification with deep convolutional neural networks. In *Advances in neural information processing systems* (pp. 1097-1105).

[13] Girshick, R., Donahue, J., Darrell, T., & Malik, J. (2014, June). Rich feature hierarchies for accurate object detection and semantic segmentation. In *Computer Vision and Pattern Recognition (CVPR), 2014 IEEE Conference on* (pp. 580-587). IEEE.

[14] Eyben, F., Wöllmer, M., & Schuller, B. (2010, October). Opensmile: the Munich versatile and fast open-source audio feature extractor. In *Proceedings of the international conference on Multimedia* (pp. 1459-1462). ACM.

[15] Abhinav Dhall, O. V. Ramana Murthy, Roland Goecke, Jyoti Joshi and Tom Gedeom, Video and Image based Emotion Recognition Challenges in the Wild: EmotiW 2015, ICMI 2015.

[16] Lazebnik, S., Schmid, C., & Ponce, J. (2006). Beyond bags of features: Spatial pyramid matching for recognizing natural scene categories. In *Computer Vision and Pattern Recognition, 2006 IEEE Computer Society Conference on* (Vol. 2, pp. 2169-2178). IEEE.

[17] Sikka, K., Wu, T., Susskind, J., & Bartlett, M. (2012, January). Exploring bag of words architectures in the facial expression domain. In *Computer Vision–ECCV 2012. Workshops and Demonstrations* (pp. 250-259). Springer Berlin Heidelberg.

[18] Sikka, K., Dykstra, K., Sathyanarayana, S., Littlewort, G., & Bartlett, M. (2013, December). Multiple kernel learning for emotion recognition in the wild. In *Proceedings of the 15th ACM on International conference on multimodal interaction* (pp. 517-524). ACM.

[19] Wang, J., Yang, J., Yu, K., Lv, F., Huang, T., & Gong, Y. (2010, June). Locality-constrained linear coding for image classification. In *Computer Vision and Pattern Recognition (CVPR), 2010 IEEE Conference on* (pp. 3360-3367). IEEE.

[20] Vedaldi, A., & Fulkerson, B. (2010, October). VLFeat: An open and portable library of computer vision algorithms. In *Proceedings of the international conference on Multimedia* (pp. 1469-1472). ACM.

[21] LeCun, Y., Bottou, L., Bengio, Y., & Haffner, P. (1998). Gradient-based learning applied to document recognition. *Proceedings of the IEEE*, *86*(11), 2278-2324.

[22] LeCun, Y., Bengio, Y., & Hinton, G. (2015). Deep learning. *Nature*,*521*(7553), 436-444.

[23] Russakovsky, O., Deng, J., Su, H., Krause, J., Satheesh, S., Ma, S., ... & Fei-Fei, L. (2014). Imagenet large scale visual recognition challenge. *International Journal of Computer Vision*, 1-42.

[24] Fan, R. E., Chang, K. W., Hsieh, C. J., Wang, X. R., & Lin, C. J. (2008). LIBLINEAR: A library for large linear classification. *The Journal of Machine Learning Research*, *9*, 1871-1874.

[25] Sun, B., Li, L., Zuo, T., Chen, Y., Zhou, G., & Wu, X. (2014, November). Combining multimodal features with hierarchical classifier fusion for emotion recognition in the wild. In *Proceedings of the 16th International Conference on Multimodal Interaction* (pp. 481-486). ACM.

[26] Kahou, S. E., Bouthillier, X., Lamblin, P., Gulcehre, C., Michalski, V., Konda, K., ... & Bengio, Y. (2015). EmoNets: Multimodal deep learning approaches for emotion recognition in video. *arXiv preprint arXiv:1503.01800.*

[27] Jia, Y., Shelhamer, E., Donahue, J., Karayev, S., Long, J., Girshick, R., ... & Darrell, T. (2014, November). Caffe: Convolutional architecture for fast feature embedding. In *Proceedings of the ACM International Conference on Multimedia* (pp. 675-678). ACM.

[28] Varma, M., & Babu, B. R. (2009, June). More generality in efficient multiple kernel learning. In *Proceedings of the 26th Annual International Conference on Machine Learning* (pp. 1065-1072). ACM.

Emotion Recognition in the Wild via Convolutional Neural Networks and Mapped Binary Patterns

Gil Levi
The Open University of Israel
gil.levi100@gmail.com

Tal Hassner
USC / Information Sciences Institute
hassner@isi.edu
and
The Open University of Israel

ABSTRACT

We present a novel method for classifying emotions from static facial images. Our approach leverages on the recent success of Convolutional Neural Networks (CNN) on face recognition problems. Unlike the settings often assumed there, far less labeled data is typically available for training emotion classification systems. Our method is therefore designed with the goal of simplifying the problem domain by removing confounding factors from the input images, with an emphasis on image illumination variations. This, in an effort to reduce the amount of data required to effectively train deep CNN models. To this end, we propose novel transformations of image intensities to 3D spaces, designed to be invariant to monotonic photometric transformations. These are applied to CASIA Webface images which are then used to train an ensemble of multiple architecture CNNs on multiple representations. Each model is then fine-tuned with limited emotion labeled training data to obtain final classification models. Our method was tested on the Emotion Recognition in the Wild Challenge (EmotiW 2015), Static Facial Expression Recognition sub-challenge (SFEW) and shown to provide a substantial, 15.36% improvement over baseline results (40% gain in performance).

Categories and Subject Descriptors

I.5.4 [**Pattern Recognition**]: Applications—*Computer Vision*

Keywords

Emotion Recognition; Deep Learning; Local Binary Patterns; EmotiW 2015 Challenge

1. INTRODUCTION

Facial expressions play a vital role in social communications between humans. It is therefore unsurprising that automatic facial emotion recognition has become a subject of much recent research. Additional motivation comes from potential applications of effective systems for emotion recognition, with some examples including affect-sensitive Man-Machine-Interaction systems and auto tutors [12, 11, 29]. Yet despite this work, present automatic capabilities are still far from meeting the needs of commercial systems. This gap in performance is especially noteworthy when considering the substantial leaps in performance recently reported for the related task of face recognition (e.g., [33, 38, 37]).

Possible reasons for this performance gap between expression and face recognition systems include the significant difference in the data available for developing, training and testing automatic systems: Much of the recent achievements in machine face recognition have been due to deep Convolutional Neural Networks (CNN) which require massive amounts of labeled training data [33], and these are not yet available for emotion recognition. Exacerbating this is the particular nature of the emotion recognition problem, which involves large intra-class and small inter-class appearance variations. These are added to the many confounding factors of face image analysis under unconstrained *in-the-wild* conditions, such as those considered here.

We propose a method designed to jointly address two of the key challenges of automatic emotion recognition from still images. The first is the small amount of labeled data available for training deep CNN models and the second is appearance variation, specifically, illumination variability. We

Figure 1: Image intensities (left) are converted to Local Binary Pattern (LBP) codes (middle), shown here as grayscale values. We propose to map these values to a 3D metric space (right) in order to use them as input for Convolutional Neural Network (CNN) models. 3D codes in the right image are visualized as RGB colors.

EmotiW'15, November 9, 2015, Seattle, WA, USA.
© 2015 ACM. ISBN 978-1-4503-3983-4/15/11 ...$15.00.
DOI: http://dx.doi.org/10.1145/2823327.2823333.

define a novel mapping from intensities to illumination invariant, 3D spaces, based on the well-known Local Binary Patterns (LBP) feature transform [25, 27, 26]. Unlike LBP codes, our mapping produces values in a metric space which can be processed by CNN models (Fig. 1). Transformed images from the CASIA webface collection are used to train an ensemble of CNN models using different network architectures and applied to different representations. These are then fine-tuned on a substantially smaller set of emotion-labeled face images. We test our method on the Emotion Recognition in the Wild Challenge (EmotiW 2015), Static Facial Expression Recognition sub-challenge (SFEW) [10]. Our results demonstrate a remarkable 15.36% improvement over baseline scores (40% gain in performance).

2. RELATED WORK

Automatic facial emotion recognition has received increasing interest in the last two decades. The nature of the problems considered by previous work is reflected in the benchmarks used to measure and report performances. For example, early relevant data-sets such as those of [23, 18, 30] contained only constrained images taken in laboratory controlled conditions. More recently, unconstrained, in-the-wild photos have been considered with the release of the EmotiW challenge [9].

In [36] a Boosted-LBP descriptor was proposed, designed by learning the most discriminative LBP features using AdaBoost. Images represented using these features were then classified for different emotions using Support Vector Machines (SVM) [8]. In [5] a novel classification tree, based on sparse coding [24] was presented. The authors of [22] proposed a deep architecture which models face expressions by utilizing a set of local Action Unit features. Finally, the authors of [16] suggest using high-dimensional image features produced by dense census transformed vectors [44] based on locations defined by fiducial landmark detections.

Similar to some of the methods listed above, our own also uses deep CNNs. Unlike them, we propose applying these networks to pre-processed images, transformed in a manner designed to reduce variability due to illumination changes. Furthermore, we use network ensembles, rather than just single networks, where each one is trained using different image representations (different pre-processing applied to the input images) as well as different network architectures. Rigorous testing shows that these different networks provide complementary information which, when combined, provides a substantial boost to recognition performance.

Deep CNNs. Though CNNs have been introduced more than three decades ago [20], it is only recently that they become a predominant method in image classification tasks. With the emergence of very large classification data-sets, the increase in computation power and algorithmic improvements in training those models, the huge number of model parameters is no longer a limiting factor in applying CNNs in practical settings. Thus, in recent years, deep CNNs have been applied in various image classification problems, including, e.g., object recognition [19], scene recognition [45], face verification [33, 38, 37], age and gender classification [21], and more.

Local Binary Patterns. Local Binary Patterns (LBP) were originally developed as a means of describing texture images [25, 27, 26]. They have since been successfully applied to a wide range of other image recognition tasks, most notably face recognition [1, 41], age estimation [6] and gender classification [35]. To our knowledge, we are the first to propose the use of LBP features as input to CNN models. We show that doing so boosts performance well beyond that obtained with CNN models trained on RGB alone.

3. METHOD

We next describe the various components of our approach. We assume that images have been preprocessed by converting them to gray scale and cropping them to the region of the face. We further assume that faces are in-plane aligned. Though frontalization [14] may presumably be used here to reduce appearance variability further, we have not tested this approach in our pipeline. In practice, we use the images provided by the EmotiW 2015 challenge [10], aligned using the Zhu and Ramanan facial feature detector [46].

Each face image is processed as follows:

1. We begin by applying LBP encoding to the pixels of each image using different values for the LBP radius parameter (Section 3.1). Each encoding converts image intensity values to one of 256 LBP code values.

2. LBP codes are mapped to a 3D space using the mapping obtained by applying Multi Dimensional Scaling (MDS) using code-to-code dissimilarity scores based on an approximation to the Earth Mover's Distance (Section 3.2).

3. The original RGB image, along with the mapped code images, are then used to train multiple, separate CNN models to predict one of seven emotion classes. A final classification is obtained by a weighted average over the outputs of the network ensemble taking the predicted emotion class to be the one with the maximum average probability (Section 3.3).

Each of these steps is described in detail next.

3.1 LBP code extraction

LBP codes have been widely used for nearly two decades; we refer to previous work for detailed description of how these are produced and of their various properties [25, 27, 26]. Here, we provide a cursory overview related to their use in our work.

LBP codes capture local image micro-textures. They are produced by applying thresholds on the intensity values of the pixels in small neighborhoods using the intensity of each neighborhood's central pixel as the threshold. The resulting pattern of 0s (lower than the threshold) and 1s (higher than the threshold) is then treated as the pixel's representation or *code*. When the neighborhood contains eight other pixels, this binary string is treated as an eight-bit number between 0 and 255. These codes are typically pooled over image regions using a histogram of code frequencies. Histograms are then used to represent the image region (see, e.g., [42]). In our work we use these codes in an entirely different manner.

Before continuing, we stop to consider specific advantage of LBP codes and the reason for their use here. By basing each pixel's encoding on a threshold value applied to its neighbors, the resulting representation is inherently invariant to monotonic photometric transformations; that is, any photometric transformation which does not change the order of image intensities. This includes, but is not limited to, additive and multiplicative intensity transformations, gamma correction and contrast manipulations.

Used with Support Vector Machines (SVM) classifiers, LBP code histograms have been key to the success of face recognition systems [41, 42, 14]. In contrast to these earlier methods, we wish to process LBP codes directly, without pooling, using CNN models. LBP codes, however, are, by their nature, not well suited as CNN inputs.

To understand why, note that the basic operation performed by a CNN on its input values is a convolution, which is equivalent to a weighted average of these values. When these values are codes from an unordered set, the outcome of a convolution is meaningless. To illustrate this, consider the following three LBP codes: $a = (0,0,0,0,0,0,0,0)$, $b = (1,0,0,0,0,0,0,0)$ and $c = (0,0,0,0,0,0,0,1)$. Both b and c differ from a by just one bit, meaning the distance in the binary LBP space between a and b is the same as the distance between a and c. This can be taken to imply that they represent very similar local arrangements of pixel values. Simply treating these codes as eight-bit integer values, however, we get that $a = 0$, $b = 128$ and $c = 1$. Hence, the euclidean distance between b and a is much larger than the euclidean distance between c and a. Our mapping, described next, addresses this very issue.

3.2 Mapping LBP codes

The key to our LBP code mapping is the use of *Multi Dimensional Scaling* (MDS) [2, 34] to transform the unordered LBP code values to points in a metric space. In this way, transformed points may be averaged together using convolution operations yet their distances approximate the original code-to-code distances.

To this end, we first define a distance (dissimilarity) $\delta_{i,j}$ between LBP codes, $C_i, C_j \in 2_2^8$. This distance should reflect the underlying similarity of the image intensity patterns used to produce each LBP code string. A full dissimilarity matrix, representing the distances between all possible code values, can then be defined as:

$$\Delta := \begin{bmatrix} \delta_{11} & \delta_{12} & \delta_{13} & \dots & \delta_{1n} \\ \delta_{21} & \delta_{22} & \delta_{23} & \dots & \delta_{2n} \\ \vdots & \vdots & \vdots & \ddots & \vdots \\ \delta_{d1} & \delta_{d2} & \delta_{d3} & \dots & \delta_{dn} \end{bmatrix},$$

For a given dissimilarity matrix Δ, MDS seeks a mapping of the codes to a low dimensional metric space, such that:

$$\delta_{i,j} \approx \|V_i - V_j\| = \|MDS(C_i) - MDS(C_j)\|. \quad (1)$$

Here, LBP codes C_i, and C_j are mapped to V_i, V_j resp.

Defining a binary LBP pattern dissimilarity. Ostensibly, the difference between two LBP codes can be estimated by the number of different bit values they have between them; that is by their Hamming distance. This, however, may not accurately reflect the differences in the intensity patterns which produced these codes: The *locations* of differing bit values, not just their number, are also important when considering code similarity.

To illustrate this, again consider the following three binary LBP vectors: $a = (1,0,0,0,0,0,0,0)$, $b = (0,1,0,0,0,0,0,0)$ and $c = (0,0,0,0,1,0,0,0)$ (see also, Eq. 2). The number of different bits (and hence the Hamming distance) for the pair a and b is the same number as for a and c: two. The original texture patterns which produced these patterns, however, are very different: the pair a and b are related by a slight, one-pixel rotation of the pattern around the central pixel, whereas code c represents a mirror of the intensity pattern represented by a and the two are hence less similar.

$$a = \begin{bmatrix} 1 & 0 & 0 \\ 0 & \times & 0 \\ 0 & 0 & 0 \end{bmatrix} \quad b = \begin{bmatrix} 0 & 1 & 0 \\ 0 & \times & 0 \\ 0 & 0 & 0 \end{bmatrix} \quad c = \begin{bmatrix} 0 & 0 & 0 \\ 0 & \times & 0 \\ 0 & 0 & 1 \end{bmatrix} \quad (2)$$

In order to account for differences in spatial locations of pixel codes rather than Humming distance we use their *Earth Mover's Distance* (EMD) [31].

Generally speaking, EMD is defined to reflect the smallest effort required to convert one distribution into anther. It is used here as a measure of the difference between two LBP codes. Formally, the EMD between two codes, P and Q is defined as follows:

$$EMD(P,Q) = \frac{\min_{\{f_{kl}\}} \sum_{kl} f_{kl} d_{kl}}{\sum_{kl} f_{kl}}, s.t.,$$

$$0 \leq f_{kl}, \sum_{l} f_{kl} \leq P_k, \sum_{k} f_{kl} \leq Q_l, \textit{ and} \quad (3)$$

$$\sum_{kl} f_{kl} = \min\left(\sum_{k} P_k, \sum_{l} Q_l\right).$$

Intuitively, this reflects the effort required to shift values from one code to another, where $f_{kl} \in \{0,1\}$ is the flow of the value from bit k in P (P_k) to bit l in Q (Q_l), $\{f_{kl}\}$ is the entire flow from P to Q and

$$d_{kl} = ||k - l||_2, \quad (4)$$

is taken to be the standard definition of a *ground distance* between two bit positions , and represents the effort required to move the value between bit positions.

EMD approximation. In practice, rather than compute the true EMD between the two code strings (Eq. 3), we approximate it by making the (here, often untrue) assumption that both codes have the same number of bits set to 1. This allows the use of the closed form solution to EMD [40, 7]:

$$EMD(P,Q) = ||CDF(P) - CDF(Q)||_1, \quad (5)$$

with CDF being the cumulative distribution function (cumulative sum) of bit values. This not only allows faster computation than general EMD, but, more importantly, it better reflects code distances whenever the numbers of bits set to 1 is different. To illustrate this, the true EMD distance between the codes $a = (0,0,0,0,0,0,0,0)$ and $b = (1,1,1,1,1,1,1,1)$ would be 0, as there are no bit values of 1 to move from any position in a to b. This would wrongly imply that they encode similar local appearance. The value computed using Eq. 5, however, would be 36, correctly reflecting the difference in the local appearance represented by the two codes. The entire code-to-code distance matrix

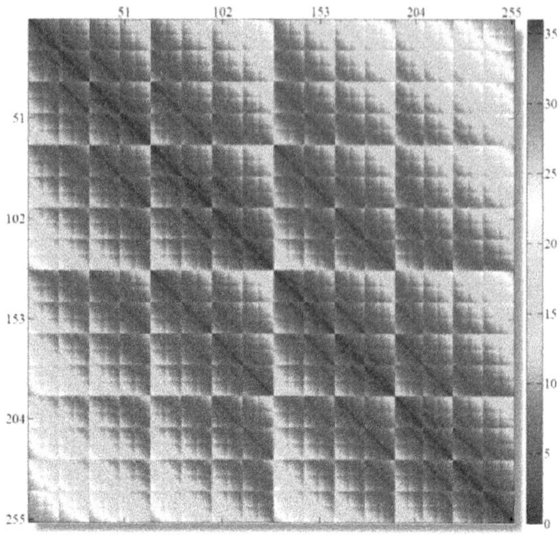

Figure 2: **Visualization of code-to-code distance matrix Δ. Left is the 256×256 matrix Δ of code distances (color coded), computed using the EMD approximation of Eq. 5. On the right is the distances color bar. Evidently, this distance penalizes two codes for different positions and different numbers of of bits.**

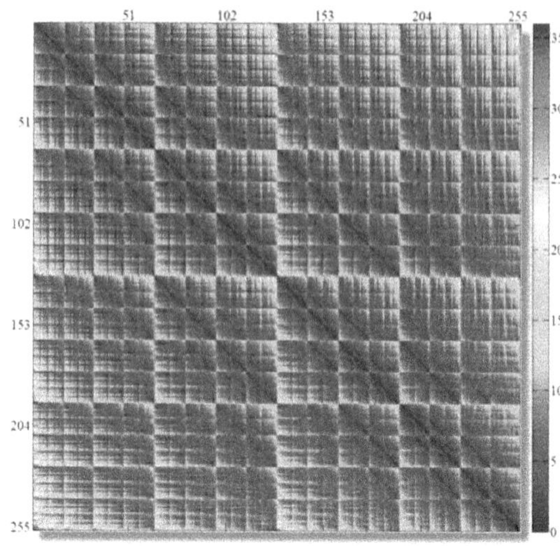

Figure 3: **Visualization of code-to-code distance matrix Δ. Left is the 256×256 matrix Δ of code distances (color coded), computed using Eq. 6 to account for the cyclic nature of LBP codes. On the right is the distances color bar. Compared with the distances visualized in Fig. 2, distances are smaller (codes are more similar) whenever codes have bits set to 1 across code rotations.**

Δ produced using this approximation is visualized in Fig. 2. Clearly, the distances between codes reflect both the difference in positions and numbers of on bits.

Distances for cyclic codes. LBP codes are cyclic by design: the least significant bit represents a pixel adjacent to the pixel represented by the most significant bit (see, e.g., Eq. 2). When using the standard EMD of Eq. 3 this can be expressed by modifying the ground distance (Eq. 4). In order to employ the approximation of Eq. 5, however, we chose the following method of accounting for the cyclic nature of LBP codes.

Given two LBP codes $P, Q \in 2_2^8$, we append a single 0-valued bit as the new least significant bit of each code (increasing code sizes to nine bits) and denote the modified codes as P' and Q', respectively. The modified, *cyclic distance*, $\delta'(P,Q)$ is defined by

$$\delta'(P,Q) = min(\delta(P',Q'), \delta(rev(P'),Q'), \delta(P', rev(Q')), \quad (6)$$

where δ is the the distance computed by Eq. 5 and $rev()$ rearranges code values in reverse order. The distances computed following this modification are illustrated in Fig. 3. A visual comparison of the distances in Fig. 3 to those in Fig. 2 demonstrates that indeed smaller distances (more similar codes) are assigned whenever bit values can be moved from one end of the code to another.

3.3 Ensemble of Deep CNN

Previous work has shown the benefits of employing multiple image representations and multiple similarity measures in face recognition tasks [41, 42]. Here, to our knowledge for the first time, we propose doing the same using multiple CNN architectures, multiple representations and multiple similarity measures.

Specifically, we employ four different, existing network architectures: the *VGG_S*, *VGG_M-2048* and *VGG_M-4096* networks presented in [4] and the BVLC *GoogleNet* network presented in [39]. Please see relevant papers for the details of each network design and architecture. In all cases, CNNs were trained to predict 7D vectors of emotion class probabilities using the labeled training data (seven different emotion classes and an additional "neutral" class).

Images were represented using both RBG values as well as by extracting LBP codes with three different radius parameter values: the default of 1, as well as 5 and 10. All three LBP variants were processed using the encoding described in Sec. 3.2 with the cyclic distance of Eq. 6. In order to compare the influence of the cyclic adaptation to the original EMD approximation (Eq. 5) LBP codes with radius set to 1 were additionally encoded using the EMD approximation directly. All told, we use four CNN architectures and five representations for an ensemble of 20 networks.

In order to predict emotion labels, we take a weighted average of the 7D output vectors produced by our 20 ensemble models. The selected class is the one with the highest probability in the resulting 7D average prediction vector. Weights reflect the relative importance of each ensemble component. These were determined empirically by random searching through different weight combinations using the training data to evaluate the quality of each combination. The best performing weights were selected for our tests and are visualized in Fig. 4. Curiously, of the top ten models, only one uses the original RGB values. Despite being the common practice for CNN based approaches, an RGB representation seems to provide inferior results than those obtained using more robust features as input.

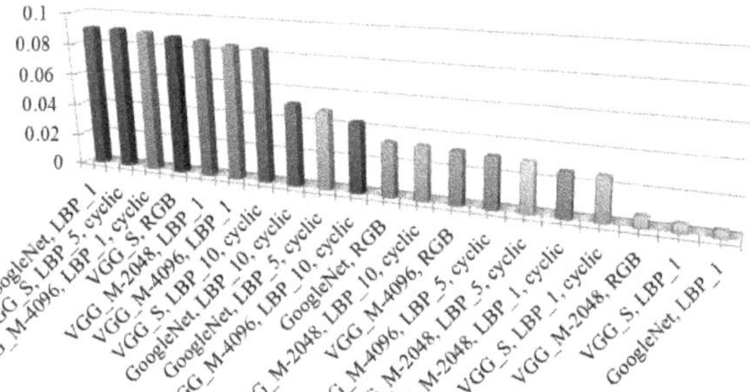

Figure 4: Relative weights of CNN ensemble components. Sorted left to right from the most important to the least. Interestingly, of the top ten most important networks, only one uses original RGB values, despite being the common practice in CNN based approaches.

Training vs. fine-tuning. Due to the huge number of model parameters, deep CNN are prone to overfitting when they are not trained with a sufficiently large training set. The EmotiW challenge contains only 891 training samples, making it dramatically smaller than other image classification data-sets commonly used for training deep networks (e.g, the Imagenet dataset [32]).

To alleviate this problem, we train our models in two steps: First, we fine-tune pre-trained object classification networks on a large face recognition data-set, namely the CASIA WebFace data-set [43]. This allows the network to learn general features relevant for face classification related problems. Then, we fine-tune the resulting networks for the problem of emotion recognition using the smaller training set given in the challenge.

Oversampling the input representations. *Oversampling* [15] is the process of providing a network with several, slightly translated versions of the same input image. In the related work of [21] oversampling was shown to provide superior age and gender classification performance on the Adience benchmark [13]. Here, we employ the same process with all representations and all CNN architectures. Specifically, our results, reported in Sec. 4 provide the performances obtained using the following techniques:

- **Center crop:** The CNN was applied to image regions of size 224×224 pixels, cropped from the center of the input representation.
- **Oversampling:** We produce five 227×227 pixel regions cropped from the input representation as follows: four regions aligned with the four corners of each input representation and one from its center. These five regions, along with their mirrored versions were presented to the CNN. The prediction values of the CNN were then averaged over all ten predictions.

As we later show, similarly to [21], oversampling generally provided better prediction accuracy and we therefore employed it with all our networks in our ensemble.

Table 1: The EmotiW SFEW 2.0 Challenge. Breakdown of the SFEW 2.0 benchmark into the different emotions classes.

	Anger	Disgust	Fear	Happy	Neutral	Sad	Surprise	Total
Train	178	52	78	184	144	161	94	891
Val	77	23	46	72	84	73	56	431

4. EXPERIMENTS

LBP encoding and mapping, as described in Sections 3.1 and 3.2, was implemented in Matlab. Training and testing the networks was done using the Caffe open source framework for Deep Convolutional Neural Networks [15]. We have used two Amazon Web Services g2.8xlarge GPU machines, each with 4 NVIDIA GRID GPUs, where each GPU has 1,536 CUDA cores and 4 GB of video memory.

Fine-tuning each of the networks on the CASIA WebFace Database [43] required approximately four days. Additional fine-tuning of the resulting networks the training set for the EmotiW 2015 data set [10] required one more day. Emotion prediction for a single image requires ≈500ms. This time, however, may potentially be substantially reduced if prediction was performed on image batches rather than individual images. Please see our project webpage[1] for code and additional details.

Our tests were performed on the EmotiW 2015 benchmark [10] which includes data from version 2.0 of the **S**tatic **F**acial **E**xpression in the **W**ild benchmark [9]. It was assembled by selecting frames from different videos of the **A**cted **F**acial **E**xpressions in the **W**ild (AFEW), and then assigning them one of the following seven emotion labels: *angry*, *disgust*, *happy*, *sad*, *surprise*, *fear* and *neutral*. Images from this data set are unconstrained and cover a wide range of head poses and ages, both genders, different occlusions and resolution qualities. Table 1 additionally provides a breakdown of the number of images in each emotion category for the training and validation subsets.

4.1 Results

Table 2 summarizes the results on the validation set for all of the different network architectures and image presentations considered. Subscripts used for the LBP representations denote the value of the radius parameter values used (default of 1, as well as 5 and 10). The use of the approximate EMD without modifying it for cyclic codes – that is, direct application of Eq. 5 to compute code-to-code distances – is referred to as "w.o. cyclic". We use "cyclic" to refer to the modified distance of Eq. 6.

Several interesting observations can be made from these results. First, in line with the ensemble weights reported in Fig. 4, using RGB values as input does not necessarily provide the best performance. This is at odds with the common practice of applying CNNs directly to input images. Presumably, pre-processing images using robust feature alleviates some of the challenges CNNs face when adopting to a particular domain; learning can better focus on information important to the recognition task, rather than filtering out confounding factors such as illumination variations.

Also important are the differences between ensembles and single CNNs. In all cases, whether by combining differ-

[1]Available: `http://www.openu.ac.il/home/hassner/projects/cnn_emotions`

Table 2: **Emotion classification results. The accuracy over all emotion classes is listed. Subscripts for the LBP representations denote the values used for their radius parameters; *w.o. cyclic* refers to the use of the approximate EMD of Eq. 5; and finally, *cyclic* refers to the modified distance of Eq. 6.**

			Validation			Test
	RGB	LBP_1, w.o. cyclic	LBP_1, cyclic	LBP_5, cyclic	LBP_{10}, cyclic	
Baseline (provided by the Challenge authors)			35.33%			39.13%
GoogleNet - single crop	41.68%	39.34%	41.45%	41.68%	40.28%	—
GoogleNet - Oversampling	41.21%	39.57%	40.98%	40.98%	41.45%	—
VGG_S - single crop	41.45%	39.34%	41.92%	41.92%	39.34%	—
VGG_S - Oversampling	40.04%	43.79%	42.38%	43.09%	41.21%	—
VGG_M-2048 - single crop	37.93%	38.17%	36.06%	40.98%	32.31%	—
VGG_M-2048 - Oversampling	40.74%	42.62%	36.76%	42.62%	33.72%	—
VGG_M-4096 - single crop	37.00%	41.92%	40.28%	40.28%	37.47%	—
VGG_M-4096 - Oversampling	37.93%	42.85%	44.73%	42.85%	40.98%	—
Ensemble	46.13	48.94	47.3	47.54	47.3	—
Ensemble of all methods			51.75%			54.56%

ent networks applied to the same representation or different representations used with the same architectures, ensembles seem superior in performance than single networks. Though this should come as no surprise, considering earlier related work (e.g., [42]), evidence of the advantages provided by CNN ensembles are still scares.

Finally, modifying the approximate EMD distance in order to address rotations of the LBP codes slightly degrades results. On the other hand, combining all distances appears to provide complementary information and contributes to improving overall accuracy.

Our results should be compared against the baseline performance for the benchmark. These were obtained using features produced from pyramids of Histogram of Gradients [3] and Local Phase Quantization [28] extracted from the aligned faces and classified using a fusion of separate support vector machines. In the majority of cases, our individual models outperformed the baseline, though not by large margins. Ensemble results, however, boosted performance substantially, by a remarkable 40% gain in performance (15.36% improvement).

Tables 3 and 4 provide confusion matrices for the validation and test sets respectively. Evidently, the *disgust* emotion was never classified correctly. This is consistent with results previously reported for the 2013 Emotion Recognition in the Wild Challenge (e.g., [17]). This performance may be due to the class being inherently more challenging to classify or simply due to the relatively small number of examples available for the class (see Table 1).

Finally, we provide a selection of correct and wrong classification results for all of the remaining six classes is provided in Fig. 5. These show that at least in some cases, poor performance may be traced to failures in the face alignment step, rather than the recognition pipeline.

5. CONCLUSIONS

We present a substantial improvement over existing baseline results on the Emotion Recognition in the Wild Challenge (EmotiW 2015), Static Facial Expression Recognition sub-challenge (SFEW). To achieve this performance boost, we make a number of novel contributions: We propose to apply CNNs to pre-processed images rather than RGB, in order to eliminate confounding factors and focus the network's efforts on variations due to class labels. To this end, we convert images to LBP codes, designed to be robust to illumination changes. In order to apply CNNs to these binary codes, we further describe a unique mapping of codes to metric space by applying an approximation of the EMD. Finally, multiple CNN architectures and representations are combined in an ensemble by a weighted average of their predictions. Our results clearly demonstrate the advantage of looking beyond RGB as the input space for CNNs, as well as the complementary information offered by multiple representations and network architectures.

Acknowledgments

This research is based upon work supported in part by the Office of the Director of National Intelligence (ODNI), Intelligence Advanced Research Projects Activity (IARPA), via IARPA 2014-14071600010. The views and conclusions contained herein are those of the authors and should not be interpreted as necessarily representing the official policies or endorsements, either expressed or implied, of ODNI, IARPA, or the U.S. Government. The U.S. Government is authorized to reproduce and distribute reprints for Governmental purpose notwithstanding any copyright annotation thereon.

6. REFERENCES

[1] T. Ahonen, A. Hadid, and M. Pietikainen. Face description with local binary patterns: Application to face recognition. *Trans. Pattern Anal. Mach. Intell.*, 28(12):2037–2041, 2006.

[2] I. Borg and P. J. Groenen. *Modern multidimensional scaling: Theory and applications.* Springer Science & Business Media, 2005.

[3] A. Bosch, A. Zisserman, and X. Munoz. Representing shape with a spatial pyramid kernel. In *Proc. Int. Conf. on Image and video retrieval*, pages 401–408. ACM, 2007.

[4] K. Chatfield, K. Simonyan, A. Vedaldi, and A. Zisserman. Return of the devil in the details: Delving deep into convolutional nets. *arXiv preprint arXiv:1405.3531*, 2014.

[5] H.-C. Chen, M. Z. Comiter, H. Kung, and B. McDanel. Sparse coding trees with application to emotion classification. In *Proc. Conf. Comput. Vision Pattern Recognition Workshops*. IEEE, 2015.

[6] S. E. Choi, Y. J. Lee, S. J. Lee, K. R. Park, and J. Kim. Age estimation using a hierarchical classifier based on global and local facial features. *Pattern Recognition*, 44(6):1262–1281, 2011.

Table 3: *Validation* set confusion matrix

	Anger	Disgust	Fear	Happy	Neutral	Sad	Surprise
Anger	**48.04**	0.	16.67	12.22	3.3	10.42	6.25
Disgust	5.88	**0.**	0.	5.56	6.59	5.21	3.12
Fear	17.65	0.	**41.67**	3.33	6.59	8.33	15.62
Happy	2.94	0.	0.	**64.44**	2.2	8.33	3.12
Neutral	7.84	50.	8.33	2.22	**58.24**	13.54	15.62
Sad	5.88	0.	8.33	6.67	12.09	**43.75**	12.5
Surprise	11.76	50.	25.	5.56	10.99	10.42	**43.75**

Table 4: *Test* set confusion matrix

	Anger	Disgust	Fear	Happy	Neutral	Sad	Surprise
Anger	**54.55**	66.67	22.58	3.16	4.48	9.26	11.9
Disgust	2.6	**0.**	0.	8.42	4.48	5.56	2.38
Fear	16.88	16.67	**19.35**	3.16	4.48	12.96	19.05
Happy	10.39	16.67	9.68	**75.79**	4.48	14.81	0.
Neutral	2.6	0.	16.13	0.	**62.69**	14.81	2.38
Sad	5.19	0.	25.81	6.32	16.42	**37.04**	14.29
Surprise	7.79	0.	6.45	3.16	2.99	5.56	**50.**

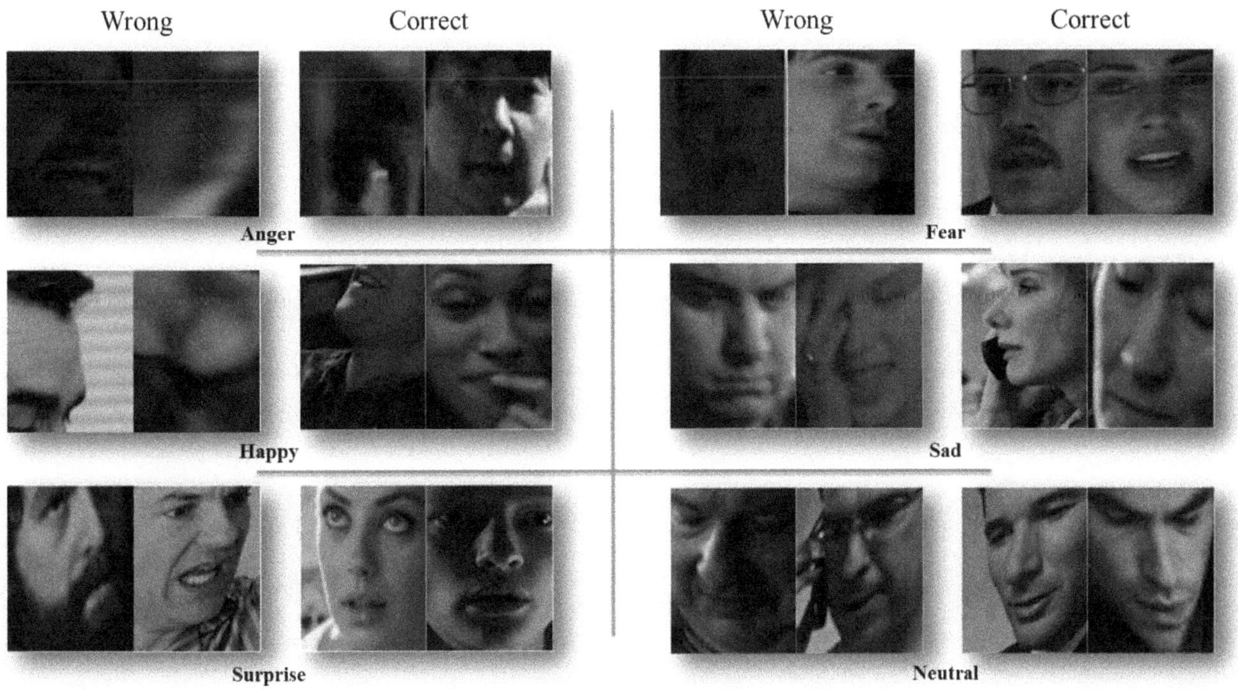

Figure 5: Example prediction results. For each emotion the left pair is a wrong classification and the right is a correct classification result.

[7] S. Cohen and L. Guibas. The earth mover's distance: Lower bounds and invariance under translation. Technical report, DTIC Document, 1997.

[8] C. Cortes and V. Vapnik. Support-vector networks. *Machine Learning*, 20(3):273–297, 1995.

[9] A. Dhall, R. Goecke, S. Lucey, and T. Gedeon. Static facial expression analysis in tough conditions: Data, evaluation protocol and benchmark. In *Proc. Int. Conf. Comput. Vision Workshops*, pages 2106–2112. IEEE, 2011.

[10] A. Dhall, O. R. Murthy, R. Goecke, J. Joshi, and T. Gedeon. Video and image based emotion recognition challenges in the wild: EmotiW 2015. In *Int. Conf. on Multimodal Interaction*. ACM, 2015.

[11] S. DâĂŹMello, N. Blanchard, R. Baker, J. Ocumpaugh, and K. Brawner. Affect-sensitive instructional strategies. *Design Recommendations for Intelligent Tutoring Systems: Volume 2-Instructional Management*, 2:35, 2014.

[12] S. D'Mello, R. W. Picard, and A. Graesser. Toward an affect-sensitive autotutor. *Intelligent Systems*, (4):53–61, 2007.

[13] E. Eidinger, R. Enbar, and T. Hassner. Age and gender estimation of unfiltered faces. *Trans. on Inform. Forensics and Security*, 9(12), 2014.

[14] T. Hassner, S. Harel, E. Paz, and R. Enbar. Effective face frontalization in unconstrained images. In *Proc. Conf. Comput. Vision Pattern Recognition*, 2015.

[15] Y. Jia, E. Shelhamer, J. Donahue, S. Karayev, J. Long, R. Girshick, S. Guadarrama, and T. Darrell. Caffe: Convolutional architecture for fast feature embedding. *arXiv preprint arXiv:1408.5093*, 2014.

[16] S. E. Kahou, P. Froumenty, and C. Pal. Facial expression analysis based on high dimensional binary features. In *European Conf. Comput. Vision*, pages 135–147. Springer, 2014.

[17] S. E. Kahou, C. Pal, X. Bouthillier, P. Froumenty, Ç. Gülçehre, R. Memisevic, P. Vincent, A. Courville, Y. Bengio, R. C. Ferrari, et al. Combining modality specific deep neural networks for emotion recognition in video. In *Int. Conf. on Multimodal Interaction*, pages 543–550. ACM, 2013.

[18] T. Kanade, J. F. Cohn, and Y. Tian. Comprehensive database for facial expression analysis. In *Automatic*

Face and Gesture Recognition, pages 46–53. IEEE, 2000.

[19] A. Krizhevsky, I. Sutskever, and G. E. Hinton. Imagenet classification with deep convolutional neural networks. In *Neural Inform. Process. Syst.*, pages 1097–1105, 2012.

[20] Y. LeCun, B. Boser, J. S. Denker, D. Henderson, R. E. Howard, W. Hubbard, and L. D. Jackel. Backpropagation applied to handwritten zip code recognition. *Neural computation*, 1(4):541–551, 1989.

[21] G. Levi and T. Hassner. Age and gender classification using convolutional neural networks. In *Proc. Conf. Comput. Vision Pattern Recognition Workshops*, June 2015.

[22] M. Liu, S. Li, S. Shan, and X. Chen. AU-aware deep networks for facial expression recognition. In *Automatic Face and Gesture Recognition*. IEEE, 2013.

[23] M. J. Lyons, S. Akamatsu, M. Kamachi, J. Gyoba, and J. Budynek. The japanese female facial expression (jaffe) database, 1998.

[24] J. Mairal, F. Bach, J. Ponce, and G. Sapiro. Online dictionary learning for sparse coding. In *Int. Conf. Mach. Learning*, pages 689–696. ACM, 2009.

[25] T. Ojala, M. Pietikäinen, and D. Harwood. A comparative study of texture measures with classification based on featured distributions. *Pattern recognition*, 29(1):51–59, 1996.

[26] T. Ojala, M. Pietikäinen, and T. Mäenpää. A generalized local binary pattern operator for multiresolution gray scale and rotation invariant texture classification. In *Int. Conf. Pattern Recognition*, volume 1, pages 397–406. Springer, 2001.

[27] T. Ojala, M. Pietikäinen, and T. Mäenpää. Multiresolution gray-scale and rotation invariant texture classification with local binary patterns. *Trans. Pattern Anal. Mach. Intell.*, 24(7):971–987, 2002.

[28] V. Ojansivu and J. Heikkilä. Blur insensitive texture classification using local phase quantization. In *Image and signal processing*, pages 236–243. Springer, 2008.

[29] M. Pantic and L. J. Rothkrantz. Toward an affect-sensitive multimodal human-computer interaction. *Proceedings of the IEEE*, 91(9):1370–1390, 2003.

[30] M. Pantic, M. Valstar, R. Rademaker, and L. Maat. Web-based database for facial expression analysis. In *Int. Conf. on Multimedia and Expo*. IEEE, 2005.

[31] Y. Rubner, C. Tomasi, and L. J. Guibas. The earth mover's distance as a metric for image retrieval. *Int. J. Comput. Vision*, 40(2):99–121, 2000.

[32] O. Russakovsky, J. Deng, H. Su, J. Krause, S. Satheesh, S. Ma, Z. Huang, A. Karpathy, A. Khosla, M. Bernstein, et al. Imagenet large scale visual recognition challenge. *Int. J. Comput. Vision*, pages 1–42, 2014.

[33] F. Schroff, D. Kalenichenko, and J. Philbin. Facenet: A unified embedding for face recognition and clustering. In *Proc. Conf. Comput. Vision Pattern Recognition*, pages 815–823, 2015.

[34] G. A. Seber. *Multivariate observations*, volume 252. John Wiley & Sons, 2009.

[35] C. Shan. Learning local binary patterns for gender classification on real-world face images. *Pattern Recognition Letters*, 33(4):431–437, 2012.

[36] C. Shan, S. Gong, and P. W. McOwan. Facial expression recognition based on local binary patterns: A comprehensive study. *Image and Vision Computing*, 27(6):803–816, 2009.

[37] Y. Sun, D. Liang, X. Wang, and X. Tang. Deepid3: Face recognition with very deep neural networks. *arXiv preprint arXiv:1502.00873*, 2015.

[38] Y. Sun, X. Wang, and X. Tang. Deeply learned face representations are sparse, selective, and robust. *arXiv preprint arXiv:1412.1265*, 2014.

[39] C. Szegedy, W. Liu, Y. Jia, P. Sermanet, S. Reed, D. Anguelov, D. Erhan, V. Vanhoucke, and A. Rabinovich. Going deeper with convolutions. *arXiv preprint arXiv:1409.4842*, 2014.

[40] M. Werman, S. Peleg, and A. Rosenfeld. A distance metric for multidimensional histograms. *Computer Vision, Graphics, and Image Processing*, 32(3):328–336, 1985.

[41] L. Wolf, T. Hassner, and Y. Taigman. Descriptor based methods in the wild. In *European Conf. Comput. Vision Workshops*, 2008.

[42] L. Wolf, T. Hassner, and Y. Taigman. Effective unconstrained face recognition by combining multiple descriptors and learned background statistics. *Trans. Pattern Anal. Mach. Intell.*, 33(10):1978–1990, 2011.

[43] D. Yi, Z. Lei, S. Liao, and S. Z. Li. Learning face representation from scratch. *arXiv preprint arXiv:1411.7923*, 2014.

[44] R. Zabih and J. Woodfill. Non-parametric local transforms for computing visual correspondence. In *European Conf. Comput. Vision*, pages 151–158. Springer, 1994.

[45] B. Zhou, A. Lapedriza, J. Xiao, A. Torralba, and A. Oliva. Learning deep features for scene recognition using places database. In *Neural Inform. Process. Syst.*, pages 487–495, 2014.

[46] X. Zhu and D. Ramanan. Face detection, pose estimation, and landmark localization in the wild. In *Proc. Conf. Comput. Vision Pattern Recognition*, pages 2879–2886. IEEE, 2012.

Quantification of Cinematography Semiotics for Video-based Facial Emotion Recognition in the EmotiW 2015 Grand Challenge

Albert C. Cruz
acruz@cs.csubak.edu
Department of Computer and Electrical Engineering & Computer Science
California State University, Bakersfield
Bakersfield, CA 93311

ABSTRACT

The Emotion Recognition in the Wild challenge poses significant problems to state of the art auditory and visual affect quantification systems. To overcome the challenges, we investigate supplementary meta features based on film semiotics. Movie scenes are often presented and arranged in such a way as to amplify the emotion interpreted by the viewing audience. This technique is referred to as mise en scéne in the film industry and involves strict and intentional control of color palette, light source color, and arrangement of actors and objects in the scene. To this end, two algorithms for extracting mise en scéne information are proposed. Rule of thirds based motion history histograms detect motion along rule of thirds guidelines. Rule of thirds color layout descriptors compactly describe a scene at rule of thirds intersections. A comprehensive system is proposed that measures expression, emotion, vocalics, syntax, semantics, and film-based meta information. The proposed mise en scéne features have a higher classification rate and ROC area than LBP-TOP features on the validation set of the EmotiW 2015 challenge. The complete system improves classification performance over the baseline algorithm by 3.17% on the testing set.

Categories and Subject Descriptors

I.5.4 [**Pattern Recognition**]: Applications; I.4.m [**Image Processing and Computer Vision**]: Miscellaneous

Keywords

Mise en Scéne; syntax and semantics; EmotiW 2015 Challenge

ICMI 2015, November 9–13, 2015, Seattle, WA, USA.

ACM 978-1-4503-3912-4/15/11 ...$15.00.
DOI: http://dx.doi.org/10.1145/2818346.2830592.

1. INTRODUCTION

Emotion recognition is the study of computer algorithms that infer the underlying affect of a human from visual and auditory cues. We propose a comprehensive system for the Emotion Recognition in the Wild Challenge 2015 (EmotiW 2015) AFEW subchallenge [1] that combines vocalics, syntax, semantics, apparent expression, universal affect features, as well as features derived from cinematographic meta information. Publicly available data sets and grand challenges have energized the advancements to state of the art methods in the field of video-based affect recognition. Among the first such standard databases was the Japanese Female Facial Expression dataset (JAFFE) [2]. Later, it was realized that the expressions in most datasets were posed. Naturalistically expressed emotion must be captured so that a computer vision system can learn an accurate model to predict emotion in the wild [3]. The facial Emotion Recognition and Analysis challenge [4] was among the first such grand challenges to offer professionally acted data. Following this effort, the Audio Visual Emotion Challenge [5] and EmotiW [3] also offered more natural data. EmotiW is distinct from other challenges in that clips from AFEW are professionally acted scenes from movies. This is key to the novel methods presented in this approach.

Films use established semiotics to communicate a story to the viewing audience. As Frank Capra, a famous director, once said, "Film is one of three universal languages, the other two, mathematics and music." Clips in the data convey an emotion with more than just visual and auditory information. Nearly standard cues, referred to as *signs* in cinematography, supplement the ability of the audience to understand the affect of the actor [6]. Some techniques are so overused that they are cliché. We make significant contributions to the baseline approach including the incorporation of contextual information from object placement and lighting from cinematography semiotics, referred to as *mise en scéne* [6].

The rest of this work is organized as follows. Section 2 contains related work, motivation and contributions. Section 3 gives the technical approach and mise en scéne features are given in Section 3.1. Section 4 gives experimental parameters and results. Section 5 discusses the results. Section 6 concludes the paper and summarizes the key findings of the method.

2. RELATED WORK

In the following section, we summarize the top performers from previous EmotiW challenges.

EmotiW 2013 Challenge: M. Liu et al. [7] identified face regions with a PCA subspace approach, carried out subspace learning of appearance features with a Grassmannian manifold, and predicted labels with multiple one versus all partial less squares classifiers. S. Kahou et al. [8] applied different neural networks for each modality: a deep convolutional neural network for facial expression, a deep belief network for audio, a deep autoencoder for human actions, and a shallow network for mouth-specific features. K. Sikka et al. [9] combined SIFT, GIST and audio features, and carried out prediction with Multiple Kernel Learning and Support Vector Machine (SVM).

EmotiW 2014 Challenge: M. Liu et al. [10] computed histogram of oriented gradients, SIFT, and a convolution neural network. These features were projected into a Riemannian manifold before classification. J. Chen et al. [11] proposed histogram of orientated gradients of three orthogonal planes, and applied multiple kernel learning with SVM for classification. Sun et al. [12] extracted SIFT, LBP-TOP, pyramid of histograms of oriented gradients, and audio features from the openSMILE toolkit [13]. Prediction of affect was carried out at the decision level with a tiered re-voting scheme.

2.1 Motivation of Approach

Because the clips are from movies, actors in the scene will express their emotion in an overt way that can be understood by the audience. Despite this requirement, EmotiW 2015 still poses difficult challenges to state of the art facial emotion recognition methods. There are multiple characters in the same scene. There is no guarantee that the frame will focus on the person of interest who is expressing the emotion that needs to be predicted. The scene may abruptly shift from the subject's face. In at least one video, the majority of the clip is not focused on the face of the subject. There are greatly varying extrinsic imaging conditions that pose difficulties to face region of interest extraction algorithms. E.g., it may be too dark, the face region of interest may be too small or the face pose angle can be too great. All these factors are significant challenges to a video-only based affect recognition system.

Auditory cues provide discriminative information that can supplement an affect recognition system. However, multiple actors can speak in the same segment. For at least a few videos, the subject actor is silent and another actor is speaking. Additionally, since the clips are from movies, there may be a musical score and a glut of sound effects to immerse the viewing audience in the scene. These factors inhibit the ability of accurate quantification of auditory cues from the actor of focus.

Instead, we investigate the commonly used signs from the mise en scéne concept in cinematography and how they can supplement the auditory and visual affect projected in the scene. Consider a scene of an actor expressing fear, e.g. training set fear video # 010845040, a scene from Harry Potter (Figure 1-a). The actors eyebrows are raised in an expression of fear and there is an eerie voice. While this may be enough information to infer fear, there are a number of signs that contribute to this feeling. For instance, Harry Potter is gazing out of the window at something which is out of view of the audience–viewers can only guess what he is looking at and thinking about. The camera angle is spiraling toward his face indicating a loss of power-control affect. The tonal distribution of the image tends toward darkness and the color palette is limited to blues and greens. This is an example of how specific configurations of mise en scéne amplify the emotion being interpreted by the viewing audience. Proper execution of mise en scéne is entailed by strict and intentional control of lighting, costume, setting, color palette, props and the placement of objects and actors in the scene–referred to as *theatrical blocking* [6].

Previous work has explored encoding the emotional identity of movies from light source color [14]. In the Audio Visual Emotion Challenge 2014 [15], Kächele et al. outperformed the baseline approach focusing on meta information rather than features derived from audio or video. E.g., the ID of the subject, the length of the video, general motion and pixel differences, approximate weight, approximate age, and semantic content. In Dhall et al. [3], social event information, location and proximity of individuals in the scene were used for group affect analysis. To the best of our knowledge, we are the first to fuse cinematography-based meta information in a comprehensive system with vocalics, syntax, semantics, expression and emotion features.

(a)

(b)

Figure 1: This figure should be viewed in color. Applications of key and color in cinematography. In general, the proportion of lighter tones are correlated with the valence conveyed in the scene. Projected affect is further controlled by the temperature of the light source. (a) Frame with letterboxing removed. A low keyed scene (dark with some light highlights) and cold tones from a high temperature light source convey fear and suspense. (b) A high keyed scene (very light with some dark highlights) and a low temperature light source used in a scene conveying happiness.

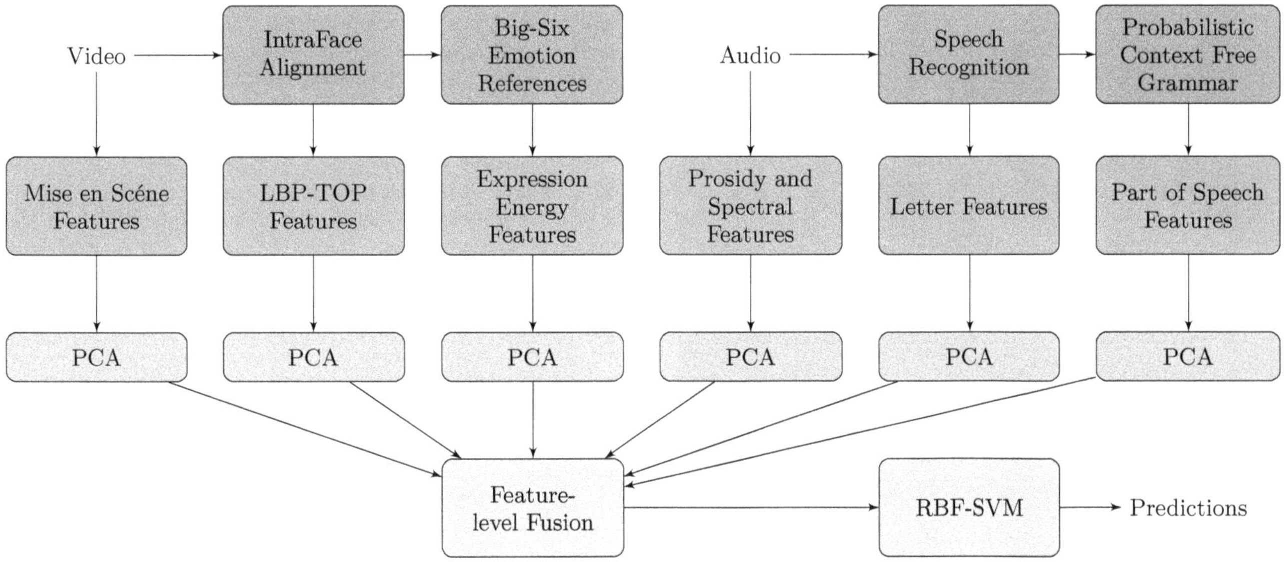

Figure 2: Overview of the approach. Features from left to right: mise en scéne configuration is leveraged as cinematographic meta information, apparent expression is extracted with LBP-TOP, emotion similarities are computed from references of faces expressing big six emotions, vocalics are extracted with prosidy and speech features, syntax is quantified with a letter histogram and semantics are quantified with a part of speech histogram. Fusion of modalities is carried out at the feature level and a SVM predicts emotion labels.

2.2 Contribution

We are the first to incorporate mise en scéne based meta information in a facial emotion recognition system. Lighting, color and theatrical blocking features supplement vocalic, semantic, expression and emotion features. Two new features are proposed: (1) rule of thirds based motion history histograms that capture motion at rule of thirds guidelines and (2) rule of thirds based color layout descriptors that compactly represent the scene at rule of thirds intersections.

3. TECHNICAL APPROACH

For mise en scéne features, key and overall color are measured with max-RGB and shades of gray color constancy algorithms. The proposed rule of thirds motion history histogram algorithm measures motion at the lines and intersections of rule of thirds guidelines. A color layout descriptor is computed at the rule of thirds guideline intersections to quantify the overall tone at these locations. For audio features, vocalics, syntax and semantics are extracted. openSMILE vocalic features are supplemented by additional features from the VoiceSauce toolbox [16]. The audio waveforms are parsed for syntax with Dragon Dictate for Mac, then further parsed for semantics by the Stanford Parser package [17]. For visual features, expression level and emotion level features are extracted. Apparent expression information is captured with LBP-TOP features. Similarities to big six reference emotions are computed with expression energy [18]. A system overview is given in Figure 2.

3.1 Mise en Scéne Features

The video clips from the AFEW dataset are segments from professionally filmed movies that follow specific patterns expected by the audience. A general example of this are genre films, such as action, fantasy, mystery, etc., that follow a specific story pattern. Cinematographers also follow rules of thumb when filming scenes to augment the emotion being projected to the audience. It is not just conveyed through the expressions, vocalics and semantics of the actor of focus, but also how the scene is presented to the movie goer. The actors are expected to act and speak in a conspicuous or typical way based on the affective state of the character they are acting out, and so to must the properties of a scene be arranged to convey a specific emotion. E.g., if the director intends to convey fear, the scene will be poorly lit. If the cinematographer intends to convey happiness, the scene will be well lit and vibrantly colored. We consider two concepts of mood lighting: key and color.

Key is the proportion of light and dark in an image. High keyed scenes have a higher proportion of light tones and convey a feeling of warmth and energy. This is accomplished by having the entire scene well lit. E.g., the Wizard of Oz (1939) is full of vibrant colors. Low key lighting is the opposite, with a higher proportion of dark tones. Low key lighting conveys melodrama and suspense. Continuing with the Wizard of Oz example, low key lighting was used when the characters first met the evil antagonist of the story, the witch. These are serious scenes intended to convey apprehension. E.g., in Figure 1-a, low keyed lighting is used in a scene with fear.

When filming a movie, the director will use a specific color palette that fits the emotion being conveyed in the movie to augment the affect being expressed by the actors. Cinematographers generalize colors in terms of warm, such as red, yellow and orange, or cool, such as blue, green and violet. Scenes which are warm convey feelings of positive valence and positive attention. Scenes which are cool convey feelings of negative valence and negative predictability. When filming, this is achieved by using a color correction

(a)

(b)

Figure 3: Applications of rule of thirds in cinematography. In a scene, points of interest are generally placed near two sets of equally spaced lines, with the sets perpendicular to each other. (a) Frame with letterboxing removed. The face of the actor is placed near the intersection in the upper left-hand corner. (b) The actor's body is placed along the right line.

gel to achieve a specific light source temperature. E.g., in Figure 1-b, a low temperature light source is used.

Another cinematographic technique considered in our approach is theatrical blocking, specifically rule of thirds. This concept asserts that an image should be divided into nine equally sized sub-regions by two equally spaced vertical lines and two equally spaced horizontal lines. Points of interest in the scene are placed along the lines or intersections of the lines. E.g. the face of the actor is often placed at the intersection of the guide lines, see Figure 3. A summary of the features used in the method follows:

- Normalized color histogram of the entire video, summed across all frames
- Light source tone computed with max-RGB, averaged across all frames
- Light source tone computed with shades of gray, averaged across all frames
- Motion history histogram weighted by distance to rule of thirds guidelines
- Color layout descriptor computed at each rule of thirds intersection

3.1.1 Color Palette and Key Features

The first feature extracted is a color histogram with each channel quantized to sixteen bins. This gives overall key and color of the frame. However, in filmography, the color palette is managed by color temperature of light sources, motivating more in depth representation of the colors in the frame. This information is not provided with the data and must be estimated. Color constancy is the study of object tones measured independently of light source color. Methods attempt to estimate the light source tone and use this information to correct the tones in the image. We apply the methods which compute the light source color $\mathbf{l}$. Assuming that the average light reflectance in the scene is achromatic:

$$k \int_{\lambda} l(\lambda)\, \mathbf{c}(\lambda)\, d\lambda = k\mathbf{l} \tag{1}$$

where λ is the wavelength, k is a constant based on the incident light and $\mathbf{c}$ is the camera sensitivity.

With the max-RGB color constancy method [19] this is estimated as:

$$k\mathbf{l} = \max_{\mathbf{p}} \mathbf{f}(\mathbf{p}) = \left| \max_{\mathbf{p}} f_r(\mathbf{p}), \max_{\mathbf{p}} f_g(\mathbf{p}), \max_{\mathbf{p}} f_b(\mathbf{p}) \right| \tag{2}$$

where f_r, f_g, and f_b are the red, green and blue channels of the image $\mathbf{f}$ respectively. Each channel is separately searched for the lightest tone, and the maximum value in each of these channels is taken to be the respective light source color component. The second method employed is called shades of gray. It computes the light source color as a function of the L_p norm of the tone:

$$k\mathbf{l} = \left(\frac{1}{N_{\mathbf{p}}} \sum_{\mathbf{p}} \mathbf{f}(\mathbf{p})^p \right)^{1/p} \tag{3}$$

where p is the value of the L_p norm and $N_{\mathbf{p}}$ is the number of pixels. For $p = \infty$, Equation 3 is equal to Equation 2 [20]. The results of these two equations are computed on a frame by frame basis.

3.1.2 Rule of Thirds Based Features

Theatrical blocking is measured by extracting features of the scene at the lines and intersections of the rule of thirds guidelines. Objects that the viewing audience should focus on are placed at the lines and intersections of these guidelines. When assuming this model, regions far from the guidelines are background and not a part of the regions of interest.

The first feature proposed quantifies activity of the actor by measuring motion along the rule of thirds guidelines. Frequently used approaches involve quantifying motion with optical flow or with a feature-descriptor matching process. However, these methods can be computationally undesirable given the large resolution of the frames. Instead, we use motion history images and histograms because of their ability to succinctly represent spatiotemporal information. Among the earliest uses of motion history images was [21], where motion history images (MHI) were used to describe action scenes as a single image representation. Variations of the motion image concept continue to be used for emotion recognition (MHH in depression recognition [22]). The motion energy image is computed as:

$$m_t(\mathbf{p}) = \begin{cases} 1 & |\mathbf{f}_t(\mathbf{p}) - \mathbf{f}_{t-1}(\mathbf{p})| > \tau \\ 0 & \text{Otherwise} \end{cases} \tag{4}$$

where m_t is the motion history image at time t. $\mathbf{f}_t$ is the frame color at time t. We modify the MHI concept to focus

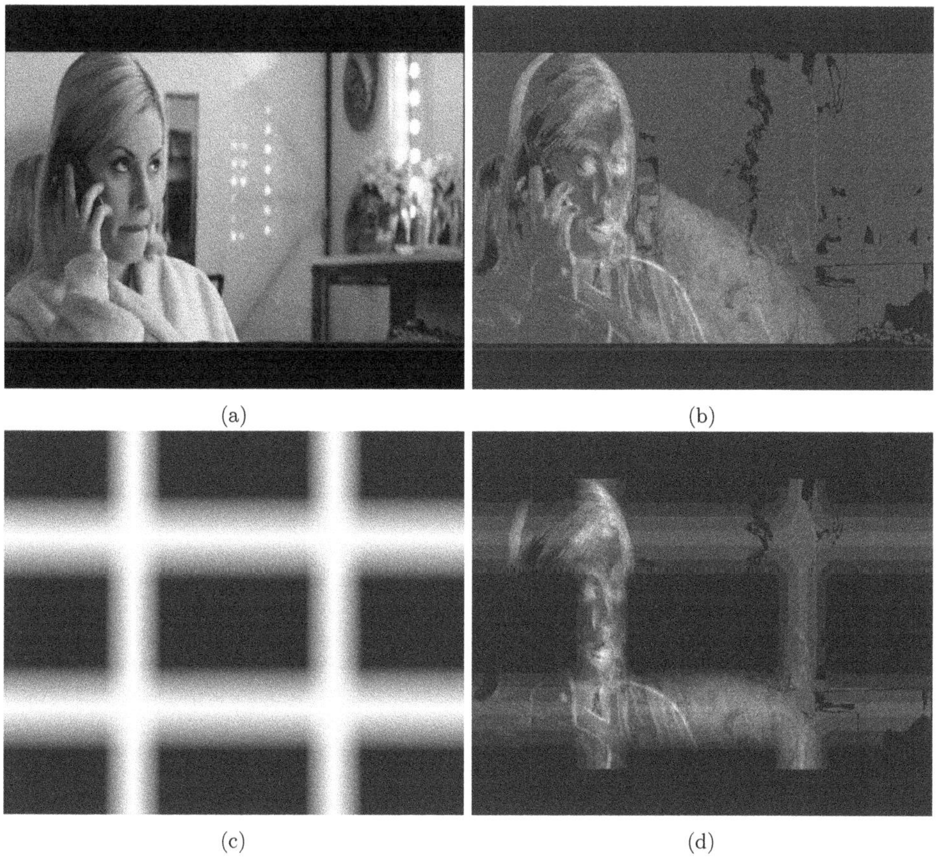
(a) (b) (c) (d)

Figure 4: Rule of thirds motion history histogram. (a) Original frame. (b) Summation of motion history images. (c) Weighting scheme based on rule of thirds guidelines. (d) Result of weighting (b) with (c).

strictly on temporal changes near the rule of thirds guidelines (spatial information is handled with the CLD descriptor below). The time dimension in Equation 4 is marginalized, and weighted:

$$\tilde{m}(\mathbf{p}) = \sum_{k} g(\mathbf{p})\, m_k(\mathbf{p}) \tag{5}$$

where $g(\mathbf{p})$ is an image containing the weight values. A pixel is weighted inversely proportional to its distance to one of the rule of thirds guidelines (see Figure 4-c). As the final step, a histogram is taken of $\tilde{m}$. The proposed method is significantly different from previous MHI and MHH algorithms. The output of this method is a motion magnitudes histogram capturing temporal motion of theatrical blocking. Previous MHI algorithms captured spatiotemporal motion represented as an image. An example of the method is given in Figure 4. Letterboxing is removed before computing the locations of the guidelines. Note that this feature only measures motion. The following feature measures color palette.

Spatial information is quantified at the rule of thirds intersections with color layout descriptors. Color layout descriptors were defined with the MPEG-7 standard as a method for quantification of tone of a video at a glance [23]. First, an image is reduced to 8×8 resolution for each channel by averaging the tone of the regions before subsampling. Then, the image is converted to YCbCr color channels. The DCT of each channel is taken, and a zig-zag traverse re-orders components by frequency. Typically, some high frequency components are removed. In this work, we do not reduce the amount of information at this stage; PCA is used to compute the most variant axes later on. It should remove high frequency components as most energy is located in the lower frequency spectrum. This feature captures theatrical blocking as well as color palette information and keying.

3.2 Audio Features

3.2.1 Vocalic Features

We supplement the baseline audio features from openSMILE with features from the VoiceSauce toolbox [16]. Features are computed for the entire video then averaged to produce a single feature vector. A summary of these features are as follows:

- All baseline audio features
- Fundamental frequency, fundamental frequency frequencies and bandwidths of the first four formants
- Amplitudes of harmonics
- Root mean square of waveform at every frame over a variable window equal to five pitch pulses
- Ceptral peak prominence
- Subharmonic-to-harmonic ratio

Table 1: Results on EmotiW 2015 for varying modalities, fusion results and results on the testing fold. CR: classification rate. FPR: false positive rate. Bold: best performer for set. Underline: second best performer for set.

Validation Set						
	CR	FPR	Precision	Recall	F-measure	ROC Area
Vocalics (openSMILE, VoiceSauce)	0.272	0.140	0.274	0.272	0.235	0.530
Syntax + Semantics (Dragon, Stanford Parser)	0.232	0.151	**0.350**	0.232	0.134	0.515
Expression (LBP-TOP)	0.315	**0.129**	0.266	<u>0.315</u>	<u>0.267</u>	0.528
Emotion (Expression Energy)	0.237	0.152	0.173	0.237	0.174	0.526
Meta information (Mise en Scéne)	<u>0.324</u>	0.152	0.231	0.286	0.227	<u>0.587</u>
Feature-level Fusion	**0.361**	<u>0.130</u>	<u>0.300</u>	**0.335**	**0.301**	**0.668**
Testing Set						
	CR	FPR	Precision	Recall	F-measure	ROC Area
Feature-level Fusion	0.425	0.103	0.625	0.203	0.282	-

3.2.2 Syntax and Semantic Features

The focus of facial affect recognition is the prediction of emotion from non-verbal cues. However, a significant part of communication is delivered via language. Thus, we supplement the approach with a system that computes the syntactic and semantic meaning of speech uttered in the video. As stated previously, because the video clips are from movies, the actors can be expected to act and speak in a conspicuous or typical way. E.g., if a person is angry they will curse. To compute these features, syntax is extracted from vocalics and then the syntax is processed into a parse tree to find parts of speech. Both the syntactic and semantic features are used for the approach.

Dragon commercial software was successfully employed in the Audio Visual Emotion Challenge 2014 for speech recognition [15]. In this work, we use Dragon Dictate for Mac to compute the words from the video clips. At this stage in syntax and semantic processing, a letter histogram is computed as a feature. The sentences from the commercial software are parsed into a tree with an unlexicalized probabilistic context-free grammar method [17]. A histogram counting the frequency of parts of speech is used as a feature. A summary of the features in this component of the algorithm are as follows:

- Unnormalized letter histogram with non-alpha character omitted
- Unnormalized histogram of specific parts of speech: coordinating conjunction, cardinal number, determiner, existential there, preposition or subordinating conjunction, adjective, comparative adjective, superlative adjective, model, singular noun, plural noun, singular proper noun, plural proper noun, predeterminer, progressive ending, personal pronoun, possessive pronoun, adverb, comparative adverb, superlative adverb, particle, symbol, interjection, base form verb , past tense verb, present participle verb, past participle verb, non-3rd person singular present verb, 3rd person singular present verb, Wh-determiner, Wh-pronoun, possessive wh-pronoun, and wh-adverb
- Unnormalized histogram of general parts of speech: adjectives, nouns, verbs, and adverbs

3.3 Video Features

Low-level facial information is extracted with baseline LBP-TOP features. The reader is referred to [24] for an in-depth explanation of the algorithm. These features are supplemented with higher-level facial emotion information that computes each frame's similarity to one of the six basic emotions. The similarity is computed to a reference face that is generated from training. The reference face represents the typical expression of one of the big six emotions. A summary of the visual features used in the approach are as follows:

- LBP-TOP features from baseline
- Six similarity scores to big six emotion references

3.3.1 Emotion Features

In this section, we discuss the expression energy method that computes the similarity to one of the big six emotions. This method was first proposed in [25] and was shown to have promising generalization performance in a person-independent setting. The face image $\mathbf{f}$ is compared to reference faces of six-basic emotions. Because the six-basic emotions are universal, comparisons to representations of the six-basic emotions may be a more reliable encoding of affective cues than apparent facial information.

Let Φ be the set of references: $\Phi = \{$happy, sad, fearful, angry, surprised, disgusted$\}$. Let e be one of the emotions in Φ. Let r_e be the reference of a characteristically expressed emotion e. In [25], $\mathbf{f}$ was binary classified as either a given reference e or not: $\Phi - \{e\}$. This was carried out with a SVM, and the decision value was used as a feature for r_e. This was carried out once for each emotion in Φ. In our method, we compute the expression energy of $\mathbf{f}$ directly to each emotion in Φ and take the scores to be the feature vector. The score is a comparison of $\mathbf{f}$ to one of the emotions in Φ:

$$x_e = d(\mathbf{f}, r_e) \tag{6}$$

where e is the emotion.

The avatar reference image concept [26] is used to create a reference of a face from the training data. Avatar reference images originally created an expressionless reference face for registration purposes. Instead, we generate a reference of each r_e that positively expresses e.

Let $\mathbf{f}_e$ be an image expressing e. To estimate r_e we take the mean:

$$r_e(\mathbf{p}) = \frac{1}{N} \sum_{\mathcal{D}_e} \mathbf{f}_e(\mathbf{p}) \tag{7}$$

where $\mathcal{D}_e$ is the set of face regions of interest images positively expressing e, and N is the number of images in $\mathcal{D}_e$.

Then, SIFT-Flow [27] aligns each face in $\mathcal{D}_e$ to r_e. The process iterates by rewarping $\mathcal{D}_e$ to the avatar reference image.

We calculate d in Equation 6 as the energy of warping $\mathbf{f}$ to r_e with a dense warp of SIFT features. Let $\mathbf{w}$ be the flow field calculated with a modified SIFT Flow objective function:

$$E(\mathbf{w}(\mathbf{p})) = \sum_{\mathbf{p}} \|\mathbf{s}_{r_e}(\mathbf{p}) - \mathbf{s}_{\mathbf{f}}(\mathbf{p} + \mathbf{w}(\mathbf{p}))\|_1 \qquad (8)$$
$$+\alpha \sum_{\mathbf{p}} \left((u(\mathbf{p}) - \mu_x)^2 + v(\mathbf{p} - \mu_y)^2\right)$$

where E is the objective function that is minimized. α is a parameter. $\mathbf{s}_{\mathbf{f}}(\mathbf{p} + \mathbf{w}(\mathbf{p}))$ is the dense SIFT feature of $\mathbf{f}$ at $\mathbf{p}$ offset by $\mathbf{w}(\mathbf{p})$. μ_x and μ_y are the mean motion in the horizontal and vertical directions of $\mathbf{w}$ respectively. After optimal warp, Equation 8 is taken to be d.

The first term reduces the error of r_e and a candidate SIFT feature in $\mathbf{f}$. If the SIFT features are equal, the first term is zero. Non-zero values capture the changes from r_e to $\mathbf{f}$. The second term constrains the flow field by minimizing the magnitude of all of the flow vectors. We subtract the mean from the magnitude to account for slight translation errors from region of interest detection. Otherwise, translation errors would falsely approximate dissimilarity proportional to the size of the image. Because we are subtracting the mean, the effects of whole plane translation errors are reduced, and a fine registration process is not required. Non-zero values of Equation 8 approximate dissimilarity to reference r_e.

4. RESULTS

For mise en scéne features, τ in Equation 4 is 13. For avatar reference image, we iterated the algorithm three times because it was the optimal parameter found in [26]. RBF SVM was implemented with LibSVM [28]. For the SVM, the cost c was 3.5481 and γ was 0.3162. These values were selected with a grid search on the validation set. For rule of thirds color layout descriptor (CLD), CLD is computed in 100×100 sub-regions of the image placed at the rule of thirds intersections.

Results are given in Table 4 for varying modalities on the validation set, feature-level fusion on the validation set, and final results on the testing set. ROC area is not available for the testing fold results because the labels are not public. Expression (LBP-TOP) features are the same features provided in the baseline, except the classifier stage involves PCA dimensionality reduction and an RBF-SVM for classification. In depth results with classification rate, false positive rate, precision, recall, F-measure and ROC area give a full understanding of performance for each modality. Fusion of all modalities and mise en scéne features give the best classification rate. Fusion and expression give the least number of false positives. Semantics and fusion give the best precision. Expression and fusion give the best recall, F-measure. Fusion and mise en scéne features give the best ROC area. A confusion matrix of the testing results is given in Table 2.

5. DISCUSSION

The syntax and semantic features were the worst performers. There is no mechanism to isolate the significant speaker in the scene, so vocalic features measured background noise

Table 2: Confusion matrix of results from the EmotiW 2015 challenge. Ang.: angry. Dis.: disgust. Hap.: happy. Neut.: neutral. Sur.: surprise.

	Ang.	Dis.	Fear	Hap.	Neut.	Sad	Sur.
Ang.	45	1	5	15	6	4	3
Dis.	4	0	2	7	13	3	0
Fear	9	0	33	10	7	6	1
Hap.	15	2	3	46	33	8	1
Neut.	6	1	14	31	85	21	1
Sad	14	1	6	9	20	19	2
Sur.	1	0	3	8	9	5	1

Table 3: Q-statistic values for each modality. Positive values of $q_{i,j}$ approaching 1 indicate disparate classifications, showing promise for fusion. i = Mise en Scéne.

Modality j	$\tilde{q}_{00}$	$\tilde{q}_{01}$	$\tilde{q}_{01}$	$\tilde{q}_{11}$	$q_{i,j}$
Vocalics	234	73	48	16	0.033
Syntax + Semantics	259	48	50	14	0.203
Expression	222	85	37	27	0.312
Emotion	264	43	44	20	0.472

and music. In line with the mise en scéne concept, musical score key should predict apparent affect. However, a number of the videos did not have music. Additionally, some background music had lyrics which were parsed by the semantics modality.

The proposed mise en scéne features outperformed the baseline LBP-TOP features when comparing the modalities without fusion. But, there were still a significant number of misclassifications. Expressionist films are heavily stylized, with extremely typical and discriminative configurations of mise en scéne. However, a movie does not have to follow expressionist style. The scene can be presented as-is with no distortions to light, color, etc. This style of cinematography is referred to as realism. Additionally, artistic value can be generated from intentionally violating cliché mise en scéne patterns. Movie style can also vary from director to director. Meta information estimating the cinematography style or director identity could further supplement mise en scéne features for movie-based affect recognition.

We further investigate the impact of mise en scéne features with a Q-statistic [29]:

$$q_{i,j} = \frac{(\tilde{q}_{00}\tilde{q}_{11} - \tilde{q}_{10}\tilde{q}_{01})}{(\tilde{q}_{00}\tilde{q}_{11} + \tilde{q}_{10}\tilde{q}_{01})} \qquad (9)$$

The Q-statistic compares the success and failure rates of two different single modality feature methods, i and j. $\tilde{q}_{00}$ is the number of videos where both algorithms failed. $\tilde{q}_{11}$ is the number of videos where both algorithms succeeded. $\tilde{q}_{01}$ is the number of videos where i failed and j succeeded, and vise versa. $q_{i,j}$ is valued $[-1, 1]$. Values approaching -1 indicate that both i and j made identical decisions. Values approaching 1 indicate that i and j made opposite decisions, and should compliment each other if fused. Q-statistic results are given in Table 3. There is promise for pairing of mise en scéne with semantics, syntax, expression and emotion modalities. There are no negative values.

6. CONCLUSION

We proposed a multimodal system that measured expression, emotion, vocalics, syntax, semantics, and film-based meta information, referred to as mise en scéne features. Two algorithms for extracting mise en scéne information were proposed. Rule of thirds based motion history histograms detected motion along rule of thirds guidelines. Rule of thirds color layout descriptors compactly described a scene at rule of thirds intersections. The system improved classification performance over the baseline algorithm by 3.17% on the testing set.

7. REFERENCES

[1] A. Dhall, O. R. Murthy, R. Goecke, J. Joshi, and T. Gedeon, "Video and image based emotion recognition challenges in the wild: Emotiw 2015," in *ACM ICMI Workshops*, 2015.

[2] M. J. Lyons, "Automatic classification of single facial images," *IEEE Trans. PAMI*, vol. 21, no. 12, pp. 1357–1362, 1999.

[3] A. Dhall, R. Goecke, S. Lucey, and T. Gedeon, "Collecting large, richly annotated facial-expression databases from movies," *IEEE Multimedia*, vol. 19, no. 3, pp. 34–41, 2012.

[4] M. F. Valstar, M. Mehu, B. Jiang, M. Pantic, and K. Scherer, "Meta-analysis of the first facial expression recognition challenge," *IEEE Trans. SMC, Part B: Cybernetics*, vol. 42, no. 4, pp. 966–979, 2012.

[5] B. Schuller, M. Valstar, F. Eyben, G. McKeown, R. Cowie, and M. Pantic, "AVEC 2011 - The first international audio/visual emotion challenge," in *Affective Computing and Intelligent Interaction Workshops*, vol. 6975, pp. 415–424, 2011.

[6] R. Edgar-Hunt, J. Marland, and S. Rawle, *The Language of Film*. Fairchild Books, 2005.

[7] M. Liu, R. Wang, Z. Huang, S. Shan, and X. Chen, "Partial least squares regression on grassmannian manifold for emotion recognition," in *ACM ICMI Workshops*, pp. 525–530, 2013.

[8] S. E. Kahou, C. Pal, X. Bouthillier, P. Froumenty, R. Memisevic, P. Vincent, A. Courville, and Y. Bengio, "Combining modality specific deep neural networks for emotion recognition in video," in *ACM ICMI Workshops*, pp. 543–550, 2013.

[9] K. Sikka, K. Dykstra, S. Sathyanarayana, G. Littlewort, and M. Bartlett, "Multiple kernel learning for emotion recognition in the wild," in *ACM ICMI Workshops*, pp. 517–524, 2013.

[10] M. Liu, R. Wang, S. Li, S. Shan, Z. Huang, and X. Chen, "Combining multiple kernel methods on Riemannian manifold for emotion recognition in the wild," in *ACM ICMI Workshops*, pp. 494–501, 2014.

[11] J. Chen, Z. Chen, Z. Chi, and H. Fu, "Emotion recognition in the wild with feature fusion and multiple kernel learning," in *ACM ICMI Workshops*, pp. 508–513, 2014.

[12] B. Sun, L. Li, T. Zuo, Y. Chen, G. Zhou, and X. Wu, "Combining multimodal features with hierarchical classifier fusion for emotion recognition in the wild," in *ACM ICMI Workshops*, pp. 481–486, 2014.

[13] F. Eyben, F. Weninger, F. Gross, and B. Schuller, "Recent developments in openSMILE, the munich open-source multimedia feature extractor," in *ACM Multimedia*, pp. 835–838, 2013.

[14] L. Canini, S. Benini, P. Migliorati, and R. Leonardi, "Emotional identity of movies," in *IEEE Int'l. Conf. Image Processing*, pp. 1821–1824, 2009.

[15] M. Kächele and M. Schels, "Inferring depression and affect from application dependent meta knowledge," in *ACM Multimedia Workshops*, pp. 41–48, 2014.

[16] Y.-L. Shue, P. Keating, C. Vicenik, and K. Yu, "Voicesauce: A program for voice analysis," in *Int'l. Congress of Phonetic Sciences*, pp. 1846–1849, 2011.

[17] D. Chen and C. D. Manning, "A fast and accurate dependency parser using neural networks," in *Conf. Empirical Methods on Natural Language Processing*, 2014.

[18] A. C. Cruz, B. Bhanu, and N. Thakoor, "Facial emotion recognition with expression energy," in *ACM ICMI Workshops*, pp. 457–464, 2012.

[19] E. H. Land, "The retinex theory of color vision," in *Edwin H. Land's Essays* (M. McCann, ed.), pp. 53–60, Society for Imaging Science & Technology, 1993.

[20] J. Weijer, T. Gevers, and A. Gijsenij, "Edge-Based Color Constancy," *IEEE Trans. on Image Processing*, vol. 16, no. 9, pp. 2207–2214, 2007.

[21] J. W. Davis, "Recognizing Movement using Motion Histograms," Tech. Rep. 487, MIT, 1998.

[22] H. Meng, D. Huang, H. Wang, H. Yang, M. AI-Shuraifi, and Y. Wang, "Depression Recognition Based on Dynamic Facial and Vocal Expression Features Using Partial Least Square Regression," in *ACM ICMI Workshops*, pp. 21–30, 2013.

[23] E. Kasutani and A. Yamada, "The mpeg-7 color layout descriptor: a compact image feature description for high-speed image/video segment retrieval," in *IEEE Int'l. Conf. Image Processing*, vol. 1, pp. 674–677 vol.1, 2001.

[24] G. Zhao and M. Pietikainen, "Dynamic texture recognition using local binary patterns with an application to facial expressions," *IEEE Trans. PAMI*, vol. 29, no. 6, pp. 1–14, 2007.

[25] A. Cruz, B. Bhanu, and N. Thakoor, "One shot emotion scores for facial emotion recognition," in *IEEE Int'l. Conf. Image Processing*, pp. 1376–1380, Oct 2014.

[26] S. Yang and B. Bhanu, "Understanding discrete facial expressions in video using an emotion avatar image," *IEEE Trans. SMC, Part B: Cybernetics*, vol. 42, no. 4, pp. 920–992, 2011.

[27] C. Liu, J. Yuen, and A. Torralba, "SIFT flow: dense correspondence across scenes and its applications," *IEEE Trans. PAMI*, vol. 33, no. 5, pp. 978–994, 2011.

[28] C.-C. Chang and C.-J. Lin, "LIBSVM: A library for support vector machines," *ACM Trans. Intelligent Systems and Technology*, vol. 2, pp. 27:1–27:27, 2011.

[29] X. Zhou and B. Bhanu, "Integrating face and gait for human recognition at a distance in video," *IEEE Trans. SMC, Part B: Cybernetics*, vol. 37, no. 5, pp. 1119–1137, 2007.

Affect Recognition using Key Frame Selection based on Minimum Sparse Reconstruction

Mehmet Kayaoglu, Cigdem Eroglu Erdem
Department of Electrical and Electronics Engineering
Bahcesehir University
34343, Besiktas, İstanbul, Turkey
Phone: +90 212 381 0895
mehmet.kayaoglu@stu.bahcesehir.edu.tr, cigdem.eroglu@eng.bahcesehir.edu.tr

ABSTRACT
In this paper, we present the methods used for Bahcesehir University team's submissions to the 2015 Emotion Recognition in the Wild Challenge. The challenge consists of categorical emotion recognition in short video clips extracted from movies based on emotional keywords in the subtitles. The video clips mostly contain expressive faces (single or multiple) and also audio which contains the speech of the person in the clip as well as other human voices or background sounds/music. We use an audio-visual method based on video summarization by key frame selection. The key frame selection uses a minimum sparse reconstruction approach with the goal of representing the original video in the best possible way. We extract the LPQ features of the key frames and average them to determine a single feature vector that will represent the video component of the clip. In order to represent the temporal variations of the facial expression, we also use the LBP-TOP features extracted from the whole video. The audio features are extracted using OpenSMILE or RASTA-PLP methods. Video and audio features are classified using SVM classifiers and fused at the score level. We tested eight different combinations of audio and visual features on the AFEW 5.0 (Acted Facial Expressions in the Wild) database provided by the challenge organizers. The best visual and audio-visual accuracies obtained on the test set are 45.1% and 49.9% respectively, whereas the video-based baseline for the challenge is given as 39.3%.

Categories and Subject Descriptors
I.5.4 [Pattern Recognition]: Applications, computer vision, signal processing; I.4.m [Image Processing and Computer Vision]: Miscellaneous

General Terms
Algorithms, Human Factors, Experimentation.

ICMI'15, November 09-13, 2015, Seattle, WA, USA
©2015 ACM. ISBN 978-1-4503-3912-4/15/11 $15.00
DOI: http://dx.doi.org/10.1145/2818346.2830594

Keywords
Emotion Recognition; EmotiW 2015 Challenge; Video Summarization; Affect Recognition; Affective Computing

1. INTRODUCTION
In daily human-to-human interactions, our facial expressions convey non-verbal messages about our emotions and mental states that complement our verbal messages. In the future, human-computer interaction scenarios are also expected to have the ability to recognize emotions to provide more natural man-machine interaction and ubiquitous computing applications such as health care [13], education, psychology [20] and security [18].

In order to test and benchmark automatic affect recognition algorithms, affective databases are needed. Early databases used were mostly acted and recorded in laboratory conditions under controlled head pose and illumination variations. Recently, more spontaneous and close-to-real world databases have been collected [1], [4], [7], [8], [26], several of which have been used in challenges, such as FERA 2015 [22], AVEC 2014 [23], and EmotiW 2015 [5].

The third Emotion Recognition in the Wild (EmotiW 2015) challenge consists of categorical audio-video based emotion recognition based on the Acted Facial Expression in Wild database (AFEW 5.0). The AFEW database contains short audio-visual clips collected from movies and labeled using a semi-automatic approach described in [4]. This challenge is a continuation of the EmotiW 2013 and 2014 challenges and the task is to assign a single emotion label to the video clip from the seven emotions (Anger, Disgust, Fear, Happiness, Neutral, Sad and Surprise). The AFEW database is quite challenging since the video clips contain variability in illumination and head pose, as well as severe occlusion and complex background.

The audio-visual emotion recognition methods in the literature have shown the advantages of fusing audio and video modalities [1], [3], [12], [14], [24], [28]. In this paper, we also present a multimodal affect recognition method using facial expressions and the speech signal. Given a video with an emotional expression, the frames in the video generally reflect the emotion with different intensities. Moreover, some parts of the video might have little motion, which makes subsequent frames to be very similar to each other. Therefore, we aim to select key frames, which will summarize the content of the video effectively. We adopt a recent video summarization method [15] for the problem of selecting key frames from affective videos. Then, static appearance-based facial features are extracted from the selected key frames and averaged to describe the visual content of the whole video. We also intend to capture the temporal variations of facial expressions using LBP-TOP features. We use the audio features extracted by several approaches (OpenSMILE [8], [10], RASTA-PLP [11] etc.) and fuse with the video-based features at the score level. The experimental results on the AFEW 5.0 test database gave an accuracy of 45.1% using visual features and 49.9% using audio-visual features whereas the video based baseline was given as 39.3% [5] .

The organization of the paper is as follows. In Section 2, we give the details of the proposed multimodal emotion recognition system focusing on the key frame selection method using minimum sparse reconstruction. In Section 3, experimental results using various fusion cases are presented. Finally, in Section 4, conclusions are given.

2. EMOTION RECOGNITION SYSTEM

In this section, we first present the methods used for feature extraction from video and speech. Then, we present the classification and fusion methods utilized.

2.1 Feature Extraction from Video

An audio-visual video with an emotional expression consists of many frames, where each frame represents the emotion with a different intensity. Therefore, one way of recognizing the emotion in the video is to select and classify the facial expression on the "key frames" selected from the video. The key frames are selected so that they summarize the content of the video in the best way. This is based on the assumption that there is a single emotion in the sequence, which is true for most databases in the literature including the AFEW 5.0 database.

As a preprocessing step, the face regions in all frames of a video are detected and aligned. We use the aligned and cropped face provided by the challenge organizers. Face detection is achieved using the mixture of parts framework of Zhu and Ramanan [29], which is followed by face tracking using IntraFace method [21]. The face regions are aligned and cropped using the tracked feature points.

Below, in Section 2.1.1 we give the details of the key frame selection method used in this paper. Once the key frames are selected, the LPQ features (explained in Section 2.1.2) are computed and averaged over them to represent the visual component of the whole video. Another feature set that we tested is the LBP-TOP feature, which captures the temporal variation of the facial feature expression as well, which is explained in Section 2.1.3.

2.1.1 Key Frame Selection using Minimum Sparse Reconstruction

The assumption behind the utilized key frame selection method is that set of key frames are the most representative frames in the sequence among others and also the conceptual information of the sequence is mostly covered by key frames [15]. Therefore, we view the key frame selection as a similar problem to video summarization. In [15], video summarization is formulated as a problem of selecting the minimum number of frames to reconstruct the entire video as accurately as possible. Video summarization is actually a ranking process of the frames considering how well they represent the video. We adopted this video summarization method to emotional videos to select the key frames from a video with an emotional expression.

Given a video with n frames, each frame is a candidate to be a key frame. Let $\mathbf{F} = [\mathbf{f}_1, \mathbf{f}_2, \ldots, \mathbf{f}_n] \in R^{d \times n}$, where $\mathbf{f}_i \in \mathrm{R}^{\mathrm{d}}$ denotes the feature vector corresponding to frame i. The goal of key frame selection is to select an optimal subset $\boldsymbol{F_K} = [\mathbf{f}_{k_1}, \mathbf{f}_{k_2}, \ldots, \mathbf{f}_{k_m}] \in R^{d \times m}$ such that $k_1, k_2, \ldots, k_m \in [1,2, \ldots, n]$. There are two goals when the subset is formed: i) The original video is reconstructed accurately and ii) the number of key frames is as small as possible. That is, the following minimum sparse reconstruction (MSR) expression is minimized:

$$\min_{\mathbf{S}} \frac{1}{2} \|\mathbf{F} - \mathbf{F}_K \mathbf{A}\|_2 + \lambda \|\mathbf{S}\|_0 \tag{1}$$

s.t. $\mathbf{F}_K = \mathbf{FS}$

$\mathbf{A} = f(\mathbf{F}, \mathbf{F}_K)$

where $\mathbf{S}$ is a diagonal selection matrix that models the selection of keyframes from the original video:

$$S_{ij} = \begin{cases} 0, & i \neq j \\ 0 \text{ or } 1, & i = j \end{cases} \tag{2}$$

and $\|\mathbf{S}\|_0$ is the L_0 norm of the selection matrix, which is the number of nonzero elements indicating the number of key frames selected. Therefore, sparsity is ensured by the L_0 norm. In (1), $\mathbf{A}$ represents the reconstruction coefficients of $\mathbf{F}$ by the matrix $\mathbf{F}_K$ which are computed using the reconstruction function $f(.,.)$, $\|.\|_2$ represents the L_2 norm, and λ is a weighting coefficient. The first term in (1) tries to minimize the least-square reconstruction error (LSRE), while the second term minimizes the number of key frames selected.

Assuming that m keyframes have been selected, the next keyframe chosen should maximally decrease LSRE. Therefore, the frame which gives the maximum LSRE at the current iteration should be selected as the next key frame:

$$\mathbf{f}_{k_{m+1}} = \arg\max_{\mathbf{f}_j \in \mathbf{F}/\mathbf{F}_K} \left\| f_j - \mathbf{F}_K \mathbf{a}_j \right\|_2, \tag{3}$$

where $\mathbf{a}_j$ represents the reconstruction coefficient for the jth frame and $\mathbf{F}/\mathbf{F}_K$ represents the set of all non-keyframes. This is equivalent to selecting the worst reconstructed frame, after normalization by the vector magnitude:

$$\mathbf{f}_{k_{m+1}} = \arg\min_{\mathbf{f}_j \in \mathbf{F}/\mathbf{F}_K} \frac{\|\mathbf{F}_K \mathbf{a}_j\|_2}{\|\mathbf{f}_j\|_2}. \tag{4}$$

In order to determine the reconstruction coefficients, the orthogonal subspace projection (OSP) method is used [15] by projecting all frames to the space spanned by $\mathbf{F}_K$, which gives:

$$\mathbf{a}_j = (\mathbf{F}_K^T \mathbf{F}_K)^{-1} \mathbf{F}_K^T \mathbf{f}_j = \mathbf{P}_K \mathbf{f}_j \tag{5}$$

The algorithm continues to select new key frames as long as the percentage of reconstruction error (POR) of any frame is below a predetermined threshold, i.e.:

$$POR_j = \frac{\|\mathbf{F}_K \mathbf{a}_j\|_2}{\|\mathbf{f}_j\|_2} < T_P \tag{6}$$

The overall algorithm that we use for key frame selection can be summarized as follows:

Algorithm 1. Minimum sparse reconstruction based key frame selection algorithm.

Input: The expressive video $\mathbf{F} \in R^{d \times n}$ with n frames, where each frame is represented by the LPQ features extracted from the face region.

Output: The key frame set $\mathbf{F}_K \in R^{d \times m}$.

1. Initialize the key frame set using the first frame of the sequence as $\mathbf{F}_K = [\boldsymbol{f}_{k_1}]$ and set $m = 1$.
2. Calculate the POR for all frames in set $\mathbf{F}/\mathbf{F}_K$ using (6).
3. Repeat steps 4-6 while POR of any frame is smaller than T_P.
4. Select the next key frame using (4).
5. Increase m by one.
6. Calculate the POR for all frames in set $\mathbf{F}/\mathbf{F}_K$ using (6).

After the iterations terminate, we discard the first frame selected at the initialization step. Two examples for the key frame selection results are shown in Figure 1 and Figure 2. We can observe that the minimum number of frames that represent the whole video have been selected.

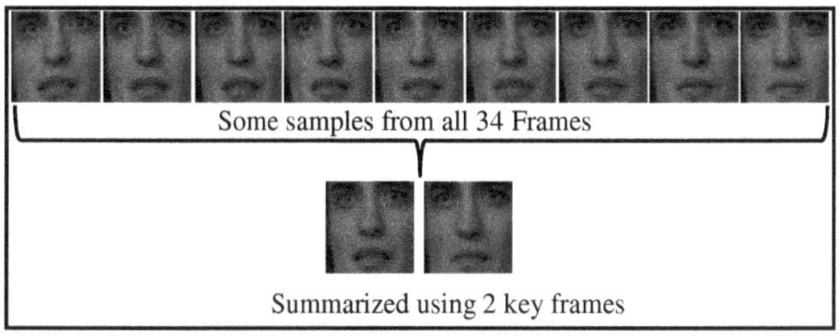

Figure 1: An example of video summarization from the AFEW 5.0 database for a sequence labeled with "sad".

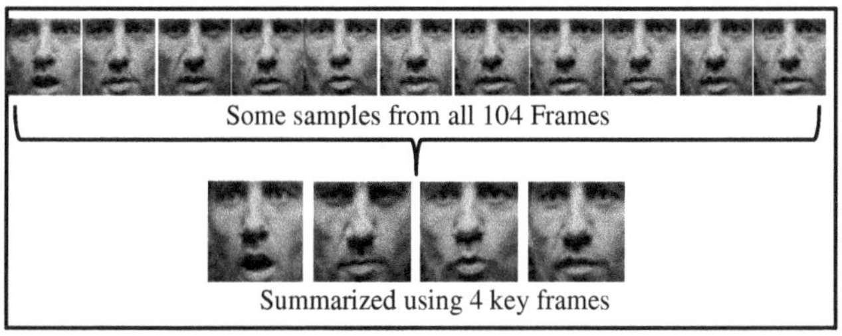

Figure 2: An example of video summarization from the test set of AFEW 5.0 database.

2.1.2 LPQ

Local Phase Quantization (LPQ) features have been originally used for blur-insensitive texture classification [17], which has also been used for facial expression recognition with success [6], [25]. LPQ features are based on computing the 2D short–term DFT of the image in a window around each pixel. Then the DFT is sampled at four frequencies, which are then decorrelated and quantized. The quantized local phase vectors are represented as integer values between 0-255. Finally, 256 bin histograms of these numbers in sub-blocks of the face region are concatenated and used as a feature vector (see Figure 3).

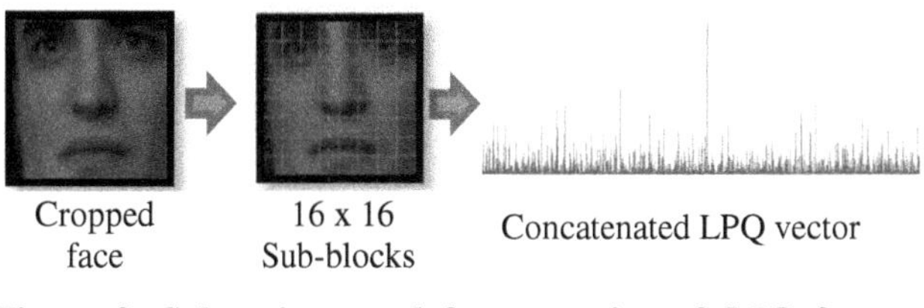

Figure 3: Sub-regions used for extraction of LPQ feature vectors.

2.1.3 LBP-TOP

Local Binary Pattern (LBP) operator considers pixels in a neighborhood and labels them by thresholding to encode local primitives such as uniform regions, edges, corners and spots etc. [16]. It has also been used for facial expression recognition [19]. LBP static descriptor was extended to describe dynamic textures and has been demonstrated to be successful for facial expression recognition [27]. LBP-TOP utilizes three orthogonal spatio-temporal planes around a pixel and computes the LBP features on the planes to obtain XY-LBP, XT-LBP and YT-LBP features, which are then concatenated to obtain a single feature vector.

2.2 Feature Extraction from Audio

In order to extract audio features for emotion recognition, we used Mel-Frequency Cepstral Coefficients (MFCC) and relative spectral features (RASTA) based on perceptual linear prediction (PLP) [11]. Before extraction of audio features, first we detected the endpoints of speech signals to estimate the starting and ending points of the speech in a given audio file. Then, we calculated the MFCC and RASTA-PLP features using filters with an order of 12 and 20, respectively, using a window of length 25msec and 50% overlap ratio. Then, we appended the 12 MFCC and 13 RASTA-PLP coefficients with their first and second time derivatives. The final audio-based feature vector was extracted by applying nine statistical functions (max, min, maximum position, minimum position, mean, variance, range, kurtosis and skewness) to the 75 elements of the MFCC and RASTA-PLP vector.

We also tested the audio features extracted using the OpenSMILE toolbox [9], [10], which were provided by the challenge organizers [5].

2.3 Classification and Fusion

We used a Support Vector Machine (SVM) classifier using chi-square and exponential chi-square kernels with one-vs-all strategy to classify the video and audio features [2], [29].

We used a score level fusion technique, where we combine the probabilities for each class, which are estimated using each modality separately. We tested several approaches for combining the probabilities [1] estimated using the SVM classifiers and the best results were obtained using the product rule [24], in which the probabilities obtained from the classification of each modality is multiplied for a given test vector and we predict the final label as the one which gives the maximum product:

$$P(\omega_k \mid x) = \prod_{i=1}^{2} P(\tilde{\omega}_k \mid x, \lambda_i) \ , k = 1,...,6 \tag{7}$$

$$\omega^* = \max_k \{P(\omega_k \mid x)\}, \quad \text{k} = 1,...,6 \tag{8}$$

where x represents the audio-visual feature vector of the test video, ω and $\tilde{\omega}$ represent the predicted output labels after and before fusion, $P(\tilde{\omega}_k \mid x, \lambda_i)$ is the probability of class k for each individual classifier λ_i and ω^* is the final estimated class of the test video. In order to fuse the LPQ and LBP-TOP based features for the video modality, we utilized a similar approach as well (see Figure 4 and Figure 5).

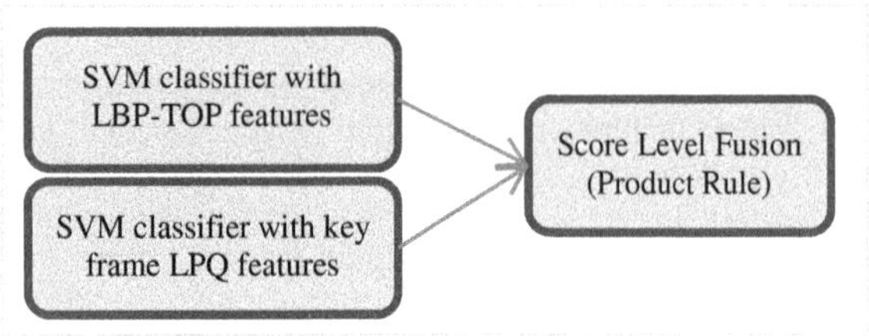

Figure 4: Fusion of LBP-TOP and LPQ video features

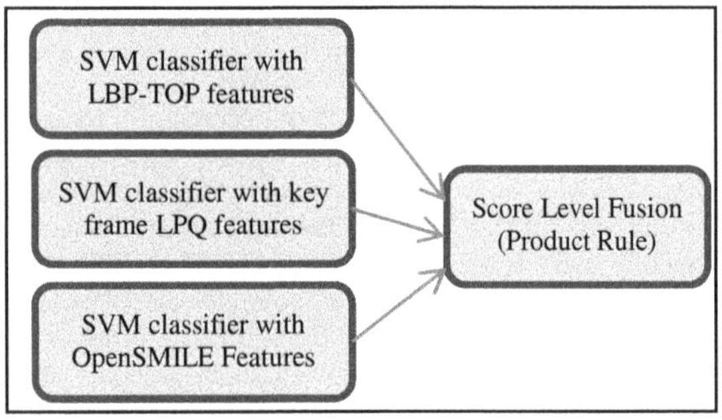

Figure 5: Fusion of LBP-TOP, LPQ based video and OpenSMILE audio features

3. EXPERIMENTAL RESULTS

3.1 EmotiW 2015 Challenge

The challenge is based on the AFEW 5.0 (Acted Facial Expressions in the Wild) database, which is divided into three parts for training, validation and testing. The numbers of samples for each emotion in each set are shown in Table 1. The labels of the test set are not given to the participants of the challenge.

The organizers of the EmotiW 2015 challenge provide the LBP-TOP feature set on the AFEW 5.0 database. After the pre-processing step for aligning and cropping the face region, LBP-TOP features are extracted from non-overlapping spatial 4x4 blocks. The LBP-TOP features from each block are concatenated to create one feature vector of size 1 × 2832 for each frame of a video.

Table 1: The numbers of samples for each emotion in AFEW 5.0 database for the EmotiW 2015 Challenge.

	Anger	Disg.	Fear	Happy	Neut.	Sad	Surp
Train	118	72	77	145	131	107	73
Valid.	64	40	46	63	63	61	46
Test	79	29	66	108	159	71	27

The video only baseline classification accuracy provided by the challenge organizers using an SVM classifier with Chi square kernel on the validation set is 36.08%. Similarly, baseline classification accuracy on the test set is 39.33% (see Table 2).

We would like to note that while the database comes with Zhu's [29] face tracking results, the difficult and close-to-real-world conditions cause problems even in the early stages of the processing pipeline. Some examples of incorrectly detected and tracked face images are illustrated in Figure 6.

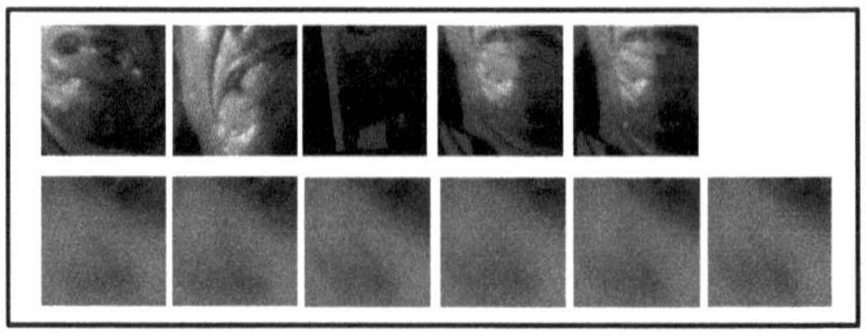

Figure 6: Noisy face detection and tracking results of two different sequences from train and validation sets of AFEW 5.0 dataset.

3.2 Experimental Setup

In our tests, we used the aligned faces provided by the challenge organizers. The size of a face region is 128×128 pixels. We divide the aligned faces into non-overlapping sub-blocks of size 16×16 and obtain 64 sub-blocks for feature extraction as shown in Figure 3. In the created sub-regions, we extract the 256 bin histogram of LPQ features of each region. The LPQ features of the 64 sub-blocks are concatenated into a single feature vector of length 1×16384.

During the key frame extraction phase, LPQ features are used as the feature vector for each frame. The threshold for percentage of reconstruction (POR), i.e. the T_P parameter has been selected as 0.80. After key frames are selected by the method explained in section 2.1.1, average LPQ features of the selected key frames are calculated and used to represent the whole video feature of the sequence.

The audio features include the first 12 MFCC features. As a common practice, delta and double-delta MFCCs (sometimes referred to as first and second derivatives, respectively) are calculated to capture local dynamics, forming a 1×36 dimensional feature vector. Then, nine statistical functions and their first and second time derivatives are applied to the first 12 MFCCs in order to get a vector of length 1×324 representing MFCC features. We also calculated 13 RASTA-PLP coefficients by using a filter of order 20 and augmented by their delta and double delta features. The same statistical parameters as in MFCCs are used for the RASTA-PLPs, giving a 1×351 dimensional feature vector. The MFCC and RASTA-PLP feature vectors are then concatenated to get an audio feature vector of length 1×675 for the a video clip.

3.3 Test Cases

We evaluated the performance of video features (LBP-TOP and LPQ`s from key frames) and audio features (OpenSMILE and MFCC & RASTA-PLP features) on the validation and test sets. The emotion recognition results of eight combinations on validation and test sets are illustrated in Table 2. The configuration used for each test case is explained below.

Case 1: Video based experiment, where key frames of all video sequences are selected using T_P as 0.80. For each video sequence, average LPQ feature vector of all key frames is used to represent the whole video. An SVM with a chi-square kernel is trained.

Case 2: Video based experiment combining case 1 and a second chi-square kernel SVM, which is trained using LBP-TOP features. Then score level fusion is applied using the product rule.

Case 3: Video based experiment, which is same as case 2 but the parameter T_P has been selected as 0.85.

Case 4: Same as case 3 with the SVM classifier trained using both the training and the validation sets of AFEW 5.0 dataset.

Case 5: Audio based experiment using feature level fusion of MFCC and RASTA-PLP features. An SVM classifier with an exponential chi-square kernel is used.

Case 6: Audio based experiment using the OpenSMILE feature set. An SVM classifier with an exponential chi-square kernel is used.

Case 7: Audio-visual experiment using score level fusion of Case 2 and Case 5.

Case 8: Audio-visual experiment using score level fusion of Case 2 and Case 6.

Table 2: Overall accuracies of the 8 test cases on validation and test sets. Numbers are given in percentages.

Case	Methods		Accuracy	
			Val.	Test
Video Based Baseline			36.08	39.33
1	Video Based	LPQ (T_P = 0.80)	40.70	41.37
2		LBP-TOP + LPQ (T_P = 0.80)	43.40	45.08
3		LBP-TOP + LPQ (T_P = 0.85)	44.47	44.71
4		LBP-TOP + LPQ (trained by train + val. set) (T_P = 0.80)	-	43.23
5	Audio Based	MFCC & RASTA-PLP	24.02	33.40
6		OpenSMILE	31.85	33.21
7	Video + Audio Based	LBP-TOP + LPQ + MFCC & RASTA-PLP	41.24	47.68
8		LBP-TOP + LPQ + OpenSMILE	40.70	49.91

The best classification accuracy on the test set is achieved for Case 8, using score level fusion of LBP-TOP, key frame LPQ's and OpenSMILE audio features, which is 49.91%. The confusion matrices of this case for the validation and test sets are shown in Table 3 and Table 4, respectively.

Table 3: Confusion matrix of Case 8 (audio-visual) on validation set. Numbers are given in percentages.

	Ang	Disg	Fear	Hap	Neut	Sad	Surp
Ang	67.8	0.00	0.00	13.5	6.78	8.47	3.39
Disg	20.5	7.69	0.00	23.08	25.64	17.95	5.13
Fear	34.0	0.00	11.3	15.91	20.45	9.09	9.09
Hap	4.7	1.59	0.00	79.37	9.52	4.76	0.00
Neut	4.92	0.00	4.92	26.23	55.74	8.20	0.00
Sad	11.8	3.39	8.47	18.64	32.20	25.42	0.00
Surp	28.2	2.17	10.8	13.04	30.43	6.52	8.70

Table 4: Confusion matrix of Case 8 (audio-visual) on test set. Numbers are given in percentages.

	Ang	Disg	Fear	Hap	Neut	Sad	Surp
Ang	73.42	1.27	3.80	6.33	12.66	2.53	0.00
Disg	13.79	0.00	0.00	37.93	17.24	20.69	10.34
Fear	31.82	3.03	18.18	7.58	10.61	16.67	12.12
Hap	5.56	0.93	0.93	73.15	8.33	9.26	1.85
Neut	5.03	2.52	0.63	15.72	55.35	18.87	1.89
Sad	12.68	4.23	2.82	21.13	14.08	42.25	2.82
Surp	22.22	0.00	7.41	14.81	29.63	18.52	7.41

Table 5: Confusion matrix of Case 2 (visual) on test set. Numbers are given in percentages.

	Ang	Disg	Fear	Hap	Neut	Sad	Sur
Ang	73.42	2.53	5.06	6.33	6.33	6.33	0.00
Disg	10.34	17.24	3.45	17.24	13.79	24.14	13.79
Fear	27.27	3.03	15.15	6.06	15.15	18.18	15.15
Hap	9.26	2.78	0.93	68.52	4.63	12.04	1.85
Neut	10.69	3.14	3.14	15.72	43.40	18.87	5.03
Sad	12.68	7.04	5.63	22.54	11.27	33.80	7.04
Surp	37.04	0.00	7.41	14.81	18.52	11.11	11.11

Table 6: Confusion matrix of Case 6 (audio) on test set. Numbers are given in percentages.

	Ang	Disg	Fear	Hap	Neut	Sad	Surp
Ang	55.70	0.00	11.39	20.25	7.59	3.80	1.27
Disg	13.79	0.00	3.45	31.03	34.48	17.24	0.00
Fear	25.76	1.52	18.18	21.21	21.21	10.61	1.52
Hap	14.81	0.93	0.00	43.52	25.93	12.04	2.78
Neut	6.29	0.63	5.66	33.33	36.48	16.35	1.26
Sad	15.49	0.00	5.63	25.35	26.76	23.94	2.82
Surp	11.11	3.70	3.70	18.52	33.33	25.93	3.70

We can see that happiness and anger have the highest accuracies. In Table 5 and Table 6, we give the confusion matrices of Case 2 (video only) and Case 6 (audio only), as well.

4. CONCLUSIONS

We presented a multimodal categorical emotion recognition method based on key frame selection from video. The key frames are selected so that they represent the content of the whole video clip in the best possible way. The video and audio features are fused at the score level using multiplication rule. We tested eight different combinations of audio and visual features on the AFEW 5.0 (Acted Facial Expressions in the Wild) database provided by the challenge organizers. The best visual and audio-visual accuracies obtained on the test set are 45.1% and 49.9% respectively, which are above the baseline accuracy of 39.3%.

5. ACKNOWLEDGMENTS

This work was partially supported by The Scientific and Technological Research Council of Turkey (TUBITAK) under project number EEAG-110E056.

6. REFERENCES

[1] Atrey, P. K., Hossain, M. A., El Saddik, A. and Kankanhalli, M. S. 2010. Multimodal fusion for multimedia analysis: a survey, *Multimedia Systems,* 16 (6), 345-379.

[2] Chang, C. C. and Lin, C. J. 2011. LIBSVM: a library for support vector machines, *ACM Transactions on Intelligent Systems and Technology (TIST)*, 2, 27.

[3] Cruz, A., Bhanu, B., and Yang, S. 2011. A psychologically-inspired match-score fusion model or video-based facial expression recognition, *Proc. Int. Conf. Affective Computing and Intelligent Interaction (ACII)*, 341-350.

[4] Dhall, A., Goecke, R., Lucey, S. and Gedeon, T. 2012. Collecting large, richly annotated facial-expression databases from movies. *IEEE Multimedia,* 19(3), 34-41.

[5] Dhall, A., Ramana Murthy, O. V., Goecke, R., Joshi, J., and Gedeon, T., 2015. Video and image based emotion recognition challenges in the wild: EmotiW 2015, *ACM Int. Conf. on Multimodal Interaction (ICMI 2015).*

[6] Dhall, A., Asthana, A., Goecke R., Gedeon T. 2011. Emotion recognition using PHOG and LPQ features. In *Proceedings of the workshop on Facial Expression Recognition and Analysis Challenge FERA2011, IEEE Automatic Face and Gesture Recognition Conference FG2011.* Santa Barbara.

[7] Douglas-Cowie, E., Cowie, R., Schoder, M. 2000. A new emotion database: Considerations, resources and scope. *In Proceedings ISCA ITRW on Speech and Emotion*, 39–44.

[8] Erdem, C. E., Turan, C., and Aydın, Z. 2015. BAUM-2: A multilingual audio-visual affective face database. *Multimedia Tools and Applications*, 74, 18 (2015), 7429- 7459.

[9] Eyben, F., Wöllmer, M., and Schuller, B. 2010. OpenSMILE - The Munich versatile and fast open-source audio feature extractor. In *Proc. s of the 18th ACM Int. Conf. on Multimedia (ACM'MM 2010)* (Florence, Italy), 1459-1462.

[10] Eyben,F., Weninger, F., Groß, F., and Schuller, B. Recent developments in openSMILE, the Munich open-source multimedia feature extractor, In *Proceedings of the 21st ACM International Conference on Multimedia (ACM'MM 2013)* (Barcelona, Spain, October 2013), 835-838.

[11] Hermansky, H. and Morgan, N. 1994. RASTA processing of speech," *IEEE Transactions on Speech and Audio Processing*, 2, 4, 578–589. DOI=10.1109/89.326616

[12] Khou, S. E., Pal, C., Bouthillier, X., Froumenty, P., Gulcehre, C., Memisevic, R., Vincent, P., Courville, A., Bengio, Y. et. al.2013. Combining modality specific deep neural networks for emotion recognition in video. *In Proc. of the 15th ACM on Int. Conf. on Multimodal Interaction* (Sydney, December 9-13, ICMI'13), 543-550.

[13] Littlewort, G. C., Bartlett, M. S., and Lee, K. 2009. Automatic coding of facial expressions displayed during posed and genuine pain, *Image and Vision Computing,* 27 (12), 1797-1803.

[14] Liu, M., Wang, R., Li, S., Shan, S., Huang, Z., Chen, X., 2014. Combining Multiple Kernel Methods on Riemannian Manifold for Emotion Recognition in the Wild, *ICMI 2014,* In *Proceedings of the 15th ACM on Int. Conf. on Multimodal Interaction,* 494 - 501.

[15] Mei, S., Guan, G., Wang, Z., Wan, S., He, M., and Feng, D. D. 2015. Video summarization via minimum sparse reconstruction. *Pattern Recognition*, 48, 522-533.

[16] Ojala T., Pietikainen M., Maenpaa T. 2002.Multiresolution gray-scale and rotation invariant texture classification with local binary patterns. *IEEE Trans. Pattern Anal Mach. Intell.* 24 (7), 971–987.

[17] Ojansivu V., Heikkil J. 2008. Blur insensitive texture classification using local phase quantization. *Lecture Notes in Computer Science*, 5099:236–243.

[18] Ryan, A., Cohn, J. F., Lucey, S., Saragih, J., Lucey, P., and De la Torre, F. *et al.*, 2009. Automated facial expression recognition system, *Int'l Conf. on Security Technology,* 172-177. DOI=10.1109/AFGR.1998.670980"

[19] Shan, C., Gong, S., and McOwan, P.W. 2009. Facial expression recognition based on local binary patterns: A comprehensive study. *Image and Vision Computing*, 27, 6, 803-816. DOI=10.1016/j.imavis.2008.08.005

[20] Sloan, D. M., and Kring, A. M. 2007. Measuring changes in emotion during psychotherapy: Conceptual and methodological issues. *Clinical Psy.: Science and Practice,* 14, 307-322. DOI=10.1111/j.1468-2850.2007.00092.x

[21] Xiong, X. and De La Torre, F. 2013. Supervised descent method and its application to face alignment. *IEEE Conf. on Computer Vision and Pattern Recognition (CVPR), 532-539.*

[22] Valstar, M. F., Almaev, T., Girard, J. M., McKeown, G., Mehu, M., Yin, L., Pantic, M., Cohn, J. F. 2015. Second facial expression recognition and analysis challenge, *IEEE Int. Conf. and Workshops on Automatic Face and Gesture Recognition*, Ljubljana, Slovenia.

[23] Valstar, M., Schuller, B., Smith, K., Almaev, T., Eyben, F., Krajewski, J., Cowie, R., Pantic, M. 2014. AVEC 2014: 3 dimensional affect and depression recognition challenge. In *Proceedings of the 4th Int. Workshop on Audio/Visual Emotion Challenge (AVEC), ACM Multimedia, 3-10.*

[24] Wang, Y., Guan, L. and Venetsanopoulos, A. N. 2012. Kernel cross-modal factor analysis for information fusion with application to bimodal emotion recognition, *IEEE Transactions on Multimedia* , 14 (3), 597-607.

[25] Yang, S. and Bhanu, B. 2011. Facial expression recognition using emotion avatar image, in *IEEE International Conference on Automatic Face & Gesture Recognition and Workshops*, 866-871. DOI=10.1109/FG.2011.5771364

[26] Zeng, Z. H. , Pantic, M., Roisman, G. I., Huang, T. S., 2009. A survey of affect recognition methods: audio, visual, and spontaneous expressions. *IEEE Trans. on Pattern Analysis and Machine Intelligence* 31(1), 39 – 58.

[27] Zhao, G., and Pietikäinen, M. 2007. Dynamic texture recognition using local binary patterns with an application to facial expressions. *IEEE Transactions on Pattern Analysis and Machine Intelligence* 29(6), 915–928.

[28] Zhalehpour, S., Akhtar Z., and Erdem, C. E. 2014. Multimodal emotion recognition with automatic peak frame selection, in *IEEE International Symposium on Innovations in Intelligent Systems and Applications (INISTA) Proceedings*, Alberobello, Italy, June 23-25, 2014, 116-121.

[29] Zhu, X. and Ramanan, D., 2012. Face detection, pose estimation, and landmark localization in the wild. *IEEE Conf. on Computer Vision and Pattern Recognition (CVPR),* pp. 2879-2886.

[30] LibSVM http://wmii.uwm.edu.pl/~ksopyla/libsvm_chi2

2015 Multimodal Learning and Analytics Grand Challenge

Marcelo Worsley
Rossier School of Education
& Institute for Creative Technologies
University of Southern California
Los Angeles, CA, USA
worsley@usc.edu

Katherine Chiluiza
Escuela Superior Politécnica del Litoral
Guayaquil, Ecuador
kchilui@espol.edu.ec

Joseph F. Grafsgaard
Department of Psychology
North Carolina State University
Raleigh, NC, USA
jfgrafsg@ncsu.edu

Xavier Ochoa
Centro de Tecnologías de Información
Escuela Superior Politécnica del Litoral
Guayaquil, Ecuador
xavier@cti.espol.edu.ec

ABSTRACT
Multimodality is an integral part of teaching and learning. Over the past few decades researchers have been designing, creating and analyzing novel environments that enable students to experience and demonstrate learning through a variety of modalities. The recent availability of low cost multimodal sensors, advances in artificial intelligence and improved techniques for large scale data analysis have enabled researchers and practitioners to push the boundaries on multimodal learning and multimodal learning analytics. In an effort to continue these developments, the 2015 Multimodal Learning and Analytics Grand Challenge includes a combined focus on new techniques to capture multimodal learning data, as well as the development of rich, multimodal learning applications.

Categories and Subject Descriptors
H.5.m [**Information Interfaces and Presentation**]: Miscellaneous
J.4 [**Computer Applications**]: Social and Behavioral Sciences

General Terms
Performance, Design, Human Factors

Keywords
Design Challenge, Learning Environments, Human Computer Interaction

1. INTRODUCTION
The 21st century has seen an expansion in the set of tools available for assessing the quality of a given learning environment or experience (i.e., [2,3,16]. A number of the traditional tools, test and quiz performance, speeches and essays, are modes of expression that have been around for centuries and remain the more privileged forms of assessment. For all of their pedagogical shortcomings, these forms of assessment have the benefit of being widely accepted and easy to interpret. However, contemporary learning sciences research is increasingly concerned with additional constructs: motivation, engagement, collaboration, creativity, critical thinking, and problem solving, for example [1,13,17,34]. These are constructs that tend to be much harder to quantify using traditional testing instruments [8] and often necessitate adopting an alternative approach that more closely aligns with the design of said learning environment [22,27]. Fortunately, recent advances in multimodal human perception and low-cost multimodal sensory technology have made it possible to study complex human-human and human-machine interactions [15,18,23,28]. Multimodal learning analytics [5,24,32] works to leverage these advances in multimodal processing in order to address the challenges of studying a variety of complex learning-relevant constructs. In fact, recent reports have identified multimodal learning analytics [12,21], and multimodal evaluations [1], as important emerging areas of research. Multimodality allows researchers and practitioners to triangulate among the various ways that students may evidence learning while also allowing for a more complete and contextualized description of each student's experience and development.

ICMI '15, November 09-13, 2015, Seattle, WA, USA
© 2015 ACM. ISBN 978-1-4503-3912-4/15/11...$15.00
DOI: http://dx.doi.org/10.1145/2818346.2829995

Taking a multimodal perspective becomes increasingly salient in complex learning environments (e.g., Makerspaces, Collaborative Tangible User Interfaces). To this end, recent research in multimodal learning analytics has been particularly useful in studying non-traditional learning activities: collaborative mathematics problem-solving [19,20,33]; makerspaces [30,31]; computer programming [4,9,10], oral presentations [6,7,14] and collaborative tangible user interfaces learning [25,26]. Across these studies, researchers have used multimodal analytic techniques to model student performance, predict student learning, and, more importantly, construct models of student-student/student-artifact interactions. By constructing models of student-student interactions, as well as student-artifact interactions, multimodal learning analytics has been useful for better understanding the intricate learning processes that emerge in complex learning environments.

However, a significant hindrance to advancing multimodal learning analytics is the lack of high quality multimodal data capture tools that researchers and practitioners can easily use to collect meaningful process-oriented data. To address this, the 2015 Multimodal Learning and Analytics Grand Challenge focused on two design challenges that will hopefully advance the field's ability to capture and analyze high quality multimodal data. Both challenges are situated in the domain of multimodal teaching and learning, and should lend to the continuation of data driven challenges in future years.

2. CHALLENGE DESCRIPTIONS

Participation was solicited in two design categories: Multimodal Capture of Learning Environments and Multimodal Learning Applications: Incorporating Human Movement

2.1 Multimodal Capture of Learning Environments

The Multimodal Capture of Learning Environments challenge addresses the need to develop multimodal tools that can be used to effectively gather data from unstructured environments. While multimodal data capture can reasonably be completed in laboratory settings, with a small number of students, undertaking classroom wide multimodal data capture and analysis in authentic, everyday learning settings is quite challenging. However, we believe that the current availability of high quality multimodal sensor technology can significantly improve the state-of-the-art in this area. Furthermore, advances in this specific scenario should have applications across a variety of domains and scenarios outside of education. Submissions in this category were evaluated based on the quality, quantity and diversity of the data captured. Additionally, submissions were evaluated based on their ability to generalize to a variety of classroom learning contexts. Finally, authors were asked to focus on one or more areas for application optimization: data quality, cost, scalability, flexibility and intrusiveness. More specific details concerning submission evaluation guide can be found in the Evaluation and Guidelines section.

2.2 Multimodal Learning Applications: Incorporating Human Movement

The Multimodal Learning Application category sought submissions of software and/or hardware solutions that enable multimodal teaching and learning for one or more users. We were particularly interested in soliciting submissions that include recent low-cost motion sensors (e.g., Microsoft Kinect, Leap Motion, Myo). The low-cost motion sensors can easily be coupled with sensors from other modalities (Eye Tribe, Q-sensor/Empatica E4, etc.) Additionally, we encouraged participants to leverage existing software applications that ease the process of software development (e.g. the Institute of Creative Technology's Virtual Human Toolkit [11] and the LITE Lab's Generalized Intelligent Framework for Tutoring [29]).

For this design challenge, submissions were evaluated based on: how naturalistic the interactions are, the extent to which the affordances of the platform align with the learning goals, the quality of the learning (learning will be considered in the broad sense to include cognitive, socio-emotional, intuitive, etc.) that is taking place and how well the platform is able to record and leverage meaningful multimodal data in real-time. Authors were asked to include quantitative and/or qualitative results from a preliminary user study. A specific set of questions to ask of pilot test participants was provided in the Multimodal Learning Applications Evaluation and Design Guide. Additionally, solutions were rated based on the scalability of the platform (how easily can it be developed across multiple geographies and for multiple students) as well as its ability to offer real-time feedback.

3. EVALUATION CRITERIA

Each submission was evaluated by at least three reviewers that came from a variety of disciplines. Specific evaluation guidelines were provided for each sub-challenge. In the case of the Multimodal Capture of Learning Environments, submissions were evaluated based on the quality and quantity of data captured, and the ease with which that data could be interpreted and analyzed. For the Multimodal Learning Application challenge, submissions were evaluated based on how naturalistic the learning experience was, the quality of the learning gained from the interaction, and the platform's ability to capture and analyze rich multimodal data in real-time. More specific guidelines for the Multimodal Capture of Learning Environments category can be found below.

3.1 Multimodal Capture of Learning Environments Evaluation Guidelines

Capturing multimodal data that can effectively be used for learning analytics research can be challenging. In the submission guide, we provided some suggestions around the types and quality of data needed to conduct meaningful analyses. The suggestions for the modalities and data quality were based on prior work.

3.1.1 Cost

The total cost (both in economic and human resources) is an important variable that determines the feasibility of replicating and applying the capture design. Authors were asked to provide a rough estimate of the total cost of procuring, installing and operating the proposed solution.

3.1.2 Scalability

Learning environments vary widely in terms of size, from small working groups involving just two students to large auditoria with hundreds of students. Authors should report on how feasible it is for their design to adapt to larger or smaller settings.

3.1.3 Flexibility

Learning environments also vary widely in terms of disposition and arrangement, from traditional lecture settings with the instructor in front and students sitting at desks, to more active modes with workgroups of students sitting around tables and a group of instructors roaming among them. The authors should report how feasible it is for their design to adapt to different classroom arrangements.

3.1.4 Intrusiveness

Ideally, multimodal recording solutions for the classroom should be transparent for both the instructor and the students. In reality, different solutions create some level of intrusion (cameras pointing at participants, using special devices to conduct activities, wearing sensor or markers, etc.). As the natural behavior in the classroom could be altered by the recording setup, the authors should provide a small reflection on the intrusiveness of their designs.

3.2 Data Quality

3.2.1 Multimodal Fusion

Across all of the data there is an expectation that each data stream can be resolved to a specific individual (or, in some cases, a pair or triad of students), and to a properly synchronized point in time. Several audio/video, and software based approaches can be used for doing data synchronization, but this information should be clearly reflected in the submission text, as synchronization dramatically impacts data quality. The specific fusion strategy is based on the nature of the tasks and the data streams.

3.2.2 Skeletal Tracking (and Motion)
Skeletal tracking from the Kinect sensor should be frontal. For alternative motion data capture tools (e.g., 2D/3D computer vision algorithms, motion capture with markers) authors were instructed to see the appropriate guidelines on collecting high quality data as described in their documentation.

3.2.3 Audio
Prior work in speech and audio process has established a minimum frequency of 8Hz for speech recognition, and higher frequencies, between 12 Hz and 24 Hz, for conducting prosodic and spectral analysis. Additionally, in order to identify various learning relevant constructs (e.g. collaboration quality, voice quality and individual development) the audio captured should have the capability of being resolved to an individual speaker.

3.2.4 Video
One reason for capturing video data is to do facial expression analysis and head pose estimation. Facial expression analysis using computer-automated techniques typically requires a minimum ear to ear width of 64 pixels. A minimum size of 128 x 96 pixels is recommended, as some facial analysis software requires larger images in order to increase accuracy of detection. Additionally, a frontal view is required for being able to conduct facial expression and head pose analysis. However, the data capture environment is free to determine the appropriate frequency of frontal face capture, provided this is a modality of interest.

4. ACCEPTED PAPERS

4.1 Multimodal Capture of Learning Environments
Submissions in this category ranged from using multiple microphones to capture high quality audio data from classrooms (for the purpose of using ASR and studying dialogic patterns), to leveraging a Multimodal Recording Device that students can use to take multimodal selfies. From these two examples, we begin to see the breadth of approaches that can be used, and some of the technological, as well as ethical considerations that need to be taken into account when proposing the capture and analysis of multimodal data in a learning environment.

A third paper in this category provided an in-depth discussion of the current capabilities of depth sensors, and some of the analytic strategies that can help improve how researchers and designers use depth cameras to support learning.

4.2 Multimodal Learning Applications
Both accepted papers in this category were related to public speaking skills, one of the topics discussed during the 2014 Multimodal Learning Analytics Workshop and Grand Challenge. One paper focused on detecting different body postures (closed versus open) and sought to provide visual feedback to the user when they were exhibited closed poses. In this preliminary study, participants used more open poses when they were provided with the visual feedback about their body pose. The other paper looked at body posture in conjunction with audio-based features (effective use of pauses and presenter volume). It used a combination of visual, haptic and audio channels, in order to provide feedback to the user. These two papers are among of foray of research being conducted in the oral presentation and communication space, and will hopefully contribute to increasingly informative systems that can model and support good public speaking skills.

5. CONCLUSION
This year's challenge offered a noticeable change from previous years. As we look to advance the area of multimodal learning analytics, we need to simultaneously, or perhaps preemptively, push the boundaries in the area of multimodal data capture. The current work in laboratory settings is useful, but there is a need to transition this research to more authentic environments. Furthermore, there is an opportunity to take the work of multimodal learning analytics beyond traditional learning environments, into multimodal learning environments. These multimodal learning environments are not merely spaces where students continue their everyday classroom practices of doing algebra problems, or writing an essay. Multimodal learning environments transform learning by requiring students to employ a variety of modalities in order to effectively complete the task or assignment. It is our hypothesis that as multimodal learning environments are increasingly developed and used, research in multimodal learning and analytics will produce novel benefits for learners and new insights into learning processes above and beyond that of traditional learning.

6. REFERENCES

1. D Atkins, J Bennett, J S Brown, et al. 2010. Transforming American education: Learning powered by technology (National Educational Technology Plan 2010). *Washington, DC: US Department of Education, Office of Educational Technology.*

2. Ryan S J D Baker and Kalina Yacef. 2009. The state of educational data mining in 2009: A review and future visions. *JEDM-Journal of Educational Data Mining* 1, 1, 3–17.

3. Marie Bienkowski, Mingyu Feng, and Barbara Means. 2012. Enhancing teaching and learning through educational data mining and learning analytics: An issue brief. *US Department of Education, Office of Educational Technology*, 1–57.

4. Paulo Blikstein, Marcelo Worsley, Chris Piech, Mehran Sahami, Steve Cooper, and Daphne Koller. 2014. Programming pluralism: Using learning analytics to detect patterns in the learning of computer programming. *Journal of Learning Sciences.*

5. Paulo Blikstein and Marcelo Worsley. (in press) Multimodal Learning Analytics: a methodological framework for research in constructivist learning. *Journal of Learning Analytics.*

6. Lei Chen, Chee Wee Leong, Gary Feng, and Chong Min Lee. 2014. Using Multimodal Cues to Analyze MLA'14 Oral Presentation Quality Corpus: Presentation Delivery and Slides Quality. *Proceedings of the 2014 ACM Workshop on Multimodal Learning Analytics Workshop and Grand Challenge*, ACM, 45–52. http://doi.org/10.1145/2666633.2666640

7. Vanessa Echeverría, Allan Avendaño, Katherine Chiluiza, Aníbal Vásquez, and Xavier Ochoa. 2014. Presentation Skills Estimation Based on Video and Kinect Data Analysis. *Proceedings of the 2014 ACM Workshop on Multimodal Learning Analytics Workshop and Grand Challenge*, ACM, 53–60. http://doi.org/10.1145/2666633.2666641

8. JS Gorin and RJ Mislevy. 2013. Inherent Measurement Challenges in the Next Generation Science Standards for Both Formative and Summative Assessment. September. Retrieved March 17, 2014 from http://www.k12center.org/rsc/pdf/gorin-mislevy.pdf

9. Joseph F Grafsgaard, Joseph B Wiggins, Kristy Elizabeth Boyer, Eric N Wiebe, and James C Lester. 2014. Predicting Learning and Affect from Multimodal Data Streams in Task-Oriented Tutorial Dialogue. *7th International Conference on Educational Data Mining*, 122–129.

10. Joseph F Grafsgaard. 2014. Multimodal Analysis and Modeling of Nonverbal Behaviors During Tutoring. *Proceedings of the 16th International Conference on Multimodal Interaction*, ACM, 404–408. http://doi.org/10.1145/2663204.2667611

11. Arno Hartholt, David Traum, Stacy C Marsella, et al. 2013. All together now. *Intelligent Virtual Agents*, 368–381.

12. Larry Johnson, Samantha Adams, Malcolm Cummins, Victoria Estrada, Alex Freeman, and Holly Ludgate. 2013. The NMC horizon report: 2013 higher education edition.

13. Linda Katehi, Greg Pearson, and Michael Feder. 2009. The status and nature of K-12 engineering education in the United States. *The Bridge* 39, 3, 5–10.

14. Gonzalo Luzardo, Bruno Guamán, Katherine Chiluiza, Jaime Castells, and Xavier Ochoa. 2014. Estimation of Presentations Skills Based on Slides and Audio Features. *Proceedings of the 2014 ACM Workshop on Multimodal Learning Analytics Workshop and Grand Challenge*, ACM, 37–44. http://doi.org/10.1145/2666633.2666639

15. Marwa Mahmoud, Louis-Philippe Morency, and Peter Robinson. 2013. Automatic multimodal descriptors of rhythmic body movement. *Proceedings of the 15th ACM on International conference on multimodal interaction - ICMI '13*, 429–436. http://doi.org/10.1145/2522848.2522895

16. Taylor Martin and Bruce Sherin. 2013. Learning analytics and computational techniques for detecting and evaluating patterns in learning: An introduction to the special issue. *Journal of the Learning Sciences* 22, 4, 511–520.

17. National Research Council. 2012. *A Framework for K-12 Science Education: Practices, Crosscutting Concepts, and Core Ideas*. National Academies Press.

18. Jiquan Ngiam, Aditya Khosla, Mingyu Kim, Juhan Nam, Honglak Lee, and Andrew Y Ng. 2011. Multimodal deep learning. *Proceedings of the 28th International Conference on Machine Learning (ICML-11)*, 689–696.

19. Xavier Ochoa, Katherine Chiluiza, Gonzalo Méndez, Gonzalo Luzardo, Bruno Guamán, and James Castells. 2013. Expertise estimation based on simple multimodal features. *Proceedings of the 15th ACM on International conference on multimodal interaction - ICMI '13*, 583–590. http://doi.org/10.1145/2522848.2533789

20. S Oviatt and A Cohen. 2013. Written and multimodal representations as predictors of expertise and problem-solving success in mathematics. *Proceedings of the 15th ACM International Conference on Multimodal Interaction – ICMI '13*, ACM, 599-606. http://dx.doi.org/10.1145/2522848.2533793

21. Roy Pea. 2014. THE LEARNING ANALYTICS Workgroup A Report on Building the Field of Learning Analytics.

22. Jean Piaget. 1973. To understand is to invent: the future of education (G. Roberts, Trans.). *NY: Grossman Publishers*.

23. Stefan Scherer, Michael Glodek, Georg Layher, et al. 2012. A generic framework for the inference of user states in human computer interaction. *Journal on Multimodal User Interfaces* 6, 3-4, 117–141.

24. Stefan Scherer, Marcelo Worsley, and Louis-Philippe Morency. 2012. 1st international workshop on multimodal learning analytics. *ICMI*, 609–610.

25. Bertrand Schneider and Paulo Blikstein. Unraveling Students' Interaction Around a Tangible Interface using Multimodal Learning Analytics. *Journal of Educational Data Mining*.

26. Bertrand Schneider, Jenelle Wallace, Paulo Blikstein, and Roy Pea. 2013. Preparing for future learning with a tangible user interface: the case of neuroscience. *Learning Technologies, IEEE Transactions on* 6, 2, 117–129.

27. Daniel L Schwartz. 1992. Constructivism in an age of non-constructivist assessments.

28. Yale Song, Louis-Philippe Morency, and Randall Davis. 2012. Multimodal human behavior analysis: learning correlation and interaction across modalities. *Proceedings of the 14th ACM international conference on Multimodal interaction*, 27–30.

29. Robert A Sottilare, Keith W Brawner, Benjamin S Goldberg, and Heather K Holden. 2012. The generalized intelligent framework for tutoring (GIFT).

30. Marcelo Worsley and Paulo Blikstein. 2013. Towards the Development of Multimodal Action Based Assessment. *Proceedings of the Third International Conference on Learning Analytics and Knowledge*, ACM, 94–101. http://doi.org/10.1145/2460296.2460315

31. Marcelo Worsley and Paulo Blikstein. 2015. Leveraging Multimodal Learning Analytics to Differentiate Student Learning Strategies. *Proceedings of the Fifth International Conference on Learning Analytics And Knowledge*, ACM, 360–367. http://doi.org/10.1145/2723576.2723624

32. Marcelo Worsley. 2012. Multimodal learning analytics: enabling the future of learning through multimodal data analysis and interfaces. *Proceedings of the 14th ACM international conference on Multimodal interaction*, 353–356.

33. Jianlong Zhou, Kevin Hang, Sharon Oviatt, Kun Yu, and Fang Chen. 2014. Combining Empirical and Machine Learning Techniques to Predict Math Expertise Using Pen Signal Features. *Proceedings of the 2014 ACM Workshop on Multimodal Learning Analytics Workshop and Grand Challenge*, ACM, 29–36. http://doi.org/10.1145/2666633.2666638

34. 2013. Next Generation Science Standards: For States, By States.

Providing Real-time Feedback for Student Teachers in a Virtual Rehearsal Environment

Roghayeh Barmaki
Computer Science Division
University of Central Florida
Orlando, FL, USA
barmaki@cs.ucf.edu

Charles E. Hughes
Computer Science Division
University of Central Florida
Orlando, FL, USA
ceh@cs.ucf.edu

ABSTRACT

Research in learning analytics and educational data mining has recently become prominent in the fields of computer science and education. Most scholars in the field emphasize student learning and student data analytics; however, it is also important to focus on teaching analytics and teacher preparation because of their key roles in student learning, especially in K-12 learning environments. Nonverbal communication strategies play an important role in successful interpersonal communication of teachers with their students. In order to assist novice or practicing teachers with exhibiting open and affirmative nonverbal cues in their classrooms, we have designed a multimodal teaching platform with provisions for online feedback. We used an interactive teaching rehearsal software, TeachLivE^{TM}, as our basic research environment. TeachLivE employs a digital puppetry paradigm as its core technology. Individuals walk into this virtual environment and interact with virtual students displayed on a large screen. They can practice classroom management, pedagogy and content delivery skills with a teaching plan in the TeachLivE environment.

We have designed an experiment to evaluate the impact of an online nonverbal feedback application. In this experiment, different types of multimodal data have been collected during two experimental settings. These data include talk-time and nonverbal behaviors of the virtual students, captured in log files; talk time and full body tracking data of the participant; and video recording of the virtual classroom with the participant. 34 student teachers participated in this 30-minute experiment. In each of the settings, the participants were provided with teaching plans from which they taught. All the participants took part in both of the experimental settings. In order to have a balanced experiment design, half of the participants received nonverbal online feedback in their first session and the other half received this feedback in the second session. A visual indication was used for feedback each time the participant exhibited a closed, defensive posture. Based on recorded full-body tracking data, we observed that only those who received feedback in their first session demonstrated a significant number of open postures in the session containing no feedback. However, the post-questionnaire information indicated that all participants were more mindful of their body postures while teaching after they had participated in the study.

ICMI '15, November 09-13, 2015, Seattle, WA, USA
©2015 ACM. ISBN 978-1-4503-3912-4/15/11 ... $15.00
DOI: http://dx.doi.org/10.1145/2818346.2830604

Categories and Subject Descriptors

H.5.1. [**Information Interfaces and Presentation (e.g. HCI)**]: Multimedia Information Systems

Keywords

Immersive teaching rehearsal environment; Teacher training; Posture recognition; Mutimodal data analytics;

1. INTRODUCTION

Communication involves both verbal and nonverbal components. Nonverbal communication (NVC) is all of the elements of communication excluding the words [20]. Paralanguage (pitch, volume, etc.) is the vocal element of nonverbal communication. On the other hand, body language (gestures and movements, facial expressions, eye contact, etc.) is the nonvocal element of nonverbal communication [16]. Upwards of 65 percent of the meaning derived in interactions comes from nonverbal communication [20, 11].

Gestures, the primary focus of this research, are a form of nonverbal communication in which visible body movements and poses are used to communicate important messages, either in place of speech or together and in parallel with spoken words [15]. The context in which we consider gestures is the student-teacher interaction that occurs in a classroom setting. Here, NVC is known to play a central role in the successful interaction that occurs between student and teacher [6]. The research indicates that teachers' gestures have an impact, both positive and negative, on student comprehension and student learning, specifically in instructional discourses [29, 21]. Thus, to be effective in the classroom, teachers must not only be aware of their own nonverbal cues but also must be cognizant of those being transmitted by the students [6].

This paper reports the results of an investigation of the nonverbal behaviors (body movements, especially gestures and postures) of participants in an immersive rehearsal environment. In this experiment different modalities have been captured, such as event-logs and video captures from participant and virtual classroom; however the main focus was to perceive the relations of a participant's teaching experience with body posture feedback exhibited in a simulated classroom. In addition, the participants were asked to take pre and post questionnaires during the experiment to determine their perception of the experience. The eventual goal of the research is to design a semi-automated annotation system for body language and gesture tracking of participants in the virtual classroom environment that leads to multimodal assessment and reflection procedures for professional development.

2. BACKGROUND AND RELATED WORK

2.1 The Teaching Rehearsal Environment

Our test-bed environment, TeachLivE, is a teaching and learning environment that was developed to provide an interactive learning experience for teachers to rehearse and hone their classroom skills. The environment uses a virtual classroom setting that is typically inhabited by five or six virtual students, commonly called avatars. Each virtual student has behaviors that reflect their personalities and backstories. A single human, called an interactor, uses a combination of agency and digital puppeteering to orchestrate the behaviors of all students in a manner that reflects how each would react to the teacher participant's actions. Figure 1 depicts the core architecture of the TeachLivE system [22], with some features that have been added to support the research reported here.

In the TeachLivE paradigm, users of the system, typically university faculty members or school district coaches, specify subject matter, a teaching plan, student behaviors (e.g., cooperative, needing encouragement, terribly distracted) and other desired attributes at least two weeks in advance of a planned use of the environment.

Over its almost decade of evolution, TeachLivE has gone from a local resource to a system used at over 55 universities in the training of some 12,000 teacher candidates during the 2014–15 academic year. In addition to its use as a pedagogical tool, partnering universities have carried out significant research projects within the TeachLivE environment. One of the largest of these studies was funded by the Bill and Melinda Gates Foundation. This study involved approximately 150 in-service teachers and demonstrated that four ten-minute sessions in the simulated classroom were sufficient to charge a small set of targeted behaviors that have been shown to be critical elements of effective teaching [8].

In one of our previous formative studies [4], we used an after-action review tool-set as an interface for manual annotation of the nonverbal behaviors (body language (open versus closed poses) and head movement (nodding)) for a group of teachers. That data, along with automated recording of proximity and talk time (teacher versus students) were used as a first step (proof of concept) in our research plan. The currently reported research employs the Microsoft Kinect V2 SDK and 3D-sensor technology [2] to automate the nonverbal communication coding procedure. We discuss details of the modality and features of the recording process in the method section.

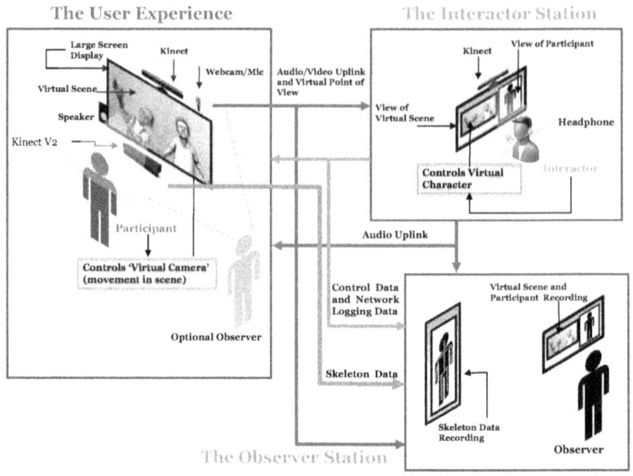

Figure 1: The test-bed environment with some adjustments from the original architecture. The recorded streams are: (I) skeleton data (IR, depth and body frame) shown with orange arrow and (II) virtual scene paired with user experience recording from the observer station (video stream) with red arrow and (III) network logging data including virtual classroom's verbal and nonverbal behaviors with green arrow.

2.2 Nonverbal Communication

Nonverbal communication has been divided into nine categories: kinesics, more commonly referred to as body language and physical appearance; chronemics or communication through time; proxemics or communication using space; para-language, communication through tone of voice; artifacts, communication by physical objects; haptics, communication through touch; facial expressions; olfactics, communication by means of smells; and oculesics, more commonly referred to as eye contact [27]. The presented research focuses on kinesics and body language, especially gestures from defined NVC categories.

McNeill categorizes gestures into four main types [19]. Iconics are related to semantic content of speech; metaphorics tie to an abstract concept; deictics or pointing gestures relate to the identity of individuals to whom the utterances refer; and beats keep the rhythm of speech [13, 19].

NVC plays an important role in several professions. In the case of physician-patient interaction, scholars presented results on the relation of nonverbal communication skill of the physicians and the patient satisfaction [7, 9]. In the classroom environment, the successful student-teacher communication is also affected by the NVC skills of the teacher [17, 6].

2.2.1 *Nonverbal Communication in Immersive Environments*

There is extensive research on the impact and application of gestures in virtual and interactive environments. The context of deictic expressions and the impact of pointing gestures in virtual immersive environment have been investigated in [26]. Two participants were asked to play an object identification game together and the session was recorded and annotated based on gaze finger pointing and index-finger pointing to analyze the success rate of object identification. In a similar study [10] from the same research lab the applications of iconic gestures to express shape-related references to objects in a virtual construction environment were investigated. They showed how to make use of the Imagistic Description Tree (IDT) formalism to enhance virtual construction parts with shape-related information.

In [12], the scholars introduced an automated system for social skills training called MACH (My Automated Conversation CoacH). The system includes a virtual agent that reads facial expressions, speech, and prosody (tone, pitch) of the participant and responds with verbal and nonverbal behaviors in real-time. As an example application, the developers of MACH created an interview trainer that asks questions appropriate for a job interview, automatically mimicking certain behaviors displayed by the user, and exhibiting appropriate nonverbal behaviors [12].

2.2.2 Nonverbal Communication in Classroom
Nonverbal communication strategies are consistently noted in successful approaches to teacher training [18]. The effects of strategies like eye contact, prolonged gaze, and proximity can have positive or negative effects on student behavior and classroom management, depending on the situation and context [17].

Teachers can use gesture to be effective in several fundamental aspects of their profession, including communication, assessment of student knowledge, and the ability to instill a profound understanding of abstract concepts in traditionally difficult domains such as language and mathematics [13].

There is a significant body of research on the impact of gestures in the classroom. Kelly et al. showed that employing iconic gestures during teaching had a significant impact on English-speaking adults attempting to learn new Japanese words [14]. In a recent study from Wang and Loewen [31] the employment of nonverbal behaviors of teachers as feedback in second language acquisition was investigated. They explored teachers' nonverbal behaviors in corrective feedback during 48 observations (about 65 hours of recordings) of nine classrooms for English as a second language. The results indicated that teachers used a variety of nonverbal behaviors in their corrective feedback, including hand gestures (specifically iconics, metaphorics, deictics, and beats), head movements, affect displays, kinetographs, and emblems.

Alibali et al. [3] observed that teachers use gestures in an effort to scaffold student's understanding, especially on abstract concepts. In this research, they worked on a 20-minute sixth-grade mathematics lesson session that focused on algebraic relations [3]. They manually annotated the gestures and transcribed the teacher's conversation in the study and used the annotation data to analyze the nonverbal behavior of the teacher.

In [5], we investigated the way teachers use gestures in the virtual classroom settings of TeachLivE. Our research had been developed based on the hypothesis reported in [3]. Biology and algebra teachers were evaluated in this study. Analysis of video recordings from real and virtual classroom environments indicated that algebra teachers gesture significantly more often than biology teachers [5].

2.2.3 Multimodal Discourse Analysis (MDA)
Employing a multimodal approach to classroom analysis has implications for teaching and learning as well as teacher training and development. Multimodal discourse analysis (MDA) is an emerging paradigm in discourse studies which extends the study of language per se to the study of language in combination with other resources, such as images, scientific symbolism, gesture, action, music and sound [25]. In a project done in a classroom in Singapore [24], the meanings made in the multimodal pedagogic discourse, specifically in language, gesture, positioning and movement were investigated. Their project particularly focused on proxemics to multimodal classroom discourse analysis as well as material distance socio-semiotic meanings.

2.2.4 Nonverbal Behavior Annotation
Manual annotation of nonverbal behaviors using the video recordings by experts can provide accurate annotations; however it is extremely time consuming [23, 28]. Hence, some automated techniques were presented for gesture/posture recognition from video clips and other resources. In general, most of gesture recognition engines have a set of training data to learn and extract the patterns of the gesture from the training set and then use the trained engine for recognition. In this research, we use a similar technique with skeleton data in the Visual Gesture Builder environment [2]. This approach is fast and inexpensive in comparison to the hand-coded procedure.

3. METHOD AND MATERIALS

3.1 Recording Specifications
Different types of data were recorded during the experiment. (I) full-body tracking data (IR, depth and body frame), (II) virtual scene paired with user experience from the observer station (video recording) and finally (III) network logging data including virtual students' verbal (talk-time) and their nonverbal behaviors in the experiment session. Figure 1 presents the room setting and data collection specifications. The skeletal data of the participants were recorded using the Kinect V2 sensor and Kinect Studio utility application. The recorded clips with the Kinect Studio are required as data inputs to Visual Gesture Builder (VGB) to do automated tagging of gestures [2]. Further details are presented in the following subsection.

The second type of recorded data was the virtual classroom scene (from the observer workstation) paired with user experience (participant's front view as seen through the Skype application) in mp4 format that was recorded with a window recording application-Bandicam. Lastly, the network traffic data was recorded to keep track of interactions of the virtual characters. Virtual avatars' NVC signals and their talk-time were recorded in a log-file with comma-delimited format in an observer station for future multimodal analysis such as revealing the correlations of the teacher's wait-time with the student's talk-time or the teacher's talk-time with teacher's body movement data in the two settings.

3.1.1 VGB Automated Tagging and its Input Corpus

VGB generates gesture databases that are used by applications to perform real-time gesture detection. In the technical document reported by Microsoft team [2], VGB is defined as a data driven machine learning solution for gesture detection. Visual Gesture Builder uses skeleton tracking data (25 body points in Kinect V2) representing body movements, and AdaBoost ensemble classifier (for discrete gestures) or Random Forest Regression (for continuous gestures).

First of all, for each gesture, some clips from different subjects must be recorded with Kinect Studio. Every clip contains an individual facing the Kinect (and within the Kinect's field of view) who exhibits the gesture (with some variations) 5 to 15 times. Then, the VGB tool is used to give meaning to the recorded clips. All the frames in the recordings that define a gesture, must be tagged manually. For each gesture, a project as a binary classifier is trained. All the frames exhibiting the gesture get the label of 1 and the remaining frames in the clip get the value of -1.

At this point, the problem is similar to a supervised binary classification, in which the classifier will recognize the frames in which a gesture is performed. Depending on the number of gestures that we intend to recognize, the gesture recognition engine will have binary classifiers. After the training step, VGB is able to generate the tags automatically in the analysis step from the test clips. In the following subsection we discuss more details about targeted gestures to recognize according to interpersonal communication perspective.

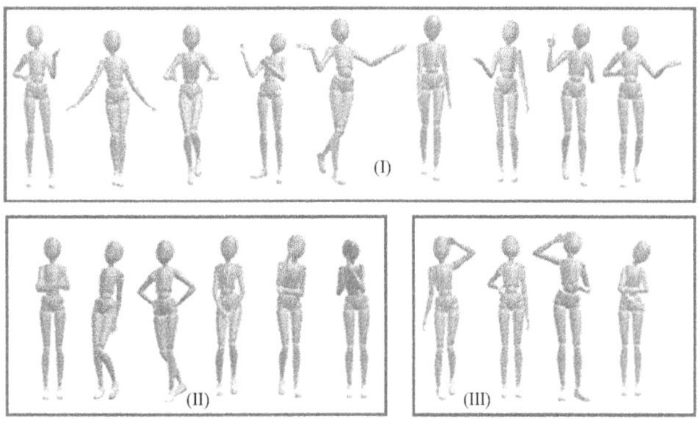

Figure 2: Reference example of (I) open poses, (II) closed poses; left to right: unreceptive (arms folded in front), seductive (hands clasped in back) skeptical (hands placed on hips) protective (hands clasped in lower front) pensive (thoughtful pose) submissive (hands clasped in upper front), and (III) ambivalent poses.

Some of the most common and interesting postures from the teaching evaluation literature [6] and from our previous study [4] are shown in Figure 2. Caswell and Neill in [6] present results on body language of competent teachers. Using reference poses as a communication medium, they recommend that teachers employ open rather than closed or ambivalent poses in their classroom. Closed poses indicate defensiveness and avoidance by the speaker/teacher of the listener [30]. In addition, ambivalent poses, which are mainly a combination of both closed and open poses, cause confusion and misconception about the speaker's behavior and intention in the listeners'/students' mind.

A corpus of closed body poses (reference poses in figure 2.II and some variations of them) was recorded from the performances of three male and two female students using the Microsoft Kinect V2. Subjects for the main study were not involved in the corpus collection. The corpus was used as training clips in the Visual Gesture Builder (VGB) application. All the clips were hand-coded and tagged in order to feed the automated analysis procedure of the participant's clips. There were six targeted closed gestures/postures to train/evaluate in this research. For training each posture, some 30-sec clips were manually annotated and added to the gesture database. 7 x 5 short clips were manually annotated in total since the thinking or pensive gesture is a sided-gesture, and we needed to record left and right versions for that gesture. Hence, we had seven classifiers rather than six at the end of training for the initial six gestures. The process of creating the gesture recognition engine [2] is shown in figure 3.

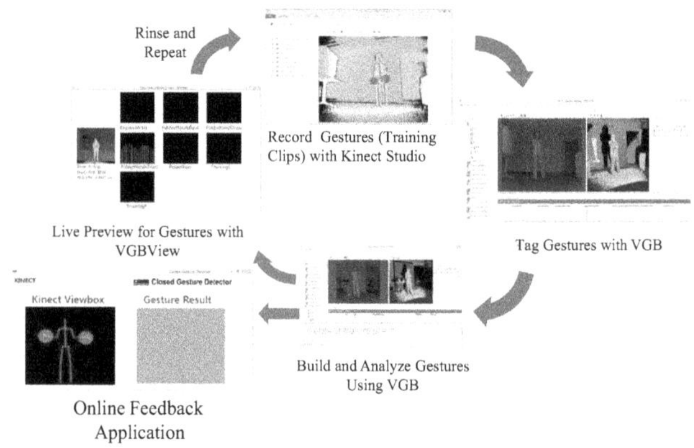

Figure 3: The data-driven and incremental process of creating a gesture detector using the Microsoft SDK 2.0 and the VGB utility[2]. The proposed online feedback application is developed on top of the gesture detector database.

3.2 Recruitment Procedure

In this experiment, 34 student participants were recruited. Only those College of Education students who had seen the TeachLivE environment before the experiment were eligible to be recruited. Participants were ones over age 18 years from the affiliated university community and each participant had a basic level of English proficiency, with some teaching experience to be able to talk and interact with the virtual students in the TeachLivE.

All participants were from the students who were registered for a classroom management and strategies class in the TESOL (Teaching English to Speakers of Other Languages) program taught in the summer semester at the College of Education. All the students had an assignment prior to the experiment using the TeachLivE environment. The experiment was mandatory for all of the registered students as a classroom activity because of its perfect overlap with the course goals. Students did not get compensation or credit for their participation. Individuals were expected to spend approximately 30 minutes for the experiment (two 7-minute sessions for the teaching plus three 5-minutes intervals for questionnaires).

3.3 Design Details

The experiment was designed to have two treatments: with and without feedback provision to participants in the virtual classroom session (7-minutes long each). Feedback was in the form of a visual indication each time the participant exhibits a closed stance while interacting with the virtual students. Figure 4 indicates the multiple settings for the experiment. The feedback application is designed based on an existing closed body posture corpus and a new interface for automated online (real-time) feedback. All the participants experienced both of the treatments. The experiment is designed based on 2x2 Latin-squares in order to balance the experimental design; therefore half the participants received real-time feedback (treatment or setting 2) during this first session while the other half received no feedback (setting 1) during this session.

Participants were given a consent form, a pre-questionnaire and a teaching plan before their first experience. After completing the pre-questionnaire and reviewing the teaching plan and consent form, the participants taught their first session. Afterwards, all participants filled out a post-questionnaire. They then reentered the virtual classroom to present the same teaching plan and had their second treatment accordingly. All participants were then asked to complete the same post-questionnaire that they filled out after the first session.

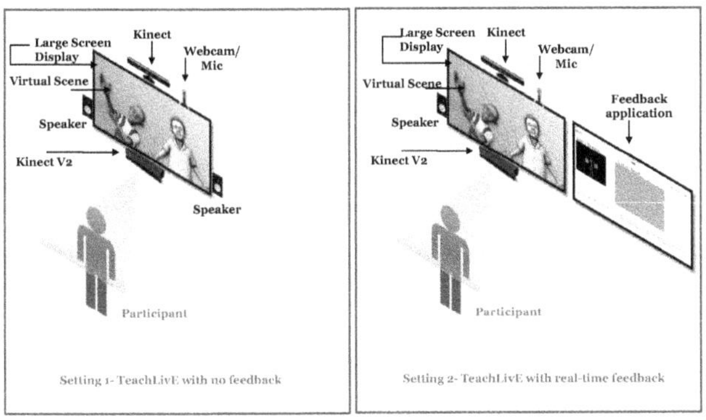

Figure 4: The settings of the experiment.

3.3.1 Questionnaires

This experiment had one pre-questionnaire and one post-questionnaire. In the pre-questionnaire, participants were asked to indicate their age, gender, ethnicity, major and highest level of education, teaching experience and related teaching topics, and finally their particular experience with the TeachLivE environment.

The post-questionnaire was designed based on the multimodal learning application evaluation and design guide with some changes[1]. There were different types of questions about naturalness of use, boredom, intrusiveness, likelihood of use during spare time, learning experience, comparison with traditional learning methods, the novelty of the system and some open-ended questions. Based on the different nature of our experiment (teacher evaluation rather than student evaluation), there were some questions in the original questionnaire that were not applicable to our experiment, therefore we removed them from our post questionnaire. We also modified some of the questions slightly to match our proposed application.

3.3.2 Teaching Plan

The teaching plan we employed is designed to enhance science literacy and is aligned with disciplinary core ideas and cross-cutting concepts from the Next Generation Science Standards[2], as well as the Common Core Standards for Literacy in Science [3]. The lesson is based on the 5E instructional model and has been validated and field-tested in high school Biology classrooms as part of a larger module from the NIH Curriculum Supplement Series "Using Technology to Study Cellular and Molecular Biology"[1]. The title of the teaching plan was: "What is Technology?" In this teaching plan, some questions were mentioned to discuss with virtual students by the participant. The participant, as the teacher, was expected to ask virtual students about their personal definition of technology, what does technology do for human beings, what technologies are available in the room, and the impact of technology in diseases. The participants were free to discuss any concept they preferred within the topic of this teaching plan.

3.3.3 Room Setting

The room was equipped with required laptops and wired network connection for the experiment. Three laptops were used for the experiment: one as an observer workstation, one for skeletal data recording and visualized feedback, and the last one for the participant's workstation. Figure 1 and figure 4 present further details about the room setting. The virtual classroom's students were high-school avatars (three males and two females with their own predefined characteristics). Their level of misbehavior was set to zero which means no misbehavior in the classroom-side. We also scheduled the same interactor for all the experiment sessions in order to minimize the confounding conditions related to the inter-actor change.

Next to the participant's large TV display, we posted all the teaching plan's main questions on a board as reference for participants. This was a very important step, since all of the participants requested to keep this sheet of paper in their hands during the interaction. We asked them to leave the teaching plan and use the reference board instead. This was critical as the gestures of participants were affected negatively while they were holding an object (even a sheet of paper) in their hands.

3.3.4 Feedback Application

As mentioned before, feedback was in the form of a visual indication each time the participant exhibited a closed, defensive stance. We used the Kinect V2 and the closed-postures

[1]http://sigmla.org/mla2015/ApplicationGuidelines.pdf accessed on August 2015.

[2]http://www.nextgenscience.org accessed on August 2015.

[3]http://www.corestandards.org/ELA-Literacy/RST accessed on August 2015.

corpus as input to this application. The feedback application ran independently from the TeachLivE program.

Figure 5 presents the feedback user interface in more details than figure 4. Most of the participants changed their body movements in the feedback setting to prevent the orange box from showing.

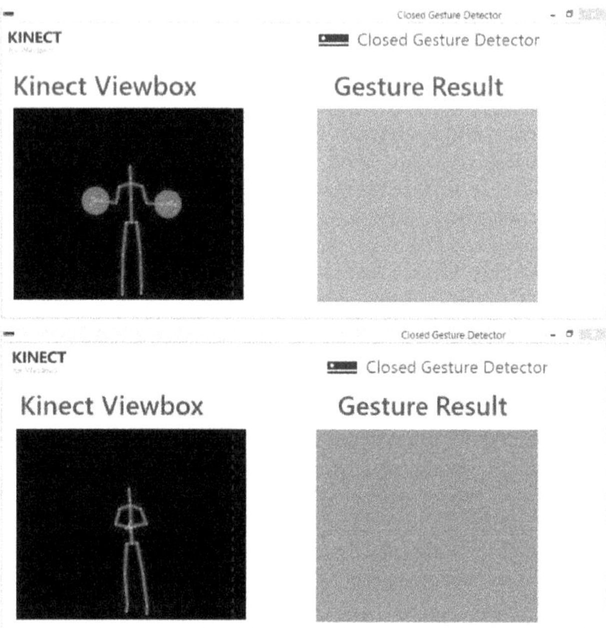

Figure 5: The feedback application user-interface for two different body postures. The user can see his/her body posture in real-time in the Kinect ViewBox. Whenever the participant exhibits one of the closed gestures that were targeted, the Gesture Result window become orange from green automatically.

3.4 Preliminary Observations

As might be expected, those who received body posture feedback in their first session displayed more awareness of their nonverbal messaging (significant employment of open postures) in the second session. In contrast, those who received no feedback in first session showed only slight improvement in the second, despite the availability of real-time feedback. We hypothesize that this small improvement came from their increased comfort with the TeachLivE environment. Interestingly, members of both groups indicated in the post-questionnaire that they had gained an awareness of the messages they were sending through their body poses and expressed the intent to employ these strategies in their teaching.

In addition, there was a difference between experienced teachers and novice teachers in their body language. We observed that experienced teachers did not exhibit closed gestures as often as students who had no teaching experience. Also, among the detected gestures, submissive and seductive gestures were the most frequent closed gestures exhibited by participants.

4. FUTURE STEPS

We intend to complete the data analysis and reporting the correlations from the multimodal assessment point-of-view. This phase involves multimodal signal processing: data synchronization, data fusion and data mining.

Recruiting the participants who already had this experience after one-semester (or later) and observing their potential body movement changes is another interesting direction to follow, since most of the participants were very motivated to experience the environment one more time. In addition, most of the participants indicated valuable information in their post-questionnaire about how to improve the application. For example, most of the students requested to have a more immersive experience. This might be done by using Head-Mounted-Displays (HMD) for instance, although HMDs introduce an additional confound by changing people's sense of being in a physical environment.

4.1 Acknowledgments

The authors wish to thank Drs. Lisa Dieker, Michael Hynes, Cynthia Hutchinson, Joyce Nutta, Thomas Owens, Jacqueline Rodriguez, Guo-Jun Qi, Carrie Straub, and the entire TeachLivE team including Pam Jones and Michael Hopper for their support during the data collection and analysis processes. Their insights and their assistance with subject recruitment were invaluable. We also wish to express our appreciation for the support of the interactors and the study participants. Finally we wish to acknowledge support for the evolution of the TeachLivE project from the Bill & Melinda Gates Foundation (OPP1053202) and the National Science Foundation (CNS1051067, IIS1116615). Any opinions, findings, and conclusions or recommendations expressed in this material are those of the authors and do not necessarily reflect the views of the sponsors.

5. REFERENCES

[1] Using technology to study cellular and molecular biology. http://1.usa.gov/1LKos30. Accessed 2015-8-5.

[2] Visual gesture builder: A data-driven solution to gesture detection. http://aka.ms/k4wv2vgb, July 2014. Accessed 2015-8-8.

[3] M. W. Alibali and M. J. Nathan. Teachers' gestures as a means of scaffolding students' understanding: Evidence from an early algebra lesson. *Video research in the learning sciences*, pages 349–365, 2007.

[4] R. Barmaki. Nonverbal communication and teaching performance. In *Proceedings of the Eighth International Conference on Educational Data Mining*, EDM '14, pages 441–443, 2014.

[5] R. Barmaki and C. E. Hughes. A case study to track teacher gestures and performance in a virtual learning environment. In *Proceedings of the Fifth International Conference on Learning Analytics And Knowledge*, LAK '15, pages 420–421, New York, USA, 2015.

[6] C. Caswell and S. Neill. *Body language for competent teachers*. Routledge, 2003.

[7] L. G. Collins, A. Schrimmer, J. Diamond, and J. Burke. Evaluating verbal and non-verbal communication skills, in an ethnogeriatric osce. *Patient education and counseling*, 83(2):158–162, 2011.

[8] L. A. Dieker, C. L. Straub, C. E. Hughes, M. C.

Hynes, and S. Hardin. Learning from virtual students. *Educational Leadership*, 71(8):54–58, 2014.

[9] M. R. DiMatteo, R. D. Hays, and L. M. Prince. Relationship of physicians' nonverbal communication skill to patient satisfaction, appointment noncompliance, and physician workload. *Health Psychology*, 5(6):581, 1986.

[10] C. Fröhlich, P. Biermann, M. E. Latoschik, and I. Wachsmuth. Processing iconic gestures in a multimodal virtual construction environment. In *Gesture-Based Human-Computer Interaction and Simulation*, pages 187–192. Springer, 2009.

[11] L. K. Guerrero and K. Floyd. *Nonverbal communication in close relationships*. Routledge, 2006.

[12] M. E. Hoque, M. Courgeon, J.-C. Martin, B. Mutlu, and R. W. Picard. Mach: My automated conversation coach. In *Proceedings of the 2013 ACM international joint conference on Pervasive and ubiquitous computing*, pages 697–706. ACM, 2013.

[13] S. D. Kelly, S. M. Manning, and S. Rodak. Gesture gives a hand to language and learning: Perspectives from cognitive neuroscience, developmental psychology and education. *Language and Linguistics Compass*, 2(4):569–588, 2008.

[14] S. D. Kelly, T. McDevitt, and M. Esch. Brief training with co-speech gesture lends a hand to word learning in a foreign language. *Language and Cognitive Processes*, 24(2):313–334, 2009.

[15] A. Kendon. *Gesture: Visible action as utterance*. Cambridge University Press, 2004.

[16] M. Knapp, J. Hall, and T. Horgan. *Nonverbal communication in human interaction*. Cengage Learning, 2013.

[17] R. Laslett and C. Smith. *Effective classroom management: a teacher's guide*. Routledge, 2002.

[18] J. Mahon, B. Bryant, B. Brown, and M. Kim. Using second life to enhance classroom management practice in teacher education. *Educational Media International*, 47(2):121–134, 2010.

[19] D. McNeill. *Hand and mind: What gestures reveal about thought*. University of Chicago Press, 1992.

[20] A. Mehrabian. Communication without words. *Psychological today*, 2:53–55, 1968.

[21] P. W. Miller. Body language in the classroom. *Techniques: Connecting Education and Careers*, 8:28–30, 2005.

[22] A. Nagendran, R. Pillat, A. Kavanaugh, G. Welch, and C. Hughes. A unified framework for individualized avatar-based interactions. *Presence: Teleoperators and Virtual Environments*, 23(2):109–132, 2014.

[23] L.-V. Nguyen-Dinh, A. Calatroni, and G. Tröster. Robust online gesture recognition with crowdsourced annotations. *The Journal of Machine Learning Research*, 15(1):3187–3220, 2014.

[24] K. L. O'Halloran. Multimodal analysis and digital technology. In *Interdisciplinary Perspectives on Multimodality: Theory and Practice, Proceedings of the Third International Conference on Multimodality, Palladino, Campobasso*, 2009.

[25] K. L. O'Halloran. Multimodal discourse analysis. *Companion to discourse*, pages 120–137, 2011.

[26] T. Pfeiffer, M. E. Latoschik, and I. Wachsmuth. Conversational pointing gestures for virtual reality interaction: implications from an empirical study. In *Virtual Reality Conference, 2008. VR'08. IEEE*, pages 281–282. IEEE, 2008.

[27] V. P. Richmond, J. C. McCroskey, and M. L. Hickson III. Nonverbal behavior in interpersonal relations. 2014.

[28] D. Roggen, A. Calatroni, M. Rossi, T. Holleczek, K. Forster, G. Troster, P. Lukowicz, D. Bannach, G. Pirkl, A. Ferscha, et al. Collecting complex activity datasets in highly rich networked sensor environments. In *Networked Sensing Systems (INSS)*, pages 233–240. IEEE, 2010.

[29] H. A. Smith. Nonverbal communication in teaching. *Review of Educational Research*, 49(4):631–672, 1979.

[30] J. S. Tucker and S. L. Anders. Adult attachment style and nonverbal closeness in dating couples. *Journal of Nonverbal Behavior*, 22(2):109–124, 1998.

[31] W. Wang and S. Loewen. Nonverbal behavior and corrective feedback in nine esl university-level classrooms. *Language Teaching Research*, pages 1–20, 2015.

Presentation Trainer, your Public Speaking Multimodal Coach

Jan Schneider, Dirk Börner, Peter van Rosmalen and Marcus Specht
Welten Institute, Open University of the Netherlands
Valkenburgerweg 177, 6419 AT Heerlen
+(31)45 576 2222
{jan.schneider, dirk.boerner, peter.vanrosmalen, marcus.specht}@ou.nl

ABSTRACT

The Presentation Trainer is a multimodal tool designed to support the practice of public speaking skills, by giving the user real-time feedback about different aspects of her nonverbal communication. It tracks the user's voice and body to interpret her current performance. Based on this performance the Presentation Trainer selects the type of intervention that will be presented as feedback to the user. This feedback mechanism has been designed taking in consideration the results from previous studies that show how difficult it is for learners to perceive and correctly interpret real-time feedback while practicing their speeches. In this paper we present the user experience evaluation of participants who used the Presentation Trainer to practice for an elevator pitch, showing that the feedback provided by the Presentation Trainer has a significant influence on learning.

Categories and Subject Descriptors

H.5.2 [**User Interfaces**]: Graphical user interfaces (GUI), Haptic I/O; K3.0 [Computers and Education]: general.

General Terms

Design, Experimentation, Human Factors.

Keywords

Immediate Feedback; Multimodal Interfaces; Sensors; Public Speaking; Presentation Training.

1. INTRODUCTION

"Practice does not make perfect. Only perfect practice makes perfect." Is a famous quote by Vince Lombardi, one of the most successful coaches in the history of Professional Football [12]. A key factor to achieve this "perfect practice" required for the development and improvement skills is feedback, which has also been identified as one of the most influential interventions in learning [13]. Having a human tutor providing us with high quality feedback whenever we have time to practice our skills is neither an affordable nor a feasible solution.

ICMI '15, November 09 - 13, 2015, Seattle, WA, USA

ACM 978-1-4503-3912-4/15/11...$15.00
DOI: http://dx.doi.org/10.1145/2818346.2830603

In our effort to study an affordable solution for this feedback availability challenge, we explored the topic 'public speaking skills'. Where we followed a design based research methodology [1] developing different prototypes of the *Presentation Trainer* (PT). The PT is an example of an automated feedback tool that tracks the learners' voice and body. It provides them with feedback about their nonverbal communication, with the purpose to support them with the development of their public speaking skills.

In this article we describe the current version of the PT, and present the user experience evaluation of a study, where participants had to prepare themselves for an elevator pitch. This study followed a quasi-experimental set-up where we explored the learning effects of the feedback provided by the PT.

2. Related Work

Research has proven that feedback provided by a tutor influences the development of public speaking skills [15] and that the magnitude of this influence depends on how this feedback is given to the learner. An important factor that has an effect in the development of these skills is the timing in which feedback is given. For aspects that can be corrected immediately, such as the nonverbal communication of the speaker, immediate feedback has proven to be far more efficient [16].

The nonverbal communication of a speaker is composed of multiple aspects such as: different qualities of the voice, use of gestures, postures, eye contact, facial expressions, etc. All these communication aspects are transmitted simultaneously to the audience; therefore our PT, in order to identify and give feedback about these communication aspects, needs to be a multimodal system.

Multimodal systems first appear in 1980 with the "Put That There" system [6], which opened the exploration of new human computer interactions designed to recognize naturally occurring forms of human language and behavior [19]. Hence, we can find this type of systems in different type of educational settings that range from the creation of collaborative diagrams through multimodal speech, pen and gesture interactions [2, 8]; to helping kids to learn biology through pen and audio interaction [10]. In the particular case of systems presenting some learning support through feedback, a technology that has been used for a vast number of learning applications, is the one of sensors. Sensor systems are able to track the learner's performance through one or multiple modalities, analyze this tracked data, and present the results of this analysis in the form of feedback [21].

Automated feedback has already been used to support nonverbal communication for scenarios such as job interviews [4, 14] and public speaking. The studies of tools designed to support public speaking, can be divided in two groups. The first group supports the performance of the public speaker while giving a speech. Studies falling in this category researched how to present support by using augmented reality feedback for specific nonverbal communication factors [9], improving the voice quality of the presenter by using a smart synthesizer [17], improving the timing of a presentation by giving haptic feedback [24], etc. The second group studies how to support the training of public speaking skills. The tool studied in [3] has been designed to help learners to overcome their public speaking anxiety by giving presentations in front of a virtual audience; this system is also able to make an assessment of some nonverbal aspects of the presentations. The study in [22] showed a tool able to provide learners with some exercises designed to improve their nonverbal skills for public speaking and a dashboard interface giving immediate feedback about some nonverbal communication aspects while learners practice their presentations. This study also indicated that a dashboard interface is too difficult to follow while practicing for a presentation.

In order to come up with an effective tool to train public speaking skills, we decided to build upon the assumption that immediate feedback is proven to be more effective for training nonverbal communication [16], and that a dashboard interface to provide this feedback has been shown to be far from ideal [22]. Therefore the version of the PT described in this article has the capability analyze the user's performance, and to accordingly select at most one nonverbal communication aspect to be presented as feedback.

3. Presentation Trainer

In terms of likeability for face-to-face communication, the nonverbal communication is far more important than the words itself [18]. The Presentation Trainer (PT) is a tool designed for anyone who wants to practice and foster some basic nonverbal skills for a special type of face-to-face communication, which is public speaking. We developed the PT following a design based research methodology [1], in which we have iteratively designed, developed and tested different prototypes of the PT. In this chapter of the article we describe the current third version of the PT. This version of the PT supports the practice of basic public speaking skills by presenting trainees in public speaking feedback about the following nonverbal communication aspects: body posture, use of gestures, voice volume, use of pauses, use of phonetic pauses, and ability to stay grounded without shifting the weight from one foot to the other making movements that resemble the ones of dancing. This set of aspects does not cover all the nonverbal communication factors that influence a speech; however, these aspects are commonly mentioned in public speaking textbooks and manuals [5,11,25] and we consider them sufficient to help us studying the feedback mechanism of the PT. The following subsections of this article explain how the PT generates Presentation Actions about these aspects, and how these Presentation Actions are mapped into the feedback presented to the user.

3.1 Presentation Actions.

In this subsection of the article we describe the analysis done by the PT about different nonverbal communication aspects, and explain how it generates specific Presentation Actions about them. One of these nonverbal aspects is the body posture of the speaker. The body posture of the speaker is a tool that helps to convey confidence, openness and attentiveness towards the audience, in order to do so, it is recommended to stand up in an upright position facing the audience and with the hands inside of the acceptable box space; in front of the body without covering it, and preferably above the hips [5]. The PT uses the Microsoft Kinect sensor V2[1] to track the learner's body. This body tracking allows the PT to get the coordinates of different learner's joints. By knowing these coordinates the PT is able to infer the learner's body posture. Even when the learner stays still, these coordinates still flicker, however this flickering is usually not big enough to interfere with the posture identification. In order to improve this level of accuracy to a degree where the PT is able to detect all predefined postures without giving false positives, we added a time threshold to distinguish between postures and movements. Through some tuning we set this time threshold to 0.3 seconds. Meaning that the PT recognizes a posture if the tracked body coordinates of the learner remain inside of some predefined posture values for a period longer than the time threshold. Whenever the recognized posture violates the preset posture rules, the PT generates a body posture Presentation Action.

Hand gestures in public speaking enhance a speech in different ways such as: strengthening the audience's understanding of verbal messages, painting vivid pictures in the listeners' minds, conveying the speaker's feelings and attitudes, dissipate nervous tension, enhance audience attentiveness and retention, etc. [25]. The current version of the PT does not identify specific gestures. It only recognizes whether gestures are being used and gives feedback to the user whenever she has been speaking without using any gesture after a predefined amount of time. It recognizes if a gesture has been used, by using the input of the Microsoft Kinect V2 to capture the coordinates of the user's joints and keeping track of the angles between forearms and arms, and between arms and shoulder blades. The PT takes notice of the increment and decrement of all the angles. Whenever angles stop decreasing and start increasing, or the opposite way around, stop increasing and start decreasing a "pre-gesture" is identified. If the total amount of increment or decrement from the tracked angles is greater than 5° then a gesture is identified. The use of this strategy allowed us to identify new gestures accurately, without having to worry about the constant flickering of the body coordinates tracked by the Kinect sensor, because the angles between the tracked user's limbs remain stable when the user is not moving. If the user is speaking and no new gestures appear or the angles do not change sufficiently for a predefined time set to six seconds, a Presentation Action about gestures is created. The 5° of angle change and six seconds of speaking time have been obtained by tuning up the PT. We identified than when users move their hands and arms to make a gesture angles are much higher than 5°. Also identified that while not making any gestures the angles never changed more than 5°. We set the threshold to six seconds because while tuning the PT, we identified that a gesture rarely takes longer than six seconds, and that people who stays longer than six seconds without using gestures generally remains a whole presentation without using them.

Having a good voice volume modulation while public speaking is fundamental to transmit a clear message and keeping the audience attention [11]. The PT captures the sound through a microphone at a rate of 16 kHz and stores the absolute volume values in a buffer 0.64 seconds long. To interpret the voice volume of the learner the PT makes use of three thresholds that can be defined manually during runtime in order to adapt them to the acoustic needs of the room where the PT is used. These thresholds are: speaking threshold, soft speaking threshold, loud speaking threshold. The PT interprets silence when the average volume stored in the buffer is below the speaking threshold. It generates a soft volume

[1] https://www.microsoft.com/en-us/kinectforwindows/

Presentation Action whenever the volume of the buffer is in between the speaking threshold and the low volume threshold. Finally the PT generates a loud volume Presentation action whenever the average volume in the buffer is above the loud speaking threshold.

A foremost important skill for public speaking is the use of pauses [5]. When used correctly, pauses allow the audience to take a breathe when information is dense in content or emotion, create spaces for the audience to refocus on the given information, prepare the audience for the following subject, and can add dramatic emphasis during the presentation [25]. Whenever the average value of the sound buffer is below the speaking threshold longer than the predefined time of 0.25 seconds a pause is detected. In the case where no pauses are detected after the predefined time of 15 seconds, a Presentation Action about pauses is raised. We came up with these times of 0.25 seconds and 15 seconds after analyzing the average speaking time and pausing time in 15 different Ted Talks[2].

The filler sounds or phonetic pauses as we call them are all the "ehm", "hmm", "aah", etc. sounds that express hesitation. Showing hesitation is not a good practice while public speaking and therefore during the Toastmasters gatherings[3] is common to have an Ah-counter indicating the speakers how many times they have used a filler sound. The PT uses the speech recognition capabilities of the Microsoft Kinect V2 to recognize some of these filler sounds. The accuracy of recognizing these phonetic pauses is about 20%, which is quite low, however we found it satisfactory enough to remind learners about this type of mistakes. Whenever one of these phonetic pauses is recognized a Presentation Action about phonetic pauses is raised.

While conducting our research on the PT, examining several presentations and interviewing teachers in public speaking, we identified that a common mistake that students in this field usually do is to switch weight from one leg to the other, giving the impression that they are dancing during their presentations. To track this behavior the PT uses the Microsoft Kinect sensor V2 to track the X and Z coordinates of the user's hips. The PT has a counter that takes note of how many times these coordinates have increased and decreased in more degree than the predefined threshold. After four seconds this counter is reset. We came up with this threshold while tuning the PT. In the case where the counter reaches three or more swings in four seconds a Presentation Action about staying grounded is raised.

The PT stores all the raised Presentation Actions in a list and deletes them from it once they are not longer detected. This strategy of raising Presentation Actions whenever something is detected makes the PT scalable, making it possible to add new type of "nonverbal mistakes" or "good practices" for updated versions of the tool.

3.2 Interface and Feedback

The act of practicing for a presentation in itself already requires a lot of cognitive load from the learner [23]. If on top of this we want to give her feedback, we have to carefully design it, so that this feedback can actually help her to become aware of her nonverbal communication, adapt it, and use this increased awareness to improve her skills [22]. To support the increase of self-awareness the main graphical interface of the PT shows a mirrored image of the user. Taking in consideration the cognitive load of the learner, on top of this mirrored image, the PT presents the learner with at most one real-time feedback instruction at the time. This feedback instruction is transmitted through a visual and a haptic channel, since research has shown that as the cognitive load increases more redundant multimodal communication is needed [20]. Visual feedback is displayed on the graphical interface of the PT. The haptic feedback is communicated through the feedback wristband (Figure 1) that produces some vibration whenever a feedback event is triggered.

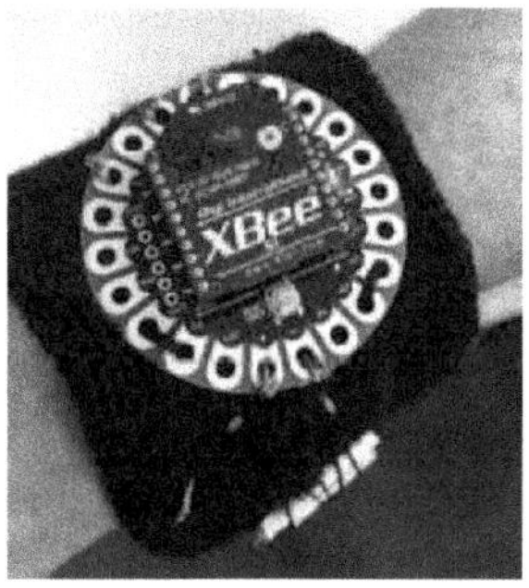

Figure 1. Wristband used to give haptic feedback.

In order to present the learner with a maximum amount of one feedback at the time, the PT executes the following procedure:

First it checks whether the time to give feedback is appropriate. In a small user study that we conducted we realized that a constant stream of feedback, even when it was only one type of feedback at the time, resulted in too much confusion for the users. Hence, the PT waits at least six seconds after the last feedback stopped being shown, in order to present the user with a new feedback.

When the time to give feedback is appropriate, the PT looks at the list of Presentation Actions and selects which one of them should be used to create a feedback event. So far we have tested two strategies to select the feedback to be displayed by the PT. The first one assigns scores to the different Presentation Actions according to their relevance. This relevance depends on the number of occasions that each Presentation Action has been on the list, amount of time inside of the list and user profiling [7]. The second strategy, which is the one that we used for this study, triggers the oldest Presentation Action stored in the list as a feedback event. Once the feedback event is triggered it keeps on being displayed until the mistake is corrected. When corrected a correction mark is shown to the user.

The PT selects the Presentation Action to be triggered as a feedback event and then decides whether it is presented as corrective or interruptive feedback. Corrective feedback indicates the user in real-time that a Presentation Action has been identified. It is presented to the user by displaying an icon and a short (maximum two words long) written statement indicating how to correct the identified mistake (Figure 2) together with a small vibration produced by the feedback wristband.

---

[2] https://www.ted.com/talks

[3] https://www.toastmasters.org/

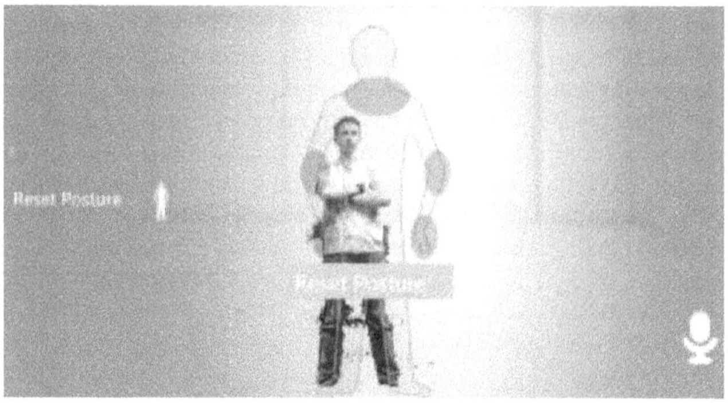

Figure 2. Immediate corrective feedback for crossing arms

Interruptive feedback is triggered whenever a mistake is considered to be severe. Examples of severe mistakes are: mistakes repeated several times, mistakes that stay for too long time without being corrected (currently a mistake repeated five times, or longer than 20 seconds without correction), and any type of predefined severe mistake. Interruptive feedback, produces some vibration, a pause sound, stops the program and displays the reason of the interruption (Figure 3). The interface of the interruption offers the user the possibility to continue practicing her presentation receiving feedback in all nonverbal aspects, or only on the aspect that she was interrupted for, so that she can focus on improving this specific skill.

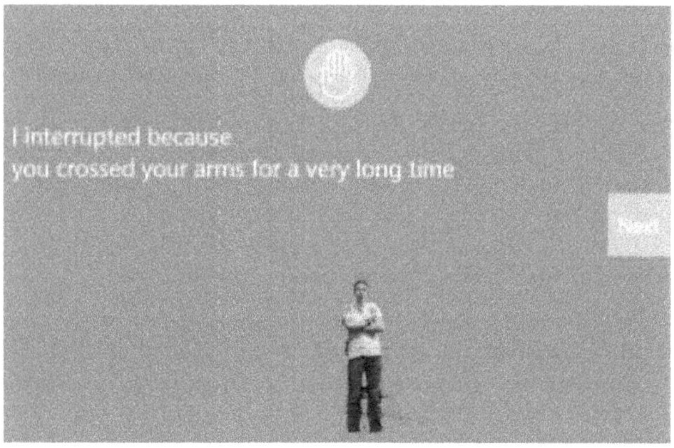

Figure 3. Interruptive feedback for crossing arms for a long time.

3.3 Presentation Trainer Architecture

The PT trainer has been developed in C# using the .NET framework 4.5[4]. In order to help people in their nonverbal skills, the PT needs to be able to track the user's voice and body; the current set-up of the PT does this tracking through the use of the Microsoft Kinect for Windows V2 sensor in conjunction with its SDK. Nevertheless its architecture shown in Figure 4 allows the inclusion of more sensor channels.

The PT receives the body and audio sensor data and stores it in the Body and Audio pre-Analysis objects respectively. The Body pre-Analysis object contains the current coordinates of the detected joints of the user's body and flags indicating whether certain postures rules, such as crossing arms are fired. The Audio pre-Analysis object contains the values of the audio buffer received from the Kinect microphones together with a flag indicating whether the user is currently speaking.

The JudgementMaker object uses the information stored in the Body and Audio pre-Analysis objects to create Presentation Actions. These Presentation-Actions are any type of nonverbal communication mistakes or good practices identified by the system. For example speaking for too long time without pausing, standing in an incorrect posture, etc.

A list of the current Presentation-Actions is passed to the RulesAnalyzer object, which according to the state of the program and performance of the user decides the feedback event to be triggered. The running operational state receives these feedback events and forwards them to the connected output channels.

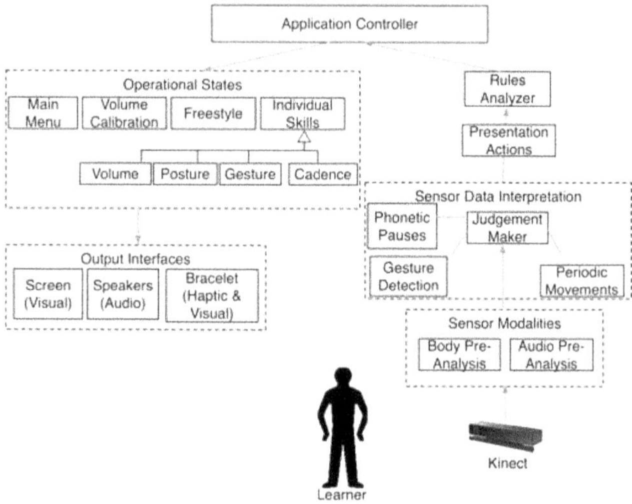

Figure 4. System Architecture.

4. Evaluation

In this study we investigated how the feedback provided by the PT has an effect on the user experience of learners practicing to give an elevator pitch. An elevator pitch is a 30 to 120 seconds long speech where one summarizes in lay terms what one does and why it is important[5]. In order to study this user experience we conducted a quasi-experiment with a treatment and a control group of participants.

4.1 Participants

For this experiment we had a total number of 40 participants. The control and the treatment group both had 11 males and 9 females. The average age of the participants was 42.6 with a range of 24-62. All participants were professionals working at our university, with a similar cultural background. We recruited them by personally asking for their willingness to take part in our experiment. Once they agreed to take part, they scheduled their experimental session themselves by selecting an available timeslot. The criteria used to accommodate them in the control or treatment group was randomly based on the number of their experimental session. Participants from odd sessions (1st, 3rd, etc.) were assigned to the treatment group, and participants arriving from even sessions (2nd, 4th, etc.) were assigned to the control group.

4.2 Apparatus and Materials

To measure the user experience of participants we used a questionnaire designed to evaluate the user experience with

[4] http://www.microsoft.com/net

[5] https://en.wikipedia.org/wiki/Elevator_pitch accessed on August 2015

multimodal learning applications[6]. The questionnaire consists of ten questions. Each of the first six questions inquires a different dimension of the user experience with multimodal learning applications. This six dimensions are: naturalness of use, boredom, invasiveness, unlikelihood of use during free time, perceived learning, and comparison against traditional classroom learning. Answers of these six questions are provided through a rating from 1 to 10 in a Likert-type scale. In addition there is one multiple-choice question about the novelty of the system, and three open questions inquiring the participants' opinion about the system, recommendations, and insights while using the system. Besides the questionnaire the PT also created a log file for each training session. This log file includes: the starting and ending time of the training session, all identified Presentation Actions (mistakes) together with their corresponding starting and ending timestamps, and all Feedback events together also with their corresponding timestamps.

4.3 Experimental Setup

Each experimental session in this study was individual. The session started with a short, five-minute, lecture about nonverbal communication for public speaking. This lecture reviewed the aspects that the PT is able to track, which are: body posture, use of hand gestures, use of voice volume, pauses, phonetic pauses and ability to stay grounded. The reason for this lecture was to assure participants have a similar baseline of basic knowledge about nonverbal communication for public speaking.

Figure 5. Training session setup with Presentation Trainer giving feedback.

Immediately after this lecture, participants had another short five-minute lecture about elevator pitches where they learned how to do an elevator pitch. Finishing the lecture the tutor showed the participants a live example of an elevator pitch. As soon as the lectures finished the participant had 5 minutes to create her own elevator pitch. Participants were free to use any topic they want for the pitch. Once the pitch was created, it was time to practice its delivery.

Participants of both groups had to practice the delivery of the pitch in five successive training sessions. Participants in the control group practiced using a version of the PT whose interface only shows a mirrored image of the user, in other words they did not receive any specific feedback. The treatment group practiced the pitch using the full version of the PT (Figure 5). They received, if necessary, both immediate and interruptive feedback.

After practicing the pitch for the fifth time, the participants were asked to answer a questionnaire about their user experience.

5. Results

The answers to the six dimensions regarding the user experience posted in the questionnaire are shown in Table 1. To calculate the significance of the results we used a t-test. A dimension that showed significant differences between the control and treatment group is the one of motivation. Participants from the control group felt significantly less motivated while using the PT scoring an average of 6.52 against an average of 3.05 scored by the treatment group. In terms of perceived learning the treatment group reported to learn significantly more with an average score of 7.47 against a 6.0. With no significant difference between groups, results indicate that participants found the interaction with the tool to be natural, not invasive, better for learning than the traditional classroom setting, and found it unlikely to use it during free time.

Table 1. Average results on the 6 dimensions of user experience extracted from the post session questionnaire (ratings from 1 to 10).

Dimension	Treatment Group	Control Group	P-Value
Naturalness *10=very natural	6.47	6.42	p = 0.92
Invasiveness *10=very invasive	2.68	3.84	p = 0.08
Boredom vs. Motivation *10=very bored	3.05	6.52	p <.01
Unlikelihood of free time use *10=very unlikely	6.05	6.05	p = 1
Learning Perception *10=learned a lot	7.47	6	p < .05
Practice using tool vs. Classroom *10=much better than classroom	6.94	6.1	p = 0.2

None of the participants from the treatment group had ever used an application similar to the PT, on the other hand one participant of the control group stated to have used a similar application, and two of them stated that maybe they have seen something similar.

When asking participants about the specific aspects learned while using the PT, most of the participants from the treatment group mentioned specific nonverbal communication aspects. The learning aspect most frequently mentioned by participants was the use of pauses; followed by the use of gestures, voice volume, posture, and finally phonetic pauses. On the other hand participants from the control group stated that they learned about self-awareness, staying calm and the importance of practice.

[6]http://www.sigmla.org/mla2015/ApplicationGuidelines.pdf accessed on August 2015

Twelve participants from the control group suggested improving the system by providing users with some real-time feedback about their performance. The suggestion for improvement from the treatment group include the use of more explicit icons for feedback, selection to practice one skill at the time, and giving a summary of the performance at the end of each training session.

The logged data generated by the PT show significant differences in the assessed performances of participants between both groups. To assess the performance of each training session, we looked at the proportion of time while the user is making a mistake (pTM), to get this value, first we added up the duration of all Presentation Actions (mistakes) because according to our criterion, one mistake that lasts for instance for an entire minute is much worse than five mistakes that in total have a duration of ten seconds.

Then we divided the total duration of the mistakes by the total time of the session. We performed this division because according to our criterion for instance 30 seconds of mistakes in a 45 seconds pitch is far worse than two minutes of mistakes in a 25 minutes long presentation. Even when the PT at maximum displays one corrective feedback at the time, it still keeps tracks and logs all Presentation Actions, meaning that the pTM value can be larger than 1, since multiple mistakes can happen simultaneously. The pTM average values for every session are listed in Table 2. In order to calculate the significance of these results we used a t-test.

Table 2. pTM average for each training session

Training Session	Treatment Group	Control Group	P-Value
1	0.51	0.92	$p < 0.05$
2	0.32	1.11	$p < 0.01$
3	0.35	1.01	$p < 0.01$
4	0.26	0.92	$p < 0.01$
5	0.25	1.002	$p < 0.01$

From the first training session, there were already significant differences between the groups with average values of 0.92 for the control and 0.51 for the treatment group. These differences (see Figure 6) increased during the sessions. The average pTM for the treatment group continued to decrease to an average of 0.25 for the fifth session, while staying considerably constant with an average of 1.002 on the fifth session for the control group.

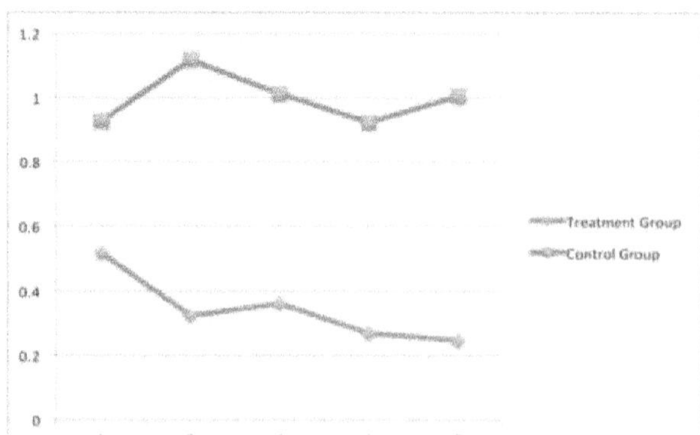

Figure 6. Reduction of ptm after 5 training sessions.

6. Discussion

Results and observations realized within this study showed that in general participants enjoyed using the PT to practice their communication skills, especially the version of the PT including feedback. Some participants stated during the firsts sessions how difficult it is to give a speech while paying attention to the feedback, however the general impression at the end of the training sessions was that it became stepwise much easier to use and that it is a very helpful tool for training nonverbal communication skills.

The answers to the questionnaire indicate that practicing with the PT is perceived by users as a better way to learn than the traditional classroom methods, particularly in the case where this practice includes feedback. This feedback apparently makes the user experience more natural and less invasive. It seems that participants that did not receive feedback and only saw their reflection, felt observed and became suspicious about what the system could be doing with all the tracked information. Participants receiving feedback experienced what the system was doing with the information and felt the interaction more natural and less invasive.

Results show how feedback can significantly motivate learners, however this feedback is not enough to motivate them to use such a tool during their free time. We have to take in consideration that none of the participants practiced public speaking as a hobby and that this version of the PT has been designed to be a learning supporting tool and not a game.

Participants that received feedback felt as if they have learned more during their practice sessions and listed concrete nonverbal communication aspects, when asked about the subjects learned while using the system. In contrast with participants from the control group, who reported to have learned more abstract subjects such as self-awareness, stay calm, etc. This difference in learning is not only shown in the reports of the participants, it has also been objectively corroborated by the performance measurements taken during the practice sessions, where from the first session the treatment group already performed much better than the control group. Moreover the performances of the treatment group kept improving considerably throughout the sessions, while the performances of control group remained stable.

A limitation of the PT is that its performance measurement mechanism cannot be directly translated to the assessment that a human would make about the quality of a presentation or an elevator pitch. These limitations of assessment start with the fact that the quality of a presentation or a pitch highly depends on its content and not only its delivery, and the PT is only able to interpret part of its nonverbal delivery. Additionally there are still limitations regarding what the sensors can perceive and what the PT can interpret out of the sensor data. In previous user tests conducted to tune the PT we learned that the identification of false positives should be avoided as much as possible. False positives lead users to believe that the system does not work properly and therefore users stop taking the feedback seriously. Thus it is better in some cases to reduce the accuracy of the system, as we did it with the phonetic pauses where the identification ration is only about 20%. Another current limitation of the PT in terms of interpreting data has to do with the interpretation of gestures; the PT cannot recognize the difference between iconic gestures, emphasis gestures, or waving hands without purpose. Fortunately waving hands without purpose is something that we have not seen during the experiments, and are hardly seen throughout presentations.

Public speaking in some cases can be seen as a performing art, where the creativity and capacity of the speaker to impress the audience play a big role in the quality of a presentation. It is perfectly acceptable for a speaker to deliberately break any rule in order to create the desired impact in the audience. The PT is not capable to interpret between deliberately broken rules or mistakes by the presenter. However, we want to stress that the PT is designed to support the practice of basic nonverbal skills, by making learners aware of the identified Presentation Actions; and this study has proven its success to do so.

7. Future work and conclusions

The presented study identified that the feedback mechanism of the PT facilitates the improvement of basic nonverbal communication skills for public speaking. As a next step we plan to do an expert study to extract a rich set of nonverbal communication aspects and rules that have an effect on the quality of a presentation, and improve the PT based on those findings. In this expert study we also want to investigate how a tool such as the PT can become a complementary tool able to support the improvement of courses in public speaking.

In this context we also want to explore how the measured assessment of the PT compares to expert, peer and self-assessment, and study how these combination of assessments can support the development of public speaking skills.

To conclude, in this article we showed how the feedback mechanism implemented in the PT has supported users with the development of their public speaking skills by helping them to significantly improve their performance during training sessions. If we consider the PT as an example of a multimodal system; and consider public speaking as an example of an activity that requires a great deal of practice with effective feedback to become proficient at it, then this study points out a way in which multimodal systems are able to contribute in getting us one step closer to a perfect practice that makes perfect.

8. ACKNOWLEDGMENTS

The underlying research project is partly funded by the METALOGUE project. METALOGUE is a Seventh Framework Programme collaborative project funded by the European Commission, grant agreement number: 611073 (http://www.metalogue.eu).

9. REFERENCES

[1] Anderson, T., Shattuck, J.: Design-Based Research A Decade of Progress in Education Research? *Educational Researcher*, 41(1) (2012), pp. 16-25

[2] Barthelmess, P. Kaiser, E., Huang, X, Demirdjian, D. Distributed pointing for multimodal collaboration over sketched diagrams. *Proceedings of the Seventh International Conference on Multimodal Interfaces*, ACM: (New York 2005), pp. 10-17.

[3] Batrinca, L., Stratou, G., Shapiro, A., Morency, L.-P., Scherer, S. Cicero - towards a multimodal virtual audience platform for public speaking training. *In Proc. IVA*, vol. 8108. Springer, 2013, 116–128.

[4] Baur, T., Damian, I., Gebhard, P., Porayska-Pomsta, K., Andre, E. A job interview simulation: Social ´ cue-based interaction with a virtual character. *In Proc. SocialCom. IEEE*, (2013), pp. 220–227.

[5] Bjerregaard, M., Compton, E. Public Speaking Handbook. Snow College, Supplement for Public Speaking (2011)

[6] Bolt, R. A. Put-that-there: Voice and gesture at the graphics interface. *Computer Graphics*, 14 (3) (1980), pp. 262-270.

[7] Brouwers, J. Implementation and Testing of an Improved Automated Presentation Trainer. Master Thesis, Maastricht University, Faculty of Humanities and Sciences, Department of Knowledge Engineering, Aug-Sept. 2015.

[8] Cohen, P.R., McGee, D. (2004) Tangible multimodal interfaces for safety critical applications. *Communications of the ACM*, vol. 47 (January 2004) 41-46.

[9] Damian I., Tan C.S.S., Baur T., Schöning J., Luyten K., André E. Augmenting Social Interactions: Realtime Behavioural Feedback using Social Signal Processing Techniques. *In CHI '15 Proceedings of the 33rd Annual ACM Conference on Human Factors in Computing Systems.* (Seul 2015), pp. 565-574.

[10] Darves, C., Oviatt, S. Talking to digital fish: Designing effective conversational interfaces for educational software. *In Evaluating Embodied Conversational Agents*, Z. Ruttkay, C. Pelachaud, Eds., (Dordrecht 2004), pp. 271-292.

[11] DeVito J.A. *The Essential Elements of Public Speaking*. Pearson (2014)

[12] ESPN Greatest coaches in NFL History. http://espn.go.com/nfl/story/_/page/greatestcoach1/greatest-coaches-nfl-history-vince-lombardi . Accessed July 2015.

[13] Hattie, J., & Timperley, H., The power of feedback. *Review of Educational Research* (2007), pp. 81–112

[14] Hoque, M. E., Courgeon, M., Martin, J., Mutlu, B., and Picard, R. W. Mach: My automated conversation coach. *In Proc. UbiComp* (2013).

[15] Kerby, D. & Romine, J.: Develop Oral Presentation Skills Through Accounting Curriculum Design and Course-Embedded Assessment. *Journal of Education for Business*. Vol. 85, Iss. 3. (2009).

[16] King, P., Young, M., & Behnke, R. Public speaking performance improvement as a function of information processing in immediate and delayed feedback interventions. *Communication Education*, 49(4) (2000), pp. 365-374.

[17] Li, X., and Rekimoto, J. Smartvoice: a presentation support system for overcoming the language barrier. *In Proc. CHI'14, ACM* (2014), pp. 1563–1570.

[18] Mehrabian, A. Nonverbal communication. Oxford, UK: Aldine-Atherton, 1972.

[19] Oviatt, S. Multimodal Interfaces. The human-computer interaction handbook. 3rd edition Lawrence Erlbaum: New Jersey, 2012.

[20] Ruiz, N., Chen, F. and Oviatt S., "Multimodal Input", *in Multimodal Signal Processing: Theory and Applications for Human-Computer Interaction.* Edited by Thiran, J.P., Marques, F. and Bourlard, H., Academic Press, 2010, Chapter 12, pp. 231-255.

[21] Schneider, J., Börner, D., van Rosmalen, P., Specht, M. Augmenting the senses: a review on sensor-based learning support. *Sensors* **15**(2) (February 2015), pp. 4097–4133.

[22] Schneider, J., Börner, D., van Rosmalen, P., Specht, M. Stand Tall and Raise your Voice! A Study on the Presentation Trainer. *In EC-TEL'15 Proceedings of the tenth European Conference on Technology enhanced learning* (Toledo 2015).

[23] Sweller, J. Cognitive Load Theory, learning difficulty, and instructional design. *Learning and Instruction* 4 (4) (1994), pp. 295–312.

[24] Tam, D., MacLean, K., McGrenere, J., and K. J. Kuchenbecker, K. J. The design and field observation of a haptic notification system for timing awareness during oral presentations. *In Proc. CHI '13*. ACM, 2013.

[25] Toastmasters International. Gestures: your body speaks. http://www.toastmasters.org/ (2011)

Utilizing Depth Sensors for Analyzing Multimodal Presentations: Hardware, Software and Toolkits

Chee Wee Leong, Lei Chen, Gary Feng, Chong Min Lee and Matthew Mulholland
Research & Development
Educational Testing Service
Princeton, New Jersey, USA
{cleong, lchen, gfeng, clee001, mmulholland}@ets.org

ABSTRACT

Body language plays an important role in learning processes and communication. For example, communication research produced evidence that mathematical knowledge can be embodied in gestures made by teachers and students. Likewise, body postures and gestures are also utilized by speakers in oral presentations to convey ideas and important messages. Consequently, capturing and analyzing non-verbal behaviors is an important aspect in multimodal learning analytics (MLA) research. With regard to sensing capabilities, the introduction of depth sensors such as the Microsoft Kinect has greatly facilitated research and development in this area. However, the rapid advancement in hardware and software capabilities is not always in sync with the expanding set of features reported in the literature. For example, though Anvil [21] is a widely used state-of-the-art annotation and visualization toolkit for motion traces, its motion recording component based on OpenNI is outdated. As part of our research in developing multimodal educational assessments, we began an effort to develop and standardize algorithms for purposes of multimodal feature extraction and creating automated scoring models. This paper provides an overview of relevant work in multimodal research on educational tasks, and proceeds to summarize our work using multimodal sensors in developing assessments of communication skills, with attention on the use of depth sensors. Specifically, we focus on the task of public speaking assessment using Microsoft Kinect. Additionally, we introduce an open-source Python package for computing expressive body language features from Kinect motion data, which we hope will benefit the MLA research community.

Categories and Subject Descriptors

H.5.1 [**Information Systems**]: Information Interfaces and Presentation—*Multimedia Information Systems*

ICMI '15 November 09 - 13, 2015, Seattle, WA, USA

DOI: http://dx.doi.org/10.1145/2818346.2830605.

Keywords

Depth sensors; Kinect; Multimodal Learning Analytics

1. INTRODUCTION

Effective communication between humans for a specific cause requires adaptive measures to convey the intent and message clearly to the other party. Kinesics are often used along with words to infer the intent of the speaker [4]. In the context of classrooms or study groups, teachers tend to teach effectively by utilizing body gestures, voice modulation, visual aids, etc, in addition to use of the blackboard. Likewise, students learn better not just by listening, but also by providing feedback through nodding, vocal acknowledgment, facial expressions, all of which are channels of feedback potentially helpful for improving pedagogic processes [7]. In fact, cognitive and communication research produced evidence that mathematical knowledge can be embodied in gestures made by teachers and students [1], along with other recent studies that lend weight to similar hypotheses that proper use of body movements and gestures can lead to instructional scaffolding to achieve better learning outcomes [23, 3].

While the above classroom scenarios are reflective of a conducive learning environment that leverages on multimodal cues, constructing automated systems for fostering such scenarios is still difficult with the current level of multimodal learning analytics research. Some of the main blocking issues relates to spatial constraints (e.g. how to mount sensors conveniently without being intrusive), background noise, lighting issues, classroom artifacts (e.g. partially occluded body due to desks and chairs), and even psychological effects (e.g. different behavioral patterns induced by the thought that one is being tracked). Nevertheless, the central goal in multimodal learning analytics relates to the effective deployment of algorithms and systems to collect and analyze similar communication cues, and build automated systems with predictive models that have good correlation with human ratings on the target learning or assessment task. Intuitively, such a system comprises the following components (1) A network of input sensors for capturing data from multiple modalities, including voice, video, haptics, etc. (2) A communication protocol to process data streams from the sensors for the purposes of time and events synchronization. (3) A set of algorithms implemented for real-time feature tracking and machine learning outcomes prediction. (4) A set of output devices rendering the learner outcomes textually, aurally, or visually or e.g. interactive avatars, audio feedback,etc. (5) A data storage protocol and devices implementing the protocol for holding persistent sensor data, feature values and learner predictions along with other metadata for offline analysis and model training.

With respect to multimodal learning analytics, there is significant ongoing work in the literature. [38] documented the study of how expertise in building stable, well-engineered structures can be identified through meaningful utterances and coordinated hand movements, which are extracted from time-series, process-oriented video and voice data. In another line of work, [15] employed automated facial expression tracking to predict time instances when students become disengaged or frustrated during interactions with tutoring systems. [30] proposed a multi-camera tracking framework for detecting engagement/disengagement of students and teaching performance in classroom. When combining this framework with other input such as after-class questionnaires and in-depth interviews, a viable system for predicting the quality of a class can be deployed. In addition, previous MLA challenges also yielded important contributions where there are efforts to extract multimodal cues from audio, video and motion traces to automatically score presentations of students [10, 13].

In this paper, we are particularly interested in the use of depth sensors for multimodal learning analytics. Specifically, we focus on the application of a low-cost depth sensor, Microsoft Kinect, to evaluate a target assessment task, public speaking, which is a core competency skill for college and workforce success. The main contribution of our work is to provide a cookbook style of discussion, where we elaborate from beginning to end how we leverage state-of-the-art sensors, toolkits and algorithms to build a preliminary presentation assessment system with good correlation with human annotations on the same task.

The paper proceeds in the following manner. First, we highlight and explain the emerging importance of depth sensors, how they operate in principle, and why they should be utilized as part of the sensing network. This is especially relevant given that traditional input sensors which are restricted to video and audio tend to limit the performance of multimodal systems [17]. With the advent of 3D depth sensors, an orthogonal form of information can be used together with information from other sensors in the same set of input features. In particular, as our depth sensor of choice, we focus on the Microsoft Kinect. Second, we provide an overview of existing integrative multimodal systems that can be leveraged to perform recording and synchronization of data streams in the data collection process, which is elaborated next with technical details via two case studies. Finally, we highlight a set of high-level features extracted from Kinect that are shown to have promising predictive power for multimodal presentation assessments. Extraction of these features from other datasets is possible through our Python scripts to be released as open-source software, which we hope to benefit the MLA research community.

2. DEPTH SENORS

A 3D depth sensor is a device that assigns distance from an anchor point in a 3D space to a 2D scene. Specifically, each pixel in the 2D scene is attached with relative depth information from the anchor point. Once calibrated, the actual physical units of distance (e.g. inches or feet) can be mapped. The role of 3D sensors has been significantly amplified over the years, graduating from its origination in research labs and increasingly finding its way into our everyday lives [39, 20, 8, 37]. This can be attributed to the continuous innovation in sensors, improvement in sensing accuracy, decreasing costs of sensor components, availability of APIs for sensors and related software libraries for developing useful applications. More importantly, since depth sensors have the ability to track body movements as the scene changes, it allows human body language understanding, a research problem proven formidably challenging with video cameras [17]. It it this enabling technology that gives rise to a new way of human computer interaction.

A brief section on the inner workings of optical depth sensors is provided here in order to create a bridge from their hardware obscurity to their practical usefulness. There are generally three principles by which these devices operate, namely structured light, time-of-flight (ToF), and stereo vision. *Structured light* sensors use a projector to produce a laser, typically Infrared (IR), that passes through a diffraction grating to produce a set of IR dots which are projected onto the scene. The projected IR pattern is random, but all the IR dots are distinct from one another, which allows differentiation between dots. Since the relative geometry between the IR projector and IR sensor is known during calibration, including the angles of the diffraction, triangulation can be used to render each dot in the image taken by the IR sensor in 3D, thus allowing depth information to be obtained. Unlike structured light, a *Time-of-Flight* depth sensor also employs laser-inducing light to illuminate the scene, but uses the actual reflected light to compute depth. Each light pulse is modulated i.e. "information" is being attached to the light by varying its amplitude or frequency, hence making it identifiable from emission to detection. Taking into account the travel time of the light pulse (hence, "time-of-flight"), the distance from from the depth sensor to a single spot in the scene can be computed. To create a 3D point cloud of the entire scene, a ToF sensor must enable the time taken for millions of light pulses to return to the sensor, typically achieved in picoseconds. In *stereo vision* sensor systems, two or more cameras mounted in parallel but separated by a short distance are utilized to collectively compute depth information. Specifically, the focal length and optical axes of each camera are parameters used to project a specific, shared 2D point on the images into 3D Cartesian space. The 3D projections from each camera are necessarily different from one another due to the difference in the geometric setup of each camera, hence the discrepancies can be plugged into a formula to compute the depth distance from the cameras to the point.

Apart from their different working principles, depth sensors can be categorized by their range of sensing and tracking ability. There are also several aspects of depth sensors that we believe are important for researching learning analytics. First, while there are depth sensors operating on similar principles that focus on scene understanding and reconstruction, such as the 3D structure sensor[1] or Intel's R200 3D sensor[2], we believe understanding human body movements to be key to valuable multimodal learning applications. These user-centric depth sensors are designed and calibrated to work optimally for motion capture and gesture tracking, ranging from the entire body skeleton to tracking

[1]http://structure.io/

[2]https://software.intel.com/en-us/articles/realsense-r200-camera

Table 1: *Technical specification summary of commonly used depth sensors*

	Microsoft Kinect v1	Microsoft Kinect v2	Intel Realsense (F200)	LEAP Motion Controller
		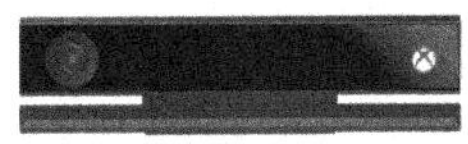		
Technology	Structured Light	Time-of-Flight	Time-of-Flight	Stereo Cameras
RGB camera	640x480 @30fps	1920x1080 @30fps	1920x1080 @30fps	undisclosed
Depth sensors	640x480 @30fps	512x424 @30fps	640x480 @60fps	undisclosed
Microphone	Quad-array microphone	Quad-array microphone	Dual array microphone	-
Range	0.4 to 4.5 m	0.5 to 4.5 m	0.2 to 1.2 m	0.03 to 0.6 m
Skeletons tracked	2	6	-	-
Horizontal Field of View (FOV)	57°	70°	70°	150°
Vertical FOV	43°	60°	43°	120°
USB	2.0	3.0	3.0	3.0
Gestures tracking	Yes	Yes	Yes	Yes
Body joints	20	25	-	-
SDK	Yes	Yes	Yes	Yes
Portability	No	No	Yes	Yes

of hands and fingers, and hence are more appropriate for our study. Second, in view of versatile learning and assessment scenarios, we consider the portability of a sensor, measured as its ability to be attached to a tablet or laptop, to be a valuable characteristic. This allows for an extension of learning environments beyond classrooms to other situations that require mobility, where feature tracking and analytics can take place on demand and on the fly. Third, the availability of a Software Development Kit (SDK) to create customized solutions is central to meeting the diverse needs of learning tasks and assessments. Such middleware allows the transformation of lower-level data streams to high-level features, many of which can be more interpretable. Hence, it yields transparency to scoring models. Table 1 shows selected 3D depth sensors noted for their relevance to user-centric sensing and tracking capabilities. It is by no means exhaustive, but rather represents sensors that have been used with groundings in research studies [12, 6, 16]. The table also summarizes important characteristics of each sensor, which collectively creates a usability scenario that can be matched against the needs of different learning tasks or assessments. For instance, in our public speaking assessment task, Microsoft Kinect is the depth sensor of choice, since it allows the capture of holistic body movements. A full, in-depth treatment of the inner workings of Kinect and how body movements can be inferred is described in [39]. Other scenarios, such as when students attending online courses via laptops require intervention at times of doubt, are probably better served by Intel Realsense. Further, it is possible to use the LEAP motion controller, a highly precise hand gesture tracker, for conducting tutorials in virtual worlds, such as mixing chemicals from test tubes in chemistry lessons.

3. INTEGRATED MOTION CAPTURE SYSTEMS

Advances in low-cost consumer-grade depth sensors such as the Kinect have highlighted the need for standardization of these natural interaction devices. OpenNI[3] is an organization established to shoulder this task. Additionally, it provides an open-source framework for the development of drivers and software for accessing and utilizing Natural User Interface (NUI) devices. Compliant devices include the Kinect and the original PrimeSense sensor, and a growing list of other depth sensors. The Kinect itself has also provided its own SDK[4] with sample code supporting gesture and voice recognition and facial tracking, among other things. To date, five versions of SDK have been released: SDK versions 1.5, 1.6, 1.7 and 1.8, supporting Kinect for Windows v1, while SDK version 2.0 supports Kinect for Windows v2. There have also been a multitude of projects in online repositories in github, kinecthacks.com and codeplex.com that address ways to capture depth sensor data. However, to our knowledge, many of these programs are created as ad hoc solutions for isolated problems e.g. [25], and did not undergo stress testing. In the context of our evaluative task, it is also imperative that the data collection system is easy to calibrate and deploy, allows for repetitive use while being fault-tolerant, and permits the interoperation of depth sensors with other sensing equipment to record synchronized data streams. The last characteristic is important to create a rich feature set spanning across multiple modalities. While it is true that the SDK of many depth sensors also captures and allows extraction of non-depth data such as video and speech, synchronous recording by other higher fidelity devices is sometimes required. For example, for higher speech recognition rates, a lapel microphone is preferred to

[3]http://openni.ru/index.html
[4]https://www.microsoft.com/en-us/kinectforwindows/develop/default.aspx

the built-in microphone array from Kinect. We may also find the need to record data using a non-traditional, non-depth sensor, such as a haptic sensor or sociometric badges for future exploitations. Here, we introduce two multimodal data collection systems that we found to be reliable for repetitive use. An attractive notion is that they are available in free, fully-functional version, and are actively supported. Both are based on the Windows operating system.

3.1 Brekel

Brekel[5] is a proprietary, integrated motion capture system that records video, speech and skeletal data streams in real-time using SDK from Kinect SDK and OpenNI and NITE. It allows for quick recognition and tracking of up to 2 persons at a time. Writing of synchronous data streams is direct to disk in FilmBox (FBX), BioVision Hierarchical (BVH) and TXT formats. In total, 58 joints covering all body parts are tracked, with major tracking points such as hips, left/right arms, left/right hands, left/right legs. While file outputs are possible, there is also direct streaming to 3D applications e.g. Autodesk MotionBuilder for creating virtual reality software. The basic version, Brekel Kinect, which supports Kinect v1, is free for research use; other Brekel packages provide enhanced tracking capabilities e.g. Brekel Pro Body v2 tracks humans using Kinect v2, while facial feature and head pose tracking is possible with Brekel Pro Face v2. The experiments reported in this paper are performed using Brekel Pro Body Kinect tracking software, which is similar to Pro Body 2 but operates with Kinect v1.

3.2 Multisense

Multisense [18] is a open-source framework for integrating data streams from multiple sensors for the purpose of audio and video sensing, as well as non-verbal behavior processing. Developed by USC ICT initially as part of the Virtual Human Architrecture[6] (VHT), it is a modular platform for generating probabilistic models for human behavior perception and understanding. Multisense is capable of tracking, in real-time or offline mode, facial expressions, body posture, acoustic and linguistic patterns, and higher levels of behavioral descriptors, such as attention span for example. This tracking is enabled via multiple input modalities including video, audio, depth streams from devices such as Kinect, webcam and high-fidelity microphones embedded into the framework. The data streams are synchronized but processed by the appropriate trackers independently e.g. CLM-Z for facial and head tracking [2], skeleton tracking by Microsoft Kinect SDK and FAAST [34] for skeleton action encoding. In total, 24 joints covering all body parts are tracked, with major tracking points such as head, neck, torso, and waist, as well as left/right shoulders, left/right knees, etc. The richness of the multimodal feature set created can lead to inference of higher-level information such as mental and emotional states. Architecturally, Multisense operates on multithreading processes allowing for the different trackers to run in parallel and in real-time. This functionality is built and improved on top of the Social Signal Interpretation (SSI) framework [36] from which MultiSense borrows basic functional elements. A compiled, basic version of Multisense is freely available at the VHT website by request. This version includes the AVRecorder application which allows for multithreaded, synchronous recording of Kinect v1, a webcam, and external microphones.

[5]http://brekel.com/

[6]https://vhtoolkit.ict.usc.edu/

4. CASE STUDIES

4.1 Task

Oral communication skills are critical to success in both learning and career development. For example, it has been consistently rated as one of the most valued workforce skills in large scale surveys [22], and its importance is also reflected in the newly developed national K-12 education standards [28]. Consequently, there is a pressing need for obtaining valid, reliable, and cost-efficient ways to evaluate oral communication skills, such as on public speaking tasks.

Public speaking involves a range of constructs, including but not limited to, content, organization, language use, vocal quality, and the effective use of non-verbal cues. Evidence for these qualities is distributed across multiple modalities, from linguistic (e.g., coherence of the message and word choice), vocal (e.g., intonation and disfluencies), facial expressions, to hand and body gestures. A competent public speaker coordinates all aspects of these modalities to achieve an engaging and effective performance. It is not surprising that most existing rubrics for public speaking skills [29, 24, 32] evaluate both verbal and nonverbal aspects of communication. Clearly, low-cost commodity depth sensors, such as Microsoft Kinect, have the potential of providing a cheap solution for tracking and understanding body postures of presenters.

From 2013 to 2014, we have worked on creating a multimodal public speaking performance corpus. Two types of public speaking tasks were used in our data collection, namely *informative* and *impromptu* presentations. In an informative speech, presenters were given a pre-prepared slides deck and up to 20 minutes to prepare their presentation deliveries. In an impromptu speech, presenters were required to advocate an idea that was not actually favorable to them. No visual aids were provided for this type of speech. The experience of the presenters in public speaking varied widely from beginners to experienced members of the Toastmasters club.

4.2 Data Collection

The selection of the hardware and software used in data collection are based on the following technical requirements:

- **complete motion recording**: in contrast to event-based motion recording, which usually lasts several seconds, a complete presentation session may last up to 5 minutes.
- **full body tracking**: full body tracking of presenters must be recorded for body language understanding and interpretation.
- **complicated background**: PowerPoint presentations were used in the informative presentation task, and therefore interfered as background "noise" lighting, affecting brightness and contrast during video recording.
- **high-resolution face videos**: facial expressions shown in presentations are important cues for detecting psychological states e.g. nervousness, which is useful for rating performance.

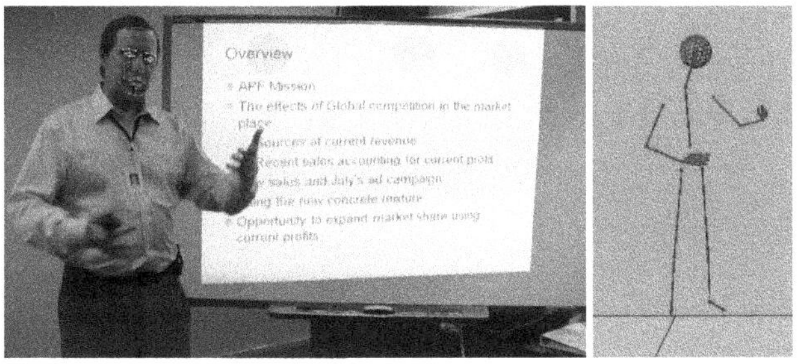

Figure 1: **Multimodal data example (informative speech) : the left panel shows a video of a subject with the tracking of facial features activated; the right panel shows the corresponding motion tracking.**

- **data streams synchronization**: multiple data streams (motion, video, and audio) may be recorded independently by different devices, hence they must be precisely synchronized.
- **simplicity of system**: in order to establish sensor setup conventions for a wider usage, we need to control for the complexity of the setup.

Our initial data collection efforts started in 2013. The first integrated motion capture system we experimented with was NUICapture which was used in [35] to record short sequences of motion on the order of seconds. However, it did not satisfy our technical constraint of complete motion recording. System crashes were frequent and disruptive to our data collection processes. Eventually, we switched our recording software to Brekel Pro Body, which turned out to be more reliable.

Consequently, our data collection system in 2013 comprised the following: One Microsoft Kinect for Windows Version 1 device was used to record 3D body motions. Brekel Pro Body Kinect tracking software (v1.30 64 bit version) was used to record 48 body joints, and the motion data was stored using the BioVision Hierarchical (BVH) format. JVC Everio GZ-HM35BUSD, a consumer-grade digital camcorder with 1080p resolution, was used for audio/video recording. Note that the camcorder was used to capture high-resolution videos for facial expression analysis, since Kinect v1 recorded at a maximum resolution of only 640x480. The Kinect and camcorder devices were mounted together on a tripod and placed 6ft away from the front of the speaking zone, which was marked on the ground. For the informative speech task, a SMART Board projector system was used to show the PowerPoint slides. Shortly after the start of each recording, each presenter was requested to perform a clapping action before the actual speaking task, which served as a synchronization signal common to all the multimodal data streams. Figure 1 provides an example of the collected video and motion tracking results. More details on other data processing steps for creating this corpus (e.g., video conversion, speech transcription and alignment) can be found in [9].

Using the above-mentioned data collection system, we successfully created our first multimodal presentation corpus by the end of 2013. The corpus contains Kinect motion traces, videos/audios recorded by Brekel software, as well as high-resolution videos/audios recorded by the camcorder. A total of 17 participants from our organization participated in the data collection. This system satisfied most of our technical requirements. Brekel Pro Body operated reliably on a laptop with modest configuration to support complete motion recording. Due to horizontal and vertical field of view constraints of Kinect v1, markers had to be placed on the ground to restrict movements of presenters to within a trapezium-like area. This prevented motion traces recording from being dropped during presentations.

However, there were other requirements that were not met fully. Since the high-resolution videos/audios and the motion traces were recorded independently by the camcorder and Kinect respectively, manual, imprecise synchronization had to be performed via the clapping action. Attempting to focus on faces of presenters using digital zooming in the camcorder would fail from time to time due to excessive pacing of the presenters.

One major issue was with lighting in the background. Due to illumination from The SMART Board used for displaying presentation slides during the informative talk task, a "lens flare" effect was generated, thereby reducing contrast on the face and subsequently hindering with facial expression analysis.

To address these issues found in 2013, in our 2014 data collection, we made several important improvements to our data collection system. Firstly, to address the challenge of precisely synchronizing multiple data streams, we utilized the MultiSense software from USC. The consumer-grade camcorder previously used was replaced with a HD webcam (Logitech C615). Similar to our 2013 setup, Kinect v1 was used for recording body traces for the presentations. Data streams from the different sensors i.e., Kinect v1 and webcam were time synchronized using the VRecorder application of Multisense, which allows for multithreaded, synchronous recording of the input sensors. USB 3.0 connections are made between the Kinect, webcam and the recording laptop. Given the large real-time data throughput requirements, a high-end mobile workstation with Intel Core i7-4800MQ quad-core processor with 8 threads, 16 GB RAM, and a 512 GB SSD hard drive was used in 2014. More details on the setup of sensors and equipment as well as the recording environment are illustrated in Figure 2.

Figure 2: The data collection setup (2014): [Left] Input sensors setup for collecting presentations [Top Right] Ground markers indicating effective area for presentations. [Bottom Right] MultiSense software running on a high-end laptop with skeleton tracking.

Secondly, to address the "lens flare" effect caused by the SMART Board, we utilized an Autocue/QTV 3 head softbox lighting kit to provide contrast adjustment for presenters. Two softbox heads, each with 85W fluorescent lamps, are placed 10 feet away from each end of the SMART Board respectively, projecting at an angle of 45°inwards toward the presenter. Using this new lighting toolkit, we conducted a pretest/posttest on facial features extraction based on CLM-Z [2] head/face tracking application, and concluded that the additional lighting significantly decreases the percentage of corrupted video frames tracked from 19.2% to 5.24%, as well lowering the mean and standard deviation of tracking uncertainty over those frames. Figure 3 shows the effect of using a lighting softbox.

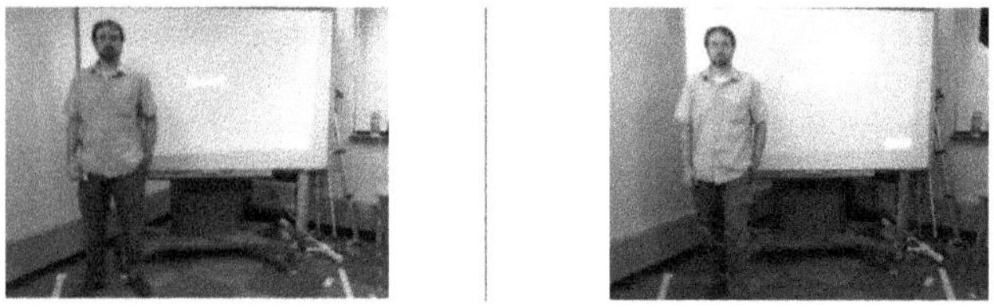

Figure 3: Applying two Autocue/QTV 3 lighting softboxes significantly improves contrast on the faces of the presenters: the left/right pictures reveal the effects before/after the softboxes are applied.

In summary, there are several technical requirements for collecting multimodal data from public speaking sessions in order to allow for a meaningful analysis and interpretation of these data for learning or assessment purposes. In our initial recording setup in 2013, we managed to address a subset of these requirements. In 2014, our improved setup has enabled us to meet all of the requirements. While the delivery of each speaking task represents a scenario in the lab, there are already significant challenges encountered, such as the inadequate field of view of Kinect v1 that led to the requirement of a marked out area for restricting presenters' movements, or the diminished contrast on presenters' faces due to the "lens flare" effect, which is still somewhat problematic for ideal facial expression analysis. Migrating the tasks delivery to a real-world classroom would inevitably bring more challenges. Nevertheless, we hope that the advancement of sensors and tracking technology would allow some of these problems to be solved. For example, Microsoft Kinect v2 boasts a larger effective FOV and should lift some of the movement restrictions. It is a prospect we are interested to pursue as part of our future work. For the remaining sections in this paper, we focus on feature extraction and machine learning experiments on the 2013 corpus.

5. OPEN-SOURCE TOOLKIT FOR GENERATING MULTIMODAL FEATURES

We hypothesize several high-level features that can be transformed from low-level sensors data that are potentially useful in a machine learning framework for our public speaking tasks assessment. To our knowledge, there are no publicly available implementations of these features, hence we hope to benefit the MLA community through the release of an open source toolkit that facilitates their extraction for evaluation of public speaking tasks, as well as other similar pedagogic tasks related to speaking. In this section, we first elaborate on details for motivating these features, and provide details on the open-source toolkit that generates them.

5.1 Motion-based Body Features

Note that, though we have a multitude of multimodal features as outputs from the sensing network, we focus on the use of the depth sensor and its efficacy in our work. While we are aware that Microsoft and OpenNI SDKs provide gestures recognition ability, they are mostly limited to a set of closed-form gestures e.g. hand swiping to the left, etc, for improving interaction with NUI devices. Such gestures have limited interpretability for evaluating public speaking, and also do not occur frequently during speaking presentations (feature sparseness problem). In contrast, we aspire to extract higher-level features that are more generalizable and applicable to measuring the constructs of speaking proficiency.

Various methods have been proposed to compute expressive features related to body language in several research areas, e.g., affective computing, virtual agents, and multimodal dialogic systems. For example, [26] systematically summarized the methods used for analyzing expressive body language performances. They categorized the extractable features into the three layers: (a) low-level, such as *hands velocity*, (b) medium-level, such as *hands symmetry*, and (c) high-level, such as gestures bearing communicational meanings. Glowinski et al. [14] presented a framework for finding a minimal representation set of affective gestures. They first processed head and hand motion data through an array of expressive feature extraction modules for measuring energy, spatial extent, smoothness, symmetry, and head posture. Next, they computed statistics such as the maximum, mean, and standard deviation (SD) from these measurements. Finally, the minimal set of representational features was obtained using PCA-based dimension reduction.

Following [14, 26], we extracted a number of visual features related to spatial, temporal and dynamic aspects from the Kinect motion data, a frame-by-frame 3D-coordinated (XYZ) recording of each body part as stored in the BVH file. Specifically, we focus on the following body parts: hip, spine, left/right forearms, and left/right hands, due to these body parts' dynamism during presentation.

- **Spatial**: for each motion data frame, (a) the distance between the hands and the body (**hands-spine**); (b) the distance between the arms and the body (**arms-spine**), and (c) the distance between the two hands (**hands**);
- **Temporal**: the first order derivatives of the above spatial measurements; the corresponding features' names contain a special token "1dv". For example, **hands-spine-1dv** indicates the first order derivative of **hands-spine**.
- **Power**: second order derivatives of the above spatial measurements; the corresponding features' names contain a special token "2dv". For example, **hands-spine-2dv** indicates the second order derivative of **hands-spine**.

Note that the temporal feature relates to the rate of change of the spatial feature e.g. the speed at which both hands are moving away from each other. Similarly, power relates to the rate of change of the temporal feature e.g. the rate at which the speed is changing when both hands are moving away from each other. In additional to the spatial features, both temporal and power features approximate "smoothness" of the movement of body parts. Furthermore, [26] also suggested several derived features to measure full-body motions, such as Kinetic Energy (KE), Posture, and Symmetry.

- **Kinetic Energy**: We postulate the KE as a measure of the power/energy exhibited by the presenter. It measures the amount of overall movement of the body, and is somewhat correlated to the speaker being "physically active" during the presentation. KE is computed based on the velocities of upper-body segments and their corresponding percentage of mass, as described in the formula below:

$$KE = 0.5 \times \sum_i m_i v_i^2$$

where m_i and v_i refer to the normalized mass and velocity of body part i respectively. In our work, we focus exclusively on body parts that are in the upper-body region – namely, hips, spine, shoulders, arms, forearms and hands – noted for their importance in a related study in Kinesiology [27], from which we also obtained the normalized mass of these body parts[7].

- **Posture**: The posture of a presenter can be approximated using the concept of a Bounding Volume (BV) described in [26], whereby using the hip as the center, we construct an imaginary, pseudo-cuboid whose length, width and height are formed by the furthest distance spanning any two arbitrary body parts in the X, Y and Z dimensions respectively. The BV of a presenter at any frame can be computed simply by taking the volume of this imaginary cuboid. Intuitively, BV provides an approximation of the degree of body "openness" shown by the presenter.

- **Symmetry**: Following [26], we compute the symmetry index (SI) of a presenter's two-handed gestures. SIs measure the degree of symmetry exhibited by both hands along a specified spatial dimension. For example, we compute X dimension's SI as

$$SI_X = \frac{\| X_P - X_L \mid - \mid X_P - X_R \|}{\mid X_L - X_R \mid}$$

where X_L and X_R are the X-dimension coordinates of the left and right hands, and X_P is the X coordinate of the pivoting body part i.e. hips. A value of 0 for SI_X suggests perfect symmetry while a value of 1 suggests perfect dissymmetry. SI for the Y and Z dimensions can be computed accordingly. Symmetry-based features were shown to be relevant for measuring affective and behavioral status, and is also concerned with detecting the underlying attitude of a speaker e.g. relaxed or tensed [14]. From symmetry measurements of the individual axes, we also derived the following averages as additional measurements: $SI_{XY} = (SI_X + SI_Y)/2$ and $SI_{XYZ} = (SI_X + SI_Y + SI_Z)/3$.

Finally, for each frame-wise measurement described above (f), a set of statistics were computed to serve as features for the entire response, including:

- **mean**: mean value, which is $mean(f)$
- **mmrt**: ratio of the max value to the mean, which is computed as $max(f)/mean(f)$
- **mean-log**: mean of log-scaled value, which is computed as $mean(log(f))$
- **mmrt-log**: ratio of max log-scaled value to the mean of log-scaled value, which is computed as $max(log(f))/mean(log(f))$
- **SD**: standard deviation, which is computed as $SD(f)$
- **SD-log**: standard deviation of log-scaled values, which is computed as $SD(log(f))$

As a way to efficiently generate these high-level features, we implemented the Visualization and Analysis for Multimodal Presentation (**VAMP**)[8] toolkit, which is a toolkit consisting of a set of scripts in Python, chosen for its fast prototyping speed for research. Currently, only processing of Kinect-based skeletal data is supported. In the future, we hope to extend support to other depth sensors, while also providing continuous updates to the library of high-level features found to have high relevance for the automated scoring of public presentation tasks.

The toolkit receives as inputs a set of synchronized video, audio and skeletal data, and transforms them into feature contours for visualization. Figure 4 shows the operating flowchart of our toolkit. The core function emphasized here is the application of a recursive parser to extract the frame-level features elaborated above using the skeletal data from Kinect. Note that there are other functions that extract multimodal cues from the other modalities as well, and these would also be available as part of the toolkit. Of those, Praat [5] can be used to determine the prosody of the speech given during the presentation, while FAVE [31] can be used to align the phones and words if an audio transcription is available. Video-based facial emotion extraction is an optional function which relies on the outputs generated by FACET[9], a state-of-the-art computer-based automated emotion recognition toolkit that requires separate licensing. A more elaborate explanation of the motivation for including these multimodal cues can be found in [11]. Finally, all feature contours from the different modalities are normalized to be range-bound for optimal display in Anvil. Standardization of codecs formatting for video and audio is performed to comply with visualization specifications. Note that, in addition to the purposes of visualization, the time-series data from each modality can also be saved to persistent storage for the purposes of further analysis and model training.

As mentioned, we used Anvil[10] as our visualization module. Originally developed as a gesture research tool, Anvil is now widely used as a video annotation toolkit in Human-Computer Interaction, Linguistics, Ethology, Anthropology, Psychotherapy, Embodied Agents, Computer Animation and

[7]When a body part listed in our BVH motion tracking result is missing from [27], we selected the normalized mass weight of the closest body part as its replacement e.g. pelvis weight is used for hips, abdomen weight is used for spine.

[8]https://github.com/EducationalTestingService/VAMP

[9]http://emotient.com/

[10]http://www.anvil-software.org/

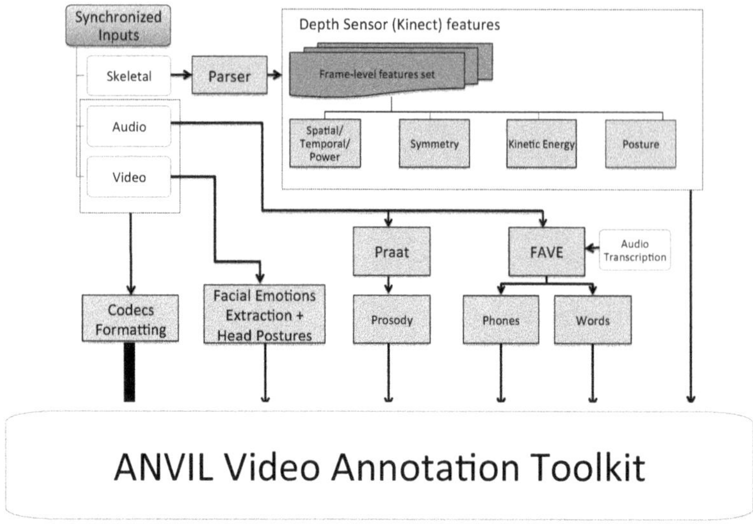

Figure 4: Figure showing the VAMP flowchart and its visualization in Anvil. Besides the high-level Kinect features, note that it is possible to generate additional contours for other modalities. Here, we show that emotion expression output computed using FACET can be visualized together with the Kinect features. Additionally, given transcriptions, it is possible to use FAVE to perform force-alignment of phones to words.

many other fields. It provides annotations that are accurately aligned with the various input modalities e.g. video, audio and skeletal. Additionally, the annotations are color-coded and hierarchically defined, and are fully customizable using the XML markup language. By visualizing the time-series data in one place, researchers can perform observation and garner intuition and evidence about the potential usefulness of certain features or feature types for building assessment or learning models. Furthermore, interesting event markers can be annotated for further discussion and analysis.

5.2 Motion-based Body Features Applied to Public Speaking Assessment

The motion-based body features have previously been used in research and have been found to be valuable for representing body language behaviors. Using our 2013 multimodal presentation corpus (containing 56 completed sessions with all data streams), we applied a well-established human rating rubric [33] to fully double-score all presentations. Due to the surprisingly low inter-rater reliability found on our corpus, we ended up using the adjudicated scores (denoted as final score), which are holistic judgments by human raters, determined by a range of presentation performance aspects, e.g., word choice, verbal expression, and also nonverbal communication. The low inter-rater reliability is probably due to the subjective nature of the scoring process itself, hence the adjudicated score is a more reliable metric for measuring presentation performance.

The adjudication process is described as follows: All presentations were double-scored by two raters using a score-scale from 1 to 4. In the cases in which the two scores differed by more than 1 point, a third scorer was called in to adjudicate. The final "operational" score is the average of all scores assigned to a given dimension in the scoring rubric for a given presenter. Consequently, a psychometric analysis of the human scores was published in [19], but is not included here since it is not the focus of this paper[11].

A correlation study has been done on the extracted Kinect data with final holistic scores that reflect overall presentation performance. Table 2 reports some representative correlations between the features extracted and the non-verbal behavior score, as well as the holistic score. $|r|$ values of more than 0.4 are regarded as significant. We find that the features we proposed and computed by using the toolkit show considerable indicative abilities for predicting overall performance. For example, a large standard deviation in hands-spine displacement and bounding volume is positively correlated to the non-verbal behavioral score. This probably indicates that the appropriate use of hands (e.g. gesturing) and body parts extension (e.g. a form of embracing) are indicative of a non-verbal behavioral style that is appealing to the audience. Despite these promising results, note that this study was based on quite a small data set ($n = 56$), and a larger dataset is needed for further validation.

These Kinect body-based, high-level features were used in a machine learning experiment for building an automatic prediction model to evaluate a presentation based on multimodal input features. In this study, a set of linguistic and speech related features were extracted from the audio streams and their corresponding transcriptions. From the visual channel, these Kinect features were used for representing body language. Furthermore, extra visual features from head orientation, gaze tracking, and facial expressions were considered as well. The visual features (including Kinect features) were found to provide supplementary support for the presentation evaluation task. More on the experimental details can be found in [11].

[11]Low to medium reliability between human raters was observed. For example, intraclass correlation coefficients (ICCs) on several key items and holistic scores are: 0.60 (Vocal expression), 0.41 (Nonverbal behavior), 0.39 (holistic score)

Feature	Type	r_{NVB}	$r_{Holistic}$
SD hands-spine-disp	Spatial	0.405	0.376
mean hands-spine-disp-1dv	Temporal	−0.292	−0.322
mean arms-spine-disp-2dv	Power	−0.429	−0.635
lg SD bounding-volume	Posture	0.499	0.354
mean kinetic-energy	Kinetic Energy	−0.315	−0.426
symm3d.mean	Symmetry	0.220	0.250

Table 2: Table showing the Pearson correlation of a few representative Kinect-based motion features to two types of human-rated scores. Note: *NVB* denotes for Non-Verbal behavior score while *Holistic* denotes overall holistic scores.

6. CONCLUSION

Multimodal learning analytics is a growing multi-disciplinary research area that leverages expertise from education, computer vision, natural language processing, linguistics, cognitive science and psychology. Expanding beyond the usage of standard sensing equipment such as video and audio, we proposed the exploitation of depth sensors for extracting construct-relevant features for modeling assessment tasks. Specifically, in this paper, we focused on the use of Microsoft Kinect to obtain motion-based, low-level data and transform them into higher-level features for measuring public speaking skills proficiency. We show how Kinect can be integrated into existing integrative recording platforms for performing data collection via two case studies, and provide technical details in those studies. The preliminary assessment of scoring models that were based on the Kinect's depth sensing capabilities and built in a machine learning framework provides promising results. While there is relevant work in the literature addressing the use of depth sensors for multimodal learning analytics, few efforts have been expended to standardize algorithms and protocols for performing learning or assessment tasks, probably due to the exploratory nature of this line of work. We aspire to create a standard toolkit that allows data transformation, feature extraction and data visualization on the most commonly used input sensor modalities for research purposes, and we hope that this contribution streamlines efforts in the MLA research community. In the future, we also hope to pursue research in other learning analytics scenarios utilizing other low-cost, commodity depth sensors, such as portable learning assessments or virtual reality applications for learning simulations. Finally, given the absence of sensors in everyday, non-experimental learning scenarios, we hope to pursue another interesting research direction that involves detailed analysis of whether their presence would have effects over the validity of the predictions of the two speaking tasks.

7. REFERENCES

[1] M. W. Alibali and M. J. Nathan. Embodiment in mathematics teaching and learning: Evidence from learners' and teachers' gestures. *Journal of the Learning Sciences*, 21(2):247–286, 2012.

[2] T. Baltrušaitis, P. Robinson, and L.-P. Morency. 3d constrained local model for rigid and non-rigid facial tracking. In *Computer Vision and Pattern Recognition (CVPR), 2012 IEEE Conference on*, pages 2610–2617. IEEE, 2012.

[3] R. Barmaki and C. E. Hughes. A case study to track teacher gestures and performance in a virtual learning environment. In *Proceedings of the Fifth International Conference on Learning Analytics And Knowledge*, pages 420–421. ACM, 2015.

[4] R. L. Birdwhistell. *Kinesics and context: Essays on body motion communication.* University of Pennsylvania press, 2010.

[5] P. Boersma and D. Weenink. Praat, a system for doing phonetics by computer. 2001.

[6] T. Breuer, C. Bodensteiner, and M. Arens. Low-cost commodity depth sensor comparison and accuracy analysis. In *SPIE Security+ Defence*, pages 92500G–92500G. International Society for Optics and Photonics, 2014.

[7] C. Caswell and S. Neill. *Body language for competent teachers.* Routledge, 2003.

[8] Y.-J. Chang, S.-F. Chen, and J.-D. Huang. A kinect-based system for physical rehabilitation: A pilot study for young adults with motor disabilities. *Research in developmental disabilities*, 32(6):2566–2570, 2011.

[9] L. Chen, G. Feng, J. Joe, C. W. Leong, C. Kitchen, and C. M. Lee. Towards automated assessment of public speaking skills using multimodal cues. In *Proceedings of the 16th International Conference on Multimodal Interaction*, pages 200–203. ACM, 2014.

[10] L. Chen, C. W. Leong, G. Feng, and C. M. Lee. Using multimodal cues to analyze mla'14 oral presentation quality corpus: Presentation delivery and slides quality. In *Proceedings of the 2014 ACM workshop on Multimodal Learning Analytics Workshop and Grand Challenge*, pages 45–52. ACM, 2014.

[11] L. Chen, C. W. Leong, G. Feng, C. M. Lee, and S. Somasundaran. Utilizing multimodal cues to automatically evaluate public speaking performance. In *Affective Computing and Intelligent Interaction*, 2015.

[12] M. Draelos, Q. Qiu, A. Bronstein, and G. Sapiro. Intel realsense = real low cost gaze. In *Proceedings of the International Conference on Image Processing.* IEEE, 2015.

[13] V. Echeverría, A. Avendaño, K. Chiluiza, A. Vásquez, and X. Ochoa. Presentation skills estimation based on video and kinect data analysis. In *Proceedings of the 2014 ACM workshop on Multimodal Learning Analytics Workshop and Grand Challenge*, pages 53–60. ACM, 2014.

[14] D. Glowinski, N. Dael, A. Camurri, G. Volpe, M. Mortillaro, and K. Scherer. Toward a minimal representation of affective gestures. *Affective*

Computing, IEEE Transactions on, 2(2):106–118, 2011.

[15] J. Grafsgaard, J. B. Wiggins, K. E. Boyer, E. N. Wiebe, and J. Lester. Automatically recognizing facial expression: Predicting engagement and frustration. In *Educational Data Mining 2013*, 2013.

[16] J. Guna, G. Jakus, M. Pogačnik, S. Tomažič, and J. Sodnik. An analysis of the precision and reliability of the leap motion sensor and its suitability for static and dynamic tracking. *Sensors*, 14(2):3702–3720, 2014.

[17] J. Han, L. Shao, D. Xu, and J. Shotton. Enhanced computer vision with microsoft kinect sensor: A review. *Cybernetics, IEEE Transactions on*, 43(5):1318–1334, 2013.

[18] A. Hartholt, D. Traum, S. C. Marsella, A. Shapiro, G. Stratou, A. Leuski, L.-P. Morency, and J. Gratch. All together now. In *Intelligent Virtual Agents*, pages 368–381. Springer, 2013.

[19] J. Joe, C. Kitchen, L. Chen, and G. Feng. A prototype public speaking skills assessment: An evaluation of human scoring quality. *ETS Research Report*, in press.

[20] K. Khoshelham and S. O. Elberink. Accuracy and resolution of kinect depth data for indoor mapping applications. *Sensors*, 12(2):1437–1454, 2012.

[21] M. Kipp. Annotation facilities for the reliable analysis of human motion. In *LREC*, pages 4103–4107, 2012.

[22] P. C. Kyllonen. Measurement of 21st century skills within the common core state standards. In *Invitational Research Symposium on Technology Enhanced Assessments. May*, pages 7–8, 2012.

[23] P. W. Miller. Body language in the classroom. *Techniques: Connecting Education and Careers*, 80(8):28–30, 2005.

[24] S. P. Morreale, M. R. Moore, D. Surges-Tatum, and L. Webster. *"The competent speaker" speech evaluation form (2nd ed.)*. National Communication Association, 2007.

[25] M. Nebeling, D. Ott, and M. C. Norrie. Kinect analysis: A system for recording, analysing and sharing multimodal interaction elicitation studies. In *Proceedings of the 7th SIGCHI Symposium on Engineering Interactive Computing Systems*. ACM, 2015.

[26] R. Niewiadomski, M. Mancini, and S. Piana. Human and virtual agent expressive gesture quality analysis and synthesis. *Coverbal Synchrony in Human-Machine Interaction*, pages 269–292, 2013.

[27] S. Plagenhoef, F. G. Evans, and T. Abdelnour. Anatomical data for analyzing human motion. *Research quarterly for exercise and sport*, 54(2):169–178, 1983.

[28] A. Porter, J. McMaken, J. Hwang, and R. Yang. Common core standards the new us intended curriculum. *Educational Researcher*, 40(3):103–116, 2011.

[29] R. L. Quianthy. *Communication is life: Essential college sophomore speaking and listening competencies*. Speech Communication Association, 1990.

[30] M. Raca and P. Dillenbourg. Holistic analysis of the classroom. In *Proceedings of the 2014 ACM workshop on Multimodal Learning Analytics Workshop and Grand Challenge*, pages 13–20. ACM, 2014.

[31] I. Rosenfelder, J. Fruehwald, K. Evanini, and J. Yuan. Fave (forced alignment and vowel extraction) program suite. *U RL http://fave. ling. upenn. edu*, 2011.

[32] L. M. Schreiber, G. D. Paul, and L. R. Shibley. The development and test of the public speaking competence rubric. *Communication Education*, 61(3):205–233, 2012.

[33] L. M. Schreiber, G. D. Paul, and L. R. Shibley. The development and test of the public speaking competence rubric. *Communication Education*, 61(3):205–233, 2012.

[34] E. Suma, B. Lange, A. S. Rizzo, D. M. Krum, M. Bolas, et al. Faast: The flexible action and articulated skeleton toolkit. In *Virtual Reality Conference (VR), 2011 IEEE*, pages 247–248. IEEE, 2011.

[35] H. Vasquez, L. E. Sucar, and H. J. Escalante. Simultaneous segmentation and recognition of gestures for human-machine interaction. In *Workshop on Ubiquitous Data Mining, IJCAI*, page 29, 2013.

[36] J. Wagner, F. Lingenfelser, T. Baur, I. Damian, F. Kistler, and E. André. The social signal interpretation (ssi) framework: multimodal signal processing and recognition in real-time. In *Proceedings of the 21st ACM international conference on Multimedia*, pages 831–834. ACM, 2013.

[37] D. Webster and O. Celik. Systematic review of kinect applications in elderly care and stroke rehabilitation. *J. Neuroeng. Rehabil*, 11(1):108, 2014.

[38] M. Worsley and P. Blikstein. Towards the development of multimodal action based assessment. In *Proceedings of the third international conference on learning analytics and knowledge*, pages 94–101. ACM, 2013.

[39] Z. Zhang. Microsoft kinect sensor and its effect. *MultiMedia, IEEE*, 19(2):4–10, 2012.

Multimodal Capture of Teacher-Student Interactions for Automated Dialogic Analysis in Live Classrooms

Sidney K. D'Mello[1], Andrew M. Olney[2], Nathan Blanchard[1], Xiaoyi Sun[3], Brooke Ward[3], Borhan Samei[2], and Sean Kelly[4]
[1]University of Notre Dame; [2]University of Memphis
[3]University of Wisconsin, Madison; [4]University of Pittsburgh
118 Haggar Hall, Notre Dame, IN, 46556, USA
sdmello@nd.edu

ABSTRACT
We focus on data collection designs for the automated analysis of teacher-student interactions in live classrooms with the goal of identifying instructional activities (e.g., lecturing, discussion) and assessing the quality of dialogic instruction (e.g., analysis of questions). Our designs were motivated by multiple technical requirements and constraints. Most importantly, teachers could be individually mic'ed but their audio needed to be of excellent quality for automatic speech recognition (ASR) and spoken utterance segmentation. Individual students could not be mic'ed but classroom audio quality only needed to be sufficient to detect student spoken utterances. Visual information could only be recorded if students could not be identified. Design 1 used an omnidirectional laptop microphone to record both teacher and classroom audio and was quickly deemed unsuitable. In Designs 2 and 3, teachers wore a wireless Samson AirLine 77 vocal headset system, which is a unidirectional microphone with a cardioid pickup pattern. In Design 2, classroom audio was recorded with dual first-generation Microsoft Kinects placed at the front corners of the class. Design 3 used a Crown PZM-30D pressure zone microphone mounted on the blackboard to record classroom audio. Designs 2 and 3 were tested by recording audio in 38 live middle school classrooms from six U.S. schools while trained human coders simultaneously performed live coding of classroom discourse. Qualitative and quantitative analyses revealed that Design 3 was suitable for three of our core tasks: (1) ASR on teacher speech (word recognition rate of 66% and word overlap rate of 69% using Google Speech ASR engine); (2) teacher utterance segmentation (F-measure of 97%); and (3) student utterance segmentation (F-measure of 66%). Ideas to incorporate video and skeletal tracking with dual second-generation Kinects to produce Design 4 are discussed.

Categories and Subject Descriptors
I.2.7 [Artificial Intelligence]: Natural Language Processing – *discourse, Speech recognition and synthesis, text analysis.*

General Terms
Algorithms, Experimentation, Human Factors.

ICMI 2015, November 9–13, 2015, Seattle, WA, USA.
© 2015 ACM. ISBN 978-1-4503-3912-4/15/11…$15.00.
DOI: http://dx.doi.org/10.1145/2818346.2830602

Keywords
Multimodal; classroom discourse; dialogic instruction

1. INTRODUCTION
A particular style of classroom discourse, known as dialogic instruction, has been found to be a powerful predictor of student achievement in middle and high-school English Language Arts and Social Studies classrooms [22-24]. Dialogic instruction focuses on the free exchange of ideas and open-ended discussion between teachers and students with the goals of provoking deeper student thought and analysis and more evenly distributing effort among students. The resultant increase in critical thinking and student engagement [13] are the mechanisms by which dialogic instruction leads to improved achievement [8].

In the first major quantitative study of dialogic instruction, Nystrand and colleagues [22] coded discourse practices involving thousands of eighth- and ninth-grade students in a diverse sample of hundreds of English Language Arts classes. Their coding scheme consisted of three key 'tracks,' of increasingly fine granularity: 1) *episodes*, which refer to the activity/topic being addressed in class (e.g., the civil war); 2) *segments*, which represent possible instructional activities used within the episode; (e.g., lecturing, discussion, group work) and 3) *questions* asked by teachers or students embedded within segments. When controlling for gender, race, ethnicity, socioeconomic status, grade level, and prior achievement in writing and reading, they found that dialogically organized instruction (indicated by the following three items) had positive effects on reading comprehension (including both recall and depth of understanding as well as response to aesthetic aspects of literature):

- *Discussion*: Open exchange of ideas among at least three participants lasting longer than 30 seconds;
- *Authentic teacher questions*: Open-ended questions without a pre-scripted answer rather than known-answer test questions; and
- *Uptake*: Speaker's incorporation of a previous answer into a subsequent question (e.g., follow up question – "what did you mean by that")

These results were replicated by Applebee, et al. [2] in a 1-year study of 974 students in 64 middle and high school English classrooms in 19 schools across 5 states. This body of research has also demonstrated that the quality of dialogic instruction can also be enhanced with teacher training programs, suggesting that dialogic instruction can be formatively assessed (by classroom observations) and improved via teacher professional development programs.

Unfortunately, the research is difficult to scale and put into practice because dialogic instruction must be manually coded by trained observers. Even with performance support tools developed by Nystrand and colleagues, including live coding CLASS 4.24

software [21], it still requires approximately 4 hours of coding time per 1 hour of classroom observation. This is an unsustainable task for scalable research and for providing day-to-day feedback for teacher professional development.

To address this key limitation, the present project (CLASS 5) is focused on automatically analyzing classroom discourse as a means of providing feedback to researchers, teachers, teacher educators, and professional development personnel. Our approach uses automatic speech recognition (ASR), natural language understanding, and machine learning, which requires collection of large volumes of data in authentic classroom settings. This poses a number of technical and logistical challenges. The purpose of this paper is to describe our data collection designs and corresponding analyses techniques to meet these challenges.

Our initial designs and experiments focus on recording multiple streams of audio in live classrooms. We emphasized audio in this initial stage of work due to the intended application and because audio is an important component modality for multimodal interactions. Once a satisfactory audio recording solution has been developed, we extend the basic designs to incorporate visual information.

In the remainder of this section, we discuss the technical requirements and constraints that motivated our design, briefly consider related work in this area, followed by an overview of our approach.

1.1 Technical Requirements and Constraints

Our design is guided by the following technical requirements and constraints:

1. *Usability*: The system is intended for use by researchers, teachers, teacher educators, and professional development personnel. These individuals might have limited technical proficiency, so no advanced technical skills should be required.
2. *Economic Cost*: Equipment cost should be between ($500 to $1,000) so that the average school can afford the system.
3. *Human Cost*: The system should run autonomously after a brief (<5 minute) setup period. No human monitoring should be necessary during data collection.
4. *Scalability*: The system should be suitable for average public classrooms in the U.S., where class sizes are an average of 21.2 students and 26.8 students for public elementary and secondary schools, respectively [20].
5. *Flexibility*: The design should accommodate common classroom designs including traditional lecture (teacher up front with students seated in rows), small group work (students sitting around tables with teacher walking around), and designs promoting discussion (students sitting around a circle/oval with teacher on the perimeter).
6. *Non-intrusiveness*: The design should be minimally intrusive in that normal classroom instruction should not be interrupted.
7. *Visual information*: Video is desirable but not required. Further, due to privacy concerns, video data must either be processed in real time so the actual images are discarded or transformed into a non-personally-identifiable form.
8. *Audio information*: The teacher can be mic'ed but students cannot be individually mic'ed.
9. *Teacher audio quality*: High quality teacher audio is required. Teacher quality should be sufficiently high for teacher utterance segmentation and ASR.
10. *Student audio quality*: Student audio quality should be sufficient for detection of student speech. ASR on student audio is desired but not required.
11. *Stream synchronization*: Audio (and potentially video) data streams need to be synchronized with millisecond accuracy. These data streams need to be synchronized with the live coding that occurs in the classrooms within a 500 ms margin of error (during data collection for development of CLASS 5).
12. *Identity resolution*: Identity only needs to be resolved to the level of teacher vs. student(s), but not to individual students.

1.2 Related Work

There is a long research history on the use of audio (and video) to study instructional practices and student behaviors in live classrooms [1, 11] - most notably see [9]. However, the recorded signals are typically processed by humans; automatic analyses of classroom video and audio are few and far between. Thus, the literature did not provide much guidance on how to instrument a live classroom in order to collect data of sufficient quality for automated analysis.

The closest related work is research by Wang, et al. [30], who recorded classroom audio in 1st to 3rd grade math classes with the goal of automatically analyzing instructional segments in order to boost the level of discussion in these classes. Their data collection design consisted of 11 teachers wearing the LENA (Language Environment Analysis [7]) recorder (a small nonintrusive device) while teaching mathematics classes. LENA is a wearable system which records and measures surface-level aspects of language produced by and directed at very young children. The LENA propriety software uses differences in volume and pitch in order to assess when teachers were speaking, students were speaking, speech was overlapping, or there was silence.

Wang, et al. [30] report impressive accuracy rates ranging from 0.95 to 0.99 for teacher utterance segmentation. However, accuracy rates for student speech segmentation were lower due to the system misclassifying student speech as teacher speech. They attribute this to small differences in pitch between teachers and elementary school students since LENA was optimized to differentiate between caregivers and very young children. In particular, LENA was designed to analyze speech produced by children between 2-48 months in age [7], but was applied for a much older age group (1st to 3rd graders) in the Wang study. To address this, they adapted the underlying algorithm, which resulted in improved student speech segmentation accuracy rates ranging from 0.70 to 0.86.

The Wang, et al. [30] study is pioneering in a number of ways. Their approach satisfies the following subset of our technical requirements and constraints: usability, human cost, scalability, non-intrusiveness, audio information, student audio quality, and identity resolution. It is agnostic with respect to visual information and stream synchronization. Adherence to the flexibility requirement is unknown. Their approach is somewhat limited in terms of economic cost because it requires customized commercial hardware and software that can be quite expensive (>>$1,000) [14]. However, the most critical concern pertains to the suitability of the teacher audio quality for ASR. Wang, et al. [30] are agnostic to this issue because they are mainly concerned with a coarse-grained analysis of instructional activities (i.e., lecturing, discussion, and group work), which can be achieved by modeling teacher-student turn-taking dynamics in a content-free manner [31]. Consequently, they do not report any ASR results. However, in addition to classifying instructional activities, our analysis of dialogic instruction requires identification of questions and classification of questions with respect to authenticity and uptake. The content of teacher speech is needed for this fine-grained level of analysis [12, 27], which is why the Wang approach is unsuitable for our project.

1.3 Proposed Approach

Our core approach emphasizes recording high-quality teacher audio given that the intended application is teacher professional development and that teachers can be individually mic'ed. Further, given that students could not be individually mic'ed, our design focused on simply identifying when students are speaking rather than identifying what they are saying. We expect that certain features of dialogic instruction can be revealed by the sequence of speakers. In particular, we believe that lecturing is more likely to have a pattern of *teacher-teacher-teacher-student* compared to question-answer segments (*teacher-student-teacher-student*). Even within question-answer segments, test recitation might have a pattern similar to *teacher-student-teacher-student*, but an authentic discussion is more likely to have a pattern encompassing transitions between students (i.e., *teacher-student-student-student-teacher)*. We also expect that the duration of student responses is another critical index of question properties in that short student responses should mark test questions whereas elaborated responses are more likely to index authentic teacher questions. Thus, our design is intended to optimize teacher audio as the primary channel. Classroom audio (and subsequently video) is considered to be a secondary channel that is primarily used to contextualize the teacher audio channel.

We identify the following three core analytic tasks motivated by our core approach. By core analytic tasks, we mean that outputs of these fundamental tasks are intended to serve as inputs towards the overall goal of automatically analyzing dialogic instruction as defined above. The three core tasks include:

- *Teacher automatic speech recognition*: Obtain text transcriptions of teacher speech.
- *Teacher utterance segmentation*: Obtain start and end times of teacher spoken utterances.
- *Student utterance segmentation*: Obtain start and end times of student spoken utterances without attempting to identify individual students.

In this paper, we discuss our approach to instrumenting the classroom for data collection suitable for automatic analysis of classroom discourse and report results pertaining to our three core tasks. Although our approach was designed for a specific application (CLASS 5), it should be beneficial for researchers interested in automatic analysis of teacher-focused classroom discourse more broadly.

The remainder of the paper is organized as follows. We discuss the three recording designs that were developed (Section 2) and used to collect data from 38 live classrooms over a two year period (Section 3). The data was analyzed with respect to the three primary tasks of automatic recognition of teacher speech, teacher speech segmentation, and student speech segmentation (Section 4). Plans for incorporating visual information into the design to produce a fourth design are discussed in Section 5.

2. RECORDING DESIGNS

We experimented with a variety of recording designs in order to satisfy the aforementioned requirements and constraints. These include omnidirectional laptop microphones, phase microphone arrays, headset microphones, and pressure-zone-microphones (PZM). We simulated classroom environments in the lab as well as collected classroom data in authentic field environments in order to evaluate these designs. These tests can be organized with respect to three recording designs as discussed below.

2.1 Design 1

2.1.1 *Omnidirectional Microphone*

We did not believe that basic omnidirectional microphones would be sufficient to record audio of sufficient quality for teacher speech recognition. Nevertheless, we collected a few sessions of classroom audio data with an omnidirectional microphone (built into a laptop) to make sure that we were correct. This was an important option to exclude because omnidirectional microphones on commodity laptops, tablets, and smartphones, if they could work, would allow us to disseminate CLASS5 on these platforms without special hardware. Qualitative evaluations conclusively revealed that this was not the case. Further, ASR using Sphinx 4 [29] and Microsoft Speech SDK 5.1 [19] on teacher speech recorded via an omnidirectional laptop mic produced gibberish. Thus, we determined that special microphone hardware was required to record adequate audio, leading us to Designs 2 and 3.

2.2 Design 2

Design 2 utilized a specialized headset microphone for teacher speech and two first-generation Kinect to record classroom audio consisting of both student and teacher speech. These devices are shown in Figure 1.

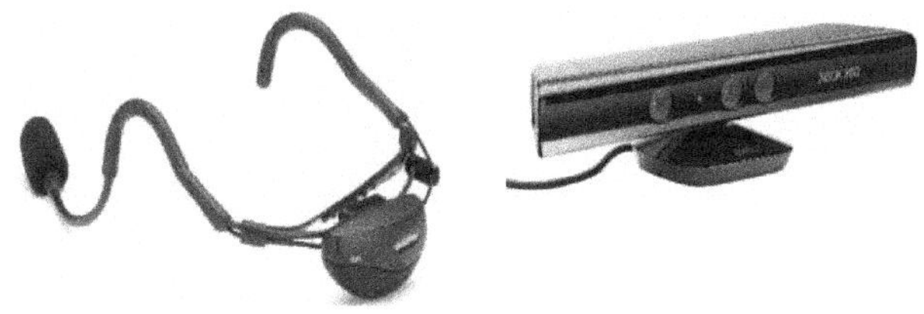

Samson 77 Airline Microphone (Teacher audio) | First- generation Kinect (Classroom audio)

Figure 1: Devices in Design 1

2.2.1 *Samson Airline Microphone (Teacher Audio)*

We selected the Samson 77 Airline microphone system (AH1 Headset Transmitter with CR77 Wireless Receiver), a wireless microphone that is also marketed for aerobics instructors. We performed qualitative evaluations using pre-recorded classroom audio as background noise. These informal analyses revealed that the noise cancellation properties of the Samson were sufficient to overcome classroom background noise even when that noise was played at 2x real levels.

2.2.2 *First-generation Kinects (Classroom Audio)*

Our design consists of two first-generation Kinect microphone arrays placed in the front corners of the classroom for recording of classroom audio (see Figure 2). Preliminary qualitative testing revealed that Kinect microphones, which are among the least expensive on the market, easily match the quality of the Acoustic Magic Voice Tracker™ array microphone. In addition to recording audio, we can also record positional information using the Kinects. More specifically, each Kinect calculates a "beam" using the difference between the arrival of sound to its microphone elements. The beam indicates the direction of the current sound. By calculating the intersection of the Kinect microphone array beams, i.e., triangulation, we can localize the sound (see Figure 3) within a 3-foot area. We hypothesize that location can serve as a proxy for identity, because students generally stay in the same seats in a given class.

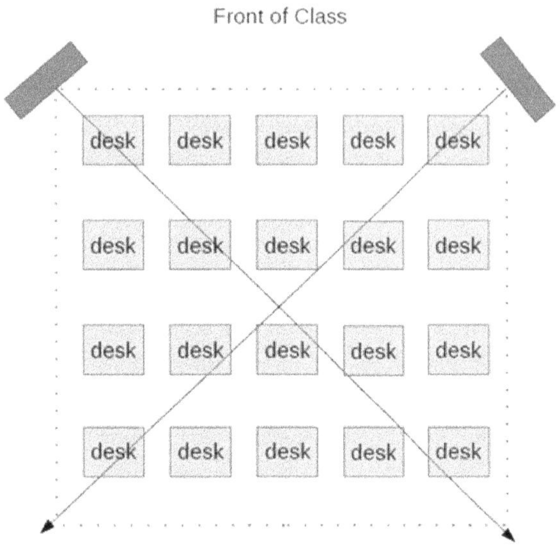

Figure 2. Kinects (shown in red) are aligned to form a coordinate plane, rotated 45 degrees

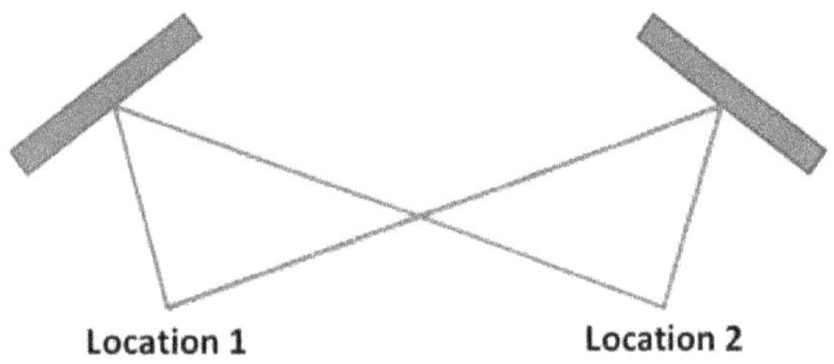

Figure 3. An example of triangulation. At any one time, the red (right) and blue (left) Kinects have a preferred direction, or beam, indicated by the colored lines. When these lines converge, they identify a unique location via triangulation.

2.2.3 *Synchronizing Streams*

Using the Microsoft Kinect SDK, we created a multithreaded software recording application that synchronized the Kinect streams and teacher audio stream. Each Kinect stream consisted of waveform audio data (i.e., wav files) and Kinect beam data (angle, timestamp, and confidence) whereas the teacher stream consisted of audio data only. All three streams were synchronized on a single laptop with dual USB hubs, which is required when simultaneously recording from two Kinects. Each Kinect performed analog/digital conversion internally. The teacher mic was interfaced using an integrated analog/digital converting XLR to USB cable. The cable utilized stock Windows 7 plug and play drivers. The synchronization software did not have the facility to adjust audio levels, so the automatic gain control (AGC) feature from Windows 7 was used to dynamically adjust volume of the teacher mic.

Synchronization of Kinect beam data was achieved with millisecond precision using hardware-defined timestamps. Specifically, each Kinect produced a sparse list of timestamps, and a dense (aligned) list of pairs was created by filling in each missing value with the preceding value in the respective series. This approach was necessary because the Kinects report beam changes rather than sampling at a fixed interval, and a sound source may change location with respect to the beam of one Kinect without changing its location with respect to the other Kinect. The accuracy and sensitivity of beam pairings was qualitatively verified by recording sound bursts at various locations in a room and matching these locations to the triangulated location derived from the paired beams.

The researchers (called coders), who were trained to perform live coding, started recording by clicking a button on the recording interface. A separate program (CLASS 4.24) was used for live coding of classroom discourse and ran on the same computer as the stream synchronization program. Thus, synchronizing the CLASS codes and data streams (waveforms, position info) simply involved automatic indexing of coded events within the data streams based on recorded start times of the streams (audio data) or time-stamped event data (live coding and position data).

2.2.4 *Evaluation of Design 2*

Design 2 was tested by collecting several months of audio in authentic classroom environments. We discuss a number of qualitative assessments here; more formal analyses are presented in Section 4.

- The noise cancellation properties of the Samson Airline Microphone were excellent. Therefore, we believe we have found a viable solution to the challenge of recording high-quality teacher speech in authentic classroom conditions.
- The plug-and-play nature of the recording setup, necessitated the use of automatic gain control (AGC). However, this was undesirable as AGC can reduce ASR accuracy by as much as 20% [16].
- Student voice quality recorded from the Kinects was short of what would be required for automatic utterance segmentation.
- The Kinects were wired, so this limited the optimal placement required for accurate sound source localization (see Figure 2). Also, teachers confounded the location information derived from the Kinects by moving about the classroom.
- The software-level synchronization was not perfect because the application was multithreaded. We observed a 0.5 to 2 second discrepancy in the lengths of the resulting audio files.

2.3 Design 3

The evaluation of the data collected with Design 2 provided evidence for the success of using the Samson 77 Airline microphone for recording audio from teachers. We also noted several limitations with the Kinect-based solution to recording classroom audio. Thus, a replacement microphone (a pressure-zone microphone or PZM-30D [6], Figure 4) was added to our classroom recording solution in order to improve classroom recording quality (combined teacher-student speech) without having to resort to mic'ing individual students (and violating a technical constraint).

2.3.1 *PZM-30D (Classroom microphone)*

A lab based study [5] was conducted to select a suitable classroom microphone for our needs. Several microphones (Perceptron 120, PZM-30D, PZM6D, SM58, Kinect, and Apple Laptop Mic) were tested in an empty classroom with variable conditions. These included either no-noise or high-noise conditions, variable microphone placement (flat on teacher's desk or propped up on chalkboard), and variable live speech (obtained by a speaker walking to four corners of a classroom's student seating area and speaking from each corner). We also evaluated an omnidirectional non-boundary microphone which acted as a baseline for unacceptable speech quality since we had previously evaluated this style of microphone to record classroom audio (see Section 2.1).

The PZM-30D (see Figure 4) was selected as the best performing mic in these tests. PZMs or pressure zone microphones are omnidirectional boundary microphones that are placed on large surfaces (e.g., a table, wall) and minimize interference from surface reflections. They are designed to record rooms of speech or music while minimizing noise. The tests also indicated that the PZM-30D worked best when placed upright. Typically this included leaning the microphone against a chalkboard, though it can also be placed upright on the teacher's desk or anywhere in the front of the room. Qualitative tests with parallel devices placed on the side walls and floors of an authentic classroom were also conducted, with no notable performance improvements. This is particularly advantageous since most classrooms have a chalkboard (or whiteboard) and a teacher's desk.

Crown PZM-30D (mounted on board) M-Audio M-Track

Figure 4: Additional devices in Design 3

2.3.2 Stream Synchronization

An audio interface device, an M-Audio M-Track (see Figure 4), was added to the classroom recording solution for stream synchronization. The M-Track has several benefits. First, the teachers' speech and the students' speech are aligned by making each a channel in a stereo recording. In other words the M-Track aligns the channels at the hardware level, rather than the software level, which ensures exact alignment of the two audio streams. This addressed the synchronization problem noted in Design 2. Second, the M-Track simplified the recording setup to a point where an open-source audio recording and editing software (Audacity) was sufficient for recording. Audacity's Timer Record feature, which allows one to specify an exact time to start recording, was used to synchronize the audio with the CLASS 4.24 coding software. Third, in lieu of automatic gain control (which is disabled in Design 3), each microphone has a volume adjustment that researchers/teachers can adjust dynamically to avoid clipping. The adjustment is done based on a live wavform (from Audacity – see Figure 5) being displayed during the first few minutes of the recordings.

2.3.3 Recording Case

Setup complexity was increased with the inclusion of the M-Track and the PZM-30D mic. Individuals needed to be able to switch classrooms between class sessions, which requires a full tear down and setup of audio equipment in a time period as short as five minutes. The solution was to build physical recording case which compactly contained all recording equipment, requiring only that a person place the case near an outlet, plug in a power cable, plug in a USB outlet into a computer, setup the teacher's headset mic, and place the PZM-30D microphone at the front of the classroom.

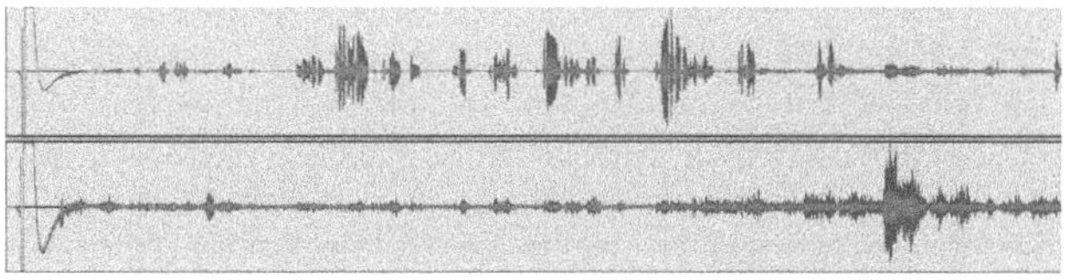

Figure 5. Teacher audio from Samson 77 Airline mic (top) and classroom audio from PZM-30 D mic (bottom)

2.3.4 Evaluation of Design 3

We collected several weeks of classroom audio from authentic classroom environment. Qualitative analyses suggested that the recording quality was acceptable and no major problems were identified. More formal analyses are discussed in Section 4.

3. DATA COLLECTION

We recorded more than 30 hours of data using the recording Designs 2 and 3. Data was collected in rural Wisconsin middle schools during literature, language arts, and civics classes. The audio streams were accompanied by human-coded observations according to the CLASS scheme using the CLASS 4.24 coding software (see Introduction for a description of the coding scheme). Table 1 provides a high-level overview of the two data sets.

Table 1. Overview of data sets collected using proposed recording designs

	Design 2	Design 3
District	District A	District B
# Schools	1	5
# Teachers	3	8
# Sessions	21	17
Hours of Data	15.6	16.7
Teacher audio mic	Samson 77 Airline	Samson 77 Airline
Class audio mic	Kinect	PZM-30D

4. DATA ANALYSIS

The overall goal of the project is to develop algorithms to replicate the human-coded CLASS codes with computer-generated codes. In this paper, we report results on three core analytic tasks that need to be addressed in order to achieve the foundational goal. These include: (1) teacher automatic speech recognition; (2) teacher utterance segmentation; and (3) student utterance segmentation. Preliminary results of (1) and (2) using teacher audio collected in Design 2 are reported in [3] and [4], respectively. Here, we increase the scope of the analyses by including teacher audio from Design 3, effectively doubling the sample size and introducing considerable more variability in terms of teachers and class sessions (see Table 1). Preliminary unpublished results on (3) obtained from data collected with Design 3 are presented here.

4.1 Automatic Recognition of Teacher Speech

Automatic speech recognition (ASR) is an important first step in recognizing questions and classifying question types from classroom audio because it enables the application of natural language understanding techniques. However, speech recognition remains a challenging research problem in noisy environments. To determine the suitability of existing ASR technologies for CLASS 5, we analyzed several out-of-the-box ASR engines that do not require training on speakers and do not require any domain-specific knowledge. We focus on questions asked by teachers because they are the most essential component of dialogic instruction (see Introduction). The goal of the analysis was to evaluate the feasibility of ASR on the current data and to identify which ASR engines are best suited for transcription of teacher speech in classrooms.

4.1.1 Method

We considered four ASR engines: Google Speech [28], Bing Speech [17], AT&T Watson [10], and Kaldi [25]. We also examined Sphinx 4 [29], Microsoft Speech SDK 5.1 [19], and RASR [32] at an early stage of this work, but these were quickly abandoned due to poor performance on our data (see [3] for details). Google Speech, Bing Speech, and AT&T Watson are query-oriented, cloud-based recognition systems primarily intended for web-queries on mobile devices (typically noisy conditions). Kaldi is a speech toolkit written in C++ and is intended for research purposes.

We processed the 1,118 questions recorded across the 38 class sessions by submitting them to each of the ASR engines. We then compared the transcriptions from the engines with human-transcriptions provided by the CLASS coders. Performance metrics were word accuracy (WAcc) and simple word overlap (SWO). WAcc is the complement of the standard ASR metric of word error rate (WER). (WAcc = 1 – WER). WER is calculated by dynamically aligning the ASR engine's hypothesized transcript with the human's transcript and dividing the number of substitutions, insertions, and deletions required to transform the transcript into the hypothesis by the number of words in the transcript. SWO is the number of words that appear in both the hypothesized transcript and the human's transcript divided by the total number of words in the human's transcript. WAcc preserves word order while SWO ignores it. WAcc is bounded on $[-\infty, 1]$ while SWO is bounded on $[0, 1]$. Higher numbers indicate better performance for both metrics.

4.1.2 Results

Table 2 presents descriptives on WAcc and SWO by ASR sorted in descending order of WAcc. This table was produced by first computing the mean WAcc or SWO for each teacher and then computing means and standard deviations across the 11 unique teachers in our sample. A repeated-measures ANOVA with teacher as the unit of analysis and ASR as a four-level factor yielded a significant main effect of ASR on WAcc, $F(3, 30) = 11.2$, $MSE = .013$, $p < .001$. Post-hoc tests indicated the following pattern of significance (at $p < .05$[1]) in the data: Google > Bing > [Kaldi = AT&T]. There was also a significant main effect of ASR on SWO, $F(3, 30) = 24.0$, $MSE = .004$, $p < .001$ with the following pattern in the data: [Google = Kaldi] > Bing > AT&T. Thus, Google Speech outperformed the other engines when word order was considered (WAcc metric), but tied with Kaldi when word order was ignored (SWO metric). Importantly, almost 70% of the words could be correctly recognized using Google Speech — no small feat given the noisy nature of the classroom environment and the conversational speaking style of the teachers.

[1] $p = .057$ the for Bing vs. Kaldi pairwise comparison.

Table 2. Mean speech recognition accuracy across questions (with standard deviations in parentheses)

ASR	Word Accuracy (WAcc)	Simple Word Overlap (SWO)
Google Speech	.655 (.081)	.690 (.075)
Bing Speech	.533 (.133)	.615 (.099)
Kaldi	.439 (.251)	.671 (.116)
AT&T Watson	.391 (.178)	.477 (.126)

We performed a follow-up analysis to study variability in WAcc and SWO as a function of teacher (coded as indicator variables representing each teacher) and speech characteristics (speech rate and verbosity of individual utterances). The analyses preceded by separately regressing WAcc and SWO on the three factors for each ASR engine. Table 3 shows the proportion of variance explained (i.e., Rsq.) in each model. We note that Google and Bing were largely robust to teacher identity and speech characteristics as they explained a mere 3% and 6% of the variability in ASR accuracy, respectively. In contrast, Kaldi and AT&T were severely affected by teacher identity and speech characteristics as these factors explained between 13% to 19% of the variability. Thus, we selected Google and Bing for further analysis as these ASRs were quite accurate and largely invariant to differences in teachers and speech characteristics.

Table 3. Proportion of variance explained (Rsq.)

ASR	Word Accuracy (WAcc)	Simple Word Overlap (SWO)
Google	.031	.028
Bing	.056	.053
Kaldi	.192	.130
AT&T Watson	.141	.126

4.2 Teacher Utterance Segmentation

The goal of this analysis was to convert the teacher audio stream into instances of teacher speech vs. no speech. We developed and validated an utterance detection method and applied it to the teacher audio recorded across the 38 class sessions (see Table 1).

4.2.1 Method

Teacher speech was recorded from a high-quality noise-canceling headset microphone. Thus, we assumed that most sound was voice and that preprocessing using advanced voice activity detection (i.e., detecting presence or absence of speech) or speaker diarization techniques (i.e., segmenting utterances in an audio stream by individual speakers) were not required[2]. Thus, a simple binary procedure was used for utterance detection. Specifically, the amplitude envelope of the teacher's low-pass filtered speech was passed through a threshold function in 20 millisecond increments. Where the amplitude envelope was above threshold, the teacher was considered to be speaking. Where the amplitude envelope was below threshold, the teacher was assumed to not be speaking. Any

[2] We also experimented with an off-the-shelf voice activity detection and speaker diarization algorithm [26] with comparable, if not slightly inferior, results.

time speech was detected, that speech was considered part of an utterance, meaning there was no minimum threshold for how short an utterance could be. Utterances were marked as complete when no speech was detected for 1000 milliseconds (1 second). An example result of this automatic utterance labeling method is depicted in Figure 6.

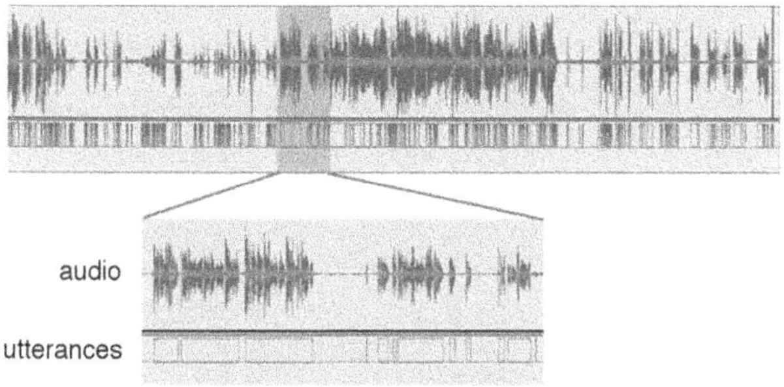

Figure 6. Example of teacher utterance segmentation. An approximately 45-minute class recording (top) with a small portion of the recording enlarged for a detailed view (bottom). The upper track visualizes the .wav form of the audio. The lower track visualizes detected utterances.

The speech delimiter and threshold were both set to be low to ensure all speech was detected, resulting in no known cases of missed speech. This process resulted in 17,298 utterances, which we call *candidate utterances*. An examination of a random subset of these candidate utterances indicated that there were a large number of false alarms. These were mainly attributed to aforementioned low threshold which made it difficult to discriminate background noise from speech. Common examples of background noise picked up by the microphone included voices of students who were being exceptionally loud, sounds from a film or audio clip being played in the classroom, and sounds of teachers' heavy breathing.

A two-step filtering approach was taken to eliminate the false alarms. First, candidate utterances less than 125 milliseconds in length (12% in all) were deemed to be too short to contain meaningful speech and were eliminated. Second, the remaining candidate utterances were submitted through an automatic speech recognizer (Bing Speech) in an effort to identify the false alarms. Bing was selected because it was one of our top performing ASR engines; the other top ASR engine, Google, is also being considered. Bing returns a recognition result and a confidence score for the transcribed utterance. Instances where Bing rejected the utterance or where it returned no transcribed text were considered to be false alarms. After eliminating the false alarms, we were left with a total of 10,426 utterances (60% of the 17,298 candidate utterances).

4.2.2 Validation

A study was conducted to evaluate the aforementioned teacher utterance detection method. A random sample of 1,000 candidate utterances was selected and manually annotated for speech/non-speech. Speech was defined to include all articulations (i.e., "um", "hm", "sh", etc.) in addition to normal spoken segments. Candidate utterances which included noise (i.e., loud students) in addition to teacher speech, were deemed as valid utterances since they contained teacher speech. In total, 59% of the candidate utterances were classified as containing teacher speech, indicating a false alarm rate of 41% prior to discarding utterances based on our filtering method.

Table 4 presents the confusion matrix obtained after the two-step filtering process on the sample of 1,000 candidate utterances. The filtering approach was highly successful, resulting in a kappa of 0.94 (agreement between computer-segmented teacher utterances and human-coded teacher utterances). Precision (96.3%) and recall (98.6%) were excellent, resulting in an F-measure of 97.4%. Thus, the present method was deemed to be sufficiently accurate for automatic teacher utterance segmentation.

Table 4. Confusion matrix for teacher utterance segmentation

	Predicted	
Actual	*Speech*	*Non-Speech*
Speech	0.963 (hit)	0.037 (false alarm)
Non-Speech	0.020 (miss)	0.980 (correct rejection)

4.3 Student Utterance Segmentation

The primary goal of student utterance segmentation is to identify student utterances from the classroom audio stream. Although high-quality speech recognition of student utterances would be ideal, our working hypothesis is that identification of student utterances and their surface properties, like duration, may be useful for dialogic question classification even when audio quality, and thus speech recognition, is poor (see Introduction). Moreover since the query-oriented ASR systems described in Section 4.1 require short duration inputs, student utterance segmentation is a necessary preprocessing step.

4.3.1 Method

The key challenge in student utterance segmentation is that the PZM channel records all classroom audio. Because the PZM mic is placed in the front of the class, the teacher's speech signal is as strong, or stronger, than the student signal. In contrast, the teacher headset microphone, due to its directional properties, proximity to the teacher's mouth, and filtering capabilities, produces a teacher speech signal that is substantially stronger than students' speech (see Figure 5). For these reasons, the relatively simple amplitude envelope followed by our two-step filtering approach used for teacher utterance segmentation (see Section 4.2.1) is unlikely to be applicable for student speech segmentation; qualitative tests quickly confirmed this suspicion.

To address this issue, we developed an alternative approach for student speech segmentation. This approach has two steps. First, we used an off-the-shelf diarizer - the LIUM diarizer [26] - to generate *candidate student segments*. The LIUM diarizer is an open source diarization system created for broadcast news. It performs diarization by extracting acoustic features, segmenting, and clustering, typically in a pipeline with interleaving and clustering stages. LIUM can perform gender identification, speaker identification, and speech/non-speech identification. However, the classroom audio under discussion is sufficiently noisy that only speech/non-speech discrimination appears to be feasible.

Our initial investigations revealed that LIUM critically depends on a few manually set parameters for minimum speech and silence lengths along with transition probability parameters for speech/music/silence segmentation. The parameters influence both the size of resulting segments and the filtration of noisy segments, such that poor parameter choices can either group multiple utterances together and filter away smaller segments or fragment single utterances into many small segments and fail to filter small segments (a classic precision/recall tradeoff). Fortunately, preliminary analyses revealed that the internal parameters, once set for a particular recording context, appeared to be fairly stable for other recordings in that context. However, this does need to be verified with more systematic analyses.

As mentioned, the resulting candidate segments from LIUM contain both teacher and student utterances, since the PZM records the entire classroom. Thus, the second step involved using the high-fidelity teacher segments to filter teacher segments from the candidate segments (student + teacher) returned by LIUM. The primary assumption of our filtering approach is that overlapping speech between teacher and student is rare, and when it occurs, we can assume that the teacher's speech has priority. Using this assumption we can filter all LIUM-obtained candidate segments that intersect the high-fidelity teacher segments by simply treating those as teacher speech. However, this naïve approach turned out to be too strict because it eliminated student segments on the boundary with teacher segments, as might occur when student segments have been marginally lengthened due to LIUM error.

Therefore, we adopted a slightly more complex approach shown in Figure 7. We used the high-fidelity teacher segments (from dedicated teacher channel) to re-segment LIUM-candidate segments. If a candidate segment intersected a teacher segment, the overlapping portion was removed, either deleting, shortening, or splitting the LIUM segment depending on the nature of the overlap. Since multiple teacher segments potentially overlap with a given candidate segment, and since the re-segmentation process itself potentially generates new segments, the re-segmentation process was recursive and terminated when every teacher segment had been applied to every candidate segment. We then merged all segments from the same speaker (remaining segments after the filtering process are now assumed to be student segments) that have less than 1 second of silence between them. After this step, segments shorter than 250 milliseconds are removed. These two parameters (1 second and 250 ms) have been fixed in these analyses but are tunable.

4.3.2 Validation

We conducted a study to evaluate the student utterance segmentation procedure. We randomly selected a subset of teacher questions and then manually coded all audio between the start of each question and the start of the next question as teacher speech, student speech, or silence, resulting in 298 annotated segments spanning 15 class sessions. We focused our analyses on student speech or silence immediately after teacher questions because these are the most interesting moments from the perspective of dialogic instruction. Thus, the 298 manually annotated segmented constitute our "gold standard."

Next, the entire PZM audio files from which these segments were drawn were submitted for teacher segmentation (using the method specified in Section 4.2.1) and to LIUM, and then the resulting segmentations from these methods were merged as specified in Section 4.3.1. For each annotated segment, the corresponding time interval in the merged segmentations was located and the interval classification was compared to the manual segment annotations. In order to take the duration of the segments into account, comparisons were done at the $1/100^{th}$ of a second level. This allowed us to consider segmentation accuracy as a standard classification problem and use precision/recall metrics, i.e. each $1/100^{th}$ of a second represented one opportunity for the "classifier" to identify whether the classroom audio reflected teacher speech, student speech, or silence (N = 99,290 in all).

The accuracy of the student utterance segmentation at the $1/100^{th}$ of a second level was fairly high, with precision of 79.6%, recall of 55.8%, and F-measure of 65.6%. The misclassifications of student segments to teacher or silence were approximately evenly distributed, suggesting that using the teacher segmentation to guide the student segmentation did not bias student segmentation according to the false alarms or misses of teacher segmentation. It appears that performance was largely limited by student utterance detection accuracy (F-measure of 65.6%). Results can be considered to be moderate given the noisy environment and technical constraints of not being able to mic individual students.

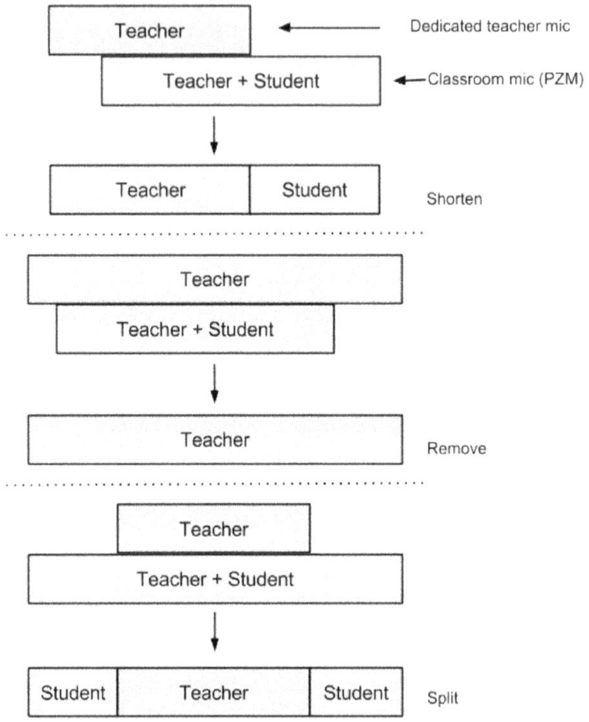

Figure 7. Student utterance segmentation. Overlap with teacher segments identified from the Airline mic shorten (top), remove (middle), or split (bottom) candidate segments recorded with the PZM mic to create student segments.

5. DESIGN 4 (Visual Information)

The key limitation in our designs to date boils down to physics (the least noisy signal must be collected close to the source) and to the practicalities of modern classrooms (instrumenting each student with a microphone is impractical). One possibility is to identify a set of verbose students and individually mic these students or to mic small groups of students. These options offer a middle ground to the current dichotomy of mic'ing individual students vs. none of the students and need to be tested more extensively. It is also worth considering what other kinds of sensors might be applicable to this problem.

In an early design we experimented with Kinects but did not use their video capability because of privacy concerns. It may be possible, however, to use the Kinects to collect visual data in a manner that would not raise privacy concerns. For example, the first-generation Kinects have the capability of collecting depth information. This depth information is sufficiently coarse that facial identification is obfuscated if not impossible. The skeleton tracking capabilities of the first-generation Kinect, which are only functional for single individuals, have been greatly expanded and made functional for small groups of individuals in the second generation Kinect. The second-generation Kinect can detect whether the eyes or mouth are open, if a person is looking away, and if the mouth has moved, for up to six people at a time [18].

In addition to using the mouth open/closed/moved information to better determine whether a student is speaking (by integrating this information with audio information collected by the microphone and PZM), the measures mentioned above could be used to estimate the students' levels of engagement. After all, the dialogic properties we are investigating are to some extent a linguistic measure of joint attention and engagement. It is an open question as to whether other measures, such as the degree to which students in the class are all looking at the teacher, are correlated with or even more predictive than linguistic measures on engagement.

In light of the aforementioned discussion, we are considering adding second-generation Kinects to Design 3, effectively producing Design 4. Design 4 will consist of the following devices and will yield the following data streams (in parentheses).

- CLASS 4.24 coding program (live codes of classroom discourse provided by humans)
- 1 Samson 77 Airline Microphone (teacher audio)
- 1 Crown PZM-30D (classroom audio)
- 2 second-generation Microsoft Kinects placed similar to Figure 2 (classroom audio, speaker position information, body tracking, and face tracking)

Synchronization of these multiple streams will likely pose a challenge. Synchronization of items 1-3 have already been completed as part of Design 3, but synchronization with the Kinects will need to be worked out, especially given previous difficulties involving synchronization of Kinects (see Section 2.2.4).

It should also be noted that the second-generation Kinects can only track up to six students simultaneously, which makes tracking the entire class impractical in terms of cabling around the classroom. This suggests that only the first and perhaps part of the second row can be successfully tracked with the proposed two Kinects. However, this limitation may represent the most pragmatic balance between the capabilities of modern sensors and the practicalities of classrooms. Moreover, there is some evidence to suggest that most question events involve the front of the class: in a within-subject study, students randomly assigned to the front asked more questions than when they were assigned to the back of the class [15]. Therefore the inability of the Kinects to track more than the front of the class may not be such a limitation after all.

6. DISCUSSION

The present project was concerned with the development of CLASS 5 – a program to autonomously code classroom discourse with respect to instructional activities (e.g., lecturing, discussion) and dialogic instruction quality (e.g., authenticity of questions; uptake). We developed and tested three recording designs in 38 live classrooms in multiple schools in the U.S. Our approach was motivated by a set of 12 technical requirements and constraints (see Section 1.1). The current most successful design (Design 3) met or exceeded the aforementioned requirements/constraints with respect to: usability, economic cost (around $875), human cost, scalability, non-intrusiveness, audio information, teacher audio quality, stream synchronization, and identity resolution. It was moderately successful in terms of flexibility and student audio quality, though the former needs to be studied more conclusively.

Analyses indicated that the data collected via Design 3 was suitable for our three core data analytic tasks: automatic speech recognition on teacher speech (word recognition rate of 66% and word overlap rate of 69%); teacher utterance segmentation (F-measure of 97%); and student utterance segmentation (F-measure of 66%). We consider these results to be promising due to the challenging nature of the classroom context in that we are instrumenting the classrooms with head-worn teacher microphones and boundary microphones, giving us a mixture of relatively clean teacher audio and extremely noisy student audio.

Importantly, the outputs of these basic tasks have been successfully applied towards the broader goal of automatic analysis of classroom discourse. As a concrete example, Blanchard, et al. [4] studied the possibility of automatically detecting question-answer segments (an example of instructional activity identification) in live classrooms based solely on audio recordings of teacher speech. Our approach had two steps. First, teacher utterances were automatically detected from the audio stream using the method specified in Section 4.2.1. Second, supervised classifiers were trained on speech-silence patterns derived from the segmented teacher utterances. We were able to detect Q&A segments in windows of 90 seconds with an AUC (Area Under the Receiver Operating Characteristic Curve) of 0.78 and in a manner that generalizes to new classes (i.e., using class-level cross validation). Similar results for identifying other instructional activities (e.g., small group work, lecturing), question detection, and question property classification, are underway and preliminary results are promising. We also have been working on using the data collected with these designs to identify questions in utterances and further identify questions with authenticity and uptake.

Despite its success, Design 3 was limited by its inability to record visual information (mainly due to privacy requirements). To address this, we proposed Design 4 which extends Design 3 to incorporate visual information from two second-generation Microsoft Kinects. We expect that the additional multimodal information available in Design 4 will help us to further improve the core task of student utterance segmentation. This, in turn, will be essential for more accurately coding classroom discourse, thereby providing valuable information to researchers, teachers, teacher educators, and professional development personnel. This information can be used to help teachers improve on their use of dialogic instruction techniques with the overall goal of improving student engagement and achievement.

7. ACKNOWLEDGMENTS

We acknowledge Mike Brady and Martin Nystrand for their contributions. This research was supported by the Institute of Education Sciences (IES) (R305A130030). Any opinions, findings and conclusions, or recommendations expressed in this paper are those of the author and do not represent the views of the IES.

8. REFERENCES

[1] Alibali, M.W., Nathan, M.J., Wolfgram, M.S., Church, R.B., Jacobs, S.A., Johnson Martinez, C. and Knuth, E.J. 2014. How teachers link ideas in mathematics instruction using speech and gesture: A corpus analysis. *Cognition and Instruction, 32* (1), 65-100.

[2] Applebee, A.N., Langer, J.A., Nystrand, M. and Gamoran, A. 2003. Discussion-based approaches to developing understanding: Classroom instruction and student performance in middle and high school English. *American Educational Research Journal, 40* (3), 685-730.

[3] Blanchard, N., Brady, M., Olney, A.M., Glaus, M., Sun, X., Nystrand, M., Samei, B., Kelly, S. and D'Mello, S. 2015. A Study of Automatic Speech Recognition in Noisy Classroom Environments for Automated Dialog Analysis. In Conati, C.,

Heffernan, N., Mitrovic, A. and Verdejo, M.F. eds. *Artificial Intelligence in Education*, Springer-Verlag, Berlin Heidelberg.

[4] Blanchard, N., D'Mello, S., Nystrand, M. and Olney, A.M. 2015. Automatic Classification of Question & Answer Discourse Segments from Teacher's Speech in Classrooms. In Romero, C., Pechenizkiy, M., Boticario, J. and Santos, O. eds. *Proceedings of the 8th International Conference on Educational Data Mining (EDM 2015)*, International Educational Data Mining Society.

[5] Brady, M.C., D'Mello, S., Blanchard, N., Olney, A. and Nystrand, M. Year. Evaluating microphones and microphone placement for signal processing and automatic speech recognition of teacher-student dialog. In *168th meeting of the Acoustical Society of America*, (Indianapolis, Indiana, 2014), 2215-2215.

[6] Crown. 2006. PZM-30D PZM-60D.

[7] Ford, M., Baer, C., Xu, D., Yapanel, U. and Gray, S. 2008. The LENA language environment analysis system, LENA Foundation Technical Report LTR-03-02., Boulder, CO.

[8] Gamoran, A. and Nystrand, M. 1992. Taking students seriously. In Newmann, F.M. ed. *Student engagement and achievement in american secondary schools*, Teachers College Press, New York, NY.

[9] Gates. 2013. Ensuring Fair and Reliable Measures of Effective Teaching: Culminating Findings from the MET Project's Three-Year Study, Bill & Melinda Gates Foundation.

[10] Goffin, V., Allauzen, C., Bocchieri, E., Hakkani-Tür, D., Ljolje, A., Parthasarathy, S., Rahim, M.G., Riccardi, G. and Saraclar, M. Year. The AT&T WATSON Speech Recognizer. In *International Conference on Acoustics, Speech and Signal Processing*, (2005), 1033-1036.

[11] Goldman, R., Pea, R., Barron, B. and Derry, S.J. (eds.). *Video research in the learning sciences*. Erlbaum, Mahwah, NJ.

[12] Graesser, A. and Person, N. 1994. Question asking during tutoring. *American Education Research Journal*, *31* (1), 104-137.

[13] Kelly, S. 2008. Race, social class, and student engagement in middle school English classrooms. *Social Science Research*, *37* (2), 434-448.

[14] LENA. 2015. LENA Research Foundation.

[15] Marx, A., Fuhrer, U. and Hartig, T. 1999. Effects of classroom seating arrangements on children's question-asking. *Learning Environments Research*, *2* (3), 249-263.

[16] Microsoft. 2010. Best Practices for Enabling Voice Recognition, Microsoft.

[17] Microsoft. 2014. The Bing Speech Recognition Control

[18] Microsoft. 2015. Kinect for Windows SDK MSDN.

[19] Microsoft. 2014. Speech SDK 5.1.

[20] NCES. 2015. Digest of Education Statistics, 2013, U.S. Department of Education, National Center for Education Statistics, Washington, DC.

[21] Nystrand, M. 2004. Classroom Language Assessment System (CLASS) 4.24, University of Wisconsin–Madison, Madison, WI.

[22] Nystrand, M. 1997. *Opening Dialogue: Understanding the Dynamics of Language and Learning in the English Classroom. Language and Literacy Series*. Teachers College Press, New York, NY.

[23] Nystrand, M. and Gamoran, A. 1991. Instructional discourse, student engagement, and literature achievement. *Research in the Teaching of English*, *25* (3), 261-290.

[24] Nystrand, M., Wu, L.L., Gamoran, A., Zeiser, S. and Long, D.A. 2003. Questions in time: Investigating the structure and dynamics of unfolding classroom discourse. *Discourse Processes*, *35* (2), 135-198.

[25] Povey, D., Ghoshal, A., Boulianne, G., Burget, L., Glembek, O., Goel, N., Hannemann, M., Motlíček, P., Qian, Y. and Schwarz, P. Year. The Kaldi speech recognition toolkit. In *IEEE Workshop on Automatic Speech Recognition and Understanding*, (2011).

[26] Rouvier, M., Dupuy, G., Gay, P., Khoury, E., Merlin, T. and Meignier, S. Year. An open-source state-of-the-art toolbox for broadcast news diarization. In *Interspeech*, (2013).

[27] Samei, B., Olney, A., Kelly, S., Nystrand, M., D'Mello, S., Blanchard, N., Sun, X., Glaus, M. and Graesser, A. 2014. Domain Independent Assessment of Dialogic Properties of Classroom Discourse. In Stamper, J., Pardos, Z., Mavrikis, M. and McLaren, B.M. eds. *Proceedings of the 7th International Conference on Educational Data Mining (EDM 2014)* International Educational Data Mining Society.

[28] Schalkwyk, J., Beeferman, D., Beaufays, F., Byrne, B., Chelba, C., Cohen, M., Kamvar, M. and Strope, B. 2010. "Your Word is my Command": Google Search by Voice: A Case Study. In Neustein, A. ed. *Advances in Speech Recognition: Mobile Environments, Call Centers, and Clinics*, Springer US, New York, NY.

[29] Walker, W., Lamere, P., Kwok, P., Raj, B., Singh, R., Gouvea, E., Wolf, P. and Woelfel, J. 2004. Sphinx-4: A flexible open source framework for speech recognition, Sun Microsystems, Inc, Mountain View, CA, USA.

[30] Wang, Z., Miller, K. and Cortina, K. 2013. Using the LENA in Teacher Training: Promoting Student Involement through automated feedback. *Unterrichtswissenschaft*, *4*, 290-305.

[31] Wang, Z., Pan, X., Miller, K.F. and Cortina, K.S. 2014. Automatic classification of activities in classroom discourse. *Computers & Education*, *78* (1), 115-123.

[32] Wiesler, S., Richard, A., Golik, P., Schluter, R. and Ney, H. 2014. RASR/NN: The RWTH neural network toolkit for speech recognition. In *IEEE International Conference on Acoustics, Speech and Signal Processing (ICASSP)* IEEE, Washington, DC.

Multimodal Selfies: Designing a Multimodal Recording Device for Students in Traditional Classrooms

Federico Domínguez
Escuela Superior Politécnica del Litoral
Vía Perimetral Km. 30.5
Guayaquil, Ecuador
fexadomi@espol.edu.ec

Vanessa Echeverría
Escuela Superior Politécnica del Litoral
Vía Perimetral Km. 30.5
Guayaquil, Ecuador
vecheverria@cti.espol.edu.ec

Katherine Chiluiza
Escuela Superior Politécnica del Litoral
Vía Perimetral Km. 30.5
Guayaquil, Ecuador
kchilui@espol.edu.ec

Xavier Ochoa
Escuela Superior Politécnica del Litoral
Vía Perimetral Km. 30.5
Guayaquil, Ecuador
xavier@cti.espol.edu.ec

ABSTRACT

The traditional recording of student interaction in classrooms has raised privacy concerns in both students and academics. However, the same students are happy to share their daily lives through social media. Perception of data ownership is the key factor in this paradox. This article proposes the design of a personal Multimodal Recording Device (MRD) that could capture the actions of its owner during lectures. The MRD would be able to capture close-range video, audio, writing, and other environmental signals. Differently from traditional centralized recording systems, students would have control over their own recorded data. They could decide to share their information in exchange of access to the recordings of the instructor, notes form their classmates, and analysis of, for example, their attention performance. By sharing their data, students participate in the co-creation of enhanced and synchronized course notes that will benefit all the participating students. This work presents details about how such a device could be build from available components. This work also discusses and evaluates the design of such device, including its foreseeable costs, scalability, flexibility, intrusiveness and recording quality.

Categories and Subject Descriptors

K.3.1 [**Computing Milieux**]: Computers and Education-Computer Uses in Education

Keywords

Multimodal Recording; Learning Analytics; Recording Quality; Data Privacy

ICMI 2015, November 9–13, 2015, Seattle, WA, USA.

ACM 978-1-4503-3912-4/15/11 ...$15.00.
DOI: http://dx.doi.org/10.1145/2818346.2830606 .

1. INTRODUCTION

The first law of technology according to Kranzberg [19] is that it is neither good nor bad, nor is it neutral. Learning Analytics, seen as an Educational Technology, also follows this law. The act of collecting data from learning environments automatically creates a balance of power between students, instructor and the educational institution [32]. While references to *Big Brother* or *Foucault's Panopticon* can be seen as extreme comparisons for the Learning Analytics practice, there are real privacy concerns that need to be addressed before implementing data-collection schemes [24]: How to maintain transparency about the use of data, who owns and controls data, who has access to (different parts of) data and how to account and assess their good use. While all these privacy dimensions are important, ownership of data is the dimension most influenced by the recording strategy. An example of the impact of data collection in the perception of privacy, the so called privacy paradox [18], is the following: the difference in reaction when a stranger takes a photo of an individual in a public space and publishes it on the Internet, versus when an individual takes a "selfie" in the same spot and uploads it to a social network, such as Twitter. The end result is the same, the picture is now public for everyone to see. However, in the first scenario, the individual could feel that its privacy has been violated, but in the second scenario, the same person could even be happy to receive comments from strangers about the picture. All other things being equal, who does the recording and who controls what and when is recorded has a direct influence on the perception of ownership of data and the perception of privacy invasion.

One of the learning environments where recordings are especially problematic from a privacy viewpoint is the traditional classroom. Differently from virtual environments or specialized settings, there is the expectation of privacy in the classroom, as recording devices have never been part of it. This problematic feature and the ethical aspects of video-recording lectures have sparked debate among educational researchers and remain controversial to these days [8] [9] [29].

Despite these dilemmas, researchers and participants of studies have pointed out the positive side of video recording in natural settings, such as classrooms [12]. The following privacy protecting solutions to gather data in classroom settings are a point of reference [13]: manual annotation, no video (least invasive); fully automated digital video capture, data is gathered at all times without teacher intervention, manual or automatic indexing is used; fully automated capture with a location-based filter, video captures individuals interacting with specific objects of interest, surrounding environment is blurred, the videos are manually or automatically indexed; fully automated capture with a subject-based filter, space around the subject remains clear while anything else is blurred; and, selective archiving of captured video, everything is captured at all times, but the archiving procedure requires manual intervention. The usage of such recordings are often related to explorative/ experimental objectives, where subjects are prompted to use artifacts, or engaged in situations or environments where they perform some activities, while data are gathered for future analyses [2]. These scenarios are monitored and set-up before the subjects participate in the experiments and teachers and learners might not be aware of the recording that takes place or the related equipment. The same applies for initiatives such as the MIT OpenCourseWare (OCW) project, where they share audio/video recordings and supporting class material. Projects like this are very popular and have generated public awareness about open content and research about its impact on informal education [33] [30] [4]. In these initiatives, the focus of the videos was usually the lecturer and her/his writing on the blackboard or the slides, not the students. The video camera is always located at the back of the classroom and the lecturer's voice was captured via a lavalier microphone. Nowadays, with the availability of mobile phones, tablets and similar devices, innovative approaches that are built-upon their ubiquitous nature have appeared. These approaches allow students to: add value to class notes shared by their lecturers and learn more from them [2], do crowd-sourcing in learning [6] [7], support teachers in their teaching [3], and many more. For instance, in [17], students can video-record themselves expressing their opinions about a task designed by their teachers. This happens in a private platform where teachers and students can interact and see what others post.

The approach of this study is to give students the opportunity to video-record their interactions, poses, emotions and notes by means of a Multimodal Recording Device (MRD). This device sits on top of the student's desk while collecting audio, video and the notes the student takes while attending a lecture. The same set of data would be gathered by other students that would like to share their interactions during and after the class. Meanwhile a video camera is recording the lecture, focusing on the lecture and the notes the instructor makes in the whiteboard or the slides. After the lecture is finished, the annotations and instructor's slides synchronize with the students' notes; thus, everyone that attended the lecture gets an enhanced set of notes and lectures. The sharing of such information is optional from the side of the students; however, all the students would have access to the recorded lecture but only those that shared their recordings would gain access to the enhanced set of information.

This paper is structured as follows: first, a review of related work is presented; next, the design of the proposed device is described, including a section about the potential applications of such device for the students, the instructors, the institutions and educational researchers; following, a set of criteria are used to analyze the proposed design. Finally, the paper closes with conclusions and next steps to implement and evaluate the MRD.

2. RELATED WORK

Recording a lecture in a traditional classroom is an activity that learners have been doing for several purposes. These recordings imply the use of one or multiple devices, dedicated to the recording of: teacher interactions, students' attention and interventions (through video cameras, microphones, digital pens and multitouch surfaces).

As mentioned in the introduction, there has been a plethora of studies where educational researchers have used video recording of lectures to gain insight on student behavior. However, only a handful of studies approaches the problem from a learning analytics perspective, that is, recording the lecture to automatically analyze the students' behavior and providing immediate feedback to the participants. These studies usually focused on the determination of the level of student attention [28] [27] [25]. The multimodal recording setting consists in a set of cameras located in the classroom to capture the teacher's interactions as well as the students' attention. Automatic descriptors, such as slide duration or question and answer duration, can be extracted from the teacher's video recordings; whereas the students' level of attention can be determined by quantifying the student's gaze direction [25] or tracking and recognizing individual student interactions [22]. Additional resources such as questionnaires and interviews from students, and an eye tracker for the teacher, are used to perform a holistic analysis of what is actually happening in the classroom [26].

Another methodology to capture the students' interaction is through the use of multi-tabletop systems (MTS). These systems have been used for supporting different stages of collaboration in group work activities [5] and for planning learning activities on the teacher's side [23] [16]. They are capable of collecting the students' writing and interaction activities with learning objects through finger or pen-based input methods [11]. More sophisticated MTS can also understand voice commands to interact with the system [14].

The solution presented in this paper differs from these works in two main points: 1) It is not based on a centralized recording setting. The distributed approach is more flexible and highly reduces privacy concerns, and 2) It is multimodal in nature, enabling a more holistic analysis of the behavior than just recording unimodal signals.

3. DESIGN

Recording a traditional classroom has usually two components: 1) capturing the actions of the instructor and the materials he or she is presenting and 2) capturing the actions and artifacts produced by the students. There are several successful designs for the first component, for example Galicaster [10], a hardware solution to record lectures and Project Matterhorn [15], a full open source suite of software to capture, edit and distribute those lectures. While these systems have not been used for research, their recordings can be easily re-purposed to analyze the behavior of the teacher in the classroom. On the other hand, as mentioned in the Related Work section, there has been very little research on how to produce automatic recordings of the students and

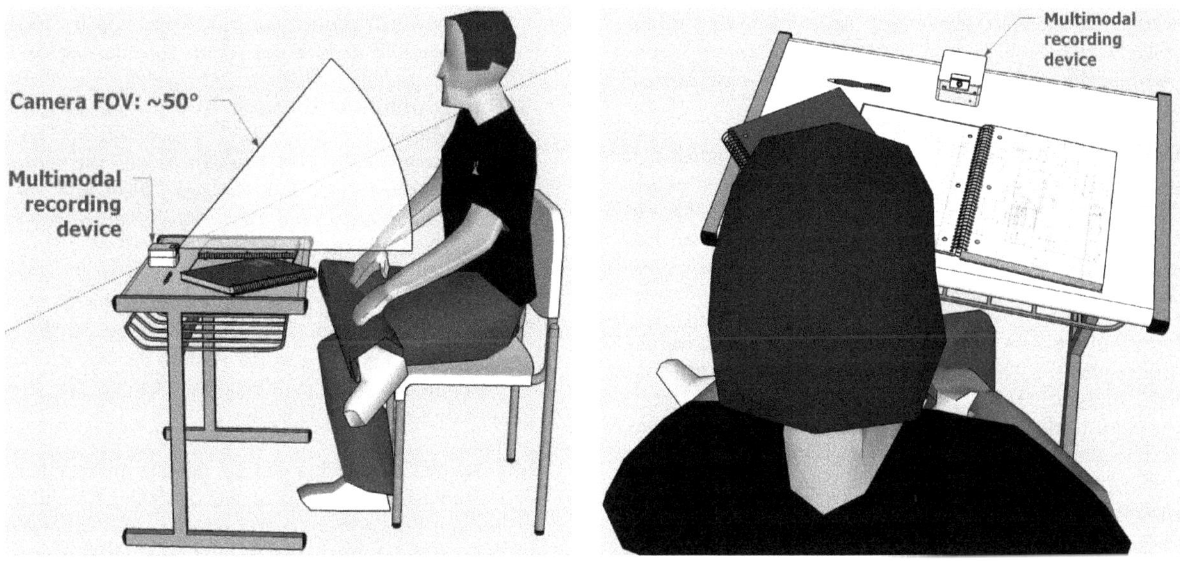

(a) MRD in the classroom (b) MRD from the student's point of view

Figure 1: The Multimodal Recording Device (MRD) is a relatively compact appliance designed to sit unnoticed on top of a student's desk. It collects video, audio, environmental parameters and notes during class. Its video camera aims at the student's head and torso.

their artifacts. The design proposed in this work, a MRD, focuses on this second component.

3.1 Design Principles

The process to design a solution to record the students during lectures was guided by the following principles:

- Privacy should be respected. The system should be owned and operated by the student and the control and ownership of the data should remain in the possession of the student that generated it. The student will always have the control of the device and can decide at any time during the lecture to start or stop recording.
- The recording device should be small and cheap enough to be taken from classroom to classroom. It should be a portable device that connects to their cellphones or laptops and should not cost more than a low-end smartphone.
- The recording device should provide a clear value to the student that uses it. Sharing the recordings produced by the device should provide some incentive to the student. Even if not shared, the recording devices should be useful *per-se*.
- It should record as many modes (video, audio, writing, temperature, movement) as feasible for future analysis. The research goal of the tool requires the recording of any relevant variable even if their usefulness is not immediately clear.
- The quality of the capture should be enough to allow advanced analysis. For example, audio recordings should be clear enough to allow speech recognition, recording of the face of the student should provide enough resolution to allow gaze and expression recognition, writing recording should be good enough to enable script and sketch recognition.

Any real device will have to compromise between all of these principles. For example, the quality of the recording will conflict with the portability of the device, the number of modes will conflict with the low-cost, and the research objectives will conflict with the privacy. The design presented in this paper is one instantiation of the different compromises between design principles and the current availability of technology.

3.2 Multimodal Streams

There are several personal devices that can be used to capture the activity of the student during the classroom. For example, digital pens to capture writing, movement tracking devices, such as Fitbit [1] and even electroencephalogram (EEG) recorders such as Emotiv [2]. These devices, however, only capture one or two modes. Several of these devices will be needed to track all relevant signals during a lecture. Figure 1 illustrates how the MRD will capture student's activity and environment within the classroom. The MRD should be placed on the student's desk, within the view of the student, and it will capture the following modes:

- **Video of the face:** The device will have a low-cost camera pointed to the student's face. The objective of capturing this mode is to establish the gaze, facial expression and head movements.
- **Close range audio:** The device will have a small microphone to capture the audio produced and heard by the student. The objective of capturing this mode

[1]Fitbit: https://www.fitbit.com
[2]Emotiv: https://www.emotiv.com

is to establish noise levels and capturing inter-student conversations and voiced opinions. The microphones can also be used to synchronize the devices through audio signals.

- **Pen strokes:** The device will integrate a digital pen to capture the pen strokes made by the student in any paper. The technology used by the digital pen should allow the capture of the strokes over any surface. The objective of capturing this mode will be to analyze the note-taking behavior and the analysis of those notes.

- **Environmental context:** The device will integrate other sensors to measure temperature, humidity and light intensity that could provide information about the environment where the lecture is taking place. These variables could be later correlated with the student's performance or attention span during class (e.g. high temperature and humidity could have a negative impact in attention span).

The MRD will connect to the classroom's WiFi infrastructure to upload and synchronize all shared data. The processing of the signals should be made in the device itself, as feasible, to avoid sharing the raw data.

3.3 Hardware Design

A first prototype for the MRD (Figure 2) to test the capabilities and usability of the device can be built with the following components:

- **Main processor:** Any micro-computer available today could serve as the main processor of the MRD. The selected component for the prototype is the Intel Edison [3]. This is a x86-compatible computer that is low-cost, has a small-form factor, low-power consumption, and has integrated WiFi and Bluetooth communications. It also provides a breakout board kit to easily connect sensors.

- **Video capture:** Video will be captured by a Micro-USB CMOS Camera. A typical CMOS camera such as the OmniVision OV7725 [4] can capture video with a 640x480 resolution at 30 fps while consuming around 100mA. It has a USB 2.0 port that will connect to the USB-OTG port on the Intel Edison Breakout Board.

- **Audio capture:** The audio will be captured by a digital MEMS microphone. These microphones are typically used in mobile phones and are cheap, small and power efficient. For example, the ICS-43432 [5] provides a good noise-bed (65db SNR), miniature size (4x3x1mm), low power consumption (1mA) and connects to the Edison's I^2S port.

- **Digital Pen:** Any digital pen based on ultrasound technology can be used to capture the pen strokes. For this prototype the Wacom Inkling [6] will be used. This pen will connect to our device via its Bluetooth interface and it does not require special paper.

- **Environmental Sensors:** Any low-cost sensor to measure temperature and humidity available for DIY projects can be connected to the Edison Board through analog inputs extensions. For the light level and the noise level, the camera and the microphone array, respectively, can be used.

- **Storage:** To store all digital streams, the device should have a non-volatile solid-state memory. In the case of the prototype, any generic Micro SD card, with at least 32Gb of capacity can be connected to the breakout board of the Intel Edison.

- **Power:** The device will be battery powered; a small Polymer Lithium Ion Battery of 2000 mAh will provide enough power for several hours (two to three sessions, depending on use). It will include a USB charger module to allow recharging with any generic mobile phone USB charger.

- **Control interface:** At minimum the prototype should provide a switch to turn on the device, a button to start or stop the recording and a multi-color LED to signal if the device is turned on and if it is recording. Future designs could include a small touch-sensing LCD screen to convert the recorder in an input device for other educational applications, such as a clicker.

The hardware mentioned is just an example of how such a device can be built with readily available parts. A more polished design will use specialized components. For example, instead of using an available digital pen, an OEM version could be integrated in the same board as the processor. This level of optimization can only be reached with high-volume production. The prototype specified in Figure 2 presents two LEDs for feedback and one single button for turning on the device (long press) and start/stop a recording (short press).

3.4 Applications for the Proposed Design

The proposed MRD has several potential applications. These applications generate and added value to the following subjects: students, teachers, institutions and researchers.

- **Value proposition for students:** The MRD could be used as a personal device, in the same way as a tablet (video, audio, photos), but the captured content (notes) can be synchronized with the rest of the signals from the lecture. Therefore, a student could know, for instance, what happened in the lecture, when she/he wrote a special symbol or note, which in other circumstances would have no meaning, when revisited by a student. Additionally, students could also share their notes and produce content summarization or highlight sections of other students' notes, that got unnoticed when she/he first "attended" to the lecture. This MRD could be used to do crowd sourcing when learning, as in [6], since it can get access to the internet and thus other participants can support students in different and innovative ways.

[3]Intel Edison: https://www-ssl.intel.com/content/www/us/en/do-it-yourself/edison.html

[4]Camera: http://www.ovt.com/products/sensor.php?id=80

[5]Microphone: http://www.invensense.com/products/digital/ics-43432/

[6]Digital Pen: http://inkling.wacom.com/

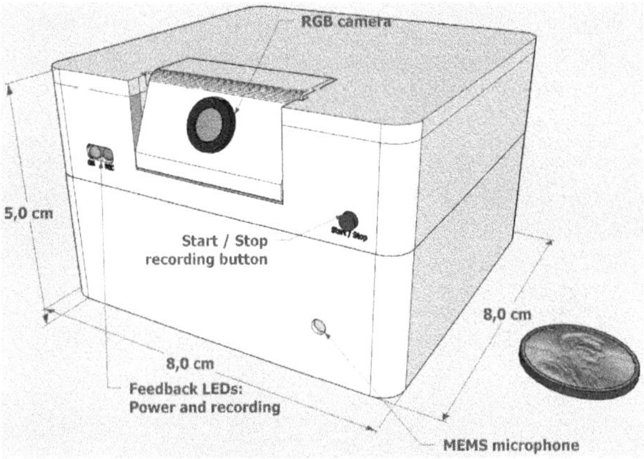

(a) Dimensions and scale diagram

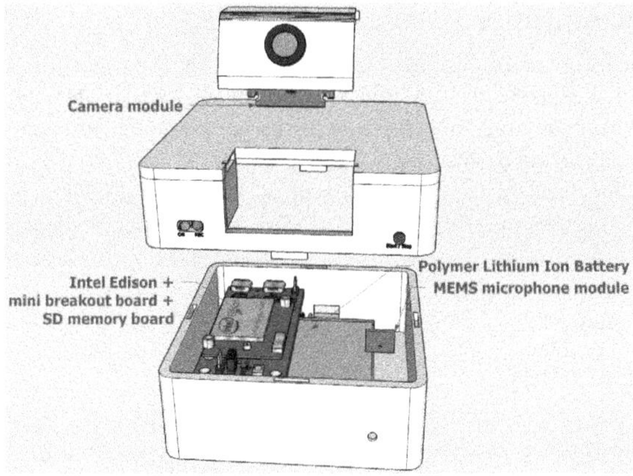

(b) Exploded view diagram

Figure 2: The MRD has a front-facing camera and microphone, a single button to start and stop recording, and two LEDs for providing feedback (green LED for power and red LED for recording activity). The device is based on the Intel Edison System on Module platform and includes a rechargeable battery with enough capacity to last for several hours.

- **Value proposition for teacher:** Teachers from all levels of expertise could benefit when using this device; for instance, they could detect when students' attention was the highest or the lowest and take further actions in their teaching plans. In parallel, the system that records the teachers' performance could get synchronized to students' signals allowing teachers to critically review their performance.
- **Value proposition for institution:** In several higher education institutions, peer-evaluation is part of the monitoring and feedback lecturers receive. Nevertheless, having another professor or colleague seated at the back of a classroom might generate tension within the class environment. The multi-sychronized signals obtained from the proposed system could be used by a third party to analyze them in a private space and to further give feedback to lecturers, which in turn would diminish anxiety from the side of novice professors.
- **Value proposition for researchers:** The large amount of data generated by the proposed system, as well as its varied diversity would be valuable resources for researchers to find patterns in behaviors observed in students and lecturers. Quality of notes, actual learning in real environments, discourses, quality of interactions between students in the classroom, quality of learning when notes are revisited, patterns of note revisions, and more, are just a few examples of the different type of topics researchers can get interested in as a consequence of using the data generated by the proposed device and its related applications.

4. ANALYSIS OF THE DESIGN

Even if not tested with students, from the description of the design of the MRD several analysis can be performed. This section will provide some discussion about the relative cost, scalability, flexibility and intrusiveness of the device. Also, it will discuss the quality of the data that can be captured.

Table 1: Bill of materials of the MRD prototype

Part	Quantity	Cost
Processor: Intel Edison + Board	1	80
Storage: Micro SD card 32 Gb	1	20
Power: LiPo 2000 mAh + Charger	1	23
Camera: OmniVision OV7725	1	35
Microphone: ICS-43432	1	12
Digital Pen: Wacom Inkling	1	80
Temp. and Humidity Sensor: RHT03	1	10
Switch	2	1
LEDs	2	1
Casing and wiring	1	10
Total	**274 USD**	

4.1 Cost

One of the design principles behind the MRD is that it should cost almost the same as a low-end smart phone (100 to 150 USD). The cost of the MRD can be estimated with a bill of materials (BOM) consisting of the discrete components described in the Hardware Design section (Table 1). The prices were obtained from consumer sites at the time of writing. As it can be seen from the table, the total cost of building the prototype is 274 USD.

While 274 is higher than the desired 100-150 range, the cost of the prototype is a ceiling of the actual cost that the device could have. Volume production and integration into a single product will bring costs down. It is expected that the final cost of such a device will be closer or inside the desired range.

The device will be owned by the student. In such an scheme, the device, even if subsidized by the educational institution, should provide a tangible value to the student in order to be attractive. The device should be marketed as a digital pen plus a lecture recorder at around 50 USD.

4.2 Scalability

One of the strong points of the design is its scalability. Due to its distributed nature, the number of students that use the device does not have a major impact in the complexity of the recording solution.

The only major scalability issue is WiFi availability as each device will be connected to the wireless network. However, if no connection is available at the moment, the transmission needed to share the recording can be made after the lecture ends.

4.3 Flexibility

The MRD provides several levels of flexibility. First, it is flexible to class configuration. As each student positions the device in front of her/him, the recording will take place regardless of the sitting scheme. It can even be adapted to other settings, such as sitting in groups or standing around a table. The only restriction for the use of the MRD is if no surface is present in front of the student (standing setup) or if there is constant movement in the classroom (walking or outdoor design).

In addition, the functionality of the MRD is flexible. While the main function of the MRD is recording video, audio, strokes and environment, it can be extended to be used as a clicker or calculator or to capture other types of modes (bio-signals or motion, for example).

Finally, the design is flexible enough to be constructed as an addition to existing devices such as cellphones or laptops. With a clever hardware design and the right software, an smart phone can be converted into a MRD.

4.4 Intrusiveness

The MRD is an intrusive device in the sense that it is not a transparent recorder of the lecture. However, given that the device provides students additional functionalities, it becomes a technological part of the classroom, such as a projector, a clicker or an electronic whiteboard. Moreover, the personal, purposeful and voluntary use of the MRD makes it as intrusive as the use of pens for note-taking.

The main sources of intrusion: setting and starting or stopping the device can be offset by a clever mechanical design and automation functions such as starting by audible tones triggered by the instructor or stopping after a period of inactivity. The device can also be controlled and configured by the student using its Bluetooth interface. Actions such as selecting which data to share, configuring WiFi or downloading notes can be implemented via this interface.

4.5 Data Quality

The main purpose of the MRD is to collect data for further learning analytics. As such, it is very important that the recorded multimodal streams have the required quality to conduct such analysis. The focus of this subsection will be the analysis of the quality of the three main signals: video, audio and pen strokes. Other captured modes are briefly discussed.

4.5.1 Video

In a common scenario, that is, the device resting on the desk, the MRD will capture video with a minimum resolution of 640x480 at the 40-60 cm range in a not-zoomed slightly low-angle shot (Figure 3). In this setup, the face dimensions take, in average, 180 pixels wide (ear-to-ear) and 200 pixels tall (hair line to chin). This resolution is enough for face recognition [34], gaze estimation [21] and basic facial expression estimation [31].

Figure 3: Example shot from 640x480 camera at 40-60 cm range

4.5.2 Audio

The microphone used in the MRD, a digital MEMS microphone, is a low cost, low-power consumption component with a dynamic range and SNR similar or better than their electret microphone counterparts [20]. The latest model can provide a 65db SNR, more than enough for prosodic analysis, speaker identification and usable speech recognition [1].

4.5.3 Pen Strokes

The current resolution of digital pens exceed the resolution for handwriting recognition and sketch recognition. Given that the MRD will use a commercial digital pen or an OEM integrated version, no temporal or spatial resolutions problems are expected.

4.5.4 Other Modes

The MRD will be able to record other signals through their respective sensor. In the prototype, humidity and temperature are sampled and recorded. The main limitations that these measurements could have are the actual analog limitations of the sensor.

In the foreseen types of analysis of contextual variables, the temporal resolution required will be in the order of seconds or minutes. Even the most basic processors can provide at least one order of magnitude faster sampling.

5. CONCLUSIONS AND FURTHER WORK

The main contribution of this design is the change of paradigm between centralized to distributed recording to establish student behavior in class. This solution has the potential to greatly reduce the privacy concerns that centralized systems raise among students and academics.

The design process of the Multimodal Recording Device showed that such a device can be built with existing technology at a relative low cost and provide the necessary quality to conduct learning analytics over the captured data. However, the introduction of such a device should be accompanied by a group of applications that provide immediate and tangible value to both students and instructors.

The next step needed to evaluate the MRD design is to test the prototype in a real lecture environment. The test will consist on taking a sizable number of multimodal recordings (at least 30) and apply state-of-the-art algorithms to automatically extract features that are likely to be part of any learning analytics application, such as attention measurement. If the error-rate of the automatic extraction of features is on par with what the state-of-the-art algorithm produces when fed with more intrusive recordings, the MRD will be proved useful to record that specific feature. Due to the variety of modes and variety of features to extract, this evaluation will require a considerable amount of work.

The most important evaluation of the MRD tool, however, does not involve the application of data-mining algorithms for automatic feature extraction. To obtain a real indication of the viability of the MRD, its usefulness for students has to be evaluated. This evaluation can only be conducted in the context of a much larger system described in the Application Design subsection. If the MRD tool can enable a collaborative note-taking system that is perceived as useful to the students, then it has the possibility of being introduced in the classroom and could produce data that can be used for learning analytics research.

Finally, this work is also meant as a discussion-starter for the design and implementation of more discrete and decentralized measurement instruments that shift the power relation that traditional data capturing schemes establish.

6. ACKNOWLEDGMENTS

The authors want to acknowledge the support of the SENESCYT Project "Andamios".

7. REFERENCES

[1] A. Acero. *Acoustical and environmental robustness in automatic speech recognition*, volume 201. Springer Science & Business Media, 2012.

[2] J. A. Brotherton and G. D. Abowd. Lessons learned from eclass: Assessing automated capture and access in the classroom. *ACM Trans. Comput.-Hum. Interact.*, 11(2):121–155, June 2004.

[3] A. Buckland and A. Quigley. Csct-computer supported cooperative teaching. In *Proceedings of The International Symposium on Pervasive Displays*, page 188. ACM, 2014.

[4] R. Buckland. Open teaching a case study on publishing lecture videos publicly. In *Proceedings of the Thirteenth Australasian Computing Education Conference - Volume 114*, ACE '11, pages 19–28, Darlinghurst, Australia, Australia, 2011. Australian Computer Society, Inc.

[5] P. Dillenbourg and M. Evans. Interactive tabletops in education. *International Journal of Computer-Supported Collaborative Learning*, 6(4):491–514, 2011.

[6] S. Dow, E. Gerber, and A. Wong. A pilot study of using crowds in the classroom. In *Proceedings of the SIGCHI Conference on Human Factors in Computing Systems*, pages 227–236. ACM, 2013.

[7] H. Du, M. B. Rosson, J. M. Carroll, and C. Ganoe. I felt like a contributing member of the class: increasing class participation with classcommons. In *Proceedings of the ACM 2009 international conference on Supporting group work*, pages 233–242. ACM, 2009.

[8] R. Flewitt*. Conducting research with young children: some ethical considerations. *Early Child Development and Care*, 175(6):553–565, 2005.

[9] R. Flewitt. Using video to investigate preschool classroom interaction: education research assumptions and methodological practices. *Visual Communication*, 5(1):25–50, 2006.

[10] E. González-Agulla, J. L. Alba-Castro, H. Canto, and V. Goyanes. Galitracker: Real-time lecturer-tracking for lecture capturing. In *Multimedia (ISM), 2013 IEEE International Symposium on*, pages 462–467. IEEE, 2013.

[11] R. Granda, V. Echeverría, K. Chiluiza, and M. Wong-Villacrés. Supporting the assessment of collaborative design activities in multi-tabletop classrooms. *Conference Proceedings in the Third Asia-Pacific Conference on Computer Aided System Engineering (APCASE). In Press.*, pages 270–275, Jul 2015.

[12] G. R. Hayes and G. D. Abowd. Tensions in designing capture technologies for an evidence-based care community. In *Proceedings of the SIGCHI Conference on Human Factors in Computing Systems*, CHI '06, pages 937–946, New York, NY, USA, 2006. ACM.

[13] G. R. Hayes, J. A. Kientz, K. N. Truong, D. R. White, G. D. Abowd, and T. Pering. Designing capture applications to support the education of children with autism. In *UbiComp 2004: Ubiquitous Computing*, pages 161–178. Springer, 2004.

[14] A. Jones, A. Kendira, D. Lenne, T. Gidel, and C. Moulin. The tatin-pic project: A multi-modal collaborative work environment for preliminary design. In *Computer Supported Cooperative Work in Design (CSCWD), 2011 15th International Conference on*, pages 154–161, June 2011.

[15] M. Ketterl, O. A. Schulte, and A. Hochman. Opencast matterhorn: A community-driven open source solution for creation, management and distribution of audio and video in academia. In *2009 11th IEEE International Symposium on Multimedia*, pages 687–692. IEEE, 2009.

[16] A. Kharrufa, M. Balaam, P. Heslop, D. Leat, P. Dolan, and P. Olivier. Tables in the wild: lessons learned from a large-scale multi-tabletop deployment. In *Proceedings of the SIGCHI Conference on Human Factors in Computing Systems*, pages 1021–1030. ACM, 2013.

[17] J. Kim, E. L. Glassman, A. Monroy-Hernández, and M. R. Morris. Rimes: Embedding interactive multimedia exercises in lecture videos. In *Proceedings of the 33rd Annual ACM Conference on Human Factors in Computing Systems*, CHI '15, pages 1535–1544, New York, NY, USA, 2015. ACM.

[18] S. Kokolakis. Privacy attitudes and privacy behaviour: A review of current research on the privacy paradox phenomenon. *Computers & Security*, 2015.

[19] M. Kranzberg. Technology and history:" kranzberg's laws". *Technology and culture*, pages 544–560, 1986.

[20] J. Lewis and P. Schreier. Low Self Noise: The First Step to High Performance MEMS Microphone Applications. Technical report, InvenSense, 2013.

[21] Y.-T. Lin, R.-Y. Lin, Y.-C. Lin, and G. C. Lee. Real-time eye-gaze estimation using a low-resolution webcam. *Multimedia tools and applications*, 65(3):543–568, 2013.

[22] Y. Mao, H. Li, and Z. Yin. Who missed the class?: Unifying multi-face detection, tracking and recognition in videos. In *Multimedia and Expo (ICME), 2014 IEEE International Conference on*, pages 1–6, July 2014.

[23] R. Martinez Maldonado, Y. Dimitriadis, J. Kay, K. Yacef, and M.-T. Edbauer. Orchestrating a multi-tabletop classroom: From activity design to enactment and reflection. In *Proceedings of the 2012 ACM International Conference on Interactive Tabletops and Surfaces*, ITS '12, pages 119–128, New York, NY, USA, 2012. ACM.

[24] A. Pardo and G. Siemens. Ethical and privacy principles for learning analytics. *British Journal of Educational Technology*, 45(3):438–450, 2014.

[25] M. Raca and P. Dillenbourg. System for assessing classroom attention. In *Proceedings of the Third International Conference on Learning Analytics and Knowledge*, LAK '13, pages 265–269, New York, NY, USA, 2013. ACM.

[26] M. Raca and P. Dillenbourg. Holistic analysis of the classroom. In *Proceedings of the 2014 ACM Workshop on Multimodal Learning Analytics Workshop and Grand Challenge*, MLA '14, pages 13–20, New York, NY, USA, 2014. ACM.

[27] M. Raca, R. Tormey, and P. Dillenbourg. Student motion and it" s potential as a classroom performance metric. In *3rd International Workshop on Teaching Analytics (IWTA)*, number EPFL-TALK-188524, 2013.

[28] M. Raca, R. Tormey, and P. Dillenbourg. Sleepers' lag - study on motion and attention. In *Proceedings of the Fourth International Conference on Learning Analytics And Knowledge*, LAK '14, pages 36–43, New York, NY, USA, 2014. ACM.

[29] B. Rosenstein. Video use in social science research and program evaluation. *International Journal of Qualitative Methods*, 1(3):22–43, 2008.

[30] M. Sabin and J. Leone. It education 2.0. In *Proceedings of the 10th ACM Conference on SIG-information Technology Education*, SIGITE '09, pages 91–99, New York, NY, USA, 2009. ACM.

[31] G. Sandbach, S. Zafeiriou, M. Pantic, and L. Yin. Static and dynamic 3d facial expression recognition: A comprehensive survey. *Image and Vision Computing*, 30(10):683–697, 2012.

[32] S. Slade and P. Prinsloo. Learning analytics ethical issues and dilemmas. *American Behavioral Scientist*, 57(10):1510–1529, 2013.

[33] S. Vahdati, C. Lange, and S. Auer. Opencourseware observatory: Does the quality of opencourseware live up to its promise? In *Proceedings of the Fifth International Conference on Learning Analytics And Knowledge*, LAK '15, pages 73–82, New York, NY, USA, 2015. ACM.

[34] W. W. Zou and P. C. Yuen. Very low resolution face recognition problem. *Image Processing, IEEE Transactions on*, 21(1):327–340, 2012.

Temporal Association Rules for Modelling Multimodal Social Signals

Thomas Janssoone
Sorbonne Universités
UPMC Univ Paris 06
CNRS UMR 7222, ISIR
F-75005, Paris, France
thomas.janssoone@isir.upmc.fr

ABSTRACT

In this paper, we present the first step of a methodology dedicated to deduce automatically sequences of signals expressed by humans during an interaction. The aim is to link interpersonal stances with arrangements of social signals such as modulations of Action Units and prosody during a face-to-face exchange. The long-term goal is to infer association rules of signals. We plan to use them as an input to the animation of an Embodied Conversational Agent (ECA). In this paper, we illustrate the proposed methodology to the SEMAINE-DB corpus from which we automatically extracted Action Units (AUs), head positions, turn-taking and prosody information. We have applied the data mining algorithm that is used to find the sequences of social signals featuring different social stances. We finally discuss our primary results focusing on given AUs (smiles and eyebrows) and the perspectives of this method.

Keywords

Social signal processing; Sequence Mining; Data Mining; Interpersonal stance; Action Unit; Prosody; Facial expression; Data processing

Categories and Subject Descriptors

I.3.6 [**Methodology and Techniques : Interaction techniques**]; H.1.2 [**User/Machine Systems : Human information processing**]; H.2.8 [**Database Applications : Data mining**]; I.2.11 [**Distributed Artificial Intelligence : Intelligent agents**]

1. INTRODUCTION

To enhance the quality of life in our modern digital society, the integration of Embodied Conversational Agents (ECAs) is a regularly proposed solution. For example, autonomous living can be eased with the help of an intelligent artifact if this one is emphatic enough to provide support. This work aims to enhance the interaction between Humans and ECAs by making it as efficient and as realistic as possible.

ICMI 2015, November 9–13, 2015, Seattle, WA, USA.

ACM 978-1-4503-3912-4/15/11 ...$15.00.
DOI: http://dx.doi.org/10.1145/2818346.2823305 .

One challenge in the domain of ECAs is to improve their believability by given them the capacity to express emotions and interpersonal stances [1]. For this purpose, the field of Social Signal Processing is thriving [2] and more and more databases are available for its study. These databases are mainly audiovisual and are used as monomodal or multimodal inputs to Machine Learning methods [3, 4, 5, 6]. The aim is to detect characteristics such as prosodic descriptors or activations of facial muscles labelled Action Units (AU see Fig1) to recognize a social expression (emotion, stance, behavior . . .). Furthermore, an external observant can annotate this data by describing his/her perception of the ongoing interaction (Antagonism, Tension, Valence, Arousal,. . .). These annotations provide different classes for the supervised machine learning algorithms.

The context of my Ph.D thesis is focused on one aspect of the interaction which is the interpersonal stance of an exchange as defined by Scherer [7] which can be seen as the "colouration" of the interaction : is it friendly or hostile ? Is someone dominated or dominant ?

The scheduling of the multimodal signals expressed by a protagonist in an intra-synchrony study will also provide information about his/her interpersonal stance. Intra-synchrony refers here to the simultaneous occurrences of the modality of one individual whereas the inter-synchrony is between two interlocutors. Intra-synchrony and inter-synchrony are linked as the social signals expressed by one speaker influence the stance of his/her interlocuteur and then the signals he/she will use as a response. Chindamo et al. [8] illustrate the importance of this intermodal dynamic of the intra-synchrony dynamic with the football example : if someone says, "*I really love football !*", this sentence will be perceived differently if told with a high pitch and a smiling face (e.g. arousal) as opposed to being expressed with low pitch and a serious face (e.g. sarcasm).

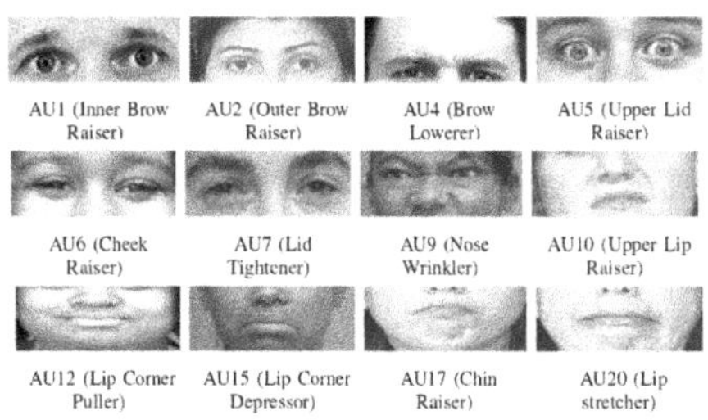

Figure 1: face and Action Unit locations, images are obtained from `http://www.cs.cmu.edu/~face/facs.htm`

We aim at investigating an automatic method based on a Sequence-Mining algorithm to analyse the dynamics of the social signals such as facial expressions, head nods, prosody, and turn-taking. The focus is put on the variations of these signals modelled as a sequence of temporal events. Our approach will propose to identify sequences of signals corresponding to a given interpersonal stance. These association rules learnt from a corpus will provide time-related information between the occurrence of the signals in a sequence and also the distribution of these sequences in an interaction. From a long term perspective, this should allow automatic temporal planing to generate a realistic model of stances for ECAs. The difficulty lies in the dependence of the intra-synchrony of these temporal signals not only on the stance but also to other constraints such as identity or bio-mechanical constraints (e.g. the speech production mechanisms involved) or the semantic contents of the given utterance [9]. For example, two persons can have a very warm exchange but one frowns because he/she is dazzled by the sun.

In this paper, the former approaches found in the literature will be first detailed. Then, the first steps of my Ph.D research will be explained : the choice of the sequence mining algorithm and its first implementation are justified. A primary study on a restricted set of social signals (smile, frown) and its results will be then reviewed. Finally, perspectives and future leads will be presented for discussion.

2. RELATED WORK

The field of interpersonal stance has been investigated during the last decades [10] and one of its application is the generation of believable interpersonal stances for ECAs. To do so, humans' expressions of these stances were studied.

Allwood et al. [11] proposes a qualitative study of verbal and gestural feedbacks during dialogues between a travel agent and customers. In this particular context, they underline the relationship between prosody and gestures. Yet, this study does not make any explicit link between the kind of feedback and the stances of the protagonists. A statistical study of the smiles as backchannels is proposed by Prepin et al. [12, 13]. It provides a link between smiles and interpersonal stances and shows that the alignment and the synchronization of smiles between two agents can modify the perception of the stances by an observer. In a study about first impression, Cafaro et al. [14] show how nonverbal immediacy cues impact the observant's feeling of the stance of a virtual character.

Lee and Marsella [15] propose to apply a Machine-Learning algorithm to study how head-nod magnitude and eyebrow movements evolve while speaking. Participants were asked to rate their immediate feeling of a virtual agent speaking while making head nods and eyebrow movements. They show that different models affect human perception but the link with interpersonal stance is not investigated. Ravenet et al. [16] create a corpus of ECAs postures according to several stances. They develop a Bayesian model to automatically generate stance which however remains static : it is a posture, not a movement.

Martinez et al. [17] and then Chollet et al.[18] explain how to use data mining algorithms to find simple sequences of non-verbal signals associated to social stances. Martinez et al. [17] linked these feature samples to emotions such as frustration in the context of video gaming. Chollet et al. [18] extract sequences of non-verbal signals characterizing different interpersonal stances using the Generalised Sequence Pattern algorithm. This algorithm extracts sequences without temporal information i.e. it can express that one event happens after another. Then, they build a model to select the most appropriate sequence for the expression of a particular stance by an ECA. Although these studies have proposed an analysis of social signal sequences, they do not consider temporal information. However, such information may change the interpretation of social signals sequences e.g. a long smile versus a short one.

3. OUR APPROACH

In the same vein, we choose to take advantage of a sequence mining algorithm that considers temporal information which is suitable for social signals. After a survey of existing Temporal Constrained Systems solutions (Chronicle, Episode, ...), we focused on The Temporal Interval Tree Association Rule Learning (Titarl) algorithm [19] because of its flexibility and its ability to express uncertainty and temporal inaccuracy of temporal events. Indeed, it can compute time relation as rules between events (before/after), negation and accurate time constraints such as *"If there is an event D at time t, then there is an event C at time t+5 "*. This temporal learning approach to find temporal associative rules from symbolic sequences allows to represent imprecise (non-deterministic) and inaccurate temporal between social signals considered as events. Furthermore, from a long-term perspective, TITARL is also linked to a meta-planner algorithm to choose good strategies for the generation of a non-verbal behaviour of an agent[20]. This algorithm takes a description of the "world", a set of doable actions (here the Titarl rules) and a set of goals and infers a plan, i.e., a description of the action to perform in order to achieve the goal.

We will now detail in the following this algorithm, and we will apply it with particular social signal data such as AUs, head nods, and prosodic events. To the best of our knowledge, this is the first attempt to use a sequence mining algorithm with temporal information to find association rules between social signals events in the context of behaviour analysis and modelling.

A temporal rule gives information about the relation between symbolic events with a temporal aspect. In our case, the events are the social signals (AUs, head nods, ...) considered as discrete events after a preprocessing step of symbolization. For example, with the input of Fig.2, a temporal pattern could be :
If an event "activation of AU4" happens at time t while state Speak is active, then an event "activation of AU9" will be triggered between t+Δt and t+3Δt with a uniform distribution which can be symbolized by the rule shown in (1) :

$$\underset{Speaking}{AU4_{activation}} \xrightarrow{\mathscr{U}_{\Delta t,3\Delta t}} AU9_{activation} \qquad (1)$$

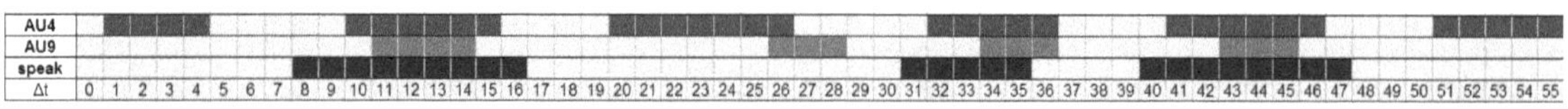

Figure 2: example of social signal input for TITARL

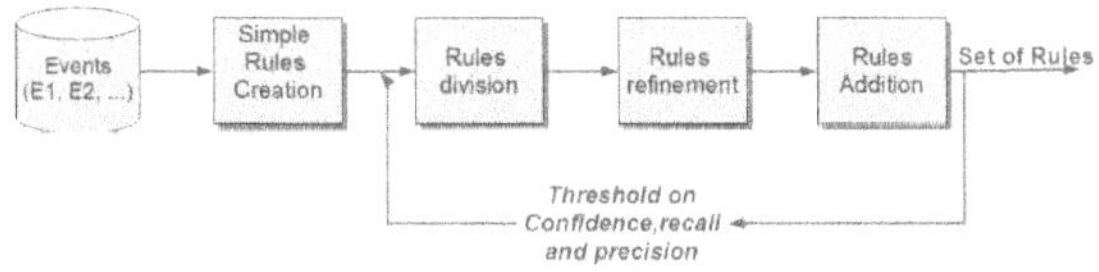

Figure 3: pipeline of the TITARL algorithm

Δt represents here a time-step due to the training data such as the video frame rate. However, the output of the Titarl algorithm models the duration of the interval between consecutive changes.

A rule is composed by a head, here the $AU9_{activation}$, a tree of temporal constraints, here the $AU4_{activation}$, a temporal distribution, $\underset{Speaking}{}$ here the $\mathscr{U}_{\Delta t, 3\Delta t}$.

Some characteristics of a rule can be computed to validate its interest. If we look at the following rule r defined in (2) :

$$A \xrightarrow{\mathscr{U}_{\Delta t_{min}, \Delta t_{max}}} B \qquad (2)$$

then the confidence of a rule is the probability of a prediction of the rule to be true (see 3a). We are also interested in the support of a rule which is the percentage of events explained by the rule (see 3b). Finally, TITARL ensures a good precision in the rule that is the temporal accuracy of the prediction, i.e., a low dispersal of the events A (standard deviation) verifying the rule r (see 3c).

$$conf = P(B(t')|A(t)), t' - t \in [\Delta t_{min}, \Delta t_{max}] \qquad (3a)$$

$$support = \frac{\# B, \exists A \text{ such that } (A \rightarrow B) \text{ true}}{\# B} \qquad (3b)$$

$$precision = \frac{1}{\text{standard deviation of rule r}} \qquad (3c)$$

The structure of the TITARL pipeline, shown in the Fig.3, has two major parts. With the set of input events, characterized by a name, a session, a character and a time, a first process will generate simple rules with a structure like in 2 and a very large temporal distribution. These rules have a high confidence and support but a very low precision.

The three steps of TITARL are recursively applied : division of the rule, refinement and addition of conditions.
The division step will produce more accurate rules by dealing with co-occurence of events. For example, if we have an event A at time t, an event B at time $t + 5\Delta t$ and an event B at time $t + 15\Delta t$, we can have the rule $A \xrightarrow{\mathscr{U}_{5\Delta t, 15\Delta t}} B$ or the two rules $A \xrightarrow{\mathscr{U}_{5\Delta t}} B$ and $A \xrightarrow{\mathscr{U}_{15\Delta t}} B$. This division step will allow to choose between the two possibilities.
The refinement of a rule aims at increasing its precision : it observes the temporal distribution of the events verifying the rule and decreases their variance with a threshold on its histogram of distribution.
The addition of a condition to a rule is done to maximize the information gain. To do so, given a rule $A \rightarrow B$, the algorithm observes all the simple rules like $B \rightarrow C$. It will combine them as $A \rightarrow B \rightarrow C$ if its number of occurrences remains over a fixed threshold. This step will stop in case of a loop in the chain of events.

These last steps are carried on while the product of the confidence, the support and the precision remains over a threshold. More details about the TITARL algorithm can be found in [19].

4. PRELIMINARY RESULTS

In order to validate the first step of our methodology, TITARL is used to compute association rules with temporal information on social signals found in the literature. From [21, 16], we defined prior connections. These papers explain that friendliness involves AU6 and AU12 (smile and cheek raiser) while hostility is linked to AU1/2 and AU4 (brow lowerer). For this preliminary study, we only focus on these Action Units.

Therefore, we applied TITARL on the SEMAINE database [22] restricted to our purpose. This corpus proposes video and audio data streams of a Face-to-Face interaction between an user and an operator acting an agent with very specific characters. Due to computation time, for this preliminary study, we only focus here on two roles of the operator part, one friendly, Poppy, and one hostile, Spike. This represents 11 sessions of $3-4$ minutes recording, 7 with Poppy, 4 with Spike.

We then processed these sessions of operators in order to get facial Action Units activation detected using the solution proposed by Nicolle et al. [23] and symbolized as three states : inactivate, low activation and high activation.
Some results can be seen in Table1 : association rules are shown with their confidence, support and score as defined in eq4 from [19].

$$score = \frac{conf_r^4 . supp_r^2}{range_r} \qquad (4)$$

We chose to present in the first two rows the most complex rules obtained after the addition part. We can see that Poppy is most likely to smile and that its smiles implies the activation of cheek raiser and lasts longer. In the four other rows are presented simple rules (just division and refinement) focused on eyebrows with the highest score over Spike, the hostile agent, and Poppy, the friendly one. As expected, they are found in Spike results and we see that Poppy is less likely to use its eyebrows while Spike will frown them 82% of the time.

These results allow us not only to validate our methodology as they are in agreement with the literature but also to provide temporal information and confidence. Indeed, the empirical and theoretical research have shown that friendly stances imply more smiles and eyebrow together out of anger are perceived as threatening and hostile. Moreover, our study enables us to identify more precisely the duration of the social signals. Such information is essential to synthesize the stance of an ECA.

5. CONCLUSION AND FUTURE WORK

This paper presents the methodology planned to automatically extract temporal rules of multimodal signals. The preliminary results shows that such methodology can be used to identify sequences of social signals as well as temporal information associated to specific stances. We will now discuss the various tracks we want to investigate during the rest of my Ph.D research.

Evaluation : the evaluation and the validation of the association rules remain an open question. We are currently investigating two

	rule ($body \xrightarrow{\Delta t_{min};\Delta t_{max}} head$)	confidence	support	score
Poppy	$AU6_{off} \xrightarrow{0.0s;6.5s} AU12_{off} \xrightarrow{1.1s;2.3s} AU12_{low}$	0.41	0.23	5.10^{-3}
Spike	$AU12_{off} \xrightarrow{5.0s;13.1s} AU6_{off} \xrightarrow{0.2s;3.5s} AU6_{low}$	0.34	0.22	1.10^{-4}
Poppy	$AU6_{off} \xrightarrow{1.6s;6.1s} AU6_{low}$	0.60	0.30	1.10^{-3}
Spike	$AU6_{off} \xrightarrow{0.0s;0.1s} AU6_{low}$	0.47	0.47	3.10^{-4}
Poppy	$AU1+2_{off} \xrightarrow{1.2s;2.3s} AU1+2_{low}$	0.32	0.26	3.10^{-3}
Spike	$AU1+2_{off} \xrightarrow{0.5s;2.2s} AU1+2_{low}$	0.82	0.76	6.10^{-3}

Table 1: Sample of results with their confidence, support and score. The two first rows are "complex" rules but the four others, due to computation delay, are simple rules obtained after the division and refinement steps.

possibilities. First a Leave One Subject Out validation will be done were the rule learnt with one actor will be compared to the ones learnt on the other actors in the corpus. Second, a subjective validation will be performed to check if a rule correspond to the desired stance evolution such as explained in [18] : an ECA will play the sequence of social signals and an annotator will rate the stance variation.

Scoring : for this preliminary study, the score defined in [19] is used and we obtained the expected results. However, we are not fully satisfied with this formula because, as seen in Table1, it does not take into account the complexity of the rule and the number of occurrences of a signal. For these reasons, we think that some improvements need to be made.

Multimodality : we plan to quickly extend this study to other modalities than Action Unit. We already processed the Semaine corpus in order to get features like the head nod, the turn taking and the prosody. The first issue deals with the symbolisation of these continuous signals. As a first step, we are investigating the Symbolic Aggregate Algorithm [24] to do so. The second one is technical : the more inputs Titarl has, the more time consuming its execution is.

Temporal Association Rule of social signal events for a specific stance : in order to find association rules that are specific to a stance, we plan to use a text mining method such as Term Frequency Inverse Document Frequency (tf-idf). The rules will be considered as words and the sessions as documents. This metric appears to be relevant to our purpose because it will evaluate how important a rule is to the corpus and also should find bio-mechanical rules as they are not specific to a character. Nevertheless, we are open to all suggestions and discussions to improve this selection.

Temporal analysis of the Temporal Association Rules : as explained by Chindamo et al. [8], interpersonal stance is built over the turns of an interaction. Thus, we think that it will be interesting to analyse the temporal distribution of the association rules found by Titarl and their evolutions over the time. For example, we could investigate whether smiles last longer at the beginning or at the end of an interaction. This raises the issue of defining temporal parts of an interaction like its beginning, its end or its middle for instance..

Strategy building : the Meta Planner Titarl algorithm can be used with the (Meta) Titarl planner, also introduced by Guillame-Bert et al. [20]. This algorithm can provide an efficient temporal planning from a goal which, here, could be a specific stance. It is designed to deal with and predictable but imprecisely time located exogenous events. Therefore, we would like to use it to provide a model of interpersonal stance generation.

Intra and inter synchrony model : as explained in the introduction, the focus here is on the simultaneous occurrences of the modality of one individual which refers to his/her intra-synchrony. However, an interaction is built over two or more protagonists and their actions will modify their stances. Some studies have investigated these mechanisms such as smile alignment [21] so improve the association rules with the inter-personal synchrony will be an improvement for the strategy building as a second step.

6. ACKNOWLEDGEMENT

I would like to thank my advisors, Chloé Clavel, Magalie Ochs, Kévin Bailly and Gaël Richard, for their support and guidance. This work was performed within the Labex SMART supported by French state funds managed by the ANR within the Investissements dÁvenir programme under reference ANR-11-IDEX-0004-0.

7. REFERENCES

[1] Alessandro Vinciarelli, Maja Pantic, and Hervé Bourlard. Social signal processing : Survey of an emerging domain. *Image and Vision Computing*, 27(12) :1743–1759, 2009.

[2] Alessandro Vinciarelli, Maja Pantic, Dirk Heylen, Catherine Pelachaud, Isabella Poggi, Francesca D'Errico, and Marc Schröder. Bridging the gap between social animal and unsocial machine : A survey of social signal processing. *Affective Computing*, 3(1) :69–87, 2012.

[3] Ognjen Rudovic, Mihalis A Nicolaou, and Vladimir Pavlovic. 1 machine learning methods for social signal processing.

[4] Alex Pentland. Social dynamics : Signals and behavior. In *ICDL*, volume 5, 2004.

[5] Georgia Sandbach, Stefanos Zafeiriou, and Maja Pantic. Markov random field structures for facial action unit intensity estimation. In *ICCVW, 2013*, pages 738–745. IEEE, 2013.

[6] Arman Savran, Haichuan Cao, Ani Nenkova, and Rajesh Verma. Temporal bayesian fusion for affect sensing : Combining video, audio, and lexical modalities. 2014.

[7] Klaus R Scherer. What are emotions ? and how can they be measured ? *Social science information*, 44(4) :695–729, 2005.

[8] Massimo Chindamo, Julian Allwood, and Elisabeth Ahlsen. Some suggestions for the study of stance in communication. In *PASSAT, 2012 and SocialCom 2012*, pages 617–622. IEEE, 2012.

[9] Elisabetta Bevacqua and Catherine Pelachaud. Expressive audio-visual speech. *Computer Animation and Virtual Worlds*, 15(3-4) :297–304, 2004.

[10] Qiuhua Fu, R op den Akker, and M Bruijnes. A literature review of typical behavior of different interpersonal attitude. *Capita Selecta HMI, University of Twente*, 2014.

[11] Jens Allwood and Loredana Cerrato. A study of gestural feedback expressions. In *First nordic symposium on multimodal communication*, pages 7–22. Copenhagen, 2003.

[12] Ken Prepin, Magalie Ochs, and Catherine Pelachaud. Mutual stance building in dyad of virtual agents : Smile alignment and synchronisation. In *PASSAT, 2012 and SocialCom, 2012*, pages 938–943. IEEE, 2012.

[13] Ken Prepin, Magalie Ochs, and Catherine Pelachaud. Beyond backchannels : co-construction of dyadic stancce by reciprocal reinforcement of smiles between virtual agents. In *International Conference CogSci*, 2013.

[14] Angelo Cafaro, Hannes Högni Vilhjálmsson, Timothy Bickmore, Dirk Heylen, Kamilla Rún Jóhannsdóttir, and Gunnar Steinn Valgardsson. First impressions : UsersâĂŹ judgments of virtual agentsâĂŹ personality and interpersonal attitude in first encounters. In *IVA*, pages 67–80. Springer, 2012.

[15] Jina Lee and Stacy Marsella. Modeling speaker behavior : A comparison of two approaches. In *IVA*, pages 161–174. Springer, 2012.

[16] Brian Ravenet, Magalie Ochs, and Catherine Pelachaud. From a user-created corpus of virtual agentâĂŹs non-verbal behavior to a computational model of interpersonal attitudes. In *IVA*, pages 263–274. Springer, 2013.

[17] Héctor P Martínez and Georgios N Yannakakis. Mining multimodal sequential patterns : a case study on affect detection. In *Proc. 13th ICMI*, pages 3–10. ACM, 2011.

[18] Mathieu Chollet, Magalie Ochs, and Catherine Pelachaud. From non-verbal signals sequence mining to bayesian networks for interpersonal attitudes expression. In *IVA*, pages 120–133. Springer, 2014.

[19] Mathieu Guillame-Bert and James L Crowley. Learning temporal association rules on symbolic time sequences. In *ACML*, pages 159–174, 2012.

[20] Mathieu Guillame-Bert and James L Crowley. Planning with inaccurate temporal rules. In *ICTAI, 2012*, volume 1, pages 492–499. IEEE, 2012.

[21] Magalie Ochs and Catherine Pelachaud. Model of the perception of smiling virtual character. In *Proc. 11th International Conference on AAMAS*, pages 87–94. International Foundation for Autonomous Agents and Multiagent Systems, 2012.

[22] Gary McKeown, Michel Valstar, Roddy Cowie, Maja Pantic, and Marc Schröder. The semaine database : Annotated multimodal records of emotionally colored conversations between a person and a limited agent. *Affective Computing*, 3(1) :5–17, 2012.

[23] Jeremie Nicolle, Kevin Bailly, and Mohamed Chetouani. Facial action unit intensity prediction via hard multi-task metric learning for kernel regression. In *FERA Challenge In : IEEE International Conference on Automatic Face and Festure Recognition*, 2015.

[24] Jessica Lin, Eamonn Keogh, Li Wei, and Stefano Lonardi. Experiencing sax : a novel symbolic representation of time series. *Data Mining and knowledge discovery*, 15(2) :107–144, 2007.

Detecting and Synthesizing Synchronous Joint Action in Human-Robot Teams

Tariq Iqbal and Laurel D. Riek
Computer Science and Engineering, University of Notre Dame
{tiqbal,lriek}@nd.edu

ABSTRACT

To become capable teammates to people, robots need the ability to interpret human activities and appropriately adjust their actions in real time. The goal of our research is to build robots that can work fluently and contingently with human teams. To this end, we have designed novel nonlinear dynamical methods to automatically model and detect synchronous joint action (SJA) in human teams. We also have extended this work to enable robots to move jointly with human teammates in real time. In this paper, we describe our work to date, and discuss our future research plans to further explore this research space. The results of this work are expected to benefit researchers in social signal processing, human-machine interaction, and robotics.

Categories and Subject Descriptors

I.2.9 [**Artificial Intelligence**]: Robotics

1. INTRODUCTION

Humans and robots are increasingly working side-by-side across many disciplines, ranging from manufacturing and agriculture, to education and home healthcare [27]. However, for a robot to be useful to human teammates, it needs to understand the activities occurring around it, as well as their context [19]. If a robot can better interpret its surroundings, its interaction with humans is more likely to reach to a higher level of coordination, and will lead to a *fluent* meshing of their actions over time [5, 8, 3]. Therefore, it is important for robots to possess the ability to interpret the high-level activities happening around them from its sensor data, and to predict future activities in order to inform their own actions [9, 7].

Many fields, such as robotics and computer vision, have been working on improving the automatic understanding of human activities, as well as the dynamics of a group. This work include advances in both exo-centric and ego-centric processing, used to detect activities from buttering toast to social interaction [20, 4]. Recent work has built upon this high-level human activity detection to automatically characterize the dynamics and interaction patterns of a group [26, 2].

This work is useful for many situations; however, in human-robot teamwork, it can be challenging for a robot to understand and contextualize human activity as it happens. Solely relying on high-level human activity detection may not provide robots sufficient contextual information to characterize the situation and environment. Furthermore, it is challenging to sense and respond to people when both are in motion, due to sensor occlusion, camera shake, noise, etc. [9]. However, employing a lower-level, dynamical approach to group behavior and motion understanding may help robots overcome these limitations.

Synchronous joint action (SJA) is a common phenomenon observed during human-human interaction (HHI). This is a form of social interaction where two or more participants coordinate their actions both in space and time while making changes to their environment [21]. Understanding joint action in a human-robot interaction (HRI) scenario is also important, as a robot may make decisions about its actions to improve its overall engagement as a team member. For example, a robot can be a more effective team member by anticipating a human teammate's motion and acting appropriately in collaborative manipulation tasks [23, 22].

Researchers in the fields of cognitive science, psychology and music have explored different methods to measure joint action in HHI [15, 1, 18]. Recently, it also has attracted the attention of the HRI community [13, 6]. Most of this research has focused on dyadic HRI (one human, one robot), and focused mostly on manipulation tasks, such as handovers and assembly. However, it is important for a robot to extend the notion of understanding joint action beyond this dyadic HRI, such as when working in a team with multiple people and robots. In the case of synchronous group activities, such as collaborative climbing, running, or dancing, a robot needs to understand the motion of its co-humans and predict their future actions to move "in-step" with the rest of the group.

This leads us to explore several research questions. First, can we automatically *measure* the degree of synchronous joint action in a group from the high-level activities of the group members? As SJA is an important indicator of the group cohesiveness, and enables an understanding of a group's affective behavior, answering this research question would help machines more accurately characterize group dynamics [12, 25, 18]. Moreover, addressing this question would be helpful for a robot to understand the dynamics of a human group more accurately, even when everyone is continuously in motion.

Second, can this method be used to *synthesize* joint activity in real-time while robots are moving within synchronous human-robot teams? Addressing this question would mean that the robot not only will be able to understand the behavior of the group, but also can inform its own activities appropriately.

Addressing these research questions is important, because this will lead us to build intelligent robots which will both be able to understand human teams, and interact contingently within them.

ICMI '15, November 9–13, 2015, Seattle, WA, USA

DOI: http://dx.doi.org/10.1145/2818346.2823315.

In our research, we developed a novel method to automatically detect SJA in a group from multi-modal data streams. This nonlinear, dynamical-systems approach takes multiple types of task-level events into account, and is able to work with non-periodic time series data as it estimates SJA [12, 9]. In the next Section, we describe our SJA measurement method, and briefly present a human-human and human-robot validation study. Then, we describe a method to enable a robot to synchronously move within a human-robot team using the SJA measure. Finally, we discuss our research contribution and plan in the last Section.

2. MEASURING SJA IN A TEAM

Several researchers have worked on measuring synchronization within a group, such as Varni et al. [26]. These methods typically only incorporate a single modality and a single type of event when calculating synchrony of a group (e.g., only gross body motion, or only EEG signals). However, there are cases where multiple types of events are associated with a group activity. Usually to assess these events, analysis of multimodal data streams is necessary. For example, in the case of a repetitive manufacturing process, humans need to perform different types of tasks, and all these types of tasks need to incorporate together if we want to measure the synchronization of the group. In these cases, it is necessary to incorporate all these different types of events together, instead of just one, when measuring group synchrony [12].

To address this gap, we developed a new method that builds on event synchronization work by Quian Quiroga et al. [16] and Varni et al. [26]. Our method considers multiple types of task-level events together to measure SJA (group synchrony), and can also incorporate multiple types of sensor data (i.e., depth, RGB, audio). In addition to this contribution, it is also more accurate than single-event based methods, and able to work with real-world sensor data. The detailed description of the method can be found in [12, 9].

In our method, we employ the following six high-level steps to measure group synchronization [12, 10]:

1. Automatically detect the high-level events during the group activity from the multimodal data stream,
2. Express all of the detected events of each group member with a time series,
3. Measure the pair-wise synchronization index (*PSync*) for each pair of group members, taking all types of events into account together,
4. Build a group topology graph (*CTG*) of the group based on the *PSync* values,
5. Calculate the individual synchronization index (*ISync*) of each group member from the *PSync* and the *CTG*,
6. Determine the group synchronization index (*GSync*) from the *ISync* values and the *CTG*.

To detect the task-level events associated with a group task, we can use different sensor data together. After detecting the multiple types of events, we can present those in a time series. Now, suppose x_n and y_n are the two time series, where $n = 1, \ldots, N$ (N samples). For each event type $e_i \in E$, $m_x(e_i)$ and $m_y(e_i)$ are the number of events occurring in x and y respectively, where E is the set of all events. Now, for each event type $e_i \in E$, we calculate the pairwise synchronization index ($Q(e_i)$) [12, 9].

$Q(e_i)$ represents the synchronization of event event type e_i in two time series. We normalized this value, thus $Q(e_i) = 1$ means all the events are fully synchronous, whereas, $Q(e_i) = 0$ means, the events are not synchronous at all. Then, the overall pairwise synchronization index (Q) considering all events is calculated as:

$$\forall e_i \in E : Q = \frac{\sum [Q(e_i) \times [m_x(e_i) + m_y(e_i)]]}{\sum [m_x(e_i) + m_y(e_i)]} \qquad (1)$$

After detecting Q, we build a group topology graph (CTG), which is a undirected weighted graph. In this graph, each time series is represented by a vertex, and each pair of vertices are connected by an edge weighted by the Q value of that pair. Based on this graph, and the value of Q, we measure the individual synchronization index (*ISync*) of each member of the group. Individual synchronization index represents how well a member is synchronous with the rest of the group. Then, based the *ISync* values and the *CTG*, we determine the group synchronization index (*GSync*) [12, 9, 10].

3. VALIDATION OF THE METHOD

We validated our method by applying it to two group activities that involve SJA. The first activity involved only humans, while the second activity included both humans and robots. We briefly describe the experimental studies below, though they are explained in detail in [12, 9].

3.1 Human-Human Validation Study

First, we validated the method by applying it to a multiple, event-based, rhythmic group game called "The Cup Game" [12]. During this game, the players stand at a table, perform a sequential and rhythmic activity with their hands and a cup, and pass the cup to their neighbor at the end of an iteration (see Fig. 1-A). We chose this task due to the fact that each player performs a periodic activity, and each player's movements influences the others. This task helped us to address our first research question.

Two Microsoft Kinect sensors were connected to two time synchronized computers running Robot Operating System. We recorded the RGB video and the skeletal data of the players during the games. The events during the game (clap, pass or move the cup) were detected from the hand joint positions of each player and the cup positions. We tracked the hands using the Kinect's skeletal data. The cups were tracked using the standard RGB-based blob tracking techniques from the RGB data. From these events, we measured the *GSync* index for each game using the method described previously [12].

In this study, a total of 22 people participated (50% female) in groups of four players per session, yielding a total of six experimental sessions. Each group had a learning and practice session, followed by two games. After the two games, each group member rated on a Discrete Visual Analog Scale (DVAS) how well-synchronized they felt each game was, and which game was more synchronous [12].

The results suggest that the group synchronization indices produced by our method agreed with the perception of the majority of participants in all of the sessions. The results further suggest that our method is more accurate in estimating SJA than other methods described in the literature. Full experimental details and result analyses are available in [12], though we present an analysis of one of the sessions in Fig 2-A.

3.2 Human-Robot Validation Study

In the second validation experiment, we employed our proposed method on a human-robot teamwork scenario to automatically measure SJA of the group [12, 9]. In this study, two people performed a high-march action down a hallway across four scenarios (see Fig 1-B). The first performer acted as the leader, and wore noise-canceling headphones playing "Stars and Stripes Forever", a march by John Philip Sousa, to help them march at a consistent pace.

Figure 1: Our research explores psychomotor entrainment between groups of people and robots, where we work toward enabling robots to automatically sense and respond to synchronous group behavior.

The second performer acted as the follower, and was approximately two feet behind the leader to their right. The follower adjusted their steps either synchronously or asynchronously as directed by the experimenter per condition of the experiment. Two autonomous mobile robots (Turtlebots) were programmed to follow the respective performers [9].

We defined two types of task-level events based on the positions of the legs of the performers. These events occurred when a performer began to raise their leg from the ground, and when a leg reached its maximum height. As a result, a total of four types of events occurred during this marching activity (two for each leg) [9].

To detect the events, the feet of each performer were tracked using standard RGB-based blob tracking techniques, as captured from the robots' Kinect sensors. These blobs corresponded to the four unique squares of colored paper attached to the performers' feet. Detecting these events were challenging, as both the humans and the robots were in motion during this activity. From these events, we measured the *GSync* index for each marching session [9].

In the study, we recorded data from a total of four scenarios, which corresponded to the four experimental conditions, and yielded four unique marching patterns. We expected to see high synchronization index values when the performers marched synchronously, and low values when they were asynchronously. As demonstrated by Fig 2-B, our measured experimental results for each scenario reasonably match the expected synchronization indices. The detailed analysis can be found in Iqbal et al. [9, 11].

4. SYNTHESIZING SJA IN A TEAM

It is important for a robot to make appropriate decisions based on its understanding of the activities occurring around it using its sensor data. In the previous Section, we described methods for a robot to understand group activity and behavior from multiple types of task-level events. In this Section, we describe two methods for a robot to anticipate future activities and actions of the other group members. We also describe methods to generate appropriate actions for a robot based on these anticipations. This study was aimed to address our second research question.

We used a synchronous group dance performed by a human-robot team as an experimental test bed for studying SJA tasks. Three human performers along with a mobile robot (i.e., a Turtlebot robot) performed a dance to the song "Smooth Criminal" by Michael Jackson (see Fig 1-C). With the help of an experienced dancer, we choreographed a routine for the participants to perform. The dance is iterative, and performed cyclically in a counter-clockwise manner. Each phase includes four iterations of the following steps in order: move forward, move backward, move forward, move backward, clap, and a 90-degree turn [17].

To acquire the movement data of the humans during the dance sessions, we used four Microsoft Kinect for Windows version 2 sensors. Each Kinect sensor was connected to a computer to capture and process depth, infrared and skeletal data. One of the main challenges of a multi-sensor and multi-client setup is to maintain a consistent time reference across all the client machines. To maintain a time reference for all the machines, we implemented a client-server architecture for communication between the clients with Kinect sensors and the server [17].

The clients periodically synchronized their clocks with the server, giving a global accuracy to the timestamps recorded with detected events. When a client determined that an event had occurred, it sent a message to the server indicating the classification of the event, the time at which it occurred to millisecond precision, and other information relevant to the particular event [17].

Each client processed the data streams captured by the attached Kinect sensor, and sent the processed data to the server. The server received the data, and generated predictions for the movements of the robot client. The robot client was also connected to the server. The robot node ran on the Robot Operating System (ROS) platform to control a Turtlebot's movements based on instructions received from the server [17].

The clients detected five high-level events from the performers' movements during the dance performance: start and stop moving forward, start and stop moving backward, and clap. These events were detected from the change in 3-D skeleton joint positions of the dancers. The start and the stop of the forward and backward motion was detected when there was a sufficient change in the z component of the human performer's skeletal joint coordinates. A clap was detected when the hand joint positions of the human performer reached a sufficiently small local minima within a time window [17].

From these detected events, in the server, we employed two methods to anticipate the future action of the humans, and generate necessary commands for the robot to perform appropriate actions in a timely fashion. The first method that we employed was an *Event Cluster based Anticipation (ECA)* method for predicting the timing of future group events and informing the robot to perform the actions accordingly. Then, relying on our previously proposed event-based method for measuring the degree of synchrony of a group, we used a *Synchronization Index based Anticipation (SIA)* method to inform robot's movements.

The ECA method relied on the assumption that the movement events of one iteration are more or less similar to the events that happened in the previous iteration. This was a valid assumption because this dance is rhythmic and iterative in nature. Thus, the event timing of one iteration was taken into consideration to predict the event timing of the next iteration. First, we clustered all the similar types of events together that happened relatively closer in

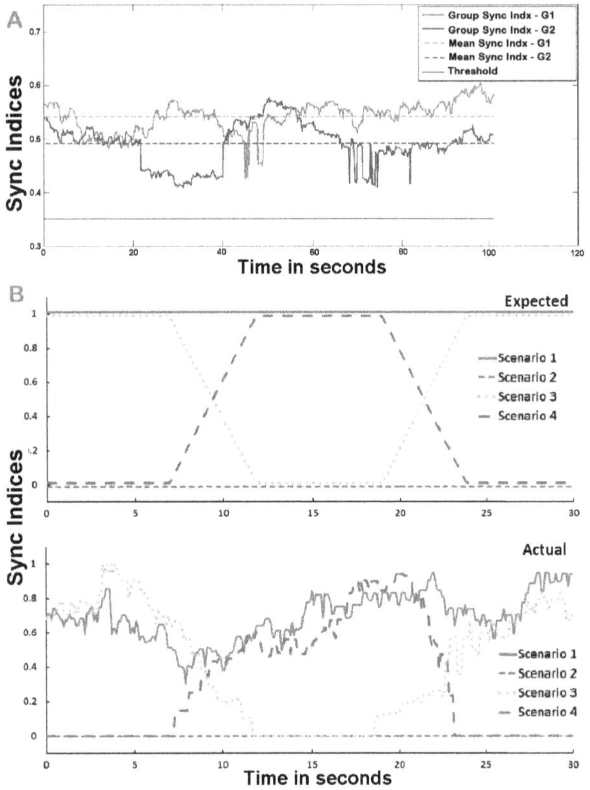

Figure 2: A) Group Synchronization Indices over time during a cup game session [12], B) Expected and Actual synchronization indices for all four experimental scenarios of the human-robot marching study [9].

time. Then, we calculated the average time of all the events and used that time as the timing of the event for the next iteration.

Alternatively, the SIA method takes the group's internal dynamics into account while generating movements for the robot. The method operates under the assumption that a person, who was synchronous with the rest of the group members in the previous iterations, is more likely to be synchronous with the rest of the group members during this iteration of the dance as well. Thus, if the robot follows the movements of that person during this iteration of the dance, it is more likely that the robot would also be synchronous with the rest of the group during this iteration.

We recruited a total of 9 groups (27 participants, 3 persons per group) for our study. Each group had a learning and practice session, and then participated in three dance sessions. During the first dance session, only the humans participated in the dance movements, while the robot joined the humans in the dance during the last two sessions.

During the last two sessions, the robot joined the group. We used the anticipation methods in different sessions. To reduce the bias due to the ordering of the methods, we counterbalanced the anticipation methods. However, we did not disclose which method was in use to the participants during the dance.

Following the experiment, participants completed a short questionnaire asking them to rate which of the two dance sessions they felt was more synchronous. A detailed description of this study can be found in [17].

Our initial data analysis shows some promising results. The results suggest that most of the groups were more synchronous when the SIA method was used as the anticipation method for the robot, than the ECA method. These results might support the robustness of the SIA method over the ECA method, as SIA the method takes the group's internal dynamics into account while anticipating future events.

5. RESEARCH CONTRIBUTIONS AND RESEARCH PLAN

The aim of this research project is to build intelligent robots, able to fluently interact with human teams. To summarize, we have made the following contributions:

1. The creation of a nonlinear, dynamical systems inspired approach to measure the degree of SJA in a group from the multiple types of task-level activities of the group members [12, 10].
2. The employment of this method to a human-robot teamwork scenario, where both the humans and the robots were in motion [9].
3. The application of this method on a robot to anticipate the actions of group members, and to perform appropriate actions depending on their dynamics [17].

Building on this foundation, we plan to develop and incorporate methods to detect high-level activities of the humans using the local multimodal sensors of the robot. Incorporating both local and global sensor data of a robot will be helpful for better high-level event detection, which will lead the robot perceiving group dynamics more accurately. However, as the local sensor data may be more noisy in nature due to camera shake or occlusion, it will be more challenging to incorporate this data to detect high-level human activities. To overcome this problem, we plan to use an activity recognition approach similar to Ryoo et al. [20], which uses a first-person view to detect high level events. By combining the events from both the local and global sensors, we will then use our proposed algorithm to detect the SJA of a group.

Additionally, humans are skilled at synchronizing their movements with event sequences containing continuous tempo changes [24]. Models like ADAM (ADaptation and Anticipation Model) have been proposed in literature to model this behavior by combining adaptation and anticipation during an activity [24]. It will be beneficial for a robot to have this ability to be more acceptable by the human counterparts in a team. We also might explore the adaptation mechanism such as those proposed in ADAM, but in the context of a human-robot team. We might extend the error correction mechanism, and can integrate this with our SIA algorithm. This integration might make the SIA algorithm more robust in anticipating and synthesizing future activities more accurately.

After exploring this, the next step of our research will be to extend our model to work for activities beyond SJA, which are not necessarily synchronous, such as human-robot collaboration tasks in industrial environments, like to Wilcox et al. [27], Nikolaidis et al. [14]. Teams working in these settings have specific sequences of activities to perform over time, some of which might be independent, and might not have to happen synchronously. We are planning to extend our proposed algorithm to work during these kind of activities, by incorporating this ordering of events into account. The extended method might be useful to modify SIA to anticipate future activities of the group.

Our current research will directly support other researchers exploring multimodal interaction in the human-robot interaction domain. This method can enable robots to have an automatic understanding of high-level group behavior by processing multimodal sensor streams, and to inform its own actions in response. This also can play a role in handovers, joint action, and collaborative manipulation in HRI, which are all current topics in the field [9]. Moreover, this research is directly applicable in fields beyond HRI, such as social signal processing [12]. Our hope is that this research will help machines to be more socially aware, as well as be more acceptable to people.

6. REFERENCES

[1] S. M. Boker and J. L. Rotondo. Symmetry building and symmetry breaking in synchronized movement. *Adv Consc Res*, 2002.

[2] O. Brdiczka, J. Maisonnasse, and P. Reignier. Automatic detection of interaction groups. In *Proc. Int. Conf. Multimodal Interfaces*, 2005.

[3] M. Cakmak, S. S. Srinivasa, M. K. Lee, S. Kiesler, and J. Forlizzi. Using spatial and temporal contrast for fluent robot-human hand-overs. In *Proc. of ACM/IEEE HRI*, 2011.

[4] A. Fathi, J. K. Hodgins, and J. M. Rehg. Social interactions: A first-person perspective. *IEEE CVPR*, 2012.

[5] G. Hoffman and C. Breazeal. Cost-based anticipatory action selection for human–robot fluency. *IEEE Transactions on Robotics*, 2007.

[6] G. Hoffman and G. Weinberg. Gesture-based human-robot jazz improvisation. In *Proc. of IEEE ICRA*, 2010.

[7] T. Iqbal, M. Gonzales, and L. D. Riek. Mobile robots and marching humans: Measuring synchronous joint action while in motion. In *Proc. of AAAI Fall Symposium Series on AI-HRI*, 2014.

[8] T. Iqbal, M. J. Gonzales, and L. D. Riek. A Model for Time-Synchronized Sensing and Motion to Support Human-Robot Fluency. In *ACM/IEEE HRI, Workshop on Timing in HRI*, 2014.

[9] T. Iqbal, M. J. Gonzales, and L. D. Riek. Joint action perception to enable fluent human-robot teamwork. In *Proc. of IEEE RO-MAN*, 2015.

[10] T. Iqbal and L. Riek. Assessing group synchrony during a rhythmic social activity: A systemic approach. In *In Proc. of ISGS*, 2014.

[11] T. Iqbal and L. D. Riek. Role distribution in synchronous human-robot joint action. In *Proc. of IEEE RO-MAN, Towards a Framework for Joint Action*, 2014.

[12] T. Iqbal and L. D. Riek. A Method for Automatic Detection of Psychomotor Entrainment. *IEEE T on Affective Computing*, 2015.

[13] S. Lallée and et al. Towards a platform-independent cooperative human-robot interaction system: Ii. perception, execution and imitation of goal directed actions. In *IROS*, 2011.

[14] S. Nikolaidis, R. Ramakrishnan, K. Gu, and J. Shah. Efficient model learning from joint-action demonstrations for human-robot collaborative tasks. In *Proc. of HRI*, 2015.

[15] L. Noy, E. Dekel, and U. Alon. The mirror game as a paradigm for studying the dynamics of two people improvising motion together. *P Natl Acad Sci USA*, 2011.

[16] R. Q. Quiroga, T. Kreuz, and P. Grassberger. Event synchronization: a simple and fast method to measure synchronicity and time delay patterns. *Phys Rev E*, 2002.

[17] S. Rack, T. Iqbal, and L. Riek. Enabling synchronous joint action in human-robot teams. In *Proc. of ACM/IEEE HRI*, 2015.

[18] M. J. Richardson, R. L. Garcia, T. D. Frank, M. Gergor, and K. L. Marsh. Measuring group synchrony: a cluster-phase method for analyzing multivariate movement time-series. *Frontiers in Physiology*, 2012.

[19] L. D. Riek. The social co-robotics problem space: Six key challenges. In *In Proc. of RSS, Robotics Challenges and Visions Workshop*, 2013.

[20] M. S. Ryoo and L. Matthies. First-Person Activity Recognition: What Are They Doing to Me? *In Proc. of IEEE CVPR*, 2013.

[21] N. Sebanz, H. Bekkering, and G. Knoblich. Joint action: bodies and minds moving together. *T. Cogn. Sci.*, 2006.

[22] K. W. Strabala and et al. Towards seamless human-robot handovers. *JHRI*, 2013.

[23] V. V. Unhelkar, H. C. Siu, and J. A. Shah. Comparative performance of human and mobile robotic assistants in collaborative fetch-and-deliver tasks. In *Proc of. HRI*, 2014.

[24] M. M. van der Steen, N. Jacoby, M. T. Fairhurst, and P. E. Keller. Sensorimotor synchronization with tempo-changing auditory sequences: Modeling temporal adaptation and anticipation. *Brain research*, 2015.

[25] G. Varni, G. Volpe, and A. Camurri. A System for Real-Time Multimodal Analysis of Nonverbal Affective Social Interaction in User-Centric Media. *IEEE T Multimedia*, 2010.

[26] G. Varni, G. Volpe, and B. Mazzarino. Towards a social retrieval of music content. In *IEEE Conference on Social Computing*, 2011.

[27] R. Wilcox, S. Nikolaidis, and J. A. Shah. Optimization of temporal dynamics for adaptive human-robot interaction in assembly manufacturing. In *Proc. of RSS*, 2012.

Micro-opinion Sentiment Intensity Analysis and Summarization in Online Videos

Amir Zadeh
Carnegie Mellon University
5000 Forbes Avenue,
Pittsburgh, PA 15213
abagherz@cs.cmu.edu

ABSTRACT
There has been substantial progress in the field of text based sentiment analysis but little effort has been made to incorporate other modalities. Previous work in sentiment analysis has shown that using multimodal data yields to more accurate models of sentiment. Efforts have been made towards expressing sentiment as a spectrum of intensity rather than just positive or negative. Such models are useful not only for detection of positivity or negativity, but also giving out a score of how positive or negative a statement is. Based on the state of the art studies in sentiment analysis, prediction in terms of sentiment score is still far from accurate, even in large datasets [27]. Another challenge in sentiment analysis is dealing with small segments or micro opinions as they carry less context than large segments thus making analysis of the sentiment harder. This paper presents a Ph.D. thesis shaped towards comprehensive studies in multimodal micro-opinion sentiment intensity analysis.

Author Keywords
Sentiment Analysis, Multimodal Machine Learning, Sentiment Summarization

ACM Classification Keywords
I.2.7 [**Artificial Intelligence**]: Natural Language Processing - language parsing and understanding.

1. INTRODUCTION
Video sharing websites such as YouTube, Vine, and Vimeo are increasingly popular. For example, more than 300 hours of video are uploaded every minute to YouTube. Many people share their opinions, stories and reviews through these online video postings. This phenomena has seen a growing attention from many companies, researchers and consumers interested in building better opinion-mining applications for summarization, question answering and video retrieval.

The automatic analysis of these online opinion videos is among the newest research challenges brought to the field of sentiment analysis. First and foremost, there is the fundamental research question on how to jointly represent spoken language and visual gestures. To simply focus on the spoken words (e.g., text-based sentiment analysis) may bring an ambiguity that would be easily resolved with the visual information. For example, the sentiment expressed by the spoken opinion "*this movie was different*" may not be clear by itself but observing a strong frown expression from the speaker can make it clear that it is negative.

A second challenge comes from the volatile and high-tempo nature of these online opinion videos where speakers will often switch between topics and opinions either for entertainment purpose or because they edited the original video footage. This phenomena requires to go beyond sentiment analysis at the whole document or video level, requiring a more fine-grained analysis at the opinion-level (i.e., subjectivity segmentation of spoken opinions, without punctuation markers).

A third challenge comes with the range and subtlety of sentiment intensities expressed in these opinion videos. We want approaches not only able to recognize the polarity of a video segment (e.g., positive or negative) but also estimate the strength of the expressed sentiment. And this approach should generalize between speakers.

The thesis presented in this paper has 3 major thrusts discussed in the next section. Section 3 discusses the related works. Section 4 discusses the research roadmap. Section 5 presents preliminary results as well as discussion about the new MOSI dataset created for multimodal sentiment intensity analysis.

2. RESEARCH THRUSTS
In general there are 3 fundamental research thrusts in my thesis:

T1: Study of verbal and nonverbal behavior descriptors: prior works have focused on using simple audio and visual features in conjunction with verbal. Features were mostly used as they were extracted and no further analysis were made on how they interact. A focus of thesis will be on investigating different structural correspondence and interaction patterns between text, audio and video. The outcome of this thrust would be a multimodal representation that captures such interactions.

T2: Sentiment analysis and study of multimodal fusion approaches: related works have used different multimodal

ICMI '15, November 09-13, 2015, Seattle, WA, USA
© 2015 ACM. ISBN 978-1-4503-3912-4/15/11...$15.00
DOI: http://dx.doi.org/10.1145/2818346.2823317

fusion techniques [19, 31]. Specifically fusion approaches that take into account temporal relations between consecutive opinions in a video will be investigated such as LSTMs [33] and Deep Recursive Neural Networks.

T3: Sentiment summarization: A specific focus of thesis will be on sentiment summarization. During videos, speakers talk about different topics and present different opinions. Aggregating and summarizing the whole video into a sentiment score based on opinions presented in the video will be studied in context of online videos.

3. BACKGROUND

Related works can be categorized in following research directions:

Text-based sentiment analysis Research in text based sentiment analysis has been an active and extremely successful field [5]. Among notable efforts are works done in automatically identifying opinion words and their sentiment polarity [30, 25, 20, 22], studies using n-grams and more complex language models [14, 8] and works addressing sentiment compositionality by using polarity shifting rules or careful feature engineering [37]. These methods have been used in many different applications including opinion mining in tweets and online forums [38], analysis of political debates [24], question answering [15], conversation summarization [13], and citation sentiment detection [1]. Recursive Neural Networks have also been successful in sentiment analysis. Socher et.al [27] presented an approach for fine-grained sentiment analysis as a 5 class classification task and managed to get accuracy of 45.7% using Recursive Neural Tensor Networks. All these approaches are primarily focusing on the (spoken or written) text, ignoring the other communicative modalities.

Multimodal Sentiment Analysis Some earlier work introduced acoustic and paralinguistic features to the text-based analysis for the purpose of subjectivity or sentiment identification [29, 28, 11, 12]. A first step to my thesis is taken in the work reported in [19, 31], where multimodal cues, including visual cues, have been used for the sentiment analysis in product and movie reviews. Their approach directly concatenated modalities in an early fusion representation with experiments performed in a speaker-dependent manner, with no analysis of sentiment intensity.

Audio-visual emotion recognition Among the related works are works done in the fields of affective computing and computer vision to detect emotions based on visual cues. Facial expressions are among the most powerful means of communicating emotions and intentions in human interactions [32]. Interesting studies discuss findings about mental state of the speaker based on facial expressions, head gestures and other visual cues [3, 21]. More recently, many challenges have been organized focusing on the recognition of emotions using audio and visual cues [2, 7], which brings the participation of many teams from around the world.

4. RESEARCH PLAN

Research plan is in three major steps aligned with the research thrusts mentioned in section 2.

4.1 Study of verbal and nonverbal behavior descriptors

Previous works in multimodal sentiment analysis uses simple low-level features in each modality. To model text, language models such as n-grams are used. For visual modality features such as FAUs [34], Ekman emotions [35] and head pose [36] are extracted from the video frames. Acoustic features such as MFCC, NAQ, Energy, Peak Slope, etc. are extracted from audio. A specific focus of the thesis will be on how these different modalities interact with each other. Previous works in text-based sentiment analysis have shown that taking dependencies into account, according to the outputs of a dependency parser, can improve the results of sentiment analysis [27]. Gestures however have mostly been analyzed in a sequence [37]. The relation between text and gestures may not be trivial but a suitable embedding method could create a joint multimodal representation that aligns gestures and words according to hypothesis on their structural correspondence.

4.2 Sentiment analysis and study of multimodal fusion approaches

The main contribution of my thesis will be implementing novel machine learning techniques that can 1) learn a suitable multimodal fusion approach for sentiment analysis; one that investigates non-trivial relations between gestures, text and voice 2) takes into account the dynamics of how opinions form the video. In a video, there can be many different opinions but the opinions are not completely independent. Speakers navigate through different opinions and discuss a topic from different perspectives. This creates a temporal dependency between opinions. Studies of these dependencies can give an insight of how speakers convey their messages through opinions and also how they build the dynamics of their speech.

4.3 Sentiment summarization

The growth of video sharing on internet means users have plenty of multimedia sources to access; But in practice going through desired videos for users may be impossible. To tackle this information overload, multimodal sentiment summarization aggregates and summarizes the opinion of a video.

Figure 1: Example snapshots of videos from our new MOSI dataset.

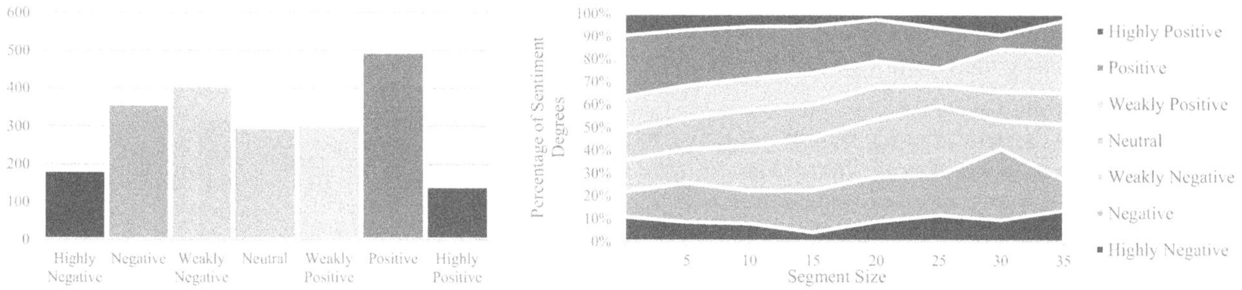

Figure 2: Histogram in the left shows the distribution of sentiment over the entire dataset. The right graph shows the percentage of each sentiment degree per segment size.

5. PRIMARY RESULTS

5.1 MOSI Dataset

As discussed in the background section, there is only limited prior works in multimodal sentiment analysis and none of these datasets include sentiment intensity annotations for opinion videos. In this section, we introduce the Multimodal Opinion-level Sentiment Intensity (MOSI) dataset which addresses three challenges: (1) multimodal observations including transcribed speech and visual gestures, (2) opinion-level subjectivity segmentation, and (3) sentiment intensity annotations with high coder agreement. The following sub-sections are describing the dataset in more details.

5.1.1 Video Acquisition Methodology

Videos were collected from the YouTube website with a focus on video-blogs, or vlogs: popular update videos used by many YouTube users to express opinions about many different subjects, often indexed by #vlog. One big advantage of this type of videos is that they usually contain only one speaker, looking primarily at the camera. The videos are recorded in diverse setups, some users have high-tech microphones and cameras, while others are using less professional recording devices. Users are in different distances from the camera. Background and lighting condition is variable between videos. We focused on vlogs centered on movie reviews. The videos were kept in their original resolution and recorded locally in MP4 format. The length of the videos varies from 2-5 minutes

A total of 93 videos were randomly selected using these guidelines. The final set of videos contained 89 distinct speakers, including 41 female and 48 male speakers. Most of the speakers were approximately between the ages of 20 and 30. Although the speakers were from different ethnic backgrounds (e.g., Caucasian, African-American, Hispanic, Asian), all speakers expressed themselves in English and the videos originated from either United States of America or United Kingdoms. Sample snapshots of our MOSI dataset[1] are shown in Figure 1.

All video clips are manually transcribed to extract spoken words as well as the start time of each spoken utterance. Our transcription methodology consisted of four stages. First, an expert transcriber manually transcribed all the videos followed by a second transcriber reviewing and correcting all the transcriptions. Our transcription scheme contained details about pause fillers (umm, uhh, etc.), stresses and speech pause. In the third stage, the text was aligned with the audio using a forced aligner called P2FA[1]. During the final stage, the results of the alignment were manually checked and if necessary corrected using PRAAT (Paul and Weenink, 2001). It must be noted that in future, transcriptions may be provided using automatic speech recognizers.

The following sub-sections present our procedure to extract subjective segments from videos, followed by sentiment intensity annotation.

5.1.2 Opinion-level Subjectivity Segmentation

As previously discussed, an important requirement of our dataset is to perform subjectivity segmentation at the opinion level so that we can achieve a fine-grained sentiment analysis. Following the work of Wiebe et.al. (2005), subjective sentences are defined as expressions of one's opinions while objective sentences express facts and truth. Although their work primarily focused on written text, our MOSI dataset contains continuous speech. This section presents the formal definition of our segmentation scheme which expands their work to extract spoken opinion segments.

We define subjectivity as an expression of a private state, one that is distinguishable by carrying an opinion, belief, thought, feeling, emotion, goal, evaluation or judgment. The following three rules are used to define subjectivity:

- Explicit mention of a private state – a direct mention of private state. Example: "*I also love the casting of Mark Strong as Sinestro.*"
- Speech events expressing private states – private state has been said or written by another. Example: "*Shia LaBeouf said that the second movie lacked um heart.*"

[1] https://github.com/srubin/p2fa-vislab

- Expressive subjective – not a direct opinion but implicit reference to an opinion. Example: "*I would never recommend watching this movie.*"

5.1.3 Sentiment Intensity Annotation

Sentiment intensity is defined from strongly negative to strongly positive with a linear scale from -3 to +3. The intensity annotations were performed using online workers from Amazon Mechanical Turk website. Only master workers with approval rate of higher than 95% were selected to participate. A total of 2199 short video clips were created from the subjective opinion segments (see Section 3.2). For each video the annotators had 8 choices: strongly positive (labeled as +3), positive (+2), weakly positive (+1), neutral (0), weakly negative (-1), negative (-2), strongly negative (-3) and also they were given a choice "uncertain" if they were not sure.

The instructions were kept simple on purpose to reduce any bias. The only tutorial was on how to use the online system (e.g., how to submit the form). The task was phrased as following: "*How would you rate the sentiment expressed in this video segment? (Please note that you may or may not agree with what the speaker says. It is imperative that you only rate the sentiment state of the speaker, not yourself)*". Each video clip was annotated by 5 different workers. The workers were offered to annotate as many video clips as they wanted (but could not annotate the same clip twice).

The inter annotator agreement between workers is 0.77 in terms of Krippendorf's Alpha. The final sentiment intensity of each segment is the average of all 5 workers. Figure 2 shows the distribution of sentiment intensities for all opinion segment in MOSI dataset on the left side. On the right side of Figure 2, we show how the distribution changes as the size of the opinion increases, where the size is defined as the number of words. It is interesting to see that the proportions are mostly constant across all segment sizes, something that text based sentiment analysis suffers from [27].

5.2 Baseline experiments

As a primary experiment, MOSI datasets has been used to train models for subjectivity analysis. The goal was to detect if a segment is subjective or objective based on features extracted from the segment. For text features the n-grams up to 3 were created. For visual features FAUs, facial landmarks and head pose were extracted. For audio, a set of 48 features including MFCC, NAQ, Peak Slope, etc. were extracted. Two models, linear SVM and MLP (two hidden layers) have been used to detect subjective segments. The results in figure 3 indicate that multimodal fusion does improve the accuracy of detecting subjective sentences.

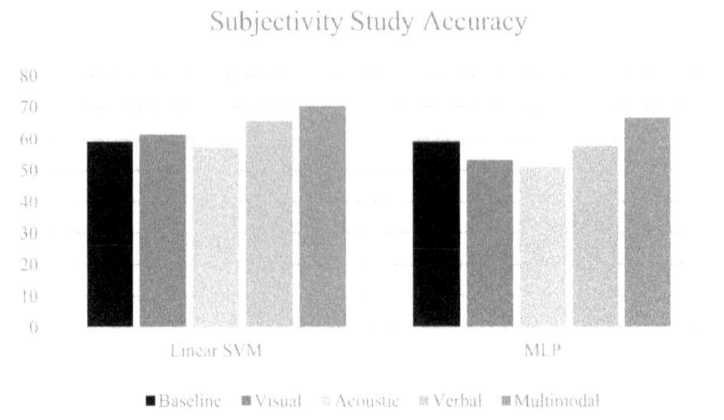

Figure 3. Results of multimodal subjectivity studies

As a baseline, MOSI dataset has been used to run preliminary studies on multimodal sentiment analysis. The results have been presented in table 1. A simple model that uses a concatenation of verbal and visual features shows improvement over each one of modalities alone. The regression model used in linear SVR. Further experiments will be according to research plan presented in section 4 and will build upon the baseline results.

Table 1. Results of multimodal sentiment intensity analysis using linear SVR

	MAE	Correlation
Baseline	1.39	-
Visual	1.24	0.36
Verbal	1.18	0.46
Verbal+Visual	1.14	0.49

6. CONCLUSION AND FUTURE WORK

My research goal is understanding how humans convey sentiment through multimodal communication means. As a focus point, I have chosen online videos to be the data source of my studies. In the first step, a new dataset, called MOSI, has been created for the research direction of multimodal sentiment intensity analysis. Baseline studies on the dataset show promising results of how multimodal studies can improve the text-only sentiment analysis while being speaker independent, which is an improvement over previous works. Extension of MOSI dataset from 93 videos to close to 1000 videos is among the short term goals of my research. This has a particular advantage; it allows me to use more complex models to capture the relations between the different modalities as well as modeling the sentiment intensity.

7. ACKNOWLEDGMENT

Special thanks to Prof. Louis-Philippe Morency, my academic mentor, for his passionate support in every stage of my Ph.D. studies.

REFERENCES

[1] A. Athar and S. Teufel. 2012. Context-enhanced cita-tion sentiment detection. In Proceedings of the 2012 Conference of the North American Chapter of the Association for Computational Linguistics: Human Language Technologies, Montr´eal, Canada, June.

[2] A. Dhall, R. Goecke, J. Joshi, K. Sikka and T. Gedeon. 2014. Emotion Recognition In The Wild Chal-lenge 2014: Baseline, Data and Protocol. In pro-ceedings of ACM International Conference on Multimodal Interaction.

[3] A. J. Calder, A. M. Burton, P. Miller, A.W. Young, and S. Akamatsu. 2001. A principal component analysis of facial expressions. Vision research, 41(9):1179– 1208, April.

[4] A.J. Smola, B. Schölkopf. "A tutorial on support vec-tor regression." Statistics and computing 14.3 (2004): 199-222.

[5] B. Pang and L. Lee. 2004. A sentimental education: Sentiment analysis using subjectivity summariza-tion based on minimum cuts. In Proceedings of the 42nd Meeting of the Association for Compu-tational Linguistics, Barcelona, Spain, July.

[6] B. Paul, D. Weenink. "Praat, a system for doing pho-netics by computer." (2001): 341-345.

[7] B. Schuller, M. Valstar, R. Cowie, and M. Pantic, edi-tors. 2011. Audio/Visual Emotion Challenge and Workshop (AVEC 2011).

[8] B. Yang and C. Cardie. 2012. Extracting opinion ex-pressions with semi-markov conditional random fields. In Proceedings of the 2012 Joint Confer-ence on Empirical Methods in Natural Language Processing and Computational Natural Language Learning, Jeju Island, Korea.

[9] C.C. Chang, C.J. Lin. "LIBSVM: a library for support vector machines." ACM Transactions on Intelli-gent Systems and Technology (TIST)2.3 (2011): 27.

[10] F. Li, S. J. Pan, O. Jin, Q. Yang, and X. Zhu. 2012. Cross-domain co-extraction of sentiment and topic lexicons. In Proceedings of the 50th Annual Meeting of the Association for Computational Linguistics, Jeju Island, Korea.

[11] F. Mairesse, J. Polifroni, and G. Di Fabbrizio. 2012. Can prosody inform sentiment analysis? Exper-iments on short spoken reviews. In Acoustics, Speech and Signal Processing (ICASSP), 2012 IEEE International Conference on, pages 5093 –5096, march.

[12] F. Metze, T. Polzehl, and M. Wagner. 2009. Fusion of acoustic and linguistic features for emotion de-tection. In Semantic Computing, 2009. ICSC '09. IEEE International Conference on, pages 153 –160, sept.

[13] G. Carenini, R. Ng, and X. Zhou. 2008. Summarizing emails with conversational cohesion and subjec-tivity. In Proceedings of the Association for Computational Linguistics: Human Language Technologies (ACLHLT 2008), Columbus, Ohio.

[14] H. Takamura, T. Inui, and M. Okumura. 2006. La-tent variable models for semantic orientations of phrases. In Proceedings of the European Chapter of the Association for Computational Linguistics.

[15] J. Oh, K. Torisawa, C. Hashimoto, T. Kawada, S. De Saeger, J. Kazama, and Y. Wang. 2012. Why question answering using sentiment analysis and word classes. In Proceedings of the 2012 Joint Conference on Empirical Methods in Natural Language Processing and Computational Natural Language Learning, Jeju Island, Korea.

[16] J. Wagner, E. Andre, F. Lingenfelser, and Jonghwa Kim. 2011. Exploring fusion methods for multi-modal emotion recognition with missing data. Affective Computing, IEEE Transactions on, 2(4):206–218, oct.-dec.

[17] J. Wiebe, T. Wilson, and C. Cardie. 2005. Annotating expressions of opinions and emotions in lan-guage. Language Resources and Evaluation, 39(2-3):165–210.

[18] K. Balog, G. Mishne, and M. de Rijke. 2006. Why are they excited? identifying and explaining spikes in blog mood levels. In Proceedings of the 11th Meeting of the European Chapter of the As soci-ation for Computational Linguistics (EACL-2006).

[19] L.P. Morency, R. Mihalcea, and P. Doshi. 2011. To-wards multimodal sentiment analysis: Harvesting opinions from the web. In Proceedings of the In-ternational Conference on Multimodal Compu-ting, Alicante, Spain.

[20] M. Hu and B. Liu. 2004. Mining and summarizing customer reviews. In Proceedings of the tenth ACM SIGKDD international conference on Knowledge discovery and data mining, Seattle, Washington.

[21] M. Rosenblum, Y. Yacoob, and L.S. Davis. 1996. Human expression recognition from motion us-ing a radial basis function network architecture. Neural Networks, IEEE Transactions on, 7(5):1121 – 1138, sep.

[22] M. Taboada, J. Brooke, M. Tofiloski, K. Voli, and M. Stede. 2011. Lexicon-based methods for senti-ment analysis. Computational Linguistics, 37(3).

[23] M. Valstar, B. Schuller, K. Smith, T. Almaev, F. Eyben, J. Krajewski, R. Cowie, and M. Pantic 2014. AVEC 2014 - 3D Dimensional Affect and Depression Recognition Challenge. In proc. 4th ACM international workshop on Audio/visual emotion challenge.

[24] P. Carvalho, L. Sarmento, J. Teixeira, and M. Silva. 2011. Liars and saviors in a sentiment annotated corpus of comments to political debates. In Pro-ceedings of the Association for Computational Linguistics (ACL 2011), Portland, OR.

[25] P. Turney. 2002. Thumbs up or thumbs down? Se-mantic orientation applied to unsupervised clas-sification of reviews. In Proceedings of the 40th Annual Meeting of the Association for Computa-tional Linguistics (ACL 2002), pages 417–424, Philadelphia

[26] R. Mihalcea, C. Banea, and J. Wiebe. 2007. Learning multilingual subjective language via cross-lingual projections. In Proceedings of the Association for Computational Linguistics, Prague, Czech Re-public.

[27] R. Socher, et al. 2013. "Recursive deep models for semantic compositionality over a sentiment tree-bank." Proceedings of the conference on empiri-cal methods in natural language processing (EMNLP). Vol. 1631. 2013.

[28] S. Raaijmakers, K. Truong, and T. Wilson. 2008. Mul-timodal subjectivity analysis of multiparty con-versation. In Proceedings of the Conference on Empirical Methods in Natural Language Pro-cessing, pages 466–474, Honolulu, Hawaii.

[29] S. Somasundaran, J. Wiebe, P. Hoffmann, and D. Litman. 2006. Manual annotation of opinion categories in meetings. In Proceedings of the Workshop on Frontiers in Linguistically Annotat-ed Corpora 2006.

[30] V. Hatzivassiloglou and K. McKeown. 1997. Predict-ing the semantic orientation of adjectives. In Proceedings of the Conference of the European Chapter of the Association for Computational Linguistics, pages 174–181.

[31] V. Perez-Rosas, R. Mihalcea, and L.-P. Morency. 2013. Multimodal sentiment analysis of spanish online videos. IEEE Intelligent Systems.

[32] Y.-I. Tian, T. Kanade, and J.F. Cohn. 2001. Recogniz-ing action units for facial expression analysis. Pattern Analysis and Machine Intelligence, IEEE Transactions on, 232):97 –115, feb.

[33] Ekman, Paul, and Wallace V. Friesen. "Facial action coding system." (1977).

[34] Ekman, Paul, et al. "Universals and cultural differences in the judgments of facial expressions of emotion." *Journal of personality and social psychology*53.4 (1987): 712.

[35] Baltrusaitis, Tadas, Peter Robinson, and Louis-Philippe Morency. "Constrained local neural fields for robust facial landmark detection in the wild." *Computer Vision Workshops (ICCVW), 2013 IEEE International Conference on*. IEEE, 2013.

[36] Morency, Louis-Philippe, Ariadna Quattoni, and Trevor Darrell. "Latent-dynamic discriminative models for continuous gesture recognition." *Computer Vision and Pattern Recognition, 2007. CVPR'07. IEEE Conference on*. IEEE, 2007.

[37] Polanyi, Livia, and Annie Zaenen. "Contextual valence shifters." *Computing attitude and affect in text: Theory and applications*. Springer Netherlands, 2006. 1-10.

[38] Agarwal, Apoorv, et al. "Sentiment analysis of twitter data." *Proceedings of the Workshop on Languages in Social Media*. Association for Computational Linguistics, 2011.

Attention and Engagement Aware Multimodal Conversational Systems

Zhou Yu
Carnegie Mellon University
Pittsburgh, USA
zhouyu@cs.cmu.edu

ABSTRACT

Despite their ability to complete certain tasks, dialog systems still suffer from poor adaptation to users' engagement and attention. We observe human behaviors in different conversational settings to understand human communication dynamics and then transfer the knowledge to multimodal dialog system design. To focus solely on maintaining engaging conversations, we design and implement a non-task oriented multimodal dialog system, which serves as a framework for controlled multimodal conversation analysis. We design computational methods to model user engagement and attention in real time by leveraging automatically harvested multimodal human behaviors, such as smiles and speech volume. We aim to design and implement a multimodal dialog system to coordinate with users' engagement and attention on the fly via techniques such as adaptive conversational strategies and incremental speech production.

Categories and Subject Descriptors

H.5.m. [**Information Interfaces and Presentation (e.g. HCI)**]: Miscellaneous; H.1.2 [**User/Machine Systems**]: Human factors

Keywords

Multimodal Analysis; Adaptive Dialog System; Engagement; Attention

1. INTRODUCTION

Nowadays dialog systems with a fixed goal have already achieved many functionalities, such as the Let's Go! [15] bus system which provides bus schedules, and Siri from Apple, which serves as a personal assistant, completing tasks like setting up an alarm clock. These spoken dialog systems, such as customer services phone lines, are not user friendly. Users get irritated throughout the interactions, and most of them prefer to talk to a real human rather than the dialog system. Even users who are able to finish the task in the end do not enjoy the conversational experience. The reason for user complaint is that dialog systems do not model users' engagement and attention throughout the conversation. We are at the point where we must consider how to make the dialog system not only achieve the task goal, but also make the conversation natural and effective.

The goal of my doctoral work is to model engagement and attention in conversations. Engagement and attention are crucial in understanding human-human dynamics, and are also important in designing autonomous dialog systems.

Engagement is not well understood in the human-human communication context, in part because it has only been pursued in the sociological and psychological communities as part of general communication studies, and in part because in artificial intelligence, much of the focus has been on language understanding and production, rather than on the fundamental problems of how to start a connection and the role of verbal and non-verbal behaviors in connecting. We define engagement as "the process by which two (or more) participants establish, maintain and end their perceived connection during interactions they jointly undertake" [17]. We use multimodal features to model engagement in a conversational setting in real time. We further plan to coordinate with users' engagement by using different conversational strategies.

Attention is another conversation metric. Much work focuses on how visual attention or gaze facilitate multiparty turn taking. However, we argue that attention is not simply about visual attention, but is also about cognitive attention, which is equally important but harder to detect and model. There are situations that users are cognitively focused on the task, but are visually looking away from the agent. We aim to model users' attention with respect to the task content. We then coordinate the agent behaviors with users' attention both cognitively and visually to achieve more natural and effective conversations [21].

We intent to make our multimodal dialog framework available to the public in a distributed cloud version.

2. RELATED WORK

Different multimodal features and machine learning algorithms are used to predict engagement or involvement in human-human conversations. Previously, people used audio features, such as intensity, fundamental frequency and speech rate [9], or combining audio feature with some visual features such as, hand blob [7] to predict engagement. Some work use more fine grained features, such as Oertel et al. [13] used gaze features obtained by an eye tracker to model engagement and involvement in multiparty conversations. However, all the engagement prediction work is conducted on human-human conversation and is all the models are trained and tested offline.

For attention modeling work, situated and multiparty systems often incorporate attention and gaze in their models for turn taking and interaction planning [18] [4]. Sciutti et al. [16] used gaze as an implicit signal for turn taking in a robotic teaching context. In

ICMI '15, November 09-13, 2015, Seattle, WA, USA
ACM 978-1-4503-3912-4/15/11.
DOI: http://dx.doi.org/10.1145/2818346.2823309

an in-car navigation setting, situated incremental speech synthesis that accommodates user's cognitive load was shown to improve user experience but not user's task performances [10]. However, no work has investigated how to coordinate speech production of the dialog system with a user's visual and cognitive attention with respect of the task.

3. PSYCHOLOGICAL CONSTRUCTS

In the work reported in [22], we propose a multimodal dyadic computational method to automatically predict friendship of the two participants in a conversation. The proposed model used a L2,1 norm to deal with the noisy and sparse features space that the multimodal signals present. This work use automatic extracted features in three modalities: text, audio and video and found friends talk in a more relaxed way (less varied pitch range), exchange turns more and have more overlaps in their speech (more conversational turns and overlap) and look into each other's eyes more during the conversation (more mutual gaze). The change of these verbal and nonverbal behaviors over time also indicates the change of the relationship.

We also look into multimodal behaviors in depression detection in the setting of human-virtual agent interactions [24] . The dialogue was conducted in a semi-structured setting, which consists of a series of adjacency pairs (i.e. question and response pair). In order to take the context into consideration, we propose a computational model, the multimodal hidden conditional random fields, that extract the commonalities among adjacency pairs to infer the psychological states of the interviewees. We find that depressed people tend to have longer speech onset time when they are prompted with intimate questions. The performance achieves 0.66 in F1-measure in predicting whether the interviewee is depressed or not with automatically harvested features.

4. TICKTOCK

With the previous knowledge of human behavior analysis in human-human and human-virtual agent conversations, we design and implement a non-task oriented dialog system, TickTock, for the purpose of studying engagement alone without task influence [23].

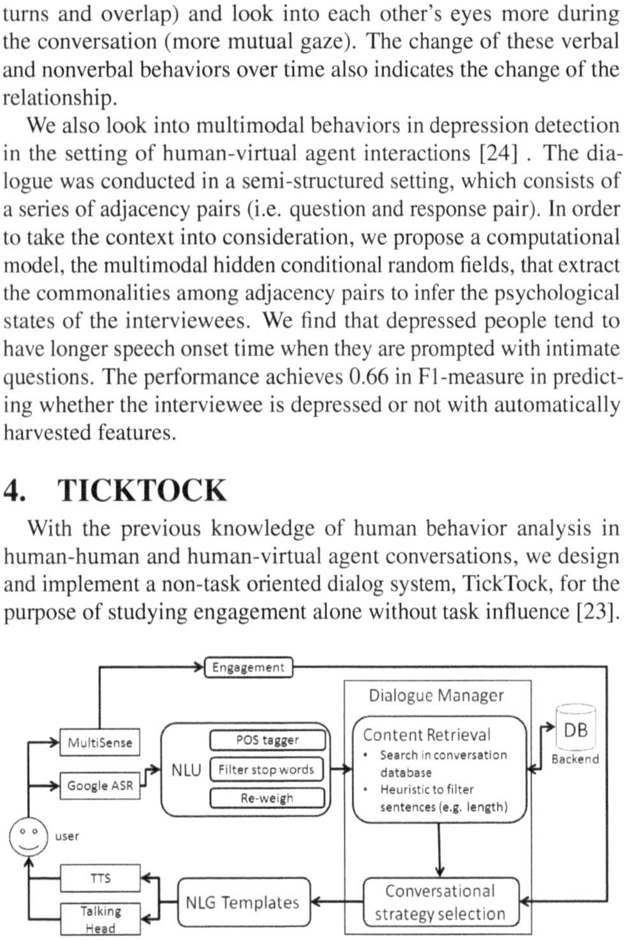

Figure 1: The architecture of TickTock

Figure 1 shows the architecture of the TickTock conversational agent; we use Google Automatic Speech Recognition (ASR), MultiSense and purpose-build Natural Language Understanding (NLU) to process the input, a RavenClaw-based dialogue manager [5] and template-based Natural Language Generation (NLG), Flite Text to Speech (TTS) [3] and an animated head for realization. An earlier version of a free-form conversational agent guided some of our design decisions [11].

Our database consists of question-answer pairs from CNN Interview Transcripts from the "Piers Morgan Tonight" Show. The corpus has 767 interviews in total and each interview is between 500 to 1,000 sentences. Key Term Matching [12] is used for content retrieval. Our goal is to generate coherent responses efficiently without deep understanding of the context, which is useful in a non-task oriented interactive system, and is motivated by lexical cohesion in modeling discourse. The coherence can be reflected by the repetition of lexicon items. The method first does shallow syntactic analysis of the input utterance and extracts keywords. These keywords are then used to search the corpus for a suitable response.

Once we retrieved the response, we select a conversational strategy, based on a heuristic (implemented in the Engagement module), i.e. a predefined threshold for the retrieval confidence score, which can be tuned to make the system appear more active or more passive. Higher thresholds correspond to more active systems. We designed two strategies for each case and at each dialogue turn, we randomly chose between the two strategies.

If the retrieval confidence score is low, meaning no good response was obtained, we use strategies to change the current topic by proposing a new topic, such as "sports" or "music" or we close the current topic using an open question, such as "Could you tell me something interesting?" If the retrieval confidence score is higher than the threshold, we choose between two strategies, one where we return the retrieved answer and another where we ask about the user's opinion, for example: "What do you think?" These simple strategies are designed as baselines to sustain the flow of conversation.

5. HUMAN BEHAVIOR QUANTIFICATION

We collected 24 five-minute interactions to form the TickTock database (TTDB). A video example of the conversation snippet is available at http://www.cs.cmu.edu/afs/cs/user/zhouyu/www/TickTock_Demo_Sync_final.mp4. We labeled how engaged the human subject is in each turn of the conversation in a five point likert scale. Please refer to [23] for the detailed annotation scheme.

We used both manual transcriptions and automatic speech recognition (ASR) output to calculate "the number of turn", "the number of words spoken per turn", and "speech rate" (number of words spoken per second). All of then are positively correlated (Pearson correlation) with engagement regardless of whether calculated in manual transcription or ASR. This indicates that the more, the faster one speaks, the more engaged one is in the conversation.

5.1 Audio Features

Firstly We automatically identify the prosodic units within a turn to calculate audio features in a precise manner. We also perform person wise normalization. Praat [14] was used to extract the intensity features and the fundamental frequency (pitch) for each automatically identified pause bounded unit in each turn.

We find that the mean intensity is positively correlated to engagement, this indicates that when people are more engaged, they speak louder. For pitch, we find that the correlation is insignificant for both databases. Our find differs from [20] which found that both intensity and pitch are positively correlated with engagement. This may be due to the fact that the two databases contain different types of content: ours is conversational data while theirs is monologue.

5.2 Vision Features

Based on the CML-Z [2] trackers' face mesh and head pose, we train our smile, head nod and shake detectors. We train a SVM classifier using the annotations in CCDb [1] as training. We find that smiles are positively correlated with engagement.

We find smile is positively correlated with engagement. Head nod is neither positively or negatively correlated with engagement. The reason is that head nod does not only signal agreement but also bacchanals, which is not considering very engagement behaviors. However head shake is positively correlation with engagement, as participants who disagree with their conversational partners are more engaged in the conversation. Still, there are participant-wise differences in the data. There is one participant who shook his head 62.7% of the turns, while there are participants who didn't shake their head at all.

5.3 Turn Taking Features

Interruptions are very differently between human-human conversations and human-dialog system conversations. When conversational partners interrupt each other, they are perceived as more engaged in the conversation. In our context, TickTock sometimes misjudges the opportunity to take a turn and interrupts the human subject, which will lead to a disruptive interruption. TickTock does not have the ability to do cooperative interruptions so far. We find that interruption is slightly negatively correlated with engagement. Speech onset time is positively correlated with engagement, which means that people who respond to each other more quickly are more engaged, and people who take less time to respond to the agent are less engaged. The reason is that the system would say "pardon me" or "excuse me" to ask people to repeat their previous responses. People who take very little time to respond in these turns are not engaged as they find it annoying. We find time since session start to be the most strongly correlated feature to engagement. One reason is that the excitement of talking to a dialog agent wears off fast, as the dialog system has defects and the impact of them accumulates over time.

6. ENGAGEMENT ASSESSMENT

We choose features with high correlations to engagement, based on our previous analysis, to develop an automatic prediction model for engagement. We exclude all the features mentioned except pitch mean, pitch variance, head nod, and interruption, as they are not correlated with engagement in either database

We use a support vector regression algorithm [6] with a rbf kernel to predict how engaged the participant is in each turn. To speed up the prediction process and reduce the variance of the model, we encode the contextual information in features instead of in the models, because models that incorporate time have more parameters to tune and we have little data for that. We find adding three previous turns as history yields a good trade-off between performance and computational complexity.

7. ENGAGEMENT STRATEGIES

Based on the TickTock Dataset (TTDB), which used a basic model of TickTock without the engagement model, we categorized the conversational strategies used in turns that have increased user engagement into five categories.

- S1: Introducing new topics.
- S2: Initiating things to do together.
- S3: Adopting famous movie script lines.
- S4: Adding humorous content.
- S5: Making fun of each other.

We will build these strategies into TickTock, and design a policy to make decisions on when to use which strategy based on the user's engagement state.

8. ATTENTION REGULATION

In the work reported in [21], we propose a model to coordinate speech production with the listeners' focus of attention in a physically situated dialog system. In human-human conversations, we find speaker's disfluencies such as pauses, restarts are correlated with listeners' gaze shifts. Goodwin [8] suggests that disfluencies are not merely speaker's cognitive production errors, they might also be a conversational strategy to attract listeners' attention. Vinciarelli et al. [19] argues that "Computer systems with capabilities to sense agreement and attention that are able to adapt or respond to these signals in an appropriate way will likely be perceived as more natural, efficacious and trustworthy". Thus we hypothesize that dialog systems that adapt to users' attention could lead to more effective and natural interactions.

We propose a three-step framework to develop an attention adaptive system. First, we want to identify the distribution of users' visual attention throughout the task. Thus we designed a coding scheme based on the knowledge of the open space the dialog system is positioned in and the task content of the dialog. We categorize the users' visual attention targets as: "Robot", "PointingDirection", "Badge", and anywhere else as "Elsewhere". We heuristically infer attention targets in real time based on the dialog state and the geometric direction of user's gaze, which is obtained via a supervised machine learning algorithm.

We then design a coordination policy to leverage the attention signal to adapt to users' attention via incremental speech production. The component regulates production based on identifying when the attention of the user does not match the demand we set for different utterances. We consider two types of attentional demands. The first one, which we refer to as onset demand, encapsulates Goodwin's observation [8] that participants in a conversation generally aim to achieve mutual orientation at the beginnings of turns. The model specifies that at system phrase onset, the listeners' attention must be on the system.

In addition, a second type of attentional demand, denoted production demand is defined at the level of the dialog act by the system developer. During certain system acts, for in stance ones that carry important content, or ones that are deemed as unexpected for the listeners, it is important for addressees to attend to the system or to certain task-relevant objects. The production demand defines where the listener's attention is expected during the production of the system's utterances, i.e., it defines a set of permitted targets. For instance, when the robot is giving directions the production demand is set to "Robot"or "PointingDirections". In contrast, other dialog acts, such as the robot asking "Where are you trying to get to?", are naturally expected, as at that point we already confirmed the user needs directions.

The coordination policy controls the speech synthesis engine and deploys various mechanisms, such as pauses, restarts, interjections, to coordinate the system's speech with the listeners' attention. If the listeners' attention does not meet the demand at the beginning of a phrase, the system will perform a sequence of actions, starting with a wait, followed by an attention drawing interjection such as "Excuse me!", followed by another wait action, followed by launching the phrase; if onset attentional demand is still not satisfied the phrase is interrupted after two words, then another wait action is taken, followed finally by launching the entire phrase. As soon as the attention supply matches the onset demand, the system launches the phrase. At the phrase end, if the production demand is not met, the robot repeats the phrase. The robot will only repeat once as too many times will annoy users.

We implemented the framework in the context of the Directions Robot, a physically situated humanoid (Aldebaran Nao) robotic system that interacts with people and provides directions inside Microsoft Research Building 99 (Bohus, Saw and Horvitz, 2014). Video snippets from natural interactions are available at http://1drv.ms/1GQ1ori.

9. FUTURE RESEARCH PLANS

We plan to implement and adjust the engagement model in TickTock to perform real time user engagement tracking. We will design and implement strategies to regulate a user's engagement level throughout the conversation.

We also plan to carry human subjective evaluations to assess if there is improved naturalness and effectiveness in the adaptive systems.

Transfer engagement knowledge from non-task-oriented dialog systems to task-oriented dialog dialog systems.

10. EXPECTED CONTRIBUTIONS

We introduce two machine learning models designed specifically to handle noisy, high dimensional and context sensitive multimodal features.

We introduce using multimodal information to model engagement and attention throughout conversations with a dialog system.

We also design and implement a multimodal non-task oriented dialog framework that can serve as a tool to understand user conversational behaviors.

In the future, we intend to make a distributed cloud based multimodal dialog system framework that can adapt to different task contents, such as language proficiency assessment, interview training, communication ability assessment, etc.

11. REFERENCES

[1] Andrew J Aubrey, David Marshall, Paul L Rosin, Jason Vandeventer, Douglas W Cunningham, and Christian Wallraven. 2013. Cardiff Conversation Database (CCDb): A database of natural dyadic conversations. In *IEEE Conference on Computer Vision and Pattern Recognition Workshops*. IEEE, 277–282.

[2] Tadas Baltrusaitis, Peter Robinson, and L Morency. 2012. 3D constrained local model for rigid and non-rigid facial tracking. In *Proceedings of International Conference on Computer Vision and Pattern Recognition (CVPR)*. IEEE, 2610–2617.

[3] Alan W Black and Kevin A Lenzo. 2001. Flite: a small fast run-time synthesis engine. In *4th ISCA Tutorial and Research Workshop (ITRW) on Speech Synthesis*.

[4] Dan Bohus and Eric Horvitz. 2011. Multiparty turn taking in situated dialog: Study, lessons, and directions. In *Proceedings of the SIGDIAL 2011 Conference*. Association for Computational Linguistics, 98–109.

[5] Dan Bohus and Alexander I Rudnicky. 2009. The RavenClaw dialog management framework: Architecture and systems. *Computer Speech & Language* 23, 3 (2009), 332–361.

[6] Chih-Chung Chang and Chih-Jen Lin. 2011. LIBSVM: a library for support vector machines. *ACM Transactions on Intelligent Systems and Technology (TIST)* 2, 3 (2011), 27.

[7] Daniel Gatica-Perez, Iain A McCowan, Dong Zhang, and Samy Bengio. 2005. Detecting group interest-level in meetings. In *Proceedings of the International Conference on Acoustics, Speech, and Signal Processing (ICASSP)*.

[8] Charles Goodwin. 1981. *Conversational organization: Interaction between speakers and hearers*. Academic Press.

[9] Joey Chiao-yin Hsiao, Wan-rong Jih, and Jane Yungjen Hsu. 2012. Recognizing continuous social engagement level in dyadic conversation by using turntaking and speech emotion patterns. In *Proceedings of the Activity Context Representation Workshop at AAAI*.

[10] Spyros Kousidis, Casey Kennington, Timo Baumann, Hendrik Buschmeier, Stefan Kopp, and David Schlangen. 2014. A Multimodal In-Car Dialogue System That Tracks The Driver's Attention. In *Proceedings of the 16th International Conference on Multimodal Interaction*. ACM, 26–33.

[11] Matthew Marge, Joao Miranda, Alan W Black, and Alexander I Rudnicky. 2010. Towards improving the naturalness of social conversations with dialogue systems. In *Proceedings of the 11th Annual Meeting of the Special Interest Group on Discourse and Dialogue*. Association for Computational Linguistics, 91–94.

[12] J. R. Martin. 2002. *Meaning beyond the clause: area: self-perspectives*. Annual Review of Applied Linguistics 22.

[13] Catharine Oertel and Giampiero Salvi. 2013. A gaze-based method for relating group involvement to individual engagement in multimodal multiparty dialogue. In *Proceedings of the International Conference on Multimodal Interaction (ICMI)*. ACM, 99–106.

[14] Boersma Paul and Weenink David. 2006. Praat: doing phonetics by computer [Computer program]. *Version 5.3. 03, retrieved 21 November 2011 from http://www. praat. org* (2006).

[15] Antoine Raux, Brian Langner, Alan W Black, and Maxine Eskenazi. 2003. LETâĂŹS GO: Improving spoken dialog systems for the elderly and non-native. In *in Eurospeech03*. Citeseer.

[16] Alessandra Sciutti, Lars Schillingmann, Oskar Palinko, Yukie Nagai, and Giulio Sandini. 2015. A Gaze-contingent Dictating Robot to Study Turn-taking. In *Proceedings of the Tenth Annual ACM/IEEE International Conference on Human-Robot Interaction Extended Abstracts*. ACM, 137–138.

[17] Candace L Sidner, Cory D Kidd, Christopher Lee, and Neal Lesh. 2004. Where to look: a study of human-robot engagement. In *Proceedings of the International Conference on Intelligent User Interfaces*. ACM, 78–84.

[18] David Traum and Jeff Rickel. 2002. Embodied agents for multi-party dialogue in immersive virtual worlds. In *Proceedings of the first international joint conference on Autonomous agents and multiagent systems: part 2*. ACM, 766–773.

[19] A. Vinciarelli, M. Pantic, and H. Bourlard. 2009. Social Signal Processing: Survey of an Emerging Domain. *Image and Vision Computing Journal* 27, 12 (2009), 1743–1759.

[20] Rob Voigt, Robert J Podesva, and Dan Jurafsky. 2014. Speaker movement correlates with prosodic indicators of engagement. In *Speech Prosody*, Vol. 7.

[21] Zhou Yu, Dan Bohus, and Eric Horvitz. 2015. Incremental Coordination: Attention-Centric Speech Production in a Physically Situated Conversational Agent. (2015).

[22] Zhou Yu, David Gerritsen, Amy Ogan, Alan W Black, and Justine Cassell. 2013. Automatic Prediction of Friendship via Multi-model Dyadic Features. (2013), 51–60.

[23] Zhou Yu, Alexandros Papangelis, and Alexander Rudnicky. 2015. TickTock: A Non-Goal-Oriented Multimodal Dialog System with Engagement Awareness. In *2015 AAAI Spring Symposium Series*.

[24] Zhou Yu, Stefen Scherer, David Devault, Jonathan Gratch, Giota Stratou, Louis-Philippe Morency, and Justine Cassell. 2013. Multimodal prediction of psychological disorders: Learning verbal and nonverbal commonalities in adjacency pairs. In *Semdial*. 160–169.

Implicit Human-computer Interaction: Two Complementary Approaches

Julia Wache

Department of Information Engineering and Computer Science (DISI)
University of Trento, Italy
Julia.Wache@disi.unitn.it

ABSTRACT

One of the main goals in Human Computer Interaction (HCI) is improving the interface between users and computers: Interfacing should be intuitive, effortless and easy to learn. We approach the goal from two opposite but complementary directions: On the one hand, computer-user interaction can be enhanced if the computer can assess users differences in an automated manner. Therefore we collected physiological and psychological data from people exposed to emotional stimuli and created a database for the community to use for further research in the context of automated learning to detect the differences in the inner states of users. We employed the data both to not only predict the emotional state of users but also their personality traits.

On the other hand, users need information dispatched by a computer to be easily, intuitively accessible. To minimize the cognitive effort of assimilating information we use a tactile device in form of a belt and test how it can be best used to replace or augment the information received from other senses (e.g., visual and auditory) in a navigation task. We investigate how both approaches can be combined to improve specific applications.

Categories and Subject Descriptors

H.1.2 [User/Machine Systems]: Human information processing; H.5.2 [User Interfaces]: Haptic I/O; I.5.2 [Pattern Recognition Design Methodology]: Pattern analysis

General Terms

Measurement; Algorithms; Verification; Human Factors

Keywords

Bio-signals; Affective Computing; Emotions; Personality recognition; Tactile device; vibrotactile feedback.

1. INTRODUCTION

Over the past decades interaction elements facilitating the interface with computers have become a common and increasingly important part of human life. Technology develops fast, constantly creating more opportunities to improve human-computer interaction. Technological gadgets are becoming cheaper and also more inclusive. New interaction designs and intuitive user concepts facilitate access to technology for different user groups. For instance even blind people can interface with a smartphone through smart voice over technologies.

ICMI '15, November 09 - 13, 2015, Seattle, WA, USA

ACM 978-1-4503-3912-4/15/11…$15.00
DOI: http://dx.doi.org/10.1145/2818346.2823311

Our general goal is to improve the intuitiveness of new technological developments to make the interaction with them easier. There are two complementary approaches that we address.

1) At first we want to better recognize the inner state of a person automatically without them having to actively provide information themselves. We employ facial expressions and physiological signals, implicit signals, as they are mostly unconscious and difficult to influence. Therefore we use sensors measuring their changes while subjects watch multimedia content that elicit different emotions. With pattern recognition and machine learning approaches we then predict emotions as well as personality traits from the collected measurements.

2) Secondly we investigate how to provide relevant information to the users in an easily comprehensible way. Therefore we choose a tactile belt as output device to provide a maximum of information with a minimum of cognitive effort.

Finally we integrate both approaches by proposing a framework in which a system uses knowledge about the inner state of a user to adapt the information output.

1.1 Understanding users' inner state

One important factor influencing human behavior is emotion. Emotions are psychological phenomena but they also have an impact on physiological signals that can be measured and analyzed (e.g. [17]). Physiological changes are induced by the Limbic System, the part of the brain controlling the autonomic nervous system. It is involved in emotional experience and sensory input processing. Hence, the current emotional state may influence the perception of a situation and the corresponding behavioral actions of people. Also further internal factors, such as personality, can have an impact.

Therefore one challenge for contemporary human-computer-interaction (HCI) systems is the ability to understand the influence that factors like the personality traits or the environment have on the emotional state of a user and to use this information to predict consequential behavioral actions. For example, in an e-learning scenario the computer might adapt the shown content depending on how easy (boring) or difficult (stressing) it is perceived by the user.

To investigate emotional states and what influences them emotional videos are preferably used because multimedia contents such as movies intend to induce certain emotions in viewers to create a specific experience. One way to understand the current emotional state of users while watching emotional stimuli is to interrupt them and directly ask them for an evaluation. Newer methods extract the emotional state without the need to interrupt the user based on their implicit reactions. Therefore one method is to record physiological responses and facial expressions during exposure to emotional content.

In this way we intend to solve the first problem – automated emotion and personality recognition. The challenge is to accurately detect physiological changes caused by affective responses and understand the correlations between physiological signals and the emotions of users. Hence it is important to i) choose a method that reliably induces similar specific emotions in people and ii) to select adequate implicit signals that correlate with those emotions.

1.2 Providing easily understandable information

The other side of an effective communication between humans and their technological devices is the ability to provide information in an easily understandable way making the processing of data effortless for the users. In a world of increasing information overload, people are often overwhelmed by the huge amount of data to be processed. Most input is usually received over the visual and audio channel. In daily life people continuously encounter an endless stream of sounds and images. To relieve eyes and ears, a further sense that can be employed for information input is the tactile sense. The sense of touch is suitable to transmit simple information in a discrete way, e.g. a mobile phone that vibrates to transmit information to its owner without attracting attention from the surrounding.

We use a tactile alternative to common output devices (visual displays, loudspeakers, earphones) for navigation tasks. As a direct application outside of the lab, tactile belts can, in combination with a smartphone, be used for navigation in unknown environments. Current navigation aids are mostly based on audio or visual instructions. Normally navigating in a new environment requires eyes and ears to be focused on the traffic to evade obstacles or other people. The usage of tactile signals elegantly circumnavigates an overload of the visual and auditory sensory modalities as it uses the tactile sense to provide information. In summary, tactile devices can be applied in real world applications to facilitate information reception.

1.3 Scientific approach

To investigate both mentioned aspects we developed and applied two experimental approaches. First, to better understand the user, we investigated how to predict the inner mental state by measuring implicit signals. We collected the physiological data of 36 participants and trained classifiers to predict both, their emotional reactions and personality traits and used correlation methods to understand their connections.

For the second aspect, to investigate how to provide easy understandable information, we selected a scenario in which we provide tactile feedback from a navigation device.

Finally we propose a setting to integrate both aspects. We use contextual information about users to adapt the information output of a navigation device and therefore improve the navigation experience.

2. PROBLEM STATEMENT

Taking into consideration the contextual situation of the user in HCI is an important aspect when interacting with intelligent systems. Therefore, adapting the interaction possibilities between computer and user according to the user's mental state can facilitate understanding between human and machine. Important aspects of the mental state are current emotions and personality traits. Emotions are correlated to implicit responses but it is yet to investigate more how personality affects this relationship.

Additionally, there is an increasing need of easy information transfer from machines to humans to avoid information overload. To achieve these goals we work on the following problems:

1. At first we need to understand which aspects influence the mental state of users. Then we try to automatically detect these aspects such as emotions and personality in users and employ them to improve interactions with intelligent systems.

Consequently the following research questions arise: How can we correlate physiological signals to emotions and personality traits? Can we predict emotional states and personality traits from them? If yes, which are the most useful signals?

2. The second problem is to find a good way to communicate information to users and make them easily understandable. They need to be transmitted in a complex context even when eyes and ears are already occupied by other tasks that require attention. We investigate whether tactile signals can overcome limitations of attention and be used to transmit information intuitively.

Here, we contribute to the following research questions: How can a tactile device in form of a belt be used best to display information for navigation purposes? How can we create an intuitive understanding of directional indications and reduce the required mental effort in orientation?

3. The final problem is a combination of both. We investigate how knowledge about the mental state of a user can be utilized by a system to provide information in a personalized way adapted to individual needs.

The example application we want to apply our results to is a navigation task. We examine whether detecting the mental state of a user can be used to adapt the directional indications provided accordingly and represent them in more easily understandable ways. Do personal and situational factors require different relevant information and ways to display them?

3. RELATED WORK

We review relevant literature about decoding aspects of the mental state such as affect and personality as well as how information can be intuitively displayed to users.

3.1 Implicit Affect Decoding

Affect is often measured employing a dimensional model [16]. Hereby users give feedback about their emotional state by rating their valence and arousal on a scale from negative to positive and low to high respectively. Over the past years Affective Computing advanced in decoding emotion by analyzing users facial expressions [7] or spontaneous physiological responses [11]. Facial expressions might be controlled willingly but other physiological reactions such as changes in heart rate, skin conductance level, blood pressure and facial Electromyogram (EMG) are barely influenceable by intention. They are used by Sinha [17] to show the differences of emotional responses to negative and neutral valence stimuli. Lisetti and Nasoz [12] review technologies and algorithms for recognizing emotions using wearable devices that measure Galvanic Skin Response (GSR), heart rate and skin temperature. Abadi et al. [1] compiled a dataset with 18 subjects collecting measurements of Magneto-Encephalogram (MEG), Electrooculogram (EOG), Electrocardiogram (ECG) and EMG responses for music and movie clips. In their conclusion movie clips proofed better results for emotion elicitation and affect prediction than music video clips.

Movie clips are intended to elicit emotions making them appropriate to evoke specific emotions that can then be utilized for analyzing the correspondent implicit signals. Koelstra et al. [11] presented music video clips in the DEAP dataset and recorded peripheral physiological signals and EEG. They correlated them with collected ratings on arousal, valence, liking, and dominance. Soleymani et al. [18] in contrary showed emotional video clips to participants when creating the MAHNOB-HCI multimodal database. Such affective datasets that comprise simultaneous data of many modalities are valuable tools for improving emotion recognition techniques [18].

Research efforts to enhance emotion recognition using facial expressions [7] and physiological responses such as brain activity, ECG and GSR have increased [3, 11, 12, 18], but the effects that personality has on emotion perception was hardly investigated by prior affect recognition studies. Our work is one of the first to also measure personality dimensions and predict them through multimodal fusion of users' implicit responses in emotional contexts.

3.2 Relation of Personality and Affect Perception

The five-factor model describes five dimensions of human personality: Extraversion (sociable vs. reserved), Agreeableness (compassionate vs. dispassionate), Conscientiousness (dutiful vs. easy-going), Neuroticism or Emotional Stability (nervous vs. confident), and Openness to Experience or Creativity (open vs. closed) [13]. Traditionally these personality dimensions have been measured by using questionnaires or self-reports. Argamon et al. [4] were one of the first to attempt automated personality estimation. To recognize Extraversion and Neuroticism they used lexical cues from informal texts. The few studies investigating the relation between personality and emotion by using explicit or implicit responses mostly work only on Neuroticism and Extroversion [11].

Unique aspects of this work in this context are: (1) The influence of personality differences on emotion perception has hardly been studied yet. (2) In contrast to personality assessment with questionnaires we work on decoding both affect and all five personality traits from implicit responses.

3.3 Intuitive Information Display

When designing interfaces the senses mostly employed are vision (e.g. screens) and hearing (speakers, earphones). This can cause an intensive information load for the visual and auditory senses in contexts where much information needs to be processed at the same time, such as during navigation. Employing the sense of touch has several advantages: First of all, simple information can be processed directly, intuitively and without requiring attention. Furthermore, tactile information can be used to inform a specific user privately without drawing other people's attention. While various applications use tactile stimulation (overview see in [8]) one specific opportunity of tactile information is the possibility to map directions onto the body. One design is a belt with integrated vibration units that can be used in navigation contexts [5, 6] and has been shown to be easily understandable [5].

4. RESEARCH OUTLINE

We already performed various studies to investigate the automated recognition of user's emotional states. Currently, we assess data to learn about the provision of easily understandable tactile information.

4.1 Affective Multimedia Analysis and Retrieval of Physiological Data

To study the relationship between personality and affect we employed physiological signals while participants were exposed to different emotional stimuli. Even though facial expressions contain also psychological aspects for simplicity we summarize them together with ECG, GSR and EEG as psychological signals in the scope of this work. After watching each video clip participants gave direct feedback of their emotional state. Afterwards they provided measures for the big-five personality dimensions (overview see Figure 1).

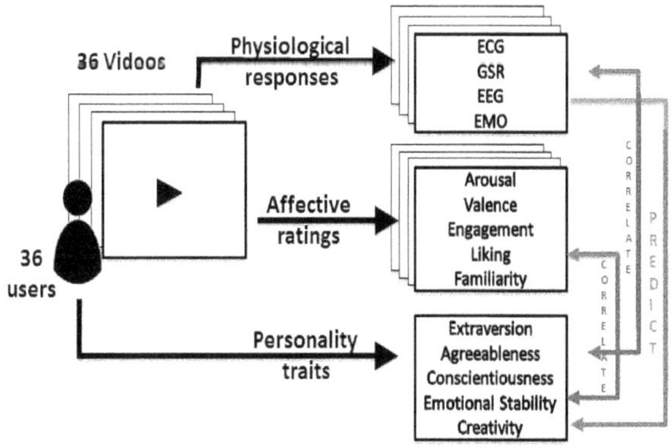

Figure 1: Overview of the experimental setting; 36 participants watch 36 movie clips and rate each along five dimensions. For each person one personality test measures five traits. Their relationship with both ratings and physiological signals is analyzed.

4.1.1 Stimuli, Subjects and Personality Scores

As stimuli we used 36 Hollywood movie clips used by Abadi et al [3] (mean length = 80s). Their valence and arousal ground truth scores were uniformly distributed along valence and arousal dimensions (9 clips per quadrant). 36 people (12 female, mean age = 29.2) took part in the study. They completed the big-five marker scale (BFMS) questionnaire [15] used to compute scores along the five personality dimensions.

4.1.2 Experimental Set-up and Procedure

Sensors to measure implicit signals (GSR, ECG and facial-EEG) were placed on the participant's body and a webcam was positioned to record the face from a frontal position. The measurements were done with portable and commercially available sensors. They watched the movie clips in a randomized order with a break in the middle. Subjects rated each clip directly after viewing on five 7-point scales expressing their current emotional state with arousal and valence ratings as well as engagement, liking, and familiarity of each video clip.

4.1.3 Feature Extraction

Throughout the experiment we collected the following signals to extract features from them:

1. GSR measures the transpiration rate of the skin similarly as in [10, 18].
2. Electroencephalography (EEG) measures small changes in the electrical field surrounding the brain. The facial-EEG responses also include the level of facial activation.
3. Following [9] we used Electrocardiogram (ECG) signals to monitor heartbeats and derive features from it.
4. Facial expressions were detected by a facial tracking module [7] that captures the displacements of 12 facial motion units (MU) in each video frame (EMO).

4.1.4 Results and Discussion

We provided baseline statistics for the dataset and did analyses to show correlation and mutual information between affective ratings, physiological responses and personality measures. Indeed we found high mutual information between physiological signals and personality and especially emotional ratings. We then divided people in high- and low-trait groups depending on the median of each personality dimension and attempted binary classification using physiological features. The objective was to predict whether each of the 36 subjects belonged to the 'high' or 'low' trait group depending on the response for all stimuli. We used the linear libSVM implementation and adopted a Leave-one-out cross-validation scheme. In Table 1 we report F1 scores that measure test accuracy considering both the precision and the recall. First we present the unimodal results achieved with the four modalities and additionally denote the results of the multimodal approach (W_{est}). Above chance recognition (F1=0.50) is achieved for three personality traits namely Extraversion (F1=0.60), Emotional Stability (F1=0.63) and Creativity (F1=0.91). The results improve when analyzing implicit signals only for homogeneous videos from one quadrant. Also recognition of Agreeableness (F1= 0.84 for high-arousal-high-valence videos) and Conscientiousness (F1= 0.74 for high-arousal-low-valence videos) reach above chance level (not visible in table). Currently we prepare a paper to publish the dataset and the results in the Journal Transactions of Affective Computing.

4.2 Inference of Personality Traits and Affect Schedule by Analysis of Spontaneous Reactions to Affective Videos

In this study [2], we additionally collected data about the Positive and Negative Affective Schedule (PANAS). PANAS [19] is used to better understand the mood of a person, which can also be an important factor for the interaction of users with computers.

We used linear regression models trained independently on each modality to predict personality traits and PANAS. They can indeed be predicted based on the 35 users' implicit responses to the affective stimuli. Physiological signals (ECG+GSR) reveal the distinction between extroverts and introverts (70%±8% F1-score) and EEG signals the distinction between creative and non-creative people (69%±6% F1-score). Also for predicting agreeableness, emotional stability, and baseline affective states significantly higher than chance-level results were achieved. We could therefore show that the collected signals are useful to predict the big-five personality traits but also PANAS.

4.3 Tactile Feedback as Intuitive Indicator for Directional Information in a Navigation Task

We used a tactile belt that is worn around the waist to display directional information (see Figure 2). 32 vibrating units were equally distributed around the body so that 360° can be mapped on the body via tactile stimulation.

	Extr	Agree	Consc	ES	Crea
ECG	0.43	**0.37**	**0.31**	**0.50**	0.54
GSR	0.14	0.34	0.28	0.20	**0.91**
EMO	**0.59**	0.34	0.11	0.37	0.26
EEG	0.34	0.28	0.13	**0.50**	0.50
W_{est}	**0.60**	**0.37**	**0.31**	**0.63**	**0.91**

Table 1: Emotion and Personality classification considering responses to all stimuli. Maximum F1-scores obtained using unimodal and multimodal methods are shown in bold.

Two different kinds of directional information can be provided to facilitate navigation. (1) With the compass function general cardinal information is provided. To indicate the north always one unit vibrates, namely the one pointing towards north. (2) With the turn-by-turn navigation function one vibrating unit always indicates where to go next. The vibrating unit in front of the waist signals the user a straight path. If a turn is coming up, the vibrating signal digresses to the appropriate side towards which the turn should be made. Turning the body towards the indicated direction will bring the tactile signal back to the front.

In one experiment we tested whether the compass function improves navigation abilities. We displayed north so that always one unit vibrated namely the one pointing towards north. We conducted a pointing study to test whether orientation performance increases. Over the course of two weeks 18 participants were introduced to three different large-scale areas unknown to them with six landmarks each. Upon arriving at each landmark, participants were asked to point towards the location of the previously visited landmark(s). We measured the pointing error, i.e. the difference between pointed direction and actual beeline direction. We hypothesized that given the additional information participants learn to use the belt's north signal and improve their navigation performance. First results indicate that while some people improved their performance significantly within the short time others did not improve as much. Currently we are still analyzing the data in more detail.

Figure 2: Tactile belt with 32 vibration units (provided by the feelSpace group at University Osnabrück)

4.4 Remaining work

The previous experiment suggests that personal differences play an important role when handling new technologies. We will investigate in more detail what aspects contribute to the differences of performance between participants. Possible factors are the personality of users (e.g. whether they are open towards new experiences) or their emotional state (e.g. whether they were bored or stresses by the tasks). Contextual information of the individual are often neglected but might well contribute to the success of interaction with new technologies. We plan to integrate both belt functions enabling users to use it with both, the compass and the turn-by-turn navigation function. Then we investigate how we can automatically adapt the functions individually depending on the current state of the user.

5. CONTRIBUTION AND PERSPECTIVE

In conclusion, we approach HCI from two different perspectives: On the one hand we work on better understanding the users without them having to actively provide much information and on the other hand, we investigate a method to provide information in a way that requires little conscious effort and does not compromise the input of other senses such as hearing or seeing.

We collected and analyzed physiological data in emotional contexts together with personality data. We created a database for the community to analyze correlations between emotional and physiological states, thus providing the basis for automated learning of the inner states of a user. In a second experiment, we also included PANAS data [2]. To make the setting ecological valid we used portable and commercially available sensors and continue to learn which methods and sensors compose the most effective and least invasive combination for emotion and personality detection.

Currently, we use a tactile navigation device to provide easily understandable directional signals in an orientation task. Our goal is to find out the best way tactile feedback can be used to display information, aiming at real world application e.g. as an intuitive navigation system for the blind that adapts automatically to the current individual situation.

Both approaches will finally be integrated to investigate how and in which contexts we can use the results to actually improve the user experience in real life settings. When people are navigating during high traffic volume, detecting their mental state (tired, distracted, etc.) and providing adequate feedback cannot only be helpful but could even be lifesaving

Coming from an interdisciplinary background we encourage a holistic viewpoint on HCI. While often single aspects are investigated and taken into account, a broader understanding of the interactions can help to improve HCI experiences.

6. ACKNOWLEDGMENTS

I thank my advisor Nicu Sebe for constant support with my thesis. I am also grateful for the support of my colleagues from the feelSpace group as well as M. Khomami Abadi, R. Subramanian and all the participants of the experiments.

7. REFERENCES

[1] Abadi, M.K. et al. 2013. Decoding Affect in Videos Employing the MEG Brain Signal. *2013 10th IEEE International Conference and Workshops on Automatic Face and Gesture Recognition (FG)*. (Apr. 2013), 1–6.

[2] Abadi, M.K. et al. 2015. Inference of Personality Traits and Affect Schedule by Analysis of Spontaneous Reactions to Affective Videos. *Automatic Face and Gesture Recognition* (2015).

[3] Abadi, M.K. et al. 2013. User-centric Affective Video Tagging from MEG and Peripheral Physiological Responses. *2013 Humaine Association Conference on Affective Computing and Intelligent Interaction* (2013), 582–587.

[4] Argamon, S. et al. 2005. Lexical predictors of personality type. *Interface and the Classification Society of North America*. (Jan. 2005).

[5] Van Erp, J.B.F. et al. 2005. Waypoint navigation with a vibrotactile waist belt. *ACM Transactions on Applied Perception*. 2, 2 (2005), 106–117.

[6] Ho, C. et al. 2006. Assessing the effectiveness of "intuitive" vibrotactile warning signals in preventing front-to-rear-end collisions in a driving simulator. *Accident Analysis and Prevention*. 38, 5 (2006), 988–996.

[7] Joho, H. et al. 2011. Looking at the Viewer: Analysing Facial Activities to Detect Personal Highlights of Multimedia Contents. *Multimedia Tools and Applications*. 51, 2 (2011), 505–523.

[8] Jones, L.A. and Sarter, N.B. 2008. Tactile Displays: Guidance for Their Design and Application. *Human Factors*. 50, 1 (2008), 90–111.

[9] Kim, J. and André, E. 2008. Emotion recognition based on physiological changes in music listening. *IEEE transactions on pattern analysis and machine intelligence*. 30, 12 (Dec. 2008), 2067–83.

[10] Kim, K.H. et al. 2004. Emotion recognition system using short-term monitoring of physiological signals. *Medical & biological engineering & computing*. 42, 3 (May 2004), 419–27.

[11] Koelstra, S. et al. 2012. DEAP: A Database for Emotion Analysis Using Physiological Signals. *IEEE Transactions on Affective Computing*. 3, 1 (2012), 18–31.

[12] Lisetti, C. and Nasoz, F. 2004. Using Noninvasive Wearable Computers to Recognize Human Emotions from Physiological Signals. *EURASIP Journal on Advances in Signal Processing*. 2004, 11 (2004), 1672–1687.

[13] McCrae, R.R. and John, O.P. 1992. An introduction to the five-factor model and its applications. *Journal of personality*. 60, 2 (Jun. 1992), 175–215.

[14] Ng, W. 2009. Clarifying the relation between neuroticism and positive emotions. *Personality and Individual Differences*. 47, 1 (Jul. 2009), 69–72.

[15] Perugini, M. and Blas, L. Di 2002. Analyzing personality-related adjectives from an etic–emic perspective: The Big Five Marker Scales (BFMS) and the Italian AB5C taxonomy. *Big Five Assessment*. (2002), 281–304.

[16] Russell, J.A. and Mehrabian, A. 1977. Evidence for a three-factor theory of emotions. *Journal of Research in Personality*. 11, 3 (1977), 273–294.

[17] Sinha, R. 1996. Multivariate Response Patterning of Fear and Anger. *Cognition & Emotion*. 10, 2 (Mar. 1996), 173–198.

[18] Soleymani, M. et al. 2012. A Multimodal Database for Affect Recognition and Implicit Tagging. *IEEE Transactions on Affective Computing*. 3, 1 (Jan. 2012), 42–55.

[19] Watson, D. et al. 1988. Development and validation of brief measures of positive and negative affect: the PANAS scales. *Journal of personality and social psychology*. 54, 6 (Jun. 1988), 1063–70

Instantaneous and Robust Eye-Activity Based Task Analysis

Hoe Kin Wong
University of New South Wales
Sydney, Australia
hoekin.wong@unsw.edu.au

ABSTRACT

Task analysis using eye-activity has previously been used for estimating cognitive load on a per-task basis. However, since pupil size is a continuous physiological signal, eye-based classification accuracy of cognitive load can be improved by considering cognitive load at a higher temporal resolution and incorporating models of the interactions between the task-evoked pupillary response (TEPR) and other pupillary responses such as the Pupillary Light Reflex into the classification model.

In this work, methods of using eye-activity as a measure of continuous mental load will be investigated. Subsequently pupil light reflex models will be incorporated into task analysis to investigate the possibility of enhancing the reliability of cognitive load estimation in varied lighting conditions. This will culminate in the development and evaluation of a classification system which measures rapidly changing cognitive load. Task analysis of this calibre will enable interfaces in wearable optical devices to be constantly aware of the user's mental state and control information flow to prevent information overload and interruptions.

Author Keywords

task evoked pupillary responses; cognitive load estimation; human computer interaction

ACM Classification Keywords

H.5.2. Information interfaces and presentation (e.g., HCI): Miscellaneous; I.4.9. Image Processing and Computer Vision: Applications;

MOTIVATION AND KEY RESEARCH QUESTIONS

Until recently, advancements in computing have not significantly addressed the challenges associated with maximising productivity in a human-device relationship. The importance of considering the human agent as a dynamic biological entity with limited processing ability has been largely ignored. Information overload is a multifaceted problem which is becoming prevalent in the workforce due to the increased uptake of technology [3].

ICMI '15, November 09 - 13, 2015, Seattle, WA, USA

ACM 978-1-4503-3912-4/15/11…$15.00
DOI: http://dx.doi.org/10.1145/2818346.2823312

The sheer number of information channels with which people are intermittently interacting facilitates diverse types of information to be readily accessible and thus improve productivity. However, electronic devices also act as sources of interference and disruption due to their ability to provide notifications which demand users' attention and thus when neglected or improperly managed, these notifications inadvertently result in breaks of concentration and subsequently reduced efficacy in completing tasks.

Physiologically attentive user interfaces have been touted as a key ingredient for solving some aspects of information overload in the context of human computer interaction, including the management of multiple channels of information. Various sources of physiological signals have been researched and investigated as useful input for interfaces including electroencephalography, electrocardiography (ECG), galvanic skin response and eye-activity [2], the last having the advantage of being simple to obtain and process, but not fully understood.

The research questions of this thesis are:

1. Investigate methods of estimating *instantaneous* cognitive load using eye-activity
2. Develop cognitive load classification systems which incorporate models of the Pupillary Light Reflex (PLR) to further understand the interaction of the task evoked pupillary response and PLR
3. Evaluate and enhance the performance of existing methods of pupil size measurement and blink detection
4. Investigate the feasibility of task analysis in real world settings (i.e. in stimuli rich environments with everyday tasks without predefined contexts).

LITERATURE REVIEW

Cognitive Load Theory

The Cognitive Load Theory (CLT) provides a framework for understanding learning processes in terms of long term and short term memory and its connection to task instructional design and complexity [12]. In this theory cognitive load is defined as the "total amount of mental activity imposed on working memory at an instance in time".

Other researchers have extended CLT, increasing its precision and detail to facilitate more accurate task analysis and mental load classification. For example, Xie and

Salvendy introduced several concepts including notions of instantaneous workload and average workload to account for the effects of individual and task type differences in task response [14]. These concepts though appealing due to their mathematical intuition, have not been fully verified in experiments due to the lack of task paradigms which enable control of instantaneous cognitive load.

Cognitive Load Estimation and Induction

Due to the complexity and incomplete understanding of cognitive load, developing an accurate measure of cognitive load has proven a difficult task for researchers. Since cognitive load is inherently connected to a person's perception of a task, a method involving subjective rating is an obvious and natural consideration. Gopher and Braune determined that subjects could reliably report their perceived level of mental load on a numerical scale [5]. However, the use of subjective ratings relies on several assumptions, such as participants being able to introspect on their thought processes and provide a quantitative assessment of the degree of mental exertion. Multidimensional rating systems which consider multiple factors associated with cognitive load, such as mental stress and fatigue are widely considered the best means of obtaining subjective feedback for cognitive load estimation. Two such well-known systems are the National Aeronautics and Space Administration's Task Load Index (TLX) and the Subjective Workload Assessment Technique (SWAT). Both the TLX and SWAT are recognised to have merit in prediction of experienced workload and accounting for variations in individuals [9]. In the problem of mental load classification, it is apparent that the role of subjective ratings would be confined to the development, evaluation and configuration of the system and not in the actual classification, considering that the objective of the system is effectively to predict the would-be subjective rating of the user.

A diverse assortment of task types has been used to induce various forms of mental load including cognitive load. For example, artificial short-term memory tasks such as digit span memorisation and real life tasks like air traffic control have been used by researchers to induce mental load and observe and record subject performances and responses [10]. Tasks which require complex processing such as mental arithmetic, lingual translation and Stroop tasks have been frequently used to induce mental load while measuring not only TEPRs, but also other physiological signals. Mental arithmetic tasks can be designed to invoke various loads on short-term and long-term memory by adjusting the lengths of numbers to be operated on and the magnitudes of the pairs of digits, hence changing the number of carry over digits to be memorised. Researchers such as Ryu and Myung used this technique to maximise the difference in difficulty between two levels of tasks and were able to observe statistically significant differences in the physiological responses of heart rate variability and pupillary dilation [11]. Tasks designed to induce cognitive load levels are effective for verifying and developing theories on cognition but practical task analysis systems will more frequently classify complex tasks. Complex tasks are ubiquitous in everyday life situations and the collective effect of the operations involved on physiological responses can be measured to distinguish tasks of different load levels. However the extent to which physiological responses can be deconstructed and analysed to identify the underlying operations involved in a task remains uncertain.

Physiological signals derived from ECG, functional magnetic resonance imaging and positron emission tomography and eye-activity have been shown to be strong correlates of cognitive load. However, eye-activity is superior because it can be measured non-intrusively [2].

Task Evoked Pupillary Response

The task evoked pupillary response (TEPR) refers to changes in pupil size due to mental load induced by a task. One of the earliest and most prominent findings in the field is Hess and Polt's discovery that pupil dilation could be empirically correlated with task difficulty in the context of solving simple arithmetic problems [6]. Subsequent research over the decades has reinforced and built upon this knowledge through investigations of the TEPR in a diverse range of tasks and contexts. The method Hess and Polt used to analyse the change in pupil size, by obtaining the difference of the pupil sizes at the time of control and response, has been used extensively by various researchers [10]. However, many aspects of the TEPR have not been fully determined, such as its temporal resolution, ability to reflect in-task variation and most significantly, the nature and observability of the TEPR during the presence of pupillary responses to light, emotion and other stimuli. Research such as that of Chen and Epps supports the notion that accurate task analysis in emotion stimulating environments is indeed possible, since they determined empirically that emotional factors did not affect TEPRs [2].

Hardware

Eye tracking systems are predominantly used for gaze tracking solutions, but they are also becoming the choice of data collection apparatus for TEPR investigations. There are both remote and head-mounted systems in the form of glasses. The disadvantage of head-mounted trackers over remote eye trackers is the discomfort and obstruction of vision caused by wearing frames with an attached camera, which some researchers believe results in distress and thus affects TEPRs [8]. While remote eye trackers have the advantage of not interfering with participants at all, they tend not to be able to capture the same amount of detail as head-mounted tracking systems and the data captured requires extra processing such as facial recognition and head movement compensation to accurately record pupil data. Furthermore, remote-eye trackers are stationary, meaning that they will only operate when the subject is positioned in the tracker's field of vision. With all of these aspects given due consideration, a head-mounted eye tracker is better positioned to address the problems in mobile mental load classification systems.

Eye-Activity Data Processing

Various algorithms have been developed for pupil tracking in near-field eye video sequences. Their operations can be categorised into three stages: image pre-processing, segmentation of the pupil and iris and pupil ellipse fitting.

Some image pre-processing techniques such as linear and non-linear filtering are used to remove artefacts and noise in order to reduce the probability of false detections and thus improve accuracy, while others such as greyscale conversion serve to reduce the computation time required by more intensive operations. While pre-processing techniques can play an important role of enhancing the accuracy of the pupil tracking, the differences of the accuracy, robustness to camera or illumination conditions and computational requirements between algorithms lies in the approach used to segment the pupil and iris.

There have been vastly different approaches to the pupil iris segmentation task, but all of them rely on the basic assumption that the pupil is a low intensity blob which mostly resembles a circle or ellipse, surrounded by a higher intensity iris. Li's Starburst Algorithm, for example, searches radially from a pupil point areas of high contrast, corresponding ideally to the pupil iris boundary [7]. Swirski's algorithm obtains pupil blob points by *k*-means clustering the pupil region of the image, separating the pupil blob from the iris [13]. While these two methods require an approximate location of the pupil region and adjustments to a considerable number of parameters to achieve the desired trade-off between accuracy and performance, Chen's self-tuning threshold algorithm is superior as it does not require background knowledge of the pupil region and only one parameter needs to be adjusted to achieve the desired trade-off [1]. Although the developers of these algorithms have reported respectable performances in terms of accuracy and reliability in less than ideal conditions, no comprehensive study has been conducted to compare the performance of all these algorithms.

To measure pupillary behaviour, a representation of the pupil is required, and ellipse fitting methods are extensively used. One method commonly used is least squares, which calculates the parameters of the ellipse equation by solving the matrix equation which minimises the sum of the errors squared [4]. The Random Sample Consensus (RANSAC) Fitting paradigm is a more complex method which iteratively estimates the best fitting ellipse by applying the least squares method to small, random subsets of points (at least five points to define a unique ellipse) and choosing the ellipse which agrees the most with the whole set of pupil points [13]. Swirski's version of RANSAC incorporates a support function favouring inliers with gradients matching the image gradients and performs additional checks allow for early exits [13]. It is more intelligent and computationally faster than Li's basic version because of the image sensitive support function and fewer iterations are performed in general [13]. However, the least squares algorithm is computationally faster given that it performs only one iteration of calculations and results in sufficiently accurate ellipse fitting if no false pupil edge points are present [1].

METHODOLOGY – RESEARCH PLATFORM

Figure 1 depicts the scope of the technical problem. The system to be developed in order to investigate the questions outlined will capture eye data in form of near-field videos, process the video frames to extract eye features and use those features to perform classification and output a description of mental state. The components of this system are described in detail in the following subsections.

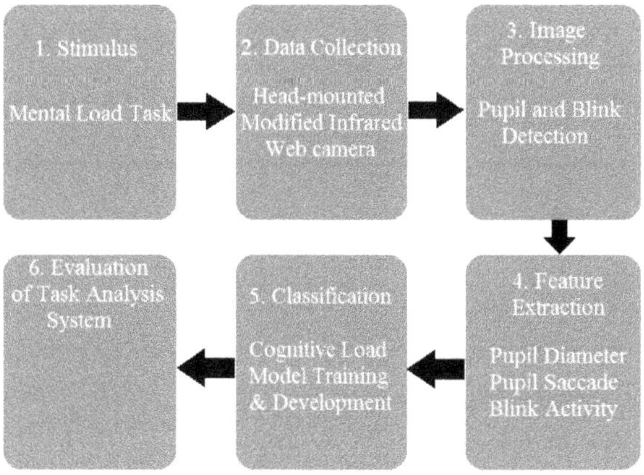

Figure 1. Scope of Technical Problem

Head-Mounted Eye Tracker

For the reasons outlined in the Hardware subsection of the Literature Review, a head-mounted modified infrared camera set up was chosen as the means of collecting video sequences of eye data. Commercially available systems, which come in packages with custom made software are arguably superior due to their integration of components. However the packages are unsuitable for pupil based task analysis because they are designed primarily for gaze tracking and not pupil size measurement. Additionally, they offer unnecessary polish, functionality and connectivity which results in exorbitant costs upwards of USD $10,000.

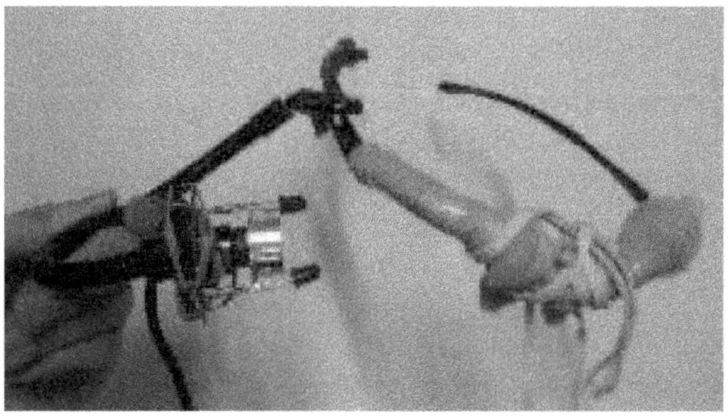

Figure 2. Head-Mounted Infrared Web Camera System

The USB web camera used is a low cost 5MP sensor capable of capturing 30 frames per second. Following the principles used by researchers such as Li [7], Chen [2] and Swirski [13], two IR LEDs were soldered onto the camera's printed circuit board which contains pre-existing through-hole pairs for additional LEDs. Two IR LEDs were determined to be sufficient to illuminate the eye region of each video frame. The IR filter block in the lens was removed and replaced with a piece of floppy disk film to filter out visible light (see Figure 2). These steps ensure maximum IR detection and thus clear distinction between the pupil and iris.

Algorithm for Data Processing

The algorithm used by Chen [1], which includes the previously mentioned self-tuning threshold algorithm was selected as the main method of processing the near-field video sequences for the reasons outlined in the Eye-Activity Data Processing subsection. It performs pupil blob analysis iteratively across a set of binary threshold images and extracts the pupil blobs and computes their bounding boxes [1]. Five vectors describing characteristics of the bounding boxes are formed. These are the area $A(t)$, uppermost coordinate $H_{up}(t)$, lowermost coordinate $H_{down}(t)$, leftmost coordinate $V_{left}(t)$ and rightmost coordinate $V_{right}(t)$ of the bounding box. Then a new vector $E(t)$ is computed from which the optimum threshold t_{opt} is determined and the corresponding pupil blob points are used (see (1) and (2)).

$$E(t) = |\nabla A| + |\nabla H_{up}| + |\nabla H_{down}| + |\nabla V_{left}| + |\nabla V_{right}| \quad (1)$$

$$t_{opt} = \arg\min_t(E(t)) \quad (2)$$

Convex hull is then applied to exclude any pupil edge points corresponding to the edge of corneal reflections before obtaining an ellipse using least squares fitting [1].

Feature Extraction

Similarly to Chen's work, features of all three classes of eye activity: pupillary size, eye movement and blink activity, will be extracted from datasets to analyse the responses of participants [2]. However, these features will not necessarily be used directly to build the classification model for task analysis but primarily to assist in the development of mathematical models describing the transient responses of task behaviours.

METHODOLOGY – EXPERIMENTAL WORK

Continuous Cognitive Load Estimation

The first research question of this PhD research requires a dataset of responses to tasks which can be designed to arbitrarily induce continuously varying or fixed difficulty levels of cognitive load for arbitrary time periods. Thus, an aurally presented digit span memorisation task paradigm was designed and implemented in MATLAB (see Figure 3). The digit span memorisation task paradigm used by others such as Peavler [10] was identified to be a suitable paradigm because of its documented usefulness in inducing TEPRs, its simplicity and potential to be modified and extended (see under Cognitive Load Estimation and Induction). In addition to the total number of digits to memorise, two methods were identified as means of varying the cognitive load induced in a task:

- Varying the presentation rate of presented digits
- Issuing a drop command to forget memorised digits.

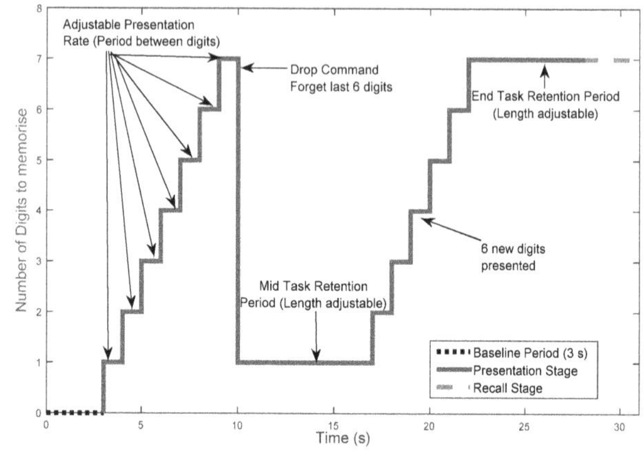

Figure 3. Induced Cognitive Load Level during a 7 Digit Span Memorisation Task

These methods will induce significant changes of within-task cognitive load which require higher temporal resolution analysis to be detected.

A set of tasks with carefully chosen parameter combinations was used to generate a dataset of TEPRs from 20 participants. From the analysis of this dataset, it is anticipated that two aspects of instantaneous cognitive load estimation will be observable, namely:

1. The TEPR indexes the *rate of increase* in induced cognitive load.
2. *Within-task reduction* of cognitive load is reflected in transient pupil diameter response of exponential decay.

Application of statistical methods including Analysis of Variance (ANOVA) in conjunction with mathematical modelling techniques of linear and non-linear least squares fitting on the TEPR data will confirm whether the TEPR is a strong index of instantaneous cognitive load.

Cognitive Load Estimation in the Presence of PLR

The second research question first requires the collection of TEPRs and PLR responses under dynamic lighting conditions. Simplified models of the PLR using 2nd order transient responses will be then developed and verified using the PLR dataset. If subtraction of the modelled PLR responses from TEPRs improves the accuracy of cognitive load estimation, then this finding will support the argument that the TEPR is robust to variations in lighting conditions.

Investigating Data Processing Algorithms

To evaluate the effectiveness of different pupil detection algorithms in terms of robustness, sets of pupil ellipses output by the algorithms will be compared against a ground truth set formed by manually fitted ellipses of video frames under conditions such as poor illumination due to low infrared (IR) contrast, highly off-axis camera angles and occlusion due to eyelashes. Two metrics, Hausdorff Distance and Mean Square Error of pupil diameter, will be used to generate a quantitative assessment of how similar the output ellipse is to the ground truth ellipse.

Task Analysis System Development

For the development of the task analysis system, a ground truth set of models based on the analysis of a comprehensive set of features from eye data will be computed from training datasets. These features will include those used by Chen in her work. The models are anticipated to be 1st or 2nd order time equations with lag and should form the basis of the task analysis system. Then, classification will be performed on unseen datasets of TEPRs of real-life everyday tasks. Classification accuracy of the system and computational speeds of training and classification will also be determined.

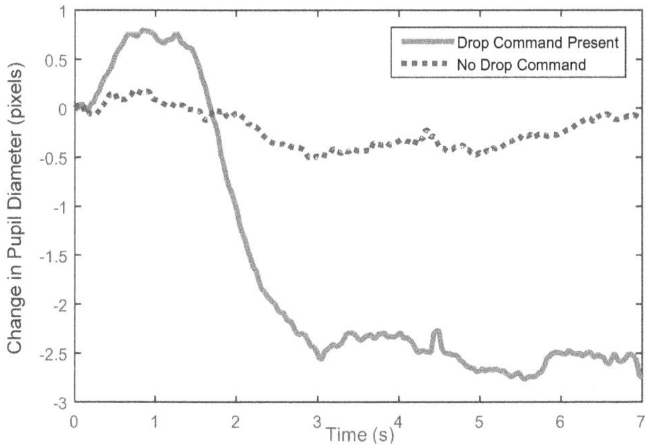

Figure 4. Averages of Mid Task Retention Period Pupillary Responses across all participants

COMPLETED WORK

Preliminary analysis of the dataset collected for the first investigation question has thus far shown that there is a significant decrease in pupil diameter resulting from a "drop command" during the Mid Task Retention Periods of tasks compared to Periods in which users continued memorising the total number of digits (see Figure 3). 18 out of 20 participants had average Mid Task Retention Periods responses which were consistent with the aforementioned hypothesis, as depicted in Figure 4. This finding is the first which gives an explicit indication of a transient response of exponential decay of pupil diameter between a loaded and unloaded cognitive level. Models can be then developed and used for continuous cognitive load classification.

EXPECTED CONTRIBUTION

This work will determine the extent to which eye activity reflects instantaneous cognitive load. The ability to perform cognitive load classification in the presence of the interfering effect of the PLR will also be evaluated. A pupil tracking algorithm which is more accurate and robust to variations in hardware conditions than existing methods will be developed and verified.

REFERENCES

1. Siyuan Chen and Julien Epps. 2014. Efficient and Robust Pupil Size and Blink Estimation from Near-Field Video Sequences for Human – Machine Interaction. *IEEE Trans. Cyb.* 44, 12, 2356–2367.
2. Siyuan Chen. 2014. *Cognitive Load Measurement from Eye Activity : Acquisition , Efficacy , and Real-time System Design.* Ph.D. Dissertation. University of New South Wales, New South Wales.
3. J. Eppler, M. & Mengis. 2004. The Concept of Information Overload: A Review of Literature. *The Info Soc: An Int J* 20, 5, 325–344.
4. Andrew W Fitzgibbon, Robert B Fisher, Forrest Hill, and Edinburgh Eh. 1999. Direct Least Squres Fitting of Ellipses. *IEEE Trans Pattn Anlys Mach Intelligence* 21, 5, 476-480.
5. D. Gopher and R. Braune. 1984. On the psychophysics of workload - Why bother with subjective measures? 26, 5, 519–532.
6. Eckhard H. Hess and James M Polt. 1960. Pupil Size as Related to Interest Value of Visual Stimuli. *Science* 132, 3423, 349–350.
7. Dongheng Li, Jason Babcock, and Dj Parkhurst. 2006. openEyes: a low-cost head-mounted eye-tracking solution. *Proc of the 2006 symposium on Eye tracking research & applications* 1, March, 27–29.
8. S.P. Marshall. 2002. The Index of Cognitive Activity: measuring cognitive workload. *Proceedings of the IEEE 7th Conf on Hum Fac and Power Plants*, 5–9.
9. T.E. Nygren. 1991. Psychometric properties of subjective work- load measurement techniques: Implications for their use in the assessment of perceived mental workload. *Hum Fac: J of Hum Fac Ergonom. Soc.* 33, 1, 17 – 33.
10. W. Peavler. 1974. Pupil Size, Information Overload, and Performance Differences. *Psychophysiology 11*, 559–566.
11. Kilseop Ryu and Rohae Myung. 2005. Evaluation of mental workload with a combined measure based on physiological indices during a dual task of tracking and mental arithmetic. *Int J Ind Ergonom* 35, 11, 991–1009.
12. John Sweller, Jeroen J G Van Merrienboer, and Fred G W C Paas. 1998. Cognitive Architecture and Instructional Design. *Educational Psychology Review* 10, 3, 251–296.
13. Lech Swirski, Andreas Bulling, and Neil Dodgson. 2001. Robust real-time pupil tracking in highly off-axis images. *Eye Tracking Research & Apps 2012*, 1–4.
14. Bin Xie and Gavriel Salvendy. 2000. Prediction of Mental Workload in Single and Multiple Tasks Environments. *Int J Cogn Ergonom* 4, 3, 213–242.

Challenges in Deep Learning for Multimodal Applications

Sayan Ghosh
Institute for Creative Technologies
University of Southern California
Los Angeles, USA
sghosh@ict.usc.edu

ABSTRACT

This consortium paper outlines a research plan for investigating deep learning techniques as applied to multimodal multi-task learning and multimodal fusion. We discuss our prior research results in this area, and how these results motivate us to explore more in this direction. We also define concrete steps of enquiry we wish to undertake as a short-term goal, and further outline some other challenges of multimodal learning using deep neural networks, such as inter and intra-modality synchronization, robustness to noise in modality data acquisition, and data insufficiency.

Author Keywords

Multimodal fusion; multi-task; deep learning; classification; neural networks

ACM Classification Keywords

I.5 [Pattern Recognition]: Models – *Neural nets*
I.2 [Artificial Intelligence]: Learning – *Parameter learning, Connectionism and neural nets*

INTRODUCTION

Multimodality is an emerging field with different applications in domains as varied as human behavior analytics, health informatics, virtual reality, affective computing and multimedia understanding. There has also been an increase in new technologies for acquisition of multimodal data, along with improved computational power, which would provide a big research and development boost for this field. Recent advances in machine learning, particularly deep learning has also led to several breakthroughs in the automated understanding of individual modalities such as video, speech and text.

However, there has been limited investigation into exploration of such approaches to multimodal applications. This proposal discusses prior state-of-the-art results in multimodal understanding using neural networks, along with common challenges of multimodal systems, and how we attempt to address those challenges using deep learning in the future.

We discuss our prior work in multimodal fusion for psychological distress prediction, deep learning for facial Action Unit (AU) detection, and how the insights we obtain from our results can be applied to multimodal deep learning. As a short term research plan, we particularly focus on two main challenges in multimodal analysis – (1) Design of multimodal, multi-task neural networks and (2) Early/Late fusion of modalities. We also discuss other related challenges in the design of multimodal systems, such as inter and intra-modality synchronization, data scarcity and robustness to multimodal sensor acquisition, and how deep neural networks can be effectively employed to address those issues.

PRIOR WORK IN MULTIMODAL DEEP LEARNING

Ngiam et al. [1] use sparse restricted Boltzmann machines for cross modality learning, shared representation learning and multimodal fusion using standard datasets of digit and letter utterances. They report impressive results on audio-visual speech classification. Srivastava et al. [2] applied multimodal deep Boltzmann machines to learn a generative model of images and text for image retrieval tasks, and compared their performance to other deep networks such as auto-encoders and deep belief networks. Srivastava and Salakhutdinov [3] applied multimodal deep belief networks to learn joint multimodal representations which outperformed standard classifiers such as support vector machines (SVM).

Martinez [4] used convolutional auto-encoders to integrate continuous multimodal signals of skin conductance with video game events (enemy collision and pellet collection) to predict affective attributes such as anxiety, challenge and frustration. The winning submission to the EmotiW [5] (Emotion Recognition in the Wild) challenge at ICMI 2013 was from the University of Montreal, who used an ensemble of deep learning models to perform emotion recognition from short movie clips. Karpathy [6] introduced a system to learn multimodal embeddings using recurrent neural networks (RNN) and convolutional neural networks (CNN).

ICMI '15, November 09 - 13, 2015, Seattle, WA, USA

ACM 978-1-4503-3912-4/15/11...$15.00
DOI: http://dx.doi.org/10.1145/2818346.2823313

Table 1. Classification performances of unimodal and multimodal classifiers for distress classification

Experimental Condition		Precision	Recall	F1-Scores	Accuracy
Unimodal	Text	0.675	0.605	0.6380	63.02%
	Audio	0.622	0.593	0.6071	58.63%
	Video	0.607	0.628	0.6171	58.00%
Audio, Video	Late	0.635	0.628	0.6315	60.50%
	Early	0.642	0.605	0.6227	60.50%
Text, Audio, Video	Late	0.705	0.648	**0.6751**	**66.40%**
	Early	0.700	0.651	0.6746	66.14%
Majority Baseline		-	-	-	53.86%

Experiments on image retrieval tasks show state-of-the-art results on datasets such as Flickr8k, and Flickr30k. Even though there has been a lot of work in this domain, there are several shortcomings in the previous literature. Firstly, multimodal recognition systems are not only multi-input but also multi-task in nature. An example is affective computing, where multimodal inputs such as facial images, speech utterances and physiological signals are predictive of multiple attributes such as emotion, mental depression and personality traits. Secondly, there is no systematic study of how deep learning techniques can be used to address common challenges of designing multimodal systems such as early/late fusion, multi-input architectures, multimodal synchronization of heterogeneous inputs, or data insufficiency due to difficulty in acquisition. In this extended abstract, we describe our hypotheses and define a set of research goals for systematic study in this direction.

OUR PRIOR WORK AND MAIN RESULTS

Prediction of Psychological Distress

In our prior work on prediction of psychological distress from multimodal cues using context dependent information [7], we performed a multimodal analysis of conversations between human participant and a virtual human health-screening agent. The virtual human asks questions designed to create rapport with the participant and elicit emotional responses, such as "So how are you doing today?" and "Have you been getting a good night's sleep?" Each question is annotated with polarity and intimacy scores, which indicate the context of the question, for example positive/negative sentiment, or high intimacy (more personal questions).

We extracted features not only from the audio and visual modalities, but also verbal features, and experimented with different fusion models. From the audio modality, voice quality features such as NAQ (Normalized Amplitude Quotient), F0 (Fundamental Frequency) and spectral slope [20] were extracted, and for video we mainly looked at features describing head rotation, facial expressions (such as

Table 2. Classification performances of multi-label CNN on DISFA and BP4D datasets (Accuracy and 2AFC scores)

Approach		Accuracy	2AFC scores
DISFA	Multi-label CNN	84.6	0.757
	Baseline [19]	86.8	0.760
BP4D	Multi-label CNN BP4D	75.6	0.751
	Baseline-BP4D [12]	72.0	0.427

anger, sad, and happy) and Action Units. The LIWC (Linguistic Inquiry and Word Count) program [21] was used for feature extraction from the verbal modality, where each category of features corresponded to social, cognitive and affective processes. We implemented early fusion (stacked concatenation of features), and a weighted late fusion scheme, where we used a two-layer hierarchical model. We trained separate classifiers on each modality, and then trained a second layer combiner using stacked generalization [8] and EM (Expectation Maximization) algorithm. Table 1 shows performance in terms of F-scores for both early and weighted late-fusion approaches. We observe that the verbal modality performs the best in unimodal classification, with an F1-score of 0.6380, and a late fusion of audio, video and verbal features outperforms the unimodal results, with an F1-score of 0.6751.

Even though we did not use a deep network, our weighted late fusion approach outperformed early fusion when applied to detection of depression and PTSD (Post Traumatic Stress Disorder) on human subjects. We also examined the weights learnt by the combiner, and find that the verbal modality was given higher importance in the late fusion. This would imply that verbal features are more discriminative of psychological distress than the audio or video modalities.

We also observed that usage of contextual information could improve performance. Features extracted only from the intimate-positive category of questions are the most discriminative, with 0.72 F1-score on distress classification. This indicates that responses to certain categories of questions are more predictive of psychological distress, as compared to aggregating the human participant's response to all questions asked.

Detection of Action Units using Multi-label CNN

A recent paper by us [9], which has been accepted for publication at ACII (Affective Computing and Intelligent Interaction) describes our experiments in modeling Action Unit (AU) detection from facial images as a multi-label classification task. In particular, we approached the task in the following way: let us assume that there are C AU categories, N data points $\{ \boldsymbol{x}_i \}$, where each $\boldsymbol{x}_i$ denotes the

Table 3. Cross-dataset generalization performances of multi-label CNN on DISFA, BP4D and CK+ datasets (Accuracy and 2AFC scores)

Source dataset	Target dataset	Accuracy	2AFC scores
DISFA	BP4D	77.34	0.690
	CK+	88.14	0.780
BP4D	DISFA	80.34	0.730
	CK+	77.77	0.759

i-th image and $y_{ij} \in \{0,1\}$ is a label denoting presence or absence of the j-th AU. Let $f(\boldsymbol{x}_i)$ be the transformation learnt by the neural network at the hidden layer just prior to computation of the loss function. Similar to [10], we define the multi-label soft-max classification loss as:

$$J = -\frac{1}{N}\sum_{i=1}^{N}\sum_{j=1}^{C} y_{ij}\log(\widehat{p_{ij}}) = -\frac{1}{N}\sum_{i=1}^{N}\sum_{j=1}^{C_+}\log(\widehat{p_{ij}})$$

Where C_+ is the number of AUs actually present in image $\boldsymbol{x}_i$, $\widehat{p_{ij}}$ are the prediction probabilities from the last soft-max layer for the i-th input image and the j-th AU, obtained as:

$$\widehat{p_{ij}} = \frac{\exp(f_j(\boldsymbol{x}_i))}{\sum \exp(f_j(\boldsymbol{x}_i))}$$

We train a multi-label CNN (Convolutional Neural Network) on two datasets of AUs – DISFA (Denver Intensity of Spontaneous Facial Expressions) [11], and FERA 2015 BP4D-Spontaneous Dataset [12]. Testing is performed in a leave-one-subject-out fashion on the same dataset used for training, as well as across datasets (The CK+ dataset [13] is for example used only for testing). Our multi-label CNN achieves results comparable to state-of-the-art baselines in terms of accuracy and 2AFC (Two Alternative Forced Choice) scores, as shown in Table 2. Table 3 also indicates that the CNN generalizes well for cross-dataset training and evaluation. . We observe that the CNN trained on DISFA can generalize to BP4D, and vice-versa.

FUTURE WORK AND HYPOTHESES

We obtain several promising results in our prior research, which would also help us decide on future short-term research directions. There are several challenges and open research directions in deep learning for multimodal applications, among which we mainly describe (1) multimodal multi-task learning of deep representations, and (2) fusion strategies such as early, late or hybrid fusion.

Multimodal multi-task learning

In multi-task learning, a set of related tasks are learnt, along with a primary task. It is expected that data for the secondary tasks could have information which would also be discriminative in learning the first task. Many multimodal applications are also multi-task in nature. For example, prediction of emotion, affective states, and personality traits can be done together from the same audio-visual stream.

Our prior work [9], while being unimodal, is significant step towards multimodal, multi-task learning since it allows us to address two interesting research questions. Firstly, since the prediction of AUs is jointly addressed using a single multi-label loss function, taking all the outputs from the topmost layer of the CNN is an effective strategy. Our results also indicate that certain AUs are much easier to classify compared to the others. For example, AUs 12 (Lip corner puller) and 20 (Lip stretcher) yield the highest detection accuracies, whereas AUs 15 and 17 are much harder to classify.

We hypothesize that a deeper network might be needed to detect more complex AUs, whereas the prediction of easier AUs may be possible only from the lower layer activations. For example, AUs from the lower facial region (such as AU 27 for mouth stretch, and AU 15 for lip corner depressor) might need relatively less non-linearity for detection compared to subtle AUs from eyebrows (such as AU 2 and 4). This would justify detectors for AU 2 and AU 4 being placed at a higher layer of the network. Use of this hierarchical multi-task structure might reduce the number of parameters to be learnt and combat over-fitting.

Secondly, the cross-dataset generalization capabilities of the network also merit further investigation. Not all AU datasets have the same labels, and are also acquired under different conditions of lighting, pose and background. As a future step, we plan to investigate whether training of the network using a subset of AUs on a particular dataset can enable it to learn mid-layer activations, which might be discriminative of unseen AUs on another dataset. This would enable us to combine datasets with different AUs to train a powerful network, which would be able to adapt to different datasets, and also to AUs for which it has scarce training data.

In the longer term, we also intend to explore other general properties of multi-task networks, such as weighting of different tasks during training, including whether the weights should be selected through validation, or can be learnt automatically from data. Subsequently we wish to go towards generalized MIMO (Multi-Input Multi-Output) networks, where multiple modalities are fused to predict multiple attributes.

Early/Late Fusion of modalities

In most literature on multimodal fusion, modalities can be fused through early or late fusion [14]. In early fusion, all features from modalities are concatenated together, and used as a single unified feature stream to the learning algorithm. In late fusion, a separate model is learnt for each modality, and then the predictions are combined together to form a final decision. We have experimented with both early and late fusion in [7], where we have trained a hierarchical weighted late-fusion approach and obtained promising results. This shows that a multi-layer fusion system could be a possible step forward.

Similar to shallow models, in deep neural networks, early fusion can be implemented through feature concatenation. Late fusion can be implemented with two possible approaches: (1) Create a large model with split feature inputs, and then jointly train the entire network using back-propagation, including the higher layer combiner, or (2) Train separate networks for each modality, and then learn the combiner, which could also be a shallower neural network.

Hybrid fusion is also possible, where certain modalities could be inserted into the network at intermediate layers. From the results we obtained in our prior work [7], we hypothesize that if a modality is more discriminative of a higher-level attribute (for example, the verbal features were more relevant in the distress classification task), then that relevant modality could be processed at a higher layer of the network.

As a next step, we plan to explore and validate different neural network topologies for standard fusion tasks, which would involve deriving back-propagation algorithms for layers with multimodal inputs, or inserting sparse constraints into weight activations. We intend to make use of standard deep learning libraries, such as Caffe [15] or Torch [16] and modify the algorithms, which will enable us to perform fast prototyping of models, by retaining comparability and compatibility with existing algorithms.

OTHER CHALLENGES IN MULTIMODAL SYSTEMS

In the previous sections, we have described our results, and also discussed the major steps forward. There are also other related challenges in multimodal understanding which we can address using deep learning techniques, and we discuss them in this section.

Inter and intra-modality synchronization

Input features in an input modality may be correlated, where the correlation can occur within each modality, or between different modalities. If an input modality is a temporal or a spatial signal, adjacent pixels (or samples) may be correlated, which happens as in natural images or speech signals. In deep networks, temporal correlation can be modeled using an RNN (recursive neural network) which can handle long-range dependencies, or by insertion of an HMM (Hidden Markov Model) or CRF (Conditional Random Field) after the deep network. Inter-modality correlation poses a bigger challenge. Jia et al. [17] introduced the concept of group sparsity in latent variable models for capturing modality correlations. However it still remains an open research problem to integrate latent variables along with discriminative neural networks. We propose to explore neural network topologies, in which groupings can be learnt, along with the weights, where certain sets of neurons can only be activated by groups of modalities.

Robustness to acquisition of modalities

It is commonly observed in multimodal acquisition that certain modalities could be missing during data capture, or severely corrupted, where we would also have access to a sensor confidence stream recording the certainty in the data acquisition process. For example, in health and behavioral applications, each data point could correspond to a human subject, where certain types of acquisition would be turned off at a request for the subject's privacy.

There are several potential approaches to train deep models in presence of modality absence and uncertainty, which could include (1) Using sensor confidence as an explicit features stream in the neural network, where different thresholding techniques can be employed to control neuron activations based on the confidence values. (2) Setting neuron activations to data-driven defaults for missing modalities. Latent variable models are also efficient at learning from missing features, particularly through EM (Expectation-Maximization) [18]. It would also be an interesting open problem to explore neural network learning, drawing parallels to EM-style algorithms, and then explore training with missing/low-confidence modalities.

Data insufficiency in multimodal deep learning

Deep learning has been shown to perform best when trained on very large amounts of data, and particularly for multimodal applications, the amount of data must be proportional to the complexity of the deep network. This is suitable for multimodal tasks, for which unlimited data can be downloaded from the web, such as image retrieval. However, there are low-data applications, particularly those where data is acquired from a human subject. However, deep learning techniques can be applied to such domains by using standard techniques to combat over-fitting, such as dropout, and L-1 regularization. Another approach would be to train an unsupervised neural network, such as an auto-encoder on large amounts of out-of-domain data (unlabeled speech corpora such as audiobooks, or a large dataset of facial images), and then initialize a supervised network (such as a CNN) with those weights. Deep learning for resource scarce applications is understudied, and would be a potential topic for further research.

CONCLUSIONS

In this extended abstract, we have described prior work by us and other authors in the field of deep learning for multimodal understanding. We have also identified short-term research goals related to two main challenges in the design of multimodal systems – multimodal multi-task learning, and fusion of modalities. We also discuss other open problems which we believe would be important considerations in the design of multimodal interfaces and analysis systems.

ACKNOWLEDGEMENTS

The author would like to acknowledge his thesis advisors Prof. Louis-Philippe Morency and Prof. Stefan Scherer for their constructive comments while writing this extended research abstract, and the University of Southern California Viterbi Graduate School Fellowship for financially supporting his doctoral program. The work depicted here is sponsored by the U.S. Army Research Laboratory (ARL) under contract number W911NF-14-D-0005.

REFERENCES

1. Ngiam, Jiquan, Aditya Khosla, Mingyu Kim, Juhan Nam, Honglak Lee, and Andrew Y. Ng. "Multimodal deep learning." In *Proceedings of the 28th international conference on machine learning (ICML-11)*, pp. 689-696.
2. Srivastava, Nitish, and Ruslan R. Salakhutdinov. "Multimodal learning with deep boltzmann machines." In *Advances in neural information processing systems*, pp. 2222-2230. 2012.
3. Srivastava, Nitish, and Ruslan Salakhutdinov. "Learning representations for multimodal data with deep belief nets." In *International Conference on Machine Learning Workshop*. 2012.
4. Martínez, Héctor P., and Georgios N. Yannakakis. "Deep Multimodal Fusion: Combining Discrete Events and Continuous Signals." In *Proceedings of the 16th International Conference on Multimodal Interaction*, pp. 34-41. ACM, 2014.
5. Kahou, Samira Ebrahimi, Christopher Pal, Xavier Bouthillier, Pierre Froumenty, Çaglar Gülçehre, Roland Memisevic, Pascal Vincent et al. "Combining modality specific deep neural networks for emotion recognition in video." In *Proceedings of the 15th ACM on International conference on multimodal interaction*, pp. 543-550. ACM, 2013.
6. Karpathy, Andrej, Armand Joulin, and Fei Fei F. Li. "Deep fragment embeddings for bidirectional image sentence mapping." In *Advances in neural information processing systems*, pp. 1889-1897. 2014.
7. Ghosh, Sayan, Moitreya Chatterjee, and Louis-Philippe Morency. "A multimodal context-based approach for distress assessment." In *Proceedings of the 16th International Conference on Multimodal Interaction*, pp. 240-246. ACM, 2014.
8. Wolpert, David H. "Stacked generalization." *Neural networks* 5, no. 2 (1992): 241-259.
9. Ghosh, Sayan, Eugene Laksana, Stefan Scherer, Louis-Philippe Morency, "A Multi-label Convolutional Neural Network Approach to Cross-Domain Action Unit Detection", accepted for publication in *Proceedings of Affective Computing and Intelligent Interaction Conference*, 2015
10. Gong, Yunchao, Yangqing Jia, Thomas Leung, Alexander Toshev, and Sergey Ioffe. "Deep convolutional ranking for multilabel image annotation." *arXiv preprint arXiv:1312.4894* (2013).
11. Mavadati, S. Mohammad, Mohammad H. Mahoor, Kevin Bartlett, Philip Trinh, and Jeffrey F. Cohn. "Disfa: A spontaneous facial action intensity database." *IEEE Transactions on Affective Computing,* 4, no. 2 (2013): 151-160.
12. Valstar, M., J. Girard, T. Almaev, Gary McKeown, Marc Mehu, Lijun Yin, Maja Pantic, and J. Cohn. "FERA 2015-second facial expression recognition and analysis challenge." *Proc. IEEE ICFG* (2015).
13. Lucey, Patrick, Jeffrey F. Cohn, Takeo Kanade, Jason Saragih, Zara Ambadar, and Iain Matthews. "The Extended Cohn-Kanade Dataset (CK+): A complete dataset for action unit and emotion-specified expression." In *Computer Vision and Pattern Recognition Workshops (CVPRW), 2010 IEEE Computer Society Conference on*, pp. 94-101.
14. Natarajan, Pradeep, Shuang Wu, Shiv Vitaladevuni, Xiaodan Zhuang, Stavros Tsakalidis, Unsang Park, Rohit Prasad, and Premkumar Natarajan. "Multimodal feature fusion for robust event detection in web videos." In *IEEE Conference on Computer Vision and Pattern Recognition (CVPR), 2012*, pp. 1298-1305. IEEE, 2012.
15. Jia, Yangqing, Evan Shelhamer, Jeff Donahue, Sergey Karayev, Jonathan Long, Ross Girshick, Sergio Guadarrama, and Trevor Darrell. "Caffe: Convolutional architecture for fast feature embedding." In *Proceedings of the ACM Multimedia*, pp. 675-678. ACM, 2014.
16. Collobert, Ronan, Samy Bengio, and Johnny Mariéthoz. *Torch: a modular machine learning software library*. EPFL-REPORT-82802. IDIAP, 2002.
17. Jia, Yangqing, Mathieu Salzmann, and Trevor Darrell. "Factorized latent spaces with structured sparsity." In *Advances in Neural Information Processing Systems*, pp. 982-990. 2010.
18. Moon, Tood K. "The expectation-maximization algorithm." *IEEE Signal processing magazine,* 13, no. 6 (1996): 47-60.
19. Song, Yale, Daniel McDuff, Deepak Vasisht, and Ashish Kapoor. "Exploiting Sparsity and Co-occurrence Structure for Action Unit Recognition.", *International Conference on Automatic Face and Gesture Recognition.* May 2015.
20. Cummins, Nicholas, Stefan Scherer, Jarek Krajewski, Sebastian Schnieder, Julien Epps, and Thomas F. Quatieri. "A review of depression and suicide risk assessment using speech analysis." *Speech Communication* 71 pp. 10-49, 2015.
21. Pennebaker, James W., Martha E. Francis, and Roger J. Booth. "Linguistic inquiry and word count: LIWC 2001", *Mahway: Lawrence Erlbaum Associates* 71, 2001.

Exploring Intent-driven Multimodal Interface for Geographical Information System

Feng Sun
College of Information Sciences and Technology
Pennsylvania State University
University Park, PA 16802
fzs122@psu.edu

ABSTRACT

Geographic Information Systems (GIS) offers a large amount of functions for performing spatial analysis and geospatial information retrieval. However, off-the-shelf GIS remains difficult to use for occasional GIS experts. The major problem lies in that its interface organizes spatial analysis tools and functions according to spatial data structures and corresponding algorithms, which is conceptually confusing and cognitively complex. Prior work identified the usability problem of conventional GIS interface and developed alternatives based on speech or gesture to narrow the gap between the high-functionality provided by GIS and its usability. This paper outlined my doctoral research goal in understanding human-GIS interaction activity, especially how interaction modalities assist to capture spatial analysis intention and influence collaborative spatial problem solving. We proposed a framework for enabling multimodal human-GIS interaction driven by intention. We also implemented a prototype GeoEASI (Geo-dialogue Environment for Assisted Spatial Inquiry) to demonstrate the effectiveness of our framework. Further work will evaluate the effectiveness of our framework, improve the reliability and flexibility of the system, extend the GIS interface for supporting multiple users, and integrate the system into GeoDeliberation. We will concentrate on how multimodality technology can be adopted in these circumstances and explore the potentials of it. The study aims to demonstrate the feasibility of building a GIS to be both useful and usable by introducing an intent-driven multimodal interface, forming the key to building a better theory of spatial thinking for GIS.

Categories and Subject Descriptors

H.5.m. [**Information Interfaces and Presentation**]: Miscellaneous

Keywords

Multimodal interface; geographical information systems; user interface design; geospatial analysis; agents and intelligent systems; usability

ICMI 2015, November 9–13, 2015, Seattle, WA, USA.
© 2015 ACM. ISBN 978-1-4503-3912-4/15/11 ...$15.00.
DOI: http://dx.doi.org/10.1145/2818346.2823304.

1. INTRODUCTION

As a high-functionality computer system [7], GIS is capable of offering plentiful functionalities. Meanwhile, the argument "GIS is hard to use" made by Traynor et al. [24] almost two decades ago still remains accurate nowadays. Current GIS interface organize functions and operations according to geospatial algorithms and data structure, rather than straightforward conceptual analytical intention [8], making it difficult for users to explore and locate the desirable operation. It is passively driven by each single functional request through menus and buttons controlled by keyboards and mice [21]. User has to remember all kinds of operation names and evoke them explicitly. This is especially the case for occasional GIS users who can express their spatial intentions but possess little expertise and limited spatial understanding.

Efforts have been made in designing a more usable user interface. Some researchers incorporated different kinds of communication modalities into GIS [23, 17, 20, 21, 25]. Among them, speech, gestures and stylus are most prevailing. Speech is generally popular in human-computer interaction. Gestures and stylus are widely adopted in human-GIS interaction because of the nature of geospatial information. However, they usually merely consider these modalities as alternatives to conventional WIMP (windows, icons, menus, and pointers) interface. Few of them employ multimodality technology in the context of spatial analysis tasks and corresponding intentions.

To exploit the potentials of multimodality technology in GIS interface design, we introduce the concept of intention and proposed a framework for designing a multimodal GIS interface driven by it. We also implemented a prototype called GeoEASI as a proof-of-concept. Intention is the purpose of a spatial analysis task and it provides a reason for performing a specific action or conveying a content [13]. It serves as a context for a spatial analysis task and can guide multimodality interaction process. By this high-level abstraction, our framework hides the implementation details of GIS functions, conceals execution procedures and relieves users from remembering unintelligible terminologies. In addition, it is able to infer knowledge from existing information in the context and make certain proactive actions. With all kinds of input modalities, one intention might be achieved through multiple implementation strategies. When making an error progress, it can gracefully move back and try another possible action instead of starting from scratch.

My doctoral research has made or will make the following contributions:

- Proposed a framework in which multimodality driven by intention serves as a promising alternative for interacting with GIS. Developed a prototype called GeoEASI as a proof of concept.

- Confirm that multimodal interface driven by intention can facilitate a more intuitive and straightforward human-GIS interaction style.
- Investigate how human-GIS interaction modalities change when more than one user is involved.
- Integrate the interface to other GIS-related scenarios and demonstrate its effectiveness in those situations.
- Enable thinking spatial problems at intentional level, form the foundation to having a comprehensive understanding and build a better theory of spatial thinking.

2. RELATED WORK

As an important method to facilitate interaction between the user and GIS, GIS interface serves as a bridge to connect the user and GIS. Many research about GIS interface attempted to improve human-GIS from a single perspective. Hedley et al. applied augmented reality technology to GIS and enhanced collaborative geographic data visualization through hybrid user interfaces [15]. A recent work utilized Kinect, which is capable of capturing gestures and voices, to provide GIS with a natural user interface. It allows users to interact with map in the air [1]. Hecht et al. pointed out the problem results from lack of communication between scholars in geography and HCI and proposed that the two groups need to collaborate to apply HCI technologies to GIS [14]. However, limited work has focused on intention-driven or agent-based GIS interface.

Rauschert et al. designed a multimodal, multi-user GIS interface [22], which provides real time geospatial data retrieval on demand, especially useful in emergency management. In their design, the conventional WIMP interface is replaced with one that supports free-hand gestures and natural language interaction. A knowledge-based dialogue management system is used for storing and retrieving geospatial data. However, their system follows the conventional GIS design philosophy. Essentially the user has to invoke the function at operational level, which requires the user to have a very good understanding of GIS.

Goodchild discovered the usability problem of GIS results from its poor-defined framework, confusing spatial concepts and chaotic function organization [9]. He explained the necessity of a better GIS interface and emphasized the importance of spatial thinking. His following work tried to integrate spatial thinking by a GIS interface that translates spatial concepts into a sequence of GIS functions [10]. While it can answer simple GIS questions, it cannot support real spatial thinking because it fall short of a activity modal that takes human factors into consideration.

Cai et al. [2] proposed a natural conversational GIS interface, called GeoDialogue, that enables users to interact with geospatial databases through dialogue. GeoDialogue realized the interface by mapping natural language to GIS functions. Later on, Cai et al. [5] improved the interface by modeling interaction with a GIS as human-GIS collaborative spatial analytical activities between a user and an intelligent agent. The agent communicates the spatial analysis intention with the user, reasons about the required procedures, and assists users with spatial problem solving.

GeoEASI extends the work of Cai et al. [6], an intention-based GIS interface called CAGA, in which a conversational agent for GIS analysis is embedded. CAGA is capable of communicating the human GIS analyst at intentional level and assist the user to perform GIS functions. GeoEASI extends CAGA by integrating all kinds of reasoning strategies, enhancing communication flexibility, providing correction mechanism and supporting more complicated task.

3. HYPOTHESIS STATEMENT

My doctoral research project is aimed at mediating the usefulness and usability dilemma inside current GIS. It is composed of three main hypotheses:

H1: A multimodal GIS interface driven by intention provide occasional GIS users with a better user experience than other conventional interfaces when performing spatial analysis. Meanwhile, it offers enough functionality.

H2: Multimodality plays an important role in human-GIS interaction that involves more than one user

H3: A multimodal GIS interface driven by intention can assist participants to address geographically complex problems in online deliberation and thus contribute to expanding and deepening civic engagement.

4. PRELIMINARY RESULTS

To present the feasibility of improving the usability of GIS by introducing an intent-driven multimodal interface, we implemented a prototype called GeoEASI. The section describes the framework and illustrates several important feature of GeoEASI.

4.1 Framework

Our framework is proposed to guide the development of GIS interface for occasional users. The framework includes a user, who can express spatial analysis intention clearly, while might be able to operate GIS software proficiently. The framework also includes an agent, who can capture the user's spatial analysis intention and construct a partial plan for achieving the intention. During the human-GIS collaboration process, the agent is able to elaborate the plan through interacting with users, and evoke proper GIS functions.

In this framework, capabilities and knowledge are distributed across different agents, thus neither the user nor the agent is capable of completing spatial analysis alone. They need to contribute their own piece and construct plan collaboratively in order to achieving the intention. Communication is the key point in the process and a multimodal interface provides such ability.

4.2 System overview

The architecture of GeoEASI is shown as Figure 1. GeoEASI consists of a multimodal inputs component, a semantic interpretation component, a cooperative planning component, a response generation component and a knowledge base. A user is able to propose her intention by interacting with GeoEASI the same way interacting with an actual human GIS expert. Once a user expresses her intention by words and gestures, GeoEASI performs speech and gesture recognition and fuse these multimodal inputs. Then intention is extracted by interpreting these inputs semantically using rule-based language processing technique (Speech Recognition Grammar Specification). Current plan will be updated according to the new perceiving information, along with the existing one acquired from knowledge base. Based on the updated plan, a proper response, in forms of speech and voice, is generated and presented to the user. If it is highly possible that a user may request a further operation in order to complete the intention, GeoEASI will perform it proactively. User always has the chance to rollback and requests another one once the user is misunderstood.

As shown in Figure 2, we employ a Microsoft Kinect sensor to track gestures and speech. Participants interact with a 27-inch monitor. Kinect is mounted on the top of the monitor. The GeoEASI software is running on that desktop.

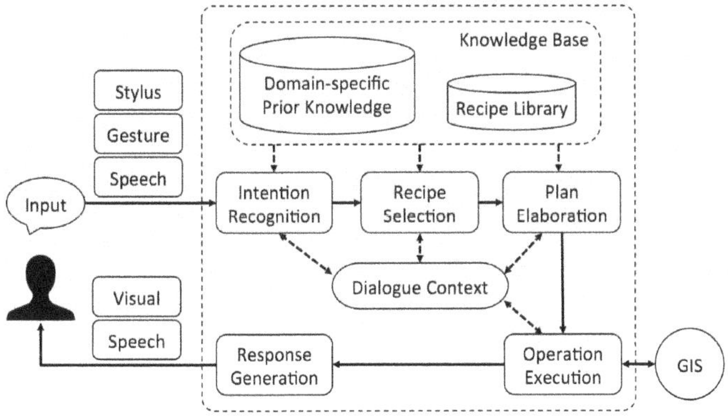

Figure 1: GeoEASI system overview

Figure 2: Student workstation with Kinect sensor and GeoEASI

The main graphical user interface generally follows the conventional design of popular map-based systems, such as Google Maps and Esri ArcMap, to lower the entrance bar to get started by meeting the users' expectations with regard to common operations, for examples, zooming, panning and selection. The map view serves as the main part of the GUI so that it attracts attention all the time. The skeleton of the user appears on the upper right corner when being tracked and the lower right window keeps a log of run-time status information. The design goal of GeoEASI GUI is to be as straightforward and intuitive as possible, meanwhile, maintain all the necessary functionality and information accessible. The Map can be manipulated in the conversational way through WIMP (windows, icons, menus and pointer) interfaces when necessary. Buttons and menus are placed in single line on top of the map view.

4.3 Human-GIS collaboration model

In GeoEASI, the communication context of a human-GIS interaction process is represented as PlanGraph, an agent-based computational model. PlanGraph model is built on computational collaborative discourse theory [13] and SharedPlan theory [11, 12]. It also adopts the agent-based computational model, named RecipeGraph [16]. The core of PlanGraph lies in constructing and elaborating a collaborative plan among users and GIS during the process of a conversation. It is established and executed based on the participants' mutual understanding and knowledge. Both system and user have their own plan for completing a task and would like to contribute their knowledge and capability to achieve it. However, the user might has the idea of making a general plan without any knowledge about how each step is performed in details. Meanwhile, the system has the knowledge, along with capability of executing GIS operations. In order to realize their common goal, the system needs to reason about the way in which it assists the user during the process. There is probably more than one recipe for achieving one intention but each time only one is implemented. Readers can refer to Cai's work [3] for more details on PlanGraph.

4.4 Evaluation

We conducted a lab study to evaluate the effectiveness of our prototype system. We recruited 6 students as participants. They are able to express spatial analysis intention, while they have not learned any professional GIS software before. The participants were asked to perform a predefined spatial analysis task through both GeoEASI and conventional GIS interface provided by ArcGIS 10. We observed their behavior and performance during the process. We also interviewed them after the process. The lab study showed that GeoEASI is able to improve human-GIS interaction experience for occasional GIS users.

However, the scope our study is still limited now. We plan to expand experiment from laboratory study to field study once the current system is reliable enough. We also plan to utilize more data collection methods, such as video recording, screen recording and input logging, so that we can perform more comprehensive data analyses.

5. RESEARCH PLAN

There are still some limitations in our current work. Further work in my doctoral research will concentrate on improving current system to be more reliable and flexible. A system that allows multiple users to interact with GIS will be developed. We will also try to apply this system to other scenario. We are considering the following three aspects as the major directions to improve and extend our current work:

- **Larger recipe library with more flexibility**

  At the present, we refer to GIS textbooks [18, 19] for recipe library construction. We draw knowledge from them for their organizing its contents and materials according to spatial analysis intentions. The highest-level spatial analysis intentions can be generally classified into *Where Things Are, Mapping the Most and Least, Mapping Density, Finding What's Inside, Finding What's Nearby*, and *Mapping Change*. GeoEASI is able to capture two of them, while more intentions should be included in the recipe library so that GeoEASI is capable of collaborating with users in more complicated spatial analysis tasks. We are seeking methods to automate the process of constructing recipe library.

  In addition, we will apply machine learning approaches to learn from previously collected data during human-GIS interaction as well. By doing this, the system can learn from the previous data and provide users with more personalized and appropriate recommendations, leading to a better GIS interface with more reliability and flexibility.

- **Multi-user support**

  So far we only considered single user scenario. However, many circumstances, for example, city planning and emergency response, might include more than one person. Several users might interact with GIS collaboratively at the same time. Besides, the latest Kinect sensor is equipped with function that is able to perform facial recognition, which establishes the foundation for GeoEASI to support multiple users in the future.

In such case, we need to not only take care of human-GIS interaction, but also take human-human interaction into consideration. New challenges, such as capturing common spatial analysis intention, constructing a shared plan and coordinating interactions among users are introduced. We will explore how to coordinate and facilitate collaboration, and investigate how human-GIS interaction modalities change when more than one user is involved.

- **GeoDeliberation integration**

  Geodeliberation is project that aims to expand and deepen civic engagement of local communities in deliberating geographically complex problems. Concerning the characteristics of these problems, we are trying to improve the process by taking advantage of geographical information system and online deliberation technologies [4]. Nevertheless, many of the participants are not GIS experts and they are not incapable of analyzing spatial problems using GIS since GIS is difficult to use for untrained people.

  By adapting the interface to GeoDeliberation online forum, we anticipate participants can initiate spatial analysis simply by expressing their intentions and perform actions through speech, gesture and stylus rather than remembering names of a large amount of GIS operation and evoking them explicitly, which allows participants to get a deeper insight of the problem and in turn improves the quality of deliberation. We plan to investigate the application of intent-driven multimodal interface in this scenario.

6. CONCLUSION

To reduce the gap between the high functionality GIS provides and the usability of its user interface, an alternative interface is necessary for GIS to make it more accessible. My doctoral research project aims to improve human-GIS interaction, especially human-GIS collaborative problem solving process concerning spatial analysis problem. To achieve this purpose, we proposed a framework that modals such activity and can exploit the potentials of multimodality technology. We also implemented a prototype system GeoEASI following the framework. GeoEASI is capable of communicating with users with multiple modalities, such as speech and gesture and stylus, and the visual and audio information returned by the system. One characteristic of the system is its ability of fusing information from multiple modalities in context of the captured intention.

The next step of this doctoral research project is to continue to construct the recipe library for spatial analysis to make it more reliable and flexible. By doing this, the system is able to process more complicated situation. In addition, we plan to extend the system to support multiple users, which is usually the case in real life, and examine the role multimodal interaction plays in such situation. Also, we plan to incorporate the system into an online deliberation forum so as to allow participants, who are not GIS experts, to get a deeper insight on topic concerning geospatial information.

7. ACKNOWLEDGMENTS

I would like to express my deepest gratitude to my research advisor, Professor Guoray Cai, for his support and guidance in every stage of my Ph.D. endeavor.

8. REFERENCES

[1] Maged N Kamel Boulos, Bryan J Blanchard, Cory Walker, Julio Montero, Aalap Tripathy, and Ricardo Gutierrez-Osuna. 2011. Web GIS in practice X: a Microsoft Kinect natural user interface for Google Earth navigation. *International journal of health geographics* 10, 1 (Jan. 2011), 45.

[2] Guoray Cai, Hongmei Wang, Alan M. MacEachren, and Sven Fuhrmann. 2005a. Natural Conversational Interfaces to Geospatial Databases. *Transactions in GIS* 9, 2 (March 2005), 199–221.

[3] Guoray Cai, Hongmei Wang, Alan M MacEachren, and Sven Fuhrmann. 2005b. Natural conversational interfaces to geospatial databases. *Transactions in GIS* 9, 2 (2005), 199–221.

[4] Guoray Cai and Bo Yu. 2009. Spatial annotation technology for public deliberation. *Transactions in GIS* 13, s1 (2009), 123–146.

[5] Guoray Cai, Bo Yu, and Dong Chen. 2013a. Modeling and Communicating the Conceptual Intent of Geo-Analytical Tasks for Human-GIS Interaction. *Transactions in GIS* 17, 3 (June 2013), 353–368.

[6] Guoray Cai, Bo Yu, and Dong Chen. 2013b. Modeling and Communicating the Conceptual Intent of Geo-Analytical Tasks for Human-GIS Interaction. *Transactions in GIS* 17, 3 (2013), 353–368.

[7] Gerhard Fischer. 1987. Making computers more useful and more usable. In *HCI (2)*. 97–104.

[8] Michael F Goodchild. 2011a. Spatial thinking and the gis user interface. *Procedia-Social and Behavioral Sciences* 21 (2011), 3–9.

[9] Michael F. Goodchild. 2011b. Spatial Thinking and the GIS User Interface. *Procedia - Social and Behavioral Sciences* 21 (Jan. 2011), 3–9.

[10] Michael F. Goodchild. 2013. Asking Spatial Questions to Identify GIS Functionality. *2013 Fourth International Conference on Computing for Geospatial Research and Application* (July 2013), 106–110.

[11] Barbara J Grosz and Sarit Kraus. 1996. Collaborative plans for complex group action. *Artificial Intelligence* 86, 2 (1996), 269–357.

[12] Barbara J Grosz and Sarit Kraus. 1999. The evolution of SharedPlans. In *Foundations of rational agency*. Springer, 227–262.

[13] Barbara J Grosz and Candace L Sidner. 1986. Attention, intentions, and the structure of discourse. *Computational linguistics* 12, 3 (1986), 175–204.

[14] Brent Hecht, Johannes Schöning, Thomas Erickson, and Reid Priedhorsky. 2011. Geographic human-computer interaction. *Proceedings of the 2011 annual conference extended abstracts on Human factors in computing systems - CHI EA '11* (2011), 447.

[15] Nicholas R. Hedley, Mark Billinghurst, Lori Postner, Richard May, and Hirokazu Kato. 2002. Explorations in the Use of Augmented Reality for Geographic Visualization. *Presence: Teleoper. Virtual Environ.* 11, 2 (April 2002), 119–133.

[16] Karen E Lochbaum. 1998. A collaborative planning model of intentional structure. *Computational Linguistics* 24, 4 (1998), 525–572.

[17] Ishantha Lokuge and Suguru Ishizaki. 1995. Geospace: An interactive visualization system for exploring complex information spaces. In *Proceedings of the SIGCHI conference*

on Human factors in computing systems. ACM Press/Addison-Wesley Publishing Co., 409–414.

[18] A Mitchell. 1999. *The ESRI Guide to GIS analysis, Volume 1: Geographic patterns and relationship*. Redlands, Calif: ESRI.

[19] A Mitchell. 2005. *The ESRI Guide to GIS analysis, Volume 2: Spartial measurements and statistics*. Redlands, Calif: ESRI.

[20] Sharon Oviatt. 1996. Multimodal interfaces for dynamic interactive maps. In *Proceedings of the SIGCHI Conference on Human Factors in Computing Systems*. ACM, 95–102.

[21] Ingmar Rauschert, Pyush Agrawal, Rajeev Sharma, Sven Fuhrmann, Isaac Brewer, and Alan MacEachren. 2002a. Designing a human-centered, multimodal GIS interface to support emergency management. In *Proceedings of the 10th ACM international symposium on Advances in geographic information systems*. ACM, 119–124.

[22] Ingmar Rauschert, Pyush Agrawal, Rajeev Sharma, Sven Fuhrmann, Isaac Brewer, and Alan MacEachren. 2002b. Designing a human-centered, multimodal GIS interface to support emergency management. In *Proceedings of the tenth ACM international symposium on Advances in geographic information systems - GIS '02*. ACM Press, New York, New York, USA, 119.

[23] SC Shapiro, H Chalupski, and HC Chou. 1991. Linking ARC/INFO with snactor. *Santa Barbara, California.: National Center for geographic Information and Analysis* (1991).

[24] Carol Traynor and Marian G Williams. 1995. Why are geographic information systems hard to use?. In *Conference companion on Human factors in computing systems*. ACM, 288–289.

[25] Hongmei Wang, Guoray Cai, and Alan M MacEachren. 2008. GeoDialogue: a software agent enabling collaborative dialogues between a user and a conversational GIS. In *Tools with Artificial Intelligence, 2008. ICTAI'08. 20th IEEE International Conference on*, Vol. 2. IEEE, 357–360.

Software Techniques for Multimodal Input Processing in Realtime Interactive Systems

Martin Fischbach
University of Würzburg
Würzburg, Germany
martin.fischbach@uni-wuerzburg.de

ABSTRACT

Multimodal interaction frameworks are an efficient means of utilizing many existing processing and fusion techniques in a wide variety of application areas, even by non-experts. However, the application of these frameworks to highly interactive application areas like VR, AR, MR, and computer games in a reusable, modifiable, and modular manner is not straightforward. It currently lacks some software technical solutions that (1) preserve the general decoupling principle of platforms and at the same time (2) provide the required close temporal as well as semantic coupling of involved software modules and multimodal processing steps. This thesis approches current challenges and aims at providing the research community with a framework that fosters repeatability of scientific achievements and the ability to built on previous results.

Categories and Subject Descriptors

D.2.11 [**Software Engineering**]: Software Architectures

Keywords

multimodal processing; multimodal fusion; software architecture; Realtime Interactive Systems; Virtual Reality

1. INTRODUCTION

New technical solutions for multimodal interfaces have been introduced for over three decades. Frameworks and accompanying demonstrators begin with Bolt's "Put that there" [1] and range from Neal and Thielmann's "Cubricon" [28], Wahlster's "Xtra" [31], Koon's "ICONIC" [19] and Cohen's "Quickset" [5] to Latoschik's "PrOSA" showcased by the *virtuelle Werkstatt* [26, 24], Bouchet's "ICARE" [2], Johnston and Bangalore's finit state multimodal integration [17], Serrano's "OpenInterface"[29], Dumas' "HephaisTK" [7] and Hoste's "Mudra" [15]. Over these years features and complexity have increased and different application areas have been explored, promoting multimodal processing to a mature technology [22].

However, this maturity does not apply equally for all application areas. While most of the frameworks support non-functional software quality requirements to counter the negative impacts of ad-hoc tailored application-specific solutions, their application to the area of highly interactive systems is not as straightforward as one would expect [24, 22, 27, 25]. These so-called Realtime Interactive Systems (RIS) are characterized by dynamically changing scenes and user perspectives. Therefore, they typically exhibit a complex temporal interplay of the involved software modules and—more importantly—require a close temporal as well as semantic coupling of many multimodal processing steps. If not considered carefully, an implementation of these requirements can quickly entail poor maintainability, i.e. reusability, modifiability, or modularity [16], on platform scope.

In fact, this circumstance led to a situation where sophisticated demonstrations like Latoschik's *virtuelle Werkstatt* [24] have no running build or successor. This is mostly due to the fact that simulation modules are closely coupled. Outdated or unsupported core software modules (like the rendering module) entail enormous efforts for the maintenance of the platform or the reuse of single modules, like the multimodal processing framework. In other words, neither the respective module(s) can be exchanged, nor single modules be reused, without a re-implementation of almost the whole RIS platform. On a greater scope, this circumstance hinders scientific progress, since it prevents repeatability and the ability to build on previous results. Here, alternative software models for multimodal processing frameworks are desirable to satisfy the general decoupling principle of platforms. The key research motivation of the presented thesis thus is the identification, design, development, and evaluation of software techniques for multimodal processing that enhance maintainability and API usability and specifically target the challenging requirements of highly interactive applications in Virtual Reality (VR), Augmented Reality (AR), Mixed Reality (MR), and computer games.

ICMI '15 Seattle, Washington USA
© 2015 ACM. ISBN 978-1-4503-3912-4/15/11 ...$15.00.
DOI: http://dx.doi.org/10.1145/2818346.2823308.

2. BACKGROUND AND RELATED WORK

Multimodal processing frameworks provide different sets of methods for multimodal processing and fusion at data-, feature-, and decision-level. Generally, these frameworks foster maintainability by utilizing software engineering methods like modularization and composition [15], component models [2, 30, 29], software agents [5, 7], or explicit interface definitions [24]. However, current application-independent

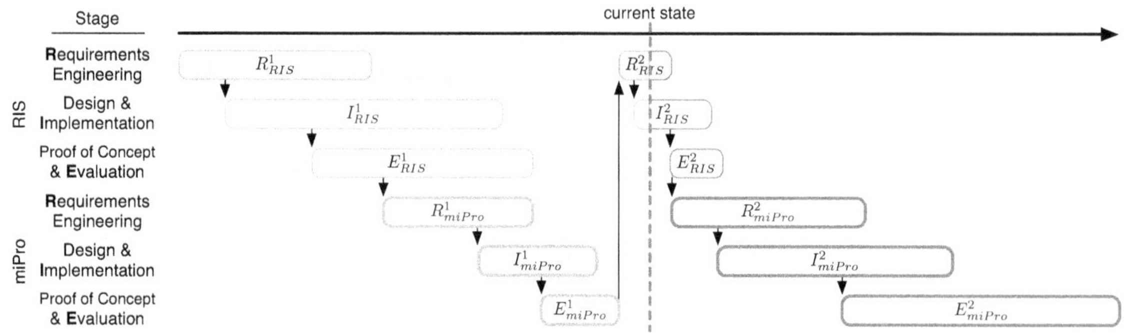

Figure 1: The main stages of the presented thesis, comprising the development of a RIS platform and of software techniques for multimodal processing.

frameworks leave the task of implementing a scheme to access the application state to the application developers. This lack of a unified access scheme is a potential source for ad-hoc implementations with poor reusability, modifiability, and modularity. Still, this problem can often be neglected for low-interactive applications. In these, state access is infrequent and the respective API often only consists of a few methods that are rarely called and at well-defined execution times. It becomes mission-critical for RIS applications. Multimodal frameworks tailored for RIS applications [24] usually provide an application state access scheme. Yet, such frameworks often exhibit a close coupling to other main modules of the underlying RIS platform. This coupling dilemma [27] is a prominent problem in the RIS area and makes the maintainability of multimodal frameworks indirectly dependent on the software quality characteristics of the underlying RIS platform.

Besides these technical aspects, the human centered requirement *API usability* [4, 6], e.g. programmability or readability [8], plays a critical part in supporting maintainability. Current multimodal processing frameworks utilize high-level graphical [2, 29] or text-based [15, 30, 24, 7] languages to increase usability for developers and allow non-experts to design multimodal interfaces. Despite this importance, conducted evaluations primarily focus user interface usability [21] or the quality of multimodal processing techniques [18]. However, there are contributions to the evaluation of API usability in other domains [4, 6] that should be considered for the evaluation of APIs for multimodal frameworks.

Altogether, multimodal processing for RIS still lacks techniques to support high maintainability and API usability, built upon a platform that supports the same software quality requirements while fostering mutual access between multimodal processing and application state. One approach to a solution of this dilemma is the *Simulator X* research platform [23], which is co-developed within the scope of this thesis. In addition to own results, its development resulted in contributions that promote the realization of multimodal processing techniques, though they do not explicitly address this domain [33, 34].

3. SCOPE

The targeted application area is constituted of highly interactive systems (i.e. RIS) and clearly differentiated from low-interactive applications that require few to no mutual access between multimodal processing and application state. It is characterized by dynamically changing scenes and user perspectives and typically incorporates stereoscopic rendering as well as motion parallax.

Under these conditions users interact with the system using multiple modalities in a synergistic manner. Targeted modalities include, but are not limited to, speech and deictic, iconic, as well as mimetic gestures. These gestures range from static postures to dynamic movements that have to be continuously mapped to some application properties. For example, a user utters "Turn [pointing gesture] the wheel [begin rotation gesture] like this [end rotation gesture]." (as in [24]), expecting the system to rotate the wheel around the same axis and in the same direction and speed as she shows. The complex temporal interplay between the detection and fusion stages of multimodal processing and the application's state can further be illustrated by a second example. The user moves around exploring the virtual scene and then utters "Take the item left of [pointing gesture] this pole." Here, the resolution of the pointing gesture as well as the user's position are required to resolve the spatial relation "left of". Both calculations have to be done with respect to the time when "this" was uttered. Since multimodal processing will take some time and should not block the application's rendering and simulation loops, access to past application states, e.g. the user's position $300ms$ ago, is essential. This requirement gets even more critical if the scene is dynamically changing.

Considering this application area as well as the current challenges of multimodal frameworks described before, the following research question drives the efforts of this thesis:

What software techniques enhance the maintainability and API usability of multimodal processing frameworks for highly interactive applications in the area of in VR, AR, MR, and computer games?

The investigation of this research question is subdivided into four aspects that are elaborated in the process of this thesis: (1) An approach to a solution to the RIS coupling dilemma that fosters maintainability as well as (2) the semantics-based mutual access between multimodal processing and application state. (3) A general and uniform interface for multimodal processing steps that explicitly targets (4) API usability. While (1) is a necessary prerequisite to the latter aspects and (3) has been alternatively addressed by other contributions [29, 15, 30], (2) and (4) are unique characteristics of the presented thesis.

4. RESEARCH PLAN

In order to adress those aspects, a RIS research platform will be developed first. This platform serves as a testbed for the exploration and evaluation of potential software techniques for multimodal processing. Subsequently, a general framework for multimodal processing (miPro) is built upon this platform. The research plan follows an iterative approach (see next section) of incremental refinement as illustrated in Figure 1:

$\mathbf{R}^1_{\mathbf{RIS}}$ Analysis and identification of requirements for RIS platforms supporting multimodal processing tasks. A modular software design, reusability, and modifiability of mission-critical interface components are paramount.

$\mathbf{I}^1_{\mathbf{RIS}}$ Implementation of core functionality for RIS, based on the results of the previous stage, including software solutions for concurrency and parallelism, a distributed application state and execution scheme, as well as intra- and interprocess communication capabilities. *These stages were performed within the externally founded project Semantic Reflection for Realtime Interactive Systems together with two colleagues.*

$\mathbf{E}^1_{\mathbf{RIS}}$ Production of early prototypes as proof of concept verification of functional aspects of the platform. In addition, utilization of the platform for teaching and student projects to evaluate its maintainability.

$\mathbf{E}^1_{\mathbf{miPro}}$ Analysis and identification of basic requirements for multimodal processing in highly interactive applications. Interaction use cases include static postures and simple dynamic movements as proposed by Bolt [1], Neal and Thielmann [28], Wahlster [31], Koon [20, 19] or Cohen [5].

$\mathbf{I}^1_{\mathbf{miPro}}$ Implementation of core functionality for multimodal processing within the developed platform prototype.

$\mathbf{E}^1_{\mathbf{miPro}}$ Creation of early prototypes as proof of concept verification of functional aspects of miPro. In addition, utilization of miPro for teaching and student projects to gather preliminary evaluation results regarding its maintainability and API usability.

$[\mathbf{R},\mathbf{I},\mathbf{E}]^2_{\mathbf{RIS}}$ Utilization of the results of the first development loop for a quick refinement of the underlying platform. Results of both preceding evaluation stages are taken into account.

$\mathbf{R}^2_{\mathbf{miPro}}$ Analysis and identification of advanced requirements for multimodal processing in highly interactive applications. Interaction use cases include deictic, iconic, and mimetic gestures as proposed by Latoschik [24] and Hoste [15].

$\mathbf{I}^2_{\mathbf{miPro}}$ Implementation of sophisticated functionality for multimodal input processing within the developed platform prototype. The implementation extends the software solutions of the previous stages.

$\mathbf{E}^2_{\mathbf{miPro}}$ Realization of one complex demonstration containing interaction examples as showcased in Latoschik's *virtuelle Werkstatt* [24] as well as the *World Builder* short film [3]. In addition, conduction of a detailed evaluation including students as well as computer science researchers targeting the maintainability and API usability of miPro.

5. APPROACH AND METHODOLOGY

The presented research plan consists of four iterative software engineering tasks, all of which are constituted of a requirements engineering phase R, a design and implementation phase I, and a proof of concept and evaluation phase E. Two key software development methodologies serve as guiding principles: (1) Agile software development as the method of choice for the scientific environment with its reliance on self-organization and collaboration of people with different expertises. (2) User centered design to ensure API usability and validity, by treating students and colleagues as end-users and giving them early access to prototypes that they can use for their exercises, projects, and research. In addition to these general approaches, the following methods are applied for each of the three development phases:

R Review of literature covering RIS platforms in general as well as multimodal processing frameworks, approaches and techniques in particular. Definition of use cases based on the analyzed literature, fine grained definition of functional and non-function requirements as well as of milestones. For the development of the RIS platform: additional moderated expert discussions with colleagues and supervisors.

I Iterative and incremental development of milestones. Iterative production of proof of concept prototypes that utilize the features of finished milestones. Integration of fixes for bugs reported from E. For the development of the RIS platform: additional application of the *SCRUM* process as well as moderated expert code reviews with other researchers.

E Verification of defined features by means of the proof of concept prototypes. Evaluation of feedback from the utilization of platform prototypes for the practical part of lecture modules and student projects on multimodal interaction as well as research projects (see next section). Execution of a white-box review by domain experts as well as execution of a survey based on a questionnaire in the course of at least one lecture module in the course of the final stage E^2_{miPro}.

6. RESULTS AND REMAINING WORK

The elaboration of the presented research plan has resulted in the following contributions so far:

$\mathbf{R}^1_{\mathbf{RIS}}$, $\mathbf{I}^1_{\mathbf{RIS}}$ The RIS research platform *Simulator X* has been analyzed, designed and implemented. It serves as testbed for ongoing implementations and evaluations. A core-level integrated semantic binding of elements for later semantic interpretation steps as well as reactive information processing have been identified as corner stones for the design of this platform.

$\mathbf{E}^1_{\mathbf{RIS}}$, $\mathbf{R}^1_{\mathbf{miPro}}$ Its usefulness has been demonstrated by the proof of concept demonstration *SiXton's Curse* [11]. Its key technical design approaches have been evaluated in terms of an expert review [32]. Multiple series of proof of concept prototypes demonstrated functional and non-functional aspects of Simulator X and explored use cases for multimodal input processing, namely the *smARTbox* hardware setup as showcased by several demonstrations [13, 12, 9] and the *XRoads* project [14]. In addition, Simulator X is used in practical parts of lecture modules and student projects [35].

$\mathbf{I}^1_{\mathbf{miPro}}$ A first prototype of the multimodal processing framework *miPro* [25] has been designed and implemented. The implementation includes semantic-based definition of requirements and produced results, software solutions for general processing steps, as well as interfaces dedicated to application developers and interaction designers.

$\mathbf{E}^1_{\mathbf{miPro}}$ Its usefulness has been explored by means of an early prototype [10]. In addition, miPro is used in practical parts of lecture modules and ongoing student projects.

The rest of work that still has to be done consists of:

$[\mathbf{R}, \mathbf{I}, \mathbf{E}]^2_{\mathbf{RIS}}$ A full development loop for the refinement of Simulator X based on accumulated insights.

$\mathbf{R}^2_{\mathbf{miPro}}$ An extended literature review as well as the definition of complex use cases.

$\mathbf{I}^2_{\mathbf{miPro}}$ Design of an improved API. Implementation of extended functionality and a large scale demonstration.

$\mathbf{E}^2_{\mathbf{miPro}}$ Identification good methodologies to evaluate the maintainability and API usability. Execution of a white-box review with domain experts as well as execution of a survey with students on these subjects.

7. CONCLUSION

The presented thesis targets the identification, design, development, and evaluation of software techniques for multimodal processing in highly interactive applications that enhance maintainability and API usability. So far, Simulator X, a research platform for applications in the target area has been co-developed and a first prototype of the multimodal processing framework miPro has been developed. Simulator X and miPro are in use for various research and teaching projects.

Although these results provide highly valuable insight into final requirements, some key ideas of the miPro framework are not yet implemented and the realization of a larger scale demonstration as well as a detailed evaluation are still missing. The Doctoral Consortium could contribute to the pending second half of the PhD research by revealing directions on currently unsolved issues, like (1) the concrete interface design of future miPro versions, (2) suitable use cases for demonstrations, and—most importantly—(3) good methodologies to evaluate the maintainability and API usability of such an specialized system.

The completed implementation of Simulator X and miPro will provide the research community with a framework that fosters repeatability as well as the ability to build on previous results. It will constitute a general testbed for evaluating and comparing multimodal processing techniques. The latter has repeatedly been identified to be a necessary requirement for future research in the field of multimodal processing [8, 22].

8. ACKNOWLEDGEMENTS

The author wants to thank his supervisor, Prof. Dr. Marc Erich Latoschik, for his advice, insights, and guidance.

9. REFERENCES

[1] R. A. Bolt. „put-that-there": Voice and gesture at the graphics interface. In *Proceedings of the 7th Annual Conference on Computer Graphics and Interactive Techniques*, pages 262–270. ACM, 1980.

[2] J. Bouchet, L. Nigay, and T. Ganille. Icare software components for rapidly developing multimodal interfaces. In *Proceedings of the 6th International Conference on Multimodal Interfaces*, pages 251–258. ACM, 2004.

[3] B. Branit. World builder, 2007.

[4] S. Clarke. Measuring API usability. *Dr. Dobb's Journal*, 2004.

[5] P. R. Cohen, M. Johnston, D. McGee, S. Oviatt, J. Pittman, I. Smith, L. Chen, and J. Clow. Quickset: Multimodal interaction for distributed applications. In *Proceedings of the Fifth International Conference on Multimedia*, pages 31–40. ACM, 1997.

[6] J. M. Daughtry, U. Farooq, J. Stylos, and B. A. Myers. Api usability: Chi'2009 special interest group meeting. In *CHI '09 Extended Abstracts on Human Factors in Computing Systems*, CHI EA '09, pages 2771–2774. ACM, 2009.

[7] B. Dumas, D. Lalanne, and R. Ingold. Hephaistk: A toolkit for rapid prototyping of multimodal interfaces. In *Proceedings of the 2009 International Conference on Multimodal Interfaces*, pages 231–232. ACM, 2009.

[8] B. Dumas, D. Lalanne, and S. Oviatt. Multimodal Interfaces: A Survey of Principles, Models and Frameworks. In *Human Machine Interaction*, pages 3–26. Springer, 2009.

[9] M. Fischbach, M. E. Latoschik, G. Bruder, and F. Steinicke. smARTbox: Out-of-the-Box Technologies for Interactive Art and Exhibition. In *Proceedings of the 2012 Virtual Reality International Conference*, pages 19:1–19:7. ACM, 2012.

[10] M. Fischbach, M. Neff, I. Pelzer, J.-L. Lugrin, and M. E. Latoschik. Input device adequacy for multimodal and bimanual object manipulation in virtual environments. In *Virtuelle und Erweiterte Realität, 10. Workshop der GI-Fachgruppe VR/AR*, pages 145–156. Shaker Verlag, 2013.

[11] M. Fischbach, D. Wiebusch, A. Giebler-Schubert, M. E. Latoschik, S. Rehfeld, and H. Tramberend. SiXton's curse - Simulator X demonstration. In *Virtual Reality Conference (VR), 2011 IEEE*, pages 255–256, 2011.

[12] M. Fischbach, D. Wiebusch, M. E. Latoschik, G. Bruder, and F. Steinicke. Blending real and virtual worlds using self-reflection and fiducials. In *Proceedings of the 11th international conference on Entertainment Computing*, pages 465–468, Berlin, Heidelberg, 2012. Springer-Verlag.

[13] M. Fischbach, D. Wiebusch, M. E. Latoschik, G. Bruder, and F. Steinicke. smARTbox A Portable Setup for Intelligent Interactive Applications. In *Mensch & Computer Workshopband*, pages 521–524. Oldenbourg Verlag, 2012.

[14] M. Fischbach, C. Zimmerer, A. Giebler-Schubert, and M. E. Latoschik. DEMO Exploring multimodal interaction techniques for a mixed reality digital

surface. In *IEEE International Symposium on Mixed and Augmented Reality (ISMAR)*, 2014.

[15] L. Hoste, B. Dumas, and B. Signer. Mudra: A Unified Multimodal Interaction Framework. In *Proceedings of the 13th International Conference on Multimodal Interfaces*, pages 97–104. ACM, 2011.

[16] ISO. Systems and software engineering – systems and software quality requirements and evaluation (square) – system and software quality models. ISO ISO/IEC 25010:2011, International Organization for Standardization, Geneva, Switzerland, 2011.

[17] M. Johnston and S. Bangalore. Finite-state multimodal integration and understanding. *Natural Language Engineering*, 11(02):159–187, 2005.

[18] E. Kaiser, A. Olwal, D. McGee, H. Benko, A. Corradini, X. Li, P. Cohen, and S. Feiner. Mutual Disambiguation of 3D Multimodal Interaction in Augmented and Virtual Reality. In *Proceedings of the 5th International Conference on Multimodal Interfaces*, pages 12–19. ACM, 2003.

[19] D. B. Koons and C. J. Sparrell. Iconic: Speech and depictive gestures at the human-machine interface. In *Conference Companion on Human Factors in Computing Systems*, pages 453–454. ACM, 1994.

[20] D. B. Koons, C. J. Sparrell, and K. R. Thorisson. Intelligent multimedia interfaces. chapter Integrating Simultaneous Input from Speech, Gaze, and Hand Gestures, pages 257–276. American Association for Artificial Intelligence, 1993.

[21] D. M. Krum, O. Omoteso, W. Ribarsky, T. Starner, and L. F. Hodges. Evaluation of a Multimodal Interface for 3D Terrain Visualization. In *Proceedings of the Conference on Visualization '02*, VIS '02, pages 411–418. IEEE Computer Society, 2002.

[22] D. Lalanne, L. Nigay, P. Palanque, P. Robinson, J. Vanderdonckt, and J.-F. Ladry. Fusion engines for multimodal input: A survey. In *Proceedings of the 2009 International Conference on Multimodal Interfaces*, pages 153–160. ACM, 2009.

[23] M. Latoschik and H. Tramberend. Simulator X: A Scalable and Concurrent Architecture for Intelligent Realtime Interactive Systems. In *Virtual Reality Conference (VR), 2011 IEEE*, pages 171–174, 2011.

[24] M. E. Latoschik. A User Interface Framework for Multimodal VR Interactions. In *Proceedings of the 7th International Conference on Multimodal Interfaces*, pages 76–83. ACM, 2005.

[25] M. E. Latoschik and M. Fischbach. Engineering Variance: Software Techniques for Scalable, Customizable, and Reusable Multimodal Processing. In *Proceedings of the HCI International Conference*, pages 308–319. Springer, 2014.

[26] M. E. Latoschik, M. Fröhlich, B. Jung, and I. Wachsmuth. Utilize speech and gestures to realize natural interaction in a virtual environment. In *Proceedings of the annual Conference of the IEEE Industrial Electronics Society*, IECON'98, pages 2028–2033, 1998.

[27] M. E. Latoschik and H. Tramberend. Short Paper: Engineering Realtime Interactive Systems: Coupling & Cohesion of Architecture Mechanisms. In *Proceedings of the 16th Eurographics Conference on Virtual Environments & Second Joint Virtual Reality*, pages 25–28. Eurographics Association, 2010.

[28] J. G. Neal, C. Y. Thielman, Z. Dobes, S. M. Haller, and S. C. Shapiro. Natural language with integrated deictic and graphic gestures. In *Proceedings of the Workshop on Speech and Natural Language*, pages 410–423. Association for Computational Linguistics, 1989.

[29] M. Serrano, L. Nigay, J.-Y. L. Lawson, A. Ramsay, R. Murray-Smith, and S. Denef. The Openinterface Framework: A Tool for Multimodal Interaction. In *Extended Abstracts on Human Factors in Computing Systems*, pages 3501–3506. ACM, 2008.

[30] J. Wagner, F. Lingenfelser, T. Baur, I. Damian, F. Kistler, and E. André. The Social Signal Interpretation (SSI) Framework: Multimodal Signal Processing and Recognition in Real-time. In *Proceedings of the 21st ACM International Conference on Multimedia*, pages 831–834. ACM, 2013.

[31] W. Wahlster. User and discourse models for multimodal communication. In *Intelligent User Interfaces*, pages 45–67. ACM Press, 1991.

[32] D. Wiebusch, M. Fischbach, M. E. Latoschik, and H. Tramberend. Evaluating Scala, Actors, & Ontologies for Intelligent Realtime Interactive Systems. In *Proceedings of the 18th ACM Symposium on Virtual Reality Software and Technology*, VRST '12, pages 153–160. ACM, 2012.

[33] D. Wiebusch and M. E. Latoschik. A uniform semantic-based access model for realtime interactive systems. In *7th Workshop on Software Engineering and Architectures for Realtime Interactive Systems (SEARIS)*, 2014.

[34] D. Wiebusch and M. E. Latoschik. Decoupling the Entity-Component-System Pattern using Semantic Traits for Reusable Realtime Interactive Systems. In *Workshop on Software Engineering and Architectures for Realtime Interactive Systems*, IEEE VR, 2015.

[35] C. Zimmerer, M. Fischbach, and M. E. Latoschik. Fusion of mixed reality tabletop and location-based applications for pervasive games. In *Proceedings of the 2014 ACM International Conference on Interactive Tabletops and Surfaces*. ACM, 2014.

Gait and Postural Sway Analysis, A Multi-Modal System

Hafsa Ismail
University of Canberra, Australia
hafsa.ismail@canberra.edu.au

ABSTRACT

Detecting a fall before it actually happens will positively affect lives of the elderly. While the main causes of falling are related to postural sway and walking, determining abnormalities in one of these activities or both of them would be informative to predicting the fall probability. A need exists for a portable gait and postural sway analysis system that can provide individuals with real-time information about changes and quality of gait in the real world, not just in a laboratory. In this research project I aim to build a multi-modal system that finds the correlation between vision extracted features and accelerometer and force plate data to determine a general gait and body sway pattern. Then this information is used to assess a difference to normative age and gender relevant patterns as well as any changes over time. This could provide a core indicator of broader health and function in ageing and disease.

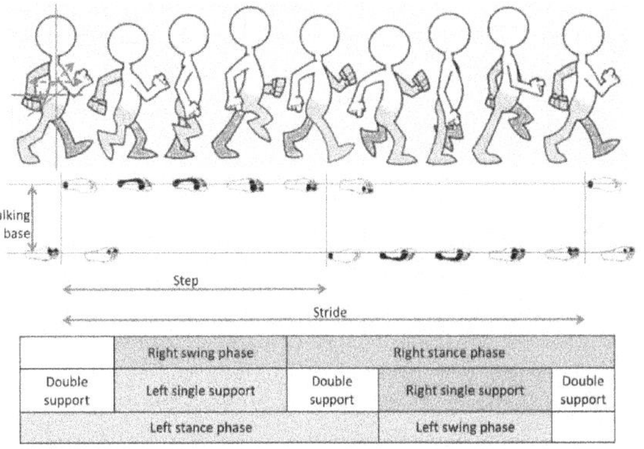

Figure 1: Gait Cycle: walking base, stride length and single lemb support time are the main changes in elderly gait. Body sway: side-to-side and forward-backword body movement, illustrated by the red arrows on the first graph on the left.

Categories and Subject Descriptors

I.2.10 [**Vision and Scene Understanding: Video Analysis**]; I.4 [**Image Processing and Computer Vision**]; I.5 [**Pattern Recognition**]; J.3 [**Life and Medical Sciences**]

Keywords

Multi-modal system; 3D pose; Sway pattern; Gait analysis

1. MOTIVATION

Maintaining a high standard of life for the elderly enables them to live their lives with minimum fear of sudden accidents. Falling is one of the most important problems that affect elderly lives. It causes injuries that may be deadly or decrease the functional ability and the quality of life. Predicting falls before they happen makes a critical difference, enabling optimal self-care for elderly adults.

This work aims to develop an application for self monitoring of an individuals based on vision and accelerometer data. Capturing changes in the movement patterns as persons age enables them to intervene if they detect deterioration in movement performance and seek help if needed before a serious fall happens. The research is innovative in that there is no current method of evaluating change in movement performance in walking that can be applied at the individual level that references normative population data. Current assessment of sway, in particular the lateral sway, which is particularly relevant to falls, relies on the use of force platforms. While these have become less expensive in recent years, it is unlikely that these will be omnipresent in homes any time soon.

Our methodology is to build a multi-modal algorithm to link vision data, wearable sensor (accelerometer) and force plate data altogether and to explore the correlation between them. A focus of this algorithm will be on measuring the changes in the lateral sway and quantifying these changes.

First, related work is viewed. The methodology, which includes data collecting and processing, is presented. Finally, our contributions and the time-line of the study are discussed.

2. RELATED WORK

An accurate, inexpensive and easily accessible tool for quantitatively measuring postural sway is needed and must be suitable to be used with daily activities. If such a tool was available, it could enable earlier detection, better ongoing monitoring and immediate assessment of treatment interventions of balance disturbances in elderly and could lead to a reduction in the probability of injuries related to falls.

In clinical research, specially related to falls in aged people, assessing a fall takes typically place after it already happened to address the causes and circumstances of falls in the elderly. The most frequent cause of falling was incorrect weight shifting and walking

ICMI 2015, November 9–13, 2015, Seattle, WA, USA.
 ISBN 978-1-4503-3912-4/15/11 ...$15.00.
DOI: http://dx.doi.org/10.1145/2818346.2823310.

was the activity that was associated with the highest ratio of falls, followed by standing quietly [10].

Gait and postural sway are reflections for the brain signals that generated to control balance and the main keys to fall prevention. Many different parameters and techniques have been identified to measure gait and postural sway.

For the human gait, cycle time (cadence), stride length and speed are the general gait parameters that provide the simplest form of objective gait evaluation [19]. In most locomotor disabilities, general gait parameters tend to change together. The general gait parameters are easy to be determined from a video recording. These parameters give a guide for the walking ability, but little specific information. In the elderly people, pathological conditions and the affect of age influence the gait of the elderly [19]. Under these conditions, the elderly gait changes to improve walking security. Maintaining balance while walking can be obtained by both decreasing the stride length and increasing the walking base. Increasing the step cycle time leads to reduction in the percentage of the gait cycle for which there is only single limb support. Figure 1 illustrates main gait parameters that are interested regards to elderly, such as: walk base, step and stance.

More than twenty gait factors, in addition to the general gait parameters were presented and defined in [7] in addition to methods and technologies used for measuring such parameters. Gait parameters were classified into five primary domains in [4]. (1) Rhythm Domain, which contains cadence and temporal parameters, *e.g.* stride time. (2) Phase domain, which is characterized by distance divisions such as stance. (3) Variability domain, which is characterized by gait cycle and step variability parameters such as stride length variability. (4) Space domain, which contains gait speed, step length and stride length parameters. Finally, (5) base of support domain, which contains step width and step width variability parameters. Variability domain parameters are considered to be the best fall indicator in elderly.

A quantitative gait markers are identified in [14] for incident fall risk in older adults. Quantitative gait markers, such as speed, cadence, and swing time variability, are independent predictors of falls in older adults. Studying gait speed and other markers, specially variability, could improve current fall risk assessments and develop new interventions.

The postural sway (body sway) maintains balance position with slight postural movement to assess body balance [16], illustrated in Figure 1. Falls in the elderly are related to the difficulties in adapting body balance. Postural sway can be measured by the total displacement of the body centre of mass relative to the base of support over time. When self-induced shifting of body weight cause the centre of gravity (same as centre of mass) moved outside the base of support of the human body, the incorrect transfer or incorrect shifting of body weight occurs, which is the main cause of fall in elderly regarding to [10]. As people age, maintaining balance becomes increasingly difficult and postural sway, both lateral and anterior-posterior, increases with time.

For recognizing and analysing human gait and body sway, three different approaches are used: image processing, floor sensors and sensors placed on the body (wearable sensors)[4]. These approaches are used to measure gait parameters with 1) semi-subjective analysis techniques and 2) objective analysis techniques. Semi-objective methods usually consist of analyses carried out in clinical conditions by a specialist. This is time consuming and expensive. On the other hand, objective techniques are based on the use of different devices to capture and measure information related to the various gait parameters. With the improvement in all aspects of life, new technologies and approaches are proposed to make the measurements and the assessments easier, faster and more reliable.

A force platform is used to measure the postural sway by measuring the movement of the centre of pressure COP. COP position references the base of support, anterior-posterior and lateral sway, the length of sway path, sway velocity and sway area, which are considered as postural sway parameters. Different balance tests were developed as discriminative measures for postural sway to identify balance deficits that may cause fall. Balance tests such as: Standing test for imbalance and disequilibrium (SIDE)[13] and balance error scoring system (BESS)[2], are take place on the force plate to measure body sway parameters.

Automatic, continuous and long-term physical activity measurement in a free-living environment are enabled to be monitored using accelerometry techniques [20]. Modern smart phones contain accelerometers and gyroscopes, which enable exquisitely sensitive measures of human movement performance beyond simple step detection in devices that are ubiquitous. Accelerometers allow the examination of fine details of movement performance that have not previously been available outside of laboratory-based environments and have been shown to be valid and reliable in the assessment of gait variability [6]. This type of data enables analysis of the accelerations of the individual's trunk movements utilising measures such as harmonic ratio, index of harmonicity, multi-scale entropy and recurrence quantification analysis as in [9].

Computer vision techniques can be used to make the process more time-efficient, more cost-effective and, most importantly, more reliable. Body silhouettes were used in [1] to detect if the observed walking pattern appears to be normal or not. A homeomorphism between 2D lattices and silhouette shapes is presented to address the requirement of abstracting gait characteristics that allow gait classification across individuals. Extracted silhouette from videos as well as the frame-to-frame optical flow were used in [18] to determine different styles of walking and detect the deviation from usual walking patterns.

A marker-less, model-free study, based on the block matching algorithm is presented in [3]. The method consisted of tracking the relevant points on the human silhouette, followed by the evaluation of the rotations of the principal body segments, and estimation of centre of mass (COM) trajectories. Another method for analysing body sway from a three dimensional voxel reconstruction from silhouette is presented in [16]. Using two inexpensive calibrated webcams to extract sway parameters from both standing and walking subjects. The voxel person was built from back-projected silhouettes extracted from multiple camera views as in [17]. A Vicon marker-based motion capture was used as ground truth. A good agreement is obtained for body sway during standing. For walking, the overall agreement were lower. An inexpensive depth camera in-home is used to assess gait and fall risk in [11, 12] offering an opportunity for elderly to safely and independently as they age.

In this work, a normative gait dataset over different age groups will be collected to overcome the deficiencies of the gait data. This dataset will contain high definition video recordings as the vision data. Data will also be collected from accelerometers and force plates for determining the postural sway for the participants. Fusing the visual features with the accelerometer and force plates data to get to an efficient and reliable gait and sway pattern representation is one of this study aims.

3. METHODOLOGY

In this section, I describe the whole system of gait and body sway analysis, which can be used to predict the sway patterns of individ-

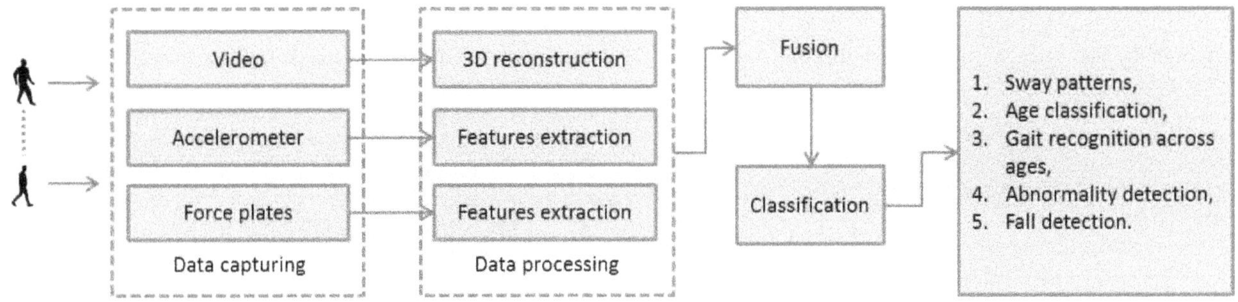

Figure 2: Framework overview: From left to right, the phases of the multi-modal system, which consists of data capturing, extracting the features, fusing the vision based features with the other sensors measurements toward the output classification.

uals, detect the abnormality in their walking/sway and increase the ability to prevent their falling as shown in Figure 2.

To start with, the process of recording the data and the devices to be used in this study are briefly described. Three devices are used to collect the data: (1) cameras to collect the visual evidences of the individuals, (2) accelerometers to monitor periodicity of the walking style and (3) a force plate, to measure the postural sway of the individuals. Then, the processes of extracting the features, constructing the sway pattern, detecting the abnormality in the walking and predicting the fall are summarised.

3.1 Multi-modal gait and postural sway dataset

One contribution of this study is to provide a complete multi-modal gait analysis dataset from both the cameras and other sensors, such as accelerometers and force plates while walking and performing balance test. Validating data and ground truth will be recorded.

High Definition cameras are employed to record the participants' movement during the proposed activities. This will help in extracting the gait parameters from the visual cues of the participants' images through time. These visual cues are represented by low-level features, mid-level features, high-level features or combination of them as will be discussed in the next section. Motion capture cameras (vicon) are used to build an accepted accuracy ground truth for the collected data to compare with.

Force plates are used to assess human body balance improvement. They are low cost and portable device for measuring COP of the human body. The displacement of the COP can measure the postural stability, which is an important feature that protect people from a fall and helps to complete the desired actions [5]. Recording and analysing COP data help us to assess the degree of human body balance and postural sway.

Gait variability parameters (in addition to the body sway) can be measured by the accelerometers that placed at the participant's back. Accelerometer data enables the analysis of the individual's postural sway as it measures the trunk movements over the time.

Data recording studio is illustrated in Figure 3. The activities area is the same. Vicon cameras are used in the case of ground truth with addition to the video cameras. Only video cameras are used for validating data.

The data for each participant will be collected on three stages: 1) Baseline stage, 2) Medium line stage, three months later, and 3) Final stage, six months later. At each stage, a balance test will take a place on the force plate and normal walk for about five meters will be performed. During these activities, an accelerometer will be hanged to the participant's waist and the camera(s) will be recording.

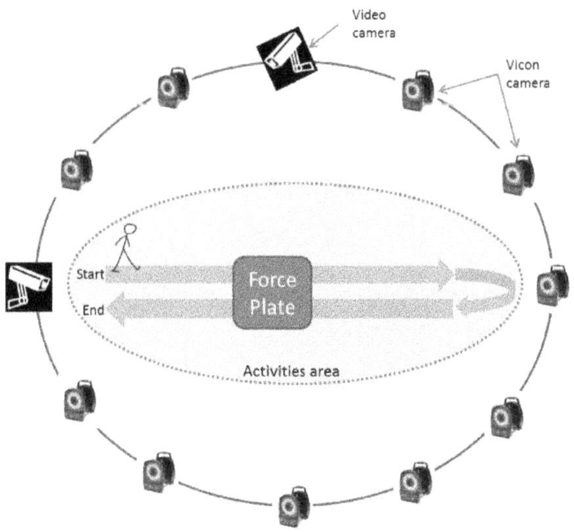

Figure 3: Data recording. Activities area, where walking and balance test will take place (red area). For ground truth, Vicon and video cameras are used. For the validating data, only video cameras are used.

The Balance Error Scoring System (BESS) is an example of clinical balance tests. BESS provides an objective method to assess the static postural stability. The normal BESS needs to be completed on two testing surfaces: ground/floor and foam pad. The foam pad creates an unstable surface witch is a more challenging balance task. Three stance posture are required to be taken for 30 seconds on each surface: 1) double leg stance with feet side by side, 2) single leg stance on the non-dominate foot (the opposite leg of the preferred kicking leg), and 3) tandem stance (standing heel to toe with non-dominate foot in the back). For all positions, the eyes are closed and the hands are on the hips.

In this work, the considered BESS part is the stance postures. These positions will take place on the force plate to measure the postural sway for the participants during the test. The BESS goes as follows:

- Double leg stance: Standing with feet side by side (touching) for 30 seconds.
- Single leg stance: Standing on the non-dominant foot for 30 seconds.

- Tandem Stance: Standing heel to toe with the non-dominate foot in the back. Heel of the dominant foot should be touching the toe of the non-dominant foot.

The participants will be asked to walk normally with their own speed with no assistance for about 5 metres with performing 180-degree turn. Figure 3 illustrates the data recording scenario for the data set.

To have a normative data set over time, the same activities will be recorded for the participants after three and six months from the baseline stage.

3.2 3D pose Reconstruction

Recovering the 3D structures of the deformable objects (*e.g.* human body) from monocular sequences is well-known challenge in the computer vision. In our study, the 3D human poses of the individuals are discriminative representation to infer the gait parameters from the monocular videos. So that the second contribution of this doctoral study is to tackle this problem and to provide a solid representations from the human sequences. Which if fused with the other data from the accelerometers and force plates, would efficiently, lead to determining the sway patterns, discovering the abnormality in the gait of the individuals and detecting the possibility of falling toward reducing it.

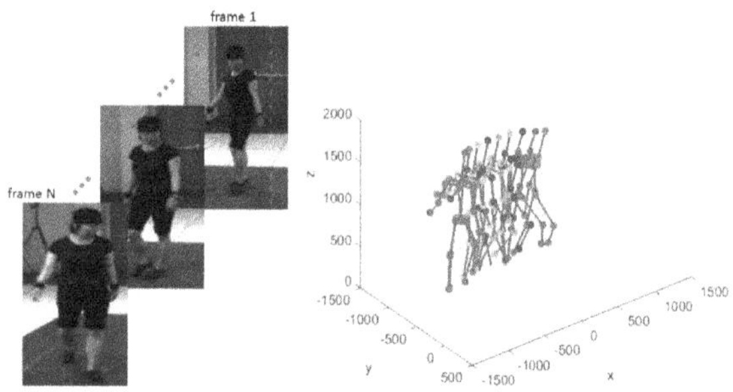

Figure 4: Construct 3D pose from video. To the left, selected frames from walking action in Human Eva dataset. To the right, the initial result for the constructed 3D pose from single view.

The 3D pose reconstruction from monocular videos is an ill-posed problem as any 3D pose can be projected to multiple 2D instances [15, 8]. The need for having strong 3D motion prior may lead to reduce the search space of the recovery and may result in accurate 3D reconstruction. In my study, I plan to learn set of 3D base poses from the state-of-the-art databases (*e.g.* CMU Mocap dataset[1]). Then, use these bases with the kinematic constraints to recover the 3D pose and learn the camera parameters. I already have started an experiment based on this idea and initial qualitative results are shown in Figure 4. The estimated 3D poses will be fused with the others parameters measured from accelerometers and force plates to estimate the gait parameters and detect the abnormality in the sway of the individuals.

3.2.1 Fusion

During training, the 3D pose is constructed from each video frame by selecting the most discriminative features. I will correlate the estimated 3D pose with measurements from accelerometer and force plate data to build the gait and sway pattern for each age group and determine the normal patterns for gait and body sway. During testing, after extracting the 3D pose for video frames, classification method, such as support vector machine SVM, is used on a feature or decision level to determine the age group and the sway pattern for the participant, detect if there is abnormality in an individual's gait, and detect falling likelihood.

[1]http://mocap.cs.cmu.edu/

4. THESIS CONTRIBUTIONS

The proposed contributions of this PhD are:

1 Build a normative data set for gait and body sway patterns across ages,

2 Measure gait and body sway parameters from constructed 3D pose,

3 Using 3D pose to study the discriminative features for gait abnormality, and

4 Determine if cameras and accelerometer are accurate enough to determine abnormality in the gait and sway patterns to predict a fall months in advance.

5. RESEARCH TIMELINE

- First year, research background, ethical clearance and start data recording with the base-line stage. Also recording the ground truth.
- Second year, begin pre-processing on the collected data (3D pose reconstruction from single video). Fusion 3D pose with features extracted from other sensors. Also recording data for other stages when required.
- Third year, finalize the experiments for gait and sway patterns classification to determine the abnormalities and fall probabilities. Thesis Writing.

6. ACKNOWLEDGEMENT

I would like to thank Ibrahim Radwan, Roland Goecke and Gordon Waddington for there help and support.

7. REFERENCES

[1] C. Bauckhage, J. K. Tsotsos, and F. E. Bunn. Automatic detection of abnormal gait. *Image and Vision Computing*, 27(1):108–115, 2009.

[2] J. T. Finnoff, V. J. Peterson, J. H. Hollman, and J. Smith. Intrarater and interrater reliability of the balance error scoring system (bess). *PM&R*, 1(1):50–54, 2009.

[3] M. Goffredo, M. Schmid, S. Conforto, and T. DŠAlessio. A markerless sub-pixel motion estimation technique to reconstruct kinematics and estimate the centre of mass in posturography. *Medical engineering & physics*, 28(7):719–726, 2006.

[4] J. H. Hollman, E. M. McDade, and R. C. Petersen. Normative spatiotemporal gait parameters in older adults. *Gait & posture*, 34(1):111–118, 2011.

[5] C.-W. Huang, P.-D. Sue, M. F. Abbod, B. C. Jiang, and J.-S. Shieh. Measuring center of pressure signals to quantify human balance using multivariate multiscale entropy by designing a force platform. *Sensors*, 13(8):10151–10166, 2013.

[6] S. Lord, T. Howe, J. Greenland, L. Simpson, and L. Rochester. Gait variability in older adults: a structured review of testing protocol and clinimetric properties. *Gait & posture*, 34(4):443–450, 2011.

[7] A. Muro-de-la Herran, B. Garcia-Zapirain, and A. Mendez-Zorrilla. Gait analysis methods: An overview of wearable and non-wearable systems, highlighting clinical applications. *Sensors*, 14(2):3362–3394, 2014.

[8] I. Radwan, A. Dhall, and R. Goecke. Monocular image 3d human pose estimation under self-occlusion. In *Computer Vision (ICCV), 2013 IEEE International Conference on*, pages 1888–1895. IEEE, 2013.

[9] F. Riva, M. Toebes, M. Pijnappels, R. Stagni, and J. van Dieën. Estimating fall risk with inertial sensors using gait stability measures that do not require step detection. *Gait & posture*, 38(2):170–174, 2013.

[10] S. N. Robinovitch, F. Feldman, Y. Yang, R. Schonnop, P. M. Leung, T. Sarraf, J. Sims-Gould, and M. Loughin. Video capture of the circumstances of falls in elderly people residing in long-term care: an observational study. *The Lancet*, 381(9860):47–54, 2013.

[11] E. Stone and M. Skubic. Evaluation of an inexpensive depth camera for in-home gait assessment. *Journal of Ambient Intelligence and Smart Environments*, 3(4):349–361, 2011.

[12] E. E. Stone and M. Skubic. Evaluation of an inexpensive depth camera for passive in-home fall risk assessment. In *Pervasive Computing Technologies for Healthcare (PervasiveHealth), 2011 5th International Conference on*, pages 71–77. IEEE, 2011.

[13] T. Teranishi, I. Kondo, S. Sonoda, Y. Wada, H. Miyasaka, G. Tanino, W. Narita, H. Sakurai, M. Okada, and E. Saitoh. Validity study of the standing test for imbalance and disequilibrium (side): Is the amount of body sway in adopted postures consistent with item order? *Gait & posture*, 34(3):295–299, 2011.

[14] J. Verghese, R. Holtzer, R. B. Lipton, and C. Wang. Quantitative gait markers and incident fall risk in older adults. *The Journals of Gerontology Series A: Biological Sciences and Medical Sciences*, 64(8):896–901, 2009.

[15] B. Wandt, H. Ackermann, and B. Rosenhahn. 3d human motion capture from monocular image sequences. In *Proceedings of the IEEE Conference on Computer Vision and Pattern Recognition Workshops*, pages 1–8, 2015.

[16] F. Wang, M. Skubic, C. Abbott, and J. M. Keller. Body sway measurement for fall risk assessment using inexpensive webcams. In *Engineering in Medicine and Biology Society (EMBC), 2010 Annual International Conference of the IEEE*, pages 2225–2229. IEEE, 2010.

[17] F. Wang, E. Stone, W. Dai, M. Skubic, and J. Keller. Gait analysis and validation using voxel data. In *Engineering in Medicine and Biology Society, 2009. EMBC 2009. Annual International Conference of the IEEE*, pages 6127–6130. IEEE, 2009.

[18] L. Wang. Abnormal walking gait analysis using silhouette-masked flow histograms. In *Pattern Recognition, 2006. ICPR 2006. 18th International Conference on*, volume 3, pages 473–476. IEEE, 2006.

[19] M. Whittle. *Gait Analysis: An Introduction.* Butterworth-Heinemann, 2007.

[20] C.-C. Yang and Y.-L. Hsu. A review of accelerometry-based wearable motion detectors for physical activity monitoring. *Sensors*, 10(8):7772–7788, 2010.

A Computational Model of Culture-Specific Emotions for Artificial Agents in the Learning Domain

Ganapreeta Renunathan Naidu
Universiti Sains Malaysia
Penang
Malaysia
+6012 412 5590
grn14_com028@student.usm.my

ABSTRACT

Nowadays intelligent agents are expected to be affect-sensitive as agents are becoming essential entities that supports computer-mediated tasks, especially in teaching and training. These agents use common natural modalities—such as facial expressions, gestures and eye gaze in order to recognize a user's affective state and respond accordingly. However, these nonverbal cues may not be universal as emotion recognition and expression differ from culture to culture.

It is important that intelligent interfaces are equipped with the abilities to meet the challenge of cultural diversity to facilitate human-machine interaction particularly in Asia. Asians are known to be more passive and possess certain traits such as indirectness and non-confrontationalism, which lead to emotions such as (culture-specific form of) shyness and timidity. Therefore, a model based on other culture may not be applicable in an Asian setting, out-rulling a one-size-fits-all approach. This study is initiated to identify the discriminative markers of culture-specific emotions based on the multimodal interactions.

Categories and Subject Descriptors

C.3. **[Special-purpose application-based systems]:** Real-time and embedded systems. H.5.1, H.5.m. **[Information interfaces and presentation]:** Artificial, augmented, and virtual realities, human–computer interaction (HCI).

General Terms

Algorithms, Design, Reliability, Experimentation, Human Factors

Keywords

Multimodal interaction, human–computer interaction (HCI), affective computing, intelligent agents, culture-specific, learning domain.

1. INTRODUCTION

Multimodal interaction is an important attribute in Human Computer Interaction (HCI).

People mostly depend on interaction with each other to establish relationship by recognizing and interpreting multimodal signals of their correspondent with little or no effort. However design and development of an automated system that accomplishes these tasks is rather difficult.

Automatic detection of culture-specific emotions such as colourings of shyness, passiveness, specific form of frustration and masking will be highly valuable in the learning domain which requires a reliable emotion recognition model. An emotion recognition model that is based on one culture may not reliably predict emotion from other culture as recognition of emotion across culture varies, and so does expressions of emotion that is projected through different display rules.

Emotion recognition models are not only task-based, but it is also dependent on a specific culture because the way certain task are carried out may differ from culture to culture. In order to construct a prediction or recognition model that is tailored to a specific culture, one should quantify and convert the culture-specific emotional concepts into a computational entity to enable prediction and recognition of the particular culture-specific emotions. For example, self-conscious emotions such as shyness or timidity and traits such as face saving, indirectness and non-confrontationalism seems to be more apparent in Asia especially among South East Asians. Study based on Malaysian learners by Hamid [1], shows that the concept of shyness or "malu" is highly prevalent within the Malaysian society - in academic, professional, as well as inter-personal spheres. Thus applying a model based on data from other cultures in the local settings in teaching and learning may impact the emotion recognition rate.

This research focuses on the learning domain in Malaysia where learners are more timid, passive, shy and tend to mask their real state of emotion. As a result, affect-sensitive agents in learning that are not equipped with the ability to recognize culture-specific emotions may fail to achieve the ultimate goal of improving learner's emotional experience with machines.

2. KEY RESEARCH QUESTIONS AND MOTIVATION

i. Are traits such as indirectness/non-confrontationalness that subsequently lead to certain emotions (e.g., colourings of shyness, passiveness, specific form of frustration, masking) a form of culturally specific emotions that are related to Malaysians?

ii. What is the solution to improve emotion recognition in the teaching and learning domain?

ICMI 2015, November 9–13, 2015, Seattle, WA, USA.
© 2015 ACM. ISBN 978-1-4503-3912-4/15/11…$15.00.DOI: http://dx.doi.org/10.1145/2818346.2823307

3. BACKGROUND

Now with the mass appeal of artificially-mediated communication, higher expectations are being placed upon artificial agents - they are expected not only to deliver the information or the actions desired by the users [2,3] but also required to have the social abilities that humans naturally demonstrate in their daily interactions. Thus real-time automatic detection of emotion is vital to any affect-sensitive interface, especially in the learning domain. In line with this, Atkison et al. [4] and Moreno [5] revealed that increased scores were shown for participants who interacted with an affect-sensitive agent compared to those working on their own.

Cole et al. [6] showed that even though their artificial agent was only a disembodied head and lacking natural facial expressions, it still engaged and helped participants respond. However empirically researchers found that the performance of learners could be improved further when agents are incorporated with emotional intelligence. This is because agents with emotional intelligence can create a more empathetic learning environment.

Within the learning domain, Wang et al. [7] proved that empathetic agents stimulate learner's interest and hence created more conducive learning environment. In a similar vein, Acosta [8] revealed that an artificial consultant in the varsity that is equipped with emotional intelligence gained better rapport with students than one that is not. When agents are able to adapt to the learner's emotion and engage the learner to perform a given tasks, the objective of the model is achieved. An affect-sensitive agent that could help assess students' cognitive, affective, and motivational states will keep students engaged, boost self-confidence, heighten interest, and is likely to maximize learning, D'mello [9].

According to Sabourin and collegues [10] affect plays an increasingly important role in intelligent tutoring systems as an effort to increase the effectiveness of tutorial interactions and ultimately, learning. Forbes-Riley and colleagues [11] focused on detecting learners' uncertainty – in which their automated spoken dialogue computer tutor, UNCITSPOKEWOZ detects and adapts to learner's uncertainty through the multimodal interactions established by the learners. Once uncertainty is detected, the tutor reacts by providing correctness feedback to the learner and then initiates a sub-dialogue to remediate the learner's uncertainty results. This adaptation leads to an improved learning environment.

However, an agent should not only be affect-sensitive but also culture-sensitive. This is because emotion recognition and expression differ from culture to culture [12]. Incorporating a localized model can further enhance the believability of an agent among learners. Rossen et al. [13] showed that in an experimental medical interview conducted using artificial agents, less user empathy was displayed towards a character with a dark skin tone as compared to a light one. Likewise, Lee and Nass [14] showed that a localized synthetic speech of an agent from the same ethnic background as the interlocutor is perceived to be more socially attractive and trustworthy than those from different backgrounds. Another study by Lutfi and colleagues [15] proved that infusing a more familiarized set of emotions into a Text-to-System whose users are natives, are less offensive and hence mitigated negative emotions from users, namely confusion, annoyance and aggravation. These reasons motivate this study to explore the potentials in identifying culture-sensitive patterns of emotions, towards the discovery of culture-specific emotion model that could underlie affective and culturally-sensitive artificial interfaces that are more suitable for local learners. Malaysian learners tend to show more subtle, self-conscious emotions such as shyness, passiveness, specific form of frustration, and emotion masking which may lead to misperceptions when interacting with outgroups. "Malaysian students don't feel that they have the "right" to question what is being taught until they have completely understood all aspects of it. Moreover, they avoid being critical out of respect for the teacher, so that the teacher will not lose "face" in front of other students, and to preserve harmony in the classroom, so that everything runs smoothly. There is also an element of preserving their own "face", Chuah [16]. Correspondingly, Saleh et al. [17] described adult learners as shy and fearful due to the intrinsic nature of Malaysians.

In a case study on the challenges and adjustments of expatriates in Malaysia, Tahir and Ismail [18] pointed out that almost all expatriates that were interviewed reached a consensus that Malaysians are indirect and non-confrontational in expressing their personal opinions, especially towards others and this "attitude" caused difficulties in obtaining solutions for problems because "they either be positive or impartial towards the issue at hand" Tahir and Ismail [18]. Furthermore, Zabid and Ling [19] reported that foreigners perceive Malaysians as shy and passive, and added that these caused poor communication skills among the latter, especially students. Indirectness and non-confrontationalism could be variants of the introvert category within the Big Five model; however, it is unclear whether Malaysian extroverts also behave similarly. Asma [20] and Zabid and Ling [19] pointed out that this is a "face saving" mechanism (e.g., avoiding embarrassments), which suggests that the abovementioned behavior may be culture-specific, regardless of personality. Consequently, this might have led to a culturally-specific form of shyness, or timidity. Therefore the understanding, prediction and detection of such emotions may be flawed – one of the reasons that motivate the efforts to identify the patterns of culture-specific emotions and to provide an empirical base to reject the one-size-fits-all approach in emotion modelling in learning.

4. HYPOTHESES

i. There are significant differences in patterns of specific emotions (e.g., colourings of shyness, passiveness, specific form of frustration, masking) among the different races of Malaysian learners.

ii. A culture-specific model of emotion contributes to an improved emotion recognition rate when detecting in-group learners emotions compared to out-group learners emotions, out-ruling the one-size-fits-all approach.

5. METHODOLOGY

Identifying the discriminative markers of culture specific emotions implicitly demands a twofold effort; first, a carefully designed stimuli for data collection purposes and analysis strategy. Secondly, the application of robust pattern recognition techniques to identify significant markers of culture-specific emotion towards a culture-sensitive emotion recognition model. We will draw upon examples from the localized context of Malaysian learners, particularly patterns that indicate culturally specific form of shyness and timidity.

5.1 Phase 1

Stimuli and Data Collection

A group of 30 - 40 subjects comprising of local learners, will be students of University Sains Malaysia (USM). Demographic details (sex, age, and ethnicity) of all participants will be collected prior to the experiment. All participation is to be on a voluntary basis.

At Phase 1, the subjects will be given a set of questionnaires to measure the personality traits through personality questionnaire NEO-PI-R [21, 22] which was adapted and used in a previous work of Ahmad [23]. A self-report of the questionnaires given will be collected.

The stimuli used to simulate the subjects for feature extraction and data collection has not been finalized. However the author is considering to adapt the Wizard of Oz (WoZ) method [24].

This method will be used as a stimuli where subjects will be made believe they are interacting with the real e-tutor in a learning platform. The learners will be asked to interact with the e-tutor in a learning environment with aim to capture the emotions expressed by the learner during a learning session

The "wizard" will create interactions that will induce targeted emotions (e.g., colourings of shyness) from the subjects. For example, the "wizard" would praise the subject in front of fellow participants, as praise induces shyness among Asians [25]. Another example would be to ask subjects to speak out (e.g., give opinion) in front of the class in the local leaners second language – English. In an experiment conducted by Salleh et al. [17] with adult learners, showed that majority of the subjects identified themselves as being shy and afraid to use the English language especially in presence of others. The "wizard" could also create a situation where subjects are asked for opinion (few actors could be fixed as subject) and when the participating student voice out his/her opinion, the actors could show disagreement. This scenario might induce the subject to display cues indicating shyness as Asians are afraid of voicing out their real opinion on certain issues (e.g., politics) fear of contradicting views with the majority of people around them [25].

This experiment is intended to be conducted as a group rather than one-to-one as most likely subjects will tend to display shyness and mask their real emotions with the presence of others. Study by Bahiyah [25] showed that most Malaysian learners prefer to 'hide' in silence rather than participate in on-going face-to-face oral interaction among friends, between students, lecturers and strangers.

The emotions expressed by the subjects through facial expression, vocal and gesture during the interaction will be recorded.

The verbal (linguistic) and nonverbal emotion data (facial and task-based features) will be collected through the recordings.

Task-based features are features related to the tutorial, such as difficulty of question, level of question, time taken to answer etc. Analyses on the verbal and task-based features extracted from the dataset in order to investigate what types of qualitative and affective aspects of social interaction are relevant in determining culturally related emotion (e.g., colourings of shyness; passiveness, form of frustration, masking). Specifically, this is to identify the relevant nonverbal multimodal cues (such as facial expressions, voice and gestures) that correlate with qualitative and affective aspects of behavior.

A pilot experiment with a small group of subjects will be conducted to ensure the effectiveness of the stimuli. Findings will be compared between in-group learners and out-group learners to determine statistically significant differences in culture-sensitive emotional patterns.

5.2 Phase 2

Annotation and Labeling

Several independent annotators will be labelling the videos of learners using the stimuli. Annotation conducted will be both web-based which consist of 25 annotators and 25 non-expert annotators among Malaysians and non-Malaysians annotators. The labels of emotions are based on primary multimodal cues that comprises facial, gesture, vocal, dialogue and task-based features. Kappa inter-annotator agreement computation on the labelled emotion category will be carried out to analyse the agreements among annotators. The output of this phase are emotion datasets that are labelled.

5.3 Phase 3

Feature Extraction, Training and Testing

Based on the annotated datasets, standard classification techniques in which several classifier schemes will be utilized with the intention to determine the best performance. Cross validation technique will be used for all the classification tasks to automatically assess culturally related qualitative and affective aspects of the emotional behavior.

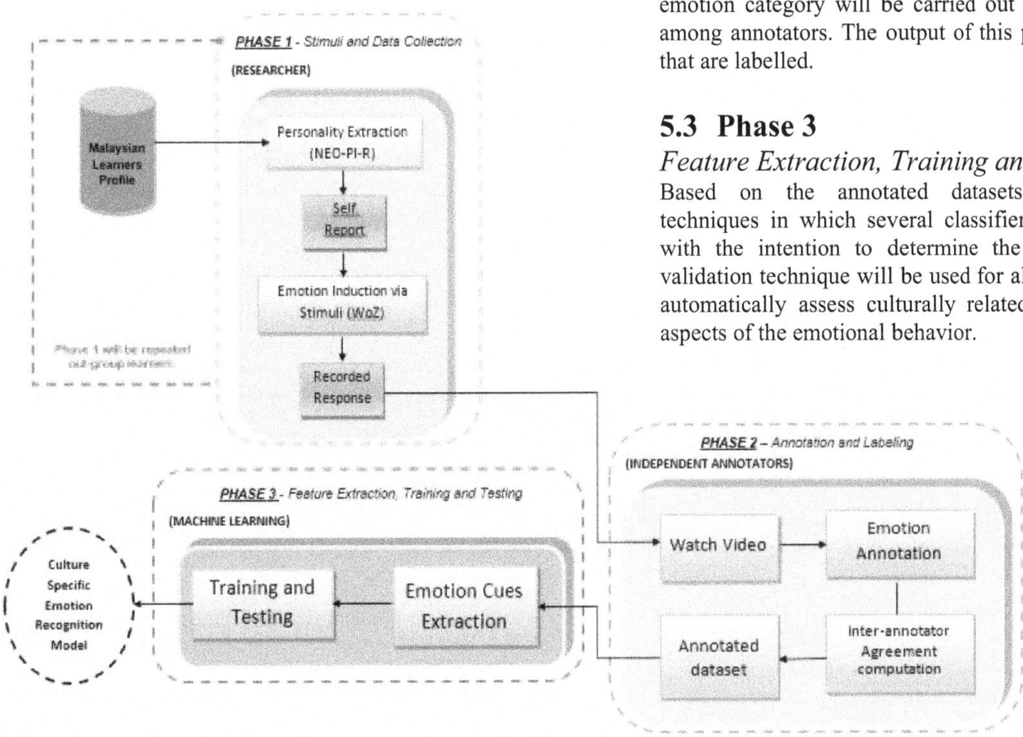

Figure 1. High level framework of the culture-specific emotion recognition.

Feature extraction process is carried out to find the significant predictors of culture-specific emotion. The outcome of this process are datasets with a reduced dimensionality space. A number of prominent features for classification in distinguishing culture-specific and non-culture-specific emotions will be selected.

Training and testing will be carried out using machine learning approach – loosely following the methods in the previous work of Lutfi [26] and Mokhtar [27]. Statistical Analysis will be carried out to investigate the significance of the feature selections.

Comparisons will be done to search for a predictive pattern in emotion recognition between in-group learners and out-group learners. The output of the model will be incorporated with a virtual tutor and tested with USM students.

The flow of the proposed method is illustrated in Figure 1.

6. CONCLUSION

Researches in the field of HCI has shown that adding emotions in artificial agents could mitigate user frustration and ultimately increase user satisfaction towards the agent. However, by modelling and incorporating a culture-sensitive emotion detection (and ultimately a localized response model, or expression model) into artificial agents, users trust and acceptance towards the agent could be increased as well. This would especially benefit the use of artificial agents in persuasion related domains, such as in learning (artificial tutors).

This research area is a rare and new field that has not been explored extensively in our country. In this study, we attempt to address this challenge by using multimodal cues such as facial expressions and gestures in a robust machine learning approach to identify the patterns of emotion markers that indicates colorings of culture-sensitive emotion for example, shyness and timidity in a Malaysian context. This effort is towards the bigger aim of achieving an emotion recognition model that would underlie artificial agents to be more socially intelligent in facilitating human-computer interaction in learning.

7. ACKNOWLEDGMENTS

The author would like to thank Universiti Sains Malaysia (USM) for the funding of this work from the grant no. 304/PKOMP/6312153. The author also would like to acknowledge and convey special thanks to her advisor Dr. Syaheerah Lebai Lutfi her continuous support and guidance.

8. REFERENCES

[1] Hamid, B. A. (2001). Malu. *Shyness and Shyness Behaviour in the English Language Classroom: Who, What, Where, When, How and Why. The English Teacher, 21.*

[2] Dautenhahn, K. (2004). Socially intelligent agents in human primate culture. *In Payr, S. and Trappl, R., editors, Agent Culture: Human Agent Interaction in a Multicultural World,* pages 45–71. Lawrence Erlbaum Associates, Mahwah, New Jersey.

[3] Lisetti, C., Nasoz, F., LeRouge, C., Ozyer, O., and Alvarez, K. (2003). Developing multimodal intelligent affective interfaces for tele-home health care. *Int. J. Hum. Comput. Stud.,* 59(2003):245–225.

[4] Atkinson, R., Foshee, C., Harrison, C., Lin, L., Joseph, S., & Christopherson, R. (2009). Does the type and degree of animation present in a visual representation accompanying narration in a multimedia environment impact learning? *In World Conference on Educational Multimedia, Hypermedia and Telecommunications* (Vol. 2009, No. 1, pp. 726-734).

[5] Moreno, R. (2010). Cognitive load theory: More food for thought. *Instructional Science, 38*(2), 135-141.

[6] Cole, J., Lloyd, J. W., & Ng, K. S. (2003). Symbolic learning for adaptive agents. *In Proceedings of the Annual Partner Conference, Smart Internet Technology Cooperative Research Centre*

[7] Wang, H., Chignell, M., & Ishizuka, M. (2006, March). Empathic tutoring software agents using real time eye tracking. *In Proceedings of the 2006 symposium on Eye tracking research & applications* (pp. 7378). ACM.

[8] Acosta, J. C. (2009). Using emotion to gain rapport in a spoken dialog system. *In Proceedings of Human Language Technologies: The 2009 Annual Conference of the North American Chapter of the Association for Computational Linguistics, Companion Volume: Student Research Workshop and Doctoral Consortium* (pp. 4954).Association for Computational Linguistics.

[9] D'Mello, S. K. & Graesser, A. C. (2012). AutoTutor and Affective AutoTutor: Learning by Talking with Cognitively and Emotionally Intelligent Computers that Talk Back, *ACM Transactions on Interactive Intelligent Systems*, 2(4), 23:223:39.

[10] Sabourin, J., Rowe, J. P., Mott, B. W., & Lester, J. C. (2011, January). When off task is on task:The affective role of off task behavior in narrative centered learning environments. *In Artificial Intelligence in Education* (pp. 534536). Springer Berlin Heidelberg.

[11] ForbesRiley, K., & Litman, D. (2011). Benefits and challenges of real time uncertainty detection and adaptation in a spoken dialogue computer tutor. *Speech Communication*, 53(9), 11151136.

[12] Matsumoto, D, Juang, L. (1991) Cultural Influences –on Facial Expressions of Emotion. Cross Cultural Research on the Emotions – *The Southern Communication Journal*

[13] Rossen, B; Lok, B; Johnsen, K; Lind, S & Eladisma, A (2008) Virtual Humans Elicit Skin Tone Bias Consistent with Real World Skin Tone Biases.

[14] Lee, E. J., & Nass, C. (2002). Experimental Tests of Normative Group Influence and Representation Effects in Computer - Mediated Communication. *Human Communication Research*, 28(3), 349381

[15] Lutfi, S. L., Montero, J. M., Ainon, R. N., Don, Z. M. (2008). eXTRA: A Culturally Enriched Malay Text to Speech System. *Proc. of AISB 2008 Symposium on Affective Language in Human and Machine* Vol 2, pp. 7783, (ISBN 1 902956 61 3).

[16] Chuah, S. H. (2010). *Teaching East-Asian Students: Some Observations.* Retrieved September 10, 2015. http://www.economicsnetwork.ac.uk/showcase/chuah_international

[17] Salleh, B. M., Esa, A., Selamat, A., Othman, H., Sulaiman, A., & Suhaimy, K. A. (2010). Computer-mediated communication as a tool for improving the English language among adult learners in TVET programme.

[18] Tahir, A. H. M, Ismail, M. (2007). Cross Cultural Challenges and Adjustments of Expatriates: A Case Study in Malaysia. Alternatives: *Turkish Journal of International Relations*, Vol. 6, No.3 &4, Fall & Winter 2007

[19] Zabid, A. M., & Ling, C. N. (2010). Malaysian employer perceptions about local and foreign MBA graduates. *Journal of Education for Business*, 79(2), 111117.

[20] Asma, A. (2001). Understanding the Malaysian workforce: Guidelines for managers. Malaysian Institute of Management. Malaysia.

[21] Costa, P. T., Jr., & McCrae, R. R. (1992). Revised NEO Personality Inventory (NEO-PI–R)

[22] Dahlbäck, N., Jönsson, A. & Ahrenberg, L.: Wizard of Oz Studies – Why and How. *Proceedings of Intelligent User Interfaces* (1993) 193-200

[23] Dahlbäck, N., Jönsson, A. & Ahrenberg, L.: Wizard of Oz Studies – Why and How. Proceedings of Intelligent User Interfaces (1993) 193-200

[24] Ahmad, Z. (2015) Prediction Models of extraversion and neuroticism of Malaysian facebook users. *Unpublished master's thesis*, University Sains Malaysia.

[25] Bahiyah, A. H. (1992). Malu. Shyness and Shyness Behaviour in the English Language Classroom. *The English Teacher,* 21, 97-107.

[26] Lutfi, S. L., Fernández-Martínez, F., Lucas-Cuesta, J. M., Lopez-Lebon, L., & Montero, J. M. (2013). A satisfaction-based model for affect recognition from conversational features in spoken dialog systems. *Speech Communication*, 55(7), 825-840.

[27] Mokhtar, N. S. (2015) A Computational Model of Affect Detection in Learning. *Unpublished master's thesis,* University Sains Malaysia.

Record, Transform & Reproduce Social Encounters in Immersive VR - An Iterative Approach

Jan Kolkmeier
University of Twente
P.O. Box 217, 7500 AE, Enschede, The Netherlands
j.kolkmeier@utwente.nl

ABSTRACT

Immersive Virtual Reality Environments that can be accessed through multimodal natural interfaces will bring new affordances to mediated interaction with virtual embodied agents and avatars. Such interfaces will measure, amongst others, users' poses and motion which can be copied to an embodied avatar representation of the user that is situated in a virtual or augmented reality space shared with autonomous virtual agents and human controlled or semi-autonomous avatars. Designers of such environments will be challenged to facilitate believable social interactions by creating agents or semi-autonomous avatars that can respond meaningfully to users' natural behaviors, as captured by these interfaces. In our future research, we aim to realize such interactions to create rich social encounters in immersive Virtual Reality. In this current work, we present the approach we envisage to analyze and learn agent behavior from human-agent interaction in an iterative fashion. We specifically look at small-scale, 'regulative' nonverbal behaviors. Agents inform their behavior on previous observations, observing responses that these behaviors elicit in new users, thus iteratively generating corpora of short, situated human-agent interaction sequences that are to be analyzed, annotated and processed to generate socially intelligent agent behavior. Some choices and challenges of this approach are discussed.

Categories and Subject Descriptors

H.5.1 [**Multimedia Information Systems**]: Artificial, augmented, and virtual realities.

Keywords

Non-verbal Behaviors; Multimodal Interactive Systems; Virtual Reality

1. INTRODUCTION

In the Smart Social Systems and Spaces for Living Well project (S4Living, [1]), we are interested in employing smart mixed and virtual reality environments to improve the lifestyle of people. In such environments, artificial agents, avatars and their hybrids [6] could facilitate social encounters with remote visitors, as simulated companions or as intelligent actors in serious games as part of virtual reality training. Moreover, through natural, multimodal interfaces, users can be present in shared virtual spaces to collaborate with other remotely connected users.

The effectiveness of agents and avatars employed in such environments depends on more than their capabilities to engage in and facilitate conversation. They also need to understand and employ non-verbal behaviors during social interaction, such as facial expressions, gaze, gestures, posture and proxemics, but also touch and prosodics of speech. These behaviors can be employed to signal the agents' attention and intentions, to express agents' emotions and to affect how the agents' personalities are perceived - and of course, if the agent acts as an avatar, to extend these states and attributes from their controller to other agents and avatars.

How elaborate and interactive the implementations of such behaviors for artificial agents need to be depends on the affordances of the user interface through which one interacts with these agents. To illustrate this, consider a serious game where the user controls a virtual policeman that has to interrogate a virtual agent (VA) that acts as a suspect in a crime. The objective of the game is to teach the user that different non-verbal behaviors can be used to affect interpersonal stances between suspect and interrogator, which can be used as part of the interrogation strategy[1]. Now, if the user presses the 'intimidate'-key, the user's avatar may perform an 'intimidating' animation, signalizing a change in stance. This animation is metaphoric for a dominant stance. The keystroke does not allow the user to add or change qualities of this action. For the suspect agent to respond, only a single, predetermined animation that signals 'being intimidated' suffices and the interaction unfolding on the screen is understood by the user. We find that non-verbal behaviors of other agents need to respond appropriately to the capabilities that the interface translates to the user's avatar on the screen. In this case, they need to respond appropriately to the predetermined animation triggered by a keystroke.

In immersive Virtual Reality Environments (iVREs) however, the user is situated in a virtual space shared equally with those agents, taking a true first-person perspective. One ambition of iVR is the attempt to simulate reality [7]. To this end, natural interfaces such as those using full-body tracking will increase the user's capabilities to manipulate the environment and express him- or herself in a natural fashion using multiple channels of communication. Given the perspective, actions directed towards virtual interaction partners are more immediate, and VAs have higher immediacy when directing their actions towards the user. With sensors that can accurately estimate behavioral cues such as pose, gaze, or proxemics, there is

[1]This scenario serves as an example and is taken from a related project. It is not (yet) a definitive scenario in our own work.

ICMI '15, November 09-13, 2015, Seattle, W A, USA
 ISBN 978-1-4503-3912-4/15/11...$15.00.
DOI: http://dx.doi.org/10.1145/2818346.2823314

Figure 1: Two virtual agents manipulating their interpersonal distance and gaze behaviors in our previous study in iVR.

an opportunity to have agents interactively respond to these cues using their own channels of communication.

If the interrogation game was realized in iVR, a user should be able to take an intimidating pose by changing his physical pose only, not needing to make this explicit otherwise. The virtual suspect should respond by adjusting his or her pose appropriately, not by playing an animation metaphoric for 'being intimidated'. Effects of nuances in the user's behavior must be preserved. If a user modulates his interpersonal gaze while taking the intimidating pose, the agents gaze behavior and possible behaviors in other channels should adjust accordingly, for example to seek or avoid eye-contact.

The challenge is to design intelligent agents that can meaningfully employ such multimodal behaviors, that are interactive and continuous rather than metaphoric and static. To realize interaction, we must be aware what channels we can use in agent behavior, the channels used by users to response to such behavior, and their relationship. To some extend, we have addressed this in our previous work, which we present in the following section.

2. PREVIOUS WORK

In our previous work we examined the effects and relationships of agent behavior manipulations on avatar perception and behavioral responses of users. In [4], we situated virtual humanoid agents in augmented reality. Agents could exhibit social touch through the congruent visual and haptic cues of the VA touching the user's arm and the actuation of a haptic display on the user's arm. In a collaborative setting, touching agents were rated higher on affective attributes than non-touching agents. In our study in iVR [5], we examined the single and joint effects of gaze and proxemic behaviors during social interaction. Gaze and proxemic behaviors of two virtual humanoid agents (see Figure 1) were manipulated dynamically in terms of the perceived intimacy they elicit. Participants' gaze and proxemic responses were measured on-line. Participants showed strongest gaze and proxemic responses when agents manipulated both proxemic and gaze manipulations at the same time. More intimate manipulations such as standing closer and seeking more mutual gaze elicited gaze aversion and increase of personal distance from the participants. Less intimate manipulations such as increasing distance and averting gaze elicited more mutual gaze and reduction of personal distance from the participants. Agents that only manipulated gaze elicited weaker responses compared to agents that only manipulated proxemics. Agents with more intimate behaviors were rated higher in intimacy-related attributes, but lower on those related to warmth and trustworthiness.

Concluding from this previous work, there exists cross-channel interaction between agent and user behaviors in mixed and virtual reality settings, and these behaviors affect how agents' personalities are perceived. To build on this, our future research could contribute by disentangling this relationship even further for multiple modalities to allow agents to formulate and realize responses to detected cues in the appropriate channels during human-agent interaction. In the following section, we outline the envisaged method to approach our research.

3. MULTIMODAL SOCIAL INTERACTION ANALYSIS

We are interested in creating virtual agents and avatars that regulate non-verbal behaviors in an interactive fashion during social encounters in iVREs. With the increased equality of users' and agents' capabilities in such environments, agents could learn directly from the behaviors expressed by human users. The envisaged approach is to reproduce previously observed human behavior towards new users in an iVRE, and then learn from the response behaviors by these new users. Contingencies of these responses can further be examined by procedurally creating variations of behaviors as well as by comparing different responses between users.

3.1 Recording & Reproducing

'Equality of capabilities' means that whatever a user can do in VR, the agent can do as well. Given our approach of agents reproducing observed behaviors, we formulate an 'equality requirement', satisfied only by those communication channels in which users' activities can be recorded and later reproduced in VAs without significant loss in quality of the signal. Two examples of technologies that could satisfy the equality requirement for some modalities are motion capture and facial expression recognition to animate pose and facial expressions in the agent. Combinations of haptic interfaces and displays may also qualify here, measuring and displaying aspects of social touch. Emotions detected in speech prosody could be reproduced in agents speech using speech synthesizers.

3.2 Considered Behaviors & Cues

Not all conceivable behaviors may be meaningfully captured and reproduced in our approach. Recordings of highly contextual behaviors such as manipulating objects, pointing, miming or even laughing may not be suitable for reproduction unless we are also able to consistently reproduce the relevant context. Behaviors that we expect to be feasible and meaningful to reproduce and learn from are small-scale behaviors that are continuously and subconsciously regulated by humans. Think of regulation of interpersonal distance and gaze, posture, foot placement or the harmonic properties in the overall kinetic channels such as shakiness or calmness.

Detecting these behaviors is challenging. It is necessary to constrain this problem to a given context. For example, if we aim to realize an agent such as the virtual suspect from the example in the introduction, we may want to inform our method based on theories that describe the nonverbal cues during interrogation situations. For example, reducing interpersonal distance while engaging in eye-contact may be labeled as aggressive or competing user behavior when interrogating a virtual suspect agent.

3.3 Context & Scenario

As mentioned above, constraining the context of the interaction is crucial in managing the complexity of the problem. As of yet, we have not decided on a particular context or scenario for our research or for the application in which we want to demonstrate our results.

For the time being, the police interrogation scenario with the virtual suspect agent serves as our use-case. However, we aim keep the generalization of the method in mind, so that it is not confined to a solution for a single scenario.

3.4 Iterative Corpus Creation

To create a corpus that is suitable for learning, data needs to be collected where interaction between the considered behaviors can be observed. The classical virtual reality approach to examining interaction is to create a controlled environment with a virtual agent whose behavior is the same towards each participant in a given condition. This way, the VAs function as standardized interaction partners that make it possible to observe more than one response to the exact same behavior trigger.

The specified 'equality requirement' allows us to extend on this method as we may include observed responses in our agent's repertoire of behavior triggers. Again, this is only sensible for those behaviors that can be reproduced meaningfully without also reproducing the entire context of the original recording. One consequence of this approach is that we need to treat these regulative behaviors as equal. That is, an observed response behavior is from the same set of classes as the behavior that triggered this observed behavior. For example, mirroring [3] would translate to both the trigger and the response behavior being of the same class. If we observe a behavior response, we need to decide whether it belongs to an existing class, or whether we need to assign a new class to it, and then add it to the agent's repertoire for the next iteration of data collection.

Data collection is complete when we have a broad enough repertoire of behavior classes, and when we observed sufficient samples of responses to (each of) these behaviors.

3.5 Personality

We may expect variance in the responses to behaviors. One approach to explain this variance is to consider more contextual information. For the virtual suspect agent, a measure of the user's personality may be a good predictor of the user's response. For example, introvert users may respond to aggressive behavioral cues with submissive behavior, whereas extrovert users may respond with aggressive behavior. Such information may further be used to eventually let agents portray a given personality by learning responses from users with that personality.

3.6 Learning to Respond

For our agent to be able to respond dynamically to a user's behavior regulation, we need to train a classifier that separates the classes of known behaviors. Then it must classify observed user behavior online. If a known behavior is detected, the agent's response is a realization of a behavior class with the highest response probability given the contextual information such as the personality that the agent portrays.

3.7 Cross Modality

So far, we have treated behavior as a holistic, single signal. In practice, we may expect the considered behaviors to be multimodal. Some cues might only be mediated through a single channel, whereas others are only meaningful when all channels are considered at the same time. Further, as we have found in our previous work, regulating behaviors do not need to be symmetric across channels, but can also be cross channel. For example, a reduction in interpersonal distance may cause a regulating response in gaze behavior, such as averted gaze. This concept is to be integrated more carefully into our approach, as it will certainly inform architectural and methodological choices.

4. CHALLENGES

One fundamental challenge is to determine, once we have selected a context for our study, whether or not the relevant behaviors can be captured and preserved in the reproduction. Subsequently, can we conceive a scenario for data collection in which triggers elicit meaningful response behaviors reliably, rather than just noise.

Another challenge is the annotation of behavior segments. During interaction, the start and end of a segment needs to be determined. Behaviors from different channels related to the same action may have different starting and ending times. Then, behavior segments between interaction partners need to be related to each other to determine which segment is a response to a given earlier event. This does not only require to setup labeling guidelines for annotators, but also the integration (and possibly extension) of annotation tools into the process.

In our previous work, we manipulated the behavior of agents with an explicit goal in mind, such as being perceived as more intimate. In the proposed approach however, goals or intentions behind observed (and then reproduced) behavior segments may not be known. We therefore need to evaluate and annotate these segments. Some labels, such as those related to the current task, may be automatically computed on-line. Other labels, such as those related to the internal, emotional or cognitive state of the user, require rigorous manual annotation or off-line computation.

For meaningful reproduction, we may require further transformation of the observed data. As [8] points out, the intrinsic value of some measures such as the absolute gaze direction of a users may be limited. In terms of gaze behavior, the object that the user is looking at or the angle that the user's gaze is averted from the face of an agent may be more valuable than the absolute gaze direction.

There are also several technical challenges. The amount of data generated by capturing high-dimensional motion captures at high frame-rates must be stored and retrieved. Others even have suggested (soft) real time requirements for transmitting and reproducing activities in such applications [6].

5. RESEARCH PLAN

To develop our approach further, we focus on kinetic channels, such as gaze and pose. Intensive literature reviews on previous, related approaches and specifically on the machine learning aspects are still required.

Besides the literature study, in our first year we aim for the realization of a demonstrator that provides real-time mimicry agent, much as in [2]. Such a study would give insight to the feasibility of several aspects of our approach, such as the quality to be expected from reproducing behaviors, and a first insight to the technical challenges. Follow up studies would focus on selecting a context and on labeling processes of observations inside that context.

During the second year, we plan to employ the mimicry setup in a specific scenario. Recordings are to be annotated, to create a first corpus. Next we implement capabilities to retrieve earlier observations at runtime, to have users in a second iteration interact with agents that reproduce behaviors of other (previous) users. Besides growing our corpus, studies on including contextual information such as 'personality' could be used to evaluate the success of the approach. One research question could be to what extend we can have agents portray a given personality by selecting responses by previous users with that personality.

During the third year, we plan to implement a system that can automatically select and realize appropriate responses in a given context. For evaluation, we test again whether the chosen personality is perceived by the user - now with the agent acting autonomously.

From there, possible future studies could address the possibilities of hybrid avatar/agent approaches, specifically extending the learning and generation of behaviors from observations, the transformation of observations to non-human agents.

6. CONCLUSIONS

Natural interfaces in iVR bring new affordances and opportunities to social interaction with virtual agents and avatars. Our research aims to answer these affordances by having agents learn directly from user activity.

We contribute an extension of the classical virtual reality method of controlled behavior analysis by exploiting the possibility of having equal communication capabilities that allow recording and reproduction of multimodal behaviors by the artificial agents. Through controlled reproduction towards multiple other users, corpora of elicited responses are to be created iteratively and are to be used for teaching agents to predict and respond to future cues. Several challenges of this approach have been highlighted and need to be addressed in future research. An overall proposed plan has been presented.

7. REFERENCES

[1] 3TU. 2015. Smart Social Systems and Spaces for Living Well. (30 7 2015). http://www.3tu.nl/ht/en/research/research-programme/s4living/.

[2] Jeremy N Bailenson, Nick Yee, Kayur Patel, and Andrew C Beall. 2008. Detecting digital chameleons. *Comput. Human Behav.* 24, 1 (Jan. 2008), 66–87. DOI: http://dx.doi.org/10.1016/j.chb.2007.01.015

[3] Tanya L Chartrand and John A Bargh. 1999. The chameleon effect: the perception–behavior link and social interaction. *J. Pers. Soc. Psychol.* 76, 6 (1999), 893.

[4] Gijs Huisman, Jan Kolkmeier, and Dirk Heylen. 2014. With Us or Against Us: Simulated Social Touch by Virtual Agents in a Cooperative or Competitive Setting. In *Intell. Virtual Agents*. Springer, 204–213.

[5] Jan Kolkmeier. 2015. *Intimacy is Induced and Regulated Through Proxemic & Gaze Behaviour - A Study in Immersive Virtual Reality*. Master thesis. University of Twente.

[6] Daniel Roth, Marc E Latoschik, Kai Vogeley, and Gary Bente. 2015. Hybrid Avatar-Agent Technology - A Conceptual Step Towards Mediated "Social" Virtual Reality and its Respective Challenges. *i-com* 14, 2 (2015), 107–114.

[7] Mel Slater. 2014. Grand Challenges in Virtual Environments. *Front. Robot. AI* 1, May (2014), 1–4. DOI: http://dx.doi.org/10.3389/frobt.2014.00003

[8] William Steptoe and Anthony Steed. 2012. Multimodal Data Capture and Analysis of Interaction in Immersive Collaborative Virtual Environments. *Presence-Teleoperators Virtual Environ.* 21, 4 (2012), 388–405. DOI: http://dx.doi.org/10.1162/PRES_a_00123

Multimodal Affect Detection in the Wild: Accuracy, Availability, and Generalizability

Nigel Bosch
University of Notre Dame
384 Fitzpatrick Hall,
Notre Dame, IN 46556, USA
pbosch1@nd.edu

ABSTRACT

Affect detection is an important component of computerized learning environments that adapt the interface and materials to students' affect. This paper proposes a plan for developing and testing multimodal affect detectors that generalize across differences in data that are likely to occur in practical applications (e.g., time, demographic variables). Facial features and interaction log features are considered as modalities for affect detection in this scenario, each with their own advantages. Results are presented for completed work evaluating the accuracy of individual modality face- and interaction- based detectors, accuracy and availability of a multimodal combination of these modalities, and initial steps toward generalization of face-based detectors. Additional data collection needed for cross-culture generalization testing is also completed. Challenges and possible solutions for proposed cross-cultural generalization testing of multimodal detectors are also discussed.

Author Keywords

Affect detection; detector generalization; classroom data; in the wild.

ACM Classification Keywords

H.5.m. Information interfaces and presentation (e.g., HCI): Miscellaneous.

INTRODUCTION

Many techniques have been employed to improve learning in computerized education, including methods from the field of human-computer interaction. Affect sensitivity in interfaces is one such technique and has been shown to be useful for improving learning [11]. There are many ways in which an interface can leverage affect sensitivity for increasing learning. For example, bored and disengaged students may be directed to new learning tasks to help them re-engage, while students who are frequently frustrated due to excessively difficult tasks might be presented with material more appropriate to their knowledge levels. Affect detection is a key component of such affect-sensitive systems, because responding to affect requires accurate detection of affect.

The present focus is on multimodal affect detection, so unimodal detection will not be considered in detail. D'Mello and Kory [12] recently provided a review and meta-analysis of 90 multimodal affect detection systems. Their review revealed that two of the most common modalities for affect detection were facial features and audio features, which were used in 76.7% (face) and 82.2% (audio) of surveyed studies. Audiovisual affect detection is clearly the most prominent multimodal fusion approach. However, audio features are limited to interfaces that support spoken interaction.

The current paper proposes taking a somewhat different approach by employing a fusion of facial features and interaction log features, two potentially complementary modalities that have only rarely been considered together. The proposed affect detectors are designed to operate in computer-enabled classrooms, a context that is rife with noisy and missing data, thereby providing additional challenges for multimodal affect detection. Furthermore, the current paper considers challenges and solutions for cross-culture generalization of detectors, which may be mitigated in part by using interaction features. To that end we primarily consider face- and interaction- based affect detection approaches in educational contexts as related work, along with detector generalizability work.

BACKGROUND AND RELATED WORK

Affect detection from facial features and interaction log data has been studied deeply in recent years [1,12]. In this section we briefly review some of the research related to individual face- and interaction- based affect detection, followed by multimodal and generalization work.

Unimodal Affect Detection

Face-based affect detection has been studied in a variety of learning contexts in recent years. For example, Whitehill et al. [18] discriminated four levels of engagement at a fine-grained level in students as they used cognitive skills training software. Grafsgaard et al. [6] used facial features to detect a variety of affect-related variables such as perceived temporal demand (hurriedness), performance,

ICMI '15, November 09-13, 2015, Seattle, WA, USA
© 2015 ACM. ISBN 978-1-4503-3912-4/15/11…$15.00
DOI: http://dx.doi.org/10.1145/2818346.2823316

and frustration. A variety of computer vision methods have been used for affect detection, such as texture, shape, and motion features extracted from faces. A full review of methods is beyond the scope of this paper, but recent review articles cover it in detail (e.g., [12]).

Interaction-based affect detection has been increasingly studied over the last decade [1,14]. Unlike physical sensor-based detectors, which rely upon the physical reactions of the student, these detectors infer affective states from students' interactions with computerized learning systems. Their unobtrusive and cost-efficient nature also makes it feasible to apply interaction-based detectors at scale, leading to a growing field of research regarding discovery with models.

Multimodal Affect Detection

As noted above, there have been a large number of studies that have considered face- and interaction- features independently. However, multimodal combinations of these features are few and far between. These studies are reviewed below, with a special emphasis on affect detection in learning environments – the context of the present work.

In one of the first such studies, Kapoor et al. [9] used multimodal techniques with face- and posture- based features collected from naturalistic data to create a detector of student interest. Facial features such as detected head nods, shakes, and smiles were combined with posture features gathered from a pressure-sensitive chair and interaction log features from the learning environment. They classified interest/disinterest with 87% accuracy (chance being 52%).

More recently, Grafsgaard et al. [7] developed multimodal affect detectors that utilized both facial features and student interaction features (as well as tutor-student dialog) from a dialog-based computerized learning environment designed to teach Java computer programming. They predicted engagement, frustration, and learning (all self-reported by the students) using linear regression with leave-one-student-out cross validation. A combination of facial features and interaction features predicted engagement (R^2 = .112) and frustration (R^2 = .134) more accurately than unimodal features (best R^2 = .048 and -.010 respectively for engagement and frustration). Adding tutor-student dialogue features improved results even further, to R^2 = .282 and R^2 = .520 respectively. This shows the potential for a fusion of features to outperform individual modalities. However, affect detection was done at a course-grained level across an entire learning session, which limits its applicability to drive real-time interventions.

Affect Detector Generalization

The unimodal and multimodal detectors previously discussed have been demonstrated in a variety of contexts and are often cross validated at the student level, demonstrating generalization to new students within the same population. In this section selected works that demonstrate generalizability across time or demographic variables are also discussed.

Prior work has demonstrated cross-corpus generalization of affect detection in some contexts, especially using audio features (e.g., [15,17]). Audio, though useful for affect detection, is not considered in the current research. The generalizability of speech-based affect detection across languages is an important but large goal that is beyond the scope of the current project.

Interaction data from log-files have shown promise for building affect detectors that generalize across time. Pardos et al. [14] used interaction data collected over the span of a few days in 2010 to build affect detectors. These detectors were then applied to a separate, previously collected dataset from two school years (Fall 2004-Spring 2006). The detectors' predictions were correlated with students' scores on a standardized test. Several of these correlations demonstrated the consistency of detectors across two school years. Predicted boredom ($r = -.119, p < .01$ for year 1; $r = -.280, p < .01$ for year 2), confusion ($r = -.165, p < .01$; $r = -.089, p < .05$), and gaming the system ($r = -.431, p < .01$; $r = -.301, p < .01$) negatively correlated with test score in both school years, while engaged concentration ($r = .449, p < .01$; $r = .258, p < .01$) positively correlated in both years. However, they did not directly test cross-year generalization by building detectors on one year of data and testing on the other.

The previously discussed face-based engagement detection work by Whitehill et al. (see above) also investigated generalization of engagement detection across ethnicity in a small separate sample. Their training set consisted of 26 black students from a Historically Black College/University (HBCU) while the generalization testing set consisted of 8 Caucasian-Americans and Asian-Americans. Their best result for cross-ethnicity testing was AUC = .691, versus .729 for training/testing on the same sample. Thus they demonstrated above-chance detection accuracy across ethnicity, with a slight reduction in accuracy. However, their testing set was small, only considered engagement, and tested only one direction of generalization (Caucasian and Asian → Black).

PROPOSED RESEARCH

The literature review revealed a variety of affect detection methods and some work that has been done to investigate issues of generalization for affect detectors. In this doctoral consortium paper we propose a series of studies and contributions intended to develop answers to some remaining key research questions related to multimodal methods for cross-population affect detection in the wild. Each of these questions is partially addressed in the current paper, though much work remains to be done.

First, there are questions of the feasibility of affect detection in the wild, specifically for educational technology in a computer-enabled classroom. Factors such as conversation, movement, posture, and lighting occur in classroom environments, which cannot be as easily controlled as laboratory contexts. These factors have undesirable effects on affect detection (e.g., missing or noisy data for face-based affect detection). In the proposed research we consider facial features and interaction log data (e.g., clicks, response times) as two modalities for affect detection in this context, each with their own advantages.

Second, it is important to explore the potential benefits of multimodal techniques for improving affect detection in a computer-enabled classroom context. Facial features capture expressions of affective states at brief time scales compared to interaction features, while interaction data may be more indicative of affective states with less active facial expressions, such as boredom. Additionally, facial feature detection is highly influenced by factors such as lighting and movement, which may also cause missing data. Interaction log data on the other hand is available as long as students continue to interact with the educational interface, and may thus complement face-based affect detection in situations where facial features cannot be extracted.

Third, there are questions of generalizability for affect detection methods in computer-enabled classroom contexts. Student-independent cross-validation techniques have become commonplace in affect detection research, but there are aspects of generalization not specifically tested by student-level generalization that may be important for applying affect detection techniques in an educational interface. Additional dimensions of generalization include time (applying detectors at a different time than when they were trained), gender, ethnicity, and culture. A multimodal approach to affect detection in the wild should be explicitly tested across these dimensions if such an approach can be applied in a computer-enabled classroom context to students in a new population.

PROPOSED METHOD

We collected a dataset and employed machine learning techniques that have served to answer some (but not all) of the proposed research questions.

Current Dataset

Students played an educational physics game (see [16] for information about the game) in their school's computer-enabled classroom, while videos of their faces were recorded and their interaction (mouse and keyboard) behaviors were logged. The sample consisted of 137 8th and 9th grade students (57 male, 80 female) who were enrolled in a public school in a medium-sized city in the Southeastern U.S. There were about 20 students per class period (four periods) on four different days (55 minutes per period). For affect detection we considered data from the second and third days (roughly two hours total) when students were only playing the game and not being tested.

Students' affective states were "live" annotated during their interactions with Physics Playground using the Baker-Rodrigo Observation Method Protocol (BROMP) field observation system (see [2] for details). These observations served as ground truth labels for affect detection. Affective states of interest were boredom, confusion, delight, engaged concentration, and frustration. This list of states was selected based on previous research [10] and from observing students during the first day of data collection (these data were not used when creating detectors).

Affect Detection Method

We employed supervised machine learning to build affect detectors trained and tested on the dataset collected. Specifically, we have developed methods for face- and interaction- based detectors, multimodal fusions of these modalities, and cross-validation methods for testing some aspects of generalization.

Details of face-based detection methods (classifiers, features, etc.) are available in a recent publication [2]. In brief, facial features were extracted using FACET computer vision software for each frame of video, and aggregated across a window of time leading up to the BROMP-coded affect label. Gross body movement features were extracted from the videos using a previously validated method. A variety of classification models were evaluated by training and testing using student-independent cross-validation.

Interaction-based affect detectors were built using similar methods [8]. Features extracted from the interaction log data consisted of features specific to the learning environment, such as the number of recently occurring events in the game, as well as more general features such as variability of mouse clicks throughout time. These features were also aggregated across time leading up to the affect labels, and student-independent detectors were built.

Generalization across time (to new days and new times of day) was tested for face-based detectors (and will be for interaction-based detectors) by developing cross-validation methods that preserved student independence while training a detector on one day of data and testing it on data from a different day [3]. Similar techniques were employed for testing across time of day, gender, and ethnicity within the sample of students collected (publication currently in review). In the future a similar method will be used to test cross-cultural generalization, by training a detector on data from students in one country and testing on students from a different country.

CURRENT RESULTS

We have completed work toward answering some, but not all of the broad questions posed in the previous section. We collected a dataset in a computer-enabled classroom environment, which was then used to develop interaction- and face- based affect detectors, analyze the benefits of multimodal techniques in this context, and tested generalization of affect detectors across some of the proposed generalization dimensions. In this section we very briefly review the results obtained thus far (Table 1).

Table 1. Summary of Current Results.

	Mean AUC	Availability	Generalization Effect
Face-based	.687	65%	-2.19%
Interaction-based	.608	94%	
Multimodal	.637	98%	

Face-based Affect Detection

Area Under the ROC Curve (AUC) was used to measure classification accuracy, where chance level is .500 and perfect accuracy is 1.00. Boredom (AUC = .610), confusion (.649), delight (.867), engagement (.679), and frustration (.631) were all detected with better than chance-level accuracy [2].

Interaction-based Affect Detection

Interaction-based affect detectors were not as accurate as face-based detectors on average (.608 vs. .687), though still above chance level. Interaction-based boredom detection was slightly more accurate than face-based detection (AUC = .629), while confusion (.588), delight (.679), engagement (.586), and frustration (.559) were not as accurate [8].

Multimodal Fusion

We explored several methods for creating multimodal affect detectors with the face and interaction data, using late fusion. First, we created models using only instances where both face and interaction data were available, to provide a direct comparison of face, interaction, and multimodal techniques. Face-based affect detection was more accurate than interaction-based affect detection on average (AUC = .667 vs. .574), and multimodal fusion performed at least as well (AUC = .671) as face-based detection.

The benefit of multimodal fusion in this context was more apparent in subsequent analyses of detector availability and accuracy. Interaction log data were available in 94% of instances, while facial features were available in just 65% of instances. By training an additional classifier on the outputs of detectors from the individual modalities, we created affect detectors with average AUC = .637, close to face-based detectors (.687), notably better than interaction-based detectors (.608), and with 98% availability.

Detector Generalization

Thus far we have investigated aspects of generalization for face-based affect detection only. Average accuracy was not severely diminished by testing generalization across different dimensions. Accuracy was reduced by 1.89% when cross-validating across time of day, 1.51% across days, and 1.81% across gender, and 3.53% when testing across ethnicities.

REMAINING WORK

Results thus far suggested that multimodal affect detection was possible in a noisy computer-enabled classroom context. Face-based affect detection also appeared to generalize well across time and demographic variables tested. The remaining work will focus on generalizability aspects of multimodal affect detectors. Toward this end we have collected data in another country to enable generalization testing across populations with differing cultures. In this section we identify key cross-culture generalization challenges and propose potential solutions.

Perhaps the most well-studied challenge in cross-culture generalization is the variation in facial expression of affect between cultures. Classic studies of this problem have shown that people of one culture can recognize affect from people of another culture at above chance levels [4]. However, there is also research demonstrating a within-group advantage, i.e. people are better at recognizing the facial expressions of people from their own culture [5]. This may also indicate a within-group advantage for automatic affect detectors built with. We plan to expand face-based feature extraction methods (texture-based and motion-based features) with geometric shape-based features. We will divide features into groups based on categories, such as representation (e.g., shape-based) and area of the face (e.g., mouth), building separate models for these categories to determine which features may be most generalizable across cultures. Additionally, the interaction-based predictions may be less influenced by cultural norms, which could prove to be an added multimodal advantage.

Observing and labeling affecting states poses a related challenge when collecting data from multiple cultures. The observers should be members of the students' culture to exploit in-group recognition advantage. However, this creates a challenge because observers will differ between datasets, and may have slightly different interpretations of the labels (as they should if there are cultural differences). We will examine frequently misclassified cross-cultural instances from each affective state to determine if there are salient differences that could not only be adapted for, but also shed light on cross-cultural expressions of affect.

Another issue related to the affect labels is the fact that prior proportions of affect could be quite different between datasets collected in different cultures. Differing data distributions between training and testing sets can cause problems for machine learning methods. For example, detectors built on one dataset might be too biased toward or away from some affective states when applied to another dataset. We propose applying methods from transfer learning [13], designed to solve distribution-related issues, in order to adapt models from one culture to the other.

Future improvements to affect detection will also include information about affect developing through time. For example, long short-term memory (LSTM) recurrent neural networks have shown improved affect classification performance compared to traditional methods [19]. LSTM is capable of capturing patterns that evolve over long periods of time, which is relevant to affect detection.

CONCLUSION

Applying affect detection methods to new data collected in a different country will serve as a thorough test of multimodal face- and interaction- based affect detectors. If detectors trained on data collected in year 2013 in the Southeastern U.S. successfully detect affect at above-chance levels in data collected two or more years later in a different country, these detectors can indeed by applied to computer-enabled classroom contexts with confidence that detectors are robust to potential sources of systematic bias. The work already completed as well as the results of cross-cultural generalization testing will serve as the central theme of a PhD dissertation for the author.

ACKNOWLEDGEMENTS

I would like to thank my advisor, Sidney D'Mello, for his guidance on this research. This research was supported by the National Science Foundation (NSF) (DRL 1235958) and the Bill & Melinda Gates Foundation. Any opinions, findings and conclusions, or recommendations expressed in this paper do not necessarily reflect the views of the NSF or the Bill & Melinda Gates Foundation.

REFERENCES

1. Ryan Baker and Jaclyn Ocumpaugh. 2015. Interaction-based affect detection in educational software. In *The Oxford Handbook of Affective Computing*, Rafael Calvo, Sidney D'Mello, J. Gratch and A. Kappas (eds.). New York: Oxford University Press, 233–245.
2. Nigel Bosch, Sidney D'Mello, Ryan Baker, et al. 2015. Automatic detection of learning-centered affective states in the wild. *Proceedings of the 2015 International Conference on Intelligent User Interfaces (IUI 2015)*, New York, NY: ACM, 379–388.
3. Nigel Bosch, Sidney D'Mello, Ryan Baker, Jaclyn Ocumpaugh, and Valerie J. Shute. 2015. Temporal generalizability of face-based affect detection in noisy classroom environments. *Proceedings of the 17th International Conference on Artificial Intelligence in Education (AIED 2015)*, Berlin Heidelberg: Springer-Verlag, 44–53.
4. Paul Ekman. 1994. Strong evidence for universals in facial expressions: a reply to Russell's mistaken critique. *Psychological bulletin* 115, 2: 268–287.
5. Hillary Anger Elfenbein and Nalini Ambady. 2002. On the universality and cultural specificity of emotion recognition: a meta-analysis. *Psychological bulletin* 128, 2: 203.
6. Joseph F. Grafsgaard, Joseph B. Wiggins, Kristy Elizabeth Boyer, Eric N. Wiebe, and James C. Lester. 2013. Automatically recognizing facial expression: Predicting engagement and frustration. *Proceedings of the 6th International Conference on Educational Data Mining.*
7. Joseph F. Grafsgaard, Joseph B. Wiggins, Alexandria Katarina Vail, Kristy Elizabeth Boyer, Eric N. Wiebe, and James C. Lester. 2014. The additive value of multimodal features for predicting engagement, frustration, and learning during tutoring. *Proceedings of the 16th International Conference on Multimodal Interaction*, ACM, 42–49.
8. Shiming Kai, Luc Paquette, Ryan Baker, et al. 2015. Comparison of face-based and interaction-based affect detectors in physics playground. *Proceedings of the 8th International Conference on Educational Data Mining (EDM 2015)*, International Educational Data Mining Society, 77–84.
9. Ashish Kapoor and Rosalind W. Picard. 2005. Multimodal affect recognition in learning environments. *Proceedings of the 13th Annual ACM International Conference on Multimedia*, ACM, 677–682.
10. Sidney D'Mello. 2013. A selective meta-analysis on the relative incidence of discrete affective states during learning with technology. *Journal of Educational Psychology* 105, 4: 1082–1099.
11. Sidney D'Mello, Nathan Blanchard, Ryan Baker, Jaclyn Ocumpaugh, and Keith Brawner. 2014. I feel your pain: A selective review of affect-sensitive instructional strategies. In *Design Recommendations for Intelligent Tutoring Systems - Volume 2: Instructional Management*, Robert Sottilare, Art Graesser, Xiangen Hu and Benjamin Goldberg (eds.). 35–48.
12. Sidney D'Mello and Jacqueline Kory. 2015. A review and meta-analysis of multimodal affect detection systems. *ACM Computing Surveys* 47, 3: 43:1–43:36.
13. Sinno Jialin Pan and Qiang Yang. 2010. A Survey on Transfer Learning. *IEEE Transactions on Knowledge and Data Engineering* 22, 10: 1345–1359.
14. Zachary A. Pardos, Ryan S. J. D. Baker, Maria O. C. Z. San Pedro, Sujith M. Gowda, and Supreeth M. Gowda. 2013. Affective states and state tests: Investigating how affect throughout the school year predicts end of year learning outcomes. *Proceedings of the Third International Conference on Learning Analytics and Knowledge*, ACM, 117–124.
15. B. Schuller, B. Vlasenko, F. Eyben, et al. 2010. Cross-corpus acoustic emotion recognition: Variances and strategies. *IEEE Transactions on Affective Computing* 1, 2: 119–131.
16. Valerie Shute and Matthew Ventura. 2013. *Measuring and supporting learning in games: Stealth assessment.* The MIT Press, Cambridge, MA.
17. Marie Tahon, Agnes Delaborde, and Laurence Devillers. 2011. Real-life emotion detection from speech in human-robot interaction: Experiments across diverse corpora with child and adult voices. *INTERSPEECH*, 3121–3124.
18. J. Whitehill, Z. Serpell, Yi-Ching Lin, A Foster, and J.R. Movellan. 2014. The faces of engagement: Automatic recognition of student engagement from facial expressions. *IEEE Transactions on Affective Computing* 5, 1: 86–98.
19. Martin Wöllmer, Moritz Kaiser, Florian Eyben, Björn Schuller, and Gerhard Rigoll. 2013. LSTM-modeling of continuous emotions in an audiovisual affect recognition framework. *Image and Vision Computing* 31, 2: 153–163.

Multimodal Assessment of Teaching Behavior in Immersive Rehearsal Environment - TeachLivE™

Roghayeh Barmaki
Computer Science Division
University of Central Florida
Orlando, FL, USA
barmaki@eecs.ucf.edu

ABSTRACT

Nonverbal behaviors such as facial expressions, eye contact, gestures, and body movements in general have strong impacts on the process of communicative interactions. Gestures play an important role in interpersonal communication in the classroom between student and teacher. To assist teachers with exhibiting open and positive nonverbal signals in their actual classroom, we have designed a multimodal teaching application with provisions for real-time feedback in coordination with our TeachLivE test-bed environment and its reflective application; ReflectLivE.

Individuals walk into this virtual environment and interact with five virtual students shown on a large screen display. The recent research study is designed to have two settings (7-minute long each). In each of the settings, the participants are provided lesson plans from which they teach. All the participants are asked to take part in both settings, with half receiving automated real-time feedback about their body poses in the first session (group 1) and the other half receiving such feedback in the second session (group 2).

Feedback is in the form of a visual indication each time the participant exhibits a closed stance. To create this automated feedback application, a closed posture corpus was collected and trained based on the existing TeachLivE teaching records. After each session, the participants take a post-questionnaire about their experience. We hypothesize that visual feedback improves positive body gestures for both groups during the feedback session, and that, for group 2, this persists into their second unaided session but, for group 1, improvements occur only during the second session.

Categories and Subject Descriptors

H.5.1. [**Information Interfaces and Presentation (e.g. HCI)**]: Multimedia Information Systems

ICMI '15, November 09-13, 2015, Seattle, WA, USA
©2015 ACM. ISBN 978-1-4503-3912-4/15/11 ... $15.00
DOI: http://dx.doi.org/10.1145/2818346.2830604

Keywords

Immersive rehearsal environment; Teacher preparation; Gesture recognition; Reflection; Mutimodal Analytics

1. INTRODUCTION

Interpersonal communication includes verbal and nonverbal elements. Nonverbal communication (NVC) refers to all of the components of communication excluding the actual words used [19]. Para-language (pitch, volume, etc.) is the vocal element of nonverbal communication. On the other hand, body language (gestures and movements, facial expressions, eye contact, etc.) is the nonvocal element of nonverbal communication[14]. Upwards of 65 percent of the meaning derived in interactions comes from nonverbal communication [19, 10].

In the classroom and student-teacher communication, NVC also plays a critical role in successful interaction [20]. Teachers are required to comprehend the nonverbal cues they are sending and receiving in the classroom setting [6]. Teachers may use NVC in the classroom for different purposes. Alibali et al. [2] indicated that teachers' gestures have impact on student comprehension and student learning, specifically in instructional discourses. Gestures are defined as a form of nonverbal communication that associated visible bodily actions are used to communicate messages, either in place of speech or together and in parallel with spoken words [13].

The presented research investigates the nonverbal behaviors (body movements, especially gestures and postures) of participants in an immersive rehearsal environment - TeachLivE. The objective is to perceive the relations of participant's teaching experience with NVC feedback provision in simulated classroom. In addition, the participants are asked to take pre and post questionnaires during the experiment to determine their perception of the experience. The eventual goal of the research is to design a semi-automated annotation system from multimodal features including the body language and gesture tracking of participants in the TeachLivE environment that leads to assessment and reflection procedures for professional development. There have been one completed and one ongoing case studies related to the research topic that is covered in this paper. The methodology details and results of the first case study along with the design and preliminary results the second case study are described after the background section.

2. BACKGROUND

2.1 TeachLivE Rehearsal Environment

TeachLivE is a teaching and learning environment that was developed at the University of Central Florida to provide an interactive learning experience for teachers to rehearse and hone their classroom skills. It is an avatar-mediated system that consists of at least five student avatars in a virtual classroom setting. A human in the loop (interactor), orchestrates the behaviors of student avatars in response to a participant's actions. Figure 1 shows the architecture of the TeachLivE system [21] with some extended features that is explained in methodology section. TeachLivE has been widely used for training purposes. Over 12,000 users at 70 universities in the U.S, experienced the environment in 2014-15. Many of these universities have carried out research projects that use TeachlivE as the basic study environment. One of the largest of these studies was funded by the Bill & Melinda Gates Foundation. The results showed positive changes in teaching strategies after just four ten-minute sessions in the simulated classroom [9].

In the previous study [4], we used TeachAARS (TeachLivE After Action Review System) for manual annotation of nonverbal behaviors including proximity, body language (open versus closed postures) and head movement (nodding). Moving forward in our research, the nonverbal communication coding procedure is supported by the Microsoft Kinect V2 and 3D-sensor technology [1]. In addition, a new application, called ReflectLivE, is integrated into TeachLivE for multimodal data collection of participants' experiences.

2.2 Nonverbal Communication in Context

Communication scholars have compartmentalized nonverbal communication into nine categories: kinesics, more commonly referred to as body language and physical appearance; chronemics or communication through time; proxemics or communication using space; para-language, communication through tone of voice; artifacts, communication by physical objects; haptics, communication through touch; facial expressions; olfactics, communication by means of smells; and oculesics, more commonly referred to as eye contact [23]. The presented research focuses on kinesics and body language, especially gestures from defined NVC categories. McNeill defines gestures as four main types. Iconics are related to semantic content of speech; metaphorics tie to an abstract concept; deictics or pointing gestures relate to the identity of individuals to whom the utterances refer; and beats keep the rhythm of speech [18].

NVC plays important role in various professions. In the case of physician-patient interaction, scholars presented results on the relation of nonverbal communication skill of the physicians and the patient satisfaction [7]. Also in the classroom environment, the successful student-teacher communication is affected by the NVC skills of the teacher [15, 20].

2.2.1 *NVC and Immersive Environments*

There exist an extensive amount of work on the impact and application of gestures in virtual and interactive environments. The context of deictic expressions and the impact of pointing gestures in virtual immersive environment have been investigated by Pfeiffer et al. [22]. Two participants were asked to play an object identification game together and the session was recorded and annotated based on gaze finger pointing and index-finger pointing to analyze the success rate of object identification.

In another research [11], scholars introduced an automated system for social skills training called MACH (My Automated Conversation CoacH). The system includes a virtual agent that reads facial expressions, speech, and prosody (tone, pitch) of the participant and responds with verbal and nonverbal behaviors in real-time. During the interview training session as an example application, MACH asks interview questions, automatically mimics certain behavior issued by the user, and exhibits appropriate nonverbal behaviors [11].

2.2.2 *NVC and Classroom*

Nonverbal communication strategies is as expressive as verbal communication skills and this has been also noted in teacher training [16]. The strategies like eye contact, prolonged gaze, and proximity can have positive or negative effects on student behavior and classroom management, depending on the situation and context [15, 6]. Teachers can use gesture to be effective in several fundamental aspects of their profession, including communication, assessment of student knowledge, and the ability to instill a profound understanding of abstract concepts in traditionally difficult domains such as teaching foreign languages and mathematics [12].

Alibali et al. showed that teachers use gestures in an effort to scaffold students' understanding, especially on abstract concepts. They worked on a mathematics lesson session that focused on algebraic relations [3]. They manually annotated the gestures and transcribed the teacher's conversation in the study and used the annotation data to analyze the nonverbal behavior of the teacher. In [5], we investigated the way teachers use gestures in the virtual classroom settings of TeachLivE. Our research had been developed based on the hypothesis reported in [3]. Analysis of video recordings from real and virtual classroom environments form biology and algebra teachers indicated that algebra teachers gesture significantly more often than biology teachers.

3. METHOD: GESTURE RECOGNITION

Manual annotation on video recordings by experts can provide accurate annotations; however it is extremely time consuming and sometimes costly. Hence, some automated techniques have been presented for gesture recognition from video clips and other resources. In general, most gesture recognition techniques have a set of training data to learn and extract the patterns of the gesture from the training set and then use the trained engine for recognition. In this research, we also use a similar technique with skeletal data in the Visual Gesture Builder (VGB) environment [1]. This approach is fast and inexpensive in comparison to the manual gesture annotation procedure.

VGB generates gesture databases that are used by applications to perform run-time gesture detection. VGB is defined as a data driven machine learning solution for gesture detection. Visual Gesture Builder uses skeleton tracking data (25 body points in Kinect V2) representing body movements, and AdaBoost ensemble classifier (for discrete gestures) or Random Forest Regression (for continuous gestures). At first, for each gesture, some clips from different subjects must be recorded with the Kinect Studio application from the Microsoft Kinect V2 Software Developement Kit. Every clip contains an individual in front of the Kinect who exhibits the gesture (with some variations) 15 to 25 times. Then, the VGB tool is used to give meaning to the recorded clips. All the frames in the recordings that define a gesture, must be tagged manually. All the frames exhibiting the gesture get the label of 1 and the remaining frames in the clip get the label of -1 [1]. At this point, the problem is similar to a supervised binary classification, in which the classifier will recognize the frames in which a gesture is performed. For each gesture, the recognition engine have an associate's binary classifier. After the training step, VGB is able to generate the tags automatically in the analysis step from the test clips. In the following section, we discuss more details about the case studies and the targeted gestures to recognize according to interpersonal communication perspective.

3.1 Case Study 1

3.1.1 Participants and Study Setting

The experiment was a within-subjects study, fitting in a single session lasting at most 12 minutes (session range = 8-12 min., mean= 10 min.). The subjects were self-selected from a group of visiting UCF scholars composed of instructors and university students. Participants were given a consent form and a pre-questionnaire that were used to determine demographic information, teaching and educational background, English speaking level, and topic of interest for the teaching session. The participants (n=14, 6 female, 8 male) had an average age of 28.1 years and all were Hispanic/Latino with English as their second language. Two of the subjects majored in English Language Teaching (ELT). Six of 14 subjects had taught for at least five years. The other eight subjects were students with no teaching experience. Half of the participants selected Spanish Language as a teaching topic and the others picked different topics from science, marketing and algebra. All of the participants, except one, were novices in the TeachLivE environment. Each participant was introduced to the virtual classroom prior to the recording procedure and then were asked to start their teaching session.

3.1.2 Recording

Two types of data were recorded during the study. (I) skeleton data (IR, depth and body frame) and (II) virtual scene paired with the user experience from the observer station (video recording). Figure 1 presents the TeachLivE setting for the study and data collection specifications. The skeleton data of the participants were recorded using a Kinect V2 sensor and the Kinect Studio utility application. The recorded clips with Kinect Studio are required as data inputs to Visual Gesture Builder (VGB) to do automated tagging of gestures [1]. The second type of recorded data was the virtual scene paired with the user experience from the classroom in mp4 format. This was used for teaching proficiency analysis by experts.

Some of the closed postures from previous work [4] are shown in Figure 2. Caswell and Neill in their study on effects of

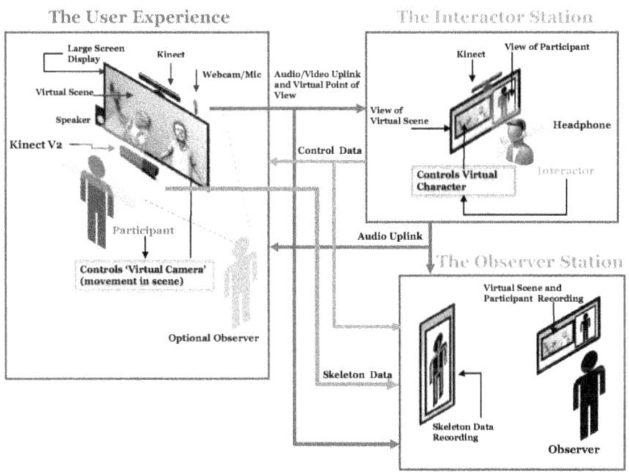

Figure 1: TeachLivE setting with some adjustments from the original architecture [21]. Two types of recorded streams are: (I) skeleton data (IR, depth and body frame) shown with orange arrow and (II) virtual scene paired with user experience recording from the observer station (video stream) with red arrow.

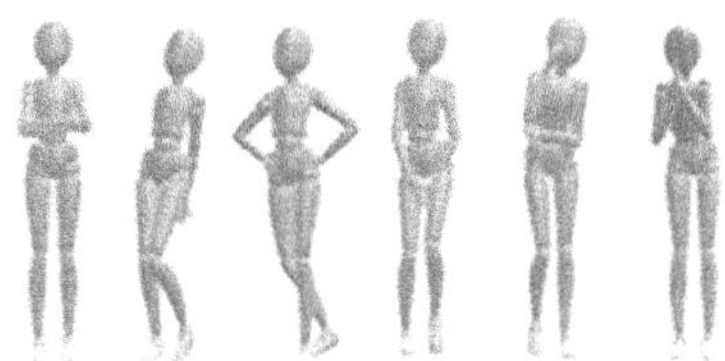

Figure 2: Reference example of closed postures/gestures; left to right: unreceptive (arms folded in front), seductive (hands clasped in back), skeptical (hands placed on hips), protective (hands clasped in lower front), pensive (thoughtful pose), and submissive (hands clasped in upper front).

body language of competent teachers showed that using reference postures as a communication medium, teachers employ open instead of closed poses in their classroom [6]. They also hypothesized in their study that closed poses indicate defensiveness and avoidance of the speaker/teacher to listener. A corpus of closed body poses (reference poses in figure 2 and some variations of them) was recorded from the performances of three male and two female students using the Microsoft Kinect V2. Subjects for the main study were not involved in the corpus collection. The corpus was used as training clips in the Visual Gesture Builder (VGB) application. All the clips were hand-coded and tagged in order to feed the automated analysis procedure of the participant's clips. There were six targeted closed gestures/poses to train/evaluate in this research. For training each pose, four 30-sec clips were manually annotated and added to the gesture database. 7 x 5 short clips were annotated; a thinking or pensive gesture is a sided-gesture, and we needed to record left and right versions of that gesture. Hence, we had seven classifiers rather than six at the end of training for the targeted six gestures. The process of creating the gesture recognition engine is shown in reference [1].

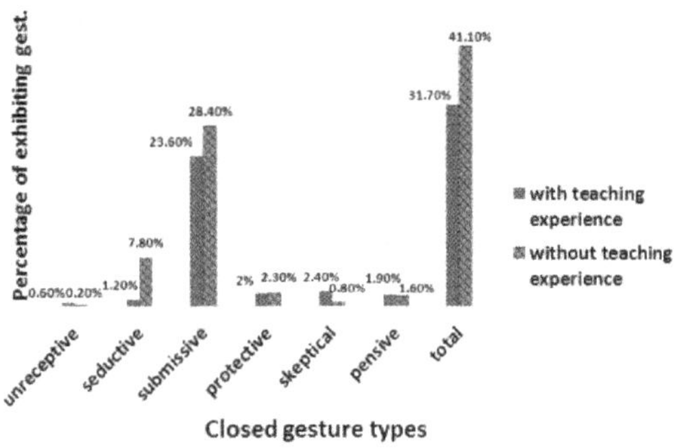

Figure 3: The average time of exhibiting closed gesture for two different groups in the study.

3.1.3 Performance Measures

The raw data from the user experience recordings (video clips) were reviewed by two supervisors to measure the teaching proficiency aspect and the communication aspect as an interested sub-domain of teaching evaluation framework. There are some teaching frameworks [8, 17] as evaluation instruments of teachers in real classrooms, but due to the specifications of TeachLivE as a virtual classroom, some domains may not be measurable. We created a teaching and communication proficiency checklist as a reference for observers with some adjustments to existing teaching evaluation frameworks. The checklist from the observers are available at the TeachLive web site (TeachlivE.org). Space limitations prevented them from being included here.

3.1.4 Results

All valid clips were added to the VGB solution created with different projects trained for each closed gesture. The automatically tagged data were reviewed to minimize the tagging error. For each clip of the participant, the length of exhibiting gesture(s) was reported as a percentage of the total session time. Figure 3 presents the average time of exhibiting six different closed gestures for teachers (n=6) and students (n=8) who participated in the case study.

This bar chart indicates that experienced teachers did not exhibit closed gestures as much as students who had no teaching experiences, considering the total time of having closed gesture (shown in the last two columns of figure 3). In addition, submissive gesture was employed frequently rather than other closed gestures by all participants. On the other hand, experienced teachers exhibited skeptical gesture more than students. As figure 3 shows, the results for all of the gestures, except for the seductive and submissive, were close to each other for both of the groups.

From a performance prospective, there was a significance positive correlation between some demographics data and teaching proficiency (TP) and communication proficiency (CP) scores reported by observers. For instance, there was a significant correlation for those in the ELT major, having teaching experience, and being older ($p < 0.01$ for all these variables) with TP score. For CP, age and English speaking level had significant correlations. Other demographics had weak correlations with TP and CP.

3.1.5 Discussion

In this pilot study, we hypothesized that there is a relation between teaching/communication proficiency and a subject's body movements/gestures during the interactive experiment. Among the detected gestures, submissive and seductive gestures were much more prevalent than other closed gestures. There might be cultural and personal influences for the prevalence of submissive and skeptical gestures among participants. In addition, since English was not the participants' first spoken language, they frequently used beat gestures to keep the rhythm of the speech [18]. There was significant correlation between a subject's teaching experience, age and TP/CP scores.

There may be multiple confounding factors involved in this study. All of the subjects except one were new to the simulated classroom and the experiment was single-session. All the participants were non-native English speakers with average level of English proficiency. The other limitation was the small number of participants and also having selective open topic for teaching sessions because the sample was from a group of convenience.

3.2 Case Study 2

3.2.1 Study Setting

In this case study, which is an ongoing project, a maximum of 50 student participants will be recruited from the affiliated University. Only those College of Education students who have seen the TeachLivE environment before are eligible to be recruited. Participants will be ones to have a native level of English proficiency, with some teaching experience to be able to talk and interact with virtual students in the TeachLivE simulator.

The new case study is designed to have two settings with and without feedback provision to participants (7-minute long each). Feedback is in the form of a visual or perhaps haptic indication each time the participant exhibits a closed posture. The feedback application is designed based on an existing closed body-posture corpus and a new interface for automated online feedback provision during the sessions. All the participants experience both of the settings. Half the participants receive real-time feedback (setting 2) during this first session while the other half receive no feedback (setting 1) during this session. After the first teaching session, all participants fill out a post-questionnaire. They reenter the virtual classroom then to present the same lesson plan. During this second session, those who did not receive real-time feedback in the first session will receive it during the second, and those who received it in the first will receive none during the second. All participants will then be asked to complete the same post-questionnaire that they filled out after the first session.

3.2.2 Recording

In the new experiment, in addition to full-body and video recording, we will keep a track of virtual classroom's interactions as well. Virtual avatars' NVC signals and their talk-time will be recorded in a log-file using the comma-delimited format in an observer station for further multimodal analysis such as understanding the correlations of teacher's wait-time, student's talk-time or teacher's talk-time with teacher's body movement data in the two settings or groups. We are using our reflection tool called ReflectLivE for saving and analyzing the related log-data.

3.2.3 Preliminary Results and Analysis

We have recruited 12 participants so far. As mentioned before, half (6) of the participants received automated real-time feedback about their body poses in the first session and the other half received such feedback in the second session. Based on recorded skeletal data, we observed that only those who received feedback in their first session demonstrated a significant number of open poses in the session containing no feedback. However, the post-questionnaire information indicated that most of the participants were more mindful of their body poses while teaching after they had participated in the study. Some strict adjustments about the case study 2 recruitment group has been made. The discussion section from case study 1 explains the reasons for those changes to minimize the negative effect of confounding conditions.

4. FUTURE WORK

For future steps, we intend to complete the new experiment phase. Multimodal data analysis will be performed next, and correlations will be reported. This phase involves multimodal signal processing and related machine learning approaches.

5. ACKNOWLEDGMENTS

The author wish to thank TeachLivE principal investigators Drs. Lisa A. Dieker, Michael Hynes and Charles E. Hughes (faculty supervisor), as well as Cynthia Hutchinson, Joyce Nutta, Thomas Owens, Jacqueline Rodriguez, Mrs. Pam Jones and Mr. Michael Hopper for their support during the data collection and analysis processes. Their insights and their assistance with subject recruitment were invaluable. I also wish to express my appreciation for the support of the entire TeachLivE team and the participants. Finally I wish to acknowledge support for the evolution of the TeachLivE project from the Bill & Melinda Gates Foundation (OPP1053202) and the National Science Foundation (CNS1051067, IIS1116615). Any opinions, findings, and conclusions or recommendations expressed in this material are those of the authors and do not necessarily reflect the views of the sponsors.

6. REFERENCES

[1] Visual gesture builder: A data-driven solution to gesture detection, July 2014.

[2] M. W. Alibali, S. Kita, and A. J. Young. Gesture and the process of speech production: We think, therefore we gesture. *Language and cognitive processes*, 15(6):593–613, 2000.

[3] M. W. Alibali and M. J. Nathan. Teachers' gestures as a means of scaffolding students' understanding: Evidence from an early algebra lesson. *Video research in the learning sciences*, pages 349–365, 2007.

[4] R. Barmaki. Nonverbal communication and teaching performance. In P. Z. M. M. M. B. M. Stamper, J., editor, *Educational Data Mining 2014*, pages 441–443, 2014.

[5] R. Barmaki and C. E. Hughes. A case study to track teacher gestures and performance in a virtual learning environment. In *Proceedings of the Fifth International Conference on Learning Analytics And Knowledge*, LAK '15, pages 420–421, New York, NY, USA, 2015. ACM.

[6] C. Caswell and S. Neill. *Body language for competent teachers.* Routledge, 2003.

[7] L. G. Collins, A. Schrimmer, J. Diamond, and J. Burke. Evaluating verbal and non-verbal communication skills, in an ethnogeriatric osce. *Patient education and counseling*, 83(2):158–162, 2011.

[8] C. Danielson. *The framework for teaching evaluation instrument.* Danielson Group, 2011.

[9] L. A. Dieker, C. L. Straub, C. E. Hughes, M. C. Hynes, and S. Hardin. Learning from virtual students. *Educational Leadership*, 71(8):54–58, 2014.

[10] L. K. Guerrero and K. Floyd. *Nonverbal communication in close relationships.* Routledge, 2006.

[11] M. E. Hoque, M. Courgeon, J.-C. Martin, B. Mutlu, and R. W. Picard. Mach: My automated conversation coach. In *Proceedings of the 2013 ACM international joint conference on Pervasive and ubiquitous computing*, pages 697–706. ACM, 2013.

[12] S. D. Kelly, S. M. Manning, and S. Rodak. Gesture gives a hand to language and learning: Perspectives from cognitive neuroscience, developmental psychology and education. *Language and Linguistics Compass*, 2(4):569–588, 2008.

[13] A. Kendon. *Gesture: Visible action as utterance.* Cambridge University Press, 2004.

[14] M. Knapp, J. Hall, and T. Horgan. *Nonverbal communication in human interaction.* Cengage Learning, 2013.

[15] R. Laslett and C. Smith. *Effective classroom management: a teacher's guide.* Routledge, 2002.

[16] J. Mahon, B. Bryant, B. Brown, and M. Kim. Using second life to enhance classroom management practice in teacher education. *Educational Media International*, 47(2):121–134, 2010.

[17] R. J. Marzano and M. D. Toth. *Teacher evaluation that makes a difference: A new model for teacher growth and student achievement.* ASCD, 2013.

[18] D. McNeill. *Hand and mind: What gestures reveal about thought.* University of Chicago Press, 1992.

[19] A. Mehrabian. Communication without words. *Psychological today*, 2:53–55, 1968.

[20] P. W. Miller. Body language in the classroom. *Techniques: Connecting Education and Careers*, 8:28–30, 2005.

[21] A. Nagendran, R. Pillat, A. Kavanaugh, G. Welch, and C. Hughes. A unified framework for individualized avatar-based interactions. *Presence: Teleoperators and Virtual Environments*, 23(2):109–132, 2014.

[22] T. Pfeiffer, M. E. Latoschik, and I. Wachsmuth. Conversational pointing gestures for virtual reality interaction: implications from an empirical study. In *Virtual Reality Conference, 2008. VR'08. IEEE*, pages 281–282. IEEE, 2008.

[23] V. P. Richmond, J. C. McCroskey, and M. L. Hickson III. Nonverbal behavior in interpersonal relations. 2014.

Author Index

www.ingramcontent.com/pod-product-compliance
Ingram Content Group UK Ltd.
Pitfield, Milton Keynes, MK11 3LW, UK
UKHW051418290926
15471UKWH00009B/1672

9 781450 341080